Subscriber Update Service

BECOME A SUBSCRIBER!
Did you purchase this product from a bookstore?

If you did, it's important for you to become a subscriber. John Wiley & Sons, Inc. may publish, on a periodic basis, supplements and new editions to reflect the latest changes in the subject matter that you *need to know* in order stay competitive in this ever-changing industry. By contacting the Wiley office nearest you, you'll receive any current update at no additional charge. In addition, you'll receive future updates and revised or related volumes on a 30-day examination review.

If you purchased this product directly from John Wiley & Sons, Inc., we have already recorded your subscription for this update service.

To become a subscriber, please call **1-877-762-2974** or send your name, company name (if applicable), address, and the title of the product to:

mailing address: **Supplement Department**
John Wiley & Sons, Inc.
One Wiley Drive
Somerset, NJ 08875

e-mail: **subscriber@wiley.com**
fax: **1-732-302-2300**
online: **www.wiley.com**

For customers outside the United States, please contact the Wiley office nearest you:

Professional & Reference Division
John Wiley & Sons Canada, Ltd.
22 Worcester Road
Etobicoke, Ontario M9W 1L1
CANADA
Phone: 416-236-4433
Phone: 1-800-567-4797
Fax: 416-236-4447
E-mail: canada@wiley.com

John Wiley & Sons Australia, Ltd.
33 Park Road
P.O. Box 1226
Milton, Queensland 4064
AUSTRALIA
Phone: 61-7-3859-9755
Fax: 61-7-3859-9715
E-mail: brisbane@johnwiley.com.au

John Wiley & Sons, Ltd.
The Atrium
Southern Gate, Chichester
West Sussex, PO19 8SQ
ENGLAND
Phone: 44-1243-779777
Fax: 44-1243-775878
E-mail: customer@wiley.co.uk

John Wiley & Sons (Asia) Pte. Ltd.
2 Clementi Loop #02-01
SINGAPORE 129809
Phone: 65-64632400
Fax: 65-64634604/5/6
Customer Service: 65-64604280
E-mail: enquiry@wiley.com.sg

WILEY

2012 Interpretation and Application of

International Financial Reporting Standards

Bruce Mackenzie   Tapiwa Njikizana

Danie Coetsee   Raymond Chamboko

Blaise Colyvas   Brandon Hanekom

WILEY

JOHN WILEY & SONS, INC.

CONTENTS

PREFACE

This edition of *IFRS: Interpretation and Application of International Financial Reporting Standards* provides detailed, analytical explanations and illustrations of all current accounting principles promulgated by the IASB that are applicable to the 2012 financial reporting period of reporting entities. The focus of the book is to provide sufficient guidelines for entities that prepare their 2012 financial statements. New developments that are applicable to periods after 2012 are identified and briefly discussed separately from the main text in each chapter.

The book integrates the accounting principles set out in International Financial Reporting Standards (IFRS) including Interpretations issued by the IFRS Interpretations Committee. These materials have been synthesized into a user-oriented topical format, eliminating the need for readers to first be familiar with the names or numbers of the salient professional standards.

The stated goal of the IFRS Foundation and the IASB is to develop, in the public interest, a single set of high-quality, understandable, enforceable, and globally accepted financial reporting standards based upon clearly articulated principles. More and more global economies are adopting IFRS. In fact, the IASB acknowledges that all major economies have established time lines to converge with or adopt IFRS in the near future. The US Securities and Exchange Commission is also in the process of making a decision whether to phase out US GAAP in favor of IFRS.

The primary objective of this book is to assist the practitioner, user, or preparer in navigating the myriad practical problems faced in applying IFRS. Accordingly, the paramount goal has been to incorporate meaningful, real-world-type examples in guiding users in the application of IFRS to the complex fact situations that must be dealt with in the actual practice of accounting. In addition to this emphasis, a major strength of this book is that it does explain the theory of IFRS in sufficient detail to serve as a valuable adjunct to, or substitute for, accounting textbooks. Much more than a reiteration of currently promulgated IFRS, it provides the user with an understanding of the underlying conceptual basis for the rules, to enable the reasoning by analogy that is so necessary in dealing with a complex, fast-changing world of commercial arrangements and structures using principles-based standards. Since IFRS is by design less prescriptive than many national GAAP, practitioners have been left with a proportionately greater challenge in actually applying the rules. This book is designed to bridge the gap between these less detailed standards and application problems encountered in practice.

Each chapter of this book, or major section thereof, provides a detailed discussion of the topic, with examples, as it relates to the 2012 financial reporting period, as well as a short overview of both new standards applicable after the 2012 financial reporting period and proposed new developments. At the end of each applicable chapter, a short US GAAP comparison is provided, detailing the main areas in which US GAAP differs from IFRS. A comprehensive checklist following the main text offers practical guidance to preparing financial statement disclosures in accordance with IFRS. The book features examples of actual informative disclosures made by companies currently reporting under IFRS.

The authors' wish is that this book will serve practitioners, faculty, and students as a reliable reference tool, to facilitate their understanding of, and ability to apply, the complexities of the authoritative literature. Comments from readers, both as to errors and omissions and as to proposed improvements for future editions, should be addressed to John Wiley & Sons, Inc., 155 N. 3rd Street, Suite 502, DeKalb, Illinois 60115, for consideration in future editions.

Bruce Mackenzie
Danie Coetsee
Tapiwa Njikizana
Raymond Chamboko
Brandon Hannekom

December 2011

ABOUT THE AUTHORS

Bruce Mackenzie, CA (SA), FCCA, RA, JSE Registered IFRS Advisor, is a member of the IASB SME Implementation Group (SMEIG) and a partner at W Consulting (www.wconsulting.co.za), a global IFRS consulting and training company. He has held positions at Deloitte both in South Africa and the United Kingdom in the IFRS Centers of Excellence.

Danie Coetsee, CA (SA), is Professor of Accounting at the University of Johannesburg, specializing in financial accounting.

Tapiwa Njikizana, CA (SA), RA, JSE Registered IFRS Advisor, is a technical partner at W Consulting. After qualifying with Coopers & Lybrand, he spent time internationally with Ernst & Young and Anderson.

Raymond Chamboko, CA (SA), JSE Registered IFRS Advisor, is a technical partner at W Consulting. He was previously with Ernst & Young and SizweNtsalubaVSP where he handled accounting technical issues.

Blaise Colyvas, CA (SA), RA, is a technical director at W Consulting. He was previously the Head of Technical Accounting at an audit consultancy, and an audit manager with Grant Thornton.

Brandon Hanekom, CA (SA), is a technical manager at W Consulting. He completed his articles at RSM Betty & Dickson where he has gained three years public practice experience on audits for large listed companies, large privately owned groups, trusts, and various associations.

ABOUT THE ONLINE RESOURCES

Because you have purchased this print edition of *Wiley IFRS 2012: Interpretation and Application of International Financial Reporting Standards*, you are eligible to download a free e-Book version of it (in e-PDF format). Please see the inside back cover of this book to find your unique ACCESS CODE giving you online access to the e-Book file.

Please Note

Your unique ACCESS CODE is located on the back of the printed card sealed on the inside back cover of this book. Once the stop label is torn, this print book is nonreturnable.

In addition, this offer only provides the e-Book of *IFRS 2012* in e-PDF format (which can be viewed by using Adobe Digital Editions).

1 INTRODUCTION TO INTERNATIONAL FINANCIAL REPORTING STANDARDS

INTRODUCTION

The stated goal of the IFRS Foundation and the International Accounting Standards Board (IASB) is to develop, in the public interest, a single set of high-quality, understandable, enforceable and globally accepted financial reporting standards based upon clearly articulated principles.

There were once scores of unique sets of financial reporting standards among the more developed nations ("national GAAP"). The year 2005 marked the beginning of a new era in global conduct of business, and the fulfillment of a thirty-year effort to create the financial reporting rules for a worldwide capital market. For during that year's financial reporting cycle, the 27 European Union (EU) member states, plus many others in countries such as Australia, New Zealand, Russia, and South Africa adopted International Financial Reporting Standards (IFRS).

Since then, many countries, such as Argentina, Brazil, and Canada, have adopted IFRS. Mexico is adopting IFRS in 2012. China has substantially converted their national standards in line with IFRS. All other major economies, such as Japan and United States have established time lines to converge with or adopt IFRS in the near future.

2007 and 2008 proved to be watershed years for the growing acceptability of IFRS. In 2007, one of the most important developments was that the SEC dropped the reconciliation (to US GAAP) requirement that had formerly applied to foreign private registrants; thereafter, those reporting in a manner fully compliant with IFRS (i.e., without any exceptions to the complete set of standards imposed by IASB) do not have to reconcile net income and shareholders' equity to that which would have been presented under US GAAP. In effect, the US SEC was acknowledging that IFRS was fully acceptable as a basis for accurate, transparent, meaningful financial reporting.

This easing of US registration requirements for foreign companies seeking to enjoy the benefits of listing their equity or debt securities in the US led, quite naturally, to a call by domestic companies to permit them to also freely choose between financial reporting under US GAAP and IFRS. By late 2008 the SEC had begun the process of acquiescence, first for the largest companies in those industries having (worldwide) the preponderance of IFRS adopters, and later for all publicly held companies. A new SEC chair took office in 2009, expressing a concern that the move to IFRS, if it were to occur, should perhaps move more slowly than had previously been indicated. In the authors' view, however, any revisiting of the earlier decision to move decisively toward mandatory use of IFRS for public company financial reporting in the US will create only a minor delay, if any. Simply put, the world-wide trend to uniform financial reporting standards (for which role the only candidate is IFRS) is inexorable and will benefit all those seeking to raise capital and all those seeking to invest.

It had been highly probable that nonpublicly held US entities would have remained bound to only US GAAP for the foreseeable future, both from habit and because no other set of standards would be viewed as being acceptable. However, the body that oversees the private-sector auditing profession's standards in the US amended its rules in 2008 to fully recognize IASB as an accounting standard-setting body (giving it equal status with the FASB), meaning that auditors and other service providers in the US may now opine (or provide other levels of assurance, as specified under pertinent guidelines) on IFRS-based financial statements. This change, coupled with the promulgation by IASB of a long-sought standard providing simplified financial reporting rules for privately held entities (described later in this chapter), has probably increased the likelihood that a broad-based move to IFRS will occur in the US within the next several years. The SEC commissioner and chair recently confirmed that they are committed to a single set of global standards and are on schedule for the 2011 determination whether to incorporate IFRS in the US for US issuers.

The impetus for the convergence of historically disparate financial reporting standards has been, in the main, to facilitate the free flow of capital so that, for example, investors in the United States will become more willing to finance business in, say, China or the Czech Republic. Having access to financial statements that are written in the same "language" would eliminate what has historically been a major impediment to engendering investor confidence, which is sometimes referred to as "accounting risk," which adds to the already existing risks of making such cross-border investments. Additionally, the permission to list a company's equity or debt securities on an exchange has generally been conditioned on making filings with national regulatory authorities, which have historically insisted either on conformity with local GAAP or on a formal reconciliation to local GAAP. Since either of these procedures was tedious and time-consuming, and the human resources and technical knowledge to do so were not always widely available, many otherwise anxious would-be registrants forwent the opportunity to broaden their investor bases and potentially lower their costs of capital.

The historic 2002 Norwalk Agreement—between the US standard setter, FASB, and the IASB—called for "convergence" of the respective sets of standards, and indeed a number of revisions of either US GAAP or IFRS have already taken place to implement this commitment, with more changes expected in the immediate future. The aim of the Boards was to complete the milestone projects of the Memorandum of Understanding (MOU) by the end of June 2011. These milestone projects include

- Financial instruments
- Consolidations
- Derecognition
- Fair value measurement
- Revenue recognition

- Leases
- Financial instruments with characteristics of equity
- Financial statement presentation
- Other MOU projects
- Other joint projects

Details of these and other projects of the standard setters are included in a separate section in each relevant chapter of this book. Although the Boards were committed to complete the milestone projects by June 2011, certain projects such as financial instruments (impairment and hedge accounting), revenue recognition and leases have been deferred due to the complexity of the projects and obtaining consensus views.

Only after these projects are completed will the US make a final decision on the adoption of IFRS in the US. Although the target date to make the decision was for 2011, at date of completion of this book no decision was made. Until this issue is resolved, IFRS and US GAAP will remain the two comprehensive financial reporting frameworks in the world, with IFRS gaining more and more momentum.

ORIGINS AND EARLY HISTORY OF THE IASB

Financial reporting in the developed world evolved from two broad models, whose objectives were somewhat different. The earliest systematized form of accounting regulation developed in continental Europe in 1673. Here a requirement for an annual fair value statement of financial position was introduced by the government as a means of protecting the economy from bankruptcies. This form of accounting at the initiative of the state to control economic actors was copied by other states and later incorporated in the 1807 Napoleonic Commercial Code. This method of regulating the economy expanded rapidly throughout continental Europe, partly through Napoleon's efforts and partly through a willingness on the part of European regulators to borrow ideas from each other. This "code law" family of reporting practices was much developed by Germany after its 1870 unification, with the emphasis moving away from market values to historical cost and systematic depreciation. It was used later by governments as the basis of tax assessment when taxes on business profits started to be introduced, mostly in the early twentieth century.

This model of accounting serves primarily as a means of moderating relationships between the individual company and the state. It serves for tax assessment, and to limit dividend payments, and it is also a means of protecting the running of the economy by sanctioning individual businesses that are not financially sound or were run imprudently. While the model has been adapted for stock market reporting and group (consolidated) structures, this is not its main focus.

The other model did not appear until the nineteenth century and arose as a consequence of the industrial revolution. Industrialization created the need for large concentrations of capital to undertake industrial projects (initially, canals and railways) and to spread risks between many investors. In this model the financial report provided a means of monitoring the activities of large businesses in order to inform their (nonmanagement) shareholders. Financial reporting for capital markets purposes developed initially in the UK, in a common-law environment where the state legislated as little as possible and left a large degree of interpretation to practice and for the sanction of the courts. This approach was rapidly adopted by the US as it, too, became industrialized. As the US developed the idea of groups of companies controlled from a single head office (towards the end of the nineteenth century), this philosophy of financial reporting began to become focused on consolidated accounts and the group, rather than the individual company. For different reasons, neither the UK nor the US governments saw this reporting framework as appropriate for income tax purposes, and in this tradition, while the financial reports inform the assessment process, taxation retains a separate stream of law, which has had little influence on financial reporting.

The second model of financial reporting, generally regarded as the Anglo-Saxon financial reporting approach, can be characterized as focusing on the relationship between the business and the investor, and on the flow of information to the capital markets. Government still uses reporting as a means of regulating economic activity (e.g., the SEC's mission is to protect the investor and ensure that the securities markets run efficiently), but the financial report is aimed at the investor, not the government.

Neither of the two above-described approaches to financial reporting is particularly useful in an agricultural economy, or to one that consists entirely of microbusinesses, in the opinion of many observers. Nonetheless, as countries have developed economically (or as they were colonized by industrialized nations) they have adopted variants of one or the other of these two models.

IFRS are an example of the second, capital market-oriented, systems of financial reporting rules. The original international standard setter, the International Accounting Standards Committee (IASC) was formed in 1973, during a period of considerable change in accounting regulation. In the US the Financial Accounting Standards Board (FASB) had just been created, in the UK the first national standard setter had recently been organized, the EU was working on the main plank of its own accounting harmonization plan (the Fourth Directive), and both the UN and the OECD were shortly to create their own accounting committees. The IASC was launched in the wake of the 1972 World Accounting Congress (a five-yearly get-together of the international profession) after an informal meeting between representatives of the British profession (Institute of Chartered Accountants in England and Wales—ICAEW) and the American profession (American Institute of Certified Public Accountants). A rapid set of negotiations resulted in the professional bodies of Canada, Australia, Mexico, Japan, France, Germany, the Netherlands, and New Zealand being invited to join with the US and UK to form the international body. Due to pressure (coupled with a financial subsidy) from the UK, the IASC was established in London, where its successor, the IASB, remains today.

The actual reasons for the IASC's creation are unclear. A need for a common language of business was felt, to deal with a growing volume of international business, but other more political motives abounded also. For example, some believe that the major motivation was that the British wanted to create an international standard setter to trump the regional initiatives within the EU, which leaned heavily to the Code model of reporting, in contrast to what was the norm in the UK and almost all English-speaking nations.

In the first phase of its existence, the IASC had mixed fortunes. Once the International Federation of Accountants (IFAC) was formed in 1977 (at the next World Congress of Accountants), the IASC had to fight off attempts to become a part of IFAC. It managed to resist, coming to a compromise where IASC remained independent but all IFAC members were automatically members of IASC, and IFAC was able to nominate the membership of the standard-setting Board.

Both the UN and OECD were active in international rule making in the 1970s, but the IASC was successful in persuading them to leave establishment of recognition and measurement rules to the IASC. However, having established itself as the unique international rule maker, IASC encountered difficulty in persuading any jurisdiction or enforcement agency to use its rules. Although member professional bodies were theoretically committed to pushing for the use of IFRS at the national level, in practice few national bodies were influential in standard setting in their respective countries (because standards were set by taxation or other governmental bodies), and others (including the US and UK) preferred their national standards to whatever IASC might propose. In Europe, IFRS were used by some reporting entities in Italy and Switzerland, and national standard setters in some countries such as Malaysia began to use IFRS as an input to their national rules, while not necessarily adopting them as written by the IASC or giving explicit recognition to the fact that IFRS were being adopted in part as national GAAP.

IASC's efforts entered a new phase in 1987, which led directly to its 2001 reorganization, when the then-Secretary General, David Cairns, encouraged by the US SEC, negotiated an agreement with the International Organization of Securities Commissions (IOSCO). IOSCO was interested in identifying a common international "passport" whereby companies could be accepted for secondary listing in the jurisdiction of any IOSCO member. The concept was that, whatever the listing rules in a company's primary stock exchange, there would be a common minimum package which all stock exchanges would accept from foreign companies seeking a secondary listing. IOSCO was prepared to endorse IFRS as the financial reporting basis for this passport, provided that the international standards could be brought up to a quality and comprehensiveness level that IOSCO stipulated.

Historically, a major criticism of IFRS had been that it essentially endorsed all the accounting methods then in wide use, effectively becoming a "lowest common denominator" set of standards. The trend in national GAAP had been to narrow the range of acceptable alternatives, although uniformity in accounting had not been anticipated as a near-term result. The IOSCO agreement energized IASC to improve the existing standards by removing the many alternative treatments that were then permitted under the standards, thereby improving comparability across reporting entities. The IASC launched its Comparability and Improvements Project with the goal of developing a "core set of standards" that would satisfy IOSCO. These were complete by 1993, not without difficulties and spirited disagreements among the members, but then—to the great frustration of the IASC—these were not accepted by IOSCO. Rather than endorsing the standard-setting process of IASC, as was hoped for, IOSCO seemingly wanted to cherry-pick individual standards. Such a process could not realistically result in near-term endorsement of IFRS for cross-border securities registrations.

Ultimately, the collaboration was relaunched in 1995, with IASC under new leadership, and this began a further period of frenetic activities, where existing standards were again reviewed and revised, and new standards were created to fill perceived gaps in IFRS. This time the set of standards included, among others, IAS 39, on recognition and measurement of financial instruments, which was endorsed, at the very last moment and with great difficulty, as a compromise, purportedly interim standard.

At the same time, the IASC had undertaken an effort to consider its future structure. In part, this was the result of pressure exerted by the US SEC and also by the US private sector standard setter, the FASB, which were seemingly concerned that IFRS were not being developed by "due process." While the various parties may have had their own agendas, in fact the IFRS were in need of strengthening, particularly as to reducing the range of diverse but accepted alternatives for similar transactions and events. The challenges presented to IASB ultimately would serve to make IFRS stronger.

If IASC was to be the standard setter endorsed by the world's stock exchange regulators, it would need a structure that reflected that level of responsibility. The historical Anglo-Saxon standard-setting model—where professional accountants set the rules for themselves—had largely been abandoned in the twenty-five years since the IASC was formed, and standards were mostly being set by dedicated and independent national boards such as the FASB, and not by profession-dominated bodies like the AICPA. The choice, as restructuring became inevitable, was between a large, representative approach—much like the existing IASC structure, but possibly where national standard setters appointed representatives—or a small, professional body of experienced standard setters which worked independently of national interests.

The end of this phase of the international standard setting, and the resolution of these issues, came about within a short period in 2000. In May of that year, IOSCO members voted to endorse IASC standards, albeit subject to a number of reservations (see discussion later in this chapter). This was a considerable step forward for the IASC, which itself was quickly exceeded by an announcement in June 2000 that the European Commission intended to adopt IFRS as the requirement for primary listings in all member states. This planned full endorsement by the EU eclipsed the lukewarm IOSCO approval, and since then the EU has appeared to be the more influential body insofar as gaining acceptance for IFRS has been concerned. Indeed, the once-important IOSCO endorsement has become of little importance given subsequent developments, including the EU mandate and convergence efforts among several standard-setting bodies.

In July 2000, IASC members voted to abandon the organization's former structure, which was based on professional bodies, and adopt a new structure: beginning in 2001, standards would be set by a professional board, financed by voluntary contributions raised by a new oversight body.

THE CURRENT STRUCTURE

The formal structure put in place in 2000 has the IFRS Foundation, a Delaware corporation, as its keystone (this was previously known as the IASC Foundation). The Trustees of the IFRS Foundation have both the responsibility to raise funds needed to finance standard setting, and the responsibility of appointing members to the International Accounting Standards Board (IASB), the International Financial Reporting Interpretations Committee (IFRIC) and the Standards Advisory Council (SAC). The structure changed by incorporating the Monitoring Board in 2009, renaming and incorporating the SME Implementation Group in 2010 as follows:

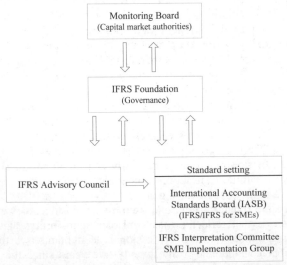

The Monitoring Board is responsible to ensure that the Trustees of the IFRS Foundation discharge their duties as defined by the IFRS Foundation Constitution and to approve the appointment or reappointment of Trustees. The Monitoring Board consists of the Emerging

Markets and Technical Committees of the International Organization of Securities Commissions (IOSCO), the European Commission, the Financial Services Agency of Japan (JFSA), and US Securities and Exchange Commission (SEC). The Basel Committee on Banking Supervision currently only participates as an observer.

The IFRS Foundation is governed by trustees and reports to the Monitoring Board. The IFRS Foundation has fundraising responsibilities and oversees the standard-setting work, the IFRS structure and strategy. It is also responsible for the review of the Constitution.

The IFRS Advisory Council (formerly the SAC) is the formal advisory body to the IASB and the Trustees of the IFRS Foundation. Members consist of user groups, preparers, financial analysts, academics, auditors, regulators, professional accounting bodies and investor groups.

The IASB is an independent body that is solely responsible for establishing International Financial Reporting Standards (IFRS), including IFRS for SMEs. The IASB also approves new interpretations.

The IFRS Interpretations Committee (IFRIC) is a committee comprised mostly of technical partners in audit firms but also includes preparers and users. IFRIC's function is to answer technical queries from constituents about how to interpret IFRS — in effect, filling in the cracks between different rules. In recent times it has also proposed modifications to standards to the IASB, in response to perceived operational difficulties or need to improve consistency. IFRIC liaises with the US Emerging Issues Task Force and similar bodies and standard setters, to try to preserve convergence at the level of interpretation.

Working relationships are set up with local standard setters who have adopted or converged with International Financial Reporting Standards (IFRS), or are in the process of adopting or converging with IFRS. The statement of working relationship sets out a range of activities that should be undertaken to facilitate the adoption and use of IFRS.

PROCESS OF IFRS STANDARD SETTING

The IASB has a formal due process which is set out in the *Preface to IFRS*, and *The Due Process Handbook of the IASB*. At a minimum, a proposed standard should be exposed for comment, and these comments should be reviewed before issuance of a final standard, with debates open to the public. However, this formal process is rounded out in practice, with wider consultation taking place on an informal basis.

The IASB's agenda is determined in various ways. Suggestions are made by the Trustees, the IFRS Advisory Council, liaison standard setters, the international audit firms, and others. These are debated by IASB and tentative conclusions are discussed with the various consultative bodies. The IASB also has a joint agenda committee with the FASB. Long-range projects are first put on the research agenda, which means that preliminary work is being done on collecting information about the problem and potential solutions. Projects can also arrive on the current agenda outside that route.

The agenda was largely driven in the years immediately after 2001 by the need to round out the legacy standards, to ensure that there would be a full range of standards for European companies moving to IFRS in 2005. Also, it was recognized that there was an urgent need to effect modifications to many standards in the name of convergence (e.g., acquisition accounting and goodwill) and to make needed improvements to other existing standards. These needs were largely met by mid-2004.

Once a project reaches the current agenda, the formal process is that the staff (a group of about 20 technical staff permanently employed by the IASB) drafts papers which are then discussed by IASB in open meetings. Following that debate, the staff rewrites the paper, or writes a new paper which is then debated at a subsequent meeting. In theory there is an internal process where the staff proposes solutions, and IASB either accepts or rejects them. In practice the process is more involved: sometimes (especially for projects such as financial instruments) individual Board members are delegated special responsibility for the project, and they discuss the problems regularly with the relevant staff, helping to build the papers that come to the Board. Equally, Board members may write or speak directly to the staff outside of the formal meeting process to indicate concerns about one thing or another.

The due process comprises six stages: (1) setting the agenda; (2) planning the project; (3) developing and publishing the discussion paper; (4) developing and publishing the Exposure Draft; (5) developing and publishing the standard and (6) the stages after the standard is issued. The process also includes discussion of Staff Papers outlining the principal issues and analysis of comments received on Discussion Papers and Exposure Drafts. Final draft standards are sometimes provided to certain individuals or entities for final comments before the final ballot.

Final ballots on the standard are carried out in secret, but otherwise the process is quite open, with outsiders able to consult project summaries on the IASB Web site and attend Board meetings if they wish. Of course, the informal exchanges between staff and Board on a day-to-day basis are not visible to the public, nor are the meetings where IASB takes strategic and administrative decisions.

The basic due process can be modified in different circumstances. The Board may decide not to issue Discussion Papers or to reissue Discussion Papers and Exposure Drafts.

The IASB also has regular public meetings with the Analyst Representative Group (ARG) and the Global Preparers Forum (GPF), among others. Special groups such as the Financial Crisis Advisory Group are set up from time to time. Formal working groups are established for certain major projects to provide additional practical input and expertise. Apart from these formal consultative processes, IASB also carries out field trials of some standards (as it recently did on performance reporting and insurance), where volunteer preparers apply the proposed new standards. The IASB may also hold some form of public consultation during the process, such as roundtable discussions. The IASB engages closely with stakeholders around the world such as investors, analysts, regulators, business leaders, accounting standard setters, and the accountancy profession.

CONVERGENCE: THE IASB AND FINANCIAL REPORTING IN THE US

Although IASC and FASB were created almost contemporaneously, FASB largely ignored IASB until the 1990s. It was only then that FASB became interested in IASC, when IASC was beginning to work with IOSCO, a body in which the SEC has always had a powerful voice. In effect, both the SEC and FASB were starting to consider the international financial reporting area, and IASC was also starting to take initiatives to encourage standard setters to meet together occasionally to debate technical issues of common interest.

IOSCO's efforts to create a single passport for secondary listings, and IASC's role as its standard setter, while intended to operate worldwide, would have the greatest practical significance for foreign issuers in terms of the US market. It was understood that if the SEC were to accept IFRS in place of US GAAP, there would be no need for a Form 20-F reconciliation, and access to the US capital markets by foreign registrants would be greatly facilitated. The SEC has therefore been a key factor in the later evolution of IASC. It encouraged IASC to build a relationship with IOSCO in 1987, and also observed that too many options for diverse accounting were available under IAS. SEC suggested that it would be more favorably inclined to consider acceptance of IAS (now IFRS) if some or all of these alternatives were reduced. Shortly after IASC restarted its IOSCO work in 1995, the SEC issued a statement (April 1996) to the effect that, to be acceptable, IFRS would need to satisfy the following three criteria:

1. It would need to establish a core set of standards that constituted a comprehensive basis of accounting;
2. The standards would need to be of high quality, and would enable investors to analyze performance meaningfully both across time periods and among different companies; and
3. The standards would have to be rigorously interpreted and applied, as otherwise comparability and transparency could not be achieved.

IASC's plan was predicated on its completion of a core set of standards, which would then be handed over to IOSCO, which in turn would ask its members for an evaluation, after which IOSCO would issue its verdict as to acceptability. It was against this backdrop that the SEC issued a "concept release" in 2000, that solicited comments regarding the acceptability of the core set of standards, and whether there appeared to be a sufficiently robust compliance and enforcement mechanism to ensure that standards were consistently and rigorously applied by preparers, whether auditors would ensure this, and whether stock exchange regulators would verify such compliance.

This last-named element remains beyond the control of IASB, and is within the domain of national compliance bodies or professional organizations in each jurisdiction. The IASC's Standards Interpretations Committee (SIC, which was later succeeded by IFRIC) was formed to help ensure uniform interpretation, and IFRIC has taken a number of initiatives to establish liaison channels with stock exchange regulators and national interpretations bodies—but the predominant responsibilities remain in the hands of the auditors, the audit oversight bodies, and the stock exchange oversight bodies.

The SEC's stance at the time was that it genuinely wanted to see IFRS used by foreign registrants, but that it preferred convergence (so that no reconciliation would be necessary) over the acceptance of IFRS as they were in 2000 without reconciliation. In the years since, the SEC has in many public pronouncements supported convergence and, as promised, waived reconciliations in 2008 for registrants fully complying with IFRS. Thus, for example, the SEC welcomed various proposed changes to US GAAP to converge with IFRS.

Relations between FASB and IASB have grown warmer since IASB was restructured, perhaps influenced by the growing awareness that IASB would assume a commanding position in the financial reporting standard-setting domain. The FASB had joined the IASB for informal meetings as long ago as the early 1990s, culminating in the creation of the G4+1 group of Anglophone standard setters (US, UK, Canada, Australia and New Zealand, with the IASC as an observer), in which FASB was an active participant. Perhaps the most significant event was when IASB and FASB signed the Norwalk Agreement in October 2002, which set out a program for the convergence of their respective sets of financial reporting standards. The organizations' staffs have worked together on a number of vital projects, including business combinations and revenue recognition, since the Agreement was signed and, later, supplemented by the 2006 and 2008 Memorandum of Understandings (MOU) between these bodies. The two boards have a joint agenda committee whose aim is to harmonize the timing with which the boards discuss the same subjects. The boards are also committed to meeting twice a year in joint session.

In June 2010 the Boards announced a modification to their convergence strategy, responding to concerns from some stakeholders regarding the volume of draft standards due for publication in close proximity. The strategy retained the June 2011 target date to complete those projects for which the need for improvement was the most urgent. In line with this strategy, the Boards completed the consolidation (including joint arrangements) and fair value measurement project before the June 2011 target date. The derecognition project was cancelled and only disclosure amendments were incorporated in the standard. Projects on financial instruments (impairment, hedging and offsetting), leases and revenue were extended to create significant time for reconsultation after comments were received. Standards on most of these are only expected in 2012. The Boards also decided to amend the timetable for projects that are important but less urgent. The projects affected are Financial Statement Presentation (the replacement of IAS 1 and IAS 7), Financial Instruments with Characteristics of Equity, Emissions Trading Schemes, Liabilities (IAS 37 amendments) and Income Taxes. The Boards do not expect to return to these topics until the June 2011 targeted projects are completed.

However, certain convergence problems remain, largely of the structural variety. FASB operates within a specific national legal framework, while IASB does not. Equally, both have what they term "inherited" GAAP (i.e., differences in approach that have a long history and are not easily resolved). FASB also has a tradition of issuing very detailed, prescriptive ("rules-based) standards that give bright-line accounting (and, consequently, audit) guidance, which are intended to make compliance control easier and remove uncertainties. Notwithstanding that detailed rules had been ardently sought by preparers and auditors alike for many decades, in the post-Enron world, after it became clear that some of these highly prescriptive rules had been abused, interest turned toward developing standards that would rely more on the expression of broad financial reporting objectives, with far less detailed instruction on how to achieve them ("principles-based" standards). This was seen as being superior to the US GAAP approach, which mandated an inevitably doomed effort to prescribe responses to every conceivable fact pattern to be confronted by preparers and auditors.

This exaggerated rules-based vs. principles-based dichotomy was invoked particularly following the frauds at US-based companies WorldCom and Enron, but before some of the more prominent European frauds, such as Parmalat (Italy) and Royal Ahold (the Netherlands) came to light, which would suggest that neither the use of US GAAP nor IFRS could protect against the perpetration of financial reporting frauds if auditors were derelict in the performance of their duties or even, on rare occasions, complicit in managements frauds. As an SEC study (which had been mandated by the Sarbanes-Oxley Act of 2002) into principles-based standards later observed, use of principles alone, without detailed guidance, reduces comparability. The litigious environment in the US also makes companies and auditors reluctant to step into areas where judgments have to be taken in uncertain conditions. The SEC's solution: "objectives-based" standards that are both soundly based on principles and inclusive of practical guidance.

Events in the mid- to late-2000s have served to accelerate the pressure for full convergence between US GAAP and IFRS. In fact, the US SEC's decision in late 2007 to waive reconciliation requirements for foreign registrants complying with "full IFRS" was a clear indicator that the outright adoption of IFRS in the US is on the horizon, and that the convergence process may be made essentially redundant if not actually irrelevant. The SEC has since granted qualifying US registrants (major players in industry segments, the majority of whose worldwide participants already report under IFRS) the limited right to begin reporting under IFRS in 2009, after which (in 2011) it has indicated it will determine the future path toward the supercession of US GAAP by IFRS.

In late 2008, the SEC proposed its so-called "roadmap" for a phased-in IFRS adoption, setting forth four milestones that, if met, could lead to wide-scale adoption beginning in 2014. Under the new leadership, which assumed office in 2009, the SEC may act with less urgency on this issue, and achievement of the "milestones"—which include a number of subjective measures such as improvement in standards and level of IFRS training and awareness among US accountants and auditors—leaves room for later balking at making the final commitment to IFRS. Notwithstanding these possible impediments to progress, the authors believe that there is an inexorable move toward universal adoption of IFRS, and that the leading academic and public accounting (auditing) organizations must, and will, take the necessary steps to ensure that this can move forward. For example, in the US the principal organization of academicians is actively working on standards for IFRS-based accounting curricula, and the main organization representing independent accountants is producing Web-based materials and live conferences to educate practitioners about IFRS matters.

While the anticipated further actions by the US SEC will only directly promote or require IFRS adoption by multinational and other larger, publicly held business entities, and later by even small, publicly held companies, in the longer run, even medium- and smaller-sized entities will probably opt for IFRS-based financial reporting. There are several reasons to predict this "trickle down" effect. First, because some involvement in international trade is increasingly a characteristic of all business operations, the need to communicate with customers, creditors, and potential partners or investors will serve to motivate "one language" financial reporting. Second, the notion of reporting under "second-class GAAP" rather than under the standards employed by larger competitors will eventually prove to be unappealing. And thirdly, IASB's issuance of a one-document comprehensive standard on financial reporting by entities having no public reporting responsibilities (IFRS for SMEs, discussed later in this chapter), coupled with formal recognition under US auditing standards that financial reporting rules established by IASB are a basis for an expression of an auditor's professional opinion may actually find enthusiastic support among smaller US reporting entities and their professional services providers, even absent immediate adoptions among publicly held companies.

In a March 2010 statement, the SEC stated that staff has been directed to develop a work plan to enhance both the understanding of the SEC's purpose and public transparency regarding the incorporation of IFRS in the US. The execution of this work plan and the completion of the projects in the MOU by 2011 will position the SEC to make a decision regarding such an incorporation of IFRS. However, if the SEC determines late 2011 or early 2012 to incorporate IFRS in the US, the first time that US issuers will report under IFRS is foreseen to be only in 2015 or 2016, thus extending the initial proposal to implement IFRS by 2014.

THE IASB AND EUROPE

Although France, Germany, the Netherlands and the UK were founding members of predecessor organization IASC and have remained heavily involved with IASB, the European Commission as such has generally had a fitful relationship with the international standard setter. The EC did not participate in any way until 1990, when it finally became an observer at Board meetings. It had had its own regional program of harmonization since the 1960s and in effect only officially abandoned this in 1995, when, in a policy paper, it recommended to member states that they seek to align their rules for consolidated financial statements on IFRS. Notwithstanding this, the Commission gave IASB a great boost when it announced in June 2000 that it wanted to require all listed companies throughout the EU to use IFRS beginning in 2005 as part of its initiative to build a single European financial market. This intention was made concrete with the approval of the IFRS Regulation in June 2002 by the European Council of Ministers (the supreme EU decision-making authority).

The EU decision was all the more welcome given that, to be effective in legal terms, IFRS have to be enshrined in EU statute law, creating a situation where the EU is in effect ratifying as laws the set of rules created by a small, self-appointed, private-sector body. This proved to be a delicate situation, which was revealed within a very short time to contain the seeds of unending disagreements, as politicians were being asked in effect to endorse something over which they had no control. They were soon being lobbied by corporate interests that had failed to effectively influence IASB directly, in order to achieve their objectives, which in some cases involved continued lack of transparency regarding certain types of transactions or economic effects, such as fair value changes affecting holding of financial instruments. The process of obtaining EU endorsement of IFRS was at the cost of exposing IASB to political pressures in much the same way that the US FASB has at times been the target of congressional manipulations (e.g., over stock-based compensation accounting rules in the mid-1990s, the derailing of which arguably contributed to the practices that led to various backdating abuse allegations made in more recent years).

The EU created an elaborate machinery to mediate its relations with IASB. It preferred to work with another private-sector body, created for the purpose, the European Financial Reporting Advisory Group (EFRAG), as the formal conduit for EU inputs to IASB. EFRAG was formed in 2001 by a collection of European representative organizations (for details see www.efrag.org), including the European Accounting Federation (FEE) and a European employer organization (UNICE). EFRAG in turn formed the small Technical Expert Group (TEG) that does the detailed work on IASB proposals. EFRAG consults widely within the EU, and particularly with national standard setters and the European Commission to canvass views on IASB proposals, and provides input to IASB. It responds formally to all discussion papers and Exposure Drafts.

At a second stage, when a final standard is issued, EFRAG is asked by the Commission to provide a report on the standard. This report is to state whether the standard has the requisite quality and is in conformity with European company law directives. The European Commission then asks another entity, the Accounting Regulation Committee (ARC), whether it wishes to endorse the standard. ARC consists of permanent representatives of the EU member state governments. It should normally only fail to endorse IFRS if it believes they are not in conformity with the overall framework of EU law, and should not take a strategic or policy view. However, the European Parliament also has the right to independently comment, if it so wishes. If ARC fails to endorse a standard, the European Commission may still ask the Council of Ministers to override that decision.

Experience has shown that the system suffers from a number of problems. First, although EFRAG is intended to enhance EU inputs to IASB, it may in fact isolate people from IASB, or at least increase the costs of making representations. For example, when IASB revealed its intention to issue a standard on stock options, it received nearly a hundred comment letters from US companies (who report under US GAAP, not IFRS), but only one from EFRAG, which in the early 2000s effectively represented about 90% of IASB's constituents. It is possible, however, that EFRAG is seen at IASB as being only a single respondent, and if so, that people who have made the effort to work through EFRAG feel underrepresented. In addition, EFRAG inevitably will present a distillation of views, so it is already filtering respondents' views before they even reach IASB. The only recourse is for respondents to make representations not only to EFRAG but also directly to IASB.

However, resistance to the financial instruments standards, IAS 32 and IAS 39, put the system under specific strain. These standards were already in existence when the European Commission announced its decision to adopt IFRS for European listed companies, and they had each been exhaustively debated before enactment. European adoption again exposed these particular standards to strenuous debate.

The first task of EFRAG and ARC was to endorse the existing standards of IASB. They did this—but excluded IAS 32 and 39 on the grounds that they were being extensively revised as part of IASB's then-ongoing *Improvements Project*.

During the exposure period of the improvements proposals—which exceptionally included roundtable meetings with constituents—the European Banking Federation, under particular pressure from French banks, lobbied IASB to modify the standard to permit special accounting for macrohedging. The IASB agreed to do this, even though that meant the issuance of another Exposure Draft and a further amendment to IAS 39 (which was finally issued in March 2004). The bankers did not like the terms of the amendment, and even as it was still under discussion, they appealed to the French president and persuaded him to intervene. He wrote to the European Commission in July 2003, saying that the financial instruments standards were likely to cause banks' reported earnings to be more volatile and would destabilize the European economy, and thus that the proposed standard should not be approved. He also argued that the Commission did not have sufficient input to the standard-setting process.

This drive to alter the requirements of IAS 39 was intensified when the European Central Bank complained in February 2004 that the "fair value option," introduced to IAS 39 as an improvement in final form in December 2003, could be used by banks to manipulate their *prudential ratios* (the capital to assets ratios used to evaluate bank safety), and asked IASB to limit the circumstances in which the option could be used. IASB agreed to do this, although this meant issuing another Exposure Draft and a further amendment to IAS 39 which was not finalized until mid-2005. When IASB debated the issue, it took a pragmatic line that no compromise of principle was involved, and that it was reasonable that the principal bank regulator of the Board's largest constituent by far should be accommodated. The fact that the European Central Bank had not raised these issues at the original Exposure Draft stage was not discussed, nor was the legitimacy of a constituent deciding unilaterally it wanted to change a rule that had just been approved. The Accounting Standards Board of Japan lodged a formal protest, and many other constituents were not pleased at this development.

Ultimately, ARC approved IAS 32 and IAS 39, but a "carve out" from IAS 39 was prescribed. Clearly the EU's involvement with IFRS is proving to be a mixed blessing for IASB, both exposing it to political pressures that are properly an issue for the Commission, not IASB, and putting its due process under stress. Some commentators speculated that the EU might even abandon IFRS, but this is not a realistic possibility, given the worldwide movement toward IFRS and the fact that the EU had already tried and rejected the regional standard-setting route.

A better observation is that this is merely part of a period of adjustment, with regulators and lobbyists both being uncertain as to how exactly the system does and should work, and both testing its limits, but with some *modus vivendi* evolving over time. However, it is severe distraction for IASB that financial instruments, arguably the area of greatest accounting controversy in the 1990s, is one that is still causing concern to the present date, in part exacerbated by the worldwide financial crisis of 2007-2009. Some believe that financial instruments accounting issues should have been fully resolved years ago, so that IASB could give its undivided attention to such crucial topics as revenue recognition, performance reporting and insurance contracts.

The EC decision to impose "carve-outs" has most recently had the result that the US SEC's historic decision to eliminate reconciliation to US GAAP for foreign private issuers has been restricted to those registrants that file financial statements that comply with "full IFRS" (which implies that those using "Euro-IFRS" and other national modifications of IFRS promulgated by the IASB will not be eligible for this benefit). Registrants using any deviation from pure IFRS, and those using any other national GAAP, will continue to be required to present a reconciliation to US GAAP. Over time, it can be assumed that this will add to the pressure to report under "full IFRS," and that even the EU may line up behind full and complete adherence to officially promulgated IFRS. In November 2009 the EFRAG decided to defer the endorsement of IFRS 9, although in principle they agree with the management approach adopted in IFRS 9. They believe that more time should be taken to consider the outcome of other sections of the financial instrument project and that the sections should be endorsed as a package.

In June 2010 the EFRAG issued a new *Strategy for European Proactive Financial Reporting Activities*. This strategy of proactive activities enhances EFRAG's role in influencing standard setting by early engagement with European constituents to provide effective and timely input to the IASB's work. This demonstrates that EFRAG is positively committed to the standard-setting process.

IFRS FOR SMES

The *IFRS for SMEs* was issued by the IASB in July 2009 to reduce the financial reporting burden of small and medium-sized entities. In the process, many of the recognition and measurement principles in full IFRS have been simplified, disclosures significantly reduced and topics not relevant to SMEs omitted. Appendix B attached to this chapter provides discussion of these differences.

The standard is a stand-alone document with only one optional cross-reference to full IFRS for financial instruments, which provides a choice regarding the treatment of financial instruments. The standard is appropriate for general-purpose financial statements. General-purpose financial statements are directed towards the common information needs of a wide range of users, for example, shareholders, creditors, employees, and the public at large.

IFRS for SMEs is intended for entities that do not have public accountability. An entity has public accountability—and therefore would not be permitted to use the full IFRS—if it meets either of the following conditions: (1) it has issued debt or equity securities in a public market; or (2) it holds assets in a fiduciary capacity, as its primary purpose of business, for a broad group of outsiders. The latter category of entity would include banks, insurance companies, securities broker/dealers, pension funds, mutual funds, and investment banks.

The responsibility lies with each jurisdiction to determine which entities should apply the *IFRS for SMEs*. Comprehensive training material is in the process of being developed for SMEs by the IFRS Foundation and a SME Implementation Group is set up to deal with financial reporting issues regarding SMEs. However, the IASB has indicated that the *IFRS for SMEs* will only be updated every three years.

The application of the *IFRS for SMEs* standard has not been covered in this publication. However, there is a detailed accounting manual available that addresses the requirements, application, and interpretation of this standard—*Applying IFRS for SMEs* (available from Wiley).

Appendix A:
Current International Financial Reporting Standards (IAS/IFRS) and Interpretations (SIC/IFRIC)

IAS 1	Presentation of Financial Statements
IAS 2	Inventories
IAS 7	Statement of Cash Flows
IAS 8	Accounting Policies, Changes in Accounting Estimates and Errors
IAS 10	Events After the Reporting Period
IAS 11	Construction Contracts
IAS 12	Income Taxes
IAS 16	Property, Plant, and Equipment
IAS 17	Accounting for Leases
IAS 18	Revenue
IAS 19	Employee Benefits
IAS 20	Accounting for Government Grants and Disclosure of Government Assistance
IAS 21	The Effects of Changes in Foreign Exchange Rates
IAS 23	Borrowing Costs
IAS 24	Related-Party Disclosures
IAS 26	Accounting and Reporting by Retirement Benefit Plans
IAS 27	Separate Financial Statements (Consolidation part replaced by IFRS 10, *Consolidated Financial Statements*, effective 2013)
IAS 28	Investments in Associates and Joint Ventures (Joint ventures included effective 2013)
IAS 29	Financial Reporting in Hyperinflationary Economies
IAS 31	Financial Reporting of Interests in Joint Ventures (replaced by IFRS 11 and IAS 28, effective 2013)
IAS 32	Financial Instruments: Presentation
IAS 33	Earnings Per Share
IAS 34	Interim Financial Reporting
IAS 36	Impairments of Assets
IAS 37	Provisions, Contingent Liabilities, and Contingent Assets
IAS 38	Intangible Assets
IAS 39	Financial Instruments: Recognition and Measurement

IAS 40   Investment Property

IAS 41   Agriculture

IFRS 1   First-Time Adoption of IFRS

IFRS 2   Share-Based Payment

IFRS 3   Business Combinations

IFRS 4   Insurance Contracts

IFRS 5   Noncurrent Assets Held for Sale and Discontinued Operations

IFRS 6   Exploration for and Evaluation of Mineral Resources

IFRS 7   Financial Instruments: Disclosures

IFRS 8   Operating Segments

IFRS 9   Financial Instruments

IFRS 10   Consolidated Financial Statements

IFRS 11   Joint Arrangements

IFRS 12   Disclosure of Interest in Other Entities

IFRS 13   Fair Value Measurement

SIC 7   Introduction of the Euro

SIC 10   Government Assistance—No Specific Relation to Operating Activities

SIC 12   Consolidation—Special-Purpose Entities (replaced by IFRS 10, effective 2013)

SIC 13   Jointly Controlled Entities—Nonmonetary Contributions by Venturers (replaced by IAS 28, effective 2013)

SIC 15   Operating Leases—Incentives

SIC 25   Income Taxes—Changes in the Tax Status of an Enterprise or Its Shareholders

SIC 27   Evaluating the Substance of Transactions Involving the Legal Form of a Lease

SIC 29   Disclosure—Service Concession Arrangements

SIC 31   Revenue—Barter Transactions Involving Advertising Services

SIC 32   Intangible Assets—Web Site Costs

IFRIC 1   Changes in Existing Decommissioning, Restoration and Similar Liabilities

IFRIC 2   Members' Shares in Cooperative Entities and Similar Instruments

IFRIC 4   Determining Whether an Arrangement Contains a Lease

IFRIC 5   Rights to Interests Arising from Decommissioning, Restoration and Environmental Rehabilitation Funds

IFRIC 6   Liabilities Arising from Participating in a Specific Market—Waste Electrical and Electronic Equipment

IFRIC 7   Applying the Restatement Approach under IAS 29, *Financial Reporting in Hyperinflationary Economies*

IFRIC 10   Interim Financial Reporting and Impairment

IFRIC 11   IFRS 2: Group and Treasury Share Transactions

IFRIC 12   Service Concession Arrangements

IFRIC 13   Customer Loyalty Programs

IFRIC 14   IAS 19—The Limit on a Defined Benefit Asset, Minimum Funding Requirements, and Their Interaction

IFRIC 15   Agreements for the Construction of Real Estate

IFRIC 16   Hedges of a Net Investment in a Foreign Operation

IFRIC 17   Distributions of Noncash Assets to Owners

IFRIC 18   Transfer of Assets from Customers

IFRIC 19   Extinguishing Financial Liabilities with Equity Instruments

Appendix B:
Projects Completed the Previous Year (October 2010 to September 2011)

Project	Issue date	Nature	Effective date
Derecognition – Disclosures	October 2010	Improve disclosure requirements in IFRS 7 of transferred financial assets	July 1, 2011
IFRS 9, Financial Instruments (Part II)	October 2010	Financial liabilities elected to be measured at fair value	January 1, 2013
IFRS 1 Severe Hyperinflation	December 2010	Resumes presenting financial statements in accordance with IFRS after period unable to comply with IFRS	January 1, 2013
Management Commentary	December 2010	A broad, nonbinding framework for the presentation of narrative reporting to accompany financial statements	Immediately
Deferred Tax: Recovery of Underlying Assets	December 2010	Practical solution to the rate applicable to the fair value model in IAS 40, *Investment Property*, when calculating deferred tax under IAS 12	July 1, 2011
IFRS 10, *Consolidated Financial Statements*	May 2011	A single consolidation model that identifies control as the basis for consolidation for all types of entities	January 1, 2013
IFRS 11, *Joint Arrangements*	May 2011	Establishes principles for the financial reporting by parties to a joint arrangement	January 1, 2013
IFRS 12, *Disclosure of Interests in Other Entities.*	May 2011	Combines, enhances, and replaces the disclosure requirements for subsidiaries, joint arrangements, associates and unconsolidated structured entities	January 1, 2013
IAS 27, *Separate Financial Statements*	May 2011	Deals only with separate financial statements	January 1, 2013

IAS 28, *Investments in Associates and Joint Ventures*	May 2011	Recognition and measurement model for associates and joint ventures	January 1, 2013
IFRS 13, *Fair Value Measurement*	May 2011	Defines fair value, sets out a framework for measuring fair value and related disclosures	January 1,2013
Post-employment Benefits	June 2011	Improve the recognition and disclosure requirements for defined benefit plans under IAS 19	July 1, 2012.
Financial Statement Presentation	June 2011	Improve presentation of components of other comprehensive income under IAS 1	July 1,2012

Appendix C:
IFRS for SMEs

A long-standing debate among professional accountants, users and preparers—between those advocating for some form of simplified financial reporting standards for (variously defined) smaller or nonpublicly responsible entities, and those arguing that all reporting entities purporting to adhere to officially mandated accounting standards do so with absolute faithfulness—has now been resolved. On July 9, 2009, IASB published *International Financial Reporting Standards (IFRS) for Small and Medium-Sized Entities (IFRS for SMEs)*. Notwithstanding the name, it is actually intended as an optional, somewhat simplified and choice-limited comprehensive financial reporting standard for enterprises not having public accountability.

A parallel debate raged in the UK, the US, and in other national GAAP domains for decades. In the US a number of inchoate proposals have been offered over at least the past thirty years, but no serious proposal was forthcoming, largely because the idea of differential recognition or measurement standards for smaller entities was seen as conceptually unappealing, leaving the relatively trivial issue of differential disclosures as the focus of discussion. Apart from a limited number of disclosure topics, such as segment results and earnings per share, and some pension obligation details, this proved to not be a very productive line of inquiry, and no sweeping changes were ever adopted or even proposed.

In the UK, the story was different. A single, comprehensive standard, *Financial Reporting Standards for Smaller Entities* (FRSSE), was successfully implemented over a decade ago, and then revised several times, employing a periodic updating strategy that IASB now appears likely to emulate. Rather than impose different recognition or measurement concepts on smaller entities, the approach taken, in the main, was to slim down the standards, eliminate much of the background and illustrative materials, and in some cases narrow or eliminate the alternative methods that users of full UK GAAP could elect to apply, with some concomitant simplifications to informative disclosures. Since this was deemed to have been successful in the UK, IASB determined to emulate it, beginning with a Discussion Paper in 2004, and continuing through an early-2007 Exposure Draft and a final standard in mid-2009.

In August 2009 the UK Accounting Standards Board (ASB) issued a consultation paper to adopt *IFRS for SMEs* in the UK. Good support was received to adopt *IFRS for SMEs* as a second-tier standard. FRSSE should be retained as an interim measure for third-tier standard. The next step for the ASB is to develop an Exposure Draft outlining the recommendations for the future of UK GAAP.

The enthusiasm and support that was shown for the *IFRS for SMEs* project from national accounting standard setters throughout the world stemmed mostly from the widely acknowledged complexity of the full body of IFRS, and from the different statutory requirements for financial reporting in many countries, which in many instances demands that audited financial statements, without any qualifications, be submitted to tax or other authorities. For example, in the European Union about 7,000 listed companies were implementing IFRS in 2005, but more than 5 million SMEs are required to prepare their financial statements in accordance with various national GAAP, resulting in lack of comparability across this sector of financial reporting entities. Reportedly, more than 50 different sets of standards govern private reporting in the 27 EU nations. EFRAG has not decided whether the *IFRS for SMEs* should be endorsed in Europe, although most countries have responded positively to such an implementation.

It had long been asserted, although often without solid evidence, that the complexity of the full body of IFRS (and, even more so, of full US GAAP) imposes a high and unwelcome cost on implementing and applying these standards, and that many or most external users of the resulting financial statements did not see value commensurate with the cost and effort associated with their preparation. Whether or not this is true, many now believe that *IFRS for SMEs* will provide companies with an easier transition to the full IFRS, thus serving to accomplish, in the longer term, a more thorough and broadly based move toward universal reporting under a single set of financial reporting standards.

Opponents of a separate set of standards for SMEs believe that all entities should follow the same basic set of accounting principles for the preparation of general-purpose financial statements, whether that set of standards be IFRS or US GAAP. Some have noted that complexity in accounting is merely a symptom—the inevitable result of the ever-increasing complexity of transactional structures, such as the widespread use of "engineered" financial products. Based on observations of the difficulties faced by companies implementing and applying the full IFRS, others have concluded that the problem is not that SMEs need simpler accounting, but that all reporting entities would benefit from reporting requirements that are less complex and more principles-based. Since this latter goal seemed to be perpetually unattainable, momentum ultimately shifted in favor of having a simplified stand-alone standard for either smaller or nonpublic companies. *IFRS for SMEs*, available for use by non-publicly accountable entities of any size, is the solution that has been rendered by IASB to this chronic problem.

Because the IASB lacks the power to require any company to use its standards, the adoption of *IFRS for SMEs* is a matter for each country to decide. The issue must be resolved by a country's government legislators and regulators, or by an independent standards setter, or by a professional accountancy body. Each country will need to establish criteria to determine eligibility of reporting entities seeking to qualify under this new standard as a "small or medium-sized" entity.

Definition of SMEs

IFRS for SMEs is intended for entities that do not have public accountability. An entity has public accountability—and therefore would not be permitted to use the full IFRS—if it meets either of the following conditions: (1) it has issued debt or equity securities in a public market; or (2) it holds assets in a fiduciary capacity, as its primary purpose of business, for a broad group of outsiders. The latter category of entity would include banks, insurance companies, securities broker/dealers, pension funds, mutual funds, and investment banks. The standard does not impose a size test in defining SMEs, notwithstanding the nomenclature used.

The standard also states that the standard is intended for entities that publish financial statements for external users; as with IFRS and US GAAP, in other words, the standard is not intended to govern internal or managerial reporting (although there is nothing to prevent such reporting from fully conforming to such standards).

A subsidiary of an entity that employs full IFRS, or an entity that is part of a consolidated entity that reports in compliance with IFRS may report, on a stand-alone basis, in accordance with *IFRS for SMEs*, if the financial statements are so identified, and if the subsidiary does not have public accountability itself. If this is done, that standard must be fully complied with, which could mean that the subsidiary's stand-alone financial statements would differ from how they are presented within the parent's consolidated financial statements; for example, in the subsidiary's financial statements prepared in accordance with *IFRS for SMEs*, borrowing costs incurred in connection with construction of long-lived assets would be expensed as incurred, but those same borrowing costs would be capitalized in the consolidated financial statements, since IAS 23 as most recently revised no longer provides the option of immediate expensing. In the authors' view, this would not be optimal financial reporting, and the goals of consistency and comparability would be better served if the stand-alone financial statements of the subsidiary also were based on full IFRS.

IFRS for SMEs Is a Complete, Self-Contained Set of Requirements

IFRS for SMEs is a complete and comprehensive standard, and accordingly contains much or most of the vital guidance provided by the full IFRS. For example, it defines the qualities that are needed for IFRS-compliant financial reporting (reliability, understandability, et al.), the elements of financial statements (assets, liabilities, et al.), the required minimum captions in the required full set of financial statements, the mandate for comparative reporting, and so forth. There is no need for an entity reporting under this standard to refer elsewhere (other than for guidance in IAS 39, discussed below), and indeed it would be improper to do so.

An entity having no public accountability that elects to report in conformity with *IFRS for SMEs* must make an "explicit and unreserved" declaration to that effect in the notes to the financial statements. As with a representation that the financial statements comply with (full) IFRS, if this representation is made, the entity must comply fully with all relevant requirements in the standard(s).

Many options under full IFRS remain under *IFRS for SMEs*. For example, a single statement of comprehensive income can be presented, with profit or loss being an intermediate step in the derivation of the period's comprehensive income or loss, or alternatively a separate statement of income can be displayed, with profit or loss (the "bottom line" in that statement) then being the opening item in the separate statement of comprehensive income. Likewise, most of the mandates under full IFRS, such as the need to consolidate special-purpose entities that are controlled by the reporting entity, also exist under *IFRS for SMEs*.

Modifications of Full IFRS Made for *IFRS for SMEs*

Compared to the full IFRS, the aggregate length of the standards, in terms of number of words, has been reduced by more than 90%. This was achieved by eliminating topics deemed to not be generally relevant to SMEs, by eliminating certain choices of accounting treatments, and by simplifying methods for recognition and measurement. These three sets of modifications to the content of the full IFRS, which are discussed below, respond to both the perceived needs of users of SMEs' financial statements and to cost-benefit concerns. According to the IASB, the set of standards in the *IFRS for SMEs* will be suitable for a typical enterprise having 50 employees, and will also be valid for so-called microentities having only a single or a few employees. However, no size limits are stipulated in the standard, and thus even very large entities could conceivably elect to apply *IFRS for SMEs*, assuming they have no public accountability as defined in the standard, and that no objections are raised by their various other stakeholders, such as lenders, customers, vendors, or joint venture partners.

Omitted topics. Certain topics covered in the full IFRS were viewed as not being relevant to typical SMEs (e.g., rules pertaining to transactions that were thought to be unlikely to occur in an SME context), and have accordingly been omitted from the standard. This leaves open the question of whether SMEs could optionally seek expanded guidance in the full IFRS. Originally, when the Exposure Draft of *IFRS for SMEs* was released, cross-references to the full IFRS were retained, so that SMEs would not be precluded from applying any of the financial reporting standards and methods found in IFRS, essentially making the *IFRS for SMEs* standard entirely optional on a component-by-component basis. However, in the final *IFRS for SMEs* standard all of these cross-references have been removed, with the exception of a reference to IAS 39, *Financial Instruments: Recognition and Measurement*, thus making *IFRS for SMEs* a fully stand-alone document, not to be used in conjunction with the full IFRS. An entity that would qualify for use of *IFRS for SMEs* must therefore make a decision to use full IFRS or *IFRS for SMEs* exclusively.

Topics addressed in the full IFRS that are entirely omitted from the IFRS for SME standard are as follows:

- Earnings per share;
- Interim reporting;
- Segment reporting;
- Special accounting for assets held for sale;
- Insurance (since, because of public accountability, such entities would be precluded from using *IFRS for SMEs* in any event).

Thus, for example, if a reporting entity concluded that its stakeholders wanted presentation of segment reporting information, and the entity's management wished to provide that to them, it would elect to prepare financial statements in conformity with the full set of IFRS, eschewing use of *IFRS for SMEs*.

Only the simpler option included. Where full IFRS provide an accounting policy choice, generally only the simpler option is included in *IFRS for SMEs*. SMEs will not be permitted to employ the other option(s) provided by the full IFRS, as had been envisioned by the Exposure Draft that preceded this standard, as all cross-references to the full IFRS have been eliminated.

The simpler options selected for inclusion in *IFRS for SMEs* are as follows, with the excluded alternatives noted:

- For investment property, measurement is driven by circumstances rather than a choice between the cost and fair value models, both of which are permitted under IAS 40, *Investment Property*. Under provisions of *IFRS for SMEs*, if the fair value of investment property can be measured reliably without undue cost or effort, the fair value model must be used. Otherwise, the cost method is required.
- Use of the cost-amortization-impairment model for property, plant, and equipment and intangibles is required; the revaluation model set forth by IAS 16, *Property, Plant, and Equipment*, and IAS 38, *Intangible Assets*, is not allowed.
- Immediate expensing of borrowing costs is required; the capitalization model stipulated under revised IAS 23 is not deemed appropriate for SMEs.
- Jointly controlled entities cannot be accounted for under the proportionate consolidation method under *IFRS for SMEs*, but can be under full IFRS as they presently exist. *IFRS for SMEs* does permit the use of the fair-value-through-earnings method as well as the equity method, and even the cost method can be used when it is not possible to obtain price or value data.
- Entities electing to employ *IFRS for SMEs* are required to expense development costs as they are incurred, together with all research costs. Full IFRS necessitates making a distinction between research and development costs, with the former expensed and the latter capitalized and then amortized over an appropriate period receiving economic benefits.

It should be noted that the Exposure Draft that preceded *IFRS for SMEs* would have required that the direct method for the presentation of operating cash flows be used, to the exclusion of the less desirable, but vastly more popular, indirect method. The final standard has retreated from this position and permits both methods, so it includes necessary guidance on application of the indirect method, which was absent from the draft.

All references to full IFRS found in the draft of this standard have been eliminated, except for the reference to IAS 39, which may be used, optionally, by entities reporting under *IFRS for SMEs*. The general expectation is that few reporting entities will opt to do this, since the enormous complexity of that standard was a primary impetus to the development of the streamlined *IFRS for SMEs*.

It is inevitable that some financial accounting or reporting situations will arise for which *IFRS for SMEs* itself will not provide complete guidance. The standard provides a hierarchy, of sorts, of additional literature upon which reliance could be placed, in the absence of definitive rules contained in *IFRS for SMEs*. First, the requirements and guidance that is set forth for highly similar or closely related circumstances would be consulted within *IFRS for SMEs*. Second, the *Concepts and Pervasive Principles* section (Section 2) of the standard would be consulted, in the hopes that definitions, recognition criteria, and measurement concepts (e.g., for assets, revenues) would provide the preparer with sufficient guidance to reason out a valid solution. Third and last, full IFRS is identified explicitly as a source of instruction. Although reference to US (or other) GAAP is not suggested as a tactic, since full IFRS permits preparers to consider the requirements of national GAAP, if based on a framework similar to full IFRS, this omission may not be fully dispositive.

Recognition and measurement simplifications. For purposes of *IFRS for SMEs*, IASB has made significant simplifications to the recognition and measurement principles included in full IFRS. Examples of the simplifications to the recognition and measurement principles found in IFRS are as follows:

1. Financial instruments:

   a. *Classification of financial instruments.* Only two categories for financial assets (cost or amortized cost, and fair value through profit or loss) are provided, rather than the four found in full IFRS. Because the available-for-sale and held-to-maturity classifications under IAS 39 are not available, there will be no need to deal with all of the "intent-driven" held-to-maturity rules, or related "tainting" concerns, with no need for an option to recognize changes in value of available-for-sale securities in current profit or loss instead of as an item of other comprehensive income.

   (1) *IFRS for SMEs* requires an amortized cost model for most debt instruments, using the effective interest rate as of initial recognition. The effective rate should consider all contractual terms, such as prepayment options. Investments in nonconvertible and nonputtable preference shares and nonputtable ordinary shares that are publicly traded or whose fair value can otherwise be measured reliably are to be measured at fair value with changes in value reported in current earnings. Most other basic financial instruments are to be reported at cost less any impairment recognized. Impairment or uncollectibility must always be assessed, and, if identified, recognized immediately in profit or loss; recoveries to the extent of losses previously taken are also recognized in profit or loss.

   (2) For more complex financial instruments (such as derivatives), fair value through profit or loss is generally the applicable measurement method, with

cost less impairment being prescribed for those instruments (such as equity instruments lacking an objectively determinable fair value) for which fair value cannot be ascertained.

(3) Assets that would generally not meet the criteria as being basic financial instruments include (a) asset-backed securities, such as collateralized mortgage obligations, repurchase agreements and securitized packages of receivables; (b) options, rights, warrants, futures contracts, forward contracts and interest rate swaps that can be settled in cash or by exchanging another financial instrument; (c) financial instruments that qualify and are designated as hedging instruments in accordance with the requirements in the standard; (d) commitments to make a loan to another entity; and (e) commitments to receive a loan if the commitment can be net settled in cash. Such instruments would include (a) an investment in another entity's equity instruments other than nonconvertible preference shares and nonputtable ordinary and preference shares; (b) an interest rate swap that returns a cash flow that is positive or negative, or a forward commitment to purchase a commodity or financial instrument that is capable of being cash-settled and that, on settlement, could have positive or negative cash flow: (c) options and forward contracts, because returns to the holder are not fixed; (d) investments in convertible debt, because the return to the holder can vary with the price of the issuer's equity shares rather than just with market interest rates; and (e) a loan receivable from a third party that gives the third party the right or obligation to prepay if the applicable taxation or accounting requirements change.

b. *Derecognition.* In general, the principle to be applied is that, if the transferor retains any significant risks or rewards of ownership, derecognition is not permitted, although if full control over the asset is transferred, derecognition is valid even if some very limited risks or rewards are retained. The complex "pass-through testing" and "control retention testing" of IAS 39 thus can be omitted, unless full IAS 39 is optionally elected by the reporting entity. For financial liabilities, derecognition is permitted only when the obligation is discharged, cancelled, or expires.

c. *Simplified hedge accounting.* Much more simplified hedge accounting and less strict requirements for periodic recognition and measurement of hedge effectiveness are specified than those set forth by IAS 39.

d. *Embedded Derivatives.* No separate accounting for embedded derivatives is required.

(1) *Goodwill impairment*: An indicator approach has been adopted to supersede the mandatory annual impairment calculations in IFRS 3, *Business Combinations*. Additionally, goodwill and other indefinite-lived assets are considered to have finite lives, thus reducing the difficulty of assessing impairment.

(2) *All research and development costs are expensed* as incurred (IAS 38 requires capitalization after commercial viability has been assessed).

(3) *The cost method or fair value through profit or loss of accounting for associates and joint ventures* may be used (rather than the equity method or proportionate consolidation).

(4) *Simplified accounting for deferred taxes*: The "temporary difference approach" for recognition of deferred taxes under IAS 12, *Income Taxes*, is al-

lowed with a minor modification. Current and deferred taxes are required to be measured initially at the rate applicable to undistributed profits, with adjustment in subsequent periods if the profits are distributed.

(5) *Less use of fair value for agriculture* (being required only if fair value is readily determinable without undue cost or effort).

(6) *Defined benefit plans*. Two of the four options available under IAS 19, *Employee Benefits*, are allowed, that is, to recognize actuarial gains and losses in full in profit and loss when they occur, or to recognize these in full directly in other comprehensive income when they occur. The complex "corridor approach" has been deleted under *IFRS for SMEs*.

(7) *Share-based payment*: Equity-settled share-based payments should always be recognized as an expense and the expense should be measured on the basis of observable market prices, if available. When there is a choice of settlement, the entity should account for the transaction as a cash-settled transaction, except under certain circumstances.

(8) *Finance leases*: A simplified measurement of lessee's rights and obligations is prescribed.

(9) *First-time adoption*. Less prior period data would have to be restated than under IFRS 1, *First-time Adoption of International Financial Reporting Standards*. An impracticability exemption has also been included.

Because the default measurement of financial instruments would be fair value through profit and loss under *IFRS for SMEs*, some SMEs may actually be required to apply more fair value measurements than do entities reporting under full IFRS.

Disclosure Requirements under *IFRS for SMEs*

There are indeed certain reductions in disclosure requirements under *IFRS for SMEs* vis-à-vis full IFRS, but these are relatively minor and alone would not drive a decision to adopt this standard. Furthermore, key stakeholders, such as banks, often prescribe supplemental disclosures (e.g., major contracts, compensation agreements) that transcend what is required under IFRS, and this would likely continue to be true under *IFRS for SMEs*.

Maintenance of the *IFRS for SMEs*

SMEs have expressed concerns not only over the complexity of IFRS, but also about the frequency of changes to standards. To respond to these issues, IASB intends to update *IFRS for SMEs* approximately once every three years via an "omnibus" standard, with the expectation that any new requirements would not have mandatory application dates sooner than one year from issuance. Users are thus being assured of having a moderately stable platform of requirements.

SME Implementation Group

The mission of the SME Implementation Group (SMEIG) is to support the international adoption of the *IFRS for SMEs* and monitor its implementation. The SMEIG has two main responsibilities:

- Consider implementation questions raised by users of the *IFRS for SMEs*, and develop proposed guidance in the form of questions and answers (Q&As) that would be made publicly available. The Q&As are intended to be non-mandatory guidance.
- Consider, and make recommendations to the IASB on the need to amend the *IFRS for SMEs*.

To date one Q&A has been issued on the use of the *IFRS for SMEs* in a parent's separate financial statements.

Implications of the *IFRS for SMEs*

IFRS for SMEs is a significant development that may have real impact on the future accounting and auditing standards issued by organizations participating in the standard-setting process.

On March 6, 2007, the FASB and the AICPA announced that the newly established Private Company Financial Reporting Committee (PCFRC) will address the financial reporting needs of private companies and of the users of their financial statements. The primary objective of PCFRC will be to help the FASB determine whether and where there should be specific differences in prospective and existing accounting standards for private companies.

In many Continental European countries a close link exists between the statutory financial statements and the results reported for income tax purposes. The successful implementation of SME Standards will require breaking the traditional bond between the financial statements and the income tax return, and may well trigger a need to amend company laws.

Since it is imperative that international convergence of accounting standards be accompanied by convergence of audit standards, differential accounting for SMEs will affect regulators such as the Public Company Accounting Oversight Board (PCAOB) and the SEC. *IFRS for SMEs* may be a welcome relief for auditors as it will decrease the inherent risk that results from the numerous choices and judgment required by management when utilizing the full version of IFRS. The success of *IFRS for SMEs* will depend on the extent to which users, preparers and their auditors believe the standards meet their needs.

2 CONCEPTUAL FRAMEWORK

INTRODUCTION

The IASB inherited the IASC's *Framework for the Preparation and Presentation of Financial Statements* that was issued in July 1998. Like the other current conceptual frameworks among Anglo-Saxon standard setters, this derives mainly from the US conceptual framework.

IASB and FASB have been, since 2005, revisiting their respective conceptual frameworks to build on them by refining and updating them and developing them into a common framework that both can use in developing accounting standards. The objective of the conceptual framework project is to create a sound foundation for future accounting standards that are principles-based, internally consistent, and internationally converged. The new framework builds on existing IASB and FASB frameworks. The IASB *Framework* is, for instance, relatively silent on measurement issues. The three paragraphs that address this matter merely mention that several different measurement bases are available and that historical cost is the most common.

The Boards completed Phase A of the new Conceptual Framework, the *Objectives and Qualitative Characteristics,* in September 2010. Both the Boards will amend sections of their conceptual frameworks as they complete individual phases of the project. The IASB issued a new framework, *Conceptual Framework for Financial Reporting 2010,* containing the two new chapters and the rest of the previous framework that was not adjusted. FASB issued Concepts Statement 8 to replace Concepts Statements 1 and 2. This chapter provides a review of the new framework issued in September 2010, the future phases of the framework project and IFRS Practice Statement Management Commentary that was issued in December 2010.

CONCEPTUAL FRAMEWORK FOR FINANCIAL REPORTING 2010

Purpose and Status

The purpose of the conceptual framework is to set out the concepts that underlie the preparation and presentation of financial statements. The preparation of financial statements is based on estimates, judgments and models rather than exact depictions. The conceptual framework provides the concepts on which these uncertainties are based.

The main aim is therefore to help the IASB preparing new standards and reviewing existing standards. The conceptual framework also helps national standard-setters, preparers, auditors, users and others interested in IFRS in completing their tasks. The conceptual framework is, however, not regarded as an IFRS and can therefore not override any IFRS although there might be potential conflicts. The IASB believes that over time any such conflicts will be removed.

The Accounting Model

The introduction to the conceptual framework states that accounting statements are most commonly prepared in accordance with an accounting model based on recoverable historical cost and the nominal financial capital maintenance concept. Other models and concepts may be more appropriate but there is currently no consensus for change. The conceptual framework is prepared to be applicable to a wide range of accounting models and concepts of capital and capital maintenance. It is envisaged that the objective and qualitative characteristics in the conceptual framework will be used to make the appropriate decisions.

The Objective of General Purpose Financial Statements

The objective of general-purpose financial statements in the conceptual framework is defined as follows:

> The objective of general-purpose financial reporting is to provide financial information about the reporting entity that is useful to existing and potential investors, lenders, and other creditors in making decisions about providing resources to the entity.

The objective confirms the decision-useful orientation on which financial reporting is based. It is clearly stated that financial reporting does not provide information regarding the value of a reporting entity, but assists in making such valuations. The information needs of investors, lenders, and other creditors are the main focus. They are the primary users since they cannot require direct information from the reporting entity. They make decisions regarding the purchase or sale of equity and debt instruments or to provide finance to the entity.

The conceptual framework holds that users need to evaluate the prospects for future net cash inflows to an entity. To assess these net inflows information is needed of an entity's resources, claims to those resources, and the ability of management and governing board to discharge their responsibility to use the resources. Assessing stewardship is thus included in the ability of users to assess the net cash flows of an entity.

General-purpose financial statements provide information about the financial position of an entity, its resources, and claims against the resources. The financial position is affected by the economic resources controlled by the entity, its financial structure, its liquidity and solvency, and its capacity to adapt to changes in the environment in which it operates. Information is provided about the strengths and weaknesses of an entity and its ability to acquire finance.

Changes in an entity's resources and claims are a result of an entity's financial performance and are derived from other transactions such as issuing debt and equity instruments. Financial performance is assessed both through the process of accrual accounting and changes in cash flows. This helps users to understand the return on the resources of an entity and how well management has discharge their stewardship responsibilities. Both these changes and the implications of these changes reflected in the historical information help to assess future performance.

Qualitative Characteristics of Useful Financial Information

The qualitative characteristics identify the information that is most useful in financial reporting. Financial reporting includes information in financial statements and financial information that is provided by other means. The qualitative characteristics are divided into fundamental qualitative characteristics and enhancing qualitative characteristics. The fundamental qualitative characteristics are relevance and faithful representation. The enhancing qualitative characteristics are comparability, verifiability, timeliness, and understandability.

No hierarchy of applying the qualitative characteristics is determined. The application is, however, a process. The fundamental characteristics are applied by following a three-step process. Identify the economic phenomenon that has a potential to be useful. Then identify the type of information regarding the phenomenon that is most relevant that could be faithfully represented. Thirdly, determine whether the information is available and could be faithfully represented. After that the enhancing characteristics are applied to confirm or enhance the quality of the information. The different qualitative characteristics are explained as follows:

Relevant financial information is capable of making a difference in decision making. Information is capable of making a difference if it has predictive value, confirmatory value or both. Financial information has predictive value if it can be used as input in the process to predict future outcomes, and has confirmatory value if it provides feedback about previous evaluations. Materiality is included in relevance. Information is material if omitting it or misstating it could influence the decisions of users.

Faithful representation faithfully represents the phenomena it purports to represent. It includes three characteristics: complete, neutral, and free from error. A complete depiction includes all information needed to understand the phenomena. A neutral depiction is without bias. Free from error means that there are no errors or omissions in the description of the phenomena and in the process applied.

Comparability refers to the ability to identify similarities in, and differences among, items. *Consistency* (the use of the same accounting policies and procedures within an entity from period to period, or in a single period across entities) aids comparability.

Verifiability helps to assure users that information represents faithfully the economic phenomena that it purports to represent. It implies that knowledgeable and independent observers could reach a general consensus (but not necessarily absolute agreement) that the information does represent faithfully the economic phenomena it purports to represent without material error or bias, or that an appropriate recognition or measurement method has been applied without material error or bias. It means that independent observations would yield essentially the same measure or conclusions.

Timeliness means that the information is provided in time to be capable of influencing decisions.

Understandability is classifying, characterizing and presenting information clearly and concisely. Understandability enables users who have a reasonable knowledge of business and economic and financial activities and financial reporting, and who apply reasonable diligence to comprehend the information, to gain insights into the reporting entity's financial position and results of operations, as intended.

The cost constraint is the only constraint included regarding the information provided in useful financial reports. The question is whether the benefits of providing information exceed the cost of providing and using the information. Presumably this will constrain the imposition of certain new requirements, although this is a relative concept, and as information technology continues to evolve and the cost of preparing and distributing financial and other information declines, this constraint conceivably will be relaxed as well.

The 1989 Framework: The Remaining Text

The current guidance of the IASB's 1989 framework, not changed by the new objective and qualitative characteristics, is included in chapter 4 of the 2010 conceptual framework. More detailed discussions of the remaining text are included in other chapters of this book. For instance, the definitions of assets, liabilities, and equity are discussed in greater detail in Chapter 4, *Statement of Financial Position.* Only a brief discussion follows below.

The going concern assumption is retained. Financial statements are prepared on the assumption that the entity is a going concern and will continue its operation in the future.

Elements determining the financial position are still assets, liabilities and equity. The current definitions in the 1989 framework are retained: An asset is "a resource controlled by the entity as a result of past events and from which future economic benefits are expected to flow to the entity." A liability is a "present obligation of the entity arising from past events, the settlement of which is expected to result in an outflow from the entity of resources embodying future benefits." Equity is simply a residual arrived at by deducting the liabilities from assets.

The elements determining financial position are income and expenses. Elements are identified based on the substance and economic reality of the transaction or events and not based on the legal form. Elements are only recognized in the financial statements when they are probable and have a cost or value that can be measured reliably, which means that some assets and liabilities may go unrecognized.

Measurement is the assignment of a monetary amount to an element. The following measurement basis is identified, without determining when they should be applied: Historical cost, current cost, realizable value and present value. Currently, in IFRS other measurement bases, such as amortized cost and fair value, are applied that are not mentioned in the conceptual framework.

Finally the financial capital maintenance and the physical capital maintenance are still identified as the concepts of capital maintenance.

CONCEPTUAL FRAMEWORK PROJECT

The remaining phases of the conceptual framework project will only be considered after the June 2011 MOU projects are completed. The Boards have considered the comments they received on the Exposure Draft for Phase D, *Reporting Entity,* but have decided that they will need more time to finalize this chapter than they initially anticipated. The Reporting Entity Exposure Draft describes a reporting entity as follows:

A reporting entity is a circumscribed area of economic activities whose financial information has the potential to be useful to existing and potential equity investors, lenders and other creditors who cannot directly obtain the information they need in making decisions about providing resources to the entity and in assessing whether management and the governing board of that entity have made efficient and effective use of the resources provided.

The Reporting Entity Exposure Draft clarifies that the existence of a legal entity is neither necessary nor sufficient to identify a reporting entity. Further, a reporting entity can include more than one entity or it can be a portion of a single entity.

This Exposure Draft confirms that if an entity controls one or more entities, it should present consolidated financial statements. An entity controls another entity when it has the power to direct the activities of that other entity to generate benefits for (or limit losses to) itself. However, if one entity has *significant influence* over another entity, it specifically does not control that other entity. "Parent-only" financial statements may be presented provided they are presented with consolidated financial statements. Combined financial statements may be prepared for commonly controlled entities in a group. The final chapter on the reporting entity is not expected in the near future.

Discussion has since moved on to the elements of financial statements recognition and measurement principles. The elements and recognition phase will revise and clarify the definition of assets and liabilities, resolve differences regarding other elements and their definitions, and revise the recognition criteria.

The objective of the measurement phase is to provide guidance to select measurement bases that satisfy the objectives and qualitative characteristics of financial reporting. A mixed measurement basis will still be applied in IFRS.

Other components of the conceptual framework project will address presentation and disclosure, purpose and status, application to not-for-profit entities, and possible other issues.

HIERARCHY OF STANDARDS

The conceptual framework is used by IASB members and staff in their debate, and they expect that those commenting on Exposure Drafts will articulate their arguments in terms of the conceptual framework. However, the conceptual framework is not normally intended to be used directly by preparers and auditors in determining their accounting methods. In the 2003 revision of IAS 8 the IASB introduced a hierarchy of accounting rules that should be followed by preparers in seeking solutions to accounting problems. This hierarchy says that the most authoritative guidance is IFRS, and the preparer should seek guidance as follows:

1. IAS/IFRS and SIC/IFRIC Interpretations, when these specifically apply to a transaction or condition.
2. In the absence of such a directly applicable standard, judgment is to be used to develop and apply an accounting policy that conforms to the definitions, recognition criteria, and measurement concepts for assets, liabilities, income, and expense set forth in the *Framework*.
3. If this is not possible, the preparer should then look to recent pronouncements of other standard setters which use a similar conceptual framework to develop its standards, as well as other accounting literature and industry practices that do not conflict with guidance in IFRS dealing with the same or similar circumstances or with definitions set forth in the *Framework*.

IFRS PRACTICE STATEMENT MANAGEMENT COMMENTARY

Nature and Scope

IFRS Practice Statement *Management Commentary* was issued in December 2010 and is prospectively applicable from December 8, 2010. The Practice Statement provides a broad, nonbinding framework for the presentation of narrative reporting to accompany financial statements prepared in accordance with IFRS. It is therefore not an IFRS standard, and local authorities may voluntarily choose to implement the Practice Statement. However, it is foreseen that many countries will not implement the Practice Statement and will implement the developments regarding integrated reporting instead. Further, many local authorities have similar local guidance.

Management commentary is a narrative report that provides the content within the financial position, financial performance, and cash flows of an entity that needs to be interpreted. Management also has the opportunity to explain its objectives and strategies applied to fulfill those objectives. Management commentary falls in the scope of financial reporting and thus the conceptual framework, and should be read in conjunction with the conceptual framework. The Practice Statement provides the principles, elements, and qualitative characteristics of decision-useful information regarding management commentary, and therefore assists management in presenting management commentary.

Management needs to identify the extent of applying the Practice Statement. Full compliance can only be claimed if an entity complies with all the requirements. In applying the Practice Statement, management must consider the needs of the primary users of financial statements. The primary users are similar to the 2010 conceptual framework: existing and potential investors, lenders and other creditors.

Principles

Management commentary is based on the principles of management view and supplement and compliment information. Management commentary should include forward-looking information as prescribed by the qualitative characteristics of the conceptual framework. The principles of management view present management perspective and should be derived from the information important to management decision making.

Supplemental and complimented information explain the amounts provided in financial statements and the conditions and events forming that information. It includes all information that is important in understanding the financial statements.

Regarding forward-looking information, it must provide management perspective regarding the entity's direction. It does not predict the future, but focuses more on the entity's objectives and strategies to achieve those objectives. Forward-looking information is provided regarding uncertainties, trends and factors that could influence an entity's revenue, performance, liquidity and capital resources. Forward-looking information is provided through both narrative descriptions and quantitative data and must include disclosures of the assumptions used.

Qualitative Characteristics

The conceptual framework fundamental qualitative characteristics of relevance and faithful representation are applied and the enhancing qualitative characteristics of comparability, verifiability, timeliness and understandability should be maximized. Management should include all information that is material to its management commentary.

Presentation

The presentation of management commentary should be clear and straightforward. Management commentary should be consistent with the related financial statements, avoid duplication, and avoid generic disclosure. To assess the performance of an entity, include the entity's risk exposures, the risk strategies and how effective the strategies are, how resources recognized could affect the financial performance, and how nonfinancial information affects the financial statements.

Elements

The following main elements should be included:

Nature of business;
Management's objectives and strategies to achieve the objectives;
The most important sources, risks and relationships;
The entity's results of operations and prospects; and
The critical performance measures and indicators used.by management to assess the performance against objectives.

A description of the business to understand the entity and its environment is the starting point of management commentary. It include information about the entity's industry, its market and competition, the legal, regulative and macroeconomic environment, its main projects, services, business processes and distribution channels, structure and how it creates value.

Objectives and strategies, and changes thereof, must be disclosed in a way that users can understand the priorities and the resources used to achieve them. This includes performance indicators and the time frame over which success is measured. Relationships between objectives, strategies, management actions and executive remunerations are also helpful.

A clear description of the most important resources, risks and relationships that affect entity's value and how they are managed is needed. This includes analysis of financial and nonfinancial resources, capital structure, financial needs, liquidity and cash flows and human and intellectual capital. Risk disclosure includes principle risk exposures, changes therein, uncertainties, means of mitigating risks and effectiveness of risk strategies. Risk disclosure could be divided in principle strategic, commercial, operational and financial risks. Significant relationship with stakeholders that are value driven and managed should also be disclosed.

A clear description of financial and nonfinancial performances and prospects should be included. A description of performance and progress during the year helps to predict the future by identifying main trends and factors affecting the business. Comparison of financial position, performance, liquidity and financial position with previous years is essential.

Performance measures and indicators (financial and nonfinancial) used by management should be disclosed and the reasons why they change over time. This increases comparability of management commentary over time.

US GAAP COMPARISON

The FASB Framework consists of different concept statements. Chapters one and two of the new joint framework have also been included in the FASB Framework. Both frameworks focus on the asset and liability approach and define assets and liabilities similarly. The IASB *Framework* only defines two elements of changes in assets and liabilities, namely income and expenses. The FASB Framework GAAP identifies more elements such as investments by owners, distributions to owners and other comprehensive income, and subdivides comprehensive income into revenue, expenses, gains and losses. The FASB Framework does not identify probability as a recognition criterion, but includes relevance as a recognition criterion. The FASB Framework separates measurement in (1) a selection of the monetary unit and (2) choice of attribute. Both frameworks provide a list of measurement attributes but provide no guideline on when each should be applied. Both frameworks also do not have an adequate concept of the reporting entity.

3 PRESENTATION OF FINANCIAL STATEMENTS

INTRODUCTION

As set forth by the IASB's *Conceptual Framework for Financial Reporting 2010,* the objective of general-purpose financial reporting is to provide financial information about the reporting entity that is useful to existing and potential investors, lenders and other creditors in making decision about providing resources to the entity. Although financial statements prepared for this purpose meet the needs of these specific users, they do not provide all the information that the users may need to make economic decisions since they largely portray the financial effects of past events and do not necessarily provide nonfinancial information.

In the past, many considered the lack of guidance on the presentation of the financial statements under IFRS to be a significant impediment to the achievement of comparability among the financial statements. Users previously expressed concerns that information in financial statements was highly aggregated and inconsistently presented, making it difficult to fully understand the relationship among the financial statements and financial results of the reporting entity.

The revised IAS 1 presented in this chapter resulted from the IASB's deliberations on Phase A of the Financial Statement Presentation project and brings IAS 1 largely into line with the corresponding US standard—Statement of Financial Accounting Standards 130 (FAS 130), *Reporting Comprehensive Income.* The FASB decided that it would not publish a separate standard on this phase of the project but will expose issues pertinent to this and the next phase together in the future. The revised IAS 1 was effective for annual periods beginning on or after January 1, 2009.

IAS 1 is discussed in this chapter, while the structure and content of the financial statements are discussed in Chapter 4 (Statement of Financial Position), Chapter 5 (Statement of

Comprehensive Income and Statement of Changes in Equity), and Chapter 6 (Statement of Cash Flows).

Sources of IFRS
Conceptual Framework for Financial Reporting 2010
IAS 1, 7, 8, 10, 12, 18, 24, 27, 33, 34   *IFRS* 5, 8

AMENDMENTS EFFECTIVE DURING 2012

In June 2011 the IASB issued an amendment to IAS 1 titled *Presentation of Items of Other Comprehensive Income,* which is effective for annual periods beginning on or after July 1, 2012. The amendment improves the consistency and clarity of items recorded in other comprehensive income. Components of other comprehensive income are grouped together on the basis of whether they are subsequently reclassified to profit or loss or not. The Board highlighted the importance of presenting profit or loss and other comprehensive together and with equal prominence. The name of the statement of comprehensive income is changed to statement of profit or loss and other comprehensive income.

SCOPE

IAS 1, *Presentation of Financial Statements,* is applicable to all general-purpose financial statements prepared and presented in accordance with IFRS. IAS 1 is applicable to both consolidated and separate financial statements, but is not applicable to the structure and content of interim financial statements (see Chapter 34). The general features of IAS 1 are, however, applicable to interim financial statements.

IAS 1 is developed for profit-orientated entities. Entities with not-for-profit activities or public sector entities may apply this standard, provided that appropriate adjustments are made to particular line items in the financial statements. Entities whose share capital is not classified as equity (such as mutual funds) may also apply IAS 1 provided the member's interest is appropriately disclosed.

DEFINITIONS OF TERMS

General-purpose financial statements. The financial statements intended to meet the needs of users who are not in a position to require an entity to prepare reports tailored to their particular information needs.

Impracticable. Applying a requirement is impracticable when the entity cannot apply it after making every reasonable effort to do so.

International Financial Reporting Standards (IFRS). Standards and Interpretations adopted by the International Accounting Standards Board (IASB) which comprise

1. International Financial Reporting Standards;
2. International Accounting Standards issued by the former International Accounting Standards Committee (IASC); and
3. Interpretations developed by the International Financial Reporting Interpretations Committee (IFRIC) or the former Standing Interpretations Committee (SIC).

Material omissions or misstatements. Those omissions and misstatements that could, individually or collectively, influence the economic decisions that users make on the basis of the financial statements. Materiality depends on the size and nature of the omission or misstatement judged in the surrounding circumstances. The size or nature of the item, or a combination of both, could be the determining factor.

Notes. Information provided in addition to that presented in the financial statements, which comprise a summary of significant accounting policies and other explanatory information, including narrative descriptions or disaggregation of items presented in those statements as well as information about items that do not qualify for recognition in those statements.

Other comprehensive income. The total of income less expenses (including reclassification adjustments) that are not recognized in profit or loss as required or permitted by other IFRS or Interpretations. The components of other comprehensive income include

1. Changes in revaluation surplus (IAS 16 and IAS 38);
2. Actuarial gains and losses on defined benefit plans (IAS 19);
3. Translation gains and losses (IAS 21);
4. Gains and losses on remeasuring available-for-sale financial assets (IAS 39) and
5. The effective portion of gains and losses on hedging instruments in a cash flow hedge (IAS 39).

Owners. Holders of instruments classified as equity.

Profit or loss. The total of income less expenses, excluding the components of other comprehensive income.

Reclassification adjustments. Amounts reclassified to profit or loss in the current period that were recognized in other comprehensive income in the current or previous periods.

Total comprehensive income. The change in equity during a period resulting from transactions and other events, other than those changes resulting from transactions with owners in their capacity as owners. It comprises all components of "profit or loss" and of "other comprehensive income."

FINANCIAL STATEMENTS

Financial statements are a central feature of financial reporting—a principal means through which an entity communicates its financial information to those outside it. The IASB *Framework* describes the basic concepts by which financial statements are prepared. It does so by defining the objective of financial statements; identifying the qualitative characteristics that make information in financial statements useful; and defining the basic elements of financial statements and the concepts for recognizing and measuring them in financial statements.

The elements of financial statements are the broad classifications and groupings which convey the substantive financial effects of transactions and events on the reporting entity. To be included in the financial statements, an event or transaction must meet definitional, recognition, and measurement requirements, all of which are set forth in the *Framework*.

How an entity presents information in its financial statements, for example, how assets, liabilities, equity, revenues, expenses, gains, losses and cash flows should be grouped into line items and categories and which subtotals and totals should be presented, is of great importance in communicating financial information to those who use that information to make decisions (e.g., capital providers).

Objective

IAS 1 prescribes the basis for presentation of general-purpose financial statements to ensure comparability both with the entity's financial statements of previous periods and with the financial statements of other entities. It sets out overall requirements for the presentation of financial statements, guidelines for their structure, and minimum requirements for their content. In revising IAS 1, the IASB's main objective was to aggregate information in the financial statements on the basis of shared characteristics. Other sources of guidance on the financial statement presentation can be found in IAS 7, 8, 10, 12, 18, 24, 27, 34, and IFRS 5.

Purpose of Financial Statements

IAS 1 refers to financial statements as "a structured representation of the financial position and financial performance of an entity" and elaborates that the objective of financial statements is to provide information about an entity's financial position, its financial performance, and its cash flows, which is then utilized by a wide spectrum of end users in making economic decisions. In addition, financial statements also show the results of management's stewardship of the resources entrusted to it. All this information is communicated through a complete set of financial statements that provide information about an entity's

1. Assets;
2. Liabilities;
3. Equity;
4. Income and expenses, including gains and losses;
5. Contributions by and distributions to owners in their capacity as owners; and
6. Cash flows.

All this information, and other information presented in the notes, helps users of financial statements to predict the entity's future cash flows and their timing and certainty.

GENERAL FEATURES

Fair Presentation and Compliance with IFRS

In accordance with IFRS, financial statements should present fairly the financial position, financial performance and cash flows of an entity. Fair presentation means faithful representation of the effects of transactions, other events and conditions in accordance with the definitions and recognition criteria for assets, liabilities, income and expenses set out in the *Framework*. As stated in IAS 1, the application of IFRS, with additional disclosure when necessary, should result in financial statements achieving fair presentation. However, in extremely rare circumstances where management concludes that compliance with a requirement in an IFRS would be so misleading that it would conflict with the objective of financial statements as set out in the *Framework,* the entity can depart from that requirement if the relevant regulatory framework requires, or otherwise does not prohibit, such a departure, and the entity discloses all of the following:

1. Management has concluded that the financial statements present fairly the entity's financial position, financial performance, and cash flows;
2. The entity has complied with all applicable IFRS, except that it has departed from a particular requirement to achieve a fair presentation;
3. The title of the IFRS from which the entity has departed, the nature of the departure, including the treatment that the IFRS would require, the reason why that treatment

would be so misleading in the circumstances that it would conflict with the objective of financial statements set out in the *Framework,* and the treatment adopted; and

4. For each period presented, the financial effect of the departure on each item in the financial statements that would have been reported in complying with the requirement.

When an entity has departed from a requirement of an IFRS in a prior period, and that departure affects the amounts recognized in the current period, it shall make the disclosures as in 3. and 4. above.

The standard notes that deliberately departing from IFRS might not be permissible in some jurisdictions, in which case the entity should comply with the standard in question and disclose in the notes that it believes this to be misleading, and show the adjustments that would be necessary to avoid this distorted result. In extremely rare circumstances where management concludes that compliance with a requirement in an IFRS would be so misleading that it would conflict with the objective of financial statements as set out in the *Framework,* but the relevant regulatory framework prohibits departure from the requirement, to the maximum extent possible, the entity is required to reduce the perceived misleading aspects of compliance by disclosing all of the following:

1. The title of the IFRS in question, the nature of the requirement, and the reason why management has concluded that complying with that requirement is so misleading in the circumstances that it conflicts with the objective of financial statements as set out in the *Framework,* and
2. For each period presented, the adjustments to each item in the financial statements that management has concluded would be necessary to achieve a fair presentation.

When assessing whether complying with a specific requirement in an IFRS would be so misleading that it would conflict with the objective of financial statements as set out in the *Framework,* management should consider the following:

1. Why the objective of financial statements is not achieved in the particular circumstances; and
2. How the entity's circumstances differ from those of other entities that comply with the requirement. If other entities in similar circumstances comply with the requirement, there is a rebuttable presumption that the entity's compliance with the requirement would not be so misleading that it would conflict with the objective of financial statements as set out in the *Framework.*

An entity presenting financial statements in accordance with IFRS must include an explicit and unreserved statement of compliance with all the requirements of IFRS in the notes.

Going concern. When preparing financial statements, management makes an assessment regarding the entity's ability to continue in operation for the foreseeable future (as a going concern). Financial statements should be prepared on a going concern basis unless management either intends to liquidate the entity or to cease trading, or has no realistic alternative but to do so. If the result of the assessment casts significant doubt upon the entity's ability to continue as a going concern, management is required to disclose that fact, together with the basis on which it prepared the financial statements and the reason why the entity is not regarded as a going concern. When the financial statements are prepared on the going concern basis it is not necessary to disclose this basis.

Most accounting methods are based on this assumption. For example, the cost principle would be of limited usefulness if we assume potential liquidation of the entity. Using a liquidation approach, fixed assets would be valued at net realizable value (sale price less cost to sell) rather than at amortized cost. The concept of depreciation, amortization and depletion is justifiable and appropriate only if we assume that the entity will have a long life.

Accrual basis of accounting. Financial statements, except for the statement of cash flow, are to be prepared using the accrual basis of accounting. Under the accrual basis of accounting, an entity recognizes the elements of the financial statements (items such as assets, liabilities, income and expenses) when they meet the definition and recognition criteria for those elements in the *Framework*. Consequently, transactions and events are recognized when they occur and they are recorded in the accounting records and presented in the financial statements in the periods when they occur (and not when cash is received or paid). For example, revenues are recognized when earned and expenses are recognized when incurred, without regard to the time of receipt or payment of cash.

Materiality and aggregation. An entity should present separately each material class of similar items as well as present separately material items of dissimilar nature or function. If a line item is not individually material, it is aggregated with other items either in those statements or in the notes. An item that is considered immaterial to justify separate presentation in the financial statements may warrant separate presentation in the notes. It is not necessary for an entity to provide a specific disclosure required by an IFRS if the information is not material.

In general, an item presented in the financial statements is material—and therefore is also relevant—if its omission or misstatement would influence or change the economic decisions of users made on the basis of the financial statements. Materiality depends on the relative size and nature of the item or error judged in the particular circumstances. For example, preparers and auditors sometimes adopt the rule of thumb that anything under 5% of total assets or net income is considered immaterial. Although the US SEC indicated that a company may use this percentage for an initial assessment of materiality, other factors, quantitative as well as qualitative, must also be considered. For example, the fact of breaking the environmental law (or any laws) could be significant in principle, even if the amount is small.

Financial statements are the result of processing, aggregating and classifying a large number of transactions or other events based on their nature or function, and presenting condensed and classified data, which represent individual line items. If a line item is not individually material, it can be aggregated either in the statements or in the notes (for example, disaggregating total revenues into wholesale revenues and retail revenues), but only to the extent that this will enhance the usefulness of the information in predicting the entity's future cash flows. An entity should disaggregate similar items that are measured on different bases and present them on separate lines; for example, an entity should not aggregate investments in debt securities measured at amortized cost and investments in debt securities measured at fair value.

Offsetting. Assets and liabilities, or income and expenses, may not be offset against each other, unless required or permitted by an IFRS. Offsetting in the statement of comprehensive income (or income statement, if presented separately) or statement of financial position is allowed in rare circumstances when it reflects better the substance of the transaction or other event. For example, IAS 37 allows netting warranty expenditure against the related reimbursement (under a supplier's warranty agreement). There are other examples when IFRSs "require or permit" offsetting; for example, IAS 18 defines revenue and requires measurement at fair value of the consideration received or receivable, less any trade discounts or volume rebates (see Chapter 20); or in IAS 11 contract costs plus/less profits/losses are offset against progress billings to determine the amount due from customers (see Chapter 20). In addition, an entity can present on a net basis certain gains and losses arising from a group of similar transactions, for example, foreign exchange gains and losses or gains or losses on financial instruments held for trading (unless material).

In general, the IASB's position is that offsetting detracts from the ability of users both to understand the transactions and other events and conditions that have occurred, and to assess the entity's future cash flows. However, the reduction of accounts receivable by the allowance for doubtful accounts, or of property, plant, and equipment by the accumulated depreciation, are acts that reduce these assets by the appropriate valuation accounts and are not considered to be offsetting assets and liabilities.

Frequency of reporting. An entity should present a complete set of financial statements (including comparative information) at least annually. If the reporting period changes such that the financial statements are for a period longer or shorter than one year, the entity should disclose the reason for the longer or shorter period and the fact that the amounts presented are not entirely comparable.

There is a presumption that financial statements will be presented annually, at a minimum. The most common time period for the preparation of financial statements is one year. However, if for practical reasons some entities prefer to report, for example, for a 52-week period, IAS 1 does not preclude this practice.

Comparative information. Unless IFRS permit or require otherwise, comparative information of the previous period should be disclosed for all amounts presented in the current period's financial statements. Comparative narrative and descriptive information should be included when it is relevant to an understanding of the current period's financial statements. As a minimum, two statements of financial position, as well as two statements of comprehensive income, changes in equity, cash flows and related notes should be presented.

Comparability is the quality of information that enables users to compare the financial statements of an entity through time (among periods), to identify trends in its financial position and performance, as well as across entities. Comparability should not be confused with uniformity; for information to be comparable, like things must look alike and unlike things must look different, and users should be able to identify similarities in and differences between two sets of economic phenomena.

In addition, users must be aware of the accounting policies applied in the preparation of the financial statements as well as of any changes in those policies and the effects of such changes. Consequently, an entity is required to include a statement of financial position as at the beginning of the earliest comparative period whenever an entity retrospectively applies an accounting policy, or makes a retrospective restatement of items in its financial statements, or when it reclassifies items in its financial statements. In those limited circumstances, an entity is required to present, as a minimum, three statements of financial position and related notes, as at

1. The end of the current period;
2. The end of the previous period (which is the same as the beginning of the current period); and
3. The beginning of the earliest comparative period.

When the entity changes the presentation or classification of items in its financial statements, the entity should reclassify the comparative amounts, unless reclassification is impractical. In reclassifying comparative amounts, the required disclosure includes

1. The nature of the reclassification;
2. The amount of each item or class of items that is reclassified; and
3. The reason for the reclassification.

In situations where it is impracticable to reclassify comparative amounts, an entity should disclose:

1. The reason for not reclassifying the amounts and
2. The nature of the adjustments that would have been made if the amounts had been reclassified.

It should be noted that IAS 8, *Accounting Policies, Changes in Accounting Estimates and Errors,* sets out the adjustments to comparative information needed if changes constitute a change in accounting policy or correction of error (see Chapter 7).

Note, however, that in circumstances where no accounting policy change is being adopted retrospectively, and no restatement (to correct an error) is being applied retrospectively, the statement of financial position as of the *beginning* of the earliest comparative period included is not required to be presented. There is no prohibition against doing so, on the other hand.

The related footnote disclosures must also be presented on a comparative basis, except for items of disclosure that would be not meaningful, or might even be confusing, if set forth in such a manner. Although there is no official guidance on this issue, certain details, such as schedules of debt maturities as of the end of the previous reporting period, would seemingly be of little interest to users of the current statements and would be largely redundant with information provided for the more recent year-end. Accordingly, such details are often omitted from comparative financial statements. Most other disclosures, however, continue to be meaningful and should be presented for all years for which basic financial statements are displayed.

To increase the usefulness of financial statements, many companies include in their annual reports five- or ten-year summaries of condensed financial information. This is not required by IFRS. These comparative statements allow investment analysts and other interested readers to perform comparative analysis of pertinent information. The presentation of comparative financial statements in annual reports enhances the usefulness of such reports and brings out more clearly the nature and trends of current changes affecting the entity.

Such presentation emphasizes the fact that the statements for a series of periods are far more significant than those for a single period and that the accounts for one period are but an installment of what is essentially a continuous history.

Consistency of presentation. The presentation and classification of items in the financial statements should be consistent from one period to the next. A change in presentation and classification of items in the financial statements may be required when there is a significant change in the nature of the entity's operations, another presentation or classification is more appropriate (having considered the criteria of IAS 8), or when an IFRS requires a change in presentation. When making such changes in presentation, an entity should reclassify its comparative information and present adequate disclosures (see comparable information above). As stated in the ED *An Improved Conceptual Framework for Financial Reporting,* consistency refers to the use of the same accounting policies and procedures, either from period-to-period within an entity or in a single period across entities. Comparability is the goal and consistency is a means to achieve that goal.

STRUCTURE AND CONTENT

Complete Set of Financial Statements

IAS 1 defines a complete set of financial statements to be comprised of the following:

1. A **statement of financial position** as at the reporting date (end of the reporting period). The previous version of IAS 1 used the title "balance sheet";
2. A statement of profit or loss and other comprehensive income for the period (the name "statement of comprehensive income" may still be used);

   a. Components of **profit or loss** may be presented either as part of a single statement of profit or loss and other comprehensive income or in a separate income statement.
   b. A single statement of comprehensive income for the reporting period is preferred and presents all items of income and expense reported in **profit or loss** (a subtotal in the statement of comprehensive income) as well as items of **other comprehensive income** recognized during the reporting period.
   c. A separate statement of profit or loss and a separate statement of comprehensive income (two separate statements—dual presentation). Under this method of presentation, the statement of comprehensive income should begin with profit or loss and then report items of other comprehensive income.

3. A statement of changes in equity for the reporting period;
4. A statement of cash flows for the reporting period;

   a. The previous version of IAS 1 used the title "cash flow statement."

5. Notes, comprising a summary of significant accounting policies and other explanatory information; and
6. A statement of financial position as at the beginning of the earliest comparative period when the reporting entity applies an accounting policy retrospectively or makes a retrospective restatement of items in its financial statements, or when it reclassifies items in its financial statements. This requirement is part of the revised IAS 1.

Financial statements, except for cash flow information, are to be prepared using the accrual basis of accounting. Illustrative examples of the format of the statements of financial position, comprehensive income and changes in equity based on the guidance provided in the appendix to IAS 1 have been provided at the end of this chapter.

The standard provides the structure and content of financial statements and minimum requirements for disclosure on the face of the relevant financial statement or in the notes. These topics are dealt with in the next three chapters (Chapters 4, 5, and 6).

Notes. In accordance with IAS 1, the notes should (1) present information about the basis of preparation of the financial statements and the specific accounting policies used; (2) disclose the information required by IFRS that is not presented elsewhere in the financial statements, and (3) provide information that is not presented elsewhere in the financial statements, but is relevant to an understanding of any of them.

An entity should present notes in a systematic manner and should cross-reference each item in the statements of financial position and of profit or loss and other comprehensive income, in the separate statement of profit or loss (if presented), and in the statements of changes in equity and of cash flows to any related information in the notes.

An entity normally should present notes in the following order, to help users to understand the financial statements and to compare them with financial statements of other entities:

1. Statement of compliance with IFRS
2. Summary of significant accounting policies applied
3. Supporting information for items presented in the financial statements
4. Other disclosures, including contingent liabilities and unrecognized contractual commitments; and nonfinancial disclosures (e.g., the entity's financial risk management objectives and policies).

Statement of compliance with IFRS. IAS 1 requires an entity whose financial statements comply with IFRS to make an explicit and unreserved statement of such compliance in the notes. Financial statements should not be described as complying with IFRS unless they comply with all the requirements of IFRS.

An entity might refer to IFRS in describing the basis on which its financial statements are prepared without making this explicit and unreserved statement of compliance with IFRS. For example, the EU mandated a carve-out of the financial instruments standard and other jurisdictions have carved out or altered other IFRS standards. In some cases, these differences may significantly affect the reported financial performance and financial position of the entity. This information should be disclosed in the notes.

Accounting policies. The policy note should begin with a clear statement on the nature of the comprehensive basis of accounting used. A reporting entity may only claim to follow IFRS if it complies with every single IFRS in force as of the reporting date. The EU made certain amendments to IFRS when endorsing them (a carve-out from IAS 39), and those EU companies following these directives cannot claim to follow IFRS, and instead will have to acknowledge compliance with IFRS as endorsed by the EU.

Financial statements should include clear and concise disclosure of all significant accounting policies that have been used in the preparation of those financial statements. Management must also indicate the judgments that it has made in the process of applying the accounting policies that have the most significant effect on the amounts recognized. The entity must also disclose the key assumptions about the future and any other sources of estimation uncertainty that have a significant risk of causing a material adjustment to later be made to the carrying amounts of assets and liabilities.

IAS 1 requires an entity to disclose in the summary of significant accounting policies:

1. The measurement basis (or bases) used in preparing the financial statements; and
2. The other accounting policies applied that are relevant to an understanding of the financial statements.

Measurement bases may include historical cost, current cost, net realizable value, fair value or recoverable amount. Other accounting policies should be disclosed if they could assist users in understanding how transactions, other events, and conditions are reported in the financial statements.

In addition, an entity should disclose the judgments that management has made in the process of applying the entity's accounting policies and that have the most significant effect on the amounts recognized in the financial statements. Management makes judgments which can significantly affect the amounts reported in the financial statements, for example, when making decisions whether investments in securities should be classified as trading, available for sale or held to maturity, or whether lease transactions transfer substantially all the significant risks and rewards of ownership of financial assets to another party.

Determining the carrying amounts of some assets and liabilities requires estimating the effects of uncertain future events on those assets and liabilities at the end of the reporting period in measuring, for example, the recoverable values of different classes of property, plant, and equipment, or future outcome of litigation in progress. The reporting entity should disclose information about the assumptions it makes about the future and other major sources of estimation uncertainty at the end of the reporting period, which have a significant risk of resulting in a material adjustment to the carrying amount of assets and liabilities within the next financial year. The notes to the financial statements should include the nature and the carrying amount of those assets and liabilities at the end of the period.

Financial statement users must be made aware of the accounting policies used by reporting entities, so that they can better understand the financial statements and make comparisons with the financial statements of others. The policy disclosures should identify and describe the accounting principles followed by the entity and methods of applying those principles that materially affect the determination of financial position, results of operations, or changes in cash flows. IAS 1 requires that disclosure of these policies be an integral part of the financial statements.

IAS 8 (as discussed in Chapter 7) provides criteria for making accounting policy choices. Policies should be relevant to the needs of users and should be reliable (representationally faithful, reflecting economic substance, neutral, prudent, and complete).

Fairness exception under IAS 1. Accounting standard setters have commonly recognized the fact that even full compliance with promulgated financial reporting principles may, on rare occasions, still not result in financial statements that are accurate, truthful, or fair. Therefore many, but not all, standard-setting bodies have provided some form of exception whereby the higher demand of having fair presentation of the entity's financial position and results of operations may be met, even if doing so might require a technical departure from the codified body of GAAP.

In the US, this provision historically has been found in the profession's auditing literature (the "Rule 203 exception"), but under various other national GAAP there commonly was found a "true and fair view" requirement that captured this objective. Under revised IAS 1, an approach essentially identical to the true and fair view requirement (which is codified in the EU's Fourth Directive) has been formalized, as well. The rule under IFRS should be narrowly construed, with only the more serious situations dealt with by permitting departures from IFRS in order to achieve appropriate financial reporting objectives.

This matter has been addressed in greater detail above. In the authors' view, having such a fairness exception is vital for the goal of ensuring accurate and useful financial reporting under IFRS. However, extreme caution is urged in reaching any decision to depart from the formal requirements of IFRS, since these exceptions may have not been transposed into stock exchange regulations.

Reporting comparative amounts for the preceding period. IAS 1 requires that financial statements should present corresponding figures for the preceding period. When the presentation or classification of items is changed, the comparative data must also be changed, unless it is impracticable to do so.

When an entity applies an accounting policy retrospectively or makes a retrospective restatement of items in its financial statements, or when it reclassifies items in its financial statements, at a minimum, three statements of financial position, two of each of the other statements, and related notes are required. The three statements of financial position presented are as at

1. The end of the current period;
2. The end of the previous period (which is the same as the beginning of the current period); and
3. The beginning of the earliest comparative period.

Note, however, that in circumstances where no accounting policy change is being adopted retrospectively, and no restatement (to correct an error) is being applied retrospectively, the statement of financial position as of the *beginning* of the earliest comparative period included is not required to be presented. There is no prohibition against doing so, on the other hand.

When the entity changes the presentation or classification of items in its financial statements, the entity should reclassify the comparative amounts, unless reclassification is impractical. In reclassifying comparative amounts, the required disclosure includes

1. The nature of the reclassification;
2. The amount of each item or class of items that is reclassified; and
3. The reason for the reclassification.

In situations where it is impracticable to reclassify comparative amounts, an entity should disclose

1. The reason for not reclassifying the amounts; and
2. The nature of the adjustments that would have been made if the amounts had been reclassified.

To increase the usefulness of financial statements, many companies include in their annual reports five- or ten-year summaries of condensed financial information. This is not required by IFRS. These comparative statements allow investment analysts and other interested readers to perform comparative analysis of pertinent information. The presentation of comparative financial statements in annual reports enhances the usefulness of such reports and brings out more clearly the nature and trends of current **changes affecting the entity.**

Such presentation emphasizes the fact that the statements for a series of periods are far more significant than those for a single period and that the accounts for one period are but an installment of what is essentially a continuous history.

Other disclosures required by IAS 1. The reporting entity is required to provide details of any dividends proposed or declared before the financial statements were authorized for issue but not charged to equity. It should also indicate the amount of any cumulative preference dividends not recognized in the statement of changes in equity.

If not otherwise disclosed within the financial statements, these items should be reported in the notes:

1. The domicile and legal form of the entity, its country of incorporation, and the address of the registered office (or principal place of business, if different);
2. A description of the nature of the reporting entity's operations and its principal activities; and
3. The name of the parent entity and the ultimate parent of the group.

These disclosures (which have been modeled on those set forth by the Fourth and Seventh EU Directives) are particularly of interest given the multinational character of many entities reporting in accordance with IFRS.

FUTURE DEVELOPMENTS

Since mid-2004, the IASB and the FASB have been jointly pursuing a project on *Financial Statement Presentation* (originally titled *Performance Reporting*, and conducted independently by the IASB and FASB prior to April 2004) that should culminate in a common, high-quality standard for presentation of information in the basic financial statements, including the classification and display of line items and the aggregation of line items into subtotals and totals. The objective of this joint project is to develop standards guiding the presentation of financial statements that would provide information to investors, creditors, and other financial statement users that is useful in assessing an entity's

- Present and past financial position;
- Business (operating, investing), financing and other activities that caused changes in an entity's financial position (and their components); and
- Amounts, timing, and uncertainty of future cash flows.

The project on financial statement presentation is being conducted in three phases.

- **Phase A** addressed what constitutes a complete set of financial statement and requirements to present comparative information (absent from US GAAP). The IASB and FASB have completed deliberations on this Phase, and the current IAS 1 revised in 2007, in effect from 2009, is the result of the undertaking.
- **Phase B** addresses more fundamental issues for presenting information on the face of the financial statements, including: consistent principles for aggregating information in each financial statement; the totals and subtotals that should be reported in each financial statement; and whether the direct or the indirect method of presenting operating cash flows provides more useful information. In late 2008 a Discussion Paper was issued on this phase of the project, following two years' development. It is uncertain when an Exposure Draft on this phase is expected.
- **Phase C** will address interim financial reporting. As of late, the IASB has not yet begun deliberations on this topic.

In October 2008, the IASB and FASB published for public comment a Discussion Paper, *Preliminary Views on Financial Statement Presentation*, which is discussed later in this chapter. The DP represents the first step in the development of a standard that would require entities to present financial statements in a manner that clearly communicates an integrated financial picture of the entity.

Based on the working principles of this project, financial statements should present information in a manner that reflects a cohesive financial picture of an entity's activities by

- Presenting separately an entity's financing activities from its business and other activities and further separating financing activities with owners from all other financing activities;
- Disaggregating information so that it is useful in predicting an entity's future cash flows;
- Assisting users in assessing an entity's liquidity and financial flexibility; and
- Assisting users in understanding the bases used for measuring assets and liabilities, the uncertainty in measurements and the difference between cash-based accounting and accrual accounting.

In order to achieve all three objectives for financial statement presentation, (1) cohesiveness, (2) disaggregation, and (3) liquidity and financial flexibility, the DP proposed the following format for the financial statements, which is presented below.

Statement of Financial Position	Statement of Comprehensive Income	Statement of Cash Flows
Business • Operating assets and liabilities • Investing assets and liabilities	**Business** • Operating income and expenses • Investing income and expenses	**Business** • Operating cash flows • Investing cash flows
Financing • Financing assets • Financing liabilities	**Financing** • Financing asset income • Financing liability expenses	**Financing** • Financing asset cash flows • Financing liability cash flows
Income taxes	**Income taxes** On continuing operations (business and financing)	**Income taxes**
Discontinued operations	**Discontinued operations** Net of tax	**Discontinued operations**
	Other comprehensive income Net of tax	
Equity		**Equity**

Notes:
* *Section names are in bold type; required categories within sections are indicated by bullet points.*
* *Sections and categories within a section can be presented in a different order as long as this order is the same in each statement.*
* *Each section and category within a section should have a subtotal.*
* *The statement of comprehensive income would include a subtotal for profit or loss (or net income) and a total for comprehensive income.*
* *The statement of changes in equity is not included in the table because it would not include the sections and categories used in the other financial statements.*

The new proposed financial statement presentation model requires an entity to disclose, as a matter of accounting policy, the bases used for classifying assets and liabilities in the operating, investing and financing categories and any changes in those classifications. In addition, information related to the liquidity and financial flexibility objective of financial statement presentation should be disclosed (e.g., contractual maturity schedules).

ILLUSTRATIVE FINANCIAL STATEMENTS

IAS 1 sets out the format and content of the individual financial statements, minimum requirements for disclosure in the statements of financial position, comprehensive income and changes in equity, as well as other information that may be presented either in the financial statements or in the notes. The illustrative financial statements, prepared based on the guidance provided in the appendix to IAS 1 are presented below. According to the IASB, each entity can change the content, sequencing and format of presentation and the descriptions used for line items to achieve a fair presentation in that entity's particular circumstances. For example, the illustrative statement of financial position presents noncurrent assets followed by current assets, and presents equity followed by noncurrent liabilities and then by current liabilities (most liquid items are presented last), but many entities use to reverse this sequencing (e.g., most liquid items to be presented first).

The illustrative financial statements illustrate the presentation of comprehensive income in two separate statements—the statement of profit or loss presented separately, followed by the statement of comprehensive income beginning with profit or loss and then reporting items of other comprehensive income. All expenses in the statement of profit or loss are classified by nature. Alternatively, the single statement of profit or loss and comprehensive income could be presented, displaying all items of profit and loss as well as other comprehensive items in one statement. Also, expenses could be classified by function, instead of by nature.

These examples do not illustrate a complete set of financial statements, which would also include a statement of cash flows, a summary of significant accounting policies, and other explanatory information.

ABC Group
Statement of Financial Position as at December 31, 2012
(in thousands of currency units)

	2012	2011
Assets		
Noncurrent assets:		
Property, plant & equipment	384,000	384,349
Goodwill	22,210	23,430
Other intangibles	203,720	203,720
Investments in associates	91,040	102,430
Available-for-sale financial assets	125,620	153,400
Total noncurrent assets	826,590	867,329
Current assets:		
Inventories	143,500	141,101
Trade receivables	74,390	97,260
Other current assets	21,040	10,450
Cash and cash equivalent	281,030	303,040
Total current assets	519,960	551,851
Total assets	1,346,550	1,419,180
Equity & liabilities		
Equity attributable to owner:		
Share capital	320,000	300,000
Retained earnings	168,600	114,800
Other components of equity	42,600	31,000
	531,200	445,800
Noncontrolling interests	189,800	170,950
Total equity	721,000	616,750
Noncurrent liabilities:		
Long-term borrowings	130,000	160,000
Deferred tax	33,300	21,400
Long-term provisions	37,758	43,270
Total noncurrent liabilities	201,058	224,670

	2012	*2011*
Current liabilities:		
Trade and other payables	142,042	226,430
Short-term borrowings	200,000	250,000
Current portion of long-term borrowings	40,000	51,000
Current tax payable	32,000	39,500
Short-term provisions	10,450	10,830
Total current liabilities	424,492	577,760
Total liabilities	625,550	802,430
Total equity and liabilities	1,346,550	1,419,180

ABC Group
Statement of profit or loss
For the year ended December 31, 2012
(Presentation of comprehensive income in two statements and
classification of expenses within profit by nature)
(in thousands of currency units)

	2012	*2010*
Revenue	250,000	200,000
Other income	20,000	10,000
Changes in inventories of finished goods	(30,000)	(25,000)
Changes in inventories of work in progress	(20,000)	(15,000)
Work performed by the entity and capitalized	20,000	18,000
Raw material and consumables used	(60,000)	(55,000)
Employee benefits expense	(50,000)	(46,000)
Depreciation and amortization expense	(21,000)	(20,000)
Impairment of property, plant, and equipment	(5,000)	--
Other expenses	(8,000)	(7,000)
Finance costs	(10,000)	(12,000)
Share of profit of associates[1]	30,000	20,000
Profit before tax	116,000	68,000
Income tax expense	(29,000)	17,000
Profit for the year from continuing operations	87,000	51,000
Loss for the year from discontinued operations	--	(9,000)
Profit for the year	87,000	42,000
Profit attributable to		
Owners of the parent (80%)	69,600	33,600
Non-controlling interest (20%)	17,400	8,400
	87,000	42,000
Earnings per share		
Basic and dilluted	x.xx	x.xx

[1] *Share of associates' profit attributable to owners, after tax and noncontrolling interests in the associates.*

ABC Group
Statement of profit or loss and other comprehensive income
For the year ended December 31, 2012
(Presentation of comprehensive income in two statements)
(in thousands of currency units)

	2012	2011
Profit for the year	87,000	42,000
Other comprehensive income:		
Items that will not be reclassified in profit or loss		
Gains on property revaluation	4,000	14,000
Actuarial gains (losses) on defined benefit pension plans	(10,000)	(8,000)
Share of other comprehensive income of associates[2]	2,000	(1,000)
Income tax relating to components of other comprehensive income[3]	1,500	(1,750)
	(2,500)	3,250
Items that may be reclassified subsequently to profit or loss		
Exchange differences on translation of foreign operations	20,000	16,000
Available for sale assets	(5,000)	24,000
Cash flow hedges	(2,000)	(1,000)
Income tax related to items that may be reclassified	(3,250)	(9,500)
	9,750	29,500
Other comprehensive income for the year, net of tax	7,250	32,750
Total comprehensive income for the year	94,250	74,750
Total comprehensive income attributable to		
Owners of the parent	75,400	59,800
Non-controlling interest	18,850	14,950
	94,250	74,750

[2] *Share of associates' other comprehensive income attributable to owners of the associates, after tax and noncontrolling interests in the associates.*
[3] *The income tax relating to each component of other comprehensive income is disclosed in the notes.*

ABC Group
Disclosure of components of other comprehensive income[4]
Notes
Year ended December 31, 2012
(in thousands of currency units)

	2012		2011	
Other comprehensive income				
Exchange differences on translating foreign operations[5]		20,000		16,000
Available-for-sale financial assets:				
Gains arising during the year	(12,000)		(30,000)	
Less: Reclassification adjustments for gains (losses) included in profit or loss	(7,000)	(5,000)	(6,000)	24,000
Cash flow hedges:				
Gains (losses) arising during the year	(4,000)		(1,000)	
Less: Reclassification adjustments for gains (losses) included in profit or loss	1,800		--	
Less: Adjustments for amounts transferred to initial carrying amount of hedged items	200	(2,000)	--	(1,000)
Gains on property revaluation		4,000		14,000
Actuarial gains (losses) on defined benefit pension plans		(10,000)		(8,000)
Share of other comprehensive income of associates		2,000		(1,000)
Other comprehensive income		9,000		44,000
Income tax relating to components of other comprehensive income[6]		(1,750)		(11,250)
Other comprehensive income for the year		7,250		32,750

[4] When an entity chooses an aggregated presentation in the statement of comprehensive income, the amounts for reclassification adjustments and current year gain or loss are presented in the notes.

[5] There was no disposal of a foreign operation and therefore, there is no reclassification adjustment for the years presented.

[6] The income tax relating to each component of other comprehensive income is disclosed in the notes.

ABC Group
Disclosure of tax effects relating to each component of other comprehensive income
Notes
Year ended December 31, 2012
(in thousands of currency units)

	2012			2011		
	Before-tax amount	*Tax (expense) benefit*	*Net-of-tax amount*	*Before-tax amount*	*Tax (expense) benefit*	*Net-of-tax amount*
Exchange differences on translating foreign operations	20,000	(5,000)	15,000	16,000	(4,000)	12,000
Available-for-sale financial assets	(5,000)	1,250	(3,750)	24,000	(6,000)	18,000
Cash flow hedges	(2,000)	500	(1,500)	(1,000)	250	(750)
Gains on property revaluation	4,000	(1,000)	3,000	14,000	(3,500)	10,500
Actuarial gains (losses) on defined benefit pension plans	(10,000)	2,500	(7,500)	(8,000)	2,000	(6,000)
Share of other comprehensive income of associates	2,000	--	2,000	(1,000)	--	(1,000)
Other comprehensive income	9,000	(1,750)	7,250	44,000	(11,250)	32,750

ABC Group
Statement of Changes in Equity
For the year ended December 31, 2012
(in thousands of currency units)

	Share capital	Retained earnings	Translation of foreign operations	Available-for-sale financial assets	Cash flow hedges	Revaluation surplus	Total	Minority interest	Total equity
Balance at January 1, 2011	300,000	91,000	(2,000)	1,000	1,000	--	391,000	156,000	547,000
Changes in accounting policy	--	--	--	--	--	--	--	--	--
Restated balance	300,000	91,000	(2,000)	1,000	1,000	--	391,000	156,000	547,000
Changes in equity for 2011									
Dividends		(5,000)					(5,000)	--	(5,000)
Total comprehensive income for the year[7]		38,400	9,600	14,400	(525)	7,400	69,275	14,950	84,225
Balance at December 31, 2011	300,000	124,400	7,600	15,400	475	7,400	455,275	170,950	626,225
Changes in equity for 2012									
Issue of share capital	20,000						20,000	--	20,000
Dividends		(10,000)					(10,000)	--	(10,000)
Total comprehensive income for the year[8]		75,600	12,000	(14,400)	1,200	4,400	78,800	18,850	97,650
Transfer to retained earnings		200				(200)			
Balance at December 31, 2012	320,000	190,200	19,600	1,000	1,675	11,600	544,075	189,800	733,875

[7] The amount included in retained earnings for 2011 of 38,400 represents profit attributable to owners of the parent of 33,600 plus actuarial gains on defined benefit pension plans of 4,800 (8,000 less tax 2,000, less minority interest 1,200). The amount included in the translation, available-for-sale and cash flow hedge reserves represents other comprehensive income for each component, net of tax and minority interest, (e.g., other comprehensive income related to translation of foreign operations for 2011 of 9,600 is 16,000, less tax 4,000, less minority interest 2,400). The amount included in the revaluation surplus of 7,400 represents the share of other comprehensive income of associates of (1,000) plus gains on property revaluation of 8,400 (14,000, less tax 3,500, less minority interest 2,100). Other comprehensive income of associates relates solely to gains or losses on property revaluation.

[8] The amount included in retained earnings for 2012 of 75,600 represents profit attributable to owners of the parent of 69,600 plus actuarial losses on defined benefit pension plans of 7,500 (10,000, less tax 2,500, less minority interest 1,500). The amount included in the translation, available-for-sale and cash flow hedge reserves represents other comprehensive income for each component, net of tax and minority interest (e.g., other comprehensive income related to the available-for-sale financial assets for 2012 of 12,000 is 20,000, less tax 5,000, less minority interest 3,000). The amount included in the revaluation surplus of 4,400 represents the share of other comprehensive income of associates of 2,400 (4,000, less tax 1,000, less minority interest 600). Other comprehensive income of associates relates solely to gains or losses on property revaluation.

US GAAP COMPARISON

US GAAP has no single pronouncement that defines presentation of financial statements. The format and content are prescribed by presentation requirements in the respective standards and by Securities Exchange Commission rule.

4 STATEMENT OF FINANCIAL POSITION

INTRODUCTION

The statement of financial position (sometimes called the balance sheet) is a statement that presents an entity's assets, liabilities, and equity (net assets) at a given point in time (i.e., as of a specific date). During the early era of financial reporting standard setting, throughout the nineteenth century and first half of the twentieth century, the emphasis of legislation was almost entirely on the statement of financial position but by the mid-twentieth century owners were asking for more and more information about operating performance, leading to presentations of an increasingly complete income statement (sometimes called the profit and loss account).

There is a continuing tension between the two financial statements, since—because of double entry bookkeeping conventions—they are linked together and cannot easily serve differing objectives. The stock markets look primarily at earnings expectations, which are largely based on historic performance, as measured by the income statement. If earnings measurement drives financial reporting, this means that, of necessity, the statement of financial position carries the residuals of the earnings measurement process. For example, assets such as motor vehicles with service potential that is used up over several accounting periods will have their costs allocated to these periods through the depreciation process, with the statement of financial position left to report a residual of that allocation process, which may or may not reflect the value of those assets at the end of the reporting period. However, if reporting were truly statement of financial position driven, the reporting entity would value the vehicles at the end of each reporting period—for example by reference to their replacement costs in current condition—and the change in statement of financial position values from one year to another would be reflected in the statement of comprehensive income.

By the 1960s many national GAAP standards were being promulgated to overtly favor the income statement over the balance sheet, but the pendulum began to swing back to a balance sheet–oriented strategy when standard setters—first, the FASB in the US; later others, including the International Accounting Standards Committee, predecessor of the current

IASB—developed conceptual frameworks intended to serve as the fundamental theory of financial reporting. Undertaking that exercise had the result of causing accounting theory to revert to the original purpose—namely, to measure economic activity—and to implicitly adopt the definition of income as the change in wealth from period to period. With this in mind, measurement of that wealth, as captured in the balance sheet, became more central to new standards development efforts.

In practice, IFRS as currently written are a mixture of both approaches, depending on the transaction being recognized, measured, and reported. This mixed attribute approach is partially a legacy of earlier financial reporting rule making, but also reflects the practical difficulties of value measurement for many categories of assets and liabilities. For example, many financial instruments are remeasured at the end of each reporting period, whereas property, plant, and equipment are normally held at original cost and are depreciated systematically over estimated useful lives, subject to further adjustment for impairment, as necessary.

However, while existing requirements are not entirely consistent regarding financial statement primacy, both the IASB and the FASB, when developing new accounting standards, now are formally committed to a statement of financial position (balance sheet)–oriented approach. The conceptual framework is expressed in terms of measuring assets and liabilities, and reportedly the two standard-setting bodies and their respective staffs analyze transactions affected by proposed standards from the perspective of whether they increase or diminish the assets and liabilities of the entity. Overall, the IASB sees financial reporting as being based on the measuring of assets and liabilities, and has the overall goal of requiring the reporting of all changes to them (other than those which are a result of transactions with owners, such as the payment of dividends) in a statement of comprehensive income.

The focus on earnings in the capital markets does not mean that the statement of financial position is irrelevant; clearly the financial structure of the company is an important aspect of the company's risk profile, which in turn is important to evaluating the potential return on an investment from the perspective of a current or potential shareholder. Lenders have an even greater interest in the entity's financial structure. This is why companies sometimes go to great lengths to keep some transactions off the statement of financial position, for example by using special-purpose entities and other complex financing structures. IAS 32 considers that any instrument that gives rise to a right to claim assets from an entity is a liability.

IAS 1 states that "each material class of similar items" should be presented separately in the financial statements. In addition, "items of dissimilar nature or function" should be presented separately, unless they are immaterial. The standard expresses a preference for a presentation based on the current/noncurrent distinction, but allows a presentation by liquidity if that is more reliable and relevant. An asset or liability is current if it is part of the reporting entity's normal operating cycle (e.g., customer receivables) or if it will be realized or settled within twelve months after the reporting period. Only one of these conditions needs to be satisfied—so, for example, inventory that remains on hand for two years should still be classified as current, while long-term liabilities should be reclassified as current for the final year before settlement. IAS 1 includes a sample of illustrative financial statement structure in its *Guidance on Implementing IAS 1,* but use of this format is optional.

Sources of IFRS	
IAS 1, 8, 10, 24, 32, 36, 38, 39, 40, 41	*IFRS* 5, 6

SCOPE

This chapter discusses the format and content of the statement of financial position by incorporating guidance form the conceptual framework, IAS 1 and other standards

DEFINITIONS OF TERMS

The IASB conceptual framework describes the basic concepts by which financial statements are prepared. It does so by defining the objective of financial statements; identifying the qualitative characteristics that make information in financial statements useful; and defining the basic elements of financial statements and the concepts for recognizing and measuring them in financial statements.

The elements of financial statements are the broad classifications and groupings which convey the substantive financial effects of transactions and events on the reporting entity. To be included in the financial statements, an event or transaction must meet definitional, recognition, and measurement requirements, all of which are set forth in the conceptual framework.

The elements of a statement of financial position are

An **asset** is *a resource controlled by the entity as a result of past events and from which future economic benefits are expected to flow to the entity.*

The following three characteristics must be present for an item to qualify as an asset:

1. The asset must provide probable future economic benefit that enables it to provide future net cash inflows.
2. The entity is able to receive the benefit and restrict other entities' access to that benefit.
3. The event that provides the entity with the right to the benefit has occurred.

In addition, the asset must be capable of being measured reliably. The *conceptual framework* states that reliable measurement means that the number must be free from material error and bias and can be depended upon by users to represent faithfully. In the Basis for Conclusions of IFRS 2, the IASB notes that the use of estimates is permitted, and that there may be a trade-off between the characteristics of being free from material error and having representational faithfulness.

Assets have features that help identify them in that they are exchangeable, legally enforceable, and have future economic benefit (service potential). It is that potential that eventually brings in cash to the entity and that underlies the concept of an asset.

A **liability** is *a present obligation of the entity arising from past events, the settlement of which is expected to result in an outflow from the entity of resources embodying future benefits.*

The following three characteristics must be present for an item to qualify as a liability:

1. A liability requires that the entity settle a present obligation by the probable future transfer of an asset on demand when a specified event occurs or at a particular date.
2. The obligation cannot be avoided.
3. The event that obligates the entity has occurred.

Liabilities are similarly recognized subject to the constraint that they can be measured reliably.

Liabilities usually result from transactions that enable entities to obtain resources. Other liabilities may arise from nonreciprocal transfers, such as the declaration of dividends to the owners of the entity or the pledge of assets to charitable organizations.

An entity may involuntarily incur a liability. A liability may be imposed on the entity by government or by the court system in the form of taxes, fines, or levies. A liability may arise from price changes or interest rate changes. Liabilities may be legally enforceable or they may be equitable obligations that arise from social, ethical, or moral requirements. Liabilities continue in existence until the entity is no longer responsible for discharging them.

The diagram that follows, which is taken from one of the statements, produced from the conceptual framework project by the US standard setter, the FASB, identifies the three classes of events that affect an entity, and shows the relationship between assets and liabilities, on the one hand, and comprehensive income, on the other.

> **Equity**—*The residual interest in the assets that remains after deducting its liabilities. In a business enterprise, the equity is the ownership interest.*

Equity arises from the ownership relation and is the basis for distributions of earnings to the owners. Distributions of entity assets to owners are voluntary. Equity is increased by owners' investments and comprehensive income and is reduced by distributions to owners.

In practice, the distinction between equity and liabilities may be difficult to determine. Securities such as convertible debt and certain types of preference shares may have characteristics of both equity (residual ownership interest) and liabilities (nondiscretionary future sacrifices). For both the IASB and the FASB, equity, aside from exchanges with owners, is a residual of the asset/liability recognition model.

Statement of financial position. A statement of financial position (balance sheet) presents an entity's assets, liabilities, and equity as of a specific date.

GENERAL CONCEPTS, STRUCTURE AND CONTENT

General Concepts

Under IFRS, assets and liabilities are recorded at fair value at inception in financial statements, which for assets and liabilities arising from arm's-length transactions will be equal to negotiated prices. Subsequent measurement is usually under the historical cost principle, although in many cases subsequent changes in values are also recognized. All assets are now subject to impairment testing. IAS 36, *Impairment of Assets,* requires assets to be reduced in value if their carrying value exceeds the higher of fair value or value in use (expected future cash flows from the asset). IAS 39, *Financial Instruments: Recognition and Measurement,* IAS 40, *Investment Property,* and IAS 41, *Agriculture,* all include some element of subsequent measurement at fair value. Where assets are classified as held for sale, they are carried at the lower of their carrying amount or fair value less selling costs (IFRS 5).

Historical exchange prices, and the amortized cost amounts that are later presented, are sometimes cited as being useful because these amounts are objectively determined and capable of being verified independently. However, critics point out that, other than at transaction date, historical cost does not result in presenting in the statement of financial position numbers that are comparable between companies, so while they are reliable, they may not be relevant for decision-making purposes. This captures the fundamental conflict regarding accounting information: absolutely reliable or objective information may not be very relevant to current decision making.

All transactions and other events and circumstances that affect a business enterprise during a period

A. All changes in assets and liabilities not accompanied by changes in equity

1. Exchanges of assets for assets
2. Exchanges of liabilities for liabilities
3. Acquisitions of assets by incurring liabilities
4. Settlements of liabilities by transferring assets

B. All changes in assets or liabilities accompanied by changes in equity

1. Comprehensive income
2. All changes in equity from transfers between a business enterprise and its owners

a. Revenues
b. Gains
c. Expenses
d. Losses

a. Investments by owners
b. Distributions to owners

C. Changes within equity that do not affect assets or liabilities

Structure and Content

The titles commonly given to the primary financial statement that presents an entity's financial position include the statement of financial position, also known as the balance sheet or the statement of financial condition. The revised IAS 1 changed the title of the "balance sheet" to the "statement of financial position," the title used throughout this publication. The IASB concluded that "statement of financial position" better reflects the function of the statement and is consistent with the conceptual framework. In addition, the title "balance sheet" simply reflected the convention that double entry bookkeeping requires all debits to equal credits, and did not identify the content or purpose of the statement. According to the IASB, the term "financial position" was a well-known and accepted term, and had already been used in auditors' opinions internationally for more than 20 years to describe what "the balance sheet" presents.

The three elements that are always to be displayed in the heading of a statement of financial position are

1. The entity whose financial position is being presented
2. The title of the statement
3. The date of the statement

The entity's name should appear exactly as written in the legal document that created it (e.g., the certificate of incorporation, partnership agreement, etc.). The title should also clearly reflect the legal status of the entity as a corporation, partnership, sole proprietorship, or division of some other entity.

The statement of financial position presents a "snapshot" of the resources (assets) and claims to resources (liabilities and equity) as of a specific date. The last day of a month is normally used as the statement date (in jurisdictions where a choice is allowed) unless the entity uses a fiscal reporting period always ending on a particular day of the week, such as a Friday or Sunday (e.g., the last Friday in December, or the Sunday falling closest to December 31). In these cases, the statement of financial position can appropriately be dated accordingly (i.e., December 26, October 1, etc.). In all cases, the implication is that the statement of financial position captures the pertinent amounts as of the close of business on the date noted.

Statements of financial position should generally be uniform in appearance from one period to the next, as indeed should all of the entity's financial statements. The form, terminology, captions, and pattern of combining insignificant items should be consistent. The goal is to enhance usefulness by maintaining a consistent manner of presentation unless there are good reasons to change these and the changes are duly reported.

IAS 1 does not prescribe the sequence or format in which items should be presented in the statement of financial position. Thus, for example, in a standard classified statement of financial position noncurrent assets may be presented before or after current assets, and within the current assets cash can be presented as the first or the last line item. However, the standard stipulates the following list of minimum line items that are sufficiently different in nature or function to justify separate presentation in the statement:

1. Property, plant, and equipment;
2. Investment property;
3. Intangible assets;
4. Financial assets;
5. Investments accounted for using the equity method;
6. Biological assets;
7. Inventories;

8. Trade and other receivables;
9. Cash and cash equivalents;
10. The total of assets classified as held for sale and assets included in disposal groups classified as held for sale in accordance with IFRS 5, *Noncurrent Assets Held for Sale and Discontinued Operations*;
11. Trade and other payables;
12. Provisions;
13. Financial liabilities:
14. Liabilities and assets for current tax, as defined in IAS 12, *Income Taxes*;
15. Deferred tax liabilities and deferred tax assets, as defined in IAS 12;
16. Liabilities included in disposal groups classified as held for sale in accordance with IFRS 5;
17. Noncontrolling interest, presented within equity; and
18. Issued capital and reserves attributable to owners of the parent.

The format of the statement of financial position as illustrated by the appendix to IAS 1 is similar to the following:

XYZ Limited
Consolidated Statement of Financial Position
December 31, 2012
(in thousands of currency units)

	2012	2011
Assets		
Noncurrent assets:		
Property, plant, and equipment	x	x
Goodwill	x	x
Other intangible assets	x	x
Investments in associates	x	x
Available-for-sale investments	x	x
	x	x
Current assets:		
Inventories	x	x
Trade and other receivables	x	x
Other current assets	x	x
Cash and cash equivalents	x	x
Total assets	x	x
Equity and Liabilities		
Equity attributable to owners of the parent		
Share capital (Note _____)	x	x
Other reserves (Note _____)	x	x
Retained earnings	x	x
	x	x
Noncontrolling interest	x	x
Total equity	x	x
Noncurrent liabilities:		
Long-term borrowings	x	x
Deferred taxes	x	x
Long-term provisions	x	x
Total noncurrent liabilities		

Wiley IFRS 2012

	2012	2011
Current liabilities:		
Trade and other payables	X	X
Short-term borrowings	X	X
Current portion of long-term borrowings	X	X
Current tax payable	X	X
Short-term provisions	X	X
Total current liabilities	X	X
Total liabilities	X	X
Total equity and liabilities	X	X

CLASSIFICATION OF ASSETS

Assets, liabilities, and equity are presented separately in the statement of financial position. In accordance with IAS 1, companies should make a distinction between current and non-current assets and liabilities, except when a presentation based on liquidity provides information that is more reliable or relevant. As a practical matter, the liquidity exception is primarily invoked by banks and some other financial organizations, for which fixed investments (e.g., in property and equipment) are dwarfed by financial instruments and other assets and liabilities.

Current assets. An asset should be classified as a current asset when it satisfies any one of the following:

1. It is expected to be realized in, or is held for sale or consumption in, the normal course of the entity's operating cycle;
2. It is held primarily for trading purposes;
3. It is expected to be realized within twelve months of the end of the reporting period;
4. It is cash or a cash equivalent asset that is not restricted in its use.

If a current asset category includes items that will have a life of more than twelve months, the amount that falls into the next financial year should be disclosed in the notes. All other assets should be classified as noncurrent assets, if a classified statement of financial position is to be presented in the financial statements.

Thus, current assets include cash, cash equivalents and other assets that are expected to be realized in cash, or sold or consumed during one normal operating cycle of the business. The operating cycle of an entity is the time between the acquisition of materials entering into a process and its realization in cash or an instrument that is readily convertible into cash. Inventories and trade receivables should still be classified as current assets in a classified statement of financial position even if these assets are not expected to be realized within twelve months from the end of the reporting period. However, marketable securities could only be classified as current assets if they are expected to be realized (sold, redeemed, or matured) within twelve months after the end of the reporting period, even though most would deem marketable securities to be more liquid than inventories and possibly even than receivables. Management intention takes priority over liquidity potential. The following items would be classified as current assets:

1. **Inventories** are assets held, either for sale in the ordinary course of business or in the process of production for such sale, or in the form of materials or supplies to be consumed in the production process or in the rendering of services (IAS 2). The basis of valuation and the method of pricing, which is limited to FIFO or weighted-average cost, should be disclosed.

Inventories—at the lower of cost (FIFO) or net realizable value $xxx

In the case of a manufacturing concern, raw materials, work in process, and finished goods should be disclosed separately on the statement of financial position or in the footnotes.

Inventories:
Finished goods	$xxx	
Work in process	xxx	
Raw materials	xxx	$xxx

2. **Receivables** include accounts and notes receivable, receivables from affiliate companies, and officer and employee receivables. The term *accounts receivable* represents amounts due from customers arising from transactions in the ordinary course of business. Allowances due to expected lack of collectibility and any amounts discounted or pledged should be stated clearly. The allowances may be based on a relationship to sales or based on direct analysis of the receivables. If material, the receivables should be analyzed into their component parts. The receivables section may be presented as follows:

Receivables:
Customer accounts	$xxx		
Customer notes/commercial paper	xxx	$xxxx	
Less allowance for doubtful accounts		(xxx)	$xxxx
Due from associated companies			xxx
Due from officers and employees			xxx
Total			$xxxx

3. **Prepaid expenses** are assets created by the prepayment of cash or incurrence of a liability. They expire and become expenses with the passage of time, use, or events (e.g., prepaid rent, prepaid insurance and deferred taxes). This item is frequently aggregated with others on the face of the statement of financial position with details relegated to the notes, since it is rarely a material amount.

4. **Trading investments** are those that are acquired principally for the purpose of generating a profit from short-term fluctuations in price or dealer's margin. A financial asset should be classified as held-for-trading if it is part of a portfolio for which there is evidence of a recent actual pattern of short-term profit making. Trading assets include debt and equity securities and loans and receivables acquired by the entity with the intention of making a short-term profit. Derivative financial assets are always deemed held-for-trading unless they are designed as effective hedging instruments.

    As required by IAS 39, a financial asset held for trading should be measured at fair value, with changes in value reflected currently in earnings. There is a presumption that fair value can be reliably measured for financial assets that are held for trading.

5. **Cash** and cash equivalents include cash on hand, consisting of coins, currency, and undeposited cheques; money orders and drafts; and deposits in banks. Anything accepted by a bank for deposit would be considered cash. Cash must be available for a demand withdrawal; thus, assets such as certificates of deposit would not be considered cash because of the time restrictions on withdrawal. Also, to be classified as a current asset, cash must be available for current use. According to IAS 1, cash that is restricted in use and whose restrictions will not expire within the operating cycle, or cash restricted for a noncurrent use, would not be included in current assets.

According to IAS 7, cash equivalents include short-term, highly liquid investments that (1) are readily convertible to known amounts of cash, and (2) are so near their maturity (original maturities of three months or less) that they present negligible risk of changes in value because of changes in interest rates. Treasury bills, commercial paper, and money market funds are all examples of cash equivalents.

Noncurrent assets. IAS 1 uses the term "noncurrent" to include tangible, intangible, operating, and financial assets of a long-term nature. It does not prohibit the use of alternative descriptions, as long as the meaning is clear. The European Union (EU) uses the term *fixed assets* (which derives from nineteenth-century balance sheets, which drew a distinction between fixed and circulating assets). Noncurrent assets include held-to-maturity investments, investment property, property, plant and equipment, intangible assets, assets held for sale, and miscellaneous other assets.

Other assets. An all-inclusive heading for accounts that do not fit neatly into any of the other asset categories (e.g., long-term deferred expenses that will not be consumed within one operating cycle, and deferred tax assets).

CLASSIFICATION OF LIABILITIES

The liabilities are normally displayed in the statement of financial position in the order of payment due dates.

Current liabilities. According to IAS 1, a liability should be classified as a current liability when

1. It is expected to be settled in the normal course of business within the entity's operating cycle;
2. It is due to be settled within twelve months of the date of the statement of financial position;
3. It is held primarily for the purpose of being traded; or
4. The entity does not have an unconditional right to defer settlement beyond twelve months

An improvement effective for annual periods beginning on or after January 1, 2010, states that an entity should classify a liability as current when it does not have an unconditional right to defer settlement of the liability for at least twelve months after the reporting period. The amendment clarifies that terms of a liability that could, at the option of the counterparty, result in its settlement by the issue of equity instruments do not affect its classification.

Financial assets and financial liabilities that are classified as held for trading in accordance with IAS 39 need not necessarily be presented as current assets or current liabilities.

All other liabilities should be classified as noncurrent liabilities. Obligations that are due on demand or are callable at any time by the lender are classified as current regardless of the present intent of the entity or of the lender concerning early demand for repayment. Current liabilities also include

1. Obligations arising from the acquisition of goods and services entering into the entity's normal operating cycle (e.g., accounts payable, short-term notes payable, wages payable, taxes payable, and other miscellaneous payables).
2. Collections of money in advance for the future delivery of goods or performance of services, such as rent received in advance and unearned subscription revenues.

3. Other obligations maturing within the current operating cycle, such as the current maturity of bonds and long-term notes.

Certain liabilities, such as trade payables and accruals for operating costs, which form part of the working capital used in the normal operating cycle of the business, are to be classified as current liabilities even if they are due to be settled after more than twelve months from the date of the statement of financial position.

Other current liabilities which are not settled as part of the operating cycle, but which are due for settlement within twelve months of the date of the statement of financial position, such as dividends payable and the current portion of long-term debt, should also be classified as current liabilities. However, interest-bearing liabilities that provide the financing for working capital on a long-term basis and are not scheduled for settlement within twelve months should not be classified as current liabilities.

IAS 1 provides another exception to the general rule that a liability due to be repaid within twelve months from the end of the reporting period should be classified as a current liability. If the original term was for a period longer than twelve months and the entity intended to refinance the obligation on a long-term basis prior to the date of the statement of financial position, and that intention is supported by an agreement to refinance, or to reschedule payments, which is completed before the financial statements are approved, then the debt is to be reclassified as non-current as of the date of the statement of financial position.

However, an entity would continue to classify as current liabilities its long-term financial liabilities when they are due to be settled within twelve months, if an agreement to refinance on a long-term basis was made after the date of the statement of financial position. Similarly if long-term debt becomes callable as a result of a breach of a loan covenant, and no agreement with the lender to provide a grace period of more than twelve months has been concluded by the date of the statement of financial position, the debt must be classified as current.

The distinction between current and non-current liquid assets generally rests upon both the ability and the intent of the entity to realize or not to realize cash for the assets within the traditional one-year concept. Intent is not of similar significance with regard to the classification of liabilities, however, because the creditor has the legal right to demand satisfaction of a currently due obligation, and even an expression of intent not to exercise that right does not diminish the entity's burden should there be a change in the creditor's intention. Thus, whereas an entity can control its use of current assets, it is limited by its contractual obligations with regard to current liabilities, and accordingly, accounting for current liabilities (subject to the two exceptions noted above) is based on legal terms, not expressions of intent.

Noncurrent liabilities. Obligations that are not expected to be settled within the current operating cycle, including

1. Obligations arising as part of the long-term capital structure of the entity, such as the issuance of bonds, long-term notes, and lease obligations;
2. Obligations arising out of the normal course of operations, such as pension obligations, decommissioning provisions, and deferred taxes; and
3. Contingent obligations involving uncertainty as to possible expenses or losses. These are resolved by the occurrence or nonoccurrence of one or more future events that confirm the amount payable, the payee, and/or the date payable. Contingent obligations include such items as product warranties (see the section on provisions below).

For all long-term liabilities, the maturity date, nature of obligation, rate of interest, and description of any security pledged to support the agreement should be clearly shown. Also, in the case of bonds and long-term notes, any premium or discount should be reported separately as an addition to or subtraction from the par (or face) value of the bond or note. Long-term obligations which contain certain covenants that must be adhered to are classified as current liabilities if any of those covenants have been violated and the lender has the right to demand payment. Unless the lender expressly waives that right or the conditions causing the default are corrected, the obligation is current.

Offsetting assets and liabilities. In general, assets and liabilities may not be offset against each other. However, the reduction of accounts receivable by the allowance for doubtful accounts, or of property, plant, and equipment by the accumulated depreciation, are acts that reduce these assets by the appropriate valuation accounts and are not considered to be the result of offsetting assets and liabilities.

Only where there is an actual right of setoff is the offsetting of assets and liabilities a proper presentation. This right of setoff exists only when *all* the following conditions are met:

1. Each of the two parties owes the other determinable amounts (although they may be in different currencies and bear different rates of interest).
2. The entity has the right to set off against the amount owed by the other party.
3. The entity intends to offset.
4. The right of setoff is legally enforceable.

In particular cases, laws of certain countries, including some bankruptcy laws, may impose restrictions or prohibitions against the right of setoff. Furthermore, when maturities differ, only the party with the nearest maturity can offset because the party with the longer maturity must settle in the manner determined by the earlier maturity party.

The question of setoff is sometimes significant for financial institutions which buy and sell financial instruments, often repackaging them as part of the process. IAS 39 provides detailed rules for determining when derecognition is appropriate and when assets and liabilities must be retained on the statement of financial position.

CLASSIFICATION OF SHAREHOLDERS' EQUITY

Shareholders' equity represents the interests of the owners in the net assets of a corporation. It shows the cumulative net results of past transactions and other events affecting the entity since its inception.

Share capital. This consists of the par or nominal value of preference and ordinary shares. The number of shares authorized, the number issued, and the number outstanding should be clearly shown. For preference share capital, the preference features must also be stated, as the following example illustrates:

6% cumulative preference shares, $100 par value, callable at $115, 15,000 shares authorized, 10,000 shares issued and outstanding	$ 1,000,000
Ordinary shares, $10 par value per share, 2,000,000 shares authorized, 1,500,000 shares issued and outstanding	$15,000,000

Preference share capital that is redeemable at the option of the holder may not be considered a part of equity—rather, it should be reported as a liability. IAS 32 makes it clear that substance prevails over form in the case of compound financial instruments; any instrument which includes a contractual obligation for the entity to deliver cash is considered to be a liability.

Retained earnings. This represents the accumulated earnings since the inception of the entity, less any earnings distributed to owners in the form of dividends. In some jurisdictions, notably in continental Europe, the law requires that a portion of retained earnings, equivalent to a small proportion of share capital, be set aside as a legal reserve. Historically, this was intended to limit dividend distributions by young or ailing businesses. This practice is expected to wane, and in any event is not congruent with financial reporting in accordance with IFRS and with the distinction made between equity and liabilities.

Also included in the equity section of the statement of financial position is treasury stock representing issued shares that have been reacquired by the issuer, in jurisdictions where the purchase of the entity's own shares is permitted by law. These shares are generally stated at their cost of acquisition, as a reduction from shareholders' equity.

Finally, some elements of comprehensive income, the components of other comprehensive income, are reported in equity. These components of other comprehensive income include net changes in the fair values of available-for-sale securities portfolios, and unrealized gains or losses on translations of the financial statements of subsidiaries denominated in a foreign currency, net changes in revaluation surplus, actuarial gains and losses on defined benefit plans, and the effective portion of gains and losses on hedging instruments in a cash flow hedge. In accordance with the revised IAS 1, net changes in all items of other comprehensive income should be reported in a new statement called "statement of comprehensive income," and accumulated balances in these items are reported in equity. (For a detailed discussion on statement of comprehensive income, refer to Chapter 5.)

Noncontrolling interests should be shown separately from owners' equity of the parent company in group accounts (i.e., consolidated financial statements), but are included in the overall equity section.

Disclosure of share capital. An entity is required to disclose information that enables users of its financial statements to evaluate the entity's objectives, policies, and processes for managing capital. This information should include a description of what it manages as capital, the nature of externally imposed capital requirements, if there are any, as well as how those requirements are incorporated into the management of capital. Additionally, summary quantitative data about what it manages as capital should be provided as well as any changes in the components of capital and methods of managing capital from the previous period. The consequences of noncompliance with externally imposed capital requirements should also be included in the notes. All these disclosures are based on the information provided internally to key management personnel.

An entity should also present either in the statement of financial position or in the statement of changes in equity, or in the notes, disclosures about each class of share capital as well as about the nature and purpose of each reserve within equity. Information about share capital should include the number of shares authorized and issued (fully paid or not fully paid); par value per share or that shares have no par value; the rights, preferences and restrictions attached to each class of share capital, shares in the entity held by the entity (treasury shares) or by its subsidiaries or associates; and shares reserved for issue under options and contracts.

FUTURE DEVELOPMENT

The financial statement presentation project (discussed in Chapter 3) should fundamentally change the format of the statement of financial position. Major changes proposed in the 2008 DP with regard to the statement of financial position are as follows:

1. **Disaggregation by major activities.** A main difference is that individual items on the statement of financial position would be grouped by major activities (operating, investing, and financing), and not by assets, liabilities and equity, as it is today. The assets and liabilities would be presented in the following sections:

    a. Business (includes operating and investing categories)
    b. Financing (includes only financing assets and liabilities)
    c. Income taxes (includes current and deferred income tax assets and liabilities)
    d. Discontinued operations (includes all amounts related to discontinued operations, as defined in IFRS 5); and
    e. Equity

2. **Disaggregation into short-term and long-term subcategories.** Assets and liabilities are to be classified within each of the major categories (operating, investing, financing) as either short-term or long-term, based on a one-year distinction rather than the length of an entity's operating cycle (except when a presentation of assets and liabilities in increasing or decreasing order of liquidity would provide more relevant information). In practice today, a classified statement of financial position requires that assets and liabilities are presented in current and noncurrent categories, and this distinction is based on the length of an entity's operating cycle.

3. **Disaggregation by different measurement bases.** The DP proposes that assets and liabilities that are measured on different bases would be presented in separate line items on the statement of financial position. For example, investments in debt securities measured at amortized cost should not be aggregated with investments in debt securities measured at fair value and the total presented in a single line item.

4. **Totals and subtotals.** Entities would have to present total assets and total liabilities, as well as total short-term assets, total long-term assets, total short-term liabilities and total long-term liabilities either in the statement of financial position or in the notes to the financial statements. A total for each category and section in the financial statement should be presented, and operating assets should be clearly distinguished from operating liabilities.

The element and recognition phase of the conceptual framework project should change the definitions of elements in the conceptual framework. No expected date is set for the first consultative document regarding the elements.

US GAAP COMPARISON

The balance sheet is usually presented in order of most liquid or current to least. This is usually the opposite of the order in IFRS. US GAAP contains captions for long-term assets and liabilities and not for noncurrent assets and liabilities. Noncurrent debt that matures within one year can be classified as noncurrent if refinancing for a term of greater than one year is completed before the financial statements are issued. Current portions of deferred tax assets and liabilities are shown as current.

5 STATEMENT OF PROFIT OR LOSS AND OTHER COMPREHENSIVE INCOME, AND CHANGES IN EQUITY

INTRODUCTION

The IASB's conceptual framework emphasizes the importance of information about the performance of an entity, which is useful to assess potential changes in the economic resources that are likely to control in the future, predict future cash flows, and form judgments about the effectiveness with which the entity might employ additional resources. Since mid-2004, the IASB and the FASB have been collaboratively pursuing projects on *Financial Statement Presentation* (originally entitled *Performance Reporting),* which has resulted in fundamental changes to the format and content of what is commonly referred to as the income statement (or the profit or loss account). This joint effort has been bifurcated. The first phase of the project addressed what constitutes a complete set of financial statements and a requirement to present comparative financial statements (absent from US GAAP), and culminated in the issuance of revised IAS 1 in 2007, effective in 2009.

IAS 1, *Presentation of Financial Statements,* as revised in 2007, brings IAS 1 largely into line with the US standard—Statement of Financial Accounting Standards 130 (FAS 130), *Reporting Comprehensive Income.* The standard requires all nonowner changes in equity (i.e., comprehensive income items) to be presented either in one statement of comprehensive income or else in two statements, a separate income statement and a statement of comprehensive income. Components of comprehensive income are not permitted to be presented in the statement of changes in equity As a combined statement of income and comprehensive income became mandatory (or at least preferable), this represented a triumph of the *all-inclusive concept* of performance reporting. While this approach has been officially endorsed by world standard setters for many decades, in fact many standards promulgated over the years (e.g., IAS 39 requiring the exclusion of temporary changes in the fair value of investments other than trading securities from current income) have deviated from adherence to this principle. While IAS 1 encourages the presentation of comprehensive income in a single statement, with net income being an intermediate caption, it remains acceptable to instead report in a two-statement format, with a separate income statement and a separate statement of comprehensive income. The statement of comprehensive income will report all nonowner changes in equity separately from owner changes in equity (investments by or distributions to owners).

IAS 1 in its current incarnation thus marks a notable return to an all inclusive concept of performance reporting, which had been eroded in recent decades as items such as unrealized gains and losses on available-for-sale investments and defined benefit plan actuarial gains or losses became reportable directly in the equity section of the statement of financial position—a practice which generated understandable confusion regarding the identity of the reporting entity's "real" results of operations.

Concepts of performance and measures of income have changed over the years, and current reporting still largely focuses on *realized* income and expense. However, *unrealized* gains and losses also reflect real economic transactions and events and are of great interest to decision makers. Under current IFRS, some of these unrealized gains and losses are *recognized*, while others are *unrecognized*. Both the financial reporting entities themselves and the financial analyst community go to great lengths to identify those elements within reported income which are likely to be continuing into the future, since expected earnings and cash flows of future periods are main drivers of share prices.

IFRS rules for the presentation of income are based on a so-called "mixed attribute model." It thus reflects a mixture of traditional realized income reporting, accompanied by fair value measures applied to unrealized gains and losses meeting certain criteria (e.g., financial instruments are accounted for differently from plant assets). For example, unrealized gains and losses arising from the translation of the foreign currency–denominated financial statements of foreign subsidiaries do not flow through the income statement. IAS 1 requires that all owner changes in equity should be reported separately from nonowner changes (deriving from performance), in a separate *statement of changes in equity*.

The traditional income statement has been known by many titles. IFRS refer now to this statement as the statement of profit or loss, which reports all items entering into the determination of periodic earnings, but excluding other comprehensive income items which are reported in the other comprehensive income section of the comprehensive statement of profit or loss and other comprehensive income.

For many years, the income statement had been widely perceived by investors, creditors, management, and other interested parties as the single most important of an entity's basic financial statements. In fact, beginning in the mid-twentieth century, accounting theory development was largely driven by the desire to present a meaningful income statement, even to the extent that the balance sheet sometimes became the repository for balances of various accounts, such as deferred charges and credits, which could scarcely meet any reasonable definitions of assets or liabilities. This was done largely to serve the needs of investors, who are commonly thought to use the past income of a business as the most important input to their predictions for entities' future earnings and cash flows, which in turn form the basis for their predictions of future share prices and dividends.

Creditors look to statement of profit or loss for insight into the borrower's ability to generate the future cash flows needed to pay interest and eventually to repay the principal amounts of the obligations. Even in the instance of secured debt, creditors do not look primarily to the statement of financial position (balance sheet), inasmuch as the seizure and liquidation of collateral is never the preferred route to recovery of the lender's investment. Rather, generation of cash flows from operations—which is generally closely correlated to income—is seen as the primary source for debt service.

Management, then, must be concerned with the statement of profit or loss by virtue of the importance placed on it by investors and creditors. In many large corporations, senior management receives substantial bonuses relating to either profit targets or share price performance. Consequently, managements sometimes devote considerable efforts to massaging what appears in the income statement, in order to present the most encouraging view of the reporting entity's future prospects. This means that standard setters need to bear in mind the abuse possibilities of the rules they impose, and for that matter, the rules have been imposed in response to previous financial reporting abuses.

The importance placed on income measurement has, as is well known, influenced behavior by some management personnel, who have sought to manipulate results to, say, meet Wall Street earnings estimates. The motivation for this improper behavior is readily understandable when one observes that recent markets have severely punished companies that missed earnings estimates by as little as a penny per share. One very popular vehicle for earnings management has centered on revenue recognition. Historically, certain revenue recognition situations, such as that involving prepaid service revenue, have lacked specific financial reporting rules or have been highly subject to interpretation, opening the door to aggressive accounting by some entities. While in many businesses the revenue earning cycle is simple and straightforward and therefore difficult to manipulate, there are many other situations where it is a matter of interpretation as to when the revenue has actually been earned. Examples have included recognition by lessor of lease income from long-term equipment rental contracts that were bundled with supplies and maintenance agreements, and accruals of earnings on long-term construction contracts or software development projects having multiple deliverables.

The information provided by the statement of profit or loss, relating to individual items of income and expense, as well as to the relationships between and among these items (such as the amounts reported as gross margin or profit before interest and taxes), facilitates financial analysis, especially that relating to the reporting entity's historical and possible future profitability. Even with the ascendancy of the statement of financial position as the premier financial statement, financial statement users will always devote considerable attention to the statement of profit or loss

Sources of IFRS
Conceptual Framework for Financial Reporting 2010

IAS 1, 8, 14, 16, 18, 19, 21, 36, 37, 38, 39, 40	*IFRS* 1, 5	*SIC* 29

AMENDMENTS EFFECTIVE DURING 2011

In June 2011 the IASB issues an amendment to IAS 1 titled *Presentation of Items of Other Comprehensive Income,* which is effective for annual periods beginning on or after 1 July 2012. The amendment improves the consistency and clarity of items recorded in other comprehensive income. Other comprehensive income is group together on the basis of whether or not they are subsequently reclassified to profit or loss. The Boards highlighted the importance of presenting profit or loss and other comprehensive together and with equal prominence. The name of the *statement of comprehensive income* is changed to *statement of profit or loss and other comprehensive income*.

SCOPE

This chapter focuses on key income measurement issues and on matters of comprehensive income, statement presentation and disclosure. It also explains and illustrates the presentation of the *statement of profit or loss and other comprehensive income* and the *statement of changes in equity*. The chapter incorporates information from the *Conceptual Framework for Financial Reporting 2010,* IAS 1, and other standards.

DEFINITIONS OF TERMS

Elements of Financial Statements

Comprehensive income. The change in equity (net assets) of an entity during a period from transactions and other events and circumstances from nonowner sources. It includes all changes in net assets during a period, except those resulting from investments by owners and distributions to owners. It comprises all components of "profit or loss" and "other comprehensive income" presented in the statement of comprehensive income.

Expenses. Decreases in economic benefits during the accounting period in the form of outflows or depletions of assets or incurring liabilities that result in decreases in equity, other than those relating to distributions to equity participants. The term *expenses* is broad enough to include *losses* as well as normal categories of expenses; thus, IFRS differs from the corresponding US GAAP standard, which deems losses to be a separate and distinct element to be accounted for, denoting decreases in equity from peripheral or incidental transactions.

Income. Increases in economic benefits during the accounting period in the form of inflows or enhancements of assets that result in increases in equity, other than those relating to contributions from equity participants. The IASB's *Framework* clarifies that this definition of income encompasses both revenue and gains. As with expenses and losses, the corresponding US accounting standard holds that revenues and gains constitute two separate elements of financial reporting, with gains denoting increases in equity from peripheral or incidental transactions.

Other comprehensive income. Items of income and expense (including reclassification adjustments) that are not recognized in profit or loss as required or permitted by other IFRS. The components of other comprehensive income include (1) changes in revaluation surplus (IAS 16 and 38); (2) actuarial gains and losses on defined benefit plans (IAS 19); (3) translation gains and losses (IAS 21); (4) gains and losses on remeasuring available-for-sale financial assets (IAS 39); and (5) the effective portion of gains and losses on hedging instruments in a cash flow hedge (IAS 39).

Profit or loss. The total of income less expenses, excluding the components of other comprehensive income.

Reclassification adjustments. Amounts reclassified to profit or loss in the current period that were recognized in other comprehensive income in the current or previous periods.

Statement of changes in equity As prescribed by IAS 1, an entity should present, as a separate financial statement, a statement of changes in equity showing

1. Total comprehensive income for the period (reporting separately amounts attributable to owners of the parent and to noncontrolling interest);

2. For each component of equity, the effect of retrospective application or retrospective restatement recognized in accordance with IAS 8;
3. The amounts of transactions with owners in their capacity as owners, showing separately contributions by and distributions to owners; and
4. A reconciliation for each component of equity (each class of share capital and each reserve) between the carrying amounts at the beginning and the end of the period, separately disclosing each movement.

Statement of profit or loss and other comprehensive income. the statement of profit or loss and other comprehensive income presents all components of "profit or loss" and "other comprehensive income" in a single statement, with net income being an intermediate caption. Alternatively, IAS 1 permits the use of a two-statement format, with separate statement of profit or loss and statement of comprehensive income.

Other Terminology

Discontinued operations. IFRS 5 defines a "discontinued operation" as a component of an enterprise that has been disposed of, or is classified as held for sale, and

1. Represents a separate major line of business or geographical area of operations;
2. Is part of a single coordinated disposal plan;
3. Is a subsidiary acquired exclusively with a view to resale.

Component of an entity In the context of discontinued operations, IFRS 5 currently defines a component of an entity as operations and cash flows that can be clearly distinguished, operationally and for financial reporting purposes, from the rest of the entity—a cash-generating unit, or group of cash-generating units.

Net assets. Net assets are total assets minus total liabilities (which is thus equivalent to owners' equity).

Realization. The process of converting noncash resources and rights into money or, more precisely, the sale of an asset for cash or claims to cash.

Recognition. The process of formally recording or incorporating in the financial statements of an entity items that meet the definition of an element and satisfy the criteria for recognition.

Operating segment. A component of an entity (1) that engages in business activities from which it may earn revenues and incur expenses (including revenues and expenses relating to transactions with other components of the same entity); (2) whose operating results are regularly reviewed by the entity's chief operating decision maker to make decisions about resources to be allocated to the segment and assess its performance; and (3) for which discrete financial information is available.

CONCEPTS OF INCOME

Economists have generally employed a wealth maintenance concept of income. Under this concept (as specified by Hicks), income is the maximum amount that can be consumed during a period and still leave the entity with the same amount of wealth at the end of the period as existed at the beginning. Wealth is determined with reference to the current market values of the net productive assets at the beginning and end of the period. Therefore, the economists' definition of income would fully incorporate market value changes (both increases and decreases in wealth) in the determination of periodic income and this would correspond to measuring assets and liabilities at fair value, with the net of all the changes in net assets equating to comprehensive income.

Accountants, on the other hand, have traditionally defined income by reference to specific transactions that give rise to recognizable elements of revenue and expense during a reporting period. The events that produce reportable items of revenue and expense comprise a subset of economic events that determine economic income. Many changes in the market values of wealth components are deliberately excluded from the measurement of accounting income but are included in the measurement of economic income, although those exclusions have grown fewer as the use of fair values in financial reporting has been more widely embraced in recent years.

The discrepancy between the accounting and economic measures of income are the result of a preference on the part of accountants and financial statement users for information that is reliable, and also considerations of measurement of income for tax purposes in many jurisdictions. Since many fluctuations in the market values of assets are matters of conjecture, accountants have preferred to retain the historical cost/realization model, which generally postpones the recognition of value changes until there has been a completed transaction. While both accountants and economists understand that the earnings process occurs throughout the various stages of production, sales, and final delivery of the product, accountants have tended to stress the difficulty of measuring the precise rate at which this earnings process is taking place. That, coupled with a desire to not pay tax any earlier than necessary, has led accountants to conclude that income should be recognized only when it is fully realized.

Nonetheless, an application of the conceptual framework approach of recognizing assets and liabilities when they can be measured reliably enough is leading standard setters to experiment with the idea of recognizing transactions that are incomplete. This can be seen in IAS 39, where the changes in market value of some financial instruments are recognized, and in IAS 41, where the change in value of biological assets is recognized although not realized.

RECOGNITION AND MEASUREMENT

Income. According to the IASB's conceptual framework

Income is increases in economic benefits during the accounting period in the form of inflows or enhancements of assets or decreases of liabilities that result in increases in equity, other than those relating to contributions from equity participants. The definition of income encompasses both revenue and gains, and revenue arises in the course of ordinary activities of an enterprise and is referred to by different names, such as sales, fees, interest, dividends, royalties, and rent.

IAS 18 is the standard that deals with the accounting for revenue. It says that revenue is the gross inflow of economic benefits during the period (excluding transactions with owners).

The measurement basis is that revenue be measured at the fair value of the consideration received or receivable. *Fair value* is defined as

The amount for which an asset could be exchanged, or a liability settled, between knowledgeable, willing parties in an arm's-length transaction.

The historical cost measurement basis involves recognizing a completed marketplace transaction, in other words measuring at fair value at initial recognition. Revenue recognition is discussed in detail in Chapter 20.

Expenses. According to the IASB's conceptual framework

Expenses are decreases in economic benefits during an accounting period in the form of outflows or depletions of assets or incurrences of liabilities, other than those relating to distributions to equity participants.

Expenses are expired costs, or items that were assets but are no longer assets because they have no future value. The matching principle requires that all expenses incurred in the generating of revenue be recognized in the same accounting period as the related revenues are recognized.

Costs such as materials and direct labor consumed in the manufacturing process are relatively easy to identify with the related revenue elements. These cost elements are included in inventory and expensed as cost of sales when the product is sold and revenue from the sale is recognized. This is associating cause and effect.

Some costs are more closely associated with specific accounting periods. In the absence of a cause and effect relationship, the asset's cost should be allocated to the benefited accounting periods in a systematic and rational manner. This form of expense recognition involves assumptions about the expected length of benefit and the relationship between benefit and cost of each period. Depreciation of fixed assets, amortization of intangibles, and allocation of rent and insurance are examples of costs that would be recognized by the use of a systematic and rational method.

All other costs are normally expensed in the period in which they are incurred. This would include those costs for which no clear-cut future benefits can be identified, costs that were recorded as assets in prior periods but for which no remaining future benefits can be identified, and those other elements of administrative or general expense for which no rational allocation scheme can be devised. The general approach is first to attempt to match costs with the related revenues. Next, a method of systematic and rational allocation should be attempted. If neither of these measurement principles is beneficial, the cost should be immediately expensed.

Gains and losses. The *conceptual framework* defines the term *expenses* broadly enough to include losses. IFRS include no definition of gains and losses that enables them to be separated from income and expense. Traditionally, gains and losses are thought by accountants to arise from purchases and sales outside the regular business trading of the company, such as on disposals of noncurrent assets that are no longer required. IAS 1 used to include an extraordinary category for display of items that were clearly distinct from ordinary activities. The IASB removed this category in its 2003 Improvements Project, concluding that these items arose from the normal business risks faced by an entity and that it is the nature or function of a transaction or other event, rather than its frequency that should determine its presentation within the statement of comprehensive income.

According to the IASB's *Framework*

Gains (losses) represent increases (decreases) in economic benefits and as such are no different in nature from revenue (expenses). Hence they are not regarded as separate elements in IASB's Framework. Characteristics of gains and losses include the following:

1. *Result from peripheral transactions and circumstances that may be beyond entity's control*
2. *May be classified according to sources or as operating and nonoperating*

STATEMENT OF PROFIT OR LOSS AND OTHER COMPREHENSIVE INCOME

The IASB's *conceptual framework* states that comprehensive income is the change in the entity's net assets over the course of the reporting period arising from nonowner sources. An entity has the option of presenting comprehensive income in a period either in one statement (the single-statement approach) or in two statements (the two-statement approach). The IASB initially intended to introduce the single-statement approach for the statement of comprehensive income, but during discussions with constituents, many of them were opposed to the concept of a single statement, stating that it could result in undue focus on the "bottom line" of the statement. Consequently, the IASB decided that presentation in a single statement was not as important as its fundamental decision that all nonowner changes in equity should be presented separately from owner changes in equity. However, the IASB prefers a one-statement approach. If an entity presents the components of profit or loss in a separate statement, this separate statement of profit or loss (income statement) forms part of a complete set of financial statements and should be displayed immediately before the statement of comprehensive income.

Although IAS 1 uses the terms "profit or loss," "other comprehensive income," and "total comprehensive income," an entity may use other terms to describe the totals, as long as the meaning is clear. For example, an entity may use the term "net income" to describe profit or loss.

Comprehensive income comprises all components of "profit or loss" and of "other comprehensive income."

An entity has a choice of presenting all components of comprehensive income recognized in a period either

1. In a single statement of profit or loss and other comprehensive income, in which all items of income and expense are recognized in the period (the single-statement approach); or
2. In two statements (the two-statement approach)

   a. A statement displaying components of profit or loss (separate statement of profit or loss);
   b. A second statement beginning with profit or loss and displaying components of other comprehensive income.

Total comprehensive income for the period reported in a statement of profit or loss and other comprehensive income is the total of all items of income and expense recognized during the period (including the components of profit or loss and other comprehensive income).

Other comprehensive income is the total of income less expenses (including reclassification adjustments) that are not recognized in profit or loss as required or permitted by other IFRS or Interpretations.

The components of *other comprehensive income* comprise

1. Changes in revaluation surplus (see IAS 16, *Property, Plant, and Equipment,* and IAS 38, *Intangible Assets*);
2. Actuarial gains and losses on defined benefit plans recognized in accordance with paragraph 93A of IAS 19, *Employee Benefits;*
3. Gains and losses arising from translating the financial statements of foreign operation (see IAS 21, *The Effects of Changes in Foreign Exchange Rates*);

4. Gains and losses on remeasuring available-for-sale financial assets (see IAS 39, *Financial Instruments: Recognition and Measurement*);

5. The effective portion of gains and losses on hedging instruments in a cash flow hedge (see IAS 39, *Financial Instruments: Recognition and Measurement*).

The statement of profit and loss and other comprehensive income must in addition to the profit and loss and other comprehensive section disclose the following totals:

1. Profit and loss
2. Total other comprehensive income
3. Comprehensive income for the year (total of 1. and 2.)

IAS 1 stipulates that, in addition to items required by other IFRS, the profit and loss section of the statement of profit or loss must include line items that present the following amounts for the period (if they are pertinent to the entity's operations for the period in question):

1. Revenue
2. Finance costs
3. Share of the profit or loss of associates and joint ventures accounted for by the equity method
4. Tax expense
5. A single amount for the total of discontinued operations

In addition, an entity should disclose the following items on the face of the statement of profit or loss and other comprehensive income as allocations of

1. Profit or loss for the period attributable to

   a. Noncontrolling interest, and
   b. Owners of the parent

2. Total comprehensive income for the period attributable to

   a. Noncontrolling interest, and
   b. Owners of the parent

Items 1-5 listed above and disclosure of profit or loss attributable to noncontrolling interest and owners of the parent (listed in 1.) can be presented on the face of a separate statement of profit or loss (income statement).

The foregoing items represent the barest minimum of acceptable detailing in the statement of comprehensive income: the standard states that additional line items, headings, and subtotals should be presented on the face of the statement when this is relevant to an understanding of the entity's financial performance This requirement cannot be dealt with by incorporating the items into the notes to the financial statements. When items of income or expense are material, disclosures segregating their nature and amount are required in the statement of comprehensive income or in the notes.

PRESENTATION IN THE PROFIT OR LOSS SECTION

In accordance with IAS 1, if an entity presents the components of profit or loss in a separate statement of profit or loss, this separate statement should be displayed immediately before the statement of comprehensive income. The following also need to be disclosed.

Statement title. The legal name of the entity must be used to identify the financial statements and the correct title used to distinguish the statement from other information presented in the annual report.

Reporting period. The period covered by the statement of profit or loss must clearly be identified, such as "year ended December 31, 2011." Or "six months ended September 30, 2011." Income statements are normally presented annually (i.e., for a period of twelve months or a year). However, in some jurisdictions they may be required at quarterly or six-month intervals, and in exceptional circumstances (such as a newly acquired subsidiary harmonizing its account dates with those of its new parent), companies may need to prepare statement of profit or loss for periods in excess of one year or for shorter periods as well. IAS 1 requires that when financial statements are presented for periods other than a year, the following additional disclosures should be made:

1. The reason for presenting the statement of profit or loss (and other financial statements, such as the statement of cash flows, statement of changes in equity, and notes) for a period other than one year; and
2. The fact that the comparative information presented (in the statement of profit or loss, statement of changes in equity, statement of cash flows, and notes) is not truly comparable.

Entities whose operations form a natural cycle may have a reporting period end on a specific day of the week (e.g., the last Friday of the month). Certain entities (typically retail enterprises) may prepare income statements for a fiscal period of fifty-two or fifty-three weeks instead of a year (thus, to always end on a day such as Sunday, on which no business is transacted, so that inventory may be taken). These entities should clearly state that the income statement has been presented, for instance, "for the fifty-two-week period ended March 30, 2009." IAS 1 states that it is deemed to be unlikely that the financial statements thus presented would be materially different from those that would be presented for one full year.

In order that the presentation and classification of items in the statement of profit or loss be consistent from period to period, items of income and expenses should be uniform both with respect to appearance and categories from one time period through the next. If a decision is made to change classification schemes, the comparative prior period financials should be restated to conform and thus to maintain comparability between the two periods being presented together. Disclosure must be made of this reclassification, since the earlier period financial statements being presented currently will differ in appearance from those nominally same statements presented in the earlier year.

ABC Group
Statement of Profit or Loss
For the Year Ended December 31, 2012
(classification of expense by nature)
(in thousands of currency units)

Revenue		800,000
Other income		100,000
Changes in inventories of finished goods and work in progress	50,000	
Work performed by the entity and capitalized	60,000	
Raw materials and consumables used	110,000	
Employee benefits expense	350,000	
Depreciation expense	200,000	
Other expense	10,000	
Finance costs	30,000	

Total expenses	810,000
Profit before tax	90,000

An example of the income statement (profit or loss) classification by the "function of expense" method is as follows:

Statement of Profit or Loss
For the Year Ended December 31, 2012
(classification of expense by function)
(in thousands of currency units)

Revenue	800,000
Cost of sale	500,000
Gross profit	300,000
Other income	100,000
Distribution (selling) costs	100,000
Administrative expenses	170,000
Other expenses	10,000
Finance costs	30,000
Profit before tax	90,000

Under the "function of expense" or "cost of sales" method an entity should report, at a minimum, its cost of sales separately from other expenses. This method can provide more relevant information to the users of the financial statements than the classification under the "nature of expense" method, but allocating costs to functions may require arbitrary allocations based on judgment.

IAS 1 furthermore stipulates that if a reporting entity discloses expenses by function, it must also provide information on the nature of the expenses, including depreciation and amortization and staff costs (salaries and wages). The standard does not provide detailed guidance on this requirement, but companies need only provide a note indicating the nature of the allocations made to comply with the requirement.

IFRS 5 governs the presentation and disclosures pertaining to discontinued operations. This is discussed later in this chapter.

While IAS 1 does not require the inclusion of subsidiary schedules to support major captions in the statement of income, it is commonly found that detailed schedules of line items are included in full sets of financial statements. These will be illustrated in the following section to provide a more expansive discussion of the meaning of certain major sections of the statement of income.

Revenue. Companies typically show their regular trading operations first and then present any items to which they wish to direct analysts' attention.

1. **Sales or other operating revenues** are charges to customers for the goods and/or services provided to them during the period. This section of the statement of income should include information about discounts, allowances, and returns, to determine net sales or net revenues.
2. **Cost of goods sold** is the cost of the inventory items sold during the period. In the case of a merchandising firm, net purchases (purchases less discounts, returns, and allowances plus freight-in) are added to beginning inventory to obtain the cost of goods available for sale. From the cost of goods available for sale amount, the ending inventory is deducted to compute cost of goods sold.

Example of schedule of cost of goods sold

ABC Group
Schedule of Cost of Goods Sold
For the Year Ended December 31, 2012

Beginning inventory			$xxx
Add: Purchases		$xxx	
Freight-in		xxx	
Cost of purchases		xxx	
Less: Purchase discounts	$xx		
Purchase returns and allowances	xx	(xxx)	
Net purchases			xxx
Cost of goods available for sale			xxx
Less: Ending inventory			(xxx)
Cost of goods sold			$xxx

A manufacturing enterprise computes the cost of goods sold in a slightly different way. Cost of goods manufactured would be added to the beginning inventory to arrive at cost of goods available for sale. The ending finished goods inventory is then deducted from the cost of goods available for sale to determine the cost of goods sold. Cost of goods manufactured is computed by adding to raw materials on hand at the beginning of the period the raw materials purchases during the period and all other costs of production, such as labor and direct overhead, thereby yielding the cost of goods placed in production during the period. When adjusted for changes in work in process during the period and for raw materials on hand at the end of the period, this results in the calculation of goods produced.

Example of schedules of cost of goods manufactured and sold

ABC Group
Schedule of Cost of Goods Manufactured
For the Year Ended December 31, 2012

Direct materials inventory, January 1	$xxx	
Purchases of materials (including freight-in and deducting purchase discounts)	xxx	
Total direct materials available	$xxx	
Direct materials inventory, December 31	(xxx)	
Direct materials used		$xxx
Direct labor		xxx
Factory overhead:		
Depreciation of factory equipment	$xxx	
Utilities	xxx	
Indirect factory labor	xxx	
Indirect materials	xxx	
Other overhead items	xxx	xxx
Manufacturing cost incurred in 2012		$xxx
Add: Work in process, January 1		xxx
Less: Work in process, December 31		(xxx)
Cost of goods manufactured		$xxx

ABC Group
Schedule of Cost of Goods Sold
For the Year Ended December 31, 2012

Finished goods inventory, January 1	$xxx
Add: Cost of goods manufactured	xxx
Cost of goods available for sale	$xxx
Less: Finished goods inventory, December, 31	(xxx)
Cost of goods sold	$xxx

3. **Operating expenses** are primary recurring costs associated with central operations, other than cost of goods sold, which are incurred to generate sales. Operating expenses are normally classified into the following two categories:

   a. Distribution costs (or selling expenses)
   b. General and administrative expenses

   Distribution costs are those expenses related directly to the company's efforts to generate sales (e.g., sales salaries, commissions, advertising, delivery expenses, depreciation of store furniture and equipment, and store supplies). General and administrative expenses are expenses related to the general administration of the company's operations (e.g., officers and office salaries, office supplies, depreciation of office furniture and fixtures, telephone, postage, accounting and legal services, and business licenses and fees).

4. **Other revenues and expenses** are incidental revenues and expenses not related to the central operations of the company (e.g., rental income from letting parts of premises not needed for company operations).

5. **Separate disclosure items** are items that are of such size, nature, or incidence that their disclosure becomes important in order to explain the performance of the enterprise for the period. Examples of items that, if material, would require such disclosure are as follows:

   a. Write-down of inventories to net realizable value, or of property, plant, and equipment to recoverable amounts, and subsequent reversals of such write-downs
   b. Costs of restructuring the activities of an enterprise and any subsequent reversals of such provisions
   c. Costs of litigation settlements
   d. Other reversals of provisions

6. **Income tax expense.** The total of taxes payable and deferred taxation adjustments for the period covered by the income statement.

7. **Discontinued operations.** IFRS 5, *Noncurrent Assets Held for Sale and Discontinued Operations,* was issued by the IASB as part of its convergence program with US GAAP,

IFRS 5 created a new "held for sale" category of asset into which should be put assets, or "disposal groups" of assets, and liabilities that are to be sold. Such assets or groups of assets are to be valued at the lower of carrying value and fair value, less selling costs. Any resulting write-down appears, net of tax, as part of the caption "discontinued operations" in the statement of income.

The other component of this line is the posttax profit or loss of discontinued operations. A discontinued operation is defined as a component of an entity that either has been disposed of, or has been classified as held for sale. It must also

- Be a separate major line of business or geographical area of operations,
- Be a part of a single coordinated plan for disposal, or
- Is a subsidiary acquired exclusively with a view to resale.

The two elements of the single line of statement of income have to be analyzed in the notes, breaking out the related income tax expense between the two, as well as showing the components of revenue, expense, and pretax profit of the discontinued items.

For the asset or disposal group to be classified as held for sale, and its related earnings to be classified as discontinued, IFRS 5 says that sale must be highly probable, the asset must be saleable in its current condition, and the sale price must be reasonable in relation to its fair value. The appropriate level of management in the group must be committed to a plan to sell the asset and an active program has been embarked upon. Sale should be expected within one year of classification and the standard sets out stringent conditions for any extension of this, which are based on elements outside of the control of the entity.

Where an operation meets the criteria for classification as discontinued, but will be abandoned within one year rather than be sold, it should also be included in discontinued operations. Assets or disposal groups categorized as held for sale are not depreciated further.

Example of disclosure of discontinued operations under IFRS 5

ABC Group
Statement of Income
For the Years Ended December 31, 2012 and 2011
(in thousands of euros)

	2012	2011
Continuing Operations (Segments X & Y):		
Revenue	10,000	5,000
Operating expenses	(7,000)	(3,500)
Pretax profit from operating actives	3,000	1,500
Interest expense	(300)	(200)
Profit before tax	2,700	1,300
Income tax expense	(540)	(260)
Profit after taxes	2,160	1,040
Discontinuing operation (Segment Z):		
Discontinued operations (note)	(240)	80
Total enterprise:		
Profit (loss) attributable to owners	1,920	1,120

The relevant note is as follows:

Discontinued Operations		
Revenue	3,000	2000
Operating expenses	(1,800)	(1400)
Provision for end-of-service benefits	(900)	--
Interest expense	(100)	(100)
Pretax profit	200	500
Income tax	(40)	(100)
Discontinued earnings	160	400
Impairment loss	(500)	(400)
Income tax	100	80
Write-down of assets	(400)	(320)
Discontinued operations, net	(240)	(80)

Aggregating items. Aggregation of items should not serve to conceal significant information, as would the netting of revenues against expenses, or the combining of other elements that are individually of interest to readers, such as bad debts and depreciation. The categories "other" or "miscellaneous expense" should contain, at maximum, an immaterial total amount of aggregated, individually insignificant elements. Once this total approaches, for example, 10% of total expenses (or any other materiality threshold), some other aggregations, together with appropriate explanatory titles, should be selected.

Information is material if its omission or misstatement or nondisclosure could influence the economic decisions of users taken on the basis of the financial statements. Materiality depends on the size of the item judged in the particular circumstances of its omission (according to IASB's *Framework*). But it is often forgotten that materiality is also linked with understandability and the level of precision in which the financial statements are to be presented. For instance, the financial statements are often rendered more understandable by rounding information to the nearest thousand currency units (e.g., US dollars). This obviates the necessity of loading the financial statements with unnecessary detail. However, it should be borne in mind that the use of the level of precision that makes presentation possible in the nearest thousands of currency units is acceptable only as long as the threshold of materiality is not surpassed.

Offsetting items of revenue and expense. Materiality also plays a role in the matter of allowing or disallowing offsetting of the items of income and expense. IAS 1 addresses this issue and prescribes rules in this area. According to IAS 1, assets and liabilities or income and expenses may not be offset against each other, unless required or permitted by an IFRS. Usually, when more than one event occurs in a given reporting period, losses and gains on disposal of noncurrent assets or foreign exchange gains and losses are seen reported on a net basis, due to the fact that they are not material individually (compared to other items on the income statement). However, if they were material individually, they would need to be disclosed separately according to the requirements of IAS 1.

However, the reduction of accounts receivable by the allowance for doubtful accounts, or of property, plant, and equipment by the accumulated depreciation, are acts that reduce these assets by the appropriate valuation accounts and are not considered to be offsetting assets and liabilities.

Views differ as to the treatment of disposal gains and losses arising from the routine replacement of noncurrent assets. Some experts believe that these should be separately disclosed as a disposal transaction, whereas others point out that if the depreciation schedule is estimated correctly, there should be no disposal gain or loss. Consequently, any difference between carrying value and disposal proceeds is akin to an adjustment to previous depreciation, and should logically flow through the income statement in the same caption where the depreciation was originally reported. Here again, the issue comes down to one of materiality: does it affect users' ability to make economic decisions?

IAS 1 further clarifies that when items of income or expense are offset, the enterprise should nevertheless consider, based on materiality, the need to disclose the gross amounts in the notes to the financial statements. This standard gives the following examples of transactions that are incidental to the main revenue-generating activities of an enterprise and whose results when presented by offsetting or reporting on a net basis, such as netting any gains with related expenses, reflect the substance of the transaction:

1. Gains or losses on the disposal of noncurrent assets, including investments and operating assets, are reported by deducting from the proceeds on disposal the carrying amounts of the asset and related selling expenses.
2. Expenditure related to a provision that is reimbursed under a contractual arrangement with a third party may be netted against the related reimbursement.

OTHER COMPREHENSIVE INCOME

Under IAS 1, *other comprehensive income* (OCI) includes items of income and expense (including reclassification adjustments) that are not recognized in profit or loss as may be required or permitted by other IFRS. The components of OCI include (1) changes in revaluation surplus (IAS 16 and IAS 38); (2) actuarial gains and losses on defined benefit plans (IAS 19); (3) translation gains and losses (IAS 21); (4) gains and losses on remeasuring available-for-sale financial assets (IAS 39); and (5) the effective portion of gains and losses on hedging instruments in a cash flow hedge (IAS 39).

The above items and an entity's share of other comprehensive of any associate must be classified in those that

1. Will not be reclassified subsequently to profit or loss: and
2. Will be reclassified subsequently to profit or loss.

The amount of income tax relating to each component of OCI, including reclassification adjustments, should be disclosed either on the face of the statement of comprehensive income or in the notes.

Components of OCI can be presented in one of two ways

1. Net of related tax effects; or
2. Before related tax effects with one amount shown for the aggregate amount of income tax relating to those components.

Other IFRS specify whether and when amounts previously recognized in OCI are reclassified to profit or loss. The purpose of this requirement is to avoid double-counting of OCI items in total comprehensive income when those items are reclassified to profit or loss in accordance with other IFRS. Under IFRS, some items of OCI are subject to recycling while other items are not (under US GAAP, always recycle). For example, gains realized on the disposal of a foreign operation are included in profit or loss of the current period. These amounts may have been recognized in OCI as unrealized foreign currency translation (CTA) gains in the current or previous periods. Those unrealized gains must be deducted from OCI in the period in which the realized gains are included in profit or loss to avoid double-counting them. In the same manner, for instance, unrealized gains or losses on available-for-sale (AFS) financial assets should not include realized gains or losses from the sale of AFS financial assets during the current period, which are reported in profit or loss. Reclassification adjustments arise, for example, on the following components:

- On disposal of a foreign operation (IAS 21)
- On derecognition of available-for-sale financial assets (IAS 39)
- When a hedged forecast transaction affects profit or loss (IAS 39)

Reclassification adjustments *do not* arise on the following components, which are recognized in OCI, but are not reclassified to profit or loss in subsequent periods:

- On changes in revaluation surplus (IAS 16; IAS 38)
- On changes in actuarial gains or losses on defined benefit plans (IAS 19)

In accordance with IAS 16 and IAS 38, changes in revaluation surplus may be transferred to retained earnings in subsequent periods when the asset is sold or when it is derecognized. Actuarial gains and losses are reported in retained earnings in the period that they are recognized as OCI (IAS 19).

Reclassification Adjustments: An Example

In general, the reporting of unrealized gains and losses on available-for-sale (AFS) securities in comprehensive income is straightforward unless the company sells securities during the year. In such a case, double-counting results when a company reports realized gains and losses as part of profit or loss (net income), but also shows the amounts as part of other comprehensive income (OCI) in the current period or in previous periods.

When a sale of securities occurs, a reclassification adjustment is necessary to ensure that gains and losses are not counted twice. To illustrate, assume that ABC Group has the following two AFS securities in its portfolio at the end of 2011, its first year of operations:

Investments	*Cost*	*Fair value*	*Unrealized holding gain (loss)*
Radar Ltd	€105,000	€125,000	€20,000
Konini Ltd	260,000	300,000	40,000
Total value of portfolio	265,000	425,000	60,000
Previous (accumulated) securities fair value adjustment balance			0
Securities fair value adjustment (Dr)			€60,000

ABC Group reports net income of €650,000 in 2011 and presents a statement of profit or loss and other comprehensive income as follows:

ABC Group
Statement of Profit or Loss and Other Comprehensive Income
For the Year Ended December 31, 2011

Profit or loss	€650,000
Other comprehensive income	
Holding gains on available-for-sale securities	60,000
Comprehensive income	€710,000

During 2012, ABC Group sold 50% of the shares of the Konini Ltd common stock for €150,000 and realized a gain on the sale of €20,000 (€150,000 – €130,000). At the end of 2012, ABC Group reports its AFS securities as follows:

Investments	*Cost*	*Fair value*	*Unrealized holding gain (loss)*
Radar Ltd	€105,000	€130,000	€25,000
Konini Ltd	130,000	160,000	30,000
Total value of portfolio	235,000	290,000	55,000
Previous (accumulated) securities fair value adjustment balance			(60,000)
Securities fair value adjustment (Dr)			€ (5,000)

ABC Group should report an unrealized holding loss of €(5,000) in comprehensive income in 2012 and realized gain of €20,000 on the sale of the Konini common stock. Consequently, ABC recognizes a total holding gain in 2012 of €15,000 (unrealized holding loss of €5,000 plus realized holding gain of €20,000).

ABC reports net profit of €830,000 in 2012 and presents the components of holding gains (losses) as follows:

ABC Group
Statement of Profit or Loss and Other Comprehensive Income
For the Year Ended December 31, 2012

Net income (includes €20,000 realized gain on Konini shares)		€830,000
Other comprehensive income		
Total holding gains (€5,000 + €20,000)	€15,000	
Less: Reclassification adjustment for realized gains included		
in net income	(20,000)	(5,000)
Comprehensive income		€815,000

In 2011, ABC included the unrealized gain on the Konini common stock in comprehensive income. In 2012, ABC sold the stock and reported the realized gain on sale in profit, which increased comprehensive income again. To prevent double-counting of this gain of €20,000 on the Konini shares, ABC makes a reclassification adjustment to eliminate the realized gain from the computation of comprehensive income in 2012.

An entity may display reclassification adjustments on the face of the financial statement in which it reports comprehensive income or disclose them in the notes to the financial statements. The IASB's view is that separate presentation of reclassification adjustments is essential to inform users clearly of those amounts that are included as income and expenses in two different periods—as income or expenses in other comprehensive income in previous periods and as income or expenses in profit or loss (net income) in the current period.

STATEMENT OF CHANGES IN EQUITY

Equity (owners', partners', or shareholders') represents the interest of the owners in the net assets of an entity and shows the cumulative net results of past transactions and other events affecting the entity since its inception. The statement of changes in equity reflects the increases and decreases in the net assets of an entity during the period. In accordance with IAS 1, all changes in equity from transactions with owners are to be presented separately from nonowner changes in equity.

IAS 1 requires an entity to present a statement of changes in equity including the following components on the face of the statement:

1. Total comprehensive income for the period, segregating amounts attributable to owners and to noncontrolling interest;
2. The effects of retrospective application or retrospective restatement in accordance with IAS 8, separately for each component of equity;
3. Contributions from and distributions to owners; and
4. A reconciliation between the carrying amount at the beginning and the end of the period, separately disclosing each change, for each component of equity.

The amount of dividends recognized as distributions to equity holders during the period, and the related amount per share should be presented either on the face of the statement of changes in equity or in the notes.

According to IAS 1, except for changes resulting from transactions with owners (such as equity contributions, reacquisitions of the entity's own equity instruments, dividends, and costs related to these transactions with owners), the change in equity during the period represents the total amount of income and expense (including gains and losses) arising from activities other than those with owners.

The following should be disclosed, either in the statement of financial position or the statement of changes in equity, or in the notes:

1. For each class of share capital

   - Number of shares authorized;
   - Number of shares issued and fully paid, and issued but not fully paid;
   - Par value per share, or that the shares have no par value;
   - Recognition of the number of shares outstanding at the beginning and at the end of the periods;
   - Any rights, preferences and restrictions attached;
   - Shares in the entity held by the entity or its subsidiaries; and
   - Shares reserved for issue under options and contracts for the sale of shares, including terms and amounts.

2. A description of the nature and purpose of each reserve within equity

FUTURE DEVELOPMENTS

The second phase of the financial statement presentation project should change the structure and format of the statement of comprehensive income (see Chapter 2). The 2008 Discussion Paper (DP) proposes the following changes:

1. **Single-statement presentation.** All entities should present a single (stand-alone) statement of comprehensive income displaying all items of income and expense that are recognized in profit or loss (which is a subtotal in the statement of comprehensive income) and other comprehensive income items (OCI), presented in a separate section. Consequently, the current option available to present a separate income statement (two-statement approach) would be eliminated. Existing guidance on presentation of OCI items would remain unchanged as well as the recycling mechanism.

2. **Disaggregation by activities, function and nature.** In the statement of comprehensive income, an entity would be required to present the items of income and expense and OCI items in separate sections, based on the primary activities (functions) in which it engages.

   a. Business ("operating income and expenses" and "investing income and expenses" presented separately);
   b. Financing (financing asset income and financing liability expense presented separately);
   c. Income taxes on continuing operations;
   d. Discontinued operations (net of tax); and
   e. Equity

   An entity should further disaggregate each of those activities (except discontinued operations and taxes) on the basis of their function within those categories, and then, by nature, but only to the extent that this disaggregation would help users in predicting the entity's future cash flows;

   f. Function (e.g., selling, manufacturing, advertising, business administration).
   g. Nature (e.g., disaggregating total revenues into wholesale revenues and retail revenues).

Changes are also foreseen regarding discontinued operations. The objective of the discontinued operations project is to develop jointly with the FASB a common definition of discontinued operations and to require common disclosures relating to disposals of components of entities.

US GAAP COMPARISON

The US GAAP income statement is presented in basically the same order, but differences in presentation and captions result in some substantive differences. For example, US GAAP includes an income statement caption entitled, "Extraordinary Items" for infrequent and unusual events. IFRS does not allow for any extraordinary items.

Other Comprehensive Income is presented as part of the Statement of Equity, as opposed to single or consecutive statements under IFRS. In the OCI section, tax effects can be shown parenthetically or gross with a single tax amount at the bottom.

6 STATEMENT OF CASH FLOWS

INTRODUCTION

IAS 7, *Cash Flow Statements,* became effective in 1994. IAS 7 had originally required that reporting entities prepare the statement of changes in financial position (commonly referred to as the funds flow statement), which was once a widely accepted method of presenting changes in financial position, as part of a complete set of financial statements. The IASB has amended the title of IAS 7 from *Cash Flow Statements* to *Statement of Cash Flows* (the title used in the US) as a consequence of the latest revision of IAS 1, *Presentation of Financial Statements,* a result of the IASB and the FASB deliberations on the first phase of the Financial Statement Presentation project. The statement of cash flows is now universally accepted and required under most national GAAP as well as IFRS. While there are some variations in terms of presentation (most of which pertain to the section in which certain captions appear), the approach is highly similar across all current sets of standards.

The purpose of the statement of cash flows is to provide information about the operating cash receipts and cash payments of an entity during a period, as well as providing insight into its various investing and financing activities. It is a vitally important financial statement, because the ultimate concern of investors is the reporting entity's ability to generate cash flows which will support payments (typically but not necessarily in the form of dividends) to the shareholders. More specifically, the statement of cash flows should help investors and creditors assess:

1. The ability to generate future positive cash flows
2. The ability to meet obligations and pay dividends

3. Reasons for differences between profit or loss and cash receipts and payments
4. Both cash and noncash aspects of entities' investing and financing transactions

Sources of IFRS
IAS 7

SCOPE

The statement of cash flows is prepared in terms of IAS 7 and must be presented as an integral part of the financial statements in the form of a separate statement.

DEFINITIONS OF TERMS

Cash. Cash on hand and demand deposits with banks or other financial institutions.

Cash equivalents. Short-term highly liquid investments that are readily convertible to known amounts of cash and which are subject to an insignificant risk of changes in value. Treasury bills, commercial paper, and money market funds are all examples of cash equivalents.

Direct method. A method that derives the net cash provided by or used in operating activities from major components of operating cash receipts and payments.

Financing activities. The transactions and other events that cause changes in the size and composition of an entity's capital and borrowings.

Indirect (reconciliation) method. A method that derives the net cash provided by or used in operating activities by adjusting profit (loss) for the effects of transactions of a noncash nature, any deferrals or accruals of past or future operating cash receipts or payments, and items of income or expense associated with investing or financing activities.

Investing activities. The acquisition and disposal of long-term assets and other investments not included in cash equivalents. An amendment effective for annual periods beginning on or after January 1, 2010, states explicitly that only expenditures that result in a recognized asset in the statement of financial position are eligible for classification as investing activities. Examples of expenditures that in certain instances do not result in the recognition of assets are exploration and evaluation activities; also expenditures on advertising and promotional activities, staff training, and research and development could raise such an issue.

Operating activities. The transactions and other events not classified as financing or investing activities. In general, operating activities are principal revenue-producing activities of an entity that enter into the determination of profit or loss, including the sale of goods and the rendering of services.

BACKGROUND

Benefits of Statement of Cash Flows

The perceived benefits of presenting the statement of cash flows in conjunction with the statement of financial position and the statement of profit or loss and comprehensive income have been highlighted by IAS 7 to be as follows:

1. It provides an insight into the financial structure of the entity (including its liquidity and solvency) and its ability to affect the amounts and timing of cash flows in order to adapt to changing circumstances and opportunities.

The statement of cash flows discloses important information about the cash flows from operating, investing, and financing activities, information that is not available or as clearly discernible in either the statement of financial position or the statement of profit or loss and comprehensive income. The additional disclosures which are either recommended by IAS 7 (such as those relating to undrawn borrowing facilities or cash flows that represent increases in operating capacity) or required to be disclosed by the standard (such as that about cash held by the entity but not available for use) provide a wealth of information for the informed user of financial statements. Taken together, the statement of cash flows coupled with these required or recommended disclosures provide the user with vastly more insight into the entity's performance and position, and its probable future results, than would the statement of financial position and statement of comprehensive income alone.

2. It provides additional information to the users of financial statements for evaluating changes in assets, liabilities, and equity of an entity.

When comparative statements of financial position are presented, users are given information about the entity's assets and liabilities at the end of each of the years. Were the statement of cash flows not presented as an integral part of the financial statements, it would be necessary for users of comparative financial statements either to speculate about how and why certain amounts reported in the statement of financial position changed from one period to another, or to compute (at least for the latest year presented) approximations of these items for themselves. At best, however, such a do-it-yourself approach would derive the net changes (the increase or decrease) in the individual assets and liabilities and attribute these to normally related accounts in the statement of comprehensive income. (For example, the net change in accounts receivable from the beginning to the end of the year would be used to convert reported sales to cash-basis sales or cash collected from customers.)

While basic changes in the statement of financial position can be used to infer cash flow implications, this is not universally the case. More complex combinations of events (such as the acquisition of another entity, along with its accounts receivables, which would be an increase in that asset which was not related to sales to customers by the reporting entity during the period) would not immediately be comprehensible and might lead to incorrect interpretations of the data unless an actual statement of cash flows were presented.

3. It enhances the comparability of reporting of operating performance by different entities because it eliminates the effects of using different accounting treatments for the same transactions and events.

There was considerable debate even as early as the 1960s and 1970s over accounting standardization, which led to the emergence of cash flow accounting. The principal argument in support of cash flow accounting by its earliest proponents was that it avoids the difficult to understand and sometimes seemingly arbitrary allocations inherent in accrual accounting. For example, cash flows provided by or used in operating activities are derived, under the indirect method, by adjusting profit (or loss) for items such as depreciation and amortization, which might have been computed by different entities using different accounting methods. Thus, accounting standardization will be achieved by converting the accrual-basis profit or loss to cash-basis profit or loss, and the resultant figures will become comparable across entities.

4. It serves as an indicator of the amount, timing, and certainty of future cash flows. Furthermore, if an entity has a system in place to project its future cash flows, the statement of cash flows could be used as a touchstone to evaluate the accuracy of past projections of those future cash flows. This benefit is elucidated by the standard as follows:

    a. The statement of cash flows is useful in comparing past assessments of future cash flows against current year's cash flow information, and
    b. It is of value in appraising the relationship between profitability and net cash flows, and in assessing the impact of changing prices.

Exclusion of Noncash Transactions

The statement of cash flows, as its name implies, includes only actual inflows and outflows of cash and cash equivalents. Accordingly, it excludes all transactions that do not directly affect cash receipts and payments. However, IAS 7 does require that the effects of transactions not resulting in receipts or payments of cash be disclosed elsewhere in the financial statements. The reason for not including noncash transactions in the statement of cash flows and placing them elsewhere in the financial statements (e.g., the notes) is that it preserves the statement's primary focus on cash flows from operating, investing, and financing activities. It is thus important that the user of financial statements fully appreciate what this financial statement does—and does not—attempt to portray.

Components of Cash and Cash Equivalents

Cash and cash equivalents include unrestricted cash (meaning cash actually on hand, or bank balances whose immediate use is determined by the management), other demand deposits, and short-term investments whose maturities at the date of acquisition by the entity were three months or less. Equity investments do not qualify as cash equivalents unless they fit the definition above of short-term maturities of three months or less, which would rarely, if ever, be true. Preference shares carrying mandatory redemption features, if acquired within three months of their predetermined redemption date, would meet the criteria above since they are, in substance, cash equivalents. These are very infrequently encountered circumstances, however.

Bank borrowings are normally considered as financing activities. However, in some countries, bank overdrafts play an integral part in the entity's cash management, and as such, overdrafts are to be included as a component of cash equivalents if the following conditions are met:

1. The bank overdraft is repayable on demand, and
2. The bank balance often fluctuates from positive to negative (overdraft).

Statutory (or reserve) deposits by banks (i.e., those held with the central bank for regulatory compliance purposes) are often included in the same statement of financial position caption as cash. The financial statement treatment of these deposits is subject to some controversy in certain countries, which becomes fairly evident from scrutiny of published financial statements of banks, as these deposits are variously considered to be either a cash equivalent or an operating asset. If the latter, changes in amount would be presented in the operating activities section of the statement of cash flows, and the item could not then be combined with cash in the statement of financial position. Since the appendix to IAS 7, which illustrates the application of the standard to statement of cash flows of financial institutions, does not include statutory deposits with the central bank as a cash equivalent, the authors have concluded that there is little logic to support the alternative presentation of this item as a cash equivalent. Given the fact that deposits with central banks are more or less permanent (and in fact would be more likely to increase over time than to be diminished, given a going concern assumption about the reporting financial institution) the presumption must be that these are not cash equivalents in normal practice.

PRESENTATION

Classifications in the Statement of Cash Flows

The statement of cash flows prepared in accordance with IAS 7 requires classification into these three categories:

1. *Investing activities* include the acquisition and disposition of property, plant, and equipment and other long-term assets and debt and equity instruments of other entities that are not considered cash equivalents or held for dealing or trading purposes. Investing activities include cash advances and collections on loans made to other parties (other than advances and loans of a financial institution).
2. *Financing activities* include obtaining resources from and returning resources to the owners. Also included is obtaining resources through borrowings (short-term or long-term) and repayments of the amounts borrowed.
3. *Operating activities,* which can be presented under the (IFRS-preferred) direct or the indirect method, include all transactions that are not investing and financing activities. In general, cash flows arising from transactions and other events that enter into the determination of profit or loss are operating cash flows. Operating activities are principal revenue-producing activities of an entity and include delivering or producing goods for sale and providing services.

The following are examples of the statement of cash flows classification under the provisions of IAS 7:

	Operating	*Investing*	*Financing*
Cash inflows	• Receipts from sale of goods or rendering of services	• Principal collections from loans and sales of other entities' debt instruments	• Proceeds from issuing share capital
	• Sale of loans, debt, or equity instruments carried in trading portfolio	• Sale of equity instruments of other entities and from returns of investment in those instruments	• Proceeds from issuing debt (short-term or long-term)
	• Returns on loans (interest)	• Sale of plant and equipment	• Not-for-profits' donor-restricted cash that is limited to long-term purposes
	• Returns on equity securities (dividends)		
Cash outflows	• Payments to suppliers for goods and other services	• Loans made and acquisition of other entities' debt instruments	• Payment of dividends
	• Payments to or on behalf of employees	• Purchase of equity instruments* of other entities	• Repurchase of company's shares

Operating	*Investing*	*Financing*
• Payments of taxes	• Purchase of plant and equipment	• Repayment of debt principal, including capital lease obligations
• Payments of interest		
• Purchase of loans, debt, or equity instruments carried in trading portfolio		

* *Unless held for trading purposes or considered to be cash equivalents.*

Noncash investing and financing activities should, according to IAS 7, be disclosed in the notes to financial statements ("elsewhere" is how the standard actually identifies this), but apparently are not intended to be included in the statement of cash flows itself. Examples of significant noncash financing and investing activities might include

1. Acquiring an asset through a finance lease
2. Conversion of debt to equity
3. Exchange of noncash assets or liabilities for other noncash assets or liabilities
4. Issuance of stock to acquire assets

Basic example of a classified statement of cash flows

ABC Group
Statement of Cash Flows
For the Year Ended December 31, 2012

Net cash flows from operating activities		
Cash receipts from customers	€ xxx	
Cash paid to suppliers and employees	(xxx)	
Interest paid	(xx)	
Income taxes paid	(xx)	
Net cash **provided** by operation activities		€xxxx
Cash flows from investing activities:		
Purchase of property, plant, and equipment	€ (xxx)	
Sale of equipment	xx	
Collection of notes receivable	xx	
Net cash **used** in investing activities		(xx)
Cash flows from financing activities:		
Proceeds from issuance of share capital	xxx	
Repayment of long-term debt	(xx)	
Reduction of notes payable	(xx)	
Net cash **provided** by financing activities		xx
Effect of exchange rate changes on cash		xx
Net increase in cash and cash equivalents		€ xxx
Cash and cash equivalents at beginning of year		xxx
Cash and cash equivalents at end of year		€xxxx

Footnote Disclosure of Noncash Investing and Financing Activities

Note 4: Supplemental Statement of Cash Flows Information

Significant noncash investing and financing transactions:	
Conversion of bonds into ordinary shares	€ xxx
Property acquired under finance leases	xxx
	€ xxx

Reporting Cash Flows from Operating Activities

Direct vs. indirect methods. The operating activities section of the statement of cash flows can be presented under the direct or the indirect method. However, IFRS has expressed a preference for the direct method of presenting net cash from operating activities. For their part, most preparers of financial statements have chosen overwhelmingly to ignore the recommendation of the IASC, preferring by a very large margin to use the indirect method in lieu of the recommended direct method.

The *direct method* shows the items that affected cash flow and the magnitude of those cash flows. Cash received from, and cash paid to, specific sources (such as customers and suppliers) are presented, as opposed to the indirect method's converting accrual-basis profit (or loss) to cash flow information by means of a series of add-backs and deductions. Entities using the direct method are required by IAS 7 to report the following major classes of gross cash receipts and gross cash payments:

1. Cash collected from customers
2. Interest and dividends received[1]
3. Cash paid to employees and other suppliers
4. Interest paid[2]
5. Income taxes paid
6. Other operating cash receipts and payments

Given the availability of alternative modes of presentation of interest and dividends received, and of interest paid, it is particularly critical that the policy adopted be followed consistently. Since the face of the statement of cash flows will in almost all cases make it clear what approach has been elected, it is not usually necessary to spell this out in the accounting policy note to the financial statements, although this certainly can be done if it would be useful to do so.

An important advantage of the direct method is that it permits the user to better comprehend the relationships between the entity's profit or loss and its cash flows. For example, payments of expenses are shown as cash disbursements and are deducted from cash receipts. In this way the user is able to recognize the cash receipts and cash payments for the period. Formulas for conversion of various statement of profit or loss and comprehensive income amounts for the direct method presentation from the accrual basis to the cash basis are summarized below.

Accrual basis	*Additions*	*Deductions*	*Cash basis*
Net sales	+ Beginning AR	− Ending AR AR written off	= Cash received from customers
Cost of goods sold	+ Ending inventory Beginning AP	− Depreciation and amortization* Beginning inventory Ending AP	= Cash paid to suppliers
Operating expenses	+ Ending prepaid expenses Beginning accrued expenses	− Depreciation and amortization Beginning prepaid expenses Ending accrued expenses payable Bad debts expense	= Cash paid for operating expenses

* *Applies to a manufacturing entity only*

---

[1] *Alternatively, interest and dividends received may be classified as investing cash flows rather than as operating cash flows because they are returns on investments.*

[2] *Alternatively, IAS 7 permits interest paid to be classified as a financing cash flow, because this is the cost of obtaining financing.*

From the foregoing it can be appreciated that the amounts to be included in the operating section of the statement of cash flows, when the direct approach is utilized, are derived amounts that must be computed (although the computations are not onerous); they are not, generally, amounts that exist as account balances simply to be looked up and then placed in the statement. The extra effort needed to prepare the direct method operating cash flow data may be a contributing cause of why this method has been distinctly unpopular with preparers.

The *indirect method* (sometimes referred to as the reconciliation method) is the most widely used means of presentation of cash from operating activities, primarily because it is easier to prepare. It focuses on the differences between net operating results and cash flows. The indirect format begins with the amount of profit or loss for the year, which can be obtained directly from the statement of profit or loss and comprehensive income. Revenue and expense items not affecting cash are added or deducted to arrive at net cash provided by operating activities. For example, depreciation and amortization would be added back because these expenses reduce profit or loss without affecting cash.

The statement of cash flows prepared using the indirect method emphasizes changes in the components of most current asset and current liability accounts. Changes in inventory, accounts receivable, and other current accounts are used to determine the cash flow from operating activities. Although most of these adjustments are obvious (most preparers simply relate each current asset or current liability on the statement of financial position to a single caption in the statement of comprehensive income), some changes require more careful analysis. For example, it is important to compute cash collected from sales by relating sales revenue to both the change in accounts receivable and the change in the related bad debt allowance account.

As another example of possible complexity in computing the cash from operating activities, the change in short-term borrowings resulting from the purchase of equipment would not be included, since it is not related to operating activities. Instead, these short-term borrowings would be classified as a financing activity. Other adjustments under the indirect method include changes in the account balances of deferred income taxes, noncontrolling interest, unrealized foreign currency gains or losses, and the profit or loss from investments under the equity method.

IAS 7 offers yet another alternative way of presenting the cash flows from operating activities. This could be referred to as the *modified indirect method*. Under this variant of the indirect method, the starting point is not profit or loss but rather revenues and expenses as reported in the statement of comprehensive income. In essence, this approach is virtually the same as the regular indirect method, with two more details: revenues and expenses for the period.

The following summary, actually simply an expanded statement of financial position equation, may facilitate understanding of the adjustments to profit or loss necessary for converting accrual-basis profit or loss to cash-basis profit or loss when using the indirect method.

	Current assets*	−	Fixed assets	=	Current liabilities	+	Long-term liabilities	+	Profit or loss	Accrual profit adjustment to convert to cash flow
1.	Increase			=					Increase	Decrease
2.	Decrease			=					Decrease	Increase
3.				=	Increase				Decrease	Increase
4.				=	Decrease				Increase	Decrease

* *Other than cash and cash equivalents*

For example, using row 1 in the above chart, a credit sale would increase accounts receivable and accrual-basis profit but would not affect cash. Therefore, its effect must be removed from the accrual profit to convert to cash profit. The last column indicates that the increase in a current asset balance must be deducted from profit to obtain cash flow.

Similarly, an increase in a current liability, row three, must be added to profit to obtain cash flows (e.g., accrued wages are in the statement of profit or loss and comprehensive income as an expense, but they do not require cash; the increase in wages payable must be added back to remove this noncash flow expense from accrual-basis profit).

The major drawback to the indirect method involves the user's difficulty in comprehending the information presented. This method does not show from where the cash was received or to where the cash was paid. Only adjustments to accrual-basis profit or loss are shown. In some cases the adjustments can be confusing. For instance, the sale of equipment resulting in an accrual-basis loss would require that the loss be added to profit to arrive at net cash from operating activities. (The loss was deducted in the computation of profit or loss, but because the sale will be shown as an investing activity, the loss must be added back to profit or loss.)

Although the indirect method is more commonly used in practice, the IASB encourages entities to use the direct method. As pointed out by IAS 7, a distinct advantage of the direct method is that it provides information that may be useful in estimating or projecting future cash flows, a benefit that is clearly not achieved when the indirect method is utilized instead. Both the direct and indirect methods are presented below.

Direct method

Cash flows from operating activities:		
Cash received from sale of goods	€xxx	
Cash dividends received*	xxx	
Cash provided by operating activities		€ xxx
Cash paid to suppliers	(xxx)	
Cash paid for operating expenses	(xxx)	
Cash paid for income taxes**	(xxx)	
Cash disbursed for operating activities		€ (xxx)
Net cash flows from operating activities		€ xxx

* *Alternatively, could be classified as investing cash flow.*

** *Taxes paid are usually classified as operating activities. However, when it is practical to identify the tax cash flow with an individual transaction that gives rise to cash flows that are classified as investing or financing activities, then the tax cash flow is classified as an investing or financing activity as appropriate.*

Indirect method

Cash flows from operating activities:	
Profit before income taxes	€ xx
Adjustments for:	
Depreciation	xx
Unrealized loss on foreign exchange	xx
Interest expense	xx
Operating profit before working capital changes	xx
Increase in accounts receivable	(xx)
Decrease in inventories	xx
Increase in accounts payable	xx
Cash generated from operations	xx
Interest paid	(xx)
Income taxes paid (see note**above)	(xx)
Net cash flows from operating activities	€xxx

OTHER REQUIREMENTS

Gross vs. net basis. The emphasis in the statement of cash flows is on gross cash receipts and cash payments. For instance, reporting the net change in bonds payable would obscure the financing activities of the entity by not disclosing separately cash inflows from issuing bonds and cash outflows from retiring bonds.

IAS 7 specifies two exceptions where netting of cash flows is allowed. Items with quick turnovers, large amounts, and short maturities may be presented as net cash flows. Cash receipts and payments on behalf of customers when the cash flows reflect the activities of the customers rather than those of the entity may also be reported on a net rather than a gross basis.

Foreign currency cash flows. Foreign operations must prepare a separate statement of cash flows and translate the statement to the reporting currency using the exchange rate in effect at the time of the cash flow (a weighted-average exchange rate may be used if the result is substantially the same). This translated statement is then used in the preparation of the consolidated statement of cash flows. Noncash exchange gains and losses recognized in the statement of profit or loss and comprehensive income should be reported as a separate item when reconciling profit or loss and operating activities. For a more detailed discussion about the exchange rate effects on the statement of cash flows, see Chapter 23.

Cash flow per share. There is presently no requirement under IFRS to disclose such information in the financial statements of an entity, unlike the requirement to report earnings per share (EPS). In fact, cash flow per share is a somewhat disreputable concept, since it was sometimes touted in an earlier era as being indicative of an entity's "real" performance, when of course it is not a meaningful alternative to earnings per share because, for example, entities that are self-liquidating by selling productive assets can generate very positive total cash flows, and hence, cash flows per share, while decimating the potential for future earnings. Since, unlike a comprehensive statement of cash flows, cash flow per share cannot reveal the components of cash flow (operating, investing, and financing), its usage could be misleading.

While cash flow per share is not well regarded, it should be noted that in recent years a growing number of entities have resorted to displaying a wide range of pro forma amounts, some of which roughly correspond to cash-based measures of operating performance. These non-IFRS categories should be viewed with great caution, both because they convey the message that IFRS-based measures of performance are somehow less meaningful, and also because there are no standard definitions of the non-IFRS measures, opening the door to possible manipulation.

Net Reporting by Financial Institutions.

IAS 7 permits financial institutions to report cash flows arising from certain activities on a net basis. These activities, and the related conditions under which net reporting would be acceptable, are as follows:

1. Cash receipts and payments on behalf of customers when the cash flows reflect the activities of the customers rather than those of the bank, such as the acceptance and repayment of demand deposits;
2. Cash flows relating to deposits with fixed maturity dates;
3. Placements and withdrawals of deposits from other financial institutions; and
4. Cash advances and loans to banks customers and repayments thereon.

Reporting Futures, Forward Contracts, Options, and Swaps

IAS 7 stipulates that cash payments for and cash receipts from futures contracts, forward contracts, option contracts, and swap contracts are normally classified as investing activities, except:

1. When such contracts are held for dealing or trading purposes and thus represent operating activities; or
2. When the payments or receipts are considered by the entity as financing activities and are reported accordingly.

Further, when a contract is accounted for as a hedge of an identifiable position, the cash flows of the contract are classified in the same manner as the cash flows of the position being hedged.

Reporting Extraordinary Items in the Statement of Cash Flows

Under IFRS, prior to revisions to IAS 1 in 2005, cash flows associated with extraordinary items were to be disclosed separately as arising from operating, investing, or financing activities in the statement of cash flows, as appropriate. Revised IAS 1 has eliminated the categorization of gains or losses as being extraordinary in character, so this no longer will impact the presentation of the statement of cash flows under IFRS.

Reconciliation of Cash and Cash Equivalents

An entity should disclose the components of cash and cash equivalents and should present a reconciliation of the difference, if any, between the amounts reported in the statement of cash flows and equivalent items reported in the statement of financial position.

Acquisitions and Disposals of Subsidiaries and Other Business Units

IAS 7 requires that the aggregate cash flows from acquisitions and from disposals of subsidiaries or other business units should be presented separately as part of the investing activities section of the statement of cash flows. The following disclosures have also been prescribed by IAS 7 in respect to both acquisitions and disposals:

1. The total consideration included;
2. The portion thereof discharged by cash and cash equivalents;
3. The amount of cash and cash equivalents in the subsidiary or business unit acquired or disposed; and
4. The amount of assets and liabilities (other than cash and cash equivalents) acquired or disposed, summarized by major category.

DISCLOSURE AND EXAMPLES

Other Disclosures Required or Recommended by IAS 7

Certain additional information may be relevant to the users of financial statements in gaining an insight into the liquidity or solvency of an entity. With this objective in mind, IAS 7 sets forth other disclosures that are required or in some cases, recommended.

1. **Required disclosure**—The amount of significant cash and cash equivalent balances held by an entity that are not available for use by the group should be disclosed along with a commentary by management.

2. **Recommended disclosures**—The disclosures that are encouraged are the following:

   a. The amount of undrawn borrowing facilities, indicating restrictions on their use, if any;

   b. In the case of investments in joint ventures, which are accounted for using proportionate consolidation, the aggregate amount of cash flows from operating, investing and financing activities that are attributable to the investment in the joint venture;

   c. The aggregate amount of cash flows that are attributable to the increase in operating capacity separately from those cash flows that are required to maintain operating capacity; and

   d. The amount of the cash flows arising from the operating, investing and financing activities of each reportable segment determined in accordance with IFRS 8. (See Chapter 28).

The disclosures above recommended by IAS 7, although difficult to present, are useful in enabling the users of financial statements to better understand the entity's financial position.

Basic example of preparation of the statement of cash flows under IAS 7 using a worksheet approach

Using the following financial information for ABC Ltd., preparation and presentation of the statement of cash flows according to the requirements of IAS 7 are illustrated. (Note that all figures in this example are in thousands of euros.)

ABC Ltd.
Statements of Financial Position
December 31, 2012 and 2011

	2012	*2011*
Assets		
Cash and cash equivalents	€ 3,000	€ 1,000
Accounts receivable	5,000	2,500
Inventory	2,000	1,500
Prepaid expenses	1,000	1,500
Due from associates	19,000	19,000
Property, plant, and equipment, at cost	12,000	22,500
Accumulated depreciation	(5,000)	(6,000)
Property, plant, and equipment, net	7,000	16,500
Total assets	€37,000	€42,000
Liabilities		
Accounts payable	€ 5,000	€12,500
Income taxes payable	2,000	1,000
Deferred taxes payable	3,000	2,000
Total liabilities	10,000	15,500
Shareholders' equity		
Share capital	6,500	6,500
Retained earnings	20,500	20,000
Total shareholders' equity	27,000	26,500
Total liabilities and shareholders' equity	€37,000	€42,000

ABC Ltd.
Statement of Profit or Loss and Comprehensive Income
For the Year Ended December 31, 2012

Sales	€ 30,000
Cost of sales	(10,000)
Gross profit	20,000
Administrative and selling expenses	(2,000)
Interest expense	(2,000)
Depreciation of property, plant and equipment	(2,000)
Amortization of intangible assets	(500)
Investment income	3,000
Profit before taxation	16,500
Taxes on income	(4,000)
Profit	€ 12,500

The following additional information is relevant to the preparation of the statement of cash flows:

1. Equipment with a net book value of €7,500 and original cost of €10,500 was sold for €7,500.
2. All sales made by the company are credit sales.
3. The company received cash dividends (from investments) amounting to €3,000, recorded as income in the statement of comprehensive income for the year ended December 31, 2011.
4. The company declared and paid dividends of €12,000 to its shareholders.
5. Interest expense for the year 2012 was €2,000, which was fully paid during the year. All administration and selling expenses incurred were paid during the year 2012.
6. Income tax expense for the year 2012 was provided at €4,000, out of which the company paid €2,000 during 2012 as an estimate.

A worksheet can be prepared to ease the development of the statement of cash flows, as follows:

Cash Flow Worksheet

	2012	*2011*	*Change*	*Operating*	*Investing*	*Financing*	*Cash and equivalents*
Cash and equivalents	3,000	1,000	2,000				2,000
Accounts receivable	5,000	2,500	2,500	(2,500)			
Inventories	2,000	1,500	500	(500)			
Prepaid expenses	1,000	1,500	(500)	500			
Due from associates	19,000	19,000	0				
Property, plant, and equipment	7,000	16,500	(9,500)	2,000	7,500		
Accounts payable	5,000	12,500	7,500	(7,500)			
Income taxes payable	2,000	1,000	1,000	1,000			
Deferred taxes payable	3,000	2,000	1,000	1,000			
Share capital	6,500	6,500	0				
Retained earnings	20,500	20,000	500	9,500	3,000	(12,000)	--
				3,500	10,500	(12,000)	2,000

ABC Ltd.
Statement of Cash Flows
For the Year Ended December 31, 2012
(Direct method)

Cash flows from operating activities		
Cash receipts from customers	€ 27,500	
Cash paid to suppliers and employees	(20,000)	
Cash generated from operations	7,500	
Interest paid	(2,000)	
Income taxes paid	(2,000)	
Net cash flows from operating activities		€ 3,500
Cash flows from investing activities		
Proceeds from the sale of equipment	7,500	
Dividends received	3,000	
Net cash flows from investing activities		10,500
Cash flows from financing activities		
Dividends paid	(12,000)	
Net cash flows used in financing activities		(12,000)
Net increase in cash and cash equivalents		2,000
Cash and cash equivalents, beginning of year		1,000
Cash and cash equivalents, end of year		€ 3,000

Details of the computations of amounts shown in the statement of cash flows are as follows:

Cash received from customers during the year		
Credit sales	€30,000	
Plus: Accounts receivable, beginning of year	2,500	
Less: Accounts receivable, end of year	(5,000)	
Cash received from customers during the year		€27,500
Cash paid to suppliers and employees		
Cost of sales	10,000	
Less: Inventory, beginning of year	(1,500)	
Plus: Inventory, end of year	2,000	
Plus: Accounts payable, beginning of year	12,500	
Less: Accounts payable, end of year	(5,000)	
Plus: Administrative and selling expenses paid	2,000	
Cash paid to suppliers and employees during the year		€20,000
Interest paid equals interest expense charged to profit or loss (per additional information)		€ 2,000
Income taxes paid during the year		
Tax expense during the year (comprising current and deferred portions)	4,000	
Plus: Beginning income taxes payable	1,000	
Plus: Beginning deferred taxes payable	2,000	
Less: Ending income taxes payable	(2,000)	
Less: Ending deferred taxes payable	(3,000)	
Cash paid toward income taxes		€ 2,000
Proceeds from sale of equipment (per additional information)		€ 7,500
Dividends received during 2011 (per additional information)		€ 3,000
Dividends paid during 2011 (per additional information)		€12,000

ABC Ltd.
Statement of Cash Flows
For the Year Ended December 31, 2012
(Indirect method)

Cash flows from operating activities		
Profit before taxation	€ 16,500	
Adjustments for:		
Depreciation of property, plant and equipment	2,000	
Decrease in prepaid expenses	500	
Investment income	(3,000)	
Interest expense	2,000	
Increase in accounts receivable	(2,500)	
Increase in inventories	(500)	
Decrease in accounts payable	(7,500)	
Cash generated from operations	7,500	
Interest paid	(2,000)	
Income taxes paid	(2,000)	
Net cash from operating activities		€ 3,500
Cash flows from investing activities		
Proceeds from sale of equipment	7,500	
Dividends received	3,000	
Net cash from investing activities		10,500
Cash flows from financing activities		
Dividends paid	(12,000)	
Net cash used in financing activities		(12,000)
Net increase in cash and cash equivalents		2,000
Cash and cash equivalents, beginning of year		1,000
Cash and cash equivalents, end of year		€ 3,000

CONSOLIDATED STATEMENT OF CASH FLOWS

A consolidated statement of cash flows must be presented when a complete set of consolidated financial statements is issued. The consolidated statement of cash flows would be the last statement to be prepared, as the information to prepare it will come from the other consolidated statements (consolidated statement of financial position, statement of profit or loss and comprehensive income, and statement of changes in equity). The preparation of these other consolidated statements is discussed in Chapter 15.

The preparation of a consolidated statement of cash flows involves the same analysis and procedures as the statement for an individual entity, with a few additional items. The direct or indirect method of presentation may be used. When the indirect method is used, the additional noncash transactions relating to the business combination, such as the differential amortization on group level, must also be reversed. Furthermore, all transfers to subsidiaries must be eliminated, as they do not represent a cash inflow or outflow of the consolidated entity.

All unrealized intragroup profits should have been eliminated in preparation of the other statements; thus, no additional entry of this sort should be required. Any profit allocated to noncontrolling parties would need to be added back, as it would have been eliminated in computing consolidated profit but does not represent a true cash outflow. Finally, any dividend payments should be recorded as cash outflows in the financing activities section.

In preparing the operating activities section of the statement by the indirect method following a purchase business combination, the changes in assets and liabilities related to operations since acquisition should be derived by comparing the consolidated statement of financial position as of the date of acquisition with the year-end consolidated statement of financial position. These changes will be combined with those for the acquiring company up to the date of acquisition as adjustments to profit. The effects due to the acquisition of these assets and liabilities are reported under investing activities.

FUTURE DEVELOPMENTS

Phase B of the *Financial Statement Presentation* project will address more fundamental issues for presenting information on the face of the financial statements (refer to Chapter 3). Major changes proposed are as follows:

1. **Presentation of movements in cash.** The 2008 DP proposes that the cash line item in the statement of financial position should no longer include cash equivalents. Consequently, the statement of cash flows should present information on movements of cash only and the concept of cash in this statement would no longer include cash equivalents. Also, an entity's statement of cash flows would also reconcile the beginning and ending amounts of cash (rather than of cash and equivalents). Cash will be presented only in one category, unless cash is used differently in two or more reportable segments. Net amounts of receipts and payments related to items previously classified as cash equivalents will be presented in the statement of cash flows.
2. **Direct method of presenting operating cash flows.** An entity should present all its cash flows directly, including its operating cash flows. The indirect method to present major classes of operating cash receipts and payments in an entity's statement of cash flows will no longer be permitted (only a *direct method* can be applied). Historically, of course, the direct method has been strongly endorsed, yet employed by very few reporting entities. The Boards recommend the direct method since it is more consistent with the proposed objectives of financial statement presentation.
3. **Disaggregation by major activities.** The statement of cash flows would have the same sections and categories as the statements of financial position and comprehensive income (operating, investing financing), discontinued operations, taxes and equity. The classification of cash flows into the operating, investing and financing activities in the proposed model is based on the classification of the related asset or liability. Consequently, if property, plant, and equipment were classified as operating assets in the statement of financial position, then cash flows related to those assets would be presented as operating cash flows in the statement of cash flows.
4. **A new schedule** that reconciles cash flows to comprehensive income which should be included in the notes to financial statements. This reconciliation schedule disaggregates income into its cash, accruals other than remeasurements, and remeasurement components (for example, fair value changes), which can help users in predicting future cash flows and assessing earnings quality.

US GAAP COMPARISON

Under US GAAP dividends and interest received are always included in operating cash flows. Dividends paid are always classified as financial cash flows.

7 ACCOUNTING POLICIES, CHANGES IN ACCOUNTING ESTIMATES, AND ERRORS

INTRODUCTION

It is axiomatic that a true picture of an entity's performance only emerges after a series of fiscal periods' results have been reported and reviewed. The information set forth in an entity's financial statements over a period of years must, accordingly, be comparable if it is to be of value to users of those statements. Users of financial statements usually seek to identify trends in the entity's financial position, performance, and cash flows by studying and analyzing the information contained in those statements. Thus it is imperative that, to the maximum extent possible, the same accounting policies be applied from year to year in the preparation of financial statements, and that any necessary departures from this rule be clearly disclosed. This fundamental theorem explains why IFRS requires restatement of prior periods' financial statements for corrections of accounting errors and retrospective application of new accounting principles.

Financial statements are impacted by the choices made from among different, acceptable accounting principles and methodologies. Companies select those accounting principles and methods that they believe depict, in their financial statements, the economic reality of their financial position, results of operations, and changes in financial position. While the IASB has made great progress in narrowing the range of acceptable alternative accounting for given economic events and transactions (e.g., elimination of LIFO inventory costing), there still remain choices that can impair the ability to compare one entity's position and results with another (e.g., FIFO versus weighted-average inventory costing; or cost versus revaluation basis of accounting for property, plant, and equipment and for intangible assets).

Lack of comparability among entities and within a given entity over time can result because of changes in the assumptions and estimates underlying the application of the accounting principles and methods, from changes in the details in acceptable principles made by a promulgating authority, such as an accounting standard-setting body, and for other reasons. While there is no preventing these various factors from causing changes to occur, it is important that changes be made only when they result in improved financial reporting, or when necessitated by imposition of new financial reporting requirements. Whatever the reason for introducing change, and hence the risk of noncomparability, to the financial reporting process, adequate disclosures must be made to achieve transparency in financial reporting so that users of the financial statements are able to comprehend the effects and compensate for them in performing financial analyses.

IAS 8 deals with accounting changes (i.e., changes in accounting estimates and changes in accounting principles) and also addresses the accounting for the correction of errors. A principal objective of IAS 8 is to prescribe accounting treatments and financial statement disclosures that will enhance comparability, both within an entity over a series of years, and with the financial statements of other entities. IAS 8 has been amended by the revisions made to IAS 23 (March 2007), IAS 1 (September 2007) and *Improvements to IFRSs* issued in May 2008.

Even though the correction of an error in financial statements issued previously is not considered an accounting change, it is discussed by IAS 8, and therefore is covered in this chapter.

In the preparation of financial statements there is an underlying presumption that an accounting policy, once adopted, should not be changed, but rather is to be uniformly applied in accounting for events and transactions of a similar type. This consistent application of accounting policies enhances the decision usefulness of the financial statements. The presumption that an entity should not change an accounting policy may be overcome only if the reporting entity justifies the use of an alternative acceptable accounting policy on the basis that it is preferable under the circumstances.

The IASB's *Improvements Project* resulted in significant changes being made to IAS 8. It now requires retrospective application of voluntary changes in accounting policies and retrospective restatement to correct prior period errors with the earliest reported retained earnings balance being adjusted for any effects of a correction of an error or of a voluntary change in accounting policy on earlier years. The only exception to this rule occurs when retrospective application or restatement would be impracticable to accomplish, and this has intentionally been made a difficult criterion to satisfy. The revised standard removed the allowed alternative in the previous version of IAS 8 (1) to include in profit or loss for the current period the adjustment resulting from changing an accounting policy or correcting a prior period error, and (2) to present unchanged comparative information from financial statements of prior periods.

The *Improvements Project* also resulted in some reorganization of materials in the standards, specifically relocating certain guidance between IAS 1 and IAS 8. As revised, certain presentational issues have been moved to IAS 1, while guidance on accounting policies, previously found in IAS 1, has been moved to IAS 8. In addition, included in revised IAS 8 is a newly established hierarchy of criteria to be applied in the selection of accounting policies.

As amended, IAS 8 incorporates the material formerly found in SIC 18, *Consistency—Alternative Methods*, which requires that an entity select and apply its accounting policies for a period consistently for similar transactions, other events and conditions, unless a standard or an interpretation specifically requires or permits categorization of items for which different policies may be appropriate, in which case an appropriate accounting policy shall be selected and applied consistently to each category. Simply stated, the expectation is that, in the absence of changes in promulgated standards, or changes in the character of the transactions being accounted for, the reporting entity should continue to use accounting policies from one period to the next without change, and use them for all transactions and events within a given class or category without exception.

When IFRS are revised or new standards are developed, they often are promulgated a year or more prior to the date set for mandatory application. Disclosure of future changes in accounting policies must be made when the reporting entity has yet to implement a new standard that has been issued but that has not yet come into effect. In addition, disclosure is now required of the planned date of adoption, along with an estimate of the effect of the change on the entity's financial position, except if making such an estimate requires undue cost or effort.

Sources of IFRS
IAS 8

SCOPE

IAS 8 is applied in the selection of accounting policies and in the accounting for changes in accounting policies, changes in estimates and corrections of prior year errors. This chapter addresses the criteria for selecting and changing accounting policies, together with the accounting treatment and disclosure of changes in accounting policies, changes in accounting estimates, and corrections of errors in accordance with IAS 8.

DEFINITIONS OF TERMS

Accounting policies. Specific principles, bases, conventions, rules, and practices adopted by an entity in preparing and presenting financial statements. Management is required to adopt the accounting policies that result in a fair, full, and complete presentation of financial position, performance, and cash flows of the reporting entity.

Change in accounting estimate. An adjustment of the carrying amount of an asset or liability, or related expense, resulting from reassessing the present status of, and expected future benefits and obligations associated with that asset or liability. Prospective application applies to changes in estimates resulting from new information or new developments (which, therefore, are not corrections of errors). The use of reasonable estimates is an essential part of the financial statement preparation process and does not undermine their reliability.

Change in accounting policy. A change in accounting policy that either (1) is required by an IFRS or (2) is a change that results in the financial statements providing faithfully represented and more relevant information about the effects of transactions, other events or conditions on the entity's financial position, financial performance or cash flows.

Impracticable. Applying a requirement is impracticable when the entity cannot apply it after making every reasonable effort to do so. For management to assert that it is impracticable to apply a change in an accounting policy retrospectively or to make a retrospective restatement to correct an error, one or more of the following conditions must be present: (1) after making every reasonable effort the effect of the retrospective application or restatement is not determinable; (2) the retrospective application or restatement requires assumptions regarding what management's intent would have been in that period; or (3) the retrospective application or retrospective restatement requires significant estimates of amounts and it is impossible to develop objective information that would have been available at the time the original financial statements for the prior period (or periods) were authorized for issue to provide evidence of circumstances that existed at that time regarding the amounts to be measured, recognized, and/or disclosed by retrospective application.

International Financial Reporting Standards (IFRS). Standards and Interpretations adopted by the International Accounting Standards Board (IASB). They comprise International Financial Reporting Standards, International Accounting Standards (IAS), and Interpretations developed by the International Financial Reporting Interpretations Committee (IFRIC) or the former Standing Interpretations Committee (SIC).

Material. Omissions or misstatements of items are material if they could, individually or collectively, influence the economic decisions that users make on the basis of the financial statements. Materiality depends on the size and nature of the omission or misstatement judged in the surrounding circumstances.

Prior period errors. Omissions from, and misstatements in, the entity's financial statements for one or more prior periods arising from a failure to use, or misuse of, reliable information that (1) was available when financial statements for those periods were authorized for issue and (2) could reasonably be expected to have been obtained and taken into account in the preparation and presentation of those financial statements. Such errors include the effects of mathematical mistakes, mistakes in applying accounting principles, oversight or misuse of available facts, use of unacceptable GAAP, and fraud.

Prospective application. The method of reporting a change in accounting policy and of recognizing the effect of a change in an accounting estimate, respectively, by (1) applying the new accounting policy to transactions, other events, and conditions occurring after the date as at which the policy is changed and (2) recognizing and disclosing the effect of the change in the accounting estimate in the current and future periods affected by the change.

Retrospective application. Applying a new accounting policy to past transactions, other events and conditions as if that policy has always been applied.

Retrospective restatement. Correcting the recognition, measurement, and disclosure of amounts of elements of financial statements as if a prior period error had never occurred.

IMPORTANCE OF COMPARABILITY AND CONSISTENCY IN FINANCIAL REPORTING

Accounting principles—whether various IFRS or national GAAP—have long held that an important objective of financial reporting is to encourage comparability among financial statements produced by essentially similar entities. This is necessary to facilitate informed economic decision making by investors, creditors, regulatory agencies, vendors, customers, prospective employees, joint venturers, and others. While full comparability will not be achieved as long as alternative principles of accounting and reporting for like transactions and events remain acceptable, a driving force in developing new accounting standards has been to enhance comparability. The IASB's convergence objective is to remove alternatives both within IFRS and between IFRS and US GAAP, in order to arrive at a single set of international, high-quality, financial reporting rules, with few exceptions and alternatives other than those demanded by the vicissitudes among the underlying facts and circumstances of the items or transactions being accounted for.

Comparability is one of the key qualitative characteristics of financial reporting information identified in the IABS's *Framework*. It is similarly cited in the underlying foundational documents of various national GAAP, such as US GAAP *Statements of Financial Reporting Concepts*.

An important implication of comparability is that users be informed about the accounting policies that were employed in the preparation of the financial statements, any changes in those policies, and the effects of such changes. While historically some accountants opposed the focus on comparability, on the grounds that uniformity of accounting removes the element of judgment needed to produce the most faithful representation of an individual entity's financial position and performance, others have expressed concern that overemphasis on comparability might be an impediment to the development of improved accounting methods. Increasingly, however, the paramount importance of comparability is being recognized, to which the current convergence efforts strongly attest.

The *Conceptual Framework for Financial Reporting 2010* lists *comparability* as one of the enhancing qualitative characteristics of accounting information (also included as such characteristics are *verifiability*, *timeliness*, and *understandability*) that are complementary to the fundamental qualitative characteristics: *relevance* and *representational faithfulness*. Comparability is explained as follows:

> **Comparability** refers to the ability to identify similarities in, and differences among, items.

In addition, comparability should not be confused with uniformity; for information to be comparable, like things must look alike and different things must look different. The quality of consistency enhances the decision usefulness of financial statements to users by facilitating analysis and the understanding of comparative accounting data.

Strict adherence to IFRS or any other set of standards obviously helps in achieving comparability, since a common accounting language is employed by all reporting parties. According to IAS 1,

> *The presentation and classification of items in the financial statements should be retained from one period to the next unless it is apparent that, following a significant change in the nature of the entity's operations or a review of its financial statements, that another presentation or classification would be more appropriate with regard to the criteria for the selection and application of accounting policies in IAS 8; or an IFRS requires a change in presentation.*

It is, however, inappropriate for an entity to continue accounting for transactions in the same manner if the policies adopted lack qualitative characteristics of relevance and reliability. Thus, if more reliable and relevant accounting policy alternatives exist, it is better for the entity to change its methods of accounting for defined classes of transactions with, of course, adequate disclosure of both the nature of the change and of its effects.

ACCOUNTING POLICY

In accordance with IAS 1, the reporting entity's management is responsible for selecting and applying accounting policies that

1. Present fairly financial position, results of operations, and cash flows of an entity, as required by IFRS
2. Provide information in a manner that provides relevant, reliable, comparable and understandable information
3. Present additional disclosures that enable users to understand the impact of particular transactions, other events, and conditions on the entity's financial position and performance

Under IFRS management is required to disclose, in the notes to the financial statements, a description of all significant accounting policies of the reporting entity. In theory, if only one method of accounting for a type of transaction is acceptable, it is not necessary to explicitly cite it in the accounting policies note, although many entities do routinely identify all accounting policies affecting the major financial statement captions.

The "summary of significant accounting policies" is customarily, but not necessarily, the first note disclosure included in the financial statements.

Selecting Accounting Policies

IAS 8 has established a hierarchy of accounting guidance for selecting accounting policies in accordance with IFRS. This is comparable to the "hierarchy of GAAP" established under US auditing standards many years ago (which recently has been superseded by guidance in the FASB Accounting Standards Codification), and provides a logical ordering of authoritativeness for those instances when competing and possibly conflicting guidance exists. Given the relative paucity of authoritative guidance under IFRS (which is, of course, seen as a virtue by those who prefer "principles-based" standards, vis-à-vis the more "rules-based" standards arguably exemplified by US GAAP), heavy reliance is placed on reasoning by analogy from the existing standards and from materials found in various nonauthoritative sources.

According to IAS 8, when selecting accounting policies with regard to an item in the financial statements, authoritative sources of such policies are included *only* in IFRS (they comprise International Financial Reporting Standards, International Accounting Standards [IAS], and Interpretations developed by the International Financial Reporting Standards Interpretations Committee [IFRIC] or the former Standing Interpretations Committee [SIC]). IFRS also provide guidance to assist management in applying their requirements. *Improvements to IFRS*, published in May 2008, clarified that only guidance that is an integral part of IFRS is mandatory. Guidance that is not an integral part of IFRS does not provide requirements for financial statements.

When there is *not* any IFRS standard or Interpretation that specifically applies to an item in the financial statements, transaction, other event or condition, management must use judgment in developing and applying an accounting policy. This should result in information that is both

1. Relevant to the decision-making needs of users; and
2. Reliable in the sense that the resulting financial statements—

   a. Will represent faithfully the financial position, performance, and cash flows of the entity;
   b. Will reflect the economic substance of transactions, other events, and conditions, and not merely their legal form;
   c. Are neutral (i.e., free from bias);
   d. Are prudent; and
   e. Are complete in all material respects.

In making this judgment, management must give consideration to the following sources, listed in descending order of significance:

1. The requirements in IFRS and in Interpretations dealing with similar and related issues; and
2. The definitions, recognition criteria and measurement concepts for assets, liabilities, income and expenses set out in the *Framework*.

Note that when developing a policy where IFRS does not provide guidance, IAS 8 also requires an entity to consider the most recent pronouncements of other standard-setting bodies that use a similar conceptual framework to develop accounting standards, other accounting literature and accepted industry practices, to the extent that these do not conflict with the sources detailed in the preceding paragraph. In practice, this means that many IFRS reporters will look to US GAAP guidance where IFRS does not provide guidance.

CHANGES IN ACCOUNTING POLICIES

A change in an accounting policy means that a reporting entity has exchanged one accounting principle for another. According to IAS 8, the term *accounting policy* includes the accounting principles, bases, conventions, rules and practices used. For example, a change in inventory costing from "weighted-average" to "first-in, first-out" would be a change in accounting policy. Other examples of accounting policy options in IFRS include cost versus revaluation basis of accounting for property, plant, and equipment and for intangible assets (IAS 16, IAS 38); cost versus fair value basis of accounting for investment property (IAS 40); proportionate consolidation versus equity accounting of jointly controlled entities (IAS 31); and fair value versus proportionate share of the value of net assets acquired for valuing a noncontrolling interest in business combinations (IFRS 3). Changes in accounting policy are permitted if

1. The change is required by a standard or an interpretation, or
2. The change in accounting principle will result in a more relevant and reliable presentation of events or transactions in the financial statements of the entity.

IAS 8 does not regard the following as changes in accounting policies:

1. The adoption of an accounting policy for events or transactions that differ in substance from previously occurring events or transactions; and
2. The adoption of a new accounting policy to account for events or transactions that did not occur previously or that were immaterial in prior periods

The provisions of IAS 8 are not applicable to the initial adoption of a policy to carry assets at revalued amounts, although such adoption is indeed a change in accounting policy. Rather, this is to be dealt with as a revaluation in accordance with IAS 16 or IAS 38, as appropriate under the circumstances.

Applying changes in accounting policies. Generally, IAS 8 provides that a change in an accounting policy should be reflected in financial statements by retrospective application to all prior periods presented as if that policy had always been applied, unless it is impracticable to do so. When a change in an accounting policy is made consequent to the enactment of a new IFRS, it is to be accounted for in accordance with the transitional provisions set forth in that standard.

An entity should account for a change in accounting policy as follows:

1. In general, initial application of an IFRS should be accounted for in accordance with the specific transitional provisions, if any, in that IFRS.
2. Initial application of an IFRS that does not include specific transitional provisions applying to that change, should be applied *retrospectively*.
3. Voluntary changes in accounting policy should be applied *retrospectively*.

Retrospective application. In accordance with IAS 8, retrospective application of a new accounting principle involves (1) adjusting the opening balance of each affected component of equity for the earliest prior period presented and (2) presenting other comparative amounts disclosed for each prior period as if the new accounting policy had always been applied.

Retrospective application to a prior period is required if it is practicable to determine the effect of the correction on the amounts in both the opening as well as closing statements of financial position for that period. Adjustments are made to the opening balance of each affected component of equity, usually to retained earnings.

For example, assume that a change is adopted in 2011 and comparative 2010 and 2009 financial statements are to be presented with the 2011 financial statements. The change in accounting policy also affects previously reported 2007-2008 financial position and financial performance, but these are not to be presented in the current financial report. Therefore, since other components of equity are not affected, the cumulative adjustment (i.e., the cumulative amount of expense or income which would have been recognized in years prior to 2009) as of the beginning of 2009 is made to opening retained earnings in 2009.

Retrospective application is accomplished by the following steps.

At the beginning of the first period presented in the financial statements,

Step 1 -   Adjust the carrying amounts of assets and liabilities for the cumulative effect of changing to the new accounting principle on periods prior to those presented in the financial statements.

Step 2 -   Offset the effect of the adjustment in Step 1 (if any) by adjusting the opening balance of each affected component of equity (usually opening balance of retained earnings).

For each individual prior period that is presented in the financial statements,

Step 3 -   Adjust the financial statements for the effects of applying the new accounting principle to that specific period.

Example of retrospective application of a new accounting principle

Dallas is a manufacturing business. During the 2012 financial year, the directors reviewed Dallas' accounting policies and identified inventories as an area where it could change the current accounting policy with respect to inventory to better reflect the actual economic substance of its business.

The directors decide to change the valuation method used for raw material from the weighted-average cost method to the first-in-first-out (FIFO) method.

The value of the inventories is as follows:

	Weighted-average	*FIFO*
December 31, 2011	160,000	140,000
December 31, 2012	190,000	160,000

Dallas was unable to obtain figures as at January 1, 2011, for inventory in terms of FIFO as it was determined to be impracticable. Ignore any income tax effects.

The changes in the closing carrying amounts of inventories due to the change in the accounting policy are calculated as follows:

	Weighted-average	*FIFO*	*Decrease in values*
December 31, 2011	160,000	140,000	(20,000)
December 31, 2012	190,000	160,000	(30,000)

Due to the change in the accounting policy, the carrying values of inventories decreased at the beginning of the period with CU20,000 and the end of the period with CU30,000 (i.e., the period ended December 31, 2012). The effect of this decrease is an increase in the cost of sales of CU10,000 (CU30,000 – CU20,000) for the period ended December 31, 2011.

Journals
December 31, 2012

Cost of sales (P/L)	10,000	
Retained earnings—opening balance (Equity)	20,000	
Inventories (SFP)		30,000

Accounting for the retrospective application of the new accounting policy.

NOTE: *Had the figures for January 2011 been available, then the comparative statement of comprehensive income would also have been restated retrospectively for the change in accounting policy.*

It is important to note that, in presenting the previously issued financial statements, the caption "as adjusted" is included in the column heading.

Indirect effects. Changing accounting principles sometimes results in indirect effects from legal or contractual obligations of the reporting entity, such as profit sharing or royalty arrangements that contain monetary formulas based on amounts in the financial statements. For example, if an entity had an incentive compensation plan that required it to contribute 15% of its pretax income to a pool to be distributed to its employees, the adoption of a new accounting policy could potentially require the entity to provide additional contributions to the pool computed.

Contracts and agreements are often silent regarding how such a change might affect amounts that were computed (and distributed) in prior years.

IAS 8 specifies that irrespective of whether the indirect effects arise from an explicit requirement in the agreement or are discretionary, if incurred they are to be recognized in the period in which the reporting entity makes the accounting change, which is 2012 in the example above.

Impracticability exception. Comparative information presented for a particular prior period need not be restated if doing so is *impracticable*. IAS 8 includes a definition of "impracticability" (see Definitions of Terms in this chapter) and guidance on its interpretation.

The standard states that applying a requirement is impracticable when the entity cannot apply it after making every reasonable effort to do so. In order for management to assert that it is impracticable to retrospectively apply the new accounting principle, one or more of the following conditions must be present:

1. Management has made every reasonable effort to determine the retrospective adjustment and is unable to do so because the effects of retrospective application are not determinable (e.g., where the information is not available because it was not captured at the time).
2. If it were to apply the new accounting principle retrospectively, management would be required to make assumptions regarding its intent in a prior period that would not be able to be independently substantiated.
3. If it were to apply the new accounting principle retrospectively, management would be required to make significant estimates of amounts for which it is impossible to develop objective information that would have been available at the time the original financial statements for the prior period (or periods) were issued to provide evidence of circumstances that existed at that time regarding the amounts to be measured, recognized, and/or disclosed by retrospective application.

Inability to determine period-specific effects. If management is able to determine the adjustment to the opening balance of each affected component of equity as at the beginning of the earliest period for which retrospective application is practicable, but is unable to determine the period-specific effects of the change on all of the prior periods presented in the financial statements, IAS 8 requires the following steps to adopt the new accounting principle:

1. Adjust the carrying amounts of the assets and liabilities for the cumulative effect of applying the new accounting principle at the beginning of the earliest period presented for which it is practicable to make the computation, which may be the current period.
2. Any offsetting adjustment required by applying step 1. is made to each affected component of equity (usually to beginning retained earnings) of that period.

Inability to determine effects on any prior periods. If it is impracticable to determine the effects of adoption of the new accounting principle on any prior periods, the new principle is applied prospectively as of the earliest date that it is practicable to do so. One example could be when management of a reporting entity decides to change its inventory costing assumption from first-in, first-out (FIFO) to weighted-average (WA), as illustrated in the following example:

Example of change from FIFO to the weighted-average method

During 2012 Waldorf Corporation (WC) decided to change the inventory costing formula from FIFO to weighted-average (WA). The inventory values are as listed below using both FIFO and WA methods. Sales for the year were €15,000,000 and the company's total purchases were €11,000,000. Other expenses were €1,200,000 for the year. The company had 1,000,000 ordinary shares outstanding throughout the year.

Inventory values

	FIFO	*WA*	*Difference*
12/31/11 Base year	€ 2,000,000	€2,000,000	€ --
12/31/12	4,000,000	1,800,000	2,200,000
Variation	€ 2,000,000	€ (200,000)	€ 2,200,000

The computations for 2012 would be as follows:

	FIFO	*WA*	*Difference*
Sales	€15,000,000	€15,000,000	€ --
Cost of goods sold			
Beginning inventory	2,000,000	2,000,000	--
Purchases	11,000,000	11,000,000	--
Goods available for sale	13,000,000	13,000,000	--
Ending inventory	4,000,000	1,800,000	2,200,000
	9,000,000	11,200,000	(2,200,000)
Gross profit	6,000,000	3,800,000	2,200,000
Other expenses	1,200,000	1,200,000	--
Net income	€ 4,800,000	€ 2,600,000	€2,200,000

The following is an example of the required disclosure in this circumstance.

Note A: Change in Method of Accounting for Inventories

During 2012, management changed the company's method of accounting for all of its inventories from first-in, first-out (FIFO) to weighted-average (WA). The change was made because management believes that the WA method provides a better matching of costs and revenues. In addition, with the adoption of WA, the company's inventory pricing method is consistent with the method predominant in the industry. The change and its effect on net income (€000 omitted except for per share amounts) and earnings per share for 2012 are as follows:

	Profit or loss	*Earnings per share*
Profit or loss before the change	€4,800	€4.80
Reduction of net income due to the change	2,200	2.20
Profit or loss as adjusted	€2,600	€2.60

Management has not retrospectively applied this change to prior years' financial statements because beginning inventory on January 1, 2012, using WA is the same as the amount reported on a FIFO basis at December 31, 2011. As a result of this change, the current period's financial statements are not comparable with those of any prior periods. The FIFO cost of inventories exceeds the carrying amount valued using WA by €2,200,000 at December 31, 2012.

Changes in amortization method. Tangible or intangible long-lived assets are subject to depreciation or amortization, respectively, as set forth in IAS 16 and IAS 38. Changes in methods of amortization may be implemented in order to more appropriately recognize amortization or depreciation as an asset's future economic benefits are consumed. For example, the straight-line method of amortization may be substituted for an accelerated method when it becomes clear that the straight-line method more accurately reports the consumption of the asset's utility to the reporting entity.

While a change in amortization method would appear to be a change in accounting policy and thus subject to the requirements of IAS 8 as revised, in fact special accounting for this change is mandated by IAS 16 and IAS 38.

Under IAS 16, which governs accounting for property, plant, and equipment (long-lived tangible assets), a change in the depreciation method is a change in the technique used to apply the entity's accounting policy to recognize depreciation as an asset's future economic benefits are consumed. Therefore it is deemed to be a change in an accounting estimate, to be accounted for as described below. Similar guidance is found in IAS 38, pertaining to intangible assets. These standards are discussed in greater detail in Chapters 9 and 11.

The foregoing exception applies when a change is made to the method of amortizing or depreciating existing assets. A different result obtains when only newly acquired assets are to be affected by the new procedures.

When a company adopts a different method of amortization for newly acquired identifiable long-lived assets, and uses that method for all new assets of the same class without changing the method used previously for existing assets of the same class, this is to be accounted for as a change in accounting policy. No adjustment is required to comparative financial statements, nor is any cumulative adjustment to be made to retained earnings at the beginning of the current or any earlier period, since the change in principle is being applied prospectively only. In these cases, a description of the nature of the method changed and the effect on profit or loss and related per share amounts should be disclosed in the period of the change.

In the absence of any specific transitional provisions in a standard, a change in an accounting policy is to be applied retrospectively in accordance with the requirements set forth in IAS 8 for voluntary changes in accounting policy, as described below.

When applying the transitional provisions of a standard has an effect on the current period or any prior period presented, the reporting entity is required to disclose

1. The fact that the change in accounting policy has been made in accordance with the transitional provisions of the standard, with a description of those provisions;
2. The amount of the adjustment for the current period and for each prior period presented;

3. The amount of the adjustment relating to periods prior to those included in the comparative information; and
4. The fact that the comparative financial information has been restated, or that restatement for a particular prior period has not been made because it was impracticable.

If the application of the transitional provisions set forth in a standard may be expected to have an effect in future periods, the reporting entity is required to disclose the fact that the change in an accounting policy is made in accordance with the prescribed transitional provisions, with a description of those provisions affecting future periods.

Although the "impracticability" provision of revised IAS 8 may appear to suggest that restatement of prior periods' results could easily be avoided by preparers of financial statements, this is not an accurately drawn implication of these rules. The objective of IFRS in general, and of revised IAS 8 in particular, is to enhance the interperiod comparability of information, since doing such will assist users in making economic decisions, particularly by allowing the assessment of trends in financial information for predictive purposes. There is accordingly a general presumption that the benefits derived from restating comparative information will exceed the resulting cost or effort of doing so—and that the reporting entity would make every reasonable effort to restate comparative amounts for each prior period presented.

In circumstances where restatement is deemed impracticable, the reporting entity will disclose the reason for not restating the comparative amounts.

In certain circumstances, a new standard may be promulgated with a delayed effective date. This is done, for example, when the new requirements are complex and IASB wishes to give adequate time for preparers and auditors to master the new materials. If, as of a financial reporting date, the reporting entity has not elected early adoption of the standard, it must disclose (1) the nature of the future change or changes in accounting policy; (2) the date by which adoption of the standard is required; (3) the date as at which it plans to adopt the standard; and (4) either (a) an estimate of the effect that the change(s) will have on its financial position, or (b) if such an estimate cannot be made without undue cost or effort, a statement to that effect. Chapter 1 lists the standards that are currently issued and not yet effective. For an updated list, you can refer to www.wconsulting.co.za where an updated list of standards issued and not yet effective is published.

CHANGES IN ACCOUNTING ESTIMATES

The preparation of financial statements requires frequent use of estimates—for such items as asset service lives, residual values, fair values of financial assets or financial liabilities, likely collectability of accounts receivable, inventory obsolescence, accrual of warranty costs, provision for pension costs, and so on. These future conditions and events and their effects cannot be perceived with certainty; therefore, changes in estimates will be highly likely to occur as new information and more experience is obtained. IAS 8 requires that changes in estimates be *recognized prospectively* by "including it in a profit or loss in

1. The period of change if the change affects that period only; or
2. The period of change and future periods if the change affects both."

For example, on January 1, 2010, a machine purchased for €10,000 was originally estimated to have a ten-year useful life, and a salvage value of €1,000. On January 1, 2015 (five years later), the asset is expected to last another ten years and have a salvage value of €800. As a result, both the current period (this year ending December 1, 2010) and subsequent periods are affected by the change.   Annual depreciation expense over the estimated remaining useful life is computed as follows:

Original cost	€10,000
Less estimated salvage (residual) value	(1,000)
Depreciable amount	9,000
Accumulated depreciation, based original assumptions (10-year life)	
2010	900
2011	900
2012	900
2013	900
2014	900
	4,500
Carrying value at 1/1/2015	5,500
Revised estimate of salvage value	(800)
Depreciable amount	4,700
Remaining useful life at 1/1/2015	10 years
	€ 470 depreciation per year
Effect on 2015 net income	€ 470 – €900 = €430 increase

The annual depreciation charge over the remaining life would be computed as follows:

$$\frac{\text{Book value of asset} - \text{Residual value}}{\text{Remaining useful life}} = \frac{€5,500 - €800}{10 \text{ years}} = €470/\text{yr}.$$

An impairment affecting the cost recovery of an asset should not be handled as a change in accounting estimate but instead should be treated as a loss of the period (See the discussion in Chapter 9).

In some situations it may be difficult to distinguish between changes in accounting policy and changes in accounting estimates. For example, a company may change from deferring and amortizing a cost to recording it as an expense as incurred because the future benefits of the cost have become doubtful. In this instance, the company is changing its accounting principle (from deferral to immediate recognition) because of its change in the estimate of the future utility of a particular cost incurred currently.

According to IAS 8, when it is difficult to distinguish a change in an accounting policy from a change in an accounting estimate, the change is treated as a change in an accounting estimate.

CORRECTION OF ERRORS

Although good internal control and the exercise of due care should serve to minimize the number of financial reporting errors that occur, these safeguards cannot be expected to completely eliminate errors in the financial statements. As a result, it was necessary for the accounting profession to promulgate standards that would ensure uniform treatment of accounting for error corrections.

IAS 8 deals with accounting for error corrections. Under earlier versions of this standard, so-called "fundamental errors" could be accounted for in accordance with either benchmark or allowed alternative approaches to effecting corrections. The IASB's *Improvements Project* resulted in the elimination of the concept of fundamental error, and also the elimination of what had formerly been the allowed alternative treatment. Under revised IAS 8, therefore, the only permitted treatment is "retrospective restatement" as a prior period adjustment (subject to an exception when doing so is impracticable, as described below).

Prior periods must be restated to report financial position and financial performance as they would have been displayed had the error never taken place.

There is a clear distinction between errors and changes in accounting estimates. Estimates by their nature are approximations that may need revision as additional information becomes known. For example, when a gain or loss is ultimately recognized on the outcome of a contingency that previously could not be estimated reliably, this does not constitute the correction of an error and cannot be dealt with by restatement. However, if the estimated amount of the contingency had been miscomputed from data available when the financial statements were prepared, at least some portion of the variance between the accrual and the ultimate outcome might reasonably be deemed an error. An error requires that information available, which should have been taken into account, was ignored or misinterpreted.

Errors are defined by revised IAS 8 as omissions from and other misstatements of the entity's financial statements for one or more prior periods that are discovered in the current period and relate to reliable information that (1) was available when those prior period financial statements were prepared; and (2) could reasonably be expected to have been obtained and taken into account in the original preparation and presentation of those financial statements. Errors include the effects of mathematical mistakes, mistakes in applying accounting policies, oversights or misinterpretations of facts, and the effects of financial reporting fraud.

IAS 8 specifies that, when correcting an error in prior period financial statements, the term "restatement" is to be used. That term is exclusively reserved for this purpose so as to effectively communicate to users of the financial statements the reason for a particular change in previously issued financial statements.

An entity should correct material prior period errors retrospectively in the first set of financial statements authorized for issue after their discovery by (1) "restating the comparative amounts for the prior periods presented in which the error occurred or (2) if the error occurred before the earliest prior period presented, restating the opening balances of assets, liabilities and equity for the earliest prior period presented."

Restatement consists of the following steps:

Step 1 - Adjust the carrying amounts of assets and liabilities at the beginning of the first period presented in the financial statements for the amount of the correction on periods prior to those presented in the financial statements.

Step 2 - Offset the amount of the adjustment in Step 1 (if any) by adjusting the opening balance of retained earnings (or other components of equity or net assets, as applicable to the reporting entity) for that period.

Step 3 - Adjust the financial statements of each individual prior period presented for the effects of correcting the error on that specific period (referred to as the period-specific effects of the error).

Example of the correction of a material error

Assume that Belmont Corporation (BC) had overstated its depreciation expense by €50,000 in 2010 and €40,000 in 2011, both due to mathematical mistakes. The errors affected both the financial statements and the income tax returns in 2010 and 2011 and are discovered in 2012. For this example, assume that only one comparative statement of financial position is given (note that the amendments to IAS 1 would require two comparative years to be given where there is a restatement as a result of an error).

BC's statements of financial position and statements of comprehensive income and retained earnings as of and for the year ended December 31, 2011, prior to the restatement were as follows:

Belmont Corporation
Statement of Comprehensive Income and Retained Earnings
Prior to Restatement
Year Ended December 31, 2011

	2011
Sales	€2,000,000
Cost of sales	
Depreciation	750,000
Other	390,000
	1,140,000
Gross profit	860,000
Selling, general, and administrative expenses	450,000
Income from operations	410,000
Other income (expense)	10,000
Income before income taxes	420,000
Income taxes	168,000
Profit or loss	252,000
Retained earnings, beginning of year	6,463,000
Dividends	(1,200,000)
Retained earnings, end of year	€5,515,000

Belmont Corporation
Statement of Financial Position
Prior to Restatement
December 31, 2011

	2011
Assets	
Current assets	€ 540,000
Property and equipment	
Cost	3,500,000
Accumulated depreciation and amortization	(430,000)
	3,070,000
Total assets	€5,610,000
Liabilities and stockholders' equity	
Income taxes payable	€ --
Other current liabilities	12,000
Total current liabilities	12,000
Noncurrent liabilities	70,000
Total liabilities	82,000
Shareholders' equity	
Ordinary share	13,000
Retained earnings	5,515,000
Total shareholders' equity	5,528,000
Total liabilities and shareholders' equity	€5,610,000

The following steps are followed to restate BC's prior period financial statements:

Step 1 - Adjust the carrying amounts of assets and liabilities at the beginning of the first period presented in the financial statements for the cumulative effect of correcting the error on periods prior to those presented in the financial statements.

    The first period presented in the financial statements is 2011. At the beginning of that year, €50,000 of the mistakes had been made and reflected on both the income tax return and financial statements. Assuming a flat 40% income tax rate and ignoring the effects of penalties and interest that would be assessed on the amended income tax returns, the following adjustment would be made to assets and liabilities at January 1, 2011:

Decrease in accumulated depreciation	€50,000
Increase in income taxes payable	(20,000)
	€30,000

Step 2 - Offset the effect of the adjustment in Step 1 by adjusting the opening balance of retained earnings (or other components of equity or net assets, as applicable to the reporting entity) for that period.

Retained earnings at the beginning of 2011 will increase by €30,000 as the offsetting entry resulting from Step 1.

Step 3 - Adjust the financial statements of each individual prior period presented for the effects of correcting the error on that specific period (referred to as the period-specific effects of the error).

The 2011 prior period financial statements will be corrected for the period-specific effects of the restatement as follows:

Decrease in depreciation expense and accumulated depreciation	€40,000
Increase in income tax expense and income taxes payable	(16,000)
Increase 2011 profit or loss	€24,000

The restated financial statements are presented below.

Belmont Corporation
Statements of Comprehensive Income Retained Earnings
As Restated
Years Ended December 31, 2011

	2011 *Restated*
Sales	€ 2,000,000
Cost of sales	
Depreciation	710,000
Other	390,000
	1,100,000
Gross profit	900,000
Selling, general, and administrative expenses	450,000
Income from operations	450,000
Other income (expense)	10,000
Income before income taxes	460,000
Income taxes	184,000
Profit or loss	276,000
Retained earnings, beginning of year, as originally reported	6,463,000
Restatement to reflect correction of depreciation (Note X)	30,000
Retained earnings, beginning of year, as restated	6,493,000
Dividends	(1,200,000)
Retained earnings, end of year	€ 5,569,000

Belmont Corporation
Statements of Comprehensive Income Retained Earnings
As Restated
Years Ended December 31, 2011

	2011 *Restated*
Assets	
Current assets	€2,540,000
Property and equipment	
Cost	3,500,000
Accumulated depreciation and amortization	(340,000)
	3,160,000
Total assets	€5,700,000
Liabilities and shareholders' equity	
Income taxes payable	€ 36,000
Other current liabilities	12,000
Total current liabilities	48,000
Noncurrent liabilities	70,000
Total liabilities	118,000
Shareholders' equity	
Ordinary share	13,000
Retained earnings	5,569,000
Total shareholders' equity	5,582,000
Total liabilities and shareholders' equity	€5,700,000

When restating previously issued financial statements, management is to disclose

1. The fact that the financial statements have been restated
2. The nature of the error
3. The effect of the restatement on each line item in the financial statements
4. The cumulative effect of the restatement on retained earnings (or other applicable components of equity or net assets)

These disclosures need not be repeated in subsequent periods.

The correction of an error in the financial statements of a prior period discovered subsequent to their issuance is reported as a prior period adjustment in the financial statements of the subsequent period. In some cases, however, this situation necessitates the recall or withdrawal of the previously issued financial statements and their revision and reissuance.

Impracticability exception. IAS 8 stipulates that the amount of the correction of an error is to be accounted for retrospectively. As with changes in accounting policies, comparative information presented for a particular period need not be restated, if restating the information is impracticable. As a result, when it is impracticable to determine the cumulative effect, at the beginning of the current period, of an error, on all prior periods, the entity changes the comparative information as if the error had been corrected, prospectively from the earliest date practicable.

However, because the value ascribed to truly comparable data is high, this exception is not to be viewed as an invitation to not restate comparable periods' financial statements to remove the effects of most errors. The standard sets out what constitutes impracticability, as discussed earlier in this chapter, and this should be strictly interpreted. When comparative information for a particular prior period is not restated, the opening balance of retained earnings for the next period must be restated for the amount of the correction before the beginning of that period.

In practice, the major criterion for determining whether or not to report the correction of the error is the materiality of the correction. There are many factors to be considered in determining the materiality of the error correction. Materiality should be considered for each correction individually as well as for all corrections in total. If the correction is determined to have a material effect on profit or loss, or the trend of earnings, it should be disclosed in accordance with the requirements set forth in the preceding paragraph.

The prior period adjustment should be presented in the financial statements as follows:

Retained earnings, January 1, 2012, as reported previously	€xxx
Correction of error (description) in prior period(s) (net of €xx tax)	xxx
Adjusted balance of retained earnings at January 1, 2012	xxx
Profit or loss for the year	xxx
Retained earnings December 31, 2012	€xxx

In comparative statements, prior period adjustments should also be shown as adjustments to the beginning balances in the retained earnings statements. The amount of the adjustment on the earliest statement shall be the amount of the correction on periods prior to the earliest period presented. The later retained earnings statements presented should also show a prior period adjustment for the amount of the correction as of the beginning of the period being reported on.

Because it is to be handled retrospectively, the correction of an error—which by definition relates to one or more prior periods—is excluded from the determination of profit or loss for the period in which the error is discovered. The financial statements are presented as if the error had never occurred, by correcting the error in the comparative information for the prior period(s) in which the error occurred, unless impracticable. The amount of the correction relating to errors that occurred in periods prior to those presented in comparative information in the financial statements is adjusted against the opening balance of retained earnings of the earliest prior period presented. This treatment is entirely analogous to that now prescribed for changes in accounting policies.

When an accounting error is being corrected, the reporting entity is to disclose the following:

1. The nature of the error;
2. The amount of the correction for each prior period presented;
3. The amount of the correction relating to periods prior to those presented in comparative information; and
4. That comparative information has been restated, or that the restatement for a particular prior period has not been made because it would require undue cost or effort.

US GAAP COMPARISON

Under US GAAP, the Accounting Standards Codification (ASC) is the single source of authoritative literature. The ASC "grandfathered" certain guidance that existed before the codification in 2009 that allowed superseded policies to remain in effect for transactions or events that occurred before the release of the respective standard. This was done to provide consistency among prior periods and later periods in which the effect of the transaction or event continued.

There is no single standard that addresses accounting policies in US GAAP similar to IAS 8. However, similar to IFRS, accounting policies must be in accordance with existing GAAP and be applied consistently. Changes in accounting policy must be based on either a change required by an updated Accounting Standards, or a substantive argument that the new policy is superior to the current due to improved representational faithfulness.

Errors and changes in accounting policies are applied retrospectively for all the periods presented in a set of financial statements. The effect of errors and changes that occurred prior to the earliest period presented are included in the opening balances of equity for the earliest period presented. If it is impracticable to determine the financial effects of prior periods, the effect is presented for the most recent period that is practicable. Reasons why it is impracticable are disclosed.

Similar to IFRS, policies need not be applied to items that are immaterial. Materiality is defined in US GAAP very similarly to IFRS, which is the inclusion or omission of information from financial statements that would affect the decisions of users. The concept includes changes in the trend of earnings or other measures that otherwise would be considered material. The threshold for materiality for errors for interim financial statements is made on the relevant measure (i.e., income) for the year. However, errors that are material to the quarter must be disclosed.

One significant difference from IFRS is that the FASB Concepts Statements, the equivalent of the IFRS *Framework*, are prohibited from being used to determine accounting treatment. Under US GAAP, the accounting policies for subsidiaries do not need to be uniform.

8 INVENTORY

INTRODUCTION

The accounting for inventories is a major consideration for many entities because of its significance on both the statement of profit or loss (cost of goods sold) and the statement of financial position. Inventories are defined by IAS 2 as items that are

> ...held for sale in the ordinary course of business; in the process of production for such sale; or in the form of materials or supplies to be consumed in the production process or in the rendering of services.

The complexity of accounting for inventories arises from several factors:

1. The high volume of activity (or turnover) in the account;
2. The various cost flow alternatives that are acceptable; and
3. The classification of inventories.

There are two types of entities for which the accounting for inventories must be considered. The merchandising entity (generally, a retailer or wholesaler) has a single inventory account, usually entitled *merchandise inventory*. These are goods on hand that are purchased for resale. The other type of entity is the manufacturer, which generally has three types of inventory: (1) raw materials, (2) work in process, and (3) finished goods. *Raw materials inventory* represents the goods purchased that will act as inputs in the production process leading to the finished product. *Work in process* (WIP) consists of the goods entered into production but not yet completed. *Finished goods inventory* is the completed product that is on hand awaiting sale.

In the case of either type of entity the same basic questions need to be resolved.

1. At what point in time should the items be included in inventory (ownership)?
2. What costs incurred should be included in the valuation of inventories?
3. What cost flow assumption should be used?
4. At what value should inventories be reported (net realizable value)?

The standard that addresses these questions is IAS 2, which has been revised several times since it was first promulgated. IAS 2 discusses the definition, valuation, and classification of inventory.

Sources of IFRS
IAS 2, 18, 34, 41

DEFINITIONS OF TERMS

Absorption (full) costing. Inclusion of all manufacturing costs (fixed and variable) in the cost of finished goods inventory.

By-products. Goods that result as an ancillary product from the production of a primary good; often having minor value when compared to the value of the principal product(s).

Consignments. Marketing method in which the consignor ships goods to the consignee, who acts as an agent for the consignor in selling the goods. The inventory remains the property of the consignor until sold by the consignee.

Direct (variable) costing. Inclusion of only variable manufacturing costs in the cost of ending finished goods inventory. While often used for management (internal) reporting, this method is not deemed acceptable for financial reporting purposes.

Finished goods. Completed but unsold products produced by a manufacturing firm.

First-in, first-out (FIFO). Cost flow assumption; the first goods purchased or produced are assumed to be the first goods sold.

Goods in transit. Goods being shipped from seller to buyer at year-end.

Gross profit method. Method used to estimate the amount of ending inventory based on the cost of goods available for sale, sales, and the gross profit percentage.

Inventory. Assets held for sale in the normal course of business, or which are in the process of production for such sale, or are in the form of materials or supplies to be consumed in the production process or in the rendering of services.

Joint products. Two or more products produced jointly, where neither is viewed as being more important; in some cases additional production steps are applied to one or more joint products after a split-off point.

Last-in, first-out (LIFO). Cost flow assumption; the last goods purchased are assumed to be the first goods sold.

Lower of cost and net realizable value. Inventories must be valued at lower of cost or realizable value.

Markdown. Decrease below original retail price. A markdown cancellation is an increase (not above original retail price) in retail price after a markdown.

Markup. Increase above original purchase price. A markup cancellation is a decrease (not below original purchase price) in retail price after a markup.

Net realizable value. Estimated selling price in the ordinary course of business less the estimated costs of completion and the estimated costs necessary to make the sale.

Periodic. Inventory system where quantities are determined only periodically by physical count.

Perpetual. Inventory system where up-to-date records of inventory quantities are kept.

Raw materials. For a manufacturing firm, materials on hand awaiting entry into the production process.

Replacement cost. Cost to reproduce an inventory item by purchase or manufacture. In lower of cost or market computations, the term *market* means replacement cost, subject to the ceiling and floor limitations.

Retail method. Inventory costing method that uses a cost ratio to reduce ending inventory (valued at retail) to cost.

Specific identification. Inventory system where the seller identifies which specific items have been sold and which ones remain in the closing inventory.

Standard costs. Predetermined unit costs, which are acceptable for financial reporting purposes if adjusted periodically to reflect current conditions. While useful for management (internal) reporting under some conditions, this is not an acceptable costing method for financial statements presented in accordance with IFRS.

Weighted-average. Periodic inventory costing method where ending inventory and cost of goods sold are priced at the weighted-average cost of all items available for sale.

Work in process. For a manufacturing firm, the inventory of partially completed products.

RECOGNITION AND MEASURMENT

Basic Concept of Inventory Costing

IFRS (IAS 2) established that the lower of cost and net realizable value should be the basis for the valuation of inventories. In contrast to IFRS dealing with property, plant, and equipment (IAS 16) or investment property (IAS 40), there is no option for revaluing inventories to current replacement cost or other measure of fair value, presumably due to the far shorter period of time over which such assets are held, thereby limiting the cumulative impact of inflation or other economic factors on reported amounts.

The cost of inventories of items that are ordinarily interchangeable, and goods or services produced and segregated for specific projects, are generally assigned carrying values by using the specific identification method. For most goods, however, specific identification is not a practical alternative. In cases where there are a large number of items of inventory and where the turnover is rapid, the extant standard prescribes two inventory costing formulas, namely the first-in, first-out (FIFO) and the weighted-average methods. A third alternative formerly endorsed by IFRS, the LIFO costing method, has now been designated as being unacceptable.

FIFO and weighted-average cost are now the only acceptable cost flow assumptions under IFRS. Either method can be used to assign cost of inventories, but once selected an entity must apply that cost flow assumption consistently (unless the change to the other method can be justified under the criteria set forth by IAS 8). Furthermore, an entity is constrained from applying different cost formulas to inventories having similar nature and use to the entity. On the other hand, for inventories having different natures or uses, different cost formulas may be justified. Mere difference in location, however, cannot be used to justify applying different costing methods to otherwise similar inventories.

Ownership of Goods

Inventory can only be an asset of the reporting entity if it is an economic resource of the entity at the date of the statement of financial position. In general, an entity should record purchases and sales of inventory when legal title passes. Although strict adherence to this rule may not appear to be important in daily transactions, a proper inventory cutoff at the end of an accounting period is crucial for the correct determination of periodic results of operations. Thus, for accounting purposes, to obtain an accurate measurement of inventory quantity and corresponding monetary representation of inventory and cost of goods sold in the financial statements, it is necessary to determine when title passes.

The most common error made in this regard is to assume that title is synonymous with possession of goods on hand. This may be incorrect in two ways:

1. The goods on hand may not be owned, and
2. Goods that are not on hand may be owned.

There are four matters that may cause confusion about proper ownership:

1. Goods in transit,
2. Consignment sales,
3. Product financing arrangements, and
4. Sales made with the buyer having generous or unusual right of return.

Goods in transit. At year-end, any *goods in transit* from seller to buyer may properly be includable in one, and only one, of those parties' inventories, based on the terms and conditions of the sale. Under traditional legal and accounting interpretation, goods are included in the inventory of the firm financially responsible for transportation costs. This responsibility may be indicated by shipping terms such as FOB, which is used in overland shipping contracts, and by FAS, CIF, C&F, and ex-ship, which are used in maritime transport contracts.

The term *FOB* stands for "free on board." If goods are shipped FOB destination, transportation costs are paid by the seller and title does not pass until the carrier delivers the goods to the buyer; thus these goods are part of the seller's inventory while in transit. If goods are shipped FOB shipping point, transportation costs are paid by the buyer and title passes when the carrier takes possession; thus these goods are part of the buyer's inventory while in transit. The terms *FOB destination* and *FOB shipping point* often indicate a specific location at which title to the goods is transferred, such as FOB Milan. This means that the seller retains title and risk of loss until the goods are delivered to a common carrier in Milan who will act as an agent for the buyer.

A seller who ships *FAS* (free alongside) must bear all expense and risk involved in delivering the goods to the dock next to (alongside) the vessel on which they are to be shipped. The buyer bears the cost of loading and of shipment; thus title passes when the carrier takes possession of the goods.

In a *CIF* (cost, insurance, and freight) contract the buyer agrees to pay in a lump sum the cost of the goods, insurance costs, and freight charges. In a CIF contract, the buyer promises to pay a lump sum that includes the cost of the goods and all freight charges. In either case, the seller must deliver the goods to the carrier and pay the costs of loading; thus both title and risk of loss pass to the buyer upon delivery of the goods to the carrier.

A seller who delivers goods *ex-ship* bears all expense and risk until the goods are unloaded, at which time both title and risk of loss pass to the buyer.

The foregoing is meant only to define normal terms and usage; actual contractual arrangements between a given buyer and a given seller can vary widely. The accounting treatment should in all cases strive to mirror the substance of the legal terms established between the parties.

Examples of accounting for goods in transit

The Vartan Gyroscope Company is located in VeraCruz, Mexico, and obtains precision jeweled bearings from a supplier in Switzerland. The standard delivery terms are free alongside (FAS) a container ship in the harbor in Nice, France, so that Vartan takes legal title to the delivery once possession of the goods is taken by the carrier's dockside employees for the purpose of loading the goods on board the ship. When the supplier delivers goods with an invoiced value of 1,200,000 Mexican pesos to the wharf, it e-mails an advance shipping notice (ASN) and invoice to Vartan via an electronic data interchange (EDI) transaction, itemizing the contents of the delivery. Vartan's computer system receives the EDI transmission, notes the FAS terms in the supplier file, and therefore automatically logs it into the company computer system with the following entry:

Inventory	1,200,000	
Accounts payable		1,200,000

The goods are assigned an "In Transit" location code in Vartan's perpetual inventory system. When the precision jeweled bearings delivery eventually arrives at Vartan's receiving dock, the receiving staff records a change in inventory location code from "In Transit" to a code designating a physical location within the warehouse.

Vartan's secondary precision jeweled bearings supplier is located in Vancouver, British Columbia, and ships overland using free on board (FOB) VeraCruz terms, so the supplier retains title until the shipment arrives at Vartan's location. This supplier also issues an advance shipping notice by EDI to inform Vartan of the estimated arrival date, but in this case Vartan's computer system notes the FOB VeraCruz terms, and makes no entry to record the transaction until the goods arrive at Vartan's receiving dock.

Consignment sales. There are specifically defined situations where the party holding the goods is doing so as an agent for the true owner. In *consignments,* the consignor (seller) ships goods to the consignee (buyer), which acts as the agent of the consignor in trying to sell the goods. In some consignments, the consignee receives a commission; in other arrangements, the consignee "purchases" the goods simultaneously with the sale of the goods to the final customer. Goods out on consignment are properly included in the inventory of the consignor and excluded from the inventory of the consignee. Disclosure may be required of the consignee, however, since common financial analytical inferences, such as days' sales in inventory or inventory turnover, may appear distorted unless the financial statement users are informed. However, IFRS does not explicitly address this.

Example of a consignment arrangement

The Random Gadget Company ships a consignment of its wireless media control devices to a retail outlet of the Consumer Products Corporation. Random Gadget's cost of the consigned goods is €3,700, and it shifts the inventory cost into a separate inventory account to track the physical location of the goods. The entry is as follows:

Consignment out inventory	3,700	
Finished goods inventory		3,700

A third-party shipping company ships the cordless phone inventory from Random Gadget to Consumer Products. Upon receipt of an invoice for this €550 shipping expense, Random Gadget charges the cost to consignment inventory with the following entry:

Consignment out inventory	550	
Accounts payable		550

To record the cost of shipping goods from the factory to Consumer Products Corporation

Consumer Products sells half the consigned inventory during the month for €2,750 in credit card payments, and earns a 22% commission on these sales, totaling €605. According to the consignment arrangement, Random Gadget must also reimburse Consumer Products for the 2% credit card processing fee, which is €55 (€2,750 × 2%). The results of this sale are summarized as follows:

Sales price to Consumer Product's customer earned on behalf of Random Gadget	€2,750
Less: Amounts due to Consumer Product in accordance with arrangement	
22% sales commission	605
Reimbursement for credit card processing fee	55
	660
Due to Random Gadget	€2,090

Upon receipt of the monthly sales report from Consumer Products, Random Gadget records the following entries:

Accounts receivable	2,090	
Cost of goods sold	55	
Commission expense	605	
Sales		2,750

To record the sale made by Consumer Product acting as agent of Random Gadget, the commission earned by Consumer Product and the credit card fee reimbursement earned by Consumer Product in connection with the sale

Cost of goods sold	2,125	
Consignment out inventory		2,125

To transfer the related inventory cost to cost of goods sold, including half the original inventory cost and half the cost of the shipment to Consumer Product [(€3,700 + €550 = €4,250) × ½ = €2,125]

Right to return purchases. A related inventory accounting issue that deserves special consideration arises in the situation that exists when the buyer is granted an exceptional right to return the merchandise acquired. This is not meant to address the normal sales terms found throughout commercial transactions (e.g., where the buyer can return goods, whether found to be defective or not, within a short time after delivery, such as five days). Rather, this connotes situations where the return privileges are well in excess of standard practice, so as to place doubt on the veracity of the purported sale transaction itself.

IAS 18 notes that when the buyer has the right to rescind the transaction under defined conditions and the seller cannot, with reasonable confidence, estimate the likelihood of this occurrence, the retention of significant risks of ownership makes this transaction not a sale. The sale is to be recorded if the future amount of the returns can reasonably be estimated. If the ability to make a reasonable estimate is precluded, the sale is not to be recorded until further returns are unlikely. Although legal title has passed to the buyer, the seller must continue to include the goods in its measurement and valuation of inventory.

In some situations, a "side agreement" may grant the nominal customer greatly expanded or even unlimited return privileges, when the formal sales documents (bill of sale, bill of lading, etc.) make no such reference. These situations would be highly suggestive of financial reporting irregularities, in an apparent attempt to overstate revenues in the current period (and risk reporting high levels of sales returns in the following period, if customers do indeed avail themselves of the generous terms). In such circumstances, these sales should in all likelihood not be recognized, and the goods nominally sold should be returned to the reporting entity's inventories.

Accounting for Inventories

The major objectives of accounting for inventories are the matching of appropriate costs against revenues in order to arrive at the proper determination of periodic income, and the accurate representation of inventories on hand as assets of the reporting entity at the end of the reporting period.

The accounting for inventories is done under either a periodic or a perpetual system. In a *periodic inventory system,* the inventory quantity is determined periodically by a physical count. Next, a cost formula is applied to the quantity so determined to calculate the cost of ending inventory. Cost of goods sold is computed by adding beginning inventory and net purchases (or cost of goods manufactured) and subtracting ending inventory.

Alternatively, a *perpetual inventory system* keeps a running total of the quantity (and possibly the cost) of inventory on hand by recording all sales and purchases as they occur. When inventory is purchased, the inventory account (rather than purchases) is debited. When inventory is sold, the cost of goods sold and reduction of inventory are recorded. Periodic physical counts are necessary only to verify the perpetual records and to satisfy the tax regulations in some jurisdictions (tax regulations may require that a physical inventory count be undertaken at least annually).

Valuation of Inventories

According to IAS 2, the primary basis of accounting for inventories is cost. *Cost* is defined as the sum of all costs of purchase, costs of conversion, and other costs incurred in bringing the inventories to their present location and condition. This definition allows for significant interpretation of the costs to be included in inventory.

For raw materials and merchandise inventory that are purchased outright and not intended for further conversion, the identification of cost is relatively straightforward. The cost of these purchased inventories will include all expenditures incurred in bringing the goods to the point of sale and putting them in a salable condition. These costs include the purchase price, transportation costs, insurance, and handling costs. Trade discounts, rebates, and other such items are to be deducted in determining inventory costs; failure to do so would result in carrying inventory at amounts in excess of true historical costs.

The impact of interest costs as they relate to the valuation of inventories (IAS 23) is discussed in Chapter 10. As most recently revised, IAS 23 requires capitalization of financing costs incurred during the manufacture, acquisition or construction of qualifying assets. However, borrowing costs will generally not be capitalized in connection with inventory acquisitions, since the period required to ready the goods for sale will generally not be significant. On the other hand, when a lengthy production process is required to prepare the goods for sale, the provisions of IAS 23 would be applicable and a portion of borrowing costs would become part of the cost of inventory. In practice, such situations are rare and IAS 23 allows an exemption for inventories that are manufactured, or otherwise produced, in large quantities on a repetitive basis.

Conversion costs for manufactured goods should include all costs that are directly associated with the units produced, such as labor and overhead. The allocation of overhead costs, however, must be systematic and rational, and in the case of fixed overhead costs (i.e., those which do not vary directly with level of production) the allocation process should be based on normal production levels. In periods of unusually low levels of production, a portion of fixed overhead costs must accordingly be charged directly to operations, and not taken into inventory.

Costs other than material and conversion costs are capitalized only to the extent they are necessary to bring the goods to their present condition and location. Examples might include certain design costs and other types of preproduction expenditures if intended to benefit specific classes of customers. On the other hand, all research costs and most development costs (per IAS 38, as discussed in Chapter 11) would typically *not* become part of inventory costs. Also generally excluded from inventory would be such costs as administrative and selling expenses, which must be treated as period costs; the cost of wasted materials, labor, or other production expenditures; and most storage costs. Included in overhead, and thus allocable to inventory, would be such categories as repairs, maintenance, utilities, rent, indirect labor, production supervisory wages, indirect materials and supplies, quality control and inspection, and the cost of small tools not capitalized.

Example of recording raw material or component parts cost

Accurate Laser-Guided Farm Implements, Inc. purchases lasers, a component that it uses in manufacturing its signature product. The company typically receives delivery of all its component parts and uses them in manufacturing its finished products during the fall and early winter, and then sells its stock of finished goods in the late winter and spring. The supplier invoice for a January delivery of lasers includes the following line items:

Lasers	€5,043
Shipping and handling	125
Shipping insurance	48
Sales tax	193
Total	€5,409

Since Accurate is using the lasers as components in a product that it resells, it will not pay the sales tax. However, both the shipping and handling charge and the shipping insurance are required for ongoing product acquisition, and so are included in the following entry to record receipt of the goods:

Inventory—components	5,216	
Accounts payable		5,216

To record purchase of lasers and related costs (€5,043 + €125 + €48)

On February 1, Accurate purchases a €5,000, two-month shipping insurance (known as "inland marine") policy that applies to all incoming supplier deliveries for the remainder of the winter production season, allowing it to refuse shipping insurance charges on individual deliveries. Since the policy insures all inbound components deliveries (not just lasers) it is too time-consuming to charge the cost of this policy to individual components deliveries using specific identification, the controller can estimate a flat charge per delivery based on the number of expected deliveries during the two-month term of the insurance policy as follows:

€5,000 insurance premium ÷ 200 expected deliveries during the policy term = €25 per delivery and then charge each delivery with €25 as follows:

Inventory—components	25	
Prepaid insurance		25

To allocate cost of inland marine coverage to inbound insured components shipments

In this case, however, the controller determined that shipments are expected to occur evenly during the two-month policy period and therefore will simply make a monthly standard journal entry as follows:

Inventory—components	2,500	
Prepaid insurance		2,500

To amortize premium on inland marine policy using the straight-line method

Note that the controller must be careful, under either scenario, to ensure that perpetual inventory records appropriately track unit costs of components to include the cost of shipping insurance. Failure to do so would result in an understatement of the cost of raw materials inventory on hand at the end of any accounting period.

Joint products and by-products. In some production processes, more than one product is produced simultaneously. Typically, if each product has significant value, they are referred to as *joint products*; if only one has substantial value, the others are known as *by-products*. Under IAS 2, when the costs of each jointly produced good cannot be clearly determined, a rational allocation among them is required. Generally, such allocation is made by reference to the relative values of the jointly produced goods, as measured by ultimate selling prices. Often, after a period of joint production the goods are split off, separately incurring additional costs before being completed and ready for sale. The allocation of joint costs should take into account the additional individual product costs yet to be incurred after the point at which joint production ceases.

By-products by definition are products that have limited value when measured with reference to the primary good being produced. IAS 2 suggests that by-products be valued at net realizable value, with the costs allocated to by-products thereby being deducted from the cost pool, being otherwise allocated to the sole or several principal products.

For example, products A and B have the same processes performed on them up to the split-off point. The total cost incurred to this point is €80,000. This cost can be assigned to products A and B using their relative sales value at the split-off point. If A could be sold for €60,000 and B for €40,000, the total sales value is €100,000. The cost would be assigned on the basis of each product's relative sales value. Thus, A would be assigned a cost of €48,000 (60,000/100,000 × 80,000) and B a cost of €32,000 (400,000/100,000 × 80,000).

If inventory is exchanged with another entity for similar goods, the earnings process is generally not culminated. Accordingly, the acquired items are recorded at the recorded, or book, value of the items given up. In terms of IAS 18, such an exchange is not deemed to be a revenue-generating transaction and, as such, the transaction is accounted for as a straight exchange, unless it can be argued that the transaction undertaken lacks commercial substance.

In some jurisdictions, the categories of costs that are includable in inventory for tax purposes may differ from those that are permitted for financial reporting purposes under IFRS. To the extent that differential tax and financial reporting is possible (i.e., that there is no statutory requirement that the taxation rules constrain financial reporting) this situation will result in deferred taxation. This is discussed more fully in Chapter 26.

Direct costing. The generally accepted method of allocating fixed overhead to both ending inventory and cost of goods sold is commonly known as *(full) absorption costing.* IAS 2 requires that absorption costing be employed. However, often for managerial decision-making purposes an alternative to absorption costing, known as *variable or direct costing,* is utilized. Direct costing requires classifying only direct materials, direct labor, and variable overhead related to production as inventory costs. All fixed costs are accounted for as period costs. The virtue of direct costing is that under this accounting strategy there will be a predictable, linear effect on marginal contribution from each unit of sales revenue, which can be useful in planning and controlling the business operation. However, such a costing method does not result in inventory that includes all costs of production, and therefore this is deemed not to be in accordance with IAS 2. If an entity uses direct costing for internal budgeting or other purposes, adjustments must be made to develop alternative information for financial reporting purposes.

Differences in inventory costing between IFRS and tax requirements. In certain tax jurisdictions, there may be requirements to include or exclude certain overhead cost elements which are handled differently under IFRS for financial reporting purposes. For example, in the US the tax code requires elements of overhead to be allocated to inventory, while IFRS demands that these be expensed currently as period costs. Since tax laws do not dictate IFRS, the appropriate response to such a circumstance is to treat these as temporary differences, which will create the need for interperiod income tax allocation under IAS 12. Deferred tax accounting is fully discussed in Chapter 26.

METHODS OF INVENTORY COSTING UNDER IAS 2

Specific Identification

The theoretical basis for valuing inventories and cost of goods sold requires assigning the production and/or acquisition costs to the specific goods to which they relate. For example, the cost of ending inventory for an entity in its first year, during which it produced ten items (e.g., exclusive single family homes), might be the actual production cost of the first, sixth, and eighth unit produced if those are the actual units still on hand at the date of the statement of financial position. The costs of the other homes would be included in that year's profit or loss as cost of goods sold. This method of inventory valuation is usually referred to as *specific identification*.

Specific identification is generally not a practical technique, as the product will generally lose its separate identity as it passes through the production and sales process. Exceptions to this would generally be limited to those situations where there are small inventory quantities, typically having high unit value and a low turnover rate. Under IAS 2, specific identification must be employed to cost inventories that are not ordinarily interchangeable, and goods and services produced and segregated for specific projects. For inventories meeting either of these criteria, the specific identification method is mandatory and alternative methods cannot be used.

Because of the limited applicability of specific identification, it is more likely to be the case that certain assumptions regarding the cost flows associated with inventory will need to be made. One of accounting's peculiarities is that these cost flows may or may not reflect the physical flow of inventory. Over the years, much attention has been given to both the flow of physical goods and the assumed flow of costs associated with those goods. In most jurisdictions, it has long been recognized that the flow of costs need not mirror the actual flow of the goods with which those costs are associated. For example, a key provision in an early US accounting standard stated that

> ...cost for inventory purposes shall be determined under any one of several assumptions as to the flow of cost factors; the major objective in selecting a method should be to choose the one which, under the circumstances, most clearly reflects periodic income.

Under the current IFRS on inventories, IAS 2, there are two acceptable cost flow assumptions. These are: (1) first-in, first-out (FIFO) method and (2) the weighted-average method. There are variations of each of these cost flow assumptions that are sometimes used in practice, but if an entity presents its financial statements under IFRS it has to be careful not to apply a variant of these cost flow assumptions that would represent a deviation from the requirements of IAS 2. Furthermore, in certain jurisdictions, other costing methods, such as the last-in, first-out (LIFO) method and the base stock method, continue to be permitted. The LIFO method was an allowed alternative method of costing inventories under IAS 2 until the revision that became effective in 2005, at which time it was banned. Certain jurisdictions such as the US still allow the use of the LIFO method, and since use of LIFO for tax purposes necessitates use for financial reporting, the elimination of LIFO in the US is a controversial topic and may hinder full convergence with IFRS. (Note, however, that since the US Congress has frequently debated banning the use of the LIFO inventory costing method, this impediment to convergence may be eliminated as an issue.)

First-In, First-Out (FIFO)

The FIFO method of inventory valuation assumes that the first goods purchased will be the first goods to be used or sold, regardless of the actual physical flow. This method is thought to parallel most closely the physical flow of the units for most industries having moderate to rapid turnover of goods. The strength of this cost flow assumption lies in the inventory amount reported in the statement of financial position. Because the earliest goods purchased are the first ones removed from the inventory account, the remaining balance is composed of items acquired closer to period end, at more recent costs. This yields results similar to those obtained under current cost accounting in the statement of financial position, and helps in achieving the goal of reporting assets at amounts approximating current values.

However, the FIFO method does not necessarily reflect the most accurate or decision-relevant income figure when viewed from the perspective of underlying economic performance, as older historical costs are being matched against current revenues. Depending on the rate of inventory turnover and the speed with which general and specific prices are changing, this mismatching could potentially have a material distorting effect on reported income. At the extreme, if reported earnings are fully distributed to owners as dividends, the entity could be left without sufficient resources to replenish its inventory stocks due to the impact of changing prices. (This problem is not limited to inventory costing; depreciation based on old costs of plant assets also may understate the true economic cost of capital asset consumption, and serve to support dividend distributions that leave the entity unable to replace plant assets at current prices.)

The following example illustrates the basic principles involved in the application of FIFO:

	Units available	*Units sold*	*Actual unit cost*	*Actual total cost*
Beginning inventory	100	--	€2.10	€210
Sale	--	75	--	--
Purchase	150	--	2.80	420
Sale	--	100	--	--
Purchase	50	--	3.00	150
Total	300	175		€780

Given these data, the cost of goods sold and the ending inventory balance are determined as follows:

	Units	*Unit cost*	*Total cost*
Cost of goods sold	100	€2.10	€210
	75	2.80	210
	175		€420
Ending inventory	50	3.00	€150
	75	2.80	210
	125		€360

Notice that the total of the units in cost of goods sold and ending inventory, as well as the sum of their total costs, is equal to the goods available for sale and their respective total costs.

The unique characteristic of the FIFO method is that it provides the same results under either the periodic or perpetual system. This will not be the case for any other costing method.

Weighted-Average Cost

The other acceptable method of inventory valuation under revised IAS 2 involves averaging and is commonly referred to as the weighted-average cost method. The cost of goods available for sale (beginning inventory and net purchases) is divided by the units available for sale to obtain a weighted-average unit cost. Ending inventory and cost of goods sold are then priced at this average cost. For example, assume the following data:

	Units available	Units sold	Actual unit cost	Actual total cost
Beginning inventory	100	--	€2.10	€210
Sale	--	75	--	--
Purchase	150	--	2.80	420
Sale	--	100	--	--
Purchase	50	--	3.00	150
Total	300	175		€780

The weighted-average cost is €780/300, or €2.60. Ending inventory is 125 units at €2.60, or €325; cost of goods sold is 175 units at €2.60, or €455.

When the weighted-average assumption is applied to a perpetual inventory system, the average cost is recomputed after each purchase. This process is referred to as a moving average. Sales are costed at the most recent average. This combination is called the moving-average method and is applied below to the same data used in the weighted-average example above.

	Units on hand	Purchases in euros	Sales in euros	Total cost	Inventory unit cost
Beginning inventory	100	€ --	€ --	€210.00	€2.10
Sale (75 units @ €2.10)	25	--	157.50	52.50	2.10
Purchase (150 units, €420)	175	420.00	--	472.50	2.70
Sale (100 units @ €2.70)	75	--	270.00	202.50	2.70
Purchase (50 units, €150)	125	150.00	--	352.50	2.82

Cost of goods sold is 75 units at €2.10 and 100 units at €2.70, or a total of €427.50.

Net Realizable Value

As stated in IAS 2

Net realizable value is the estimated selling price in the ordinary course of business less the estimated costs of completion and the estimated costs necessary to make the sale.

The utility of an item of inventory is limited to the amount to be realized from its ultimate sale; where the item's recorded cost exceeds this amount, IFRS requires that a loss be recognized for the difference. The logic for this requirement is twofold: first, assets (in particular, current assets such as inventory) should not be reported at amounts that exceed net realizable value; and second, any decline in value in a period should be reported in that period's results of operations in order to achieve proper matching with current period's revenues. Were the inventory to be carried forward at an amount in excess of net realizable value, the loss would be recognized on the ultimate sale in a subsequent period. This would mean that a loss incurred in one period, when the value decline occurred, would have been deferred to a different period, which would clearly be inconsistent with several key accounting concepts.

IAS 2 states that estimates of net realizable value should be applied on an item-by-item basis in most instances, although it makes an exception for those situations where there are groups of related products or similar items that can be properly valued in the aggregate. As a general principle, item-by-item comparisons of cost to net realizable value are required, lest unrealized "gains" on some items (i.e., where the net realizable values exceed historical costs) offset the unrealized losses on other items, thereby reducing the net loss to be recognized. Since recognition of unrealized gains in profit or loss is generally proscribed under IFRS, evaluation of inventory declines on a grouped basis would be an indirect or "backdoor" mechanism to recognize gains that should not be given such recognition. Accordingly, the basic requirement is to apply the tests on an individual item basis.

Recoveries of previously recognized losses. IAS 2 stipulates that a new assessment of net realizable value should be made in each subsequent period; when the reason for a previous write-down no longer exists (i.e., when net realizable value has improved), it should be reversed. Since the write-down was taken into income, the reversal should also be reflected in profit or loss. As under prior rules, the amount to be restored to the carrying value will be limited to the amount of the previous impairment recognized.

Other Valuation Methods

There are instances in which an accountant must estimate the value of inventories. Whether for interim financial statements or as a check against perpetual records, the need for an inventory valuation without an actual physical count is required.

Retail method. IAS 2 notes that the retail method may be used by certain industry groups but does not provide details on how to employ this method, nor does it address the many variations of the technique. The conventional retail method is used by retailers as a method to estimate the cost of their ending inventory. The retailer can either take a physical inventory at retail prices or estimate ending retail inventory and then use the cost-to-retail ratio derived under this method to convert the ending inventory at retail to its estimated cost. This eliminates the process of going back to original invoices or other documents to determine the original cost for each inventoriable item. The retail method can be used under either of the two cost flow assumptions discussed earlier: FIFO or weighted-average cost. As with ordinary FIFO or weighted-average cost, the lower of cost or net realizable value (LCNRV) rule can also be applied to the retail method when either one of these two cost assumptions is used.

The key to applying the retail method is determining the cost-to-retail ratio. The calculation of this number varies depending on the cost flow assumption selected. Essentially, the cost-to-retail ratio provides a relationship between the cost of goods available for sale and the retail price of these goods. This ratio is used to convert the ending retail inventory back to cost. Computation of the cost-to-retail ratio for each of the available methods is described below.

1. **FIFO cost**—The concept of FIFO indicates that the ending inventory is made up of the latest purchases; therefore, beginning inventory is excluded from computation of the cost-to-retail ratio, and the computation becomes net purchases divided by their retail value adjusted for both net markups and net markdowns.

2. **FIFO (using a lower of cost or net realizable approach)**—The computation is basically the same as FIFO cost except that markdowns are excluded from the computation of the cost-to-retail ratio.

3. **Average cost**—Average cost assumes that ending inventory consists of all goods available for sale. Therefore, the cost-to-retail ratio is computed by dividing the cost of goods available for sale (Beginning inventory + Net purchases) by the retail value of these goods adjusted for both net markups and net markdowns.

4. **Average cost (using a lower of cost or net realizable approach)**—This is computed in the same manner as average cost except that markdowns are excluded for the calculation of the cost-to-retail ratio.

A simple example illustrates the computation of the cost-to-retail ratio under both the FIFO cost and average cost methods in a situation where no markups or markdowns exist.

	FIFO cost		*Average cost*	
	Cost	*Retail*	*Cost*	*Retail*
Beginning inventory	€100,000	€ 200,000	€100,000	€ 200,000
Net purchases	500,000	800,000	500,000	800,000
Total goods available for sale	€600,000	1,000,000	€600,000	1,000,000
Sales at retail		(800,000)		(800,000)
Ending inventory at retail		€ 200,000		€ 200,000

$$\text{Cost-to-retail ratio} \quad \frac{500,000}{800,000} = 62.5\% \quad \frac{600,000}{1,000,000} = 60\%$$

Ending inventory at cost
$200,000 \times 0.625$ € 125,000
$200,000 \times 0.60$ € 120,000

Note that the only difference in the two examples is the numbers used to calculate the cost-to-retail ratio.

As shown above, the lower of cost or market aspect of the retail method is a result of the treatment of net markups and net markdowns. *Net markups* (defined as markups less markup cancellations) are net increases above the original retail price, which are generally caused by changes in supply and demand. *Net markdowns* (markdowns less markdown cancellations) are net decreases below the original retail price. An approximation of lower of cost or market is achieved by including net markups but excluding net markdowns from the cost-to-retail ratio.

To understand this approximation, assume that a toy is purchased for €6 and the retail price is set at €10. It is later marked down to €8. A cost-to-retail ratio including markdowns would be €6 divided by €8 or 75%, and ending inventory would be valued at €8 times 75%, or €6 (original cost). A cost-to-retail ratio excluding markdowns would be €6 divided by €10 or 60%, and ending inventory would be valued at €8 times 60%, or €4.80 (on a lower of cost or market basis). The write-down to €4.80 reflects the loss in utility that is evidenced by the reduced retail price.

The application of the lower of cost or market rule is illustrated for both the FIFO and average cost methods in the example below. Remember, if the markups and markdowns below had been included in the preceding example, *both* would have been included in the cost-to-retail ratio.

	FIFO cost (LCNRV)		Average cost (LCNRV)	
	Cost	Retail	Cost	Retail
Beginning inventory	€100,000	€ 200,000	€100,000	€ 200,000
Net purchases	500,000	800,000	500,000	800,000
Net markups	--	250,000	--	250,000
Total goods available for sale	€600,000	1,250,000	€600,000	1,250,000
Net markdowns		(50,000)		(50,000)
Sales at retail		(800,000)		(800,000)
Ending inventory at retail		€ 400,000		€ 400,000

$$\text{Cost-to-retail ratio} \quad \frac{500,000}{1,050,000} = 47.6\% \quad \frac{600,000}{1,250,000} = 48\%$$

Ending inventory at cost
400,000 × 0.476   € 190,400
400,000 × 0.48   € 192,000

Notice that under the FIFO (LCNRV) method all of the markups are considered attributable to the current period purchases. Although this is not necessarily accurate, it provides the most conservative estimate of the ending inventory.

There are a number of additional inventory topics and issues that affect the computation of the cost-to-retail ratio and, therefore, deserve some discussion. Purchase discounts and freight affect only the cost column in this computation. The sales figure that is subtracted from the adjusted cost of goods available for sale in the retail column must be gross sales after adjustment for sales returns. If sales are recorded at gross, deduct the gross sales figure. If sales are recorded at net, both the recorded sales and sales discount must be deducted to give the same effect as deducting gross sales (i.e., sales discounts are not included in the computation). Normal spoilage is generally allowed for in the firm's pricing policies, and for this reason it is deducted from the retail column after calculation of the cost-to-retail ratio. Abnormal spoilage, on the other hand, should be deducted from *both* the cost and retail columns *before* the cost-to-retail calculation, as it could distort the ratio. It is then generally reported as a loss separate from the cost of goods sold section. Abnormal spoilage is generally considered to arise from a major theft or casualty, while normal spoilage is usually due to shrinkage or breakage. These determinations and their treatments will vary depending on the firm's policies.

When applying the retail method, separate computations should be made for any departments that experience significantly higher or lower profit margins. Distortions arise in the retail method when a department sells goods with varying margins in a proportion different from that purchased, in which case the cost-to-retail percentage would not be representative of the mix of goods in ending inventory. Also, manipulations of income are possible by planning the timing of markups and markdowns.

The retail method is an acceptable method of valuing inventories for tax purposes in some, but not all, jurisdictions. The foregoing examples are not meant to imply that the method would be usable in any given jurisdiction; readers should ascertain whether or not it can be used.

Standard costs. Standard costs are predetermined unit costs used by many manufacturing firms for planning and control purposes. Standard costs are often incorporated into the accounts, and materials, work in process, and finished goods inventories are all carried on this basis of accounting. The use of standard costs in financial reporting is acceptable if adjustments are made periodically to reflect current conditions and if its use approximates one of the recognized cost flow assumptions.

Fair value as an inventory costing method. In general, inventories are to be carried at cost, although, as has been explained in the preceding sections of this chapter, cost may be ascertained by a variety of methods under IAS 2, and when recoverable amounts do not equal cost there is the further need to write down inventory to reflect such impairment. However, under defined circumstances, inventories may be carried at fair value, in excess of the actual cost of production or acquisition. Currently, IAS 41 provides that agricultural products that are carried in inventory are to be reported at fair value, subject to certain limitations.

Under the provisions of IAS 41, all biological assets are to be measured at fair value less expected point-of-sale costs at each date of the statement of financial position, unless fair value cannot be measured reliably. Agricultural produce is to be measured at fair value at the point of harvest less expected point-of-sale costs. Because harvested produce is a marketable commodity, there is no "measurable reliability" exception for produce.

Furthermore, the change in fair value of biological assets occurring during a reporting period is reported in net profit or loss, notwithstanding that these are "unrealized" as of the date of the statement of financial position. IAS 41, however, does provide an exception to this fair value model for biological assets for situations where there is no active market at time of recognition in the financial statements, and no other reliable measurement method exists. In such instances, it provides that the cost model is to be applied to the specific biological asset for which such conditions hold, only. These biological assets should be measured at depreciated cost less any accumulated impairment losses.

More generally, the quoted market prices in active markets will represent the best measure of fair value of biological assets or agricultural produce. If an active market does not exist, IAS 41 provides guidance for choosing another measurement basis. Fair value measurement stops at the moment of harvest. IAS 2 applies after that date.

The details of IAS 41 are described in Chapter 31, Agriculture.

Other Cost Topics

Inventories valued at net realizable value. In exceptional cases, inventories may be reported at net realizable value in accordance with well-established practices in certain industries. Such treatment is justified when cost is difficult to determine, quoted market prices are available, marketability is assured, and units are interchangeable. IAS 2 stipulates that producers' inventories of agricultural and forest products, agricultural produce after harvest, and minerals and mineral products, to the extent that they are measured at net realizable value in accordance with well-established practices, are to be valued in this manner. IAS 41 subsequently addressed this matter for biological assets only. When inventory is valued above cost, revenue is recognized before the point of sale; full disclosure in the financial statements would, of course, be required.

Inventories valued at fair value less costs to sell. In case of commodity broker-traders' inventories, IAS 2 stipulates that these inventories be valued at fair value less costs to sell. While allowing this exceptional treatment for inventories of commodity broker-traders, IAS 2 makes it mandatory that in such cases the fair value changes should be reported in profit and loss account for the period of change.

Disclosure Requirements

IAS 2 sets forth certain disclosure requirements relative to inventory accounting methods employed by the reporting entity. According to this standard, the following must be disclosed:

1. The accounting policies adopted in measuring inventories, including the costing methods (e.g., FIFO or weighted-average) employed

2. The total carrying amount of inventories and the carrying amount in classifications appropriate to the entity
3. The carrying amount of inventories carried at fair value less costs to sell (inventories of commodity broker-traders)
4. The amount of inventories recognized as expense during the period
5. The amount of any write-down of inventories recognized as an expense in the period
6. The amount of any reversal of any previous write-down that is recognized in profit or loss for the period
7. The circumstances or events that led to the reversal of a write-down of inventories to net realizable value
8. The carrying amount of inventories pledged as security for liabilities

The type of information to be provided concerning inventories held in different classifications is somewhat flexible, but traditional classifications, such as raw materials, work in progress, finished goods, and supplies, should normally be employed. In the case of service providers, inventories (which are really akin to unbilled receivables) can be described as work in progress.

In addition to the foregoing, the financial statements should disclose either the cost of inventories recognized as an expense during the period (i.e., reported as cost of sales or included in other expense categories), or the operating costs, applicable to revenues, recognized as an expense during the period, categorized by their respective natures.

Costs of inventories recognized as expense includes, in addition to the costs inventoried previously and attaching to goods sold currently, the excess overhead costs charged to expense for the period because, under the standard, they could not be deferred to future periods.

EXAMPLES OF FINANCIAL STATEMENT DISCLOSURES

Nokia Corporation and Subsidiaries
Annual Report 2010

Notes to the Consolidated Financial Statements

1. Accounting Principles

Inventories. Inventories are stated at the lower of cost or net realizable value. Cost is determined using standard cost, which approximates actual cost, on a FIFO basis. Net realizable value is the amount that can be realized from the sale of the inventory in the normal course of business after allowing for the costs of realization. In addition to the cost of materials and direct labor, an appropriate proportion of production overhead is included in the inventory values. An allowance is recorded for excess inventory and obsolescence is based on the lower of cost or net realizable value.

18. Inventories

	2010 EURm	2009 EURm
Raw material, supplies and other	762	409
Work in progress	642	681
Finished goods	1,119	775
Total	2,523	1,865

Lectra S.A.
Annual Report 2010

Accounting Policies

Inventories. Inventories of raw materials are valued at the lower of purchase cost (based on weighted average cost, including related costs) and their net realizable value. Finished goods and work-in-progress are valued at the lower of standard industrial cost (adjusted at year-end on an actual cost basis) and their net realizable value.

Net realizable value is the estimated selling price in the normal course of business, less the estimated cost of completion or upgrading of the product and unavoidable selling costs.

Inventory cost does not include interest expense.

A write-down is recorded if net realizable value is less than the book value.

Write-downs on inventories of spare parts and consumables are calculated by comparing book value and probable net realizable value considering a specific analysis of the rotation and obsolescence of inventory items, taking into account the utilization of items for maintenance and after-sales services activities, and changes in the range of products marketed.

Notes to the Consolidated Financial Statements

7. Inventories

€ in thousands	2010	2009
Raw materials	17,683	18,424
Finished goods and works-in-progress [(1)]	11,001	10,186
Inventories, gross value	28,684	28,610
Raw materials	(5,281)	(5,251)
Finished goods and work-in-progress [(1)]	(4,066)	(4,911)
Write-downs	(9,348)	(10,162)
Raw materials	12,402	13,173
Finished goods and work-in-progress [(1)]	6,934	5,275
Inventories, net value	19,336	18,448

[(1)] Including demonstration and second-hand equipment.

€1,624,000 of inventory fully written down was scrapped in the course of 2010 (€2,063,000 in 2009), thereby diminishing the gross value and write-downs by the same amount.

The sharp rebound in orders led to an increase in production level and resulted in a slight increase in inventories in 2010.

Progress made in the utilization of the new production and inventory management software programs since their deployment on January 1, 2007, and since the deployment of modules of these software programs dedicated to the subsidiaries, had resulted in a sharp reduction in Group inventories in 2009.

Inventory write-downs charged for the year amounted to €3,036,000 (€3,275,000 in 2009). Reversals of previous write-downs relating to sales transactions amounted to €2,076,000 (€1,542,000 in 2009), booked against the charges for the period.

US GAAP COMPARISON

Accounting for inventory under US GAAP is essentially the same except for inherent differences in measurement of costs (i.e., fair value where applicable, capitalized interest where applicable). The last-in-first-out cost method (LIFO) is permitted under US GAAP. This cost method is used primarily for oil & gas companies to minimize taxable income. The US Tax code contains a concept called book-tax conformity that would prohibit deductions under LIFO if it is not the primary cost model.

US GAAP measures all inventory at the lower of cost or market value. IAS 2 requires that where inventories are held primarily for the purpose of trading, they are measured at fair value. US GAAP does not permit write-backs of previously recognized write-downs to net realizable value. The written down value is the new basis.

9 PROPERTY, PLANT, AND EQUIPMENT

INTRODUCTION

Long-lived tangible and intangible assets (which include property, plant, and equipment as well as development costs, various intellectual property intangibles, and goodwill) hold the promise of providing economic benefits to an entity for a period greater than that covered by the current year's financial statements. Accordingly, these assets must be capitalized rather than immediately expensed, and their costs must be allocated over the expected periods of benefit for the reporting entity. IFRS for long-lived assets address matters such as the determination of the amounts at which to initially record the acquisitions of such assets, the amounts at which to present these assets at subsequent reporting dates, and the appropriate method(s) by which to allocate the assets' costs to future periods. Under current IFRS, while historical cost is normally assumed to be the basis for financial reporting, it is also acceptable to periodically revalue long-lived assets if certain defined conditions are met.

Long-lived nonfinancial assets are primarily operational in character, (i.e., actively used in the business rather than being held as passive investments), and they may be classified into two basic types: tangible and intangible. *Tangible assets,* which are the subject of the present chapter, have physical substance and can be further categorized as follows:

1. Depreciable assets
2. Depletable assets
3. Other tangible assets

Intangible assets, on the other hand, have no physical substance. The value of an intangible asset is a function of the rights or privileges that its ownership conveys to the business entity. Intangible assets, which are explored at length in Chapter 11, can be further categorized as being either (1) identifiable, or (2) unidentifiable (i.e., goodwill), and further subcategorized as being finite-life assets and indefinite-life assets.

Long-lived assets are sometimes acquired in nonmonetary transactions, either in exchanges of assets between the entity and another business organization, or else when assets are given as capital contributions by shareholders to the entity. IAS 16 requires such transactions to be measured at fair value, unless they lack commercial substance.

Hitherto, IFRS has not addressed situations where agreements are entered into in which an entity receives from a customer an item of property, plant, and equipment that the entity must then use either to connect the customer to a network or to provide the customer with ongoing access to a supply of goods or services, or to agreements in which an entity receives cash from a customer when that amount of cash must be used only to construct or acquire an item of property, plant, and equipment and the entity must then use the item of property, plant, and equipment either to connect the customer to a network or to provide the customer with ongoing access to a supply of goods or services. To this end, IFRIC 18, *Transfers of Assets from Customers,* was issued with an effective date of July 1, 2009.

It is increasingly the case that assets are acquired or constructed with an attendant obligation to dismantle, restore the environment, or otherwise clean up after the end of the assets' useful lives. Decommissioning costs have to be estimated at initial recognition of the asset and recognized, in most instances, as additional asset cost and as a provision, thus causing the costs to be spread over the useful lives of the assets via depreciation charges.

Measurement and presentation of long-lived assets subsequent to acquisition or construction involves both systematic allocation of cost to accounting periods, and possible special write-downs. Concerning cost allocation to periods of use, IFRS now requires a "components approach" to depreciation. Thus, significant elements of an asset (in the case of a building, such components as the main structure, roofing, heating plant, and elevators, for instance) are to be separated from the cost paid for the asset, and amortized over their various appropriate useful lives.

It has long been held that an entity's statement of financial position should never present assets at amounts in excess of some threshold level of economic utility; under different national GAAP standards, this was variously defined in terms of market value or an amount which could be recovered from future revenues to be derived from utilization of the asset.

However, such rules were only infrequently formalized and less often enforced. For many years, there was no specific guidance within IFRS on how to account for any diminution in the value of long-lived assets that may have occurred during the reporting period. IAS 36, *Impairment of Assets*, which was introduced in 1998, significantly altered the accounting landscape by providing thorough coverage of this subject. IAS 36 is equally applicable to tangible and intangible long-lived assets, and will be accordingly addressed in both this and the immediately succeeding chapters.

Sources of IFRS			
IFRS 5, 8	*IAS* 16, 36, 37	*SIC* 21	*IFRIC* 1, 17, 18

DEFINITIONS OF TERMS

Accumulated depreciation. The total of all prior year deductions for depreciation taken to write off the value of a fixed asset over its estimated useful life. The accumulated depreciation account is a contra asset account, which reduces the value of total property, plant and equipment in the statement of financial position.

Asset held for sale. A noncurrent asset or a group of assets (disposal group) to be disposed of in a single transaction, together with directly associated liabilities. Assets classified as held for sale are not subject to depreciation and are carried at the lower of carrying amount and fair value less costs to sell. Separate classification of "assets and liabilities held for sale" in the statement of financial position is required.

Carrying amount (book value). The value reported for an asset or liability in the statement of financial position. For assets, this is either cost, revalued amount, or cost minus offsets such as depreciation or allowance for bad debts. Carrying amount of property, plant, and equipment is the amount at which an asset is recognized after deducting any accumulated depreciation and accumulated impairment losses. Carrying amount is often different from market value because depreciation is a cost allocation rather than a means of valuation. For liabilities, the carrying amount is the amount of the liability minus offsets such as any sums already paid or bond discounts.

Cash-generating unit. The smallest identifiable group of assets that generates cash inflows from continuing use that are largely independent of the cash inflows associated with other assets or groups of assets; used for impairment testing purposes.

Commercial substance. The ability to change an entity's future cash flows; used in determining the accounting for certain nonmonetary exchanges.

Component depreciation. The systematic allocation of the cost of each part of an item of property, plant, and equipment when this cost is significant in relation to the total cost of the item. An entity should allocate the amount initially recognized as an item of property, plant, and equipment to its significant parts and depreciate separately each such part.

Component of an entity. Operations and cash flows that can be clearly distinguished, operationally and for financial reporting purposes, from the rest of the entity.

Corporate assets. Assets, excluding goodwill, that contribute to future cash flows of both the cash-generating unit under review for impairment as well as other cash-generating units of the entity.

Cost. Amount of cash or cash equivalent paid or the fair value of the other consideration given to acquire an asset at the time of its acquisition or construction or, where applicable, the amount attributed to that asset when initially recognized in accordance with the specific requirements of other IFRS (e.g., IFRS 2, *Share-Based Payment*).

Costs of disposal. The incremental costs directly associated with the disposal of an asset; these do not include financing costs or related income tax effects (IAS 36).

Costs to sell. The incremental costs directly attributed to a disposal of an asset (or disposal group), excluding finance costs and income tax expense (IFRS 5).

Current asset. An asset should be classified as a current asset when it satisfies any one of the following:

1. It is expected to be realized in, or is held for sale or consumption in, the normal operating course of the entity's operating cycle;
2. It is held primarily for trading purposes;
3. It is expected to be realized within twelve months after the reporting period; or
4. It is cash or a cash equivalent (as defined in IAS 7) that is not restricted in its use.

Decommissioning costs. The costs of dismantling an asset and restoring the land on which it was sited, and any other affected assets to their previous state.

Depreciable amount. Cost of an asset or the other amount that has been substituted for cost, less the residual value of the asset.

Depreciation. The process of allocating the depreciable amount (cost less residual value) of an asset over the expected useful life of the asset. This process reduces the carrying amount of an asset as a result of wear and tear, age, or obsolescence, and recognizes depreciation expense in profit or loss. Similar to amortization, depreciation is a method of measuring the "consumption" of the carrying amount of long-term assets. It is not intended to be a valuation process. The amount allocated to depreciation expense is based on one of several accounting depreciation methods (IAS 16, IAS 36)

Depreciation method. A method of allocating the depreciable amount of an asset on a systematic basis over its useful life. IAS 16 states that the depreciation method should reflect the pattern in which the asset's future economic benefits are expected to be consumed by the entity, and that appropriateness of the method should be reviewed at least annually in case there has been a change in the expected pattern. Beyond that, the standard leaves the choice of method to the entity, even though it does cite the following methods; straight-line, diminishing balance, and units of production methods.

Discontinued operation. A component of an entity that either has been disposed of or is classified as held for sale and satisfies any one of the following:

1. It is a separate major line of business or geographical area of operations,
2. It is part of a single coordinated plan to dispose of a separate major line of business or geographical area of operations, or
3. It is a subsidiary acquired exclusively with a view to resale.

Disposal group. A group of assets (and liabilities associated with those assets) to be disposed of, by sale or otherwise, together as a group in a single transaction. Goodwill acquired in a business combination is included in the disposal group if this group is a cash-generating unit to which goodwill has been allocated in accordance with IAS 36 or if it is an operation within such a cash-generating unit.

Exchange. Reciprocal transfer between an entity and another entity that results in the acquisition of assets or services, or the satisfaction of liabilities, through a transfer of other assets, services, or other obligations.

Fair value. Amount that would be obtained for an asset in an arm's-length exchange transaction between knowledgeable, willing parties.

Fair value less costs to sell. The amount obtainable from the sale of an asset in an arm's-length transaction between knowledgeable, willing parties, less the costs of disposal.

Firm purchase commitment. An agreement with an unrelated party, binding on both parties and usually legally enforceable, that (1) specifies all important terms, including the price and timing of the transactions, and (2) includes a disincentive for nonperformance (sufficiently large) making performance highly probable.

Highly probable. Significantly more likely than probable.

Impairment loss. The excess of the carrying amount of an asset or a cash-generating unit over its recoverable amount.

Impairment test. Recoverability test, comparing the carrying amount of an asset in the statement of financial position to its recoverable amount to ensure that no asset is carried at more than its fair value. In general, impairment occurs when a company can no longer generate sufficient future cash inflows to recover the value of an asset.

Intangible assets. Identifiable nonmonetary assets, without physical substance.

Monetary assets. Money held and assets to be received in fixed or determinable amounts of money. Examples are cash, accounts receivable, and notes receivable.

Noncurrent asset. An asset not meeting the definition of a current asset.

Nonmonetary assets. Assets other than monetary assets. Examples are inventories; investments in equity instruments; and property, plant, and equipment.

Nonmonetary transactions. Exchanges and nonreciprocal transfers that involve little or no monetary assets or liabilities.

Nonreciprocal transfer. Transfer of assets or services in one direction, either from an entity to its owners or another entity, or from owners or another entity to the entity. An entity's reacquisition of its outstanding stock is a nonreciprocal transfer.

Property, plant, and equipment. Tangible assets that are expected to be used during more than one period, and that are held for use in the process of producing goods or services for sale, or for rental to others, or for administrative purposes; also referred to as fixed assets.

Probable. More likely than not.

Provision. A liability established to recognize a probable outflow of resources, whose timing or value is uncertain, where the reporting entity has a present obligation arising out of a past event.

Qualifying asset. An asset that necessarily requires a substantial period of time to get ready for its intended use or sale. (See Chapter 10.)

Recoverable amount. The greater of an asset's fair value less costs to sell or its value in use.

Residual (salvage) value. Estimated amount that an entity would currently obtain from disposal of the asset, net of estimated costs of disposal, if the asset were already of the age and in the condition expected at the end of its useful life.

Similar productive assets. Productive assets that are of the same general type, that perform the same function, or that are employed in the same line of business.

Useful life. Period over which an asset is expected to be available for use by an entity, or the number of production or similar units expected to be obtained from the asset by an entity.

Value in use. The present value of estimated future cash flows expected to be realized from the continuing use of an asset and from its disposal at the end of its useful life.

RECOGNITION AND MEASUREMENT

Property, Plant, and Equipment

Property, plant and equipment (also variously referred to as plant assets, fixed tangible assets, fixed assets or PP&E) is the term most often used to denote tangible assets to be used in the production or supply of goods or services, for rental to others, or for administrative purposes and that will benefit the entity during more than one accounting period.. This term is meant to distinguish these assets from intangibles, which are long-term, generally identifiable assets that do not have physical substance, or whose value is not fully indicated by their physical existence. Property, plant, and equipment does not include biological assets related to agricultural activity and mineral rights and mineral reserves (which subject matter is covered in Chapters 31 and 32 respectively). An item of property, plant, and equipment should be recognized as an asset only if two conditions are met: (1) it is probable that future economic benefits associated with this item will flow to the entity; and (2) the cost of this item can be determined reliably.

There are four concerns to be addressed in accounting for long-lived assets.

1. The amount at which the assets should be recorded initially on acquisition;
2. How value changes subsequent to acquisition should be reflected in the financial statements, including questions of both value increases and possible decreases due to impairments;
3. The rate at which the amount the assets are recorded should be allocated as an expense to future periods; and
4. The recording of the ultimate disposal of the assets.

Initial measurement. All costs required to bring an asset into working condition should be recorded as part of the cost of the asset. Elements of such costs include

1. Its purchase price, including legal and brokerage fees, import duties, and nonrefundable purchase taxes, after deducting trade discounts and rebates;
2. Any directly attributable costs incurred to bring the asset to the location and operating condition as expected by management, including the costs of site preparation, delivery and handling, installation, setup and testing; and
3. Estimated costs of dismantling and removing the item and restoring the site.

These costs are capitalized and are not to be expensed in the period in which they are incurred, as they are deemed to add value to the asset and indeed were necessary expenditures to obtain the asset.

The costs required to bring acquired assets to the place where they are to be used includes such ancillary costs as testing and calibrating, where relevant. IAS 16 aims to draw a distinction between the costs of getting the asset to the state in which it is in a condition to be exploited (which are to be included in the asset's carrying amount) and costs associated with the start-up operations, such as staff training, down time between completion of the asset and the start of its exploitation, losses incurred through running at below normal capacity etc., which are considered to be operating expenses. Any revenues that are earned from the asset during the installation process are netted off against the costs incurred in preparing the asset for use. As an example, the standard cites the sales of samples produced during this procedure.

IAS 16 distinguishes the situation described in the preceding paragraph from other situations where incidental operations unrelated to the asset may occur before or during the construction or development activities. For example, it notes that income may be earned through using a building site as a car parking lot until construction begins. Because incidental operations such as this are not necessary to bring the asset to the location and working condition necessary for it to be capable of operating in the manner intended by management, the income and related expenses of incidental operations are to be recognized in current earnings, and included in their respective classifications of income and expense in profit or loss. These are not to be presented net, as in the earlier example of machine testing costs and sample sales revenues.

Administrative costs, as well as other types of overhead costs, are not normally allocated to fixed asset acquisitions, despite the fact that some such costs, such as the salaries of the personnel who evaluate assets for proposed acquisitions, are in fact incurred as part of the acquisition process. As a general principle, administrative costs are expensed in the period incurred, based on the perception that these costs are fixed and would not be avoided in the absence of asset acquisitions. On the other hand, truly incremental costs, such as a consulting fee or commission paid to an agent hired specifically to assist in the acquisition, may be treated as part of the initial amount to be recognized as the asset cost.

While interest costs incurred during the construction of certain *qualifying* assets must be added to the cost of the asset under (see Chapter 10), if an asset is purchased on deferred payment terms, the interest cost, whether made explicit or imputed, is *not* part of the cost of the asset. Accordingly, such costs must be expensed currently as interest charges. If the purchase price for the asset incorporates a deferred payment scheme, only the cash equivalent price should be capitalized as the initial carrying amount of the asset. If the cash equivalent price is not explicitly stated, the deferred payment amount should be reduced to present value by the application of an appropriate discount rate. This would normally be best approximated by use of the entity's incremental borrowing cost for debt having a maturity similar to the deferred payment term, taking into account the risks relating to the asset under question that a financier would necessarily take into account.

Decommissioning costs included in initial measurement. The elements of cost to be incorporated in the initial recognition of an asset are to include the estimated costs of its eventual dismantlement ("decommissioning costs"). That is, the cost of the asset is "grossed up" for these estimated terminal costs, with the offsetting credit being posted to a liability account. It is important to stress that recognition of a liability can only be effected when all the criteria set forth in IAS 37 for the recognition of provisions are met. These stipulate that a provision is to be recognized only when (1) the reporting entity has a *present* obligation, whether legal or constructive, as a result of a *past* event; (2) it is *probable* that an outflow of resources embodying economic benefits will be required to settle the obligation; and (3) a reliable estimate can be made of the amount of the obligation.

For example, assume that it were necessary to secure a government license in order to construct a particular asset, such as a power generating plant, and a condition of the license is that at the end of the expected life of the property the owner would dismantle it, remove any debris, and restore the land to its previous condition. These conditions would qualify as a present obligation resulting from a past event (the construction of the plant), which will probably result in a future outflow of resources. The cost of such future activities, while perhaps challenging to estimate due to the long time horizon involved and the possible intervening evolution of technology, can normally be accomplished with a requisite degree of accuracy. Per IAS 37, a best estimate is to be made of the future costs, which is then to be discounted to present value. This present value is to be recognized as an additional cost of acquiring the asset.

The cost of dismantlement and similar legal or constructive obligations do not extend to operating costs to be incurred in the future, since those would not qualify as "present obligations." The precise mechanism for making these computations is addressed in Chapter 18.

If estimated costs of dismantlement, removal, and restoration are included in the cost of the asset, the effect will be to allocate this cost over the life of the asset through the depreciation process. Each period the discounting of the provision should be "unwound," such that interest cost is accreted each period. If this is done, at the expected date on which the expenditure is to be incurred it will be appropriately stated. The increase in the carrying amount of the provision should be reported as interest expense or a similar financing cost.

Examples of decommissioning or similar costs to be recognized at acquisition

Example 1—Leased premises. In accordance with the terms of a lease, the lessee is obligated to remove its specialized machinery from the leased premises prior to vacating those premises, or to compensate the lessor accordingly. The lease imposes a contractual obligation on the lessee to remove the asset at the end of the asset's useful life or upon vacating the premises, and therefore in this situation an asset (i.e., deferred cost) and liability should be recognized. If the lease is a finance lease, it is added to the asset cost; if an operating lease (less likely), a deferred charge would be reported.

Example 2—Owned premises. The same machinery described in Example 1 is installed in a factory that the entity owns. At the end of the useful life of the machinery, the entity will either incur costs to dismantle and remove the asset or will leave it idle in place. If the entity chooses to do nothing (i.e., not remove the equipment), this would adversely affect the fair value of the premises should the entity choose to sell the premises on an "as is" basis. Conceptually, to apply the matching principle in a manner consistent with Example 1, the cost of asset retirement should be recognized systematically and rationally over the productive life of the asset and not in the period of retirement. However, in this example, there is no *legal obligation* on the part of the owner of the factory and equipment to retire the asset and, thus, a cost would *not* be recognized at inception for this possible future loss of value.

Example 3—Promissory estoppel. Assume the same facts as in Example 2. In this case, however, the owner of the property sold to a third party an option to purchase the factory, exercisable at the end of five years. In offering the option to the third party, the owner verbally represented that the factory would be completely vacant at the end of the five-year option period and that all machinery, furniture, and fixtures would be removed from the premises. The property owner would reasonably expect that the purchaser of the option relied to the purchaser's detriment (as evidenced by the financial sacrifice of consideration made in exchange for the option) on the representation that the factory would be vacant. While the legal status of such a promise may vary depending on local custom and law, in general this is a constructive obligation and should be recognized as a decommissioning cost and related liability.

Example of timing of recognition of decommissioning cost

Teradactyl Corporation owns and operates a chemical company. At its premises, it maintains underground tanks used to store various types of chemicals. The tanks were installed when Teradactyl Corporation purchased its facilities seven years prior. On February 1, 2011, the legislature of the nation passed a law that requires removal of such tanks when they are no longer being used. Since the law imposes a legal obligation on Teradactyl Corporation, upon enactment, recognition of a decommissioning obligation would be required.

Example of ongoing additions to the decommissioning obligation

Jermyn Manufacturing Corporation operates a factory. As part of its normal operations it stores production by-products and used cleaning solvents on-site in a reservoir specifically designed for that purpose. The reservoir and surrounding land, all owned by Jermyn, are contaminated with these chemicals. On February 1, 2011, the legislature of the nation enacted a law that requires cleanup and disposal of hazardous waste from existing production processes upon retirement of the facility. Upon the enactment of the law, immediate recognition would be required for the decommissioning obligation associated with the contamination that had already occurred. In addition, liabilities will continue to be recognized over the remaining life of the facility as additional contamination occurs.

Changes in decommissioning costs. IFRIC 1 addresses the accounting treatment to be followed where a provision for reinstatement and dismantling costs has been created when an asset was acquired. The Interpretation requires that where estimates of future costs are revised, these should be applied prospectively only, and there is no adjustment to past years' deprecation. IFRIC 1 is addressed in Chapter 18 of this publication.

Initial recognition of self-constructed assets. Essentially the same principles that have been established for recognition of the cost of purchased assets also apply to self-constructed assets. All costs that must be incurred to complete the construction of the asset can be added to the amount to be recognized initially, subject only to the constraint that if these costs exceed the recoverable amount (as discussed fully later in this chapter), the excess must be expensed as an impairment loss. This rule is necessary to avoid the "gold-plated hammer syndrome," whereby a misguided or unfortunate asset construction project incurs excessive costs that then find their way into the statement of financial position, consequently overstating the entity's current net worth and distorting future periods' earnings. Of course, internal (intragroup) profits cannot be allocated to construction costs. The standard specifies that "abnormal amounts" of wasted material, labor, or other resources may not be added to the cost of the asset.

Self-constructed assets should include, in addition to the range of costs discussed earlier, the cost of borrowed funds used during the period of construction. Capitalization of borrowing costs, as set forth by IAS 23, is discussed in Chapter 10.

Exchanges of assets. IAS 16 discusses the accounting to be applied to those situations in which assets are exchanged for other similar or dissimilar assets, with or without the additional consideration of monetary assets. This topic is addressed later in this chapter, under the heading "Nonmonetary (Exchange) Transactions."

Costs incurred subsequent to purchase or self-construction. Costs that are incurred subsequent to the purchase or construction of the long-lived asset, such as those for repairs, maintenance, or betterments, may involve an adjustment to the carrying amount, or may be expensed, depending on the precise facts and circumstances.

To qualify for capitalization, cost must meet the recognition criteria of an asset. For example, modifications to the asset made to extend its useful life (measured either in years or in units of potential production) or to increase its capacity (e.g., as measured by units of output per hour) would be capitalized. Similarly, if the expenditure results in an improved quality of output, or permits a reduction in other cost inputs (e.g., would result in labor savings), it is a candidate for capitalization. Where a modification involves changing part of the asset (e.g., substituting a mightier power source), the cost of the part that is removed should be derecognized (treated as a disposal).

For example, roofs of commercial buildings, linings of blast furnaces used for steel making, and engines of commercial aircraft all need to be replaced or overhauled before the related buildings, furnaces, or airframes themselves must be replaced. If componentized depreciation was properly employed, the roofs, linings, and engines were being depreciated over their respectively shorter useful lives, and when the replacements or overhauls are performed, on average, these will have been fully depreciated. To the extent that undepreciated costs of these components remain, they would have to be removed from the account (i.e., charged to expense in the period of replacement or overhaul) as the newly incurred replacement or overhaul costs are added to the asset accounts, in order to avoid having, for financial reporting purposes, "two roofs on one building."

It can usually be assumed that ordinary maintenance and repair expenditures will occur on a ratable basis over the life of the asset and should be charged to expense as incurred. Thus, if the purpose of the expenditure is either to maintain the productive capacity anticipated when the asset was acquired or constructed, or to restore it to that level, the costs are not subject to capitalization.

A partial exception is encountered if an asset is acquired in a condition that necessitates that certain expenditures be incurred in order to put it into the appropriate state for its intended use. For example, a deteriorated building may be purchased with the intention that it be restored and then utilized as a factory or office facility. In such cases, costs that otherwise would be categorized as ordinary maintenance items might be subject to capitalization. Once the restoration is completed, further expenditures of similar type would be viewed as being ordinary repairs or maintenance, and thus expensed as incurred.

However, costs associated with required inspections (e.g., of aircraft) could be capitalized and depreciated. These costs would be amortized over the expected period of benefit (i.e., the estimated time to the next inspection). As with the cost of physical assets, removal of any undepreciated costs of previous inspections would be required. The capitalized inspection cost would have to be treated as a separate component of the asset.

Depreciation of property, plant, and equipment. The costs of property, plant, and equipment are allocated through depreciation to the periods that will have benefited from the use of the asset. Whatever method of depreciation is chosen, it must result in the systematic and rational allocation of the depreciable amount of the asset (initial cost less residual value) over the asset's expected useful life. The determination of the useful life must take a number of factors into consideration. These factors include technological change, normal deterioration, actual physical use, and legal or other limitations on the ability to use the property. The method of depreciation is based on whether the useful life is determined as a function of time or as a function of actual physical usage.

IAS 16 states that, although land normally has an unlimited useful life and is not to be depreciated, where the cost of the land includes estimated dismantlement or restoration costs, these are to be depreciated over the period of benefits obtained by incurring those costs. In some cases, the land itself may have a limited useful life, in which case it is to be depreciated in a manner that reflects the benefits to be derived from it.

Since, under the historical cost convention, depreciation accounting is intended as a strategy for cost allocation, it does not reflect changes in the market value of the asset being depreciated (except in some cases where the impairment rules have been applied in that way—as discussed below). Thus, with the exception of land, which has indefinite useful life, all tangible property, plant, and equipment must be depreciated, even if (as sometimes occurs, particularly in periods of general price inflation) their nominal or real values increase.

Furthermore, if the recorded amount of the asset is allocated over a period of time (as opposed to actual use); it should be the expected period of usefulness to the entity, not the physical or economic life of the property itself that governs. Thus, such concerns as technological obsolescence, as well as normal wear and tear, must be addressed in the initial determination of the period over which to allocate the asset cost. The reporting entity's strategy for repairs and maintenance will also affect this computation, since the same physical asset might have a longer or shorter useful life in the hands of differing owners, depending on the care with which it is intended to be maintained.

Similarly, the same asset may have a longer or shorter useful life, depending on its intended use. A particular building, for example, may have a fifty-year expected life as a facility for storing goods or for use in light manufacturing, but as a showroom would have a shorter period of usefulness, due to the anticipated disinclination of customers to shop at entities housed in older premises. Again, it is not physical life, but useful life, that should govern.

Compound assets, such as buildings containing such disparate components as heating plant, roofs, and other structural elements, are most commonly recorded in several separate accounts, to facilitate the process of depreciating the different elements over varying periods. Thus, a heating plant may have an expected useful life of twenty years, the roof a life of fifteen years, and the basic structure itself a life of forty years. Maintaining separate ledger accounts eases the calculation of periodic depreciation in such situations, although for financial reporting purposes a greater degree of aggregation is usual.

IAS 16, as revised in 2003, requires a component approach for depreciation, where, as described above, each material component of a composite asset with different useful lives or different patterns of depreciation is accounted for separately for the purpose of depreciation and accounting for subsequent expenditure (including replacement and renewal). Thus, rather than recording a newly acquired, existing office building as a single asset, it is recorded as a building shell, a heating plant, a roof, and perhaps other discrete mechanical components, subject to a materiality threshold. Allocation of cost over useful lives, instead of being based on a weighted-average of the varying components' lives, is based on separate estimated lives for each component.

IAS 16 states that the depreciation method should reflect the pattern in which the asset's future economic benefits are expected to be consumed by the entity, and that appropriateness of the method should be reviewed at least annually in case there has been a change in the expected pattern. Beyond that, the standard leaves the choice of method to the entity, even though it does cite straight-line, diminishing balance, and units of production methods.

Depreciation methods based on time.

1. Straight-line—Depreciation expense is incurred evenly over the life of the asset. The periodic charge for depreciation is given as

$$\frac{\text{Cost or amount substituted for cost, less residual value}}{\text{Estimated useful life of asset}}$$

2. Accelerated methods—Depreciation expense is higher in the early years of the asset's useful life and lower in the later years. IAS 16 only mentions one accelerated method, the diminishing balance method, but other methods have been employed in various national GAAP under earlier or contemporary accounting standards.

    a. Diminishing balance—the depreciation rate is applied to the net carrying amount of the asset, resulting in a diminishing annual charge. There are various ways to compute the percentage to be applied. The formula below provides a mathematically correct allocation over useful life.

$$\text{Rate \%} = \left(1 - \sqrt[n]{\text{Residual value/cost}}\right) \times 100$$

    Where n is the expected useful life in years. However, companies generally use approximations or conventions influenced by tax practice, such as a multiple of the straight-line rate times the net carrying amount at the beginning of the year.

$$\text{Straight-line rate} = \frac{1}{\text{Estimated useful life}}$$

Example

Double-declining balance depreciation (if salvage value is to be recognized, stop when carrying amount = estimated salvage value)

$$\text{Depreciation} = 2 \times \text{Straight-line rate} \times \text{Book value at beginning of year}$$

Another method to accomplish a diminishing charge for depreciation is the sum-of-the-years' digits method, which is commonly employed in the United States and certain other venues.

b. Sum-of-the-years' digits (SYD) depreciation =

(Cost less salvage value) × Applicable fraction

$$\text{Where applicable fraction} = \frac{\text{Number of years of estimated life remaining as of the beginning of the year}}{\text{SYD}}$$

$$\text{and SYD} = \frac{n(n + 1)}{2} \text{ and } n = \text{estimated useful life}$$

Example

An asset having a useful economic life of 5 years and no salvage value would have 5/15 (= 1/3) of its cost allocated to year 1, 4/15 to year 2, and so on.

In practice, unless there are tax reasons to employ accelerated methods, large companies tend to use straight-line depreciation. This has the merit that it is simple to apply, and where a company has a large pool of similar assets, some of which are replaced each year, the aggregate annual depreciation charge is likely to be the same, irrespective of the method chosen (consider a trucking company that has ten trucks, each costing €200,000, one of which is replaced each year: the aggregate annual depreciation charge will be €200,000 under any mathematically accurate depreciation method).

Partial-year depreciation. Although IAS 16 is silent on the matter, when an asset is either acquired or disposed of during the year, the full year depreciation calculation should be prorated between the accounting periods involved. This is necessary to achieve proper matching. However, if individual assets in a relatively homogeneous group are regularly acquired and disposed of, one of several conventions can be adopted, as follows:

1. Record a full year's depreciation in the year of acquisition and none in the year of disposal.
2. Record one-half year's depreciation in the year of acquisition and one-half year's depreciation in the year of disposal.

Example of partial-year depreciation

Assume the following:

Taj Mahal Milling Co., a calendar-year entity, acquired a machine on June 1, 2011, that cost €40,000 with an estimated useful life of four years and a €2,500 salvage value. The depreciation expense for each *full* year of the asset's life is calculated as follows:

	Straight-line			Double-declining balance					Sum-of-years' digits		
Year 1	€37,500* ÷ 4 = €9,375	50%	×	€40,000	=	€20,000	4/10	×	€37,500*	=	€15,000
Year 2	€9,375	50%	×	€20,000	=	€10,000	3/10	×	€37,500	=	€11,250
Year 3	€9,375	50%	×	€10,000	=	€ 5,000	2/10	×	€37,500	=	€ 7,500
Year 4	€9,375	50%	×	€ 5,000	=	€ 2,500	1/10	×	€37,500	=	€ 3,750

* *€40,000 – €2,500.*

Because the first full year of the asset's life does not coincide with the company's fiscal year, the amounts shown above must be prorated as follows:

	Straight-line			Double-declining balance					Sum-of-years' digits		
2011	7/12 × 9,375 = €5,469	7/12	×	€20,000	=	€11,667	7/12	×	€15,000	=	€ 8,750
2012	€9,375	5/12	×	€20,000	=	€ 8,333	5/12	×	€15,000	=	€ 6,250
		7/12	×	€10,000	=	€ 5,833	7/12	×	€11,250	=	€ 6,563
						€14,166					€12,813
2013	€9,375	5/12	×	€10,000	=	€ 4,167	5/12	×	€11,250	=	€ 4,687
		7/12	×	€ 5,000	=	€ 2,917	7/12	×	€ 7,500	=	€ 4,375
						€ 7,084					€ 9,062
2014	€9,375	5/12	×	€ 5,000	=	€ 2,083	5/12	×	€ 7,500	=	€ 3,125
		7/12	×	€ 2,500	=	€ 1,458	7/12	×	€ 3,750	=	€ 2,188
						€ 3,541					€ 5,313
2015	5/12 × 9,375 = €3,906	5/12	×	€ 2,500	=	€ 1,042	5/12	×	€ 3,750	=	€ 1,562

Depreciation method based on actual physical use—Units of production method. Depreciation may also be based on the number of units produced by the asset in a given year. IAS 16 identifies this as the units of production method, but it is also known as the sum of the units approach. It is best suited to those assets, such as machinery, that have an expected life that is most rationally defined in terms of productive output; in periods of reduced production (such as economic recession) the machinery is used less, thus extending the number of years it is likely to remain in service. This method has the merit that the annual depreciation expense fluctuates with the contribution made by the asset each year. Furthermore, if the depreciation finds its way into the cost of finished goods, the unit cost in periods of reduced production would be exaggerated and could even exceed net realizable value unless the units of production approach to depreciation was taken.

$$\text{Depreciation rate} = \frac{\text{Cost less residual value}}{\begin{array}{c}\text{Estimated number of units to be produced}\\ \text{by the asset over its estimated useful life}\end{array}}$$

$$\begin{array}{c}\text{Units of production}\\ \text{depreciation}\end{array} = \text{Depreciation rate} \times \begin{array}{c}\text{Number of units produced}\\ \text{during the period}\end{array}$$

Other depreciation methods. Although IAS 16 does not discuss other methods of depreciation (nor even all the variations noted in the foregoing paragraphs), at different times and in various jurisdictions other methods have been used. Some of these are summarized as follows:

1. **Retirement method**—Cost of asset is expensed in period in which it is retired.
2. **Replacement method**—Original cost is carried in accounts and cost of replacement is expensed in the period of replacement.
   (Neither the retirement nor replacement methods would be acceptable under IAS 16 because they do not reflect the pattern of consumption.)

3. **Group (or composite) method**—Averages the service lives of a number of assets using a weighted-average of the units and depreciates the group or composite as if it were a single unit. A group consists of similar assets, while a composite is made up of dissimilar assets.

$$\text{Depreciation rate} = \frac{\text{Sum of the straight-line depreciation of individual assets}}{\text{Total asset cost}}$$

$$\text{Depreciation expense} = \text{Depreciation rate} \times \text{Total group (composite) cost}$$

A peculiarity of the composite approach is that gains and losses are not recognized on the disposal of an asset, but rather, are netted into accumulated depreciation. This is because it is a presumption of this method that although dispositions of individual assets may yield proceeds greater than or less than their respective carrying amounts, the ultimate gross proceeds from a group of assets will not differ materially from the aggregate carrying amount thereof, and accordingly, recognition of those individual gains or losses should be deferred and effectively netted out.

4. **Revenue method**—The future cash flows expected to be derived from the asset are estimated, and a percentage is calculated which reflects the cost of the asset as a proportion of its expected revenue. When revenue is received, that percentage is applied to it as a depreciation charge. This is used, for example, for films, and could be considered to be a variant on the units of production method.

Residual value. Most depreciation methods discussed above require that depreciation is applied not to the full cost of the asset, but to the "depreciable amount": that is, the historical cost or amount substituted therefor (i.e., fair value) less the estimated residual value of the asset. As IAS 16 points out, residual value is often not material and in practice is frequently ignored, but it may impact upon some assets, particularly when the entity disposes of them early in their life (e.g., rental vehicles) or where the residual value is so high as to negate any requirement for depreciation (some hotel companies, for example, claim that they have to maintain their premises to such a high standard that their residual value under historical cost is higher than the original cost of the asset).

Under IAS 16, residual value is defined as the estimated amount that an entity would currently obtain from disposal of the asset, after deducting the estimated costs of disposal, if the asset were already of the age and in the condition expected at the end of its useful life. Residual value should, however, be measured net of any expected costs of disposal. In some cases, assets will have a negative residual value, as for example when the entity is likely to incur costs to dispose of the asset, or to return the property to an earlier condition, as in the case of certain operations, such as strip mines, that are subject to environmental protection or other laws. In such instances, periodic depreciation should total more than the asset's original cost, such that at the expected disposal date, an estimated liability has been accrued equal to the negative residual value. The residual value is, like all aspects of the depreciation method, subject to at least annual review.

If the revaluation method of measuring property, plant, and equipment is chosen, residual value must be assessed anew at the date of each revaluation of the asset. This is accomplished by using data on realizable values for similar assets, ending their respective useful lives at the time of the revaluation, after having been used for purposes similar to the asset being valued. Again, no consideration can be paid to anticipated inflation, and expected future values are not to be discounted to present values to give recognition to the time value of money.

Useful lives. Useful life is affected by such things as the entity's practices regarding repairs and maintenance of its assets, as well as the pace of technological change and the market demand for goods produced and sold by the entity using the assets as productive inputs. If it is determined, when reviewing the depreciation method, that the estimated life is greater or less than previously believed, the change is handled as a change in accounting estimate, not as a correction of an accounting error. Accordingly, no restatement is to be made to previously reported depreciation; rather, the change is accounted for strictly on a prospective basis, being reflected in the period of change and subsequent periods.

Example of estimating the useful life

An asset with a cost of €100,000 was originally estimated to have a productive life of 10 years. The straight-line method is used, and there was no residual value anticipated. After 2 years, management revises its estimate of useful life to a total of 6 years. Since the net carrying amount of the asset is €80,000 after 2 years (= €100,000 × 8/10), and the remaining expected life is 4 years (2 of the 6 revised total years having already elapsed), depreciation in years 3 through 6 will be €20,000 (= €80,000/4) each.

Tax methods. The methods of computing depreciation discussed in the foregoing sections relate only to financial reporting under IFRS. Tax laws in different nations of the world vary widely in terms of the acceptability of depreciation methods, and it is not possible for a general treatise such as this to address those in any detail. However, to the extent that depreciation allowable for income tax reporting purposes differs from that required or permitted for financial statement purposes, deferred income taxes would have to be computed. Interperiod income tax allocation is discussed more fully in Chapter 26.

Leasehold improvements. Leasehold improvements are improvements to property not owned by the party making these investments. For example, a lessee of office space may invest its funds to install partitions or to combine several suites by removing certain interior walls. Due to the nature of these physical changes to the property (done with the lessor's permission, of course), the lessee cannot remove or undo these changes and must abandon them upon termination of the lease, if the lessee does not remain in the facility.

A frequently encountered issue with respect to leasehold improvements relates to determination of the period over which they are to be amortized. Normally, the cost of long-lived assets is charged to expense over the estimated useful lives of the assets. However, the right to use a leasehold improvement expires when the related lease expires, irrespective of whether the improvement has any remaining useful life. Thus, the appropriate useful life for a leasehold improvement is the lesser of the useful life of the improvement or the term of the underlying lease.

Some leases contain a fixed, noncancelable term and additional renewal options. When considering the term of the lease for the purposes of depreciating leasehold improvements, normally only the initial fixed noncancelable term is included. There are exceptions to this general rule, however. If a renewal option is a bargain renewal option, which means that it is probable at the inception of the lease that it will be exercised and, therefore, the option period should be included in the lease term for purposes of determining the amortizable life of the leasehold improvements. Additionally, under the definition of the lease term there are other situations where it is probable that an option to renew for an additional period would be exercised. These situations include periods for which failure to renew the lease imposes a penalty on the lessee in such amount that a renewal appears, at the inception of the lease, to be reasonably assured. Other situations of this kind arise when an otherwise excludable renewal period precedes a provision for a bargain purchase of the leased asset or when, during periods covered by ordinary renewal options, the lessee has guaranteed the lessor's debt on the leased property.

Example

  Mojo Corporation occupies a warehouse under a five-year operating lease commencing January 1, 2011, and expiring December 31, 2015. The lease contains three successive options to renew the lease for additional five-year periods. The options are not bargain renewals as they call for fixed rentals at the prevailing fair market rents that will be in effect at the time of exercise. When the initial calculation was made to determine whether the lease is an operating lease or a capital lease, only the initial noncancelable term of five years was included in the calculation. Consequently, for the purpose of determining the depreciable life of any leasehold improvements made by Mojo Corporation, only the initial five-year term is used. If Mojo Corporation decides, at the beginning of year four of the lease, to make a substantial amount of leasehold improvements to the leased property, it could be argued that it would now be probable that Mojo would exercise one or more of the renewal periods, since not doing so would impose the substantial financial penalty for abandoning expensive leasehold improvements. This would trigger accounting for the lease by treating the period or periods for which it is likely that the lessee will renew as a new agreement and require testing to determine whether the lease, prospectively, qualifies as a finance or operating lease.

Revaluation of Property, Plant, and Equipment

IAS 16 provides for two acceptable alternative approaches to accounting for long-lived tangible assets. The first of these is the historical cost method, under which acquisition or construction cost is used for initial recognition, subject to depreciation over the expected useful life and to possible write-down in the event of a permanent impairment in value. In many jurisdictions this is the only method allowed by statute, but a number of jurisdictions, particularly those with significant rates of inflation, do permit either full or selective revaluation and IAS 16 acknowledges this by also allowing what it calls the "revaluation model." Under the revaluation model, after initial recognition as an asset, an item of property, plant and equipment whose fair value can be measured reliably should be carried at a revalued amount, being its fair value at the date of the revaluation less any subsequent accumulated depreciation and subsequent accumulated impairment losses.

The logic of recognizing revaluations relates to both the statement of financial position and the measure of periodic performance provided by the statement of comprehensive income. Due to the effects of inflation (which even if quite moderate when measured on an annual basis can compound dramatically during the lengthy period over which property, plant, and equipment remain in use) the statement of financial position can become a virtually meaningless agglomeration of dissimilar costs.

Furthermore, if the depreciation charge to income is determined by reference to historical costs of assets acquired in much earlier periods, profits will be overstated, and will not reflect the cost of maintaining the entity's asset base. Under these circumstances, a nominally profitable entity might find that it has self-liquidated and is unable to continue in existence, at least not with the same level of productive capacity, without new debt or equity infusions. IAS 29, *Financial Reporting in Hyperinflationary Economies,* addresses adjustments to depreciation under conditions of hyperinflation. Use of the revaluation method is typically encountered in economies that from time to time suffer less significant inflation than that which necessitates application of the procedures specified by IAS 29.

Under the revaluation model the frequency of revaluations depends upon the changes in fair values of the items being revalued and, consequently, when the fair value of a revalued asset differs materially from its carrying amount, a further revaluation is required. Since the revaluation model is more costly to maintain than the historical cost model, the results of the survey conducted by the Institute of Chartered Accountants in England and Wales in 2005 (ICAEW, 2007) indicated that a mere 4% of EU companies used revaluation for buildings (none for other property and equipment) and only 28% of EU companies with investment property used fair value (revaluation) method for that class of assets.

Fair value. As the basis for the revaluation method, the standard stipulates that it is *fair value* (defined as the amount for which the asset could be exchanged between knowledgeable, willing parties in an arm's-length transaction) that is to be used in any such revaluations. Furthermore, the standard requires that, once an entity undertakes revaluations, they must continue to be made with sufficient regularity that the carrying amounts in any subsequent statements of financial position are not materially at variance with then-current fair values. In other words, if the reporting entity adopts the revaluation method, it cannot report obsolete fair values in the statements of financial position that contain previous years' comparative data, since that would not only obviate the purpose of the allowed treatment, but would actually make it impossible for the user to meaningfully interpret the financial statements. Accordingly, the IASB recommends that a class of assets should be revalued on a rolling basis provided revaluation of the class of assets is completed within a short period and provided the revaluations are kept up-to-date.

In accordance with IAS 16, fair value is usually determined by appraisers, using market-based evidence. Market values can also be used for machinery and equipment, but since such items often do not have readily determinable market values, particularly if intended for specialized applications, they may instead be valued at depreciated replacement cost. Until recently, the term fair value was employed by several IFRS without reference to any detailed guidance as to how it is applied. This changed with the issuance of IFRS 13, *Fair Value Measurements*, in May 2011 which is effective for annual periods commencing on or after January 1, 2013. The new standard, which is presented in further detail in Chapter 25, introduces a new definition for the term "fair value," and identifies three levels of fair value. It cites as the highest (Level 1 inputs) quoted prices in active markets for identical assets; the second best (Level 2 inputs) being directly or indirectly observable prices in active markets for similar assets; and the final (Level 3 inputs) being the use of unobservable inputs, that should reflect assumptions that market participants would use in pricing the assets, including assumptions about risk.

Alternative concepts of current value. A number of different concepts have been proposed over the years to achieve accounting adjusted for inflation. Methods that address changes in specific prices, in contrast to those that attempt to adjust for general purchasing power changes, have measured reproduction cost, replacement cost, sound value, exit value, entry value, and net present value.

In brief, *reproduction cost* refers to the actual current cost of exactly reproducing the asset, essentially ignoring changes in technology in favor of a strict bricks-and-mortar concept. Since the same service potential could be obtained currently, in many cases, without a literal reproduction of the asset, this method fails to fully address the economic reality that accounting should ideally attempt to measure.

Replacement cost, in contrast, deals with the service potential of the asset, which is after all what truly represents value for its owner. An obvious example can be found in the realm of computers. While the cost to reproduce a particular mainframe machine exactly might be the same or somewhat lower today versus its original purchase price, the computing capacity of the machine might easily be replaced by one or a small group of microcomputers that could be obtained for a fraction of the cost of the larger machine. To gross up the statement of financial position by reference to reproduction cost would be distorting, at the very least.

Instead, the replacement cost of the service potential of the owned asset should be used to accomplish the revaluation contemplated by IAS 16.

Furthermore, even replacement cost, if reported on a gross basis, would be an exaggeration of the value implicit in the reporting entity's asset holdings, since the asset in question has already had some fraction of its service life expire. The concept of sound value addresses this concern. Sound value is the equivalent of the cost of replacement of the service potential of the asset, adjusted to reflect the relative loss in its utility due to the passage of time or the fraction of total productive capacity that has already been utilized.

Example of depreciated replacement cost (sound value) as a valuation approach

An asset acquired January 1, 2011, at a cost of €40,000 was expected to have a useful life of 10 years. After three years, on January 1, 2014, it is appraised as having a gross replacement cost of €50,000. The sound value, or depreciated replacement cost, would be 7/10 × €50,000, or €35,000. This compares with a book, or carrying, value of €28,000 at that same date. Mechanically, to accomplish a revaluation at January 1, 2014, the asset should be written up by €10,000 (i.e., from €40,000 to €50,000 gross cost) and the accumulated depreciation should be proportionally written up by €3,000 (from €12,000 to €15,000). Under IAS 16, the net amount of the revaluation adjustment, €7,000, would be credited to other comprehensive income and accumulated in equity as revaluation surplus.

An alternative accounting procedure is also permitted by the standard, under which the accumulated depreciation at the date of the revaluation is written off against the gross carrying amount of the asset. In the foregoing example, this would mean that the €12,000 of accumulated depreciation at January 1, 2014, immediately prior to the revaluation, would be credited to the gross asset amount, €40,000, thereby reducing it to €28,000. Then the asset account would be adjusted to reflect the valuation of €35,000 by increasing the asset account by €7,000 (= €35,000 – €28,000), with the offset to other comprehensive income (and accumulated in the revaluation surplus in shareholders' equity). In terms of total assets reported in the statement of financial position, this has exactly the same effect as the first method.

Revaluation applied to all assets in the class. IAS 16 requires that if any assets are revalued, all other assets in those groupings or categories must also be revalued. This is necessary to prevent the presentation in a statement of financial position that contains an unintelligible and possibly misleading mix of historical costs and fair values, and to preclude selective revaluation designed to maximize reported net assets. Coupled with the requirement that revaluations take place with sufficient frequency to approximate fair values at the end of each reporting period, this preserves the integrity of the financial reporting process. In fact, given that a statement of financial position prepared under the historical cost method will, in fact, contain noncomparable values for similar assets (due to assets having been acquired at varying times, at differing price levels), the revaluation approach has the possibility of providing more consistent financial reporting. Offsetting this potential improvement, at least somewhat, is the greater subjectivity inherent in the use of fair values, providing an example of the conceptual framework's trade-off between relevance and reliability.

Although IAS 16 requires revaluation of all assets in a given class, the standard recognizes that it may be more practical to accomplish this on a rolling, or cyclical, basis. This could be done by revaluing one-third of the assets in a given asset category, such as machinery, in each year, so that at the end of any reporting period one-third of the group is valued at current fair value, another one-third is valued at amounts that are one year obsolete, and another one-third are valued at amounts that are two years obsolete. Unless values are changing rapidly, it is likely that the statement of financial position would not be materially distorted, and therefore, this approach would in all likelihood be a reasonable means to facilitate the revaluation process.

According to the IASB, annual revaluation is necessary for those items of property, plant, and equipment which experience significant and volatile changes in fair value; items with only insignificant changes in fair value may be revalued only every three or five years.

Revaluation adjustments. In general, revaluation adjustments increasing an asset's carrying amount are recognized in other comprehensive income and accumulated in equity as *"revaluation surplus."* However, the increase should be recognized in profit or loss to the extent that it reverses a revaluation decrease (impairment) of the same asset previously recognized in profit or loss. If a revalued asset is subsequently found to be impaired, the impairment loss is recognized in other comprehensive income only to the extent that the impairment loss does not exceed the amount in the revaluation surplus for the same asset. Such an impairment loss on a revalued asset is first offset against the revaluation surplus for that asset, and only when that has been exhausted, it is recognized in profit or loss.

Revaluation adjustments decreasing an asset's carrying amount, in general, are recognized in profit or loss. However, the decrease should be recognized in other comprehensive income to the extent of any credit balance existing in the revaluation surplus in respect of that asset. The decrease recognized in other comprehensive income reduces the amount accumulated in equity in the revaluation surplus account.

Under the provisions of IAS 16, the amount credited to revaluation surplus can either be transferred directly to retained earnings (but *not* through profit or loss!) as the asset is being depreciated, or it can be held in the revaluation surplus account until such time as the asset is disposed of or retired from service. Any transfer to retained earnings is limited to the amount equal to the difference between depreciation based on the revalued carrying amount of the asset and depreciation based on the asset's original cost. In addition, revaluation surplus may be transferred directly to retained earnings when the asset is derecognized. This would involve transferring the whole of the surplus when the asset is retired or disposed of.

Initial revaluation. Under the revaluation model in IAS 16, at the date of initial revaluation of an item of property, plant, and equipment, revaluation adjustments are accounted for as follows:

1. Increases in an asset's carrying amount are credited to other comprehensive income (gain on revaluation); and
2. Decreases in an asset's carrying amount are charged to profit or loss as this is deemed to be an impairment recognized on the related asset.

Example—Initial revaluation

Assume Henan Corporation (HC) acquired a building with a cost of €100,000. After one year the building is appraised as having a current fair value of €110,000. The journal entry to increase the carrying amount of the building to its fair value is as follows:

Building	10,000	
Other comprehensive income—gain on revaluation		10,000

At the end of the fiscal period, the increase in the carrying amount of the building is accumulated in the "revaluation surplus" in the shareholders' equity section of the statement of financial position.

Subsequent revaluation. In accordance with IAS 16, in subsequent periods, revaluation adjustments are accounted for as follows:

1. Increases in an asset's carrying amount (upward revaluation) should be recognized as income in profit or loss to the extent of the amount of any previous impairment loss recognized, and any excess should be credited to equity through other comprehensive income;
2. Decreases in an asset's carrying amount (downward revaluation) should be charged to other comprehensive income to the extent of any previous revaluation surplus, and any excess should be debited to profit or loss as an impairment loss.

Example—Subsequent revaluation

In the following year, Henan Corporation determines that the fair value of the building is no longer €110,000. Assuming the fair value decreased to €95,000, the following journal entry is made to record downward revaluation:

Other comprehensive income—loss on revaluation	10,000	
Impairment loss—building (expense)	5,000	
Building		15,000

Methods of adjusting accumulated depreciation at the date of revaluation. When an item of property, plant and equipment is revalued, any accumulated depreciation at the date of the revaluation is treated in one of the following ways:

1. Restate accumulated depreciation proportionately with the change in the gross carrying amount of the asset (so that the carrying amount of the asset after revaluation equals its revalued amount); or
2. Eliminate the accumulated depreciation against the gross carrying amount of the asset.

Example—Accumulated depreciation

Konin Corporation (KC) owns buildings with a cost of €200,000 and estimated useful life of five years. Accordingly, depreciation of €40,000 per year is anticipated. After two years, KC obtains market information suggesting that a current fair value of the buildings is €300,000 and decided to write the buildings up to a fair value of €300,000. There are two approaches to apply the revaluation model in IAS 16: the asset and accumulated depreciation can be "grossed up" to reflect the new fair value information, or the asset can be restated on a "net" basis. These two approaches are illustrated below. For both illustrations, the net carrying amount (carrying amount or depreciated cost) immediately prior to the revaluation is €120,000 [€200,000 – (2 × €40,000)]. The net upward revaluation is given by the difference between fair value and net carrying amount, or €300,000 – €120,000 = €180,000.

Option 1. Applying the **"gross up" approach,** since the fair value after two years of the five-year useful life have already elapsed is found to be €300,000, the gross fair value (gross carrying amount) must be 5/3 × €300,000 = €500,000. In order to have the net carrying amount equal to the fair value after two years, the balance in accumulated depreciation needs to be €200,000. Consequently, the buildings and accumulated depreciation accounts need to be restated upward as follows: buildings up €300,000 (€500,000 – €200,000) and accumulated depreciation €120,000 (€200,000 – €80,000). Alternatively, this revaluation could be accomplished by restating the buildings account and the accumulated depreciation account so that the ratio of net carrying amount to gross carrying amount is 60% (€120,000/€200,000) and the net carrying amount is $300,000. New gross carrying amount is calculated €300,000/.60 = x; x = €500,000.

The following journal entry and table illustrate the restatement of the accounts:

Buildings	300,000	
Accumulated depreciation		120,000
Other comprehensive income—gain on revaluation		180,000

	Original cost		*Revaluation*		*Total*	*%*
Gross carrying amount	€200,000	+	€300,000	=	€500,000	100
Accumulated depreciation	80,000	+	120,000	=	200,000	40
Net carrying amount	€120,000	+	€180,000	=	€300,000	60

After the revaluation, the carrying amount of the buildings is €300,000 (= €500,000 – 200,000) and the ratio of net carrying amount to gross carrying amount is 60% (= €300,000/ €500,000). This method is often used when an asset is revalued by means of applying an index to determine its depreciated replacement cost.

Option 2. Applying the **"netting" approach,** KC would eliminate accumulated depreciation of €80,000 and then increase the building account by €180,000 so the net carrying amount is €300,000 (= €200,000 – €80,000 + €180,000):

Accumulated depreciation	80,000	
Buildings		80,000
Buildings	180,000	
Other comprehensive income—gain on revaluation		180,000

This method is often used for buildings. In terms of total assets reported in the statement of financial position, option 2 has exactly the same effect as option 1.

However, many users of financial statements, including credit grantors and prospective investors, pay heed to the ratio of net property and equipment as a fraction of the related gross amounts. This is done to assess the relative age of the entity's productive assets and, indirectly, to estimate the timing and amounts of cash needed for asset replacements. There is a significant diminution of information under the second method. Accordingly, the first approach described above, preserving the relationship between gross and net asset amounts after the revaluation, is recommended as the preferable alternative if the goal is meaningful financial reporting.

Deferred tax effects of revaluations. As described in detail in Chapter 26, the tax effects of temporary differences must be provided. Where assets are depreciated over longer lives for financial reporting purposes than for tax reporting purposes, a deferred tax liability will be created in the early years and then drawn down in later years. Generally speaking, the deferred tax provided will be measured by the expected future tax rate applied to the temporary difference at the time it reverses; unless future tax rate changes have already been enacted, the current rate structure is used as an unbiased estimator of those future effects.

In the case of revaluation of assets, it may be that taxing authorities will not permit the higher revalued amounts to be depreciated for purposes of computing tax liabilities. Instead, only the actual cost incurred can be used to offset tax obligations. On the other hand, since revaluations reflect a holding gain, this gain would be taxable if realized. Accordingly, a deferred tax liability is still required to be recognized, even though it does not relate to temporary differences arising from periodic depreciation charges.

SIC 21 confirms that measurement of the deferred tax effects relating to the revaluation of nondepreciable assets must be made with reference to the tax consequences that would follow from recovery of the carrying amount of that asset through an eventual sale. This is necessary because the asset will not be depreciated, and hence, no part of its carrying amount is considered to be recovered through use. As a practical matter this means that if there are differential capital gain and ordinary income tax rates, deferred taxes will be computed with reference to the former. This guidance of SIC 21 has now been incorporated into IAS 12 as part of a December 2010 amendment, which becomes effective for annual periods commencing on or after January 1, 2012. SIC 21 is consequently withdrawn with effect from that date.

IMPAIRMENT

Impairment of Property, Plant, and Equipment

Until the promulgation of IAS 36, there had been a wide range of practices dealing with impairment recognition and measurement. Many European jurisdictions had statutory obligations to compare the carrying amount of assets with their market value, but these requirements were not necessarily applied rigorously. Some jurisdictions, typically those with a British company law tradition, had no requirement to reflect impairment unless it was permanent and long-term. The much more rigorous approach of IAS 36 reflects awareness by regulators that this has been a neglected area in financial reporting.

Principal requirements of IAS 36. In general, the standard provides the procedures that an entity is required to apply to ensure that its assets are not carried at amounts higher than their recoverable amount. If an asset's carrying amount is more than its recoverable amount (the amount to be recovered through use or sale of the asset), an impairment loss is recognized. IAS 36 requires an entity to assess at the end of each reporting period whether there is any indication that an asset may be impaired. Tests for impairment are only necessary when there is an indication that an asset might be impaired (but annually for intangible assets having an indefinite useful life, intangible assets not yet available for use, and goodwill). When carried out, the test is applied to the smallest group of assets for which the entity has identifiable cash flows, called a "cash-generating unit." The carrying amount of the asset or assets in the cash-generating unit is compared with the recoverable amount, which is the higher of the asset's (or cash-generating unit's) fair value less costs to sell and the present value of the cash flows expected to be generated by using the asset ("value in use"). If the higher of these future values is lower than the carrying amount, an impairment loss is recognized for the difference.

IAS 36 does not apply to

- Inventories (IAS 2);
- Assets arising from construction contracts (IAS 11);
- Deferred tax assets (IAS 12);
- Assets arising from employee benefits (IAS 19);
- Financial assets within the scope of IAS 39 or IFRS 9;
- Investment property measured at fair value (IAS 40);
- Biological assets related to agricultural activity measured at fair value less costs to sell (IAS 41);
- Deferred acquisition costs and intangible assets under insurance contracts (IFRS 4); and
- Noncurrent assets (or disposal groups) classified as held for sale (IFRS 5).

Identifying impairments. According to IAS 36, at each financial reporting date the reporting entity should determine whether there are conditions that would indicate that impairments may have occurred. Note that this is *not* a requirement that possible impairments be calculated for all assets at the end of each reporting period, which would be a formidable undertaking for most entities. Rather, it is the existence of conditions that might be suggestive of a heightened risk of impairment that must be evaluated. However, if such indicators are present, then further analysis will be necessary.

The standard provides a set of indicators of potential impairment and suggests that these represent a minimum array of factors to be given consideration. Other more industry- or entity-specific gauges could be devised by the reporting entity.

At a minimum, the following external and internal signs of possible impairment are to be given consideration on an annual basis:

- Market value declines for assets, beyond the declines expected as a function of asset aging and use;
- Significant changes in the technological, market, economic, or legal environments in which the entity operates, or the specific market to which the asset is dedicated;
- Increases in the market interest rate or other market-oriented rate of return such that increases in the discount rate to be employed in determining value in use can be anticipated, with a resultant enhanced likelihood that impairments will emerge;
- Declines in the entity's market capitalization suggest that the aggregate carrying amount of assets exceeds the perceived value of the entity taken as a whole;
- There is specific evidence of obsolescence or of physical damage to an asset or group of assets;
- There have been significant internal changes to the organization or its operations, such as product discontinuation decisions or restructurings, so that the expected remaining useful life or utility of the asset has seemingly been reduced; and
- Internal reporting data suggest that the economic performance of the asset or group of assets is, or will become, worse than previously anticipated.

The mere fact that one or more of the foregoing indicators suggests that there might be cause for concern about possible asset impairment does not necessarily mean that formal impairment testing must proceed in every instance, although in the absence of a plausible explanation why the signals of possible impairment should not be further considered, the implication would be that some follow-up investigation is needed.

Computing recoverable amounts—General concepts. IAS 36 defines impairment as the excess of carrying amount over recoverable amount, and defines recoverable amount as the greater of two alternative measures: fair value less costs to sell and value in use. The objective is to recognize impairment when the economic value of an asset (or cash-generating unit comprised of a group of assets) is truly below its book (carrying) value. In theory, and for the most part in practice also, an entity making rational choices would sell an asset if its net selling price (fair value less costs to sell) were greater than the asset's value in use, and would continue to employ the asset if value in use exceeded salvage value. Thus, the economic value of an asset is most meaningfully measured with reference to the greater of these two amounts, since the entity will either retain or dispose of the asset, consistent with what appears to be its highest and best use. Once recoverable amount has been determined, this is to be compared to carrying amount; if recoverable amount is lower, the asset has been impaired, and this impairment must be given accounting recognition. It should be noted that value in use is an entity-specific value, in contrast to fair value, which is based on market price. Value in use is thus a much more subjective measurement than is fair value, since it takes account of factors available only to the individual business, which may be difficult to validate. If either an asset's fair value less costs to sell or its value in use exceeds the asset's carrying amount, the asset is not impaired and it is not necessary to estimate the other amount.

Determining fair value less costs to sell. The determination of the fair value less costs to sell (i.e., net selling price) and the value in use of the asset being evaluated will typically present some difficulties. For actively traded assets, fair value can be ascertained by reference to publicly available information (e.g., from price lists or dealer quotations), and costs of disposal will either be implicitly factored into those amounts (such as when a dealer quote includes pick-up, shipping, etc.) or else can be readily estimated. Most common productive tangible assets, such as machinery and equipment, will not easily be priced, however, since active markets for used items will either not exist or be relatively illiquid. It will often be necessary to reason by analogy (i.e., to draw inferences from recent transactions in similar assets), making adjustments for age, condition, productive capacity, and other variables. For example, a five-year-old machine having an output rate (for a given component) of 2,000 units per day, and an estimated useful life of eight years, might be valued at 30% (=3/8 × .8) of the cost of a new replacement machine having a capacity of 2,500 units per day. In many industries, trade publications and other data sources can provide a great deal of insight into the market value of key assets.

Computing value in use. The computation of value in use involves a two-step process: first, future cash flows must be estimated; and second, the present value of these cash flows must be calculated by application of an appropriate discount rate. These will be discussed in turn in the following paragraphs.

Projection of future cash flows must be based on reasonable assumptions. Exaggerated revenue growth rates, significant anticipated cost reductions, or unreasonable useful lives for plant assets must be avoided if meaningful results are to be obtained. In general, recent past experience is a fair guide to the near-term future, but a recent sudden growth spurt should not be extrapolated to more than the very near-term future. For example, if growth over the past five years averaged 5%, but in the latest year equaled 15%, unless the recent rate of growth can be identified with factors that demonstrate it as being sustainable, a future growth rate of 5%, or slightly higher, would be more supportable.

Typically, extrapolation cannot be made to a greater number of future periods than the number of "base periods" upon which the projection is built. Thus, a five-year projection, to be sound, should be based on at least five years of actual historical performance data. Also, since no business can grow exponentially forever—even if, for example, a five-year historical analysis suggests a 20% annual (inflation-adjusted) growth rate—beyond a horizon of a few years a moderation of that growth must be hypothesized. (Reversion to the mean growth rate for the industry as a whole, or of some other demographic trend, such as population growth, is usually assumed.) This is even more important for a single asset or small cash-generating unit, since physical constraints and the ironclad law of diminishing marginal returns makes it virtually inevitable that a plateau will be reached, beyond which further growth will be strictly constrained. Basic economic laws suggest that, if exceptional returns are being reaped from the assets used to produce a given product line, competitors will enter the market, driving down prices and limiting future profitability.

IAS 36 stipulates that steady or declining growth rates must be utilized for periods beyond those covered by the most recent budgets and forecasts. It further states that, barring an ability to demonstrate why a higher rate is appropriate, the growth rate should not exceed the long-term growth rate of the industry in which the entity participates.

The guidance offered by IAS 36 suggests that only normal, recurring cash inflows and outflows from the continuing use of the asset being evaluated should be considered, to which would be added any estimated salvage value at the end of the asset's useful life. Noncash costs, such as depreciation of the asset, obviously must be excluded from this calculation, since, in the case of depreciation, this would in effect double count the very item being measured. Furthermore, projections should always exclude cash flows related to financing the asset—for example, interest and principal repayments on any debt incurred in acquiring the asset—since operating decisions (e.g., keeping or disposing of an asset) are to be evaluated separately from financing decisions (borrowing, leasing, buying with equity capital funds). Also, cash flow projections must relate to the asset in its existing state and in its current use, without regard to possible future enhancements. Income tax effects are also to be disregarded (i.e., the entire analysis should be on a pretax basis). An entity should translate the present value of future cash flows estimated in the foreign currency using the spot exchange rate at the date of the value-in-use calculation.

Cash-generating units. Under IAS 36, when cash flows cannot be identified with individual assets, (as will frequently be the case), assets must be grouped in order to permit an assessment of future cash flows. The requirement is that this grouping be performed at the lowest level possible, which would be the smallest aggregation of assets for which discrete cash flows can be identified, and which are independent of other groups of assets. In practice, this unit may be a department, a product line, or a factory, for which the output of product and the input of raw materials, labor, and overhead can be identified.

Thus, while the precise contribution to overall cash flow made by, say, a given drill press or lathe may be impossible to surmise, the cash inflows and outflows of a department which produces and sells a discrete product line to an identified group of customers can be more readily determined. To comply with IFRS, the extent of aggregation must be the minimum necessary to develop cash flow information for impairment assessment, and no greater.

A too-high level of aggregation is prohibited for a very basic reason: doing so could permit some impairments to be concealed, by effectively offsetting impairment losses against productivity or profitability gains derived from the expected future use of other assets. Consider an entity which is, overall, quite profitable and which generates positive cash flow, although certain departments or product lines are significantly unprofitable and cash drains. If aggregation at the entity level were permitted, there would be no impairment to be recognized, which would thwart IAS 36's objectives. If impairment testing were done at the departmental or product line level, on the other hand—consistent with IAS 36 requirements— then some loss-producing assets would be written down for impairment, while the cash-generating assets would continue to be accounted for at depreciated historical cost.

Put another way, excessive aggregation results (when there are both cash-generating and cash-using groups of operating assets, departments, or product lines) in the recognition of unrealized gains on some assets that nominally are being accounted for on the historical cost basis, which violates IFRS. These gains, while concealed and not reported as such, offset the impairment losses on assets (or groups of assets) whose value have suffered diminutions in value. IAS 36 does not permit this result to be obtained.

IAS 36 requires that cash-generating units be defined consistently from period to period. In addition to being necessary for consistency in financial reporting from period to period, which is an important objective per se, it is also needed to preclude the opportunistic redefining of cash-generating groups affected in order to minimize or eliminate impairment recognition.

Discount rate. The other measurement issue in computing value in use comes from identifying the appropriate discount rate to apply to projected future cash flows. The discount rate is comprised of subcomponents. The base component of the discount rate is the current market rate, which should be identical for all impairment testing at any given date. This must be adjusted for the risks specific to the asset, which thus adds the second component of discount rate.

In practice, this asset class risk adjustment can be built into the cash flows. Appendix A to the standard discusses what it describes as the *traditional approach* to present value calculation, where forecast cash flows are discounted using a rate that is adjusted for uncertainties. It also describes the *expected cash flow* method, where the forecast cash flows are directly adjusted to reflect uncertainty and then discounted at the market rate. These are alternative approaches and care must be exercised to apply one or the other correctly. Most importantly, risk should not be adjusted for twice in computing the present value of future cash flows.

IAS 36 suggests that identifying the appropriate risk-adjusted cost of capital to employ as a discount rate can be accomplished by reference to the implicit rates in current market transactions (e.g., leasing transactions), or from the weighted-average cost of capital of publicly traded entities operating in the same industry grouping. Such statistics are available for certain industry segments in selected (but not all) markets. The entity's own recent transactions, typically involving leasing or borrowing to buy other long-lived assets, will be highly salient information in estimating the appropriate discount rate to use.

When risk-adjusted rates are not available, however, it will become necessary to develop a discount rate from surrogate data. The two steps to this procedure are

1. To identify the pure time value of money for the requisite time horizon over which the asset will be utilized: and
2. To add an appropriate risk premium to the pure interest factor, which is related to the variability of future cash flows.

Regarding the first component, the life of the asset being tested for impairment will be critical; short-term obligations almost always carry a lower rate than intermediate- or long-term ones, although there have been periods when "yield curve inversions" have been dramatic. As to the second element, projected future cash flows having greater variability (which is the technical definition of risk) will be associated with higher risk premiums.

Of these two discount rate components, the latter is likely to prove the more difficult to determine or estimate, in practice. IAS 36 provides a fairly extended discussion of the methodology to utilize, however, and this should be carefully considered before embarking on this procedure. It addresses such factors as country risk, currency risk, cash flow risk, and pricing risk.

The interest rate is considered to include an inflation risk component (i.e., to represent nominal rates, rather than real or inflation-adjusted rates), and to calculate present value consistent with this fact, the forecast cash flows should reflect the monetary amounts expected to be received in the future, rather than being adjusted to current price levels.

The interest rate to apply must reflect current market conditions as of the end of the reporting period. This means that during periods when rates are changing rapidly the computed value in use of assets will also change, perhaps markedly, even if projected cash flows before discounting remain stable. This is not a computational artifact, however, but rather it reflects economic reality: as discount (interest) rates decline, holdings of productive assets become more economically valuable, holding all other considerations constant; and as rates rise, such holdings lose value because of the erosion of the value of their future cash flows. The accounting implication is that long-lived assets that were unimpaired one year earlier may fail an impairment test in the current period if rates have risen during the interim.

Corporate assets. Corporate assets, such as headquarters buildings and shared equipment, which do not themselves generate identifiable cash flows, need to be tested for impairment as with all other long-lived assets. However, these present a particular problem in practice due to the inability to identify cash flows deriving from the future use of these assets. A failure to test corporate assets for impairment would permit such assets to be carried at amounts that could, under some circumstances, be at variance with requirements under IFRS. It would also permit a reporting entity to deliberately evade the impairment testing requirements by opportunistically defining certain otherwise productive assets as being corporate assets.

To avoid such results, IAS 36 requires that corporate assets be allocated among or assigned to the cash-generating unit or units with which they are most closely associated. For a large and diversified entity, this probably implies that corporate assets will be allocated among most or all of its cash-generating units, perhaps in proportion to annual turnover (revenue). Since ultimately an entity must generate sufficient cash flows to recover its investment in all long-lived assets, whether assigned to operating divisions or to administrative groups, there are no circumstances in which corporate assets can be isolated and excluded from impairment testing.

Accounting for impairments. If the recoverable amount of the cash-generating unit is lower than its carrying amount, an impairment must be recognized. The mechanism for recording an impairment loss depends upon whether the entity is accounting for long-lived assets on the historical cost subject to depreciation or revaluation basis. Impairments computed for assets carried at historical cost will be recognized as charges against current period profit or loss, either included with depreciation for financial reporting, or identified separately in the statement of profit or loss, if prepared separately, or in the statement of comprehensive income.

For assets grouped into cash-generating units, it will not be possible to determine which specific assets have suffered impairment losses when the unit as a whole has been found to be impaired, and so IAS 36 prescribes a formulaic approach. If the cash-generating unit in question has been allocated any goodwill, any impairment should be allocated fully to goodwill, until its carrying amount has been reduced to zero. Any further impairment would be allocated proportionately to all the other assets in that cash-generating unit. In practice, the impairment loss is allocated against the nonmonetary assets that are carried, as the carrying amount of monetary assets usually approximates actual.

The standard does not specify whether the impairment should be credited to the asset account or to the accumulated depreciation (contra asset) account. Of course, either approach has the same effect: net carrying amount is reduced by the accumulated impairment recognized. European practice has generally been to add impairment provisions to the accumulated depreciation account. This is consistent with the view that reducing the asset account directly would be a contravention of the general prohibition on offsetting.

If the entity employs the revaluation method of accounting for long-lived assets, the impairment adjustment will be treated as the partial reversal of a previous upward revaluation. However, if the entire revaluation account is eliminated due to the recognition of an impairment, any excess impairment should be charged to expense (and thus be closed out to profit or loss). In other words, the revaluation account cannot contain a net debit balance.

Example of accounting for impairment

Xebob Corporation (XC) has one of its (many) departments that performs machining operations on parts that are sold to contractors. A group of machines have an aggregate carrying amount at the end of the latest reporting period (December 31, 2011) totaling €123,000. It has been determined that this group of machinery constitutes a cash-generating unit for purposes of applying IAS 36.

Upon analysis, the following facts about future expected cash inflows and outflows become apparent, based on the diminishing productivity expected of the machinery as it ages, and the increasing costs that will be incurred to generate output from the machines:

Year	Revenues	Costs, *excluding* depreciation
2012	€ 75,000	€ 28,000
2013	80,000	42,000

Year	Revenues	Costs, **excluding** depreciation
2014	65,000	55,000
2015	20,000	15,000
Totals	€240,000	€140,000

The fair value of the machinery in this cash-generating unit is determined by reference to used machinery quotation sheets obtained from a prominent dealer. After deducting estimated disposal costs, the fair value less costs to sell is calculated as €84,500.

Value in use is determined with reference to the above-noted expected cash inflows and outflows, discounted at a risk rate of 5%. This yields a present value of about €91,981, as shown below.

Year	Cash flows	PV factors	Net PV of cash flows
2012	€47,000	.95238	€44,761.91
2013	38,000	.90703	34,467.12
2014	10,000	.86384	8,638.38
2015	5,000	.82270	4,113.51
Total			€91,980.91

Since value in use exceeds fair value less costs to sell, value in use is selected to represent the recoverable amount of this cash-generating unit. This is lower than the carrying amount of the group of assets, however, and thus an impairment must be recognized as of the end of 2011, in the amount of €123,000 – €91,981 = €31,019. This will be included in operating expenses (either depreciation or a separate caption in the statement of comprehensive income or in the statement of profit or loss, if prepared separately) for 2011.

Reversals of previously recognized impairments under historical cost method of accounting. IFRS provides for recognition of reversals of previously recognized impairments. In order to recognize a recovery of a previously recognized impairment, a process similar to that which led to the original loss recognition must be followed. This begins with consideration, at the end of each reporting period, of whether there are indicators of possible impairment recoveries, utilizing external and internal sources of information. Data relied upon could include that pertaining to material market value increases; changes in the technological, market, economic or legal environment or the market in which the asset is employed; and the occurrence of a favorable change in interest rates or required rates of return on assets which would imply changes in the discount rate used to compute value in use. Also to be given consideration are data about any changes in the manner in which the asset is employed, as well as evidence that the economic performance of the asset has exceeded expectations and/or is expected to do so in the future.

If one or more of these indicators is present, it will be necessary to compute the recoverable amount of the asset in question or, if appropriate, of the cash-generating unit containing that asset, in order to determine if the current recoverable amount exceeds the carrying amount of the asset, where it had been previously reduced for impairment.

If that is the case, a recovery can be recognized under IAS 36. The amount of recovery to be recognized is limited, however, to the difference between the carrying amount and the amount which would have been the current carrying amount had the earlier impairment not been given recognition. Note that this means that restoration of the full amount at which the asset was carried at the time of the earlier impairment cannot be made, since time has elapsed between these two events and further depreciation of the asset would have been recognized in the interim.

Example of impairment recovery

To illustrate, assume an asset had a carrying amount of €40,000 at December 31, 2010, based on its original cost of €50,000, less accumulated depreciation representing the one-fifth, or two years, of its projected useful life of ten years which already has elapsed. The carrying amount of €40,000 is after depreciation for 2010 has been computed, but before impairment has been addressed. At that date, a determination was made that the asset's recoverable amount was only €32,000 (assume this was properly computed and that recognition of the impairment was warranted), so that an €8,000 adjustment must be made. For simplicity, assume this was added to accumulated depreciation, so that at December 31, 2010, the asset cost remains €50,000 and accumulated depreciation is stated as €18,000.

At December 31, 2011, before any adjustments are posted, the carrying amount of this asset is €32,000. Depreciation for 2011 would be €4,000 (= €32,000 carrying amount ÷ 8 years remaining life), which would leave a net carrying amount, after current period depreciation, of €28,000. However, a determination is made that the asset's recoverable amount at this date is €37,000. Before making an adjustment to reverse some or all of the impairment loss previously recognized, the carrying amount at December 31, 2011, as it would have existed had the impairment not been recognized in 2009 must be computed.

December 31, 2010 preimpairment carrying amount	€40,000
2011 depreciation based on above	5,000
Indicated December 31, 2011 carrying value	€35,000

The December 31, 2011 carrying value would have been €40,000 – €5,000 = €35,000; this is the maximum carrying value which can be reflected in the December 31, 2011 statement of financial position. Thus, the full recovery cannot be recognized; instead, the 2011 statement of profit or loss will reflect (net) a *negative* depreciation charge of €35,000 – €32,000 = €3,000, which can be thought of (or recorded) as follows:

Actual December 31, 2010 carrying amount	€32,000
2011 depreciation based on above	4,000 (a)
Indicated December 31, 2011 carrying amount	€28,000
Indicated December 31, 2011 carrying amount	€28,000
Actual December 31, 2011 carrying amount	35,000
Recovery of previously recognized impairment	€ 7,000 (b)

Thus, the net effect in 2011 profit or loss is (a) – (b) = €(3,000). The asset cannot be restored to its indicated recoverable amount at December 31, 2011, amounting to €37,000, as this exceeds the carrying amount that would have existed at this date had the impairment in 2010 never been recognized.

Where a cash-generating unit including goodwill has been impaired, and the impairment has been allocated first to the goodwill and then pro rata to the other assets, *only* the amount allocated to nongoodwill assets can be reversed. The standard specifically prohibits the reversal of impairments to goodwill, on the basis that the goodwill could have been replaced by internally generated goodwill, which cannot be recognized under IFRS.

Reversals of previously recognized impairments under revaluation method of accounting. Reversals of impairments are accounted for differently if the reporting entity employed the revaluation method of accounting for long-lived assets. Under this approach, assets are periodically adjusted to reflect current fair values, with the write-up being recorded in the asset accounts and the corresponding credit reported in other comprehensive income and accumulated in the revaluation surplus in shareholders' equity, and not include in profit or loss. Impairments are viewed as being downward adjustments of fair value in this scenario, and accordingly are reported in other comprehensive income as reversals of previous revaluations (to the extent of any credit balance in the revaluation surplus for that asset) and not charged against profit unless the entire remaining, unamortized portion of the revaluation surplus is eliminated as a consequence of the impairment. Any further impairment is reported in profit or loss.

When an asset (or cash-generating group of assets) had first been revalued upward, then written down to reflect impairment, and then later adjusted to convey a recovery of the impairment, the required procedure is to report the recovery as a reversal of the impairment, as with the historical cost method of accounting for long-lived assets. Since in most instances impairments will have been accounted for as reversals of upward revaluations, a still-later reversal of the impairment will be seen as yet another upward revaluation and accounted for as a credit to other comprehensive income and cumulative amount in revaluation surplus in equity, not to be reported through profit or loss. In the event that impairment will have eliminated the entire revaluation surplus account, and an excess loss will have been charged against profit, then a later recovery will be reported in profit to the extent the earlier write-down had been so reported, with any balance recorded as a credit to other comprehensive income.

Example of impairment recovery—revaluation method

To illustrate, assume an asset was acquired January 1, 2010, and it had a net carrying amount of €45,000 at December 31, 2011, based on its original cost of €50,000, less accumulated depreciation representing the one-fifth, or two years, of its projected useful life of ten years, which has already elapsed, plus a revaluation write-up of €5,000, net. The increase in carrying amount was recorded a year earlier, based on an appraisal showing the asset's then fair value was €56,250.

At December 31, 2012, impairment is detected, and the recoverable amount at that date is determined to be €34,000. Had this not occurred, depreciation for 2012 would have been (€45,000 ÷ 8 years remaining life =) €5,625; carrying amount after recording 2012 depreciation would have been (€45,000 – €5,625 =) €39,375. Thus the impairment loss recognized in 2012 is (€39,375 – €34,000 =) €5,375. Of this loss amount, €4,375 represents a reversal of the net amount of the previously recognized valuation increase remaining (i.e., undepreciated) at the end of 2012, as shown below.

Gross amount of revaluation at December 31, 2010	€6,250
Portion of the above allocable to accumulated depreciation	625
Net revaluation increase at December 31, 2010	5,625
Depreciation taken on appreciation for 2011	625
Net revaluation increase at December 31, 2011	5,000
Depreciation taken on appreciation for 2012	625
Net revaluation increase at December 31, 2012, before recognition of impairment	4,375
Impairment recognized as reversal of earlier revaluation	4,375
Net revaluation increase at December 31, 2012	€ 0

The remaining €1,000 impairment loss is recognized at December 31, 2012, in profit or loss, since it exceeds the available amount of revaluation surplus.

In 2013 there is a recovery of value that pertains to this asset; at December 31, 2013, it is valued at €36,500. This represents a €2,500 increase in carrying amount from the earlier year's balance, net of accumulated depreciation. The first €1,000 of this recovery in value is credited to profit, since this is the amount of previously recognized impairment that was charged against profit; the remaining €1,500 of recovery is accounted for as other comprehensive income and accumulated in the revaluation surplus in shareholders' equity.

Deferred tax effects. Recognition of an impairment for financial reporting purposes will most likely not be accompanied by a deduction for current tax purposes. As a consequence of the nondeductibility of most impairment charges, the carrying amount and tax basis of the impaired assets will diverge, with the difference thus created to gradually be eliminated over the remaining life of the asset, as depreciation for tax purposes varies from that which is recognized for financial reporting. Following the dictates of IAS 12, deferred taxes must be recognized for this new discrepancy. The accounting for deferred taxes is discussed in Chapter 26 and will not be addressed here.

Impairments that will be mitigated by recoveries or compensation from third parties. Impairments of tangible long-lived assets may result from natural or other damages, such as from floods or windstorms, and in some such instances there will be the possibility that payments from third parties (typically commercial insurers) will mitigate the gross loss incurred. The question in such circumstances is whether the gross impairment must be recognized, or whether it may be offset by the actual or estimated amount of the recovery to be received by the reporting entity.

IAS 16 holds that when property is damaged or lost, impairments and claims for reimbursements should be accounted for separately (i.e., not netted for financial reporting purposes). Impairments are to be accounted for per IAS 36 as discussed above; disposals (of damaged or otherwise impaired assets) should be accounted for consistent with guidance in IAS 16. Compensation from third parties, which are gain contingencies, should be recognized as profit only when the funds become receivable. The cost of replacement items or of restored items is determined in accordance with IAS 16.

Disclosure requirements. For each class of property, plant, and equipment, the amount of impairment losses recognized in profit or loss for each period being reported upon must be stated, with an indication of where in the statement of comprehensive income it has been presented (i.e., as part of depreciation or with other charges). For each class of asset, the amount of any reversals of previously recognized impairment must also be stipulated, again with an identification of where in the statement of comprehensive income that this has been presented. If any impairment losses were recognized in other comprehensive income and in revaluation surplus in equity (i.e., as a reversal of a previously recognized upward revaluation), this must be disclosed. Finally, any reversals of impairment losses that were recognized in other comprehensive income and in equity must be stated.

If the reporting entity is reporting financial information by segment (in accordance with IFRS 8 as discussed in more detail in Chapter 28), the amounts of impairments and of reversals of impairments, recognized in profit or loss and in other comprehensive income during the year for each reportable segment, must also be stated. Note that the segment disclosures pertaining to impairments need not be categorized by asset class, and the location of the charge or credit in the statement of profit or loss need not be stated (but will be understood from the disclosures relating to the primary financial statements themselves).

IAS 36 further provides that if an impairment loss for an individual asset or group of assets categorized as a cash-generating unit is either recognized or reversed during the period, in an amount that is material to the financial statements taken as a whole, disclosures should be made of the following:

- The events or circumstances that caused the loss or recovery of loss;
- The amount of the impairment loss recognized or reversed;
- If for an individual asset, the nature of the asset and the reportable segment to which it belongs, as defined under IFRS 8;
- If for a cash-generating unit, a description of that unit (e.g., defined as a product line, a plant, geographical area, etc.), the amount of impairment recognized or reversed by class of asset and by reportable segment based on the primary format, and, if the unit's composition has changed since the previous estimate of the unit's recoverable amount, a description of the reasons for such changes;

- Whether fair value less costs to sell or value in use was employed to compute the recoverable amount;
- If recoverable amount is fair value less costs to sell, the basis used to determine it (e.g., whether by reference to active market prices or otherwise); and
- If the recoverable amount is value in use, the discount rate(s) used in the current and prior period's estimate.

Furthermore, when impairments recognized or reversed in the current period are material in the aggregate, the reporting entity should provide a description of the main classes of assets affected by impairment losses or reversals of losses, as well as the main events and circumstances that caused recognition of losses or reversals. This information is not required to the extent that the disclosures above are given for individual assets or cash-generating units.

DERECOGNITION

An entity should derecognize an item of property, plant, and equipment (1) on disposal, or (2) when no future economic benefits are expected from its use or disposal. In such cases an asset is removed from the statement of financial position. In the case of long-lived tangible assets, both the asset and the related contra asset, accumulated depreciation, should be eliminated. The difference between the net carrying amount and any proceeds received will be given immediate recognition as a gain or loss arising on the derecognition.

If the revaluation method of accounting has been employed, and the asset and the related accumulated depreciation account have been adjusted upward, if the asset is subsequently disposed of before it has been fully depreciated, the gain or loss computed will be identical to what would have been determined had the historical cost method of accounting been used. The reason is that, at any point in time, the net amount of the revaluation (i.e., the step-up in the asset less the unamortized balance in the step-up in accumulated depreciation) will be offset exactly by the remaining balance in the revaluation surplus account. Elimination of the asset, contra asset, and revaluation surplus accounts will balance precisely, and there will be no gain or loss on this aspect of the disposition transaction. The gain or loss will be determined exclusively by the discrepancy between the net carrying amount, based on historical cost, and the proceeds from the disposition. Thus, the accounting outcome is identical under cost and revaluation methods.

Examples of accounting for asset disposal

On January 1, 2009, Zara Corp. acquired a machine at a cost of €12,000; it had an estimated life of six years, no residual value, and was expected to provide a level pattern of utility to the entity. Thus, straight-line depreciation in the amount of €2,000 was charged to operations. At the end of four years, the asset was sold for €5,000. Accounting was done on a historical cost basis. The entries to record depreciation and to report the ultimate disposal on January 1, 2013, are as follows:

1/1/09	Machinery	12,000	
	Cash, etc.		12,000
12/31/09	Depreciation expense	2,000	
	Accumulated depreciation		2,000
12/31/10	Depreciation expense	2,000	
	Accumulated depreciation		2,000

12/31/11	Depreciation expense	2,000	
	Accumulated depreciation		2,000
12/31/12	Depreciation expense	2,000	
	Accumulated depreciation		2,000
1/1/13	Cash	5,000	
	Accumulated depreciation	8,000	
	Machinery		12,000
	Gain on asset disposal		1,000

Now assume the same facts as above, but that the revaluation method is used. At the beginning of year four (2012) the asset is revalued at a gross replacement cost of €7,500. A year later it is sold for €5,000. The entries are as follows (note in particular that the remaining revaluation surplus is transferred directly to retained earnings):

1/1/09	Machinery	12,000	
	Cash, etc.		12,000
12/31/09	Depreciation expense	2,000	
	Accumulated depreciation		2,000
12/31/10	Depreciation expense	2,000	
	Accumulated depreciation		2,000
12/31/11	Depreciation expense	2,000	
	Accumulated depreciation		2,000
1/1/12	Machinery	3,000	
	Accumulated depreciation		1,500
	Other comprehensive income –		1,500
	revaluation surplus		
12/31/12	Depreciation expense	2,500	
	Accumulated depreciation		2,500
	Revaluation surplus	500	
	Retained earnings		500
1/1/13	Cash	5,000	
	Accumulated depreciation	10,000	
	Revaluation surplus	1,000	
	Machinery		15,000
	Retained earnings		1,000

NONCURRENT ASSETS HELD FOR SALE

As part of its ongoing efforts to converge IFRS with US GAAP, the IASB issued IFRS 5, *Noncurrent Assets Held for Sale and Discontinued Operations*. This introduced new and substantially revised guidance for accounting for long-lived tangible (and other) assets that have been identified for disposal, as well as new requirements for the presentation and disclosure of discontinued operations.

IFRS 5 states that where management has decided to sell an asset, or disposal group, these should be classified in the statement of financial position as "held-for-sale" and should be measured at the lower of carrying amount or fair value less cost to sell. After reclassification, these assets will no longer be subject to systematic depreciation. The measurement basis for noncurrent assets classified as held-for-sale is to be applied to the group as a whole, and any resulting impairment loss will reduce the carrying amount of the noncurrent assets in the disposal group.

Assets and liabilities which are to be disposed of together in a single transaction are to be treated as a *disposal group*. In accordance with the standard, a disposal group is a group of assets (and liabilities directly associated with those assets) to be disposed of, by sale or otherwise, together as a group in a single transaction. Goodwill acquired in a business combination is included in the disposal group if this group is a cash-generating unit to which goodwill has been allocated in accordance with IAS 36 or if it is an operation within such a cash-generating unit.

Held-for-sale classification. The reporting entity would classify a noncurrent asset (or disposal group) as held-for-sale if its carrying amount will be recovered principally through a sale transaction rather than through continuing use. The criteria are as follows:

1. For an asset or disposal group to be classified as held-for-sale, the asset (or asset group) must be available for immediate sale in its present condition and its sale must be *highly probable*.
2. In addition, the asset (or disposal group) must be currently being marketed actively at a price that is reasonable in relation to its current fair value.
3. The sale should be completed, or expected to be so, within a year from the date of the classification. IFRS 5 does however allow for some exceptions to this principle, which are discussed below.
4. The actions required to complete the planned sale will have been made, and it is unlikely that the plan will be significantly changed or withdrawn. For this purpose, factors such as, for example, shareholders' approval should be considered as part of the assessment of whether the sale is highly probable.
5. For the sale to be highly probable, management must be committed to selling the asset and must be actively looking for a buyer.
6. In the case that the sale may not be completed within one year, the asset could still be classified as held-for-sale if the delay is caused by events beyond the entity's control and the entity remains committed to selling the asset.

Extension of the period beyond one year is allowable in the following situations:

- The reporting entity has committed itself to sell an asset, and it expects that others may impose conditions on the transfer of the asset that could not be completed until after a firm purchase commitment has been made, and a firm purchase commitment is highly probable within a year.
- A firm purchase commitment is made but a buyer unexpectedly imposes conditions on the transfer of the asset held for sale; timely actions are being taken to respond to the conditions, and a favorable resolution is anticipated.
- During the one-year period, unforeseen circumstances arise that were considered unlikely, and the asset is not sold. Necessary action to respond to the change in circumstances should be taken. The asset should be actively marketed at a reasonable price and the criteria set out for the asset to be classified as held-for-sale should have been met.

Occasionally companies acquire noncurrent assets exclusively with a view to disposal. In these cases, the noncurrent asset will be classified as held-for-sale at the date of the acquisition only if it is anticipated that it will be sold within the one-year period and it is highly probably that the held-for-sale criteria will be met within a short period of the acquisition date. This period normally will be no more than three months. Exchanges of noncurrent assets between companies can be treated as held for sale when such an exchange has commercial substance in accordance with IAS 16.

If the criteria for classifying a noncurrent asset as held-for-sale occur *after* the reporting date, the noncurrent asset should *not* be shown as held-for-sale. Nonetheless, certain information should be disclosed about these noncurrent assets.

Operations that are expected to be wound down or abandoned do not meet the definition of held for sale. However, a disposal group that is to be abandoned may meet the definition of a discontinued activity. *Abandonment* means that the noncurrent asset (disposal group) will be used to the end of its economic life, or the noncurrent asset (disposal group) will be closed rather than sold. The reasoning behind this is that the carrying amount of the noncurrent asset will be recovered principally through continued usage. A noncurrent asset that has been temporarily taken out of use or service cannot be classified as being abandoned.

Measurement of noncurrent assets held for sale. Assets that are classified as being held for disposal are measured differently and presented separately from other noncurrent assets. In accordance with IFRS 5, the following general principles would apply in measuring noncurrent assets that are held for sale:

- Just before an asset is initially classified as held-for-sale, it should be measured in accordance with the applicable IFRS.
- When noncurrent assets or disposal groups are classified as held-for-sale, they are measured at the *lower of the carrying amount and fair value less costs to sell.*
- When the sale is expected to occur in greater than a year's time, the entity should measure the cost to sell at its present value. Any increase in the present value of the cost to sell that arises from the passage of time should be shown in profit and loss as finance cost.
- Any impairment loss is recognized in profit or loss on any initial or subsequent write-down of the asset or disposal group to fair value less cost to sell.
- Any subsequent increases in fair value less cost to sell of an asset can be recognized in profit or loss to the extent that it is *not in excess of the cumulative impairment loss* that has been recognized in accordance with IFRS 5 (or previously in accordance with IAS 36).
- Any impairment loss recognized for a disposal group should be applied in the order set out in IAS 36.
- Noncurrent assets or disposal groups classified as held-for-sale should not be depreciated.

Any interest or expenses of a disposal group should continue to be provided for.

The standard stipulates that, for assets not previously revalued (under IAS 16), any recorded decrease in carrying amount (to fair value less cost to sell or value in use) would be an impairment loss taken as charge against income; subsequent changes in fair value would also be recognized, but not increases in excess of impairment losses previously recognized.

For an asset that is carried at a revalued amount (as permitted under IAS 16), revaluation under that standard will have to be effected immediately before it is reclassified as held-for-sale under this proposed standard, with any impairment loss recognized in profit or loss. Subsequent increases or decreases in estimated costs to sell the asset will be recognized in profit or loss. On the other hand, decreases in estimated fair value would be offset against revaluation surplus created under IAS 16, (recognized in other comprehensive income and accumulated in equity under the heading of revaluation surplus), and subsequent increases in fair value would be recognized in full as a revaluation increase under IAS 16, identical to the accounting required before the asset was reclassified as held-for-sale.

A disposal group, as defined under IFRS 5, may include some assets which had been accounted for by the revaluation method. For such disposal groups subsequent increases in fair value are to be recognized, but only to the extent that the carrying amounts of the noncurrent assets in the group, after the increase has been allocated, do not exceed their respective fair value less costs to sell. The increase recognized would continue to be treated as a revaluation increase under IAS 16.

Finally, IFRS 5 states that noncurrent assets classified as held-for-sale are not to be depreciated. This is logical: the concept objective of depreciation accounting is to allocate asset cost to its useful economic life, and once an asset is denoted as being held for sale, this purpose is no longer meaningful. The constraints on classifying an asset as held-for-sale are, in part, intended to prevent entities from employing such reclassification as a means of avoiding depreciation. Even after classification as held-for-sale, however, interest and other costs associated with the asset are still recognized as expenses as required under IFRS.

Change of plans. If the asset held for sale is not later disposed of, it is to be reclassified to the operating asset category it is properly assignable to. The amount to be initially recognized upon such reclassification would be the lower of

1. The asset's carrying amount before the asset (or disposal group) was classified as held-for-sale, adjusted for any depreciation or amortization that would have been recognized during the interim had the asset (disposal group) not been classified as held-for-sale, and
2. The *recoverable amount* at the date of the subsequent decision not to sell.

If the asset is part of a cash-generating unit (as defined under IAS 36), its recoverable amount will be defined as the carrying amount that would have been recognized after the allocation of any impairment loss incurred from that same cash-generating unit.

Under the foregoing circumstance, the reporting entity would include, as part of income from continuing operations in the period in which the criteria for classification as held-for-sale are no longer met, any required adjustment to the carrying amount of a noncurrent asset that ceases to be classified as held-for-sale. That adjustment would be presented in income from continuing operations. It is not an adjustment to prior period results of operations under any circumstances.

If an individual asset or liability is removed from a disposal group classified as held-for-sale, the remaining assets and liabilities of the disposal group still to be sold will continue to be measured as a group only if the group meets the criteria for categorization as held-for-sale. In other circumstances, the remaining noncurrent assets of the group that individually meet the criteria to be classified as held-for-sale will need to be measured individually at the lower of their carrying amounts or fair values less costs to sell at that date.

Presentation and disclosure. IFRS 5 specifies that noncurrent assets classified as held-for-sale and the assets of disposal group classified as held-for-sale must be presented separately from other assets in the statement of financial position. The liabilities of a disposal group classified as held-for-sale are also presented separately from other liabilities in the statement of financial position.

Several disclosures are required, including a description of the noncurrent assets of a disposal group, a description of the facts and circumstances of the sale, and the expected manner and timing of that disposal. Any gain or loss recognized for impairment or any subsequent increase in the fair value less costs to sell should also be shown in the applicable segment in which the noncurrent assets or disposal group is presented in accordance with IFRS 8 (Chapter 28).

IFRS 5 was amended in the 2009 Improvements Project and now specifies the disclosures required in respect of noncurrent assets (or disposal groups) classified as held-for-sale or discontinued operations. It provides that the disclosure requirements in other IFRS do not apply to such assets (or disposal groups) unless those IFRS require

1. Specific disclosures in respect of noncurrent assets (or disposal groups) classified as held-for-sale or discontinued operations; or
2. Disclosures about measurement of assets and liabilities within a disposal group that are not within the scope of the measurement requirement of IFRS 5 and such disclosures are not already provided in the other notes to the financial statements.

It also provides that where additional disclosures about noncurrent assets (or disposal groups) classified as held-for-sale or discontinued operations are necessary in order to comply with the general requirements of IAS 1, then such disclosures must still be made.

DISCONTINUED OPERATIONS

Presentation and disclosure. IFRS requires an entity to present and disclose information that enables users of the financial statements to evaluate the financial effects of discontinued operations. A *discontinued operation* is a part of an entity that has either been disposed of or is classified as held-for-sale and meets the following requirements:

1. Represents a separate major line of business or geographical area of operations;
2. Is part of a single coordinated plan to dispose of separate major line of business or geographical area of operations; or
3. Is a subsidiary acquired exclusively with a view to resale.

An entity should present in the statement of comprehensive income a single amount comprising the total of

- The after-tax profit or loss of discontinued operations, and
- The after-tax gain or loss recognized on the measurement to fair value less costs to sell (or on the disposal) of the assets or disposal groups classified as discontinued operations.

IFRS 5 requires detailed disclosure of revenue, expenses, pretax profit or loss, and the related income tax expense, either in the notes or on the face of the statement of comprehensive income. If this information is presented on the face of the statement of comprehensive income (or separate statement of profit or loss if the two-statement alternative is used), the information should be separately disclosed from information relating to continuing operations. Regarding the presentation in the statement of cash flows, the net cash flows attributable to the operating, investing, and financing activities of the discontinued operation should be shown separately on the face of the statement or disclosed in the notes.

Any disclosures should cover both the current and all prior periods that have been shown in the financial statements. Retrospective classification as a discontinued operation, where the criteria are met after the statement of financial position date, is prohibited by IFRS. In addition, adjustments made in the current accounting period to amounts that have previously been disclosed as discontinued operations from prior periods must be separately disclosed. If an entity ceases to classify a component as held-for-sale, the results of that element must be reclassified and included in the results from continuing operations.

Example—Presentation of discontinued operations in the statement of comprehensive income

IFRS 5 requires an entity to disclose a single amount in the statement of comprehensive income for discontinued operations, presented after profit for the period from continuing operations, with an analysis in the notes or in a section of the statement of comprehensive income separate from continuing operations:

Discontinued operations	*2011*	*2012*
Profit for the period from discontinued operations*	€600,000	€700,000
Profit for the period		
Attributable to		
Owners of the parent (80%)		
Profit for the period from discontinued operations	480,000	560,000
Discontinued operations		
Noncontrolling interests (20%)		
Profit for the period from discontinued operations	120,000	140,000

*The required analysis would be provided in the notes

Forthcoming changes in accounting for discontinued operations. In September 2008, the IASB issued an Exposure Draft (ED), *Discontinued Operations,* proposing amendments to IFRS 5, *Noncurrent Assets Held for Sale and Discontinued Operations.* The ED is part of the joint project by the IASB and the US FASB to develop a common definition of discontinued operations as well as common presentation and disclosures. The ED proposed that a disposal activity should be characterized as discontinued operations only when an entity has made a strategic shift in its operations.

The IASB proposed a change in the definition of *discontinued operation,* which should be based on operation segments, best presenting a strategic shift in operations. The new definition would hold that a discontinued operation is a *component of an entity* that

- Is an operating segment (as defined in IFRS 8) and either has been disposed of or is classified as held-for-sale, or
- Is a business (as defined in IFRS 3) that meets the criteria to be classified as held-for-sale on acquisition. The proposed change would bring IFRS 5 into conformity with IFRS 8 (which requires segment reporting by publicly accountable entities).

The new rules would apply to all entities; thus, reporting entities that have not previously been required to disclose segment information (i.e., privately held companies) would be required to determine whether the component to be disposed of meets the definition of an operating segment. Also, the information to be reported with respect to discontinued operations would be based on the amounts presented in the statement of comprehensive income (or separate statement of profit or loss, where presented), even if the segment information disclosed by an entity to comply with IFRS 8 is prepared on a different basis (i.e., the amounts reported to the chief operating decision maker, as is permitted under IFRS 8).

Some additional disclosures would be required for all *components* of an entity (as defined above) disposed of or classified as held-for-sale—regardless of whether or not they are presented as discontinued operations.

After considering the comments received from respondents, both the IASB and the FASB decided to adopt a common definition of a discontinued operation based on the current definition in IFRS 5. As such, they decided to reexpose their proposals for public comment. In May 2010, the boards decided to align the project timetable with the main financial statement presentation project. The boards now plan to publish an Exposure Draft in late 2011 of a converged definition of a discontinued operation and related disclosures, with a revision to the standard expected the following year.

Special industry situations. Accounting for property, plant and equipment in specialized industries such as agriculture or mineral extraction is dealt with in Chapters 31 and 32 respectively.

DISCLOSURES

The disclosures required under IAS 16 for property, plant, and equipment, and under IAS 38 for intangibles, are similar. Furthermore, IAS 36 requires extensive disclosures when assets are impaired or when formerly recognized impairments are being reversed. The requirements that pertain to property, plant, and equipment are as follows:

For each class of tangible asset, disclosure is required of

1. The measurement basis used (cost or revaluation approaches)
2. The depreciation method(s) used
3. Useful lives or depreciation rates used
4. The gross carrying amounts and accumulated depreciation at the beginning and at the end of the period
5. A reconciliation of the carrying amount from the beginning to the end of the period, showing additions, dispositions, acquisitions by means of business combinations, increases or decreases resulting from revaluations, reductions to recognize impairments, amounts written back to recognize recoveries of prior impairments, depreciation, the net effect of translation of foreign entities' financial statements, and any other material items. (An example of such a reconciliation is presented below.) This reconciliation need be provided for only the current period even if comparative financial statements are being presented.

In addition, the statements should also disclose the following facts:

1. Any restrictions on titles and any assets pledged as security for debt
2. The accounting policy regarding restoration costs for items of property, plant, and equipment
3. The expenditures made for property, plant, and equipment, including any construction in progress
4. The amount of outstanding commitments for property, plant, and equipment acquisitions

In addition, the statements should also disclose the following facts:

1. Whether, in determining recoverable amounts, future projected cash flows have been discounted to present values
2. Any restrictions on titles and any assets pledged as security for debt
3. The amount of outstanding commitments for property, plant, and equipment acquisitions

---

Example of reconciliation of asset carrying amounts

Date	Gross cost	Accumulated depreciation	Net carrying amount
1/1/12	€4,500,000	€2,000,000	€2,500,000
Acquisitions	3,000,000	-	3,000,000
Disposals	(400,000)	(340,000)	(60,000)
Impairment		600,000	(600,000)
Depreciation		200,000	(200,000)
12/31/12	€7,100,000	€2,460,000	€4,640,000

Nonmonetary (Exchange) Transactions

Businesses sometimes engage in nonmonetary exchange transactions, where tangible or intangible assets are exchanged for other assets, without a cash transaction or with only a small amount of cash "settle-up." These exchanges can involve productive assets such as machinery and equipment, which are not held for sale under normal circumstances, or inventory items, which are intended for sale to customers.

IAS 16 provides authoritative guidance to the accounting for nonmonetary exchanges of tangible assets. It requires that the cost of an item of property, plant, and equipment acquired in exchange for a similar asset is to be measured at *fair value*, provided that the transaction has commercial substance. The concept of a purely "book value" exchange, formerly employed, is now prohibited under most circumstances.

Commercial substance is a new notion under IFRS, and is defined as the event or transaction causing the cash flows of the entity to change. That is, if the expected cash flows after the exchange differ from what would have been expected without this occurring, the exchange has commercial substance and is to be accounted for at fair value. In assessing whether this has occurred, the entity has to consider if the amount, timing and uncertainty of the cash flows from the new asset are different from the one given up, or if the entity-specific portion of the company's operations will be different. If either of these is significant, then the transaction has commercial substance.

If the transaction does not have commercial substance, or the fair value of neither the asset received nor the asset given up can be measured reliably, then the asset acquired is valued at the carrying amount of the asset given up. Such situations are expected to be rare.

If there is a settle-up paid or received in cash or a cash equivalent, this is often referred to as *boot;* that term will be used in the following example.

Example of an exchange involving dissimilar assets and no boot

Assume the following:

1. Jamok, Inc. exchanges an automobile with a carrying amount of €2,500 with Springsteen & Co. for a tooling machine with a fair market value of €3,200.
2. No boot is exchanged in the transaction.
3. The fair value of the automobile is not readily determinable.

In this case, Jamok, Inc. has recognized a gain of €700 (= €3,200 – €2,500) on the exchange, and the gain should be included in the determination of net income. The entry to record the transaction would be as follows:

Machine	3,200	
Automobile		2,500
Gain on exchange of automobile		700

Nonreciprocal transfers. In a nonreciprocal transfer, one party gives or receives property without the other party doing the opposite. Often these involve an entity and the owners of the entity. Examples of nonreciprocal transfers with owners include dividends paid-in-kind, nonmonetary assets exchanged for common stock, split-ups, and spin-offs. An example of a nonreciprocal transaction with parties other than the owners is a donation of property either by or to the entity.

The accounting for most nonreciprocal transfers should be based on the fair market value of the asset given (or received, if the fair value of the nonmonetary asset is both objectively measurable and would be clearly recognizable under IFRS). The same principle also applies to distributions of noncash assets (e.g., items of property, plant and equipment, businesses as defined in IFRS 3, ownership interest in another entity, or disposal groups as defined in IFRS 5); and also to distributions that give owners a choice of receiving either noncash assets or a cash alternative. IFRIC 17 was issued in January 2009 to address the accounting that should be followed in such situations and provides that the assets involved must be measured at their fair value and any gains or losses taken to profit or loss. The Interpretation also provides guidance on the measurement of the dividend payable in that the dividend payable is measured at the fair value of the assets to be distributed. If the entity gives its owners a choice of receiving either a noncash asset or a cash alternative, the entity should estimate the dividend payable by considering both the fair value of each alternative and the associated probability of owners selecting each alternative. At the end of each reporting period and at the date of settlement, the entity is required to review and adjust the carrying amount of the dividend payable, with any changes in the carrying amount of the dividend payable recognized in equity as adjustments to the amount of the distribution.

This approach differs from the previous approach, which permitted the recording of transactions that resulted in the distribution of nonmonetary assets to owners of an entity in a spin-off or other form of reorganization or liquidation being accounted for based on their recorded amount.

Example of accounting for a nonreciprocal transfer

Assume the following:

1. Salaam distributed property with a carrying amount of €10,000 to its shareholder as a dividend during the current year.
2. The property had a fair market value of €17,000 at the date of the transfer.

The transaction is to be valued at the fair market value of the property transferred, and any gain or loss on the transaction is to be recognized. Thus, Salaam should recognize a gain of €7,000 (= €17,000 – €10,000) in the determination of the current period's profit or loss. The entry to record the transaction would be as follows:

Dividend paid	17,000	
Property		10,000
Gain on transfer of property		7,000

Transfers of Assets from Customers

IFRIC 18, *Transfers of Assets from Customers,* addresses the accounting that must be applied to transfers of items of property, plant, and equipment by entities that receive such transfers from their customers. The Interpretation addresses agreements in which the entity receives from a customer an item of property, plant, and equipment that it must then use either to connect the customer to a network or to provide the customer with ongoing access to a supply of goods or services, or to do both. This Interpretation also applies to agreements in which the entity, rather than receiving property, plant, and equipment, instead receives cash from a customer and that amount of cash must be used only to construct or acquire an item of property, plant, and equipment that will then be used in the delivery of goods and services to the customer. The Interpretation does not apply to agreements in which the transfer is either a government grant as defined in IAS 20 or infrastructure used in a service concession arrangement that is within the scope of IFRIC 12.

Where an asset is received, such asset is accounted for at its fair value, provided that it meets the definition of an asset as contained in the *Framework*. Simultaneously, the entity must identify its obligations to its customer and identify the credit side of the transaction as an obligation to provide goods and services. Revenue from the rendering of such goods and services will then be recognized over the period of time that the obligation is discharged, in accordance with the terms of the agreement entered into with the customer.

Examples of Financial Statement Disclosures

Novartis AG
Annual Report 2010

1. Accounting policies

Property, plant, and equipment

Land is recorded at acquisition cost less accumulated impairment, if any. Prepayments for long-term leasehold land agreements are amortized over the life of the lease. Other items of property, plant, & equipment are recorded at acquisition cost or production cost and are depreciated on a straight-line basis to the income statement over the following estimated useful lives:

Buildings	20 to 40 years
Machinery and equipment	7 to 20 years
Furniture and vehicles	5 to 10 years
Computer hardware	3 to 7 years

Additional costs that enhance the future economic benefit of property, plant, & equipment are capitalized. Government grants for construction activities and equipment are deducted from the carrying value of the assets. With effect from January 1, 2009, as required by IAS 23, borrowing costs associated with the construction of new property, plant, and equipment projects are capitalized. Such costs related to projects commencing prior to January 1, 2009, have been expensed. Property, plant, & equipment is reviewed for impairment whenever events or changes in circumstances indicate that the balance sheet carrying amount may not be recoverable.

Property, plant, & equipment that are financed by leases giving Novartis substantially all risks and rewards of ownership are capitalized at the lower of the fair value of the leased asset or the present value of minimum lease payments at the inception of the lease. These are depreciated in the same manner as other assets over the shorter of the lease term or their useful life. Leases in which a significant portion of the ownership risks and rewards are retained by the lessor are classified as operating leases. These are charged to the consolidated income statement over the life of the lease, generally, on a straight-line basis

Notes to the Novartis Group Consolidated Financial Statements

10. Property, plant, and equipment movements

	Land USD millions	Buildings USD millions	Construction in progress USD millions	Machinery & other equipment USD millions	Total USD millions
2010					
Cost					
January 1	**709**	**9,380**	**2,176**	**13,635**	**25,900**
Impact of business combinations	95	474	244	606	1,419
Reclassifications[1]	12	616	(1,407)	779	
Additions	3	62	1,260	328	1,653
Disposals	(2)	(49)	(28)	(295)	(374)
Currency translation effects	10	191	82	76	359
December 31	**827**	**10,674**	**2,327**	**15,129**	**28,957**

	Land USD millions	Buildings USD millions	Construction in progress USD millions	Machinery & other equipment USD millions	Total USD millions
Accumulated depreciation					
January 1	**(13)**	**(3,869)**	**(8)**	**(7,935)**	**(11,825)**
Reclassifications[1]		5		(5)	
Depreciation charge	(4)	(343)		(1,016)	(1,363)
Depreciation on disposals		29		264	293
Impairment charge		(3)	(2)	(9)	(10)
Currency translation effects	(2)	(137)		(73)	(212)
December 31	**(19)**	**(4,318)**	**(6)**	**(8,774)**	**(13,117)**
Net book value at December 31	**808**	**6,356**	**2,321**	**6,355**	**15,840**
Insured value at December 31					32,288
Net book value of property, plant, & equipment under finance lease contracts					4
Commitments for purchases of property, plant, & equipment					597

[1] *Reclassifications between various asset categories due to competition of plant and other equipment under construction.*

The Group was awarded government grants in the United States for the construction of a manufacturing facility to produce flu vaccines.

The contracts included a maximum of USD 294 million cost reimbursement for construction activities and equipment, of which USD 185 million was received by December 31, 2010. These grants were deducted in arriving at the carrying value of the assets since the receipt of the respective government grant is reasonably assured.

There are no onerous contracts or unfulfilled conditions in connection with this grant.

Borrowing costs on new additions to property, plant and equipment have been capitalized since January 1, 2009 and amounted to USD 1 million in 2010 (2009: USD 1 million).

	Land USD millions	Buildings USD millions	Construction in progress USD millions	Machinery & other equipment USD millions	Total USD millions
2009					
Cost					
January 1	**658**	**8,560**	**2,440**	**12,315**	**23,973**
Impact of business combinations	2	21	2	39	64
Reclassifications[1]	50	782	(1,809)	977	
Additions	5	93	1,453	332	1,883
Disposals	(19)	(259)	(7)	(375)	(660)
Currency translation effects	13	183	97	347	640
December 31	**709**	**9,380**	**2,176**	**13,635**	**25,900**

	Land USD millions	Buildings USD millions	Construction in progress USD millions	Machinery & other equipment USD millions	Total USD millions
Accumulated depreciation					
January 1	**(18)**	**(3,727)**	**(1)**	**(7,127)**	**(10,873)**
Reclassifications[1]		5		(5)	
Depreciation charge	(2)	(318)		(921)	(1,241)
Depreciation on disposals	7	251		327	585
Impairment charge		(1)	(7)	(1)	(9)
Currency translation effects		(79)		(208)	(287)
December 31	**(13)**	**(3,869)**	**(8)**	**(7,935)**	**(11,825)**
Net book value at December 31	696	5,511	2,168	5,700	14,075
Insured value at December 31					27,147
Net book value of property, plant, & equipment under finance lease contracts					4
Commitments for purchases of property, plant, & equipment					548

[1] *Reclassifications between various asset categories due to competition of plant and other equipment under construction.*

Lectra SA
Financial Report 2010

Summary of significant accounting policies and scope of consolidation

Property, plant, and equipment. Property, plant, and equipment is carried at cost less accumulated depreciation and impairment, if any. When a tangible asset comprises significant components with different useful lives, the latter are analyzed separately. Consequently, costs incurred in replacing or renewing a component of a tangible asset are booked as a distinct asset. The carrying value of the component replaced is written off. Moreover, the Group considers that there is no residual value on its assets. At each closing date, the useful life of assets is reviewed and adjusted as required. Subsequent expenditures relating to a tangible asset are capitalized if they increase the future economic benefits of the specific asset to which they are attached. All other costs are expensed directly at the time they are incurred.

Financial expense is not included in the cost of acquisition of tangible assets. Investment grants received are deducted from the value of tangible assets. Losses or gains on disposals of assets are recognized in the income statement under caption "Selling, general and administrative expenses."

Depreciation is computed on the straight-line method over their estimated useful lives as follows:

- Buildings and building main structures: 20-35 years;
- Secondary structures and building installations: 15 years;
- Fixtures and installations: 5-10 years;
- Land arrangements: 5-10 years;
- Technical installations, equipment and tools: 4-10 years;
- Office equipment and computers: 3-5 years;
- Office furniture: 5-10 years.

Fixed asset impairment–impairment tests

When events or changes in the market environment, or internal factors, indicate a potential impairment of value of goodwill, other intangible assets or property, plant, and equipment, these are subjected to detailed scrutiny. In the case of goodwill, impairment tests are carried out systematically at least once a year. Goodwill is tested for impairment by comparing its carrying value with its recoverable amount, which is defined as the higher of the asset's fair value less costs to sell and value in use determined as the present value of future cash flows attached to them, excluding interest and tax. The results utilized are derived from the Group's three-year plan. Beyond the time frame of the three-year plan, cash flows are projected to infinity, the assumed growth rate being dependent on the growth potential of the markets and/or products concerned by the impairment test. The discount rate is computed under the Weighted-Average Cost of Capital (WACC) method, the cost of capital being determined by applying the Capital Asset Pricing Model (CAPM). If the impairment test reveals an impairment of value relative to the carrying value, an irreversible impairment loss is recognized to reduce the carrying value of the goodwill to its recoverable amount. This charge, if any, is recognized under "Goodwill impairment" in the income statement. Other intangible assets and property, plant, and equipment are tested by comparing the carrying value of each relevant group of assets (which may be an isolated asset or a cash-generating unit) with its recoverable amount. If the latter is lower than the carrying value, an impairment charge equal to the difference between these two amounts is recognized. In the case of Lectra's new information system, impairment testing consists in periodically verifying that the initial assumptions regarding the useful life and functions of the system remain valid. The base and the schedule of amortization/depreciation of the assets concerned are reduced if a loss is recognized, the resulting charge being recorded as an amortization/depreciation charge under "Cost of goods sold," "Research and development expenses," or "Selling, general and administrative expenses" in the income statement depending on the nature and use of the assets concerned.

Notes to the consolidated financial statements

Note 3. Property, plant, and equipment

	Land and buildings	Fixtures and fittings	Equipment and other	Total
(in thousands of euros) **2009**				
Gross value at January 1, 2009	9,478	14,120	23,238	46,836
Additions	-	48	799	847
Write-offs and disposals	-	(327)	(494)	(821)
Transfers	-	343	(343)	-
Exchange rate differences	-	(42)	65	23
Gross value at December 31, 2009	9,478	14,120	23,265	46,885
Accumulated depreciation at December 31, 2009	(6,610)	(8,726)	(19,094)	(34,430)
Net value at December 31, 2009	2,868	5,416	4,171	12,455
(in thousands of euros) **2010**				
Gross value at January 1, 2010	9,478	14,142	23,265	46,885
Additions	-	311	760	1,071
Write-offs and disposals	-	(710)	(982)	(1,692)
Transfers	-	5	7	12
Exchange rate differences	-	185	424	609
Gross value at December 31, 2010	9,478	13,933	23,474	46,885
Accumulated depreciation at December 31, 2010	(6,670)	(9,239)	(19,910)	(35,819)
Net value at December 31, 2010	2,808	4,694	3,564	11,066

Changes in depreciation:

	Land and buildings	Fixtures and fittings	Equipment and other	Total
(in thousands of euros)				
2009				
Accumulated depreciation at January 1, 2009	**(6,546)**	**(7,929)**	**(17,941)**	**(32,416)**
Additional depreciation	(64)	(990)	(1,592)	(2,646)
Write-offs and disposals	-	178	480	658
Exchange rate differences	-	15	(41)	(26)
Accumulated depreciation at December 31, 2009	**(6,610)**	**(8,726)**	**(19,094)**	**(34,430)**
(in thousands of euros)				
2010				
Accumulated depreciation at January 1, 2010	**(6,610)**	**(8,726)**	**(19,094)**	**(34,430)**
Additional depreciation	(60)	(872)	(1,375)	(2,307)
Write-offs and disposals	-	460	908	1,368
Transfers	-	1	(13)	(12)
Exchange rate differences	-	(102)	(336)	(438)
Accumulated depreciation at December 31, 2010	**(6,670)**	**(9,239)**	**(19,910)**	**(35,819)**

"Land and buildings" pertain solely to the Group's industrial facilities in Bordeaux–Cestas (France), amounting to €9,478,000, net of investment grants received. The facility covers an area of 11.4 hectares (28.5 acres) and the buildings represent 27,300m2 (295,000 sq.ft.). Land and buildings were partly purchased outright by the company, and partly under financial leases. These have been paid for in full. The assets purchased outright by the company (excluding fixtures and fittings) represent €5,022,000, of which €2,516,000 has been depreciated.

The assets (including fixtures and fittings) purchased under finance leases are valued at €4,745,000 including €4,272,000 for the buildings, depreciated in full, and €473,000 for the land. In October 2002, the company became owner of the entire Bordeaux–Cestas land and buildings facilities. No acquisitions of new equipment were made using finance leases in 2010 or 2009.

Other fixed assets purchased in 2010 and 2009 mainly concerned manufacturing molds and tools for the Bordeaux–Cestas industrial facility. Eliminations from property, plant, and equipment arise mainly from the moves from the Paris–Chaussée d'Antin and Toulouse premises, and from the scrapping of obsolete machine tools.

Nestlé S.A.
Annual Report 2010

Accounting policies

Property, plant, and equipment. Property, plant, and equipment are shown in the balance sheet at their historical cost. Depreciation is provided on components that have homogenous useful lives by using the straight-line method so as to depreciate the initial cost down to the residual value over the estimated useful lives. The residual values are 30% on head offices and nil for all other asset types. The useful lives are as follows:

Buildings	20–40 years
Machinery and equipment	10–25 years
Tools, furniture, information technology, and sundry equipment	3–10 years
Vehicles	3-8 years

Land is not depreciated.

Useful lives, components and residual amounts are reviewed annually. Such a review takes into consideration the nature of the assets, their intended use including but not limited to the closure of facilities and the evolution of the techno logy and competitive pressures that may lead to technical obsolescence. Depreciation of property, plant and equipment is allocated to the appropriate headings of expenses by function in the income statement. Borrowing costs incurred during the course of construction are capitalised if the assets under construction are significant and if their construction requires a substantial period to complete (typically more than one year). The capitalization rate is determined on the basis of the short term borrowing rate for the period of construction. Premiums capitalised for leasehold land or buildings are amortised over the length of the lease. Government grants are recognised in accordance with the deferral method, whereby the grant is set up as deferred income which is released to the income statement over the useful life of the related assets. Grants that are not related to assets are credited to the income statement when they are received.

Notes to the consolidated financial statements

7. Property, plant, and equipment

	Land and buildings	Machinery and equipment	Tools, furniture and other equipment	Vehicles	Total
Gross value					
At January 1	13,105	24,711	7,510	865	46,191
Currency retranslations	120	408	139	(5)	
Capital expenditure[a]	914	2,519	1,094	114	4,641
Disposals	(167)	(914)	(457)	(71)	(1,609)
Reclassified as held for sale	(977)	(1,047)	(555)	(23)	(2,602)
Modification of the scope of consolidation	(64)	(115)	(14)	(4)	(197)
At December 31	**12,931**	**25,562**	**7,717**	**876**	**47,086**
Accumulated depreciation and impairments					
At January 1	(5,012)	(14,321)	(5,288)	(473)	(25,094)
Currency retranslations	(52)	(268)	(103)	2	
Depreciation	(376)	(1,372)	(859)	(106)	(2,713)
Impairments	(38)	(127)	(5)	-	(170)
Disposals	114	791	457	71	1,433
Reclassified as held for sale	309	592	388	9	1,298
Modification of the scope of consolidation	41	109	26	4	180
At December 31	**(5,014)**	**(14,596)**	**(5,384)**	**(493)**	**(25,487)**
Net at December 31	**7,917**	**10,966**	**2,333**	**383**	**(21,599)**

[a] *Including borrowing costs.*

At December 31, 2009, property, plant and equipment include CHF 775 million of assets under construction. Net property, plant, and equipment held under finance leases amount to CHF 262 million. Net property, plant, and equipment of CHF 101 million are pledged as security for financial liabilities. Fire risks, reasonably estimated, are insured in accordance with domestic requirements.

	Land and buildings	Machinery and equipment	Tools, furniture and other equipment	Vehicles	Total
Gross value					
At January 1	12,931	25,562	7,717	876	47,086
Currency retranslations	(961)	(2,722)	(670)	(95)	(4,448)
Capital expenditure[a]	872	2,469	893	151	4,384
Disposals	(137)	(688)	(541)	(65)	(1,431)

	Land and buildings	Machinery and equipment	Tools, furniture and other equipment	Vehicles	Total
Reclassified as held for sale	(48)	(31)	(5)	-	(84)
Modification of the scope of consolidation	148	186	(9)	2	327
At December 31	**12,805**	**24,775**	**7,385**	**869**	**45,834**

Accumulated depreciation and impairments

At January 1	(5,014)	(14,596)	(5,384)	(493)	(25,487)
Currency retranslations	434	1,461	512	52	2,459
Depreciation	(370)	(1,319)	(765)	(98)	(2,552)
Impairments	(38)	(131)	(17)	-	(186)
Disposals	107	641	492	56	1,296
Reclassified as held for sale	30	29	4	-	63
Modification of the scope of consolidation	-	1	10	-	11
At December 31	**(4,851)**	**(13,914)**	**(5,148)**	**(483)**	**(24,396)**
Net at December 31	**7,954**	**10,861**	**2,237**	**386**	**21,438**

(a) *Including borrowing costs.*

At December 31, 2010, property, plant, and equipment include CHF 802 million of assets under construction. Net property, plant, and equipment held under finance leases amount to CHF 240 million. Net property, plant, and equipment of CHF 112 million are pledged as security for financial liabilities. Fire risks, reasonably estimated, are insured in accordance with domestic requirements.

Impairment

Impairment of property, plant, and equipment arises mainly from the plans to optimize industrial manufacturing capacities by closing or selling inefficient production facilities.

Commitments for expenditure

At 31 December 2010, the Group was committed to expenditure amounting to CHF 624 million (2009: CHF 605 million).

US GAAP COMPARISON

US GAAP and IFRS are very similar with regard to property, plant, and equipment. Generally, expenditures that qualify for capitalization under IFRS are also eligible under US GAAP.

Initial measurement can differ for internally constructed asset. US GAAP permits only eligible interest to be capitalized, whereas IFRS includes other borrowing costs. There are also some differences regarding what borrowings are included to compute a capitalization rate.

Component accounting is not prescribed under US GAAP, but neither is it prohibited. This disparity can result in a different "mix" of depreciation and maintenance expense on the income statement. Only major upgrades to PPE are capitalized under US GAAP, whereas the replacement of a component under IFRS is characterized as accelerated depreciation and additional capital expenditures. Consequently, the classification of expenditures on the statement of cash flows can differ.

Most oil and gas companies use US GAAP for exploration assets since there is no substantial IFRS for the oil & gas industry. IFRS 6 permits entities to disregard the hierarchy of application prescribed in IAS 8 and use another standard (usually US GAAP) immediately.

The accounting for asset retirement obligations assets is largely the same but the difference in the discount rate used to measure them creates an inherent difference in the carrying cost. US GAAP uses a risk-free rate adjusted for the entity's credit risk to discount the obligation. IFRS uses the time value of money rate adjusted for specific risks of the liability. Also, assets and obligations are not adjusted for period-to-period changes in the discount. The discount rate applied to each increment of an accrual, termed "layers" in US GAAP, remains with that layer through increases and decreases.

Impairment under US GAAP is a two-step process. The first step is to compare the undiscounted future cash flows, termed the recoverable amount, of the asset being testing to the carrying value. If the recoverable amount is less than the carrying value, the second step is taken that results in a write-down of the excess of the fair value of the asset over the carrying value. Impairments cannot be reversed.

US GAAP does not permit the revaluation method. Disclosures of PP&E are less extensive under US GAAP.

10 BORROWING COSTS

INTRODUCTION

Property (such as factory buildings) is often constructed by an entity over an extended period of time, and during this interval, when the property has yet to be placed in productive service, the entity may incur interest cost on funds borrowed to finance the construction. IAS 23 provides that such cost must be added to the carrying amount of the asset under construction; the formerly available benchmark treatment option to expense financing costs as incurred was eliminated as a consequence of an amendment to IAS 23 in 2007. European companies had historically generally expensed such costs as period costs as they were incurred, because this had a more tax-efficient strategy. While IFRS does not dictate tax requirements, unless divergence between tax and financial reporting is permitted in the reporting entity's tax jurisdiction, this will no longer be an available strategy.

Sources of IFRS
IAS 23

DEFINITIONS OF TERMS

Borrowing costs. Interest and other costs that an entity incurs in connection with the borrowing of funds. Borrowing costs that are directly attributable to the acquisition, construction or production of qualifying assets (defined as those taking a substantial period of time to prepare for intended use or sale) are capitalized to the cost of those assets. Borrowing costs may include interest expense calculated using the effective interest method (IAS 39), finance charges in respect of finance leases (IAS 17), or certain exchange differences arising from foreign currency borrowings.

Carrying amount (book value). The value reported for an asset or liability in the statement of financial position. For assets, this is either cost, revalued amount, or cost minus offsets such as depreciation or allowance for bad debts. Carrying amount of property, plant and equipment is the amount at which an asset is recognized after deducting any accumulated depreciation and accumulated impairment losses. Carrying amount is often different from market value because depreciation is a cost allocation rather than a means of valuation. For liabilities, the carrying amount is the amount of the liability minus offsets such as any sums already paid or bond discounts.

Qualifying asset. An asset that necessarily requires a substantial period of time to get ready for its intended use or sale. Qualifying assets can be inventories, plant and equipment, intangibles, and investment properties, unless the assets are accounted for at fair value. Financial assets or inventories produced over a very short period of time in a repetitive process are *not* qualifying assets.

RECOGNITION AND MEASUREMENT

Capitalization of Borrowing Costs

Accounting literature says that the cost of an asset should include all the costs necessary to get the asset set up and functioning properly for its intended use in the place it is to be used. There has long been, however, a debate about whether borrowing costs should be included in the definition of all costs necessary, or whether instead such costs should be treated as purely a period expense. The concern is that two otherwise identical entities might report different asset costs simply due to decisions made regarding the financing of the entities, with the leveraged (debt issuing) entity having a higher reported asset cost. A corollary issue is whether an imputed cost of capital for equity financing should be treated as a cost to be capitalized, which would reduce or eliminate such a discrepancy in apparent asset costs.

The principal purposes to be accomplished by the capitalization of interest costs are as follows:

1. To obtain a more accurate original asset investment cost; and
2. To achieve a better matching of costs deferred to future periods with revenues of those future periods.

In the US, the FASB took the position (in FAS 34) that borrowing costs, under defined conditions, are to be added to the cost of long-lived tangible assets (and inventory also, under very limited circumstances). However, the implicit cost of equity capital may not be similarly treated as an asset cost. This treatment, where defined criteria are met, is mandatory under US GAAP. Historically, the IASB has taken a different approach, offering the US GAAP rule as one alternative treatment, optional at the reporting entity's election, until the revised IAS 23 was issued in 2007.

IAS 23, as revised in 2007. In March 2007, the IASB issued the revised IAS 23, *Borrowing Costs*, which eliminated the option of recognizing borrowing costs immediately as an expense, to the extent that they are directly attributable to the acquisition, construction, or production of a qualifying asset. This revision was a result of the Short-Term Convergence project with the FASB. The revised standard provides that a reporting entity should capitalize those borrowing costs that are directly attributable to the acquisition, construction, or production of a qualifying asset as part of the initial carrying amount of that asset, and that all other borrowing costs should be recognized as an expense in the period in which the entity incurs them.

Key changes introduced by this revised standard include

- All borrowing costs must be capitalized if they are directly attributable to the acquisition, construction or production of a qualifying asset. The previous benchmark treatment, recognizing immediately all such financing costs as period expenses, is eliminated. Under the new approach, which was an allowable alternative treatment in the past, all these costs must be added to the carrying amount of the assets, when it is probable that they will result in future economic benefits to the entity and the costs can be measured reliably.

- Borrowing costs that do not require capitalization relate to

  - Assets measured at fair value (for example, a biological asset), although an entity can present items in profit or loss as if borrowing costs had been subject to capitalization, before measuring them at their fair values.
  - Inventories that are manufactured, or otherwise produced, in large quantities on a repetitive basis, even if they take a substantial period of time to get ready for their intended use or sale.

Borrowing costs are defined as interest and other costs directly attributable to the acquisition, construction or production of qualifying assets (defined below). Such costs may include interest expense calculated using the effective interest rate method as described in IAS 39, finance charges related to finance leases (in accordance with IAS 17, *Leases*), and exchange differences arising from foreign currency borrowings to the extent they are treated as an adjustment to interest costs.

A qualifying asset is an asset that necessarily takes a substantial period of time to get ready for its intended use and may include inventories, manufacturing plants, power generation facilities, intangible assets, properties that will become self-constructed investment properties once their construction or development is complete, and investment properties measured at cost that are being redeveloped. Other investments, and inventories that are routinely manufactured or otherwise produced in large quantities on a repetitive basis over a short period of time, as well as assets that are ready for their intended use or sale when acquired, are not qualifying assets.

Borrowing costs eligible for capitalization, directly attributable to the acquisition, construction, or production of a qualifying asset, are those borrowing costs that would have been avoided if the expenditure on this asset had not been made. They include actual borrowing costs incurred less any investment income on the temporary investment of those borrowings.

The amount of borrowing costs eligible for capitalization is determined by applying a capitalization rate to the expenditures on that asset. The capitalization rate is the weighted-average of the borrowing costs applicable to the borrowings of the entity that are outstanding during the period, other than borrowings made specifically for the purpose of obtaining a qualifying asset. The amount of borrowing costs capitalized during a period cannot exceed the amount of borrowing costs incurred.

IAS 23 does not deal with the actual or imputed cost of equity, including preferred capital not classified as a liability.

Qualifying assets are those that normally take an extended period of time to prepare for their intended uses. While IAS 23 does not give further insight into the limitations of this definition, many years' experience with FAS 34 provided certain insights that may prove germane to this matter. In general, interest capitalization has been applied to those asset acquisition and construction situations in which

1. Assets are being constructed for an entity's own use or for which deposit or progress payments are made;
2. Assets are produced as discrete projects that are intended for lease or sale; or
3. Investments are being made that are accounted for by the equity method, where the investee is using funds to acquire qualifying assets for its principal operations which have not yet begun.

Generally, inventories and land that are not undergoing preparation for intended use are not qualifying assets. When land is in the process of being developed, it is a qualifying asset. If land is being developed for lots, the capitalized interest cost is added to the cost of the land. The related borrowing costs are then matched against revenues when the lots are sold. If, on the other hand, the land is being developed for a building, the capitalized interest cost should instead be added to the cost of the building. The interest cost is then matched against future revenues as the building is depreciated.

The capitalization of interest costs would probably *not* apply to the following situations:

1. The routine production of inventories in large quantities on a repetitive basis;
2. For any asset acquisition or self-construction, when the effects of capitalization would not be material, compared to the effect of expensing interest;
3. When qualifying assets are already in use or ready for use;
4. When qualifying assets are not being used and are not awaiting activities to get them ready for use;
5. When qualifying assets are not included in a consolidated statement of financial position;
6. When principal operations of an investee accounted for under the equity method have already begun;
7. When regulated investees capitalize both the cost of debt and equity capital; or
8. When assets are acquired with grants and gifts restricted by the donor to the extent that funds are available from those grants and gifts.

If funds are borrowed specifically for the purpose of obtaining a qualified asset, the interest costs incurred thereon should be deemed eligible for capitalization, net of any interest earned from the temporary investment of idle funds. It is likely that there will not be a perfect match between funds borrowed and funds actually applied to the asset production process, at any given time, although in some construction projects funds are drawn from the lender's credit facility only as vendors' invoices, and other costs, are actually paid. Only the interest incurred on the project should be included as a cost of the project, however.

In other situations, a variety of credit facilities may be used to generate a pool of funds, a portion of which is applied to the asset construction or acquisition program. In those instances, the amount of interest to be capitalized will be determined by applying an average borrowing cost to the amount of funds committed to the project. Interest cost could include the following:

1. Interest on debt having explicit interest rates;
2. Interest related to finance leases; or
3. Amortization of any related discount or premium on borrowings, or of other ancillary borrowing costs such as commitment fees.

The amount of interest to be capitalized is that portion that could have been avoided if the qualifying asset had not been acquired. Thus, the capitalized amount is the incremental amount of interest cost incurred by the entity to finance the acquired asset. A weighted-average of the rates of the borrowings of the entity should be used. The selection of borrowings to be used in the calculation of the weighted-average of rates requires judgment. In resolving this problem, particularly in the case of consolidated financial statements, the best criterion to use is the identification and determination of that portion of interest that could have been avoided if the qualifying assets had not been acquired.

The base (which should be used to multiply the weighted-average rate by) is the average amount of accumulated net capital expenditures incurred for qualifying assets during the relevant reporting period. Capitalized costs and expenditures are not synonymous terms. Theoretically, a capitalized cost financed by a trade payable for which no interest is recognized is not a capital expenditure to which the capitalization rate should be applied. Reasonable approximations of net capital expenditures are acceptable, however, and capitalized costs are generally used in place of capital expenditures unless there is a material difference.

If the average capitalized expenditures exceed the specific new borrowings for the time frame involved, the *excess* expenditures amount should be multiplied by the weighted-average of rates and not by the rate associated with the specific debt. This requirement more accurately reflects the interest cost that is actually incurred by the entity in bringing the long-lived asset to a properly functioning condition and location.

The interest being paid on the underlying debt may be either simple or subject to compounding. Simple interest is computed on the principal alone, whereas compound interest is computed on principal and on any accumulated interest that has not been paid. Compounding may be yearly, monthly, or daily. Most long-lived assets will be acquired with debt having interest compounded, and that feature should be considered when computing the amount of interest to be capitalized.

The total amount of interest actually incurred by the entity during the relevant time frame is the ceiling for the amount of interest cost capitalized. Thus, the amount capitalized cannot exceed the amount actually incurred during the period. On a consolidated financial reporting basis, this ceiling is defined as the sum of the parent's interest cost plus that incurred by its consolidated subsidiaries. If financial statements are issued separately, the interest cost capitalized should be limited to the amount that the separate entity has incurred, and that amount should include interest on intercompany borrowings, which of course would be eliminated in consolidated financial statements. The interest incurred is a gross amount and is not netted against interest earned except in rare cases.

Example of accounting for capitalized interest costs

Assume the following:

1. On January 1, 2012, Gemini Corp. contracted with Leo Company to construct a building for €20,000,000 on land that Gemini had purchased years earlier.
2. Gemini Corp. was to make five payments in 2012, with the last payment scheduled for the date of completion.
3. The building was completed December 31, 2012.
4. Gemini Corp. made the following payments during 2012:

January 1, 2012	€ 2,000,000
March 31, 2012	4,000,000
June 30, 2012	6,100,000
September 30, 2012	4,400,000
December 31, 2012	3,500,000
	€20,000,000

5. Gemini Corp. had the following debt outstanding at December 31, 2012:

   a. A 12%, 4-year note dated 1/1/10 with interest compounded quarterly. Both principal and interest due 12/31/2013 (relates specifically to building project) — €8,500,000

   b. A 10%, 10-year note dated 12/31/06 with simple interest and interest payable annually on December 31 — €6,000,000

   c. A 12%, 5-year note dated 12/31/08 with simple interest and interest payable annually on December 31 — €7,000,000

The amount of interest to be capitalized during 2012 is computed as follows:

Average Accumulated Expenditures

Date	Expenditure	Capitalization period*	Average accumulated expenditures
1/1/12	€ 2,000,000	12/12	€2,000,000
3/31/12	4,000,000	9/12	3,000,000
6/30/12	6,100,000	6/12	3,050,000
9/30/12	4,400,000	3/12	1,100,000
12/31/12	3,500,000	0/12	--
	€20,000,000		€9,150,000

* *The number of months between the date when expenditures were made and the date on which interest capitalization stops (December 31, 2011).*

Potential Interest Cost to Be Capitalized

(€8,500,000	×	1.12551)*	– €8,500,000	=	€1,066,840
650,000	×	0.1109**		=	72,020
€9,150,000					€1,138,860

* *The principal, €8,500,000, is multiplied by the factor for the future amount of €1 for 4 periods at 3% to determine the amount of principal and interest due in 2012.*
** *Weighted-average interest rate*

	Principal	Interest
10%, 10-year note	€ 6,000,000	€ 600,000
12%, 5-year note	7,000,000	840,000
	€13,000,000	€1,440,000

$$\frac{\text{Total interest}}{\text{Total principal}} = \frac{€\ 1,440,000}{€13,000,000} = 11.08\%$$

The actual interest is

12%, 4-year note [(€8,500,000 × 1.12551) – €8,500,000]	=	€1,066,840
10%, 10-year note (€6,000,000 × 10%)	=	600,000
12%, 5-year note (€7,000,000 × 12%)	=	840,000
Total interest		€2,506,840

The interest cost to be capitalized is the lesser of €1,138,860 (avoidable interest) or €2,506,840 (actual interest). The remaining €1,367,980 (= €2,506,840 – €1,138,860) must be expensed.

Determining the time period for capitalization of borrowing costs. An entity should begin capitalizing borrowing costs on the commencement date. Three conditions must be met before the capitalization period should begin:

1. Expenditures for the asset are being incurred;
2. Borrowing costs are being incurred; and
3. Activities that are necessary to prepare the asset for its intended use are in progress.

As long as these conditions continue, borrowing costs can be capitalized. Expenditures incurred for the asset include only those that have resulted in payments of cash, transfers of other assets or the assumption of interest-bearing liabilities, and are reduced by any progress payments and grants received for that asset.

Necessary activities are interpreted in a very broad manner. They start with the planning process and continue until the qualifying asset is substantially complete and ready to function as intended. These activities may include technical and administrative work prior to actual commencement of physical work, such as obtaining permits and approvals, and may continue after physical work has ceased. Brief, normal interruptions do not stop the capitalization of interest costs. However, if the entity intentionally suspends or delays the activities for some reason, interest costs should not be capitalized from the point of suspension or delay until substantial activities in regard to the asset resume.

If the asset is completed in a piecemeal fashion, the capitalization of interest costs stops for each part as it becomes ready to function as intended. An asset that must be entirely complete before the parts can be used as intended can continue to capitalize interest costs until the total asset becomes ready to function.

Suspension and cessation of capitalization. If there is an extended period during which there is no activity to prepare the asset for its intended use, capitalization of borrowing costs should be suspended. As a practical matter, unless the break in activity is significant, it is usually ignored. Also, if delays are normal and to be expected given the nature of the construction project (such as a suspension of building construction during the winter months), this would have been anticipated as a cost and would not warrant even a temporary cessation of borrowing cost capitalization.

Capitalization would cease when the project has been substantially completed. This would occur when the asset is ready for its intended use or for sale to a customer. The fact that routine minor administrative matters still need to be attended to would not mean that the project had not been completed, however. The measure should be *substantially* complete, in other words, not absolutely finished.

Costs in excess of recoverable amounts. When the carrying amount or the expected ultimate cost of the qualifying asset, including capitalized interest cost, exceeds its recoverable amount (if property, plant or equipment) or net realizable value (if an item held for resale), it will be necessary to record an adjustment necessary to write the asset carrying amount down. Any excess interest cost is thus an impairment, to be recognized immediately in expense.

In the case of plant, property, and equipment, a later write-up may occur due to use of the allowed alternative (i.e., revaluation) treatment, recognizing fair value increases, in which case, as described earlier, recovery of a previously recognized loss will be reported in earnings.

Disclosure requirements. With respect to an entity's accounting for borrowing costs, the financial statements must disclose

1. The amount of borrowing costs capitalized during the period; and
2. The capitalization rate used to determine the amount of borrowing costs eligible for capitalization.

As noted, this rate will be the weighted-average of rates on all borrowings included in an allocation pool or the actual rate on specific debt identified with a given asset acquisition or construction project.

US GAAP COMPARISON

US GAAP and IFRS are nearly identical with regard to capitalized interest. Both have essentially the same definition of eligible assets, when the capitalization can begin, and when it ends. However, US GAAP permits only eligible interest to be capitalized, whereas IFRS includes other borrowing costs. There are also some differences regarding what borrowings are included to compute a capitalization rate. US GAAP allows an entity to choose a mix of rates that best reflects the incremental interest cost that would not have been incurred if not for constructing the eligible asset.

With the exception of tax-exempt borrowings, US GAAP does not permit offsetting of interest income against interest expense to determine the amount to capitalize. The interest income can only be that which was earned on the tax-exempt borrowing. US GAAP does not permit capitalization of interest for inventories that are routinely manufactured or otherwise produced in large quantities on a repetitive basis (ASC 835-20-15-6[g]).

11 INTANGIBLE ASSETS

INTRODUCTION

Long-lived assets are those that will provide economic benefits to an entity for a number of future periods. Accounting standards regarding long-lived assets involve determination of the appropriate cost at which to record the assets initially, the amount at which to measure the assets at subsequent reporting dates, and the appropriate method(s) to be used to allocate the cost over the periods being benefited, if that is appropriate.

Long-lived nonfinancial assets may be classified into two basic types: tangible and intangible. Tangible assets have physical substance, while intangible assets either have no physical substance, or have a value that is not conveyed by what physical substance they do have. For example, the value of computer software is not reasonably measured by the cost of the diskettes or CDs on which these are contained.

The value of an intangible asset is a function of the rights or privileges that its ownership conveys to the business entity.

The accounting treatment of intangible assets is not yet in a fully settled and agreed mode. The nineteenth-century model from which we draw many of our financial reporting practices was developed when productive capacity was defined by manufacturing plant and equipment. In the postindustrial, knowledge-based economy in which the more developed nations operate today there is a different perspective on what constitutes value for a business. Intellectual property, such as patents and trade names, may be more vital than manufacturing capacity to modern growth companies, typified by Dell Computers, which is a selling organization with a brand name, and whose manufacturing is done by subcontractors in lower-cost nations.

The recognition and measurement of intangibles such as brand names is problematic because many brands are internally generated, over a number of years, and there is little or no historical cost to be recognized under IFRS or most national GAAP standards. Thus, the Dell brand does not appear on Dell's statement of financial position, nor does the Nestlé brand appear on Nestlé's statement of financial position. Concepts, designs, sales networks, brands, and processes are all important elements of what enables one company to succeed while another fails, but the theoretical support for representing them on the statement of financial position is at an early stage of development. For that matter, few companies even attempt to monitor such values for internal management purposes, so it is hardly surprising that the external reporting is still evolving.

We can draw a distinction between internally generated intangibles which are difficult to measure and thus to recognize in the statement of financial position, such as research and development assets and brands, and those that are purchased externally by an entity and therefore have a purchase price. While an intangible can certainly be bought individually, most intangibles arise from acquisitions of other companies, where a bundle of assets and liabilities are acquired.

In this area of activity, we can further distinguish between identifiable intangibles and unidentifiable ones.

Identifiable intangibles include patents, copyrights, brand names, customer lists, trade names, and other specific rights that typically can be conveyed by an owner without necessarily also transferring related physical assets. Goodwill, on the other hand, is a residual which incorporates all the intangibles that cannot be reliably measured separately, and is often analyzed as containing both these and benefits that the acquiring entity expected to gain from the synergies or other efficiencies arising from a business combination and cannot normally be transferred to a new owner without also selling the other assets and/or the operations of the business.

Accounting for goodwill is addressed in IFRS 3, and is discussed in Chapter 15 in this publication, in the context of business combinations. In this chapter we will address the recognition and measurement criteria for identifiable intangibles. This includes the criteria for separability and treatment of internally generated intangibles, such as research and development costs.

The subsequent measurement of intangibles depends upon whether they are considered to have indefinite economic value or a definable useful life. The standard on impairment of assets (IAS 36) pertains to both tangible and intangible long-lived assets. This chapter will consider the implications of this standard for the accounting for intangible, separately identifiable assets.

Sources of IFRS		
IFRS 3	*IAS* 23, 36, 38	*SIC* 32

SCOPE

IAS 38 applies to all reporting entities. It prescribes the accounting treatment for intangible assets, including development costs, but does not address intangible assets covered by other IFRS. For instance, deferred tax assets are covered under IAS 12; leases fall within the purview of IAS 17; goodwill arising in a business combination is dealt with by IFRS 3; assets arising from employee benefits are covered by IAS 19; and financial assets are defined by IAS 32 and covered by IAS 27, 28, 31, and 39. IAS 38 also does not apply to intangible assets arising in insurance companies from contracts with policyholders within the scope of IFRS 4, nor to exploration and evaluation assets in the extractive industries subject to IFRS 6, nor to intangible assets classified as held-for-sale under IFRS 5.

DEFINITIONS OF TERMS

Active market. A market in which all the following conditions exist:

1. The items traded in the market are homogeneous;
2. Willing buyers and sellers can normally be found at any time; and
3. Prices are available to the public.

Amortization. Systematic allocation of the depreciable amount of an intangible asset on a systematic basis over its useful life.

Asset. A resource that is

1. Controlled by an entity as a result of past events, and
2. From which future economic benefits are expected to flow to the entity.

Carrying amount. The amount at which an asset is recognized in the statement of financial position, net of any accumulated amortization and accumulated impairment losses thereon.

Cash-generating unit. The smallest identifiable group of assets that generates cash inflows from continuing use, largely independent of the cash inflows associated with other assets or groups of assets.

Corporate assets. Assets, excluding goodwill, that contribute to future cash flows of both the cash-generating unit under review for impairment and other cash generating units.

Cost. Amount of cash or cash equivalent paid or the fair value of other consideration given to acquire an asset at the time of its acquisition or construction or, where applicable, the amount attributed to that asset when initially recognized in accordance with the specific requirements of other IFRS (e.g., IFRS 2, *Share-Based Payment*).

Depreciable amount. Cost of an asset or the other amount that has been substituted for cost, less the residual value of the asset.

Development. The application of research findings or other knowledge to a plan or design for the production of new or substantially improved materials, devices, products, processes, systems, or services prior to commencement of commercial production or use. This should be distinguished from *research*, which must be expensed whereas development costs are capitalized.

Entity-specific value. Present value of the cash flows an entity expects to arise from the continuing use of an asset and from its disposal at the end of its useful life or expects to incur when settling a liability.

Fair value. Amount that would be obtained for an asset in an arm's-length exchange transaction between knowledgeable willing parties.

Goodwill. An intangible asset representing the future economic benefits arising from other assets acquired in a business combination that are not individually identified and separately recognized.

Impairment loss. The excess of the carrying amount of an asset over its recoverable amount.

Intangible assets. Identifiable nonmonetary assets without physical substance.

Monetary assets. Money held and assets to be received in fixed or determinable amounts of money. Examples are cash, accounts receivable, and notes receivable.

Net selling price. The amount that could be realized from the sale of an asset by means of an arm's-length transaction, less costs of disposal.

Nonmonetary transactions. Exchanges and nonreciprocal transfers that involve little or no monetary assets or liabilities.

Nonreciprocal transfer. Transfer of assets or services in one direction, either from an entity to its owners or another entity, or from owners or another entity to the entity. An entity's reacquisition of its outstanding stock is a nonreciprocal transfer.

Recoverable amount. The greater of an asset's or a cash-generating unit's fair value less costs to sell and its value in use.

Research. The original and planned investigation undertaken with the prospect of gaining new scientific or technical knowledge and understanding. This should be distinguished from *development*, since the latter is capitalized whereas research costs must be expensed.

Residual value. Estimated amount that an entity would currently obtain from disposal of the asset, net of estimated costs of disposal, if the asset were already of the age and in the condition expected at the end of its useful life.

Useful life. Period over which an asset is expected to be available for use by an entity; or the number of production or similar units expected to be obtained from the asset by an entity.

RECOGNITION AND MEASUREMENT

Background

Over the years, the role of intangible assets has grown ever more important for the operations and prosperity of many types of businesses, as the "knowledge-based" economy becomes more dominant. However, until recently, accounting standards have tended to give scant attention to, or ignore entirely, the appropriate means of reporting upon such assets.

IFRS first addressed accounting for intangibles in a thorough way with IAS 38, which was promulgated in 1998. Research and development costs had earlier been addressed by IAS 9 (issued in 1978) and goodwill arising from a business combination was dealt with by IAS 22 (issued in 1983).

IAS 38 is the first comprehensive standard on intangibles and it superseded IAS 9. It established recognition criteria, measurement bases, and disclosure requirements for intangible assets. The standard also stipulates that impairment testing for intangible assets (as specified by IAS 36) is to be undertaken on a regular basis. This is to ensure that only assets having *recoverable values* will be capitalized and carried forward to future periods as assets of the business.

IAS 38 was modified in 2004 to acknowledge that intangible assets could have indefinite useful lives. It had been the intent, when developing IAS 38, to stipulate that intangibles should have a maximum life of twenty years, but when this standard was finally approved, it included a rebuttable presumption that an intangible would have a life of no more than twenty years. The most recent amendment to IAS 38 removed the rebuttable presumption as to maximum economic life. IAS 38 now includes a list of intangibles that should normally be given separate recognition, and not merely grouped with goodwill, which is to denote only the unidentified intangible asset acquired in a business combination.

The IASB and FASB have placed on their long-term joint agendas a project on accounting for intangibles.

Nature of Intangible Assets

Identifiable intangible assets include patents, copyrights, licenses, customer lists, brand names, import quotas, computer software, marketing rights, and specialized know-how. These items have in common the fact that there is little or no tangible substance to them, and they have a useful life of greater than one year. In many but not all cases, the asset is separable; that is, it could be sold or otherwise disposed of without simultaneously disposing of or diminishing the value of other assets held.

Intangible assets are, by definition, assets that have no physical substance. However, there may be instances where intangibles also have some physical form. For example

- There may be tangible evidence of an asset's existence, such as a certificate indicating that a patent had been granted, but this does not constitute the asset itself;
- Some intangible assets may be contained in or on a physical substance such as a compact disc (in the case of computer software); and
- Identifiable assets that result from research and development activities are intangible assets because the tangible prototype or model is secondary to the knowledge that is the primary outcome of those activities.

In the case of assets that have both tangible and intangible elements, there may be uncertainty about whether classification should be as tangible or intangible assets. For example, the IASB has deliberately not specified whether mineral exploration and evaluation assets should be considered as tangible or intangible, but rather, in IFRS 6 (see Chapter 32) has established a requirement that a reporting entity consistently account for exploration and evaluation assets as either tangible or intangible.

As a rule of thumb, an asset that has both tangible and intangible elements should be classified as an intangible asset or a tangible asset based on the relative dominance or comparative significance of the tangible or the intangible components of the asset. For instance, computer software that is not an integral part of the related hardware equipment is treated as software (i.e., as an intangible asset). Conversely, certain computer software, such as the operating system, that is essential and an integral part of a computer, is treated as part of the hardware equipment (i.e., as property, plant, and equipment as opposed to an intangible asset).

Recognition Criteria

Identifiable intangible assets have much in common with tangible long-lived assets (property, plant, and equipment), and the accounting for them is accordingly very similar. Recognition depends on whether the *Framework* definition of an asset is satisfied. The key criteria for determining whether intangible assets are to be recognized are

1. Whether the intangible asset can be identified separately from other aspects of the business entity;
2. Whether the use of the intangible asset is controlled by the entity as a result of its past actions and events;
3. Whether future economic benefits can be expected to flow to the entity; and
4. Whether the cost of the asset can be measured reliably.

Identifiability. IAS 38 states that an intangible meets the identifiability requirement if

1. It is separable (i.e., is capable of being separated or divided from the entity and sold, transferred, licensed, rented or exchanged, either individually or together with a related contract, asset or liability); *or*

2. It arises from contractual or other legal rights, regardless of whether those rights are transferable or separable from the entity or from other rights and obligations.

The nature of intangibles is such that, as discussed above, many are not recognized at the time that they come into being. The costs of creating many intangibles are typically expensed year by year (e.g., as research costs or other period expenses) before it is clear that an asset has been created. The cost of internal intangible asset development cannot be capitalized retrospectively, and this means that such assets remain off the statement of financial position until and unless the entity is acquired by another entity. The acquiring entity has to allocate the acquisition price over the bundle of assets and liabilities acquired, irrespective of whether those assets and liabilities had been recognized in the acquired company's statement of financial position. For that reason, the notion of identifiability is significant in enabling an allocation of the cost of a business combination to be made.

The IASB prefers that as many individual assets be recognized as possible in a business acquisition, because the residual amount of unallocated acquisition cost is treated as goodwill, which provides less transparency to investors and other financial statement users. Furthermore, since goodwill is no longer subject to amortization, and its continued recognition—notwithstanding the impairment testing provision—can be indirectly justified by the creation of internally generated goodwill, improperly combining identifiable intangibles with goodwill can have long-term effects on the representational faithfulness of the entity's financial statements.

The revised IFRS 3, *Business Combinations,* issued in January 2008, introduced new approaches to measuring and recognizing the assets acquired and the liabilities assumed in business combinations. The standard reinforces the presumption that the acquirer should recognize, separately from goodwill, the acquisition-date fair value of an intangible asset acquired in a business combination if it meets the criteria provided in revised IAS 38. (This matter is discussed in detail in Chapter 15).

Inasmuch as the IASB advocates the recognition of the individual assets that may have been acquired in a business combination, it did acknowledge in the 2009 Improvements Project the difficulty that reporters may face in separating the intangible assets acquired. In this regard, the standard was amended to take into account that an intangible asset acquired in a business combination might be separable, but only together with a related contract or liability. In such cases, the acquirer recognizes the intangible asset separately from goodwill but together with the related item. The acquirer may recognize a group of complementary intangible assets as a single asset provided the individual assets in the group have similar useful lives. For example, the terms "brand" and "brand name" are often used as synonyms for trademarks and other marks. However, the former are general marketing terms that are typically used to refer to a group of complementary assets such as a trademark (or service mark) and its related trade name, formulas, recipes, and technological expertise.

Control. The provisions of IAS 38 require that an entity should be in a position to control the use of any intangible asset that is to be presented in the entity's statement of financial position. Control implies the power to both obtain future economic benefits from the asset as well as restrict others' access to those benefits. Normally, entities register patents, copyrights, etc. to ensure control over these intangible assets, although entities often have to engage in litigation to preserve that control.

A patent provides the registered owner (or licensee) the exclusive right to use the underlying product or process without any interference or infringement from others. In contrast with these, intangible assets arising from technical knowledge of staff, customer loyalty, long-term training benefits, etc., will have difficulty meeting this recognition criteria in spite of expected future economic benefits to be derived from them. This is due to the fact that the entity would find it impossible to fully control these resources or to prevent others from controlling them.

For instance, even if an entity expends considerable resources on training that will supposedly increase staff skills, the economic benefits from skilled staff cannot be controlled, since trained employees could leave their current employment and move on in their career to other employers. Hence, staff training expenditures, no matter how material in amount, do not qualify as an intangible asset.

Future economic benefits. Generally an asset is recognized only if it is *probable* that future economic benefits specifically associated therewith will flow to the reporting entity, and the cost of the asset can be *measured reliably*. Traditionally, the probability issue acts as an on-off switch. If the future cash flow is *more likely than not* to occur, the item is recognized, but if the cash flow is less likely to occur, nothing is recognized. However, under IFRS 3, where an intangible asset is acquired as part of a business combination, it is valued at fair value, and the fair value computation is affected by the probability that the future cash flow will occur. Under the fair value approach the recorded amount is determined as the present value of the cash flow, adjusted for the likelihood of receiving it, as well as for the time value of money. Even with a low probability of cash flow ultimately occurring, fair value will have some positive measure, and an asset will be recognized.

The IASB acknowledged in the IFRS 3 Basis for Conclusions that there is a discrepancy between this standard and the concept expressed in the *Framework*, but it took the view that this will most likely be resolved in due course by amending the *Framework*. In other words, there will be a more general movement to incorporating the concept of probability in the measurement of assets, instead of using likelihood as a recognition threshold criterion.

The future economic benefits envisaged by the standard may take the form of revenue from the sale of products or services, cost savings, or other benefits resulting from the use of the intangible asset by the entity. A good example of other benefits resulting from the use of the intangible asset is the use by an entity of a secret formula (which the entity has protected legally) that leads to reduced levels of competition in the marketplace, thus enhancing the prospects for substantial and profitable future sales and reduced expenditures on such matters as product development and advertising.

Measurement of the Cost of Intangibles

The conditions under which the intangible asset has been acquired will determine the measurement of its cost.

The cost of an intangible asset acquired separately is determined in a manner largely analogous to that for tangible long-lived assets as described in Chapter 9. Thus, the cost of a separately acquired intangible asset includes

1. Its purchase price, including legal and brokerage fees, import duties, and nonrefundable purchase taxes, after deducting trade discounts and rebates, and
2. Any directly attributable costs incurred to prepare the asset for its intended use. Directly attributable costs would include fully loaded labor costs, thus including employee benefits arising directly from bringing the asset to its intended use.

It would also include outside professional fees incurred in bringing the asset to its working condition, costs of testing whether the asset is functioning properly, and other incremental costs.

As with tangible assets, capitalization of costs ceases at the point when the intangible asset is ready to be placed in service in the manner intended by management. Any costs incurred in using or redeploying intangible assets are accordingly to be excluded from the cost of those assets. Thus, any costs incurred while the asset is capable of being used in the manner intended by management, but while it has yet to be placed into service, would be expensed, not capitalized. Similarly, initial operating losses, such as those incurred while demand for the asset's productive outputs is being developed, cannot be capitalized. Examples of expenditures that are not part of the cost of an intangible asset include costs of introducing a new product or service, costs of conducting business in a new location or with a new class of customers, and administration and other general overhead costs. On the other hand, further costs incurred for the purpose of improving the asset's level of performance would qualify for capitalization. In all these particulars, guidance under IAS 38 mirrors that under IAS 16.

According to IAS 38, the cost of an intangible asset acquired as part of a business combination is its fair value as at the date of acquisition. If the intangible asset can be freely traded in an active market, then the quoted market price is the best measurement of cost. If the intangible asset has no active market, then cost is determined based on the amount that the entity would have paid for the asset in an arm's-length transaction at the date of acquisition. If the cost of an intangible asset acquired as part of a business combination cannot be measured reliably, then that asset is not separately recognized, but rather, is included in goodwill. This fall-back position is to be used only when direct identification of the intangible asset's value cannot be accomplished.

If payment for an intangible asset is deferred beyond normal credit terms, its cost is the cash price equivalent. The difference between this amount and the total payments is recognized as financing cost over the period of credit unless it is capitalized in accordance with IAS 23. IAS 23, as amended in 2007, eliminated the former option of recognizing financing costs immediately as an expense, to the extent that they are directly attributable to the acquisition, construction, or production of a qualifying asset. (See Chapter 10.)

Intangibles acquired through an exchange of assets. In other situations, intangible assets may be acquired in exchange or partly *in exchange for other dissimilar intangible* or other assets. The same *commercial substance* rules under IAS 16 apply under IAS 38. If the exchange will affect the future cash flows of the entity, then it has commercial substance, and the acquired asset is recognized at its fair value, and the asset given up is also measured at fair value. Any difference between carrying amount of the asset(s) given up and those acquired will be given recognition as a gain or loss. However, if there is no commercial substance to the exchange, or the fair values cannot be measured reliably, then the value used is that of the asset given up.

Internally generated goodwill is not recognized as an intangible asset because it fails to meet recognition criteria including

- Reliable measurement of cost,
- An identity separate from other resources, and
- Control by the reporting entity.

In practice, accountants are often confronted with the reporting entity's desire to recognize internally generated goodwill based on the premise that at a certain point in time the market value of an entity exceeds the carrying amount of its identifiable net assets. However, IAS 38 categorically states that such differences cannot be considered to represent the cost of intangible assets *controlled by the entity,* and hence could not meet the criteria for recognition (i.e., capitalization) of such an asset in the accounts of the entity. Nonetheless, standard setters are concerned that when an entity tests a cash-generating unit for impairment, internally generated goodwill cannot be separated from acquired goodwill, and that it forms a cushion against impairment of acquired goodwill. In other words, when an entity has properly recognized goodwill (i.e., that acquired in a business combination), implicitly there is the likelihood that internally generated goodwill may well achieve recognition in later periods, to the extent that this offsets the impairment of goodwill.

Intangibles acquired at little or no cost by means of government grants. If the intangible is acquired without cost or by payment of nominal consideration, as by means of a government grant (e.g., when the government grants the right to operate a radio station) or similar means, and assuming the historical cost treatment is being utilized to account for these assets, obviously there will be little or no amount reflected as an asset. If the asset is important to the reporting entity's operations, however, it must be adequately disclosed in the notes to the financial statements.

If the revaluation method of accounting for the asset is used, as permitted under IAS 38, the fair value should be determined by reference to an active market. However, given the probable lack of an active market, since government grants are virtually never transferable, it is unlikely that this situation will be encountered. If an active market does not exist for this type of an intangible asset, the entity must recognize the asset at cost. Cost would include those that are directly attributable to preparing the asset for its intended use. Government grants, the accounting for which is under review, are addressed in Chapter 21.

Internally Generated Intangibles other than Goodwill

In many instances, intangibles are generated internally by an entity, rather than being acquired via a business combination or some other acquisitions. Because of the nature of intangibles, the measurement of the cost (i.e., the initial amounts at which these could be recognized as assets) is constrained by the fact that many of the costs have already been expensed by the time the entity is able to determine that an asset has indeed been created. For example, when launching a new magazine, an entity may have to operate the magazine at a loss in its early years, expensing large promotional and other costs which all flow through profit or loss, before such time as the magazine can be determined to have become established, and have branding that might be taken to represent an intangible asset. At the point the brand is determined to be an asset, all the costs of creating it have already been expensed, and no retrospective adjustment is allowed to create a recognized asset.

IAS 38 provides that internally generated intangible assets are to be capitalized and amortized over the projected period of economic utility, provided that certain criteria are met.

Expenditures pertaining to the creation of intangible assets are to be classified alternatively as being indicative of, or analogous to, either research activity or development activity. Per IAS 38,

1. Costs incurred in the *research* phase are expensed immediately; and
2. If costs incurred in the *development* phase meet the recognition criteria for an intangible asset, such costs should be capitalized. However, once costs have been expensed during the development phase, they cannot later be capitalized.

In practice, distinguishing research-like expenditures from development-like expenditures might not be easily accomplished. This would be especially true in the case of intangibles for which the measurement of economic benefits cannot be accomplished in anything approximating a direct manner. Assets such as brand names, mastheads, and customer lists can prove quite resistant to such direct observation of value (although in many industries there are rules of thumb, such as the notion that a customer list in the securities brokerage business is worth $1,500 per name, implying the amount of promotional costs a purchaser of a customer list could avoid incurring itself).

Thus, entities may incur certain expenditures in order to enhance brand names, such as engaging in image-advertising campaigns, but these costs will also have ancillary benefits, such as promoting specific products that are being sold currently, and possibly even enhancing employee morale and performance. While it may be argued that the expenditures create or add to an intangible asset, as a practical matter it would be difficult to determine what portion of the expenditures relate to which achievement, and to ascertain how much, if any, of the cost may be capitalized as part of brand names. Thus, it is considered to be unlikely that threshold criteria for recognition can be met in such a case. For this reason IAS 38 has specifically disallowed the capitalization of internally generated assets like brands, mastheads, publishing titles, customer lists, and items similar in substance to these.

Apart from the prohibited items, however, IAS 38 permits recognition of internally created intangible assets to the extent the expenditures can be analogized to the development phase of a research and development program. Thus, internally developed patents, copyrights, trademarks, franchises, and other assets will be recognized at the cost of creation, exclusive of costs which would be analogous to research, as further explained in the following paragraphs. The Basis for Conclusion to IAS 38 notes that "some view these requirements and guidance as being too restrictive and arbitrary" and that they reflect the standard setter's interpretation of the recognition criteria, but it agrees that they reflect the fact that it is difficult in practice to determine whether there is an internally generated asset separate from internally generated goodwill.

When an internally generated intangible asset meets the recognition criteria, the cost is determined using the same principles as for an acquired tangible asset. Thus, cost comprises all costs directly attributable to creating, producing, and preparing the asset for its intended use. IAS 38 closely mirrors IAS 16 with regard to elements of cost that may be considered as part of the asset, and the need to recognize the cash equivalent price when the acquisition transaction provides for deferred payment terms. As with self-constructed tangible assets, elements of profit must be eliminated from amounts capitalized, but incremental administrative and other overhead costs can be allocated to the intangible and included in the asset's cost provided these can be directly attributed to preparing the asset for use. Initial operating losses, on the other hand, cannot be deferred by being added to the cost of the intangible, but rather must be expensed as incurred.

The standard takes this view based on the premise that an entity cannot demonstrate that the expenditure incurred in the research phase will generate probable future economic benefits, and consequently, that an intangible asset has been created (therefore, such expenditure should be expensed). Examples of research activities include: activities aimed at obtaining new knowledge; the search for, evaluation, and final selection of applications of research findings; and the search for and formulation of alternatives for new and improved systems, etc.

The standard recognizes that the development stage is further advanced towards ultimate commercial exploitation of the product or service being created than is the research stage. It acknowledges that an entity can possibly, in certain cases, identify an intangible asset and demonstrate that this asset will probably generate future economic benefits for the organization. Accordingly, IAS 38 allows recognition of an intangible asset during the development phase, provided the entity can demonstrate *all* of the following:

- Technical feasibility of completing the intangible asset so that it will be available for use or sale;
- Its intention to complete the intangible asset and either use it or sell it;
- Its ability to use or sell the intangible asset;

- The mechanism by which the intangible will generate probable future economic benefits;
- The availability of adequate technical, financial and other resources to complete the development and to use or sell the intangible asset; and
- The entity's ability to reliably measure the expenditure attributable to the intangible asset during its development.

Examples of development activities include: the design and testing of preproduction models; design of tools, jigs, molds, and dies; design of a pilot plant which is not otherwise commercially feasible; design and testing of a preferred alternative for new and improved systems, etc.

Recognition of internally generated computer software costs. The recognition of computer software costs poses several questions.

1. In the case of a company developing software programs for sale, should the costs incurred in developing the software be expensed, or should the costs be capitalized and amortized?
2. Is the treatment for developing software programs different if the program is to be used for in-house applications only?
3. In the case of purchased software, should the cost of the software be capitalized as a tangible asset or as an intangible asset, or should it be expensed fully and immediately?

In view of IAS 38's provisions the position can be clarified as follows:

1. In the case of a software-developing company, the costs incurred in the development of software programs are research and development costs. Accordingly, all expenses incurred in the research phase would be expensed. That is, all expenses incurred before *technological feasibility* for the product has been established should be expensed. The reporting entity would have to demonstrate both technological feasibility and a probability of its commercial success. Technological feasibility would be established if the entity has completed a detailed program design or working model. The entity should have completed the planning, designing, coding, and testing activities and established that the product can be successfully produced. Apart from being capable of production, the entity should demonstrate that it has the intention and ability to use or sell the program. Action taken to obtain control over the program in the form of copyrights or patents would support capitalization of these costs. At this stage the software program would be able to meet the criteria of identifiability, control, and future economic benefits, and can thus be capitalized and amortized as an intangible asset.
2. In the case of software internally developed for in-house use—for example, a computerized payroll program developed by the reporting entity itself—the accounting approach would be different. While the program developed may have some utility to the entity itself, it would be difficult to demonstrate how the program would generate future economic benefits to the entity. Also, in the absence of any legal rights to control the program or to prevent others from using it, the recognition criteria would not be met. Further, the cost proposed to be capitalized should be recoverable. In view of the impairment test prescribed by the standard, the carrying amount of the asset may not be recoverable and would accordingly have to be adjusted. Considering the above facts, such costs may need to be expensed.

3. In the case of purchased software, the treatment could differ and would need to be evaluated on a case-by-case basis. Software purchased for sale would be treated as inventory. However, software held for licensing or rental to others should be recognized as an intangible asset. On the other hand, cost of software purchased by an entity for its own use and which is integral to the hardware (because without that software the equipment cannot operate), would be treated as part of cost of the hardware and capitalized as property, plant, or equipment. Thus, the cost of an operating system purchased for an in-house computer, or cost of software purchased for computer-controlled machine tool, is treated as part of the related hardware.

The costs of other software programs should be treated as intangible assets (as opposed to being capitalized along with the related hardware), as they are not an integral part of the hardware. For example, the cost of payroll or inventory software (purchased) may be treated as an intangible asset provided it meets the capitalization criteria under IAS 38. In practice, the conservative approach would be to expense such costs as they are incurred, since their ability to generate future economic benefits will always be questionable. If the costs are capitalized, useful lives should be conservatively estimated (i.e., kept brief) because of the well-known risk of technological obsolescence.

Example of software developed for internal use

The Hy-Tech Services Corporation employs researchers based in countries around the world. Employee time is the basis upon which charges to many customers are made. The geographically dispersed nature of its operations makes it extremely difficult for the payroll staff to collect time records, so the management team authorizes the design of an in-house, Web-based timekeeping system. The project team incurs the following costs:

Cost type	Charged to expense	Capitalized
Concept design	€ 2,500	
Evaluation of design alternatives	3,700	
Determination of required technology	8,100	
Final selection of alternatives	1,400	
Software design		€ 28,000
Software coding		42,000
Quality assurance testing		30,000
Data conversion costs	3,900	
Training	14,000	
Overhead allocation	6,900	
General and administrative costs	11,200	
Ongoing maintenance costs	6,000	
Totals	€57,700	€100,000

Thus, the total capitalized cost of this development project is €100,000. The estimated useful life of the timekeeping system is five years. As soon as all testing is completed, Hy-Tech's controller begins amortizing using a monthly charge of €1,666.67. The calculation is as follows:

€100,000 capitalized cost ÷ 60 months = €1,666.67 amortization charge

Once operational, management elects to construct another module for the system that issues an e-mail reminder for employees to complete their timesheets. This represents significant added functionality, so the design cost can be capitalized. The following costs are incurred:

Labor type	Labor cost	Payroll taxes	Benefits	Total cost
Software developers	€11,000	€ 842	€1,870	€13,712
Quality assurance testers	7,000	536	1,190	8,726
Totals	€18,000	€1,378	€3,060	€22,438

The full €22,438 amount of these costs can be capitalized. By the time this additional work is completed, the original system has been in operation for one year, thereby reducing the amortization period for the new module to four years. The calculation of the monthly straight-line amortization follows:

$$\text{€22,438 capitalized cost} \div 48 \text{ months} = \text{€467.46 amortization charge}$$

The Hy-Tech management then authorizes the development of an additional module that allows employees to enter time data into the system from their cell phones using text messaging. Despite successfully passing through the concept design stage, the development team cannot resolve interface problems on a timely basis. Management elects to shut down the development project, requiring all of the €13,000 of programming and testing costs to be expensed in the current period.

Costs Not Satisfying the IAS 38 Recognition Criteria

The standard has specifically provided that expenditures incurred for nonfinancial intangible assets should be recognized as an expense unless

1. It relates to an intangible asset dealt with in another IFRS;
2. The cost forms part of the cost of an intangible asset that meets the recognition criteria prescribed by IAS 38; or
3. It is acquired in a business combination and cannot be recognized as an identifiable intangible asset. In this case, this expenditure should form part of the amount attributable to goodwill as at the date of acquisition.

As a consequence of applying the above criteria, the following costs are expensed as they are incurred:

- Research costs;
- Preopening costs for a new facility or business, and plant start-up costs incurred during a period prior to full-scale production or operation, unless these costs are capitalized as part of the cost of an item of property, plant, and equipment;
- Organization costs such as legal and secretarial costs, which are typically incurred in establishing a legal entity;
- Training costs involved in operating a business or a product line;
- Advertising and related costs;
- Relocation, restructuring, and other costs involved in organizing a business or product line;
- Customer lists, brands, mastheads, and publishing titles that are internally generated.

In some countries entities have previously been allowed to defer and amortize setup costs and preoperating costs on the premise that benefits from them flow to the entity over future periods as well. IAS 38 does not condone this view.

The criteria for recognition of intangible assets as provided in IAS 38 are rather stringent, and many entities will find that expenditures either to acquire or to develop intangible assets will fail the test for capitalization. In such instances, all these costs must be expensed as period costs when incurred. Furthermore, once expensed, these costs cannot be resurrected and capitalized in a later period, even if the conditions for such treatment are later met. This is not meant, however, to preclude correction of an error made in an earlier period if the conditions for capitalization were met but interpreted incorrectly by the reporting entity at that time.

Improvements to IFRS published by the IASB in May 2008 included two amendments to IAS 38. One improvement clarifies that certain expenditures are recognized as an expense when the entity either has access to the goods or has received the services. Examples of expenditures that are recognized as an expense when incurred include research costs, expenditure on start-up activities, training activities, advertising and promotional activities, and on relocating or reorganizing part or all of an entity. Advertising and promotional activities now specifically include mail-order catalogues. Logically, these expenditures have difficult-to-measure future economic benefits (e.g., advertising), or are not controlled by the reporting entity (e.g., training), and therefore do not meet the threshold conditions for recognition as assets. For some entities this amendment may result in expenditures being recognized as an expense earlier than in the past.

In addition, a second improvement to IAS 38 removed the reference to the use of anything other than the straight-line method of amortization being rare, and makes it clear that entities may use the unit of production method of amortization even if it results in a lower amount of accumulated amortization than does the straight-line method. This would specifically apply to some service concession arrangements, where an intangible asset for the right to charge users for public service is created. Consequently, entities will have more flexibility as to the method of amortization of intangible assets and will need to evaluate a pattern of future benefits arising from those assets when selecting the method.

Improvements to IFRS made in 2009 included several clarifying revisions to IAS 38. One group of wording changes was made to reflect clearly the IASB's decisions on the accounting for intangible assets acquired in a business combination, as set forth by revised IFRS 3 (discussed in Chapter 15), which was also briefly mentioned earlier in this chapter.

The other changes were to clarify the description of valuation techniques commonly used to measure intangible assets at fair value when assets are not traded in an active market. The IASB also decided that these amendments should be applied prospectively, notwithstanding the general retrospective prescription under IAS 8, because retrospective application might require some entities to remeasure fair values associated with previous transactions, a process that inadvertently could involve the use of hindsight in those circumstances. This matter is addressed below.

Subsequently Incurred Costs

Under the provisions of IAS 38, the capitalization of any subsequent costs incurred on recognized intangible assets are subject to the same recognition criteria as initial costs. In practice, capitalization of subsequent expenditure is often difficult to justify. This is because the nature of an intangible asset is such that, in many cases, it is not possible to determine whether subsequent costs are likely to enhance the specific economic benefits that will flow to the entity from those assets. Provided they meet the recognition criteria for intangible assets, any subsequent expenditure on an intangible after its purchase or its completion should be capitalized along with its cost. The following example should help to illustrate this point better.

Example

An entity is developing a new product. Costs incurred by the R&D department in 2011 on the "research phase" amounted to €200,000. In 2012, technical and commercial feasibility of the product was established. Costs incurred in 2012 were €20,000 personnel costs and €15,000 legal fees to register the patent. In 2012, the entity incurred €30,000 to successfully defend a legal suit to protect the patent. The entity would account for these costs as follows:

- Research and development costs incurred in 2011, amounting to €200,000, should be expensed, as they do not meet the recognition criteria for intangible assets. The costs do not result in an identifiable asset capable of generating future economic benefits.
- Personnel and legal costs incurred in 2012, amounting to €35,000, would be capitalized as patents. The company has established technical and commercial feasibility of the product, as well as obtained control over the use of the asset. The standard specifically prohibits the reinstatement of costs previously recognized as an expense. Thus €200,000, recognized as an expense in the previous financial statements, cannot be reinstated and capitalized.
- Legal costs of €30,000 incurred in 2012 to defend the entity in a patent lawsuit should be expensed. These could be considered as expenses incurred to maintain the asset at its originally assessed standard of performance, would not meet the recognition criteria under IAS 38.
- Alternatively, if the entity were to lose the patent lawsuit, then the useful life and the recoverable amount of the intangible asset would be in question. The entity would be required to provide for any impairment loss, and in all probability, even to fully write off the intangible asset. What is required must be determined by the facts of the specific situation.

Measurement subsequent to Initial Recognition

IAS 38 acknowledges the validity of two alternative measurement bases: the cost model and the revaluation model. This is entirely comparable to what is prescribed under IAS 16 relative to tangible long-lived assets.

Cost model. After initial recognition, an intangible asset should be carried at its cost less any accumulated amortization and any accumulated impairment losses.

Revaluation model. As with tangible assets, the standard for intangibles permits revaluation subsequent to original acquisition, with the asset being written up to fair value. Inasmuch as most of the particulars of IAS 38 follow IAS 16 to the letter, and were described in detail in Chapter 9, these will not be repeated here. The unique features of IAS 38 are as follows:

1. If the intangibles were not initially recognized (i.e., they were expensed rather than capitalized) it would not be possible to later recognize them at fair value.
2. Deriving fair value by applying a present value concept to projected cash flows (a technique that can be used in the case of tangible assets under IAS 16) is deemed to be too unreliable in the realm of intangibles, primarily because it would tend to commingle the impact of identifiable assets and goodwill. Accordingly, fair value of an intangible asset should *only* be determined by reference to an active market in that type of intangible asset. Active markets providing meaningful data are not expected to exist for such unique assets as patents and trademarks, and thus it is presumed that revaluation will not be applied to these types of assets in the normal course of business. As a consequence, the standard effectively restricts revaluation of intangible assets to freely tradable intangible assets.

As with the rules pertaining to property, plant, and equipment under IAS 16, if some intangible assets in a given class are subjected to revaluation, all the assets in that class should be consistently accounted for unless fair value information is not or ceases to be available. Also in common with the requirements for tangible fixed assets, IAS 38 requires that revaluations be recognized in other comprehensive income and accumulated in equity in the revaluation surplus account for that asset, except to the extent that previous impairments had been recognized by a charge against profit, in which case the recovery would also be recognized in profit. If recovery is recognized in profit, any revaluation above what the carrying amount would have been in the absence of the impairment is to be recognized in other comprehensive income.

Example of revaluation of intangible assets

A patent right is acquired July 1, 2010, for €250,000; while it has a legal life of 15 years, due to rapidly changing technology, management estimates a useful life of only five years. Straight-line amortization will be used. At January 1, 2011, management is uncertain that the process can actually be made economically feasible, and decides to write down the patent to an estimated market value of €75,000. Amortization will be taken over three years from that point. On January 1, 2013, having perfected the related production process, the asset is now appraised at a sound value of €300,000. Furthermore, the estimated useful life is now believed to be six more years. The entries to reflect these events are as follows:

7/1/10	Patent	250,000	
	Cash, etc.		250,000
12/31/10	Amortization expense	25,000	
	Patent		25,000
1/1/11	Loss from asset impairment	150,000	
	Patent		150,000
12/31/11	Amortization expense	25,000	
	Patent		25,000
12/31/12	Amortization expense	25,000	
	Patent		25,000
1/1/13	Patent	275,000	
	Gain on asset value recovery		100,000
	Other comprehensive income		175,000

Certain of the entries in the foregoing example will be explained further. The entry at year-end 2010 is to record amortization based on original cost, since there had been no revaluations through that time; only a half-year amortization is provided [(€250,000/5) × 1/2]. On January 1, 2011, the impairment is recorded by writing down the asset to the estimated value of €75,000, which necessitates a €150,000 charge against profit (carrying amount, €225,000, less fair value, €75,000).

In 2011 and 2012, amortization must be provided on the new lower value recorded at the beginning of 2011; furthermore, since the new estimated life was three years from January 2011, annual amortization will be €25,000.

As of January 1, 2013, the carrying amount of the patent is €25,000; had the January 2011 revaluation not been made, the carrying amount would have been €125,000 (€250,000 original cost, less two-and-one-half years amortization versus an original estimated life of five years). The new appraised value is €300,000, which will fully recover the earlier write-down and add even more asset value than the originally recognized cost. Under the guidance of IAS 38, the recovery of €100,000 that had been charged to expense should be recognized as profit; the excess will be recognized in other comprehensive income and increases the revaluation surplus for the asset in equity.

Improvements made in 2009 include changes to IAS 38 to address situations where no active market exists for an intangible asset, so that its fair value must be assessed as the amount that the entity would have paid for the asset, at the acquisition date, in an arm's-length transaction between knowledgeable and willing parties, on the basis of the best information available. According to IAS 38, in determining this amount, the reporting entity is to consider the outcome of recent transactions for similar assets. The 2009 amendment adds an example of how an entity may, in making such a determination, apply multiples reflecting current market transactions to factors that drive the profitability of the asset (such as revenue, operating profit or earnings before interest, tax, depreciation and amortization).

The amendment provides further guidance for entities that are involved in the purchase and sale of intangible assets, which entities will possibly have developed techniques for estimating their fair values indirectly. These techniques may be used for initial measurement of an intangible asset acquired in a business combination if their objective is to estimate fair value and if they reflect current transactions and practices in the industry to which the asset belongs. As specified by the 2009 improvements, these techniques may include discounting estimated future net cash flows from the asset, or estimating the costs the entity avoids by owning the intangible asset and thus not needing to either (1) license it from another party in an arm's-length transaction (as in the "relief from royalty" approach, using discounted net cash flows) or (2) recreate or replace it (as in the cost approach).

These changes are to be applied prospectively for annual periods beginning on or after July 1, 2009. Earlier application is permitted, although, if applied for an earlier period, the reporting entity must disclose that fact.

Development costs as a special case. Development costs pose a special problem in terms of the application of the revaluation method under IAS 38. In general, it will not be possible to obtain fair value data from active markets, as is required by IAS 38. Accordingly, the expectation is that the cost method will be almost universally applied for development costs.

Example of development cost capitalization

Assume that Creative, Incorporated incurs substantial research and development costs for the invention of new products, many of which are brought to market successfully. In particular, Creative has incurred costs during 2010 amounting to €750,000, relative to a new manufacturing process. Of these costs, €600,000 was incurred prior to December 1, 2010. As of December 31 the viability of the new process was still not known, although testing had been conducted on December 1. In fact, results were not conclusively known until February 15, 2011, after another €75,000 in costs was incurred post–January 1. Creative, Incorporated's financial statements for 2010 were issued February 10, 2011, and the full €750,000 in research and development costs was expensed, since it was not yet known whether a portion of these qualified as development costs under IAS 38. When it is learned that feasibility had, in fact, been shown as of December 1, Creative management asks to restore the €150,000 of post–December 1 costs as a development asset. Under IAS 38 this is prohibited. However, the 2011 costs (€75,000 thus far) would qualify for capitalization, in all likelihood, based on the facts known.

If, however, it is determined that fair value information derived from active markets is indeed available, and the entity desires to apply the revaluation method of accounting to development costs, then it will be necessary to perform revaluations on a regular basis, such that at any reporting date the carrying amounts are not materially different from the current fair values. From a mechanical perspective, the adjustment to fair value can be accomplished either by "grossing up" the cost and the accumulated amortization accounts proportionally, or by netting the accumulated amortization, prior to revaluation, against the asset account and then restating the asset to the net fair value as of the revaluation date. In either case, the net effect of the upward revaluation will be recognized in other comprehensive income and accumulated in equity; the only exception would be when an upward revaluation is in effect a reversal of a previously recognized impairment which was reported as a charge against profit or a revaluation decrease (reversal or a yet earlier upward adjustment) which was reflected in profit or loss.

The accounting for revaluations is illustrated below.

Example of accounting for revaluation of development cost

Assume Breakthrough, Inc. has accumulated development costs that meet the criteria for capitalization at December 31, 2010, amounting to €39,000. It is estimated that the useful life of this intangible asset will be six years; accordingly, amortization of €6,500 per year is anticipated. Breakthrough uses the allowed alternative method of accounting for its long-lived tangible and intangible assets. At December 31, 2012, it obtains market information regarding the then-current fair value of this intangible asset, which suggests a current fair value of these development costs is €40,000; the estimated useful life, however, has not changed. There are two ways to apply IAS 38: the asset and accumulated amortization can be "grossed up" to reflect the new fair value information, or the asset can be restated on a "net" basis. These are both illustrated below. For both illustrations, the carrying amount (amortized cost) immediately prior to the revaluation is €39,000 – (2 × €6,500) = €26,000. The net upward revaluation is given by the difference between fair value and carrying amount, or €40,000 – €26,000 = €14,000.

If the "gross up" method is used: Since the fair value after two years of the six-year useful life have already elapsed is found to be €40,000, the gross fair value must be 6/4 × €40,000 = €60,000. The entries to record this would be as follows:

Development cost (asset)	21,000	
Accumulated amortization—development cost		7,000
Other comprehensive income		14,000

If the "netting" method is used: Under this variant, the accumulated amortization as of the date of the revaluation is eliminated against the asset account, which is then adjusted to reflect the net fair value.

Accumulated amortization—development cost	13,000	
Development cost (asset)		13,000
Development cost (asset)	14,000	
Other comprehensive income—revaluation surplus		14,000

The existing balance in other comprehensive income is closed at the end of the year and its balance accumulated in equity in the revaluation surplus account.

Amortization Period

IAS 38 requires the entity to determine whether an intangible has a finite or indefinite useful life. An indefinite future life means that there is no foreseeable limit on the period during which the asset is expected to generate future cash flows. The standard lists a number of factors to be taken into account:

1. The expected usage by the entity;
2. Typical product life cycles for the asset;
3. Technical, technological, commercial or other types of obsolescence;
4. The stability of the industry in which the asset operates;
5. Expected actions by competitors;
6. The level of maintenance expenditures required to generate the future economic benefits, and the company's ability and intention to reach such a level;
7. The period of control over the asset and legal or similar limits on the use of the asset;
8. Whether the useful life of the asset is dependent on the useful life of other assets.

Assets having a finite useful life must be amortized over that useful life, and this may be done in any of the usual ways (pro rata over time, over units of production, etc.). If control over the future economic benefits from an intangible asset is achieved through legal rights for a finite period, then the useful life of the intangible asset should not exceed the period of legal rights, unless the legal rights are renewable and the renewal is a virtual certainty. Thus, as a practical matter, the shorter legal life will set the upper limit for an amortization period in most cases.

The amortization method used should reflect the pattern in which the economic benefits of the asset are consumed by the entity. Amortization should commence when the asset is available for use and the amortization charge for each period should be recognized as an expense unless it is included in the carrying amount of another asset (e.g., inventory). Intangible assets may be amortized by the same systematic and rational methods that are used to depreciate property, plant, and equipment. Thus, IAS 38 would seemingly permit straight-line, diminishing balance, and units of production methods. If a method other than straight-line is used, it must accurately mirror the expiration of the asset's economic service potential.

IAS 38 offers several examples of how useful life of intangibles is to be assessed. These include the following types of assets:

Customer lists. Care is urged to ensure that amortization is only over the expected useful life of the acquired list, ignoring the extended life that may be created as the acquirer adds to the list by virtue of its own efforts and costs, after acquisition. In many instances the initial, purchased list will erode in value rather quickly, since contacts become obsolete as customers migrate to other vendors, leave business, and so forth. These assets must be constantly refreshed, and that will involve expenditures by the acquirer of the original list (and whether those costs justify capitalization and amortization is a separate issue). For example, the acquired list might have a useful economic life of only two years (i.e., without additional expenditures, the value will be fully consumed over that time horizon). Two years would be the amortization period, therefore.

Patents. While a patent has a legal life (depending on jurisdiction of issuance) of as long as several decades, realistically, due to evolving technology and end-product obsolescence or changing customer tastes and preferences, the useful economic life may be much less. IAS 38 offers an example of a patent having a 15-year remaining life and a firm offer to acquire by a third party in five years, at a fixed fraction of the original acquirer's cost. In such a situation (which is probably unusual, however), amortization of the fraction not to be recovered in the subsequent sale, over a 5-year period, would be appropriate.

In other situations, it would be necessary to estimate the economic life of the patent and amortize the entire cost, in the absence of any firmly established residual value, over that period. It should be noted that there is increasing activity involving the monetizing of intellectual property values, including via the packaging of groups of patents and transferring them to special-purpose entities which then license them to third-party licensees. This shows promise of becoming an important way for patent holders to reap greater benefits from existing pools of patents held by them, but is in its infancy at this time and future success cannot be reliably predicted. Amortization of existing acquired patents or other intellectual property (intangible assets) should not be based on highly speculative values that might be obtained from such arrangements.

Additionally, whatever lives are assigned to patents for amortization purposes, these should regularly be reconsidered. As necessary, changes in useful lives should be implemented, which would be changes in estimate affecting current and future periods' amortization only, unless an accounting error had previously been made.

Copyrights. In many jurisdictions copyrights now have very lengthy terms, but for most materials so protected the actual useful lives will be very much shorter, sometimes only a year or two.

Renewable license rights. In many situations the entity may acquire license rights, such as broadcasting of radio or television signals, which technically expire after a fixed term but which are essentially renewable with little or no cost incurred as long as minimum performance criteria are met. If there is adequate evidence to demonstrate that this description is accurate and that the reporting entity has indeed been able, previously, to successfully accomplish this, then the intangible will be deemed to have an indefinite life and not be subjected to periodic amortization. However, this makes it more vital that impairment be regularly reviewed, since even if control of the rights remains with the reporting entity, changes in technology or consumer demand may serve to diminish the value of that asset. If impaired, a charge against earnings must be recognized, with the remaining unimpaired cost (if any) continuing to be recognized as an indefinite life intangible.

Similar actions would be warranted in the case of airline route authority. If readily renewable, without limitation, provided that minimal regulations are complied with (such as maintaining airport terminal space in a prescribed manner), the standard suggests that this be treated as an indefinite-life intangible. Annual impairment testing would be required, as with all indefinite-life intangibles (more often if there is any indication of impairment).

IAS 38 notes that a change in the governmental licensing regime may require a change in how these are accounted for. It cites an example of a change that ends perfunctory renewal and substitutes public auctions for the rights at each former renewal date. In such an instance, the reporting entity can no longer presume to have any right to continue after expiration of the current license, and must amortize its cost over the remaining term.

Residual Value

Tangible assets often have a positive residual value before considering the disposal costs because tangible assets can generally be sold, at least, for scrap, or possibly can be transferred to another user that has less need for or ability to afford new assets of that type. Intangibles, on the other hand, often have little or no residual worth. Accordingly, IAS 38 requires that a zero residual value be presumed unless an accurate measure of residual value is possible. Thus, the residual value is presumed to be zero *unless*

- There is a commitment by a third party to acquire the asset at the end of its useful life; *or*
- There is an active market for that type of intangible asset, and residual value can be measured reliably by reference to that market and it is probable that such a market will exist at the end of the useful life.

IAS 38 specifies that the residual value of an intangible asset is the estimated net amount that the reporting entity currently expects to obtain from disposal of the asset at the end of its useful life, after deducting the estimated costs of disposal, if the asset were of the age and in the condition expected at the end of its estimated useful life. Changes in estimated selling prices or other variables that occur over the expected period of use of the asset are not to be included in the estimated residual value, since this would result in the recognition of projected future holding gains over the life of the asset (via reduced amortization that would be the consequence of a higher estimated residual value).

Residual value is to be assessed at the end of each reporting period. Any change to the estimated residual, other than that resulting from impairment (accounted for under IAS 36) is to be accounted for prospectively, by varying future periodic amortization. Similarly, any change in amortization method (e.g., from accelerated to straight-line), based on an updated understanding of the pattern of future usage and economic benefits to be reaped therefrom, is dealt with as a change in estimate, again to be reflected only through changes in future periodic charges for amortization.

Periodic review of useful life assumptions and amortization methods employed. As for tangible assets accounted for in conformity with IAS 16, the standard on intangibles requires that the amortization period be reconsidered at the end of each reporting period, and that the method of amortization also be reviewed at similar intervals. There is the expectation that due to their nature intangibles are more likely to require revisions to one or both of these judgments. In either case, a change would be accounted for as a change in estimate, affecting current and future periods' reported earnings but not requiring restatement of previously reported periods.

Intangibles being accounted for as having an indefinite life must furthermore be reassessed periodically, as management plans and expectations almost inevitably vary over time. For example, a trademarked product, despite having wide consumer recognition and acceptance, can become irrelevant as tastes and preferences alter, and a limited horizon, perhaps a very short one, may emerge with little warning. Business history is littered with formerly valuable franchises that, for whatever reason—including management missteps become valueless.

Impairment Losses

Where an asset is determined to have an indefinite useful life, the entity must conduct impairment tests annually, as well as whenever there is an indication that the intangible may be impaired. Furthermore, the presumption that the asset has an indefinite life must also be reviewed.

The impairment of intangible assets other than goodwill (such as patents, copyrights, trade names, customer lists, and franchise rights) should be considered in precisely the same way that long-lived tangible assets are dealt with. The impairment loss under IAS 36 is the amount by which carrying amount exceeds recoverable amount. Carrying amount must be compared to recoverable amount (the greater of fair value less costs to sell or value in use) when there are indications that an impairment may have been suffered. Net selling price is the price of an asset in an active market less disposal costs, and value in use is the present value of estimated future cash flows expected to arise from the continuing use of an asset and from its disposal.

IAS 36 permits reversals of impairment losses on assets other than goodwill under defined conditions. The effects of impairment recognitions and reversals will be reflected in profit or loss, if the intangible assets in question are being accounted for in accordance with the cost method.

On the other hand, if the revaluation method of accounting for intangible assets is followed (use of which is possible only if strict criteria can be met), impairments will normally be recognized in other comprehensive income to the extent that revaluation surplus exists, and only to the extent that the loss exceeds previously recognized valuation surplus will the impairment loss be reported as a charge against profit. Recoveries are handled consistent with the method by which impairments were reported, in a manner entirely analogous to the explanation in Chapter 9 dealing with impairments of property, plant and equipment.

Unlike other intangible assets that are individually identifiable, goodwill is amorphous and cannot exist, from a financial reporting perspective, apart from the tangible and identifiable intangible assets with which it was acquired and remains associated. Thus, a direct evaluation of the recoverable amount of goodwill is not actually feasible. Accordingly, IAS 36 requires that goodwill be combined with other assets which together define a cash-generating unit, and that an evaluation of any potential impairment be conducted on an aggregate basis annually. A cash-generating unit (CGU) is the smallest identifiable group of assets that generates cash inflows that are largely independent of the cash inflows from other assets or groups of assets.

A more detailed consideration of goodwill is presented in Chapter 15.

Improvements to IFRS issued in 2009 amended the requirements for allocating goodwill to cash-generating units as described in IAS 36, since the definition of operating segments introduced in IFRS 8 affects the determination of the largest unit permitted for goodwill impairment testing in IAS 36. For the purpose of impairment testing, goodwill acquired in a business combination should, from the acquisition date, be allocated to each of the acquirer's cash-generating unit (or groups of cash-generating units) that is expected to benefit from synergies resulting from combination, irrespective of whether other assets or liabilities are allocated to this unit (or units).

Each cash-generating unit should

1. Represent the lowest level of the entity at which management monitors goodwill (which should be the same as the lowest level of operating segments at which the chief operating decision maker regularly reviews operating results in accordance with IFRS 8), and
2. Not be larger than the operating segment, as defined in IFRS 8, before any permitted aggregation. An entity is to apply these amendments prospectively for annual periods beginning on or after January 1, 2010.

Derecognition of Intangible Assets

An intangible asset should be derecognized (1) on disposal or (2) when no future economic benefits are expected from its use or disposal. With regard to questions of accounting for the disposals of assets, the guidance of IAS 38 is consistent with that of IAS 16. A gain or loss arising from the derecognition of an intangible asset, determined as the difference between its carrying amount and the net disposal proceeds, is recognized in profit or loss (unless IAS 17 requires otherwise on a sale and leaseback) when the asset is derecognized. The 2004 amendment to IAS 38 observes that a disposal of an intangible asset may be effected either by a sale of the asset or by entering into a finance lease. The determination of the date of disposal of the intangible asset is made by applying the criteria in IAS 18 for recognizing revenue from the sale of goods, or IAS 17 in the case of disposal by a sale and leaseback. As for other similar transactions, the consideration receivable on disposal of an intangible asset is to be recognized initially at fair value. If payment for such an intangible asset is deferred, the consideration received is recognized initially at the cash price equivalent, with any difference between the nominal amount of the consideration and the cash price equivalent to be recognized as interest revenue under IAS 18, using the effective yield method.

Web Site Development and Operating Costs

With the advent of the Internet and of "e-commerce," most businesses now have their own Web sites. Web sites have become integral to doing business and may be designed either for external or internal access. Those designed for external access are developed and maintained for the purposes of promotion and advertising of an entity's products and services to their potential consumers. On the other hand, those developed for internal access may be used for displaying company policies and storing customer details.

With substantial costs being incurred by many entities for Web site development and maintenance, the need for accounting guidance became evident. SIC 32, issued in 2002, concluded that such costs represent an internally generated intangible asset that is subject to the requirements of IAS 38, and that such costs should be recognized if, and only if, an entity can satisfy the requirements set forth in IAS 38. Therefore, Web site costs have been likened to "development phase" (as opposed to "research phase") costs.

Thus the stringent qualifying conditions applicable to the development phase, such as "ability to generate future economic benefits," have to be met if such costs are to be recognized as an intangible asset. If an entity is not able to demonstrate how a Web site developed solely or primarily for promoting and advertising its own products and services will generate probable future economic benefits, all expenditure on developing such a Web site should be recognized as an expense when incurred.

Any internal expenditure on development and operation of the Web site should be accounted for in accordance with IAS 38. Comprehensive additional guidance is provided in the Appendix to SIC 32 and is summarized below.

1. Planning stage expenditures, such as undertaking feasibility studies, defining hardware and software specifications, evaluating alternative products and suppliers, and selecting preferences, should be expensed;

2. Application and infrastructure development costs pertaining to acquisition of tangible assets, such as purchasing and developing hardware, should be dealt with in accordance with IAS 16;

3. Other application and infrastructure development costs, such as obtaining a domain name, developing operating software, developing code for the application, installing developed applications on the Web server and stress testing, should be expensed when incurred unless the conditions prescribed by IAS 38 are met;

4. Graphical design development costs, such as designing the appearance of Web pages, should be expensed when incurred unless recognition criteria prescribed by IAS 38 are met;

5. Content development costs, such as expenses incurred for creating, purchasing, preparing, and uploading information onto the Web site, to the extent that these costs are incurred to advertise and promote an entity's own products or services, should be expensed immediately, consistent with how other advertising and related costs are to be accounted for under IFRS. Thus, these costs are not deferred, even until first displayed on the Web site, but are expensed when incurred;

6. Operating costs, such as updating graphics and revising content, adding new functions, registering Web site with search engines, backing up data, reviewing security access and analyzing usage of the Web site should be expensed when incurred, unless in rare circumstances these costs meet the criteria prescribed in IAS 38, in which case such expenditure is capitalized as a cost of the Web site; and

7. Other costs, such as selling and administrative overhead (excluding expenditure which can be directly attributed to preparation of Web site for use), initial operating losses and inefficiencies incurred before the Web site achieves its planned operating status, and training costs of employees to operate the Web site, should all be expensed as incurred as required under IFRS.

DISCLOSURES

The disclosure requirements set out in IAS 38 for intangible assets and those imposed by IAS 16 for property, plant, and equipment are very similar, and both demand extensive details to be disclosed in the financial statement footnotes. Another marked similarity is the exemption from disclosing "comparative information" with respect to the reconciliation of carrying amounts at the beginning and end of the period. While this may be misconstrued as a departure from the well-known principle of presenting all numerical information in comparative form, it is worth noting that it is in line with the provisions of IAS 1. IAS 1 categorically states that "unless a Standard permits or requires otherwise, comparative information should be disclosed in respect of the previous period for all numerical information in the financial statements…." (Another standard that contains a similar exemption from disclosure of comparative reconciliation information is IAS 37—which is dealt with in Chapter 18.)

For each class of intangible assets (distinguishing between internally generated and other intangible assets), disclosure is required of:

1. Whether the useful lives are indefinite or finite and if finite, the useful lives or amortization rates used;
2. The amortization method(s) used;
3. The gross carrying amount and accumulated amortization (including accumulated impairment losses) at both the beginning and end of the period;
4. A reconciliation of the carrying amount at the beginning and end of the period showing additions (analyzed between those acquired separately and those acquired in a business combination), assets classified as held for sale, retirements, disposals, acquisitions by means of business combinations, increases or decreases resulting from revaluations, reductions to recognize impairments, amounts written back to recognize recoveries of prior impairments, amortization during the period, the net effect of translation of foreign entities' financial statements, and any other material items; and
5. The line item in the statement of comprehensive income (or statement of profit or loss, if presented separately) in which the amortization charge of intangible assets is included.

The standard explains the concept of "class of intangible assets" as a "grouping of assets of similar nature and use in an entity's operations." Examples of intangible assets that could be reported as separate classes are

1. Brand names;
2. Licenses and franchises;
3. Mastheads and publishing titles;
4. Computer software;
5. Copyrights, patents and other industrial property rights, service and operating right;
6. Recipes, formulae, models, designs and prototypes; and
7. Intangible assets under development.

The above list is only illustrative in nature. Intangible assets may be combined (or disaggregated) to report larger classes (or smaller classes) of intangible assets if this results in more relevant information for financial statement users.

In addition, the financial statements should also disclose the following:

1. For any asset assessed as having an indefinite useful life, the carrying amount of the asset and the reasons for considering that it has an indefinite life and the significant factors used to determine this;
2. The nature, carrying amount, and remaining amortization period of any individual intangible asset that is material to the financial statements of the entity as a whole;
3. For intangible assets acquired by way of a government grant and initially recognized at fair value, the fair value initially recognized, their carrying amount, and whether they are carried under the cost or revaluation method for subsequent measurement;
4. Any restrictions on title and any assets pledged as security for debt; and
5. The amount of outstanding commitments for the acquisition of intangible assets.

Where intangibles are carried using the revaluation model, the entity must disclose the effective date of the revaluation, the carrying amount of the assets, and what their carrying amount would have been under the cost model, the amount of revaluation surplus applicable to the assets and the significant assumptions used in measuring fair value.

The financial statements should also disclose the aggregate amount of research and development expenditure recognized as an expense during the period. The entity is encouraged but not required to disclose any fully amortized assets still in use and any significant assets in use but not recognized because they did not meet the IAS 38 recognition criteria.

Examples of Financial Statement Disclosures

Novartis AG
For the fiscal year ending December 31, 2010

Accounting policies

Intangible assets

Goodwill

The excess of the consideration transferred to obtain a controlling interest and the fair value of any previous noncontrolling interest in the acquiree, over the fair value of the Group's share of net identifiable assets in a business combination, is recorded as goodwill in the balance sheet and is denominated in the functional currency of the related acquisition. Goodwill is allocated to an appropriate cash-generating unit which is defined as the smallest group of assets that generates independent cash inflows that support the goodwill. All goodwill is tested for impairment at least annually. In addition, goodwill is evaluated for impairment at each reporting date for each cash-generating unit with any resulting goodwill impairment charge recorded under Other Expense in the consolidated income statement. When evaluating goodwill for a potential impairment, the Group estimates the recoverable amount based on the "fair value less costs to sell" of the cash-generating unit containing the goodwill. In certain circumstances, its "value in use" to the Group is estimated if this value is higher than the "fair value less costs to sell." If the carrying amount exceeds the recoverable amount, an impairment loss for the difference is recognized. Considerable management judgment is required to estimate the discounted future cash flows and appropriate discount rates used to make these calculations. Accordingly, actual cash flows and values could vary significantly from forecasted cash flows and related values derived using discounting techniques.

Other intangible assets

All identifiable intangible assets acquired in a business combination are recognized at their fair value. Furthermore, all acquired Research & Development assets, including upfront and milestone payments on licensed or acquired compounds, which are deemed to enhance the intellectual property of Novartis, are capitalized at cost as intangible assets, when it is probable that future economic benefits will arise, even though some uncertainties exist as to whether the R&D projects will ultimately be successful in producing a commercial product. All Novartis intangible assets are allocated to cash-generating units. In-Process Research & Development (IPR&D) and the Alcon brand name are the only classes of separately identified intangible assets that are not amortized. Both are tested for impairment on an annual basis or when facts and circumstances warrant an impairment test. Any impairment charge is recorded in the consolidated income statement under "Research & Development expenses" for IPR&D and under "Other Expense" for the Alcon brand name. Once a project included in IPR&D has been successfully developed and is available for use, it is amortized over its useful life in the income statement under "Cost of Goods Sold," where any related impairment charges are also recorded. All other intangible assets are amortized over their estimated useful lives once they are available for use. The useful lives assigned to acquired intangible assets are based on the period over which they are expected to generate economic benefits, commencing in the year in which they first generate sales or are used in development. Acquired intangible assets are amortized on a straight-line basis over the following periods:

Trademarks	Over their estimated economic or legal life with a maximum of 20 years
Currently marketed products and marketing know-how	5 to 20 years
Technology	10 to 30 years
Software	3 to 5 years
Others	3 to 5 years
Alcon brand name	Indefinite useful life, not amortized

Amortization of trademarks, product and marketing rights is charged in the income statement to "Cost of Goods Sold" over their useful lives. Technology, which represents identified and separable acquired know-how used in the research, development and production process, is amortized in the income statement under "Cost of Goods Sold" or "Research & Development." Any impairment charges are recorded in the income statement in the same functional cost lines as the related amortization charges.

Intangible assets, other than the Alcon brand name and IPR&D, are reviewed for impairment whenever facts and circumstances indicate their carrying value may not be recoverable. When evaluating an intangible asset for a potential impairment, the Group estimates the recoverable amount based on the intangible asset's "fair value less costs to sell" using the estimated future cash flows a market participant could generate with that asset or, in certain circumstances, the "value in use" of the intangible asset to the Group, whichever is higher. If the carrying amount of the asset exceeds the recoverable amount, an impairment loss for the difference is recognized.

For purposes of assessing impairment, assets are grouped at the lowest level for which there are separately identifiable cash-generating units. Considerable management judgment is necessary to estimate the discounted future cash flows and appropriate discount rates used to make these calculations. Accordingly, actual cash flows and values could vary significantly from forecasted cash flows and related values derived using discounting techniques.

11. Goodwill and intangible asset movements

2010
Cost

	Goodwill USD millions	Acquired research & development USD millions	Aicon brand name USD millions	Technologies USD millions	Currently marketed products & marketing know-how USD millions	Other intangible assets USD millions	Total of intangible assets other than goodwill USD millions
January 1	12,624	3,216		1,271	11,737	954	17,178
Impact of business combinations	17,986	1,418	2,980	5,460	16,521	44	26,423
Reclassifications[1]		(474)			474		
Additions		344			62	89	495
Disposals		(24)			(184)	(13)	(221)
Currency translation effects	(349)	147		(32)	90	61	266
December 31	30,261	4,627	2,980	6,699	28,700	1,135	44,141

Accumulated amortization

	Goodwill USD millions	Acquired research & development USD millions	Aicon brand name USD millions	Technologies USD millions	Currently marketed products & marketing know-how USD millions	Other intangible assets USD millions	Total of intangible assets other than goodwill USD millions
January 1	(585)	(547)		(273)	(5,395)	(632)	(6,847)
Reclassifications[1]				(16)		16	
Amortization charge				(91)	(970)	(74)	(1,135)
Amortization on disposals		22			95	12	129
Impairment charge		(991)			(14)	(13)	(1,018)
Reversal of impairment charge		2			105		107
Currency translation effects	16	(51)		10	(75)	(30)	(146)
December 31	(569)	(1,565)		(370)	(6,254)	(721)	(8,910)
Net book value at December 31	29,692	3,062	2,980	6,329	22,446	414	35,231

1 Reclassification between various asset categories as a result of product launches of acquired In-Process Research & Development

11. Goodwill and intangible asset movements (continued)

	Goodwill USD millions	Acquired research & development USD millions	Technologies USD millions	Currently marketed products & marketing know-how USD millions	Other intangible assets USD millions	Total of intangible assets other than goodwill USD millions
2009						
Cost						
January 1	11,976	3,028	754	10,599	942	15,323
Impact of business combinations	548	161	427	241		829
Reclassifications[1]		(790)	60	724	6	
Additions	57	758		104	48	910
Disposals	(128)	(21)	(1)	(52)	(59)	(133)
Currency translation effects	171	80	31	121	17	249
December 31	12,624	3,216	1,271	11,737	954	17,178
Accumulated amortization						
January 1	(691)	(477)	(201)	(4,561)	(550)	(5,789)
Reclassifications[1]			(6)	6		
Amortization charge			(51)	(875)	(99)	(1,025)
Amortization on disposals		21		34	59	114
Impairment charge	122	(71)		(33)	(28)	(132)
Reversal of impairment charge		6		100		106
Currency translation effects	(16)	(26)	(15)	(66)	(14)	(121)
December 31	(585)	(547)	(273)	(5,395)	(632)	(6,847)
Net book value at December 31	12,039	2,669	998	6,342	322	10,331

1 Reclassification between various asset categories as a result of product launches of acquired In-Process Research & Development

Goodwill, the Alcon brand name and acquired In-Process R&D are tested for possible impairment annually and whenever events or changes in circumstances indicate the value may not be fully recoverable. If the initial accounting for an intangible asset acquired in the reporting period is only provisional, it is not tested for impairment unless an impairment indicator exists, and not included in the calculation of the net book values at risk from changes in the amount of discounted cash flows. An impairment is recognized when the consolidated balance sheet carrying amount is higher than the greater of "fair value less costs to sell" and "value in use." Novartis has adopted a uniform method for assessing goodwill for impairment and any other intangible asset indicated as possibly impaired. Under this method, the "fair value less costs to sell" of the related cash-generating unit is calculated and only if it is lower than the consolidated balance sheet carrying amount is the value in use determined. Novartis uses the Discounted Cash Flow (DCF) method to determine the "fair value less costs to sell" of a related cash-generating unit, which starts with a forecast of all expected future net cash flows. Generally, for intangible assets Novartis uses cash flow projections for the whole useful life of these assets, and for goodwill cash flow projections for the next five years are utilized based on a range of management forecasts, with a terminal value using sales projections in line or lower than inflation thereafter. Three probability-weighted scenarios are typically used. These cash flows, which reflect the risks and uncertainties associated with the asset, are discounted at an appropriate rate to net present value. The net present values involve highly sensitive estimates and assumptions specific to the nature of the Group's activities with regard to

- The amount and timing of projected future cash flows;
- The tax and discount rate selected;
- The outcome of R&D activities (compound efficacy, results of clinical trials, etc.);
- The amount and timing of projected costs to develop the IPR&D into commercially viable products;
- The probability of obtaining regulatory approval;
- Long-term sales forecasts for periods of up to 20 years;
- Sales price erosion rates after the end of patent protection and timing of the entry of generic competition; and
- The behavior of competitors (launch of competing products, marketing initiatives, etc.).

Factors that could result in shortened useful lives or impairment include entry into the market of generic or alternative products, lower than expected sales for acquired products or for sales associated with patents and trademarks; or lower than anticipated future sales resulting from acquired IPR&D. Changes in the discount rates used for these calculations also could lead to impairments.

Additionally, impairments of IPR&D and product and marketing rights may also result from events such as the outcome of R&D activity, obtaining regulatory approval and the launch of competing products.

The discount rates used are based on the Group's weighted-average cost of capital which is considered to be a good proxy for the capital cost of a market participant, which is adjusted for specific country and currency risks associated with the cash flow projections.

Due to the above factors, actual cash flows and values could vary significantly from the forecasted future cash flows and related values derived using discounting techniques.

The recoverable amount of a cash-generating unit and related goodwill is based on the higher of fair value less costs to sell or value in use. The following assumptions are used in the calculations:

	Pharmaceuticals %	Vaccines and Diagnostics %	Sandoz %	Consumer Health %
Sales growth rate assumptions after forecast period	0.6	2.0	0 to 2.0	(10.0) to 2.0
Discount rate	7.0	7.0	7.0	7.0

There has been no triggering event concerning Alcon between the date of acquisition of majority ownership of August 25, 2010, and December 31, 2010, that indicates that an impairment is necessary of any values determined as part of the final allocation of the purchase price as of August 25, 2010. In 2010, Novartis recorded impairment charges totaling USD 1.0 billion. These relate to impairment charges of USD 356 million for Mycograb, USD 250 million for PTZ601, USD 228 million for albinterferon alfa-2b and USD 120 million for ASA404 as Novartis decided to discontinue the related development projects. Additonally, USD 40 million were recorded for various other impairment charges in the Pharmaceuticals Division. Novartis also recorded various impairment charges of USD 24 million in the Sandoz and Consumer Health Divisions.

In 2009, impairment charges of USD 132 million were recorded, mainly for terminated development projects or for where the anticipated cash flows from future sales no longer supported the carrying value of the intangible assets. These related to various impairment charges of USD 88 million, mainly for upfront and milestone payments in the Pharmaceuticals Division and USD 44 million in the Vaccines and Diagnostics, Sandoz and Consumer Health Divisions.

Changes in circumstances of products impaired in prior years led to reversals in 2010 that amounted to USD 107 million mainly relating to Famvir product rights (2009: USD 106 million).

US GAAP COMPARISON

Internally-generated intangible assets are not recognized under US GAAP with the exception of some Web site developments costs. The underlying reason is that these assets do not have objectively measurable value.

12 INVESTMENT PROPERTY

INTRODUCTION

An investment in real estate held with the intention of earning rentals or for capital appreciation or both, is described as an investment property. An investment property is capable of generating cash flows independently of other assets held by the entity. Investment property is sometimes referred to as being a "passive" investment, to distinguish it from actively managed property such as plant assets, the use of which is integrated with the rest of the entity's operations. This characteristic is what distinguishes investment property from owner-occupied property, which is property held by the entity or a lessee under a finance lease, for use in its business (i.e., for use in production or supply of goods or services or for administrative purposes).

Revised IAS 40, effective in 2005, for the first time permits property interests held in the form of operating leases to be classified and accounted for as investment property. This may be done if

1. The other elements of the definition of investment property (see below) are met;
2. The operating lease is accounted for as if it were a finance lease in accordance with IAS 17 (that is, it is capitalized); and
3. The lessee uses the fair value model set out in IAS 40 for the asset recognized.

This classification option to report the lessee's property interest as investment property is available on a property-by-property basis. On the other hand, IAS 40 requires that all investment property should be consistently accounted for, employing either the fair value or cost model. Given these requirements, it is held that once the investment alternative is selected for one leased property, all property classified as investment property must be accounted for consistently, on the fair value basis.

Sources of IFRS	
IAS 40	*IFRIC* 5

DEFINITIONS OF TERMS

Carrying amount. The amount at which an asset is currently presented in the statement of financial position.

Cost. The amount of cash or cash equivalents paid or the fair value of other consideration given to acquire an asset at the time of its acquisition or construction or, where applicable, the amount attributed to that asset when initially recognized in accordance with the specific requirements of other IFRS.

Fair value. The amount for which an asset could be exchanged between a knowledgeable, willing buyer and seller in an arm's-length transaction.

Investment. An asset held by an entity for purposes of accretion of wealth through distributions of interest, royalties, dividends, and rentals, or for capital appreciation or other benefits to be obtained.

Investment property. Property (land or a building, or part of a building, or both), held (by the owner or by the lessee under a finance lease), to earn rentals or for capital appreciation purposes or both, as opposed to being held as

- An owner-occupied property (i.e. for use in the production or supply of goods or services or for administrative purposes); or
- Property held for sale in the ordinary course of business.

Owner-occupied property. Property held by the owner (i.e., the entity itself) or by a lessee under a finance lease, for use in the production or supply of goods or services or for administrative purposes.

IDENTIFICATION

The best way to understand what investment property constitutes is to look at examples of investments that are considered by the standard as investment properties, and contrast these with those investments that do not qualify for this categorization.

According to the standard, examples of investment property are

- Land held for long-term capital appreciation as opposed to short-term purposes like land held for sale in the ordinary course of business;
- Land held for an undetermined future use;
- A building owned by the reporting entity (or held by the reporting entity under a finance lease) and leased out under one or more operating leases; and
- A vacant building held by an entity to be leased out under one or more operating leases.
- Property under construction or being developed for future use as investment property (amended as part of the Improvements to IFRS issued in May 2008).

According to IAS 40, investment property does *not* include

- Property employed in the business, (i.e., held for use in production or supply of goods or services or for administrative purposes, the accounting for which is governed by IAS 16);
- Property occupied by employees (whether or not the employees pay rent at market rates);

- Property being constructed or developed on behalf of others, the accounting of which is outlined in IAS 11; and
- Property held for sale in the ordinary course of the business, the accounting for which is specified by IAS 2.

Apportioning property between investment property and owner-occupied property. In many cases it will be clear what constitutes investment property as opposed to owner-occupied property, but in other instances making this distinction might be less obvious. Certain properties are not held entirely for rental purposes or for capital appreciation purposes. For example, portions of these properties might be used by the entity for manufacturing or for administrative purposes. If these portions, earmarked for different purposes, could be sold, or leased under a finance lease, separately, then the entity is required to account for them separately. However, if the portions cannot be sold, or leased under a finance lease, separately, the property would be deemed as investment property if an insignificant portion is held by the entity for business use. An example would include that of a shopping mall, in which the landlord maintains an office for the purposes of managing and administering the commercial building, which is rented to tenants.

When ancillary services are provided by the entity and these ancillary services are a relatively insignificant component of the arrangement, as when the owner of a residential building provides maintenance and security services to the tenants, the entity treats such an investment as investment property. On the other hand, if the service provided is a comparatively significant component of the arrangement, then the investment would be considered as an owner-occupied property.

For instance, an entity that owns and operates a motel and also provides services to the guests of the motel would be unable to argue that it is an investment property in the context of IAS 40. Rather, such an investment would be classified as an owner-occupied property. Judgment is therefore required in determining whether a property qualifies as investment property. It is so important a factor that if an entity develops criteria for determining when to classify a property as an investment property, it is required by this standard to disclose these criteria in the context of difficult or controversial classifications.

Property leased to a subsidiary or a parent company. Property leased to a subsidiary or its parent company is considered an investment property from the perspective of the entity in its separate financial statements. However, for the purposes of consolidated financial statements, from the perspective of the group as a whole, it will not qualify as an investment property, since it is an owner-occupied property when viewed from the group perspective. This will necessitate the processing of appropriate adjustments to account for the difference in classification when preparing the consolidated accounts.

RECOGNITION AND MEASUREMENT

Recognition and initial cost. Investment property will be recognized when it becomes probable that the entity will enjoy the future economic benefits which are attributable to it, and when the cost or fair value can be reliably measured. In general, this will occur when the property is first acquired or constructed by the reporting entity. In unusual circumstances where would it be concluded that the owner's likelihood of receipt of the economic benefits would be less than probable, the costs incurred would not qualify for capitalization and would consequently have to be expensed.

Initial measurement will be at cost, which is usually equivalent to fair value, assuming that the acquisition was the result of an arm's-length exchange transaction. Included in the purchase cost will be such directly attributable expenditure as legal fees and property transfer taxes, if incurred in the transaction. IAS 40 does not provide explicit guidance on measuring cost for a self-constructed investment property. However, IAS 16 provides that the cost of a self-constructed asset is determined using the same principles as for an acquired asset. If an entity makes similar assets for sale in the normal course of business, the cost of the asset is usually the same as the cost of constructing an asset for sale (inventory), which would therefore include overhead charges which can be allocated on a reasonable and consistent basis to the construction activities. To the extent that the acquisition cost includes an interest charge, if the payment is deferred, the amount to be recognized as an investment asset should not include the interest charges, unless the asset meets the definition of a qualifying asset under IAS 23, which requires borrowing costs to be capitalized. Furthermore, start-up costs (unless they are essential in bringing the property to its working condition), initial operating losses (incurred prior to the investment property achieving planned level of occupancy) or abnormal waste (in construction or development) do not constitute part of the capitalized cost of an investment property. If an investment property is acquired in exchange for equity instruments of the reporting entity, the cost of the investment property is the fair value of the equity instruments issued, although the fair value of the investment property received is used to measure its cost if it is more clearly evident than the fair value of the equity instruments issued.

Subsequent expenditures. In some instances there may be further expenditure incurred on the investment property after the date of initial recognition. Consistent with similar situations arising in connection with property, plant and equipment (dealt with under IAS 16), if the costs meet the recognition criteria discussed in the paragraph above, then those costs may be added to the carrying amount of the investment property. Costs of the day-to-day servicing of an investment property (essentially repairs and maintenance) would not ordinarily meet the recognition criteria, and would therefore be recognized in profit or loss as period costs when incurred. Costs of day-to-day servicing would include the cost of labor and consumables, and may include the cost of minor parts.

Sometimes, the appropriate accounting treatment for subsequent expenditure would depend upon the circumstances that were considered in the initial measurement and recognition of the investment property. For example, if a property (e.g., an office building) is acquired for investment purposes in a condition that makes it incumbent upon the entity to perform significant renovations thereafter, then such renovation costs (which would constitute subsequent expenditures) will be added to the carrying amount of the investment property when incurred later.

Fair value vs. cost models. Analogous to the financial reporting of plant and equipment under IAS 16, IAS 40 provides that investment property may be reported at either fair value or at depreciated cost less accumulated impairment. The cost model is the benchmark treatment prescribed by IAS 16 for plant assets. The fair value approach under IAS 40 more closely resembles that used for financial instruments than it does the allowed alternative (revaluation) method for plant assets, however. Also, under IAS 40 if the cost method is used, fair value information must nonetheless be determined and disclosed.

Fair value. When investment property is carried at fair value, at each subsequent financial reporting date the carrying amount must be adjusted to the then-current fair value, with the adjustment being reported in the profit or loss for the period in which it arises. The inclusion of the value adjustments in earnings—in contrast to the revaluation approach under IAS 16, whereby adjustments are generally reported in other comprehensive income—is a reflection of the different roles played by plant or owner-occupied assets and by other investment property. The former are used, or consumed, in the operation of the business, which is often centered upon the production of goods and services for sale to customers. The latter are held for possible appreciation in value, and hence those value changes are highly germane to the assessment of periodic operating performance. With this distinction in mind, the decision was made to not only permit fair value reporting, but to require value changes to be included in profit or loss.

IAS 40 represents the first time that fair value accounting is being embraced as an accounting model for nonfinancial assets. This has been a matter of great controversy, and to address the many concerns voiced during the exposure draft stage, the IASC added more guidance on the subject to the final standard. This standard is quite comprehensive, and it includes some very insightful and practical hints on determining fair value. However, with the issue of IFRS 13 *Fair Value Measurements* in 2011, much of the fair value guidance in IAS 40 will be superseded with that of IFRS 13 once the new standard becomes effective from January 1, 2013. (See Chapter 25.)

Under the current IAS 40, fair value is defined as the price at which the property could be exchanged between knowledgeable, willing parties in an arm's length transaction, which should reflect market conditions at the end of the reporting period. Fair value would therefore not be appropriately measured with reference to either a past or a future date. Further, the definition envisions "knowledgeable, willing parties" as being the arbiters of fair value. This presupposes that both the buyer and seller are willing to enter into the transaction, and that they each have reasonable knowledge about the nature and characteristics of the investment property, its potential uses, and the state of the market as of the valuation date. Put another way, fair value presumes that neither the buyer nor the seller is acting under coercion; and fair value is not a price that is based on a "distress sale."

The standard goes into great detail to explain the concept of a "willing buyer" (i.e., one who is motivated but not compelled to buy) and a "willing seller" (i.e., one who is neither overeager nor a forced seller). For instance, in explaining the concept of a "willing seller," the standard clarifies that the motivation to sell at market terms for the best price obtainable in the open market is derived "after proper marketing." This expression has been explained very eloquently by the standard to mean that in order to be considered as "after proper marketing," the investment property would need to be "exposed to the market" in the most appropriate manner to effect its disposal at the best price obtainable. The length of exposure time, according to the standard, must be "sufficient" to allow the investment property to be brought to the attention of an "adequate number" of potential purchasers.

As if there were not enough unknowns in the equation, the standard further qualifies this by stating that the "exposure period" is assumed to occur "prior to the end of the reporting period." With respect to the length of the exposure period, the standard opines that "it may vary with market conditions." Some may find this an example of "overkill" which confuses, rather than clarifies the standard and impedes attempts to apply it. However, given that this is the maiden attempt by the IASC to mandate fair value accounting for nonfinancial assets, it may in hindsight be warranted.

The standard *encourages* (but does not require) an entity to determine the fair value based on a valuation by an independent valuer who holds a recognized and relevant professional qualification and who has had recent experience in the location and category of the investment property being valued. While terms such as "relevant" are not defined, IAS 40 does offer a significant amount of practical guidance on issues relating to the determination of fair values. These practical hints will likely greatly facilitate the correct application of the principles enshrined in the standard. They are summarized as follows:

- Factors that could distort the value, such as the incorporation of particularly favorable or unfavorable financing terms, the inclusion of sale and leaseback arrangements, or any other concession by either buyer or seller, are not to be given any consideration in the valuation process;

- On the other hand, the actual conditions in the marketplace at the valuation date, even if these represent somewhat atypical climatic factors, will govern the valuation process. For example, if the economy is in the midst of a recession and rental properties' prices are depressed, no attempt should be made to normalize fair value, since that would add a subjective element and depart from the concept of fair value as of the end of the reporting period;
- Fair values should be determined without any deduction for transaction costs that the entity may incur on the sale or other disposal of the investment property;
- Fair value should reflect the actual state of the market and circumstances as of the end of the reporting period, not as of either a past or a future date;
- In the absence of current prices on an active market, an entity should use information from a variety of sources, including

  - Current prices on an active market of dissimilar properties with suitable adjustments for the differences, recent prices on less active markets, with necessary adjustments; and
  - Discounted cash flow projections based on reliable estimates of future cash flows using an appropriate discount rate

- Fair value differs from "value in use" as defined in IAS 36. Whereas fair value is reflective of market knowledge and estimates of participants in the market in general, value in use reflects the entity's knowledge and estimates that are entity-specific and are thus not applicable to entities in general. In other words, value in use is an estimate at the entity level or at a "microlevel," while fair value is a "macrolevel" concept that is reflective of the perceptions of the market participants in general;
- Entities are alerted to the possibility of double counting in determining the fair value of certain types of investment property. For instance, when an office building is leased on a furnished basis, the fair value of office furniture and fixtures is generally included in the fair value of the investment property (in this case the office building). The IASC's apparent rationale is that the rental income relates to the furnished office building; when fair values of furniture and fixtures are included along with the fair value of the investment property, the entity does not recognize them as separate assets; and
- Lastly, the fair value of investment property should neither reflect the future capital expenditure (that would improve or enhance the property), nor the related future benefits from this future expenditure.

Inability to measure fair value reliably. There is a rebuttable presumption that, if an entity acquires or constructs property that will qualify as investment property under this standard, it will be able to assess fair value reliably on an ongoing basis. In rare circumstances, however, when an entity acquires for the first time an investment property (or when an existing property first qualifies to be classified as investment property when there has been change of use), there may be clear evidence that the fair value of the investment property cannot reliably be determined, on a continuous basis.

Under such exceptional circumstances, the standard stipulates that the entity should measure that investment property using the benchmark (cost) treatment in IAS 16 until the disposal of the investment property. According to IAS 40, the residual value of such investment property measured under the benchmark treatment in IAS 16 should be presumed to be zero. The standard further states that under the exceptional circumstances explained above, in the case of an entity that uses the fair value model, the entity should measure the other investment properties held by it at fair values. In other words, notwithstanding the fact that one of the investment properties, due to exceptional circumstances, is being carried under the benchmark (cost) treatment in IAS 16, an entity that uses the fair value model should continue carrying the other investment properties at fair values. While this results in a mixed measure of the aggregate investment property, it underlines the perceived importance of the fair value method.

Transfers to or from investment property. Transfers to or from investment property should be made only when there is demonstrated "change in use" as contemplated by the standard. A change in use takes place when there is a transfer

- From investment property to owner-occupied property, when owner-occupation commences;
- From investment property to inventories, on commencement of development with a view to sale;
- From an owner-occupied property to investment property, when owner-occupation ends;
- Of inventories to investment property, when an operating lease to a third party commences; or
- Of property in the course of development or construction to investment property, at end of the construction or development.

In the case of an entity that employs the cost model, transfers between investment property, owner-occupied property and inventories do not change the carrying amount of the property transferred and thus do not change the cost of that property for measurement or disclosure purposes. When the investment property is carried under the fair value model, vastly different results follow as far as recognition and measurement is concerned. These are explained below.

1. **Transfers from (or to) investment property to (or from) property, plant and equipment (in the case of investment property carried under the fair value model).** In some instances, property that at first is appropriately classified as investment property under IAS 40 may later become property, plant and equipment as defined under IAS 16. For example, a building is obtained and leased to unrelated parties, but at a later date the entity expands its own operations to the extent that it now chooses to utilize the building formerly held as a passive investment for its own purposes, such as for the corporate executive offices. The amount reflected in the accounting records as the fair value of the property as of the date of change in status would become the cost basis for subsequent accounting purposes. Previously recognized changes in value, if any, would not be reversed.

   Similarly, if property first classified as owner-occupied property and treated as property, plant and equipment under the benchmark treatment of IAS 16 is later redeployed as investment property, it is to be measured at fair value at the date of the change in its usage. If the value is lower than the carrying amount (i.e., if there is a previously unrecognized decline in its fair value) then this will be reflected in profit or loss in the period of redeployment as an investment property. On the other hand, if there has been an unrecognized increase in value, the accounting will depend on whether this is a reversal of a previously recognized value impairment. If the increase is a reversal of a decline in value, the increase should be recognized in profit or loss; the amount so reported, however, should not exceed the amount needed to restore the carrying amount to what it would have been, net of depreciation, had the earlier impairment not occurred.

     If, on the other hand, there was no previously recognized impairment which the current value increase is effectively reversing (or, to the extent that the current increase exceeds the earlier decline), then the increase should be recognized in other comprehensive income. If the investment property is later disposed of, any surplus in equity should be transferred to retained earnings without being recognized through profit or loss.

2. **Transfers from inventory to investment property (in the case of investment property carried under the fair value model).** It may also happen that property originally classified as inventory, originally held for sale in the normal course of the business, is later redeployed as investment property. When reclassified, the initial carrying amount should be fair value as of that date. Any gain or loss resulting from this reclassification would be reported in profit or loss.

3. **Investment property to be sold.** IAS 40 does not contemplate reclassification from investment property to inventory. When the entity determines that property held as investment property is to be sold, that property should be classified as a noncurrent asset held for sale in accordance with IFRS 5. It should not be derecognized (eliminated from the statement of financial position) or transferred to an inventory classification. The treatment of noncurrent assets held for sale is discussed in further detail in Chapter 9. However, in the case of investment property held for sale, these continue to be measured at fair value in accordance with IAS 40 up to the point of sale, unlike for example, property, plant and equipment which is measured at the lower of carrying amount or fair value less costs to sell while held for sale.

     Disposal and retirement of investment property. An investment property should be derecognized (i.e., eliminated from the statement of financial position of the entity) on disposal or when it is permanently withdrawn from use and no future economic benefits are expected from its disposal. The word "disposal" has been used in the standard to mean not only a sale but also the entering into of a finance lease by the entity. Any gains or losses on disposal or retirement of an investment property should be determined as the difference between the net disposal proceeds and the carrying amount of the asset and should be recognized in profit or loss for the period.

Deferred Tax

     A December 2010 amendment to IAS 12, *Income Taxes,* was introduced to provide a practical approach for measuring deferred tax liabilities and deferred tax assets when investment property is measured using the fair value model. Under IAS 12, the measurement of deferred tax liabilities and deferred tax assets depends on whether an entity expects to recover an asset by using it or by selling it. However, it is often difficult and subjective to determine the expected manner of recovery when the investment property is measured at fair value. The amendment introduced a rebuttable presumption that the carrying amount of an investment property measured at fair value will be recovered entirely through sale. This presumption is rebutted if the investment property is held within a business model whose objective is to consume substantially all of the economic benefits embodied in the investment property over time, rather than through sale.

DISCLOSURES

Disclosure requirements. It is anticipated that in certain cases investment property will be property that is owned by the reporting entity and leased to others under operating-type lease arrangements. The disclosure requirements set forth in IAS 17 (and discussed in Chapter 22) continue unaltered by IAS 40. In addition, IAS 40 stipulates a number of new disclosure requirements set out below.

1. **Disclosures applicable to all investment properties**

   - When classification is difficult, an entity that holds an investment property will need to disclose the criteria used to distinguish investment property from owner-occupied property and from property held for sale in the ordinary course of business.
   - The methods and any significant assumptions that were used in ascertaining the fair values of the investment properties are to be disclosed as well. Such disclosure also includes a statement about whether the determination of fair value was supported by market evidence or relied heavily on other factors (which the entity needs to disclose as well) due to the nature of the property and the absence of comparable market data.
   - If investment property has been revalued by an independent appraiser, having recognized and relevant qualifications, and who has recent experience with properties having similar characteristics of location and type, the extent to which the fair value of investment property (either used in case the fair value model is used or disclosed in case the cost model is used) is based on valuation by such a qualified independent valuation specialist. If there is no such valuation, that fact should be disclosed as well.
   - The following should be disclosed in the statement of comprehensive income:

     - The amount of rental income derived from investment property;
     - Direct operating expenses (including repairs and maintenance) arising from investment property that generated rental income;
     - Direct operating expenses (including repairs and maintenance) arising from investment property that did not generate rental income;
     - The existence and the amount of any restrictions which may potentially affect the realizability of investment property or the remittance of income and proceeds from disposal to be received; and
     - Material contractual obligations to purchase or build investment property or for repairs, maintenance or improvements thereto.

2. **Disclosures applicable to investment property measured using the fair value model**

   - In addition to the disclosures outlined above, the standard requires that an entity that uses the fair value model should also present a reconciliation of the carrying amounts of the investment property, from the beginning to the end of the reporting period. The reconciliation will separately identify additions resulting from acquisitions, those resulting from business combinations, and those deriving from capitalized expenditures subsequent to the property's initial recognition. It will also identify disposals, gains or losses from fair value adjustments, the net exchange differences, if any, arising from the translation of the financial statements

of a foreign entity, transfers to and from inventories and owner-occupied properties, and any other movements. (Comparative reconciliation data for prior periods
need not be presented).
- Under exceptional circumstances, due to lack of reliable fair value, when an entity measures investment property using the benchmark (cost) treatment under
IAS 16, the above reconciliation should disclose amounts separately for that investment property from amounts relating to other investment property. In addition, an entity should also disclose

  - A description of such a property,
  - An explanation of why fair value cannot be reliably measured,
  - If possible, the range of estimates within which fair value is highly likely to
    lie, and
  - On disposal of such an investment property, the fact that the entity has dis-
    posed of investment property not carried at fair value along with its carrying
    amount at the time of disposal and the amount of gain or loss recognized.

3. **Disclosures applicable to investment property measured using the cost model**

- In addition to the disclosure requirements outlined in 1. above, the standard requires that an entity that applies the cost model should also disclose

  - The depreciation methods used
  - The useful lives or the depreciation rates used
  - The gross carrying amount and the accumulated depreciation (aggregated with
    accumulated impairment losses) at the beginning and end of the period.

- It should also disclose a reconciliation of the carrying amount of investment property at the beginning and the end of the period showing the following details:

  - Additions resulting from acquisitions, those resulting from business combina-
    tions, and
  - Those deriving from capitalized expenditures subsequent to the property's
    initial recognition.

- It should also disclose disposals, depreciation, impairment losses recognized and
reversed, the net exchange differences, if any, arising from the translation of the
financial statements of a foreign entity, transfers to and from inventories and
owner-occupied properties, and any other movements. (Comparative reconciliation data for prior periods need not be presented.)
- The fair value of investment property carried under the cost model should also be
determined and disclosed. In exceptional cases, when the fair value of the investment property cannot be reliably estimated, the entity should instead disclose

  - A description of such property,
  - An explanation of why fair value cannot be reliably measured, and
  - If possible, the range of estimates within which fair value is highly likely to
    lie.

Examples of Financial Statement Disclosures

Sirius Real Estate Limited
Annual Report 2011

Accounting policies
Investment properties

Investment properties are properties owned by the Group which are held either for long-term rental income or for capital appreciation or both.

Investment properties are initially recognized at cost, including transaction costs. The carrying amount includes the cost of replacing part of an existing investment property at the time that cost is incurred if the recognition criteria are met and excludes the costs of day-to day servicing of an investment property. Subsequent to initial recognition, investment properties are stated at fair value, which reflects market conditions at the reporting date.

Gains or losses arising from changes in the fair values of investment properties are included in the statement of comprehensive income in the period in which they arise.

The fair value of the Group's investment properties at 31 March 2011 has been arrived at on the basis of a valuation carried out at that date by DTZ Zadelhoff Tie Leung GmbH, an independent valuer. The valuations are in accordance with standards complying with the Royal Institution of Chartered Surveyors' ("RICS") approval and the conceptual framework that has been settled by the International Valuation Standards Committee ("IVSC").

Investment property under construction

Property that is being constructed or developed for future use as investment property is accounted for as an investment property under construction until construction or development is complete and which is then reclassified as investment property.

Investment property under construction will be carried at fair value at the earlier of when the fair value first becomes reliably measurable and the date of completion of the property. Any gain or loss will be recognized in the statement of comprehensive income, consistent with the policy adopted for all other investment properties carried at fair value.

Notes to the consolidated financial statements

12. Investment properties

	2011	2010
	€000	*€000*
Opening balance	500,010	500,400
Additions	5,857	29,579
Deficit on revaluation	(367)	(29,969)
Closing balance	505,500	500,010

The fair value of the Group's investment properties at March 31, 2011 has been arrived at on the basis of a valuation carried out by DTZ Zadelhoff Tie Leung GmbH, an independent value.

The value of each of the properties has been assessed in accordance with the RICS Valuation Standards on the basis of market value. Market value was primarily derived using a ten-year discounted cash flow model supported by comparable evidence. The discounted cash flow calculation is a valuation of rental income considering nonrecoverable costs and applying a discount rate for the current income risk over a ten-year period. After ten years, a determining residual value (exit scenario) is calculated. A cap rate is applied to the more uncertain future income, discounted to a present value.

The weighted-average lease duration was 3.1 years.

As a result of the level of judgment used in arriving at the market valuations, the amounts which may ultimately be realized in respect of any given property may differ from the valuations shown in the statement of financial position.

13. Investment property under construction

	2011 €000	2010 €000
Opening balance	--	2,222
Additions	--	--
Transfers	--	(2,222)
Closing balance	--	--

US GAAP COMPARISON

No US GAAP standard is issued on investment properties. All properties are held at cost.

13 INTERESTS IN ASSOCIATES

INTRODUCTION

Accounting for investments over which the investor has significant influence is provided for in IAS 28, *Associates*. The standard allows for the carrying of investments in associate companies either at cost or at fair value in the separate financial statements of the investor (in terms of IAS 27, *Consolidations*) and provides for the accounting for the investment in associate using the equity method when preparing consolidated financial statements. A number of IFRIC Interpretations have also been issued that relate to such investments and are noted and discussed below.

Sources of IFRS	
IAS 27, 28	*IFRIC* 5, 9, 10

DEFINITIONS OF TERMS

Associate. An entity, including an unincorporated entity such as a partnership, over which an investor has significant influence but which is neither a subsidiary nor a joint venture of the investor company.

Carrying amount. The amount at which an asset is currently presented in the statement of financial position.

Consolidated financial statements. Financial statements of a group presented as those of a single economic entity.

Control. The power to govern the financial and operating policies of an entity so as to obtain benefits from its activities and increase, maintain, or protect the amount of those benefits.

Cost. The amount of cash or cash equivalents paid or the fair value of other consideration given to acquire an asset at the time of its acquisition or construction or, where applicable, the amount attributed to that asset when initially recognized in accordance with the specific requirements of other IFRS, (e.g., IFRS 2, *Share-Based Payment*).

Cost method. A method of accounting for investment whereby the investment is recorded at cost; the statement of comprehensive income reflects income from the investment only to the extent that the investor receives distributions (dividends) from the investee's accumulated net profits arising after the date of acquisition. Distributions received in excess of accumulated profits are regarded as a recovery of investment and are recognized as a reduction of the cost of the investment.

Equity method. A method of accounting whereby the investment is initially recorded at cost and subsequently adjusted for the postacquisition change in the investor's share of net assets of the investee. The investor's income from investment includes the investor's share of the investee's profit or loss as well as the investor's share of the investee's other comprehensive income.

Fair value. The amount for which an asset could be exchanged between a knowledgeable, willing buyer and seller in an arm's-length transaction.

Goodwill. An intangible asset acquired in a business combination representing the future economic benefits expected to be derived from the business combination that are not allocated to other individually identifiable and separately recognizable assets acquired.

Investee. An entity that issued voting share that is held by an investor.

Investment. An asset held by an entity for purposes of accretion of wealth through distributions of interest, royalties, dividends, and rentals, or for capital appreciation or other benefits to be obtained.

Investor. A business entity that holds an investment in the voting shares of another entity.

Separate financial statements. Financial statements presented by a parent, an investor in an associate, or a venturer in a jointly controlled entity, in which the investments are accounted for on the basis of the direct equity interest rather than on the basis of the reported results and net assets of the investees.

Significant influence. The power of the investor to participate in the financial and operating policy decisions of the investee, which may be gained by share ownership, statute or agreement; however, this is less than the ability to control those policies.

RECOGNITION AND MEASUREMENT

Equity Method of Accounting for Investments

The equity method of accounting is applied to investment situations where the investor is able to exercise significant influence over an investee. It was developed as a method of applying the concept of substance over form in the accounting for such investments. There was recognition that the actual determination of the existence of significant influence could be difficult and that, to facilitate such recognition, there might be a need to set out a bright line against which significant influence would be measured. To this end, a somewhat arbitrary, refutable presumption of such influence was set at a 20% voting interest in the investee. This has been held out as the de facto standard on assessing significant influence, and thus an investee accounts for such an investment as an associate unless it can prove otherwise.

The necessity of applying a method of accounting such as the equity method, when significant influence over the investee is held by the investor, can easily be understood when one considers how readily manipulation of the investor's financial position and results of operations could be achieved in its absence. If an investee has substantial profit or loss, but the investor, employing the cost method of accounting for the investment, uses its influence to defer the investee's declaration of dividends, the result would be that the investor would not be reporting its share of the investee's economic operating results, even though it had been in a position to influence the distribution of dividends, had it chosen to do so. This might be motivated, for example, by a desire to put aside future earnings to compensate for an expected, or feared, decline in the investor's own operations.

Conversely, the investor could effect or encourage a dividend distribution even in the absence of earnings by the investee. This could be motivated by a need for reportable earnings, perhaps to offset disappointing performance in the investor's own operations. In either case, the opportunity to manipulate reported results of operations would be of great concern.

More importantly, however, the use of the cost method would simply not reflect the economic reality of the investor's interest in an entity whose operations were indicative, in part at least, of the reporting entity's (i.e., the investor's) management decisions and operational skills. Thus, the clearly demonstrable need to reflect substance, rather than mere form, made the development of the equity method highly desirable. This is in keeping with the thinking that is currently driving IFRS that all activities that have a potential impact on the financial position and performance of an entity must be reported, including those that are deemed to be off-balance sheet-type transactions.

The equity method permits an entity (the investor) controlling a certain share of the voting interest in another entity (the investee) to incorporate its pro rata share of the investee's operating results into its profit or loss. However, rather than include its share of each component of the investee's revenues, expenses, assets and liabilities into its financial statements, the investor will only include its share of the investee's profit or loss as a separate line item in its statement of comprehensive income. Similarly, only a single line in the investor's balance is presented, but this reflects, to a degree, the investor's share in each of the investee's assets and liabilities.

It is important to recognize that the bottom-line impact on the investor's financial statements is identical whether the equity method or full consolidation is employed; only the amount of detail presented within the statements will differ. An understanding of this principle will be useful as the need to identify the "goodwill" component of the cost of the investment is explained below.

Equity method as prescribed by IAS 28. The equity method is not available to be used as a substitute for consolidation. Consolidation is required when a majority voting interest is held by the reporting entity (the parent) in another entity (the subsidiary). The equity method is intended for use where the reporting entity (the investor) has significant influence over the operations of the other entity (the investee), but lacks control.

In general, significant influence is inferred when the investor owns between 20% and 50% of the investee's voting shares. However, the 20% threshold stipulated in IAS 28 is not an absolute one. Specific circumstances may suggest that significant influence exists even though the investor's level of ownership is under 20%, in which case the equity method should be applied. In other instances, significant influence may be absent despite a level of ownership above 20%. Therefore, the existence of significant influence in the 20% to 50% ownership range should be treated as a refutable presumption.

In considering whether significant influence exists, IAS 28 identifies the following factors as evidence that such influence is present:

1. There is investor representation on the board of directors or its equivalent,
2. The investor participates in the policy-making processes of the investee,
3. There are material transactions that are undertaken between the investor and investee,
4. There is an interchange of managerial personnel between the investor and the investee; and
5. There is provision of essential technical information between the investor and the investee, which might not have occurred under normal circumstances.

There may be other factors present that suggest a lack of significant influence, such as organized opposition by the other shareholders, majority ownership by a small group of shareholders that is not inclusive of the investor, and inability to achieve representation on the board or to obtain information on the operations of the investee. Whether sufficient contrary evidence exists to negate the presumption of significant influence is a matter of judgment and requires a careful evaluation of all pertinent facts and circumstances, over an extended period of time in some cases.

When equity method is required. IAS 28 stipulates that the equity method should be employed by the investor for all investments in associates, unless the investment is acquired and held exclusively with a view to its disposal within twelve months from acquisition in which case it is accounted for in terms of IFRS 5, *Noncurrent Assets Held for Sale and Discontinued Operations.*

IAS 28 also excludes from its scope the accounting for any investments that may meet the associate entity accounting criteria but are held by venture capital organizations, mutual funds, unit trusts, and similar entities. Such investments are measured and carried at fair value in accordance with IFRS 9 or IAS 39, when such measurement is well-established practice in those industries. When those investments are measured at fair value, changes in fair value are included in profit or loss in the period of the change.

A complicating factor in ascertaining whether the reporting entity has significant influence over the investee is that the investor may own instruments such as share warrants, share call options, or other debt or equity instruments that are convertible into ordinary shares, or other similar instruments that have the potential, if exercised or converted, to give the entity additional voting power or reduce another party's relative power over the financial and operating policies of another entity (i.e., potential voting rights). The existence and effect of potential voting rights that are currently exercisable or currently convertible, including potential voting rights held by other entities, must be considered when assessing whether an entity has the power to have significant influence in the financial and operating policy decisions of the investee. This issue is discussed in greater detail later in this chapter.

The standard does distinguish between the accounting for investments in associates in consolidated financials and that in separate financials of the investor. IAS 28 provides that in the separate financials of the investor, the investment in the associate may be carried at either cost or in terms of IAS 39 (or IFRS 9 once it becomes effective). This is an accounting policy choice that the investor must make and apply consistently across all investments in associate companies that it holds.

Complications in applying equity method accounting. Complexities in the use of the equity method may arise in two areas. First, the cost of the investment to the investor might not be equal to the fair value of the investor's share of investee net assets; this is similar to the existence of goodwill in a business combination under IFRS 3. Or the fair value of the investor's share of the investee's net assets may not be equal to the book value thereof; this situation is similar to the cost allocation problem in consolidations. Since the ultimate statement of comprehensive income result from the use of equity method accounting must generally be the same as full consolidation, an adjustment must be made for each of these differentials.

Example of a simple case ignoring deferred taxes

Assume the following information:

On January 2, 2011, Regency Corporation (the investor) acquired 40% of Elixir Company's (the investee) voting shares on the open market for €100,000. Unless demonstrated otherwise, it is assumed that Regency Corporation can exercise significant influence over Elixir Company's operating and financing policies. On January 2, Elixir's shareholders' equity is comprised of the following accounts:

Shares, par €1, 100,000 shares authorized, 50,000 shares issued and outstanding	€ 50,000
Additional paid-in capital/ Share premium*	150,000
Retained earnings	50,000
Total shareholders' equity	€250,000

  * *Note that IAS 1 (revised 2007) does not require any distinction between share capital and any excess over a stated value, historically called additional paid-in capital or share premium. However, some legal jurisdictions may distinguish between these and thus this bifurcation will be maintained in these examples.*

Note that the cost of Elixir Company common shares was equal to 40% of the book value of Elixir's net assets. Assume also that there is no difference between the book value and the fair value of Elixir Company's assets and liabilities. Accordingly, the balance in the investment account in Regency's records represents exactly 40% of Elixir's shareholders' equity (net assets). Assume further that Elixir Company reported a 2011 net profit of €30,000 and paid cash dividends of €10,000. Its shareholders' equity at year-end would be as follows:

Shares, par €1, 100,000 shares authorized, 50,000 shares issued and outstanding	€ 50,000
Additional paid-in capital/ Share premium	150,000
Retained earnings	70,000
Total shareholders' equity	€270,000

Regency Corporation would record its share of the increase in Elixir Company's net assets during 2011 as follows:

Investment in Elixir Company	12,000	
Equity in Elixir profit or loss (€30,000 × 40%)		12,000
Cash	4,000	
Investment in Elixir Company (€10,000 × 40%)		4,000

When Regency's statement of financial position is prepared at December 31, 2011, the balance reported in the investment account would be €108,000 (= €100,000 + €12,000 − €4,000). This amount represents 40% of the book value of Elixir's net assets at the end of the year (40% × €270,000). Note also that the equity in Elixir profit or loss is reported as one amount on Regency's income statement under the caption "Other income and expense."

IAS 12 established the requirement that deferred income taxes be provided for the tax effects of temporary differences. Under this standard, discussed in detail in Chapter 26, the liability method must be employed, under which the provision of a net deferred tax asset or liability is adjusted at the end of each reporting period to reflect the current expectations regarding the amount that ultimately is to be received or paid.

In order to compute the deferred tax effects of profit or loss recognized by an investor employing the equity method of accounting for its investment, it must make an assumption regarding the means by which undistributed earnings of its investee will be realized. Earnings can generally be realized either through subsequent receipt of dividends, or by disposition of the investment at a gain, which presumably would reflect the investee's undistributed earnings as of that date. In many jurisdictions, these alternative modes of income realization will have differing tax implications. For example, in many jurisdictions the assumption of future dividends may result in taxes at the investor's marginal income tax rate (net of any dividends received deduction or exclusion permitted by the local taxing authorities). If the sale of the investment is expected to be the route by which earnings are realized, this may result in a capital gain, which in some jurisdictions is taxed at a different rate, or not taxed at all.

Accounting for a differential between cost and book value. The simple examples presented thus far have avoided the major complexity of equity method accounting, the allocation of the differential between the cost to the investor and the investor's share in the net equity (net assets at book value) of the investee. Since the net impact of equity method accounting must equal that of full consolidation accounting, this differential must be analyzed into the following components and accounted for accordingly:

1. The difference between the book and fair values of the investee's net assets at the date the investment is made.
2. The remaining difference between the fair value of the net assets and the cost of the investment, that is generally attributable to goodwill.

According to IAS 28, any difference between the cost of the investment and the investor's share of the fair values of the net identifiable assets of the associate should be identified and accounted for in accordance with IFRS 3 (as detailed in Chapter 15). Thus, the differential should be allocated to specific asset categories, and these differences will then be amortized to the income from investee account as appropriate, for example, over the economic lives of property, plant, and equipment whose fair values exceeded book values. The difference between fair value and cost will be treated like goodwill and, in accordance with the provisions of IFRS 3 not subject to amortization, but rather will be reviewed for impairment on a regular basis, with write-downs taken for any impairment identified, to be included in earnings of the investor in the period of impairment.

Example of a complex case ignoring deferred taxes

Assume again that Regency Corporation acquired 40% of Elixir Company's shares on January 2, 2011, but that the price paid was €140,000. Elixir Company's assets and liabilities at that date had the following book and fair values:

	Book value	*Fair value*
Cash	€ 10,000	€ 10,000
Accounts receivable (net)	40,000	40,000
Inventories (FIFO cost)	80,000	90,000
Land	50,000	40,000
Plant and equipment (net of accumulated depreciation)	140,000	220,000
Total assets	€320,000	€400,000
Liabilities	(70,000)	(70,000)
Net assets (shareholders' equity)	€250,000	€330,000

The first order of business is the calculation of the differential, as follows:

Regency's cost for 40% of Elixir's ordinary share   €140,000

Book value of 40% of Elixir's net assets (€250,000 × 40%)   (100,000)
Total differential   € 40,000

Next, the €40,000 is allocated to those individual assets and liabilities for which fair value differs from book value. In the example, the differential is allocated to inventories, land, and plant and equipment, as follows:

Item	Book value	Fair value	Difference debit (credit)	40% of difference debit (credit)
Inventories	€ 80,000	€ 90,000	€ 10,000	€ 4,000
Land	50,000	40,000	(10,000)	(4,000)
Plant and equipment	140,000	220,000	80,000	32,000
Differential allocated				€32,000

The difference between the allocated differential of €32,000 and the total differential of €40,000 is essentially identical to goodwill of €8,000. As shown by the following computation, goodwill represents the excess of the cost of the investment over the fair value of the net assets acquired.

Regency's cost for 40% of Elixir's ordinary share   €140,000
40% of Elixir's net assets (€330,000 × 40%)   (132,000)
Excess of cost over fair value (goodwill)   €   8,000

At this point it is important to note that the allocation of the differential is not recorded formally by either Regency Corporation or Elixir Company. Furthermore, Regency does not remove the differential from the investment account and allocate it to the respective assets, since the use of the equity method does not involve the recording of individual assets and liabilities. Regency leaves the differential of €40,000 in the investment account, as part of the balance of €140,000 at January 2, 2011. Accordingly, information pertaining to the allocation of the differential is maintained by the investor, but this information is outside the formal accounting system, which is comprised of journal entries and account balances.

After the differential has been allocated, the amortization pattern is developed. To develop the pattern in this example, assume that Elixir's plant and equipment have 10 years of useful life remaining and that Elixir depreciates its property, plant and equipment on a straight-line basis. Under the provisions of IFRS 3, Regency may not amortize the unallocated differential, which is akin to goodwill, but must consider its possible impairment whenever preparing financial statements to conform with IFRS. Regency would prepare the following amortization schedule:

Item	Differential debit (credit)	Useful life	Amortization 2010	2011	2012
Inventories (FIFO)	€ 4,000	Sold in 2011	€4,000	€ --	€ --
Land	(4,000)	Indefinite	--	--	--
Plant and equipment (net)	32,000	10 years	3,200	3,200	3,200
Goodwill	8,000	N/A	--	--	--
Totals	€40,000		€7,200	€3,200	€3,200

Note that the entire differential allocated to inventories is amortized in 2010 because the cost flow assumption used by Elixir is FIFO. If Elixir had been using weighted-average costing instead of FIFO, amortization might have been computed on a different basis. Note also that the differential allocated to Elixir's land is not amortized, because land is not a depreciable asset. Goodwill likewise is not subject to amortization.

The amortization of the differential, to the extent required under IFRS, is recorded formally in the accounting system of Regency Corporation. Recording the amortization adjusts the equity in Elixir's income that Regency recorded based on Elixir's statement of comprehensive income. Elixir's income must be adjusted because it is based on Elixir's book values, not on the cost that Regency incurred to acquire Elixir. Regency would make the following entries in 2011, assuming that Elixir reported profit of €30,000 and paid cash dividends of €10,000:

1.	Investment in Elixir	12,000	
	Equity in Elixir income (€30,000 × 40%)		12,000
2.	Equity in Elixir income (amortization of differential)	7,200	
	Investment in Elixir		7,200
3.	Cash	4,000	
	Investment in Elixir (€10,000 × 40%)		4,000

The balance in the investment account on Regency's records at the end of 2011 is €140,800 [= €140,000 + €12,000 − (€7,200 + €4,000)], and Elixir's shareholders' equity, as shown previously, is €270,000. The investment account balance of €140,000 is not equal to 40% of €270,000. However, this difference can easily be explained, as follows:

Balance in investment account at December 31, 2011		€140,800
40% of Elixir's net assets at December 31, 2011		108,000
Difference at December 31, 2011		€ 32,800
Differential at January 2, 2011	€40,000	
Differential amortized during 2011	(7,200)	
Unamortized differential at December 31, 2011		€ 32,800

As the years go by, the balance in the investment account will come closer and closer to representing 40% of the book value of Elixir's net assets. After twenty years, the remaining difference between these two amounts would be attributed to the original differential allocated to land (a €4,000 credit) and the amount similar to goodwill (€8,000), unless written off due to impairment. This €4,000 difference on the land would remain until Elixir sold it.

To illustrate how the sale of land would affect equity method procedures, assume that Elixir sold the land in the year 2030 for €80,000. Since Elixir's cost for the land was €50,000, it would report a gain of €30,000, of which €12,000 (= €30,000 × 40%) would be recorded by Regency, when it records its 40% share of Elixir's reported profit, ignoring income taxes. However, from Regency's viewpoint, the gain on sale of land should have been €40,000 (€80,000 − €40,000) because the cost of the land from Regency's perspective was €40,000 at January 2, 2010. Therefore, besides the €12,000 share of the gain recorded above, Regency should record an additional €4,000 gain [(= €40,000 − €30,000) × 40%] by debiting the investment account and crediting the equity in Elixir income account. This €4,000 debit to the investment account will negate the €4,000 differential allocated to land on January 2, 2010, since the original differential was a credit (the fair value of the land was €10,000 less than its book value).

Intercompany transactions between investor and investee. Transactions between the investor and the investee may require that the investor make certain adjustments when it records its share of the investee earnings. In terms of the concept that governs realization of transactions, profits can be recognized by an entity only when realized through a sale to outside (unrelated) parties in arm's-length transactions (sales and purchases) between the investor and investee. Similar problems can arise when sales of property, plant, and equipment between the parties occur. In all cases, there is no need for any adjustment when the transfers are made at book value (i.e., without either party recognizing a profit or loss in its separate accounting records).

In preparing consolidated financial statements, all intercompany (parent-subsidiary) transactions are eliminated. However, when the equity method is used to account for investments, only the *profit component* of intercompany (investor-investee) transactions is eliminated. This is because the equity method does not result in the combining of all statement of comprehensive income accounts (such as sales and cost of sales) and therefore will not cause the financial statements to contain redundancies. In contrast, consolidated statements would include redundancies if the gross amounts of all intercompany transactions were not eliminated.

IAS 28 as originally issued was not explicit regarding the percentage of unrealized profits on investor-investee transactions to be eliminated. Logical arguments can be made to eliminate 100% of intercompany profits not realized through a subsequent transaction with unrelated third parties that would replicate the approach used when preparing consolidated financial statements. However, good arguments can also be presented for the elimination of only the percentage held by the investor and this also applies to unrealized profits and losses arising for both "upstream" and "downstream" transactions (i.e., sales from investee to investor, and from investor to investee) which should be eliminated to the extent of the investor's interest in the investee.

Elimination of the investor's interest in the investee, rather than the entire unrealized profit on the transaction, is based on the logic that in an investor-investee situation, the investor does not have control (as would be the case with a subsidiary), and thus the nonowned percentage of profit is effectively realized through an arm's-length transaction. This is essentially the same logic as is set forth in IAS 31, dealing with joint venture accounting. For joint ventures, IAS 31 allows for proportionate consolidation, which implies likewise that profits on intercompany transactions be eliminated only to the extent of the investor's interest in the venture. However, notwithstanding the use of proportionate elimination of intercompany profits, to the extent that losses are indicative of impairment in the value of the investment, this rule would not apply.

For purposes of determining the percentage interest in unrealized profit or loss to be eliminated, a group's interest in an associate is the aggregate of the holdings in that associate by the parent and its subsidiaries (excluding any interests held by minority interests of subsidiaries). Any holdings of the group's other associates (i.e., equity method investees) or joint ventures are ignored for the purpose of applying the equity method. When an associate has subsidiaries, associates, or joint ventures, the profits or losses and net assets taken into account in applying the equity method are those recognized in the associate's consolidated financial statements (including the associate's share of the profits or losses and net assets of its associates and joint ventures), after any adjustments necessary to give effect to the investor's accounting policies.

Example of accounting for intercompany transactions

Continue with the same information from the previous example and also assume that Elixir Company sold inventory to Regency Corporation in 2011 for €2,000 profit. Thirty percent of this inventory remains unsold by Regency at the end of 2011. Elixir's net profit for 2011, including the gross profit on the inventory sold to Regency, is €20,000; Elixir's income tax rate is 34%. Regency should make the following journal entries for 2011 (ignoring deferred taxes):

1.	Investment in Elixir	8,000	
	Equity in Elixir income (€20,000 × 40%)		8,000
2.	Equity in Elixir income (amortization of differential)	3,600	
	Investment in Elixir		3,600
3.	Equity in Elixir income	158	
	Investment in Elixir (€2,000 × 30% × 66% × 40%)		158

The amount in the last entry needs further elaboration. Since 30% of the inventory remains unsold, only €600 of the intercompany profit is unrealized at year-end. This profit, net of income taxes, is €396. Regency's share of this profit (€158) is included in the first (€8,000) entry recorded. Accordingly, the third entry is needed to adjust or correct the equity in the reported net income of the investee.

Eliminating entries for intercompany profits in property, plant, and equipment are similar to those in the examples above. However, intercompany profit is realized only as the assets are depreciated by the purchasing entity. In other words, if an investor buys or sells property, plant, and equipment from or to an investee at a price above book value, the gain would only be realized piecemeal over the asset's remaining depreciable life. Accordingly, in the year of sale the pro rata share (based on the investor's percentage ownership interest in the investee, regardless of whether the sale is upstream or downstream) of the unrealized portion of the intercompany profit would have to be eliminated. In each subsequent year during the asset's life, the pro rata share of the gain realized in the period would be added to income from the investee.

Example of eliminating intercompany profit on property, plant, and equipment

Assume that Radnor Co., that owns 25% of Empanada Co., sold to Empanada an item of property, plant, and equipment having a five-year remaining life, at a gain of €100,000. Radnor Co. expects to remain in the 34% marginal tax bracket. The sale occurred at the end of 2011; Empanada Co. will use straight-line depreciation to amortize the asset over the years 2012 through 2016.

The entries related to the foregoing are

2011

1.	Gain on sale of property, plant, and equipment	25,000	
	Deferred gain		25,000
	To defer the unrealized portion of the gain		
2.	Deferred tax benefit	8,500	
	Income tax expense		8,500
	Tax effect of gain deferral		

Alternatively, the 2011 events could have been reported by this single entry.

Equity in Empanada income	16,500	
Investment in Empanada Co.		16,500

2012 through 2016 (each year):

1.	Deferred gain	5,000	
	Gain on sale of property, plant, and equipment		5,000
	To amortize deferred gain		
2.	Income tax expense	1,700	
	Deferred tax benefit		1,700
	Tax effect of gain realization		

The alternative treatment would be

Investment in Empanada Co.	3,300	
Equity in Empanada income		3,300

In the example above, the tax currently paid by Radnor Co. (34% × €25,000 taxable gain on the transaction) is recorded as a deferred tax benefit in 2011 since taxes will not be due on the book gain recognized in the years 2012 through 2016. Under provisions of IAS 12, deferred tax benefits should be recorded to reflect the tax effects of all deductible temporary differences. Unless Radnor Co. could demonstrate that future taxable amounts arising from existing temporary differences exist, this deferred tax benefit might be offset by an equivalent valuation allowance in Radnor Co.'s statement of financial position at year-end 2011, because of the doubt that it will ever be realized. Thus, the deferred tax benefit might not be recognizable, net of the valuation allowance, for financial reporting purposes unless other temporary differences not specified in the example provided future taxable amounts to offset the net deductible effect of the deferred gain.

NOTE: The deferred tax impact of an item of income for book purposes in excess of tax is the same as a deduction for tax purposes in excess of book.

This is discussed more fully in Chapter 26.

Accounting for a partial sale or additional purchase of the equity investment. This section covers the accounting issues that arise when the investor either sells some or all of its equity or acquires additional equity in the investee. The consequence of these actions could involve discontinuation of the equity method of accounting, or resumption of the use of that method.

Example of accounting for a discontinuance of the equity method

Assume that Plato Corp. owns 10,000 ordinary shares (30%) of Xenia Co. for which it paid €250,000 ten years ago. On July 1, 2011, Plato sells 5,000 Xenia shares for €375,000. The balance in the Investment in Xenia Co. account at January 1, 2011, was €600,000. Assume that all the original differential between cost and book value has been amortized. To calculate the gain (loss) on the sale of 5,000 shares, it is necessary first to adjust the investment account so that it is current as of the date of sale. Assuming that the investee reported net profit of €100,000 for the six months ended June 30, 2011, the investor should record the following entries:

1.	Investment in Xenia Co.	30,000	
	Equity in Xenia income (€100,000 × 30%)		30,000
2.	Income tax expense	2,040	
	Deferred tax liability (€30,000 × 20% × 34%)		2,040

The gain on sale can now be computed, as follows:

Proceeds on sale of 5,000 shares	€375,000
Book value of the 5,000 shares (€630,000 × 50%)	315,000
Gain from sale of investment in Xenia Co	€ 60,000

Two entries will be needed to reflect the sale: one to record the proceeds, the reduction in the investment account, and the gain (or loss); the other to record the tax effects thereof. Recall that the investor must have computed the deferred tax effect of the undistributed earnings of the investee that it had recorded each year, on the basis that those earnings either would eventually be paid as dividends or would be realized as capital gains. When those dividends are ultimately received or when the investment is disposed of, the deferred tax liability recorded previously must be amortized.

The gains (losses) from sales of investee equity instruments are reported on the investor's income statement in the other income and expense section, assuming that an entity presents the components of profit or loss in a separate income statement.

According to IAS 28, an investor should discontinue use of the equity method when it ceases to have significant influence in an associate while retaining some or all of its investment. When the equity method of accounting is discontinued due to a loss of significant influence, the investor is required to measure at fair value any investment it retains in the former associate. Any difference between the fair value of any retained investment and any proceeds from disposing of the part interest in the associate and the carrying amount of the investment at the date when significant influence is lost in recognized in profit or loss.

An entity may hold an investment in another entity's ordinary share that is below the level that would create a presumption of significant influence, which it later increases so that the threshold for application of the equity method is exceeded. The guidance of IAS 28 would suggest that when the equity method is first applied, the difference between the carrying value of the investment and the fair value of the underlying net identifiable assets must be computed (as described earlier in the chapter). Even though IAS 39's fair value provisions were being applied, there will likely be a difference between the fair value of the passive investment (gauged by market prices for publicly-traded instruments) and the fair value of the investee's underlying net assets (which are driven by the ability to generate cash flows, etc.). Thus, when the equity method accounting threshold is first exceeded for a formerly passively held investment, determination of the "goodwill-like" component of the investment will typically be necessary.

Investor accounting for investee capital transactions. Investor accounting for investee capital transactions that affect the worth of the investor's investment is not addressed by IAS 28. However, given that ultimately the effect of using equity method accounting is intended to be similar to full consolidation, it is reasonable that investee transactions of a capital nature, which affect the investor's share of the investee's shareholders' equity, should be accounted for as if the investee were a consolidated subsidiary. These transactions principally include situations where the investee purchases treasury shares from, or sells unissued shares or shares held in the treasury to, outside shareholders (i.e., owners other than the reporting entity). (Note that, if the investor participates in these transactions on a pro rata basis, its percentage ownership will not change and no special accounting would be necessary.) Similar results will be obtained when holders of outstanding options or convertible instruments acquire additional investee ordinary shares via exercise or conversion.

When the investee engages in one of the foregoing capital transactions, the investor's ownership percentage will be altered. This gives rise to a gain or loss, depending on whether the price paid (for treasury shares acquired) or received (for shares issued) is greater or lesser than the per share carrying value of the investor's interest in the investee. However, since no gain or loss can be recognized on capital transactions, these purchases or sales will be reflected in paid-in capital and/or retained earnings directly, without being reported in the investor's profit or loss. This method is consistent with the treatment that would be accorded to a consolidated subsidiary's capital transactions.

Example of accounting for an investee capital transaction

Assume that Roger Corp. purchases, on February 1, 2011, 25% (2,000 shares) of Energetic Corp.'s outstanding shares for €80,000. The cost is equal to both the book and fair values of Roger's interest in Energetic's underlying net assets (i.e., there is no differential to be accounted for as goodwill). One week later, Energetic Corp. acquires 1,000 own shares from other shareholders for €50,000. Since the price paid (€50/share) exceeded Roger Corp.'s per share carrying value of its interest, (€80,000 ÷ 2,000 shares =) €40, Roger Corp. has in fact suffered economic harm by virtue of this transaction. Also, Roger's percentage ownership of Energetic Corp. has increased, because the number of shares held by third parties, and total shares outstanding, have been reduced.

Roger Corp.'s new interest in Energetic's net assets is

$$\frac{2{,}000 \text{ shares held by Roger Corp}}{7{,}000 \text{ shares outstanding in total}} \times \text{Energetic Corp net assets}$$

$$= .2857 \times (\text{€}320{,}000 - \text{€}50{,}000)$$

$$= \text{€}77{,}143$$

The interest held by Roger Corp. has thus been diminished by €80,000 − €77,143 = €2,857. Therefore, Roger Corp. should make the following entry:

Paid-in capital (or retained earnings)	2,857	
Investment in Energetic Corp.		2,857

Roger Corp. should charge the loss against paid-in capital only if paid-in capital from past transactions of a similar nature exists; otherwise, the debit must be made to retained earnings. Had the transaction given rise to a gain, it would have been credited to paid-in capital only (never to retained earnings) following the accounting principle that transactions in one's own shares cannot produce reportable earnings and are accounted for in equity.

Note that the amount of the charge to paid-in capital (or retained earnings) in the entry above can be verified as follows: Roger Corp.'s share of the posttransaction net equity (2/7) multiplied by the excess price paid to outside interests (€50 – €40 = €10) multiplied by the number of shares purchased = $2/7 \times €10 \times 1,000 = €2,857$.

Other-than-temporary impairment in value of equity method investments. IAS 28 provides that if there is a decline in value of an investment accounted for by the equity method which is determined to be "other-than-temporary" in nature, the carrying value of the investment should be adjusted downward. This criterion must be applied on an individual investment basis. As goodwill forms part of the carrying amount of an associate and is not recognized separately, the entire carrying amount is tested for impairment and not the goodwill specifically. Furthermore, should an impairment be recognized and conditions change in subsequent periods such that a reversal of the impairment is required, no limitation shall be placed on the extent of that reversal on the basis that part of the carrying amount impaired implicitly related to goodwill, which creates a difference, conceptually, with the impairment of goodwill for subsidiaries.

In determining any potential impairment, an entity should consider

1. Its share of the present value of the estimated future cash flows expected to be generated by the investee as a whole, including the cash flows from the operations of the investee and the proceeds on the ultimate disposal of the investment; or
2. The present value of the estimated future cash flows that are expected to arise from dividends to be received from the investment and from its ultimate disposal.

Under appropriate assumptions (given a perfectly functioning capital market), both methods give the same result. Any resulting impairment loss for the investment is allocated in accordance with IAS 36. Accordingly, it would first be allocated to that component of the investment carrying value that reflects any underlying, remaining goodwill, as described earlier in this chapter.

Other Requirements of IAS 28

Disclosure of ownership interests. The standard requires that there be disclosure of the percentage of ownership that is held by the investor in each investment and, if it differs, the percentage of voting rights that are controlled. The method of accounting that is being applied to each significant investment should also be identified.

Consistency of accounting policies. Accounting policies will differ from entity to entity as will the assumptions that are applied in preparing the financial statements, As such, there may have been certain assumptions or adjustments made in developing the information to which the equity accounting method is applied. For example, the investee may have used different accounting principles than the investor, for which the investor made allowances in determining its share of the investee's operating results. The reported results of an investee that formerly used average costing method of accounting for inventory, for instance, may have been adjusted by the investor to conform to its first-in, first-out costing method.

Coterminous year-end dates. An investee's fiscal year may differ from the investor's, and the investor may convert this to its fiscal year by making necessary adjustments to period data accounted for. IAS 28 requires that a fiscal year-end difference of no more than three months is permissible if unadjusted investee financial statements are to be employed. In any such case, if the impact is material, the fact of having made these adjustments should be disclosed, although it would be unusual to report the actual amount of such adjustments to users of the investor's financial statements.

Treatment of cumulative preferred shares. If an associate has outstanding cumulative preferred shares, held by interests other than the investor, the investor should compute its equity interest in the investee's earnings after deducting dividends due to the preferred shareholders, whether or not declared. If material, this should be explained in the investor's financial statements.

Treatment of investor's recognition of recurring investee losses. When, due to the investor's recognition of recurring investee losses, the carrying value of the equity method investment has been reduced to zero, normally the investor will not recognize any share of further investee losses. If an investor ceases recognition of its share of losses of an investee, disclosure must be made in the notes to the financial statements of the unrecognized share of losses, both incurred during the current reporting period and cumulatively to date. The reason for the disclosure of cumulative unrecognized losses is that this is a measure of the amount of future investee earnings that will have to be realized before any further income will be reported in earnings by the investor.

There are certain exceptions to this rule. If the investor has incurred obligations or made payments on behalf of the associate to satisfy obligations of the associate that the investor has guaranteed or to which it is otherwise committed, whether funded or not, it should record further losses up to the amount of the guarantee or other commitment that it has made.

Impact of Potential Voting Interests on Application of Equity Method Accounting for Investments in Associates

Historically, actual voting interests in equity method investees has been the criterion used to determine

1. If equity method accounting for investees is to be employed; and
2. What percentage to apply in determining the allocation of the equity method investee's earnings to be included in the earnings of the equity method investor.

A potential interest may exist in the form of options, warrants, convertible shares, or a contractual arrangement to acquire additional shares, including shares that it may have sold to another shareholder in the investee or to another party, with a right or contractual arrangement to reacquire the shares transferred.

As to whether the potential shares should be considered in reaching a decision as to whether significant influence is present, and thus whether reporting entity is to be regarded as the equity method investor and should therefore apply equity method accounting, IAS 28 holds that this is indeed a factor to weigh and, thus, the existence and effect of potential voting rights that are presently exercisable or presently convertible should be considered when assessing whether an entity has significant influence over another. All potential voting rights should be considered, including potential voting rights held by other entities (which would counter the impact of the reporting entity's potential voting interest).

For example, an entity holding a 15% voting interest in another entity, but having options, not counterbalanced by options held by another party, to acquire another 15% voting interest, would thus effectively have a 30% current and potential voting interest, and would thus make use of the equity method in accounting for the investment required.

The proportion of profits or losses and share of other comprehensive income allocated to an investor that accounts for its investment using the equity method under IAS 28 should be determined based solely on present ownership interests.

DISCLOSURE REQUIREMENTS

IAS 28 provides for extensive disclosures. These include

1. The fair value of investments in associates for which there are published price quotations;
2. Summarized financial information of associates, including the aggregated amounts of assets, liabilities, revenues, and profit or loss;
3. The reasons why the presumption that an investor does not have significant influence is overcome if the investor holds, directly or indirectly through subsidiaries, less than 20% of the voting or potential voting power of the investee but concludes that it has significant influence;
4. The reasons why the presumption that an investor has significant influence is overcome if the investor holds, directly or indirectly through subsidiaries, 20% or more of the voting or potential voting power of the investee but concludes that is does not have significant influence;
5. The reporting date of the financial statements of an associate when such financial statements are used in applying the equity method and are as of a reporting date or for a period that is different from that of the investor, and the reasons for using a different reporting date or different period;
6. The nature and extent of any restrictions on the ability of associates to transfer funds to the investor in the form of cash dividends, repayment of loans or advances (i.e., borrowing arrangements, regulatory restraint, etc.);
7. The unrecognized share of net losses of an associate, both for the period and cumulatively, if an investor has discontinued recognition of its share of losses of an associate.

Investments in associates accounted for using the equity method must be classified as long-term assets and disclosed as a separate item in the statement of financial position. The investor's share of the after-tax profit or loss of such associates investments should be disclosed as a separate item in the statement of comprehensive income. The investor's share of any discontinuing operations of such associates also should be separately disclosed. Furthermore, the investor's share of changes in the associate's equity recognized directly in equity by the investor is to be disclosed in the statement of changes in equity required by IAS 1.

To comply with the requirements of IAS 37, the investor must disclose

1. Its share of the contingent liabilities of an associate for which it is also contingently liable; and
2. Those contingent liabilities that arise because the investor is severally liable for all liabilities of the associate.

FUTURE DEVELOPMENTS

IASB Project: Consolidation

In May 2011, the IASB issued standards that came to be known as the "gang of five"— essentially all standards that deal with aspects of consolidation and the reporting of interests held in other entities. The standards that were issued or amended as part of this process were IFRS 10, *Consolidated Financial Statements;* IFRS 11, *Joint Arrangements;* IFRS 12,

Disclosure of Interests in Other Entities; IAS 27, *Separate Financial Statements;* and IAS 28, *Investments in Associates and Joint Ventures.* The scope of IAS 28 as we have hitherto known it was extended to include investees over which an investor has joint control and is required to equity-account its investment in terms of IFRS 11. Effectively, the scope of IAS 28 now extends over all investees that an entity has significant influence over as well as all joint arrangements whereby the parties that have joint control of the arrangement have rights to the net assets of the arrangement. The principles applied in the current version of IAS 28 in respect of the process followed in equity accounting remain unchanged, however.

The standard is applicable for annual periods beginning on or after 1 January 2013. Earlier application is permitted. However, if an entity applies this Standard earlier, it is required to disclose that fact and apply IFRS 10, IFRS 11, IFRS 12 and IAS 27 (as amended in 2011) at the same time.

Examples of Financial Statement Disclosures

SAB Miller plc
Annual Report 2011

Accounting principles

Associates

Associates are entities in which the group has a long-term interest and over which the group has directly or indirectly significant influence, where significant influence is the ability to influence the financial and operating policies of the entity.

The associate, Distell Group Ltd., has a statutory accounting reference date of June 30. In respect of each year ending March 31, this company is included based on financial statements drawn up to the previous December 31, but taking into account any changes in the subsequent period from January 1 to March 31 that would materially affect the results. All other associates are included on a coterminous basis.

Notes to the consolidated financial statements

Investments in associates

A list of the group's significant investments in associates, including the name, county of incorporation and proportion of ownership interest is given in note 35 to the consolidated financial statements.

	US $m
At April 1, 2009	1,787
Exchange adjustments	90
Investments in associates	76
Repayment of investments by associates	337
Share of results retained	(3)
Repayment of investments by associates	337
Share of gains recognized in other comprehensives income	2
Dividends receivable	(109)
Transfer from other assets	33
At March 31, 2010	2,213
Exchange adjustments	136
Investments in associates	168
Repayment of investments by associates	(68)
Share of results retained	357
Share of gains recognized in other comprehensives income	2
Dividends receivable	(89)
March 31, 2011	2,719

2011

On February 24, 2011, the Tsogo Sun Group merged with Gold Reef Resorts Ltd., (GRR), a Johannesburg Stock Exchange listed business, through an all share merger. The transaction was effected through the acquisition by GRR of Tsogo Sun, and the group exchanged its entire 49% shareholding in Tsogo Sun for a 39.68% shareholding in the listed enlarged entity and resulted in a profit of US $159 million on the partial disposal of the group's shareholding in Tsogo Sun and a loss of US $26 million being the group's share of the associate's loss on the merger transaction. The increase in the investments in associates in the year included US $159 million being the group's share of the fair value uplift on the investment in the enlarged entity.

On November 4, 2010, Tsogo Sun Gaming (Pty) Ltd., a wholly owned subsidiary of the group's associate, Tsogo Sun, repaid the R490 million (US$68 million) preference shares issued to SABSA Holding (Pty) Ltd., a wholly owned subsidiary of the group.

2010

On October 12, 2009, SABSA Holding (Pty) Ltd. Subscribed for R490 million (US$63 million) preference share in Tsogo Sun Gaming (Pty) Ltd., as the group's share of the funding for the 30% increase in the Tsogo Sun group's effective interest in Tsogo Sun KwaZulu-Natal (Pty) Ltd., the licensee and operator of the Suncoast Casino in Durban.

The analysis of associated undertakings between listed and unlisted investment is shown below:

	2011 US $m	2010 US $m
Listed	662	189
Unlisted	2,057	2,024
	2,719	2,213

The market value of listed investments included above is

Distell Group Ltd	624	547
Delta Corporation Ltd	188	126
Gold Reef Resorts Ltd	1,028	--

Summarized financial information for associates for total assets, total liabilities, revenue and profit or loss on a 100% basis is shown below.

	2011 US $m	2010 US $m
Total assets	14,046	10,020
Total liabilities	(5,730)	(3,745)
Revenue	10,921	9,363
Net profit	1,276	1,321

Delta Corporation Ltd., a listed associate undertaking of the group which operates in Zimbabwe, was included within the group's results with effect from April 1, 2010, following the effective "dollarization" of the economy in 2009, the end of hyperinflation, and the stabilization of the local economy. Some of the group's investment in associated undertakings which operate in African countries are also subject to local exchange control regulations. These local exchange control regulations provide for restrictions on exporting capital from those countries, other than through normal dividends.

35. Principal subsidiaries, associates and joint ventures

Associates and joint ventures

The principal associates and joint ventures of the group as at March 31 are set out below. Where the group's interest in an associated or a joint venture is held by a subsidiary undertaking which is not wholly owned by the group the subsidiary undertaking is indicated in a note below.

Name	Country of incorporation	Nature of relationship	Principal activity	Effective interest 2011	Effective interest 2010
European operations					
Grolsch (UK) Ltd	United Kingdom	Associate	Brewing	50%	50%
North American operations					
MillerCoors LLC[1]	USA	Joint venture	Brewing	58%	58%
African operations					
Brasseries Internationales Holding Ltd[2]	Gibraltar	Associate	Holding company for subsidiaries principally located in Africa	20%	20%
Sociëtë des Brasseries et Glacieres Internationales[2]	France	Associate	Holding company for subsidiaries principally located in Africa	20%	20%
Algerienne de Bavaroise[2,3]	Algeria	Associate	Brewing	40%	40%
Delta Corporation Ltd[4,5]	Zimbabwe	Associate	Brewing / Soft drinks	23%	23%
Empresa Cervejas De N'Gola SARL	Angola	Associate	Brewing	28%	28%
Kenya Breweries Ltd[5,6]	Kenya	Associate	Brewing	12%	12%
Marocaine d'Investissements et de Services[2,7]	Morocco	Associate	Brewing	40%	40%
Skikda Bottling Company[2,3]	Algeria	Associate	Soft drinks	40%	40%
Sociëtë de Boissons de l'Ouest, Algerien[2,3]	Algeria	Associate	Soft drinks	40%	40%
Sociëtë des Nouvelles Brasseries[2,3]	Algeria	Associate	Brewing	40%	40%
Asian operations					
China Resources Snow Breweries Ltd[2]	British Virgin Islands	Associate	Holding company for brewing subsidiaries located in China	49%	49%
Pacific Beverages (Pty) Ltd[2]	Australia	Joint venture	Sales and distribution	50%	50%

US GAAP COMPARISON

US GAAP requires similarly to IFRS the equity method of accounting for investments in associates over which the investors have significant influence. Significant influence is presumed at equity ownership percentages between 20% and 50%, unless it can be demonstrated that the investor cannot exercise such influence. US GAAP uses the term equity-accounted subsidiary. The application of the equity method of accounting is similar to IFRS.

US GAAP contains very prescriptive guidance concerning the resumption of recognizing profits from an equity-method investee after the recognition had been suspended due to cumulative losses exceeding the investor's base. If an investor has both equity and debt in an equity-method investee, after the balance of the equity investment is reduced to zero, other instruments are reduced. Upon recovery, the basis of the other investments is restored in order of claim.

14 INTERESTS IN JOINT VENTURES

INTRODUCTION

Accounting for investments over which the investor has joint control is carried out in terms of IAS 31 *Joint Ventures*. This method of accounting proposes an additional option of accounting for joint ventures which can be exercised at the option of the investor. This method of accounting is termed the proportionate consolidation method which can be employed by a reporter as an alternative to the equity method which is also acceptable.

Sources of IFRS	
IAS 31	*SIC* 13

DEFINITIONS OF TERMS

Carrying amount. The amount at which an asset is currently presented in the statement of financial position.

Consolidated financial statements. Financial statements of a group presented as those of a single economic entity.

Control. The power to govern the financial and operating policies of an entity so as to obtain benefits from its activities and increase, maintain, or protect the amount of those benefits.

Cost. The amount of cash or cash equivalents paid or the fair value of other consideration given to acquire an asset at the time of its acquisition or construction or, where applicable, the amount attributed to that asset when initially recognized in accordance with the specific requirements of other IFRS, (e.g., IFRS 2, *Share-Based Payment*).

Cost method. A method of accounting for investment whereby the investment is recorded at cost; the statement of comprehensive income reflects income from the investment only to the extent that the investor receives distributions (dividends) from the investee's accumulated net profits arising after the date of acquisition. Distributions received in excess of accumulated profits are regarded as a recovery of investment and are recognized as a reduction of the cost of the investment.

Differential. The difference between investment cost and the book value of underlying net assets of the investee.

Equity method. A method of accounting whereby an interest in a jointly controlled entity is initially recorded at cost and adjusted thereafter for the post-acquisition change in the venturer's share of net assets of the jointly controlled entity. The profit or loss of the venturer includes the venturer's share of the profit or loss of the jointly controlled entity.

Fair value. The amount for which an asset could be exchanged between a knowledgeable, willing buyer and seller in an arm's-length transaction.

Goodwill. An intangible asset acquired in a business combination representing the future economic benefits expected to be derived from the business combination that are not allocated to other individually identifiable and separately recognizable assets acquired.

Investee. An entity that issued voting share that is held by an investor.

Investment. An asset held by an entity for purposes of accretion of wealth through distributions of interest, royalties, dividends, and rentals, or for capital appreciation or other benefits to be obtained.

Investor. A business entity that holds an investment in the voting shares of another entity.

Joint arrangement. A contractual arrangement whereby two or more parties undertake an economic activity together and share decision making relating to the activity. Joint arrangements can be classified into three types—joint operations, joint assets and joint ventures.

Joint control. The contractually agreed-on joint sharing of control over the operations and/or assets of an economic activity; exists only when the strategic financial and operating decisions relating to the activity require the unanimous consent of the parties sharing control (the venturers).

Joint venture. A contractual arrangement whereby two or more parties undertake an economic activity subject to their joint control.

Proportionate consolidation. A method of accounting whereby an investor's share of each of the assets, liabilities, income and expenses of the investee is combined line by line with similar items in the investor's financial statements or reported as separate line items in the investor's financial statements.

Separate financial statements. Financial statements presented by a parent, an investor in an associate, or a venturer in a jointly controlled entity, in which the investments are accounted for on the basis of the direct equity interest rather than on the basis of the reported results and net assets of the investees.

Significant influence. The power of the investor to participate in the financial and operating policy decisions of the investee, which may be gained by share ownership, statute or agreement; however, this is less than the ability to control those policies.

Undistributed investee earnings. The investor's share of investee earnings in excess of dividends paid.

Venturer. A party to a joint venture that has control over that joint venture.

RECOGNITION AND MEASUREMENT

Accounting for Investments in Joint Ventures

IFRS address accounting for interests in joint ventures as a topic separate from accounting for other investments. Joint ventures share many characteristics with investments that are accounted for by the equity method: The investor clearly has significant influence over the investee but does not have absolute control, and hence full consolidation is typically unwarranted. According to the provisions of IAS 31, two different methods of accounting are possible, although not as true alternatives for the same fact situations: the proportionate consolidation method and the equity method.

Joint ventures can take many forms and structures. Joint ventures may be created as partnerships, as corporations, or as unincorporated associations. The standard identifies three distinct types, referred to as jointly controlled operations, jointly controlled assets, and jointly controlled entities. Notwithstanding the formal structure, all joint ventures are characterized by certain features: having two or more venturers that are bound by a contractual arrangement, and by the fact that the contractual agreement establishes joint control of the entity.

The contractual provision(s) establishing joint control most clearly differentiates joint ventures from other investment scenarios in which the investor has significant influence over the investee. In fact, in the absence of such a contractual provision, joint venture accounting would not be appropriate, even in a situation in which two parties each have 50% ownership interests in an investee. The actual existence of such a contractual provision can be evidenced in a number of ways, although most typically it is in writing and often addresses such matters as the nature, term of existence, and reporting obligations of the joint venture; the governing mechanisms for the venture; the capital contributions by the respective venturers; and the intended division of output, income, expenses, or net results of the venture.

The contractual arrangement also establishes joint control over the venture. The thrust of such a provision is to ensure that no venturer can control the venture unilaterally. Certain decision areas will be stipulated as requiring consent by all the venturers, while other decision areas may be defined as needing the consent of only a majority of the venturers. There is no specific set of decisions that must fall into either grouping, however.

Typically, one venturer will be designated as the manager or operator of the venture. This does not imply the absolute power to govern; however, if such power exists, the venture would be a subsidiary, subject to the requirements of IAS 27 and not accounted for properly under IAS 31.

Scope exemption. IAS 31 does not apply to interests in jointly controlled entities that are held by venture capital organizations, mutual funds, unit trusts, and similar entities (whose business is investing in financial assets with a view to profiting from their total return in the form of interest or dividends and changes in fair value) that are measured at fair value in accordance with IAS 39, when such measurement is well-established practice in those industries. When such investments are measured at fair value, any changes in their fair value are included in profit or loss in the period of the change.

Specific accounting guidance is dependent on whether the entity represents jointly controlled operations, jointly controlled assets, or a jointly controlled entity.

Jointly controlled operations. This type of joint venture is characterized by the assigned use of certain assets or other resources, as opposed to the establishment of a new entity, be it a corporation or partnership. Thus, from a formal or legal perspective, this variety of joint venture may not have an existence that is separate from its sponsors; from an economic point of view, however, the joint venture can still be said to exist, which means that it may exist as an accounting entity. Typically, this form of operation will utilize assets owned by the venture partners, often including plant and equipment as well as inventories, and the partners will sometimes incur debt on behalf of the operation. Actual operations may be conducted on an integrated basis with the partners' own, separate operations, with certain employees, for example, devoting a part of their efforts to the jointly controlled operation.

IAS 31 is concerned not with the accounting by the entity conducting the jointly controlled operations, but by the venturers having an interest in the entity. Each venturer should recognize in its separate financial statements all assets of the venture that it controls, all liabilities that it incurs, all expenses that it incurs, and its share of any revenues produced by the venture. Often, since the assets are already owned by the venturers, they would be included in their respective financial statements in any event; similarly, any debt incurred will be reported by the partner even in the absence of this special rule. Perhaps the only real challenge, from a measurement and disclosure perspective, would be the revenues attributable to each venture's efforts, which will be determined by reference to the joint venture agreement and other documents.

Jointly controlled assets. In certain industries, such as oil and gas exploration and transmission and mineral extraction, jointly controlled assets are frequently employed. For example, oil pipelines may be controlled jointly by a number of oil producers, each of which uses the facilities and shares in its costs of operation. Certain informal real estate partnerships may also function in this fashion.

IAS 31 stipulates that in the case of jointly controlled assets, each venturer must report in its own financial statements its share of all jointly controlled assets, appropriately classified according to their natures. It must also report any liabilities that it has incurred on behalf of these jointly controlled assets, as well as its share of any jointly incurred liabilities. Each venturer will report any profit earned from the use its share of the jointly controlled assets, along with the pro rata expenses and any other expenses it has incurred directly.

Jointly controlled entities. The major type of joint venture is the jointly controlled entity, which is really a form of partnership (although it may well be structured legally as a corporation) in which each partner has a form of control, rather than only significant influence. The classic example is an equal partnership of two partners; obviously, neither has a majority and either can block any important action, so the two partners must effectively agree on each key decision. Although this may be the model for a jointly controlled entity, it may in practice have more than two venturers and, depending on the partnership or shareholders' agreement, even minority owners may have joint control. For example, a partnership whose partners have 30%, 30%, 30%, and 10% interests, respectively, may have entered into a contractual agreement that stipulates that investment or financing actions may be taken only if there is unanimity among the partners.

Jointly controlled entities control the assets of the joint venture and may incur liabilities and expenses on its behalf. As a legal entity, it may enter into contracts and borrow funds, among other activities. In general, each venturer will share the net results in proportion to its ownership interest. As an entity with a distinct and separate legal and economic identity, the jointly controlled entity will normally produce its own financial statements and other tax and legal reports.

IAS 31 provides alternative accounting treatments that may be applied by the venture partners to reflect the operations and financial position of the venture. The objective is to report economic substance, rather than mere form, but there is not universal agreement on how this may best be achieved.

The benchmark treatment under the standard is the use of proportionate consolidation, which requires that the venture partner reflect its share of all assets, liabilities, revenues, and expenses on its financial statements as if these were incurred or held directly. The rationale behind this being that this approach is very effective at conveying the true scope of an entity's operations, when those operations include interests in one or more jointly controlled entities.

If the venturer employs the proportionate consolidation method, it will have a choice between two presentation formats that are equally acceptable. First, the venture partner may include its share of the assets, liabilities, revenues, and expenses of the jointly controlled entity with similar items under its sole control. Thus, under this method, its share of the venture's receivables would be added to its own accounts receivable and presented as a single total in its statement of financial position. Alternatively, the items that are undivided interests in the venture's assets, and so on, may be shown on separate lines of the venture's financial statements, although still placed within the correct grouping. For example, the venture's receivables might be shown immediately below the partner's individually owned accounts receivable. In either case, the same category totals (aggregate current assets, etc.) will be presented; the only distinction is whether the venture-owned items are given separate recognition. Even if presented on a combined basis, however, the appropriate detail can still be shown in the notes to the financial statements, and indeed to achieve a fair presentation, this might be needed.

The proportionate consolidation method should be discontinued when the partner no longer has the ability to control the entity jointly. This may occur when the interest is held for disposal within twelve months from acquisition date, or when external restrictions are placed on the ability to exercise control. In some cases a partner will waive its right to control the entity, possibly in exchange for other economic advantages, such as a larger interest in the operating results. In such instances, IAS 39 should be used to guide the accounting for the investment.

Under the provisions of IAS 31, a second accounting method, the equity method, is also considered to be acceptable. The equity method in this context is as described in IAS 28 and as explained in Chapter 13. As with the proportionate consolidation method, use of the equity method must be discontinued when the venturer no longer has joint control or significant influence over the jointly controlled entity. In such a case, IAS 39 would be the relevant accounting requirement.

Change from joint control to full control status. If one of the venturers' interest in the jointly controlled entity is increased, whether by an acquisition of some or all of another of the ventures' interest, or by action of a contractual provision of the venture agreement (resulting from a failure to perform by another venturer, etc.), the proportionate consolidation method of accounting ceases to be appropriate and full consolidation will become necessary. Guidance is provided by IFRS 3 and IAS 27 and is discussed fully in Chapter 15.

Accounting for Transactions between Venture Partner and Jointly Controlled Entity

Transfers at a gain to the transferor. A general, underlying principle of financial reporting is that earnings are to be realized only by engaging in transactions with outside parties. Thus, gains cannot be recognized by transferring assets (be they productive assets or goods held for sale in the normal course of the business) to a subsidiary, affiliate, or joint venture, to the extent this really would represent a transaction by an entity with itself. Were this not the rule, entities would establish a range of related entities to sell goods to, thereby permitting the reporting of profits well before any sale to real, unrelated customers ever took place. The potential for abuse of the financial reporting process in such a scenario is too obvious to need elaboration.

IAS 31 stipulates that when a venturer sells or transfers assets to a jointly controlled entity, it may recognize profit only to the extent that the venture is owned by the other venture partners, and then only to the extent that the risks and rewards of ownership have indeed been transferred to the jointly controlled entity. The logic is that a portion of the profit has in fact been realized, to the extent that the purchase was agreed on by unrelated parties that jointly control the entity making the acquisition. For example, if venturers A, B, and C jointly control venture D (each having a 1/3 interest), and A sells equipment having a book value of €40,000 to the venture for €100,000, only 2/3 of the apparent gain of €60,000, or €40,000, may be realized. In its statement of financial position immediately after this transaction, A would report its share of the asset reflected in the statement of financial position of D, 1/3 × €100,000 = €33,333, minus the unrealized gain of €20,000, for a net of €13,333. This is identical to A's remaining 1/3 interest in the pretransaction basis of the asset (1/3 × €40,000 = €13,333). Thus, there is no step-up in the carrying value of the proportionate share of the asset reflected in the transferor's statement of financial position.

If the asset is subject to depreciation, the deferred gain on the transfer (1/3 × €60,000 = €20,000) would be amortized in proportion to the depreciation reflected by the venture, such that the depreciated balance of the asset reported by A is the same as would have been reported had the transfer not taken place. For example, assume that the asset has a useful economic life of five years after the date of transfer to D. The deferred gain (€20,000) would be amortized to profit or loss at a rate of €4,000 per year. At the end of the first posttransfer year, D would report a net carrying value of €100,000 – €20,000 = €80,000; A's proportionate interest is 1/3 × €80,000 = €26,667. The unamortized balance of the deferred gain is €20,000 – €4,000 = €16,000. Thus the net reported amount of A's share of the jointly controlled entity's asset is €26,667 – €16,000 = €10,667. This amount is precisely what A would have reported the remaining share of its asset at on this date: 1/3 × (€40,000 – €8,000) = €10,667.

Of course, A has also reported a gain of €40,000 as of the date of the transfer of its asset to joint venture D, but this represents the gain that has been realized by the sale of 2/3 of the asset to unrelated parties B and C, the coventurers in D. In short, two-thirds of the asset has been sold at a gain, while one-third has been retained and is continuing to be used and depreciated over its remaining economic life and is reported on the cost basis in A's financial statements.

The matters described above are further emphasized in SIC 13, which holds that gains or losses will result from contributions of nonmonetary assets to a jointly controlled entity *only* when significant risks and rewards of ownership have been transferred, and the gain or loss can be reliably measured. However, no gain or loss would be recognized when the asset is contributed in exchange for an equity interest in the jointly controlled entity when the asset is similar to assets contributed by the other venturers. Any unrealized gain or loss should be netted against the related assets, and not presented as deferred gain or loss in the venture's consolidated financial statements.

Transfers of assets at a loss. The foregoing illustration was predicated on a transfer to the jointly controlled entity at a nominal gain to the transferor, of which a portion was realized for financial reporting purposes. The situation when a transfer is at an amount below the transferor's carrying value is dissimilar; rather, such a transfer is deemed to be confirmation of a permanent decline in value, which must be recognized by the transferor immediately rather than being deferred. This reflects the conservative bias in accounting: Unrealized losses are often recognized, while unrealized gains are deferred.

Assume that venturer C (a 1/3 owner of D, as described above) transfers an asset it had been carrying at €150,000 to jointly controlled entity D at a price of €120,000. If the decline is deemed to be other than temporary in nature (that presumptively it is, since C would not normally have been willing to engage in this transaction if the decline were expected to be reversed in the near term), C must recognize the full €30,000 at the time of the transfer. Subsequently, C will pick up its 1/3 interest in the asset held by D (1/3 × €120,000 = €40,000) as its own asset in its statement of financial position, before considering any depreciation, and so on.

Accounting for Assets Purchased from a Jointly Controlled Entity

Transfers at a gain to the transferor. A similar situation arises when a venture partner acquires an asset from a jointly controlled entity: The venturer cannot reflect the gain recognized by the joint venture, to the extent that this represents its share in the results of the venture's operations. For example, again assuming that A, B, and C jointly own D, an asset having a book value of €200,000 is transferred by D to B for a price of €275,000. Since B has a 1/3 interest in D, it would (unless an adjustment were made to its accounting) report €25,000 of D's gain as its own, which would violate the realization concept under GAAP.

To avoid this result, B will record the asset at its cost, €275,000, less the deferred gain, €25,000, for a net carrying value of €250,000, which represents the transferor's basis, €200,000, plus the increase in value realized by unrelated parties (A and C) in the amount of €50,000.

As the asset is depreciated, the deferred gain will be amortized apace. For example, assume that the useful life of the asset in B's hands is ten years. At the end of the first year, the carrying value of the asset is €275,000 – €27,500 = €247,500; the unamortized balance of the deferred gain is €25,000 – €2,500 = €22,500. Thus the net carrying value, after offsetting the remaining deferred gain, will be €247,500 – €22,500 = €225,000. This corresponds to the remaining life of the asset (9/10 of its estimated life) times its original net carrying amount, €250,000. The amortization of the deferred gain should be credited to depreciation expense to offset the depreciation charged on the nominal acquisition price.

Transfers at a loss to the transferor. If the asset was acquired by B at a loss to D, on the other hand, and the decline was deemed to be indicative of an other-than-temporary diminution in value, B should recognize its share of this decline. This contrasts with the gain scenario discussed immediately above, and as such is entirely consistent with the accounting treatment for transfers from the venture partner to the jointly controlled venture.

For example, if D sells an asset carried at €50,000 to B for €44,000, and the reason for this discount is an other than temporary decline in the value of said asset, the venture, D, records a loss of €6,000 and each venture partner will in turn recognize a €2,000 loss. B would report the asset at its acquisition cost of €44,000 and will also report its share of the loss, €2,000. This loss will not be deferred and will not be added to the carrying value of the asset in B's hands (as would have been the case if B treated only the €4,000 loss realized by unrelated parties A and C as being recognizable).

DISCLOSURE REQUIREMENTS

A venture partner is required to disclose in the notes to the financial statements its ownership interests in all significant joint ventures, including its ownership percentage and other relevant data. If the venturer uses proportionate consolidation and merges its share of the assets, liabilities, revenues, and expenses of the jointly controlled entity with its own assets, liabilities, revenues, and expenses, or if the venturer uses the equity method, the notes should disclose the amounts of the current and long-term assets, current and long-term liabilities, revenues, and expenses related to its interests in jointly controlled ventures.

Furthermore, the joint venture partner should disclose any contingencies that the venturer has incurred in relation to its interests in any joint ventures, noting any share of contingencies jointly incurred with other joint venturers. In addition, the venturer's share of any contingencies of the joint venture (as distinct from contingencies incurred in connection with its investment in the venture) for which it may be contingently liable must be reported. Finally, those contingencies that arise because the venturer is contingently liable for the liabilities of the other partners in the jointly controlled entity must be set forth. These disclosures are a logical application of the rules set out in IAS 37, which is discussed in Chapter 18 of this publication.

A venture partner should also disclose in the notes to her/his financial statements information about any commitments s/he has outstanding in respect to interests s/he has in joint ventures. These include any capital commitments s/he has and her/his share of any joint commitments s/he may have incurred with other venture partners, as well as her/his share of the capital commitments of the joint ventures themselves, if any.

Examples of Financial Statement Disclosures

BHP Billiton Group
Annual Report 2010

Accounting principles

Joint ventures

The Group undertakes a number of business activities through joint venture. Joint ventures are established through contractual arrangements that require the unanimous consent of each of the ventures regarding the strategic financial and operating policies of the venture (joint control). The Group's joint ventures are of two types:

Jointly controlled entities

A jointly controlled entity is a corporation, partnership, or other entity in which each participant holds an interest. A jointly controlled entity operates in the same way as other entities, controlling the assets of the joint venture, earning its own income and incurring its own liabilities and expenses. Interests in jointly controlled entities are accounted for using the proportionate consolidation method, whereby the Group's proportionate interest in the assets, liabilities, revenues, and expenses of jointly controlled entities are recognized within each applicable line item of the financial statements. The share of jointly controlled entities' results is recognized in the Group's financial statements from the date that joint control commences until the date at which it ceases.

Jointly controlled assets

The Group has certain contractual arrangements with other participants to engage in joint activities that do not give rise to a jointly controlled entity. These arrangements involve the joint ownership of assets dedicated to the purposes of each venture but do not create a jointly controlled entity as the ventures directly derive the benefits of operation of their jointly owned assets, rather than deriving returns from an interest in a separate entity.

The financial statements of the Group include its share of the assets in such joint ventures, together with the liabilities, revenues, and expenses arising jointly or otherwise from those operations. All such amounts are measured in accordance with the terms of each arrangements, which are usually in proportion to the Group's interest in the jointly controlled assets.

BHP Billiton Group
Annual Report 2010

Notes to the consolidated financial statements

26. Interest in jointly controlled entities

All entities included below are subject ot joint control as a result of geverning contractual arrangements.

Major shareholdings in jointly controlled entites	*Country of incorporation*	*Principal activity*	*Reporting date[a]*	*Ownership interest[a]*	
				2010 %	*2009* %
Caesar Oil Pipeline Company LLC	US	Hydrocarbons transportation	May 31	25	25
Cleopatra Gas Gathering Company LLC	US	Hydrocarbons transporation	May 31	22	22
Ginea Alumina Corporation Ltd	British Virgin Islands	Bauxite mine and alumina refinery development	Dec 31	33.3	33.3
Mozal SARL	Mozambique	Aluminium smelting	June 30	47.1	47.1
Compania Minera Antamina SA	Peru	Copper and zinc mining	June 30	33.75	33.75
Minera Escondida Limitada [b]	Chile	Cooper mining	June 30	57.5	57.5
Phola Coal Processing Plant (Pty) Ltd	South Africa	Coal handling and processing plant	June 30	50	50
Richards Bay Minerals [c]	South Africa	Mineral sands mining and processing	Dec 31	37.76	50
Samarco Mineracao SA	Brazil	Iron ore mining	Dec 31	50	50
Carbones del Cerrejon LLC	Anguilla	Coal mining in Colombia	Dec 31	33.33	33.33
Newcastle Coal Infrastructure Group Pty Limited	Australia	Coal export terminal	June 30	35.5	35.5

	Group share	
	2010 US $m	*2009* US $m
Net assets of jointly controlled entities		
Current assets	3,352	2,813
Noncurrent assets	7,212	7,275
Current liabilities	(2,162)	(2,092)
Noncurrent liabilties	(2.388)	(2,029)
Net assets	6,014	5,967

		Group share	
	2010	2009	2008
	US $m	US $m	US $m
Share of jointly controlled entites' profit			
Revenue	8,642	6,130	10,728
Net operating costs	(4,597)	(4,103)	(3,912)
Operating profit	4,045	2,027	6,816
Net finance costs	(68)	(129)	(94)
Income tax expense	(903)	(465)	(1,418)
Profit after taxation	3,074	1,433	5,304

	Group share	
	2010	2009
	US $m	US $m
Share of continugent liabilities and expenditure commitments of jointly controlled entities		
Contingent liabilties	885	724
Capital expenditure commitments	274	152
Other expenditure commitments	1,455	1,537

(a)   The ownership interest at the Group's and the jointly controlled entity's reporting date are the same. While the annual financial reporting date may be different to the Group's, financial information is obtained as at June 30 in order to report on a consistent annual basis with the Group's reporting date.

(b)   While the group holds a 57.5% interest in Minera Escondida Limitada, the entity is subject to effective joint control due to participant and management agreements which result in the operation of an Owners' Council, whereby significant commercial and operational decisions are determined on aggregate voting interest of at least 75% of the total ownership interest. Accordingly the Group does not have the ability to unilaterally control and therefore consolidate the investment in accordance with IAS 2 7/A ASB 127, **Consolidated and Separate Financial Statements**.

(c)   Richards Bay Minerals comprises two legal entites, Richards Bay Mining (Proprietary) Limited and Richards Bay Titanium (Proprietary) Limited, in each of which the Group has a 50% interest and which function as a single economic entity. After deducting noncontrolling interests in subsidiaries of Richards Bay Minerals, the Group's economic interest in the operations of Richards Bay Minerals is 37.76%.

The principal jointly controlled assets in which the Group has an interest and which are proportionately included in the financial statements are as follows:

			The Group's effective interest	
	Country of		2010	2009
Name	incorporation	Principal activity	%	%
Atlantis	US	Hydrocarbons exploration and production	44	44
Bass Strait	Australia	Hydrocarbons exploration and production	50	50
Liverpool Bay	UK	Hydrocarbons exploration and production	46.1	46.1
Mad Dog	US	Hydrocarbons exploration and production	23.9	23.9
Minerva	Australia	Hydrocarbons exploration and production	90	90
Neptune	US	Hydrocarbons exploration and production	35	35
North West Shelf	Australia	Hydrocarbons exploration and production	8-17	8-17

Name	Country of incorporation	Principal activity	The Group's effective interest 2010 %	2009 %
Ohanet	Algeria	Hydrocarbons exploration and production	45	45
Pyrenees	Australia	Hydrocarbons exploration production and development	71.43	71.43
ROD Integrated Development	Algeria	Hydrocarbons exploration and production	45	45
Shenzi	US	Hydrocarbons exploration and production	44	44
Stybarrow	Australia	Hydrocarbons exploration and production	50	50
Greater Angostura	Trinidad and Tobago	Hydrocarbons production	45	45
Zamzama	Pakistan	Hydrocarbons exploration and production	38.5	38.5
Alumar	Brazil	Alumina refining	36	36
		Aluminium smelting	40	40
Billiton Suriname[a]	Suriname	Bauxite mining and alumina refining	--	45
Worsley	Australia	Bauxite mining and alumina refining	86	86
Central Queensland Coal Associates	Australia	Coal mining	50	50
Gregory	Australia	Coal mining	50	50
Mt Goldsworthy	Australia	Iron ore mining	85	85
Mt Newman	Australia	Iron ore mining	85	85
Yandi	Australia	Iron ore mining	85	85
EKATI	Canada	Diamond mining	80	80
Douglas/Middelburg Mine[b]	South Africa	Coal mining	--	84

	2010 US $m	2009 US $m
Share of contingent liabilties and capital expenditure commitments relating to jointly controlled assets		
Contingent liabiltieis — unsecured[c]	120	94
Contracts for capital expenditure commitments not completed[c]	4,103	4,282

[a] *Billiton Suriname was sold effective July 31, 2009.*

[b] *The Douglas/Middelburg Mine joint venture was dissolved on December 1, 2009. The mining leases, previously held jointly by Xstrata Plc, (through Tavistock Collieries Plc) and BHP Billiton Energy Coal South Africa Limited, have been divided into discrete areas which are now wholly owned and operated by Tavistock Collieries Plc and BHP Billiton Energy Coal South Africa Limited.*

[c] *Included in contingent liabilties and capital expenditure commitments for the Group. Refer to notes 21 and 22 respectively.*

SAB Miller plc
Annual Report 2011

Accounting principles

(iii) Joint ventures

Joint ventures are contractual arrangements which the group has entered into with one or more parties to undertake an economic activity that is subject to joint control. Joint control is the contractually agreed sharing of control over an economic activity, and exists only when the strategic, financial, and operating decisions relating to the activity require the unanimous consent of the parties sharing the control.

The group's share of the recognized income and expenses of associates and joint ventures are accounted for using the equity method from the date significant influence or joint control commences to the date it ceases based on present ownership interests.

The group recognizes its share of associates and joint ventures posttax results as a one-line entry before profit before tax in the income statement, and its share of associates and joint ventures equity movements as a one-line entry under other comprehensive income in the statement of comprehensive income.

When the group's interest in an associate or joint venture has been reduced to nil because the group's share of losses exceeds its interest in the associate or joint venture, the group only provides for additional losses to the extent that it has incurred legal or constructive obligations to fund such losses, or make payments on behalf of the associate or joint venture, where the investment in an associate or joint venture is disposed, the investment ceases to be equity accounted.

SAB Miller plc
Annual Report 2011

Notes to the consolidated financial statements

13. Investments in joint ventures

A list of the group's significant investments in joint ventures, including the name, country of incorporation, and proportion of ownership interest, is given in note 35 to the consolidated financial statements.

	US $m
At April 1, 2009	5,495
Exchange adjustments	11
Investments in joint ventures	353
Share of results retained	536
Share of gains recognized in other comprehensive income	134
Dividends received	(707)
At March 31, 2010	5,822
Exchange adjustments	12
Investments in joint ventures	186
Share of results retained	667
Share of losses recognized in other comprehensive income	(52)
Dividends received	(822)
At March 31, 2011	5,813

Summarized financial information for the group's interest in joint ventures is shown below.

	2011 *US $m*	2010 *US $m*
Revenue	**5,157**	5,168
Expenses	**(4,489)**	(4,631)
Profit after tax	**668**	537
Noncurrent assets	**5,837**	5,842
Current assets	**675**	649
Current liabilties	**(531)**	(564)
Noncurrent liabitlies	**(783)**	(722)

Principal subsidiaries, associates and joint ventures continued

Associates and joint ventures

The principal associates and joint ventures of the group as at March 31 are set out below. Where the group's interest in an associate or a joint venture is held by a subsidiary undertaking which is not wholly owned by the group, the subsidiary undertaking is indicated in a note below.

Name	*Country of incorporation*	*Nature of relationship*	*Principal activity*	*Effective interest* 2011	2010
European opearations					
Grolsch (UK) Ltd	United Kingdom	Associate	Brewing	**50%**	50%
North American operations					
NillerCoors LLC1	USA	Joint Venture	Brewing	**58%**	58%
African opeartions					
Brasseries Internationales Holding Ltd[2]	Gibraltar	Associate	Holding company for subsidiaries	**20%**	20%
Sociëtë des Brasseries et Glaciëres Internationales[2]	France	Associate	Holding company for subsidiaries principally located in Africa	**20%**	20%
Algerienne de Bavaroise[2,3]	Algeria	Associate	Brewing	**40%**	40%
Delta Corporation Ltd [4,5]	Zimbabwe	Associate	Brewing/Soft drinks	**23%**	23%
Empresa Cervejas De N'Gola SARL	Angola	Associate	Brewing	**28%**	28%
Kenya Breweries Ltd[5,6]	Kenya	Associate	Brewing	**12%**	12%
Marocaine d'Investissements et de Services[2,7]	Morocco	Associate	Brewing	**40%**	40%
Skikda Bottling Company[2,3]	Algeria	Associate	Soft drinks	**40%**	40%
Sociëtë de Boissons de l'Ouest Algerien[2,3]	Algeria	Assoicate	Soft drinks	**40%**	40%
Sociëtë des Nouvelles Brasseries[2,3]	Algeria	Associate	Brewing	**40%**	40%
Asian operations					
China Resources Snow Breweries Ltd[2]	British Virgin Islands	Associate	Holding company for brewing subsidiaries located in China	**49%**	49%
Pacific Beverages (Pty) Ltd[2]	Australia	Joint venture	Sales and distribution	**50%**	50%

FUTURE DEVELOPMENTS

Reconsideration of Accounting for Joint Arrangements

In May 2011, IASB issued IFRS 11, *Joint Arrangements,* which will supersede both IAS 31, *Interests in Joint Ventures,* and SIC 13, *Jointly Controlled Entities: Nonmonetary Contributions by Ventures* with effect from 1 January 2013. This standard is a result of the Board's Convergence Project with the FASB and will bring about convergence in principle with requirements set forth by US GAAP.

The main changes brought about by IFRS 11 include

1. An entity will be required to recognize only those assets that it controls and only those liabilities that are present obligations. Currently, the accounting approach under IAS 31 can lead to the recognition of assets that are not controlled and liabilities that are not obligations.
2. A choice in accounting for interests in jointly controlled ventures will be removed, improving comparability of financial reports. The standard will require the elimination of proportionate consolidation by joint venturers and that joint ventures be accounted for using the equity method set out in IAS 28 if the venturers only have a right to share in the outcome of the activities (e.g., profit or loss) and the net assets of the venture.

This new standard establishes a core principle that parties in a joint arrangement should recognize their contractual rights and obligations arising from the arrangement. It applies to joint arrangements, except interests in joint ventures held by venture capital organizations, mutual funds, unit trusts and similar entities, including investment-linked insurance funds, when those interest are measured at fair value through profit or loss or are classified as held for trading and accounted for in accordance with IAS 39 or IFRS 9.

The standard defines a "joint arrangement," subject to the requirements of proposed IFRS, as a contractual arrangement whereby two or more parties of which two or more parties have joint control. Joint control is defined as the contractually agreed sharing of control of an arrangement, which exists only when decisions about the relevant activities require the unanimous consent of the parties sharing control. Joint arrangements are classified into two types: joint operations and joint ventures, and the distinction between the two are based on the rights and obligations that arise from the contractual arrangement.

The IASB requires that the standard be applied fully retrospectively on initial adoption. Transitional provisions have been provided which will facilitate the process and provide moderate relief to reporters.

US GAAP COMPARISON

US GAAP requires the equity method of accounting for investments in joint venture except where industry practice uses proportional consolidation. In practice, proportional consolidation is used mainly in the Oil & Gas industry. To use proportional consolidation, the investor must have undivided interest, investors must make decisions on unanimous consent and be jointly and severally liable for losses.

If an investor in a joint venture makes a nonmonetary contribution to the venture, gains or losses are deferred if the investor will have continuing involvement.

Disproportionate contributions of share-based awards to a joint venture (or any equity-accounted entity) are recognized in the contributing investor's profit and loss to the extent other investors do not make equal contributions. For example, if investor A contributes 102 shares to a venture, but the other two investors do not, investor A recognizes 68 shares (2 x 34) as expense because the 68 shares benefit the other investors and not investor A.

US GAAP contains very prescriptive guidance concerning the resumption of recognizing profits from an equity-method investee after the equity method has been suspended due to cumulative losses exceeding the investor's basis. If an investor has both equity and debt in an equity-method investee, after the balances of the equity investment is reduced to zero, other instruments are reduced first. Upon recovery, the basis of the other investments is restored in order of claim seniority.

15 BUSINESS COMBINATIONS AND CONSOLIDATED FINANCIAL STATEMENTS

INTRODUCTION

Background and Historical Perspective

There has been a longstanding debate in financial reporting theory about the accounting for business combinations and about the determination of whether it is more informative and meaningful to present the financial statements of multiple entities together, as a single economic entity.

In January 2008, the IASB issued revised versions of two key standards, IFRS 3, *Business Combinations,* and IAS 27, *Consolidated and Separate Financial Statements.* These significantly change the accounting for business combinations and transactions with noncontrolling interests. The revised standards are a result of the second phase of the Business Combinations project, conducted jointly with the US Financial Accounting Standards Board (FASB), to improve financial reporting while promoting the international convergence of accounting standards. Revised IFRS 3 and IAS 27 will be denoted as IFRS 3(R) and IAS 27(R) in this chapter, for the sake of clarity, although these are not the official titles of the standards.

The first phase of the Business Combinations project, which FASB and IASB deliberated separately, concluded with the FASB issuing FAS 141, *Business Combinations,* in 2001, and the IASB issuing the original version of IFRS 3, *Business Combinations,* in 2004. Their primary conclusion in that first phase of the project was that since virtually all business combinations involve the acquisition of one entity by another, only one method of accounting for business combinations is warranted—which was denoted as the purchase method. Consequently, IFRS 3 ended the use of pooling-of-interests accounting, and treats goodwill arising from an acquisition as an intangible asset with an indefinite life, not subject to periodic amortization, but instead to be tested periodically for impairment. IFRS 3 also requires that, where there is a noncontrolling interest (formerly, minority interest), the assets and liabilities in a subsidiary are to be valued at full fair value, including the noncontrolling interest's portion. (Under US GAAP, before the recent changes made by ASC 805, the noncontrolling interest was to be valued at book value, but now it has to be presented at fair value.)

IFRS had traditionally permitted two distinct methods of accounting for business combinations. The purchase accounting method required that the actual cost of the acquisition be recognized, including any excess over the amounts allocable to the fair value of identifiable net assets, commonly known as goodwill. The pooling-of-interests method, available only when a set of stringent criteria were all met, resulted in combining the book values of the merging entities, without any adjustment to reflect the fair values of acquired assets and liabilities, and without any recognition of goodwill. Since pooling-of-interests accounting required that the mergers be achieved by means of exchanges of ordinary (common) shares, the use of this method was largely restricted to publicly held acquirers, which greatly preferred poolings since this averted step-ups in the carrying value of depreciable assets and goodwill recognition, the amortization of which would reduce future reported earnings.

IFRS 3 contained significant differences from the then-effective US GAAP standards (FAS 141 and ASC 350), and both the IASB and the FASB believed their respective standards could be improved and converged. Consequently the Boards conducted jointly the second phase of the Business Combination project to converge their respective standards, which resulted in the current versions of both standards, each of which provide guidance for applying the acquisition method of accounting for business combinations. This second phase culminated with the issuance of the revised IFRS 3(R) and IAS 27(R), which were effective prospectively for business combinations for which the acquisition date was on or after the beginning of the first annual reporting period beginning on or after July 1, 2009. While the revised IFRS more closely resemble the equivalent US GAAP standards, differences still remain. Accountants who are responsible for preparing financial statements using both sets of standards or who are responsible for reconciling or converting financial statements must be cognizant of these differences.

IFRS 3(R) and IAS 27(R) introduced a number of changes in accounting for business combinations and preparation of consolidated financial statements. These changes will impact the amounts of goodwill and noncontrolling interest recognized, and operating results in the year that acquisition occurs and future years. In accordance with the revised standards, entities will have a choice for each business combination entered into to measure noncontrolling interest in the acquiree either at its full fair value or at its proportionate share of the acquiree's identifiable net assets. This choice will result in either recognizing goodwill relating to 100% of the business (applying the full fair value option and allocating implied goodwill to noncontrolling interest) or recognizing goodwill relating only to the percentage interest acquired.

In accordance with IFRS 3(R) and IAS 27(R), all business combinations are accounted for as an acquisition. The assets acquired and liabilities assumed are recorded on the acquirer's books at their respective fair values using *acquisition accounting* (which should be distinguished from the formerly prescribed method, *purchase accounting*). Goodwill is measured initially as the difference between (1) the acquisition-date fair value of the consideration transferred plus the fair value of any noncontrolling interest in the acquiree, plus the fair value of the acquirer's previously held equity interest in the acquiree, if any; and (2) the acquisition-date fair values (or other amounts recognized in accordance with IFRS 3(R) of the identifiable assets acquired and liabilities assumed. Goodwill can arise only in the context of a business combination, and cannot arise from purchases of an asset or group of assets.

The core principles adopted in IFRS 3(R) are that an acquirer of a business recognizes assets acquired and liabilities assumed at their acquisition-date fair values, and discloses information that enables users to evaluate the nature and financial effects of the acquisition. While fair values of many assets and liabilities can readily be determined (and in an arm's-length transaction should be known to the parties), certain recognition and measurement problems do inevitably arise. Among these are the value of contingent consideration (e.g., earn-outs) promised to former owners of the acquired entity, and the determination as to whether certain expenses that arise by virtue of the transaction, such as those pertaining to elimination of duplicate facilities, should be treated as part of the transaction or as an element of postacquisition accounting.

This chapter addresses in detail the application of the acquisition method of accounting for business combinations and, to a lesser extent, the accounting for goodwill. Chapter 11 presents the accounting for all intangible assets, including goodwill, with greater specificity. This chapter addresses the two allowed options of measuring noncontrolling interest in the acquiree under IFRS 3(R):

1. The new option to measure noncontrolling interest at its fair value and to allocate implied goodwill to the noncontrolling interest, and
2. The option to measure the noncontrolling interest at its proportionate share of the acquiree's identifiable net assets—which was the only option allowable under previous IFRS 3.

Consolidation of many "special-purpose entities" (SPEs) has increased substantially under these requirements, which were in part spurred on by the financial reporting scandals of the early 2000s. Rules governing consolidation of SPEs are complex and are continuing to evolve further in response to the recent financial crisis.

The IASB recently issued a new standard on consolidation, IFRS 10, *Consolidated Financial Statements,* which addresses the basis (policy) on which a parent entity should consolidate its investments in subsidiaries and requires enhanced disclosures about consolidated and nonconsolidated entities. The new standard is effective for all financial periods commencing on or after January 1, 2013, and was issued in response to the need for a single IFRS on consolidation that would replace IAS 27, *Consolidated and Separate Financial Statements,* and SIC-12, *Consolidation—Special-Purpose Entities.* IAS 27 was amended as a result of the issuance of IFRS 10 and is now called IAS 27, *Separate Financial Statements,* and as the name implies, deals only with the accounting for investments in subsidiaries, joint ventures and associates when an entity elects, or is required by local regulations, to present separate financial statements. IFRS 10 is worded in such a manner that it provides more rigorous guidance on the concept of control, which is built on the principles and definitions established in both IAS 27(R) and SIC 12. The result is a revision of the definition of control that can be applied to all legal entities. The new standard also addresses the accounting that follows from a scenario where control might exist despite the "holding" company having control over less than a majority of the voting rights, potential voting rights, veto rights, and economic dependence. The standard also addresses the consolidation of structured entities (for example, SPEs) which are utilized for "off the books" financings, leasing activities, and other purposes. The objective is to force adherence to the "substance over form" practice of consolidating SPEs when they are, effectively, economically integrated with the reporting entity.

Major accounting issues affecting business combinations and the preparation of consolidated or combined financial statements pertain to the following:

1. The proper recognition and measurement of the assets and liabilities of the combining entities
2. The accounting for goodwill or gain from a bargain purchase (negative goodwill)
3. The elimination of intercompany balances and transactions in the preparation of consolidated financial statements
4. The manner of reporting the noncontrolling interest

The accounting for the assets and liabilities of entities acquired in a business combination is largely dependent on the fair values assigned to them at the transaction date. (The now-obsolete pooling method relied upon book values.) The US GAAP standard, FAS 157 (ASC 820), *Fair Value Measurements,* introduced a framework for measuring fair value, and its provisions provide important guidance when assigning values as part of a business combination. In essence, it favors valuations determined on the open market, but allows other methodologies if open market valuation is not practicable. The IASB added this topic to its agenda in September 2005 and decided to use the US standard as the starting point for its own deliberation. In November 2006, the IASB issued a Discussion Paper, and in May 2009 the Exposure Draft, *Fair Value Measurement,* was published. A final standard, IFRS 13, *Fair Value Measurement,* was issued in May 2011. It is aimed at establishing clear and consistent guidance for the measurement of fair value and also addressing valuation issues that arise in inactive markets. The fair value concepts and procedures are discussed in greater detail in Chapter 25.

Sources of IFRS			
IFRS 3(R)	*IAS* 27(R), 36, 37, 38	*SIC* 12, 32	*IFRIC* 5, 10

DEFINITIONS OF TERMS

Accounting consolidation. The process of combining the financial statements of a parent company and one or more legally separate and distinct subsidiaries as a single economic entity for financial reporting purposes.

Acquiree. One or more businesses in which an acquirer obtains control in a business combination.

Acquirer. An entity that obtains control over one or more businesses in a business combination. When the acquiree is a special-purpose entity (SPE), the creator or sponsor of the SPE (or the entity on whose behalf the SPE was created) may be deemed to be the acquirer.

Acquisition. A business combination in which one entity (the acquirer) obtains control over the net assets and operations of another (the acquiree) in exchange for the transfer of assets, incurrence of liability, or issuance of equity.

Acquisition date. The date on which control of the acquiree is obtained by the acquirer (i.e., the date of exchange effecting the acquisition).

Acquisition method. The method of accounting for each business combination under IFRS. Applying the acquisition method requires

1. Identifying the acquirer;
2. Determining the acquisition date;
3. Recognizing and measuring the identifiable assets acquired, the liabilities assumed, and any noncontrolling interest in the acquiree; and
4. Recognizing and measuring goodwill or a gain from a bargain purchase.

It establishes a new basis of accountability for the acquiree.

Acquisition-related costs. Costs incurred by an acquirer to enter into a business combination.

Asset. A present economic resource

1. Controlled by an entity, through an enforceable right or other means, as a result of past events; and
2. From which future economic benefits are expected to flow to the entity (*Framework,* IAS 38).

In addition, the asset must be capable of being measured reliably.

Bargain purchase. A business combination in which the net of the acquisition-date amounts of the identifiable assets acquired and the liabilities assumed, measured in accordance with IFRS 3(R), exceeds the aggregate of the acquisition-date fair value of the consideration transferred, plus the amount of any noncontrolling interest in the acquiree, plus the acquisition-date fair value of the acquirer's previously held equity interest in the acquiree.

Business. An integrated set of assets and activities capable of being conducted and managed in order to provide a return directly to investors or other owners, members, or participants. The return can be in the form of dividends, lower costs, or other economic benefits. A development stage enterprise is not precluded from qualifying as a business under this definition, and the guidance that accompanies it is provided in IFRS 3(R) (Appendix B).

Business combination. A transaction or other event that results in an acquirer obtaining control over one or more businesses. Transactions that are sometimes referred to as "true mergers" or "mergers of equals" are also considered to be business combinations with an acquirer and one or more acquirees.

Closing date. The day on which an acquirer legally transfers consideration, acquires the assets, and assumes the liabilities of an acquiree.

Consideration transferred. The acquirer measures the consideration transferred in a business combination in exchange for the acquiree (or control of the acquiree) at fair value, which is calculated as the aggregate of the acquisition-date fair values of the assets transferred, liabilities incurred to former owners of the acquiree, and the equity interests issued by the acquirer. The acquisition-date fair value of contingent consideration should also be recognized as part of the consideration transferred in exchange for the acquiree. Acquisition-related costs are expenses recognized when incurred in profit or loss.

Consolidated financial statements. The financial statements of a group (a parent and all its subsidiaries) presented as those of a single economic entity.

Contingency. An existing, unresolved condition, situation, or set of circumstances that will eventually be resolved by the occurrence or nonoccurrence of one or more future events. A potential gain or loss to the reporting entity can result from the contingency's resolution.

Contingent consideration. Generally, an acquirer's obligation to transfer additional assets or equity interests to the acquiree's former owners if specified future events occur or conditions are met. The contingent obligation is incurred as part of a business combination in order to obtain control of an acquiree. Contingent consideration might also arise when the terms of the business combination provide a requirement that the acquiree's former owners return previously transferred assets or equity interests to the acquirer under certain specified conditions.

Control. The power to govern the financing and operating policies of an entity so as to obtain benefits from its activities and increase, maintain, or protect the amount of those benefits. Control of an entity can be obtained either by

1. Obtaining ownership of a majority of its outstanding voting power; or
2. Obtaining contractual rights to receive the majority of the financial benefits and/or by assuming contractual obligations to bear the majority of the financial consequences that occur in the future from the entity outperforming or underperforming its expectations (the controlled entity being referred to as a special-purpose entity, or SPE).

IAS 27(R) indicates several circumstances which result in control even in cases where an entity owns less than one-half of the voting power of another entity.

Cost method. A method of accounting whereby the investment is recognized at cost. The investor recognizes income from the investment only to the extent that the investor receives distributions.

Creator (or sponsor) of SPE. The entity on whose behalf a special-purpose entity (SPE) was created and which retains a significant beneficial interest in the SPE's activities, even though it may own little or none of the SPE's equity.

Equity interests. For the purposes of IFRS 3(R), equity interests is used broadly to mean ownership interests (or instruments evidencing rights of ownership) of investor-owned entities. In a mutual entity, equity interests means instruments evidencing ownership, membership, or participation rights.

Fair value. The amount for which an asset could be exchanged, or a liability settled, between knowledgeable, willing parties in an arm's-length transaction.

Favorable contract. From the perspective of a counterparty, a contract is favorable if its terms are more lucrative than current market terms.

Gain from a bargain purchase. In a business combination resulting in a bargain purchase, the difference between

1. The acquisition-date fair values (or other amounts measured in accordance with IFRS 3[R]) of the identifiable assets acquired and liabilities assumed; and
2. The acquisition-date fair value of the consideration transferred plus the amount of any noncontrolling interest in the acquiree plus the acquisition-date fair value of the acquirer's previously held equity interest in the acquiree.

A gain from a bargain purchase is recognized when (1) exceeds (2). Goodwill arises when (2) exceeds (1). After the acquirer's reassessment of whether all the assets acquired and all the liabilities assumed have been correctly identified, the resulting gain from a bargain purchase is recognized in profit or loss on the acquisition date. A gain from a bargain purchase is also referred to in accounting literature as negative goodwill.

Goodwill. An intangible asset acquired in a business combination representing the future economic benefits expected to be derived from the business combination that are not allocated to other individually identifiable and separately recognizable assets acquired. In accordance with IFRS 3(R), the acquirer measures goodwill initially as the difference between:

1. The acquisition-date fair value of the consideration transferred plus the amount of any noncontrolling interest in the acquiree plus the acquisition-date fair value of the acquirer's previously held equity interest in the acquiree; and
2. The acquisition-date fair values (or other amounts measured in accordance with IFRS 3[R]) of the identifiable assets acquired and liabilities assumed.

Goodwill is recognized when (1) exceeds (2). A bargain purchase arises when (2) exceeds (1). After initial recognition, goodwill is measured at cost less any accumulated impairment losses. Entities have a choice for each business combination to measure noncontrolling interest in the acquiree either at its fair value (and recognizing goodwill relating to 100% of the business) or at its proportionate share of the acquiree's net assets.

Group. A parent and all its subsidiaries.

Identifiable asset. An asset is identifiable if it either

1. Is separable from the entity that holds it; or
2. Represents a legal and/or contractual right.

An asset is considered separable if it is capable of being separated or divided from the entity that holds it for the purpose of the asset's sale, transfer, license, rental, or exchange, by itself or together with a related contract, or other identifiable asset or liability, irrespective of whether management of the entity intends to do so. A legal and/or contractual right is considered identifiable irrespective of whether it is transferrable or separable from the entity or from other rights and obligations.

Intangible asset. An identifiable nonmonetary asset that lacks physical substance.

Leveraged buyout (LBO). A single transaction or series of transactions in which a controlling interest in the stock of a target entity is acquired from the target's owners by a financial sponsor entity often organized as a private-equity limited partnership. An LBO transaction may be structured in a variety of ways, but is typically characterized by the incurrence by the acquirer of a substantial amount of nonrecourse debt that is collateralized by the underlying assets of the acquiree. Thus, the acquiree's own assets provide the underlying collateral to the lenders, and the postacquistion operating cash flows expected to be generated by the acquiree are intended to provide the funding necessary to meet the debt service requirements. When an LBO meets its initial expectations, it can result in a substantial return on a relatively minimal initial investment by the sponsor/acquirer's investors. However, when the postacquistion activities of the acquiree do not meet the initial expectations, the potential for a default on the acquisition indebtedness is substantial and the previously successful target can end up in reorganization or outright liquidation.

Liability. A present unconditional economic obligation, the settlement of which is expected to result in an outflow from the entity of resources embodying economic benefits (IAS 37, *Framework*).

The following three characteristics must be present for an item to qualify as a liability:

1. An economic obligation is expected to result in cash outflows, or reduced cash inflows, directly or indirectly, alone or together with other economic obligations.
2. Obligations are enforceable against the entity by legal or other means and cannot be avoided.
3. The economic obligation exists at the reporting date (Conceptual Framework Project).

In addition, liabilities are recognized subject to the constraint that the amount at which the settlement will take place can be measured reliably.

Market participants. Buyers and sellers in the principal or most advantageous market for an asset or liability who are

1. Independent of the reporting entity (i.e., they are not related parties).
2. Knowledgeable to the extent that they have a reasonable understanding about the asset or liability and the transaction based on all available information, including information that is obtainable through the performance of usual and customary due diligence efforts.
3. Able to buy or sell the asset or liability.
4. Willing to enter into a transaction for the asset or liability (i.e., they are not under duress that would force or compel them to enter into the transaction).

Mutual entity. An entity that is not investor-owned, organized for the purpose of providing dividends, reduced costs, or other economic benefits directly to its owners, members, or participants. Examples of mutual entities include mutual insurance companies, credit unions, and cooperative entities.

Noncontrolling interest. The equity (net assets) in a subsidiary not directly or indirectly attributable to its parent. In accordance with IFRS 3(R), entities have a choice for each business combination entered into to measure noncontrolling interest in the acquiree either (1) at its fair value, or (2) as its proportionate share of the value of the identifiable assets and liabilities (net assets) of the acquiree, measured as required by that standard. The first choice will result in recognizing goodwill constituting all of the goodwill of the acquired business (applying the fair value option and allocating implied goodwill to noncontrolling interest), while the second choice will result in recognizing goodwill associated with only the percentage of interest acquired. Noncontrolling interests were formerly referred to in accounting literature as minority interests.

Owners. For the purposes of IFRS 3(R), the term *owners* is used broadly to include holders of equity interests (ownership interests) in investor-owned or mutual entities. Owners include parties referred to as shareholders, partners, proprietors, members, or participants.

Parent. An entity that has one or more subsidiaries.

Reporting entity. An entity for which there are users who rely on the entity's general-purpose financial statements as their major source of financial information about the entity that will be useful to them for making decisions about the allocation of resources. A reporting entity can be a single entity or a group comprising a parent and all of its subsidiaries.

Reverse acquisition. An acquisition when one entity, nominally the acquirer, issues so many shares to the former owners of the target entity that they become the majority owners of the successor entity.

Reverse spin-off. A spin-off transaction in which the nominal or legal spinnor is to be accounted for as the spinnee, in order to reflect the economic reality of the spin-off transaction.

Roll-up or put-together transaction. A business combination that is effected by two or more entities transferring the net assets of their businesses to a newly formed entity. Those transactions can also be effected by the owners of the entities transferring their equity interests in those entities to the newly formed entity.

Separate financial statements. The financial statements presented by a parent, an investor in an associate or a venture in a jointly controlled entity, in which the investments are accounted for on the basis of the direct interest rather than on the basis of the reported results and net assets of the investees. An entity accounts for such investments either (1) at cost; or (2) in accordance with IAS 39.

Special-purpose entity (SPE). An entity created to accomplish a narrow and well-defined objective (e.g., to effect a lease, research and development activities, or a securitization of financial assets), which can be a corporation, trust, partnership or unincorporated entity. SIC 12 requires consolidation when the SPE is controlled by the reporting entity (the sponsor or creator of the SPE). Under IFRS 3(R), this party is also referred to as a "parent" and the SPE is also referred to as a "subsidiary."

Spin-off. The creation of an independent entity through the sale or distribution of new shares of an existing business/division of a parent company. For example, occasionally an entity may dispose of a wholly or partially owned subsidiary, or of an investee, by transferring it unilaterally to the entity's shareholders.

Stapling arrangement. An arrangement in which two or more legal entities contractually agree to combine their securities so that they are quoted at a single price and cannot be traded or transferred independently.

Subsidiary. An entity, including an unincorporated entity such as a partnership that is controlled by another entity (known as the parent).

Unfavorable contract. From the perspective of a counterparty, a contract is unfavorable if its terms are less lucrative than current market terms. An unfavorable contract is not necessarily a contract that will result in a loss to the counterparty.

Unrealized intercompany profit. The excess of the transaction price over the carrying value of an item (usually inventory or long-lived assets) transferred from (or to) a parent to (or from) the subsidiary, or among subsidiaries, and not sold to an outside entity as of the end of the reporting period. For purposes of consolidated financial statements, recognition must be deferred until subsequent realization through a transaction with an unrelated party.

BUSINESS COMBINATIONS AND CONSOLIDATIONS

IFRS 3(R) and IAS 27(R) and International Accounting Convergence

In January 2008, the IASB issued a revised version of IFRS 3, *Business Combinations*, which in this publication is being referred to as IFRS 3(R), as well as an amended version of

IAS 27, *Consolidated and Separate Financial Statements,* which is being referred to as IAS 27(R). These standards were the product of the first major joint project undertaken by IASB and FASB

Key changes introduced by IFRS 3(R) include

- Option to measure noncontrolling interest at fair value
- Acquisition-related costs recognized in profit or loss as incurred
- In step acquisitions, any previously held equity interest in the acquiree is remeasured at its acquisition-date fair value, with the resulting gains and losses recognized in profit or loss
- Reassessing the classification or designation of all assets and liabilities acquired as required by other IFRS
- Contingent consideration measured at fair value at the date of business combination, with subsequent changes (gains, losses) recognized in profit or loss
- Reacquired rights recognized as intangible assets, separately from goodwill
- Separate accounting for preexisting relationships
- Indemnification assets measured on the same basis as the related liability

Key changes introduced by IAS 27(R) are

- Changes in a parent's controlling ownership interest that do not result in a loss of control are accounted for as equity transactions (transactions with owners in their capacity as owners). Consequently, no gain or loss, and no changes in the carrying values of the subsidiary's assets (including goodwill) or liabilities are recognized.
- Losses incurred by the subsidiary are allocated between controlling and noncontrolling interests, even if losses attributed to the noncontrolling interests exceed the noncontrolling interests in the subsidiary's equity.
- On loss of control of a subsidiary, the parent derecognizes the individual assets, liabilities, and equity related to that subsidiary (including any noncontrolling interests and amounts previously recognized in other comprehensive income). Any retained interest in the former subsidiary should be valued at fair value at the date that control is lost; any resulting gain or loss is recognized in profit or loss.

Organization of This Chapter

IFRS 3(R) and IAS 27(R) should be applied prospectively, although early application is permitted. Therefore, any business combinations that were undertaken before the effective date of IFRS 3 (R) can be accounted for using the earlier version of the standard. As the existence of such business is not expected to be commonplace at this stage, the discussion that follows does not address the superseded IFRS 3 and IAS 27; readers needing such guidance should refer to *Wiley IFRS 2009*, which presented a full discussion of those earlier standards in addition to the current standards, IFRS 3(R) and IAS 27(R).

Effective Date and Transition Provisions

IFRS 3(R) and IAS 27(R) came into effect for the first annual reporting period beginning on or after July 1, 2009. Early application was permitted, although the new pronouncements could not be applied to periods beginning prior to June 30, 2007. If an entity elected early adoption, it was necessary to adopt both IFRS 3(R) and IAS 27(R) at the same time.

Thus reporting entities must apply IFRS 3(R) prospectively to business combinations for which the acquisition date is on or after the beginning of the annual period in which the standard is adopted. Further, reporting entities are not permitted to retrospectively adjust the carrying amounts of assets and liabilities from previously recognized business combinations for the effects of the new pronouncements. Special transition provisions apply to mutual entities and with respect to amendments made to paragraph 68 of IAS 12, governing the accounting for current and deferred income taxes. After the date this IFRS is adopted, any change in a deferred tax benefit acquired in a business combination does not adjust goodwill, but is recognized in profit or loss for the period (or, if IAS 12 requires, outside profit or loss). These are discussed later in this chapter and in Chapter 26, Income Taxes.

Objectives

IFRS 3(R) and IAS 27(R) follow a revised drafting convention, intended to be more principles-based than rules-based in approach. Thus, each major section of these pronouncements is preceded by a prominent statement of the main principles embodied by that section, presented in a boldfaced font for emphasis. All paragraphs and the appendices containing implementation guidance, whether boldfaced or not, are of equal authority, however.

The overriding objective of the new standards is to improve the relevance, representational faithfulness, transparency, and comparability of information provided in financial statements about business combinations and their effects on the reporting entity by establishing principles and requirements with respect to how an acquirer, in its consolidated financial statements,

1. Recognizes and measures identifiable assets acquired, liabilities assumed, and the noncontrolling interest in the acquiree, if any,
2. Recognizes and measures acquired goodwill or a gain from a bargain purchase,
3. Determines the nature and extent of disclosures sufficient to enable the reader to evaluate the nature of the business combination and its financial effects on the consolidated reporting entity,
4. Accounts for and reports noncontrolling interests in subsidiaries, and
5. Deconsolidates a subsidiary when it ceases to hold a controlling interest in it.

Scope

Transactions or other events that meet the definition of a business combination are subject to IFRS 3(R) and IAS 27(R). Excluded from the scope of these standards, however, are

1. Formation of a joint venture
2. Acquisition of an asset or group of assets that does not represent a business
3. Combinations between entities or businesses under common control

Mutual entities (i.e., credit unions, cooperatives, etc.), those achieved by contract alone (providing control without ownership—i.e., dual-listed entities, stapled entity structures), those achieved in stages (step acquisitions), those transferring less than 100% ownership, and bargain purchases are within the scope of the revised standards.

BUSINESS COMBINATIONS

The revised standard IFRS 3(R) replaces the cost principle of accounting for business combinations with the fair value principle. Under the cost (or cost allocation) principle, which was applied under IFRS 3, the exchange transaction was to be recorded at cost. That cost was to be allocated to the assets acquired and liabilities assumed; and goodwill was to be recognized for the difference between the cost and the fair value of the identifiable net assets acquired. In contrast, applying the fair value principle means that, upon obtaining control of the subsidiary, the exchange transaction is measured at fair value. All assets, liabilities, and equity (except equity acquired by the controlling interest) of the acquired entity are measured at fair value. However, several exceptions to this principle are provided in IFRS 3(R).

Determining Fair Values

Accounting for acquisitions requires a determination of the fair value for each of the acquired entity's identifiable tangible and intangible assets and for each of its liabilities at the date of combination (except for assets which are to be resold and which are to be accounted for at fair value less costs to sell under IFRS 5; and for those items to which limited exceptions to recognition and measurement principles apply). IFRS 3(R) provides illustrative examples of how to treat certain assets, particularly intangibles, but provides no general guidance on determining fair value. The IASB recently issued IFRS 13, *Fair Value Measurement,* which addresses defines the term fair value, and sets out in a single standard a framework for measuring fair value and the concomitant disclosures. This standard is discussed in further detail in Chapter 25.

Transactions and Events Accounted for as Business Combinations

A business combination results from the occurrence of a transaction or other event that results in an acquirer obtaining control of one or more businesses. This can occur in many different ways that include the following examples individually or in some cases, in combination:

1. Transfer of cash, cash equivalents, or other assets, including the transfer of assets of another business of the acquirer,
2. Incurring liabilities,
3. Issuance of equity instruments,
4. Providing more than one type of consideration, or
5. By contract alone without the transfer of consideration, such as when

    a. An acquiree business repurchases enough of its own shares to cause one of its existing investors (the acquirer) to obtain control over it
    b. There is a lapse of minority veto rights that had previously prevented the acquirer from controlling an acquiree in which it held a majority voting interest
    c. An acquirer and acquiree contractually agree to combine their businesses without a transfer of consideration between them.

Qualifying as a Business

IFRS 3(R) substantively redefines the previous definition of a business which had been set forth for the first time in IFRS 3. This change may serve to increase the number of acquisition transactions that will be accounted for as business combinations, rather than purchases and assumptions of specific assets and liabilities, or as transactions that could be accounted for as book value combinations akin to the now-banned poolings of interests.

Under IFRS 3(R), in order to be considered a business, an integrated group of activities and assets must be *capable* of being conducted and managed to provide a return directly to investors, *owners, members, or participants.* The return can be in the form of dividends, reduced costs, or other economic benefits. The word *capable* was added to emphasize the fact that the definition does not preclude a development stage enterprise from qualifying as a business. *Other owners, members, or participants* were included to emphasize the applicability of IFRS 3(R) to mutual entities (e.g., credit unions and cooperatives) that previously used the pooling-of-interests method of accounting for business combinations and to non-corporate entities.

The definition and related guidance elaborate further that a business consists of inputs and processes applied to those inputs that have the ability to create outputs. Clarification is provided that, while outputs are usually present in a business, they are not required to qualify as a business as long as there is the *ability* to create them.

An input is an economic resource that creates or has the ability to create outputs when one or more processes are applied to it. Examples of inputs include fixed assets, intangible rights to use fixed assets, intellectual property or other intangible assets, and access to markets in which to hire employees or purchase materials.

A process is a system, protocol, convention, or rule with the ability to create outputs when applied to one or more inputs. Processes are usually documented; however, an organized workforce with the requisite skills and experience may apply processes necessary to create outputs by following established rules and conventions. In evaluating whether an activity is a process, IFRS 3(R) indicates that functions such as accounting, billing, payroll, and other administrative systems do not meet the definition. Thus, processes are the types of activities that an entity engages in to produce the products and/or services that it provides to the marketplace rather than the internal activities it follows in operating its business.

An output is simply the by-product resulting from applying processes to inputs. An output provides, or has the ability to provide, the desired return to the investors, members, participants, or other owners.

In analyzing a transaction or event to determine whether it is a business combination, it is not necessary that the acquirer retain, postcombination, all of the inputs or processes used by the seller in operating the business. If market participants could, for example, acquire the business in an arm's-length transaction and continue to produce outputs by integrating the business with their own inputs and processes, then that subset of remaining inputs and processes still meets the definition of a business from the standpoint of the acquirer.

The guidance in IFRS 3(R) provides additional flexibility by providing that it is not necessary that a business have liabilities, although that situation is expected to be rare. The broad scope of the term "capable of" requires judgment in determining whether an acquired set of activities and assets constitutes a business, to be accounted for applying the acquisition method.

As discussed previously, development stage enterprises are not precluded from meeting the criteria for being deemed a business. This is true even if they do not yet produce outputs. If there are no outputs being produced, the acquirer is to determine whether the enterprise constitutes a business by considering whether it

1. Has started its planned principal activities,
2. Has hired employees,
3. Has obtained intellectual property,
4. Has obtained other inputs,
5. Has implemented processes that could be applied to its inputs,
6. Is pursuing a plan to produce outputs,
7. Will have the ability to obtain access to customers that will purchase the outputs.

It is important to note, however, that it is not required that all of these factors be present for a given set of development stage activities and assets to qualify as a business. Again, the relevant question to ask is whether a market participant would be capable of conducting or managing the set of activities and assets as a business irrespective of whether the seller did so or the acquirer intends to do so.

Finally, IFRS 3(R) provided what it acknowledged was the circular logic of asserting that, in the absence of evidence to the contrary, if goodwill is included in a set of assets and activities, it can be presumed to be a business. The circularity arises from the fact that, in order to apply IFRS to determine whether to initially recognize goodwill, the accountant would be required to first determine whether there had, in fact, been an acquisition of a business. Otherwise, it would not be permitted to recognize goodwill. It is not necessary, however, that goodwill be present in order to consider a set of assets and activities to be a business.

Techniques for Structuring Business Combinations

A business combination can be structured in a number of different ways that satisfy the acquirer's strategic, operational, legal, tax, and risk management objectives. Some of the more frequently used structures are

1. One or more businesses become subsidiaries of the acquirer. As subsidiaries, they continue to operate as legal entities.
2. The net assets of one or more businesses are legally merged into the acquirer. In this case, the acquiree entity ceases to exist (in legal vernacular, this is referred to as a statutory merger and normally the transaction is subject to approval by a majority of the outstanding voting shares of the acquiree).
3. The owners of the acquiree transfer their equity interests to the acquirer entity or to the owners of the acquirer entity in exchange for equity interests in the acquirer.
4. All of the combining entities transfer their net assets or their owners transfer their equity interests into a new entity formed for the purpose of the transaction. This is sometimes referred to as a roll-up or put-together transaction.
5. A former owner or group of former owners of one of the combining entities obtains control of the combined entities collectively.
6. An acquirer might hold a noncontrolling equity interest in an entity and subsequently purchase additional equity interests sufficient to give it control over the investee. These transactions are referred to as step acquisitions or business combinations achieved in stages.

Accounting for Business Combinations under the Acquisition Method

The acquirer is to account for a business combination using the acquisition method. This term represents an expansion of the now-outdated term, "purchase method." The change in terminology was made in order to emphasize that a business combination can occur even when a purchase transaction is not involved.

The following steps are required to apply the acquisition method:

1. Identify the acquirer.
2. Determine the acquisition date.
3. Identify the assets and liabilities, if any, requiring separate accounting because they result from transactions that are not part of the business combination, and account for them in accordance with their nature and the applicable IFRS.
4. Identify assets and liabilities that require acquisition date classification or designation decisions to facilitate application of IFRS in postcombination financial statements and make those classifications or designations based on

   a. Contractual terms;
   b. Economic conditions;
   c. Acquirer operating or accounting policies, and
   d. Other pertinent conditions existing at the acquisition date.

5. Recognize and measure the identifiable tangible and intangible assets acquired and liabilities assumed.
6. Recognize and measure any noncontrolling interest in the acquiree.
7. Measure the consideration transferred.
8. Recognize and measure goodwill or, if the business combination results in a bargain purchase, recognize a gain from the bargain purchase.

Step 1—Identify the acquirer. IFRS 3(R), as did its predecessor standard, strongly emphasizes the concept that every business combination has an acquirer. In the "basis for conclusions" that accompanies IFRS 3(R), IASB asserts that

> ..."true mergers" or "mergers of equals" in which none of the combining entities obtain control of the others are so rare as to be virtually nonexistent...[1]

The provisions of IAS 27(R), *Consolidated and Separate Financial Statements,* should be used to identify the acquirer—the entity that obtains *control* of the acquiree. IFRS 3(R) carried forward the principle of IAS 22 that in a business combination accounted for using the acquisition method, the acquirer is the combining entity that obtains control of the other combining entities. According to the IASB, using the control concept for identifying the acquirer is consistent with using the control concept in IAS 27 to define the boundaries of the reporting entity and to provide the basis for establishing a parent-subsidiary relationship.

While IAS 27(R) provides that, in general, control is presumed to exist when the parent owns, directly or indirectly, a majority of the voting power of another entity, this is not an absolute rule to be applied in all cases. In fact, IAS 27(R) explicitly provides that in exceptional circumstances, it can be clearly demonstrated that majority ownership does not constitute control, but rather that the minority ownership may constitute control (related IFRS guidance is provided later in this chapter in the paragraph titled Presentation and Scope of Consolidated Financial Statements).

Exceptions to the general majority ownership rule include, but are not limited to the following situations:

1. An entity that is in legal reorganization or bankruptcy
2. An entity subject to uncertainties due to government-imposed restrictions, such as foreign exchange restrictions or controls, whose severity casts doubt on the majority owner's ability to control the entity
3. If the acquiree is a special-purpose entity (SPE), the creator or sponsor of the SPE is always considered to be the acquirer. Accounting for SPEs is discussed later in this chapter.

If applying the guidance in IAS 27(R) does not clearly indicate the party that is the acquirer, IFRS 3(R) provides factors to consider in making that determination under different facts and circumstances.

1. *Relative size*—Generally, the acquirer is the entity whose relative size is significantly larger than that of the other entity or entities. Size can be compared by using measures such as assets, revenues, or net income.
2. *Initiator of the transaction*—When more than two entities are involved, another factor to consider (besides relative size) is which of the entities initiated the transaction.
3. *Roll-ups or put-together transactions*—When a new entity is formed to issue equity interests to effect a business combination, one of the preexisting entities is to be

---

[1]   *IFRS 3(R), paragraph BC35.*

identified as the acquirer. If, instead, a newly formed entity transfers cash or other assets, or incurs liabilities as consideration to effect a business combination, that new entity may be considered to be the acquirer.

4. *Nonequity consideration*—In business combinations accomplished primarily by the transfer of cash or other assets, or by incurring liabilities, the entity that transfers the cash or other assets, or incurs the liabilities is usually the acquirer.

5. *Exchange of equity interests*—In business combinations that are accomplished primarily by the exchange of equity interests, the entity that issues its equity interests is generally considered to be the acquirer. One notable exception that occurs frequently in practice is sometimes referred to as a reverse acquisition, discussed in detail later in this chapter. In a reverse acquisition, the entity issuing equity interests is legally the acquirer, but for accounting purposes is considered the acquiree. There are, however, other factors that should be considered in identifying the acquirer when equity interests are exchanged. These include

   a. *Relative voting rights in the combined entity after the business combination*—Generally, the acquirer is the entity whose owners, as a group, retain or obtain the largest portion of the voting rights in the consolidated entity. This determination must take into consideration the existence of any unusual or special voting arrangements as well as any options, warrants, or convertible securities.

   b. *The existence of a large minority voting interest in the combined entity in the event no other owner or organized group of owners possesses a significant voting interest*—Generally, the acquirer is the entity whose owner or organized group of owners holds the largest minority voting interest in the combined entity.

   c. *The composition of the governing body of the combined entity*—Generally, the acquirer is the entity whose owners have the ability to elect, appoint, or remove a majority of members of the governing body of the combined entity.

   d. *The composition of the senior management of the combined entity*—Generally the acquirer is the entity whose former management dominates the management of the combined entity.

   e. *Terms of the equity exchange*—Generally, the acquirer is the entity that pays a premium over the precombination fair value of the equity interests of the other entity or entities.

Step 2—Determine the acquisition date. By definition, the acquisition date is that on which the acquirer obtains control of the acquiree. As discussed previously, this concept of control is not always evidenced by ownership of voting rights. Thus, control can be obtained contractually by an acquirer absent that party holding any voting ownership interests.

The general rule is that the acquisition date is the date on which the acquirer legally transfers consideration, acquires the assets, and assumes the liabilities of the acquiree. This date, in a relatively straightforward transaction, is referred to as the closing date. Not all transactions are that straightforward, however. All pertinent facts and circumstances are to be considered in determining the acquisition date and this includes the meeting of any significant conditions precedent. The parties to a business combination might, for example, execute a contract that entitles the acquirer to the rights and obligates the acquirer with respect to the obligations of the acquiree prior to the actual closing date. Thus, in evaluating economic substance over legal form, the acquirer will have contractually acquired the target on the date it executed the contract.

Example of acquisition date preceding closing date

In 2011, Henan Corporation (HC), a China-based holding company, purchased more than 20 wine brands and specified distribution assets from a French company. In its annual report, HC disclosed that the acquired assets were transferred to a subsidiary of the seller, in which HC received, in connection with the transaction, economic rights (these were structured as "tracker shares" in the holding subsidiary of the seller) with respect to the acquired assets prior to their actual legal transfer to the company. In addition, HC obtained the contractual right to manage the acquired assets prior to their legal transfer to HC, resulting in the acquirer obtaining control of the acquiree on the date before the closing date. Among the reasons HC cited for entering into these arrangements was their commercial desire to obtain the economic benefits associated with owning and operating the acquired assets as soon as possible after funding the purchase price for them.

Until the assets were legally transferred to HC, the transaction was accounted for under SIC 12, *Consolidation—Special-Purpose Entities*, and consequently, HC's interests in the tracker shares of the seller's subsidiary were consolidated since HC was considered the sponsor of that subsidiary. The seller's residual interest in the holding subsidiary was reported in the consolidated financial statements of HC as a noncontrolling interest.

Step 3—Recognize and measure the identifiable tangible and intangible assets acquired and liabilities assumed. In general, the measurement principle is that an acquirer measures the identifiable tangible and intangible assets acquired, and the liabilities assumed, at their fair values on the acquisition date. IFRS 3(R) provides the acquirer with a choice of two methods to measure noncontrolling interests arising in a business combination:

1. To measure the noncontrolling interest at fair value (recognizing the acquired business at fair value), or
2. To measure the noncontrolling interest at the noncontrolling interest's share of the acquiree's net assets.

Exceptions to the recognition and/or measurement principles. IFRS 3(R) provides certain exceptions to its general principles for recognizing assets acquired and liabilities assumed at their acquisition date fair values. These can be summarized as follows:

Nature of exception	*Recognition*	*Measurement*
Contingent liabilities	x	
Income taxes	x	x
Employee benefits	x	x
Indemnification assets	x	x
Reacquired rights		x
Share-based payment awards		x
Assets held for sale		x

Exceptions to the recognition principle.
Contingent liabilities of the acquiree. In accordance with IAS 37, *Provisions, Contingent Liabilities and Contingent Assets*, a contingent liability is defined as

1. A possible obligation that arises from past events and whose existence will be confirmed only by the occurrence or nonoccurrence of one or more uncertain future events not wholly within the control of the entity; or
2. A present obligation that arises from past events but is not recognized because

   a. It is not probable that an outflow of resources embodying economic benefits will be required to settle the obligation, or
   b. The amount of the obligation cannot be measured with sufficient reliability.

Under IFRS 3(R) the acquirer recognizes as of the acquisition date a contingent liability assumed in a business combination if it is a present obligation that arises from past events and its fair value can be measured reliably, regardless of the probability of cash flow arising (contrary to the principle that is established in IAS 37).

Exceptions to both the recognition and measurement principles.

Income taxes. The basic principle that applies to income tax accounting in a business combination (carried forward without change by IFRS 3[R]) is that the acquirer is to recognize in accordance with IAS 12, *Income Taxes,* as of the acquisition date, deferred income tax assets or liabilities for the future effects of temporary differences and carryforwards of the acquiree that either

1. Exist on the acquisition date, *or*
2. Are generated by the acquisition itself.

However, IAS 12 has been amended in order to accommodate the new business combinations framework and, consequently, management must carefully assess the reasons for changes in the deferred tax benefits during the measurement period. As a result of these amendments, deferred tax benefits that do not meet the recognition criteria at the date of acquisition are subsequently recognized as follows:

- Acquired deferred tax benefits recognized within the measurement period (within one year after the acquisition date) that result from new information regarding the facts and circumstances existing at the acquisition date, are accounted for as a reduction of goodwill related to this acquisition. If goodwill is reduced to zero, any remaining portion of the adjustment is recorded as a gain from a bargain purchase.
- All other acquired deferred tax benefits realized are recognized in profit or loss.

In addition, IAS 12 has been amended to require any tax benefits arising from the difference between the income tax basis and IFRS carrying amount of goodwill to be accounted for as any other temporary difference at the date of acquisition.

Employee benefits. Liabilities (and assets, if applicable), associated with acquiree employee benefit arrangements are to be recognized and measured in accordance with IAS 19, *Employee Benefits.* Any amendments to a plan (and their related income tax effects) that are made as a result of business combination are treated as a postcombination event and recognized in the acquirer's postcombination financial statements in the periods in which the changes occur.

Indemnification assets. Indemnification provisions are usually included in the voluminous closing documents necessary to effect a business combination. Indemnifications are contractual terms designed to fully or partially protect the acquirer from the potential adverse effects of an unfavorable future resolution of a contingency or uncertainty that exists at the acquisition date (e.g., legal or environmental liabilities, or uncertain tax positions). Frequently the indemnification is structured to protect the acquirer by limiting the maximum amount of postcombination loss that the acquirer would bear in the event of an adverse outcome. A contractual indemnification provision results in the acquirer obtaining, as a part of the acquisition, an indemnification asset and simultaneously assuming a contingent liability of the acquiree.

Exceptions to the measurement principle.

Reacquired rights. An acquirer and acquiree may have engaged in preacquisition business transactions such as leases, licenses, franchises, trade name or technology that resulted in the acquiree paying consideration to the acquirer to use tangible and/or intangible assets of the acquirer in the acquiree's business. The acquisition results in the acquirer reacquiring that right. The acquirer measures the value of a reacquired right recognized as an intangible asset. If the terms of the contract giving rise to a reacquired right are favorable or unfavorable compared with current terms and prices for the same or similar items, a settlement gain or loss will be recognized in profit or loss.

The IFRS accounting requirements after acquisition, on subsequently measuring and accounting for reacquired rights, contingent liabilities, and indemnification assets are discussed later in this chapter in the paragraph entitled "Postcombination measurement and accounting."

Share-based payment awards. In connection with a business combination, the acquirer often replaces acquiree's share-based payment awards with share-based payment awards of the acquirer. Obviously, there are many valid business reasons for the exchange, not the least of which is ensuring smooth transition and integration as well as retention of valued employees. The acquirer measures a liability or an equity instrument related to share-based payment transactions of the acquiree or the replacement of an acquiree's share-based payment awards with the acquirer's share-based awards in accordance with IFRS 2, *Share-Based Payment,* at the acquisition date.

Assets held for sale. Assets classified as held for sale individually or as part of a disposal group are to be measured at acquisition date fair value less cost to sell consistent with IFRS 5, *Noncurrent Assets Held for Sale and Discontinued Operations* (discussed in detail in Chapter 9). In determining fair value less cost to sell, it is important to differentiate costs to sell from expected future losses associated with the operation of the long-lived asset or disposal group to which it belongs.

In postacquisition periods, long-lived assets classified as held for sale are not to be depreciated or amortized. If the assets are part of a disposal group (discussed in Chapter 9), interest and other expenses related to the liabilities included in the disposal group are to continue to be accrued.

In determining fair value less cost to sell, it is important to differentiate costs to sell from expected future losses associated with the operation of the long-lived asset or disposal group to which it belongs.

Costs to sell are defined as the incremental direct costs necessary to transact a sale. To qualify as costs to sell, the costs must result directly from the sale transaction, incurring them needs to be considered essential to the transaction, and the cost would not have been incurred by the entity in the absence of a decision to sell the assets. Examples of costs to sell include brokerage commissions, legal fees, title transfer fees, and closing costs necessary to effect the transfer of legal title. Costs to sell are expressly not permitted to include any future losses that are expected to result from operating the assets (or disposal group) while it is classified as held for sale. If the expected timing of the sale exceeds one year from the end of the reporting period, which is permitted in limited situations by paragraph B1 of IFRS 5, the costs to sell are to be discounted to their present value.

Should a loss be recognized in subsequent periods due to a decline in the fair value less cost to sell, such losses may be restored by future periods' gains only to the extent to which the losses have been recognized cumulatively from the date the asset (or disposal group) was classified as held for sale.

IFRS guidance on recognizing and measuring the identifiable assets acquired and liabilities assumed is discussed later in this chapter in the paragraph entitled "Additional guidance in applying the acquisition method."

Step 4—Identify assets and liabilities requiring separate accounting. IFRS 3(R) provides a basic recognition principle that, as of the acquisition date, the acquirer is to recognize, separately from goodwill, the fair values of all identifiable assets acquired (whether tangible or intangible), the liabilities assumed, and, if applicable, any noncontrolling interest (previously referred to as "minority interest") in the acquiree.

In applying the recognition principle to a business combination, the acquirer may recognize assets and liabilities that had not been recognized by the acquiree in its precombination financial statements but which meet the definitions of assets and liabilities in the Conceptual Framework for Financial Reporting at the acquisition date. IFRS 3(R) continues to permit recognition of acquired intangibles (e.g., patents, customer lists) that would not be granted recognition if they were internally developed.

The pronouncement elaborates on the basic principle by providing that recognition is subject to the following conditions:

1. At the acquisition date, the identifiable assets acquired and liabilities assumed must meet the definitions of assets and liabilities as set forth in the Conceptual Framework for Financial Reporting [2]
2. The assets and liabilities recognized must be part of the exchange transaction between the acquirer and the acquiree (or the acquiree's former owners) and not part of a separate transaction or transactions.

Restructuring or exit activities. Frequently, in a business combination, the acquirer's plans include the future exit of one or more of the activities of the acquiree or the termination or relocation of employees of the acquiree. Since these exit activities are discretionary on the part of the acquirer and the acquirer is not obligated to incur the associated costs, the costs do not meet the definition of a liability and are not recognized at the acquisition date. Rather, the costs will be recognized in postcombination financial statements in accordance with other IFRS.

Boundaries of the exchange transaction. Preexisting relationships and arrangements often exist between the acquirer and acquiree prior to beginning negotiations to enter into a business combination. Furthermore, while conducting the negotiations, the parties may enter into separate business arrangements. In either case, the acquirer is responsible for identifying amounts that are not part of the exchange for the acquiree. Recognition under the acquisition method is only given to the consideration transferred for the acquiree and the assets acquired and liabilities assumed in exchange for that consideration. Other transactions outside the scope of the business combination are to be recognized by applying other relevant IFRS.

The acquirer is to analyze the business combination transaction and other transactions with the acquiree and its former owners to identify the components that comprise the transaction in which the acquirer obtained control over the acquiree. This distinction is important to ensure that each component is accounted for according to its economic substance, irrespective of its legal form.

The imposition of this condition was based on an observation that, upon becoming involved in negotiations for a business combination, the parties may exhibit characteristics of related parties. In so doing, they may be willing to execute agreements designed *primarily* for the benefit of the acquirer of the combined entity that might be designed to achieve a desired financial reporting outcome after the business combination has been consummated. Thus, the imposition of this condition is expected to curb such abuses.

---

[2]   *Assets are defined as "present economic resources: (1) controlled by an entity, through an enforceable right or other means, as a result of past events; and (2) from which future economic benefits are expected to flow to the entity" (IAS 38, **Framework**). Liabilities are defined as "present unconditional economic obligations, the settlement of which is expected to result in an outflow from the entity of resources embodying economic benefits" (IAS 37, **Framework**).*

In analyzing a transaction to determine inclusion or exclusion from a business combination, consideration should be given to which of the parties will reap its benefits. If a precombination transaction is entered into by the acquirer, or on behalf of the acquirer, or *primarily* to benefit the acquirer (or to benefit the to-be-combined entity as a whole) rather than for the benefit of the acquiree or its former owners, the transaction most likely would be considered to be a "separate transaction" outside the boundaries of the business combination and for which the acquisition method would not apply.

The acquirer is to consider the following factors, which IASB states "are neither mutually exclusive nor individually conclusive," in determining whether a transaction is a part of the exchange transaction or recognized separately:

1. *Purpose of the transaction*—Typically, there are many parties involved in the management, ownership, operation, and financing of the various entities involved in a business combination transaction. Of course, there are the acquirer and acquiree entities, but there are also owners, directors, management, and various parties acting as agents representing their respective interests. Understanding the motivations of the parties in entering into a particular transaction potentially provides insight into whether or not the transaction is a part of the business combination or a separate transaction.

2. *Initiator of the transaction*—Identifying the party that initiated the transaction may provide insight into whether or not it should be recognized separately from the business combination. IASB believes that if the transaction was initiated by the acquirer, it would be less likely to be part of the business combination and, conversely, if it were initiated by the acquiree or its former owners, it would be more likely to be part of the business combination.

3. *Timing of the transaction*—Examining the timing of the transaction may provide insight into whether, for example, the transaction was executed in contemplation of the future business combination in order to provide benefits to the acquirer or the postcombination entity. IASB believes that transactions that take place during the negotiation of the terms of a business combination may be entered into in contemplation of the eventual combination for the purpose of providing future economic benefits *primarily* to the acquirer of the to-be-combined entity and, therefore, should be accounted for separately.

IFRS 3(R) provides the following pair of presumptions after analyzing the economic benefits of a precombination transaction:

Primarily for the benefit of	*Transaction likely to be*
Acquirer or combined entity	Separate transaction
Acquiree or its former owners	Part of the business combination

IFRS 3(R) provides three examples of separate transactions that are *not* to be included in applying the acquisition method.

1. A settlement of a preexisting relationship between acquirer and acquiree,
2. Compensation to employees or former owners of the acquiree for future services, and
3. Reimbursement to the acquiree or its former owners for paying the acquirer's acquisition-related costs.

The paragraph entitled, "Determining what is part of the business combination transaction," later in this chapter, will discuss related application guidance for these transactions that are separate from the business combination (i.e., not part of the exchange for the acquiree).

In a departure from the original version of IFRS 3, acquisition-related costs are, under IFRS 3(R), generally expensed through profit or loss at the time the services are received, which will generally be prior to, or at, the date of the acquisition. This is consistent with the now-prevalent view that such costs do not increase the *value* of the assets acquired, and thus should not be capitalized.

Step 5—Classify or designate identifiable assets acquired and liabilities assumed. In order to facilitate the combined entity's future application of IFRS in its postcombination financial statements, management is required to make decisions on the acquisition date relative to the classification or designation of certain items. These decisions are to be based on the contractual terms, economic and other conditions, and the acquirer's operating and accounting policies as they exist *on the acquisition date*. Examples include, but are not limited to, the following:

1. Classification of investments in certain debt and equity securities as trading, available for sale, or held to maturity under IAS 39, *Financial Instruments: Recognition and Measurement,*
2. Designation of a derivative instrument as a hedging instrument under the provisions of IAS 39.

In applying Step 5, specific exceptions are provided for lease contracts and insurance contracts: classification of a lease contract as either an operating lease or a finance lease in accordance with IAS 17, *Leases,* and classification of a contract as an insurance contract in accordance with IFRS 4, *Insurance Contracts.* Generally, these contracts are to be classified by reference to the contractual terms and other factors that were applicable *at their inception* rather than at the acquisition date. If, however, the contracts were modified subsequent to their inception and those modifications would change their classification at that date, then the accounting for the contracts will be determined by the modification date facts and circumstances. Under these circumstances, the modification date could be the same as the acquisition date.

Step 6—Recognize and measure any noncontrolling interest in the acquiree. The term "noncontrolling interest" replaces the term "minority interest" in referring to that portion of the acquiree, if any, not controlled by the parent subsequent to the acquisition. The term "minority interest" became an inadequate descriptor because under IAS 27(R) and SIC 12, *Consolidation—Special-Purpose Entities*, an entity can possess a controlling financial interest in another entity without possessing a majority of the voting interests of that entity. Thus it would be inaccurate, in many cases, to refer to the party that does not possess a controlling financial interest as a "minority" since that party could, in fact, hold a majority of the voting equity of the acquiree.

IFRS 3(R) provides the acquirer with a choice of two methods to measure noncontrolling interests at the acquisition date arising in a business combination.

1. To measure the noncontrolling interest at *fair value* (also recognizing the acquired business at fair value), or
2. To measure the noncontrolling interest at the present ownership instruments' share in the recognized amounts of the acquiree's identifiable net assets (under this approach the only difference is that, in contrast to the approach of measuring the noncontrolling interest at fair value, no portion of imputed goodwill is allocated to the noncontrolling interest). Before the May 2010 improvement this option referred to noncontrolling interest's proportionate share of the acquiree's identifiable net assets.

In terms of the May 2010 improvement, this choice is only available for present owner-ship interest that entitles the holder to a proportionate share of the entity's net assets in the event of liquidation. All other components of noncontrolling interest are measured at the acquisition date fair value unless required otherwise by IFRS.

The choice of the method to measure the noncontrolling interest should be made sepa-rately for each business combination rather than as an accounting policy. In making this election, management must carefully consider all factors, since the two methods may result in significantly different amounts of goodwill recognized, as well as different accounting for any changes in the ownership interest in a subsidiary. One important factor would be the entity's future intent to acquire noncontrolling interest, because of the potential effects on equity when the outstanding noncontrolling interest is acquired. Contrary to the previous practice under the original IFRS 3, the subsequent acquisition of the outstanding noncontrol-ling interest under IFRS 3(R) would not result in additional goodwill being recognized, since such a transaction would be considered as taking place between shareholders.

Measuring noncontrolling interest at fair value. IFRS 3(R) allows the noncontrolling interest in the acquiree to be measured at fair value at the acquisition date, determined based on market prices for equity shares not held by the acquirer, or, if not available, by using a valuation technique. If the acquirer is not acquiring all of the shares in the acquiree and there is an active market for the remaining outstanding shares in the acquiree, the acquirer may be able to use the market price to measure the fair value of the noncontrolling interest. Other-wise, the acquirer would measure fair value using other valuation techniques. Under this approach, recognized goodwill represents all of the goodwill of the acquired business, not just the acquirer's share, as recognized under original IFRS 3.

In applying the appropriate valuation technique to determine the fair value of the non-controlling interest, it is likely that there will be a difference in the fair value per share of the noncontrolling interest and the fair value per share of the controlling interest (the acquirer's interest in the acquiree). This difference is likely to be the inclusion of a control premium in the per-share fair value of the controlling interest or, similarly, what has been referred to as a "noncontrolling interest discount" applicable to the noncontrolling shares. Obviously, an investor would be unwilling to pay the same amount per share for equity shares in an entity that did not convey control of that entity as it would pay for shares that did convey control. For this reason the amount of consideration transferred by an acquirer is not usually indica-tive of the fair value of the noncontrolling interest, since the consideration transferred by the acquirer often includes a control premium.

Example of measuring noncontrolling interest at fair value

Konin Corporation (KC) acquires a 75% interest in Bartovia Corporation (BC), in exchange for cash of €360,000. BC has 25% of its shares traded on an exchange; KC acquired the 60,000 non–publicly traded shares outstanding, at €6 per share. The fair value of BC's identifiable net as-sets is €300,000; the shares of BC at the acquisition date are traded at €5 per share.

Under the full fair value approach, the noncontrolling interest is measured based on the trad-ing price of the shares of entity BC at the date control is obtained by KC (€5 per share) and a value of €100,000 is assigned to the 25% noncontrolling interest, indicating that KC has paid a control premium of €60,000 (€360,000 – [€5 × 60,000])

Equity – Noncontrolling interest in net assets (€5 × 20,000) = €100,000

It is important to note from this analysis that, from the perspective of the acquirer, the com-putation of the acquisition-date fair value of the noncontrolling interest in the acquiree is not com-puted by simply multiplying the same fair value per share that the acquirer paid for its controlling interest. Such a calculation would have yielded a different result.

Equity – Noncontrolling interest in net assets (€6 × 20,000) = €120,000

If this method had been used, the noncontrolling interest would be overvalued by €20,000 (the difference between €120,000 and €100,000).

Under the fair value approach to measure noncontrolling interest, the acquired business will be recognized at fair value, with the controlling share of total goodwill assigned to the controlling interest and the noncontrolling share allocated to the noncontrolling interest.

Measuring noncontrolling interest at its share of the identifiable net assets of the acquiree, calculated in accordance with IFRS 3(R). Under this approach, noncontrolling interest is measured as the noncontrolling interest's proportionate interest in the value of the identifiable assets and liabilities of the acquiree, determined under current requirements of IFRS 3(R).

Example of measuring noncontrolling interest at share of net assets of the acquiree

Konin Corporation (KC) acquires a 75% interest in Bartovia Corporation (BC), in exchange for cash of €360,000. BC has 25% of its shares traded on an exchange; KC acquired the 60,000 non–publicly traded shares outstanding, at €6 per share. The fair value of BC's identifiable net assets is €300,000; the shares of entity BC at the acquisition date are traded at €5 per share. The consideration transferred indicates that KC has paid a control premium of €60,000 (€360,000 – [€5 × 60,000])

Since KC elects to measure noncontrolling interest in BC at its share of the acquiree's net assets, a value of €75,000 is assigned to the 25% noncontrolling interest.

Equity – Noncontrolling interest in net assets (€300,000 × 25%) = €75,000

Under this approach to measure noncontrolling interest, goodwill recognized will represent only the acquirer's share, as was the practice prior to the effective date of IFRS 3(R).

IAS 27(R) settles the long-controversial issue of how the noncontrolling interest is to be classified in the consolidated statement of financial position by requiring that it be reported within the equity section, separately from the equity of the parent company, and clearly identified with a caption such as "noncontrolling interest in subsidiaries." Should there be noncontrolling interests attributable to more than one consolidated subsidiary, the amounts may be aggregated in the consolidated statement of financial position.

Only equity-classified instruments issued by the subsidiary may be classified as equity in this manner. If, for example, the subsidiary had issued a financial instrument that, under applicable IFRS, was classified as a liability in the subsidiary's financial statements, that instrument would not be classified as a noncontrolling interest since it does not represent an ownership interest.

Step 7—Measure the consideration transferred. In general, consideration transferred by the acquiree is measured at its acquisition-date fair value. Examples of consideration that could be transferred include cash, other assets, a business, a subsidiary of the acquirer, contingent consideration, ordinary or preference equity instruments, options, warrants, and member interests of mutual entities. The aggregate consideration transferred is the sum of the following elements measured at the acquisition date:

1. The fair value of the assets transferred by the acquirer,
2. The fair value of the liabilities incurred by the acquirer to the former owners of the acquiree, and
3. The fair value of the equity interests issued by the acquirer subject to the measurement exception discussed earlier in this chapter for the portion, if applicable, of acquirer share-based payment awards exchanged for awards held by employees of the acquiree that is included in consideration transferred.

To the extent the acquirer transfers consideration in the form of assets or liabilities with carrying amounts that differ from their fair values at the acquisition date, the acquirer is to remeasure them at fair value and recognize a gain or loss on the acquisition date. If, however, the transferred assets or liabilities remain within the consolidated entity postcombination, with the acquirer retaining control of them, no gain or loss is recognized, and the assets or liabilities are measured at their carrying amounts to the acquirer immediately prior to the acquisition date. This situation can occur, for example, when the acquirer transfers assets or liabilities to the entity being acquired rather than to its former owners.

The structure of the transaction may involve the exchange of equity interests between the acquirer and either the acquiree or the acquiree's former owners. If the acquisition-date fair value of the acquiree's equity interests is more reliably measurable than the equity interests of the acquirer, the fair value of the acquiree's equity interests is to be used to measure the consideration transferred.

When a business combination is effected without transferring consideration—for example, by contract alone—the acquisition method of accounting also applies. Examples of such combinations include

- The acquiree repurchases a sufficient number of its own shares for an existing investor (the acquirer) to obtain control
- Minority veto rights lapse that kept the acquirer, holding the majority voting rights, from controlling an acquiree
- The acquirer and acquiree agree to combine their businesses by contract alone (e.g., a stapling arrangement or dual-listed corporation)

In a business combination achieved by contract alone, the entities involved are not under common control and the combination does not involve one of the combining entities obtaining an ownership interest in another combining entity. Consequently, there is a 100% noncontrolling interest in the acquiree's net assets since the acquirer must contribute the fair value of the acquiree's assets and liabilities to the owners of the acquiree. Depending on the option elected to measure noncontrolling interest (at fair value or share of the acquiree's net assets), this may result in recognizing goodwill allocated only to the noncontrolling interest or recognizing no goodwill at all.

Contingent consideration. In many business combinations, the acquisition price is not completely fixed at the time of the exchange, but is instead dependent on the outcome of future events. There are two major types of contingent future events that might commonly be used to modify the acquisition price: the performance of the acquired entity (acquiree), and the market value of the consideration initially given for the acquisition.

The most frequently encountered contingency involves the postacquisition performance of the acquired entity or operations. The contractual agreement dealing with this is often referred to as an "earn out" provision. It typically calls for additional payments to be made to the former owners of the acquiree if defined revenue or earnings thresholds are met or exceeded. These may extend for several years after the acquisition date, and may define varying thresholds for different years. For example, if the acquiree during its final pretransaction year generated revenues of €4 million, there might be additional sums due if the acquired operations produced €4.5 million or greater revenues in year one after the acquisition, €5 million or greater in year two, and €6 million in year three.

Contingent consideration arrangements in connection with business combinations can be structured in many different ways and can result in the recognition of either assets or liabilities under IFRS 3(R). An acquirer may agree to transfer (or receive) cash, additional equity instruments, or other assets to (or from) former owners of an acquiree after the acquisition date, if certain specified events occur in the future. In either case, according to IFRS 3(R) the acquirer is to include contingent assets and liabilities as part of the consideration transferred, measured at acquisition-date fair value, which represents a significant change from past practice under original standard IFRS 3. In accordance with IFRS 3(R), contingent consideration can only be recognized when the contingency is probable and can be reliably measured.

If the contingent consideration includes a future payment obligation, that obligation is to be classified as either a liability or equity under the provisions of

- Paragraph 11 of IAS 32, *Financial Instruments: Presentation,* or
- Other applicable IFRS.

The acquirer is to carefully consider information obtained subsequent to the acquisition-date measurement of contingent consideration. Additional information obtained during the measurement period that relates to the facts and circumstances that existed at the acquisition date result in measurement period adjustments to the recognized amount of contingent consideration and a corresponding adjustment to goodwill or gain from bargain purchase. The IFRS accounting requirements on subsequently measuring and accounting for contingent consideration in the postcombination periods is discussed later in this chapter in the paragraph entitled, "Postcombination measurement and accounting."

Step 8—Recognize and measure goodwill or gain from a bargain purchase. The last step in applying the acquisition method is the measurement of goodwill or a gain from a bargain purchase. Goodwill represents an intangible that is not specifically identifiable. It results from situations when the amount the acquirer is willing to pay to obtain its controlling interest exceeds the aggregate recognized values of the net assets acquired measured following the principles of IFRS 3(R). It arises largely from the synergies and economies of scale expected from combining the operations of the acquirer and acquiree. Goodwill's elusive nature as an unidentifiable, residual asset means that it cannot be measured directly but rather can only be measured by reference to the other amounts measured as a part of the business combination. In accordance with IFRS 3(R) management must select, for each acquisition, the option to measure the noncontrolling interest, and consequently the amount recognized as goodwill (or gain on a bargain purchase) will depend on whether noncontrolling interest is measured at fair value (option 1), or at the noncontrolling interest's share of the acquiree's net assets (option 2).

GW	=	Goodwill
GBP	=	Gain from a bargain purchase
NI	=	Noncontrolling interest in the acquiree, if any, measured at fair value (option 1); or as the noncontrolling interest's share of the acquiree's net assets (option 2)
CT	=	Consideration transferred, generally measured at acquisition-date fair value
PE	=	Fair value of the acquirer's previously held interest in the acquiree if the acquisition was achieved in stages
NA	=	Net assets acquired—consisting of the acquisition-date fair values (or other amounts recognized under the requirements of IFRS 3[R] as described in the chapter) of the identifiable assets acquired and liabilities assumed.
GW (or GBP)	=	(CT + NI + PE) – NA

Thus, when application of the formula yields an excess of the acquisition-date fair value of the consideration transferred plus the amount of any noncontrolling interest and plus fair value of the acquirer's previously held equity interest over the net assets acquired, this means that the acquirer has paid a premium for the acquisition and that premium is characterized as goodwill.

When the opposite is true, that is, when the formula yields a negative result, a gain from a bargain purchase (sometimes referred to as negative goodwill) is recognized, since the acquirer has, in fact, obtained a bargain purchase as the value the acquirer obtained in the exchange exceeded the fair value of what it surrendered.

In a business combination in which no consideration is transferred, the acquirer is to use one or more valuation techniques to measure the acquisition-date fair value of its equity interest in the acquiree and substitute that measurement in the formula for "CT," the consideration transferred. The techniques selected require the availability of sufficient data to properly apply them and are to be appropriate for the circumstances. If more than one technique is used, management of the acquirer is to evaluate the results of applying the techniques including the extent of data available and how relevant and reliable the inputs (assumptions) used are. Guidance on the use of valuation techniques is provided in the standard, IFRS 13, *Fair Value Measurement*, presented in Chapter 25.

Example of recognizing goodwill—noncontrolling interest measured at fair value

Konin Corporation (KC) acquires a 75% interest in Danube Corporation (DC), in exchange for cash of €350,000. DC has 25% of its shares traded on an exchange; KC acquired the 60,000 non–publicly traded shares outstanding. The fair value of DC's identifiable net assets is €300,000; the shares of DC at the acquisition date are traded at €5 per share. The consideration transferred indicates that KC has paid a control premium of €50,000 (€350,000 – [€5 × 60,000])

Management elects the option to measure noncontrolling interest at fair value and a value of €100,000 is assigned to the 25% noncontrolling interest. The amount of goodwill accruing to the controlling interest is €125,000, which is equal to the consideration transferred, €350,000, for the controlling interest minus the controlling interest's share in the fair value of the identifiable net assets acquired, €225,000 (€300,000 × 75%). The amount of goodwill accruing to the noncontrolling interest is €25,000 (€150,000 total goodwill less €125,000 allocated to the controlling interest). The acquirer (KC) would record its acquisition of DC in its consolidated financial statements as follows:

Identifiable net assets acquired, at fair value	300,000	
Goodwill (€450,000 – €300,000)	150,000	
Equity—Noncontrolling interest		100,000
Cash		350,000

Under the approach to measure noncontrolling interest at fair value, the acquired business is recognized at €450,000 (€350,000 + 100,000) fair value and full goodwill (€150,000 = €450,000 – €300,000) is recognized. The amount of goodwill associated with the controlling interest is €125,000 (€150,000 × 75%), and the amount of goodwill associated with noncontrolling interest is €25,000 (€150,000 × 25%).

Example of recognizing goodwill—noncontrolling interest measured at the noncontrolling interest's proportionate share of the acquiree's net assets

Konin Corporation (KC) acquires a 75% interest in Donna Corporation (DC), in exchange for cash of €350,000. DC has 25% of its shares traded on an exchange; KC acquired the 60,000 non–publicly traded shares outstanding. The fair value of DC's identifiable net assets is €300,000; the shares of DC at the acquisition date are traded at €5 per share. The consideration transferred indicates that KC has paid a control premium of €50,000 (€350,000 – [€5 × 60,000])

Management elects the option to measure noncontrolling interest at its share of the acquiree's net assets and a value assigned to the noncontrolling interest is €75,000 (€300,000 × 25%).

The amount of goodwill recognized is only €125,000 which is equal to the consideration transferred €350,000 for the controlling interest minus the controlling interest's share in the fair value of the identifiable net assets acquired €225,000 (€300,000 × 75%). No goodwill is assigned to the noncontrolling interest. The acquirer (KC) would record its acquisition of DC in its consolidated financial statement as follows:

Identifiable net assets acquired, at fair value	300,000	
Goodwill (€450,000 – 300,000)	125,000	
Equity—Noncontrolling interest		75,000
Cash		350,000

Under the approach to measure noncontrolling interest at the proportionate share of the acquiree's net assets, goodwill recognized (€125,000) represents only the acquirer's share of the goodwill.

Bargain purchases. A bargain purchase occurs when the value of net assets acquired is in excess of the acquisition-date fair value of the consideration transferred plus the amount of any noncontrolling interest and plus fair value of the acquirer's previously held equity interest. While not common, this can happen, as for example in a business combination that is a forced sale, when the seller is acting under compulsion.

Under IFRS 3(R), when a bargain purchase occurs, a gain on acquisition is recognized in the profit or loss at the acquisition date, as part of income from continuing operations.

Before recognizing a gain on a bargain purchase, IASB prescribed a verification protocol for management to follow given the complexity of the computation involved. If the computation initially yields a bargain purchase, management of the acquirer is to perform the following procedures before recognizing a gain on the bargain purchase:

1. Perform a completeness review of the identifiable tangible and intangible assets acquired and liabilities assumed to reassess whether all such items have been correctly identified. If any omissions are found, recognize the assets and liabilities that had been omitted.
2. Perform a review of the procedures used to measure all of the following items. The objective of the review is to ensure that the acquisition-date measurements appropriately considered all available information available at the acquisition date.

   a. Identifiable assets acquired
   b. Liabilities assumed
   c. Consideration transferred
   d. Noncontrolling interest in the acquiree, if applicable
   e. Acquirer's previously held equity interest in the acquiree for a business combination achieved in stages

---

Example of a bargain purchase

On January 1, 2011, Konin Corporation (KC) acquires 75% of the equity interests of Laska Corporation (LC), a private entity, in exchange for cash of €250,000. The former owners of LC were forced to sell their investments within a short period of time and unable to market LC to multiple potential buyers in the marketplace. The management of KC initially measures at the acquisition date in accordance with IFRS 3(R) the separately recognizable identifiable assets acquired at €500,000 and liabilities at €100,000. KC engages an independent valuation specialist who determines that the fair value of the 25% noncontrolling interest in LC is €110,000.

Since the amount of KC identifiable net assets (€400,000 calculated as €500,000 – €100,000) exceeds the fair value of the consideration transferred (€250,000) plus the fair value of the noncontrolling interest (€110,000), the acquisition initially results in a bargain purchase. In accordance with the requirements of IFRS 3(R), KC must perform a review to ensure whether all assets, liabilities, consideration transferred, and noncontrolling interest have been correctly measured. KC concludes that the procedures and resulting measures are correct.

The acquirer (KC) recognizes the gain on its acquisition of the 75% interest as follows:

Identifiable net assets acquired, at fair value		400,000
Less: Fair value of the consideration transferred for		
75% interest in LC	250,000	
Plus: Fair value of noncontrolling interest in LC	110,000	360,000
Gain on bargain purchase		40,000

The acquirer (KC) would record its acquisition of LC in its consolidated financial statements as follows:

Identifiable net assets acquired	400,000	
Cash		250,000
Gain on the bargain purchase		40,000
Equity—Noncontrolling interest in LC		110,000

If the acquirer (KC) elects to measure the noncontrolling interest in LC on the basis of its proportionate interest in the identifiable net assets of the acquiree, the recognized amount of the noncontrolling interest would be €100,000 (€400,000 × 25%); the gain on the bargain purchase would be €50,000 (€400,000 – [€250,000 + €100,000]).

Measurement period. More frequently than not, management of the acquirer does not obtain all of the relevant information needed to complete the acquisition-date measurements in time for the issuance of the first set of interim or annual financial statements subsequent to the business combination. If the initial accounting for the business combination has not been completed by that time, the acquirer is to report provisional amounts in the consolidated financial statements for any items for which the accounting is incomplete. IFRS 3(R) provides for a "measurement period" during which any adjustments to the provisional amounts recognized at the acquisition date are to be retrospectively adjusted to reflect new information that management obtains regarding facts and circumstances existing as of the acquisition date. Information that has a bearing on this determination must not relate to postacquisition events or circumstances. The information is to be analyzed to determine whether, if it had been known at the acquisition date, it would have affected the measurement of the amounts recognized as of that date.

In evaluating whether new information obtained is suitable for the purpose of adjusting provisional amounts, management of the acquirer is to consider all relevant factors. Critical in this evaluation is the determination of whether the information relates to facts and circumstances as they existed at the acquisition date or instead, the information results from events occurring after the acquisition date. Relevant factors include

1. The timing of the receipt of the additional information, *and*
2. Whether management of the acquirer can identify a reason that a change is warranted to the provisional amounts.

Obviously, information received shortly after the acquisition date has a higher likelihood of relevance to acquisition-date circumstances than information received months later. However, the measurement period should not exceed one year from the acquisition date.

Example of consideration of new information obtained during the measurement period

Konin Corporation (KC) acquired Automotive Industries, Inc. (AI) on September 30, 2009. KC hired independent valuation specialists to determine valuation for an asset group acquired in the combination, but the valuation was not complete by the time KC authorized for issue its 2009 consolidated financial statements. As a result, KC assigned a provisional fair value of €40 million to an asset group acquired, consisting of a factory and related machinery that manufactures engines used in large trucks and sport utility vehicles (SUVs).

As of the acquisition date, the average cost of gasoline in the markets served by the customers of AI was €4.30 per gallon. For the first six months subsequent to the acquisition, the per-gallon price of gasoline was relatively stable and only fluctuated slightly up or down on any given day. Upon further analysis, management was able to determine that, during that six-month period, the production levels of the asset group and related order backlog did not vary substantially from the acquisition date.

In April 2010, however, due to an accident on April 3, 2010, at a large refinery, the average cost per gallon skyrocketed to more than €6.00. As a result of this huge spike in the price of fuel, AI's largest customers either canceled orders or sharply curtailed the number of engines they had previously ordered.

Scenario 1: On March 31, 2010, management of KC received the independent valuation, which estimated the assets' acquisition-date fair value as €30 million. Given the fact that management was unable to identify any changes that occurred during the measurement period that would have accounted for a change in the acquisition-date fair value of the asset group, management determines that it will retrospectively reduce the provisional fair value assigned to the asset group to €30 million.

In its financial statements for the year ended December 31, 2010, KC retrospectively adjusted the 2009 prior year information as follows:

1. The carrying amount of assets is decreased by €10,600. That adjustment is measured as the fair value adjustment at the acquisition date of €10,000 plus the reduced depreciation that would have been recognized if the asset's fair value at the acquisition date had been recognized from that date (€600 for three months' depreciation)
2. The carrying amount of goodwill as of December 31, 2009 is increased by €10,000.
3. Depreciation expense for 2009 is decreased by €600.

Scenario 2: KC has not received the independent valuation of assets until May 2010. On April 15, 2010, management of KC signed a sales agreement with Jonan International (JI) to sell the asset group for €30 million. Given the intervening events that affected the price of fuel and the demand for AI's products, management determines that the €10 million decline in the fair value of the asset group from the provisional fair value it was originally assigned resulted from those intervening changes and, consequently does not adjust the provisional fair value assigned to the asset group at the acquisition date.

In addition to adjustments to provisional amounts recognized, the acquirer may determine during the measurement period that it omitted recognition of additional assets or liabilities that existed at the acquisition date. During the measurement period, any such assets or liabilities identified are also to be recognized and measured on a retrospective basis.

In determining adjustments to the provisional amounts assigned to assets and liabilities, management should be alert for interrelationships between recognized assets and liabilities. For example, new information that management obtains that results in an adjustment to the provisional amount assigned to a liability for which the acquiree carries insurance could also result in an adjustment, in whole or in part, to a provisional amount recognized as an asset representing the claim receivable from the insurance carrier. In addition, as discussed in this chapter and Chapter 26, changes in provisional amounts assigned to assets and liabilities frequently will also affect temporary differences between the items' income tax basis and IFRS carrying amount, which in turn will affect the computation of deferred income assets and liabilities.

Adjustments to the provisional amounts that are made during the measurement period are recognized retrospectively as if the accounting for the business combination had actually been completed as of the acquisition date. This will result in the revision of comparative information included in the financial statements for prior periods including any necessary adjustments to depreciation, amortization, or other effects on profit or loss or other comprehensive income related to the adjustments.

The measurement period ends on the *earlier* of

1. The date management of the acquirer receives the information it seeks regarding facts and circumstances as they existed at the acquisition date or learns that it will be unable to obtain any additional information, *or*
2. One year after the acquisition date.

After the end of the measurement period, the only revisions that are permitted to be made to the initial acquisition-date accounting for the business combination are restatements for corrections of prior period errors in accordance with IAS 8, *Accounting Policies, Changes in Accounting Estimates and Errors,* discussed in detail in Chapter 7.

Acquisition-related costs. In a departure from general practice and the requirements of original standard IFRS 3, acquisition-related costs, under IFRS 3(R), are generally to be charged to expense of the period in which the costs are incurred and the related services received. Examples of these costs include

Accounting fees	Internal acquisitions department costs
Advisory fees	Legal fees
Consulting fees	Other professional fees
Finder's fees	Valuation fees

Under the previous IFRS 3, such costs were to be included in the cost of the business combination and accordingly also included in the calculation of goodwill. In accordance with the revised standard, IFRS 3(R), because such costs are not part of the fair value exchange between the buyer and the seller for the acquired business, they are accounted for separately, as operating costs in the period in which services are received. This departure from past practice may significantly affect the operating results reported for the period of any acquisition.

IFRS 3(R) makes an exception to the general rule of charging acquisition-related costs against profit with respect to costs to register and issue equity or debt securities. These costs are to be recognized in accordance with IAS 32 and IAS 39. Share issuance costs are normally charged against the gross proceeds of the issuance (see Chapter 16). Debt issuance costs are treated as a reduction of the amount borrowed or as an expense of the period in which they are incurred; however, some reporting entities have treated these costs as deferred charges and amortized them against profit during the term of the debt (see Chapter 24).

Postcombination measurement and accounting. In general, in accordance with IFRS 3(R) in postcombination periods, an acquirer should measure and account for assets acquired, liabilities assumed or incurred and equity instruments issued in a business combination on the basis consistent with other applicable IFRS for those items, which include

- IAS 38 prescribes the accounting for identifiable intangible assets acquired in a business combination
- IAS 36 provides guidance on recognizing impairment losses
- IFRS 4 prescribes accounting for an insurance contract acquired in a business combination
- IAS 12 prescribes the postcombination accounting for deferred tax assets and liabilities acquired in a business combination.
- IFRS 2 provides guidance on subsequent measurement and accounting for share-based payment awards

- IAS 27(R) prescribes accounting for changes in a parent's ownership interest in a subsidiary after control is obtained

IFRS 3(R) provides special guidance on accounting for the following items arising in a business combination:

1. Reacquired rights,
2. Contingent liabilities recognized as of the acquisition date,
3. Indemnification assets, and
4. Contingent consideration.

After acquisition, a *reacquired right* recognized as an intangible asset is amortized over the remaining contractual term, without taking into consideration potential renewal periods. If an acquirer subsequently sells a reacquired right to a third party, the carrying amount of the right should be included in calculating the gain or loss on the sale.

In postcombination periods, until the liability is settled, cancelled or expires, the acquirer measures a *contingent liability* recognized as of the acquisition date at the higher of

1. The amount that would be recognized in accordance with IAS 37, and
2. The amount initially recognized, less, if appropriate, cumulative amortization recognized in accordance with IAS 18, *Revenue.*

This requirement would not apply to contracts accounted for under the provisions of IAS 39. In accordance with this standard, the financial liability is to be measured at fair value at each reporting date, with changes in value recognized either in profit or loss or in other comprehensive income in accordance with IAS 39.

At each reporting date subsequent to the acquisition date, the acquirer should measure an *indemnification asset* recognized as part of the business combination using the same basis as the indemnified item, subject to any limitations imposed contractually on the amount of the indemnification. If an indemnification asset is not subsequently measured at fair value (because to do so would be inconsistent with the basis used to measure the indemnified item), management is to assess the collectibility of the asset. Any changes in the measurement of the asset (and the related liability) are recognized in profit or loss.

The acquirer needs to carefully consider information obtained subsequent to the acquisition-date measurement of *contingent consideration*. Some changes in the fair value of contingent consideration result from additional information obtained during the measurement period that relates to the facts and circumstances that existed at the acquisition date. Such changes are measurement period adjustments to the recognized amount of contingent consideration and a corresponding adjustment to goodwill or gain from bargain purchase. However, changes that result from events occurring after the acquisition date, such as meeting a specified earnings target, reaching a specified share price, or reaching an agreed-upon milestone on a research and development project, do not constitute measurement period adjustments, and no longer result in changes to goodwill. This approach represents another significant change from past practice under original standard IFRS 3.

Changes in the fair value of contingent consideration that do not result from measurement period adjustments are to be accounted for as follows:

1. If the contingent consideration is classified as equity, it is not to be remeasured, and subsequent settlement of the contingency is to be reflected within equity.
2. If the contingent consideration is classified as an asset or liability that is a financial instrument within the scope of IAS 39, it is to be remeasured at fair value at each reporting date, with changes in value recognized either in profit or loss or in other comprehensive income in accordance with IAS 39.

3. If the contingent consideration is classified as an asset or liability that is not a financial instrument within the scope of IAS 39, it is to be measured in accordance with IAS 37 or other applicable standards, with changes in value recognized in profit or loss.

Since subsequent measurement and accounting for contingent consideration under IFRS 3(R) represents significant change from former practice under the original standard IFRS 3, it is important that the management provides reliable estimates of the acquisition-date fair values. The potential impact of postacquisition remeasurements on subsequent profit or loss as well as on debt covenants or management remuneration should be analyzed at the date of acquisition.

In May 2010 the IASB amended IFRS 3 through the *Improvements Project*. The amendment relates to contingent consideration recognized by the acquirer. If a business combination takes place before the effective date of the amendment (being financial years beginning on or after July 1, 2010), then adjustments to contingent consideration that are not deemed to be part of the adjustments allowed in the measurement period are recorded against goodwill or the gain from a bargain purchase. For business combinations entered into after the effective date of the amendment, adjustments to contingent consideration that are not part of the measurement period adjustments are recognized in profit and loss.

IFRS guidance on recognizing and measuring reacquired rights, contingent liabilities and indemnification assets on the acquisition date was discussed earlier in this chapter in the paragraph entitled, "Accounting for Business Combinations under the Acquisition Method, Step 5—Classify or designate the identifiable assets acquired and liabilities assumed"; and guidance on contingent consideration in "Step 7—Measure the consideration transferred."

DISCLOSURE REQUIREMENTS

The acquirer should disclose information that enables users of its financial statements to evaluate

- The nature as well as financial effect of a business combination that occurs either (1) during the current period; or (2) after the end of the reporting period but before the financial statements are authorized to issue.
- The financial effects of adjustments recognized in the current reporting period that relate to business combinations that occurred during (1) the current period; or (2) previous reporting periods.

The disclosure requirements of the new standards are quite extensive and, for the reader's convenience, are presented in detail in the disclosure checklist in Appendix A to this publication.

Additional guidance in applying the acquisition method. Due to the complexity of many business combinations and the varying structures used to effect them, IASB provided supplemental guidance to aid practitioners in applying the standard.

Recognizing and measuring the identifiable assets acquired and liabilities assumed. The following guidance is to be followed in applying the recognition and measurement principles (subject to certain specified exceptions).

Assets with uncertain cash flows (valuation allowances). Since fair value measurements take into account the effects of uncertainty regarding the amounts and timing of future cash flows, the acquirer is not to recognize a separate valuation allowance for assets subject to such uncertainties (e.g., acquired receivables, including loans). This may be a departure from current practice, especially for entities operating in the financial services industry.

Assets subject to operating leases in which the acquiree is the lessee. Irrespective of whether the acquiree is the lessee or lessor, the acquirer is to evaluate, as of the acquisition date, each of the acquiree's operating leases to determine whether its terms are favorable or unfavorable compared to the market terms of leases of identical or similar items. If the acquiree is the lessee and the lease terms are favorable, the acquirer is to recognize an intangible asset; if the lease terms are unfavorable, the acquirer is to recognize a liability.

Even when the lease is considered to be at market terms, there nevertheless may be an identifiable intangible associated with it. This would be the case if market participants would be willing to pay to obtain it (i.e., to obtain the rights and privileges associated with it). Examples of this situation are leases for favorably-positioned airport gates, or prime retail space in an economically favorable location. If, from the perspective of marketplace participants, acquiring the lease would entitle them to future economic benefits that qualify as identifiable intangible assets (discussed later in this chapter), the acquirer would recognize, separately from goodwill, the associated identifiable intangible asset.

Assets subject to operating leases in which the acquiree is the lessor. The fair value of assets owned by the acquiree that are subject to operating leases with the acquiree being the lessor are to be measured separately from the underlying lease to which they are subject. Consequently, the acquirer does not recognize a separate asset or liability if the terms of an operating lease are either favorable or unfavorable when compared with market terms, as required for leases in which the acquiree is the lessee.

Assets the acquirer plans to idle or to use in a way that is different from the way other market participants would use them. If the acquirer intends, for competitive or other business reasons, to idle an acquired asset (e.g., a research and development intangible asset) or use it in a manner that is different from the manner in which other market participants would use it, the acquirer is still required to initially measure the asset at fair value determined in accordance with its use by other market participants.

Identifiable intangibles to be recognized separately from goodwill. Intangible assets acquired in a business combination are to be recognized separately from goodwill if they meet either of two criteria to be considered *identifiable.* These criteria are

1. *Separability criterion*—The intangible asset is capable of being separated or divided from the entity that holds it, and sold, transferred, licensed, rented, or exchanged, regardless of the acquirer's intent to do so. An intangible asset meets this criterion even if its transfer would not be alone, but instead would be accompanied or bundled with a related contract, other identifiable asset, or a liability.
2. *Legal/contractual criterion*—The intangible asset results from contractual or other legal rights. An intangible asset meets this criterion even if the rights are not transferable or separable from the acquiree or from other rights and obligations of the acquiree.

Illustrative Examples to IFRS 3(R) carry forward from the original IFRS 3 a lengthy, though not exhaustive, listing of intangible assets that IASB believes have characteristics that meet one of these two criteria (legal/contractual or separability). A logical approach in practice would be for the acquirer to first consider whether the intangibles specifically included on the IASB list are applicable to the particular acquiree and then to consider whether there may be other unlisted intangibles included in the acquisition that meet one or both of the criteria for separate recognition.

IFRS 3(R) organizes groups of identifiable intangibles into categories related to or based on

1. Marketing
2. Customers or clients
3. Artistic works
4. Contractual
5. Technological

These categorizations are somewhat arbitrary. Consequently, some of the items listed could fall into more than one of the categories. Examples of identifiable intangibles included in each of the categories are as follows:

Marketing-related intangible assets.

1. *Trademarks, service marks, trade names, collective marks, certification marks.* A trademark represents the right to use a name, word, logo, or symbol that differenti- ates a product from products of other entities. A service mark is the equivalent of a trademark for a service offering instead of a product. A collective mark is used to identify products or services offered by members affiliated with each other. A certifi- cation mark is used to designate a particular attribute of a product or service such as its geographic source (e.g., Columbian coffee or Italian olive oil) or the standards under which it was produced (e.g., ISO 9000 Certified).
2. *Trade dress.* The overall appearance and image (unique color, shape, or package de- sign) of a product.
3. *Newspaper mastheads.* The unique appearance of the title page of a newspaper or other periodical.
4. *Internet domain names.* The unique name that identifies an address on the Internet. Domain names must be registered with an Internet registry and are renewable.
5. *Noncompetition agreements.* Rights to assurances that companies or individuals will refrain from conducting similar businesses or selling to specific customers for an agreed-upon period of time.

Customer-related intangible assets.

1. *Customer lists.* Names, contact information, order histories, and other information about a company's customers, that a third party, such as a competitor or a telemar- keting firm would want to use in its own business.
2. *Order or production backlogs.* Unfilled sales orders for goods and services in amounts that exceed the quantity of finished goods and work-in-process on hand for filling the orders.
3. *Customer contracts and related customer relationships.* When a company's relation- ships with its customers arise primarily through contracts and are of value to buyers who can "step into the shoes" of the sellers and assume their remaining rights and duties under the contracts, and which hold the promise that the customers will place future orders with the entity or relationships between entities and their customers for which

   a. The entities have information about the customers and have regular contact with the customers, and
   b. The customers have the ability to make direct contact with the entity.

4. *Noncontractual customer relationships.* Customer relationships that arise through means such as regular contacts by sales or service representatives, the value of which are derived from the prospect of the customers placing future orders with the entity.

Artistic-related intangible assets.

1. *Plays, operas, ballets.*
2. *Books, magazines, newspapers, and other literary works.*
3. *Musical works such as compositions, song lyrics, and advertising jingles.*
4. *Pictures and photographs.*
5. *Video and audiovisual material including motion pictures or films, music videos and television programs.*

Contract-based intangible assets.

1. *License, royalty, standstill agreements.* License agreements represent the right, on the part of the licensee, to access or use property that is owned by the licensor for a specified period of time at an agreed-upon price. A royalty agreement entitles its holder to a contractually agreed-upon portion of the income earned from the sale or license of a work covered by patent or copyright. A standstill agreement conveys assurances that a company or individual will refrain from engaging in certain activities for specified periods of time.
2. *Advertising, construction, management, service or supply contracts.* For example a contract with a newspaper, broadcaster, or Internet site to provide specified advertising services to the acquiree.
3. *Lease agreements* (irrespective of whether the acquiree is the lessee or lessor). A contract granting use or occupation of property during a specified period in exchange for a specified rent.
4. *Construction permits.* Rights to build a specified structure at a specified location.
5. *Construction contracts.* Rights to become the contractor responsible for completing a construction project and benefit from the profits it produces, subject to the remaining obligations associated with performance (including any past-due payments to suppliers and/or subcontractors).
6. *Construction management, service, or supply contracts.* Rights to manage a construction project for a fee, procure specified services at a specified fee, or purchase specified products at contractually agreed-upon prices.
7. *Broadcast rights.* Legal permission to transmit electronic signals using specified bandwidth in the radio frequency spectrum, granted by the operation of communication laws.
8. *Franchise rights.* Legal rights to engage.in a trade-named business, to sell a trade-marked good, or to sell a service-marked service in a particular geographic area.
9. *Operating rights.* Permits to operate in a certain manner, such as those granted to a carrier to transport specified commodities.
10. *Use rights, such as drilling, water, air, timber cutting and route authorities.* Permits to use specified land, property, or air space in a particular manner, such as the right to cut timber, expel emissions, or to land airplanes at specified gates at an airport.
11. *Servicing contracts.* The contractual right to service a loan. Servicing entails activities such as collecting principal and interest payments from the borrower, maintaining escrow accounts, paying taxes and insurance premiums when due, and pursuing collection of delinquent payments.
12. *Employment contract.* Contract that is beneficial from the perspective of the employer because of favorable market-related terms.
13. *Uses rights.* Rights for drilling, water, air, timber cutting and route authorities.

Technology-based intangible assets.

1. *Patented or copyrighted software.* Computer software source code, program specifications, procedures, and associated documentation that is legally protected by patent or copyright.
2. *Computer software and mask works.* Software permanently stored on a read-only memory chip as a series of stencils or integrated circuitry. Mask works may be provided statutory protection in some countries.
3. *Unpatented technology.* Access to knowledge about the proprietary processes and workflows followed by the acquiree to accomplish desired business results.
4. *Databases, including title plants.* Databases are collections of information generally stored digitally in an organized manner. A database can be protected by copyright (e.g., the database contained on the CD-ROM version of this publication). Many databases, however, represent information accumulated as a natural by-product of a company conducting its normal operating activities. Examples of these databases are plentiful and include title plants, scientific data, and credit histories. Title plants represent historical records with respect to real estate parcels in a specified geographic location.
5. *Trade secrets.* Trade secrets are proprietary, confidential information, such as a formula, process, or recipe.

One commonly cited intangible asset deliberately omitted by the IASB from its list of identifiable intangibles is an "assembled workforce." IASB decided that the replacement cost technique that is often used to measure the fair value of an assembled workforce does not faithfully represent the fair value of the intellectual capital acquired. It was thus decided that an exception to the recognition criteria would be made, and that the fair value of an acquired assembled workforce would remain part of goodwill.

Research and development assets. IFRS 3(R) requires the acquirer to recognize and measure all tangible and intangible assets used in research and development (R&D) activities acquired individually or in a group of assets as part of the business combination. This prescribed treatment is to be followed even if the assets are judged to have no alternative future use. These assets are to be measured at their acquisition-date fair values. Fair value measurements are to be made based on the assumptions that would be made by market participants in pricing the asset. Assets that the acquirer does not intend to use or intends to use in a manner that is different from the manner other market participants would use them are, nevertheless, required to be measured at fair value.

Intangible R&D assets. Upon initial recognition, the *intangible* R&D assets are to be classified as indefinite-lived assets until the related R&D efforts are either completed or abandoned. In the reporting periods during which the R&D intangible assets are classified as indefinite-lived, they are not to be amortized. Instead, they are to be tested for impairment in the same manner as other indefinite-lived intangibles. Upon completion or abandonment of the related R&D efforts, management is to determine the remaining useful life of the intangibles and amortize them accordingly. In applying these requirements, assets that are temporarily idled are not to be considered abandoned.

Tangible R&D assets. Tangible R&D assets acquired in a business combination are to be accounted for according to their nature (e.g., supplies, inventory, depreciable assets, etc.).

Determining what is part of the business combination transaction. Transactions entered into by or on behalf of the acquirer or primarily for the benefit of the acquirer or the combined entity, rather than primarily for the benefit of the acquiree (or its former owners), before the combination, are likely to be separate transactions, not accounted for under the acquisition method. In applying the acquisition method to account for a business combination, the acquirer must recognize only the consideration transferred for the acquiree and the assets acquired and liabilities assumed in the exchange for the acquiree. IFRS 3(R) provides the following examples of separate transactions that are not to be included in applying the acquisition method:

1. A transaction that in effect settles preexisting relationships between the acquirer and acquiree,
2. A transaction that remunerates employees or former owners of the acquiree for future services, and
3. A transaction that reimburses the acquiree or its former owners for paying the acquirer's acquisition-related costs.

The amount of the gain or loss measured as a result of settling a preexisting relationship will, of course, depend on whether the acquirer had previously recognized related assets or liabilities with respect to that relationship.

Example of settlement of preexisting contractual supplier relationship; contract unfavorable to acquirer

Konin Corporation (KC) and Banham Corporation (BC) are parties to a 3-year supply contract that contains the following provisions:

1. KC is required to annually purchase 3,000 flat-panel displays from BC at a fixed price of €400 per unit for an aggregate purchase price of €1,200,000 for each of the three years.
2. KC is required to pay BC the annual €1,200,000 irrespective of whether it takes delivery of all 3,000 units and the required payment is nonrefundable.
3. The contract contains a penalty provision that would permit KC to cancel it at the end of the second year for a lump-sum payment of €500,000.
4. In each of the first two years of the contract, KC took delivery of the full 3,000 units.

At December 31, 2011, the supply contract was unfavorable to KC because KC was able to purchase flat-panel displays with similar specifications and of similar quality from another supplier for €350 per unit. Therefore, KC accrued a loss of €150,000 (3,000 units remaining under the firm purchase commitment × €50 loss per unit).

On January 1, 2012, KC acquires BC for €30 million, which reflects the fair value of BC based on what other marketplace participants would be willing to pay. On the acquisition date, the €30 million fair value of BC includes €750,000 related to the contract with KC that consists of

Identifiable intangibles[3]	€600,000	Representing the remaining year of the contract, at prevailing market prices
Favorable pricing	150,000	Representing the portion of the contract price that is favorable to BC and unfavorable to KC
	€750,000	

BC has no other identifiable assets or liabilities related to the supply contract with KC. KC would compute its gain or loss on settlement of this preexisting relationship as follows:

1.	Amount of unfavorableness to acquirer (KC) at acquisition date	€150,000
2.	Lump-sum settlement amount available to KC	500,000
3.	Lessor of 1. or 2.	150,000
4.	Amount by which 1. exceeds 2.	N/A

---

[3] *In computing the valuation of BC, these amounts would represent such identifiable customer-related intangible assets as customer contract, related customer relationship, production backlog, etc.*

Since KC had already recognized an unrealized loss on the firm purchase commitment as of December 31, 2011, upon its acquisition of BC, its loss of €150,000 from recognizing the lesser of 1. and 2. above would be offset by the elimination of the liability for the unrealized loss on the firm purchase commitment in the same amount of €150,000. Thus, under these circumstances, KC would have neither a gain nor a loss on the settlement of its preexisting relationship with BC. The entries to record these events are not considered part of the business combination accounting. It is important to note that, from the perspective of KC, when it applies the acquisition method to record the business combination, it will characterize the €600,000 "at-market" component of the contract as part of goodwill and not as identifiable intangibles. This is the case because of the obvious fallacy of KC recognizing customer-relationship intangible assets that represent a relationship with itself.

Example of settlement of preexisting contractual supplier relationship; contract favorable to acquirer

Using the same facts as the KC/BC example above, assume that, instead of the contract being favorable to the acquirer KC, it was unfavorable to BC in the amount of €150,000 and that there was a cancellation provision in the contract that would permit BC to pay a penalty after year two of €100,000 to cancel the remainder of the contract.

On the acquisition date, the €30 million fair value of BC, under this scenario would include €450,000 related to the contract with KC that consists of

Identifiable intangibles	€600,000	Representing the remaining year of the contract, at prevailing market prices
Unfavorable pricing	(150,000)	Representing the portion of the contract price that is unfavorable to BC and favorable to KC
	€450,000	

Under these changed assumptions, KC would not have incurred or recorded an unrealized loss on the firm purchase commitment with BC since the contract terms were favorable to KC. The determination of KC's gain or loss would be as follows:

1.	Amount of favorability to acquirer (KC) at acquisition date	€150,000
2.	Lump-sum settlement amount available to BC	100,000
3.	Lessor of 1. or 2.	100,000
4.	Amount by which 1. exceeds 2.	50,000

Under this scenario, unless BC believed that the market would change in the near term, it would be economically advantageous, in the absence of a business combination, for BC to settle the remaining contract at the acquisition date by paying the €100,000 penalty because BC would be able to sell the remaining 3,000 units covered by the contract for an aggregate price of €150,000 more than it was committed to sell those units to KC.

At the acquisition date, KC would record a gain of €100,000 to settle its preexisting relationship with BC. The entry to record the gain is not considered part of the business combination accounting.

In addition, however, since 2. is less than 1., the €50,000 difference is included in the accounting for the business combination, since economically, in postcombination periods, the combined entity will not benefit from that portion of the acquisition date favorability of the contract.

As was the case in the first example, the portion of the purchase price allocated to the contract in the business combination accounting would be accounted for as goodwill for the same reason.

Contingent payments to employees or former owners of the acquiree. The acquirer is to assess whether arrangements to make contingent payments to employees or selling owners of the acquiree represent contingent consideration that is part of the business combination transaction or represent separate transactions to be excluded from the application of the acquisition method to the business combination. In general, the acquirer is to consider the reasons why the terms of the acquisition include the payment provision, the party that initiated the arrangement, and when (at what stage of the negotiations) the arrangement was entered into by the parties. When those considerations do not provide clarity regarding whether the transaction is separate from the business combination, the acquirer considers the following indicators:

1. *Postcombination employment*—Consideration is to be given to the terms under which the selling owners will be providing services as key employees of the combined entity. The terms may be evidenced by a formal employment contract, by provisions included in the acquisition documents, or by other documents. If the arrangement provides that the contingent payments are automatically forfeited upon termination of employment, the consideration is to be characterized as compensation for postcombination services. If, instead, the contingent payments are not affected by termination of employment, this would be an indicator that the contingent payments represent additional consideration that is part of the business combination transaction and not compensation for services.

2. *Duration of postcombination employment*—If the employee is contractually bound to remain employed for a period that equals or exceeds the period during which the contingent payments are due, this may be an indicator that the contingent payments represent compensation for services.

3. *Amount of compensation*—If the amount of the employee's compensation that is not contingent is considered to be reasonable in relation to other key employees of the combined entity, this may indicate that the contingent amounts represent additional consideration and not compensation for services.

4. *Differential between amounts paid to employees and selling owners who do not become employees of the combined entity*—If, on a per-share basis, the contingent payments due to former owners of the acquiree that did not become employees are lower than the contingent payments due to the former owners that did become employees of the combined entity, this may indicate that the incremental amounts paid to the employees are compensation.

5. *Extent of ownership*—The relative ownership percentages (e.g., number of shares, units, percentage of membership interest) owned by the selling owners who remain employees of the combined entity serve as an indicator of how to characterize the substance of the contingent consideration. If, for example, the former owners of substantially all of the ownership interests in the acquiree are continuing to serve as key employees of the combined entity, this may be an indicator that the contingent payment arrangement is substantively a profit-sharing vehicle designed with the intent of providing compensation for services to be performed postcombination. Conversely, if the former owners that remained employed by the combined entity collectively owned only a nominal ownership interest in the acquiree and all of the former owners received the same amount of contingent basis on a per-share basis, this may be an indicator that the contingent payments represent additional consideration. In considering the applicability of this indicator, care must be exercised to closely examine the effects, if any, of transactions, ownership interests, and employment relationships, precombination and postcombination, with respect to parties related to the selling owners of the acquiree.

6. *Relationship of contingent arrangements to the valuation approach used*—The payment terms negotiated in many business combinations provide that the amount of the acquisition date transfer of consideration from acquirer to acquiree (or the acquiree's former owners) is computed near the lower end of a range of valuation estimates the

acquirer used in valuing the acquiree. Furthermore, the formula for determining future contingent payments is derived from or related to that valuation approach. When this is the case, it may be an indicator that the contingent payments represent additional consideration. Conversely, if the formula for determining future contingent payments more closely resembles prior profit-sharing arrangements, this may be an indicator that the substance of the contingent payment arrangement is to provide compensation for services.

7. *Formula prescribed for determining contingent consideration*—Analyzing the formula to be used to determine the contingent consideration may provide insight into the substance of the arrangement. Contingent payments that are determined on the basis of a multiple of earnings may be indicative of being, in substance, contingent consideration that is part of the business combination transaction. Alternatively, contingent consideration that is determined as a prespecified percentage of earnings would be more suggestive of a routine profit-sharing arrangement for the purposes of providing additional compensation to employees for postcombination services rendered.

8. *Other considerations*—Given the complexity of a business combination transaction and the sheer number and girth of the legal documents necessary to effect it, the financial statements preparer is charged with the daunting, but unavoidable task of performing a comprehensive review of the terms of all the associated agreements. These can take the form of noncompete agreements, consulting agreements, leases, guarantees, indemnifications, and, of course, the formal agreement to combine the businesses. Particular attention should be paid to the applicable income tax treatment afforded to the contingent payments. The income tax treatment of these payments may be an indicator that tax avoidance was a primary motivator in characterizing them in the manner that they are structured. An acquirer might, for example, simultaneous to a business combination, execute a property lease with one of the key owners of the acquiree. If the lease payments were below market, some or all of the contingent payments to that key owner/lessor under the provisions of the other legal agreements might, in substance, be making up the shortfall in the lease and thus should be recharacterized as lease payments and accounted for separately from the business combination in the combined entity's postcombination financial statements. If this were not the case, and the lease payments were reflective of the market, this would be an indicator pointing to a greater likelihood that the contingent payment arrangements actually did represent contingent consideration associated with the business combination transaction.

Example of contingent payments to employees

Henan Corporation (HC) hired a new Accounting Director in charge of the conversion to IFRS under a five-year contract. The terms of the contract stated that HC will pay the Director €1 million annually if HC is acquired before the expiration of this contract, up to the maximum amount of €5 million. After four years, Konin Corporation (KC) acquires HC. Since the Director was still working for HC at the acquisition date, he will receive €1 million payment under the contract.

In this example, the contract for the employment of the Accounting Director was entered into much before the negotiations of the business combination were initiated, and the purpose of the contract was to receive the services of the Director. Therefore, there is no evidence that this contract was primarily entered into to provide benefits to KC or the combined entity. As a result, the liability for the payment of €1 million is included in the application of the acquisition method.

Alternatively, HC might enter into the contract at the recommendation of KC, as part of the negotiations for the business combination, with the intent to provide severance pay to the Director. Therefore, the contract may primarily benefit KC and the combined entity rather than HC or its former owners. Consequently, the acquirer KC must account for the liability of €1 million to the Director since the payment is considered a separate transaction, excluded from the application of the acquisition method to this business combination.

Replacement awards—Acquirer share-based payment awards exchanged for acquiree awards held by its employees. In connection with a business combination, the acquirer often awards share options or other share-based payments (i.e., replacement awards) to the employees of the acquiree in exchange for the employees' acquiree awards. Obviously, there are many valid business reasons for the exchange, not the least of which is ensuing smooth transition and integration, retention and motivation of valued employees, and maintaining controlling interests in the acquiree.

IFRS 3(R) provides guidance on determining whether equity instruments (e.g., share-based payments awards) issued in a business combination are part of the consideration transferred in exchange for control of the acquiree (and accounted for in accordance with IFRS 3[R]) or are in return for continued service in the postcombination periods (and accounted for under IFRS 2, *Share-Based Payment,* as a modification of a plan).

Acquirer not obligated to exchange. Accounting for the replacement awards under IFRS 3(R) is dependent on whether the acquirer is obligated to replace the acquiree awards. The acquirer is obligated to replace the acquiree awards if the acquiree or its employees can enforce replacement through rights obtained from the terms of the acquisition agreement, the acquiree awards, or applicable laws or regulations.

If the acquirer is not obligated to replace the acquiree awards, all of the market-based measure (MBM) of the replacement awards is recognized as remuneration cost in the postcombination financial statements.

Example of acquirer replacing acquiree awards without the obligation to do so

Konin Corporation (KC) acquired Henan Corporation (HC) on January 1, 2012. Because of the business combination, the share-based payment awards of the subsidiary that had been previously granted by HC to its employees expired on the acquisition date.

Although KC was not obligated, legally or contractually, to replace the expired awards, its Board of Directors approved a grant of KC awards designed so that the employees of HC would not be financially disadvantaged by the acquisition transaction.

Since the replacement awards were voluntary on the part of KC, the market-based measure of the replacement award is attributed wholly to postcombination service and therefore recognized as remuneration cost in KC's postcombination consolidated financial statements.

Acquirer obligated to replace acquiree awards. If the acquirer is obligated to replace the awards of the acquiree, either all or a portion of the market-based measure of the replacement awards are included in measuring the consideration transferred by the acquirer in the business combination. To the extent a portion of the replacement awards are not allocated to consideration transferred, they are attributable to postcombination services and therefore recognized as remuneration cost in the acquirer's consolidated financial statements, thus having no impact on goodwill and equity.

For the purposes of illustrating the allocation computations, the following conventions and abbreviations are used:

MBM_{RA} Acquisition date market-based measure of acquirer replacement award

MBM_{AA} Acquisition date market-based measure of acquiree award that is being replaced by the acquirer

VP_{AA} Original vesting period[4] of acquiree awards at acquisition date

VP_{RA} Vesting period of the acquirer replacement awards at their acquisition date

CVP_{AA} Portion of vesting period completed at the acquisition date by employees under the acquiree awards

TVP   Total vesting period—The vesting period already satisfied by the employees at the acquisition date under the acquiree awards plus the vesting period, if any, required by the acquirer replacement awards

PRE   Portion of MBM_{RA} attributable to precombination services performed by the employees of the acquiree

PRC   Postcombination remuneration cost

$$TVP = CVP_{AA} + VP_{RA}$$

The following steps are followed to determine the portion of the market-based measure of the replacement award that is to be included as part of the consideration transferred by the acquirer:

1. Compute both MBM_{RA} and MBM_{AA} by following the provision of IFRS 2, as discussed in detail in Chapter 17.
2. Compute the portion of the replacement award that is attributable to precombination services rendered by the acquiree's employees as follows:

   a. If $VP_{AA} > TVP$, then

   $$PRE = MBM_{AA}\left(\frac{CVP_{AA}}{VP_{AA}}\right)$$

   b. If $VP_{AA} < TVP$, then

   $$PRE = MBM_{AA}\left(\frac{CVP_{AA}}{TVP}\right)$$

3. Compute the portion of the nonvested replacement award attributable to postcombination service as follows:

$$PRC = MBM_{RA} - PRE$$

This amount is to be recognized as remuneration cost in the acquirer's postcombination consolidated financial statements since, at the acquisition date, the vesting conditions had not been met.

The following examples are adapted from IFRS 3(R), Illustrative Examples:

---

[4] *The term "vesting period" is defined as the period during which all the specified vesting conditions of a share-based payment arrangement are to be satisfied. Vesting conditions are the conditions that determine whether the entity receives the services that entitle the counterparty to receive cash, other assets, or equity instruments of the entity, under a share-based payment arrangement. Vesting conditions are either service conditions or performance conditions. These terms are defined in IFRS 2, discussed in detail in Chapter 17.*

> **Example 1**

Example of acquirer replacement awards requiring no postcombination services exchanges for fully vested acquiree awards where the employees have rendered all required services by the acquisition date

Acquiree awards	Vesting period *completed* before the business combination
Replacement awards	Additional employee services *are not* required after the acquisition date

Konin Corporation (KC) acquired Henan Corporation (HC) on January 1, 2012. In accordance with the acquisition agreement, KC agreed to replace share-based awards that had previously been issued by HC. Details are as follows:

	a. Acquiree awards	*b. Acquirer awards*
1. Acquisition date market-based measure of awards	$MBM_{AA} = €100$	$MBM_{RA} = €110$
2. Original vesting period of acquiree awards at their grant date	$VP_{AA} = 4$ years	--
3. Portion of 2a. completed by the acquisition date by employees of the acquiree	$CVP_{AA} = 4$ years	--
4. Vesting period of acquirer replacement awards at the acquisition date	--	$VP_{RA} = 0$
5. Total vesting period (3a. + 4b.)	--	TVP = 4 years
6. The greater of the total vesting period (5b.) or the original vesting period of the acquiree awards (2a.)	--	4 years

Since the acquiree's employees had completed all of the services required under the prior awards, applying the formula yields a result that attributes 100% of the market-based value of the acquiree award that is being replaced to precombination services rendered.

$$PRE = \text{1a.} \left(\frac{\text{3a.}}{\text{6b.}} \right)$$

$$PRE = €100 \left(\frac{4 \text{ years}}{4 \text{ years}} \right)$$

$$PRE = €100$$

The €100 result, attributed to precombination services, is included by the acquirer in its computation of the consideration transferred in exchange for control of the acquiree.

The final step in the computation is to account for the difference between the acquisition date market-based measure of the replacement awards and the acquiree awards as follows:

Market-based measure of replacement awards—MBM_{RA}	€110
– Allocated to consideration transferred per above	100
= Additional remuneration cost recognized in postcombination consolidated financial statements	€ 10

This result illustrates the basic principle in IFRS 3(R) that any excess of MBM_{RA} over the MBM_{AA} is to be attributed to postcombination services and recognized as remuneration cost in the acquirer's postcombination consolidated financial statements.

Example 2

Example of acquirer replacement awards requiring performance of postcombination services exchanged for full vested acquiree awards where the employees have rendered all required services by the acquisition date

Acquiree awards   Vesting period *completed* before the business combination

Replacement awards   Additional employee services *are* required after the acquisition date

The acquisition agreement referred to in the previous example governing the KC acquisition of HC that occurred on January 1, 2009, contained the following provisions regarding exchange of outstanding HC awards at acquisition date for KC replacement awards:

	a. Acquiree awards	*b. Acquirer awards*
1. Acquisition date market-based measure of awards	$MBM_{AA} = €100$	$MBM_{RA} = €100$
2. Original vesting period of acquiree awards at their grant date	$VP_{AA} = 4$ years	--
3. Portion of 2a. completed by the acquisition date by employees of the acquiree (the acquiree employees in this example had actually completed a total of 7 years of services by the acquisition date)	$CVP_{AA} = 4$ years	--
4. Vesting period of acquirer replacement awards at the acquisition date	--	$VP_{RA} = 1$ year
5. Total vesting period (3a. + 4b.)	--	$TVP = 5$ years
6. The greater of the total vesting period (5b.) or the original vesting period of the acquiree awards (2a.)	--	5 years

Even though the acquiree's employees had completed all the vesting period required by the acquiree's awards three years prior to the acquisition, the imposition of an additional year of required service by the acquirer's replacement awards results in an allocation between the amount attributable to precombination services and, separately, to postcombination services as follows:

$$PRE = 1a. \left(\frac{3a.}{6b.} \right)$$

$$PRE = €100 \left(\frac{4 \text{ years}}{5 \text{ years}} \right)$$

$$PRE = €80$$

The €80 result, attributed to precombination services, is included by the acquirer in its computation of the consideration transferred in exchange for control of the acquiree.

The €20 difference between the €100 market value of the replacement awards and the €80 allocated to precombination services (and included in consideration transferred) is accounted for as remuneration cost in the postcombination consolidated financial statements of KC.

Example 3

Example of acquirer replacement awards requiring performance of postcombination services exchanged for acquiree awards with remaining unsatisfied vesting period as of the acquisition date

	Acquiree awards	Vesting period *not completed* before the business combination
	Replacement awards	Additional employee services *are* required after the acquisition date

The acquisition agreement referred to in the previous examples governing the KC acquisition of HC that occurred on January 1, 2009, contained the following provisions regarding exchange of outstanding HC awards at acquisition date for KC replacement awards:

		a. Acquiree awards	b. Acquirer awards
1.	Acquisition date market-based measure of awards	$MBM_{AA} = €100$	$MBM_{RA} = €100$
2.	Original vesting period of acquiree awards at their grant date	$VP_{AA} = 4$ years	--
3.	Portion of 2a. completed by the acquisition date by employees of the acquiree	$CVP_{AA} = 2$ years	--
4.	Vesting period of acquirer replacement awards at the acquisition date	--	$VP_{RA} = 1$ year
5.	Total vesting period (3a. + 4b.)	--	$TVP = 3$ years
6.	The greater of the total vesting period (5b.) or the original vesting period of the acquiree awards (2a.)	--	4 years

The portion of the market-based measure of the replacement awards attributable to precombination services already rendered by the acquiree employees is computed as follows:

$$PRE = 1a. \left(\frac{3a.}{6b.} \right)$$

$$PRE = €100 \left(\frac{2 \text{ years}}{4 \text{ years}} \right)$$

$$PRE = €50$$

Based on the computation above, at the acquisition date, KC, the acquirer includes €50 as consideration transferred to obtain control of HC, the acquiree. The remaining €50 is attributed to postcombination services and, accordingly, recognized as remuneration cost in the postcombination consolidated financial statements of KC.

Example 4

Example of acquirer replacement awards that do not require postcombination services exchanged for acquiree awards with remaining unsatisfied vesting period as of the acquisition date

	Acquiree awards	Vesting period *completed* before the business combination
	Replacement awards	Additional employee services *are not* required after the acquisition date

The acquisition agreement referred to in the previous examples governing the KC acquisition of HC that occurred on January 1, 2012, contained the following provisions regarding exchange of outstanding HC awards at acquisition date for KC replacement awards:

		a. Acquiree awards	b. Acquirer awards
1.	Acquisition date market-based measure of awards	$MBM_{AA} = €100$	$MBM_{RA} = €100$
2.	Original vesting period of acquiree awards at their grant date	$VP_{AA} = 4$ years	--

	a. Acquiree awards	*b. Acquirer awards*
3. Portion of 2a. completed by the acquisition date by employees of the acquiree	CVP_{AA} = 2 years	--
4. Vesting period of acquirer replacement awards at the acquisition date		VP_{RA} = 0
5. Total vesting period (3a. + 4b.)	--	TVP = 2 years
6. The greater of the total vesting period (5b.) or the original vesting period of the acquiree awards (2a.)	--	4 years

Under this scenario, the terms of the replaced HC awards did not contain a change-in-control provision which would eliminate any remaining vesting period upon a change in control and would fully vest them upon the acquisition by KC. If the HC awards had included a provision eliminating any remaining vesting period upon a change in control, the guidance in Example 1 would apply and the outcome would be the same as the Example 1 (where neither the acquiree awards nor the replacement rewards required the completion of any service on the part of the acquiree's employees).

Since, at the acquisition date, the acquiree employees had completed only two out of the four years of required services and the replacement awards do not extend the duration of postcombination services required, the total vesting period (TVP) in 5b. is the 2 years already completed by the acquiree's employees under their original awards in 3a (CVP_AA).

The portion of the market-based measure of the replacement awards attributable to precombination services already rendered by the acquiree employees is computed as follows:

$$PRE = \ 1a. \ \left(\frac{3a.}{6b.} \right)$$

$$PRE = \ €100 \ \left(\frac{2 \ years}{4 \ years} \right)$$

$$PRE = \ €50$$

Consequently, €50 of the market-based measure of the replacement awards is attributable to precombination services already performed by the acquiree employees and is, therefore, included in computing the consideration transferred in exchange for obtaining control of the acquiree.

The remaining €50 of the market-based measure of the replacement awards is attributable to postcombination services. However, since the acquiree's employees are not required to provide any postcombination services under the terms of the replacement awards, the entire €50 is immediately recognized by KC, the acquirer, in its postcombination consolidated financial statements.

Although not illustrated in the preceding examples, IFRS 3(R) requires the acquirer to estimate the number of its replacement awards for which the vesting is expected to occur. To the extent that service is not expected to occur due to employees terminating prior to meeting the replacement award's vesting requirements, the portion of the market-based measure of the replacement awards included in consideration transferred in the business combination is to be reduced accordingly. For example, if the market-based measure of the portion of replacement awards attributed to precombination services is €100 and the acquirer expects that only 90% of the awards will vest, the amount included as consideration transferred in the business combination is €90. Changes in the estimated number of replacement awards expected to vest are recognized in the acquirer's postcombination financial statements in the periods in which the changes occur, not as adjustments to the amount of consideration transferred in the business combination.

Finally, it is important to note that the same requirements for apportioning the replacement award between precombination and postcombination service apply to replacement awards that are classified as equity or as liabilities in accordance with the provisions of IFRS 2. All postacquisition-date changes in the market-based measure of liability awards (and their related income tax effects recognized in accordance with the provision of IAS 12) are recognized in the acquirer's postcombination financial statements in the periods in which the changes occur.

Goodwill and Gain from a Bargain Purchase

Goodwill. Goodwill represents the difference between the acquisition-date fair value of the consideration transferred plus the amount of any noncontrolling interest in the acquiree plus the acquisition-date fair value of the acquirer's previously held equity interest in the acquiree; and the acquisition-date fair values of the identifiable assets acquired and liabilities assumed. It is presumed that when an acquiring entity pays such a premium price for the acquiree, it sees value that transcends the worth of the tangible assets and the identifiable intangibles, or else the deal would not have been consummated on such terms. This goodwill arising from acquisitions often consists largely of the synergies and economies of scale expected from combining the operations of the acquirer and acquiree. Goodwill must be recognized as an asset.

The balance in the goodwill account should be reviewed at the end of each reporting period to determine whether the asset has suffered any impairment. If goodwill is no longer deemed probable of being fully recovered through the profitable operations of the acquired business, it should be partially written down or fully written off. Any write-off of goodwill must be charged to expense. Once written down, goodwill cannot later be restored as an asset, again reflecting the concern that the independent measurement of goodwill is not possible and the acquired goodwill may, in the postacquisition periods, be replaced by internally generated goodwill, which is not to be recognized.

It should be noted that in acquisitions of less than 100% of the equity interests, IFRS 3(R) provides the acquirer with a choice of two options to measure noncontrolling interests arising in a business combination:

1. To measure the noncontrolling interest at *fair value* (also recognizing the acquired business at fair value), or
2. To measure the noncontrolling interest at *the noncontrolling interest's share of the value of net assets acquired.*

Under the fair value approach to measure noncontrolling interest, the acquired business will be recognized at fair value, with the controlling share of total goodwill assigned to the controlling interest and the noncontrolling share allocated to the noncontrolling interest. Under the second approach to measure noncontrolling interest, while the net identifiable assets attributable to the noncontrolling interest are written up to the fair values implied by the acquisition transaction, goodwill will not be imputed for the noncontrolling share.

Example of acquisition transaction—goodwill

Oman Heating Corp. acquired 100% the equity interests of Euro Boiler Manufacturing Co. on January 2, 2012, in exchange for cash of €15 million and the balance represented by a long-term note to former Euro shareholders. As of January 2, 2012, immediately prior to the transaction, Euro's statement of financial position is as follows, with both book and fair values indicated (in thousands of €):

	Book value	Fair value		Book value	Fair value
Cash	€ 1,000	€ 1,000	Current liabilities	€26,200	€26,200
Accounts receivable, net	12,200	12,000	Long-term debt	46,000	41,500
Inventory	8,500	9,750	Guarantee of debt	--	75
Other current assets	500	500			
Property, plant, and equipment, net	38,500	52,400			
Customers list	--	1,400			
Patents	2,400	3,900			
In-process research and development	--	8,600	Shareholders' equity (deficit)	(9,100)	21,775
Totals	€63,100	€89,550		€63,100	€89,550

The fair value of inventory exceeded the corresponding book value because Euro Boiler had been using LIFO for many years to cost its inventory, prior to revised IAS 2's banning this method, and actual replacement cost was therefore somewhat higher than carrying value at the date of the acquisition. The long-term debt's fair value was slightly lower than carrying value (cost) because the debt carries a fixed interest rate and the market rates have risen since the debt was incurred. Consequently, Euro Boiler benefits economically by having future debt service requirements which are less onerous than they would be if it were to borrow at current rates. Conversely, of course, the fair value of the lender's note receivable has declined since it now represents a loan payable at less than market rates. Finally, the fair values of Euro Boiler's receivables have also declined from their carrying amount, due to both the higher market rates of interest and to the greater risk of noncollectibility because of the change in ownership. The higher interest rates impact the valuation in two ways: (1) when computing the discounted present value of the amounts to be received, the higher interest rate reduces the computed present value, and (2) the higher interest rates may serve as an incentive for customers to delay payments to Euro rather than borrow the money to repay the receivables, with that delay resulting in cash flows being received later than anticipated thus causing the present value to decline.

Euro Boiler's customer list has been appraised at €1.4 million and is a major reason for the company's acquisition by Oman Heating. Having been internally developed over many years, the customer list is not recorded as an asset by Euro, however. The patents have been amortized down to €2.4 million in Euro Boiler's accounting records, consistent with IFRS, but an appraisal finds that on a fair value basis the value is somewhat higher.

Similarly, property, plant, and equipment has been depreciated down to a book value of €38.5 million, but has been appraised at a sound value (that is, replacement cost new adjusted for the fraction of the useful life already elapsed) of €52.4 million.

A key asset being acquired by Oman Heating, albeit one not formally recognized by Euro Boiler, is the in-process research and development (IPR&D), which pertains to activities undertaken over a period of several years aimed at making significant process and product improvements which would enhance Euro Boiler's market position and will be captured by the new combined operations. It has been determined that duplicating the benefits of this ongoing R&D work would cost Oman Heating €8.6 million. The strong motivation to make this acquisition, and to pay a substantial premium over book value, is based on Euro Boiler's customer list and its IPR&D. Euro Boiler has previously expensed all R&D costs incurred, as required under IFRS, since it conservatively believed that these costs were in the nature of research, rather than development.

Euro Boiler had guaranteed a €1.5 million bank debt of a former affiliated entity, but this was an "off the books" event since guarantees issued between corporations under common control were commonly deemed exempt from recognition. The actual contingent obligation has been appraised as having a fair value (considering both the amount and likelihood of having to honor the commitment) of €75,000.

Thus, although Euro Boiler's statement of financial position reflects a shareholders' deficit (including share capital issued and outstanding, and accumulated deficit) of €9.1 million, the value of the acquisition, including the IPR&D, is much higher. The preliminary computation of goodwill is as follows:

Consideration transferred		€32,000,000
Net working capital	€(2,950,000)	
Property, plant, and equipment	52,400,000	
Customer list	1,400,000	
Patents	3,900,000	
In-process research and development	8,600,000	
Guarantee of indebtedness of others	(75,000)	
Long-term debt	(41,500,000)	21,775,000
Goodwill		€10,225,000

Under IFRS 3(R), the fair value allocated to the in-process research and development must be expensed unless it is separately identifiable, is a resource that is controlled, is a probable source of future economic benefits, and has a reliably measurable fair value. Oman Heating determines that €1,800,000 of the cost of IPR&D meets all these criteria and supports capitalization. All other assets and liabilities are recorded by Oman Heating at the allocated fair values, with the excess consideration transferred being assigned to goodwill. The entry to record the acquisition (for preparation of consolidated financial statements, for example) is as follows:

Cash	1,000,000	
Accounts receivable, net	12,000,000	
Inventory	9,750,000	
Other current assets	500,000	
Property, plant, and equipment	52,400,000	
Customer list	1,400,000	
Patents	3,900,000	
Development costs capitalized	1,800,000	
Research and development expense	6,800,000	
Goodwill	10,225,000	
Current liabilities		26,200,000
Guarantee of indebtedness of others		75,000
Long-term debt		41,500,000
Notes payable to former shareholders		17,000,000
Cash		15,000,000

Note that, while the foregoing example is for a share acquisition, an asset and liability acquisition would be accounted for in the exact same manner. Also, since the debt is recorded at fair value, which will often differ from face (maturity) value, the differential (premium or discount) must be amortized using the effective yield method from acquisition date to the maturity date of the debt, and thus there will be differences between actual payments of interest and the amounts recognized in profit or loss as interest expense. Finally, note that property, plant, and equipment is recorded "net"—that is, the allocated fair value becomes the "cost" of these assets; accumulated depreciation previously recorded in the accounting records of the acquired entity does not carry forward to the postacquisition financial statements of the consolidated entity.

Impairment of goodwill. Assume that an entity acquires another entity and that goodwill arises from this acquisition. Also assume that, for purposes of impairment, it is determined that the acquired business comprises seven discrete cash-generating units. Cash-generating unit is the smallest level of identifiable group of assets that generates cash inflows that are largely independent of the cash inflows from other assets or groups of assets (not larger than an operating segment). The goodwill recorded on the acquisition must be allocated to some or all of those seven cash-generating units. If it is the case that the goodwill is associated with only some of the seven cash-generating units, the goodwill recognized in the statement of financial position should be allocated to only those assets or groups of assets.

Three steps are required for goodwill impairment testing. First, the recoverable amount of a *cash-generating unit* which is the higher of the cash-generating unit's fair value less costs to sell (net selling price) and its value in use, which is the present value of the estimated future cash flows expected to be derived from the cash-generating unit must be determined. Second, the recoverable amount of the cash-generating unit is compared to its carrying value. If the recoverable value exceeds the carrying value, then there is no goodwill impairment, and the third testing step is not required.

IAS 36 requires that if the recoverable amount is less than the carrying value, an impairment write-down must be made. In this third step in goodwill impairment testing, the recoverable value of the cash-generating unit as of the testing date is allocated to its assets (including intangible assets) and liabilities, with the remainder (if any) being assigned to goodwill. If the amount of goodwill resulting from this calculation is less than the carrying amount of goodwill, then the difference is impaired goodwill and must be charged to expense in the current period.

An impairment loss is first absorbed by goodwill, and only when goodwill has been eliminated entirely is any further impairment loss credited to other assets in the group (on a pro rata basis, unless it is possible to measure the recoverable amounts of the individual assets). This is perhaps somewhat arbitrary, but it is also logical, since the excess earnings power represented by goodwill must be deemed to have been lost if the recoverable amount of the cash-generating unit is less than its carrying amount. It is also a conservative approach, and will diminish or eliminate the display of that often misunderstood and always suspiciously viewed asset, goodwill, before the carrying values of identifiable intangible and tangible assets are adjusted.

Reversal of previously recognized impairment of goodwill. In general under IFRS, reversal of an impairment identified with a cash-generating unit is permitted. However, due to the special character of this asset, IAS 36 has imposed a requirement that reversals may not be recognized for previous write-downs in goodwill. Thus, a later recovery in value of the cash-generating unit will be allocated to assets other than goodwill. (The adjustments to those assets cannot be for amounts greater than would be needed to restore them to the carrying amounts at which they would be currently stated had the earlier impairment not been recognized—i.e., at the former carrying values less the depreciation that would have been recorded during the intervening period.)

IFRIC 10, *Interim Financial Reporting and Impairment*, addresses conflicts between the requirements of IAS 34, *Interim Financial Reporting*, and those in other standards on the recognition and reversal in the financial statements of impairment losses on goodwill and certain financial assets. In conformity with IFRIC 10, any impairment losses recognized in an interim financial statement must not be reversed in subsequent interim or annual financial statements.

Gain from a bargain purchase. In certain business combinations, the consideration transferred is less than the fair value of the net assets acquired. These are often identified as being "bargain purchase" transactions. This difference has traditionally (if illogically) been referred to as "negative goodwill." IFRS 3(R) suggests that, since arm's-length business acquisition transactions will usually favor neither party, the likelihood of the acquirer obtaining a bargain is considered remote. According to this standard, apparent instances of bargain purchases giving rise to a gain from a bargain purchase are more often the result of measurement error (i.e., where the fair values assigned to assets and liabilities were incorrect to some extent) or of a failure to recognize a contingent or actual liability (such as for employee severance payments). However, a gain from a bargain purchase can also derive from the risk of future losses, recognized by both parties and incorporated into the transaction price. (One such example was the case of the sale by BMW of its Rover car division to a consortium for £1. It did indeed suffer subsequent losses and eventually failed.)

IFRS 3(R) requires that, before a gain from a bargain purchase is recognized, the allocation of fair values is to be revisited, and that all liabilities—including contingencies—be reviewed. After this is completed, if indeed the fair values of identifiable assets acquired net of all liabilities assumed exceeds the total consideration transferred, then a gain from a bargain purchase will be acknowledged. The accounting treatment of negative goodwill has passed through a number of evolutionary stages beginning with the original IAS 22, which was later twice revised with major changes to the prescribed accounting treatment of negative goodwill.

Under IFRS 3(R), a gain from a bargain purchase is taken immediately into profit. Essentially, this is regarded, for financial reporting purposes, as a gain realized upon the acquisition transaction, and accounted for accordingly.

Example of acquisition transaction—gain from a bargain purchase

Hoegedorn Corp. acquires, on March 4, 2011, all of the outstanding ordinary shares of Gemutlicheit Co. in exchange for cash of €800,000. A formerly successful entity, Gemutlicheit had recently suffered from declining sales and demands for repayment of its outstanding bank debt, which were threatening its continued existence. Hoegedorn management perceived an opportunity to make a favorable purchase of a company operating in a related line of business, and accordingly made this modest offer, which was accepted by the shareholders of Gemutlicheit, the acquiree. Gemutlicheit's statement of financial position at the date of acquisition is as follows, with both book and fair values indicated (in thousands of €):

	Book value	Fair value		Book value	Fair value
Cash	€ 800	€ 800	Current liabilities	€ 2,875	€ 2,875
Accounts receivable, net	3,600	3,400	Long-term debt	11,155	11,155
Inventory	1,850	1,800			
Property, plant, and equipment	6,800	7,200	Shareholders'		
Net operating loss carryforwards	--	2,400	equity (deficit)	(980)	1,570
Totals	€13,050	€15,600		€13,050	€15,600

Gemutlicheit had provided a valuation allowance for the deferred income tax asset attributable to the net operating loss carryforward tax benefit, since recurring and increasing losses made it probable that these benefits would not be realized, consistent with IFRS (IAS 12). Hoegedorn Corp., which is highly profitable, is in the same line of business, and intends to continue Gemutlicheit's operation, expects to be able to realize these benefits, and therefore will have no valuation allowance against this asset.

Thus, although Gemutlicheit's statement of financial position reflects a shareholders' deficit (including share capital and accumulated deficit in retained earnings) of €980,000, the value of the acquisition is much higher, and furthermore the acquirer is able to negotiate a bargain purchase. The preliminary computation of the gain on a bargain purchase is as follows:

Net working capital	€ 3,125,000	
Property, plant, and equipment	7,200,000	
Net operating loss carryforward	2,400,000	
Long-term debt	(11,155,000)	1,570,000
Consideration transferred		800,000
Gain from bargain purchase		€ 770,000

IFRS 3(R) requires that a gain from a bargain purchase be taken into profit or loss immediately, after first verifying that all acquired or assumed liabilities, including contingencies, have been fully accounted for, and that assets acquired were not overstated. In the present example, these matters were reviewed and the amounts shown above were fully supported.

The entry to record the acquisition is therefore as follows:

Cash	800,000
Accounts receivable, net	3,400,000
Inventory	1,800,000
Property, plant, and equipment	7,200,000
Deferred income tax asset	2,400,000

Current liabilities	2,875,000
Long-term debt	11,155,000
Cash	800,000
Gain from bargain purchase	770,000

Business combinations achieved in stages (step acquisitions). *A step acquisition is a business combination in which the acquirer held an equity interest in the acquiree prior to the acquisition date on which it obtained control.* In some instances, control over another entity is not achieved in a single transaction, but rather, after a series of transactions. For example, one entity may acquire a 25% interest in another entity, followed by another 20% some time later, and then followed by another 10% at yet a later date. The last step gives the acquirer a 55% interest and, thus, control. The accounting issue is to determine at what point in time the business combination took place and how to measure the acquisition.

IFRS 3(R) requires the acquirer to remeasure its previous holdings of the acquiree's equity at acquisition-date fair value. Any gain or loss on remeasurement is recognized in profit or loss on that date.

Example of a step acquisition

On December 31, 2010, Konin Corporation (KC) owns 5% of the 30,000 outstanding voting common shares of Henan Corporation (HC). On KC's December 31, 2010 statement of financial position, it classified its investment in HC as available for sale. On March 31, 2011, KC acquired additional equity shares in HC sufficient to provide KC with a controlling interest in HC and, thus, become HC's parent company.

The following table summarizes KC's initial holdings in HC, the subsequent increase in those holdings, and the computation of the gain on remeasurement at the acquisition date of March 31, 2011:

Date	# of Shares	Percent interest	Per share Cost	Per share Fair value	Aggregate investment Cost	Aggregate investment Fair value	Unrealized appreciation included in accumulated other comprehensive income
12/31/2010	1,500	5%	$10	$16	$ 15,000	24,000	$9,000
3/31/2011	21,000	70%	20	20	420,000	420,000	
	22,500	75%					

Computation of gain (loss) on remeasurement at acquisition date:

Fair value per share on 4/1/2011	$ 20
Number of preacquisition shares	× 1,500
Aggregate fair value of preacquisition shares on 4/1/2011	30,000
Carrying amount of preacquisition shares on 4/1/2011	24,000
Appreciation attributable to the 1st quarter of 2011	6,000
Pre-2011 appreciation reclassified from accumulated OCI	9,000
Gain on remeasurement of HC stock on 3/31/2011	$ 15,000

If the acquirer had previously recognized changes in the carrying value of its equity interest in the acquiree in other comprehensive income (e.g., because the investment was classified as available for sale), that amount is to be reclassified and included in the computation of the acquisition date gain or loss from remeasurement.

Footnote Disclosure: Acquisitions

IFRS 3(R) provides an illustrative example of footnote disclosures about acquisitions which an acquirer should present in the financial statements.

Footnote XX: Acquisitions

On March 30, 2010, Konin Corporation (KC) acquired 10% of the outstanding ordinary shares of Henan Corporation (HC). On September 30, 2011 KC acquired 65% of the outstanding ordinary shares of HC and obtained control of HC. HC is the provider of electrical distribution products and as a result of the acquisition, KC is expected to be the leading provider of energy sufficiency solutions in Central and Eastern Europe.

The goodwill of €2,500 arising from the acquisition consists largely of the synergies and economies of scale expected from combining the operations of KC and HC. None of the goodwill recognized is expected to be deductible for income tax purposes.

The following information summarizes the consideration paid for HC and the fair values of the assets acquired and liabilities assumed recognized at the acquisition date, as well as the acquisition date fair value of the noncontrolling interest in HC.

Consideration (at September 30, 2011)	
Cash	€5,000
Equity instruments (65,000 ordinary shares of KC)	6,500
Contingent consideration	1,000
Total consideration transferred	12,500
Fair value of KC's equity interest in HC held before the business combination	2,000
	14,500

Acquisition-related costs (included in selling, general and administrative expenses in KC's statement of comprehensive income for the year ended December 31, 2011)	1,100

Recognized amounts of identifiable assets acquired and liabilities assumed

Financial assets	4,000
Inventory	3,000
Property, plant, and equipment	9,000
Identifiable intangible assets	2,500
Total assets	18,500
Financial liabilities	(3,500)
Contingent liability	(1,000)
Total identifiable net assets	14,000
Noncontrolling interest in HC	(3,500)
Goodwill	4,000
	14,500

The fair value of the 65,000 ordinary shares issued as part of the consideration paid for HC (€6,500) was determined on the basis of the acquisition-date closing market price of KC's ordinary shares.

The contingent consideration arrangement requires KC to pay the former owners of HC 4% of the revenues of HC in excess of €25,000 for 2012, up to a maximum amount of €2,000 (undiscounted). The potential undiscounted amount of all future payments that KC could be required to make under the contingent consideration arrangement is between €0 and €2,000. The fair value of the contingent consideration arrangement (€1,000) was estimated by applying the income approach. The fair value estimates are based on an assumed discount rate range of 15–20% and assumed probability-adjusted revenues in HC of €20,000–€30,000. As of December 31, 2011, the amount recognized for the contingent consideration and the range of outcomes and assumptions used to develop the estimates have not changed.

The fair value of the financial assets acquired includes receivables from industrial control services provided to a new customer. The gross amount due under the contracts is €2,100 of which €250 is expected to be uncollectible.

The fair value of the acquired identifiable intangibles assets (licenses) of €2,500 is based on a receipt of the final valuations for those assets.

A contingent liability of €1,000 has been recognized for expected future services to satisfy warranty claims on industrial control products sold by HC during the last four years. It is expected that the majority of this expenditure will be incurred in 2012 and that all will be incurred by the end of 2014. The estimate of potential undiscounted amount of all future payments that HC could be required to make under the warranty claims is between €750 and €1,250. As of December 31, 2011, there has been no change since September 30, 2011, in the amount estimated for the liability or any change in the range of outcomes or assumptions used to develop the estimates.

The fair value of the noncontrolling interest in HC, an unlisted company, was estimated by applying a market approach and an income approach. The fair value estimates are based on

1. An assumed discount rate range of 15–20%;
2. An assumed terminal value based on a range of terminal EBITDA multiples between 3 and 5 times (or, if appropriate, based on long-term sustainable growth rates ranging from 3 to 6%);
3. Assumed financial multiples of companies deemed to be similar to HC; and
4. Assumed adjustments because of the lack of control or lack of marketability that market participants would consider when estimating the fair value of the noncontrolling interest in HC.

KC recognized a gain of €500 as a result of measuring at fair value its 15% equity interest in HC held before the business combination. The gain is included in other income in KC's statement of comprehensive income for the year ending December 31, 2011.

The revenue included in the consolidated statement of comprehensive income since September 30, 2011, contributed by HC was €5,550 and profit of €1,100 was generated over the same period. HC reported revenue of €20,200 and profit of €3,910 for 2011.

US GAAP COMPARISON

Like IFRS, under US GAAP goodwill is recognized only upon the acquisition of a business and is not amortized but tested annually for impairment. Because goodwill is pushed down under IFRS to an operating segment or one level below (cash-generating units are not recognized under US GAAP), the grouping of cash flows used to test for impairment is almost always larger for US GAAP.

Impairment of goodwill is a two-step process. First the recoverable amount, the undiscounted cash flows from the reporting unit, is compared to the carrying value. If the recoverable amount is below the carrying value, the entity proceeds to step two. In step two, purchase accounting is essentially done using current fair values. Any remaining shortfall reduces goodwill. A recently issued accounting standards update for US GAAP permits entities to do a qualitative assessment to determine if it must execute the steps of the impairment.

CONSOLIDATED FINANCIAL STATEMENTS

The revised standard IAS 27(R) introduced a major change to accounting for noncontrolling interest and consolidated financial statements: mandatory adoption of the economic entity model. In the past, under IFRS, a mixed model was adopted with the parent entity approach used predominantly but with some elements of an economic entity approach being applied (e.g., classifying noncontrolling interest in equity). The economic entity model considers all providers of equity capital as owners of the consolidated entity, even if they are not shareholders of the parent company and have no decision-making ability. As a result, the revised standard introduced major changes to accounting for noncontrolling interest, accounting for increases and decreases in the level of controlling ownership, and accounting for the loss of control of a subsidiary.

Presentation and scope. IAS 27(R) follows the fundamental approach to consolidation of subsidiaries used in current practice in accordance with original standard IAS 27. A parent must consolidate its investments in subsidiaries. This requirement also applies to venture capital organizations, mutual funds, unit trusts, and similar organizations. There is only a limited exception available to some nonpublic entities.

IASB provides only the following four situations in which a parent need not present consolidated financial statements:

1. The parent is itself a wholly owned subsidiary, or is a partially owned subsidiary of another entity and its other owners, including those not otherwise entitled to vote, have been informed about, and do not object to, the parent not presenting consolidated financial statements;
2. The parent's debt or equity instruments are not traded in a public market (a domestic or foreign stock exchange or an over-the-counter market, including local and regional markets);
3. The parent did not file, nor is it in the process of filing, its financial statements with a securities commission or other regulatory organization for the purpose of issuing any class of instruments in a public market; and
4. The ultimate or any intermediate parent of the parent produces consolidated financial statements available for public use that comply with IFRS.

Consolidated financial statements should include all subsidiaries of the parent. While IAS 27(R) provides that, in general, control is presumed to exist when the parent owns, directly or indirectly, a majority of the voting power of another entity, this is not an absolute rule to be applied in all cases. In fact, IAS 27(R) explicitly provides that in exceptional circumstances, it can be clearly demonstrated that majority ownership does not constitute control as well as minority ownership may constitute control.

Control also exists when the parent owns one-half or less of the voting power of an entity but obtains power

1. Over more than one-half of the voting rights of the other entity by virtue of agreement with the other investors (e.g., voting trust arrangements or other contractual provisions)
2. To govern the financial and operating policies of the other entity, under a statute or agreement
3. To appoint and remove the majority of the board of directors or equivalent governing body of the other entity
4. To cast the majority of votes at meetings of the board of directors or equivalent body

Historically, actual voting interest in subsidiaries has been the criterion used to determine

1. If consolidated financial statements are to be presented; and
2. What percentage to apply in determining the allocation of a subsidiary's income, included in consolidated earnings, between the parent and the noncontrolling interests.

However, the revised standard, IAS 27(R), also addresses the situation where the parent entity has, in addition to its actual voting shareholder interest, a further potential voting interest in the subsidiary. (This was first addressed by SIC 33, which was withdrawn when IAS 27 was revised.)

A potential interest may exist due to the existence of options, warrants, convertible shares, or a contractual agreement to acquire additional shares, including shares that the investor or parent entity may have sold to another shareholder in the subsidiary or to another party, with a right or contractual arrangement to reacquire the shares transferred at a later date.

As to whether the potential shares should be considered in reaching a decision as to whether control is present, and thus whether the reporting entity is to be regarded as the parent company and should therefore prepare consolidated financial statements, IAS 27(R) holds that this is indeed a factor to weigh. It concluded that the existence and effect of potential voting rights that are *currently* exercisable or *currently* convertible should be considered, in addition to the other factors set forth in IAS 27(R), when assessing whether an entity controls another entity. All potential voting rights should be considered, including any potential voting rights held by other entities, which would mitigate or even eliminate the impact of the reporting entity's potential voting interest.

For example, an entity holding 40% voting rights in another entity, but having options to acquire another 15% voting interest, the effect of which is not offset by options held by another party, would effectively have a 55% current and potential voting interest, making consolidation required under IAS 27(R).

On the other hand, concerning whether the potential share interest should be taken into account when determining what fraction of the subsidiary's income should be allocated to the parent, the general answer is no. IAS 27(R) states that the proportion allocated to the parent and to noncontrolling interests, respectively, when preparing consolidated financial statements should be determined solely on present ownership interests. That is, potential ownership may necessitate consolidated financial reporting, but profit or loss allocation is still to be based on actual, not potential, ownership percentages.

However, the entity may, in substance, have a present ownership interest when it sells and simultaneously agrees to repurchase some of the voting shares it had held in the subsidiary. In such a situation, it does not lose control of access to economic benefits associated with an ownership interest. In this circumstance, the proportion allocated should be determined by taking into account the eventual exercise of potential voting rights and other derivatives that, in substance, give present access to the economic benefits associated with an ownership interest. Note that the right to reacquire shares alone is not enough to have those shares included for purposes of determining the percentage of the subsidiary's profit to be reported by the parent. Rather, the parent must have ongoing access to the economic benefits of ownership of those shares.

A subsidiary is not excluded from consolidation simply because the investor is a venture capital organization, mutual fund unit trust, or similar entity. Also, a subsidiary is not excluded from consolidation because its business activities are dissimilar from those of the other entities included in the group. In such cases, disclosure in accordance with IFRS 8, *Operating Segments,* helps in providing additional relevant information to investors.

Allocation of losses to noncontrolling interests. As a result of adopting the economic entity concept, the consolidated financial statements present noncontrolling interests in the profit or loss of consolidated subsidiaries for the reporting period, separately from the controlling interests (the parent's ownership interests). Also, noncontrolling interests in the net assets of consolidated subsidiaries are identified separately from the controlling interests in them.

Losses allocated to the parent and to the noncontrolling interest may exceed their respective interests in the equity of the subsidiary. When this occurs, and if it continues to occur in subsequent periods, the excess as well as any further losses are to continue to be allocated to the parent and noncontrolling interest even if this allocation results in a deficit balance in noncontrolling interest (losses in excess of the noncontrolling interests in the net assets of the subsidiary).

This is a major departure from the prior practice, since the original standard IAS 27 allowed these losses to be allocated to the noncontrolling interests only if noncontrolling interests have a binding obligation to cover the funding. Under the new approach in IAS 27(R), the controlling interests will be higher in such situations.

Noncontrolling interests in the net assets consist of (1) the amount recognized at the date of the original business combination (calculated in accordance with IFRS 3[R]), and (2) the noncontrolling interests' share of changes in equity (net assets) of the subsidiary since the date of combination.

Changes in ownership interest without loss of control. Subsequent to a business combination, the parent may increase or decrease its ownership percentage in the subsidiary. The parent entity may purchase or sell shares of the subsidiary after the acquisition date without a loss of control of the subsidiary. In addition, the subsidiary may issue new shares or repurchase some of its own shares as treasury shares or for retirement.

In accordance with IAS 27(R), changes in the parent's ownership interest that do not result in a loss of control of the subsidiary are accounted for as equity transactions (transactions with owners acting in their capacity as owners) with no gain or loss recognized in profit or loss (consolidated net income) or in other comprehensive income. Also, no change in the carrying amounts of the subsidiary's assets (including goodwill) or liabilities are to be recognized as a result of such transactions. The carrying amount of the noncontrolling interest in the subsidiary is to be adjusted to reflect the change in ownership interest. Any difference between the fair value of the consideration received or paid in the transaction and the amount by which the noncontrolling interest is adjusted is to be recognized in equity attributable to the parent.

In the past, as a result of the lack of guidance in IFRS, most common practice was to account for changes in ownership interest similar to an acquisition or disposal of goodwill. The new approach in IAS 27(R) differs significantly from this practice because the IASB acknowledged that obtaining control in a business combination is a significant event and this is the event causing the initial recognition and measurement of all the assets acquired (including goodwill) and liabilities assumed. Subsequent transactions with owners within one economic entity should not affect the measurement of those assets and liabilities. Consequently, changes in a parent's ownership interest (without loss of control) are accounted for within equity.

Example of recognizing changes in the level of the parent's controlling ownership interest

Konin Corporation (KC) owns a 75% interest in Donna Corporation (DC). KC decided to acquire an additional 10% interest in DC from the noncontrolling shareholders in exchange for cash of €100,000. DC has net assets of €800,000. KC accounts for this transaction in the consolidated financial statements as follows:

Equity—Noncontrolling interest	80,000	
Equity—Controlling interest	20,000	
Cash		100,000

In the case of a subsidiary that has accumulated other comprehensive income (OCI), if there is a change in the parent's ownership interest, the carrying amount of OCI is to be adjusted through a corresponding charge or credit to equity attributable to the parent.

Changes in ownership interest resulting in loss of control. Control of a subsidiary can be lost as a result of a parent's decision to sell its shares in the subsidiary to a third party or as a result of a subsidiary selling its shares in the marketplace. If a parent company ceases to have a controlling financial interest in a subsidiary, the parent is required to deconsolidate the subsidiary as of the date on which its control ceased. Examples of situations that can result in a parent being required to deconsolidate a subsidiary include

1. Sale by the parent of all or a portion of its ownership interest in the subsidiary resulting in the parent no longer holding a controlling financial interest,
2. Expiration of a contract that granted control of the subsidiary to the parent,
3. Issuance by the subsidiary of shares that reduces the ownership interest of the parent to a level not representing a controlling financial interest,
4. Loss of control of the subsidiary by the parent because the subsidiary becomes subject to control by a governmental body, court, administrator, or regulator.

When control of a subsidiary is lost and a noncontrolling interest is retained, consistent with the approach applied in step acquisitions, the parent should measure that retained interest at fair value and recognize, in profit or loss, a gain or loss on disposal of the controlling interest. The gain or loss is measured as follows:

FVCR = Fair value of consideration received, if any

FVNIR = Fair value of any noncontrolling investment retained by the former parent at the derecognition date (the date control is lost)

CVNI = Carrying value of the noncontrolling interest in the former subsidiary on the derecognition date, including any accumulated other comprehensive income attributable to the noncontrolling interest

CVAL = Carrying value of the former subsidiary's assets and liabilities at the derecognition date

$$(FVCR + FVNIR + CVNI) - CVAL = Gain (Loss)$$

Example of accounting for the parent's loss of control of a subsidiary

Konin Corporation (KC) owns an 85% interest in Donna Corporation (DC). On December 31, 2011, in the KC's consolidated financial statements the carrying value of DC's net assets is €1,000,000 and the carrying value of the noncontrolling interest in DC (including the noncontrolling interest's share of accumulated other comprehensive income) is €100,000. On January 1, 2012, KC decided to sell a 50% interest in DC to a third party in exchange for cash of €600,000. As a result of this transaction, KC loses control of DC but retains a 35% interest in the former subsidiary, valued at €400,000 on that date. The gain or loss on the disposal of 50% interest in DC is calculated as follows:

Cash received	€ 600,000
Fair value of retained noncontrolling interest	350,000
Carrying value of DC's noncontrolling interest	100,000
	1,050,000
Less: Carrying value of DC's net assets	1,000,000
Gain on disposal	€ 50,000

Should the parent's loss of controlling financial interest occur through two or more transactions, management of the former parent is to consider whether the transactions should be accounted for as a single transaction. In evaluating whether to combine the transactions, management of the former parent is to consider all of the terms and conditions of the transactions as well as their economic impact. The presence of one or more of the following indicators may lead to management concluding that it should account for multiple transactions as a single transaction:

1. The transactions are entered into simultaneously or in contemplation of one another,
2. The transactions, when considered in tandem, are in-substance, a single transaction designed to achieve an overall commercial objective,
3. The occurrence of one transaction depends on the occurrence of at least one other transaction,
4. One transaction, when considered on its own merits, does not make economic sense, but when considered together with the other transaction or transactions would be considered economically justifiable.

Obviously, this determination requires the exercise of sound judgment and attention to economic substance over legal form.

Separate financial statements. The revised standard IAS 27(R), in addition to consolidated financial statements, also addresses issues related to accounting for investments in subsidiaries, jointly controlled entities, and associates in separate financial statements. An entity, preparing its separate financial statements, should account for investments in subsidiaries, jointly controlled entities and associates either

1. At cost; or
2. In accordance with IAS 39.

The same accounting should be applied for each category of investments presented in separate financial statements. Investments accounted for at cost, classified as held-for-sale (or included in a disposal group that is classified as held-for-sale) are accounted for in accordance with IFRS 5, *Noncurrent Assets Held for Sale and Discontinued Operations* (measured at fair value less costs to sell). However, investments accounted for in accordance with IAS 39 are excluded from IFRS 5's measurement requirements. Consequently, an entity should continue to account for such investments in accordance with IAS 39 even if they meet the held-for-sale criteria in IFRS 5.

IASB identified an inconsistency with IFRS 5 related to the accounting by a parent in its separate financial statements for investments accounted for under IAS 39 classified as held for sale in accordance with IFRS 5. Paragraph BC13 of the Basis for Conclusions on IFRS 5 states that noncurrent assets should be excluded from the measurement scope of IFRS 5 only "if (i) they are already carried at fair value with changes in fair value recognized in profit or loss; or (ii) there would be difficulties in determining their fair value less costs to sell." The IASB acknowledged that not all financial assets within the scope of IAS 39 are recognized at fair value through profit or loss, but did not want to make more changes to the accounting for financial assets at that time. This created the need to amend paragraph 38 in IAS 27(R) by *Improvements to IFRS* issued in May 2008, which allowed the practice of accounting for such investments in accordance with IAS 39 to continue, even if they are classified as held-for-sale under IFRS 5.

The IASB noted that although the equity method provides users with some profit or loss information similar to that presented in consolidated financial statements, such information does not need to be provided to the users in separate financial statements. Since the focus in separate statements is on the performance of the investments, separate financial statements prepared using either the fair value method in accordance with IAS 39 or the cost method would be relevant.

An entity should recognize a dividend from a subsidiary, jointly controlled entity or associate in profit or loss in its separate financial statements when it has the right to receive the dividend. Under the cost model, distributions are recognized as income only if they came from postacquisition retained earnings. To apply this method retrospectively upon first-time adoption of IFRS would require information available about the subsidiary's preacquisition retained earnings in accordance with IFRS. Entities adopting IFRS for the first time ("first-time adopters") have received an exemption from restating the retained earnings of the subsidiary at the date of acquisition for the purpose of applying the cost method (*Cost of an Investment in a Subsidiary, Jointly Controlled Entity or Associate* issued in May 2004), since restating preacquisition retained earnings would be a difficult or impossible task. Consequently, the IASB decided to remove the definition of the cost method from IAS 27(R).

Disclosure requirements. IAS 27(R) has its own its own disclosure requirements in addition to those set out in IFRS 3(R) (discussed earlier in the chapter).

If an entity over which the parent does not own, directly or indirectly through subsidiaries, more than half of the voting power is included in the consolidated financial statements, the nature of the relations between the parent and a subsidiary must be explained. If any subsidiary is not included in the consolidated financial statements, the reason why the ownership, directly or indirectly through subsidiaries, more than half of the voting power or potential voting power of an investee does not constitute control, must be set forth.

The financial statements must disclose if the reporting date for a subsidiary is different from that of the parent, and if so, why this is the case. If there are any significant restrictions on the subsidiary's ability to transfer funds to the parent, this must be explained.

If a subsidiary was acquired or disposed of during the period, the effect of the event on the consolidated financial statements should be discussed. If parent-only financial statements are being presented (which is permitted, but not as a substitute for consolidated financial reporting), the method of accounting for interests in subsidiaries should be stated.

Additional disclosures introduced in the revised IAS 27(R) include the amount of any gain or loss arising on the loss of control of a subsidiary. This should include the portion of the gain or loss attributable to recognizing any investment retained in the former subsidiary at its fair value at the date when control is lost, and the line item presenting gains and losses in the statement of comprehensive income.

Also, the IASB decided to converge with the FASB to require that if a parent has equity transactions with noncontrolling interests, it should disclose in a separate schedule the effects of those transactions on the equity of the owners of the parent.

The disclosure requirements of the new standards are quite extensive and, for the reader's convenience, are presented in detail in the disclosure checklist in Appendix A to this publication.

Impact of key changes on the financial statements. The revised standards IFRS 3(R) and IAS 27(R) have a significant impact on profit or loss reported in the year of the acquisition and in future periods, as well as on the amount of goodwill recognized in the acquirer's consolidated statement of financial position. The impact of certain changes (e.g., the option to measure noncontrolling interest at fair value, or accounting for changes in a parent's controlling ownership interest accounted for as equity transactions) will depend on

1. The accounting method applied in the past to recognize the noncontrolling interest, and
2. The option chosen to measure the noncontrolling interest in accordance with the revised standards.

The revisions to accounting for contingent consideration, which is measured at the acquisition-date fair value, with subsequent changes recognized in profit or loss, may reduce future earnings and increase volatility in earnings. Additionally, expensing acquisition costs when incurred decreases current earnings. Management, taking into consideration its future intentions to acquire the noncontrolling interest, will need to elect for each business combination the appropriate option of measuring the noncontrolling interest, as a result of the potentially negative impact on equity which future acquisitions of noncontrolling interest might have.

The application of IFRS 3(R) and IAS 27(R) requires more effort (and costs) to identify and measure separately different elements in the acquisition transaction. For example, there is additional guidance on measurement and determination of whether replacement share awards are part of the consideration for the business combination or compensation for post-combination services. The revised standards have increased disclosure requirements, including information about contingent liabilities, contingent consideration, and the assumptions used in determining fair values.

Consolidation Procedures

Presentation of noncontrolling interests. In preparing consolidated financial statements an entity combines the items presented in the financial statements line by line, adding together like items of assets, liabilities, equity, income and expenses. When less than 100% of the shares of the acquired entity are owned by the acquirer, a complication arises in the preparation of consolidated statements, and a noncontrolling interest must be determined and presented. The acquired assets and liabilities are still fully included in the parent's consolidated financial statements and are valued at fair value, which has implications for the presentation of noncontrolling interest.

In order to present financial information about the group as that of a single economic entity, the following basic eliminating entries are needed:

1. The carrying amount of the parent's investment in each subsidiary is eliminated against the parent's portion of equity of each subsidiary;
2. Noncontrolling interests in the profit or loss of consolidated subsidiaries are recognized;
3. Noncontrolling interests in the net assets (equity) of consolidated subsidiaries are recognized separately from the controlling (parent's) ownership interests, measured at the acquisition-date fair value, or at the noncontrolling interest's proportionate share of the subsidiaries, net identifiable assets, plus its share of changes in equity since acquisition.

Noncontrolling interests must be presented in the consolidated statement of financial position within equity, separately from the equity of controlling interests (the owners of the parent).

Intercompany transactions and balances. In preparing consolidated financial statements, any transactions among members of the group (intragroup or intercompany transactions) must be eliminated. For example, a parent may sell merchandise to its subsidiary, at cost or with a profit margin added, before the subsidiary ultimately sells the merchandise to unrelated parties in arm's-length transactions. Furthermore, any balances due to or from members of the consolidated group at the end of the reporting period must also be eliminated. The reason for this requirement is to avoid grossing up the financial statements for transactions or balances that do not represent economic events with outside parties. Were this rule not in effect, a consolidated group could create the appearance of being a much larger entity than it is in reality, merely by engaging in multiple transactions with itself.

If assets have been transferred among the entities in the controlled group at amounts in excess of the transferor's cost, and they have not yet been further transferred to outside parties (e.g., inventories) or not yet consumed (e.g., plant assets subject to depreciation) by the end of the reporting period, the amount of profit not yet realized through an arm's-length transaction must be eliminated.

Different fiscal periods of parent and subsidiary. A practical consideration in preparing consolidated financial statements is to have information on all constituent entities current as of the parent's year-end. If the subsidiaries have different fiscal years, they may prepare updated information as of the parent's year-end, to be used for preparing consolidated statements. Failing this, IAS 27(R) permits combining information as of different dates, as long as this discrepancy does not exceed three months. Of course, if this option is elected, the process of eliminating intercompany transactions and balances may become a bit more complicated, since reciprocal accounts (e.g., sales and cost of sales) will be out of balance for any events occurring after the earlier fiscal year-end but before the later one.

Uniformity of accounting policies. There is a presumption that all the members of the consolidated group should use the same accounting principles to account for similar events and transactions. However, in many cases this will not occur, as, for example, when a subsidiary is acquired that uses cost for investment property while the parent has long employed the fair value method. IAS 27 requires that the policies of the combining entities should be uniform and therefore appropriate adjustments be made in the consolidated accounts.

If a subsidiary was acquired during the period, the results of the operations of the subsidiary should be included in consolidated financial statements only for the period it was owned. Since this may cause comparability with earlier periods presented to be impaired, there must be adequate disclosure in the accompanying footnotes to make it possible to interpret the information properly. The posttax profits or losses of operations that have been sold or classified as held for sale during the period should be disclosed separately on the face of the statement of comprehensive income as discontinued operations.

Consolidated Financial Statements with Noncontrolling Interests

When an entity acquires some, but not all, of the voting share of another entity, the shares held by third parties represent a *noncontrolling interest* in the acquired entity. Under IFRS, if a parent entity controls another entity in some other way (as discussed above), the two should be consolidated for financial statement purposes (there is only a limited exception available to some nonpublic entities). The noncontrolling interest in equity and profit of the consolidated entity must also be accounted for.

IAS 27(R) states that when consolidated financial statements are prepared, the full amount of assets and liabilities (in the statement of financial position) and income and expenses (in the statement of comprehensive income) of the subsidiary are presented. Accordingly, equity attributable to noncontrolling interest should be separately presented in the statement of financial position, representing the noncontrolling interest in consolidated equity (net assets) of the subsidiary entity. A debit (negative) balance in noncontrolling interest could result when the subsidiary has a deficit in its shareholders' equity even if the noncontrolling interests do not have a binding obligation to cover the funding. This is a major departure from the previous practice under the original IAS 27 when this negative equity attributable to noncontrolling interests would be recorded only if there is reason to believe that the noncontrolling owners will make additional capital contributions to erase that deficit. This situation could occur when the entities were closely held and the noncontrolling owners were related parties having other business relationships with the parent company and/or its shareholders; in other circumstances, a debit in noncontrolling interest would be charged against parent company retained earnings under the concept that the loss will be borne by that company.

In acquisitions of less than 100% of the equity interests in the acquired entity IFRS 3(R) provides the acquirer with a choice of two options to measure noncontrolling interests arising in a business combination: (1) to measure the noncontrolling interest at *fair value* (also recognizing the acquired business at fair value), or (2) to measure the noncontrolling interest at *the noncontrolling interest's share of the value of the net assets acquired.* Under the fair value approach to measure noncontrolling interest, the acquired business will be recognized at fair value, with the controlling share of total goodwill assigned to the controlling interest and the noncontrolling share allocated to the noncontrolling interest. Under the second approach to measure noncontrolling interest, while the net identifiable assets attributable to the noncontrolling interest are written up to the fair values implied by the acquisition transaction, goodwill will not be imputed for the noncontrolling share.

IAS 27(R) as revised stipulates that noncontrolling interest be presented in the consolidated statement of financial position as a separate component of, but within, shareholders' equity. In the past, original standard IAS 27 permitted the noncontrolling interest (then known as minority interest) to be shown in a separate caption positioned between liabilities and equity. However, IASB determined that it did not meet the definition of a liability and should be included within equity.

In accordance with IAS 27(R), income attributable to noncontrolling interest should be separately presented in the statement of comprehensive income. Generally, this is accomplished by presenting profit and total comprehensive income, attributable separately to owners of the parent (controlling interest) and noncontrolling interest.

Example of consolidation process—noncontrolling interest measured at fair value

Assume that on January 1, 2012, Alto Ltd acquired 90% of the equity interest in Bass Ltd in exchange for 5,400 shares having a fair value of €120,600 on that day. Management elects the option to measure noncontrolling interest at fair value and a value of €13,400 is assigned to the 10% noncontrolling interest[(€120,600/.90) × .10 = €13,400]. The following shows the financial positions of the companies before business combination at January 1, 2012.

Alto Ltd and Bass Ltd
Statements of Financial Position
January 1, 2012
(before combination)

	Alto Ltd	*Bass Ltd*
Assets		
Cash	€ 30,900	€ 37,400
Accounts receivable (net)	34,200	9,100
Inventories	22,900	16,100
Equipment	200,000	50,000
Less accumulated depreciation	(21,000)	(10,000)
Patents	--	10,000
Total assets	€267,000	€112,600
Liabilities and shareholders' equity		
Accounts payable	€ 4,000	€ 6,600
Bonds payable, 10%	100,000	--
Share capital	115,000	65,000
Retained earnings	48,000	41,000
Total liabilities and shareholders' equity	€267,000	€112,600

Note that in the foregoing, the net assets (equity) of Bass Ltd may be computed by one of two methods.

Method 1: Subtract the book value of the liability from the book value of the assets.

$$€112,600 - €6,600 = €106,000$$

Method 2: Add the book value of the components of Bass Ltd's shareholders' equity.

$$€50,000 + €15,000 + €41,000 = €106,000$$

At the date of the combination, the fair values of the assets and liabilities of Bass were determined by appraisal, as follows:

Bass Ltd Item	*Book value (BV)*	*Fair value (FV)*	*Difference between BV and FV*
Cash	€ 37,400	€ 37,400	€ --
Accounts receivable (net)	9,100	9,100	--
Inventories	16,100	17,100	1,000
Equipment (net)	40,000	48,000	8,000
Patents	10,000	13,000	3,000
Accounts payable	(6,600)	(6,600)	--
Totals	€106,000	€118,000	€12,000

The equipment has a book value of €40,000 (€50,000 less 20% depreciation of €10,000). An appraisal concluded that the equipment's replacement cost was €60,000 less 20% accumulated depreciation of €12,000, resulting in a net fair value of €48,000.

When a noncontrolling interest is measured at fair value, the concept employed is to record the acquired business at fair value. All the assets and liabilities of Bass Ltd are recorded at their fair values as of the date of the acquisition, including the revaluation portion accruing to the noncontrolling interest's ownership share. In addition, full goodwill will be recognized: the parent's share of total goodwill is assigned to the controlling interest and the imputed noncontrolling share of total goodwill is allocated to the noncontrolling interest.

In our example, goodwill (€16,000) is calculated as follows: consideration transferred, at fair value (€120,600) plus noncontrolling interest (€13,400) minus the net assets of Bass Ltd, at fair value (€118,000). The amount allocated to the parent's interest is €14,400 (90% × €16,000) and the amount allocated to the noncontrolling interest is €1,600 (10% × €16,000).

Bass's identifiable (i.e., before goodwill) net assets will be reported in the Alto consolidated statement of financial position at €118,000. These amounts are computed as follows:

Bass Ltd net assets, at FV	€118,000	
90% thereof (majority interest)		€106,200
Bass Ltd net assets, at FV	118,000	
10% thereof (noncontrolling interest)		11,800
Total identifiable net assets		€118,000

Goodwill is calculated as follows:

Consideration transferred (at fair value)	€120,600
Noncontrolling interest (at fair value)	13,400
Total FV of Bass Ltd	134,000
Fair value of Bass Ltd net assets	(118,000)
Goodwill (total)	16,000
Goodwill allocated to controlling interests (90%)	14,400
Goodwill allocated to noncontrolling interests (10%)	1,600

Working papers for the consolidated statement of financial position as of the date of the transaction will be as shown below.

Alto Ltd and Bass Ltd Consolidated Working Papers
As of the Date of Acquisition—1/1/12

Acquisition accounting
90% interest

	Alto Ltd	Bass Ltd	Adjustments and eliminations Debit	Adjustments and eliminations Credit	Noncontrolling interest	Consolidated balances
Statement of financial position, 1/1/12						
Cash	€ 30,900	€ 37,400				€ 68,300
Accounts receivable	34,200	9,100				43,300
Inventories	22,900	16,100	€ 1,000[b]			40,000
Equipment	200,000	50,000	10,000[b]			260,000
Accumulated depreciation	(21,000)	(10,000)		€ 2,000[b]		(33,000)
Investment in Bass Ltd	120,600			120,600[a]		
Difference between fair and book value (differential)			12,000[a]	12,000[b]		
Goodwill			16,000[a]			16,000
Patents		10,000	3,000[b]			13,000
Total assets	€387,600	€112,600				€407,600
Accounts payable	€ 4,000	€ 6,600				€ 10,600
Bonds payable	100,000					100,000
Share capital	235,600	65,000	58,500[a]		€ 6,500	235,600
Retained earnings	48,000	41,000	36,900[a]		4,100	48,000
Share of revaluation				1,200[a]	1,200	
Share of goodwill				1,600[a]		
Noncontrolling interest						13,400 NI
Total liabilities and equity	€387,600	€112,600	€137,400	€137,400		€407,600

Based on the foregoing, the consolidated statement of financial position of the date of acquisition will be as follows:

Alto Ltd and Bass Ltd
Consolidated Statement of Financial Position
January 1, 2012
(*immediately after combination*)

Assets	
Cash	€ 68,300
Accounts receivable, net	43,300
Inventories	40,000
Equipment	260,000
Less accumulated depreciation	(33,000)
Goodwill	16,000
Patents	13,000
Total assets	€407,600
Liabilities and shareholders' equity	
Accounts payable	€ 10,600
Bonds payable, 10%	100,000
Total liabilities	110,600
Share capital	235,600
Retained earnings	48,000
Owners of parent	283,600
Noncontrolling interest	13,400
Total equity	297,000
Total liabilities and equity	€407,600

1. Investment on Alto Ltd's books
    The entry to record the 90% acquisition in Bass Ltd on Alto Ltd's books was

Investment in share of Bass Ltd	120,600	
Share capital		120,600

To record the issuance of 5,400 shares of capital to acquire a 90% interest in Bass Ltd

Although share capital is issued for the consideration in our example, Alto could have transferred cash, debentures, or any other form of consideration acceptable to Bass Ltd's shareholders to make the purchase combination.

2. Allocation of step-up of Bass's net assets to fair value is calculated as follows:

Adjustment of asset values to fair values
    Book value of Bass Ltd at acquisition date

Share capital	€ 65,000		
Retained earnings	41,000		
	€106,000		
Parent's share (% stock ownership)	× 90%		
Acquired share of book value	(a) 95,400		
Allocation of step up to fair value of net assets			
Fair value of net assets	€118,000		
Book value of net assets	106,000		
Excess fair value over book value (step-up)	12,000		
Parent's share (% share ownership)	× 90%		
Parent's share of step up	(b) 10,800		
Parent's share of net assets at fair value (a) + (b)	€106,200	€106,200	
Noncontrolling interest's share of net assets at fair value		€ 1,800	

3. Elimination entries on preceding workpaper

    The workpaper elimination entry (a). The basic reciprocal accounts are the investment in subsidiary account (Bass Ltd) on the parent's books and the subsidiary's shareholders' equity accounts. Only the parent's share of the subsidiary's accounts may be eliminated as reciprocal accounts. The remaining 10% portion is allocated to the noncontrolling interest. The entries below include documentation showing the company source for the information. The workpaper entry to eliminate the basic reciprocal accounts is as follows:

Share capital—Bass Ltd.	58,500	
Retained earnings—Bass Ltd.	36,900*	
Differential	12,000	
Goodwill	16,000	
Investment in share of Bass Ltd		120,600
Noncontrolling interest in revaluation		1,200
Noncontrolling interest in goodwill		1,600

    * *90% × €41,000 = €36,900*

The Differential account is a workpaper clearing account used to balance the entry and to simplify the consolidation procedure. This account can have a debit or credit balance, depending on whether the subsidiary's net assets in the consolidation workpaper are adjusted upward or downward. The Differential represents excess of the fair value over book value of the subsidiary's assets and liabilities (net assets) as of the acquisition date. In this case, the Differential is €12,000, representing the difference between the fair value (€118,000) and book value of Bass's net assets (€106,000) on January 1, 2012, the acquisition date. The balance assigned to this account is subsequently cleared from that account with the workpaper elimination entry (b).

The noncontrolling interest column includes the 10% interest of Bass Ltd's net assets owned by outside third parties €10,600 (noncontrolling interest's proportionate share of Bass's equity) plus the noncontrolling interest's share in revaluation of net assets to fair values €1,200 (10% × €12,000) and plus imputed goodwill allocated to the noncontrolling interest (10% × €16,000).

The workpaper elimination entry (b). The amount of differential is assigned to the appropriate assets with the workpaper entry (b). This workpaper entry adjusts the various account balances to reflect the fair values of Bass's assets and liabilities at the time the parent (Alto Ltd) acquired the subsidiary (as of the date of acquisition).

Inventory	1,000	
Equipment	10,000	
Patents	3,000	
Accumulated depreciation		2,000
Differential*		12,000

   * *Differential represents excess fair value (€118,000) over book value of Bass Ltd's net assets (€106,000).*

The two workpaper eliminating entries (a) and (b) could be combined in one entry, without using the Differential clearing account. The use of the Differential account may simplify the consolidation procedure when several of the subsidiary's asset and liability accounts need to be restated to fair values.

This example does not include any other intercompany accounts as of the date of combination. If any existed, they would be eliminated to present the consolidated entity fairly. Several examples of other reciprocal accounts will be shown later for the preparation of consolidated financial statements subsequent to the date of acquisition.

Example of consolidation process—noncontrolling interest measured at the noncontrolling interest's proportionate share of the acquiree's net assets

---

Assume that on January 1, 2012, Alto Ltd acquired 90% of the equity interests in Bass Ltd in exchange for 5,400 shares having a fair value of €120,600 on that day. Management elects the option to measure noncontrolling interest at the noncontrolling interest's proportionate share of the Bass Ltd net assets. The following shows the financial positions of the companies before business combination at January 1, 2012:

Alto Ltd and Bass Ltd
Statements of Financial Position
January 1, 2012
(before combination)

	Alto Ltd	Bass Ltd
Assets		
Cash	€ 30,900	€ 37,400
Accounts receivable (net)	34,200	9,100
Inventories	22,900	16,100
Equipment	200,000	50,000
Less accumulated depreciation	(21,000)	(10,000)
Patents	--	10,000
Total assets	€267,000	€112,600
Liabilities and shareholders' equity		
Accounts payable	€ 4,000	€ 6,600
Bonds payable, 10%	100,000	--
Share capital	115,000	65,000
Retained earnings	48,000	41,000
Total liabilities and shareholders' equity	€267,000	€112,600

At the date of the combination, the fair values of the assets and liabilities of Bass Ltd were determined by appraisal, as follows:

Bass Ltd Item	Book value (BV)	Fair value (FV)	Difference between BV and FV
Cash	€ 37,400	€ 37,400	€ --
Accounts receivable (net)	9,100	9,100	--
Inventories	16,100	17,100	1,000
Equipment (net)	40,000	48,000	8,000
Patents	10,000	13,000	3,000
Accounts payable	(6,600)	(6,600)	--
Totals	€106,000	€118,000	€12,000

The equipment has a book value of €40,000 (€50,000 less 20% depreciation of €10,000). An appraisal concluded that the equipment's replacement cost was €60,000 less 20% accumulated depreciation of €12,000, resulting in a net fair value of €48,000.

When a noncontrolling interest is measured at the noncontrolling interest's proportionate share of the acquiree's net assets, the concept employed is to record all the assets and liabilities of Bass Ltd at their fair values as of the date of the acquisition, including the portion represented by the noncontrolling interest's ownership share. There will be no mixture of costs for the net identifiable assets acquired in the business combination in the consolidated statement of financial position; all items will be presented at fair values as of the acquisition date. Goodwill, however, will be assigned only to the parent (the controlling interest); there will *not* be any imputed goodwill attributable to the noncontrolling interest. This is the major difference between this approach and the approach to value noncontrolling interest at fair value, under which the amount of imputed goodwill is allocated to the noncontrolling interest.

In the present example, Bass's identifiable (i.e., before goodwill) net assets will be reported in the Alto consolidated statement of financial position at €118,000. These amounts are computed as follows:

Bass Ltd net assets, at FV	€118,000	
90% thereof (Parent's interest)		€106,200
Bass Ltd net assets, at FV	118,000	
10% thereof (noncontrolling interest)		11,800
Total identifiable net assets		€118,000

Working papers for the consolidated statement of financial position as of the date of the business combination will be as shown below.

Alto Ltd and Bass Ltd Consolidated Working Papers
As of the Date of Acquisition—1/1/12

Acquisition accounting
90% interest

	Alto Ltd	Bass Ltd	Adjustments and eliminations Debit	Credit	Noncontrolling interest	Consolidated balances
Statement of financial position, 1/1/12						
Cash	€ 30,900	€ 37,400				€ 68,300
Accounts receivable	34,200	9,100				43,300
Inventories	22,900	16,100	€ 1,000[b]			40,000
Equipment	200,000	50,000	10,000[b]			260,000
Accumulated depreciation	(21,000)	(10,000)		€ 2,000[b]		(33,000)
Investment in Bass Ltd	120,600			120,600[a]		
Difference between fair and book value (differential)			12,000[a]	12,000[b]		

	Alto Ltd	Bass Ltd	Adjustments and eliminations Debit	Credit	Noncontrolling interest	Consolidated balances
Goodwill			14,400a			14,400
Patents		10,000	3,000b			13,000
Total assets	€387,600	€112,600				€406,000
Accounts payable	€ 4,000	€ 6,600				€ 10,600
Bonds payable	100,000					100,000
Share capital	235,600	65,000	58,500a		€ 6,500	235,600
Retained earnings	48,000	41,000	36,900a		4,100	48,000
Share of revaluation				1,200a	1,200	
Noncontrolling interest					€11,800	11,800 NI
Total liabilities and equity	€387,600	€112,600	€135,800	€135,800		€406,000

Based on the foregoing, the consolidated statement of financial position of the date of acquisition will be as follows:

Alto Ltd and Bass Ltd
Consolidated Statement of Financial Position
January 1, 2012
(*immediately after combination*)

Asset

Cash	€ 68,300
Accounts receivable, net	43,300
Inventories	40,000
Equipment	260,000
Less accumulated depreciation	(33,000)
Goodwill	14,400
Patents	13,000
Total assets	€406,000

Liabilities and shareholders' equity

Accounts payable	€ 10,600
Bonds payable, 10%	100,000
Total liabilities	110,600
Share capital	235,600
Retained earnings	48,000
Owners of parent	283,600
Noncontrolling interest	11,800
Total equity	295,400
Total liabilities and equity	€406,000

1. Investment on Alto company's books

    The entry to record the 90% acquisition in Bass Ltd on Alto company's books was

Investment in share of Bass Ltd	120,600	
Share capital		120,600

    To record the issuance of 5,400 shares of capital to acquire a 90% equity interest in Bass Ltd

    Although share capital is issued for the consideration in our example, Alto could have transferred cash, debentures, or any other form of consideration acceptable to Bass Ltd's shareholders to make the purchase combination.

2. Difference between consideration transferred (at fair value) and fair value of net assets acquired.

The difference between the acquisition-date fair value of the consideration transferred and the acquisition-date fair values of the assets acquired and liabilities assumed is computed as follows:

Consideration transferred (fair value of shares)			€120,600
Computation of goodwill			
Book value of Bass Company at acquisition date			
Share capital	€ 65,000		
Retained earnings	41,000		
	€106,000		
Parent's share (% share ownership)	× 90%		
Acquired share of book value	(a) 95,400		
Allocation of step-up to fair value of net assets			
Fair value of net assets	€118,000		
Book value of net assets	106,000		
Excess fair value over book value (step-up)	12,000		
Parent's share (% share ownership)	× 90%		
Parent's share of step-up	(b) 10,800		
Parent's share of net assets at fair value (a) + (b)	€106,200	€106,200	
Goodwill to be recognized		€ 14,400	

3. Elimination entries on preceding workpaper

The workpaper elimination entry (a). The basic reciprocal accounts are the investment in subsidiary account on the parent's books and the subsidiary's shareholders' equity accounts. Only the parent's share of the subsidiary's accounts may be eliminated as reciprocal accounts. The remaining 10% portion is allocated to the noncontrolling interest. The entries below include documentation showing the company source for the information. The workpaper entry to eliminate the basic reciprocal accounts is as follows:

Share capital—Bass Ltd.	58,500	
Retained earnings—Bass Ltd.	36,900*	
Differential**	12,000	
Goodwill***	14,400	
Investment in share of Bass Co.—Alto Co.		120,600
Noncontrolling interest in revaluation		1,200

*   *€41,000 × 90%= €36,900*
** *Differential is €12,000, representing the difference between the fair value (€118,000) and book value of Bass's net assets (€106,000) on the acquisition date.*
*** *Goodwill represents only the parent's share of goodwill (=€16,000 × .90).*

Note that only 90% of Bass Ltd shareholders' equity accounts are eliminated.

The noncontrolling interest column includes the 10% interest of Bass Ltd's net assets owned by outside third parties (noncontrolling interest's proportionate share of Bass's equity) plus the noncontrolling interest's share in revaluation of net assets to fair values. Consequently, 100% of the fair values of Bass Ltd's assets and liabilities are included in the consolidated statements, but no goodwill is allocated to the noncontrolling interest.

The workpaper elimination entry (b). The amount of differential is assigned to the appropriate assets to adjust the various account balances to reflect the fair values of Bass's assets and liabilities as of the date of acquisition.

Inventory	1,000	
Equipment	10,000	
Patents	3,000	
Accumulated depreciation		2,000
Differential*		12,000

* *Differential represents excess fair value (€118,000) over book value (€106,000) of Bass Ltd's net assets.*

The two workpaper eliminating entries (a) and (b) could be combined in one entry, without using the differential clearing account. The use of the differential account may simplify the consolidation procedure when several various subsidiary's asset and liability accounts need to be restated to fair values.

This example does not include any other intercompany accounts as of the date of combination. If any existed, they would be eliminated to present the consolidated entity fairly. Several examples of other reciprocal accounts will be shown in the next paragraph presenting the preparation of consolidated financial statements subsequent to the date of acquisition.

Consolidation process in periods subsequent to acquisition. The approach followed to prepare a complete set of consolidated financial statements subsequent to a business combination is quite similar to that used to prepare a consolidated statement of financial position as of the date of acquisition. Because consolidation subsequent to a subsidiary's acquisition involves changes that take place over time, the resulting financial statements rest heavily on the concepts of consolidated comprehensive income and consolidated retained earnings.

This paragraph follows the example of the consolidation process as of the date of acquisition with noncontrolling interest measured at the noncontrolling interest's proportionate share of the acquiree's net assets, discussed in the previous section. The following additional information is available in the first year after the acquisition (2012):

1. Alto Ltd uses the partial equity method to record changes in the value of the investment account. The partial equity method means that the parent reports its share of earnings, and so on, of the subsidiary on its books using the equity method, but any differential between acquisition cost and underlying fair value of net assets, and so on, is not addressed on an ongoing basis; rather, these matters await the typical year-end accounting adjustment process.
2. During 2012, Alto Ltd sold merchandise to Bass Ltd that originally cost Alto Ltd €15,000, and the sale was made for €20,000. On December 31, 2012, Bass Ltd's inventory included merchandise purchased from Alto Ltd at a cost to Bass Ltd of €12,000.
3. Also during 2012, Alto Ltd acquired €18,000 of merchandise from Bass Ltd. Bass Ltd uses a normal markup of 25% above its cost. Alto Ltd's ending inventory includes €10,000 of the merchandise acquired from Bass Ltd.
4. Bass Ltd reduced its intercompany account payable to Alto Ltd to a balance of €4,000 as of December 31, 2012, by making a payment of €1,000 on December 30. This €1,000 payment was still in transit on December 31, 2012.
5. On January 2, 2012, Bass Ltd acquired equipment from Alto Ltd for €7,000. The equipment was originally purchased by Alto Ltd for €5,000 and had a book value of €4,000 at the date of sale to Bass Ltd. The equipment had an estimated remaining life of four years as of January 2, 2012.
6. On December 31, 2012, Bass Ltd purchased for €44,000, 50% of the outstanding bonds issued by Alto Ltd. The bonds mature on December 31, 2014, and were originally issued at par. The bonds pay interest annually on December 31 of each year, and the interest was paid to the prior investor immediately before Bass Ltd's purchase of the bonds.

The worksheet for the preparation of consolidated financial statements as of December 31, 2012, is presented on the following pages.

The investment account balance at the statement date should be reconciled to ensure that the parent company made the proper entries under the method of accounting used to account for the investment. Any adjustments (e.g., depreciation) made with respect to the step-up to fair values will be recognized only in the worksheets.

An analysis of the investment account at December 31, 2012, is as presented below.

	Investment in Share of Bass Ltd		
Original cost	120,600		
% of Bass Ltd's income			% of Bass Ltd's dividends
(€9,400 × 90%)	8,460	3,600	declared (€4,000 × 90%)
Balance, 12/31/12	125,460		

Any errors will require correcting entries before the consolidation process is continued. Correcting entries will be posted to the books of the appropriate company; eliminating entries are not posted to either company's books.

The difference between the consideration transferred in business combination and the book value of the assets acquired and liabilities assumed was determined and allocated in the preparation of the acquisition-date consolidated statements presented earlier. The same computations are used in preparing financial statements for as long as the investment is owned and the acquiree controlled.

The following adjusting and eliminating entries will be required to prepare consolidated financial statements as of December 31, 2012. Note that a consolidated statement of comprehensive income is required, and therefore, the nominal (i.e., income and expense) accounts are still open. The number or letter in parentheses to the left of the entry corresponds to the key used on the worksheets presented after the following discussion.

Step 1—Complete the transaction for any intercompany items in transit at the end of the year.

(a)	Cash	1,000	
	Accounts receivable		1,000

This adjusting entry will now properly present the financial positions of both companies, and the consolidation process may be continued.

Step 2—Prepare the eliminating entries.

(a)	Sales	38,000	
	Cost of goods sold		38,000

Total intercompany sales of €38,000 include €20,000 in a downstream transaction from Alto Ltd to Bass Ltd and €18,000 in an upstream transaction from Bass Ltd to Alto Ltd.

(b)	Cost of goods sold	5,000	
	Inventory		5,000

The ending inventories are overstated because of the unrealized profit from the intercompany sales. The debit to cost of goods sold is required because a decrease in ending inventory will increase cost of goods sold to be deducted on the income statement. Supporting computations for the entry are as follows:

	In ending inventory of	
	Alto Ltd	*Bass Ltd*
Intercompany sales not resold, at selling price	€10,000	€12,000
Cost basis of remaining intercompany merchandise		
From Bass to Alto (÷ 125%)	(8,000)	
From Alto to Bass (÷ 133 1/3%)		(9,000)
Unrealized profit	€ 2,000	€ 3,000

NOTE: When preparing consolidated working papers for 2013 (the next fiscal period), an additional eliminating entry will be required if the goods in 2012's ending inventory are sold to outsiders during 2013. The additional entry will recognize the profit for 2013 that was eliminated as unrealized in 2012. This entry is necessary since the entry at the end of 2012 was made only on the worksheet. The 2013 entry will be as follows:

Retained earnings—Bass Ltd, 1/1/13	2,000	
Retained earnings—Alto Ltd, 1/1/13	3,000	
Cost of goods sold, 2013		5,000

(c) Accounts payable	4,000	
Accounts receivable		4,000

This entry eliminates the remaining intercompany receivable/payable owed by Bass Ltd to Alto Ltd. This eliminating entry is necessary to avoid overstating the consolidated entity's statement of financial position. The receivable/payable is not extinguished, and Bass Ltd must still transfer €4,000 to Alto Ltd in the future.

(d) Gain on sale of equipment	3,000	
Equipment		2,000
Accumulated depreciation		250
Depreciation expense		750

This entry eliminates the gain on the intercompany sale of the equipment, eliminates the overstatement of equipment, and removes the excess depreciation taken on the gain. Supporting computations for the entry are as follows:

	Cost	At date of intercompany sale accum. depr.	2012 depr. exp.	End of period accum. depr.
Original basis (to seller, Alto Co.)	€5,000	€(1,000)	€ 1,000	€(2,000)
New basis (to buyer, Bass Co.)	7,000	--	1,750	(1,750)
Difference	€(2,000)		€(750)	€ 250

If the intercompany sale had not occurred, Alto Ltd would have depreciated the remaining book value of €4,000 over the estimated remaining life of four years. However, since Bass Ltd's acquisition price (€7,000) was more than Alto Ltd's basis in the asset (€4,000), the depreciation recorded on the books of Bass Ltd will include part of the intercompany unrealized profit. The equipment must be reflected on the consolidated statements at the original cost to the consolidated entity. Therefore, the write-up of €2,000 in the equipment, the excess depreciation of €750, and the gain of €3,000 must be eliminated. The ending balance of accumulated depreciation must be shown at what it would have been if the intercompany equipment transaction had not occurred. In future periods, a retained earnings account will be used instead of the gain account; however, the other concepts will be extended to include the additional periods.

(e) Bonds payable	50,000	
Investment in bonds of Alto Ltd		44,000
Gain on extinguishment of debt		6,000

This entry eliminates the book value of Alto Ltd's debt against the bond investment account of Bass Ltd. On a consolidated entity basis, this transaction must be shown as a retirement of debt, even though Alto Ltd has the outstanding intercompany debt to Bass Ltd. Any gains or losses on debt extinguishment will be reported in the statement of comprehensive income. In future periods Bass Ltd will amortize the discount, thereby bringing the investment account up to par value. In future periods the retained earnings account will be used in the eliminating entry instead of the gain account, as the gain is closed out with other nominal accounts.

(f) Equity in subsidiary's profit—Alto Ltd.   8,460
        Dividends declared—Bass Ltd.   3,600
        Investment in share of Alto Ltd.   4,860

This elimination entry adjusts the investment account back to its balance at the beginning of the period and also eliminates the subsidiary profit or loss account.

(g) Share capital—Bass Ltd.   58,500
Retained earnings—Bass Ltd.   36,900
    Noncontrolling interest in revaluation   1,200
Differential   12,000
Goodwill   14,400
    Investment in share of Bass Ltd—Alto Ltd.   120,600

This entry eliminates 90% of Bass Ltd's shareholders' equity at the beginning of the year, 1/1/12. Note that the changes during the year were eliminated in entry (f).

(h) Adjustment of asset book values to fair values
Inventory   1,000
Equipment   10,000
Patents   3,000
    Accumulated depreciation   2,000
    Differential   12,000

This entry allocates the differential (excess of fair value over the book values of the assets acquired) to step up the carrying values of Bass's net assets to their fair values. Note that this entry is similar to the allocation entry made to prepare consolidated financial statements for January 1, 2012, the date of acquisition.

(i) Cost of goods sold   1,000
Depreciation expense   2,000
Other operating expenses—patent amortization   300
    Inventory   1,000
    Accumulated depreciation   2,000
    Patents   300

The elimination entry amortizes the revaluations to fair market value made in entry (h). The inventory has been sold and therefore becomes part of cost of goods sold. The remaining revaluations will be amortized as follows:

	Revaluation	Amortization period	Annual amortization
Equipment (net)	€8,000	4 years	€2,000
Patents	3,000	10 years	300

The amortizations will continue to be made on future worksheets. For example, at the end of the next year (2013), the amortization entry (i) would be as follows:

Differential   3,300
Depreciation expense   2,000
Other operating expenses—patent amortization   300
    Inventory   1,000
    Accumulated depreciation   4,000
    Patents   600

The initial debit of €3,300 to differential is an aggregation of the prior period's charges to profit or loss (€1,000 + €2,000 + €300). During subsequent years, some accountants prefer reducing the allocated amounts in entry (h) for prior period's charges. In this case the amortization entry in future periods would reflect just that period's amortizations.

In adjusting for the noncontrolling interest in the consolidated entity's equity and earnings, the following guidelines should be observed:

1. Only the parent's share of the subsidiary's shareholders' equity is eliminated in the basic eliminating entry. The noncontrolling interest's share is presented separately.
2. The entire amount of intercompany reciprocal items is eliminated. For example, all receivables/payables and sales/cost of sales with a 90% subsidiary are eliminated.
3. For intercompany transactions in inventory and fixed assets, the possible effect on noncontrolling interest depends on whether the original transaction affected the subsidiary's profit or loss. Noncontrolling interest is adjusted only if the subsidiary is the selling entity. In this case, the noncontrolling interest is adjusted for its percentage ownership of the share capital of the subsidiary. The noncontrolling interest is not adjusted for unrealized profits on downstream sales. The effects of downstream transactions are confined solely to the parent's (i.e., controlling) ownership interests.

The noncontrolling interest's share of the subsidiary's profit is shown as a deduction on the consolidated statement of comprehensive income since 100% of the subsidiary revenues and expenses are combined, even though the parent company owns less than a 100% interest. For our example, the noncontrolling interest deduction on the income statement is computed as follows:

Bass Ltd's reported profit	€9,400
Less unrealized profit on an upstream inventory sale	(2,000)
Bass Ltd's profit for consolidated financial purposes	€7,400
Noncontrolling interest share	× 10%
Noncontrolling interest in profit	€ 740

The noncontrolling interest's share of the net assets of Bass Ltd is shown in the consolidated statement of financial position within Bass's shareholders' equity. The computation for the noncontrolling interest shown in the statement of financial position for our example is as follows:

Bass Ltd's share capital, 12/31/12	€65,000	
Noncontrolling interest share	× 10%	€ 6,500
Bass Ltd's retained earnings, 1/1/12	€41,000	
Noncontrolling interest share	× 10%	4,100
Bass Ltd's 2012 profit for consolidated purposes	€ 7,400	
Noncontrolling interest share of profit	× 10%	740
Bass Ltd's dividends during 2012	€ 4,000	
Noncontrolling interest share	× 10%	(400)
Total noncontrolling interest, 12/31/12		€10,940

Alto Ltd and Bass Ltd Consolidated Working Papers
Year Ended December 31, 2012

Acquisition accounting
90% owned subsidiary
Subsequent year

	Alto Ltd	Bass Ltd	Adjustments and eliminations Debit	Adjustments and eliminations Credit	Noncontrolling interest	Consolidated balances
Statements of comprehensive income for year ended 12/31/12						
Sales	€750,000	€420,000	€ 38,000[a]			€1,132,000
Cost of sales	581,000	266,000	5,000[b] 1,000[i]	€ 38,000[a]		815,000
Gross margin	169,000	154,000				317,000
Depreciation and interest expense	28,400	16,200	2,000[i]	750[d]		45,850
Other operating expenses	117,000	128,400	300[i]			245,700
Profit from continuing operations	23,600	9,400				25,450
Gain on sale of equipment	3,000		3,000[d]			
Gain on bonds				6,000[e]		6,000
Equity in subsidiary's profit	8,460		8,460[f]			
Noncontrolling interest in profit (€7,400 × .10)					€ 740	(740)
Profit for the year	€ 35,060	€ 9,400	€ 57,760	€ 44,750	€ 740	€ 30,710
Statement of retained earnings for year ended 12/31/12						
1/1/12 retained earnings						
Alto Ltd	€ 48,000					€ 48,000
Bass Ltd		€ 41,000	€ 36,900[g]		4,100	
Add profit (from above)	35,060	9,400	57,760	€ 44,750	740	30,710
Total	83,060	50,400			4,840	78,710
Deduct dividends	15,000	4,000		3,600[f]	400	15,000
Balance, 12/31/12	€ 68,060	€ 46,400	€ 94,660	€ 48,350	4,440	€ 63,710
Statement of financial position						
Cash	€ 45,300	€ 6,400	€ 1,000[l]			€ 52,700
Accounts receivable (net)	43,700	12,100		€ 1,000[l] 4,000[c]		50,800
Inventories	38,300	20,750	1,000[h]	5,000[b] 1,000[i]		54,050
Equipment	195,000	57,000	10,000[h]	2,000[d]		260,000
Accumulated depreciation	(35,200)	(18,900)		250[d] 2,000[h] 2,000[i]		(58,350)
Investment in share of Bass Ltd	125,460			4,860[f] 120,600[g]		
Differential			2,000[g]	2,000[h]		
Goodwill			14,400[g]			14,400
Investment in bonds of Alto Ltd		44,000		44,000[e]		
Patents		9,000	3,000[h]	300[i]		11,700
	€412,560	€130,350				€ 385,300

	Alto Ltd	Bass Ltd	Adjustments and eliminations Debit	Credit	Noncontrolling interest	Consolidated balances
Accounts payable	€ 8,900	€ 18,950	4,000c			€ 23,850
Bonds payable	100,000		50,000e			50,000
Share capital	235,600	65,000	58,500g		6,500	235,600
Retained earnings (from above)	68,060	46,400	94,660	48,350	4,440	63,710
Noncontrolling share of revaluation				1,200	1,200	
Noncontrolling interest in equity					10,940	12,140
	€412,560	€130,350	€238,560	€238,560		€385,300

The remainder of the consolidation process consists of the following worksheet techniques:

1. Take all income items across horizontally, and foot the adjustments, noncontrolling interest, and consolidated columns down to the net income line.
2. Take the amounts on the profit or loss line (on the statement of comprehensive income) in the adjustments, noncontrolling interest, and consolidated balances columns down to retained earnings items across the consolidated balances column. Foot and crossfoot the retained earnings statement.
3. Take the amounts of ending retained earnings in each of the four columns down to the ending retained earnings line in the statement of financial position. Foot the noncontrolling interest column and place its total in the consolidated balances column. Take all the statement of financial position items across to consolidated balances column.

OTHER ACCOUNTING ISSUES ARISING IN BUSINESS COMBINATIONS

Depending on the tax jurisdiction, an acquirer may or may not succeed to the available tax loss carryforward benefits of an acquired entity. IFRS requires that a liability approach be used in accounting for the tax effects of temporary differences, which includes the tax effects of tax loss carryforwards. If an acquirer is permitted to use the predecessor's tax benefits, the amount to be reflected in its statement of financial position will be measured in accordance with IAS 12, which is the amount of the benefits expected to be realized. As expectations change over time, this amount will be amended, with any such adjustments being taken into tax expense of the period in which expectations change. If the acquirer can only utilize the benefits to offset taxes on earnings of the operations acquired (i.e., it cannot shelter other sources of earnings), it will be necessary to project profitable operations to support recording this benefit as an asset.

Combined Financial Statements and Mutual Entities

When a group of entities is under common ownership, control, or management, it is often useful to present combined (or combining, showing the separate as well as the combined entities) financial statements. In this situation, the economic substance of the nominally independent entities' operations may be more important to statement users than is the legal form of those entities. When consolidated statements are not presented, combined statements may be used to show the financial position, or operating results, of a group of companies that are each subsidiaries of a common parent.

As described earlier in this chapter, the revised IFRS 3(R) and IAS 27(R) include within their scope combinations involving only mutual entities and combinations achieved by contract alone. In accordance with IFRS 3(R), mutual entities are to be accounted for in the same way as a commercial acquisition, and on the basis that one of the entities was an acquirer. Where there is no consideration, as in a combination by contract, the fair value of the assets and liabilities of the acquiree would be attributed to the noncontrolling interest (which in this scenario are actually the acquiree's unrelated shareholders). Where two mutual entities combine, the aggregate of the fair value of the acquiree's net assets and of any assets given, liabilities assumed or equity issued by the acquirer would be added to the acquirer's equity issued (contributed capital).

Accounting for Special-Purpose Entities

An issue related to the accounting for entities under common control arises when one entity has been created solely or largely for the purpose of accommodating the other's need for financing or for engaging in certain strictly limited transactions with or on behalf of the sponsoring entity. Common objectives are to effect a lease, conduct research and development activities, or to securitize financial assets. These special-purpose entities (SPE) or special-purpose vehicles (SPV) have received a good deal of attention in recent years, largely as a consequence of several notable financial frauds, which utilized SPE to conceal large amounts of the reporting entity's debt and/or to create the appearance of revenues and/or earnings which did not actually exist.

SPEs have often been used to escape the requirements of lease capitalization or other financial reporting requirements that the sponsoring entity wishes to evade. While there are often legitimate (i.e., those not driven by financial reporting) reasons for the use of special-purpose entities (SPE), at least a side effect, if not the main one, is that the sponsoring entity's apparent financial strength (e.g., leverage) will be distorted.

In many instances an adroitly structured SPE will not be owned, or majority owned, by the true sponsor. Were ownership the only criterion for determining whether entities need to be consolidated for financial reporting purposes, this factor could result in a "form over substance" decision to not consolidate the SPE with its sponsor. However, under the provisions of SIC 12, ownership is not the critical element in determining the need for consolidation; rather, a "beneficial interest" test is used to determine whether the SPE should be consolidated. Beneficial interest can take various forms, including ownership of debt instruments, or even a lessee relationship.

SIC 12 states that consolidation of an SPE should be effected if the substance of its relationship with another entity indicates that it is effectively controlled by the other entity. Control can derive from the nature of the predetermined activities of the SPE (what the interpretation refers to as being on "autopilot"), and emphatically can exist even when the sponsor has less than a majority interest in the SPE. SIC 12 specifically notes that the following conditions would suggest that the sponsor controls the SPE:

1. The activities of the SPE are conducted so as to provide the sponsor with the benefits thereof;
2. The sponsor in substance has decision-making powers to obtain most of the benefits of the SPE, or else an autopilot mechanism has been established such that the decision-making powers have been delegated;
3. The sponsor has the right to obtain the majority of the benefits of the SPE and consequently is exposed to risks inherent in the SPE activities; or
4. The sponsor retains the majority of the residual or ownership risks of the SPE or its assets, in order to obtain the benefits of the SPE activities.

SIC 12 is particularly concerned that autopilot arrangements may have been put into place specifically to obfuscate the determination of control. It cautions that although difficult to assess in some situations, control is to be attributed to the entity having the principal beneficial interest. The entity which arranged the autopilot mechanism would generally have had, and continue to have, control, and thus the need for consolidation with the sponsor for financial reporting purposes would accordingly be indicated. SIC 12 offers a number of examples of conditions which would be strongly indicative of control and thus of a need to consolidate the SPE financial statements with those of its sponsor.

Common SPE situations involve entities set up to facilitate a lease, to engage in a securitization of financial assets, or to conduct research and development activities. The concept of control used in IAS 27(R) requires having the ability to direct or dominate decision making accompanied by the objective of obtaining benefits from the SPE's activities. Thus, determining whether a given SPE should be consolidated by the sponsor or beneficiary reporting entity remains a matter of judgment under IFRS.

Some entities will separately evaluate the matter of asset derecognition, as when assets are transferred to an SPE. In certain circumstances, a transfer of assets may result in those assets being derecognized and the transfer will be accounted for as a sale, with gain or loss recognition being warranted. Even if the transfer qualifies as a sale, however, the provisions of IAS 27(R) and SIC 12 may necessitate that the entity consolidate the SPE, thus reversing or obviating sale recognition and elimination of any gain or loss. SIC 12 does not address the circumstances where sale treatment would apply for the reporting entity or when the consequences of such a sale would have to be eliminated upon consolidation. SIC 12 was modified by IFRS Interpretations Committee in late 2004 to clarify the scope exclusion for postemployment benefit plans and extend this to other long-term employee benefit plans.

The IASB is currently pursuing a project (recently renamed *Consolidation*) to address both the basis (policy) on which a parent entity should consolidate its investments in subsidiaries and enhanced disclosures about consolidated and nonconsolidated entities. The objective of the project is to publish a single IFRS on consolidation that would replace IAS 27(R), *Consolidated and Separate Financial Statements* and SIC 12, *Consolidation—Special-Purpose Entities*. The project has resulted in the issuance of IFRS 10, *Consolidated Financial Statements,* which provides a single consolidation model that identifies control as the basis for consolidation for all types of entities. The standard has an effective date of January 1, 2013 (with early adoption permitted) and will replace IAS 27, *Consolidated, and Separate Financial Statements,* and SIC-12, *Consolidation—Special-Purpose Entities*.

However, the IASB is still carrying on with another project on consolidation that will focus on the accounting to be followed by investment entities. This is discussed later on in this chapter.

Accounting for Leveraged Buyouts

Possibly one of the most complex accounting issues has been the appropriate accounting for leveraged buyouts (LBO). At the center of this issue is the question of whether a new basis of accountability is created by the LBO transaction. If so, a step-up in the reported value of assets and/or liabilities is warranted. If not, the carryforward bases of the predecessor entity should continue to be reported in the company's financial statements.

IFRS do not address this issue directly. However, guidance can be gleaned from the decisions made by the standard setters in the United States, which have dealt with this question. Although this guidance is neither definitive nor binding on preparers of IFRS-based financial reports, it is instructive.

Under relevant US GAAP, partial or complete new basis accounting is appropriate only when the LBO transaction is characterized by a change in control of voting interest in accordance with ASC Topic 805. While LBOs are not specifically mentioned in this topic, an LBO transaction can involve the same decisions that are encountered in "reverse acquisitions." Reverse acquisitions occur when the entity in a business combination that issues the shares (presumptively an indicator that the company is the acquirer) is the acquirer for accounting purposes. Topic 805 provides guidance in determining which entity is the acquirer for accounting purposes including which entity has the largest relative voting rights in the combined entity after the business combination, which includes any potential rights embodied in special voting arrangements or other instruments. The guidance also includes evaluating the composition of the senior management or control to appoint management of the combined entity.

Reverse Acquisitions

A reverse acquisition occurs when one entity, the legal parent, issues such a large proportion of its outstanding shares to the owners of the legal subsidiary that control passes to the legal subsidiary due to the number of additional shares issued by the legal parent and the owners of the subsidiary effectively become the majority owners of the combined economic entity. Thus, in a reverse acquisition, one entity—the one whose equity interests are acquired—obtains economic (although not legal) control over the other entity and is therefore the acquirer. The consequence of such a transaction is that the legal and accounting treatments will diverge, with the legal subsidiary being the accounting acquirer for financial reporting purposes. While often the legal parent (accounting acquirer) will adopt the subsidiary's name, thus alerting users of the statements to the nature of the organizational change, this does not necessarily occur, and, in any event, it will be critical that the financial statements contain sufficient disclosure so that users are not misled. This will be important particularly in the periods immediately following the transaction, and especially when comparative financial statements are presented which include some periods prior to the acquisition, since comparability will be affected.

A typical reverse acquisition would occur when a "shell" entity, which often is a publicly held but dormant company, merges with an operating company, which often will be nonpublic. The objective is for the operating entity to "go public" without the usual time-consuming and expensive registration process. However, reverse acquisitions are not limited to such situations, and there have been many such transactions involving two public or two nonpublic companies. The legal subsidiary (accounting acquirer) may have substantial operations of its own, although of lesser scope or with lower growth prospects than those of the accounting acquiree.

A number of difficult questions arise in reverse acquisitions, and there is no definitive guidance in IFRS on these important issues. Among the matters to be considered, and which will be discussed in the following paragraphs, are these:

1. What circumstances signal a reverse acquisition?
2. How should the consolidated financial statements be presented in the subsequent periods?
3. How should the acquisition cost be computed and allocated in a reverse acquisition?
4. What would the shareholders' equity section of the statement of financial position be immediately following the reverse acquisition?
5. What would be the impact on computation of earnings per share?
6. How will noncontrolling interest be presented in the financial statements?

Reverse acquisitions occur when the former shareholders of the legal subsidiary become the majority owners of the postcombination consolidated entity, and most commonly this will result when a share-for-share swap occurs. If the former owners of the legal subsidiary in a business combination become the majority owners of the consolidated entity following the transactions, it will be deemed to have been a reverse acquisition.

Following a reverse acquisition, consolidated financial statements will be presented. Although the financial statements will be identified as being those of the accounting acquiree (which will be the legal owner of the accounting acquirer), in substance these will be the financial statements of the acquiree company, with the assets and liabilities, and revenues and expenses, of the legal parent being included effective with the date of the transaction. Put another way, the legal parent will be deemed to be a continuation of the business of the legal subsidiary, notwithstanding the formal structure of the transaction or the name of the successor entity. For this reason, if the legal parent does not change its name to that of the acquiree, it would be appropriate for the financial statement titles to be captioned in a way that most clearly communicates the substance of the transaction to the readers. For example, the statements may be headed "ABC Company, Inc.—successor to XYZ Corporation."

Given the foregoing, it is clear that the shareholders' equity section of the posttransaction consolidated statement of financial position is to be that of the subsidiary, not the parent, with appropriate modification for the new shares issued in the transaction and ancillary adjustments, if any. Comparative financial statements for earlier periods, if presented, are to be consistent, meaning that these would be the financial statements of the legal subsidiary. Since in some instances the subsidiary's name is different than that shown in the heading, care must be taken to fully communicate with the readers. The fact that the prior period's financial information identified as being that of the legal parent is really that of the legal subsidiary obviously is extremely pertinent to a reader's understanding of these statements.

Consistent with the accounting imposed on other business combinations, the cost of reverse acquisitions is measured at the fair value of the net assets acquired, or the value of the consideration paid, if more determinable. A special rule is that, if fair value cannot be determined for the issuer's equity instruments, and the transaction is valued at the fair value of the issuer's net assets, no goodwill is recognized in the transaction. Clearly, in such instances there is substantial doubt about the true existence of goodwill and unusual difficulty in valuing the transaction, and this prohibition is prudent under the circumstances.

If the fair value of the shares of the legal subsidiary (accounting acquirer) is used to determine the cost of the transaction, it is suggested that a calculation be made to determine the number of shares that the acquiree would have issued in order to provide the same level of ownership in the combined entity to the shareholders of the legal parent (accounting acquiree) as they have as a consequence of the reverse acquisition. The fair value of the number of shares thus determined is used to value the transaction, as illustrated later in this section.

In some instances, the market price of acquiree shares may not be fairly indicative of the value of the transaction. In such cases, the most feasible alternative would be to use the fair value of all the outstanding shares of the ostensible acquirer, prior to the transaction, to value the purchase transaction. In some instances, adjustments would have to be made for trading volume, price fluctuations, etc., to most accurately reflect the substance of the acquisition.

In other cases, particularly where the acquirer is a dormant shell entity, market price of its shares may not be meaningful. If it is possible to determine, utilizing the fair value of the net assets of the acquirer may be a more meaningful technique.

Whatever technique is employed under the circumstances, the total purchase cost is to be allocated to the net assets of the acquirer (not the acquiree) following the principles set forth in IFRS 3. If the acquisition cost exceeds the fair value of net identifiable assets, the excess is allocated to goodwill, which will be tested for impairment, and written down or eliminated when and if impairment is detected. The financial statements of the consolidated entity following the reverse acquisition would reflect the assets and liabilities of the legal parent (nominal acquirer) at fair value, and those of the legal subsidiary (nominal acquiree) at historical cost.

Since for financial reporting purposes the accounting acquirer is the parent company, the retained earnings or deficit of the acquirer will be carried forward in the equity section of the successor entity's consolidated statement of financial position The retained earnings or deficit of the accounting acquiree will not be presented. The amount shown for issued equity interests would be measured by adding the issued equity of the legal subsidiary immediately before the business combination, plus the fair value of the consideration transferred, as described above and illustrated below. However, in the consolidated financial statements, the equity structure (e.g., the number and type of equity interests issued) must reflect the equity structure of the legal parent (which was the accounting acquiree). An example of accounting for a reverse acquisition follows.

Assume that Belmont Corporation, which is the legal subsidiary, acquires Dakar Corporation, the entity issuing equity instruments and therefore the legal parent, in a reverse acquisition.

The statements of financial position of the two entities at the end of 2010 and as of September 30, 2011, the date of the transaction, are given as follows:

	Dakar Corporation *(legal parent, accounting acquiree)*	
	December 31, 2010	*September 30, 2011*
Current assets	€ 800,000	€1,000,000
Plant, property, and equipment, net	2,400,000	2,600,000
	€3,200,000	€3,600,000
Current liabilities	€ 400,000	€ 600,000
Long-term debt	600,000	400,000
Deferred tax liabilities	200,000	200,000
	1,200,000	1,200,000
Stockholders' equity		
8% redeemable preferred stock, 2,000 shares	200,000	200,000
Common stock, 100,000 shares	600,000	600,000
Retained earnings	1,200,000	1,600,000
	€3,200,000	€3,600,000

	Belmont Corporation *(legal subsidiary, accounting acquirer)*	
	December 31, 2010	*September 30, 2011*
Current assets	€2,500,000	€1,750,000
Property, plant, and equipment, net	5,000,000	7,500,000
	€7,500,000	€9,250,000
Current liabilities	€1,250,000	€1,500,000
Long-term debt	1,750,000	2,000,000
Deferred tax liabilities	500,000	750,000
	3,500,000	4,250,000
Stockholders' equity		
Common stock, 60,000 shares	1,500,000	1,500,000
Retained earnings	2,500,000	3,500,000
	€7,500,000	€9,250,000

Dakar had profit of €400,000 for the nine months ended September 30, 2011, while Belmont Co. enjoyed earnings of €1,000,000 for that period. Neither company paid any dividends during this period.

The fair value of each share of Belmont common stock was €100 at the date of the acquisition. Dakar shares were quoted at €24 on the date.

Dakar's identifiable net assets had fair values equal to their respective book values, with the exception of the property, plant, and equipment, which were appraised at €3,000,000 at September 30, 2011.

In effecting the acquisition, Dakar issues 150,000 new shares of its common stock to the owners of Belmont in exchange for all outstanding Belmont shares. Thus, former Belmont owners become the owners of a majority of the ordinary shares of Dakar after this transaction.

To compute the cost of the reverse acquisition, the number of shares of Belmont, which would have had to have been issued to acquire Dakar, must be computed. This is done as follows:

Actual Dakar shares issued to former Belmont owners	150,000
Dakar shares outstanding prior to transaction	100,000
Total Dakar shares outstanding after transaction	250,000
Fraction held by former Belmont owners (150,000/250,000)	60%
Number of Belmont shares outstanding before transaction	60,000
Number of Belmont shares that could have been issued in transaction if 60% of total would have remained with original Belmont shareholders	40,000

Belmont would have had to issue 40,000 shares for the ratio of ownership interest in the combined entity to be the same ([60,000/.60] – 60,000).

If Belmont had issued 40,000 of its shares to effect the acquisition of Dakar, the cost would have been (given the fair value of Belmont shares at September 30, 2011) €100 × 40,000 = €4,000,000. This acquisition cost would have been allocated to Dakar's assets and liabilities as follows:

Current assets		€1,000,000
Property, plant, and equipment		3,000,000
		€4,000,000
Current liabilities	€600,000	
Long-term debt	400,000	
Deferred tax liabilities	200,000	1,200,000
		2,800,000
8% redeemable preferred stock, 2,000 shares		200,000
		2,600,000
Cost of purchase (from above)		4,000,000
Goodwill to be recognized		€1,400,000

Goodwill is measured as the excess of the fair value of the consideration effectively transferred (€4,000,000) over the net amount of Dakar's identifiable assets and liabilities (€2,600,000).

From the foregoing, the information needed to construct a consolidated statement of financial position as of the date of the transaction, September 30, 2011, can be determined.

Dakar Corporation
Consolidated Statement of Financial Position
September 30, 2011

Current assets	€ 2,750,000
Property, plant, and equipment, net	10,500,000
Goodwill	1,400,000
	€14,650,000
Current liabilities	€ 2,100,000
Long-term liabilities	2,400,000
Deferred tax liabilities	950,000
	5,450,000
Shareholders' equity	
8% redeemable preferred stock, 2,000 shares	200,000
Ordinary share, 250,000 shares (€1,500,00 + 4,000,000)	5,500,000
Retained earnings	3,500,000
	9,200,000
	€14,650,000

The amount recognized as issued equity interests in the consolidated financial statements (€5,500,000) is determined by adding the issued equity of the legal subsidiary immediately before the business combination (€1,500,000) and the fair value of the consideration transferred (€4,000,000). However, the equity structure presented in the consolidated financial statements (e.g., the number and type of shares issued) must reflect the equity structure of the legal parent, including shares issued by the legal parent to effect this combination (€100,000 + €150,000).

Computing earnings per share after a reverse acquisition poses special problems, particularly so in the year in which the transaction occurs and in any subsequent years when comparative financial statements are presented that include those of pretransaction periods.

For this purpose, the number of shares outstanding for the period from the beginning of the current reporting year until the date of the reverse acquisition is the number of shares issued by the accounting acquiree (the legal parent company) to the shareholders of the accounting acquirer (the legal subsidiary). For the period after the transaction, the number of shares considered to be outstanding is the actual number of shares of the legal parent company outstanding during that period. The average number of shares outstanding for the full year being reported upon would be computed by averaging these two amounts. Other appropriate adjustments would be made to deal with changes in numbers of shares issued during the period, as is done under other circumstances (as described in Chapter 27), if necessary. Under the current standard for computing earnings per share (IAS 33), the calculation of basic earnings per share (replacing the former measure, primary earnings per share) is simplified for all entities.

Earnings per share for any earlier periods presented for comparative purposes is likewise complicated by the occurrence of a reverse acquisition. Restated earnings for earlier periods would be calculated as the earnings of the legal subsidiary divided by the number of ordinary shares issued in the reverse acquisition.

Continuing with the Dakar-Belmont acquisition example above, earnings per share can be computed. Assume that consolidated net income for the year ended December 31, 2011, after deducting preference share dividends, equals €1,600,000. This includes Belmont's earnings for the full year 2011, plus Dakar's earnings from the date of acquisition, September 30, 2011, until year-end. Remember that, notwithstanding that the new entity is called Dakar, from an accounting perspective this is Belmont Corporation.

Earnings per share would thus be computed as follows:

Number of shares outstanding from the acquisition date (Sept. 30) to December 2011	250,000
Number of shares deemed outstanding before September 30—the number of Dakar's shares issued to Belmont	150,000
Average number of shares	

$$[(150,000 \times 9) + (250,000 \times 3)] \div 12 = 175,000$$

Earnings per share for 2011

$$€1,600,000 \div 175,000 = €9.14 \text{ per share}$$

For 2011, assuming Belmont alone had earnings of €1,400,000 for the year, earnings per share would be

$$€1,400,000 \div 150,000 = €9.33 \text{ per share}$$

Finally, there is the question of noncontrolling interest. In a reverse acquisition situation, the noncontrolling interest is comprised of the former shareholders of the legal subsidiary who do not exchange their shares for those of the new parent company, but continue on as stockholders in the legal subsidiary entity. Note that this holds even though from the accounting perspective they are shareholders in an entity that acquired another company. In other words, the identity of the noncontrolling interest is determined by the legal structure of the transaction, not the accounting substance. Since the net assets of the legal subsidiary are included in the consolidated financial statements at the old book values, noncontrolling interest is likewise computed based on the book value of the legal subsidiary's net assets.

For example, in the present case all shareholders of Belmont might not agree to tender their shares in exchange for Dakar's share, and if so they will continue on as noncontrolling owners of the legal subsidiary, Belmont. To illustrate, consider these assumed facts.

Dakar offered 2.5 shares for each share of Belmont ordinary share. In the example above, 150,000 shares of Dakar were exchanged for 60,000 Belmont shares. Now, however, assume that owners of 4,000 Belmont shares decline to participate in this transaction, so Dakar issues only 140,000 shares in exchange for 56,000 Belmont shares. After the exchange, former Belmont owners hold 140,000 of a total of 240,000 Dakar's shares, or 58.33% of the total outstanding; still a majority and thus enough to define this as a reverse acquisition.

The cost of the purchase is computed similar to what was illustrated above. Since the owners of 56,000 Belmont shares participated and the transaction resulted in these owners obtaining a 58.33% interest in the successor entity, the calculation of the number of Belmont shares hypothetically required to be issued in a "straight" acquisition of Dakar is as follows:

56,000 shares outstanding ÷ .5833 = 96,000 total shares after transaction

96,000 total shares – 56,000 shares outstanding = 40,000 new shares to be issued

Thus, it can be seen that the cost of the purchase, determined in the manner that is necessary when a reverse acquisition takes place, remains 40,000 × €100 = €4,000,000 even given the existence of the noncontrolling interest.

The noncontrolling interest is 4,000 shares ÷ 60,000 shares = 6.6667%. It consists, as of the acquisition date, of 6.6667% of the book value of Belmont ordinary share and retained earnings, as follows:

6.6667%	×	€1,500,000	=	$100,000
6.6667%	×	€3,500,000	=	233,310
Total noncontrolling interest				$333,310

The consolidated statement of financial position at the acquisition date would differ from that shown above only as follows: a noncontrolling interest of €333,310 would be presented; common stock would be only €5,400,000, comprised of 93.33% (1 – 6.66667%) of Belmont's €1,500,000, plus the €4 million purchase cost); and retained earnings would be only 93.33% or Belmont's pretransaction balance of €3.5 million, or €3,266,655. All other asset and liability account balances would be identical to the presentation above.

Spin-Offs

Occasionally, an entity disposes of a wholly or partially owned subsidiary or of an investee by transferring it unilaterally to the entity's shareholders. The proper accounting for such a transaction, generally known as a spin-off, depends on whether the assets transferred constitute a *business*. IFRS defines a business as an integrated set of activities and assets that is capable of being conducted and managed for the purpose of providing a return in the form of dividends, lower costs, or other economic benefits directly to investors or other owners, members or participants.

When a transfer of assets to shareholders constitutes a business, the effect is not merely to transfer a passive investment, but to remove the operations from the former parent and to vest them with the parent's shareholders. Although IFRS has not addressed this matter, as a point of reference, US GAAP requires that spin-offs and similar nonreciprocal transfers to owners be accounted for at the recorded book values of the assets and liabilities transferred. Under US GAAP, transfers of nonmonetary assets to owners that do not constitute a business and are nonreciprocal (meaning that the entity gets nothing in return except for its own stock), are accounted for at fair value.

If the operations (or subsidiary) being spun off are distributed during a fiscal period, it may be necessary to estimate the results of operations for the elapsed period prior to spin-off to ascertain the net book value as of the date of the transfer. Stated another way, the operating results of the subsidiary to be disposed of should be included in the reported results of the parent through the actual date of the spin-off.

Non-Sub Subsidiaries

An issue that has sometimes been of concern to accountants is the use of what have been called *non-sub subsidiaries*. This situation arises when an entity plays a major role in the creation and financing of what is often a start-up or experimental operation but does not take an equity position at the outset. For example, the parent might finance the entity by means of convertible debt or debt with warrants for the later purchase of ordinary shares. The original equity partner in such arrangements most often will be the creative or managerial talent that generally exchanges its talents for an equity interest. If the operation prospers, the parent will exercise its rights to a majority voting share position; if it fails, the parent presumably avoids reflecting the losses in its statements.

Although this strategy may seem to avoid the requirements of equity accounting or consolidation, the economic substance clearly suggests that the operating results of the subsidiary should be reflected in the financial statements of the real parent, even in the absence of ownership. In theory the control criteria of IAS 27 should apply, and where the "parent" entity's interest includes convertible debt, there may well be latent control.

FUTURE DEVELOPMENTS

IASB Project: Consolidation

The IASB is currently pursuing a project (recently renamed *Consolidation*) to address both the basis (policy) on which a parent entity should consolidate its investments in subsidiaries and enhanced disclosures about consolidated and nonconsolidated entities. The objective of the project is to publish a single IFRS on consolidation that would replace IAS 27(R), *Consolidated and Separate Financial Statements,* and SIC 12, *Consolidation—Special-Purpose Entities.* The project has resulted in the issuance of IFRS 10, *Consolidated Financial Statements,* which provides a single consolidation model that identifies control as the basis for consolidation for all types of entities. The standard has an effective date of January 1, 2013 (with early adoption permitted) and will replace IAS 27, *Consolidated and Separate Financial Statements,* and SIC-12, *Consolidation—Special-Purpose Entities.*

IFRS 10, *Consolidated Financial Statements*, requires a cohesive control-based model that would be applicable to all types of entities (including structured financing and investment vehicles, e.g., SPEs). The Standard will replace IAS 27(R), *Consolidated and Separate Financial Statements*, and SIC 12, *Consolidation—Special-Purpose Entities*, and eliminate the perceived inconsistencies that exist between these two standards (IAS 27[R] focuses on control, whereas SIC-12 puts the emphasis on risks and rewards). The ED retains the presumption in IAS 27(R) that control exists if a reporting entity owns more than half of the voting power of an entity, but control could exist through other means, including potential voting interests and the existence of a dominant shareholder (de facto control). IFRS 10 does not change the consolidation procedures or the requirement to prepare consolidated financial statements. As a result of the issuance of IFRS 10, IAS 27 has now been amended and is now entitled IAS 27, *Separate Financial Statements,* and as the name implies, deals with the preparation of separate financial statements only.

Key changes that have been made include

- A revised definition of *control*, including additional application guidance with regard to which entities should be included in consolidated financial statements, and
- New enhanced disclosure requirements (all included in a separate standard, IFRS 12, *Disclosure of Interests in Other Entities*), including extensive disclosures about entities that (correctly) are not consolidated but which can create risks for the reporting entity, and about restrictions on the assets and liabilities of the group.

The changes in consolidation principles will significantly impact the assessment of whether an entity should be consolidated, in particular, in the following areas:

- Power to control without a majority of voting rights;
- Potential voting rights (e.g., options and convertible instruments held by an investor); and
- Structured entities (e.g., special-purpose entities [SPEs] accounted for under SIC 12).

Definition of control. The standard defines control as "the power of a reporting entity to direct the activities of another entity to generate returns for the reporting entity." It replaces "benefits" with "returns," and broadens the concepts of "power" and "returns." In the new definition, the key elements are

1. The *power* to direct the activities of the other entity;
2. The right to obtain *returns*; and
3. The link between power and returns.

According to the IASB, a reporting entity has the power to direct the activities of another entity if it can determine that other entity's strategic operating and financing policies. The new definition of control is wider than the current definition of control that is contained in IAS 27 (R). The power to govern the financial and operating policies, as stated in IAS 27(R), is only one means of having power to direct the activities of another entity, but not the only way. This power can be achieved in many ways, including by having voting rights, by having options or convertible instruments to obtain voting rights, by means of contractual arrangements, or a combination of these, or by having an agent conducting activities for the benefit of the controlling entity.

The new definition of control focuses on the *ability* to exercise control rather than the actual exercise of that control. A controlling entity having the power or ability to direct the activities of another entity does not have to demonstrate that power to have control. For example, a passive dominant shareholder, having the majority of voting rights but not using its voting rights regularly, would be considered to control the entity.

Currently, the definition of control in IAS 27 focuses on the ability to obtain "benefits" from another entity. IFRS 10, however, focuses on "returns" rather than "benefits," thus [...]rns may vary according to the activities of the controlled entity and may [...] negative or positive). These returns may accrue to the reporting entity [...] as dividends, fees, cost savings, know-how or synergies.

[...]r and returns must be linked. Control assumes that an entity must use [...] benefit (or to reduce the occurrence of losses); thus, control should not [...]ne, without the ability to benefit from using that power. IFRS 10 also [...]is not shared and only one parent can control a subsidiary; although [...]s noncontrolling interests—may have rights that limit the power of the [...] reporting entity needs to conduct the assessment of control continu-

[...]holding a majority of the voting rights. IFRS 10 states that a reporting [...]n a majority of the voting rights may nonetheless have the power to [...] another entity (de facto control), if the following two conditions exist:

[...]ting rights than any other party; and
[...]ts are sufficient to give the reporting entity the ability to determine the [...]ic operating and financing policies.

[...] the list of indicators of power to direct the activities of an entity. The [...]ntrol when it has (either individually or in combination)

[...]orm of voting rights (or potential voting rights) of an investee;
[...]oint, reassign or remove members of an investee's key management [...] have the ability to direct the relevant activities;
[...]int or remove another entity that directs the relevant activities;
[...]t the investee to enter into, or veto any changes to, transactions for the [...]benefit of the investor; and

• Other rights (such as decision-making rights specified in a management contract) that give the holder the ability to direct the relevant activities.

Options and convertible instruments. Under IAS 27(R), an entity should consider potential voting rights that are currently exercisable or convertible (e.g., options, convertible instruments or other instruments that, if exercised, give voting rights) as current voting rights in its assessment of control. In IFRS 10, the Board concludes that an option holder that controls an entity has power to direct the other entity's strategic operating and financing policies irrespective of whether the options are exercised. Consequently, when assessing control, an entity should consider all facts and circumstances including the entity's power deriving from the holding of options or convertible instruments.

Structured entities. IFRS 12 uses the term "structured entities" to describe entities that are similar to SPEs, and for which control cannot be assessed in a typical manner such as by assessing voting rights or control of the entity's governing body. It defines a structured entity as one that has been designed so that voting or similar rights are not the dominant factor in deciding who controls the entity, such as when any voting rights relate to administrative tasks only and the relevant activities are directed by means of contractual arrangements. IFRS 12 requires that, when assessing control of a structured entity, all relevant facts and circumstances should be examined and considered.

Agency relationships. Currently, IAS 27(R) does not provide guidance on how agency relationships (the agent acting on behalf of another party—the principal) should be considered in the assessment of control. IFRS 10 clarifies that if the reporting entity acts exclusively as an agent, it does not control an entity because its power over the entity does not enable it to benefit from the returns of that entity.

Agents can receive a fixed fee or performance-related fee for providing services. If the remuneration to the agent is related to performance, an agency relationship may be difficult to distinguish from a control relationship, because the agent may be able to direct the activities of the entity to affect its fees. In such cases, the reporting entity must determine whether the fees and their variability are comparable to those of an investor.

Disclosures. In accordance with one of the key objectives of the Consolidation Project, IFRS 12 has been issued which requires disclosures about both consolidated and nonconsolidated entities. The new disclosure objectives are designed to enable users of the reporting entity's financial statements to evaluate the following:

- The basis of control and the related accounting consequences;
- The interest that the noncontrolling interests have in the group's activities;
- The nature and financial effect of restrictions that are a consequence of assets and liabilities being held by subsidiaries;
- The nature of, and risks associated with, the reporting entity's involvement with structured entities that the reporting entity does not control.

The disclosures are extensive and can be burdensome, especially with regard to entities that are not controlled by the reporting entity, since it could be difficult in practice for preparers to have access to this information in a timely and cost-efficient manner.

Investment entities. However, the IASB is still carrying on with another project on consolidation that will focus on the accounting to be followed by investment entities. IAS 27, *Consolidated and Separate Financial Statements,* currently requires an investment entity to consolidate all investments in entities that it controls. The project that gave rise to IFRS 10, *Consolidated Financial Statements,* did not propose to change the scope of the consolidation requirements and as such, many of the respondents to the Exposure Draft asked the IASB to consider whether investment entities should be exempt from consolidating investments in entities that are controlled.

In response to those requests, the IASB initiated a project to define an investment entity for the purpose of such an exemption. The objective of the project is to define an investment entity and to require that an investment entity should not consolidate investments in entities that it controls, but to measure those investments at fair value, with changes in fair value recognized in profit or loss. The project will be undertaken jointly with the FASB, and it is expected that an Exposure Draft will be issued in 2011.

US GAAP COMPARISON

The main consolidation premise under US GAAP is that an entity controls another when ownership is greater than 50% of the voting instruments. Like IFRS, this is a rebuttable presumption if circumstances other than voting interests determine which entity controls the other.

However, there are several exceptions to consolidation of entities even if they are controlled by another entity. These are related to investment companies and nonprofit organizations. For example, certain "capital-at-risk" ratios below a threshold can prohibit consolidation of a variable interest entity.

Unlike IFRS, potential voting rights are not considered in the assessment of control. Additionally, neither accounting policies nor year-end dates need to be the same for the consolidated entities. If a year-end of a subsidiary differs by more than three months, adjustments must be made of material amounts.

16 SHAREHOLDERS' EQUITY

INTRODUCTION

The *Framework* defines equity as the residual interest in the assets of an entity after deducting all its liabilities. Shareholders' equity is comprised of all capital contributed to the entity (including share premium, also referred to as capital paid-in in excess of par value) plus retained earnings (which represents the entity's cumulative earnings, less all distributions that have been made therefrom).

IAS 1 suggests that shareholders' interests be subcategorized into three broad subdivisions: issued share capital, retained earnings (accumulated profits or losses) and other components of equity (reserves). Depending on jurisdiction, issued share capital may need to be further categorized as par or stated capital and as additional contributed capital/ share premium. This standard also sets forth requirements for disclosures about the details of share capital for corporations and the various capital accounts of other types of entities, such as partnerships.

Equity represents an interest in the net assets (i.e., assets less liabilities) of the entity. It is, however, not a claim on those assets in the sense that liabilities are. Upon the liquidation of the business, an obligation arises for the entity to distribute any remaining assets to the shareholders, but only after the creditors are first fully paid.

Earnings are not generated by transactions in an entity's own equity (e.g., by the issuance, reacquisition, or reissuance of its common or preferred shares). Depending on the laws of the jurisdiction of incorporation, distributions to shareholders may be subject to various limitations, such as to the amount of retained (accounting basis) earnings. In other cases, limitations may be based on values not presented in the financial statements, such as the net solvency of the entity as determined on a market value basis; in such instances, IFRS-basis financial statements will not provide information needed for making such determination.

In recent years, the matter of share-based payments (e.g., share option plans and other arrangements whereby employees or others, such as vendors, are compensated via issuance of shares) has received great amounts of attention. The IASB issued a comprehensive standard, IFRS 2, *Share-Based Payment*, which requires a fair value-based measurement of all such schemes. The requirements of IFRS 2 are addressed in Chapter 17.

A major objective of the accounting for shareholders' equity is the adequate disclosure of the sources from which the capital was derived. For this reason, a number of different contributed capital accounts may be presented in the statement of financial position. The rights of each class of shareholder must also be disclosed. Where shares are reserved for future issuance, such as under the terms of share option plans, this fact must also be made known. Share option plans will be addressed in Chapter 17.

Sources of IFRS	
IAS 1, 8, 32	*IFRIC* 2

DEFINITIONS OF TERMS

Equity instrument. A contract that evidences a residual interest in the assets of an entity after deducting all of its liabilities, where liabilities are defined as the present obligations of the entity arising from past events, the settlement of which are expected to result in an outflow from the entity of resources embodying economic benefits (i.e., an outflow of cash or other assets of the entity).

Equity instrument granted. The right (conditional or unconditional) to an equity instrument of the entity conferred by the entity on another party, under a share-based payment arrangement.

Equity-settled share-based payment transaction. A share-based payment transaction in which the entity receives goods or services

1. As consideration for its own equity instruments (including shares or share options); or
2. Where it has no obligation to settle the transaction with the supplier.

Fair value. The amount for which an asset could be exchanged, a liability settled, or an equity instrument granted could be exchanged, between knowledgeable, willing parties in an arm's-length transaction.

Measurement date. The date at which the fair value of the equity instruments granted is measured for the purposes of this IFRS. For transactions with employees and others providing similar services, the measurement date is grant date. For transactions with parties other than employees (and those providing similar services), the measurement date is the date the entity obtains the goods or the counterparty renders service.

Puttable financial instruments. Shares which the holders can "put" (sell) back to the issuing entity; that is, the holders can require that the entity repurchases the shares at defined amounts that can include fair value.

RECOGNITION AND MEASUREMENT

The IASB has dealt primarily with presentation and disclosure requirements relating to shareholders' equity and are yet to fully address and resolve matters pertaining to the recognition and measurement of the various components of shareholders' equity. The issuance of IFRS 2, which thoroughly addresses the accounting for share-based payments, was a major step forward in this respect. It should be noted that in many jurisdictions, company law sets out specific requirements as regards accounting for equity, which may limit the application of IFRS.

IFRS does not always address all particular scenarios that may exist in practice, and in light of this, it provides in IAS 8 that in the absence of a standard, the preparer should refer to the *Framework* and thereafter to national GAAP based on the same conceptual framework. In the light of the project between the IASB and the FASB to converge IFRS and US GAAP, it is certainly possible that IFRS may formally adopt at least some of the US GAAP guidance, rather than attempt to create unique IFRS to deal with these matters. In the following discussion, therefore, certain guidance under US GAAP will be invoked where IFRS is silent regarding the accounting for specific types of transactions involving the entity's shareholders' equity. Since this is a rapidly evolving area, care should be taken to verify the current status of relevant developments.

PRESENTATION AND DISCLOSURE

Equity includes reserves such as statutory or legal reserves, general reserves and contingency reserves, and revaluation surplus. IAS 1 categorizes shareholders' interests in three broad subdivisions:

- Issued share capital,
- Retained earnings (accumulated profits or losses); and
- Other components of equity (reserves).

This standard also sets forth requirements for disclosures about the details of share capital for corporations and of the various capital accounts of other types of entities.

Disclosures relating to share capital.

1. *The number or amount of shares authorized, issued, and outstanding.* It is required that a company disclose information relating to the number of shares authorized, issued, and outstanding. Authorized share capital is defined as the maximum number of shares that a company is permitted to issue, according to its articles of association, its charter, or its bylaws. The number of shares issued and outstanding could vary, based on the fact that a company could have acquired its own shares and is holding them as treasury shares (discussed below under reacquired shares).

2. *Capital not yet paid in (or unpaid capital).* In an initial public offering (IPO), subscribers may be asked initially to pay in only a portion of the par value, with the balance due in installments, which are known as *calls*. Thus, it is possible that at the end of the reporting period a certain portion of the share capital has not yet been paid in. The amount not yet collected must be shown as a contra (i.e., a deduction) in the equity section, since that portion of the subscribed capital has yet to be issued. For example, while the gross amount of the share subscription increases capital, if the due date of the final call falls on February 7, 2012, following the accounting year-

end of December 31, 2011, the amount of capital not yet paid in should be shown as a deduction from shareholders' equity. In this manner, only the net amount of capital received as of the end of the reporting period will be properly included in shareholders' equity, averting an overstatement of the entity's actual equity.

IAS 1 requires that a distinction be made between shares that have been issued and fully paid, on the one hand, and those that have been issued but not fully paid, on the other hand. The number of shares outstanding at the beginning and at the end of each period presented must also be reconciled.

3. *Par value per share.* This is also generally referred to as legal value or face value per share. The par value of shares is specified in the corporate charter or bylaws and referred to in other documents, such as the share application and prospectus. Par value is the smallest unit of share capital that can be acquired unless the prospectus permits fractional shares (which is very unusual for commercial entities). In certain jurisdictions, it is also permitted for corporations to issue no-par share (i.e., shares that are not given any par value). In such cases, again depending on local corporation laws, sometimes a stated value is determined by the board of directors, which is then accorded effectively the same treatment as par value. IAS 1 requires disclosure of par values or of the fact that the shares were issued without par values.

Historically, companies often issued shares at par value in cases where shares are issued immediately on incorporation or soon thereafter. This was partially due to laws, now rare, holding share owners contingently liable in the event of business failure, up to the amount of any discount from par value at the original issuance of shares. The prohibition against issuing shares at discount was thought to protect creditors and others, who could rely on aggregate par value as having been contributed in cash to the entity. It did not restrict any subsequent sale of the shares, however. As a practical matter, par values have had a much diminished importance as corporation laws have been modernized in many jurisdictions. Additionally, often the par values will be made trivial, such as when set at €1 or even €0.01 per share, such that the concern over an original-issuance discount is made moot, since issuance prices even at inception of a new corporation will be substantially above par value.

4. *Movements in share capital accounts during the year.* This information is usually disclosed in the financial statements or the footnotes to the financial statements, generally in a tabular or statement format, although in some circumstances merely set forth in a narrative. If a statement is presented, it is generally referred to as the Statement of Changes in Shareholders' Equity. It highlights the changes during the year in the various components of shareholders' equity. It also serves the purpose of reconciling the beginning and the ending balances of shareholders' equity, as shown in the statements of financial position. Under the provisions of revised IAS 1, reporting entities must present a statement showing the changes in all the equity accounts (including issued capital, retained earnings and reserves transactions with owners are reported in this statement, while all changes other than those resulting from transactions with owners are to be reported in the statement of comprehensive income.

5. *Rights, preferences, and restrictions with respect to the distribution of dividends and to the repayment of capital.* When there is more than one class of share capital having varying rights, adequate disclosure of the rights, preferences, and restrictions attached to each such class of share capital will enhance understandability of the information provided by the financial statements.

6. *Cumulative preference dividends in arrears.* If an entity has preferred shares outstanding, and does not pay *cumulative* dividends on the preference shares annually when due, it will be required by statute to pay such arrears in later years, before any distributions can be made on common (ordinary) shares. When there are several series of preferred shares, the individual share indentures will spell out the relative preference order, so that, for example, senior preferred series may be paid dividends even though junior preferred shares are several years in arrears. Although practice varies, most preference shares are cumulative in nature. Preference shares that do not have this feature are called *noncumulative preference shares.*

7. *Reacquired shares.* Shares that are issued but then reacquired by a company are referred to as *treasury shares.* The entity's ability to reacquire shares may be limited by its corporate charter or by covenants in its loan and/or preferred share agreements (for example, it may be restricted from doing so as long as bonded debt remains outstanding). In those jurisdictions where the company law permits the repurchase of shares, such shares, on acquisition by the company or its consolidated subsidiary, become legally available for reissue or resale without further authorization. *Shares outstanding* refers to shares other than those held as treasury shares. That is, treasury shares do not reduce the number of shares issued, but affect the number of shares outstanding. It is to be noted that certain countries prohibit companies from purchasing their own shares, since to do so is considered as a reduction of share capital that can be achieved only with the express consent of the shareholders in an extraordinary general meeting, and then only under certain defined conditions.

   IAS 1 requires that shares in the entity held in its treasury or by its subsidiaries be identified for each category of share capital and be deducted from contributed capital. IAS 32 states that the treasury share acquisition transaction is to be reported in the statement of changes in equity. When later resold, any difference between acquisition cost and ultimate proceeds represents a change in equity, and is therefore not to be considered a gain or loss to be reported in the statement of comprehensive income. Accounting for treasury shares is discussed in further detail later in this chapter.

   IAS 32 also specifies that the costs associated with equity transactions are to be accounted for as reductions of equity if the corresponding transaction was a share issuance, or as increases in the contra equity account when incurred in connection with treasury share reacquisitions. Relevant costs are limited to incremental costs directly associated with the transactions. If the issuance involves a compound instrument, the issuance costs should be associated with the liability and equity components, respectively, using a rational and consistent basis of allocation.

8. *Shares reserved for future issuance under options and sales contracts, including the terms and amounts.* Companies may issue share options that grant the holder of these options rights to a specified number of shares at a certain price. Share options have become a popular means of employee remuneration, and often the top echelon of management is offered this noncash perquisite as a major part of their remuneration packages. The options grant the holder the right to acquire shares over a defined time horizon for a fixed price, which may equal fair value at the grant date or, less commonly, at a price lower than fair value. Granting options usually is not legal unless the entity has enough authorized but unissued shares to satisfy the holders' demands, if made, although in some instances this can be done, with management thus becoming bound to the reacquisition of enough shares in the market (or by other means) to enable it to honor these new commitments. If a company has shares reserved for future issuance under option plans or sales contracts, it is necessary to

disclose the number of shares, including terms and amounts, so reserved. These reserved shares are not available for sale or distribution to others during the terms of the unexercised options.

IAS 32 deals with situations in which entity obligations are to be settled in cash or in equity securities, depending on the outcome of contingencies not under the issuer's control. In general, these should be classed as liabilities, unless the part that could require settlement in cash is not genuine, or settlement by cash or distribution of other assets is available only in the event of the liquidation of the issuer. If the option holder can demand cash, the obligation is a liability, not equity.

The accounting for share options, which was introduced by IFRS 2, is dealt with in Chapter 17. As will be seen, it presents many intriguing and complex issues.

Disclosures relating to other equity.

1. *Capital contributed in excess of par value.* This is the amount received on the issuance of shares that is the excess over the par value. It is called "additional contributed capital" in the United States, while in many other jurisdictions, it is referred to as "share premium." Essentially the same accounting would be required if a stated value is used in lieu of par value, where permitted.

2. *Revaluation reserve.* When a company carries property, plant, and equipment or intangible assets under the revaluation model, as is permitted by IAS 16 and IAS 38 (revaluation to fair value), the difference between the cost (net of accumulated depreciation) and the fair value is recognized in other comprehensive income and accumulated in equity as the Revaluation Surplus.

   IAS 1 requires that movements of this reserve during the reporting period (year or interim period) be disclosed in the other comprehensive income section of the statement of comprehensive income. Increases in an asset's carrying value are recognized in other comprehensive income and accumulated in equity. Decreases are recognized in other comprehensive income only to the extent of any credit balance existing in the revaluation surplus in respect of that asset, and additional decreases are taken to profit or loss. Also, restrictions as to any distributions of this reserve to shareholders should be disclosed. Note that in some jurisdictions the directors may be empowered to make distributions in excess of recorded book capital, and this often will require a determination of fair values.

3. *Reserves.* Reserves include capital reserves as well as revenue reserves. Also, statutory reserves and voluntary reserves are included under this category. Finally, special reserves, including contingency reserves, are included herein. The use of general reserves and statutory reserves, once common or even required under company laws in many jurisdictions, is now in decline.

   Statutory reserves (or legal reserves, as they are called in some jurisdictions) are created based on the requirements of the law or the statute under which the company is incorporated. For instance, many corporate statutes in Middle Eastern countries require that companies set aside 10% of their net income for the year as a "statutory reserve," with such appropriations to continue until the balance in this reserve account equals 50% of the company's equity capital. The intent is to provide an extra "cushion" of protection to creditors, such that even significant losses incurred in later periods will not reduce the entity's actual net worth below zero, which would, were it to occur, threaten creditors' ability for repayment of liabilities.

   Sometimes a company's articles, charter, or bylaws may require that each year the company set aside a certain percentage of its net profit (income) by way of a contingency or general reserve. Unlike statutory or legal reserves, contingency reserves are based on the provisions of corporate bylaws. The use of general reserves is not consistent with IFRS.

The standard requires that movements in these reserves during the reporting period be disclosed, along with the nature and purpose of each reserve presented within owners' equity.

4. *Retained earnings.* By definition, retained earnings represent an entity's accumulated profits (or losses) less any distributions that have been made therefrom. However, based on provisions contained in IFRS, other adjustments are also made to the amount of retained earnings. IAS 8 requires the following to be shown as adjustments to retained earnings:

   a. Correction of accounting errors that relate to prior periods should be reported by adjusting the opening balance of retained earnings. Comparative information should be restated, unless it is impracticable to do so.
   b. The adjustment resulting from a change in accounting policy that is to be applied retrospectively should be reported as an adjustment to the opening balance of retained earnings. Comparative information should be restated unless it is impracticable to do so.

When dividends have been proposed but not formally approved, and hence when such intended dividends have not yet become reportable as a liability of the entity, disclosure is required by IAS 1. Dividends declared after the end of the reporting period, but prior to the issuance of the financial statements, must be disclosed but cannot be formally recognized via a charge against retained earnings (as was sometimes done in the past, and as remains normal practice in certain jurisdictions under national rules). Also, the amount of any cumulative preference dividends not recognized as charges against accumulated profits must be disclosed (i.e., arrears), either parenthetically or in the footnotes.

IAS 1 mandates that an entity should present in a statement of changes in equity the amount of total comprehensive income for the period, showing separately the total amounts attributable to owners of the parent (controlling interest) and to the noncontrolling interest. Comprehensive income includes all components of what was formerly denoted as "profit or loss" and of "other recognized income and expense." The latter category will henceforth be known as "other comprehensive income."

The components of other comprehensive income comprise

1. Changes in revaluation surplus (see IAS 16, *Property, Plant, and Equipment*, and IAS 38, *Intangible Assets*);
2. Gains and losses arising from translating the financial statements of a foreign operation (see IAS 21, *The Effects of Changes in Foreign Exchange Rates*);
3. Gains and losses on remeasuring available-for-sale financial assets (see IAS 39, *Financial Instruments: Recognition and Measurement*);
4. The effective portion of gains and losses on hedging instruments in a cash flow hedge (see IAS 39); and
5. Actuarial gains and losses on defined benefit plans recognized in accordance with paragraph 93A of IAS 19, *Employee Benefits*.

This topic is covered in more detail in a separate discussion in Chapter 5.

CLASSIFICATION BETWEEN LIABILITIES AND EQUITY

A longstanding challenge under IFRS has been to discern between instruments that are liabilities and those that truly represent permanent equity in an entity. This has been made more difficult as various hybrid instruments have been created over recent decades. IAS 32 requires that the issuer of a financial instrument should classify the instrument, or its components, as a liability or as equity, according to the substance of the contractual arrangement on initial recognition.

The standard defines a financial liability as a contractual obligation

1. To deliver cash or another financial asset to another entity, or
2. To exchange financial instruments with another entity under conditions that are potentially unfavorable.

An equity instrument, on the other hand, has been defined by the standard as any contract that evidences a residual interest in the assets of an entity after deducting all its liabilities.

A special situation arises in connection with cooperatives, which are member-owned organizations having capital which exhibits certain characteristics of debt, since it is not permanent in nature. IFRIC 2 addresses the accounting for members' shares in cooperatives. It holds that where a member of a cooperative has a contractual right to request redemption of shares, this does not necessarily require the shares to be classified as a liability. Members' shares are to be classified as equity if the entity has an unconditional right to refuse redemption, or if national law prohibits redemption. On the other hand, if the law prohibits redemption only conditionally (e.g., if minimum capital requirements are not maintained), this does not alter the general rule that cooperative shares are to be deemed a liability, not equity, of the entity.

IASB also considered the special case of shares which are puttable to the entity for a proportion of the fair value of the entity. Under then-existing IFRS, when this right was held by the shareholder, redemption could be demanded, and accordingly the shares were to be classified as a liability and to be measured at fair value. This created what was viewed by many as an anomalous situation whereby a successful entity using historical cost would have a liability that increases every year and leaves the reporting entity with, potentially, no equity at all in its statement of financial position. The logic was that, since the equity in the business would not be truly permanent in nature, and would represent a claim on the assets of the entity, it would not be properly displayed as a liability—although clearly this must be adequately explained to users of the financial statements.

In responding to the foregoing concern, the IASB issued the *Amendment to IAS 32, "Financial Instruments: Presentation," and IAS 1, "Presentation of Financial Statements, Puttable Financial Instruments and Obligations Arising on Liquidation,"* which requires that financial instruments that are puttable at fair value, as well as obligations to deliver to another entity a pro rata share of the net assets of the entity upon its liquidation, should be classified as equity. Under prior practice these instruments were classified as financial liabilities.

Puttable shares. *C*ertain puttable shares, which were classified as liabilities in the statement of financial position under a previous version of IAS 32, are now required to be presented as equity if strict conditions are met. The purpose is to avoid anomalous results when residual equity interests, which would be entitled to a pro rata share of the entity's net assets upon liquidation, are puttable throughout the life of the entity at fair value.

The conditions that must be met should limit the application of this exception to the general, and fundamental, rule that instruments that obligate the entity to the payment of cash must be reported as liabilities. The conditions are that

- The instrument's holders are entitled to their pro rata share of the entity's net assets upon the liquidation of the entity.
- The instrument is in the class of instruments that is most subordinate (i.e., is among the residual equity interests in the entity) and all instruments in that class have identical features.
- The instrument has no other features that would require classification as a liability.
- The total expected cash flows attributable to the instrument, over its life, are based substantially on profit or loss, or change in recognized net assets, or change in the fair value of recognized or unrecognized net assets; there must be no other instruments outstanding that have equivalent terms that would effectively restrict or fix the residual returns to these instrument holders.

The amendments result in equity classification of puttable shares having the foregoing characteristics, whether the shares are puttable throughout the instrument's life at fair value or only upon liquidation. Puttable instruments not meeting the criteria must be presented as liabilities.

IAS 1 has been amended to also require expanded disclosures in circumstances when puttable instruments are included in equity. These disclosures include

- Summary quantitative data about the amount classified as equity;
- The entity's objectives, policies, and processes for managing the obligation to repurchase or redeem such instruments, including changes therein;
- The expected cash outflow on redemption or repurchase; and
- Information on the means of determining such cash outflows.

Compound financial instruments. Increasingly, entities issue financial instruments that exhibit attributes of both equity and liabilities. IAS 32 stipulates that an entity that issues such financial instruments, which are technically known as compound instruments, should classify the component parts of the financial instrument separately as equity or liability as appropriate. (For a detailed discussion on financial instruments, refer to Chapter 24.) In terms of IAS 32, the full fair value of the liability component(s) must be reported as liabilities, and only the residual value, at issuance, should be included as equity.

SHARE ISSUANCES AND RELATED MATTERS

Additional Guidance Relative to Share Issuances and Related Matters

As noted, IFRS provides only minimal guidance regarding the actual accounting for share-based transactions, including the issuance of shares of various classes of equity instruments. In the following paragraphs, suggestions are made concerning the accounting for such transactions, which are within the spirit of IFRS, although largely drawn from other authoritative sources. This is done to provide guidance which conforms to the requirements under IAS 8 (hierarchy of professional standards), and to illustrate a wide array of actual transactions that often need to be accounted for.

Preferred shares. Ownership interest in an entity is made up of ordinary (common) shares and, optionally, preferred (preference) shares. The ordinary shares represent the residual risk-taking ownership of the corporation after the satisfaction of all claims of creditors and senior classes of equity. It is important that the actual common ownership be accurately identified, since the computation of earnings per share (described in Chapter 27) requires that the ultimate residual ownership class be properly associated with that calculation, regardless of what the various equity classes are nominally called.

Preferred shareholders are owners who have certain rights that are superior to those of common shareholders. These rights will pertain either to the earnings or the assets of the entity. Preferences as to earnings exist when the preferred shareholders have a stipulated dividend rate (expressed either as a dollar amount or as a percentage of the preferred share's par or stated value). Preferences as to assets exist when the preferred shares have a stipulated liquidation value. If a corporation were to liquidate, the preferred holders would be paid a specific amount before the ordinary shareholders would have a right to participate in any of the proceeds.

In practice, preferred shares are more likely to have preferences as to earnings than as to assets. Some classes of preferred shares may have both preferential rights, although this is rarely encountered. Preferred shares may also have the following features:

- Participation in earnings beyond the stipulated dividend rate;
- A cumulative feature, affording the preferred shareholders the protection that their dividends in arrears, if any, will be fully satisfied before the ordinary shareholders participate in any earnings distribution; and
- Convertibility or callability by the entity.

Whatever preferences exist must be disclosed adequately in the financial statements, either in the statement of financial position or in the notes.

In exchange for the preferences, the preferred shareholders' rights or privileges are limited. For instance, the right to vote may be limited to ordinary shareholders. The most important right denied to the preferred shareholders, however, is the right to participate without limitation in the earnings of the corporation. Thus, if the corporation has exceedingly large earnings for a particular period, these earnings would accrue to the benefit of the ordinary shareholders. This is true even if the preferred shares are participating (itself a fairly uncommon feature) because even participating preferred shares usually have some upper limitation placed on its degree of participation. For example, preferred may have a 5% cumulative dividend with a further 3% participation right, so in any one year the limit would be an 8% return to the preferred shareholders (plus, if applicable, the 5% per year prior year dividends not paid).

Occasionally, as discussed in the chapter, several classes of share capital will be categorized as ordinary (e.g., Class A ordinary, Class B ordinary, etc.). Since there can be only one class of shares that constitutes the true residual risk-taking equity interest in a corporation, it is clear that the other classes, even though described as ordinary shares, must in fact have some preferential status. Not uncommonly, these preferences relate to voting rights, as when a control group holds ordinary shares with "super voting" rights (e.g., ten votes per share). The rights and responsibilities of each class of shareholder, even if described as ordinary, must be fully disclosed in the financial statements.

Accounting for the issuance of shares. The accounting for the sale of shares by a corporation depends on whether the share capital has a par or stated value. If there is a par or stated value, the amount of the proceeds representing the aggregate par or stated value is credited to the ordinary or preferred share capital account. The aggregate par or stated value is generally defined as legal capital not subject to distribution to shareholders. Proceeds in excess of par or stated value are credited to an additional contributed capital account. The additional contributed capital represents the amount in excess of the legal capital that may, under certain defined conditions, be distributed to shareholders. A corporation selling shares below par value credits the share capital account for the par value and debits an offsetting discount account for the difference between par value and the amount actually received.

If there is a discount on original issue of share capital, it serves to notify the actual and potential creditors of the contingent liability of those investors. As a practical matter, corporations avoided this problem by reducing par values to an arbitrarily low amount. This reduction in par eliminated the chance that shares would be sold for amounts below par. Where corporation laws make no distinction between par value and amounts in excess of par, the entire proceeds from the sale of shares may be credited to the ordinary share capital account without distinction between the share capital and the additional contributed capital accounts. The following entries illustrate these concepts:

Facts: A corporation sells 100,000 shares of €5 par ordinary share for €8 per share cash.

Cash	800,000	
Ordinary share capital		500,000
Additional contributed capital/share premium		300,000

Facts: A corporation sells 100,000 shares of no-par ordinary share for €8 per share cash.

Cash	800,000	
Ordinary share capital		800,000

Preferred shares will often be assigned a par value because in many cases the preferential dividend rate is defined as a percentage of par value (e.g., 5%, €25 par value preferred share will have a required annual dividend of €1.25). The dividend can also be defined as a euro amount per year, thereby obviating the need for par values.

Share capital issued for services. If the shares in a corporation are issued in exchange for services or property rather than for cash, the transaction should be reflected at the fair value of the property or services received. If this information is not readily available, the transaction should be recorded at the fair value of the shares that were issued. Where necessary, appraisals should be obtained to properly reflect the transaction. As a final resort, a valuation by the board of directors of the shares issued can be utilized. Shares issued to employees as compensation for services rendered should be accounted for at the fair value of the shares issued. (See discussion of IFRS 2 in Chapter 17.)

Occasionally, particularly for start-up operations having limited working capital, the controlling owners may directly compensate certain vendors or employees. If shares are given by a major shareholder directly to an employee for services performed for the entity, this exchange should be accounted for as a capital contribution to the company by the major shareholder and as compensation expense incurred by the company. Only when accounted for in this manner will there be conformity with the general principle that all costs incurred by an entity, including compensation, should be reflected in its financial statements.

Issuance of share units. In certain instances, ordinary and preferred shares may be issued to investors as a unit (e.g., a unit of one share of preferred and two ordinary shares can be sold as a package). Where both of the classes of shares are publicly traded, the proceeds from a unit offering should be allocated in proportion to the relative market values of the securities. If only one of the securities is publicly traded, the proceeds should be allocated to the one that is publicly traded based on its known market value. Any excess is allocated to the other. Where the market value of neither security is known, appraisal information might be used. The imputed fair value of one class of security, particularly the preferred shares, can be based on the stipulated dividend rate. In this case, the amount of proceeds remaining after the imputing of a value of the preferred shares would be allocated to the ordinary shares.

The foregoing procedures would also apply if a unit offering were made of an equity and a nonequity security such as convertible debentures, or of shares and rights to purchase additional shares for a fixed time period.

Share subscriptions. Occasionally, particularly in the case of a newly organized corporation, a contract is entered into between the corporation and prospective investors, whereby the latter agree to purchase specified numbers of shares to be paid for over some installment period. These share subscriptions are not the same as actual share issuances, and the accounting differs accordingly. In some cases, laws of the jurisdiction of incorporation will govern how subscriptions have to be accounted for (e.g., when pro rata voting rights and dividend rights accompany partially paid subscriptions).

The amount of share subscriptions receivable by a corporation is sometimes treated as an asset in the statement of financial position and is categorized as current or noncurrent in accordance with the terms of payment. However, most subscriptions receivable are shown as a reduction of shareholders' equity in the same manner as treasury shares. Since subscribed shares do not have the rights and responsibilities of actual outstanding shares, the credit is made to a shares subscribed account instead of to the share capital accounts.

If the ordinary shares have par or stated value, the ordinary shares subscribed account are credited for the aggregate par or stated value of the shares subscribed. The excess over this amount is credited to additional contributed capital or share premium. No distinction is made between additional contributed capital relating to shares already issued and shares subscribed for. This treatment follows from the distinction between legal capital and additional contributed capital. Where there is no par or stated value, the entire amount of the ordinary share subscribed is credited to the shares subscribed account.

As the amount due from the prospective shareholders is collected, the share subscriptions receivable account is credited and the proceeds are debited to the cash account. Actual issuance of the shares, however, must await the complete payment of the share subscription. Accordingly, the debit to ordinary share subscribed is not made until the subscribed shares are fully paid for and the shares are issued.

The following journal entries illustrate these concepts:

1. 10,000 shares of €50 par preferred are subscribed at a price of €65 each; a 10% down payment is received.

Cash	65,000	
Share subscriptions receivable	585,000	
Preferred share subscribed		500,000
Additional contributed capital/share premium		150,000

2. 2,000 shares of no par ordinary shares are subscribed at a price of €85 each, with one-half received in cash.

Cash	85,000	
Share subscriptions receivable	85,000	
Ordinary share subscribed		170,000

3. All preferred subscriptions are paid, and one-half of the remaining ordinary subscriptions are collected in full and subscribed shares are issued.

Cash [€585,000 + (€85,000 × 0.50)]	627,500	
Shares subscriptions receivable		627,500

Preferred shares subscribed	500,000	
Preferred share		500,000
Ordinary shares subscribed	127,500	
Ordinary shares (€170,000 × 0.75)		127,500

When the company experiences a default by the subscriber, the accounting will follow the provisions of the jurisdiction in which the entity is incorporated. In some of these, the subscriber is entitled to a proportionate number of shares based on the amount already paid on the subscriptions, sometimes reduced by the cost incurred by the entity in selling the remaining defaulted shares to other shareholders. In other jurisdictions, the subscriber forfeits the entire investment on default. In this case the amount already received is credited to an additional contributed capital account that describes its source.

Distinguishing additional contributed capital from the par or stated value of the shares. For largely historical reasons, entities sometimes issue share capital having par or stated value, which may be only a nominal value, such as €1 or even €0.01. The actual share issuance will be at a much higher (market driven) amount, and the excess of the issuance price over the par or stated value might be assigned to a separate equity account referred to as *premium on capital (ordinary) shares* or *additional contributed (paid-in) capital*. Generally, but not universally, the distinction between ordinary shares and additional contributed capital has little legal import, but may be maintained for financial reporting purposes nonetheless.

Additional contributed capital represents all capital contributed to an entity other than that defined as par or stated value. Additional contributed capital can arise from proceeds received from the sale of ordinary and preferred shares in excess of their par or stated values. It can also arise from transactions relating to the following:

1. Sale of shares previously issued and subsequently reacquired by the entity (treasury shares)
2. Retirement of previously outstanding shares
3. Payment of share dividends in a manner that justifies the dividend being recorded at the market value of the shares distributed
4. Lapse of share purchase warrants or the forfeiture of share subscriptions, if these result in the retaining by the entity of any partial proceeds received prior to forfeiture
5. Warrants that are detachable from bonds
6. Conversion of convertible bonds
7. Other gains on the entity's own shares, such as that which results from certain share option plans

When the amounts are material, the sources of additional contributed capital should be described in the financial statements.

Examples of various transactions giving rise to (or reducing) additional contributed capital accounts are set forth below.

Examples of additional contributed capital transactions

Alta Vena Company issues 2,000 shares of ordinary shares having a par value of €1, for a total price of €8,000. The following entry records the transaction:

Cash	8,000	
Ordinary shares		2,000
Additional contributed capital		6,000

Alta Vena Company buys back 2,000 shares of its own ordinary share for €10,000 and then sells these shares to investors for €15,000. The following entries record the buyback and sale transactions, respectively, assuming the use of the cost method of accounting for treasury shares:

Treasury shares	10,000	
Cash		10,000
Cash	15,000	
Treasury shares		10,000
Additional contributed capital		5,000

Alta Vena Company buys back 2,000 shares of its own €1 par value ordinary shares (which it had originally sold for €8,000) for €9,000 and retires the shares, which it records with the following entry:

Ordinary shares	6,000	
Additional contributed capital	2,000	
Retained earnings	1,000	
Cash		9,000

Alta Vena Company issues a small share dividend of 5,000 ordinary shares at the market price of €8 per share. Each share has a par value of €1. The following entry records the transaction:

Retained earnings	40,000	
Ordinary shares		5,000
Additional contributed capital		35,000

Alta Vena Company previously has recorded €1,000 of share options outstanding as part of a compensation agreement. The options expire a year later, resulting in the following entry:

Share options outstanding	1,000	
Additional contributed capital		1,000

Alta Vena's bondholders convert a €1,000 bond with an unamortized premium of €40 and a market value of €1,016 into 127 shares of €1 par ordinary share whose market value is €8 per share. This results in the following entry:

Bonds payable	1,000	
Premium on bonds payable	40	
Ordinary shares		913
Additional contributed capital—warrants		127

Donated capital. Donated capital can result from an outright gift to the entity (e.g., a major shareholder donates land or other assets to the company in a nonreciprocal transfer) or may result when services are provided to the entity. Such a transaction may be treated as a capital contribution in the books of the receiving entity as it is received from a shareholder, the argument being that it is a capital injection from the shareholder. In situations where the asset is obtained for no consideration from a party who has no investment interest in the entity, then the terms and conditions around the asset given must be considered. Where no terms and conditions are imposed, revenue can be recognized immediately. Where terms and conditions are imposed, revenue can only be recognized as the terms and conditions set out are fulfilled.

In these situations, historical cost is not adequate to reflect properly the substance of the transaction, since the historical cost to the corporation would be zero. Accordingly, these events should be reflected at fair value. If long-lived assets are donated to the corporation, they should be recorded at their fair value at the date of donation, and the amount so recorded should be depreciated over the normal useful economic life of such assets. Disclosure will be required in the financial statements of both the assets donated and the conditions required to be met.

Example of donated capital

A board member of the for-profit organization Village Social Services donates land to the organization that has a fair market value of €1 million. Village Social Services records the donation with the following entry:

Land	1,000,000	
Revenue—donations		1,000,000

The same board member donates one year of accounting labor to Village Social Services. The fair value of services rendered is €75,000. Village Social Services records the donation with the following entry:

Salaries—accounting department	75,000	
Revenue—donations		75,000

The board member also donates one year of free rent of a local building to Village Social Services. The annual rent in similar facilities is €45,000. Village Social Services records the donation with the following entry:

Rent expense	45,000	
Revenue—donations		45,000

Finally, the board member pays off a €100,000 debt owed by Village Social Services. Village Social Services records the donation with the following entry:

Notes payable	100,000	
Revenue—donations		100,000

Following the closing of the fiscal period, the effect of all the foregoing donations will be reflected in Village Social Services' retained earnings account.

Note that IFRS explicitly addresses the proper accounting for government grants (see discussion in Chapter 21), which may differ from the foregoing illustrative example, which involved private donations only. Readers should be alert to further developments in this area.

Compound and Convertible Equity Instruments

Entities sometimes issue preferred shares which are convertible into ordinary shares. Where the preferred shares are nonredeemable, the accounting for both the preferred and ordinary shares is similar as they both represent equity in the issuer. The treatment of convertible preferred shares at its issuance is no different from that of nonconvertible preferred shares. When it is converted, the book value approach is used to account for the conversion. Use of the market value approach would entail a gain or loss for which there is no theoretical justification, since the total amount of contributed capital does not change when the share capital is converted. When the preferred shares are converted, the "Preferred shares" and related "Additional contributed capital—preferred share" accounts are debited for their original values when purchased, and "Ordinary share" and "Additional contributed capital—ordinary shares" (if an excess over par or stated value exists) are credited. If the book value of the preferred shares is less than the total par value of the ordinary shares being issued, retained earnings is charged for the difference. This charge is supported by the rationale that the preferred shareholders are offered an additional return to facilitate their conversion to ordinary share. Some jurisdictions require that this excess instead reduce additional contributed capital from other sources.

On the other hand, the issuance of debt that is convertible into equity (almost always into ordinary shares) does trigger accounting complexities. Under IAS 32, it is necessary for the issuer of nonderivative financial instruments to ascertain whether it contains both liability and equity components. If the instrument does contain both elements (e.g., debentures convertible into ordinary shares), these components must be separated and accounted for according to their respective natures.

In the case of convertible debt, the instrument is viewed as being constituted of both an unconditional promise to pay (a liability) and an option granting the holder the right, but not the obligation, to obtain the issuer's shares under a fixed conversion ratio arrangement. (Under provisions of IAS 32, unless the number of shares that can be obtained on conversion is fixed, the conversion option is not an equity instrument.) This option, at issuance date, is an equity instrument and must be accounted for as such by the issuer, whether subsequently exercised or not.

The amount allocated to equity is the residual derived by deducting the fair value of the liability component (typically, by discounting to present value the future principal and interest payments on the debt by the relevant interest rate) from the total proceeds of issuance. It would not be acceptable to derive the amount to be allocated to debt as a residual, on the other hand—a conservative rule that effectively maximizes the allocation to debt and minimizes the allocation to equity.

Retained Earnings

Accounting traditionally has clearly distinguished between equity contributed by owners (including donations from owners) and that resulting from the operating results of the reporting entity, consisting mainly of accumulated earnings since the entity's inception less amounts distributed to shareholders (i.e., dividends). Equity in each of these two categories is generically distinct from the other, and financial statement users need to be informed of the composition of shareholders' equity so that, for example, the cumulative profitability of the entity can be accurately gauged.

Legal capital (the defined aggregate par or stated value of the issued shares), additional contributed capital, and donated capital, collectively represent the contributed capital of the entity. The other major source of capital is retained earnings, which represents the accumulated amount of earnings of the entity from the date of inception (or from the date of reorganization) less the cumulative amount of distributions made to shareholders and other charges to retained earnings (e.g., from treasury share transactions). The distributions to shareholders generally take the form of dividend payments, but may take other forms as well, such as the reacquisition of shares for amounts in excess of the original issuance proceeds. They key events impacting retained earnings are as follows:

- Dividends
- Certain sales of shares held in the treasury at amounts below acquisition cost
- Certain share retirements at amounts in excess of book value
- Prior period adjustments
- Recapitalizations and reorganizations

Examples of retained earnings transactions

Baking Bread Co. declares a dividend of €84,000, which it records with the following entry:

| Retained earnings | 84,000 | |
| Dividends payable | | 84,000 |

Baking Bread acquires 3,000 shares of its own €1 par value ordinary shares for €15,000, and then resells it for €12,000. The following entries record the buyback and sale transactions, respectively, assuming the use of the cost method of accounting for treasury shares:

Treasury shares	15,000	
Cash		15,000
Cash	12,000	
Retained earnings	3,000	
Treasury shares		15,000

Baking Bread buys back 12,000 shares of its own €1 par value ordinary shares (which it had originally sold for €60,000) for €70,000 and retires the shares, which it records with the following entry:

Ordinary shares	12,000	
Additional contributed capital	48,000	
Retained earnings	10,000	
Cash		70,000

Baking Bread's accountant makes a mathematical mistake in calculating depreciation, requiring a prior period reduction of €30,000 to the accumulated depreciation account, and corresponding increases in its income tax payable and retained earnings accounts. Baking Bread's income tax rate is 35%. It records this transaction with the following entry:

Accumulated depreciation	30,000	
Income taxes payable		10,500
Retained earnings		19,500

Retained earnings are also affected by the action taken by the entity's board of directors. Appropriation serves disclosure purposes and serves to restrict dividend payments but does nothing to provide any resources for satisfaction of the contingent loss or other underlying purpose for which the appropriation has been made. Any appropriation made from retained earnings must eventually be returned to the retained earnings account. It is not permissible to charge losses against the appropriation account nor to credit any realized gain to that account. The use of appropriated retained earnings has diminished significantly over the years.

An important rule relating to retained earnings is that transactions in an entity's own shares can result in a reduction of retained earnings (i.e., a deficiency on such transactions can be charged to retained earnings) but cannot result in an increase in retained earnings (any excesses on such transactions are credited to contributed capital, never to retained earnings).

If a series of operating losses have been incurred or distributions to shareholders in excess of accumulated earnings have been made and if there is a debit balance in retained earnings, the account is generally referred to as accumulated deficit.

Dividends and Distributions

Cash dividends. Dividends represent the pro rata distribution of earnings to the owners of the entity. The amount and the allocation between the preferred and ordinary shareholders is a function of the stipulated preferential dividend rate, the presence or absence of (1) a participation feature, (2) a cumulative feature, and (3) arrears on the preferred shares, and the wishes of the board of directors. Dividends, even preferred share dividends where a cumulative feature exists, do not accrue. Depending on the jurisdiction, one may find that dividends become a liability of the entity only when they are declared by the board of directors or when members vote to accept a dividend.

Traditionally, entities were not allowed to declare dividends in excess of the amount of retained earnings. Alternatively, an entity could pay dividends out of retained earnings and additional contributed capital but could not exceed the total of these categories (i.e., they could not impair legal capital by the payment of dividends). Local company law obviously dictates, directly or by implication, the accounting to be applied in many of these situations. For example, in some jurisdictions, entities can declare and pay dividends in excess of the book amount of retained earnings if the directors conclude that, after the payment of such dividends, the fair value of the entity's net assets will still be a positive amount. Thus, directors can declare dividends out of unrealized appreciation, which, in certain industries, can be a significant source of dividends beyond the realized and recognized accumulated earnings of the entity. This action, however, represents a major departure from traditional practice and demands both careful consideration and adequate disclosure.

Three important dividend dates are

1. The declaration/ approval date
2. The record date
3. The payment date

The declaration date or approval date (depending on the jurisdiction) governs the incurrence of a legal liability by the entity. The approval date is the date when the shareholders of the entity vote on whether or not to accept the dividend declared. In some jurisdictions, the applicable legislation stipulates that an entity does not incur an obligation to pay a dividend until such time as the shareholders vote to accept a dividend payment.

The record date refers to that point in time when a determination is made as to which specific registered shareholders will receive dividends and in what amounts.

Finally, the payment date relates to the date when the distribution of the dividend takes place.

These concepts are illustrated in the following example:

Example of payment of dividends

On May 1, 2011, the directors of River Corp. declare a €75 per share quarterly dividend on River Corp.'s 650,000 outstanding ordinary shares. The dividend is payable May 25 to holders of record May 15.

May 1	Retained earnings (or Dividends)	487,500	
	Dividends payable		487,500
May 15	No entry passed		
May 25	Dividends payable	487,500	
	Cash		487,500

If a dividends account is used, it is closed directly to retained earnings at year-end.

Dividends may be made in the form of cash, property, or scrip. Cash dividends are either a given dollar amount per share or a percentage of par or stated value. Property dividends consist of the distribution of any assets other than cash (e.g., inventory or equipment). Finally, scrip dividends are either promissory notes due at some time in the future, sometimes bearing interest until final payment is made; or are the issuance of additional shares made in lieu of a cash dividend. In such a scenario, shareholders are often able to choose whether to receive a cash dividend or shares in settlement of the dividend due to them.

Occasionally, what appear to be disproportionate dividend distributions are paid to some but not all of the owners of closely held entities. Such transactions need to be analyzed carefully. In some cases these may actually represent compensation paid to the recipients. In other instances, these may be a true dividend paid to all shareholders on a pro rata basis, to which certain shareholders have waived their rights. If the former, the distribution should not be accounted for as a dividend but as compensation or some other expense category and included in the statement of comprehensive income. If the latter, the dividend should be grossed up to reflect payment on a proportional basis to all the shareholders, with an offsetting capital contribution to the company recognized as having been effectively made by those to whom payments were not made.

Upon occasion, dividends may be paid in property other than cash. For example, a merchandising firm may distribute merchandise to shareholders in lieu of cash, although this makes it more difficult to assure absolute proportionality. When, say, inventory is used to distribute earnings to shareholders, the accounting is similar to that shown above, except inventory is credited rather than cash. IFRIC 17, *Distributions of Noncash Assets to Owners,* addresses the accounting relating to the distribution of such assets to shareholders. IFRIC 17 works on the assumption that the fair value of the assets to be distributed can be determined and it is on this basis that the accounting then follows. For example, if inventory carried at cost of $100,000, and having a fair value of $125,000, is distributed to shareholders as a dividend, the entity would record profit of $25,000 and a dividend payment of $125,000.

Liquidating dividends. Liquidating dividends are not distributions of earnings, but rather, a return of capital to the investing shareholders. A liquidating dividend is normally recorded by the declarer through charging additional contributed capital rather than retained earnings. The exact accounting for a liquidating dividend is affected by the laws where the business is incorporated, and these laws vary among jurisdictions. There will often be tax implications of liquidating dividend payments, which must also be considered.

Accounting for Treasury Share Transactions

The term treasury share refers to the entity's shares that were issued but subsequently reacquired and are being held ("in the company's treasury") without having been canceled. An entity may buy back its own shares, subject to laws of the jurisdiction of incorporation, for possibly many different and legitimate business purposes, such as to have on hand for later share-based payments to employees or vendors, or to decrease the "float" of shares outstanding—which may be done to provide upward pressure on the quoted price of the share or increase the earnings per share by decreasing the number of outstanding shares.

IFRS addresses treasury shares and sets as a general principle that "earnings" cannot be created by transactions in an entity's own shares, and thus the proper accounting would be to report these as capital transactions only.

Treasury shares do not reduce the number of shares issued but do reduce the number of shares outstanding, as well as total shareholders' equity. These shares are not eligible to receive cash dividends. Treasury shares are not an asset, although in some circumstances, they may be presented as an asset if adequately disclosed. Reacquired shares that are awaiting delivery to satisfy a liability created by the firm's compensation plan or reacquired shares that are held in a profit-sharing trust may still be considered outstanding and, thus, may not be considered treasury shares. The terms and conditions of the compensation plan would need to be considered in the light of SIC 12, *Consolidation—Special Purpose Entities* which is addressed in Chapter 15.

Members' Shares in Cooperative Entities

Certain organizations are so-called membership organizations or cooperatives. These are often entities providing services to a group having common membership or interests, such as labor unions or university faculty and staff. Credit unions (a form of savings and loan association) are a common example of this form of organization. Other cooperatives may serve as marketing vehicles, as in the case of farmers' co-ops, or as buying organizations, as in co-operatives formed by merchants in certain types of businesses, generally in order to gain economies of scale and market power in order to compete with larger merchant chains. Generally, these types of organizations will refund or rebate profits to the members in proportion to the amount of business transacted over a time period, such as a year.

Ownership in cooperatives is represented by shares. Members' shares in cooperative entities have some characteristics of equity, but also, often, characteristics of debt, since they are not permanent equity which cannot be withdrawn. Members' shares typically give the holder the right to request redemption for cash, although that right may be subject to certain limitations or restrictions, imposed by law or by the terms of the membership agreement. IFRIC 2, *Members' Shares in Cooperative Entities and Similar Instruments,* gives guidance on how those redemption terms should be evaluated in determining whether the shares should be classified as financial liabilities or as equity.

Under IFRIC 2, shares for which the member has the right to request redemption are normally liabilities. Even when the intent is to leave in the equity interest for a long period, such as until the member ceases business operations, this does not qualify as true equity as defined in the *Framework.* However, the shares qualify as equity if

- The cooperative entity has an unconditional right to refuse redemption, or
- Local law, regulation, or the entity's governing charter imposes prohibitions on redemption.

However, the mere existence of law, regulation, or charter provisions that would prohibit redemption only if conditions (such as liquidity constraints) are met, or are not met, does not result in members' shares being treated as equity.

PRESENTATION OF FINANCIAL STATEMENTS

The following is an illustration of the treatment of equity that may be required in the financial statements.

Equity Section of Consolidated Statement of Financial Position

(in thousands of euros)	*2011*		*2010*	
Ordinary shares				
Authorized: 10,000,000 Par value = €1				
Issued: 6,650,000		6,650		6,585
Share premium and reserves				
Share premium	12,320		12,110	
Legal reserve	665		665	
Share options granted	724		676	
Translation adjustment	(1,854)		(2,266)	
Treasury shares	(320)		(320)	
		11,535		10,865

	2011	2010
(in thousands of euros)		
Retained earnings	4,230	3,898
Owners of the parent company	22,415	21,348
Noncontrolling interest	360	353
Total equity	22,775	21,701

Examples of Financial Statement Disclosures

SAB Miller plc
Annual Report 2011

Accounting principles

p) Share capital
Ordinary shares are classified as equity. Incremental costs directly attributable to the issue of new shares or options are shown in equity as a deduction, net of tax, from the proceeds.

SAB Miller plc
Annual Report 2011

Notes to the consolidated financial statements

26. Share capital

	2011 US$m	2010 US$m
Group and company		
Called up, allotted and fully paid share capital		
1,659,040,014 ordinary shares of 10 US cents each (2010: 1,654,749,852)	**166**	165
50,000 deferred shares of £1.00 each (2010: 50,000)	--	--
	166	165

	Ordinary shares of 10 US cents each	Deferred shares of £1 each	Nominal value US$m
At April 1, 2009	1,585,366,969	50,000	159
Issue of shares—share incentive plans	9,382,883	--	--
Issue of shares—Polish noncontrolling interest buyout transaction	60,000,000	--	6
At March 31, 2010	1,654,749,852	50,000	165
Issue of shares—share incentive plans	4,290,162	--	1
At March 31, 2011	**1,669,040,014**	**50,000**	**166**

Changes to authorized share capital
With effect from October 1, 2009, the company adopted new articles of association which removed any previous limit on the authorized share capital. Directors are still limited as to the number of shares they can at any time allot because allotment authority continues to be required under the Companies Act 2006, save in respect of employee share schemes.

Changes to issued share capital
During the year, the company issued 4,290,162 (2010: 9,382,883) new ordinary shares of 10 US cents to satisfy the exercise of options granted under the various share incentive plants, for consideration of US $73 million (2010: US $114 million)

On May 29, 2009, 60 million new ordinary shares of 10 US cents were issued as consideration for the purchase of the remaining 28.1% noncontrolling interest in the group's Polish subsidiary, Kompania Piwowarska SA.

Rights and restrictions relating to share capital

Convertible participating shares. Altria is entitled to require the company to convert its ordinary shares into convertible participating shares so as to ensure that Altria's voting shareholding does not exceed 24.99% of the total voting shareholding.

If such an event occurs, the convertible participating shares will rank pari passu with the ordinary shares in all respects and no action shall be taken by the company in relation to ordinary shares unless the same action is taken in respect of the convertible participating shares. On distribution of the profits (whether by cash dividend, dividend in specie, scrip dividend, capitalization issue or otherwise), the convertible participating shares will rank pari pasu with the ordinary shares. On a return of capital (whether winding-up or otherwise), the convertible participating shares will rank pari passu with the ordinary shares.

Altria is entitled to vote its convertible participating shares at general meetings of the company on a poll on the basis of one-tenth of a vote to every convertible participating share on all resolutions other than a resolution

(i)   Proposed by any person other than Altria, to wind-up the company
(ii) Proposed by any person other than Altria, to appoint an administrator or to approve any arrangement with the company's creditors
(iii) Proposed by the board, to sell all or substantially all of the undertaking of the company, or
(iv) Proposed by any person other than Altria, to alter any of the class rights attaching to the convertible participating shares or to approve the creation of any new class of shares,

in which case Altria shall be entitled on a poll to vote on the resolution on the basis of one vote for each convertible participating share, but for the purposes of any resolution other than a resolution mentioned in (iv) above, the convertible participating shares shall be treated as being of the same class as the ordinary shares and no separate meeting or resolution of the holders of the convertible participating share shall be required to be convened or passed.

Upon a transfer of convertible participating shares by Altria other than to an affiliate, such convertible participating shares shall convert into ordinary shares.

Altria is entitled to require the company to convert its convertible participating shares into ordinary shares if

(i)   A third party has made a takeover offer for the company and (if such offer becomes or is declared unconditional in all respects) it would result in the voting shareholding of the third party being more than 30% of the total voting shareholding; and
(ii) Altria has communicated to the company in writing its intention not itself to make an offer competing with such third party offer, provided that the conversion date shall be no earlier than the date on which the third party's offer becomes or is declared unconditional in all respects.

Altria is entitled to require the company to convert its convertible participating shares into ordinary shares if the voting shareholding of a third party should be more than 24.99%, provided that

(i)   The number of ordinary shares held by Altria following such conversion shall be limited to one ordinary share more than the number of ordinary shares held by the third party; and
(ii) Such conversion shall at no time result in Altria's voting shareholding being equal to or greater than the voting shareholding which would require Altria to make a mandatory offer in terms of Rule 9 of the City Code.

If Altria wishes to acquire additional ordinary shares (other than pursuant to a preemptive issue of new ordinary shares or with the prior approval of the board), Altria shall first convert into ordinary shares the lesser of

(i)   Such number of convertible participating shares as would result in Altria's voting shareholding being such percentage as would, in the event of Altria subsequently acquiring one additional ordinary share, require Altria to make a mandatory offer in terms of Rule 9 of City Code; and

(ii) All of its remaining convertible participating shares

The company shall use its best endeavors to procure that the ordinary shares arising on conversion of the convertible participating shares are admitted to the Official List and to trading on the London Stock Exchange's market for listed securities, admitted to listing and trading on the JSE Ltd , and admitted to listing and trading on any other stock exchange upon which the ordinary shares are from time to time listed and traded, but no admission to listing or trading shall be sought for the convertible participating shares while they remain convertible participating shares.

Deferred shares

The deferred shares do not carry any voting rights and do not entitle holders thereof to receive any dividends or other distributions. In the event of a winding-up, deferred shareholders would receive no more than the nominal value. Deferred shares represent the only nonequity share capital of the group.

a. Retained earnings

	Treasury and EBT shares US$m	Retained earnings US$m	Total US$m
At April 1, 2009	(722)	7,218	6,498
Profit for the year	--	1,910	1,910
Other comprehensive income	--	(29)	(29)
Actuarial losses taken to other comprehensive income	--	(15)	(15)
Share of associates' and joint ventures' losses recognized in other comprehensive income	--	(17)	(17)
Deferred tax credit on items taken to other comprehensive income	--	3	3
Dividends paid	--	(924)	(924)
Payment for purchase of own shares for share trusts	(8)	--	(8)
Utilization of EBT shares	57	(57)	--
Credit entry relating to share-based payments	--	80	80
At March 31, 2010	(673)	8,198	7,525
Profit for the year	--	2,408	2,408
Other comprehensive income	--	(63)	(63)
Actuarial losses taken to other comprehensive income	--	(28)	(28)
Share of associates' and joint ventures' losses recognized in other comprehensive income	--	(71)	(71)
Deferred tax credit on items taken to other comprehensive income	--	36	36
Dividends paid	--	(1,115)	(1,115)
Payment for purchase of own shares for share trusts	--	(10)	(10)
Utilization of EBT shares	16	(16)	--
Credit entry relating to share-based payments	--	246	248
At March 31, 2011	**(657)**	**9,648**	**8,991**

The group's retained earnings include amounts of US $693 million (2010: US $678 million), the distribution of which is limited by statutory or other restrictions.

Treasury and EBT shares reserve. On February 26, 2009, 77,368,338 SAB Miller plc nonvoting convertible shares were converted into ordinary shares and then acquired by the company to be held as treasury shares. While the purchase price for each share was £10.54, the whole amount of the consideration was paid between group companies. On February 15, 2010, 5,300,000 of these treasury shares were transferred to the EBT for nil consideration. These shares will be used to satisfy awards outstanding under the various share incentive plans. As of March 31, 2011, a total of 72,068,338 shares (2010: 72,068,338) were held in treasury.

The EBT holds shares in SAB Miller plc for the purposes of the various executive share incentive plans, further details of which are disclosed in the remuneration report. The shares currently rank pari passu with all other ordinary shares. At March 31, 2011, the EBT held 7,437,406 shares (2010: 8,672,331 shares) which cost US $94 million (2010: US $110 million) and had a market value of US $263 million (2010: US $255 million). These shares have been treated as a deduction in arriving at shareholders' funds. The EBT used funds provided by SAB Miller plc to purchase such of the shares as were purchased in the market. The costs of funding and administering the scheme are charged to the income statement in the period in which they relate.

BHP Billiton Group
Annual Report 2010

Notes to the consolidated financial statements

19. Share capital

	BHP Billiton Limited			BHP Billiton Plc		
	2010 US $M	2009 US $M	2008 US $M	2010 US $M	2009 US $M	2008 US $M
Share capital						
Balance at the beginning of the financial year	1,227	1,227	1,221	1,116	1,116	1,183
Exercise of Employee Share Plan Options(a)	-	-	6	-	-	-
Shares bought back and cancelled(a)	-	-	-	-	-	(67)
Balance at the end of the financial year	1,227	1,227	1,227	1,116	1,116	1,116
Treasury shares						
Balance at the beginning of the financial year	(1)	(1)	(2)	(524)	(513)	(1,455)
Purchases of shares by ESOP Trusts	(216)	(132)	(250)	(58)	(37)	(20)
Employee share awards exercised following vesting	216	132	251	58	26	29
Shares bought back(a)	-	-	-	-	-	(3,075)
Shares cancelled(a)	-	-	-	-	-	4,008
Balance at the end of the financial year	(1)	(1)	(1)	(524)	(524)	(513)

	BHP Billiton Limited			BHP Billiton Plc		
	2010 Shares(d)	2009 Shares(d)	2008 Shares(d)	2010 Shares(c)(d)	2009 Shares(c)(d)	2008 Shares(c)(d)
Share capital issued						
Ordinary shares fully paid	3,358,359,496	3,358,359,496	3,358,359,496	2,231,121,202	2,231,121,202	2,231,121,202
Comprising						
• Shares held by the public	3,358,312,376	3,358,312,376	3,358,260,180	2,206,076,344	2,206,130,916	2,206,662,027
• Treasury shares	47,120	47,120	99,316	25,044,858	24,990,286	24,459,175
Ordinary shares paid to A $1.36	110,000	110,000	195,000			
Special Voting Share of no par value(e)	1	1	1			
5.5% Preferences shares of £1 each(f)				50,000	50,000	50,000
Special Voting Share of US $0.50 par value(e)				1	1	1

BHP Billiton Limited / BHP Billiton Plc

	BHP Billiton Limited			BHP Billiton Plc		
	2010 Shares	2009 Shares	2008 Shares	2010 Shares	2009 Shares	2008 Shares
Movement in shares held by the public						
Opening number of shares	3,358,312,376	3,358,260,180	3,357,372,156	2,206,130,916	2,206,662,027	2,302,854,320
Shares issued on exercise of Employees Share Plan Options	-	-	855,923	-	-	-
Purchase of shares by ESOP Trusts	(6,304,733)	(5,274,136)	(6,550,854)	(2,081,566)	(1,447,706)	(589,802)

	BHP Billiton Limited			BHP Billiton Plc		
	2010 Shares	2009 Shares	2008 Shares	2010 Shares	2009 Shares	2008 Shares
Employee share awards exercised following vesting	6,304,733	5,326,332	6,582,955	2,026,994	916,595	1,301,595
Shares bought back[a]	-	-	-	-	-	(96,904,086)
Closing number of shares[g]	3,358,312,376	3,358,312,376	3,358,260,180	2,206,076,344	2,206,130,916	2,206,662,027

	BHP Billiton Limited			BHP Billiton Plc		
	2010 Shares	2009 Shares	2008 Shares	2010 Shares	2009 Shares	2008 Shares
Movement in treasury shares						
Opening number of shares	47,120	99,316	131,417	24,990,286	24,459,175	63,607,682
Purchase of shares by ESOP Trusts	6,304,733	5,274,136	6,550,854	2,081,566	1,447,706	589,802
Employee share awards exercised following vesting	(6,304,733)	(5,326,332)	(6,582,955)	(2,026,994)	(916,595)	(1,301,595)
Shares bought back [a]	-	-	-	-	-	96,904,086
Shares cancelled[a]	-	-	-	-	-	135,340,800
Closing number of shares	47,120	47,120	99,316	25,044,858	24,990,286	24,459,175

	BHP Billiton Limited		
	2010 Shares	2009 Shares	2008 Shares
Movement in shares partly paid to A $1.36			
Opening number of shares	110,000	195,000	195,000
Partly paid shares converted to fully paid[h]	-	(85,000)	-
Closing number of shares[i]	110,000	110,000	195,000

(a) On August 23, 2006, BHP Billiton announced a US $3 billion capital return to shareholders through an 18-month series of on-market share buybacks. On February 7, 2007, a US $10 billion extension to this program was announced. As of that date, US $1,705 million of shares in BHP Billiton Plc had been repurchased under the August program, leaving US $1,295 million to be carried forward and added to the February 2007 program. All BHP Billiton Plc. shares bought back are accounted for as Treasury shares within the share capital of BHP Billiton Plc. Details of the purchases are shown in the table below. Cost per share represents the average cost per share for BHP Billiton Plc shares and final cost per share for BHP Billiton Limited shares. Shares in BHP Billiton Plc purchased by BHP Billiton Limited have been cancelled, in accordance with the resolutions passed at the 2006 Annual General Meetings.

| | | | Cost per share and dis- | | Purchased by | | | |
| | | | | | BHP Billiton Limited | | BHP Billiton Plc | |
Year ended	Shares purchased	Number	count	Total cost US $M	Shares	US $M	Shares	US $M
June 30, 2008	BHP Billiton Plc	96,904,086	£12.37 8.7%[(i)]	3,075	96,904,086	3,075	-	-

(i) Represents the discount to the average BHP Billiton Limited share price between September 7, 2006, and December 14, 2007.
As at June 30, 2010, shares in BHP Billiton Plc bought back as part of the above program but not cancelled are held as Treasury shares. On December 14, 2007, the share buyback program was suspended in light of the Group's offers for Rio Tinto Plc and Rio Tinto Limited. On November 27, 2008, the offers lapsed. No shares were bought back under the program in the year ended June 30, 2010.

(b) An Equalization Share (US $0.50 par value) has been authorized to be issued to enable a distribution to be made by BHP Billiton Plc Group to the BHP Billiton Limited Group should this be required under the terms of the DLC merger. The Directors have the ability to issue the Equalization Share if required under those terms. The Constitution of BHP Billiton Limited allows the Directors of that Company to issue a similar Equalization Share. There has been no movement in this class of share. This share forms part of BHP Billiton Plc's total share capital.

(c) The total number of BHP Billiton Plc authorized ordinary shares of US $0.50 par value is 2,762,974,200 (2009: 2,762,974,200; 2008: 2,762,974,200).

(d) The total number of BHP Billiton Limited shares of all classes is 3,358,469,497 of which 99.99% are ordinary shares fully paid (2009: 3,358,469,497, 99.99%; 2008: 3,358,554,497, 99.99%). The total number of BHP Billiton Plc shares of all classes is 2,763,024,202, of which 99.99% are authorized ordinary shares of US $0.50 par value (2009: 2,763,024,202, 99.99%; 2008: 2,763,024, 99.99%). Any surplus remaining after payment of preferred distributions shall be payable to the holders of BHP Billiton Limited and BHP Billiton Plc ordinary shares in equal amounts per share.

(e) Each of BHP Billiton Limited and BHP Billiton Plc issued one Special Voting Share to facilitate joint voting by shareholders of BHP Billiton Limited and BHP Billiton Plc on Joint Electorate Actions. There has been no movement in these shares.

(f) Preference shares have the right to repayment of the amount paid up on the nominal value and any unpaid dividends in priority to the holders of any other class of shares in BHP Billiton Plc on a return of capital or winding-up. The holders of preference shares have limited voting rights if payment of the preference dividends are six months or more in arrears or a resolution is passed changing the rights of the preference shareholders. There has been no movement in these shares, all of which are held by JP Morgan Plc.

(g) During the period July 1, 2010, to September 7, 2010, no Executive Share Scheme partly paid shares were paid up in full, no fully paid ordinary shares (including attached bonus shares) were issued on the exercise of Employee Share Plan Options, no fully paid ordinary shares (including attached bonus shares) were issued on the exercise of Performance Share Plan Performance Rights and no fully paid ordinary shares were issued on the exercise of Group Incentive Scheme awards.

(h) During the year ended June 30, 2009, partly paid shares were converted to an equal number of fully paid shares and satisfied via on-market purchase.

(i) At June 30, 2010, 70,000 partly paid shares on issue are entitled to 79,928 bonus shares on becoming fully paid. The remaining partly paid shares are entitled to an equal number of fully paid shares upon conversion to fully paid shares.

17 SHARE-BASED PAYMENT

INTRODUCTION

The IASB's *Framework* defines equity as the residual interest in the assets of an entity after deducting all its liabilities. Shareholders' equity is comprised of all capital contributed to the entity (including share premium, also referred to as capital paid-in in excess of par value) plus retained earnings (which represents the entity's cumulative earnings, less all distributions that have been made therefrom).

In recent years, the matter of share-based payments (e.g., share option plans and other arrangements whereby employees or others, such as vendors, are compensated via issuance of shares) has received great amounts of attention. The IASB imposed a comprehensive standard, IFRS 2, *Share-Based Payment*, which requires a fair value-based measurement of all such schemes.

A major objective of the accounting for shareholders' equity is the adequate disclosure of the sources from which the capital was derived. The appropriate accounting treatment is dealt with in Chapter 16. Where shares are reserved for future issuance, such as under the terms of share option plans, this fact must also be made known. The accounting for this is addressed in this chapter.

Sources of IFRS
IFRS 2

SCOPE

IFRS 2 applies to the accounting for *all* share-based payment transactions, including

- Equity-settled share-based payment transactions,
- Cash-settled share-based payment transactions, and
- Cash-settled *or* equity-settled share-based payment transactions (when the entity has a choice to settle the transaction in cash (or other assets) or by issuing equity instruments).

This standard may also apply in the absence of specifically identifiable goods and services but when other circumstances indicate that goods or services have been (or will be) received.

Furthermore—and very importantly—IFRS 2 applies to all entities (both publicly and privately held). Also, a subsidiary using its parent's or other subsidiary's equity as consideration for goods or services is within the scope of this standard. However, an entity should *not* apply this IFRS to transactions in which the entity acquires goods as part of the net assets acquired in a business combination (transactions within the scope of IFRS 3). In such cases, it is important to distinguish share-based payments related to the acquisition from those related to employee services. Also, IFRS 2 does not apply to share-based payment contracts within the scope of IAS 32 and IAS 39.

DEFINITIONS OF TERMS

Cash-settled share-based payment transaction. A share-based payment transaction in which the entity acquires goods or services by incurring a liability to transfer cash or other assets to the supplier of those goods or services for amounts that are based on the price (or value) of equity instruments (including shares or shares options) of the entity or another group entity.

Employees and others providing similar services. Individuals who render personal services to the entity and meet one of the following additional criteria:

1. The individuals are regarded as employees for legal or tax purposes,
2. The individuals work for the entity under its direction in the same way as individuals who are regarded as employees for legal or tax purposes, or
3. The services rendered are similar to those rendered by employees. For example, the term encompasses all management personnel (i.e., those persons having authority and responsibility for planning, directing and controlling the activities of the entity, including nonexecutive directors).

Equity instrument. A contract that evidences a residual interest in the assets of an entity after deducting all of its liabilities, where liabilities are defined as the present obligations of the entity arising from past events, the settlement of which are expected to result in an outflow from the entity of resources embodying economic benefits (i.e., an outflow of cash or other assets of the entity).

Equity instrument granted. The right (conditional or unconditional) to an equity instrument of the entity conferred by the entity on another party, under a share-based payment arrangement.

Equity-settled share-based payment transaction. A share-based payment transaction in which the entity receives goods or services either

1. As consideration for its own equity instruments (including shares or share options), or
2. Where it has no obligation to settle the transaction with the supplier.

Fair value. The amount for which an asset could be exchanged, a liability settled, or an equity instrument granted could be exchanged, between knowledgeable, willing parties in an arm's-length transaction.

Grant date. The date at which the entity and another party (including an employee) agree to a share-based payment arrangement, being when the entity and the counterparty have a shared understanding of the terms and conditions of the arrangement. At grant date the entity confers on the counterparty the right to cash, other assets, or equity instruments of the entity, provided the specified vesting conditions, if any, are met. If that agreement is subject to an approval process (for example, by shareholders), grant date is the date when that approval is obtained.

Intrinsic value. The difference between the fair value of the shares to which the counterparty has the (conditional or unconditional) right to subscribe or which it has the right to receive, and the price (if any) the counterparty is (or will be) required to pay for those shares.

Market condition. A condition upon which the exercise price, vesting or exercisability of an equity instrument depends that is related to the market price of the entity's equity instruments, such as attaining a specified share price or a specified amount of intrinsic value of a share option, or achieving a specified target that is based on the market price of the entity's equity instruments relative to an index of market prices of equity instruments of other entities.

Measurement date. The date at which the fair value of the equity instruments granted is measured for the purposes of this IFRS. For transactions with employees and others providing similar services, the measurement date is grant date. For transactions with parties other than employees (and those providing similar services), the measurement date is the date the entity obtains the goods or the counterparty renders service.

Puttable financial instruments. Shares which the holders can "put" back to the issuing entity; that is, the holders can require that the entity repurchases the shares, at defined amounts that can include fair value.

Reload feature. A feature that provides for an automatic grant of additional share options whenever the option holder exercises previously granted options using the entity's shares, rather than cash, to satisfy the exercise price.

Reload option. A new share option granted when a share is used to satisfy the exercise price of a previous share option.

Share-based payment arrangement. An agreement between the entity (including its shareholder or another group entity) and another party (including an employee) to enter into a share-based payment transaction, which thereby entitles the other party to receive

1. Cash or other assets of the entity for amounts that are based on the price of equity instruments (including shares or shares options) of the entity or another group entity, or
2. Equity instruments (including shares or share options) of the entity or another group entity, provided the specified vesting conditions are met.

Share-based payment transaction. A transaction in which the entity

1. Receives goods or services from the supplier of those goods or services (including an employee) in a share-based arrangement, or
2. Incurs an obligation to settle the transaction with the supplier in a share-based payment arrangement when another group entity receives those goods or services.

Share option. A contract that gives the holder the right, but not the obligation, to subscribe to the entity's shares at a fixed or determinable price for a specified period of time.

Vest. To become an entitlement. Under a share-based payment arrangement, a counterparty's right to receive cash, other assets, or equity instruments of the entity vests upon satisfaction of any specified vesting conditions.

Vesting conditions. The conditions that must be satisfied for the counterparty to become entitled to receive cash, other assets or equity instruments of the entity, under a share-based payment arrangement. Vesting conditions may include service conditions, which require the other party to complete a specified period of service, and performance conditions, which require specified performance targets to be met (such as a specified increase in the entity's profit over a specified period of time).

Vesting period. The period during which all the specified vesting conditions of a share-based payment arrangement are to be satisfied.

OVERVIEW

Prior to the IASB's issuance of IFRS 2, *Share-Based Payment,* there had been no guidance under IFRS to the accounting for employee share-based compensation or other share-based payment situations. This was an area seriously in need of attention as the accounting for share-based payment was not commonplace and thus the accounting therefor, where it occurred, varied.

Overview. In accordance with IFRS 2, a share-based payment is a transaction in which the entity receives goods or services as consideration for its equity instruments or acquires goods or services by incurring liabilities for amounts that are based on the price of the entity's shares (or other equity instruments of the entity). The concept of share-based payments is broad and includes not only employee share options but also share appreciation rights, employee share ownership plans, employee share purchase plans, share option plans and other share arrangements. The accounting approach for the share-based payment depends on whether the transaction is settled by the issuance of

1. Equity instruments,
2. Cash, or
3. Equity and cash.

The general principle is that all share-based payment transactions should be recognized in the financial statements at fair value, with asset or expense recognized when the goods or services are received. Depending on the type of share-based payment, fair value may be determined based on the value of goods or services received, or by the value of the shares or rights to shares given up. In accordance with IFRS, the following rules should be followed:

- If the share-based payment is for goods or services other than employees, the share-based payment should be measured by reference to the fair value of goods and services;
- If the share-based payment is to employees (or those similar to employees), the transaction should be measured by reference to the fair value of the equity instruments granted at the date of grant;
- For cash-settled share-based payments, the fair value should be determined at each reporting date; and

- If the share-based payment can be settled in cash or in equity, then the equity component should be measured at the grant date only, but the cash component is measured at each reporting date.

In general, transactions in which goods or services are received as consideration for equity instruments of the entity are to be measured at the fair value of the goods or services received by the reporting entity. However, if their value cannot be readily determined (as the standard suggests is the case for employee services in limited situations) they are to be measured with reference to the fair value of the equity instruments granted.

In the case of transactions with parties other than employees, there is a rebuttable presumption that the fair value of the goods or services received is more readily determinable than is the value of the shares granted. This follows logically from the fact that, in arm's-length transactions, it should be the case that management would be highly cognizant of the value it has received (whether merchandise, plant assets, personal services, etc.) and that such data would not pose any effort to gather and utilize. Arguments to the contrary raise basic questions about managerial performance and can rarely be given much credence.

Additional guidance is also provided in the standard with regard to situations in which the entity cannot identify specifically some or all of the goods or services received. If the identifiable consideration received (if any) appears to be less than the fair value of the equity instruments granted or liability incurred, typically this situation indicates that other consideration (i.e., unidentifiable goods or services) has also been (or will be) received. The entity should measure the unidentifiable goods or services received (or to be received) at the grant date as the difference between the fair value of the share-based payment given or promised and the fair value of any identifiable goods or services received (or to be received). However, for cash-settled transactions, the liability is measured at each reporting date until it is settled.

Given the added challenge of estimating fair value for nontraded shares, this was a major point of contention among those responding to the initial draft standard. Realistically, entities granting share-based compensation to executives and other employees almost always have a sense of the value being transferred, for otherwise these bargained transactions would not make business sense, nor would they satisfy the demands or expectations of the recipients.

Where payment is made or promised in the reporting entity's shares only, the value is determined using a fair value technique that computes the cost at the date of the transaction, which is not subsequently revised, except for revised terms which increase the amount of fair value to be transferred to the recipients. In contrast, for cash-settled transactions, the liability should be remeasured at each reporting date until it is settled.

For transactions measured at the fair value of the equity instruments granted (such as compensation transactions with employees), fair value is estimated at grant date. A point of contention here has often been whether grant date or exercise date is the more appropriate reference point, but the logic of the former is that the economic decision, and the employee's contractual commitment, were made as of the grant date, and the accidents of timing of subsequent exercise (or, in some cases, forfeiture) are not indicative of the bargained-for value of the transaction. The grant date is when the employee accepts the commitment, not when the offer is first made. Accordingly, IFRS 2 requires the use of grant date to ascertain the fair value to be associated with the transaction.

When share capital is issued immediately, measurement is not generally difficult. For example, if 100 shares having a fair (market) value of €33 per share are given outright to an employee, the compensation cost is simply computed as €3,300. Since the grant vests immediately (no future service is demanded from the recipient), the expense is immediately reported.

The more problematic situation is when employees (or others) are granted *options* to later acquire shares that permit exercise over a defined time horizon. The holders' ability to wait and later assess the desirability of exercising the options has value—and the lengthier the period until the options expire, the more likely the underlying shares will increase in value, and thus the greater is the value of the option. Even if the underlying shares are publicly traded, the value of the options will be subject to some debate. Only when the options themselves are traded (which is rarely the case with employee share options, which are restricted to the grantees themselves) will fair value be directly determinable by observation. If market options on the entity's shares do trade, the value will likely exceed that to be attributed to nontradable employee share options, even if having nominally similar terms (exercise dates, prices, etc.).

The standard holds that, to estimate the fair value of a share option in the likely instance where an observable market price for that option does not exist, an *option pricing model* should be used. IFRS 2 does not specify which particular model should be used. The entity must disclose the model used, the inputs to that model, and various other information bearing on how fair value was computed. In practice, these models are all fairly sophisticated and complicated (although commercially available software promises to ease the computational complexities) and a number of the variables have inherently subjective aspects.

One issue that has to be dealt with involves the tax treatment of options, which varies across jurisdictions. In most instances the tax treatment will not comply with the fair value measurement mandated under IFRS 2, and thus there will be a need for specific guidance as to the accounting for the tax effects of granting the options and of the ultimate exercise of those options, if they are not forfeited by the option holders. This is described later in this discussion.

In respect of the appropriate tax treatment of share-based payments, the *Basis for Conclusions* of IFRS 2 notes that in jurisdictions where a tax deduction is given, the measurement of the tax deduction does not always coincide with that of the accounting deduction. Where the tax deduction is in excess of the expense reported in the statement of comprehensive income, the excess is taken directly to equity.

RECOGNITION AND MEASUREMENT

Recognition. The general recognition principle is that all share-based payment transactions should be recognized in the financial statements when the goods or services are received. An entity should recognize assets or expenses (when goods or services do not qualify for recognition as assets) with the corresponding credit to recognize an increase in

- Equity if the goods or services are received in an *equity-settled* share-based payment transaction; or
- Liability if goods or services are received in a *cash-settled* share-based payment transaction.

If the share-based payments granted to employees *vest* immediately, a presumption is that services have been provided by employees in full and employees are unconditionally entitled to those share-based payments at the grant date. If the share-based payments do not vest until the employees complete a specified period of service, the entity should recognize expenses (with a corresponding increase in equity or liabilities) as services are rendered by employees during the vesting period. IFRS 2 defines *vesting conditions* as service conditions and performance conditions only; any other features of share-based payments are not vesting conditions. Other features that are not vesting conditions are to be included in the grant date fair value measurement, which also includes market-related vesting conditions.

Measurement principle. The general principle is that all share-based payment transactions should be recognized in the financial statements at fair value, with asset or expense recognized when the goods or services are received. Depending on the type of share-based payment, fair value may be determined based on the value of goods or services received, or by the value of the shares or rights to shares given up. In accordance with IFRS, the following rules should be followed:

1. If the share-based payment is for goods or services (other than services from employees), the share-based payment should be measured by reference to the fair value of goods and services;
2. If the share-based payment is to employees (or those similar to employees), the transaction should be measured by reference to the fair value of the equity instruments granted at the grant date;
3. For cash-settled share-based payments, the fair value should be determined at each reporting date; and
4. If the share-based payment can be settled in cash or in equity, then the equity component should be measured at the grant date only, but the cash component is measured at each reporting date.

EQUITY SHARE-BASED PAYMENT TRANSACTIONS

Measurement. For equity-settled transactions, the fundamental approach is to recognize goods or services received (asset or expense), and the corresponding increase in equity, at the fair value of the goods or services received. If the fair value of the goods or services received cannot be estimated reliably, the value of goods or services received would be valued at the fair value of the equity instruments granted.

Transactions with employees and others that provide similar services are measured at the fair value of equity instruments granted since it is generally not feasible to reliably determine the fair value of the services provided by the employees. The fair value of shares is determined using the following three-tier measurement hierarchy:

1. Observable market prices if available for the equity instruments; if not available, use entity-specific observable market data such as (2) or (3)
2. Market data with reference to a recent transaction in the entity's shares, or
3. A recent independent fair valuation of the entity or its principal assets.

If entity-specific observable market data is not available or it is impracticable to obtain this data, a valuation method should be applied that would use market data to the greatest extent that is practicable. Refer to Chapter 25 for discussion of fair value measurements.

Employee share options. An entity should expense the value of share options granted to an employee over the period during which the employee is earning the option—that is, the period until the option vests (becomes unconditional). If the options vest (become exercisable) immediately, the employee receiving the grant cannot be compelled to perform future services, and accordingly the fair value of the options is compensation in the period of the grant. More commonly, however, there will be a period (several years, typically) of future services required before the options may be exercised; in those cases, compensation is to be recognized over that vesting period. There are two practical difficulties with this:

1. Estimating the value of the share options granted (true even if vesting is immediate); and

2. Allowing for the fact that not all options initially granted will ultimately vest or, if they vest, be exercised by the holders.

IFRS 2 requires that where directly observable market prices are not available (which is virtually always the case for employee share options, since they cannot normally be sold), the entity must estimate fair value using a valuation technique that is "consistent with generally accepted valuation methodologies for pricing financial instruments, and shall incorporate all factors and assumptions that knowledgeable, willing market participants would consider in setting the price." No specific valuation method is endorsed by the standard, however.

Appendix B of the standard notes that all acceptable option pricing models take into account

- The exercise price of the option
- The current market price of the share
- The expected volatility of the share price
- The dividends expected to be paid on the shares
- The risk-free interest rate
- The life of the option

In essence, the grant date value of the share option is the current market price, less the present value of the exercise price, less the dividends that will not be received during the vesting period, adjusted for the expected volatility. The time value of money, as is well understood, arises because the holder of an option is not required to pay the exercise price until the exercise date. Instead, the holder of the option can invest his funds elsewhere, while waiting to exercise the option. According to IFRS 2, the time value of money component is determined by reference to the rate of return available on *risk-free* securities. If the share pays a *dividend,* or is expected to pay a dividend during the life of the option, the value to the holder of the option from delaying payment of the exercise price is only the excess (if any) of the return available on a risk-free security over the return available from exercising the option today and owning the shares. The time value of money component for a dividend-paying share equals the discounted present value of the expected interest income that could be earned less the discounted present value of the expected dividends that will be forgone during the expected life of the option.

The time value associated with *volatility* represents the ability of the holder to profit from appreciation of the underlying shares while being exposed to the loss of only the option premium, and not the full current value of the shares. A more volatile share has a higher probability of big increases or decreases in price, compared with one having lower volatility. As a result, an option on a highly volatile share has a higher probability of a big payoff than an option on a less volatile share, and so has a higher value relating to volatility fair value component. The longer the option term, the more likely, for any given degree of volatility, that the share price will appreciate before option expiration, making exercise attractive. Greater volatility, and longer term, each contribute to the value of the option.

Volatility is the measure of the amount by which a share's price fluctuates during a period. It is expressed as a percentage because it relates share price fluctuations during a period to the share's price at the beginning of the period. Expected annualized volatility is the predicted amount that is the input to the option pricing model. This is calculated largely from the share's historical price fluctuations.

To illustrate this basic concept, assume that the present market price of the underlying shares is €20 per share, and the option plan grants the recipient the right to purchase shares at today's market price at any time during the next five years. If a risk-free rate, such as that available on government treasury notes having maturities of five years is 5%, then the present value of the future payment of €20 is €15.67 {= [€20 ÷ $(1.05)^5$]}, which suggests that the option has a value of (€20 − €15.67 =) €4.33 per share before considering the value of lost dividends. If the shares are expected to pay a dividend of €0.40 per share per year, the present value of the dividend stream that the option holder will forego until exercise five years hence is about €1.64, discounting again at 5%. Therefore, the *net* value of the option being granted, assuming it is expected to be held to the expiration date before being exercised, is (€4.33 − €1.64 =) €2.69 per share. (Although the foregoing computation was based on the full five-year life of the option, the actual requirement is to use the *expected term* of the option, which may be shorter.)

Commercial software is readily available to carry out these calculations. However, accountants must understand the theory underlying these matters so that the software can be appropriately employed and the results verified. Independent auditors, of course, have additional challenges in verifying the financial statement impacts of share-based compensation plans.

Estimating volatility does, however, involve special problems for unlisted or newly listed companies, since the estimate is usually based on an observation of past market movements, which are not available for such entities. The *Basis for Conclusions* says that IASB decided that, nonetheless, an estimate of volatility should still be made. Appendix B of IFRS 2 states that newly listed entities should compute actual volatility for whatever period this information is available, and should also consider volatility in the prices of shares of other companies operating in the same industry. Unlisted entities should consider the volatility of prices of listed entities in the same industry, or, where valuing them on the basis of a model, such as net earnings, should use the volatility of the earnings.

IASB considered the effect of the *nontransferability* on the value of the option. The standard option pricing models (such as Black-Scholes) were developed to value traded options and do not take into account any effect on value of nontransferability. It came to the view that nontransferability generally led to the option being exercised early, and that this should be reflected in the expected term of the option, rather than by any explicit adjustment for nontransferability itself.

The likelihood of the option vesting is a function of the vesting conditions. IASB concluded that these conditions should not be factored into the value of the option, but should be reflected in calculating the number of options to be expensed. For example, if an entity granted options to 500 employees, the likelihood that only 350 would satisfy the vesting conditions should be used to determine the number of options expensed, and this should be subsequently adjusted in the light of actual experience as it unfolds.

Employee share options: Valuation models. IFRS 2 fully imposes a fair value approach to measuring the effect of share options granted to employees. It recognizes that directly observable prices for employee options are not likely to exist, and thus that valuation models will have to be employee in most, or almost all, instances. The standard speaks to the relative strengths of two types of approaches: the venerable Black-Scholes (now called Black-Scholes-Merton, or BSM) option pricing model, designed specifically to price publicly traded European-style options (exercisable only at the expiration date) and subject to criticism as to possible inapplicability to nonmarketable American-style options; and the mathematically more challenging but more flexible lattice models, such as the binomial. IFRS 2 does not dictate choice of model and acknowledges that the Black-Scholes model may be validly applied in many situations.

To provide a more detailed examination of these two major types of options valuation approaches, several examples will now follow.

Both valuation models (hereinafter referred to as BSM and binomial) must take into account the following factors, at a minimum:

1. Exercise price of the option
2. Expected term of the option, taking into account several things including the contractual term of the option, vesting requirements, and postvesting employee termination behaviors
3. Current price of the underlying share
4. Expected volatility of the price of the underlying share
5. Expected dividends on the underlying share
6. Risk-free interest rate(s) for the expected term of the option

In practice, there are likely to be ranges of reasonable estimates for expected volatility, dividends, and option term. The closed form models, of which BSM is the most widely regarded, are predicated on a set of assumptions that remain invariant over the full term of the option. For example, the expected dividend on the shares on which options are issued must be a fixed amount each period over the full term of the option. In the real world, of course, the condition of invariability is almost never satisfied. For this reason, current thinking is that a lattice model, of which the binomial model is an example, would be preferred. Lattice models explicitly identify nodes, such as the anniversaries of the grant date, at each of which new parameter values can be specified (e.g., expected dividends can be independently defined each period).

Other features that may affect the value of the option include changes in the issuer's credit risk, if the value of the awards contains cash settlement features (i.e., if they are liability instruments). Also, contingent features that could cause either a loss of equity shares earned or reduced realized gains from sale of equity instruments earned, such as a "clawback" feature (for example, where an employee who terminates the employment relationship and begins to work for a competitor is required to transfer to the issuing entity shares granted and earned under a share-based payment arrangement.

Before presenting specific examples of accounting for share options, simple examples of calculating the fair value of options using both the BSM and the binomial methods are provided. First, an example of the BSM, closed-form model is provided.

BSM actually computes the theoretical value of a "European" call option, where exercise can occur only at the expiration date. "American" options, which describes most employee share options, can be exercised at any time until expiration. The value of an American-style option on dividend-paying shares is generally greater than a European-style option, since preexercise, the holder does not have a right to receive dividends that are paid on the shares. (For non-dividend-paying shares, the values of American and European options will tend to converge.) BSM ignores dividends, but this is readily dealt with, as shown below, by deducting from the computed option value the present value of expected dividend stream over the option holding period.

BSM also is predicated on constant volatility over the option term, which available evidence suggests may not be a wholly accurate description of share price behavior. On the other hand, the reporting entity would find it very difficult, if not impossible, to compute differing volatilities for each node in the lattice model described later in this section, lacking a factual basis for presuming that volatility would increase or decrease in specific future periods.

The BSM model is

$$C \quad = \quad SN(d1) - Ke^{(-rt)}N(d2)$$

Where:

C	=	Theoretical call premium
S	=	Current share price
t	=	Time until option expiration
K	=	Option striking price
r	=	Risk-free interest rate
N	=	Cumulative standard normal distribution
e	=	Exponential term (2.7183)
d_1	=	$\dfrac{\ln(S/K) + (r+s^2/2)^t}{svvt}$
d_2	=	$d_2 = d_1 - s$
s	=	Standard deviation of share returns
ln	=	Natural logarithm

The BSM valuation is illustrated with the following assumed facts; note that dividends are ignored in the initial calculation but will be addressed once the theoretical value is computed. Also note that volatility is defined in terms of the variability of the entity's share price, measured by the standard deviation of prices over the past three years, which is used as a surrogate for expected volatility over the next twelve months.

Example—Determining the fair value of options using the BSM model

BSM is a closed-form model, meaning that it solves for an option price from an equation. It computes a theoretical call price based on five parameters—the current share price, the option exercise price, the expected volatility of the share price, the time until option expiration, and the short-term risk-free interest rate. Of these, expected volatility is the most difficult to ascertain. Volatility is generally computed as the standard deviation of recent historical returns on the shares. In the following example, the shares are currently selling at €40 and the standard deviation of prices (daily closing prices can be used, among other possible choices) over the past several years was €6.50, thus yielding an estimated volatility of €6.50/€40 = 16.25%.

Assume the following facts:

S	=	€40
t	=	2 years
K	=	€45
r	=	3% annual rate
s	=	Standard deviation of percentage returns = 16.25% (based on €6.50 Standard deviation of share price compared to current €40 price)

From the foregoing data, all of which is known information (the volatility, s, is computed or assumed, as discussed above) the factors d_1 and d_2 can be computed. The cumulative standard normal variates (N) of these values must then be determined (using a table or formula), following which the BSM option value is calculated, *before the effect of dividends*. In this example, the computed amounts are

$N(d_1)$	=	0.2758
$N(d_2)$	=	0.2048

With these assumptions the value of the share options is approximately €2.35. This is derived from the BSM as follows:

$$C = SN(d_1) - Ke^{(-rt)}N(d_2)$$
$$= 40(.2758) - 45(.942)(.2048)$$
$$= 11.032 - 8.679$$
$$= 2.35$$

The foregone two-year stream of dividends, which in this example are projected to be €0.50 annually, have a present value of €0.96. Therefore, the net value of this option is €1.39 (= €2.35– .96).

Example—Determining the fair value of options using the binomial model

In contrast to the BSM, the binomial model is an open form, inductive model. It allows for multiple (theoretically, unlimited) branches of possible outcomes on a "tree" of possible price movements and induces the option's price. As compared to the BSM approach, this relaxes the constraint on exercise timing. It can be assumed that exercise occurs at any point in the option period, and past experience may guide the reporting entity to make certain such assumptions (e.g., that one-half of the options will be exercised when the market price of the shares reach 150% of the strike price). It also allows for varying dividends from period to period.

It is assumed that the common (Cox, Ross, and Rubinstein) binomial model will be used in practice. To keep this preliminary example relatively simple in order to focus on the concepts involved, a single-step binomial model is provide here for illustrative purposes. Assume an option is granted of a €20 share that will expire in one year. The option exercise price equals the share price of €20. Also, assume there is a 50% chance that the price will jump 20% over the year and a 50% chance the shares will drop 20%, and that no other outcomes are possible. The risk-free interest rate is 4%. With these assumptions there are three basic calculations.

1. Plot the two possible future share prices.
2. Translate these share prices into future options values.
3. Discount these future values into a single present value.

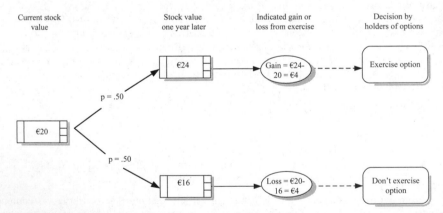

In this case, the option will only have value if the share price increases, and otherwise the option would expire worthless and unexercised. In this simplistic example, there is only a 50% chance of the option having a value of (€4 ÷ 1.04 =) €3.84, and therefore the option is worth (€3.84 × .50 =) €1.92 at grant date.

The foregoing was a simplistic single-period, two-outcome model. A more complicated and realistic binomial model extends this single-period model into a randomized walk of many steps or intervals. In theory, the time to expiration can be broken into a large number of ever-smaller time intervals, such as months, weeks, or days. The advantage is that the parameter values (volatility, etc.) can then be varied with greater precision from one period to the next (assuming, or course, that there is a factual basis upon which to base these estimates). Calculating the binomial model then involves the same three calculation steps. First, the possible future share prices are determined for each branch, using the volatility input and time to expiration (which grows shorter with each successive node in the model). This permits computation of terminal values for each branch of the tree. Second, future share prices are translated into option values at each node of the tree. Third, these future option values are discounted and added to produce a single present value of the option, taking into account the probabilities of each series of price moves in the model.

Example—Multiperiod option valuation using the binomial model

Consider the following example of a two-period binomial model. Again, certain simplifying assumptions will be made so that a manual calculation can be illustrated (in general, computer programs will be necessary to compute option values). Eager Corp. grants 10,000 options to its employees at a time when the market price of shares is €40. The options expire in two years; expected dividends on the shares will be €0.50 per year; and the risk-free rate is currently 3%, which is not expected to change over the two-year horizon. The option exercise price is €43.

The entity's past experience suggests that, after one year (of the two-year term) elapses, if the market price of the share exceeds the option exercise price, one-half of the options will be exercised by the holders. The other holders will wait another year to decide. If at the end of the second year—without regard to what the share value was at the end of the first year—the market value exceeds the exercise price, all the remaining options will be exercised. The workforce has been unusually stable and it is not anticipated that option holders will cease employment before the end of the option period.

The share price moves randomly from period to period. Based on recent experience, it is anticipated that in each period the shares may increase by €5, stay the same, or decrease by €5, with equal probability, versus the price at the period year-end. Thus since the price is €40 at grant date, one year hence it might be either €45, €40, or €35. The price at the end of the second year will follow the same pattern, based on the price when the first year ends.

Logically, holders will rather exercise their options than see them expire, as long as there is gain to be realized. Since dividends are not paid on options, holders have a motive to exercise earlier than the expiration date, which explains why historically one-half the options are exercised after one year elapses, as long as the market price exceeds the exercise price at that date, even though the exercising holders risk future market declines.

The binomial model formulation requires that each sequence of events and actions be explained. This gives rise to the commonly seen decision tree representation. In this simple example, following the grant of the options, one of three possible events occur: either the share price rises €5 over the next year, or it remains constant, or it falls by €5. Since these outcomes have equal a priori probabilities, p=1/3 is assigned to each outcome of this first year event. If the price does rise, one-half the option holders will exercise at the end of the first year, to reap the economic gain and capture the second year's dividend. The other holders will forego this immediate gain and wait to see what the share price does in the second year before making an exercise decision.

If the share price in the first year either remains flat or falls by €5, no option holders are expected to exercise. However, there remains the opportunity to exercise after the second year elapses, if the share price recovers. Of course, holding the options for the second year means that no dividends will be received.

The cost of the options granted by Eager Corp., measured by fair value using the binomial model approach is computed by the sum of the probability-weighted outcomes, discounted to present value using the risk-free rate. In this example, the rate is expected to remain at 3% per year throughout the option period, but it could be independently specified for each period—another advantage the binomial model has over the more rigid BSM. The sum of these present value computations measures the cost of compensation incorporated in the option grant, regardless of what pattern of exercise ultimately is revealed, since at the grant date, using the available information about share price volatility, expected dividends, exercise behavior and the risk-free rate, this best measures the value of what was promised to the employees.

The following graphic offers a visual representation of the model, although in practice it is not necessary to prepare such a document. The actual calculations can be made by computer program, but to illustrate the application of the binomial model, the computation will be presented explicitly here. There are four possible scenarios under which, in this example, holders will exercise the options, and thus the options will have value. All other scenarios (combinations of share price movements over the two-year horizon) will cause the holders to allow the options to expire unexercised.

First, if the share price goes to €45 in the first year, one-half the holders will exercise at that point, paying the exercise price of €43 per share. This results in a gain of €2 (= €45 – €43) per share. However, having waited until the first year-end, they lost the opportunity to receive the €0.50 per share dividend, so the net economic gain is only €1.50 (= €2.00 – €0.50) per share. As this occurs after one year, the present value is only €1.50 × 1.03^{-1} = €1.46 per share. When this is weighted by the probability of this outcome obtaining (given that the share price rise to €45 in the first year has only a 1/3 probability of happening, and given further that only one-half the option holders would elect to exercise under such conditions), the actual expected value of this outcome is [(1/3)(1/2)(€1.46) =] €0.24. More formally,

$$[(1/3)(1/2)(€2.00 – €0.50)] \times 1.03^{-1} = €0.2427$$

The second potentially favorable outcome to holders would be if the share price rises to €45 the first year and then either rises another €5 the second year or holds steady at €45 during the second year. In either event, the option holders who did not exercise after the first year's share price rise will all exercise at the end of the second year, before the options expire. If the price goes to €50 the second year, the holders will reap a gross gain of €7 (=€50 – €43) per share; if it remains constant at €45, the gross gain is only €2 per share. In either case, dividends in both years one and two will have been foregone. To calculate the compensation cost associated with these branches of the model, the first-year dividend lost must be discounted for one year, and the gross gain and the second-year dividend must be discounted for years. Also, the probabilities of the entire sequence of events must be used, taking into account the likelihood of the first year's share price rise, the proclivity of holders to wait for a second year to elapse, and the likelihood of a second-year price rise or price stability. These computations are shown below.

For the outcome if the share price rises again

$[(1/3)(1/2)(1/3)] \{[(€7.00) \times 1.03^{-2}] – [(€0.50) \times 1.03^{-1}] – [€0.50 \times 1.03^{-2}]\} =$
$[0.05544] \{€6.59 – €0.48 – €0.47\} = €0.31276$

For the outcome if the share price remains stable

$[(1/3)(1/2)(1/3)] \{[(€2.00) \times 1.03^{-2}] – [(€0.50) \times 1.03^{-1}] – [€0.50 \times 1.03^{-2}]\} =$
$[0.05544] \{€1.88 – €0.48 – €0.47\} = €0.05147$

The final favorable outcome for holders would occur if the share price holds constant at €40 the first year but rises to €45 the second year, making exercise the right decision. Note that none of the holders would exercise after the first year given that the price, €40, was below exercise price. The calculation for this sequence of events is as follows:

$[(1/3)(1/3)] \{[(€2.00) \times 1.03^{-2}] – [(€0.50) \times 1.03^{-1}] – [€0.50 \times 1.03^{-2}]\} =$
$[0.1111] \{€1.88 – €0.48 – €0.47\} = €0.10295$

Summing these values yields €0.709879 (€0.2427 + €0.31276 + €0.05147 + €0.10295), which is the expected value per optional granted. When this per-unit value is then multiplied by the number of options granted, 10,000, the total compensation cost to be recognized, €7,098.79, is derived. This would be attributed over the required service period, which is illustrated later in this section. (In the facts of this example, no vesting requirements were specified; in such cases, the employees would not have to provide future service in order to earn the right to the options, and the entire cost would be recognized upon grant.)

A big advantage of the binomial model is that it can value an option that is exercisable before the end of its term (i.e., an American-style option). This is the form that employee share-based compensation arrangements normally take. IASB appears to recognize the virtues of the binomial type of model, because it can incorporate the unique features of employee share options. Two key features that should generally be incorporated into the binomial model are vesting restrictions and early exercise. Doing so, however, requires that the reporting entity will have had previous experience with employee behaviors (e.g., gained with past employee option programs) that would provide it with a basis for making estimates of future behavior. In some instances, there will be no obvious bases upon which such assumptions can be developed.

The binomial model permits the specification of more assumptions than does the BSM, which has generated the perception that the binomial will more readily be manipulated so as to result in lower option values, and hence lower compensation costs, when contrasted to the BSM. But, this is not necessarily the case: switching from BSM to the binomial model can increase, maintain, or decrease the option's value. Having the ability to specify additional parameters, however, does probably give management greater flexibility and, accordingly, will present additional challenges for the auditors who must attest to the financial statement effects of management's specification of these variables.

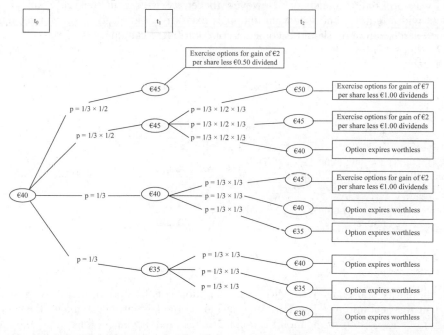

Accounting entries. Having calculated the fair value of the option at the grant date, this value then has to be expensed through the statement of comprehensive income by allocation over the financial years during which the option is vesting, since it is over that period that the grantee is presumably earning the related compensation. The corresponding credit is made to an equity account.

> Suppose a company grants 1,000 share options with a vesting period of four years to 50 employees. The fair value of each option is determined to be €20, and the company expects, in light of past experience with employee turnover and other factors, that 75% of the options will vest. Ignore graded vesting features of these options. The expense (and credit to equity) in the first year will be (50,000 options × €20 × 0.75 × 0.25 =) €187,500.

At the end of the second year, the entity now considers that 80% of the options will probably vest. As with all changes in accounting estimates, the impact of this reassessment is allocated to current and future period, with no adjustment to already-concluded fiscal periods. The expense for the current (second) year is the cumulative cost based on the new parameter values, less the amount already expensed in the first year. The cumulative amount is (50,000 options × €20 × 0.80 × 0.5 =) €400,000. The year two expense therefore will be (€400,000 – €187,500 =) €212,500.

Assume that in year three there are no changes to the estimates, and the cumulative cost over the three-year period accordingly is (50,000 × €20 × 0.80 × 0.75 =) €600,000. The annual expense in year three therefore is (€600,000 – €400,000 =) €200,000.

At the end of the four-year vesting period, 41 (or 82%) of the original employees granted options are still with the company, and their options vest. The fourth year's expense (and credit to equity) takes into account the actual options vested. The cumulative cost is (50,000 × €20 × 0.82 =) €820,000 and the fourth year's expense is (€820,000 – €600,000 =) €220,000.

At some future date some or all of the options may be exercised by the remaining employees, but this will not necessarily occur. IFRS 2 takes the view that the amount credited to equity, arising from the issue of options, is *not* to be adjusted subsequently to take account of any failure to exercise the options (which is termed a forfeiture). This is consistent with the belief that the accounting for options should be a reflection of the bargain made when the option was originally agreed to. However, the entity is free to reclassify any of these amounts within equity, and where an option is exercised, the original amount recognized, plus the exercise amount, should become part of contributed capital.

The journal entries would be

	Debit	Credit	*Memorandum cumulative equity item*
Year 1			
Employee remuneration	187,500		
Share options		187,500	187,500
Year 2			
Employee remuneration	212,500		
Share options		212,500	400,000
Year 3			
Employee remuneration	200,000		
Share options		200,000	600,000
Year 4			
Employee remuneration	220,000		
Share options		220,000	820,000

If the entity subsequently modifies the conditions of the option, then this must be reflected in the accounting. The fair value at the original grant date remains the *minimum amount to be expensed*. If the modification increases the fair value—for example, by reducing the exercise price or increasing the number of shares—the additional fair value must be expensed in the period from the modification date to the new vesting date. If the vesting conditions are changed in a way that would likely increase the probability of vesting, then this will be reflected in the number of options expected to vest. If the modification reduces the fair value, then the original fair value continues to be the basis of expensing.

If the entity cancels the option or settles it before the end of the vesting period, this should be treated as an acceleration of the vesting period, and the original fair value at grant date should be expensed over the shorter period. If a payment is made to the employee in respect of the cancellation or settlement, this is treated as a repurchase of an equity interest, and is deducted from equity. In the event that the payment exceeds the value recognized in equity, the excess is reported as an expense. If the entity settles by issuing a new option, this is treated as a modification of the original scheme and accounted for accordingly. The current IFRS 2 specifies the accounting method when an entity cancels a grant of equity instruments but does not state how cancellations by a party other than the entity should be accounted for.

Employee share options with graded vesting characteristics and service conditions. Under IFRS 2, the compensation expense for share options with graded vesting characteristics and service conditions must be made on an accelerated attribution basis. Unlike US GAAP, IFRS does not permit the straight-line method for attribution of compensation cost of share options with service conditions and graded vesting characteristics. A graded vesting plan assigns the share options to the period in which they vest. This is because IFRS 2 views each tranche of vesting as a separate grant for which service has been provided since the date of the original grant.

The mandatory use of the accelerated amortization method for stock options with graded vesting features results in a higher compensation cost in the earlier years of the vesting period as shown in the example below.

1,000 share options are granted to 100 employees at a grant price of €10 per option which gives a total share option grant value of €1,000,000. The share option plan provides for a graded vesting of these 1,000 share options, in four equal tranches over a four-year period (or 25%) at each anniversary of the grant. Ignore forfeiture rates for this example. Under the accelerated attribution method, the compensation cost for each of the four years is as follows:

	Year 1	*Year 2*	*Year 3*	*Year 4*
First year vesting 25%	€250,000			
Second year vesting 25%	125,000	€125,000		
Third year vesting 25%	83,333	83,333	€83,333	
Fourth year vesting 25%	62,500	62,500	62,500	€62,500
Total Compensation Cost for each of the years	520,833	270,833	145,833	62,500

Accordingly, options which vest in Year 2 are deemed to have a two-year vesting period and the ones which vest in Year 3 have a three-year vesting period. The accelerated attribution method shows that the compensation cost for graded options is highly front loaded from the year of grant. The straight line method of attribution followed under US GAAP would have resulted in a share option compensation expense of only €250,000 in Year 1 compared to €520,833 under IFRS.

Modifications, cancellations, and settlements. An entity may modify the terms on which equity instruments were granted during the vesting period (or after the vesting period), for example, by reducing the exercise price of an option, issuing more instruments, reducing the vesting period or modifying or eliminating a performance condition. Such modifications usually have an effect on the expense that will be recognized. Determining whether a change in terms and conditions would affect the measurement of the amount recognized as expense depends on whether the fair value of the new instruments is greater than the fair value of the original instruments at the modification date as follows:

- If the fair value of the new instruments (after the modification) is more than the fair value of the original instruments (before the modification), the incremental fair value granted should be recognized over the remaining vesting period in a manner similar to the original amount. If this modification takes place after the vesting period, the incremental value should be recognized immediately;
- If the fair value of the new instruments is less than the fair value of the original instruments and apparently is not beneficial to the employees, the amount of expense is

recognized as if that modification had not occurred, based on the original fair value of equity instruments.

Cancellations or settlements of equity-settled share-based payment awards, whether by action of the reporting entity or by other parties, should be accounted for as an acceleration of the vesting period. Any amounts not previously recognized as compensation expense (that would have been recognized over the remainder of the vesting period) are fully recognized as of the date of cancellation. Any payments made with the cancellation of settlement (up to the fair value of equity instruments) to the holder are treated as equity repurchases. Any payments made in excess of the fair value of the equity instruments granted should be expensed at the date of cancellation.

Nonemployee transactions. Share-based payments to nonemployees are fairly rare, and are perhaps encountered most frequently in connection with start-up entities, which are often cash-starved and thus willing to dilute ownership in return for the provision of vital services or goods by vendors willing to accept payment in entity shares. The basic principle of IFRS 2 is that such transactions are expensed as measured by the fair value of the goods or services received. For nonemployee transactions, there is a rebuttable presumption that the value of the goods or services can be measured reliably. That fair value is measured at the date the goods are received or the services are rendered. Per IFRS 2, only "in rare cases," if the entity concludes that it cannot measure these, should the expense be measured by reference to the fair value of the instruments granted.

It should be noted that this also has a bearing on revenue recognition by the counterparty (the entity providing the goods or services and receiving the shares). One of the abuses noted during the late 1990s "dot-com" market bubble was that the same parcel of shares, exchanged for professional services in connection with a start-up, was valued very modestly by the issuing company (for purposes of computing the expense to be recognized), but was simultaneously valued much more highly by the service provider (as revenue). If the transaction is accounted for at the fair value of the services provided, obviously that value should be exactly the same, seen from either party's perspective.

CASH-SETTLED SHARE-BASED PAYMENT TRANSACTIONS

Sometimes employees will receive a variable amount of remuneration, as part of their compensation packages that is based on the performance of the entity's shares, but resulting in an additional cash payment to the employee, rather than an equity instrument. This describes for example the issuance of share appreciation rights plans, or of shares that are redeemable by the company either mandatorily (e.g., upon cessation of employment) or at the holder's election. For cash-settled share-based payments, the goods or services received and the liability incurred are measured at the fair value of the liability. The calculation of compensation expense is to be based on the fair value of the liability when the goods and services are received, with the corresponding credit to a liability account, not to equity. Another important distinction: the liability must be remeasured at each reporting date, unlike straight option grants, which are fixed in value at the date of grant. Any changes in fair value are recognized in profit or loss for the reporting period.

Share-Based Payment Transactions with Cash Alternatives

An entity may make an arrangement where the terms provide either the entity or the employee (or other counterparty) with a choice of cash (or other assets) or equity settlement. In this case, the entity should value the option as a compound financial instrument, and value first the right to receive cash, as a liability (a cash-settled share-based transaction), and then the right to receive any additional amount as equity (an equity-settled share-based transaction). Consequently, the fair value of the compound financial instrument is the sum of the fair values of the two components: first, the fair value of the debt component is measured, and next, the fair value of the equity component—taking into consideration that the counterparty must forfeit the right to receive cash in order to receive the share option. IFRS 2 notes that in many cases the arrangement is structured so that the equity alternative has the same value as the cash alternative, in which case the whole amount is considered to be debt, since there is no extra value in the equity choice.

If the employee decides at the date of exercise to receive the equity alternative, the liability is remeasured at fair value and transferred directly into equity. If the employee takes the cash alternative, the liability is extinguished. However, if a separate equity element had been established, this remains part of equity, as with other vested options that are not exercised.

The entity should account for the share-based transaction in which the entity has a choice of whether to settle in cash or by issuing equity instruments as a cash-settled share-based transaction unless either

- The entity used to settle by issuing equity instruments in the past; or
- The settlement in cash has no commercial substance.

In some cases the choice between cash settlement and equity settlement is in the hands of the employer. Here the standard relies on the present obligation notion similar to that used in IAS 37: where the company has a past history of making cash settlements or a stated policy of doing this (i.e., where there is a reasonable expectation of cash settlement), the transaction is considered to give rise to a liability. Also, if the choice of settlement in equity instruments has no commercial substance, because for example the cash settlement bears no relationship to, and is likely to be lower in value than, the fair value of the equity instruments or the entity is legally prohibited from issuing shares, the entity has a present obligation to settle in cash. In the absence of such an obligation, the entity would account for the transaction as equity-settled. In the event that the entity ultimately decides to settle in cash, the cash payment is treated as a repurchase of equity.

SHARE-BASED TRANSACTIONS AMONG GROUP ENTITIES

The 2009 amendments to IFRS 2 incorporated the guidance contained previously in IFRIC 11 (and IFRIC 11, *Group and Treasury Share Transactions*, accordingly was withdrawn). For share-based transactions among group entities, in its separate or individual financial statements, the entity receiving the goods or services should measure the expense as either an *equity-settled* or *cash-settled* share-based transaction by assessing

1. The nature of the awards granted, and
2. Its own rights and obligations.

The entity receiving goods or services may recognize a different amount than the amount recognized by the consolidated group or by another group entity settling the share-based payment transaction.

The entity should measure the expense as an *equity-settled* share-based payment transaction (and remeasure this expense only for changes in vesting conditions) when

1. The awards granted are its own equity instruments, or
2. The entity has no obligation to settle the share-based payment transaction.

In all other cases, the expense should be measured as a *cash-settled* share-based payment transaction. Consequently, the entity should recognize the transaction as an *equity-settled* share-based transaction *only* if it is to be settled in the entity's own equity instruments (in all other circumstances the transaction is a *cash-settled* share-based payment transaction). In group transactions based on repayment arrangements that require the payment of the equity instruments to the suppliers of goods or services, the entity receiving goods or services should recognize the share-based payment expense regardless of repayment arrangements.

For example, there are various circumstances whereby a parent entity's equity shares are granted to employees of its subsidiaries. One common situation occurs where the parent is publicly traded but its subsidiaries are not (e.g., where the subsidiaries are wholly owned by the parent company), and thus the parent company's shares are the only "currency" that can be used in share-based payments to employees. If the arrangement is accounted for as an equity-settled transaction in the consolidated (group) financial statements of the parent company, the subsidiary is to measure the services under the equity-settled share-based payment transaction. A capital contribution by the parent is also recognized by the subsidiary in such situations.

Furthermore, if the employee transfers from one subsidiary to another, each is to measure compensation expense by reference to the fair value of the equity instruments at the date the rights were granted by the parent, allocated according to the relative portion of the vesting period the employee works for each subsidiary. There is no remeasurement associated with the transfer between entities. If a vesting condition other than a market condition (defined by IFRS 2, Appendix A) is not met and the share-based compensation is forfeited, each subsidiary adjusts previously recognized compensation cost to remove cumulative compensation cost from each of the subsidiaries.

On the other hand, if the subsidiary grants rights to its parent company's shares to the subsidiary's employees, that entity accounts for this as a cash-settled transaction. This means the obligation is reported as a liability, and adjusted to fair value at each reporting date.

In group transactions based on repayment arrangements that require the payment of the equity instruments to the suppliers of goods or services, the entity receiving goods or services should recognize the share-based payment expense regardless of repayment arrangements.

DISCLOSURE

IFRS 2 imposes extensive disclosure requirements, calling for an analysis of share-based payments made during the year, of their impact on earnings and financial position, and of the basis upon which fair values were measured. An entity should disclose information enabling users of the financial statements to understand the nature and extent of share-based payment transactions that occurred during the period.

Each type of share-based payment transaction that existed during the year must be described, giving vesting requirements, the maximum term of the options, and the method of settlement (but entities that have several "substantially similar" schemes may aggregate this information). The movement (i.e., changes) within each scheme must be analyzed, including the number of share options and the weighted-average exercise price for the following:

- Outstanding at the beginning of the year
- Granted during the year
- Forfeited during the year

- Exercised during the year (plus the weighted-average share price at the time of exercise)
- Expired during the year
- Outstanding at the end of the period (plus the range of exercise prices and the weighted-average remaining contractual life).
- Exercisable at the end of the period

The entity must disclose the total expense recognized in the statement of comprehensive income arising from share-based payment transactions, and a subtotal of that part which was settled by the issue of equity. Where the entity has liabilities arising from share-based payment transactions, the total amount at the end of the period must be separately disclosed, as must be the total intrinsic value of those options that had vested.

The fair value methodology disclosures apply to new instruments issued during the reporting period, or old instruments modified in that time. Regarding share options, the entity must disclose the weighted-average fair value, plus details of how fair value was measured. These will include the option pricing model used, the weighted-average share price, the exercise price, expected volatility, option life, expected dividends, the risk-free interest rate and any other inputs. The measurement of expected volatility must be explained, as must be the manner in which any other features of the option were incorporated in the measurement.

Where a modification of an existing arrangement has taken place, the entity should provide an explanation of the modifications, and disclose the incremental fair value and the basis on which that was measured (as above).

Where a share-based payment was made to a nonemployee, such as a vendor, the entity should confirm that fair value was determined directly by reference to the market price for the goods or services.

If equity instruments *other than share options* were granted during the period, the number and weighted-average fair value of these should be disclosed together with the basis for measuring fair value, and if this was not market value, then how it was measured. The disclosure should cover how expected dividends were incorporated into the value and what other features were incorporated into the measurement.

Financial Statement Presentation under IFRS

The following is an illustration of the treatment of equity that may be required in the financial statements.

Equity Section of Consolidated Statement of Financial Position

	2011		*2010*
(in thousands of euros)			
Ordinary shares			
Authorized: 10,000,000 Par value = €1			
Issued: 6,650,000		6,650	6,585
Share premium and reserves			
Share premium	12,320		12,110
Legal reserve	665		665
Share options granted	724		676
Translation adjustment	(1,854)		(2,266)
Treasury shares	(320)		(320)
		11,535	10,865
Retained earnings		4,230	3,898
Owners of the parent company		22,415	21,348
Noncontrolling interest		360	353
Total equity		22,775	21,701

Examples of Financial Statement Disclosures

SAB Miller plc
Annual Report 2011

Consolidated statement of changes in equity
For the year ended March 31

	Called up share capital US $m	Share premium account US $m	Merger relief reserve US $m	Other reserves US $m	Retained earnings US $m	Total shareholders' equity US $m	Noncontrolling interests US $m	Total equity US $m
At April 1, 2009	159	6,198	3,395	(872)	6,496	15,376	741	16,117
Total comprehensive income	-	-	-	2,194	1,881	4,075	155	4,230
Profit for the year	-	-	-	-	1,910	1,910	171	2,081
Other comprehensive income	-	-	-	2,194	(29)	2,165	(16)	2,149
Dividends paid	-	-	-	-	(924)	(924)	(162)	(1,086)
Issue of SAB Miller plc ordinary shares	6	114	1,191	-	-	1,311	-	1,311
Payment for purchase of own shares for share trusts	-	-	-	-	(8)	(8)	-	(8)
Arising on business combinations	-	-	-	-	-	-	21	21
Buyout of noncontrolling interests	-	-	-	-	-	-	(72)	(72)
Credit entry relating to share-based payments	-	-	-	-	80	80	-	80
At March 31, 2010[1]	165	6,312	4,586	1,322	7,525	19,910	683	20,593
Total comprehensive income	-	-	-	559	2,345	2,904	143	3,047
Profit for the year	-	-	-	-	2,408	2,408	149	2,557
Other comprehensive income	-	-	-	559	(63)	496	(6)	490
Dividends paid	-	-	-	-	(1,115)	(1,115)	(106)	(1,221)
Issue of SAB Miller plc ordinary shares	1	72	-	-	-	73	-	73
Proceeds from the issue of shares in subsidiaries to noncontrolling interests	-	-	-	-	-	-	34	34
Buyout of noncontrolling interests	-	-	-	-	(10)	(10)	(3)	(13)
Credit entry relating to share-based payments	-	-	-	-	246	246	-	246
At March 31, 2011	166	6,384	4,586	1,881	8,991	22,008	751	22,759

Notes to the financial statements

1. **Accounting Policies**

p) **Share capital**

Ordinary shares are classified as equity. Incremental costs directly attributable to the issue of new shares or options are shown in equity as a deduction, net of tax, from the proceeds.

q) **Investments in own shares (treasury and shares held by employee benefit trusts)**

Shares held by employee share ownership plans, employee benefit trusts and in treasury are treated as a deduction from equity until the shares are cancelled, reissued, or disposed.

Purchases of such shares are classified in the cash flow statement as a purchase of own shares for share trusts or purchase of own shares for treasury within net cash from financing activities.

Where such shares are subsequently sold or reissued, any consideration received, net of any directly attributable incremental costs and related tax effects, is included in equity attributable to the company's equity shareholders.

w) **Employee benefits**

(iv) Share-based compensation

The group operates a variety of equity-settled share-based compensation plans. These comprise share option plans (with and without market performance conditions attached), performance share award plans (with market conditions attached) and awards related to the employee element of the Broad-Based Black Economic Empowerment (BBBEE) scheme in South Africa. An expense is recognized to spread the fair value of each award granted after November 7, 2002, over the vesting period on a straight-line basis, after allowing for an estimate of the share awards that will eventually vest. A corresponding adjustment is made to equity over the remaining vesting period. The estimate of the level of vesting is reviewed at least annually, with any impact on the cumulative charge being recognized immediately. In addition the group has granted an equity-settled share-based payment to retailers in relation to the retailer element of the BBBEE scheme. A one-off charge has been recognized based on the fair value at the grant date with a corresponding adjustment to equity. The charge will not be adjusted in the future.

The charges are based on the fair value of the awards as at the date of grant, as calculated by various binomial model calculations and Monte Carlo simulations.

The charges are not reversed if the options and awards are not exercised because the market value of the shares is lower than the option price at the date of grant.

The proceeds received net of any directly attributable transaction costs are credited to share capital (nominal value) and share premium when the options are exercised.

6. **Employee and key management compensation costs**

a. **Employee costs**

	2011 US $m	2010 US $m
Wages and salaries	**1,837**	1,631
Share-based payments	**130**	80
Social security costs	**172**	168
Pension costs	**114**	106
Postretirement benefits other than pensions	**5**	13
	2,258	1,998

Of the US $2,258 million employee costs shown above, US $18 million (2010: US $13 million) has been capitalized within intangible assets and property, plant, and equipment.

26. Share capital

	2011 US $m	2010 US $m
Group and company		
Called up, allocated and fully paid share capital		
1,659,040,014 ordinary shares of 10 US cents each (2010: 1,654,749,852)	**166**	165
50,000 deferred shares of £1.00 each (2010: 50,000)	-	-
	166	165

	Ordinary share of 10 US cents each	Deferred shares of £1 each	Nominal value US $m
At April 1, 2009	1,585,366,969	50,000	159
Issue of shares—share incentive plans	9,382,883	-	-
Issue of shares—Polish noncontrolling interest buyout transaction	60,000,000	-	6
At March 31, 2010	1,654,749,852	50,000	165
Issue of shares—share incentive plans	4,290,162	-	1
At March 31, 2011	**1,659,040,014**	50,000	166

Changes to authorized share capital

With effect from October 1, 2009, the company adopted new articles of association which removed any previous limit on the authorized share capital. Directors are still limited as to the number of shares they can at any time allot because allotment authority continues to be required under the Companies Act 2006, save in respect of employee share schemes.

Changes to issued share capital

During the year, the company issued 4,290,162 (2010: 9,382,883) new ordinary shares of 10 US cents to satisfy the exercise of options granted under the various share incentive plans, for consideration of US $73 million (2010: US $114 million).

On May 29, 2009, 60 million new ordinary shares of 10 US cents were issued as consideration for the purchase of the remaining 28.1% noncontrolling interest in the group's Polish subsidiary, Kompania Piwowarska SA.

Rights and restrictions relating to share capital

Convertible participating shares. Altria is entitled to require the company to convert its ordinary shares into convertible participating shares so as to ensure that Altria's voting shareholding does not exceed 24.99% of the total voting shareholding.

If such an event occurs, the convertible participating shares will rank pari passu with the ordinary shares in all respects and no action shall be taken by the company in relation to ordinary shares unless the same action is taken in respect of the convertible participating shares. On distribution of the profits (whether by cash dividend, dividend in specie, scrip dividend, capitalization issue or otherwise), the convertible participating shares will rank pari passu with the ordinary shares. On a return of capital (whether winding-up or otherwise), the convertible participating shares will rank pari passu with the ordinary shares.

Altria is entitled to vote its convertible participating shares at general meetings of the company on a poll on the basis of one-tenth of a vote for every convertible participating share on all resolutions other than a resolution

    (i) Proposed by any person other than Altria, to wind-up the company;

    (ii) Proposed by any person other than Altria, to appoint an administrator or to approve any arrangement with the company's creditors;

    (iii) Proposed by the board, to sell all or substantially all of the undertaking of the company, or

(iv) Proposed by any person other than Altria, to alter any of the class rights attaching to the convertible participating shares or to approve the creation of any new class of shares,

In which case Altria shall be entitled on a poll to vote on the resolution on the basis of one vote for each convertible participating share, but, for the purposes of any resolution other than a resolution mentioned in (iv) above, the convertible participating shares shall be treated as being of the same class as the ordinary shares and no separate meeting or resolution of the holders of the convertible participating shares shall be required to be convened or passed.

Upon a transfer of convertible participating shares by Altria other than to an affiliate, such convertible participating shares shall convert into ordinary shares.

Altria is entitled to require the company to convert its convertible participating shares into ordinary shares if

(i) A third party has made a takeover offer for the company and (if such offer becomes or is declared unconditional in all respects) it would result in the voting shareholding of the third party being more than 30% of the total voting shareholding; and

(ii) Altria has communicated to the company in writing its intention not itself to make an offer competing with such third party offer, provided that the conversion date shall be no earlier than the date on which the third party's offer becomes or is declared unconditional in all respects.

Altria is entitled to require the company to convert its convertible participating shares into ordinary shares if the voting shareholding of a third party should be more than 24.99%, provided that

(i) The number of ordinary shares held by Altria following such conversion shall be limited to one ordinary share more than the number of ordinary shares held by the third party, and

(ii) Such conversion shall at no time result in Altria's voting shareholding being equal to or greater than the voting shareholding which would require Altria to make a mandatory offer in terms of Rule 9 of the City Code.

If Altria wishes to acquire additional ordinary shares (other than pursuant to a preemptive issue of new ordinary shares or with the prior approval of the board), Altria shall first convert into ordinary shares the lesser of

(i) Such number of convertible participating shares as would result in Altria's voting shareholding being such percentage as would, in the event of Altria subsequently acquiring one additional ordinary share, require Altria to make a mandatory offer in terms of Rule 9 of the City Code; and

(ii) All of its remaining convertible participating shares.

The company shall use its best endeavors to procure that the ordinary shares arising on conversion of the convertible participating shares are admitted to the Official List and to trading on the London Stock Exchange's market for listed securities, admitted to listing and trading on the JSE Ltd., and admitted to listing and trading on any other stock exchange upon which the ordinary shares are from time to time listed and traded, but no admission to listing or trading shall sought for the convertible participating shares while they remain convertible participating shares.

Deferred shares

The deferred shares do not carry any voting rights and do not entitle holders thereof to receive any dividends or other distributions. In the event of a winding-up deferred shareholders would receive no more than the nominal value. Deferred shares represent the only nonequity share capital of the group.

Share-based payments

The group operates various equity-settled share incentive plans. The share incentives outstanding are summarized as follows.

Scheme	2011 Number	2010 Number
GBP share options	**15,088,057**	13,515,685
ZAR share options	**13,686,079**	13,447,779
GBP stock appreciation rights (SARs)	**3,575,370**	4,297,049
GBP performance share awards	**7,364,124**	6,915,855
GBP value share awards	**3,168,200**	-
Total share incentives outstanding [1]	**42,881,830**	38,176,368

[1] *Total share incentives outstanding exclude shares relating to the BBBEE scheme.*

Further details relating to all of the share incentive schemes can be found in the remuneration report on pages 65 to 75.

The exercise prices of incentives outstanding at March 31, 2011, ranged from £22.44 and ZAR 43.09 to ZAR 225.08 (2010: £ 0 to £ 17.14 and ZAR 45.97 to ZAR 215.31). The movement in share awards outstanding is summarized in the following tables.

GBP share options

GBP share options include share options granted under the Executive Share Option Plan 2008, the Executive Share Option (No. 2) Scheme, the Approved Executive Share Option Scheme and the International Employee Share Scheme. No further grants can be made under the now closed Executive Share Option (No. 2) Scheme, the Approved Executive Share Option Scheme, or the International Employee Share Scheme; although outstanding grants may still be exercised until they reach their expiry date.

	Number of options	Weighted-average exercise price GBP	Weighted-average fair value at grant date GBP
Outstanding at April 1, 2009	16,016,731	9.61	-
Granted	3,847,500	12.36	4.29
Lapsed	(338,033)	12.19	-
Exercised	(6,010,513)	7.97	-
Outstanding at March 31, 2010	13,515,685	11.05	-
Granted	4,178,150	19.58	5.87
Lapsed	(521,316)	12.91	-
Exercised	(2,084,462)	10.27	-
Outstanding at March 31, 2011	**15,088,057**	**13.46**	**-**

ZAR share options

Share options designated in ZAR include share options granted under the South African Executive Share Option Plan 2008 and the Mirror Executive Share Purchase Scheme (South Africa). No further grants can be made under the Mirror Executive Share Purchase Scheme (South Africa) although outstanding grants may still be exercised until they reach their expiry date.

	Number of options	Weighted-average exercise price ZAR	Weighted-average fair value at grant date ZAR
Outstanding at April 1, 2009	14,336,899	126.14	-
Granted	2,903,050	203.64	104.00
Lapsed	(419,800)	163.03	-
Exercised	(3,372,370)	88.21	-

	Number of options	Weighted-average exercise price ZAR	Weighted-average fair value at grant date ZAR
Outstanding at March 31, 2010	13,447,779	151.23	-
Granted	2,943,850	222.55	88.63
Lapsed	(499,850)	176.93	-
Exercised	(2,205,700)	126.34	-
Outstanding at March 31, 2011	**13,686,079**	**169.64**	**-**

GBP SARs

GBP SARs include stock appreciation rights granted under the Stock Appreciation Rights Plan 2008 and the International Employee Stock Appreciation Rights Scheme. No further grants can be made under the now closed International Employee Stock Appreciation Rights Scheme, although outstanding grants may still be exercised until they reach their expiry date.

	Number of SARs	Weighted-average exercise price GBP	Weighted-average fair value at grant date GBP
Outstanding at April 1, 2009	7,030,030	9.07	-
Granted	84,200	12.31	3.59
Lapsed	(309,053)	12.12	-
Exercised	(2,508,128)	8.03	-
Outstanding at March 31, 2010	4,297,049	9.54	-
Granted	49,900	19.51	5.85
Lapsed	(24,036)	10.81	-
Exercised	(747,543)	9.27	-
Outstanding at March 31, 2011	**3,575,370**	**9.72**	**-**

GBP performance share awards

GBP performance share awards include awards made under the Executive Share Award Plan 2008, the Performance Share Award Scheme and the International Performance Share Award Sub-Scheme. No further awards can be made under the Performance Share Award Scheme and the International Performance Share Award Sub-Scheme, although outstanding awards remain and will vest, subject to the achievement of their respective performance conditions on their vesting date.

	Number of awards	Weighted-average exercise price GBP	Weighted-average fair value at grant date GBP
Outstanding at April 1, 2009	6,443,200	-	-
Granted	2,808,782	-	10.27
Lapsed	(725,995)	-	-
Released to participants	(1,610,132)	-	-
Outstanding at March 31, 2010	6,915,855	-	-
Granted	2,012,800	-	18.08
Lapsed	(734,088)	-	-
Released to participants	(830,443)	-	-
Outstanding at March 31, 2011	**7,364,124**	**-**	**-**

GBP value share awards

The 3,317,000 value share awards granted represent the theoretical maximum number of awards that could possibly vest in the future, although in practice it is extremely unlikely that this number of awards would be released.

	Number of value shares (per £ 10 million of additional value)	*Theoretical maximum shares at cap*	*Weighted-average exercise price GBP*	*Weighted-average fair value at grant date GBP*
Outstanding at April 1, 2010	-	-	-	
Granted	1,070	3,317,000	-	7.61
Lapsed	(48)	(148,800)	-	-
Outstanding at March 31, 2011	1,022	3,168,200	-	-

Outstanding share incentives

The following table summarizes information about share incentives outstanding at March 31.

Range of exercise prices	*Number 2011*	*Weighted-average remaining contractual life in years 2011*	*Number 2010*	*Weighted-average remaining contractual life in years 2010*
GBP share options	**229,452**	**1.9**	439,159	2.5
£4-£5	**161,070**	**1.9**	249,455	2.6
£5-£6	**501,543**	**3.1**	702,543	4.1
£6-£7	**687,427**	**4.1**	824,320	5.1
£8-£9	**116,000**	**7.6**	116,000	8.6
£9-£10	**1,345,838**	**5.5**	1,795,799	6.4
£10-£11	**1,806,653**	**6.1**	2,737,885	7.1
£11-£12	**6,213,927**	**7.7**	6,590,484	8.7
£12-£13	-	-	25,840	7.6
£13-£14	**34,200**	**8.6**	34,200	9.6
£17-£18	**3,839,997**	**9.2**	-	-
£19-£20	**71,950**	**9.7**	-	-
£20-£21	**80,000**	**9.8**	-	-
£22-£23	**15,088,057**	**7.2**	13,515,685	7.3

Consolidated Statement of Changes in Equity
For the year ended June 30, 2010

US $M	Share capital—BHP Billiton Limited	Share capital—BHP Billiton Plc	Treasury Shares	Reserves	Retained earnings	Total	Noncontrolling interests	Total equity
					Attributable to members of the BHP Billiton Group			
Balance as at July 1, 2009	1,227	1,116	(525)	1,305	36,831	39,954	757	40,711
Total comprehensive income	-	-	-	197	12,738	12,935	294	13,229
Transactions with owners:								
Purchase of shares by ESOP Trusts	-	-	(274)	-	-	(274)	-	(274)
Employee share awards exercised following vesting net of employee contributions	-	-	274	(88)	(178)	8	-	8
Employee share awards lapsed	-	-	-	(28)	28	-	-	-
Accrued employee entitlement for unvested awards	-	-	-	170	-	170	-	170
Issue of share options to noncontrolling interests	-	-	-	43	-	43	16	59
Distribution to option holders	-	-	-	(10)	-	(10)	(6)	(16)
Dividends paid	-	-	-	-	(4,618)	(4,613)	(277)	(4,895)
Transactions with owners—contributed equity	-	-	-	317	-	317	20	337
Balance as at June 30, 2010	1,227	1,116	(525)	1,906	44,801	48,525	804	49,329
Balance as at July 1, 2008	1,227	1,116	(514)	750	35,756	38,335	708	39,043
Total comprehensive income	-	-	-	404	5,742	6,146	458	6,604
Transactions with owners:								
Purchase of shares by ESOP Trusts	-	-	(169)	-	-	(169)	-	(169)
Employee share awards exercised following vesting net of employee contributions	-	-	158	(34)	(104)	20	-	20

Attributable to members of the BHP Billiton Group

US $M	Share capital– BHP Billiton Limited	Share capital–BHP Billiton Plc	Treasury Shares	Reserves	Retained earnings	Total	Noncontrolling interests	Total equity
Accrued employee entitlement for unvested awards	-	-	-	185	-	185	-	185
Dividends paid	-	-	-	-	(4,563)	(4,563)	(406)	(4,969)
Transaction with owners—contributed equity	-	-	-	-	-	-	(3)	(3)
Balance as at June 30, 2009	1,227	1,116	(525)	1,305	36,831	39,954	757	40,711
Balance as at July 1, 2007	1,221	1,183	(1,457)	991	27,729	29,667	251	29,918
Total comprehensive income	-	-	-	(368)	15,372	15,004	571	15,575
Transactions with owners:								
Exercise of Employee Share Plan Options	6	-	-	-	-	6	-	6
BHP Billiton Plc shares bought back and cancelled	-	(67)	-	67	-	-	-	-
Purchase of shares by ESOP Trusts	-	-	(250)	-	-	(250)	-	(250)
Employee share awards exercised following vesting net of employee contributions	-	-	260	(37)	(204)	19	-	19
Shares bought back	-	-	(3,075)	-	-	(3,075)	-	(3,075)
Shares cancelled	-	-	4,008	-	(4,008)	-	-	-
Accrued employee entitlement for unvested awards	-	-	-	97	-	97	-	97
Dividends paid	-	-	-	-	(3,133)	(3,133)	(113)	(3,246)
Transaction with owners—contributed equity	-	-	-	-	-	-	(1)	(1)
Balance as at June 30, 2008	1,227	1,116	(514)	750	35,756	38,335	708	39,043

Notes to the consolidated financial statements

1. Accounting Policies

Share-based payments. The fair value at grant date of equity-settled share awards granted on or after November 8, 2002, is charged to the income statement over the period for which the benefits of employee services are expected to be derived. The corresponding accrued employee entitlement is recorded in the employee share awards reserve. The fair value of awards is calculated using an option pricing model which considers the following factors:

- Exercise price
- Expected life of the award
- Current market price of the underlying shares
- Expected volatility
- Expected dividends
- Risk-free interest rate
- Market-based performance hurdles
- Nonvesting conditions

For equity-settled share awards granted on or before November 7, 2002, and that remained unvested at July 1, 2004, the estimated cost of share awards is charged to the income statement from grant date to the date of expected vesting. The estimated cost of awards is based on the market value of shares at the grant date or the intrinsic value of options awarded, adjusted to reflect the impact of performance conditions, where applicable.

Where awards are forfeited because non-market-based vesting conditions are not satisfied, the expense previously recognized is proportionately reversed. Where shares in BHP Billiton Limited or BHP Billiton Plc are acquired by on-market purchases prior to settling vested entitlements, the cost of the acquired shares is carried as treasury shares and deducted from equity. When awards are satisfied by delivery of acquired shares, any difference between their acquisition cost and the remuneration expense recognized is charged directly to retained earnings. The tax effect of awards granted is recognized in income tax expense, except to the extent that the total tax deductions are expected to exceed the cumulative remuneration expense. In this situation, the excess of the associated current or deferred tax is recognized in equity as part of the employee share awards reserve.

19. Share capital

	BHP Billiton Limited			BHP Billiton Plc		
	2010 US $M	2009 US $M	2008 US $M	2010 US $M	2009 US $M	2008 US $M
Share capital						
Balance at the beginning of the financial year	1,227	1,227	1,221	1,116	1,116	1,183
Exercise of Employee Share Plan Options(a)	-	-	6	-	-	-
Shares bought back and cancelled(a)	-	-	-	-	-	(67)
Balance at the end of the financial year	1,227	1,227	1,227	1,116	1,116	1,116
Treasury shares						
Balance at the beginning of the financial year	(1)	(1)	(2)	(524)	(513)	(1,455)
Purchases of shares by ESOP Trusts	(216)	(132)	(230)	(58)	(37)	(20)
Employee share awards exercised following vesting	216	132	231	58	26	29
Shares bought back(a)	-	-	-	-	-	(3,075)
Shares cancelled(a)	-	-	-	-	-	4,008
Balance at the end of the financial year	(1)	(1)	(1)	(524)	(524)	(513)

	BHP Billiton Limited			BHP Billiton Plc		
	2010 Shares(d)	2009 Shares(d)	2008 Shares(d)	2010 Shares(c)(d)	2009 Shares(c)(d)	2008 Shares(c)(d)
Share capital issued						
Ordinary shares fully paid	3,358,359,496	3,358,359,496	3,358,359,496	2,231,121,202	2,231,121,202	2,231,121,202
Comprising						
• Shares held by the public	3,358,312,376	3,358,312,376	3,358,260,180	2,206,076,344	2,206,130,916	2,206,662,027
• Treasury shares	47,120	47,120	99,316	25,044,858	24,990,286	24,459,175
Ordinary shares paid to A $1.36	110,000	110,000	195,000			
Special Voting Share of no par value(e)	1	1	1			
5.5% Preferences shares of £1 each(f)				50,000	50,000	50,000
Special Voting Share of US $0.50 par value(e)				1	1	1

	BHP Billiton Limited			BHP Billiton Plc		
	2010 Shares	2009 Shares	2008 Shares	2010 Shares	2009 Shares	2008 Shares
Movement in shares held by the public						
Opening number of shares	3,358,312,376	3,358,260,180	3,357,372,156	2,206,130,916	2,206,662,027	2,302,854,320
Shares issued on exercise of Employees Share Plan Options	-	-	855,923	-	-	-
Purchase of shares by ESOP Trusts	(6,304,733)	(5,274,136)	(6,550,854)	(2,081,566)	(1,447,706)	(589,802)

	BHP Billiton Limited			BHP Billiton Plc		
	2010 Shares	2009 Shares	2008 Shares	2010 Shares	2009 Shares	2008 Shares
Employee share awards exercised following vesting	6,304,733	5,326,332	6,582,955	2,026,994	916,595	1,301,595
Shares bought back(a)	-	-	-	-	-	(96,904,086)
Closing number of shares(g)	3,358,312,376	3,358,312,376	3,358,260,180	2,206,076,342	2,206,130,916	2,206,662,027
Movement in treasury shares						
Opening number of shares	47,120	99,316	131,417	24,990,286	24,459,175	63,607,682
Purchase of shares by ESOP Trusts	6,304,733	5,274,136	6,550,854	2,081,565	1,447,706	589,802
Employee share awards exercised following vesting	(6,304,733)	(5,326,332)	(6,582,955)	(2,026,994)	(916,595)	(1,301,595)
Shares bought back (a)	-	-	-	-	-	96,904,086
Shares cancelled(a)	-	-	-	-	-	(135,340,800)
Closing number of shares	47,120	47,120	99,316	25,044,857	24,990,286	24,459,175

	BHP Billiton Limited		
	2010 Shares	2009 Shares	2008 Shares
Movement in shares partly paid to A $1.36			
Opening number of shares	110,000	195,000	195,000
Partly paid shares converted to fully paid(h)	-	(85,000)	-
Closing number of shares(i)	110,000	110,000	195,000

					Purchased by			
					BHP Billiton Limited		BHP Billiton Plc	
Year ended	Shares purchased	Number	Cost per share and discount	Total cost US $M	Shares	US $M	Shares	US $M
June 30, 2008	BHP Billiton Plc	96,904,086	£12.37 8.7%(i)	3,075	96,904,086	3,075	-	-

(a) On August 23, 2006, BHP Billiton announced a US $3 billion capital return to shareholders through an 18-month series of on-market share buybacks. On February 7, 2007, a US $10 billion extension to this program was announced. As of that date, US $1,705 million of shares in BHP Billiton Plc had been repurchased under the August program, leaving US $1,295 million to be carried forward and added to the February 2007 program. All BHP Billiton Plc. shares bought back are accounted for as Treasury shares within the share capital of BHP Billiton Plc. Details of the purchases are shown in the table below. Cost per share represents the average cost per share for BHP Billiton Plc shares and final cost per share for BHP Billiton Limited shares. Shares in BHP Billiton Plc purchased by BHP Billiton Limited have been cancelled, in accordance with the resolutions passed at the 2006 Annual General Meetings.

(i) Represents the discount to the average BHP Billiton Limited share price between September 7, 2006, and December 14, 2007.
As at June 30, 2010, shares in BHP Billiton Plc bought back as part of the above program but not cancelled are held as Treasury shares. On December 14, 2007, the share buyback program was suspended in light of the Group's offers for Rio Tinto Plc and Rio Tinto Limited. On November 27, 2008, the offers lapsed. No shares were bought back under the program in the year ended June 30, 2010.

(b) An Equalization Share (US $0.50 par value) has been authorized to be issued to enable a distribution to be made by BHP Billiton Plc Group to the BHP Billiton Limited Group should this be required under the terms of the DLC merger. The Directors have the ability to issue the Equalization Share if required under those terms. The Constitution of BHP Billiton Limited allows the Directors of that Company to issue a similar Equalization Share. There has been no movement in this class of share. This share forms part of BHP Billiton Plc's total share capital.

(c) The total number of BHP Billiton Plc authorized ordinary shares of US $0.50 par value is 2,762,974,200 (2009: 2,762,974,200; 2008: 2,762,974,200).

(d) The total number of BHP Billiton Limited shares of all classes is 3,358,469,497 of which 99.99% are ordinary shares fully paid (2009: 3,358,469,497, 99.99%; 2008: 3,358,554,497, 99.99%). The total number of BHP Billiton Plc shares of all classes is 2,763,024,202, of which 99.99% are authorized ordinary shares of US $0.50 par value (2009: 2,763,024,202, 99.99%; 2008: 2,763,024, 99.99%). Any surplus remaining after payment of preferred distributions shall be payable to the holders of BHP Billiton Limited and BHP Billiton Plc ordinary shares in equal amounts per share.

(e) Each of BHP Billiton Limited and BHP Billiton Plc issued one Special Voting Share to facilitate joint voting by shareholders of BHP Billiton Limited and BHP Billiton Plc on Joint Electorate Actions. There has been no movement in these shares.

(f) Preference shares have the right to repayment of the amount paid up on the nominal value and any unpaid dividends in priority to the holders of any other class of shares in BHP Billiton Plc on a return of capital or winding-up. The holders of preference shares have limited voting rights if payment of the preference dividends are six months or more in arrears or a resolution is passed changing the rights of the preference shareholders. There has been no movement in these shares, all of which are held by JP Morgan Plc.

(g) During the period July 1, 2010, to September 7, 2010, no Executive Share Scheme partly paid shares were paid up in full, no fully paid ordinary shares (including attached bonus shares) were issued on the exercise of Employee Share Plan Options, no fully paid ordinary shares (including attached bonus shares) were issued on the exercise of Performance Share Plan Performance Rights and no fully paid ordinary shares were issued on the exercise of Group Incentive Scheme awards.

(h) During the year ended June 30, 2009, partly paid shares were converted to an equal number of fully paid shares and satisfied via on-market purchase.

(i) At June 30, 2010, 70,000 partly paid shares on issue are entitled to 79,928 bonus shares on becoming fully paid. The remaining partly paid shares are entitled to an equal number of fully paid shares upon conversion to fully paid shares.

20. Other equity

	2010 US $M	2009 US $M	2008 US $M
Reserves			
Share premium account[a]			
Balance at the beginning of the financial year	518	518	518
Balance at the end of the financial year	518	518	518
Foreign currency translation reserve[b]			
Balance at the beginning of the financial year	24	(3)	18
Exchange fluctuations on translation of foreign operations taken to equity	1	27	(21)
Exchange fluctuations on translation of foreign operations taken to the income statement	(10)	-	-
Total other comprehensive income	(9)	27	(21)
Balance at the end of the financial year	15	24	(3)
Employee share awards reserve [c]			
Balance at the beginning of the financial year	434	372	261
Deferred tax arising on accrued employee entitlement for unexercised awards	69	(89)	51
Total other comprehensive income	69	(89)	51
Accrued employee entitlement for unvested awards	170	185	97
Employee share awards exercised following vesting	(88)	(34)	(37)
Employee share awards lapsed	(28)	-	-
Balance at the end of the financial year	557	434	372
Hedging reserve–cash flow hedges[d]			
Balance at the beginning of the financial year	9	(417)	(87)
Net (loss)/gain on cash flow hedges taken to equity	(15)	710	(383)
Net realized loss on cash flow hedges transferred to the income statement	2	22	73
Net unrealized loss on cash flow hedges transferred to the income statement	-	(48)	-
Net gains on cash flow hedges transferred to initial carrying amount of hedged items	-	(26)	(190)
Deferred tax relating to cash flow hedges	4	(232)	170
Total other comprehensive income	(9)	426	(330)
Balance at the end of the financial year	-	9	(417)
Financial assets reserve[e]			
Balance at the beginning of the financial year	202	162	230
Net valuation gain/(loss) taken to equity	160	3	(76)
Net valuation losses transferred to the income statement	2	58	-
Deferred tax relating to revaluations	(16)	(21)	8
Total other comprehensive income	146	40	(68)
Balance at the end of the financial year	348	202	162
Share buy-back reserve[f]			
Balance at the beginning of the financial year	118	118	51
BHP Billiton Plc shares cancelled	-	-	67
Balance at the end of the financial year	118	118	118
Noncontrolling interest contribution reserve[g]			
Balance at the beginning of the financial year	-	-	-
Issue of share options to noncontrolling interests	43	-	-
Distribution to option holders	(10)	-	-
Transactions with owners–contributed equity	317	-	-
Balance at the end of the financial year	350	-	-
Total reserves	1,906	1,305	750

	2010 US $M	2009 US $M	2008 US $M
Retained earnings			
Balance at the beginning of the financial year	36,831	35,756	27,729
Profit for the year	12,722	5,877	15,390
Actuarial losses	(38)	(224)	(95)
Tax recognized directly in other comprehensive income	54	89	77
Total comprehensive income	12,738	5,742	15,372
Dividends paid	(4,618)	(4,563)	(3,133)
BHP Billiton Plc share buy-back–refer to note 19	-	-	(4,008)
Employee share awards exercised following vesting, net of employee contributions and lapses	(150)	(104)	(204)
Balance at the end of the financial year	44,801	36,831	35,756

	2010 US $M	2009 US $M	2008 US $M
Noncontrolling interests			
Balance at the beginning of the financial year	757	708	251
Profit for the year	287	461	572
Actuarial losses on pension and medical schemes	-	(3)	(1)
Net valuation gains taken to equity	7	-	-
Tax recognized directly in other comprehensive income	-	-	-
Total comprehensive income	294	458	571
Issue of share options to noncontrolling interests	16	-	-
Distribution to option holders	(6)	-	-
Transactions with owners–contributed equity	20	(3)	(1)
Dividends paid	(277)	(406)	(113)
Balance at the end of the financial year	804	757	708

(a) *The share premium account represents the premium paid on the issue of BHP Billiton Plc shares recognized in accordance with the UK Companies Act 2006.*

(b) *The foreign currency translation reserve represents exchange differences arising on the translation of non-US dollar functional currency operations within the Group into US dollars.*

(c) *The employee share awards reserve represents the accrued employee entitlements to share awards that have been charged to the income statement and have not yet been exercised.*

(d) *The hedging reserve represents hedging gains and losses recognized on the effective portion of cash flow hedges. The cumulative deferred gain or loss on the hedge is recognized in the income statement when the hedged transaction impacts the income statement, or is recognized as an adjustment to the cost of nonfinancial hedged items.*

(e) *The financial assets reserve represents the revaluation of available-for-sale financial assets. Where a revalued financial asset is sold or impaired, the relevant portion of the reserve is transferred to the income statement.*

(f) *The share buyback reserve represents the par value of BHP Billiton Plc shares which were purchased and subsequently cancelled. The cancellation of the shares creates a nondistributable reserve.*

(g) *The noncontrolling interest contribution reserve represents the excess of consideration received over the book value of net assets attributable to the equity instruments held by noncontrolling interests.*

US GAAP COMPARISON

IFRS and US GAAP accounting for share-based payments contain many of the same elements. However, there are differences. Like IFRS, US GAAP measures share-based payments using fair value. Both allocate the costs across the vesting periods. However, US GAAP encourages the use of Black-Sholes or the lattice method of computing fair value, whereas IFRS does not.

Certain stock-based compensation plans (e.g., ESOP) are scoped out of US GAAP, whereas IFRS includes all plans where equity is offered for products or services. US GAAP guidance for employee compensation is restricted to only those individuals that are legally employees. US GAAP includes a third type of award (in addition to employee and nonemployee) for those doing employee-type work. This method includes a date called the commitment date from which the award is marked to market until delivery of the agreement goals. In terms of measurement, US GAAP allows the use of the intrinsic value in certain circumstances for only nonpublic companies. Otherwise, fair value is used.

18 CURRENT LIABILITIES, PROVISIONS, CONTINGENCIES, AND EVENTS AFTER THE REPORTING PERIOD

INTRODUCTION

Accounting for all of a reporting entity's liabilities is clearly necessary in order to accurately convey its financial position to investors, creditors and other stakeholders. Different kinds of liabilities have differing implications: *short-term trade payables* indicate a near-term outflow, while *long-term debt* covers a wide range of periods, and *provisions* have yet other significance to those performing financial analysis. At the same time, a company with a long operating cycle will have operating liabilities that stretch for more than a year ahead, and some long-term debt may call for repayment within one year, so the distinction is not so clear, and presentation in the statement of financial position is an issue. Transparency of disclosure will also be a consideration, beyond mere questions of current or noncurrent classification.

Historically, it has long been recognized that prudence would normally necessitate the recognition of even uncertain liabilities, while uncertain assets were not to be recognized. IAS 37, the key standard on provisions, addresses the boundaries of recognition. In general, the IASB is also evolving to a new position on contingent liabilities, where the assessed probability of occurrence will be built into the measurement of liabilities, thereby changing the boundaries of accounting recognition for liabilities.

The recognition and measurement of provisions can have a major impact on the way in which the financial position of an entity is viewed. IAS 37 addresses so-called "onerous contract" provisions, which require a company to take into current earnings the entire cost of fulfilling contracts that continue into the future under defined conditions. This can be a very sensitive issue for a company experiencing trading difficulties.

Another sensitive issue is the accounting for decommissioning or similar asset retirement costs, which increasingly are becoming a burden for companies engaged in mineral extraction and manufacturing, but also potentially for those engaged in agriculture and other industry segments. Where historically it was assumed that these costs were future events to be recognized in later periods, it is now clear that these are costs of asset ownership and operation that need to be reflected over the productive lives of the assets, and that the estimated costs are to be recognized as a formal obligation of the reporting entity.

The reporting entity's financial position may also be affected by events, both favorable and unfavorable, which occur between the end of the reporting period and the date when the financial statements are authorized for issue. Under IAS 10, such events require either formal recognition in the financial statements or only disclosure, depending on the character and timing of the event in question, which are referred to as "adjusting" and "nonadjusting," respectively.

In practice, there may be some ambiguity as to when the financial statements are actually "authorized for issuance." For this reason, the revised standard recognizes that the process involved in authorizing the financial statements for issue will vary and may be dependent upon the reporting entity's management structure, statutory requirements, and the procedures prescribed for the preparing and finalizing of the financial statements. Thus, IAS 10 illustrates in detail the principles governing the determination of the financial statements' authorization date, which date is required to be disclosed.

Sources of IFRS	
IAS 1, 10, 37, 39	*IFRIC* 1, 6

DEFINITIONS OF TERMS

Adjusting events after the reporting period. Those events after the reporting period that provide evidence of conditions that existed at the end of the reporting period and require that the financial statements be adjusted.

Authorization date. The date when the financial statements would be considered legally authorized for issue.

Constructive obligation. An obligation resulting from an entity's actions such that the entity

- By an established pattern of past practice, published policies or a sufficiently specific current statement, has indicated to third parties that it will accept certain responsibilities; and
- As a result, has created a valid expectation in the minds of third parties that it will discharge those responsibilities.

Contingent asset. A possible asset that arises from past events and whose existence will be confirmed only by the occurrence or nonoccurrence of one or more uncertain future events not wholly within the control of the reporting entity.

Contingent liability. An obligation that is either

- A possible obligation arising from past events, the outcome of which will be confirmed only on the occurrence or nonoccurrence of one or more uncertain future events which are not wholly within the control of the reporting entity; or
- A present obligation arising from past events which is not recognized either because it is not probable that an outflow of resources will be required to settle an obligation, or where the amount of the obligation cannot be measured with sufficient reliability.

Current liabilities. A liability of the entity which

- The entity expects to settle in its normal operating cycle; or
- The entity holds primarily for the purpose of trading; or
- Is due to be settled within twelve months after the reporting period; or
- Allows the entity an unconditional right to defer settlement thereof for at least twelve months after the reporting period.

Events after the reporting period. Events, favorable and unfavorable, that occur between the entity's end of the reporting period and the date the financial statements are authorized for issue that would necessitate either adjusting the financial statements or disclosure. These include adjusting events and nonadjusting events.

Legal obligation. An obligation that derives from the explicit or implicit terms of a contract, or from legislation or other operation of law.

Liability. A present obligation of the entity arising from past events, the settlement of which is expected to result in an outflow from the entity of resources embodying economic benefits.

Nonadjusting events after the reporting period. Those events after the reporting period that provide evidence of conditions that arose *after* the end of the reporting period and which thus would *not* necessitate adjusting financial statements. Instead, if significant, these would require disclosure.

Obligating event. An event that creates a legal or constructive obligation that results in an entity having no realistic alternative but to settle that obligation.

Onerous contract. A contract in which the unavoidable costs of meeting the obligations under the contract exceed the economic benefits expected to be received therefrom.

Operating cycle. The operating cycle of an entity is the time between the acquisition of assets for processing and their realization in cash or cash equivalents. When the entity's normal operating cycle is not clearly identifiable, it is assumed to be twelve months.

Provision. Liabilities having uncertain timing or amount.

Restructuring. A program that is planned and controlled by management and which materially changes either the scope of business undertaken by the entity or the manner in which it is conducted.

RECOGNITION AND MEASUREMENT

Current Liabilities

Classification. IAS 1 requires that the reporting entity must present current and noncurrent assets, and current and noncurrent liabilities, as separate classifications on the face of its statement of financial position, except when a liquidity presentation provides more relevant and reliable information. In those exceptional instances, all assets and liabilities are to be presented broadly in order of liquidity. Whether classified or employing the order of liquidity approach, for any asset or liability reported as a discrete line item that combines amounts expected to be realized or settled within no more than twelve months after the reporting period and more than twelve months after the reporting period, the reporting entity must disclose the amount expected to be recovered or settled after more than twelve months.

IAS 1 also makes explicit reference to the requirements imposed by IAS 32 concerning financial assets and financial liabilities. Since such common items in the statement of financial position as trade and other receivables and payables are within the definition of financial instruments, information about maturity dates is already required under IFRS. While most trade payables and accrued liabilities will be due within thirty to ninety days, and thus are understood by all financial statement readers to be current, this requirement would necessitate additional disclosure, either in the statement of financial position or in the footnotes thereto, when this assumption is not warranted.

The other purpose of presenting a classified statement of financial position is to highlight those assets and obligations that are "continuously circulating" in the phraseology of IAS 1. That is, the goal is to identify specifically resources and commitments that are consumed or settled in the normal course of the operating cycle. In some types of businesses, such as certain construction entities, the normal operating cycle may exceed one year. Thus, some assets or liabilities might fail to be incorporated into a definition based on the first goal of reporting, providing insight into liquidity, but be included in one that meets the second goal.

As a compromise, if a classified statement of financial position is indeed being presented, the convention for financial reporting purposes is to consider assets and liabilities current if they will be realized and settled within one year or one operating cycle, whichever is longer. Since this may vary in practice from one reporting entity to another, however, it is important for users to read the accounting policies set forth in notes to the financial statements. The classification criterion should be set forth there, particularly if it is other than the rule most commonly employed: one-year threshold.

Nature of current liabilities. Current liabilities are generally perceived to be those that are payable within 12 months of reporting date. The convention has long been to use one year after the reporting period as the threshold for categorization as current, subject to the operating cycle issue for liabilities linked to operations. Examples of liabilities which are not expected to be settled in the normal course of the operating cycle but which, if due within twelve months would be deemed current, are current portions of long-term debt and bank overdrafts, dividends declared and payable, and various nontrade payables.

Current liabilities would almost always include not only obligations that are due on demand (typically including bank lines of credit, other demand notes payable, and certain overdue obligations for which forbearance has been granted on a day-to-day basis), but also the currently scheduled payments on longer-term obligations, such as installment agreements. Also included in this group would be trade credit and accrued expenses, and deferred revenues and advances from customers for which services are to be provided or product delivered within one year. If certain conditions are met (described below), short-term obligations that are intended to be refinanced may be excluded from current liabilities. A recent amendment to IAS 1, effective January 1, 2009, clarifies that terms of a liability that could, at the option of the counterparty, result in its settlement by the issue of equity instruments do not affect its classification. For example, if a liability to be settled in full in cash after 5 years also allows the lender to demand settlement in shares of the borrower at any point prior to the settlement date, that liability will be classified as noncurrent.

Like all liabilities, current liabilities may be known with certainty as to amount, due date, and payee, as is most commonly the case. However, one or more of these elements may be unknown or subject to estimation. Consistent with basic principles of accrual accounting, however, the lack of specific information on, say, the amount owed, will not serve to justify a failure to record and report on such obligations. The former commonly used term "estimated liabilities" has been superseded per IAS 37 by the term "provisions." Provisions and contingent liabilities are discussed in detail later in this chapter.

Offsetting current assets against related current liabilities. IAS 1 states that current liabilities are not to be reduced by the deduction of a current asset (or vice versa) unless required or permitted by another IFRS. In practice, there are few circumstances that would meet this requirement; certain financial instruments (to the extent permitted by IAS 32) are the most commonly encountered exceptions. As an almost universal rule, therefore, assets and liabilities must be shown "gross," even where the same counterparties are present (e.g., amounts due from and amounts owed to another entity).

Types of liabilities. Current obligations can be divided into those where

1. Both the amount and the payee are known;
2. The payee is known but the amount may have to be estimated;
3. The payee is unknown and the amount may have to be estimated; and
4. The liability has been incurred due to a loss contingency.

These types of liabilities are discussed in the following sections.

Amount and Payee Known

Accounts payable arise primarily from the acquisition of materials and supplies to be used in the production of goods or in conjunction with providing services. Payables that arise from transactions with suppliers in the normal course of business, which customarily are due in no more than one year, may be stated at their face amount rather than at the present value of the required future cash flows if the effect of discounting is immaterial.

Notes payable are more formalized obligations that may arise from the acquisition of materials and supplies used in operations or from the use of short-term credit to purchase capital assets. Monetary obligations, other than those due currently, should be presented at the present value of future payments, thus giving explicit recognition to the time value of money. Discounting, however, is only required where the impact of the discounting would be material on the financial statements. In many cases, the discounting of short-term obligations would not be material. (Note that if the obligations are interest-bearing at a reasonable rate determined at inception, discounting is not an issue.)

Dividends payable become a liability of the entity when a dividend has been approved. However, jurisdictions vary as to how this is interpreted. Under most continental European company law, only the shareholders in general meeting can approve a dividend, and so the function of the directors is to propose a dividend, which itself does not give rise to a liability. In other jurisdictions, the decision of the board of directors would trigger recognition of a liability. Since declared dividends are usually paid within a short period of time after the declaration date, they are classified as current liabilities, should a statement of financial position be prepared at a date between the two events.

Unearned revenues or advances result from customer prepayments for either performance of services or delivery of product. They may be required by the selling entity as a condition of the sale or may be made by the buyer as a means of guaranteeing that the seller will perform the desired service or deliver the product. Unearned revenues and advances should be classified as current liabilities at the end of the reporting period if the services are to be performed or the products are to be delivered within one year or the operating cycle, whichever is longer.

Returnable deposits may be received to cover possible future damage to property. Many utility companies require security deposits. A deposit may be required for the use of a reusable container. Refundable deposits are classified as current liabilities if the entity expects to refund them during the current operating cycle or within one year, whichever is longer.

Accrued liabilities have their origin in the end-of-period adjustment process required by accrual accounting. They represent economic obligations, even when the legal or contractual commitment to pay has not yet been triggered. Commonly accrued liabilities include wages and salaries payable, interest payable, rent payable, and taxes payable.

Agency liabilities result from the legal obligation of the entity to act as the collection agent for employee or customer taxes owed to various federal, state, or local government units. Examples of agency liabilities include value-added tax, sales taxes, income taxes withheld from employee salaries, and employee social security contributions, where mandated by law. In addition to agency liabilities, an employer may have a current obligation for unemployment taxes. Payroll taxes typically are not legal liabilities until the associated payroll is actually paid, but in keeping with the concept of accrual accounting, if the payroll has been accrued, the associated payroll taxes should be as well.

Obligations that are, by their terms, due on demand or will become due on demand within one year (or operating cycle, if longer) from the end of the reporting period, even if liquidation is not expected to occur within that period, must be classified as current liabilities.

However, when the reporting entity breaches an undertaking or covenant under a long-term loan agreement, thereby causing the liability to become due and payable on demand, it must be classified as current at the end of the reporting period, even if the lender has agreed, after the end of the reporting period and before the authorization of the financial statements for issue, not to demand payment as a consequence of the breach (i.e., to give forbearance to the borrower).

On the other hand, if the lender has granted an extension before the end of the reporting period (extending for at least one year from the end of the reporting period), then noncurrent classification would be warranted. Similarly, if the lender has agreed by the end of the reporting period to provide a grace period within which the entity can rectify a breach of an undertaking or covenant under a long-term loan agreement and during that time the lender cannot demand immediate repayment, the liability is to be classified as noncurrent if it is due for settlement, without that breach of an undertaking or covenant, at least twelve months after the reporting period *and either*

1. The entity rectifies the breach within the period of grace; *or*
2. When the financial statements are authorized for issue, the grace period is incomplete and it is probable that the breach will indeed be rectified.

Failure to rectify the breach confirms that current classification of the liability was warranted, and the financial statements would be adjusted to conform to that fact.

Short-term obligations expected to be refinanced. Long-term financial liabilities within twelve months of maturity are current liabilities in a classified statement of financial position. In some cases, the reporting entity has plans or intentions to refinance the debt (to "roll it over") and thus does not expect its maturity to cause it to deploy its working capital. Under provisions of IAS 1, this debt must be shown as current when due to be settled within twelve months of the end of the reporting period, notwithstanding that its original term was for a period of more than twelve months; and that an agreement to refinance, or to reschedule payments, on a long-term basis is completed after the reporting period and before the financial statements are authorized for issuance.

However, if the reporting entity has the ability, unilaterally, to refinance or "roll over" the debt for at least twelve months after the end of the reporting period, under the terms of an existing loan facility, it is classified an noncurrent, even if it is otherwise due to be repaid within twelve months of the end of the reporting period, if a "rollover" is the entity's intent. This differs from the situation in which refinancing or "rolling over" the obligation is not at the discretion of the entity (as when there is no agreement to refinance), in which case the potential to refinance (which is no more than the borrower's hope in such instance) is not considered and the obligation is classified as current.

Example of short-term obligations to be refinanced

The Marrakech Warehousing Company has obtained a €3,500,000 bridge loan to assist it in completing a new warehouse. All construction is completed by the end of the reporting period, after which Marrakech has the following three choices for refinancing the bridge loan:

- Enter into a 30-year fixed-rate mortgage for €3,400,000 at 7% interest, leaving Marrakech with a €100,000 obligation to fulfill from short-term funds. Under this scenario, Marrakech reports as current debt the €100,000, as well as the €50,000 portion of the mortgage due within one year, with the remainder of the mortgage itemized as long-term debt. The presentation follows:

  Current liabilities
Short-term notes	100,000
Current portion of long-term debt	50,000

  Noncurrent liabilities
7% mortgage note due in full by 2041	3,350,000

- Pay off the bridge loan with Marrakech's existing variable rate line of credit (LOC), which expires in two years. The maximum amount of the LOC is 80% of Marrakech's accounts receivable. Over the two-year remaining term of the LOC, the lowest level of qualifying accounts receivable is expected to be €2,700,000. Thus only €2,700,000 of the debt can be classified as long-term, while €800,000 is classified as a short-term obligation. The presentation follows:

  Current liabilities
Short-term note—variable rate line of credit	800,000

  Noncurrent liabilities
Variable rate line of credit due in 2011	2,700,000

- Obtain a loan bearing interest at 10% from Marrakech's owner, with a balloon payment due in five years. Under the terms of this arrangement, the owner can withdraw up to €1,500,000 of funding at any time, even though €3,500,000 is currently available to Marrakech. Under this approach, €1,500,000 is callable, and therefore must be classified as a short-term obligation. The remainder is classified as long-term debt. The presentation follows:

Current liabilities
    Short-term note—majority stockholder   1,500,000

Noncurrent liabilities
    10% balloon note payable to majority stock-
      holder, due in 2016   2,000,000

Long-term debt subject to demand for repayment. A lender may have the right to demand immediate or significantly accelerated repayment, or such acceleration rights vest with the lender upon the occurrence of certain events. For example, long-term (and even many short-term) debt agreements typically contain covenants, which effectively are negative or affirmative restrictions on the borrower as to undertaking further borrowings, paying dividends, maintaining specified levels of working capital, and so forth. If a covenant is breached by the borrower, the lender will typically have the right to call the debt immediately, or to otherwise accelerate repayment.

In other cases, the lender will have certain rights under a "subjective acceleration clause" inserted into the loan agreement, giving it the right to demand repayment if it perceives that its risk position has deteriorated as a result of changes in the borrower's business operations, liquidity, or other sometimes vaguely defined factors. Obviously, this gives the lender great power and subjects the borrower to the real possibility that the nominally long-term debt will, in fact, be short-term.

IAS 1 addresses the matter of breach of loan covenants, but does not address the less common phenomenon of subjective acceleration clauses in loan agreements. As to the former, it provides that continued classification of the debt as noncurrent, when one or more of the stipulated default circumstances has occurred, is contingent upon meeting two conditions: First, the lender has agreed, prior to approval of the financial statements, not to demand payment as a consequence of the breach (giving what is known as a debt compliance waiver); and second, that it is considered not probable that further breaches will occur within twelve months of the end of the reporting period. If one or both of these cannot be met, the debt must be reclassified to current status if a classified statement of financial position is, as is generally required under IAS 1, to be presented.

Logic suggests that the existence of subjective acceleration clauses convert nominally long-term debt into currently payable debt as the entity does not have an unconditional right to defer payment for 12 months from year-end. Such debt should be shown as current, with sufficient disclosure to inform the reader that the debt could effectively be "rolled over" until the nominal maturity date, at the sole discretion of the lender.

Payee Known but Amount May Need to Be Estimated

Provisions. Under IAS 37, *Provisions, Contingent Liabilities, and Contingent Assets*, those liabilities for which amount or timing of expenditure is uncertain are deemed to be provisions.

IAS 37 provides a comprehensive definition of the term "provision." It mandates, in a clear-cut manner, that a provision should be recognized *only* if

- The entity has a present obligation (legal or constructive) as a result of a past event;
- It is probable that an outflow of resources embodying economic benefits will be required to settle the obligation; and
- A reliable estimate can be made of the amount of the obligation.

Thus, a whole range of vaguely defined reserves found in financial statements in days past are clearly not permitted under IFRS. This includes the oft-manipulated restructuring reserves commonly found created during the business combination process. Now, unless there is a *present obligation* as of the purchase combination date, such reserves cannot be established—in most instances, any future restructuring costs will be recognized after the merger event and charged against the successor entity's earnings.

Many other previously employed reserves are likewise barred by the strict conditions set forth by IAS 37. However, the mere need to estimate the amount to be reflected in the provision is not evidence of a failure to qualify for recognition. If an actual obligation exists, despite one or more factors making the amount less than precisely known, recognition is required.

IAS 37 offers in-depth guidance on the topic of provisions. Each of the key words in the definition of the term "provision" is explained in detail by the standard. Explanations and clarifications offered by the standard are summarized below.

- **Present obligation.** The standard opines that in almost all cases it will be clear when a present obligation exists. The notion of an obligation in the standard includes not only a legal obligation (e.g., deriving from a contract or legislation) but also a constructive obligation. It explains that a constructive obligation exists when the entity from an established pattern of past practice or stated policy has created a valid expectation that it will accept certain responsibilities.

- **Past event.** There must be some past event which has triggered the present obligation—for example, an accidental oil spillage. An accounting provision cannot be created in anticipation of a future event. The entity must also have no realistic alternative to settling the obligation caused by the event. In other words, if the entity can avoid the expenditure through its own actions, a provision cannot be recognized (e.g., planned future maintenance on a plant).

- **Probable outflow of resources embodying economic benefits.** For a provision to qualify for recognition it is essential that it is not only a present obligation of the reporting entity, but also it should be probable that an outflow of resources embodying benefits used to settle the obligation will in fact result. For the purposes of this standard, probable is defined as "more likely than not." A footnote to the standard states that this interpretation of the term "probable" does not necessarily apply to other IFRS. The use of terms such as probable, significant, or impracticable creates problems of interpretation, both within a given set of standards (e.g., IFRS) and across different sets.

- **Reliable estimate of the obligation.** The standard recognizes that using estimates is common in the preparation of financial statements and suggests that by using a range of possible outcomes, an entity will usually be able to make an estimate of the obligation that is sufficiently reliable to use in recognizing a provision. Where no reliable estimate can be made, though, no liability is recognized.

Other salient features of provisions explained by the standard include the following:

1. **Best estimate.** For all estimated liabilities that are included within the definition of provisions, the amount to be recorded and presented in the statement of financial position should be the *best estimate*, at the end of the reporting period, of the amount of expenditure that will be required to settle the obligation. This is often referred to as the "expected value" of the obligation, which may be operationally defined as the amount the entity would pay, currently, to either settle the actual obligation or provide consideration to a third party to assume it (e.g., as a single occurrence

insurance premium). For estimated liabilities comprised of large numbers of relatively small, similar items, weighting by probability of occurrence can be used to compute the aggregate expected value; this is often used to compute accrued warranty reserves, for example. For those estimated liabilities consisting of only a few (or a single) discrete obligations, the most likely outcome may be used to measure the liability when there is a range of outcomes having roughly similar probabilities; but if possible outcomes include amounts much greater (and lesser) than the most likely, it may be necessary to accrue a larger amount if there is a significant chance that the larger obligation will have to be settled, even if that is not the most likely outcome as such.

The concept of "expected value" can be best explained through an example:

> Good Samaritan Inc. manufactures and sells pinball machines under warranty. Customers are entitled to refunds if they return defective machines with valid proof of purchase. Good Samaritan Inc. estimates that if all machines sold and still in warranty had major defects, total replacement costs would equal €1,000,000; if all those machines suffered from minor defects, the total repair costs would be €500,000. Good Samaritan's past experience, however, suggests that only 10% of the machines sold will have major defects, and that another 30% will have minor defects. Based on this information, the expected value of the product warranty costs to be accrued at year-end would be computed as follows:

> Expected value of the cost of refunds:

Resulting from major defects:	€1,000,000 × 0.10	=	€100,000
Resulting from minor defects:	€ 500,000 × 0.30	=	150,000
No defects:	€ 0 × 0.60	=	--
	Total	=	€250,000

2. **Risks and uncertainties.** The "risks and uncertainties" surrounding events and circumstances should be taken into account in arriving at the best estimate of a provision. However, as pointedly noted by the standard, uncertainty should not be used to justify the creation of excessive provisions or a deliberate overstatement of liabilities.

3. **Discounting.** The standard also addresses the use of present values or discounting (i.e., recording the estimated liability at present value, after taking into account the time value of money). While the entire subject of present value measurement in accounting has been widely debated, in practice there is a notable lack of consistency (with some standards requiring it, others prohibiting it, and many others remaining silent on the issue). IAS 37 has stood firm on the subject of present value measurement and requires the use of discounting when the effect would be material, but it can be ignored if immaterial in effect. Thus, provisions estimated to be due farther into the future will have more need to be discounted than those due currently. As a practical matter, all but trivial provisions should be discounted unless the timing is unknown (which makes discounting a computational impossibility).

IAS 37 clarifies that the discount rate applied should be consistent with the estimation of cash flows (i.e., if cash flows are projected in nominal terms). That is, if the estimated amount expected to be paid out reflects whatever price inflation is anticipated to occur between the end of the reporting period and the date of ultimate settlement of the estimated obligation, then a nominal discount rate should be used. If future cash outflows are projected in real terms, net of any price inflation, then a real interest rate should be applied. In either case, past experience must be used to ascertain likely timing of future cash flows, since discounting cannot otherwise be performed.

4. **Future events.** Future events that may affect the amount required to settle an obligation should be reflected in the provision amount where there is sufficient objective evidence that such future events will in fact occur. For example, if an entity believes that the cost of cleaning up a plant site at the end of its useful life will be reduced by future changes in technology, the amount recognized as a provision for cleanup costs should reflect a reasonable estimate of cost reduction resulting from any anticipated technological changes. However, in many instances making such estimates will not be possible.

5. **Decommissioning provisions.** IFRIC 1 mandates that changes in decommissioning provisions should be recognized prospectively (i.e., by amending future depreciation charges).

6. **Disposal proceeds.** Gains from expected disposals of assets should not be taken into account in arriving at the amount of the provision (even if the expected disposal is closely linked to the event giving rise to the provision).

7. **Reimbursements.** Reimbursements by other parties should be taken into account when computing the provision, only if it is virtually certain that the reimbursement will be received. The reimbursement should be treated as a separate asset on the statement of financial position, and not netted against the estimated liability. However, in the statement of comprehensive income or in the income statement, if prepared separately, the provision may be presented net of the amount recognized as a reimbursement. In the authors' observation, recognition of such contingent assets would be very rare in practice due to the long time horizons and concerns about the viability of the parties promising to make reimbursement payments over the long term.

8. **Changes in provisions.** Changes in provisions should be considered at the end of each reporting period, and provisions should be adjusted to reflect the current best estimate. If upon review it appears that it is no longer probable that an outflow of resources embodying economics will be required to settle the obligation, then the provision should be reversed through current period profit or loss as a change in estimate.

9. **Use of provisions recognized.** Use of a provision is to be restricted to the purpose for which it was recognized originally. A reserve for plant dismantlement, for example, cannot be used to absorb environmental pollution claims or warranty payments. If an expenditure is set against a provision that was originally recognized for another purpose, that would camouflage the impact of the two different events, distorting income performance and possibly constituting financial reporting fraud.

10. **Future operating losses.** Provisions for future operating losses cannot be recognized. This is explicitly proscribed by the standard, since future operating losses do not meet the definition of a liability at the end of the reporting period (as defined in the standard) and the general recognition criteria set forth in the standard.

11. **Onerous contracts.** Present obligations under *onerous contracts* should be recognized and measured as a provision. The standard introduces the concept of onerous contracts, which it defines as contracts under which the unavoidable costs of satisfying the obligations exceed the economic benefits expected. Executory contracts that are not onerous do not fall within the purview of this standard. In other words, the expected negative implications of such contracts (executory contracts which are not onerous) cannot be recognized as a provision.

The standard mandates that unavoidable costs under a contract represent the "least net costs of exiting from the contract." Such unavoidable costs should be measured at the *lower* of

- The cost of fulfilling the contract; *or*
- Any compensation or penalties arising from failure to fulfill the contract.

12. **Restructuring provisions.** Provisions for restructuring costs are recognized only when the general recognition criteria for provisions are met. A constructive obligation to restructure arises only when an entity has a *detailed formal plan* for the restructuring which identifies at least the following:

- The business or the part of the business concerned;
- Principal locations affected;
- Approximate number of employees that would need to be compensated for termination resulting from the restructuring (along with their function and location);
- Expenditure that would be required to carry out the restructuring; and
- Information as to when the plan is to be implemented.

Furthermore, the recognition criteria also require that the entity should have raised a valid expectation among those affected by the restructuring that it will, in fact, carry out the restructuring by starting to implement that plan or announcing its main features to those affected by it. Thus, until all the conditions mentioned above are satisfied, a restructuring provision cannot be made based upon the concept of constructive obligation. In practice, given the strict criteria of IAS 37, restructuring costs are more likely to become recognizable when actually incurred in a subsequent period.

Only *direct* expenditures arising from restructuring should be provided for. Such direct expenditures should be both necessarily incurred for the restructuring *and* not associated with the ongoing activities of the entity. Thus, a provision for restructuring would not include costs like: cost of retraining or relocating the entity's current staff members or costs of marketing or investments in new systems and distribution networks (such expenditures are in fact categorically disallowed by the standard, as they are considered to be expenses relating to the future conduct of the business of the entity, and thus are not liabilities relating to the restructuring program). Also, identifiable future operating losses up to the date of an actual restructuring are not to be included in the provision for a restructuring (unless they relate to an onerous contract). Furthermore, in keeping with the general measurement principles relating to provisions outlined in the standard, the specific guidance in IAS 37 relating to restructuring prohibits taking into account any gains on expected disposal of assets in measuring a restructuring provision, even if the sale of the assets is envisaged as part of the restructuring.

A management decision or a board resolution to restructure taken before the end of the reporting period does not automatically give rise to a constructive obligation at the end of the reporting period unless the entity has, before end of the reporting period: either started to implement the restructuring plan, or announced the main features of the restructuring plan to those affected by it in a sufficiently specific manner such that a valid expectation is raised in them (i.e., that the entity will in fact carry out the restructuring and that benefits will be paid to them).

Examples of events that may fall within the definition of restructuring are

- A fundamental reorganization of an entity that has a material effect on the nature and focus of the entity's operations;
- Drastic changes in the management structure—for example, making all functional units autonomous;
- Removing the business to a more strategic location or place by relocating the headquarters from one country or region to another; and
- The sale or termination of a line of business (if certain other conditions are satisfied, such that a restructuring could be considered a discontinued operation under IFRS 5).

DISCLOSURES

Disclosures mandated by the standard for provisions are the following:

- For each class of provision, the carrying amount at the beginning and the end of the period, additional provisions made during the period, amounts used during the period, unused amounts reversed during the period, and the increase during the period in the discounted amount arising from the passage of time and the effect of change in discount rate (comparative information is not required).
- For each class of provision, a brief description of the nature of the obligation and the expected timing of any resulting outflows of economic benefits, an indication of the uncertainties regarding the amount or timing of those outflows (including, where necessary in order to provide adequate information, disclosure of major assumptions made concerning future events), and the amount of any expected reimbursement, stating the amount of the asset that has been recognized for that expected reimbursement.
- In extremely rare circumstances, if the above disclosures as envisaged by the standard are expected to seriously prejudice the position of the reporting entity in a dispute with third parties on the subject matter of the provision, then the standard takes a lenient view and allows the reporting entity to disclose the general nature of the dispute together with the fact that, and reason why, the information has not been disclosed. This is to satisfy the concerns of those who believe that mere disclosure of certain provisions will encourage potential claimants to assert themselves, thus becoming a "self-fulfilling prophecy."

For the purposes of making the above disclosures, it may be essential to group or aggregate provisions. The standard also offers guidance on how to determine which provisions may be aggregated to form a class. As per the standard, in determining which provisions may be aggregated to report as a class, the nature of the items should be sufficiently similar for them to be aggregated together and reported as a class. For example, while it may be appropriate to aggregate into a single class all provisions relating to warranties of different products, it may not be appropriate to group and present, as a single class, amounts relating to normal warranties and amounts that are subject to legal proceedings.

Example footnote illustrating disclosures required under IAS 37 with respect to provisions

Provisions

At December 31, 2012, provisions consist of the following (all amounts in euros):

	Opening balance	Additions	Provision utilized	Unutilized provision reversed	Closing balance
Provision for environmental costs	1,000,000	900,000	(800,000)	(100,000)	1,000,000
Provision for staff bonus	2,000,000	1,000,000	(900,000)	--	2,100,000
Provision for restructuring costs	1,000,000	500,000	(100,000)	(200,000)	1,200,000
Provision for decommissioning costs	5,000,000	500,000	(2,000,000)	--	3,500,000
	9,000,000	2,900,000	(3,800,000)	(300,000)	7,800,000

Provision for environmental costs. Statutory decontamination costs relating to old chemical manufacturing sites are determined based on periodic assessments undertaken by environmental specialists employed by the company and verified by independent experts.

Provision for staff bonus. Provisions for staff bonus represents contractual amounts due to the company's middle management, based on one month's basic salary, as per current employment contracts.

Provision for restructuring costs. Restructuring provisions arise from a fundamental reorganization of the company's operations and management structure.

Provision for decommissioning costs. Provision is made for estimated decommissioning costs relating to oilfields operated by the company based on engineering estimates and independent experts' reports.

PRACTICAL EXAMPLES

The following paragraphs provide examples of provisions that would need to be recognized, based on the rules laid down by the standard. It also discusses common provisions and the accounting treatment that is often applied to these particular items.

Dry-docking costs. In some countries it is required by law, for the purposes of obtaining a certificate of seaworthiness, that ships must periodically (e.g., every three to five years) undergo extensive repairs and incur maintenance costs that are customarily referred to as "dry-docking costs." Depending on the type of vessel and its remaining useful life, such costs could be significant in amount. Before IAS 37 came into effect, some argued that dry-docking costs should be periodically accrued (in anticipation) and amortized over a period of time such that the amount is spread over the period commencing from the date of accrual to the date of payment. Using this approach, if every three years a vessel has to be dry-docked at a cost of €5 million, then such costs could be recognized as a provision at the beginning of each triennial period and amortized over the following three years.

Under the requirements set forth by IAS 37, provisions for future dry-docking expenditures cannot be accrued, since these future costs are not contractual in nature and can be avoided (e.g., by disposing of the vessel prior to its next overhaul). In general, such costs are to be expensed when incurred. However, consistent with IAS 16, if a separate component of the asset cost was recognized at inception (e.g., at acquisition of the vessel) and depreciated over its (shorter) useful life, then the cost associated with the subsequent dry-docking can likewise be capitalized as a separate asset component and depreciated over the interval until the next expected dry-docking. While the presumption is that this asset component would be included in the property and equipment accounts, in practice, some entities record major inspection or overhaul costs as a deferred charge (a noncurrent prepaid expense account) and amortize them over the expected period of benefit, which has the same impact on total assets and periodic results of operations.

Unlawful environmental damage. Cleanup costs and penalties resulting from unlawful environmental damage (e.g., an oil spill by a tanker ship which contaminates the water near the seaport) would need to be provided for in those countries which have laws requiring cleanup, since it would lead to an outflow of resources embodying economic benefits in settlement regardless of the future actions of the entity.

In case the entity which has caused the environmental damage operates in a country that has not yet enacted legislation requiring cleanup, in some cases a provision may still be required based on the principle of constructive obligation (as opposed to a legal obligation). This may be possible if the entity has a widely publicized environmental policy in which it undertakes to clean up all contamination that it causes and the entity has a clean track record of honoring its published environmental policy. The reason a provision would be needed under the second situation is that the recognition criteria have been met—that is, there is a present obligation resulting from a past obligating event (the oil spill) and the conduct of the entity has created a valid expectation on the part of those affected by it that the entity will clean up the contamination (a constructive obligation) and the outflow of resources embodying economic benefits is probable.

The issue of determining what constitutes an "obligating event" under IAS 37 has been addressed, in a highly particularized setting, by IFRIC 6, *Liabilities Arising from Participating in a Specific Market—Waste Electrical and Electronic Equipment.* This was in response to a European Union Directive on Waste Electrical and Electronic Equipment (WE&EE), which regulates the collection, treatment, recovery and environmentally sound disposal of waste equipment. Such items contain toxic metals and other materials and have become a concern in recent years, due to the large quantities (e.g., obsolete computers) of goods being dumped by household and business consumers.

The EU Directive deals only with private household WE&EE sold before August 13, 2005 ("historical household equipment"). Assuming enactment of legislation by member states, it is to be mandated that the cost of waste management for this historical household equipment will be borne by the producers of that type of equipment, with levies being assessed on them in proportion to their market shares. This will be done with reference to those manufacturers that are in the market during a period to be specified in the applicable legislation of each EU member state (the "measurement period").

The accounting issue is simply this: what is the obligating event that creates the liabilities for these producers of the defined historical household equipment, which of course all has already been sold by the producers in months and years gone by. IFRIC 6 concludes that it is participation in the market during the measurement period that will be the obligating event, rather than the earlier event (manufacture of the equipment) or a later event (incurrence of costs in the performance of waste management activities). Accordingly, initial recognition of the liability will occur when the measurement period occurs.

While IFRIC 6 was promulgated in response to a specific, and unusual, situation, it does well illustrate how significant making such determinations (the obligating event, in this instance) can be with regard to presentation in the financial statements.

Provision for restructuring costs. An entity which publicly announces, before the end of the reporting period, its plans to shut down a division in accordance with a board decision and a detailed formal plan, would need to recognize a provision for the best estimate of the costs of closing down the division. In such a case the recognition criteria are met as follows:

a present obligation has resulted from a past obligating event (public announcement of the decision to the public at large) which gives rise to a constructive obligation from that date, since it creates a valid expectation that the division will be shut down and an outflow of resources embodying economic benefits in settlement is probable.

On the other hand, if the entity had not publicly announced its plans to shut down the division before the end of the reporting period, or did not start implementing its plan before the end of the reporting period, no provision would need to be made since the board decision alone would not give rise to a constructive obligation at the end of the reporting period (since no valid expectation has in fact been raised in those affected by the restructuring that the entity will start to implement that plan). When a reporting entity commences implementation of a restructuring plan, or announces its main features to those affected, only after the end of the reporting period, disclosure is required by the provisions of IAS 10. Applying the materiality logic common in financial reporting, such disclosure would only be mandatory if the restructuring is material and if nondisclosure could reasonably be expected to influence the economic decisions made by users on the basis of the financial statements.

Onerous contracts. An entity relocates its offices to a more prestigious office complex because the old office building that it was occupying (and has been there for the last twenty years), does not suit the new corporate image it wants to project. However, the lease of the old office premises cannot be canceled at the present time since it continues for the next five years. This is a case of an onerous contract wherein the unavoidable costs of meeting the obligations under the contract exceed the economic benefits under it. A provision is thus required to be made for the best estimate of unavoidable lease payments.

Decommissioning costs. An oil company installed an oil refinery on leased land. The installation was completed before the end of the reporting period. Upon expiration of the lease contract, seven years hence, the refinery will have to be relocated to another strategic location that would ensure uninterrupted supply of crude oil. These estimated relocation or decommissioning costs would need to be recognized at the end of the reporting period. Accordingly, a provision should be recognized for the present value of the estimated decommissioning costs to take place after seven years.

In 2004, the IASB's committee dealing with implementation issues (IFRIC) issued a final interpretation, IFRIC 1, *Changes in Decommissioning, Restoration and Similar Liabilities,* which provides further guidance on this topic. Specifically, this interpretation specifies how the following matters would be accounted for:

1. Changes in the estimated outflows of resources embodying economic benefits (e.g., cash flows) required to settle the obligation;
2. Changes in current market assessments of the discount rate as defined in IAS 37 (i.e., including changes in both the time value of money and the risks specific to the liability); and
3. Increases that reflect the passage of time (also referred to as the unwinding of the discount, or as accretion of the estimated liability amount).

The interpretation holds that, regarding changes in either the estimated future cash flows or in the assessed discount rate, these would be added to (or deducted from) the related asset to the extent the change relates to the portion of the asset that will be depreciated in future periods. These charges or credits will thereafter be reflected in periodic results of operations over future periods. Thus, no prior period adjustments will be permitted in respect to such changes in estimates, consistent with IAS 8.

Regarding accretion of the discount over the asset's useful life, so that the liability for decommissioning costs reaches full value at the date of decommissioning, the interpretation holds that this must be included in current income, presumably as a finance charge. Importantly, the interpretation states that this cannot be capitalized as part of the asset cost.

Example of adjustment for changes in discount rate

To illustrate the accounting for this change, assume an oil refinery was recorded inclusive of an estimated removal cost, at present value, of €2,333,000. Now assume that, after two years have elapsed, the relevant discount rate is assessed at 6%. There have been no changes in the estimated ultimate removal costs, which are still expected to total €4,000,000. The accreted recorded liability value at this date is €2,722,000, but given the new discount rate, it needs to be adjusted to €2,989,000, for an increase of €267,000 as of the beginning of the third year. The provision account must be credited by this amount, as shown in the journal entry below.

The asset account and accumulated depreciation must also be adjusted for this change in discount rate. Under the proposed requirement, this would be done by recomputing the amount that would have been capitalized, using the initial discount rate for the first two years, followed by the new discount rate over the remaining five years (note that the new rate is not imposed on the period already elapsed, because the rate originally used was correct during those earlier periods). If the €4,000,000 future value were discounted for five years at 6% and two years at 8%, the adjusted initial present value would have been €2,563,000, instead of the €2,333,000 actually recorded. To adjust for this, the asset must be increased by (€2,563,000 – €2,333,000 =) €230,000.

Had the revised present value of the removal costs been capitalized, €732,286 (= €2,563,000 × 2/7) would have been depreciated to date, instead of the €666,571 (= €2,333,000 × 2/7) that was in fact recorded, for a net difference in accumulated depreciation of €65,715. This amount must be credited to the contra asset account.

Asset	230,000	
Expense	102,715	
Accumulated depreciation		65,715
Decommissioning liability		267,000

The remaining part of the entry above, a debit to expense totaling €102,715, is the net effect of the increase in the net book value of the asset (€230,000 – €65,715 =) €164,285, offset by the increased provision, €267,000, which is an expense of the period.

Taxes payable include federal or national, state or provincial, and local income taxes. Due to frequent changes in the tax laws, the amount of income taxes payable may have to be estimated. That portion deemed currently payable must be classified as a current liability. The remaining amount is classified as a long-term liability. Although estimated future taxes are broadly includable under the category "provisions," IAS 37 excludes tax liabilities from its scope, and specific rules in IAS 12 prohibit discounting these amounts to present values.

Property taxes payable represents the unpaid portion of an entity's obligation to a state or other taxing authority that arises from ownership of real property. Often these taxes are levied in arrears, based on periodic reassessments of value and on governmental budgetary needs. Accordingly, the most acceptable method of accounting for property taxes is a monthly accrual of property tax expense during the fiscal period of the taxing authority for which the taxes are levied. The fiscal period of the taxing authority is the fiscal period that includes the assessment or lien date.

A liability for property taxes payable arises when the fiscal year of the taxing authority and the fiscal year of the entity do not coincide or when the assessment or lien date and the actual payment date do not fall within the same fiscal year. For example, XYZ Corporation is a calendar-year corporation that owns real estate in a state that operates on a June 30 fiscal year. In this state, property taxes are assessed and become a lien against property on July 1, although they are not payable until April 1 and August 1 of the next calendar year. XYZ Corporation would accrue an expense and a liability on a monthly basis beginning on July 1.

At year-end (December 31), the firm would have an expense for six months' property tax in profit or loss and a current liability for the same amount.

Bonus payments may require estimation since the amount of the bonus payment may be affected by the amount of income taxes currently payable.

Compensated absences refer to paid vacation, paid holidays, and paid sick leave. IAS 19 addresses this issue and requires that an employer should accrue a liability for employees' compensation of future absences if the employees' right to receive compensation for future absences is attributable to employee services already rendered, the right vests or accumulates, ultimate payment of the compensation is probable, and the amount of the payment can be reasonably estimated.

If an employer is required to compensate an employee for unused vacation, holidays, or sick days, even if employment is terminated, the employee's right to this compensation is said to vest. Accrual of a liability for nonvesting rights depends on whether the unused rights expire at the end of the year in which earned or accumulated and are carried forward to succeeding years. If the rights expire, a liability for future absences should not be accrued at year-end because the benefits to be paid in subsequent years would not be attributable to employee services rendered in prior years. If unused rights accumulate and increase the benefits otherwise available in subsequent years, a liability should be accrued at year-end to the extent that it is probable that employees will be paid in subsequent years for the increased benefits attributable to the accumulated rights, and the amount can reasonably be estimated.

Pay for employee leaves of absence that represent time off for past services should be considered compensation subject to accrual. Pay for employee leaves of absence that will provide future benefits and that are not attributable to past services rendered would not be subject to accrual. Although in theory such accruals should be based on expected future rates of pay, as a practical matter these are often computed on current pay rates that may not materially differ and have the advantage of being known. Also, if the payments are to be made some time in the future, discounting of the accrual amounts would seemingly be appropriate, but again this may not often be done for practical considerations.

Similar arguments can be made to support the accrual of an obligation for post-employment benefits other than pensions if employees' rights accumulate or vest, payment is probable, and the amount can be reasonably estimated. If these benefits do not vest or accumulate, these would be deemed to be contingent liabilities. Contingent liabilities are discussed in IAS 37 and are considered later in this chapter.

Practical Examples—Payee Unknown and the Amount May Have to Be Estimated

The following are further examples of estimated liabilities, which also will fall within the definition of provisions under IAS 37.

Premiums are usually offered by an entity to increase product sales. They may require the purchaser to return a specified number of box tops, wrappers, or other proofs of purchase. They may or may not require the payment of a cash amount. If the premium offer terminates at the end of the current period but has not been accounted for completely if it extends into the next accounting period, a current liability for the estimated number of redemptions expected in the future period will have to be recorded. If the premium offer extends for more than one accounting period, the estimated liability must be divided into a current portion and a long-term portion.

Product warranties providing for repair or replacement of defective products may be sold separately or may be included in the sale price of the product. If the warranty extends into the next accounting period, a current liability for the estimated amount of warranty expense anticipated for the next period must be recorded. If the warranty spans more than the next period, the estimated liability must be partitioned into a current and long-term portion.

Example of product warranty expense accrual

The River Rocks Corporation manufactures clothes washers. It sells €900,000 of washing machines during its most recent month of operations. Based on its historical warranty claims experience, it provides for an estimated warranty expense of 2% of revenues with the following entry:

Warranty expense	18,000	
Provision for warranty claims		18,000

During the following month, River Rocks incurs €10,000 of actual labor and €4,500 of actual materials expenses to repair warranty claims, which it charges to the warranty claims provision with the following entry:

Provision for warranty claims	14,500	
Labor expense		10,000
Materials expense		4,500

River Rocks also sells three-year extended warranties on its washing machines that begin once the initial one-year manufacturer's warranty is completed. During one month, it sells €54,000 of extended warranties, which it records with the following entry:

Cash	54,000	
Unearned warranty revenue		54,000

This liability remains unaltered for one year from the purchase date, during the period of normal warranty coverage, after which the extended warranty servicing period begins. River Rocks recognizes the warranty revenue on a straight-line basis over the 36 months of the warranty period, using the following entry each month:

Unearned warranty revenue	1,500	
Warranty revenue		1,500

Contingent Liabilities

IAS 37 defines a contingent liability as an obligation that is either

- A *possible* obligation arising from past events, the outcome of which will be confirmed only on the occurrence or nonoccurrence of one or more uncertain future events which are not wholly within the control of the reporting entity; *or*
- A *present* obligation arising from past events, which is not recognized either because it is not probable that an outflow of resources will be required to settle an obligation or the amount of the obligation cannot be measured with sufficient reliability.

Under IAS 37, the reporting entity is not to give formal recognition to a contingent liability. Instead, it should disclose in the notes to the financial statements the following information:

1. An estimate of its financial effect;
2. An indication of the uncertainties relating to the amount or timing of any outflow; and
3. The possibility of any reimbursement.

Disclosure of this information is not required if the possibility of any outflow in settlement is remote, or if it is impracticable to do so.

Contingent liabilities may develop in a way not initially anticipated. Thus, it is imperative that they be reassessed continually to determine whether an outflow of resources embodying economic benefits has become probable. If the outflow of future economic benefits becomes probable, then a provision is required to be recognized in the financial statements of the period in which the change in such a probability occurs (except in extremely rare cases, when no reliable estimate can be made of the amount needed to be recognized as a provision).

Contingent liabilities must be distinguished from estimated liabilities, although both involve uncertainties that will be resolved by future events. However, an estimate exists because of uncertainty about the amount of an event requiring an acknowledged accounting recognition. The event is known and the effect is known, but the amount itself is uncertain.

In a contingency, whether there will be an impairment of an asset or the occurrence of a liability is the uncertainty that will be resolved in the future. The amount is also usually uncertain, although that is not an essential characteristic defining the contingency. Similar logic would hold for obligations related to product warranties. Both the amount and the customer are currently unknown.

Assessing the likelihood of contingent events. It is tempting to express quantitatively the likelihood of the occurrence of contingent events (e.g., an 80% probability), but this exaggerates the degree of precision possible in the estimation process. For this reason, accounting standards have not been written to require quantification of the likelihood of contingent outcomes. Rather, qualitative descriptions, ranging along the continuum from remote to probable, have historically been prescribed.

IAS 37 sets the threshold for accrual at "more likely than not," which most experts have defined as being a probability of very slightly over a 50% likelihood. Thus, if there is even a hint that the obligation is more likely to exist than to not exist, it will need to be formally recognized if an amount can be reasonably estimated for it. The impact will be both to make it much less ambiguous when a contingency should be recorded, and to force recognition of far more of these obligations at earlier dates than they are being given recognition at present.

When a loss is probable and no estimate is possible, these facts should be disclosed in the current period. The accrual of the loss should be made in the period in which the amount of the loss can be estimated. This accrual of a loss in future periods is a change in estimate. It is *not* to be presented as a prior period adjustment.

Remote contingent losses. With the exception of certain remote contingencies for which disclosures have traditionally been given, contingent losses that are deemed remote in terms of likelihood of occurrence are not accrued or disclosed in the financial statements. For example, every business risks loss by fire, explosion, government expropriation, or guarantees made in the ordinary course of business. These are all contingencies (though not necessarily contingent liabilities) because of the uncertainty surrounding whether the future event confirming the loss will or will not take place. The risk of asset expropriation exists, but this has become less common an occurrence in recent decades and, in any event, would be limited to less developed or politically unstable nations. Unless there is specific information about the expectation of such occurrences, which would thus raise the item to the possible category in any event, thereby making it subject to disclosure, these are not normally discussed in the financial statements.

Litigation. The most difficult area of contingencies accounting involves litigation. In some nations there is a great deal of commercial and other litigation, some of which exposes reporting entities to risks of incurring very material losses. Accountants must generally rely on attorneys' assessments concerning the likelihood of such events. Unless the attorney indicates that the risk of loss is remote or slight, or that the impact of any loss that does occur would be immaterial to the company, the accountant will require that the entity add explanatory material to the financial statements regarding the contingency. In cases where judgments have been entered against the entity, or where the attorney gives a range of expected losses or other amounts, certain accruals of loss contingencies for at least the minimum point of the range must be made. Similarly, if the reporting entity has made an offer in settlement of unresolved litigation, that offer would normally be deemed the lower end of the range of possible loss and, thus, subject for accrual. In most cases, however, an estimate of the contingency is unknown and the contingency is reflected only in footnotes.

Example of illustrative footnotes—contingent liabilities

1. A former plant manager of the establishment has filed a claim related to injuries sustained by him during an accident in the factory. The former employee is claiming approximately €3.5 million as damages for permanent disability, alleging that the establishment had violated a safety regulation. At the end of the reporting period, no provision has been made for this claim, as management intends to vigorously defend these allegations and believes the payment of any penalty is not probable.

2. Based on allegations made by a competitor, the company is currently the subject of a government investigation relating to antitrust matters. If the company is ultimately accused of violations of the country's antitrust laws, fines could be assessed. Penalties would include sharing of previously earned profits with a competitor on all contracts entered into from inception. The competitor has indicated to the governmental agency investigating the company that the company has made excessive profits ranging from €50 million to €75 million by resorting to restrictive trade practices that are prohibited by the law of the country. No provision for any penalties or other damages has been made at the end of the reporting period since the company's legal counsel is confident that these allegations will not be sustained in a court of law.

Financial Guarantee Contracts

Guarantees are commonly encountered in the commercial world; these can range from guarantees of bank loans made as accommodations to business associates to negotiated arrangements made to facilitate sales of the entity's goods or services. Guarantees had not been comprehensively addressed by IFRS prior to the mid-2005 amendment to IAS 39 and IFRS 4, which was made to explicitly deal with certain financial guarantee contracts.

IFRS provides guidance on the accounting for all financial guarantees—those which are in effect insurance, the accounting for which is therefore to be guided by the provisions of IFRS 4, and those which are not akin to insurance, and which are to be accounted for consistent with IAS 39. For purposes of applying this guidance, a financial guarantee contract is defined as a contract that requires the issuer to make specified payments to reimburse the holder for a loss it incurs because a specified debtor fails to make payment when due. These are generally to be accounted for under provisions of IAS 39, as follows:

- Financial guarantee contracts are initially recognized at fair value. For those financial guarantee contracts issued in stand-alone arm's-length transactions to unrelated parties, fair value at inception will be equal to the consideration received, unless there is evidence to the contrary.

- In subsequent periods, the guarantee is to be reported at the higher of (1) the amount determined in accordance with IAS 37, or (2) the amount initially recognized less, if appropriate, the cumulative amortization (to income) that was recognized in accordance with IAS 18.

If certain criteria are met, the issuer (guarantor) may elect to use the fair value option set forth in IAS 39. That is, the guarantee may be designated as simply being carried at fair value, with all changes being reported currently in profit or loss. (See Chapter 24 for discussion of the *fair value option.*)

The original (2004) proposal would have dealt with a class of arrangement that required the guarantor to make payments in response to adverse changes in the debtor's credit rating, even if no event of default occurred. However, in the amendments to IAS 39 and IFRS 4 that were actually adopted, these were excluded from the definition of financial guarantees. Rather, these credit derivatives (as they are often known) are to be accounted for at fair value under IAS 39. These are derivative financial instruments, not insurance contracts. The accounting for such derivatives is not affected by the amendments.

The language of IAS 39 observes that financial guarantee contracts can have various legal forms (e.g., a guarantee, some types of letters of credit, a credit default contract, or an insurance contract), but that the proper accounting treatment does not depend on legal form.

The basic requirement is that financial guarantee contracts, as defined, are to be accounted for under IAS 39, not under IFRS 4. However, there is an important exception: if the guarantor/issuer had previously asserted explicitly that it regarded those as insurance contracts, and had accounted for them consistently with such a declaration, then it is permitted to make a onetime election (on a contract-by-contract basis) as to whether the contracts will be accounted for as insurance or as financial instruments. This is an irrevocable election.

Apart from this special optional treatment, all financial guarantees are to be accounted for as set forth above. Free-standing guarantees (e.g., when a party other than the merchandise vendor guarantees the customer's borrowings made to effect the transaction), if arm's length, will typically be priced at fair value. For instance, if a €10,000 loan is drawn down so that the borrower can acquire machinery from a dealer, and a third party agrees to guarantee this debt to the bank for a onetime premium of €250, for a loan term of four years, that amount probably represents the fair value of the loan guarantee, which should be recorded accordingly. If it qualifies under IAS 18 for recognition as revenue on a straight-line basis, it would be amortized to income at the rate of €62.50 per year.

Assume that, subsequently, the machinery purchaser's creditworthiness is impaired by a severe downturn in its industry segment performance, so that, by the end of the second year, the fair value of this guarantee (which has two more years to run) is €200. That could be measured, among other ways, by the onetime premium that would be charged to transfer this risk to another arm's-length guarantor. Since the carrying value of the liability is €125 after two years' amortization has occurred, the *higher* of the amount determined under IAS 37 or the carrying value, €200 must be reported in the statement of financial position as the guarantee obligation. An expense of (€200 – €125 =) €75 must be recognized in the current (second) year as the cost of the additional risk borne by the reporting entity (but note that €62.50 in fee income is also being recognized in that year). The new book value, €200, will be amortized over the remaining two years ratably, assuming that no default occurs.

Note that IAS 37 stipulates that the "best estimate" of the amount to be reported as a provision is the amount that would rationally be offered to eliminate the obligation. In general, this should comport well with the notion of "fair value." Both imply a probability-weighted assessment, which may be made explicitly or implicitly depending upon the circumstances. Both also imply a present value equivalent of future resource outflows, assuming that the timing of such outflows could be estimated.

When the guarantor is not "arm's-length," determining the fair value of the guarantee at inception may be more difficult, since there is no "onetime premium" being paid to secure this arrangement. Typically, the guarantee is a sales inducement (e.g., when the machinery dealer finds it must guarantee the buyer's bank loan in order to consummate the sale), and thus is effectively a discount on the price otherwise obtainable for the merchandise (or services). The full expense would be recognized at the date of the transaction since this expense was incurred in order to generate the sale; thus it is best "matched" against revenue recognized in the current reporting period. The guarantee liability is accounted for as set forth above (adjusted to the higher of fair value or amortized original value, if amortization is appropriate under IAS 18).

Example of estimating the fair value of a guarantee

Paso Robles Company guarantees a €1,000,000 debt of Sauganash Company for the next three years in conjunction with selling equipment to Sauganash. Paso Robles evaluates its risk of payment as follows:

1. There is no possibility that Paso Robles will pay to honor the guarantee during year 1 (or, equivalently, there is zero risk of default by Sauganash in year 1).
2. There is a 15% chance that Paso Robles will pay during year 2 (i.e., that there will be a partial or complete default by Sauganash that year). If it has to pay, there is a 30% chance that it will have to pay €500,000 and a 70% chance that it will have to pay only €250,000.
3. There is a 20% chance that Paso Robles will pay during year 3. If it has to pay, there is a 25% chance that it will have to pay €600,000 and a 75% chance that it will have to pay €300,000.

The expected cash outflows from the guarantor are computed as follows:

Year 1   100% chance of paying €0 = €0

Year 2   85% chance of paying €0 and a 15% chance of paying (.30 × €500,000 + .70 × €250,000) = (€325,000 × 15%) = €48,750

Year 3   80% chance of paying €0 and a 20% chance of paying (.25 × €600,000 + .75 × €300,000) = (€375,000 × 20%) = €75,000

The present value of the expected cash flows is computed as the sum of the years' probability-weighted cash flows, here assuming an appropriate discount rate of 8%.

Year 1	€	0	×	$1/1.08$	=	€	0
Year 2	€48.750		×	$1/(1.08)^2$	=		41,795
Year 3	€75,000		×	$1/(1.08)^3$	=		59,537
	Fair value of the guarantee						€101,332

Based on the foregoing, a liability of €101,332 should be recognized at inception. This would effectively reduce the net selling price of the equipment sold to Sauganash by a like amount, thereby reducing the profit to be reported on the sale transaction. Assume that the equipment cost was €650,000; the entry recording the sale (assume specific identification is used for inventory costing) and the guarantee is as follows:

Cash	1,000,000	
Cost of goods sold	650,000	
Sales expense—guarantee of customer debt	101,332	
Revenue		1,000,000
Guarantee liability		101,332
Inventory		650,000

The profit reported in the current period would be €1,000,000 − €650,000 − €101,332 = €248,668. The guarantee liability would be amortized to income over the term of the three-year loan; if no default occurs, the dealer recovers the full sales expense it incurred by offering the discount.

Contingent Assets

Per IAS 37, a contingent asset is a possible asset that arises from past events and whose existence will be confirmed only by the occurrence or nonoccurrence of one or more uncertain future events that are not wholly within the control of the reporting entity.

Contingent assets usually arise from unplanned or unexpected events that give rise to the possibility of an inflow of economic benefits to the entity. An example of a contingent asset is a claim against an insurance company that the entity is pursuing legally.

Contingent assets should not be recognized; instead, they should be disclosed if the inflow of the economic benefits is probable. As with contingent liabilities, contingent assets need to be continually assessed to ensure that developments are properly reflected in the financial statements. For instance, if it becomes virtually certain that the inflow of economic benefits will arise, the asset and the related income should be recognized in the financial statements of the period in which the change occurs. If, however, the inflow of economic benefits has become probable (instead of virtually certain), then it should be disclosed as a contingent asset.

Example of illustrative footnotes—gain contingency/contingent asset

1. During the current year, a trial court found that a major multinational company had infringed on certain patents and trademarks owned by the company. The court awarded €100 million in damages for these alleged violations by the defendant. In accordance with the court order, the defendant will also be required to pay interest on the award amount and legal costs as well. Should the defendant appeal to an appellate court, the verdict of the trial court could be reduced or the amount of the damages could be reduced. Therefore, at the end of the reporting period, the company has not recognized the award amount in the accompanying financial statements since it is not virtually certain of the verdict of the appellate court.
2. In June 2012, the company settled its longtime copyright infringement and trade secrets lawsuit with a competitor. Under the terms of the settlement, the competitor paid the company €2.5 million, which was received in full and final settlement in October 2012, and the parties have dismissed all remaining litigation. For the year ended December 31, 2012, the company recognized the amount received in settlement as "other income," which is included in the accompanying financial statements.

Disclosures Prescribed by IAS 37 for Contingent Liabilities and Contingent Assets

An entity should disclose, for each class of contingent liability at the end of the reporting period, a brief description of the nature of the contingent liability and, where practicable, an estimate of its financial effect measured in the same manner as provisions, an indication of the uncertainties relating to the amount or timing of any outflow, and the possibility of any reimbursement.

In aggregating contingent liabilities to form a class, it is essential to consider whether the nature of the items is sufficiently similar to each other such that they could be presented as a single class.

In the case of contingent assets where an inflow of economic benefits is probable, an entity should disclose a brief description of the nature of the contingent assets at the end of the reporting period and, where practicable, an estimate of their financial effect, measured using the same principles as provisions.

Where any of the above information is not disclosed because it is not practical to do so, that fact should be disclosed. In extremely rare circumstances, if the above disclosures as envisaged by the standard are expected to seriously prejudice the position of the entity in a dispute with third parties on the subject matter of the contingencies, then the standard takes a lenient view and allows the entity to disclose the general nature of the dispute, together with the fact that, and reason why, the information has not been disclosed.

Disclosure Example

ArcelorMittal
December 31, 2010
(millions of US dollars)

Note 20: Provisions

The movements of provisions were as follows:

	Balance at December 31, 2008	Additions	Deductions/ Payments and other releases	Acquisitions	Effects of foreign exchange and other movements	Balance at December 31, 2009
Environmental (see note 24)	769	72	(131)	--	33	743
Asset retirement obligations	278	49	(2)	--	11	336
Restructuring	566	78	(131)	1	(183)	331
Voluntary separation plans[2]	935	280	(685)	--	(218)	312
Litigation (see note 24)	1,601	296	(803)	2	125	1,221
Commercial agreements and onerous contracts	855	471	(1.150)	--	(2)	174
Other[3]	631	266	(321)	3	(142)	437
	5,635	1,512	(3,223)	6	(376)	3,554
Short-term provisions	3,292					1,433
Long-term provisions	2,343					2,121
	5,635					3,554

	Balance at December 31, 2009	Additions	Deductions/ Payments and other releases	Acquisitions	Effects of foreign exchange and other movements	Balance at December 31, 2010
Environmental (see note 24)	743	95	(104)	--	(4)	730
Asset retirement obligations	336	24	(30)	--	12	342
Restructuring	331	92	(118)	--	(68)	237
Voluntary separation plans[2]	312	69	(268)	--	(32)	81
Litigation (see note 24)	1,221	327	(280)	--	(197)	1,071
Commercial agreements and onerous contracts	174	240	(221)	--	20	213
Other[3]	437	238	(143)	--	(125)	407
	3,554	1,085	(1,164)	--	(394)	3,081
Short-term provisions	1,433					1,343
Long-term provisions	2,121					1,738
	3,554					3,081

[1] *A movement of (167) is related to the transfer of provision to liabilities held for sale and distribution*

[2] *Voluntary separation plans were announced at the end of 2008 by the Group Management Board and were largely completed in 2009 and 2010. In 2010 new voluntary separation plans were announced in Mexico, Kazakhstan, Ukraine, and France. As of December 2010, the outstanding provision related to remaining plans primarily in US, France, Poland, Germany, Bosnia, Mexico, Romania, and Czech Republic.*

[3] *Other includes provision for technical warranties, and guarantees as well as other disputes.*

There are uncertainties regarding the timing and amount of the provisions above. Changes in underlying facts and circumstances for each provision could result in differences in the amounts provided for and the actual outflows. In general, provisions are presented on a nondiscounted basis due to the uncertainties regarding the timing or the short period of their expected consumption.

Environmental provisions have been estimated based on internal and third-party estimates of contaminations, available remediation technology, and environmental regulations. Estimates are subject to revision as further information develops or circumstances change. These provisions are expected to be consumed over a period of 20 years.

Restructuring provisions are mainly related to reorganizations in France and are expected to be settled within the next year.

Provisions for litigation related to probable losses that have been incurred due to a present legal or constructive obligation are expected to be settled in a period of one to four years. Discussion regarding legal matters is provided in note 24.

Provision for onerous contracts related to unavoidable costs of meeting obligations exceeding expected economic benefits under certain contracts.

In addition to existing labor agreements, voluntary separation plans which provide incentives for early retirement or separation from the Company in exchange for cash benefits, were announced at the end of 2008 and were largely completed in 2009. As of December 31, 2010, the outstanding provision relates to remaining plans primarily in France and Belgium which are expected to be settled over a period of one to four years.

Other includes provisions for technical warranties, and guarantees as well as other disputes.

REPORTING EVENTS OCCURRING AFTER THE REPORTING PERIOD

The issue addressed by IAS 10 is to what extent anything that happens between the entity's end of the reporting period and the date the financial statements are authorized for issue should be reflected in those financial statements. The standard distinguishes between events that provide information about the state of the entity existing at the end of the reporting period, and those that concern the next financial period. A secondary issue is the cutoff point beyond which the financial statements are considered to be finalized.

Authorization date. The determination of the authorization date (i.e., the date when the financial statements could be considered legally authorized for issuance, generally by action of the board of directors of the reporting entity) is critical to the concept of events after the reporting period. It serves as the cutoff point after the reporting period, up to which the events after the reporting period are to be examined in order to ascertain whether such events qualify for the treatment prescribed by IAS 10. This standard explains the concept through the use of illustrations.

The general principles that need to be considered in determining the authorization date of the financial statements are set out below.

- When an entity is required to submit its financial statements to its shareholders for approval after they have already been issued, the authorization date in this case would mean the date of original issuance and not the date when these are approved by the shareholders; and
- When an entity is required to issue its financial statements to a supervisory board made up wholly of nonexecutives, authorization date would mean the date on which management authorizes them for issue to the supervisory board.

Consider the following examples:

1. The preparation of the financial statements of Xanadu Corp. for the reporting period ended December 31, 2011, was completed by the management on February 15, 2012. The draft fi-

nancial statements were considered at the meeting of the board of directors held on February 18, 2012, on which date the Board approved them and authorized them for issuance. The annual general meeting (AGM) was held on March 28, 2012, after allowing for printing and the requisite notice period mandated by the corporate statute. At the AGM the shareholders approved the financial statements. The approved financial statements were filed by the corporation with the Company Law Board (the statutory body of the country that regulates corporations) on April 6, 2012.

Given these facts, the date of authorization of the financial statements of Xanadu Corp. for the year ended December 31, 2011, is February 18, 2012, the date when the board approved them and authorized them for issue (and not the date they were approved in the AGM by the shareholders). Thus, all post–reporting period events between December 31, 2011, and February 18, 2012, need to be considered by Xanadu Corp. for the purposes of evaluating whether or not they are to be accounted or reported under IAS 10.

2. Suppose in the above cited case the management of Xanadu Corp. was required to issue the financial statements to a supervisory board (consisting solely of nonexecutives including representatives of a trade union). The management of Xanadu Corp. had issued the draft financial statements to the supervisory board on February 16, 2012. The supervisory board approved them on February 17, 2012 and the shareholders approved them in the AGM held on March 28, 2012. The approved financial statements were filed with the Company Law Board on April 6, 2012.

In this case the date of authorization of financial statements would be February 16, 2012, the date the draft financial statements were issued to the supervisory board. Thus, all post–reporting period events between December 31, 2011, and February 16, 2012, need to be considered by Xanadu Corp. for the purposes of evaluating whether or not they are to be accounted or reported under IAS 10.

Adjusting and nonadjusting events (after the reporting period). Two types of events after the reporting period are distinguished by the standard. These are, respectively, "adjusting events after the reporting period" and "nonadjusting events after the reporting period." Adjusting events are those post–reporting period events that provide evidence of conditions that actually existed at the end of the reporting period, albeit they were not known at the time. Financial statements should be adjusted to reflect adjusting events after the reporting period.

Examples of *adjusting events*, given by the standard, are the following:

1. Resolution after the reporting period of a court case that confirms a present obligation requiring either an adjustment to an existing provision or recognition of a provision instead of mere disclosure of a contingent liability;

2. Receipt of information after the reporting period indicating that an asset was impaired or that a previous impairment loss needs to be adjusted. For instance, the bankruptcy of a customer subsequent to the end of the reporting period usually confirms the existence of loss at the end of the reporting period, and the disposal of inventories after the reporting period provides evidence (not always conclusive, however) about their net realizable value at the date of the statement of financial position;

3. The determination after the reporting period of the cost of assets purchased, or the proceeds from assets disposed of, before the reporting date;

4. The determination subsequent to the end of the reporting period of the amount of profit sharing or bonus payments, where there was a present legal or constructive obligation at the reporting date to make the payments as a result of events before that date; and

5. The discovery of frauds or errors, after the reporting period, that show that the financial statements were incorrect at the reporting date before the adjustment.

Commonly encountered situations of adjusting events are illustrated below.

- During the year 2011 Taj Corp. was sued by a competitor for €10 million for infringement of a trademark. Based on the advice of the company's legal counsel, Taj accrued the sum of €5 million as a provision in its financial statements for the year ended December 31, 2011. Subsequent to the date of the statement of financial position, on February 15, 2012, the Supreme Court decided in favor of the party alleging infringement of the trademark and ordered the defendant to pay the aggrieved party a sum of €7 million. The financial statements were prepared by the company's management on January 31, 2012, and approved by the Board on February 20, 2012. Taj Corp. should adjust the provision by €2 million to reflect the award decreed by the Supreme Court (assumed to be the final appellate authority on the matter in this example) to be paid by Taj Corp. to its competitor. Had the judgment of the Supreme Court been delivered on February 25, 2012, or later, this post–reporting period event would have occurred after the cutoff point (i.e., the date the financial statements were authorized for original issuance). If so, adjustment of financial statements would not have been required.
- Penn Corp. carries its inventory at the lower of cost and net realizable value. At December 31, 2011, the cost of inventory, determined under the first-in, first-out (FIFO) method, as reported in its financial statements for the year then ended, was €5 million. Due to severe recession and other negative economic trends in the market, the inventory could not be sold during the entire month of January 2012. On February 10, 2012, Penn Corp. entered into an agreement to sell the entire inventory to a competitor for €4 million. Presuming the financial statements were authorized for issuance on February 15, 2012, the company should recognize a write-down of €1 million in the financial statements for the year ended December 31, 2011, provided that this was determined to be an indicator of the value at year-end.

In contrast with the foregoing, *nonadjusting events* are those post–reporting period events that are indicative of conditions that arose after the reporting period. Financial statements should not be adjusted to reflect nonadjusting events after the end of the reporting period. An example of a nonadjusting event is a decline in the market value of investments between the date of the statement of financial position and the date when the financial statements are authorized for issue. Since the fall in the market value of investments after the reporting period is not indicative of their market value at the date of the statement of financial position (instead it reflects circumstances that arose subsequent to the end of the reporting period) the fall in market value need not, and should not, be recognized in the financial statements at the date of the statement of financial position.

Not all nonadjusting events are significant enough to require disclosure, however. The revised standard gives examples of nonadjusting events that would impair the ability of the users of financial statements to make proper evaluations or decisions if not disclosed. Where nonadjusting events after the reporting period are of such significance, disclosure should be made for each such significant category of nonadjusting event, of the nature of the event and an estimate of its financial effect or a statement that such an estimate cannot be made. Examples given by the standard of such significant nonadjusting post–reporting period events are the following:

1. A major business combination or disposing of a major subsidiary;
2. Announcing a plan to discontinue an operation;
3. Major purchases and disposals of assets or expropriation of major assets by government;
4. The destruction of a major production plant by fire;
5. Announcing or commencing the implementation of a major restructuring;
6. Abnormally large changes in asset prices or foreign exchange rates;
7. Significant changes in tax rates and enacted tax laws;
8. Entering into significant commitments or contingent liabilities; and

9. Major litigation arising from events occurring after the reporting period.

Dividends proposed or declared after the reporting period. Dividends on equity instruments proposed or declared after the reporting period should not be recognized as a liability at the end of the reporting period. Such declaration is a nonadjusting subsequent event, in other words. While at one time IFRS did permit accrual of post–balance sheet dividend declarations, this has not been permissible for quite some time. Furthermore, the revisions made to IAS 10 as part of the IASB's Improvements Project in late 2003 (which became effective 2005) also eliminated the display of post–reporting period dividends as a separate component of equity, as was formerly permitted. Footnote disclosure is, on the other hand, required unless immaterial.

A further clarification has been added by the 2008 *Improvements*, a collection of major and minor changes made in 2008. It states that, if dividends are declared (i.e., the dividends are appropriately authorized and no longer at the discretion of the entity) after the reporting period but before the financial statements are authorized for issue, the dividends are not recognized as a liability at the end of the reporting period, for the very simple reason that *no obligation exists at that time*. This rudimentary expansion of the language of IAS 10 was deemed necessary because it had been asserted that a *constructive obligation* could exist under certain circumstances, making formal accrual of a dividend liability warranted. The *Improvements* language makes it clear that this is never the case.

Going concern considerations. Deterioration in an entity's financial position after the end of the reporting period could cast substantial doubts about an entity's ability to continue as a going concern. IAS 10 requires that an entity should not prepare its financial statements on a going concern basis if management determines after the end of the reporting period either that it intends to liquidate the entity or cease trading, or that it has no realistic alternative but to do so. IAS 10 notes that disclosures prescribed by IAS 1 under such circumstances should also be complied with.

Disclosure requirements. The following disclosures are mandated by IAS 10:

1. The date when the financial statements were authorized for issue and who gave that authorization. If the entity's owners have the power to amend the financial statements after issuance, this fact should be disclosed;
2. If information is received after the reporting period about conditions that existed at the date of the statement of financial position, disclosures that relate to those conditions should be updated in the light of the new information; and
3. Where nonadjusting events after the reporting period are of such significance that nondisclosure would affect the ability of the users of financial statements to make proper evaluations and decisions, disclosure should be made for each such significant category of nonadjusting event, of the nature of the event and an estimate of its financial effect or a statement that such an estimate cannot be made.

Example

Altech Limited
28 February 2011

Post–Balance Sheet Events

In March 2011 the Group signed agreements to sell 25% plus one share of its interest in Altech Alcom Motomo (Pty) Limited, Altech Alcom Radio Distributors (Pty) Limited, and Altech Fleetcall (Pty) Limited to Southern Palace Group of Companies (Pty) Limited.

The empowerment consortium acquired its shareholding for a nominal consideration.

In March 2011 the Group signed agreements to sell 25% plus one share of its interest in UEC's African business to Power Matla (Pty) Limited, Empower a Thousand (Pty) Limited, and Epiworx Investment (Pty) Limited.

The empowerment consortium acquired its shareholding in UEC's African business for a nominal consideration.

FUTURE DEVELOPMENTS

In June 2005 the IASB issued an Exposure Draft (ED), *Proposed Amendments to IAS 37: Provisions, Contingent Liabilities and Contingent Assets.* On January 5, 2010, the IASB published a second ED, *IAS 37 Replacement,* that contains revised proposals for measuring liabilities within the scope of IAS 37.

The proposed amendments are principally concerned with definitions and recognition criteria in IAS 37, but have also required some amendments to the measurement requirements. The IASB proposed to eliminate the terms "provisions," "contingent liability," and "contingent asset" from the IFRS literature and replace these with a new term, "nonfinancial liabilities." The proposals provide a consistent approach to dealing with contingencies within and outside a business combination, and also provide a comprehensive approach to the accounting for nonfinancial liabilities which represents a significant change in principle for accounting for obligations. The IASB believes that "…the most significant effect of the proposed amendments is to require entities to recognize, as nonfinancial liabilities, items that were not previously recognized (and, in some cases, not considered to be liabilities)."

Provisions. Following the IASB's focus on assets and liabilities as the primary elements of the financial statements, the ED proposed that the term "provision" be eliminated and replaced with the term "nonfinancial liability," which includes items previously described as provisions as well as other liabilities. The IASB is unwilling to maintain the concept of "provision" as a separate statement of financial position item, since it believes that the current IAS 37 does not provide a clear conceptual rationale for distinguishing a provision from a liability. The IASB also clarifies that, except in specified cases, IAS 37 should be applied to all nonfinancial liabilities that are not within the scope of other Standards. Consequently, a clear distinction was made between liabilities within the scope of IAS 39 and those within the scope of IAS 37. It is also interesting to note that the ED includes a statement that IFRS do not specify how items should be described in financial statements and thus reporting entities may continue to describe some liabilities as provisions in their financial statements.

Contingent liabilities. The Exposure Draft proposes to eliminate the term "contingent liability" and to replace it with the term "nonfinancial liability." The IASB argues that liabilities arise only from unconditional (or noncontingent) obligations, and consequently a liability (i.e., an unconditional obligation) cannot be contingent or conditional.

In general, most agree that a liability should be recognized where there is a present obligation on the part of the entity as a result of past events. When there is no contingency, the point at which this occurs is determinable. In cases where there is a contingency, the ED proposed to divide the obligation into two obligations: an unconditional obligation, which is the "stand-ready" obligation, and a conditional obligation. The "stand ready" obligation requires the recognition of a liability and the conditional obligation affects the amount that will be required to settle the liability.

The application of this ED may lead to the recognition of liabilities that have a remote possibility of leading to a future outflow of economic benefits. There are certain stand-ready obligations (such as an "obligation to stand ready to perform as the court directs" of an entity that knows itself to be not guilty of the charge brought against it) that would have to be recognized under the amended guidance.

Contingent assets. As a result of analyzing items previously described as contingent assets into conditional and unconditional rights, the IASB proposed to eliminate the term "contingent assets," since it believes that the term is troublesome and confusing, and that assets arise only from unconditional (i.e., noncontingent) rights. Thus, an asset that embodies an unconditional right could not be identified as contingent or conditional. Consequently, in accordance with the *Framework*, contingent or conditional rights should not be recognized as assets, even if it is "virtually certain" that they will become unconditional or noncontingent. As a result, instead of using the term "contingent" to refer to uncertainty about whether an asset exists, the IASB decided that the term should refer to one or more uncertain future events, the occurrence (or nonoccurrence) of which affects the amount of the future economic benefits from an asset.

The ED proposes to remove the recognition requirement "virtual certainty" for reimbursement rights in IAS 37, and requires such rights to be recognized unless they cannot be measured reliably. The IASB also decided that items previously described as contingent assets under IAS 37 that satisfy the definition of an asset should be in the future within the scope of IAS 38, *Intangible Assets*. This is because such assets would be nonmonetary assets without physical form, and those which are identifiable (i.e., if separable or arise from contractual or other legal rights) meet the definition of an intangible asset.

This analysis of conditional rights and obligations can be illustrated with an example of an entity that is pursuing a lawsuit, where the outcome of this lawsuit is uncertain. In accordance with IAS 37, an entity would recognize an asset if the outcome is virtually certain. Under the proposed ED, the lawsuit would be split into two rights: (1) the entity's conditional right to receive compensation (i.e., conditional on the outcome of the legal process) and (2) the entity's unconditional right to have its claim for recovery of the damages caused by the defendant considered by the court. Consequently, although the compensation that the entity might receive as a result of a successful pursued claim is a conditional right, the pursuit of the lawsuit satisfies the definition of an asset. Therefore, the costs incurred in pursuing the lawsuit are considered an intangible asset and IAS 38 should be applied in this case.

Constructive obligations. It appears that IASB wants to heighten the threshold for, and consequently delay recognition of, constructive obligations in order to converge more with US GAAP. Under IAS 37, there must be a valid expectation in those affected that the plan will be carried out before a provision for a constructive obligation is recognized. The newly proposed definition states that there must be "a valid expectation in those parties that they can reasonably rely on it to discharge those responsibilities."

The IASB has noted that the threshold for determining whether an entity's past actions have created a constructive obligation is higher under US GAAP than under IAS 37. Under FAS 143 (ASC 410-20), which applies the doctrine of "promissory estoppel," a constructive obligation is recognized only if that obligation is a legal obligation and could be enforced by a court. However, the IASB decided that it would be premature to make such an amendment in advance of reconsidering liabilities more generally. Consequently, it proposed to introduce into a definition of a constructive obligation the notion that the counterparty should be reasonably able to rely on the entity to discharge its responsibilities.

In the Basis for Conclusions, the IASB pointed out that the "proposed amendment should not alter existing practice for well-understood examples of constructive obligations (for example, some environmental cleanup obligations and warranty obligations) because in such cases there is usually a counterparty that is relying on the entity to discharge its responsibilities. However, items that were previously determined to be constructive obligations, but leave the entity discretion to avoid settling the item, will no longer be recognized as liabilities." The ED does not provide any examples of such items or examples which could assist in developing a consistent understanding as to what type of communication is required before another party can be considered to "reasonably rely" on the entity's actions.

Probability recognition criterion. Under the current IAS 37, a provision is recognized "if it is probable that an outflow of resources embodying economic benefits will be required to settle the obligation." The IASB proposed to omit the probability recognition criterion from the Standard after having refined its analysis of items previously described as contingent liabilities. The IASB concluded that applying this criterion to "conditional obligation" conflicted with the *Framework*, which requires an entity to determine whether a liability exists before considering whether that liability should be recognized.

The ED explains that if an entity has a nonfinancial liability arising from an unconditional obligation that is accompanied by a conditional obligation, the probability recognition criterion should be applied to the unconditional obligation rather than the conditional obligation. For example, in the case of a product warranty, the criterion should be applied to the unconditional obligation to stand ready to provide warranty coverage and in such case the probability recognition criterion is always satisfied.

Measurement. In accordance with the current IAS 37, a provision should be measured at the best estimate of the expenditure required to settle the present obligation at the date of the statement of financial position. The proposed amendments to IAS 37 replaced this principle with the requirement that "a nonfinancial liability should be measured at the amount that an entity would rationally pay to settle the present obligation or to transfer it to a third party at the end of the reporting period." The ED also proposes that an expected cash flow approach can be used as the basis for measuring a nonfinancial liability for both a class of similar obligations and a single obligation. As a result, the ED moved the method of measurement of provisions (nonfinancial liabilities) from "best estimate" towards a more "fair value" approach.

Some express concerns that this measurement guidance may result in nonfinancial liabilities being recognized at their legal layoff amount (or "relief value"), the amount that has just been rejected as an appropriate measurement basis for obligations incurred within a revenue-generating context in the joint project on revenue recognition. Adopting the legal layoff approach for all nonfinancial liabilities but rejecting if for purposes of revenue recognition may create a measurement inconsistency. In light of the comments received in respect of the 2005 ED, the IASB decided during January 2010 to issue revised proposals (ED/2010/1) that include more guidance on measurement. The main provisions of the revised liability measurement ED are as follows:

- IAS 37 currently requires an entity to record an obligation as a liability only if it is probable (likelihood greater than 50%) that the obligation will result in an outflow of cash or other resources from the entity. The revised ED does not include the "probability of outflows" criterion. Instead, an entity would account for uncertainty about the amount and timing of outflows by using a measurement that reflects their expected value, namely the probability-weighted average of the outflows for the range of possible outcomes.

- Liabilities within the scope of IAS 37 would be measured at the amount that the entity would rationally pay at the measurement date to be relieved of the liability. Normally, this amount would be an estimate of the present value of the resources required to fulfill the liability, which would take into account the expected outflows of

resources, the time value of money, and the risk that the actual outflows might ultimately differ from the expected outflows.
- If the liability is to pay cash to a counterparty (for example to settle a legal dispute), the outflows would be the expected cash payments plus any associated costs, such as legal fees.
- If the liability is to undertake a service (for example, to decommission plant) at a future date, the outflows would be the amounts that the entity estimates it would pay a contractor at the future date to undertake the service on its behalf.

Reimbursement. Under the current IAS 37, when an expenditure required to settle a provision is expected to be reimbursed by another party, the reimbursement should only be recognized when it is virtually certain that the reimbursement will be received. The ED proposes to remove the recognition requirement "virtual certainty" for reimbursement rights in IAS 37 and requires such rights to be recognized unless they cannot be measured reliably.

IASB noted that most reimbursements arise from insurance contracts, indemnity clauses or suppliers' warranties. In such cases an entity has a conditional right (the reimbursement itself) and an unconditional right (e.g., the insurance contract) that satisfies the definition of an asset. As a result, any uncertainty relates to the measurement of economic benefits that will flow from the assets (and not to unconditional right).

Onerous contracts. In conformity with the current IAS 37, an onerous contract is one in which the unavoidable costs of meeting its obligations exceed the economic benefits expected. The entity should recognize as a provision the present obligation under contract, but no guidance is provided when the provision should be recognized.

The ED proposes that if a contract would become onerous as a result of an entity's own action, the liability should be recognized only when that action is taken. In the case of an onerous operating lease, the unavoidable costs of the contract should be based on the unavoidable lease commitment less any sublease rentals that the entity could reasonably obtain for the property, regardless whether the entity intends to sublease the property.

Restructuring provisions. Under the current IAS 37, an entity recognizes a restructuring provision when: (1) it has a detailed formal plan for restructuring and (2) it has raised a valid expectation in those affected that it will carry out the restructuring. The ED proposed that a nonfinancial liability for a cost associated with a restructuring should be recognized only when the definition of a liability has been satisfied for that cost. Hence, the ED removed the application guidance in IAS 37, deemphasizing the restructuring plan as the critical recognition issue; this could lead to a major change to the current practice of accounting for restructuring provisions. Following the general guidelines on constructive obligations, instead of recognizing one major restructuring provision at a specific time, in the future entities may need to recognize individual liabilities relating to the different costs occurring in restructuring, which can occur in different accounting periods.

The Exposure Drafts discussed in the preceding paragraphs have been debated at numerous IASB meetings since being proposed, but have not yet been finalized as an amended standard.

Feedback from the IASB indicates that constituents have expressed serious concerns over part of the proposed measurement guidance—in particular measuring the obligations fulfilled by undertaking a service by estimating the amount that the entity would rationally pay a contractor at the future date to undertake the service on its behalf. That proposal gained no support among constituents. Most constituents have also expressed concerns over application of risk adjustment to IAS 37 liabilities (i.e., nonfinancial liabilities).

US GAAP COMPARISION

There are substantial differences between US GAAP and IFRS with regard to provisions. US GAAP does not use the term "provisions." The term "accrual" is used in stead.

Under US GAAP, constructive obligations are only recognized for environmental obligations, decommissioning obligations, postretirement benefits, and legal disputes. Discount rates used to measure provisions at present value are a risk-adjusted risk-free rate that reflects the entity's credit standing.

When a range of estimates is available for a provision, the minimum amount is accrued under US GAAP when other estimates are equally probable, including zero. US GAAP uses the single most likely estimate to measure a provision.

Onerous contracts are not recognized as provisions. The effects are recognized upon settlement of the obligation. Exit costs are provided for only when a detailed plan is in place and recipients of severance have agreed to the terms. Costs for which employees are required to work are recognized as the work is performed.

Asset retirement obligations are largely the same, but the difference in the discount rate used to measure the obligations creates an inherent difference in the carrying value. To discount the obligation, US GAAP uses a risk-free rate adjusted for the entity's credit risk. IFRS uses the time value of money rate adjusted for specific risks of the liability. Also, period-to-period changes in the discount rate are not adjusted for. The discount rate applied to each increment of an accrual, termed "layers" in US GAAP, remains within that layer.

19 EMPLOYEE BENEFITS

INTRODUCTION

The prescribed rules for the accounting for employee benefits under IFRS have evolved markedly over the past twenty-five years. The current standard, IAS 19, was last subjected to a major revision in 1998, with further limited amendments made in 2000, 2002, 2004, and 2008, and yet a further amendment made in 2011. IAS 19 provides broad guidance, applicable to all employee benefits, not merely to pension plans. The approach set forth by IAS 19 is largely consistent with that of major national accounting standard setters. Further modifications will likely continue as the process of "convergence" moves forward.

The objective of employee benefit accounting is primarily the appropriate determination of periodic cost. Under current IAS 19, only one basic method, the "projected unit credit" variation on the *accrued benefit valuation* method, is permitted for the periodic determination of this cost. IAS 19 endorses a smoothing methodology, and thus creates a "corridor" approach to recognition of actuarial gains and losses. It requires annual valuations, whereas the earlier mandate had been for triennial valuations. It also addresses past service cost recognition and other matters that had not been given any attention in earlier standards. Revised IAS 19 is more precise in defining the extent to which components of pension cost are to be disclosed in the financial statements, and it reduces the latitude formerly given to financial statement preparers regarding amortizing certain cost elements, such as that associated with plan amendments.

IAS 19 identifies and provides accounting direction for four categories of employee benefits: short-term benefits such as wages, bonuses, and emoluments such as medical care; postemployment benefits such as pensions and other postretirement benefits; other long-term benefits such as sabbatical leave; and termination benefits. Meaningful IFRS guidance is provided on each of these, whereas the earlier standards focused only on pensions. Nonetheless, the most explicit and detailed of these instructions are for defined benefit pension and other postretirement benefits plans, with less detailed instructions given on the other types of employee benefits; this is understandable given the extreme complexity of both the plans and the accounting therefor. Another major category of employee benefit program, share-based compensation arrangements, is now dealt with by a separate standard, IFRS 2, which is addressed in detail in Chapter 17 of this publication.

Pension plans traditionally have existed in two basic varieties: defined contribution and defined benefit. The accounting for the latter is, by far, the more difficult. Given the central role that accounting estimates play in the accounting for defined benefit plans, some diversity in financial reporting will be unavoidable, and full disclosure of key assumptions and methods is the best means of preventing misunderstandings by financial statement users. Defined benefit plan accounting in particular remains a controversial subject because of the heavy impact that various management assumptions have on expense determination, and also because IAS 19 embraces the concept of expense smoothing to a much greater extent than do other accounting standards. Many believe any smoothing strategy to be inappropriate, and a number of financial reporting frauds (not related to pension accounting) uncovered in recent years used improper smoothing as a central component of their respective schemes. It remains possible that future revisions to IAS 19 and its corresponding standards under US and other national GAAP may reduce or eliminate the extent to which periodic defined benefit pension cost determinations rely on such techniques.

Because of the long-term nature of employee benefit plans, IAS 19 accepted the need for delayed recognition of certain cost components, such as those resulting from changes in actuarial estimates. Thus, certain changes are not recognized immediately but instead are recognized over subsequent years in a gradual and systematic way. Estimates and averages may be used as long as material differences are not created as a result. Explicit assumptions and estimates of future events should be made for each specified variable included in pension costs.

IAS 19 also establishes requirements for disclosures to be made by employers when defined contribution or defined benefit pension plans are settled, curtailed, or terminated. Some previously deferred amounts are required to be recognized immediately under such circumstances.

IAS 19 defines all postemployment benefits other than defined contribution plans as defined benefit plans and, thus, all the accounting complications of defined benefit pension plans are mirrored here. These difficulties may be exacerbated, in the case of postretirement health care plans, by the need to project the future escalation in health care costs over a rather lengthy time horizon, which is a famously difficult exercise to undertake.

IAS 19 was amended in mid-2002 to prohibit the recognition of gains or losses that arise solely from past service cost and actuarial losses or gains, respectively, when a surplus in the plan exists. This amendment to IAS 19 addressed what some viewed as a counterintuitive result produced by the interaction of two aspects of the standard; namely, the option to defer the gains and losses in the pension fund and the limit on the amount that can be recognized as an asset (the "asset ceiling"). The effect of the amendment, which is viewed as an interim solution only, is to prevent such counterintuitive loss or gain recognition. The asset ceiling requirement was left unchanged.

In June 2002, IASB began a limited convergence project on postemployment benefits. It resulted in the promulgation of an amendment dealing with the recognition of actuarial gain and losses, and in proposals (not acted upon) on the treatment of group defined benefit plans in the individual or separate financial statements of entities within a consolidated group, and additional disclosures. A Discussion Paper was issued in 2008, an Exposure Draft in 2010, and the final amended standard issued in 2011 with an effective date of January 1, 2013.

In July 2007, IFRIC 14 was issued, addressing the problems that arise from the interaction between the limitation on defined benefit plan asset recognition by employers/plan sponsors under IAS 19 and the statutory minimum funding requirements that exist under some jurisdictions. An amendment to IFRIC 14 was issued in November 2009 to correct an unintended consequence of that interpretation, which caused certain reporting entities, under some circumstances, to be prevented from recognizing as an asset some prepayments for minimum funding contributions.

Sources of IFRS	
IAS 19	*IFRIC* 14

DEFINITIONS OF TERMS

Accrued benefit obligation. Actuarial present value of benefits (whether vested or non-vested) attributed by the pension benefit formula to employee service rendered before a specified date and based on employee service and compensation (if applicable) prior to that date.

Accrued benefit valuation methods. Actuarial valuation methods that reflect retirement benefits based on service rendered by employees to the date of the valuation. Assumptions about projected salary levels to the date of retirement must be incorporated, but service to be rendered after the end of the reporting period is not considered in the calculation of pension cost or of the related obligation.

Accrued pension cost. Cumulative net pension cost accrued in excess of the employer's contributions.

Accrued postretirement benefit obligation. The actuarial present value of benefits attributed to employee service rendered as of a particular date. Prior to an employee's full eligibility date, the accrued postretirement benefit obligation as of a particular date for an employee is the portion of the expected postretirement benefit obligation attributed to that employee's service rendered to that date. On and after the full eligibility date, the accrued and expected postretirement benefit obligations for an employee are the same.

Actuarial gains and losses. Include (1) experience adjustments (the effects of differences between the previous actuarial assumptions and what has actually occurred); and (2) the effects of changes in actuarial assumptions.

Actuarial present value. Value, as of a specified date, of an amount or series of amounts payable or receivable thereafter, with each amount adjusted to reflect (1) the time value of money (through discounts for interest) and (2) the probability of payment (by means of decrements for events such as death, disability, withdrawal, or retirement) between the date specified and the expected date of payment.

Actuarial valuation. The process used by actuaries to estimate the present value of benefits to be paid under a retirement plan and the present values of plan assets and sometimes also of future contributions.

Amortization. Usually refers to the process of reducing a recognized liability systematically by recognizing revenues or reducing a recognized asset systematically by recognizing expenses or costs. In pension accounting, amortization is also used to refer to the systematic recognition in net pension cost over several periods of previously unrecognized amounts, including unrecognized prior service cost and unrecognized actuarial gain or loss.

Asset ceiling. The maximum amount of defined benefit asset that can be recognized is the lower of

1. The surplus or deficit in the benefit plan plus (minus) any unrecognized losses (gains) or
2. The total of

   a. Any cumulative unrecognized net actuarial losses and past service cost, and
   b. The present value of any economic benefits available in the form of refunds from the plan or reductions in future contributions to the plan, determined using the discount rate that reflects market yields at the end of the reporting period on high-quality corporate bonds or, if necessary, on government bonds.

Attribution. Process of assigning pension benefits or cost to periods of employee service.

Career-average-pay formula (career-average-pay plan). Benefit formula that bases benefits on the employee's compensation over the entire period of service with the employer. A career-average-pay plan is a plan with such a formula.

Contributory plan. Pension plan under which employees contribute part of the cost. In some contributory plans, employees wishing to be covered must contribute; in other contributory plans, employee contributions result in increased benefits.

Current service cost. The increase in the present value of the defined benefit obligation resulting from services rendered by employees during the period, exclusive of cost elements identified as past service cost, experience adjustments, and the effects of changes in actuarial assumptions.

Curtailment. Event that significantly reduces the expected years of future service of present employees or eliminates, for a significant number of employees, the accrual of defined benefits for some or all of their future services. Curtailments include (1) termination of employee's services earlier than expected, which may or may not involve closing a facility or discontinuing a segment of a business, and (2) termination or suspension of a plan so that employees do not earn additional defined benefits for future services. In the latter situation, future service may be counted toward vesting of benefits accumulated based on past services.

Defined benefit pension plan. Any postemployment benefit plan other than a defined contribution plan. These are generally retirement benefit plans under which amounts to be paid as retirement benefits are determinable, usually by reference to employees' earnings and/or years of service. The fund (and/or employer) is obligated either legally or constructively to pay the full amount of promised benefits whether or not sufficient assets are held in the fund.

Defined contribution pension plan. Benefit plans under which amounts to be paid as retirement benefits are determined by the contributions to a fund together with accumulated investment earnings thereon; the plan has no obligation to pay further sums if the amounts available cannot pay all benefits relating to employee services in the current and prior periods.

Employee benefits. All forms of consideration to employees in exchange for services rendered.

Expected long-term rate of return on plan assets. Assumption as to the rate of return on plan assets reflecting the average rate of earnings expected on the funds invested, or to be invested, to provide for the benefits included in the projected benefit obligation.

Expected postretirement benefit obligation. The actuarial present value as of a particular date of the benefits expected to be paid to or for an employee, the employee's beneficiaries, and any covered dependents pursuant to the terms of the postretirement benefit plan.

Expected return on plan assets. Amount calculated as a basis for determining the extent of delayed recognition of the effects of changes in the fair value of assets. The expected return on plan assets is determined based on the expected long-term rate of return on plan assets and the market related value of plan assets.

Experience adjustments. Adjustments to benefit costs arising from the differences between the previous actuarial assumptions as to future events and what actually occurred.

Fair value. Amount that an asset could be exchanged for between willing, knowledgeable parties in an arm's-length transaction.

Final-pay plan. A defined benefit plan that promises benefits based on the employee's remuneration at or near the date of retirement. It may be the compensation of the final year, or of a specified number of years near the end of the employee's service period.

Fund. Used as a verb, to pay over to a funding agency (as to fund future pension benefits or to fund pension cost). Used as a noun, assets accumulated in the hands of a funding agency for the purpose of meeting pension benefits when they become due.

Funding. The irrevocable transfer of assets to an entity separate from the employer's entity, to meet future obligations for the payment of retirement benefits.

Gain or loss. Change in the value of either the projected benefit obligation or the plan assets resulting from experience different from that assumed or from a change in an actuarial assumption.

Interest cost component (of net periodic pension cost). Increase in the present value of the accrued benefit obligation due to the passage of time.

Measurement date. Date as of which plan assets and obligations are measured.

Mortality rate. Proportion of the number of deaths in a specified group to the number living at the beginning of the period in which the deaths occur. Actuaries use mortality tables, which show death rates for each age, in estimating the amount of pension benefits that will become payable.

Multiemployer plans. Defined contribution plans or defined benefit plans, other than state plans, that (1) pool the assets contributed by various entities that are not under common control; and (2) use those assets to provide benefits to employees of more than one entity, on the basis that contribution and benefit levels are determined without regard to the identity of the entity that employs the employees concerned.

Net periodic pension cost. Amount recognized in an employer's financial statements as the cost of a pension plan for a period. Components of net periodic pension cost are service cost, interest cost (which is implicitly presented as part of service cost), actual return on plan assets, gain or loss, amortization of unrecognized prior service cost, and amortization of the unrecognized net obligation or asset existing at the date of initial application of IAS 19.

Other long-term employee benefits. Benefits other than postemployment, termination and stock equity compensation benefits, that are not due to be settled within twelve months after the end of the period in which service was rendered.

Past service cost. The change in the present value of the defined benefit obligation for employee services in prior periods, resulting in the current period from the introduction of, or changes to, postemployment benefits or other long-term employee benefits. Past service cost may be either positive (when benefits are introduced or changed so that the present value of the defined benefit obligation increases) or negative (when existing benefits are changed so that the present value of the defined benefit obligation decreases).

Pay-as-you-go. A method of recognizing the cost of retirement benefits only at the time that cash payments are made to employees on or after retirement.

Plan amendment. Change in terms of an existing plan or the initiation of a new plan. A plan amendment may increase benefits, including those attributed to years of service already rendered.

Plan assets. The assets held by a long-term employee benefit fund, and qualifying insurance policies. Regarding assets held by a long-term employee benefit fund, these are assets (other than nontransferable financial instruments issued by the reporting entity) that both

1. Are held by a fund that is legally separate from the reporting entity and exists solely to pay or fund employee benefits, and
2. Are available to be used only to pay or fund employee benefits, are not available to the reporting entity's own creditors (even in the event of bankruptcy), and cannot be returned to the reporting entity unless either

   a. The remaining assets of the fund are sufficient to meet all related employee benefit obligations of the plan or the entity, or
   b. The assets are returned to the reporting entity to reimburse it for employee benefits already paid by it.

Regarding the qualifying insurance policy, this must be issued by a nonrelated party if the proceeds of the policy both

1. Can be used only to pay or fund employee benefits under a defined benefit plan, and
2. Are not available to the reporting entity's own creditors (even in the event of bankruptcy) and cannot be returned to the reporting entity unless either

   a. The proceeds represent surplus assets that are not needed for the policy to meet all related employee benefit obligations, or
   b. The proceeds are returned to the reporting entity to reimburse it for employee benefits already paid by it.

Postemployment benefits. Employee benefits, other than termination benefits, which are payable after the completion of employment.

Postemployment benefit plans. Formal or informal arrangements under which an entity provides postemployment benefits for one or more employees.

Postretirement benefits. All forms of benefits, other than retirement income, provided by an employer to retirees. Those benefits may be defined in terms of specified benefits, such as health care, tuition assistance, or legal services, that are provided to retirees as the need for those benefits arises, or they may be defined in terms of monetary amounts that become payable on the occurrence of a specified event, such as life insurance benefits.

Prepaid pension cost. Cumulative employer contributions in excess of accrued net pension cost.

Present value of a defined benefit obligation. Present value, without deducting any plan assets, of expected future payments required to settle the obligation resulting from employee service in the current and prior periods.

Prior service cost. Cost of retroactive benefits granted in a plan amendment.

Projected benefit obligation. The actuarial present value as of a date of all benefits attributed by the pension benefit formula to employee service rendered prior to that date. The projected benefit obligation is measured using assumptions as to future compensation levels if the pension benefit formula is based on those future compensation levels (pay-related, final-pay, final-average-pay, or career-average-pay plans).

Projected benefit valuation methods. Actuarial valuation methods that reflect retirement benefits based on service both rendered and to be rendered by employees, as of the date of the valuation. Contrasted with accumulated benefit valuation methods, projected benefit valuation methods will result in a more level assignment of costs to the periods of employee service, although this will not necessarily be a straight-line allocation. Assumptions about projected salary levels must be incorporated. This was the allowed alternative method under the prior version of IAS 19, but is prohibited under the current standard.

Retirement benefit plans. Formal or informal arrangements whereby employers provide benefits for employees on or after termination of service, when such benefits can be determined or estimated in advance of retirement from the provisions of a document or from the employers' practices.

Retroactive benefits. Benefits granted in a plan amendment (or initiation) that are attributed by the pension benefit formula to employee services rendered in periods prior to the amendment. The cost of the retroactive benefits is referred to as prior service cost.

Return on plan assets. Interest, dividends and other revenues derived from plan assets, together with realized and unrealized gains or losses on the plan assets, less administrative costs (other than those included in the actuarial assumptions used to measure the defined benefit obligation) including taxes payable by the plan.

Service. Employment taken into consideration under a pension plan. Years of employment before the inception of a plan constitute an employee's past service; years thereafter are classified in relation to the particular actuarial valuation being made or discussed. Years of employment (including past service) prior to the date of a particular valuation constitute prior service.

Settlement. Transaction that (1) is an irrevocable action, (2) relieves the employer (or the plan) of primary responsibility for a pension benefit obligation, and (3) eliminates significant risks related to the obligation and the assets used to effect the settlement. Examples include making lump-sum cash payments to plan participants in exchange for their rights to receive specified pension benefits and purchasing nonparticipating annuity contracts to cover vested benefits.

Short-term employee benefits. Benefits other than termination and equity compensation benefits that are due to be settled within twelve months after the end of the period in which the employees rendered the related service.

Terminal funding. A method of recognizing the projected cost of retirement benefits only at the time an employee retires.

Termination benefits. Employee benefits payable as a result of the entity's termination of employment before normal retirement or the employee's acceptance of early retirement inducements.

Unrecognized prior service cost. Portion of prior service cost that has not been recognized as a part of net periodic pension cost.

Vested benefits. Those benefits which under the terms of a retirement benefit plan are not conditional on continued employment.

BACKGROUND

Importance of Pension and Other Benefit Plan Accounting

For a variety of cultural, economic, and political reasons, the existence of private pension plans has increased tremendously over the past forty years, and these arrangements are the most common and desired of the assorted "fringe benefits" offered by employers in many nations. Under the laws of some nations, employers may be required to have such programs in place for their permanent employees. For many entities, pension costs have become a very material component of the total compensation paid to employees. Unlike for wages and other fringe benefits, the timing of the payment of cash to either the plan's administrators or to the plan beneficiaries can vary substantially from the underlying economic event (that is, the plans are not always fully funded on a current basis). This creates the possibility of misleading financial statement representation of the true costs of conducting business, unless a valid accrual method is employed. For this reason, and also because of the complexity of these arrangements and the impact they have on the welfare of the workers, accounting for the cost of pension plans and similar schemes (postretirement benefits other than pensions, etc.) has received a great deal of attention from national and international standards setters.

Basic Objectives of Accounting for Pension and Other Benefit Plan Costs

Need for pension accounting rules. The principal objectives of pension accounting are to measure the compensation cost associated with employees' benefits and to recognize that cost over the employees' respective service periods. The relevant standard, IAS 19, is concerned only with the accounting aspects of pensions (and other benefit plans). The funding of pension benefits is considered to be financial management and legal concerns, and accordingly, is not addressed by this pronouncement.

When an entity provides benefits, the amounts of which can be estimated in advance, to its retired employees and their beneficiaries, the arrangement is deemed to be a pension plan. The typical plan is written, and the amounts of future benefits can be determined by reference to the plan documents. However, the plan and its provisions can also be implied from unwritten but established past practices. The accounting for most types of retirement plans is suggested by, if not heavily detailed in, IAS 19. Plans may be unfunded, insured, trust fund, defined contribution and defined benefit plans, and deferred compensation contracts, if equivalent. Independent (i.e., not employer-sponsored) deferred profit-sharing plans and pension payments which are made to selected employees on a case-by-case basis are not considered pension plans.

The establishment of a pension plan represents a long-term financial commitment to employees. Although some entities manage their own plans, this commitment usually takes the form of contributions that are made to an independent trustee or, in some countries, to a governmental agency. These contributions are used by the trustee to acquire plan assets of various kinds, although the available types of investments may be restricted by governmental regulations in certain jurisdictions. Plan assets are used to generate a financial return, which typically consists of earned interest and/or appreciation in asset values.

The earnings from the plan assets (and occasionally, the proceeds from their liquidation) provide the trustee with cash to pay the benefits to which the employees become entitled at the date of their retirements. These benefits in turn are defined by the terms of the pension plan, which is known as the plan's benefit formula. In the case of defined benefit plans, the benefit formula incorporates many factors, including the employee's current and future compensation, service longevity, age, and so on. The benefit formula is the best indicator of the plan's obligations at any point in time. It is used as the basis for determining the pension cost to be recognized each fiscal year.

BASIC PRINCIPLES OF IAS 19

Applicability: pension plans. IAS 19 is applicable to both defined contribution and defined benefit pension plans. The accounting for *defined contribution* plans is normally straightforward, with the objective of matching the cost of the program with the periods in which the employees earn their benefits. Since contributions are formula-driven (e.g., as a percentage of wages paid), typically the payments to the plan will be made currently; if they do not occur by the end of the reporting period, an accrual will be recognized for any unpaid current contribution liability. Once made or accrued, the employer has no further obligation for the value of the assets held by the plan or for the sufficiency of fund assets for payment of the benefits, absent any violation of the terms of the agreement by the employer. Employees thus suffer or benefit from the performance of the assets in which the contributions made on their behalf were invested; often the employees themselves are charged with responsibility for selecting those investments.

IAS 19 requires that disclosure be made of the amount of expense recognized in connection with a defined contribution pension plan. If not explicitly identified in the statement of profit or loss and other comprehensive income, this should therefore be disclosed in the notes to the financial statements.

Compared to defined contribution plans, the accounting for *defined benefit* plans is vastly more complex, because the employer (sponsor) is responsible not merely for the current contribution to be made to the plan on behalf of participants, but additionally for the sufficiency of the assets in the plan for the ultimate payments of benefits promised to the participants. Thus the current contribution is at best a partial satisfaction of its obligation, and the amount of actual cost incurred is not measured by this alone. The measurement of pension cost under a defined benefit plan necessarily involves the expertise of actuaries— persons who are qualified to estimate the numbers of employees who will survive (both as employees, in the case of vesting requirements which some of them may not yet have met; and as living persons who will be present to receive the promised retirement benefits), the salary levels at which they will retire (if these are incorporated into the benefit formula, as is commonly the case), their expected life expectancy (since benefits are typically payable for life), and other factors which will influence the amount of resources needed to satisfy the employer's promises. Actuarial determinations cannot be made by accountants, who lack the training and credentials, but the results of actuaries' efforts will be critical to the ability to properly account for defined benefit plan costs. Accounting for defined benefit plans is described at length in the following pages.

Applicability: other employee benefit plans. IAS 19 explicitly applies to not merely pension plans, but also three other categories of employee and postemployment benefits. These are

1. *Short-term employee benefits,* which include normal wages and salaries as well as compensated absences, profit sharing and bonuses, and such nonmonetary fringe benefits as health insurance, housing subsidies, and employer-provided automobiles, to the extent these are granted to current (not retired) employees.
2. *Other long-term employee benefits,* such as long-term (sabbatical) leave, long-term disability benefits and, if payable after twelve months beyond the end of the reporting period, profit sharing and bonus arrangements and deferred compensation.

3. *Termination benefits,* which are payments to be made upon termination of employment under defined circumstances, generally when employees are induced to leave employment before normal retirement age.

Each of the foregoing categories of employee benefits will be explained later in this chapter.

IAS 19 also addresses postemployment benefits *other than pensions,* such as retiree medical plan coverage, as part of its requirements for pension plans, since these are essentially similar in nature. These are also discussed further later in this chapter.

IAS 19 considers all plans other than those explicitly structured as defined contribution plans to be defined benefit plans, with the accounting and reporting complexities that this implies. Unless the employer's obligation is strictly limited to the amount of contribution currently due, typically driven by a formula based on entity performance or by employee wages or salaries, the obligations to the employees (and the amount of recognizable expense) will have to be estimated in accordance with actuarial principles.

Cost recognition distinguished from funding practices. Although it is arguably a sound management practice to fund retirement benefit plans on a current basis, in some jurisdictions the requirement to do this is either limited or absent entirely. Furthermore, in some jurisdictions the currently available tax deduction for contributions to pension plans may be limited, reducing the incentive to make such contributions until such time as the funds are actually needed for making payouts to retirees. Since the objective of periodic financial reporting is to match costs and revenues properly on a current basis, the pattern of funding is obviously not always going to be a useful guide to proper accounting for pension costs.

POSTEMPLOMENT BENEFIT PLANS

General discussion. Absent specific information to the contrary, it is assumed that a company will continue to provide retirement benefits well into the future. The accounting for the plan's costs should be reflected in the financial statements and these amounts should not be discretionary. All pension costs—with the exception noted below—should be charged against income. No amounts should be charged directly to retained earnings. The principal focus of IAS 19 is on the allocation of cost to the periods being benefited, which are the periods in which the covered employees provide service to the reporting entity.

As a result of a limited amendment to IAS 19 enacted in 2004, entities have the option of fully recognizing actuarial gains and losses in the period in which they occur, in other comprehensive income in the statement of comprehensive income, outside of operating results. This eliminates these gains and losses from profit or loss determination but includes them in a "middle step" statement, and not directly as charges or credits to retained earnings.

Periodic measurement of cost for defined contribution plans. Under the terms of a defined contribution plan, the employer will be obligated for fixed or determinable contributions in each period, often computed as a percentage of the wage and salary base paid to the covered employees during the period. For one example, contributions might be set at 4% of each employee's wages and salaries, up to €50,000 wages per annum. Generally, the contributions must actually be made by a specific date, such as ninety days after the end of the reporting entity's fiscal year, consistent with local law. The expense must be accrued for accounting purposes in the year the cost is incurred, whether the contribution is made currently or not.

IAS 19 requires that contributions payable to a defined contribution plan be accrued currently, even if not paid by year-end. If the amount is due over a period extending more than one year from the end of the reporting period, the long-term portion should be discounted at the rate applicable to long-term corporate bonds, if that information is known, or applicable to government bonds in the alternative.

Employers may choose to make further discretionary contributions to benefit plans in certain periods. For example, if the entity enjoys a particularly profitable year, the board of directors may vote to grant another 2% of wages as a bonus contribution to the employees' benefit plan. Normally, an entity making such a discretionary contribution does not do so simply to reward past performance by its workers. Rather, it does so in the belief that the gesture will cause its employees to be motivated to be more productive and loyal in the forthcoming years. IAS 19 addresses profit sharing and bonus plans as a subset of its requirements concerning short-term compensation arrangements; it stipulates that such a payment should be recognized only when paid or when the entity has a legal or constructive obligation to make it, and when the payment can be reliably estimated. There appears to be no basis for deferring recognition of the expense after that point, however, even though longer-term benefits to the entity might be hoped for.

Past service costs arise when a plan is amended retroactively, so that additional attribution for benefits is given to services rendered in past years. When plans are amended in this fashion, it is generally management's belief that doing so will provide an incentive for greater efforts in the future. For that reason, expense related to past service cost is recognized over the remaining period until these benefits become vested. Despite characterization as relating to past service, no adjustment or restatement is made to prior periods' reported costs, nor is a "catch-up" adjustment made in the period that the plan is amended—unless the benefit increase is fully vested when granted. The manner by which these past service costs are funded, of course, is an issue separate from the accounting for the additional expense. The measure of past service cost is the change in the pension liability resulting from the plan amendment. (In rare cases, past service cost may be a negative amount, if attribution for benefits is reduced.)

IAS 19 does not explicitly address retroactive amendments to defined contribution plans, but by analogizing from the requirements concerning similar amendments to defined benefit plans, it is clear that, if fully vested immediately (as would almost inevitably be the case), these would have to be expensed immediately.

Terminations of defined contribution plans generally provide no difficulties from an accounting perspective, since costs have been recognized currently in most instances. However, if certain costs, such as those associated with past services and with discretionary bonus contributions made in past years, have not yet been fully amortized, the remaining unrecognized portions of those costs must be expensed in the period when it becomes probable that the plan is to be terminated. This should be the period when the decision to terminate is made, which on occasion may precede the actual termination of the plan.

Periodic measurement of cost for defined benefit plans. Defined benefit plans present a far greater challenge to accountants than do defined contribution plans, since the amount of expense to be recognized currently will need to be determined on an actuarial basis. Under current IFRS, only the accrued benefit valuation method may be used to measure defined benefit plan pension cost. Furthermore, only a single variant of the accrued benefit method—the "projected unit credit" method—is permitted. A number of alternative approaches, which also fell under the general umbrella of the accrued benefit method are no longer accepted under IFRS. Accordingly, only the projected unit credit method will be discussed.

Net periodic pension cost will consist of the sum of the following six components:

1. Current (pure) service cost
2. Interest cost for the current period on the accrued benefit obligation
3. The expected return on plan assets
4. Actuarial gains and losses, to the extent recognized
5. Past service costs, to the extent recognized
6. The effects of any curtailments or settlements

Disclosures required by IAS 19 effectively require that these cost components be displayed in the notes to the financial statements.

It is important to stress that current service cost, the core cost element of all defined benefit plans, must be determined by a qualified actuary. While the other items to be computed and presented are also developed by actuaries in most cases, they can be verified or even calculated directly by others, including the entity's internal or external accountants. The current service cost, however, is not an immediately apparent computation, as it relies upon a detailed census of employees (age, expected remaining working life, etc.) and the employer's experience (turnover, etc.), and is an intricate and elaborate computational exercise in many cases. Current service cost can only be developed by this careful, employee-by-employee analysis, and this is best left to those with the expertise to complete it.

Current service cost. Current service cost must be determined by an actuarial valuation and will be affected by assumptions such as expected turnover of staff, average retirement age, the plan's vesting schedule, and life expectancy after retirement. The probable progression of wages over the employees' remaining working lives will also have to be taken into consideration if retirement benefits will be affected by levels of compensation in later years, as will be true in the case of career average and final pay plans, among others.

It is worth stressing this last point: when pension arrangements call for benefits to be based on the employees' ultimate salary levels, experience will show that those benefits will increase, and any computation based on current salary levels will surely understate the actual economic commitment to the future retirees. Accordingly, IFRS requires that, for such plans, future salary progression must be considered in determining current period pension costs. This is why the services of a consulting actuary are vital; it is not something to be assigned to accountants. While future salary progression (where appropriate to the plan's benefit formula) must be incorporated (via estimated wage increase rates), current pension cost is a function of the services provided by the employee in the reporting period, emphatically not including services to be provided in later periods.

Under IAS 19, service cost is based on the present value of the defined benefit obligation, and is attributed to periods of service without regard to conditional requirements under the plan calling for further service. Thus, vesting is not taken into account in the sense that there is no justification for nonaccrual prior to vesting. However, in the actuarial determination of pension cost, the statistical probability of employees leaving employment prior to vesting must be taken into account, lest an overaccrual of these costs result.

Example of service cost attribution

To explain the concept of service cost, assume a single employee is promised a pension of €1,000 per year for each year worked before retirement, for life, upon retirement at age 60 or thereafter. Further assume that this is the worker's first year on the job, and he is 30 years of age. The consulting actuary determines that if the worker, in fact, retires at age 60, he will have a life expectancy of 15 years, and at the present value of the required benefits (€1,000/yr × 15 years = €15,000) discounted at the long-term corporate bond rate, 8%, equals €8,560. In other words, based on the work performed thus far (one year's worth), this employee has earned the right to a lump-sum settlement of €8,560 at age 60. Since this is 30 years into the future, this amount must be reduced to present value, which at 8% is a mere €851, which is the pension cost to be recognized currently.

In year two, this worker earns the right to yet another annuity stream of €1,000 per year upon retirement, which again has a present value of €8,560 at the projected retirement age of 60. However, since age 60 is now only 29 years hence, the present value of that promised benefit at the end of the current (second) year is €919, which represents the service cost in year two. This pattern will continue: As the employee ages, the current cost of pension benefits grows apace with, for example, the cost in the final working year being €8,560, before considering interest on the previously accumulated obligation—which would, however, add another €18,388 of expense, for a total cost for this one employee in his final working year of €26,948. It should be noted, however, that in "real-life" situations for employee groups in the aggregate, this may not hold, since new younger employees will be added as older employees die or retire, which will tend to smooth out the annual cost of the plan.

Interest on the accrued benefit obligation. As noted, since the actuarial determination of current period cost is the present value of the future pension benefits to be paid to retirees by virtue of their service in the current period, the longer the time until the expected retirement date, the lower will be the service cost recognized. However, over time this accrued cost must be further increased, until at the employees' respective retirement dates the full amounts of the promised payments have been accreted. In this regard, the accrued pension liability is much like a sinking fund that grows from contributions plus the earnings thereon.

Consider the example of service cost presented in the preceding section. The €851 obligation recorded in the first year of that example will have grown to €919 by the end of the second year. This €68 increase in the obligation for future benefits due to the passage of time is reported as a component of pension cost, denoted as interest cost.

While service cost and interest are often the major components of expense recognized in connection with defined benefit plans, there are other important elements of benefit cost to be accounted for. IAS 19 identifies the expected return on plan assets, actuarial gains and losses, past service costs, and the effects of any curtailments or settlements as categories to be explicitly addressed in the disclosure of the details of annual pension cost for defined benefit plans. These will be discussed in the following sections, in turn.

The expected return on plan assets. IAS 19 has adopted the approach that since pension plan assets are intended as long-term investments, the random and perhaps sizable fluctuations from period to period should not be allowed to excessively distort the operating results reported by the sponsoring entity. This standard identifies the expected return rather than the actual return on plan assets as the salient component of pension cost, with the difference between actual and expected return being an *actuarial gain or loss* to be dealt with as described below (deferred to future periods or, if significant, partially recognized in the current period). Expected return for a given period is determined at the start of that period, and is based on long-term rates of return for assets to be held over the term of the related pension obligation. Expected return is to incorporate anticipated dividends, interest, and changes in fair value, and is furthermore to be reduced in respect of expected plan administration costs.

For example, assume that at the start of 2012 the plan administrator expects, over the long term, and based on historical performance of plan assets, that the plan's assets will receive annual interest and dividends of 6%, net of any taxes due by the fund itself, and will enjoy a market value gain of another 2.5%. It is also noted that plan administration costs will average .75% of plan assets, measured by fair value. With this data, an expected rate of return for 2012 would be computed as 6.00% + 2.50% − .75% = 7.75%. This rate would be used to calculate the return on assets, which would be used to offset service cost and other benefit plan cost components for the year 2012.

The difference between this assumed rate of return, 7.75% in this example, and the actual return enjoyed by the plan's assets would be added to or subtracted from the cumulative actuarial gains and losses. In theory, over the long run, if the expected returns are accurately estimated, these gains and losses will largely offset, inasmuch as they are the result of random, short-term fluctuations in market returns and of demographic and other changes in the group covered by the plan (such as unusual turnover, mortality, or changes in salaries). Since these are expected to largely offset, and given the very long time horizon over which pension benefit plan performance is to be judged, the notion of deferring and thus smoothing recognition of these net gains or losses was appealing, although certainly subject to criticism since actual economic results will not be reported as they occur.

Prior to a 2000 amendment to IAS 19, assets were properly considered to be plan assets only if *all* of the following three conditions were met:

1. The pension or other benefit plan is an entity which is legally separate from the sponsoring employer or entity;
2. The assets of the plan are only to be used to settle employee benefit obligations, are not available to the sponsoring entity's creditors, and either cannot be returned to the sponsor at all or can be returned only to the extent that assets remaining in the fund are sufficient to meet the plan's obligations; and
3. The sponsor will have no legal or constructive obligation to directly pay the employee benefit obligations, assuming that the fund contains sufficient assets to satisfy those obligations.

The 2000 amendment modified IAS 19's definition of plan assets to explicitly include certain insurance policies, and to eliminate the condition relating to sufficiency of assets in the funds. It also slightly amended and reworded the balance of the former definition. The new definition includes assets held by a long-term employee benefit fund, and qualifying insurance policies. Regarding assets held by a fund, these are assets (other than nontransferable financial instruments issued by the reporting entity) that both

1. Are held by a fund that is legally separate from the reporting entity and exist solely to pay or fund employee benefits, and
2. Are available to be used only to pay or fund employee benefits, are not available to the reporting entity's own creditors (even in the event of bankruptcy), and cannot be returned to the reporting entity unless either

   a. The remaining assets of the fund are sufficient to meet all related employee benefit obligations of the plan or the entity, or
   b. The assets are returned to the reporting entity to reimburse it for employee benefits already paid by it.

Regarding the qualifying insurance policy, this must be issued by a nonrelated party if the proceeds of the policy both

1. Can be used only to pay or fund employee benefits under a defined benefit plan, and
2. Are not available to the reporting entity's own creditors (even in the event of bankruptcy), and cannot be returned to the reporting entity unless either

   a. The proceeds represent surplus assets that are not needed for the policy to meet all related employee benefit obligations, or

b. The proceeds are returned to the reporting entity to reimburse it for employee benefits already paid by it.

It should be stressed that the definition of plan assets is significant for several reasons: plan assets are excluded from the sponsoring employer's statement of financial position and will also serve as the basis for determining the actual and expected rates of return, which impact on the periodic determination of pension cost. By adopting a somewhat more expansive definition of plan assets, the amended IAS 19 affected the future computation of pension costs.

The IAS 19 amendment adopted in 2000 also added certain new requirements which relate to recognition and measurement of the right of reimbursement of all or part of the expenditure to settle a defined benefit obligation. It established that only when it is virtually certain that another party will reimburse some or all of the expenditure required to settle a defined benefit obligation, the sponsoring entity would recognize its right to reimbursement as a separate asset, which would be measured at fair value. In all other respects, however, the asset (amount due from the pension plan) is to be treated in the same way as plan assets. In the statement of comprehensive income or separate income statement presented, defined benefit plan expense may be presented net of the reimbursement receivable recognized.

In some situations, a plan sponsor would be able to look to another entity to pay some or all of the cost to settle a defined benefit obligation, but the assets held by that other party were not deemed to be plan assets as defined in IAS 19 (prior to the revision in 2000). For example, when an insurance policy would match postemployment benefits, the assets of the insurer were not included in plan assets because the insurer was not established solely to pay or fund employee benefits. In such cases, the sponsor recognized its right to reimbursement as a separate asset, rather than as a deduction in determining the defined benefit liability (i.e., no right of offset was deemed to exist in such instances); in all other respects (e.g., the use of the corridor), the sponsoring entity would treat that asset in the same way as plan assets. In particular, the defined benefit liability recognized under IAS 19 had been increased (reduced) to the extent that net cumulative actuarial gains (losses) on the defined benefit obligation and on the related reimbursement remain unrecognized under this standard, as explained earlier in this chapter. A brief description of the link between the reimbursement and the related obligation would be required.

If the right to reimbursement arises under an insurance policy that exactly matches the amount and timing of some or all of the benefits payable under a defined benefit plan, the fair value of the reimbursement was formerly deemed to be present value of the related obligation (subject to any reduction required if the reimbursement was not recoverable in full).

As amended, however, qualifying insurance policies are now to be included in plan assets, arguably because those plans have similar economic effects to funds whose assets qualify as plan assets under the revised definition.

Actuarial gains and losses, to the extent recognized. Changes in the amount of the actuarially determined pension obligation and differences in the actual versus the expected yield on plan assets, as well as demographic changes (e.g., composition of the workforce, changes in life expectancy, etc.) contribute to actuarial (or "experience") gains and losses. While immediate recognition of these gains or losses could clearly be justified conceptually (because these are real and have already occurred), there are both theoretical arguments opposed to such immediate recognition (the distorting effects on the measure of current operating performance resulting from very long-term investments, much of which will reverse of their own accord over time), as well as great opposition by financial statement preparers and users. For this reason, IAS 19 does not require such immediate recognition, unless the fluctuations are so great that deferral is not deemed to be wise, and the standard defined a 10%

"corridor" as representing the range of variation deemed to be "normal." While the use of a 10% threshold is arbitrary, it does carry an aura of acceptability, since it had been employed for over a decade previously under US GAAP.

Thus, if the unrecognized actuarial gain or loss is no more than 10% of the larger of the present value of the defined benefit obligation or the fair value of plan assets, measured at the beginning of the reporting period, no recognition in the current period will be necessary (i.e., there will be continued deferral of the accumulated net actuarial gain or loss). On the other hand, if the accumulated net actuarial gain or loss exceeds this 10% corridor, the magnitude creates greater doubt that future losses or gains will offset these, and for that reason some recognition will be necessary.

It is suggested by IAS 19 that this excess be amortized over the expected remaining working lives of the then-active employee participants, but the standard actually permits any reasonable method of amortization as long as (1) recognition is at no slower a pace than would result from amortization over the working lives of participants, and (2) that the same method is used for both net gains and net losses. It is also acceptable to fully recognize all actuarial gains or losses immediately, without regard to the 10% corridor.

The corridor and the amount of any excess beyond this corridor must be computed anew each year, based on the present value of defined benefits and the fair value of plan assets, each determined as of the beginning of the year. Thus, there may have been an unrecognized actuarial gain of €450,000 at the end of year one, which exceeds the 10% corridor boundary by €210,000, and is therefore to be amortized over the average twenty-one-year remaining working life of the plan participants, indicating a €10,000 reduction in pension cost in year two. If, at the end of year two, market losses or other actuarial losses reduce the accumulated actuarial gain below the threshold implied by the 10% corridor, accordingly, in year three there will be no further amortization of the net actuarial gain. This determination, therefore, must be made at the beginning of each period. Depending on the amount of unrecognized actuarial gain or loss at the end of year three, there may or may not be amortization in year four, and so on.

The concept of the corridor has recently been removed from IAS 19. For more on this, refer to the future developments section at the end of this chapter.

Past service costs, to the extent recognized. Past service costs refer to increases in the amount of a defined benefit liability that results from the initial adoption of a plan, or from a change or amendment to an existing plan which increases the benefits promised to the participants with respect to previous service rendered. Less commonly, a plan amendment could reduce the benefits for past services, if local laws permit this. Employers will amend plans for a variety of reasons, including competitive factors in the employment marketplace, but often it is done with the hope and expectation that it will engender goodwill among the workers and thus increase future productivity. For this reason, it is sometimes the case that these added benefits will not vest immediately, but rather must be earned over some defined time period.

IAS 19 requires immediate recognition of past service cost as an expense when the added benefits vest immediately. However, when these are not immediately vested, recognition is to be on a straight-line basis over the period until vesting occurs. For example, if at January 1, 2012, the sponsoring entity grants an added €4,000 per employee in future benefits, and given the number of employees expected to receive these benefits this computes to a present value of €455,000, but vesting will not be until January 1, 2017, then a past service cost of €455,000 ÷ 5 years = €91,000 per year will be recognized. (To this amount interest must be added, as with service cost as described above.)

The effects of any curtailments or settlements. Periodic defined benefit plan expense is also affected by any curtailments or settlements which have been incurred. The standard defines a curtailment as arising in connection with isolated events such as plant closings, discontinuations of operations, or termination or suspension of a benefit plan. Curtailments may also result from changes in plan features that tie future salary progressions to benefits that will be payable for past service. Often, corporate restructurings will be accompanied by curtailments in benefit plans. Recognition can be given to the effect of a curtailment when the sponsor is demonstrably committed to make a material reduction in the number of covered employees, or it amends the terms of the plan such that a material element of future service by existing employees will no longer be covered or will receive reduced benefits. The curtailment must actually occur for it to be given recognition.

Settlements occur when the entity enters into a transaction which effectively transfers the obligation to another entity, such as an insurance company, so that the sponsor has no legal or constructive obligation to fund any benefit shortfall. Merely acquiring insurance which is intended to cover the benefit payments does not constitute a settlement, since a funding mechanism does not relieve the underlying obligation.

Under the current standard's predecessor, curtailment and settlement gains were recognized when the event occurred, but losses were to be recognized when probable of occurrence. Revised IAS 19 concluded that being *probable* was not sufficient under IFRS to warrant expense or loss recognition in the context of pension plan curtailments or settlements. Thus, both gains and losses are to be recognized when the event occurs.

The effect of a curtailment or settlement is measured with reference to the change in present value of the defined benefits, any change in fair value of related assets (normally there is none), and any related actuarial gains or losses and past service cost which had not yet been recognized. The net amount of these elements will be charged or credited to pension expense in the period the curtailment or settlement actually occurs.

Example of a settlement

Assume that a company's pension plan, at the current date, reports obligations amounting to €1,150 in vested future benefits and another €400 in nonvested benefits. It settles the €1,150 vested benefit portion of its projected benefit obligation by using plan assets to purchase a non-participating annuity contract at a cost of €1,150. After this settlement, nonvested benefits and the effects of projected future compensation levels remain in the plan. In accordance with IAS 19, a pro rata amount of the unrecognized net actuarial loss on assets and unrecognized past service cost are recognized due to settlement. Because the projected benefit obligation is reduced from €1,550 to €400, for a decrease of 74%, the pro rata amount used for recognition purposes is 74%. These changes are noted in the following table:

	Before settlement	*Effect of settlement*	*After settlement*
Assets and obligations			
Vested benefit obligation	€(1,150)	€1,150	€ 0
Nonvested benefits	(400)	0	(400)
Pension benefit obligation before salary increases projection	(1,550)	1,150	(400)
Effects of projected future salary increases	(456)	0	(456)
Pension benefit obligation	(2,006)	1,150	(856)
Plan assets at fair value	1,159	(1,150)	369

	Before settlement	Effect of settlement	After settlement
Items not yet recognized in profit or loss			
Funded status	(487)	0	(487)
Unrecognized net actuarial loss on assets	174	(129)	45
Unrecognized prior service cost	293	(217)	76
Unamortized net asset at IAS 19 adoption	(3)	0	(3)
Prepaid (accrued) benefit cost	€ (23)	€ (346)	€(369)

The entry used by the company to record this transaction does not include the purchase of the annuity contract, since the pension plan acquires the contract with existing funds. The recognition of the pro rata amount of the unrecognized net actuarial loss on assets and unrecognized prior service cost is recorded with the following entry:

Loss from settlement of pension obligation	346	
Accrued/prepaid pension cost		346

Example of a curtailment

Use information from the previous example; assume that the company shuts down one of its factories, which terminates the employment of a number of its staff. The terminated employees have nonvested benefits of €120 and a projected benefit obligation of €261. As a result of this curtailment of the plan, 19% of the pension benefit obligation has been eliminated (€381 obligation reduction resulting from the curtailment, divided by the beginning €2,006 pension benefit obligation). Accordingly, 19% of the unrecognized past service cost will also be recognized. The analysis follows:

	Before curtailment	Effect of curtailment	After curtailment
Assets and obligations			
Vested benefit obligation	€(1,150)	€ 0	€(1,150)
Nonvested benefits	(400)	120	(280)
Pension benefit obligation before salary increases projection	(1,550)	120	(1,430)
Effects of projected future salary increases	(456)	261	(195)
Pension benefit obligation	(2,006)	381	(1,625)
Plan assets at fair value	1,159		1,159
Items not yet recognized in profit or loss			
Funded status	(487)	381	(106)
Unrecognized net actuarial loss on assets	174	(33)	141
Unrecognized prior service cost	293	(56)	237
Unamortized net asset at IAS 19 adoption	(3)	0	(3)
Prepaid (accrued) benefit cost	€ (23)	€ 292	€ 269

The company records the recognition of the pro rata amount of the unrecognized prior service cost and unamortized net actuarial loss, which is offset against the net gain of €381 resulting from the reduction in the pension benefit obligation.

Accrued/prepaid pension cost	292	
Gain from curtailment of pension obligation		292

Transition adjustment. The final element of periodic pension cost under IAS 19 related to the effect of first adopting the accounting standard, which was mandatory for years beginning 1999. The transition amount was to be the present value of the benefit obligation at the date the standard was adopted, less the fair value of plan assets at that date, less any past service cost that was to be deferred to later periods, if the criterion regarding vesting period was met. If the transitional liability was greater than the liability which would have been recognized under the entity's previous policy for accounting for pension costs, it was required to make an *irrevocable* choice to either

1. Recognize the increase in the pension obligation immediately, with the expense included in employee benefit cost for the period; *or*
2. Amortize the transition amount over no longer than a five-year period, on the straight-line basis. Note that the five-year maximum transition would have concluded by 2004, if the entity adopted IAS 19 in 1999. The unrecognized transition amount was not to be formally included in the statement of financial position, but was required to be disclosed.

If the second method were elected, and the entity had a *negative* transitional liability (that is, an asset, resulting from a surplus of pension assets over the related obligation), it was limited in the amount of such asset to present in its statement of financial position to the total of any unrecognized actuarial losses plus past service cost, and the present value of economic benefits available as refunds from the plan or reductions in future contributions, with the present value determined by reference to the rate on high-quality corporate bonds. Furthermore, the amount of unrecognized transitional gain or loss at the end of each reporting period was required to have been presented, as was the amount recognized in the current period profit or loss.

Finally, if the second method was employed, recognition of actuarial gains (which did not include negative past service cost) was limited in two ways. If an actuarial gain was being recognized because it exceeded the 10% limit, or because the entity had elected a more rapid method of systematic recognition, then the actuarial gain was required to be recognized only to the extent the net cumulative gain exceeded the unrecognized transitional liability. And, in determining the gain or loss on any later settlement or curtailment, the related part of the unrecognized transitional liability was required to be incorporated.

IAS 19 also stipulated that if the transitional liability was lower than the amount which would have been recognized under previous accounting rules, the adjustment was to have been taken into profit or loss immediately (i.e., amortization was not permitted).

Upon adoption of the current revised IAS 19, the reporting entity was not permitted to retrospectively compute the effect of the 10% limit on actuarial gain or loss recognition. It was clear that retrospective application would have been impracticable to accomplish and would not have generated useful information, and that was accordingly prohibited by the revised standard.

EMPLOYER'S LIABILITY AND ASSETS

IAS 19 has as its primary concern the measurement of periodic expense incurred in connection with pension plans of employers. One source of dissatisfaction with the standard is its general failure to address the assets or liabilities that may be recognized in the employers' statements of financial position as a consequence of expense recognition, which may include deferral of certain items (e.g., past service costs). In fact, the amounts that may find their way into the statement of financial position will often not meet the strict definition of assets or liabilities, but rather, will be "deferred charges or credits." This will consist of the cumulative difference between the amount funded and the amount expensed over the life of the plan.

Thus, IAS 19 has been criticized for not requiring, under appropriate circumstances, recognition of an additional or minimum liability when plans are materially underfunded The

IASB concluded that additional measures of liability were potentially confusing and did not promise to provide relevant information. Accordingly, with the exception of any liability to be accrued under IAS 37 (regarding contingencies), the decision was made to dispense with such an item.

IAS 19 does, nonetheless, require that a defined benefit liability or asset be included in the sponsor's statement of financial position when certain conditions are met. Specifically, under the provisions of IAS 19, the amount recognized as a defined benefit liability in the employer's statement of financial position is the net total of

1. The present value of the defined benefit obligation at the end of the reporting period,
2. Any actuarial gains (less any actuarial losses) not recognized because of the "corridor" approach described elsewhere in this chapter,
3. Any past service cost not yet recognized; and
4. The fair value of plan assets at the end of the reporting period.

If this amount nets to a negative sum, it represents the defined benefit asset to be reported in the employer's statement of financial position. However, the amount of asset that can be displayed, per IAS 19, is subject to a *ceiling requirement*.

The asset ceiling defined in IAS 19 is the lower of

1. The amount computed in the preceding paragraph, or
2. The total of

    a. Any cumulative unrecognized net actuarial losses and past service cost, and
    b. The present value of any economic benefits available in the form of refunds from the plan or reductions in future contributions to the plan, determined using the discount rate that reflects market yields at the end of the reporting period on high-quality corporate bonds or, if necessary, on government bonds.

In 2002 the IASB amended IAS 19 in response to concerns raised about the perceived interaction of the deferred recognition and the asset ceiling provisions of IAS 19, and the risk that this was creating counterintuitive results. The issue affects only those entities that have, at the beginning or end of the financial reporting period, a surplus in a defined benefit plan that, based on the current terms of the plan, the entity cannot fully recover through refunds or reductions in future contributions. Such situations created financial reporting anomalies, as follows:

1. *Gains* were being reported in the financial statements based on the occurrence of actuarial *losses* in the pension plans, or
2. *Losses* were being reported on occurrence of actuarial *gains* in the pension plans.

More specifically, the issue was the wording of the asset ceiling provision in IAS 19. This wording, without regard to the limitation imposed by the amendment in 2002, sometimes caused, as a consequence of deferring the recognition of an actuarial loss (gain), the recognition of a gain (loss) in profit or loss.

The problem occurred when an entity defers recognition of actuarial losses or past service cost in determining the amount specified in IAS 19's provision for the measurement of defined benefit liability or asset, but is required to measure the defined benefit asset at the net total of

1. Any cumulative unrecognized net actuarial losses and past service cost, and
2. The present value of any economic benefits available in the form of refunds from the plan or reductions in future contributions to the plan.

In particular, the cumulative unrecognized net actuarial losses and past service cost could result in the entity recognizing an increased asset because of actuarial losses or past service cost in the period. This increase in the asset would be reported as a gain in income.

To resolve this, IAS 19 was amended to prevent gains (losses) from being recognized solely as a result of the deferred recognition of past service cost or actuarial losses (gains). This was done because it was concluded that recognizing gains (losses) arising from past service cost and actuarial losses (gains) would not be representationally faithful. The solution devised in the amendment was to require the reporting entity, to ascertain the defined benefit asset, to recognize immediately the following—but only to the extent that these items arise while the defined benefit asset is determined in accordance with the asset ceiling provision limiting it to the sum of the cumulative unrecognized net actuarial losses and past service cost and the present value of any economic benefits available in the form of refunds from the plan or reductions in future contributions to the plan:

1. The net actuarial losses of the current period and past service cost of the current period, to the extent that they exceed any reduction in the present value of the economic benefits. If there is no change or an increase in the present value of economic benefits, the entire net actuarial losses of the current period and past service cost of the current period should be recognized immediately.
2. The net actuarial gains of the current period after the deduction of past service cost of the current period to the extent that they exceed any increase in the present value of the economic benefits. If there is no change or a decrease in the present value of the economic benefits, the entire net actuarial gains of the current period after the deduction of past service cost of the current period should be recognized.

The foregoing applies to a reporting entity only if it has, at the beginning or end of the accounting period, a surplus in a defined benefit plan and cannot, based on the current terms of the plan, recover that surplus fully through refunds or reductions in future contributions. A surplus is an excess of the fair value of the plan assets over the present value of the defined benefit obligation. In such cases, past service cost and actuarial losses that arise in the period, the recognition of which is deferred, will increase the amount of the unrecognized net actuarial loss and past service cost determined in accordance with IAS 19. If that increase is not offset by an equal decrease in the present value of economic benefits identified also in IAS 19, there will be an increase in the net total specified by that provision and, hence, a recognized gain. The language added by the amendment prohibits the recognition of a gain in these circumstances.

The opposite effect arises with actuarial gains that arise in the period, the recognition of which is deferred under the standard, to the extent that the actuarial gains reduce cumulative unrecognized actuarial losses. The current language of IAS 19 prohibits the recognition of a loss in these circumstances.

The limitation on asset recognition—to the total of (1) any cumulative unrecognized net actuarial losses and past service cost, and (2) the present value of any economic benefits available in the form of refunds from the plan or reductions in future contributions to the plan—does not override the delayed recognition of certain actuarial losses and certain past service cost, except to the extent that the limitation on asset recognition is driven by the provision pertaining to basic computation of the defined benefit liability or asset in IAS 19. However, that limit does override the transitional option set forth by the standard (i.e., where straight-line amortization over a period not longer than five years is employed). The reporting entity must disclose any amount not recognized as an asset because of the limit stated at the beginning of this paragraph.

To illustrate this immediately previous matter, consider a defined benefit plan with the following characteristics:

Present value of the obligation	€ 550
Fair value of plan assets	(595)
	(45)
Unrecognized actuarial losses	(55)
Unrecognized past service cost	(35)
Unrecognized increase in the liability on initial adoption of IAS 19	(25)
Negative amount determined under defined benefit liability or asset definition	(160)
Present value of available future refunds and reductions in future contributions.	45

The limit is computed as follows:	
Unrecognized actuarial losses	55
Unrecognized past service cost	35
Present value of available future refunds and reductions in future contributions	45
Limit	€ 135

The limit, €135 in this example, is less than the amount determined under the basic definition of defined benefit asset, €160. Therefore, the reporting entity would recognize an asset of €135 and discloses that application of the limit had reduced the carrying amount of the asset by €25.

This amendment to IAS 19 added an appendix that provides several examples that illustrate how to apply this somewhat complex modification to the asset recognition ceiling under the standard.

MINIMIMUM FUNDING REQUIREMENT

IFRIC 14: IAS 19—*The Limit on a Defined Benefit Asset, Minimum Funding Requirements and Their Interaction.* In July 2007, IFRIC issued Interpretation 14 to provide guidance on the limitation on asset recognition and the statutory minimum funding requirements. IFRIC 19 was amended November 2009, effective for annual periods beginning on or after January 1, 2011. The amendment is applicable to limited circumstances where an entity is subject to minimum funding requirements and makes an early payment of contributions to cover the funding requirements. The benefit of such an early payment is regarded as an asset.

Although funding requirements would not normally affect the accounting for a defined benefit plan, however the asset ceiling test in IAS 19 limits the recognition of the net pension asset to the sum of (1) any cumulative unrecognized net actuarial losses and past service costs and (2) the present value of available to the employer economic benefits in the form of refunds from the plan or reduction in future contributions to the plan. According to IASB, the interaction of this limit and minimum funding requirement has two possible effects:

1. The minimum funding requirement may restrict the economic benefits available as a reduction in future contributions, and
2. The limit may make the minimum funding requirement onerous because contributions payable under the requirement for services already received may not be available once they have been paid, either as a refund or as a reduction in future contributions.

In some jurisdictions, there are statutory (or contractual) minimum funding requirements that require sponsors to make future contributions. This is an increasingly common phenomenon, given the public's growing awareness that many defined benefit plans have been underfunded, raising concerns that retirees will find insufficient assets to pay their benefits after, for example, the plan sponsor has ceased operations or been sold. The question raised was whether those requirements should limit the amount of plan assets the employer may report in its statement of financial position in those situations where application of IAS 19 would otherwise permit asset recognition, as discussed in the preceding paragraphs. In other words, the problem was that the IAS 19-based asset might not be available to the entity (and thus not be an asset of the reporting entity) in certain situations where future minimum funding requirements exist.

IFRIC 14 addresses the extent to which the economic benefit, via refund or reduction in future contributions, is constrained by contractual or statutory minimum funding obligations. It also addresses the calculation of the available benefits under such circumstances, as well as the effect of the minimum funding requirement on the measurement of defined benefit plan asset or liability.

IFRIC 14 addresses the following issues:

1. When refunds or reductions in future contributions should be regarded as "available to the employer"
2. The economic benefit available as a reduction in future contributions
3. The effect of a minimum funding requirement on the economic benefit available as a reduction in future contributions
4. When a minimum funding requirement may give rise to a liability

Economic benefit available as a refund. IFRIC 14 specifies that the availability of a refund of a surplus or a reduction in future contributions would be determined in accordance with the terms and conditions of the plan and any statutory requirements in its jurisdiction. An economic benefit, in the form of a refund of surplus or a reduction in future contributions, would be deemed available (and hence an asset of the sponsor) if it will be realizable at some point during the life of the plan or when the plan liabilities are finally settled. Most importantly, an economic benefit, in the form of a refund from the plan or reduction in future contributions, may still be deemed available even if it is not realizable immediately at the end of the reporting period, as long as the refunds from the plan will be realizable during the life of a plan or at final settlement.

In cases where the question to be resolved is the amount of asset that is deemed to be an economic benefit to be received via a refund, this is to be measured as the amount that will be refunded to the entity *either*

1. During the life of the plan, without assuming that the plan liabilities have to be settled in order to get the refund (e.g., in some jurisdictions, the entity may have a contractual right to a refund during the life of the plan, irrespective of whether the plan liability is settled); or
2. Assuming the gradual settlement of the plan liabilities over time until all members have left the plan; or
3. Assuming the full settlement of the plan liabilities in a single event (i.e., as a plan termination and settlement).

The amount of the economic benefit is to be determined on the basis of the approach that is the *most advantageous* to the entity. It is thus to be measured as the amount of the surplus (i.e., the fair value of the plan assets less the present value of the defined benefit obligation) that, at the end of the reporting period, the reporting entity has a right to receive as a refund after all the associated costs (such as taxes other than those on income) are paid.

If the refund is calculated using the approach in subparagraph (3) above, then the costs associated with the settlement of the plan liabilities and making the refund are to be taken into account. These could include professional fees to be paid by the plan, as well as the costs of any insurance premiums that might be required to secure the liability upon plan settlement.

Since under IAS 19 the surplus at the end of the reporting period is measured at present value, even if the refund is realizable only at a future date no further adjustment will need to be made for the time value of money.

Economic benefit available as a reduction in future contributions. When there is no minimum funding requirement for contributions relating to future service, the economic benefit available as a reduction in future contributions is the future service cost to the entity for each period over the shorter of the expected life of the plan and the expected life of the entity. The future service cost to the entity excludes amounts borne by employees.

Interpretation 14 requires that, in accordance with IAS 1, the entity disclose information about the key sources of estimation uncertainty at the end of the reporting period, if there is a significant risk of material adjustment to the carrying amount of the net asset or liability in the statement of financial position. This might include disclosure of any restrictions on the current realizability of the plan assets, or disclosure of the basis used to determine the amount of the economic benefit available as a refund.

The effect of a minimum funding requirement on the economic benefit available as a reduction in future contributions. In cases where there is a minimum funding requirement, the question to be resolved is the amount of asset that is deemed to be an economic benefit to be received via a future contribution reduction using IAS 19 assumptions applicable at the end of the reporting period. The amount is the sum of

1. Any amount that reduces future minimum funding requirement contributions for future service because the entity made a prepayment, and
2. The estimated future service cost in each period (excluding any part of the total cost that is borne by employees), *less*
3. Any future minimum funding requirement contribution that would be required for future service in those periods if no prepayment as described in 1. is applicable.

Any expected changes in the future minimum funding contributions as a result of the entity paying the minimum contributions due would be reflected in the measurement of the available contribution reduction. However, no allowance could be made for expected changes in the terms and conditions of the minimum funding requirement that are not substantively enacted at the end of the reporting period. Any allowances for expected future changes in the demographic profile of the workforce would have to be consistent with the assumptions underlying the calculation of the present value of the defined benefit obligation itself at the end of the reporting period.

If the future minimum funding requirement contribution for future service exceeds the future IAS 19 service cost in any given period, the excess would be used to reduce the amount of the economic benefit available as a future contribution reduction. The amount of the total asset available as a reduction in future contributions (point 2. above) can never be less than zero.

When a minimum funding requirement may give rise to a liability. If an entity has a statutory or contractual obligation under a minimum funding requirement to pay additional contributions to cover an existing shortfall on the minimum funding requirements in respect of services already received by the end of the reporting period, the entity would have to ascertain whether the contributions payable will be available as a refund or reduction in future contributions after they are paid into the plan. To the extent that the contributions payable will not be available once paid into the plan, the reporting entity would be required to recognize a liability. The liability would reduce the defined benefit asset or increase the defined benefit liability when the obligation arises, so that no gain or loss results when the contributions are later paid.

The adjustment to the defined benefit asset or liability in respect of the minimum funding requirement, and any subsequent remeasurement of that adjustment, would be recognized immediately in accordance with the entity's adopted policy for recognizing the effect of the limit set forth by IAS 19 (see discussion above). In particular

1. A reporting entity that recognizes the effect of the limit in profit or loss would also recognize the adjustment immediately in profit or loss, whereas
2. An entity that recognizes the effect of the limit in other comprehensive income would likewise recognize the adjustment immediately in other comprehensive income in the statement of comprehensive income.

IFRIC 14 provides a number or examples illustrating how to calculate the economic benefit available or not available when an entity has a certain funding level on the minimum funding requirement.

IFRIC 14 was applicable for annual periods beginning on or after January 1, 2008, with earlier application permitted.

OTHER PENSION CONSIDERATIONS

Multiple and multiemployer plans. If an entity has more than one plan, IAS 19 provisions should be applied separately to each plan. Offsets or eliminations are not allowed unless there clearly is the right to use the assets in one plan to pay the benefits of another plan.

Participation in a multiemployer plan (to which two or more unrelated employers contribute) requires that the contribution for the period be recognized as net pension cost and that any contributions due and unpaid be recognized as a liability. Assets in this type of plan are usually commingled and are not segregated or restricted. A board of trustees usually administers these plans, and multiemployer plans are generally subject to a collective bargaining agreement. If there is a withdrawal from this type of plan and if an arising obligation is either probable or reasonably possible, the provisions of IFRS that address contingencies (IAS 37) apply.

Some plans are, in substance, a pooling or aggregation of single employer plans and are ordinarily without collective bargaining agreements. Contributions are usually based on a selected benefit formula. These plans are not considered multiemployer plans, and the accounting is based on the respective interest in the plan.

Business combinations. When an entity that sponsors a single-employer defined benefit plan is acquired and must therefore be accounted for under the provisions of IFRS 3 (revised 2008), the purchaser should assign part of the purchase price to an asset if plan assets exceed the projected benefit obligation, or to a liability if the projected benefit obligation exceeds plan assets. The projected benefit obligation should include the effect of any expected plan curtailment or termination. This assignment eliminates any existing unrecognized components, and any future differences between contributions and net pension cost will affect the asset or liability recognized when the purchase took place.

DISCLOSURES FOR POSTEMPLOMENT BENEFIT PLANS

For defined contribution plans, IAS 19 requires only that the amount of expense included in current period earnings be disclosed. Good practice would suggest that disclosure be made of the general description of each plan, identifying the employee groups covered, and of any other significant matters related to retirement benefits that affect comparability with the previous period reported on.

For defined benefit plans, as would be expected, much more expansive disclosures are mandated. These include

1. A general description of each plan identifying the employee groups covered
2. The accounting policy regarding recognition of actuarial gains or losses
3. A reconciliation of the plan-related assets and liabilities recognized in the statement of financial position, showing at the minimum

   a. The present value of wholly unfunded defined benefit obligations
   b. The present value (gross, before deducting plan assets) of wholly or partly unfunded obligations
   c. The fair value of plan assets
   d. The net actuarial gain or loss not yet recognized in the statement of financial position
   e. The past service cost not yet recognized in the statement of financial position
   f. Any amount not recognized as an asset because of the limitation to the present value of economic benefits from refunds and future contribution reductions
   g. The amounts which are recognized in the statement of financial position

4. The amount of plan assets represented by each category of the reporting entity's own financial instruments or by property which is occupied by, or other assets used by, the entity itself
5. A reconciliation of movements (i.e., changes) during the reporting period in the net asset or liability reported in the statement of financial position
6. The amount of, and location in profit or loss of, the reported amounts of current service cost, interest cost, expected return on plan assets, actuarial gain or loss, past service cost, and effect of any curtailment or settlement
7. The total amount recognized in other comprehensive income
8. The cumulative amount of actuarial gains and losses recognized in other comprehensive income
9. The actual return earned on plan assets for the reporting period
10. The principal actuarial assumptions used, including (if relevant) the discount rates, expected rates of return on plan assets, expected rates of salary increases or other index or variable specified in the pension arrangement, medical cost trend rates, and any other material actuarial assumptions utilized in computing benefit costs for the period. The actuarial assumptions are to be explicitly stated in absolute terms, not merely as references to other indices.

Amounts presented in the sponsor's statement of financial position cannot be offset (presented on a net basis) unless legal rights of offset exist. Furthermore, even with a legal right to offset (which itself would be a rarity), unless the intent is to settle on a net basis, such presentation would not be acceptable. Thus, a sponsor having two plans, one being in a net asset position, and another in a net liability position, cannot net these in most instances.

Comprehensive example

In the following example, the various components of pension cost are reviewed in detail. Note that only a qualified actuary can compute the service cost component, which depends on numerous assumptions regarding mortality, tenure, and other factors. The remaining elements can be (but usually are not) addressed by nonactuaries, such as accountants. Amounts are keyed to summary of pension cost at end of the following discussion.

Service cost. Future compensation is considered in the calculation of the service cost component to the extent specified by the benefit formula. If part of the benefit formula, future compensation includes changes due to advancement, expected turnover of employees, inflation, etc. Indirect effects, such as predictable bonuses based on compensation levels, and automatic increases specified by the plan also need to be considered. The effect of *retroactive* amendments is included in the calculation at the point when the employer has contractually agreed to them. Service costs attributed (i.e., charged to expense) during the period increase the pension benefit obligation, since they result in additional benefits that are payable in the future.

	January 1, 2012	*2012 Service cost*
Benefit obligation based on current salary	€(1,500)	€ (90)
Effect of expected progression of salary	(400)	(24)
Actuarially determined benefit obligation	€(1,900)	€(114) (a)*

* *Component of net periodic pension cost, summarized later in this example.*

The current period service cost component is found in the actuarial report.

Interest cost. The actuarially computed benefit obligation is a discounted amount. It represents the present value, at the date of the valuation, of all benefits attributed under the plan's formula to employee service rendered prior to that date. Each year the end-of-year pension obligation becomes one year closer to the year in which the benefits attributed in prior years will begin to be paid to plan participants. Consequently, the present value of those previously attributed benefits will have increased to take into account the time value of money. This annual increment is computed by multiplying the assumed settlement discount rate times the pension obligation at the beginning of the year; this increases net periodic pension cost and the pension obligation. Since this imputed interest cost is accounted for as part of pension cost, it is not reported as interest in the financial statements, and accordingly cannot be included as interest for the purposes of computing capitalized interest under IAS 23.

	January 1, 2012	*2012 Service cost*	*2012 Interest cost*
Benefit obligation based on current salary	€(1,500)	€ (90)	€(210)
Effect of expected progression of salary	(400)	(24)	(32)
Actuarially determined benefit obligation	€(1,900)	€(114) (a)*	€(152) (b)*

* *Component of net periodic pension cost, summarized later in this example.*

In this example, the applicable discount rate has been assumed at 8%. The interest cost component is calculated by multiplying the start-of-the-year obligation balances by the 8% settlement rate. This amount is found in the actuarial report, although obviously readily computed.

Benefits paid. Benefits paid to retirees are deducted from the above to arrive at the end of the reporting period amounts of the accumulated benefit obligation and the projected benefit obligation.

	January 1, 2011	*2012 Service cost*	*2012 Interest cost*	*2012 Benefits paid*	*December 31, 2012*
Benefit obligation based on current salary	€(1,500)	€ (90)	€(120)	€160	€(1,550)
Effect of expected progression of salary	(400)	(24)	(32)	--	(456)
Actuarially determined benefit obligation	€(1,900)	€(114) (a)	€(152) (b)	€160	€(2,006)

Benefits of €160 were paid to retirees during the current year. This amount is found in the report of the pension plan trustee.

Actual return on plan assets. This component is the difference between the *fair value* of the plan assets at the end of the period and the fair value of the plan assets at the beginning of the period adjusted for contributions and payments during the period. Another way to express the result is that it is the net (realized and unrealized) appreciation and depreciation of plan assets plus earnings from the plan assets for the period.

	January 1, 2012	2012 Actual return on plan assets	2012 Employer funding	2012 Benefits paid	December 31, 2012
Plan assets	€1,376	€158 (c)*	€145	€(160)	€1,519

* *Component of net periodic pension cost, summarized later in this example.*

The actual return on plan assets of €158, cash deposited with the trustee of €145, and benefits paid (€160) are amounts found in the report of the pension plan trustee. These items increase the plan assets to €1,519 at the end of the year. For purposes of reporting periodic pension cost, however, the actual return on plan assets is adjusted to the expected long-term rate (9%, which is assumed in this example and should be based on empirical data for the classes of assets held in the plan) of return on plan assets (€1,376 × 9% = €124). The difference (€158 – €124 = €34) is an actuarial gain (loss) and is deferred as a gain (loss) to be recognized, or not recognized, in future periods (as explained below).

Gain or loss. Gains (losses) result from (1) changes in plan assumptions, (2) changes in the amount of plan assets, and (3) changes in the amount of the actuarially determined benefit obligation. As discussed previously, even though these gains or losses are economic events that impact the sponsoring entity's obligations under the plan, their immediate recognition in the sponsor's financial statements is not required by IAS 19. Instead, to provide "smoothing" of the effects of short-term fluctuations, unrecognized net gain (loss) may be amortized if the deferred amount meets the criteria specified below. Unlike under the comparable US GAAP standard, however, immediate recognition is permitted under IFRS, if the reporting entity elects to do so.

Since actuarial cost methods are based on numerous assumptions (employee compensation, mortality, turnover, earnings of the pension plan, etc.), it is not unusual for one or more of these assumptions to be invalidated by changes over time. Adjustments will invariably be necessary to bring prior estimates back in line with actual events. These adjustments are known as actuarial gains (losses). The accounting issue regarding the recognition of actuarial adjustments is their timing. All pension costs must eventually be recognized as expense. Actuarial gains (losses) are not considered prior period adjustments since they result from a refinement of estimates arising from obtaining subsequent information. Thus, under IAS 8, they are considered changes in an estimate to be recognized in current and future periods.

Plan asset gains (losses) result from both realized and unrealized amounts. They represent periodic differences between the actual return on assets and the expected return. The expected return is generated by multiplying the *expected long-term rate of return* by the *fair value* of plan assets as of the beginning of the reporting period. The expected rate of return is generally best determined by those having access to relevant data and an understanding of financial matters; this is often provided by the consulting actuary or investment advisor responsible for the pension fund asset management. Whatever method is used, it should be done consistently, which means from year to year for each asset class (i.e., bonds, equities), since different classes of assets may have their market-related value calculated in a different manner (i.e., fair value in one case, moving average in another case). There appears to be flexibility permitted under IFRS.

IFRS permits deferral of unrecognized gains or losses, but only to the extent that this does not exceed certain limits (defined as a "corridor"). This limit is the *greater* of 10% of the present value of the defined benefit obligation at the end of the preceding reporting period (before deducting plan assets), or 10% of the fair value of plan assets as of the same date.

To the extent that the unrecognized net gain (loss) exceeds this limit, the *excess* over 10% is divided by the average remaining service period of active employees and included as a component of net pension costs. Average remaining life expectancies of inactive employees may be used if that is a better measure due to the demographics of the plan participants.

Net pension costs include only the expected return on plan assets, unless immediate recognition of actuarial gains and losses is elected by the reporting entity. The difference between actual and expected returns is deferred through the gain (loss) component of net pension cost. If actual return is greater than expected return, net pension cost is increased to adjust the actual return to the lower expected return. If expected return is greater than actual return, the adjustment results in a decrease to net pension cost to adjust the actual return to the higher expected return.

As noted, if the unrecognized net gain (loss) is large enough, it is amortized. Conceptually, the expected return represents the best estimate of long-term performance of the plan's investments. In any given year, however, an unusual short-term result may occur given the volatility of financial markets.

The expected long-term rate of return used to calculate the expected return on plan assets is the average rate of return expected to be earned on invested funds to provide for pension benefits included in the defined benefit pension obligation. Present rates of return and expected future reinvestment rates of return are considered in arriving at the rate to be used.

To summarize, net periodic pension cost includes a gain (loss) component consisting of *both* of the following, if applicable:

1. As a minimum, the portion of the unrecognized net gain (loss) from previous periods that exceeds the *greater* of 10% of the beginning balances of the pension obligation *or* the fair value of plan assets, amortized over the average remaining service period of active employees expected to receive benefits (or more rapidly, if so elected).
2. The difference between the expected return and the actual return on plan assets.

	January 1, 2012	2012 Return on asset adjustment	2012 Amortization	December 31, 2012
Unrecognized actuarial gain (loss)	€(210)	€34 (d)*	€2 (d)*	€(174)

* *Component of net periodic pension cost, summarized later in this example.*

The return on asset adjustment of €34 is the difference between the actual return of €158 and the expected return of €124 on plan assets. The actuarial loss at the start of the year (€210 assumed for this example) is amortized if it exceeds a limit of the larger of 10% of the pension benefit obligation at the beginning of the period (€1,900 × 10% = €190) or 10% of the fair value of plan assets (€1,376 × 10% = €138). In this example, €20 (= €210 – €190) is amortized by dividing the years of average remaining service (twelve years assumed), with a result rounded to €2.

Past service cost. Past service costs are incurred when the sponsor adopts plan amendments (or a new plan, in its entirety) that increase plan benefits attributable to services rendered by plan participants in the past. Under IAS 19, these costs are to be recognized over the period until the benefits have become vested. Even though these pertain to past service, they are not handled as immediate charges (unless immediately vested) or as corrections of prior periods' reported results. Unlike for actuarial gains or losses, IAS 19 offers no option for more rapid recognition of these costs.

Under the rare situation where benefits are reduced, resulting in negative past service cost, this, too, is amortized (as a reduction in periodic pension cost) over the average term until vesting.

IFRS requires only that the straight-line method of amortization be used, and that this be over the vesting period. For example, if an improved benefit is granted to only employees having five years' service, the portion applicable to those workers already meeting this threshold test will be immediately expensed, while the portion applicable to those having less seniority will be amortized over the *average* term to vesting for that subgroup.

	January 1, 2012	2012 Amortization	December 31, 2012
Unrecognized prior service cost	€320	€27 (e)*	€293

* *Component of net periodic pension cost, summarized later in this example.*

Unrecognized prior service cost (€320) is amortized over the time to full vesting. In this example, that term is almost 12 years, but in practice this might be much shorter. The straight-line method must be used. These amounts are found in the actuarial report.

Transitional issues. When IAS 19 was enacted, it provided that the initial obligation was to be measured as the present value of the pension obligation, less the fair value of plan assets, less any past service cost to be amortized in later periods, as described above. When this amount exceeded what was reportable under prior GAAP used by the entity (whether an actual standard or the policy adopted by the entity in absence of definitive accounting rules), the entity had to make an irrevocable election to either immediately recognize that increased liability via a charge against profit or loss, or recognize the adjustment over a period of up to five years from date of adoption. A negative transition adjustment was to be recognized immediately in profit or loss.

Since IAS 19 was implemented effective 1999, all transition amounts should have been fully amortized by 2004, making this issue now of only historical interest. However, *solely for the purpose of completing the current comprehensive example*, the following amortization of transitional liability is included.

	January 1, 2012	2012 Amortization	December 31, 2012
Unamortized net obligation (asset) existing at IAS 19 application	€(6)	€3 (f)*	€(3)

* *Component of net periodic pension cost, summarized later in this example.*

At initial adoption of IAS 19, the "transition amount" was computed, and was being amortized using the straight-line method at a rate of €3 per year. The assumed unamortized balance at January 1, 2011, was €6 and the amortization for 2012 was €3. These amounts are found in the actuarial report.

NOTE: *All such transitions should now be complete, in actual practice.*

Summary of net periodic pension cost. The components that were identified in the above examples are summed as follows to determine the amount defined as net periodic pension cost:

		2012
Service cost	(a)	€114
Interest cost	(b)	152
Actual return on plan assets	(c)	(158)
Unrecognized gain (loss)	(d)	36
Amortization of unrecognized past service cost	(e)	27
Amortization of unrecognized net obligation (asset) existing at IAS 19 adoption	(f)	(3)
Total net periodic pension cost		€168

One possible source of confusion is the actual return on plan assets (€158) and the unrecognized gain of €36, which net to €122. The actual return on plan assets reduces pension cost. This is because, to the extent that plan assets generate earnings, those earnings help the plan sponsor subsidize the cost of providing the benefits. Thus, the plan sponsor will not have to fund benefits as they become due, to the extent that plan earnings provide the plan with cash to pay those benefits. This reduction, however, is adjusted by increasing pension cost by the difference between actual and expected return of €34 and the amortization of the excess actuarial loss of €2, for a total of €36. The net result is to include the expected return of €124 (= €158 − €34) less the amortization of the excess of €2 for a total of €122 (= €158 − €36).

In terms of reporting the results of operations, IAS 19 requires disclosure of total pension cost, with details as to the amounts of

- Current service cost
- Interest cost
- Expected return on plan assets
- Expected return on any reimbursement right recognized as an asset
- Actuarial gains and losses
- Past service cost
- The effect of any curtailment or settlement

Regarding the statement of financial position, IAS 19 requires a reconciliation of pension-related assets and liabilities presented, showing

- The present value of the defined benefit pension obligation that is wholly unfunded
- The present value of the defined benefit pension obligation that is partially or fully funded, before offsetting pension assets
- The fair value of pension assets
- Net actuarial gain or loss not recognized by the end of the reporting period
- Past service cost not recognized by the end of the reporting period
- Fair value of a reimbursement right recognized as an asset
- Any other amounts recognized in the statement of financial position

Reconciliation of Beginning and Ending Pension Obligation and Plan Assets

The following table summarizes the 2012 activity affecting the defined benefit pension obligation and the plan assets, and reconciles the beginning and ending balances per the actuarial report:

	Benefit obligation before salary progression	Effect of progression of salaries and wages	Actuarial defined benefit obligation	Fair value of plan assets
Balance, January 1, 2012	€(1,500)	€(400)	€(1,900)	€1,376
Service cost	(90)	(24)	(114) (a)	
Interest cost	(120)	(32)	(152) (b)	
Benefits paid to retired participants	160		160	(160)
Actual return on plan assets				158 (c)
Sponsor's contributions				145
Balance, December 31, 2012	€(1,550)	€(456)	€(2,006)	€1,519

OTHER EMPLOYEE BENEFITS

Short-term employee benefits. According to IAS 19, short-term benefits are those falling due within twelve months from the end of the period in which the employees render their services. These include wages and salaries, as well as short-term compensated absences (vacations, annual holiday, paid sick days, etc.), profit sharing and bonuses if due within twelve months after the end of the period in which these were earned, and such nonmonetary benefits as health insurance and housing or automobiles. The standard requires that these be reported as incurred. Since they are accrued currently, no actuarial assumptions or computations are needed and, since due currently, discounting is not to be applied.

Compensated absences may provide some accounting complexities, if accumulate and vest with the employees. Accumulated benefits can be carried forward to later periods when not fully consumed currently; for example, when employees are granted two weeks' leave per year, but can carry forward to later years an amount equal to no more than six weeks, the compensated absence benefit can be said to be subject to limited accumulation. Depending on the program, accumulation rights may be limited or unlimited; and, furthermore, the usage of benefits may be defined to occur on a last-in, first-out (LIFO) basis, which in conjunction with limited accumulation rights further limits the amount of benefits which employees are likely to use, if not fully used in the period earned.

The cost of compensated absences should be accrued in the periods earned. In some cases (as when the plans subject employees to limitations on accumulation rights with or without the further restriction imposed by a LIFO pattern of usage), it will be understood that the amounts of compensated absences to which employees are contractually entitled will exceed the amount that they are likely to actually utilize. In such circumstances, the accrual should be based on the *expected* usage, based on past experience and, if relevant, changes in the plan's provisions since the last reporting period.

Example of compensated absences

Consider an entity with 500 workers, each of whom earns two weeks' annual leave, with a carryforward option limited to a maximum of six weeks, to be carried forward no longer than four years. Also, this employer imposes a LIFO basis on any usages of annual leave (e.g., a worker with two weeks' carryforward and two weeks earned currently, taking a three-week leave, will be deemed to have consumed the two currently earned weeks plus one of the carryforward weeks, thereby increasing the risk of ultimately losing the older carried-forward compensated absence time). Based on past experience, 80% of the workers will take no more than two weeks' leave in any year, while the other 20% take an average of four extra days. At the end of the year, each worker has an average of five days' carryforward of compensated absences. The amount accrued should be the cost equivalent of $[(.80 \times 0 \text{ days}) + (.20 \times 4 \text{ days})] \times 500 \text{ workers} = 400 \text{ days' leave}$.

Other postretirement benefits. Other postretirement benefits include medical care and other benefits offered to retirees partially or entirely at the expense of the former employer. These are essentially defined benefit plans very much like defined benefit pension plans. Like the pension plans, these require the services of a qualified actuary in order to estimate the true cost of the promises made currently for benefits to be delivered in the future. As with pensions, a variety of determinants, including the age composition, life expectancies, and other demographic factors pertaining to the present and future retiree groups, and the course of future inflation of medical care (or other covered) costs (coupled with predicted utilization factors), need to be projected in order to compute current period costs. Developing these projections requires the skills and training of actuaries; the projected pattern of future medical costs has been particularly difficult to achieve with anything approaching accuracy. Unlike most defined benefit pension plans, other postretirement benefit plans are more commonly funded on a pay-as-you-go basis, which does not alter the accounting but does eliminate earnings on plan assets as a cost offset.

Other long-term employee benefits. These are defined by IAS 19 as including any benefits other than postemployment benefits (pensions, retiree medical care, etc.), termination benefits and equity compensation plans. Examples would include sabbatical leave, "jubilee" or other long-service benefits, long-term profit-sharing payments, and deferred compensation arrangements. Executive deferred compensation plans have become common in nations where these are tax-advantaged (i.e., not taxed to the employee until paid), and these give rise to deferred tax accounting issues as well as measurement and reporting questions, as benefit plans. In general, measurement will be less complex than for defined benefit pension or other postretirement benefits, although some actuarial measures may be needed.

Reportedly for reasons of simplicity, IAS 19 decided to not provide the corridor approach to nonrecognition of actuarial gains and losses for other long-term benefits, under which (as described above) only the gain or loss in excess of a threshold level has to be recognized in profit or loss. It also requires that past service cost (resulting from the granting of enhanced benefits to participants on a retroactive basis) and the transition gain or loss (from adoption of IAS 19) all must be reported in earnings in the period in which these are granted or occur. In other words, deferred recognition via amortization is not acceptable for these various long-term benefit programs.

For liability measurement purposes, IAS 19 stipulates that the present value of the obligation be presented in the statement of financial position, less the fair value of any assets that have been set aside for settlement thereof. The long-term corporate bond rate is used here, as with defined benefit pension obligations, to discount the expected future payments to present value. As to expense recognition, the same cost elements as are set forth for pension plan expense should be included, with the exceptions that, as noted, actuarial gains and losses and past service cost must be recognized immediately, not amortized over a defined time horizon.

Termination benefits. Termination benefits are to be recognized only when the employer has demonstrated its commitment either to terminate the employee or group of employees before normal retirement date, or provide benefits as part of an inducement to encourage early retirements. Generally, a detailed, formal plan will be necessary to support a representation that such a commitment exists. According to IAS 19, the plan should, as a minimum, set forth locations, functions, and numbers of employees to be terminated; the benefits for each job class or other pertinent category; and the time when the plan is to be implemented; with inception to be as soon as possible and completion soon enough to largely eliminate the chance that any material changes to the plan will be necessary.

Since termination benefits do not confer any future economic benefits on the employing entity, these must be expensed immediately. If the payments are to fall due more than twelve months after the end of the reporting period, however, discounting to present value is required (again, using the long-term corporate bond rate). Estimates, such as the number of employees likely to accept voluntary early retirement, may need to be made in many cases involving termination benefits. To the extent that accrual is based on such estimates (the possibility that greater numbers may accept, thereby triggering additional costs) further disclosure of loss contingencies may be necessary to comply with IAS 37.

EXAMPLE OF FINANCIAL STATEMENT DISCLOSURES

Vodafone plc
March 31, 2010

Postemployment benefits

Background

At March 31, 2010, the Group operated a number of pension plans for the benefit of its employees throughout the world which vary depending on the conditions and practices in the countries concerned. The Group's pension plans are provided through both defined benefit and defined contribution arrangements. Defined benefit schemes provide benefits based on the employees' length of pensionable service and their final pensionable salary or other criteria. Defined contribution schemes offer employees individual funds that are converted into benefits at the time of retirement.

The Group's principal defined benefit pension scheme in the United Kingdom, a tax-approved final salary scheme which was closed to new entrants from January 1, 2006, was closed to future accrual by current members on March 31, 2010. The assets of the scheme are held in an external trustee-administered fund. In addition, the Group operates defined benefit schemes in Germany, Ghana, Greece, India, Ireland, Italy, Turkey and the United States. Defined contribution pension schemes are currently provided in Australia, Egypt, Greece, Hungary, Ireland, Italy,

Kenya, Malta, the Netherlands, New Zealand, Portugal, South Africa, Spain, and the United Kingdom.

Income statement expense

	2010 €m	2009 €m	2008 €m
Defined contribution schemes	110	73	63
Defined benefit schemes	50	40	28
Total amount charged to the income statement (note 32)	160	113	91

Defined benefit schemes

The principal actuarial assumptions used for estimating the Group's benefit obligations are set out below:

	2010[1] %	2009[1] %	2008[1] %
Weighted-average actuarial assumptions used at March 31			
Rate of inflation	3.5	2.6	3.1
Rate of increase in salaries	4.6	3.7	4.3
Rate of increase in pensions in payment and deferred pensions	3.5	2.6	3.1
Discount rate	5.7	6.3	6.1
Expected rates of return			
Equities	8.5	8.4	8.0
Bonds[2]	5.1	5.7	4.4
Other assets	2.8	3.7	1.3

Notes:

[1] *Figures shown represent a weighted-average assumption of the individual schemes.*

[2] *For the year ended March 31, 2010, the expected rate of return for bonds consisted of a 5.5% rate of return for corporate bonds (2009: 6.1%; 2008: 4.7%) and a 4.0% rate of return for government bonds (2009: 4.0%; 2008: 3.5%).*

The expected return on assets assumptions are derived by considering the expected long-term rates of return on plan investments. The overall rate of return is a weighted average of the expected returns of the individual investments made in the group plans. The long-term rates of return on equities and property are derived from considering current risk-fee rates of return with the addition of an appropriate future risk premium from an analysis of historic returns in various countries. The long-term rates of return on bonds and cash investments are set in line with market yields currently available at the statement of financial position date.

Mortality assumptions used are consistent with those recommended by the individual scheme actuaries and reflect the latest available tables, adjusted for the experience of the Group where appropriate. The largest scheme in the Group is the UK scheme and the tables used for this scheme indicated a further life expectancy for a male/female pensioner currently aged 65 of 22.3/25.4 years (2009: 22.0/24.8 years, 2008: 22.0/24.8 years) and a further life expectancy from age 65 for a male/female nonpensioner member currently aged 40 of 24.6/27.9 years (2009: 23.2/26.0 years, 2008: 23.3/26.0 years).

Measurement of the Group's defined benefit retirement obligations are particularly sensitive to changes in certain key assumptions including the discount rate. An increase or decrease in the discount rate of 0.5% would result in a €172 million decrease or a €199 million increase in the defined benefit obligation respectively.

Charges made to the consolidated income statement and consolidated statement of comprehensive income (SOCI) on the basis of the assumptions stated above are

	2010 €m	2009 €m	2008 €m
Current service cost	29	46	53
Interest cost	77	83	69
Expected return on pension assets	(76)	(92)	(89)
Curtailment/settlement	20	3	(5)
Total included within staff costs	50	40	28
Actuarial losses recognized in the SOCI	149	220	47
Cumulative actuarial losses recognized in the SOCI	496	347	127

Fair value of the assets and present value of the liabilities of the schemes

The amount included in the statement of financial position arising from the Group's obligations in respect of its defined benefit schemes is as follows:

	2010 €m	2009 €m	2008 €m
Movement in pension assets:			
April 1	1,100	1,271	1,251
Exchange rate movements	(10)	50	50
Expected return on pension assets	76	92	89
Actuarial gains/(losses)	286	(381)	(176)
Employer cash contributions	133	98	86
Member cash contributions	12	15	13
Benefits paid	(45)	(45)	(42)
Other movements	(65)	--	--
March 31	**1,487**	**1,100**	**1,271**
Movement in pension liabilities:			
April 1	1,332	1.310	1.292
Exchange rate movements	(15)	69	60
Arising on acquisition	--	33	--
Current service cost	29	46	53
Interest cost	77	83	69
Member cash contributions	12	15	13
Actuarial losses/(gains)	435	(161)	(129)
Benefits paid	(79)	(45)	(42)
Other movements	(101)	(18)	(6)
March 31	**1,690**	**1,332**	**1,310**

An analysis of net assets/ (deficits) is provided below for the Group's principal defined benefit pension scheme in the UK and for the Group as a whole.

	UK					Group				
	2010 €m	2009 €m	2008 €m	2007 €m	2006 €m	2010 €m	2009 €m	2008 €m	2007 €m	2006 €m
Analysis of net assets/(deficits):										
Total fair value of scheme assets	1,131	755	934	954	835	1,487	1,100	1,271	1,251	1,123
Present value of funded scheme liabilities	(1,276)	(815)	(902)	(901)	(847)	(1,625)	(1,196)	(1,217)	(1,194)	(1,128)
Net (deficit)/assets for funded schemes	**(145)**	**(60)**	**32**	**53**	**(12)**	**(138)**	**(96)**	**54**	**57**	**(5)**
Present value of unfunded scheme liabilities	--	(8)	--	--	--	(65)	(136)	(93)	(98)	(96)
Net (deficit)/assets	**(145)**	**(68)**	**32**	**53**	**(12)**	**(203)**	**(232)**	**(39)**	**(41)**	**(101)**
Net (deficit)/assets are analyzed as:										
Assets	--	--	32	53	--	34	8	65	82	19
Liabilities	(145)	(68)	--	--	(12)	(237)	(240)	(104)	(123)	(120)

It is expected that contributions of €3.1 million will be paid into the Group's defined benefit retirement schemes during the year ending March 31, 2011.

Actual return on pension assets

	2010 €m	2009 €m	2008 €m
Actual return on pension assets	362	(289)	(87)
Analysis of pension assets at March 31, is as follows:	%	%	%
Equities	59.6	55.6	68.5
Bonds	37.5	41.9	17.7
Property	0.3	0.4	0.3
Other	2.6	2.1	13.5
	100.0	100.0	100.0

The schemes have no direct investments in the Group's equity securities or in property currently used by the Group.

History of experience adjustments

	2010 €m	2009 €m	2008 €m	2007 €m	2006 €m
Experience adjustments on pension liabilities:					
Amount	8	6	(5)	(2)	(4)
Percentage of pension liabilities	--	--	--	--	--
Experience adjustments on pension assets:					
Amount	286	(381)	(176)	26	121
Percentage of pension assets	19%	(35%)	(14%)	2%	11%

FUTURE DEVELOPMENTS

In June 2011, the IASB issued amendments to IAS 19. The amendment requires the immediate recognition of all actuarial gains and losses, and eliminates the use of the "corridor" approach that currently exists under IAS 19. A new presentation approach requires that service cost must be presented in profit and loss, finance cost (net interest income or expenses) as part of finance cost and remeasurement in other comprehensive income. Improved disclosures are also included in the amendments relating to the characteristics of a defined benefit plan, amounts recognized in the financial statements, arising risks, and participation in multiemployer plans.

In addition, the amended standard gives additional guidance in relation to the accounting for termination benefits. The standard assists preparers in distinguishing benefits provided in exchange for service and benefits provided in exchange for the termination of employment, and affects the recognition and measurement of termination benefits.

The standard is effective for annual periods beginning on or after January 1, 2013, with early adoption permitted.

US GAAP COMPARISON

Differences exist related to defined benefit plans. Under US GAAP, the fair value of the net defined benefit obligation or asset is reflected in full in the statement of financial position and the total change recognized in other comprehensive income. Similar to IFRS, US GAAP employs the projected unit credit method to attribute costs to years of service. Therefore the components of cost are essentially the same. However, the net periodic pension expense is offset against the total fair value changes in other comprehensive income to recognize the effect in profit or loss.

Further, no limitation is placed on the recognition of a net defined benefit asset. The corridor method to spread actuarial gains and losses is also not used. Both vested and unvested unrecognized costs are recognized immediately for a curtailment as opposed to unvested amounts being amortized over future periods as is the case under IFRS.

20 REVENUE RECOGNITION, INCLUDING CONSTRUCTION CONTRACTS

REVENUE RECOGNITION

INTRODUCTION

The standard addressing revenue recognition principles in general terms is IAS 18. It prescribes the accounting treatment for revenue arising from certain types of transactions and events and, while useful, is not a comprehensive treatise on the peculiarities on all the diverse forms of revenue and of possible recognition strategies that could be encountered. The basic premise is that revenue should be measured at the fair value of the consideration that has been received when the product or service promised has been provided to the customer. Specific guidance applies to various categories of revenues.

Thus, in the normal sale of goods, revenue is presumed to have been realized when the significant risks and rewards have been transferred to the buyer, accompanied by the forfeiture of effective control by the seller, and the amount to be received can be reliably measured. For most routine transactions (e.g., by retail merchants), this occurs when the goods have been delivered to the customer.

Revenue recognition for service transactions, as set forth in revised IAS 18, requires that the percentage-of-completion method be used unless certain defined conditions are not met. Current revenue recognition standards for services transactions closely parallel those for construction contracts under IAS 11, which is also covered in this chapter.

For interest, royalties and dividends, recognition is warranted when it is probable that economic benefits will flow to the entity. Specifically, interest is recognized on a time proportion basis, taking into account the effective yield on the asset. Royalties are recognized on an accrual basis, in accordance with the terms of the underlying agreement. Dividend income is recognized when the shareholder's right to receive payment has been established.

IAS 18 also established certain disclosure requirements, including the revenue recognition accounting policies of the reporting entity.

While the existing general guidance on revenue recognition under IAS actually exceeds that which has thus far been provided under various national standards, it nonetheless is modest given the broad importance of the topic.

Sources of IFRS
IASB's *Framework for Preparation and Presentation of Financial Statements*
IAS 11, 18   *SIC* 31   *IFRIC* 12, 13, 15, 18

DEFINITIONS OF TERMS

Fair value. An amount for which an asset could be exchanged or a liability settled, between knowledgeable, willing parties in an arm's-length transaction.

Ordinary activities. Those activities of an entity which it undertakes as part of its business and such related activities in which the entity engages in furtherance of, incidental to, or arising from those activities.

Revenue. Gross inflow of economic benefits during the period resulting from an entity's ordinary activities is considered "revenue," provided those inflows result in increases in equity, other than increases relating to contributions from owners or equity participants. Revenue refers to the gross amount (of revenue) and excludes amounts collected on behalf of third parties (such as taxes and other transactions where the entity is acting as an agent).

SCOPE

Revenue. The IASB's *Framework* defines "income" to include both revenue and gains. IAS 18 deals only with revenue. Revenue is defined as income arising from the ordinary activities of an entity and may be referred to by a variety of names including sales, fees, interest, dividends and royalties. Revenue encompasses only the gross inflow of economic benefits received or receivable by the entity, on its own account. This implies that amounts collected on behalf of others—including such items as sales tax or value added tax, which also flow to the entity along with the revenue from sales—do not qualify as revenue. Thus, these other collections should not be included in an entity's reported revenue. Put another way, gross revenue from sales should be shown net of amounts collected on behalf of third parties.

Similarly, in an agency relationship the amounts collected on behalf of the principal is not regarded as revenue for the agent. Instead, the commission earned on such collections qualifies as revenue of the agent. For example, in the case of a travel agency, the collections from ticket sales do not qualify as revenue or income from its ordinary activities. Instead, it will be the commission on the tickets sold by the travel agency that will constitute that entity's gross revenue.

Scope of the standard. IAS 18 applies to the accounting for revenue arising from

- The sale of goods;
- The rendering of services; and
- The use of the entity's assets by others, yielding (for the entity) interest, dividends and royalties.

A sale of goods encompasses *both* goods produced by the entity for sale to others and goods purchased for resale by the entity. The rendering of services involves the performance by the entity of an agreed-upon task, based on a contract, over a contractually agreed period of time.

The use of the entity's assets by others gives rise to revenue for the entity in the form of

- **Interest,** which is a charge for the use of cash and cash equivalents or for amounts due to the entity;
- **Royalties,** which are charges for the use of long-term assets of the entity such as patents or trademarks owned by the entity; and
- **Dividends,** which are distributions of profit to the holders of equity investments in the share capital of other entities.

The standard *does not* apply to revenue arising from

- Lease agreements that are subject to the requirements of IAS 17;
- Dividends arising from investments in associates which are accounted for using the equity method, which are dealt with in IAS 28;
- Insurance contracts within the scope of IFRS 4;
- Changes in fair values of financial instruments—or their disposal, which is addressed by IAS 39;
- Natural increases in herds, agriculture and forest products, which is dealt with under IAS 41;
- The extraction of mineral ores; and
- Changes in the value of other current assets.

IDENTIFICATION

While setting out clearly the criteria for the recognition of revenue under three categories—sale of goods, rendering of services and use of the entity's assets by others—the standard clarifies that these should be applied separately to each transaction. In other words, the recognition criteria should be applied to the separately identifiable components of a single transaction consistent with the principle of "substance over form."

> For example, a washing machine is sold with an after-sale service warranty. The selling price includes a separately identifiable portion attributable to the after-sale service warranty. In such a case, the standard requires that the selling price of the washing machine should be apportioned between the two separately identifiable components and each one recognized according to an appropriate recognition criterion. Thus, the portion of the selling price attributable to the after-sales warranty should be deferred and recognized over the period during which the service is performed. The remaining selling price should be recognized immediately if the recognition criteria for revenue from sale of goods (explained below) are satisfied.

Similarly, the recognition criteria are to be applied to two or more separate transactions together when they are connected or linked in such a way that the commercial effect (or substance over form) cannot be understood without considering the series of transactions as a whole. For example, Company X sells a ship to Company Y and later enters into a separate contract with Company Y to repurchase the same ship from it. In this case the two transactions need to be considered together in order to ascertain whether or not revenue is to be recognized.

MEASUREMENT

The quantum of revenue to be recognized is usually dependent upon the terms of the contract between the entity and the buyer of goods, the recipient of the services, or the users of the assets of the entity. Revenue should be measured at the fair value of the consideration received or receivable, net of any trade discounts and volume rebates allowed by the entity.

When the inflow of the consideration, which is usually in the form of cash or cash equivalents, is deferred, the fair value of the consideration will be an amount lower than the nominal amount of consideration. The difference between the fair value and the nominal value of the consideration, which represents the time value of money, is recognized as interest revenue.

When the entity offers interest-free extended credit to the buyer or accepts a promissory note from the buyer (as consideration) that bears either no interest or a below-market interest rate, such an arrangement could be construed as a financing transaction. In such a case the fair value of the consideration is ascertained by discounting the future inflows using an imputed rate of interest. The imputed rate of interest is either "the prevailing rate of interest for a similar instrument of an issuer with a similar credit rating, or a rate of interest that discounts the nominal amount of the instrument to the current cash sales price of the goods or services."

To illustrate this point, let us consider the following example:

> Hero International is a car dealership that is known to offer excellent packages for all new models of Japanese cars. Currently, it is advertising on the television that there is a special offer for all Year 2011 models of a certain make. The offer is valid for all purchases made on or before September 30, 2011. The special offer deal is either a cash payment in full of €20,000 or a zero down payment with extended credit terms of two years—24 monthly installments of €1,000 each. Thus, anyone opting for the extended credit terms would pay €24,000 in total.
>
> Since there is a difference of €4,000 between the cash price of €20,000 and the total amount payable if the car is paid for in 24 installments of €1,000 each, this arrangement is effectively a financing transaction (and, of course, a sale transaction as well). The cash price of €20,000 would be regarded as the amount of consideration attributable to the sale of the car. The difference between the cash price and the aggregate amount payable in monthly installments is interest revenue

and is to be recognized over the period of two years on a time proportion basis (using the effective interest method).

Exchanges of similar and dissimilar goods and services. When goods or services are exchanged or swapped for *similar* goods or services, the earning process is not considered being complete. Thus the exchange is not regarded as a transaction that generates revenue. Such exchanges are common in certain commodity industries, such as oil or milk industries, where suppliers usually swap inventories in various locations in order to meet geographically diverse demand on a timely basis.

In contrast, when goods or services of a *dissimilar* nature are swapped, the earning process is considered to be complete, and thus the exchange is regarded as a transaction that generates revenue. The revenue thus generated is measured at the fair value of the goods or services received or receivable. If in this process cash or cash equivalents are also transferred, then the fair value should be adjusted by the amount of cash or cash equivalents transferred. In certain cases, the fair value of the goods or services received cannot be measured reliably. Under such circumstances, fair value of goods or services given up, adjusted by the amount of cash transferred, is the measure of revenue to be recognized. Barter arrangements are examples of such exchanges involving goods that are dissimilar in nature.

RECOGNITION

According to the IASB's *Framework*, revenue is to be recognized when it is probable that future economic benefits will flow to the entity and reliable measurement of the quantum of revenue is possible. Based on these fundamental tenets of revenue recognition stated in the IASB's *Framework*, IAS 18 establishes criteria for recognition of revenue from three categories of transactions—the sale of goods, the rendering of services, and the use by others of the reporting entity's assets. In the case of the first two categories of transactions producing revenue, the standard prescribes certain additional criteria for recognition of revenue. In the case of revenue from the use by others of the entity's assets, the standard does not overtly prescribe additional criteria, but it does provide guidance on the bases to be adopted in revenue recognition from this source. This may, in a way, be construed as an additional criterion for revenue recognition from this source of revenue.

Revenue recognition from the sale of goods. Revenue from the sale of goods should be recognized if *all* of the five conditions mentioned below are met.

- The reporting entity has transferred significant risks and rewards of ownership of the goods to the buyer;
- The entity does not retain *either* continuing managerial involvement (akin to that usually associated with ownership) *or* effective control over the goods sold;
- The amount of revenue to be recognized can be measured reliably;
- The probability that economic benefits related to the transaction will flow to the entity exists; and
- The costs incurred or to be incurred in respect of the transaction can be measured reliably.

The determination of the point in time when a reporting entity is considered to have transferred the significant risks and rewards of ownership in goods to the buyer is critical to the recognition of revenue from the sale of goods. If upon examination of the circumstances of the transfer of risks and rewards of ownership by the entity it is determined that the entity could still be considered as having retained significant risks and rewards of ownership, the transaction could not be regarded as a sale.

Some examples of situations illustrated by the standard in which an entity may be considered to have retained significant risks and rewards of ownership, and thus revenue is not recognized, are when there is some degree of uncertainty around the transaction. Examples include

- A contract for the sale of an oil refinery stipulates that installation of the refinery is an integral and a significant part of the contract. Therefore, until the refinery is completely installed by the reporting entity that sold it, the sale would not be regarded as complete. In other words, until the completion of the installation, the entity that sold the refinery would still be regarded as the effective owner of the refinery even if the refinery has already been delivered to the buyer. Accordingly, revenue will not be recognized by the entity until it completes the installation of the refinery.
- Goods are sold on approval, whereby the buyer has negotiated a limited right of return. If there is uncertainty about the possibility of return, revenue is not recognized until the shipment has been formally accepted by the buyer, or the goods have been delivered as per the terms of the contract, and the time stipulated in the contract for rejection has expired.
- In the case of "layaway sales," under terms of which the goods are delivered only when the buyer makes the final payment in a series of installments, revenue is not recognized until the last and final payment is received by the entity. Upon receipt of the final installment, the goods are delivered to the buyer and revenue is recognized. However, based upon experience, if it can reasonably be presumed that most such sales are consummated, revenue may be recognized when a significant deposit is received from the buyer and goods are on hand, identified and ready for delivery to the buyer.

If the reporting entity retains only an insignificant risk of ownership, the transaction is considered a sale and revenue is recognized.

> For example, a department store has a policy to offer a refund if a customer is not satisfied. Since the entity is only retaining an insignificant risk of ownership, revenue from sale of goods is recognized. However, since the entity's refund policy is publicly announced and thus would have created a valid expectation on the part of the customers that the store will honor its policy of refunds, a provision is also recognized for the best estimate of the costs of refunds, as explained in IAS 37.

Another important condition for recognition of revenue from the sale of goods is the existence of the probability that the economic benefits will flow to the entity. For example, for several years an entity has been exporting goods to a foreign country. In the current year, due to sudden restrictions by the foreign government on remittances of currency outside the country, collections from these sales were not made by the entity. The probability of receiving the revenue must be assessed before the revenue could be recognized.

Yet another important condition for recognition of revenue from the sale of goods relates to the reliability of measuring costs associated with the sale of goods. Thus, if expenses such as those relating to warranties or other postshipment costs cannot be measured reliably, then revenue from the sale of such goods should also not be recognized. This rule is based on the principle of matching of revenues and expenses.

The IASB provides additional guidance on determining the point in time at which the entity transfers the significant risks and rewards of ownership, and thus when revenue from sale of goods is to be recognized. Since the law in different countries may determine the point in time at which the entity transfers ownership, this guidance accompanies IAS 18 but is not part of IAS 18. It includes the following:

> **Consignment sales.** Revenue is recognized by the shipper (seller or consignor), not by the recipient (buyer or consignee), when the goods are sold to a third party. Goods out on consignment remain the property of the consignor and are included in its inventory. The consignee is selling the goods on behalf of the shipper for a commission.

> **Cash on delivery sales.** In this case, revenue is recognized after delivery of goods is made and cash received.

> **Sales to intermediate parties, such as distributors, dealers or others for resale.** In general, revenue is recognized when the risks and rewards of ownership have been transferred. In situations when the buyer is acting, in substance, as an agent, the sale is treated as a consignment sale.

> **Subscriptions to publications and similar items.** Revenue is recognized on a straight-line basis over the period in which the items are dispatched (when items are of similar value); or on the basis of the sales value of items dispatched to total estimated sales value (when the items vary in value).

> **Installment sale, under which the consideration is receivable in installments.** Revenue is recognized at the present value of the consideration, determined by discounting the installments receivable at the imputed rate of interest.

> **Real estate sales.** In accordance with IFRIC 15, revenue from the construction of real estate is recognized depending on whether an agreement is for the sale of goods, the rendering of services, or a construction contract (within the scope of IAS 11 or IAS 18).

Revenue recognition from the rendering of services. When the outcome of the transaction involving the rendering of services can be estimated reliably, revenue relating to that transaction should be recognized. The recognition of revenue should be with reference to the stage of completion of the transaction at the end of the reporting period. The outcome of a transaction can be estimated reliably when each of the four conditions set out below are met.

- The amount of revenue can be measured reliably;
- The probability that the economic benefits related to this transaction will flow to the entity exists;
- The stage of completion of the transaction at the end of the reporting period can be measured reliably; and
- The costs incurred for the transaction and the costs to complete the transaction can be measured reliably.

This manner of recognition of revenue, based on the stage of completion, is often referred to as the "percentage-of-completion" method. IAS 11 also mandates recognition of revenue on this basis. Revenue is recognized only when it is probable that the economic benefits related to the transaction will flow to the reporting entity. However, when the amount of revenue cannot be estimated reliably, revenue should be recognized only to the extent of the expenses recognized that are recoverable ("cost recovery method" is fallback in this case). If there is uncertainty with regard to the collectability of an amount already included in revenue, the uncollectable amount should be recognized as an expense instead of adjusting it against the amount of revenue originally recognized.

In order to be able to make reliable estimates, an entity should agree with the other party to the following:

- Each other's enforceable rights with respect to the services provided;
- The consideration to be exchanged; and
- The manner and terms of settlement.

It is important that the entity has in place an effective internal financial budgeting and reporting system. This ensures that the entity can promptly review and revise the estimates of revenue as the service is being performed. It should be noted, however, that merely because there is a later need for revisions does not by itself make an estimate of the outcome of the transaction unreliable.

Progress payments and advances received from customers are emphatically not a measure of stage of completion. The stage of completion of a transaction may be determined in a number of ways. Depending on the nature of the transaction, the method used may include

- Surveys of work performed;
- Services performed to date as a percentage of total services to be performed; or
- The proportion that costs incurred to date bear to the estimated total costs of the transaction. (Only costs that reflect services performed or to be performed are included in costs incurred to date or in estimated total costs.)

In certain cases services are performed by an indeterminable number of acts over a specified period of time. Revenue in such a case should be recognized on a straight-line basis unless it is possible to estimate the stage of completion by some other method more reliably. Similarly when in a series of acts to be performed in rendering a service, a specific act is much more significant than other acts, the recognition is postponed until the significant act is performed.

During the early stages of the transaction it may not be possible to estimate the outcome of the transaction reliably. In all such cases, where the outcome of the transaction involving the rendering of services cannot be estimated reliably, revenue should be recognized only to the extent of the expenses recognized that are recoverable. However, in a later period when the uncertainty that precluded the reliable estimation of the outcome no longer exists, revenue is recognized as usual.

NOTE: The "percentage-of-completion" method is discussed in detail in the second part of this chapter. For numerical examples illustrating the method, please refer to the second part of this chapter relating to construction contracts.

Revenue recognition from interest, royalties, and dividends. Revenue arising from the use by others of the reporting entity's assets yielding interest, royalties and dividends should be recognized when both of the following two conditions are met:

1. It is probable that the economic benefits relating to the transaction will flow to the entity; and
2. The amount of the revenue can be measured reliably.

The bases prescribed for the recognition of the revenue are the following:

1. In the case of interest—the time proportion basis that takes into account the effective yield on the assets;
2. In the case of royalties—the accrual basis in accordance with the substance of the relevant agreement; and
3. In the case of dividends—when the shareholders' rights to receive payment are established.

According to IAS 18, "the effective yield on an asset is the rate of interest used to discount the stream of future cash receipts expected over the life of the asset to equate to the initial carrying amount of asset." Interest revenue includes the effect of amortization of any discount, premium or other difference between the initial carrying amount of a debt security and its amount at maturity.

When unpaid interest has accrued before an interest-bearing investment is purchased by the entity, the subsequent receipt of interest is to be allocated between preacquisition and postacquisition periods. Only the portion of interest that accrued subsequent to the acquisition by the entity is recognized as income. The remaining portion of interest, which is attributable to the preacquisition period, is treated as a reduction of the cost of the investment, as explained by IAS 39. Dividends earned from preacquisition profits related to equity securities purchased were previously treated as a reduction of the cost of investment. IFRS was amended to provide that dividends earned are treated as revenue in the year in which they accrue to the investee entity regardless of when the related profits were earned. However, when such a dividend payment is made and there are indicators that the carrying value of the investment may be impaired, the investee must apply IAS 36 in recognizing any impairment loss.

SPECIFIC TRANSACTIONS

Revenue recognized from the transfer of assets from customers. In some industries such as the utilities industry and entities that outsource information technology solutions, an entity may receive from its customers items of property, plant, and equipment that must be used to connect those customers to a network and/or to provide them with ongoing access to a supply of commodities and services. Alternatively, the supplier entity may receive cash from customers from the acquisition or construction of such items of property, plant, and equipment. Typically, customers will be required to pay additional amounts for the purchase of goods or services based on usage. Previously, the accounting for such transactions was wide and varied. However, in January 2009, the IFRS Interpretations Committee issued IFRIC 18, *Transfers of Assets from Customers,* to address the accounting concerns that existed. The Interpretation is applicable prospectively to transfers of assets from customers received on or after July 1, 2009. The Interpretation allows early application provided the valuations and other information needed to apply the Interpretation to past transfers were obtained at the time those transfers occurred.

IFRIC 18 addresses the following issues:

1. Is the definition of an asset met?
2. If the definition of an asset is met, how should the transferred item of property, plant, and equipment be measured on initial recognition?
3. If the item of property, plant, and equipment is measured at fair value on initial recognition, how should the resulting credit be accounted for?
4. How should the entity account for a transfer of cash from its customer?

Definition of an asset: An asset exists only if the definition of an asset as contained in the *Framework* is met. An asset is defined as "a resource controlled by the entity as a result of past events and from which future economic benefits are expected to flow to the entity." In most circumstances, the entity obtains the right of ownership of the transferred item of property, plant, and equipment. However, in determining whether an asset exists, the right of ownership is not essential. Therefore, if the customer continues to control the transferred item, the asset definition would not be met despite a transfer of ownership. Before an asset can be recognized, all the facts and circumstances that are pertinent to the arrangement must be considered fully, and should any of the requirements of ownership not be met, an asset cannot be recognized.

How should the transferred item of property, plant, and equipment be measured on initial recognition? Should the entity conclude that the definition of an asset is met, it will then recognize the transferred asset as an item of property, plant, and equipment at its fair value in accordance with IAS 16.

How should the credit be accounted for? The resultant credit is recognized in the income statement in terms of IAS 18. IAS 18 states that "When goods are sold or services are rendered in exchange for dissimilar goods or services, the exchange is regarded as a transaction which generates revenue." In this particular case, there is deemed to be an exchange of dissimilar goods and services and, as such, revenue is generated. The Interpretation also addresses scenarios where the revenue realized is earned from separately identifiable service offerings. In terms of IAS 18, such revenue streams must be recognized separately. An indicator that indicates that providing the customer with ongoing access to a supply of goods or services is a separately identifiable service to the entity is where, in the future, the customer making the transfer receives the ongoing access, the goods or services, or both at a price lower than would be charged without the transfer of the item of property, plant, and equipment. Conversely, a feature that indicates that the obligation to provide the customer with ongoing access to a supply of goods or services arises from the terms of the entity's operating license or other regulation rather than from the agreement relating to the transfer of an item of property, plant, and equipment is that customers that make a transfer pay the same price as those that do not for the ongoing access, or for the goods or services.

Where the entity identifies a single service, revenue is recognized when the service is provided based on the stage of completion method. The recognition of revenue should always take into account the obligations placed on the entity by the contract entered into. If more than one separately identifiable service is identified, IAS 18 requires the fair value of the total consideration received or receivable for the agreement to be allocated to each service and the recognition criteria applicable to each component of the contract.

If an ongoing service is identified as part of the agreement, the period over which revenue is recognized for that service is generally determined by the terms of the agreement with the customer. If the agreement does not specify a period, the revenue shall be recognized over a period no longer than the useful life of the transferred asset used to provide the ongoing service.

How should the entity account for a transfer of cash from its customer? When an entity receives a transfer of cash from a customer, it should assess whether the agreement entered into is within the scope of the Interpretation. If it is, the entity shall assess whether the constructed or acquired item of property, plant, and equipment meets the definition of an asset in accordance with the *Framework* and if the definition is met, the entity should recognize the item of property, plant, and equipment at its cost. The entity should also recognize revenue at the fair value of the cash received. Any difference is recorded as a gain or loss in the statement of comprehensive income.

A reporting entity should disclose the following:

- The accounting policies adopted for the recognition of revenue including the methods adopted to determine the stage of completion of transactions involving the rendering of services;
- The amount of each significant category of revenue recognized during the period including revenue arising from

  - The sale of goods;
  - The rendering of services; and
  - Interest, royalties, and dividends.

- The amounts of revenue arising from exchanges of goods or services included in each significant category of revenue.

Accounting for barter transactions. The much-heralded era of e-commerce (i.e., commerce conducted via Internet, based on commercial Web sites directed at end consumers ["B-to-C" business] or at intermediate consumers, such as wholesalers and manufacturers ["B-to-B" business]), although past its over-touted boom period, is now an established feature of business life. It is likely that growing percentages of business will be conducted via electronic commerce.

The "dot-com bubble" period was noteworthy for another, related trend, that of investors and others finding value in new "performance" measures such as gross sales volume and the number of "hits" registered on Web sites. Concurrently, the importance (for high technology and start-up entities in particular) of traditional measures of success, particularly profits, was often unjustifiably discounted. The confluence of these two structural changes provided an unfortunate opportunity for some entities to seek ways to inflate reported revenues, if not actual profits. One device involved barter revenues.

Specifically, it became commonplace for Web-based businesses to swap advertising with each other. With each entity "buying" advertising on others' sites and "selling" advertising opportunities on its own site to the same counterparties, a liberal interpretation of financial reporting standards could enable each of them to inflate reported revenues by attributing value to such an exchange. While the corresponding expenses of each of the counterparties were also necessarily exaggerated, so that net earnings were not at all affected (unless revenues and expenses were reported in different fiscal periods, which also occurred), with investors mesmerized by reported gross revenues and the growth thereof, the impact was to encourage overvaluation of the entities' shares in the market.

As certain financial reporting frauds have demonstrated, distortion of revenues via "swap" arrangements has hardly been constrained to the providing and acquiring of internet-based advertising. (For example, "capacity swaps" were employed by many US telecom and energy companies as a device to record immediate revenue, while amortizing the related costs over extended contract periods.). However, the bartering of advertising services came to the attention of the SIC who then issued an Interpretation, SIC 31, to address the matter.

This interpretation addresses how revenue from a barter transaction involving advertising services received or provided in a barter transaction should be reliably measured. The SIC agreed that the entity providing advertising should measure revenue from the barter transaction based on the fair value of the advertising services it has provided to its customer, and not on the value of that received. In fact, the SIC states categorically that the value of the services received cannot be used to reliably measure the revenue generated by the services provided.

Furthermore, SIC 31 holds that the fair value advertising services provided in a barter transaction can be reliably measured only by reference to nonbarter transactions that involve services similar to that in the barter transaction, when those transactions occur frequently, are expected to continue occurring after the barter transaction, represent a predominant source of revenue from advertising similar to the advertising in the barter transaction, involve cash and/or another form of consideration (e.g., marketable securities, nonmonetary assets, and other services) that has a reliably determinable fair value, and do not involve the same counterparty as in the barter transaction. All of these conditions must be satisfied in order to value the revenue to be recognized from the advertising barter transaction.

Clearly, based on the criteria mandated by SIC 31, the more common barter transactions, involving mere "swaps" of advertising among the members of the bartering group, henceforth cannot serve as a basis for revenue recognition by any of the parties thereto.

Accounting for multiple-element revenue arrangements. Presently, IAS 18 lacks guidance on the accounting for multiple-element revenue arrangements, but the IASB's project on revenue recognition does deal with this increasingly common phenomenon. When entities offer customers multiple-element arrangements, these provide for the delivery or performance of multiple products, services, or rights, which may take place at different times. For example, deregulation, innovation, and competition in the telecommunication industry resulted in complex service offerings to customers, in particular for bundled (or multiple-element) arrangements that may include a handset. Revenue recognition is one of the most complex accounting issues this industry faces. The IASB has noted that the accounting for such arrangements has been one of the most contentious practice issues of revenue recognition. As part of its current project, it examined the application of an assets and liabilities approach to revenue recognition against the cases involving multiple-element revenue arrangements, and contrasted the impact of such an approach to the positions taken by the FASB's Emerging Issues Task Force's *Accounting for Revenue Arrangements with Multiple Deliverables* (EITF Issue 00-21, which was approved by the EITF in November 2002, now codified as ASC 605-25). The IASB noted that the EITF's approach was consistent with, but more extensive than, the revenue recognition criteria in IAS 18. We discuss the IASB's Revenue project in more detail at the end of this chapter.

Reporting revenue as a principal or as an agent. IAS 18 stipulates that, when an entity is acting in the capacity of an agent, its gross inflows of cash or other economic benefits include amounts collected on behalf of the principal and which do not result in increases in equity for the entity. Since amounts collected on behalf of the principal are not revenue, the reporting entity's revenue should only be the amount of the commissions it receives. To report the gross amounts collected as revenue in such circumstances would exaggerate and greatly distort the scope or scale of the entity's actual operations.

However, determining whether an entity is acting as a principal or as an agent requires the application of judgment and consideration of all relevant facts and circumstances. IFRS previously did not offer any further guidance on making such determinations.

Improvements to IFRS adopted in 2009 provide the guidance required in determining whether an entity is acting as a principal or as an agent. As revised, IAS 18 notes that an entity is acting as a principal when it is exposed to the significant risks and rewards associated with selling goods or rendering services, and that includes having

1. Primary responsibility for providing the goods or services to the customer or for fulfilling the order;
2. Inventory risk before and after the customer order;
3. Latitude in establishing prices, either directly or indirectly; and
4. Customer's credit risk for the amount receivable from the customer.

On the other hand, an entity is acting as an agent when it is not exposed to the significant risks and rewards associated with selling goods or rendering services, for example, when compensation earned is predetermined based on either a fixed fee per transaction or a stated percentage of the amount billed to the customer. In the latter instances, the gross revenue to be reported is merely the agent's commissions received.

Sales involving customer loyalty credits. Certain sales transactions involve the granting of so-called customer loyalty credits, such that customers are granted "points" toward future purchases of goods or services. The popular airline mileage programs are perhaps the most ubiquitous of such programs, under which frequent fliers accumulate points which can be redeemed for future class upgrades or free flights. For a long time no special accounting recognition was given to these very real obligations by the airlines, which resulted in a large overhang of costly service promises. These promises clearly represented obligations (i.e., accounting liabilities) by the service providers (e.g., airlines), but were long ignored for two reasons. First, they were assumed to not be material to the service providers' statements of financial position; and second, there were legitimate concerns about how these were to be measured (i.e., whether they should have been recorded at some average of the retail value of the "free" services, or at the providers' cost to provide these services, which were to be delivered at some unspecified future date.

More recently, it had become clear that quite material amounts of such obligations had been going unreported by the service providers, with the cumulative effect of possibly materially overstating current profitability and shareholders' equity (retained earnings) and understating liabilities. In the international standards arena, this has now been definitively dealt with by the promulgation of IFRIC 13, *Customer Loyalty Programs*. It applies to a wide array of such programs, including those linked to individual and group buying activities, with goods or services due to be provided by the reporting entity itself as well as rights to be redeemed by third parties. In each such instance, customers earn the right to discounted or free goods or services, possibly after further qualifying conditions are met.

IFRIC 13 stipulates the accounting by the entity that grants the award credits. It requires that such credits be separately identified as components of the sales transactions, thus reducing the profit recognized and resulting in the creation of a liability for the future goods or services to be provided to its customers. The liability thereby created is discharged when the subsequent free or discounted service is provided, or, if a third party is to provide the later goods or services, when the third party becomes obligated to provide such goods or services. If the customer forfeits its right (e.g., by expiration of a contractual period for redemption of the credits), revenue is to be recognized at that time.

This accounting requirement is, conceptually at least, straightforward. A key issue is the proper measurement to be applied to this obligation. IFRIC 13 resolves this by specifying that the *fair value* of the award credits is the proper measure. The interpretation stipulates that this is given by reference to the fair value of the goods or services that would be offered to customers who had not accumulated credits from the initial transactions. For example, if "frequent flier" mileage points are awarded, and if, say, 25,000 mileage points result in a free round trip flight to any domestic destination, the service provider (airline) would use the average retail price of such tickets as a basis for accruing such obligations.

Where a third party assumes this responsibility, there would usually be a contractually agreed value, making recognition of the amount to be allocated to the program liability directly observable.

Since the amount to be allocated to the obligation to provide future discounted or free goods or services is determined by reference to the fair value of the goods or services, the amount allocated to this liability is a reduction in the revenue immediately recognized. It is not an expense (such as a selling expense), because that treatment would be consistent with measurement by reference to the reporting entity's cost of providing the future goods or services. Put another way, the solution prescribed by IFRIC 13 is based on a revenue recognition approach, not a cost accrual approach, to financial reporting.

The only exception to the foregoing occurs when the expected cost of delivering the free or discounted goods or services is anticipated to exceed the revenue associated with that event. Consistent with practice under other IFRS, these anticipated losses must be accrued at the date the initial transactions occur.

As noted, experience suggests that some portion of the program points will be forfeited by customers (i.e., they will be earned but never redeemed). This can occur because some customers will fail to meet other qualifying conditions, such as by reaching some defined threshold such as number of miles needed to exercise the redemption, or because of the expiration of time. With experience, the reporting entity may develop the ability to accurately project the proportion of points awarded that will not be redeemed. IFRIC 13 provides that the accrual of the obligation is to be based on the fraction of points that will eventually be redeemed. This is an estimate and ultimately the facts will differ from the estimate, and as with other changes in accounting estimates, this is accounted for prospectively; it is not an error to be corrected by retroactive restatement.

> For example, if customers earn one point for each €100 purchase, and need to accumulate 100 points to redeem them for a service having a fair value of €200, then the initial accounting need is to recognize €2 of revenue reduction (and an equivalent liability creation) for each €100 transaction. If experience shows that 25% of such loyalty program points are ultimately forfeited, then the proper subsequent accounting would be to allocate only €1.50 of each €100 transaction already undertaken to this liability. If the estimate of the proportion to be forfeited is revised in later financial reporting periods, the liability for unredeemed points is adjusted in the later periods, thereby affecting profit recognized in those periods.

A final issue, not dealt with by IFRIC 13, is whether the allocation of the transaction amount should be apportioned between the initial transaction's revenue and the deferred revenue associated with the redemption of the loyalty points based on a pro rata assignment, or whether the deferred revenue should be the fair value of the future goods or services, with the residual being assigned to the initial transaction. Thus, both approaches would be acceptable—and, as usual, the reporting entity should consistently apply one or the other.

> To illustrate this last matter, assume again that customers earn one point for each €100 purchase, and need to accumulate 100 points to redeem them for a service having a fair value of €200. Possible forfeitures are ignored in this example, for simplicity. The pro rata allocation method would assign [€100/(€100 + €2) =] €98.04 to the initial transaction, and would assign [€2/(€100 + €2) =] €1.96 to the obligation for future services, which will be recognized as revenue when the promised services are later performed. On the other hand, if the alternative method is used, the fair value of the future services, €2, is initially recorded, so the immediate transaction is reported as a €98 revenue event.

Service concession arrangements. In many countries, public-to-private service concession arrangements have evolved as a mechanism for providing public services. Under such arrangements, a private entity is used to construct, operate or maintain the infrastructure for public use such as roads, bridges, hospitals, airports, water distribution facilities and energy supply. IFRIC 12, *Service Concession Arrangements,* deals with a private sector entity (an operator) that provides a public service and operates and maintains that infrastructure (operation services) for a specified period of time. The Interpretation was published in late 2006, to be applied for financial years beginning on or after January 1, 2008. As a change in accounting policy, it was to be accounted for retrospectively, except that proved to be impracticable.

This Interpretation applies to service concession arrangements when the infrastructure for public use is constructed or acquired by the operator or given for use by the grantor and (1) the grantor controls what services operator must provide, to whom and at what price, and (2) the grantor controls any significant residual interest in the existing infrastructure at the end of the term of the service concession arrangement. Because the grantor continues to control the infrastructure assets within the scope of the interpretation, these assets are not recognized as property, plant, and equipment of the operator. The operator recognizes and measures revenue for the services it performs in accordance with IAS 11 or IAS 18. If more than one service is performed (e.g., construction or upgrade services and operation services) under a single contract or arrangement, consideration received or receivable is allocated based on relative fair values of the services provided, when the amounts are separately identifiable. The nature of the consideration the operator receives in exchange for the construction services determines its subsequent accounting treatment.

When the consideration received is a financial asset because the operator has an unconditional contractual right to receive from the grantor cash or other financial asset (e.g., a loan or receivable, available-for-sale financial asset, or, if so designated upon initial recognition, a financial asset at fair value through profit or loss), the subsequent accounting in accordance with IAS 32 and IAS 39 would apply. In this case the grantor bears the risk (demand risk) that the cash flows generated from the users will not recover the operator's investment. A financial asset is recognized during construction, giving rise to revenues from construction recovered during the period of use of the asset.

An intangible asset is recognized when the consideration the operator receives consists of rights to charge users of the public service, for example a license to charge users tolls for using roads or bridges, and it is accounted for within the scope of IAS 38. In this case, the operator bears the risk (demand risk) that the cash flows generated from the use of the public service will not recover its investment. The intangible asset received from the grantor in exchange for the construction services is used to generate cash flows from users of the public service.

Rate-regulated activities Exposure Draft. Several years ago, the IASB was first asked to consider undertaking a project on rate-regulated activities. The putative issue to be resolved was whether regulated entities could or should recognize a liability (or an asset) as a result of rate regulation by regulatory bodies or governments. This same question had also been posed to IFRIC, which declined to add this item to its agenda. As a result an Exposure Draft was issued by the IASB in July 2009.

The IASB identified two criteria for a rate regulation to be within the scope of IFRS guidance: (1) an authorized body is empowered to establish rates that bind customers; and (2) a price established by regulation (the rate) that is designed to recover the specific costs the entity incurs in providing the regulated goods or services and to earn a specified return (cost-of-service regulation). When these scope criteria are met, the entity will recognize regulatory assets and/or regulatory liabilities, in addition to the assets and liabilities recognized in accordance with other IFRS. The effect of this requirement is initially to recognize as an asset (liability) an amount that would otherwise be recognized in that period in the statement of comprehensive income as an expense (income), thus deferring income or expense recognition to a later reporting period.

A fundamental issue that was addressed was whether rate regulation can create assets or liabilities, as those terms are defined by the *Framework*. As concluded by the IASB, a regulatory asset is a right to recover previously incurred costs through rates over future periods as a result of action by a regulator. Accordingly, it will embody a right to identifiable cash flows to be received from the customer base. The unit of account is thus the customer base, as a whole, and not individual customers.

An asset created by rate regulation is neither tangible nor financial in nature, and thus more akin to an intangible, although not completely similar to other assets whose accounting is governed by IAS 38. Although such assets would be subject to separate identification, the effects of rate regulation would not be separable from the related activities, and the resulting cash flows will not be separately identifiable. For that reason, the emphasis has been on identifying the effects of rate regulation.

Any recognized rate-regulatory asset will meet some, if not all, of the criteria set forth by IAS 38, while any rate-regulatory liability will be governed by the provisions of IAS 37. The criteria in IAS 37 will serve as the principal guide. Evidence supporting the future recovery of (otherwise sunk) costs could include statutes or regulations that specifically provide for the recovery of the cost in rates, if these were immune to being overturned by future regulatory decisions; rate orders from the regulator specifically authorizing recovery of the cost in rates; previous rate orders allowing recovery for substantially similar costs (precedents) for a specific entity or other entities in the same jurisdiction; the written approval of the regulator approving future recovery in rates; uniform regulatory accounting guidance providing for the accounting treatment of various costs that is typically followed by the regulator in setting rates; written approval from the regulatory staff of the jurisdiction suggesting they will support rate recovery of the cost (albeit not legally binding); and analysis of recoverability from internal or external legal counsel.

Assets arising from the effects of rate regulation should be measured, both on initial recognition and subsequently, on the basis of the probability-weighted average of all possible outcomes. This is consistent with the measure being developed in amendments to IAS 37 expected to be issued by the time this standard on rate-regulated activities is promulgated. The proposed standard identifies the relevant risk-free rate and risk adjustments relating to the regulatory process as being factors to consider in computing the present value of future outcomes, although the decision to recognize *probability-weighted* future cash flows implies the use of risk-free discount rate, since risk should already be captured in the weighting scheme.

Any resulting recognized rate-regulatory assets and liabilities will be presented separately in the statement of financial condition from other assets and liabilities. They will not be subject to offset, and both current and noncurrent assets and liabilities would be separately recognized, if warranted. An entity may present a net regulatory asset or a net regulatory liability for each category of asset or liability subject to the same regulator.

If assets arising from rate regulation are capitalized, periodic impairment testing will also be required. At each reporting date, the reporting entity is to consider the net effect on its rates of its regulatory assets and regulatory liabilities arising from the actions of each regulator for the periods in which the regulation is expected to affect rates. It must accordingly seek to determine whether it is reasonable to assume that rates set at levels that will recover the entity's costs can be collected from its customers. Given the fact that increasing prices have a negative effect on demand for the good or service (even for such routine needs as electricity), in making this determination the entity must consider estimated changes in the level of demand or competition during the recovery period. The IASB has also contemplated requiring reporting entities to consider the overall effect of regulatory assets on future rates and its ability to generate sufficient revenue to recover them; by requiring the cash-generating unit in which the regulatory assets reside to be tested for impairment in accordance with IAS 36 if recovery of the net regulatory assets and regulatory liabilities is not reasonably assured; requiring that any impairment loss would be allocated to individual regulatory assets based on the period and amount by which estimated future cash flows are affected; and requiring reassessments in subsequent periods of the amount and timing of the estimated cash flows used to measure the asset.

An entity may also be burdened by regulatory obligations that arise because of a requirement to refund to customers amounts collected in previous periods. In effect, the entity receives revenue in advance which must ultimately be refunded to customers. In such environments, collecting amounts in excess of costs and the allowed return creates an obligation to return the payments to the aggregate customer base. Such a scenario poses a less complex accounting issue than does the situation of future cost recoveries predicated on the continuation of an existing regulatory regime.

The IASB concluded that the mere fact that certain revenue activities are regulated does not impose special financial reporting requirements on the entity. Rather, both of two criteria must be met in order to bring the entity under the proposed new standard. These criteria are as discussed in the immediately following paragraphs.

First, the entity's customers must be subject to binding pricing set by a regulatory body. This implies both that an identifiable body is authorized to set prices for the regulated goods or services it provides to its customers, and that the prices set by that body bind the entity's customers. Rate-regulated entities are not allowed to charge rates for regulated goods or services other than as approved by the regulator. Furthermore, the regulatory body will have the ability to require price reductions until a specified amount has been returned to customers through those decreases. Accordingly, regulatory assets and regulatory liabilities arise when the regulator acts on behalf of the customers who individually have no bargaining power with the regulated entity. It is this aggregate customer base that is both represented by the regulator and bound by the regulator's actions.

Second, there must be a cause-and-effect relationship between the entity's costs and the future revenue cash flows, which is the principal economic effect of regulation on the accounting for regulated entities. The regulator's action promising the recovery of a cost creates a *future economic benefit*, which is the key relevant feature in the definition of an asset. For this reason, the proposed standard only deals with regulations in which rates are designed to recover the specific costs incurred by the entity in providing the regulated goods or services, and to earn a return would result in items that meet the definitions of assets and liabilities. The IASB warns that, in some circumstances, determining whether the oversight body's action creates a cost-of-services regulation may be a matter of facts and circumstances, and a number of indicators are suggested.

Regulatory assets and liabilities may have to be tested for impairment as part of a cash-generating unit if (as seems likely) they do not generate independent cash flows. Furthermore, even if costs are allowed to be recovered for regulatory purposes, if the effect is to capitalize costs to an extent that future accounting losses are created, an impairment may have to be recognized currently.

The IASB has agreed that a reporting entity should recognize a regulatory asset for amounts the regulator permits to be included in rates associated with self-constructed assets, which may relate to indirect overheads and financing costs that would not otherwise be recognized as part of property, plant, and equipment in accordance with IAS 16.

Regarding disclosure, entities will meet the minimum disclosure requirements by providing a table showing a reconciliation, from the beginning to the end of the period, of the carrying amount in the statement of financial position of the various categories of regulatory items. This table will be required unless another format is believed to be more appropriate. The draft standard expresses the belief that this (1) enables users of the financial statements to understand the nature and the financial effects of rate regulation on the reporting entity's activities; and (2) identifies and explains the amounts of regulatory assets and regulatory liabilities, and related income and expenses, recognized in its financial statements. The reconciliation will display, in one place, the changes in the amounts recognized in the statement of comprehensive income. Such a table would be useful in helping users to understand how the entity's reported financial results and position have been affected by rate regulation. Specific disclosure requirements are proposed as follows.

For each set of operating activities subject to a different regulator, the reporting entity will have to disclose the following information:

1. If the regulator is a related party (as defined in IAS 24), a statement to that effect, together with an explanation of why the regulator is related to the entity.
2. An explanation of the approval process for the rate subject to regulation (including the rate of return), including information about how that process affects both the underlying operating activities and the specified rate of return.
3. The indicators that management considered in concluding that such operating activities are within the scope of the standard, if that conclusion requires significant judgment.
4. Significant assumptions used to measure the expected present value of a recognized regulatory asset or regulatory liability including

   a. The supporting regulatory action, for example, the issue of a formal approval for costs to be recovered pending a final ruling at a later date and that date, when known, or
   b. The entity's assessment of the expected future regulatory actions.

5. The risks and uncertainties affecting the future recovery of the regulatory asset or final settlement of the regulatory liability, including the expected timing.

The reporting entity will also have to disclose the following information for each category of regulatory asset or regulatory liability recognized that is subject to a different regulator:

1. A reconciliation from the beginning to the end of the period, in tabular format unless another format is more appropriate, of the carrying amount in the statement of financial position of the regulatory asset or regulatory liability, including at least the following elements:

   a. The amount recognized in the statement of comprehensive income relating to balances from prior periods collected or refunded in the current period.
   b. The amount of costs incurred in the current period that were recognized in the statement of financial position as regulatory assets or regulatory liabilities to be recovered or refunded in future periods.
   c. Other amounts that affected the regulatory asset or regulatory liability, such as items acquired or assumed in business combinations or the effects of changes in foreign exchange rates, discount rates or estimated cash flows. If a single cause has a significant effect on the regulatory asset or regulatory liability, the entity shall disclose it separately.

2. The remaining period over which the entity expects to recover the carrying amount of the regulatory asset or to settle the regulatory liability.
3. The amount of financing cost included in the cost of self-constructed property, plant, and equipment and internally developed intangible assets in the current period in accordance with this standard that would not have been capitalized in accordance with IAS 23.

When the reporting entity recognizes an impairment loss in accordance with this standard, it must then provide the disclosures required by IAS 36.

When an entity derecognizes regulatory assets and regulatory liabilities in accordance with this standard, because the related operating activities fail to meet the criteria set forth therein, it must make a statement to that effect, setting forth the reasons for the conclusion that the criteria in this standard are no longer being met, a description of the operating activities affected and the amount of regulatory assets and regulatory liabilities derecognized.

If the disclosures required by the standard do not meet the informational objectives set forth above, the entity is to disclose whatever additional information is necessary to meet those objectives.

If adopted in the form proposed, the standard will not require full retrospective application, but would require application to regulatory assets and liabilities existing from the beginning of the comparative period, with an adjustment being made to opening retained earnings. A consequential amendment to IFRS 1 will be required to permit entities not to restate long-lived tangible assets to recognize separately amounts that would qualify for recognition as regulatory assets. Also, there would no longer be a need for a definition of rate-regulated operations in IFRS 1 or a separate impairment test.

The May 2010 *Improvements to IFRS* amended IFRS 1 to allow entities with rate-regulated activities that hold, or previously held, items of property, plant, and equipment or intangible assets for use in such operations (and recognized them separately as regulatory assets) to elect to use the carrying amount of such items as their *deemed cost* at the date of transition to IFRS (see Chapter 36 for a detailed discussion of IFRS 1).

At its September 2010 meeting, the IASB continued its discussion on rate-regulated activities, considering comment letters and papers received to date on the Exposure Draft 2009/8, *Rate Regulated Activities*.

The IASB did not reach conclusions on any technical issues at this meeting, instead reconfirming its earlier view that the matter could not be resolved quickly, and accordingly decided that the next step should be to consider whether to include rate-regulated activities in its future agenda.

The IASB therefore decided to include in its public consultation on its future agenda a request for views on what form a future project might take, if any, to address rate-regulated activities. The feedback received will assist the IASB in setting its future agenda. The potential future steps include, but are not limited to

- A disclosure-only standard
- An interim standard, similar to IFRS 4, *Insurance Contracts*, or IFRS 6, *Exploration for and Evaluation of Mineral Resources*, to grandfather previous GAAP accounting practices with some limited improvements
- A medium-term project focused on the effects of rate regulation
- A comprehensive project on intangible assets

Example of Financial Statement Disclosures

Daimler
December 31, 2010

Accounting policies

Revenue recognition. Revenue from sales of vehicles, service parts, and other related products is recognized when the risks and rewards of ownership of the goods are transferred to the customer, the amount of revenue can be estimated reliably, and collectability is reasonably assured. Revenue is recognized net of sales reductions such as cash discounts and sales incentives granted.

Daimler uses sales incentives in response to a number of market and product factors, including pricing actions and incentives offered by competitors, the amount of excess industry production capacity, the intensity of market competition and consumer demand for the product. The Group may offer a variety of sales incentive programs at any point in time, including cash offers to dealers and consumers, lease subsidies which reduce the consumers' monthly lease payment, or reduced financing rate programs offered to customers.

Revenue from receivables from financial services is recognized using the effective interest method. When loans are issued below market rates, related receivables are recognized at present value and revenue is reduced for the interest incentive granted.

The Group offers an extended, separately priced warranty for certain products. Revenue from these contracts is deferred and recognized into income over the contract period in proportion to the costs expected to be incurred based on historical information. In circumstances in which there is insufficient historical information, income from extended warranty contracts is recognized on a straight-line basis. A loss on these contracts is recognized in the current period if the sum of the expected costs for services under the contract exceeds unearned revenue.

For transactions with multiple deliverables, such as when vehicles are sold with free or reduced in price service programs, the Group allocates revenue to the various elements based on their estimated fair values.

Sales in which the Group guarantees the minimum resale value of the product, such as sales to certain rental car companies, are accounted for similar to an operating lease. The guarantee of the resale value may take the form of an obligation by Daimler to pay any deficiency between the proceeds the customer receives upon resale in an auction and the guaranteed amount, or an obligation to reacquire the vehicle after a certain period of time at a set price. Gains or losses from the resale of these vehicles are included in gross profit.

Revenue from operating leases is recognized on a straight-line basis over the lease term. Among the assets subject to "Operating leases" are Group products which are purchased by Daimler Financial Services from independent third-party dealers and leased to customers. After revenue recognition from the sale of the vehicles to independent third-party dealers, these vehicles create further revenue from leasing and remarketing as a result of lease contracts entered into. The Group estimates that the revenue recognized following the sale of vehicles to dealers equals approximately the additions to leased assets at Daimler Financial Services. Additions to leased assets at Daimler Financial Services were approximately €5 billion in 2010 (2009: approximately €4 billion).

Barclays PLC
December 31, 2010

6. Interest, fees and commissions

Interest

Interest is recognized in interest income and interest expense in the income statement for all interest bearing financial instruments classified as held-to-maturity, available-for-sale or other loans and receivables using the effective interest method.

The effective interest method is a method of calculating the amortized cost of a financial asset or liability (or group of assets and liabilities) and of allocating the interest income or interest expense over the relevant period. The effective interest rate is the rate that exactly discounts the expected future cash payments or receipts through the expected life of the financial instrument or, when appropriate, a shorter period, to the net carrying amount of the instrument. The application of the method has the effect of recognizing income (and expense) receivable (or payable) on the instrument evenly in proportion to the amount outstanding over the period to maturity or repayment.

In calculating effective interest, the Group estimates cash flows (using projections based on its experience of customers' behavior) considering all contractual terms of the financial instrument but excluding future credit losses. Fees, including those for early redemption, are included in the calculation to the extent that they can be measured and are considered to be an integral part of the effective interest rate. Cash flows arising from the direct and incremental costs of issuing financial instruments are also taken into account in the calculation. Where it is not possible to otherwise estimate reliably the cash flows or the expected life of a financial instrument, effective interest is calculated by reference to the payments or receipts specified in the contract, and the full contractual term.

Fees and commissions

Unless included in the effective interest calculation, fees and commissions are recognized as the service is provided. Fees and commissions not integral to effective interest arising from negotiating, or participating in the negotiation of the transaction from a third party, such as the acquisition of loans, shares, or other securities, or the purchase or sale of businesses, are recognized on completion of the underlying transaction. Portfolio and other management advisory and service fees are recognized based on the applicable service contracts. Asset management fees related to investment funds are recognized over the period the service is provided. The same principle is applied to the recognition of income from wealth management, financial planning, and custody services that are continuously provided over an extended period of time.

Commitment fees, together with related direct costs, for loan facilities where drawdown is probable are deferred and recognized as an adjustment to the effective interest on the loan once drawn. Commitment fees in relation to facilities where drawdown is not probable are recognized over the term of the commitment.

Insurance premiums

Insurance premiums are recognized in the period earned.

Net trading income

Income arises from both the sale and purchase of trading positions, margins, which are achieved through market-making and customer business and from changes in fair value caused by movements in interest and exchange rates, equity prices and other market variables. Trading positions are held at fair value and the resulting gains and losses are are included in the income statement, together with interest and dividends arising from long and short positions and funding costs relating to trading activities.

Dividends

Dividends are recognized when the right to receive payments is established. In the individual financial statement of Barclays PLC, this is when the dividends are received or when the dividends are appropriately authorized by the subsidiary.

CONSTRUCTION CONTRACT ACCOUNTING

INTRODUCTION

The principal concern of accounting for long-term construction contracts involves the timing of revenue (and thus profit) recognition. It has been well accepted that, given the long-term nature of such projects, deferring revenue recognition until completion would often result in the presentation of periodic financial reports that fail to meaningfully convey the true level of activity of the reporting entity during the reporting period. In extreme cases, in fact, there could be periods of no apparent activity, and others of exaggerated amounts, when in fact the entity was operating at a rather constant rate of production during all of the periods. To avoid these distortions, the percentage-of-completion method was developed, which reports the revenues proportionally to the degree to which the projects are being completed, even in the absence of full completion and, in many cases, even in the absence of the right to collect for the work done to date.

The major challenges in using percentage-of-completion accounting are to accurately gauge the extent to which the projects are being finished, and to assess the ability of the entity to actually bill and collect for the work done. Since many projects are priced at fixed amounts, or in some other fashion prevent the passing through to the customers the full amount of cost overruns, the computation of periodic profits must be sensitive not merely to the extent to which the project is nearing completion, but also to the terms of the underlying contractual arrangements.

IAS 11 is the salient IFRS addressing the accounting for construction contracts and other situations in which the percentage-of-completion method of revenue recognition would be appropriate. This standard uses the recognition criteria established by the IASB's *Framework* as the basis for the guidance it offers on accounting for construction contracts. The various complexities in applying IAS 11, including the estimation of revenues, costs, and progress toward completion, are set forth in the following discussion.

Sources of IFRS
IAS 11, 23, 37

DEFINITIONS OF TERMS

Claims. Amounts in excess of the agreed-on contract price that a contractor seeks to collect from a customer (or another party) for customer-caused delays, errors in specifications and designs, disputed variations in contract work, or other occurrences that are alleged to be the causes of unanticipated costs.

Combining (grouping) contracts. Grouping two or more contracts, whether with a single customer or with several customers, into a single profit center for accounting purposes, provided that

1. The group of contracts is negotiated as a single package;
2. The contracts combined are so closely interrelated that, in essence, they could be considered as a single contract negotiated with an overall profit margin; and
3. The contracts combined are either executed concurrently or in a sequence.

Construction contract. Contract specifically entered into for the construction of an asset or a combination of assets that are closely interrelated or interdependent in terms of their design, technology, and function or their end use or purpose.

Construction-in-progress (CIP). Inventory account used to accumulate the construction costs of the contract project. For the percentage-of-completion method, the CIP account also includes the gross profit earned to date.

Contract costs. Comprised of costs directly related to a specific contract, costs that are attributable to the contract activity in general and can be allocated to the contract, and other costs that are specifically chargeable to the customer under the terms of the contract.

Contract revenue. Comprised of initial amount of revenue stipulated by the contract plus any variations in contract work, claims, and incentive payments, provided that these extra amounts of revenue meet the recognition criteria set by the IASB's *Framework* (i.e., regarding the probability of future economic benefits flowing to the contractor and reliability of measurement).

Cost-plus contract. Construction contract in which the contractor is reimbursed for allowable costs plus either a percentage of these costs or a fixed fee.

Estimated cost to complete. Anticipated additional cost of materials, labor, subcontracting costs, and indirect costs (overhead) required to complete a project at a scheduled time.

Fixed-price contract. Construction contract wherein the contract revenue is fixed either in absolute terms or is fixed in terms of unit rate of output; in certain cases both fixed prices being subject to any cost escalation clauses, if allowed by the contract.

Incentive payments. Any additional amounts payable to the contractor if specified performance standards are either met or surpassed.

Percentage-of-completion method. Method of accounting that recognizes income on a contract as work progresses by matching contract revenue with contract costs incurred, based on the proportion of work completed. However, any expected loss, which is the excess of total incurred and expected contract costs over the total contract revenue, is recognized immediately, irrespective of the stage of completion of the contract.

Segmenting contracts. Dividing a single contract, which covers the construction of a number of assets, into two or more profit centers for accounting purposes, provided that

1. Separate proposals were submitted for each of the assets that are the subject matter of the single contract
2. The construction of each asset was the subject of separate negotiation wherein both the contractor and the customer were in a position to either accept or reject part of the contract pertaining to a single asset (out of numerous assets contemplated by the contract)
3. The costs and revenues pertaining to each individual asset can be separately identified

Stage of completion. Proportion of the contract work completed, which may be determined using one of several methods that reliably measures it, including

1. Percentage-of-completion method
2. Surveys of work performed
3. Physical proportion of contract work completed

Variation. Instruction by the customer for a change in the scope of the work envisioned by the construction contract.

RECOGNITION AND MEASUREMENT

Construction contract revenue may be recognized during construction rather than at the completion of the contract. This "as earned" approach to revenue recognition is justified because under most long-term construction contracts, both the buyer and the seller (contractor) obtain enforceable rights. The buyer has the legal right to require specific performance from the contractor and, in effect, has an ownership claim to the contractor's work in progress. The contractor, under most long-term contracts, has the right to require the buyer to make progress payments during the construction period. The substance of this business activity is that a continuous sale occurs as the work progresses.

IAS 11 recognizes the percentage-of-completion method as the method of accounting for construction contracts (or the cost of recovery approach, when the outcome of a construction contract cannot be estimated reliably). Under an earlier version of IAS 11, both the percentage-of-completion method and the completed-contract method were recognized as being acceptable alternative methods of accounting for long-term construction activities. The completed contract method of accounting is thus no longer permitted under circumstances where application of percentage-of-completion is warranted.

Percentage-of-Completion Method

IAS 11 defines the percentage-of-completion method as follows:

Under this method contract revenue is matched with the contract costs incurred in reaching the stage of completion, resulting in the reporting of revenue, expenses and profit which can be attributed to the proportion of work completed. ...Contract revenue is recognized as revenue in the statement of comprehensive income in the accounting periods in which the work is performed. Contract costs are usually recognized as an expense in the accounting periods in which the work to which they relate is performed. However, any expected excess of total revenue for the contract is recognized as an expense immediately.

Under the percentage-of-completion method, the construction-in-progress (CIP) account is used to accumulate costs and recognized income. When the CIP exceeds billings, the difference is reported as a current asset. If billings exceed CIP, the difference is reported as a current liability. Where more than one contract exists, the excess cost or liability should be determined on a project-by-project basis, with the accumulated costs and liabilities being stated separately in the statement of financial position. Assets and liabilities should not be offset unless a right of offset exists. Thus, the net debit balances for certain contracts should not ordinarily be offset against net credit balances for other contracts.

Under the percentage-of-completion method, income should not be based on advances (cash collections) or progress (interim) billings. Cash collections and interim billings are based on contract terms that do not necessarily measure contract performance.

Costs and estimated earnings in excess of billings should be classified as an asset. If billings exceed costs and estimated earnings, the difference should be classified as a liability.

Contract costs. Contract costs comprise costs that are identifiable with a specific contract, plus those that are attributable to contracting activity in general and can be allocated to the contract and those that are contractually chargeable to a customer. Generally, contract costs would include all direct costs, such as direct materials, direct labor, and direct expenses and any construction overhead that could specifically be allocated to specific contracts.

Direct costs or costs that are identifiable with a specific contract include

1. Costs of materials consumed in the specific construction contract
2. Wages and other labor costs for site labor and site supervisors
3. Depreciation charges of plant and equipment used in the contract
4. Lease rentals of hired plant and equipment specifically for the contract
5. Cost incurred in shifting of plant, equipment, and materials to and from the construction site
6. Cost of design and technical assistance directly identifiable with a specific contract
7. Estimated costs of any work undertaken under a warranty or guarantee
8. Claims from third parties

With regard to claims from third parties, these should be accrued if they rise to the level of "provisions" as defined by IAS 37. This requires that an obligation that is subject to reasonable measurement exist at the end of the reporting period. However, if either of the above mentioned conditions is not met (and the possibility of the loss is not remote), this contingency will only be disclosed. Contingent losses are specifically required to be disclosed under IAS 11.

Contract costs may be reduced by incidental income if such income is not included in contract revenue. For instance, sale proceeds (net of any selling expenses) from the disposal of any surplus materials or from the sale of plant and equipment at the end of the contract may be credited or offset against these expenses. Drawing an analogy from this principle, it could be argued that if advances received from customers are invested by the contractor temporarily (instead of being allowed to lie idle in a current account), any interest earned on such investments could be treated as incidental income and used in reducing contract costs, which may or may not include borrowing costs (depending on how the contractor is financed, whether self-financed or leveraged). On the other hand, it may also be argued that instead of being subtracted from contract costs, such interest income should be added to contract revenue.

In the authors' opinion, the latter argument may be valid if the contract is structured in such a manner that the contractor receives lump-sum advances at the beginning of the contract (or for that matter, even during the term of the contract, such that the advances at any point in time exceed the amounts due the contractor from the customer). In these cases, such interest income should, in fact, be treated as contract revenue and not offset against contract costs. The reasoning underlying treating this differently from the earlier instance (where idle funds resulting from advances are invested temporarily) is that such advances were envisioned by the terms of the contract and as such were probably fully considered in the negotiation process that preceded fixing contract revenue. Thus, since negotiated as part of the total contract price, this belongs in contract revenues. (It should be borne in mind that the different treatments for interest income would in fact have a bearing on the determination of the percentage or stage of completion of a construction contract.)

Indirect costs or overhead expenses should be included in contract costs provided that they are attributable to the contracting activity in general and could be allocated to specific contracts. Such costs include construction overhead, cost of insurance, cost of design, and technical assistance that is not related directly to specific contracts. They should be allocated using methods that are systematic and rational and are applied in a consistent manner to costs having similar features or characteristics. The allocation should be based on the normal level of construction activity, not on theoretical maximum capacity.

Example of contract costs

A construction company incurs €700,000 in annual rental expense for the office space occupied by a group of engineers and architects and their support staff. The company utilizes this group to act as the quality assurance team that overlooks all contracts undertaken by the company. The company also incurs in the aggregate another €300,000 as the annual expenditure toward electricity, water, and maintenance of this office space occupied by the group. Since the group is responsible for quality assurance for all contracts on hand, its work, by nature, cannot be considered as being directed toward any specific contract but is in support of the entire contracting activity. Thus, the company should allocate the rent expense and the cost of utilities in accordance with a systematic and rational basis of allocation, which should be applied consistently to both types of expenditure (since they have similar characteristics).

Although the bases of allocation of this construction overhead could be many (such as the amounts of contract revenue, contract costs, and labor hours utilized in each contract) the basis of allocation that seems most rational is contract revenue. Further, since both expenses are similar in nature, allocating both the costs on the basis of the amount of contract revenue generated by each construction contract would also satisfy the consistency criteria.

Other examples of construction overhead or costs that should be allocated to contract costs are

1. Costs of preparing and processing payroll of employees engaged in construction activity
2. Borrowing costs capitalized under IAS 23.

Certain costs are specifically excluded from allocation to the construction contract, as the standard considers them as not attributable to the construction activity. Such costs may include

1. General and administrative costs that are not directly attributable to the contract
2. Costs incurred in marketing or selling
3. Research and development costs that are not directly attributable to the contract
4. Depreciation of plant and equipment that is lying idle and not used in any particular contract

Types of contract costs. Contract costs can be broken down into two categories: costs incurred to date and estimated costs to complete. The *costs incurred to date* include precontract costs and costs incurred after contract acceptance. *Precontract costs* are costs incurred before a contract has been entered into, with the expectation that the contract will be accepted and these costs will thereby be recoverable through billings. The criteria for recognition of such costs are

1. They are capable of being identified separately.
2. They can be measured reliably.
3. It is probable that the contract will be obtained.

Precontract costs include costs of architectural designs, cost of securing the contract, and any other costs that are expected to be recovered if the contract is accepted. Contract costs incurred after the acceptance of the contract are costs incurred toward the completion of the project and are also capitalized in the construction-in-progress (CIP) account. The contract does not have to be identified before the capitalization decision is made; it is only necessary that there be an expectation of the recovery of the costs. Once the contract has been accepted, the precontract costs become contract costs incurred to date. However, if the precontract costs are already recognized as an expense in the period in which they are incurred, they are not included in contract costs when the contract is obtained in a subsequent period.

Estimated costs to complete. These are the anticipated costs required to complete a project. They would be comprised of the same elements as the original total estimated contract costs and would be based on prices expected to be in effect when the costs are incurred. The latest estimates should be used to determine the progress toward completion.

Although IAS 11 does not specifically provide instructions for estimating costs to complete, practical guidance can be gleaned from other international accounting standards, as follows: The first rule is that systematic and consistent procedures should be used. These procedures should be correlated with the cost accounting system and should be able to provide a comparison between actual and estimated costs. Additionally, the determination of estimated total contract costs should identify the significant cost elements.

A second important point is that the estimation of the costs to complete should include the same elements of costs included in accumulated costs. Additionally, the estimated costs should reflect any expected price increases. These expected price increases should not be blanket provisions for all contract costs, but rather, specific provisions for each type of cost. Expected increases in each of the cost elements such as wages, materials, and overhead items should be taken into consideration separately.

Finally, estimates of costs to complete should be reviewed periodically to reflect new information. Estimates of costs should be examined for price fluctuations and should also be reviewed for possible future problems, such as labor strikes or direct material delays.

Accounting for contract costs is similar to accounting for inventory. Costs necessary to ready the asset for sale would be recorded in the construction-in-progress account, as incurred. CIP would include both direct and indirect costs but would usually not include general and administrative expenses or selling expenses since they are not normally identifiable with a particular contract and should therefore be expensed.

Subcontractor costs. Since a contractor may not be able to do all facets of a construction project, a subcontractor may be engaged. The amount billed to the contractor for work done by the subcontractor should be included in contract costs. The amount billed is directly traceable to the project and would be included in the CIP account, similar to direct materials and direct labor.

Back charges. Contract costs may have to be adjusted for back charges. Back charges are billings for costs incurred that the contract stipulated should have been performed by another party. The parties involved often dispute these charges.

Example of a back charge situation

The contract states that the subcontractor was to raze the building and have the land ready for construction; however, the contractor/seller had to clear away debris in order to begin construction. The contractor wants to be reimbursed for the work; therefore, the contractor back charges the subcontractor for the cost of the debris removal.

The contractor should treat the back charge as a receivable from the subcontractor and should reduce contract costs by the amount recoverable. If the subcontractor disputes the back charge, the cost becomes a claim. Claims are an amount in excess of the agreed contract price or amounts not included in the original contract price that the contractor seeks to collect. Claims should be recorded as additional contract revenue only if the requirements set forth in IAS 11 are met.

The subcontractor should record the back charge as a payable and as additional contract costs if it is probable that the amount will be paid. If the amount or validity of the liability is disputed, the subcontractor would have to consider the probable outcome in order to determine the proper accounting treatment.

Fixed-Price and Cost-Plus Contracts

IAS 11 recognizes two types of construction contracts that are distinguished based on their pricing arrangements: (1) fixed-price contracts and (2) cost-plus contracts.

Fixed-price contracts are contracts for which the price is not usually subject to adjustment because of costs incurred by the contractor. The contractor agrees to a fixed contract price or a fixed rate per unit of output. These amounts are sometimes subject to escalation clauses.

There are two types of cost-plus contracts.

1. **Cost-without-fee contract**—Contractor is reimbursed for allowable or otherwise defined costs with no provision for a fee. However, a percentage is added that is based on the foregoing costs.
2. **Cost-plus-fixed-fee contract**—Contractor is reimbursed for costs plus a provision for a fee. The contract price on a cost-type contract is determined by the sum of the reimbursable expenditures and a fee. The fee is the profit margin (revenue less direct expenses) to be earned on the contract. All reimbursable expenditures should be included in the accumulated contract costs account.

There are a number of possible variations of contracts that are based on a cost-plus-fee arrangement. These could include cost-plus-fixed-fee, under which the fee is a fixed monetary amount; cost-plus-award, under which an incentive payment is provided to the contractor, typically based on the project's timely or on-budget completion; and cost-plus-a-percentage-fee, under which a variable bonus payment will be added to the contractor's ultimate payment based on stated criteria.

Some contracts may have features of both a fixed-price contract and a cost-plus contract. A cost-plus contract with an agreed maximum price is an example of such a contract.

Recognition of Contract Revenue and Expenses

Percentage-of-completion accounting cannot be employed if the quality of information will not support a reasonable level of accuracy in the financial reporting process. Generally, only when the outcome of a construction contract can be estimated reliably, should the contract revenue and contract costs be recognized by reference to the stage of completion at the end of the reporting period.

Different criteria have been prescribed by the standard for assessing whether the outcome can be estimated reliably for a contract, depending on whether it is a fixed-price contract or a cost-plus contract. The following are the criteria in each case:

1. If it is a fixed-price contract

   *NOTE: **All** conditions should be satisfied.*

   a. It meets the recognition criteria set by the IASB's *Framework*; that is

      (1) Total contract revenue can be measured reliably.
      (2) It is probable that economic benefits will flow to the entity.

   b. Both the contract cost to complete and the stage of completion can be measured reliably.
   c. Contract costs attributable to the contract can be identified properly and measured reliably so that comparison of actual contract costs with estimates can be done.

2. If it is a cost-plus contract

   *NOTE: **All** conditions should be satisfied.*

   a. It is probable that the economic benefits will flow to the entity.
   b. The contract costs attributable to the contract, whether or not reimbursable, can be identified and measured reliably.

When Outcome of a Contract Cannot Be Estimated Reliably

As stated above, unless the outcome of a contract can be estimated reliably, contract revenue and costs should not be recognized by reference to the stage of completion. IAS 11 establishes the following rules for revenue recognition in cases where the outcome of a contract cannot be estimated reliably:

1. Revenue should be recognized only to the extent of the contract costs incurred that are probable of being recoverable.
2. Contract costs should be recognized as an expense in the period in which they are incurred.

Any expected losses should, however, be recognized immediately.

It is not unusual that during the early stages of a contract, the outcome cannot be estimated reliably. This would be particularly likely to be true if the contract represents a type of project with which the contractor has had limited experience in the past.

Contract Costs Not Recoverable Due to Uncertainties

When recoverability of contract costs is considered doubtful, the cost recovery method is applied and revenue is recognized only to the extent of cash collections, after all costs have first been recovered through cash collections. Recoverability of contract costs may be considered doubtful in the case of contracts that have any of the following characteristics:

1. The contract is not fully enforceable.
2. Completion of the contract is dependent on the outcome of pending litigation or legislation.
3. The contract relates to properties that are likely to be expropriated or condemned.
4. The contract is with a customer who is unable to perform its obligations, perhaps because of financial difficulties.
5. The contractor is unable to complete the contract or otherwise meet its obligation under the terms of the contract, as when, for example, the contractor has been experiencing recurring losses and is unable to get financial support from creditors and bankers and may be ready to declare bankruptcy.

In all such cases, contract costs should be expensed immediately. Although the implication is unambiguous, the determination that one or more of the foregoing conditions holds will be subject to some imprecision. Thus, each such situation needs to be assessed carefully on a case-by-case basis.

If and when these uncertainties are resolved, revenue and expenses should again be recognized on the same basis as other construction-type contracts (i.e., by the percentage-of-completion method). However, it is not permitted to restore costs already expensed in prior periods, since the accounting was not in error, given the facts that existed at the time the earlier financial statements were prepared.

Revenue Measurement—Determining the Stage of Completion

The standard recognizes that the stage of completion of a contract may be determined in many ways and that an entity uses the method that measures reliably the work performed. The standard further stipulates that depending on the nature of the contract, one of the following methods may be chosen:

1. The proportion that contract costs incurred bear to estimated total contract cost (also referred to as the cost-to-cost method)
2. Survey of work performed method
3. Completion of a physical proportion of contract work (also called units-of-work-performed) method.

NOTE: Progress payments and advances received from customers often do not reflect the work performed.

Each of these methods of measuring progress on a contract can be identified as being either an input or an output measure. The *input measures* attempt to identify progress in a contract in terms of the efforts devoted to it. The cost-to-cost method is an example of an input measure. Under the cost-to-cost method, the percentage of completion would be estimated by comparing total costs incurred to date to total costs expected for the entire job. *Output measures* are made in terms of results by attempting to identify progress toward completion by physical measures. The units-of-work-performed method is an example of an output measure. Under this method, an estimate of completion is made in terms of achievements to date. Output measures are usually not considered to be as reliable as input measures.

When the stage of completion is determined by reference to the contract costs incurred to date, the standard specifically refers to certain costs that are to be excluded from contract costs. Examples of such costs are

1. Contract costs that relate to future activity (e.g., construction materials supplied to the site but not yet consumed during construction)
2. Payments made in advance to subcontractors prior to performance of the work by the subcontractor

Example of the percentage-of-completion method

The percentage-of-completion method works under the principle that "recognized profit (should) be that percentage of estimated total profit...that incurred costs to date bear to estimated total costs." The cost-to-cost method has become one of the most popular measures used to determine the extent of progress toward completion.

Under the cost-to-cost method, the percentage of revenue to recognize can be determined by the following formula:

$$\frac{\text{Cost to date}}{\text{Cumulative costs incurred + Estimated costs to complete}} \times \text{Contract price} - \text{Revenue previously recognized} = \text{Current revenue recognized}$$

By slightly modifying this formula, current gross profit can also be determined.

$$\frac{\text{Cost to date}}{\text{Cumulative costs incurred + Estimated costs to complete}} \times \text{Expected total gross profit} - \text{Gross profit previously recognized} = \text{Current gross profit}$$

Example of the percentage-of-completion (cost-to-cost)

Assume a €500,000 contract that requires 3 years to complete and incurs a total cost of €405,000. The following data pertain to the construction period:

	Year 1	Year 2	Year 3
Cumulative costs incurred to date	€150,000	€360,000	€405,000
Estimated costs yet to be incurred at year-end	300,000	40,000	--
Progress billings made during year	100,000	370,000	30,000
Collections of billings	75,000	300,000	125,000

	Year 1		Year 2		Year 3	
Construction in progress	150,000		210,000		45,000	
Cash, payables, etc.		150,000		210,000		45,000
Contract receivables	100,000		370,000		30,000	
Billings on contracts		100,000		370,000		30,000
Cash	75,000		300,000		125,000	
Contract receivables		75,000		300,000		125,000
Construction in progress	16,667		73,333		5,000	
Cost of revenues earned	150,000		210,000		45,000	
Contract revenues earned		166,667		283,333		50,000
Billings on contracts					500,000	
Construction in progress						500,000

Statement of Comprehensive Income Presentation

	Year 1	Year 2	Year 3	Total
Contract revenues earned	€166,667*	€283,333**	€ 50,000***	€500,000
Cost of revenues earned	(150,000)	(210,000)	(45,000)	(405,000)
Gross profit	€ 16,667	€ 73,333	€ 5,000	€ 95,000

$$* \quad \frac{€150,000}{450,000} \times 500,000 \;=\; €166,667$$

$$** \quad \frac{€360,000}{400,000} \times 500,000 \;-\; 166,667 \;=\; €283,333$$

$$*** \quad \frac{€405,000}{405,000} \times 500,000 \;-\; 166,667 \;-\; 283,333 \;=\; €50,000$$

Statement of Financial Position Presentation

	Year 1	Year 2	Year 3
Current assets:			
Contract receivables		€25,000	€ 95,000	*
Costs and estimated earnings in excess of billings on uncompleted contracts			
Construction in progress	166,667**		
Less billings on long-term contracts	(100,000)	66,667	
Current liabilities:			
Billings in excess of costs and estimated earnings on uncompleted contracts, year 2 (€470,000*** – €450,000****)		20,000	

* *Since the contract was completed and title was transferred in year 3, there are no amounts reported in the statement of financial position. However, if the project is complete but transfer of title has not taken place, there would be a presentation in the statement of financial position at the end of the third year because the entry closing out the Construction-in-progress account and the Billings account would not have been made yet.*
** *€150,000 (Costs) + 16,667 (Gross profit)*
*** *€100,000 (Year 1 Billings) + 370,000 (Year 2 Billings)*
**** *€360,000 (Costs) + 16,667 (Gross profit) + 73,333 (Gross profit)*

Recognition of Expected Contract Losses

When the current estimate of total contract cost exceeds the current estimate of total contract revenue, a provision for the entire loss on the entire contract should be made. Provisions for losses should be made in the period in which they become evident under either the percentage-of-completion method or the completed-contract method. In other words, when it is probable that total contract costs will exceed total contract revenue, the expected loss should be recognized as an expense immediately. The loss provision should be computed on the basis of the total estimated costs to complete the contract, which would include the contract costs incurred to date plus estimated costs (use the same elements as contract costs incurred) to complete. The provision should be shown separately as a current liability in the statement of financial position.

In any year when a percentage-of-completion contract has an expected loss, the amount of the loss reported in that year can be computed as follows:

Reported loss = Total expected loss + All profit previously recognized

---

Example of the percentage-of-completion and completed-contract methods with loss contract

Using the previous information, if the costs yet to be incurred at the end of year 2 were €148,000, the total expected loss is €8,000 [= €500,000 – (360,000 + 148,000)], and the total loss reported in year 2 would be €24,667 (= €8,000 + 16,667). Under the completed-contract method, the loss recognized is simply the total expected loss, €8,000.

Journal entry at end of year 2	*Percentage-of-Completion*	
Loss on uncompleted long-term contract	24,667	
Construction in progress (or estimated loss on uncompleted contact)		24,667

Profit or Loss Recognized on Contract

	Year 1	*Year 2*	*Year 3*
Contract price	€500,000	€500,000	€500,000
Estimated total costs:			
Costs incurred to date	150,000	360,000	506,000*
Estimated cost yet to be incurred	300,000	148,000	--
Estimated total costs for the three-year period,			
actual for year 3	450,000	508,000	506,000
Estimated profit (loss), actual for year 3	16,667	(8,000)	(6,000)
Less profit (loss) previously recognized	--	16,667	(8,000)
Amount of estimated profit (loss) recognized			
in the current period, actual for year 3	€ 16,667	€ (24,667)	€ 2,000

* *Assumed*

Upon completion of the project during year 3, it can be seen that the actual loss was only €6,000 (= €500,000 – 506,000); therefore, the estimated loss provision was overstated by €2,000. However, since this is a change of an estimate, the €2,000 difference must be handled prospectively; consequently, €2,000 of profit should be recognized in year 3 (= €8,000 previously recognized – €6,000 actual loss).

Combining and Segmenting Contracts

The profit center for accounting purposes is usually a single contract, but under some circumstances the profit center may be a combination of two or more contracts, a segment of a contract, or a group of combined contracts. Conformity with explicit criteria set forth in IAS 11 is necessary to combine separate contracts, or segment a single contract; otherwise, each individual contract is presumed to be the profit center.

For accounting purposes, a group of contracts may be combined if they are so closely related that they are, in substance, parts of a single project with an overall profit margin. A group of contracts, whether with a single customer or with several customers, should be combined and treated as a single contract if the group of contracts

1. Are negotiated as a single package
2. Require such closely interrelated construction activities that they are, in effect, part of a single project with an overall profit margin
3. Are performed concurrently or in a continuous sequence

Segmenting a contract is a process of breaking up a larger unit into smaller units for accounting purposes. If the project is segmented, revenues can be assigned to the different elements or phases to achieve different rates of profitability based on the relative value of each element or phase to the estimated total contract revenue. According to IAS 11, a contract may cover a number of assets. The construction of each asset should be treated as a separate construction contract when

1. The contractor has submitted separate proposals on the separate components of the project
2. Each asset has been subject to separate negotiation and the contractor and customer had the right to accept or reject part of the proposal relating to a single asset
3. The cost and revenues of each asset can be separately identified

Contractual Stipulation for Additional Asset—Separate Contract

The contractual stipulation for an additional asset is a special provision in the international accounting standard. IAS 11 provides that a contract may stipulate the construction of an additional asset at the option of the customer, or the contract may be amended to include the construction of an additional asset. The construction of the additional asset should be treated as a separate construction contract if

1. The additional asset significantly differs (in design, technology or function) from the asset or assets covered by the original contract
2. The price for the additional asset is negotiated without regard to the original contract price

Changes in Estimate

Since the percentage-of-completion method uses current estimates of contract revenue and expenses, it is normal to encounter changes in estimates of contract revenue and costs frequently. Such changes in estimate of the contract's outcome are treated on a par with changes in accounting estimate as defined by IAS 8 and are therefore accounted for prospectively in the year of the change.

Agreements for the Construction of Real Estate

In June 2008, the IASB issued IFRIC 15, which deals with agreements for the construction of real estate. IFRIC 15 standardizes accounting practice across jurisdictions for the recognition of revenue by real estate developers for sales of units, such as apartments or houses before construction is complete.

The first issue the IFRIC addressed is whether the contract should be accounted for under IAS 11 or IAS 18. IFRIC 15 states that an agreement for the construction of real estate is a construction contract within the scope of IAS 11 only when the buyer is able to specify the major structural elements of the design of the real estate before construction begins and/or specify major structural changes once construction is in progress (whether it exercises that ability or not). If the buyer has that ability, then the developer should apply IAS 11 to the contract. If the buyer does not have that ability, IAS 18 should be applied.

The main impact of this interpretation is that if the developer is required to apply IAS 11, then the percentage-of-completion basis should be applied. However, if they are required to apply IAS 18, then they first need to determine whether they are selling goods or providing a service. If the developer is not providing materials for a contract, but is only delivering services for the construction project, then they may apply the rendering of services method under IAS 18. If however they are required to provide all the materials and in addition deliver the services for the construction, then they will have to apply the sale of goods criteria in IAS 18. This can be problematic for developers as under this method, revenue is only recognized when the risks and rewards of ownership pass—which is generally on completion of the construction process.

IFRIC 15 also introduces a new concept in that it concludes that in certain circumstances, a developer may meet the IAS 18 sale of goods criteria continuously, thereby transferring the construction in progress to the customer throughout the contract. However, to achieve this, IFRIC 15 states that ownership of the construction in progress should pass to the client in its current state as construction progresses. In this case, if all the criteria in paragraph 14 of IAS 18 are met continuously as construction progresses, the entity shall recognize revenue by reference to the stage of completion using the percentage-of-completion method.

DISCLOSURE

IAS 11 prescribes a number of disclosures; some of them are for all the contracts and others are only for contracts in progress at the end of the reporting period. These are summarized below.

1. Disclosures relating to all contracts

    a. Aggregate amount of contract revenue recognized in the period
    b. Methods used in determination of contract revenue recognized in the period

2. Disclosures relating to contracts in progress

    a. Methods used in determination of stage of completion (of contracts in progress)
    b. Aggregate amount of costs incurred and recognized profits (net of recognized losses) to date
    c. Amounts of advances received (at the end of the reporting period)
    d. Amount of retentions (at the end of the reporting period)

Financial Statement Presentation Requirements under IAS 11

Gross amounts due from customers should be reported as an asset. This amount is the net of

1. Costs incurred plus recognized profits, less
2. The aggregate of recognized losses and progress billings.

This represents, in the case of contracts in progress, excess of contract costs incurred plus recognized profits, net of recognized losses, over progress billings.

Gross amounts due to customers should be reported as a liability. This amount is the net of

1. Costs incurred plus recognized profits, less
2. The aggregate of the recognized losses and progress billings.

This represents, in the case of contract work in progress, excess of progress billings over contract costs incurred plus recognized profits, net of recognized losses.

Examples from Financial Statements

Group Five Ltd
June 30, 2011

1.16 Construction contracts

A construction contract is a contract specifically negotiated for the construction of an asset or a combination of assets that are closely interrelated or interdependent in terms of their design, technology, and functions, or their ultimate purpose or use.

A group of contracts is treated as a single construction contract when the group of contracts is negotiated as a single package and the contracts are so interrelated that they are, in effect, part of a single project with an overall profit margin and are performed concurrently or in a continuous sequence.

Contract costs are recognized when incurred. When the outcome of a construction contract cannot be estimated reliably, contract revenue is recognized only to the extent of contract costs incurred that are likely to be recoverable. When the outcome of a construction contract can be estimated reliably and it is probable that the contract will be profitable, contract revenue is recognized using the percentage-of-completion method. When it is probable that total contract costs will exceed total contract revenue, the expected loss is recognized as an expense immediately.

The group uses the "percentage-of-completion method" to determine the appropriate revenue to recognize in a given period. The stage of completion is measured with reference to the contract costs or major activity incurred up to the statement of financial position date as a percentage of total estimated costs or major activity for each contract. Costs incurred in the year in connection with future activity on a contract are excluded from contract costs in determining the stage of completion and are presented as contracts in progress.

The group also presents as contracts is progress the gross amount due from customers for contract work for all contracts in progress for which costs incurred plus recognized profits (less recognized losses) exceed progress billings. Progress billings not yet paid by customers and retention are included in trade and other receivables.

The group presents as a liability (excess billings over work done) the gross amount due to customers for contract work for all contracts in progress for which progress billings exceed costs incurred plus recognized profits (less recognized losses).

	Group	
16. Contracts in progress	*2011*	*2010*
Costs incurred plus profits recognized, less estimated losses relating to contracts in progress at year-end	12,520,174	7,503,849
Progress billings	(12,013,700)	(6,749,343)
	506,474	754,506

FUTURE DEVELOPMENTS

In June 2010, the IASB issued an Exposure Draft (ED), *Revenue Recognition from Contracts with Customers,* which proposes a single revenue recognition model that can be applied consistently across various industries, geographical regions, and transactions. The ED provides an overview of the main proposals that were developed jointly, and unanimously agreed upon, by the IASB and FASB. The core principle in the proposed standard is that an entity should recognize revenues in contracts to provide goods and services to customers when it satisfies its performance obligations under the contract by transferring goods or services to a customer.

The key principles that are addressed include

- *Revenue is recognized only from the transfer of goods or services to a customer*— This proposal would affect some long-term contracts currently accounted for using a percentage-of-completion method when the customer does not receive goods or services continuously (for example where construction projects and service provision contracts are being undertaken that do not result in the transfer of the product or service until it is complete). Under the proposal, an entity would be permitted to apply the percentage-of-completion method of revenue recognition if it transfers the services rendered to the customer throughout the contract. As such, the customer would need to take ownership of the work in progress as the contract is performed, should the entity wish to recognize revenue on an ongoing basis.

- *Identification of separate performance obligations for distinct goods or services*—Where a contract that is undertaken is made up of various components, the entity delivering on the contract would be required to account for all goods or services that can be identified as separate performance obligations. This proposal may result in some revenue being attributed to goods or services that may presently be considered as incidental to the contract being undertaken and might otherwise not have hitherto been accounted for. The proposal could also result in an entity identifying more performance obligations in contracts, especially on construction contracts, as compared with present practice. As a result, such accounting treatment could result in entities reporting different margins for different parts of the contract, rather than reporting a single margin for the entire contract.

- *Recognition of revenue based on the probability-weighted estimates of the consideration expected to be received*—An entity would be required to include reasonable estimates of contingent consideration in the transaction price allocated to performance obligations. This is a significant departure from current practice, and it could result in a company recognizing some revenue on the transfer of a good or service, even if the consideration amount is contingent upon the occurrence of a future event—for example, an agent that provides brokerage services in one period in exchange for an amount of consideration to be determined in future periods, depending on the customer's behavior.

- *Customer's credit risk reflected in the measurement of revenue*—When determining the amount of revenue to recognize, an entity would be required to take into account the possibility that some of the consideration may not be recoverable from the customer. This differs to some extent from the current practice, which requires there to be some certainty around the collectibity of the amount due before revenue can be recognized, in that this proposal could result in a company recognizing some revenue when it transfers a good or service to a customer even if there is uncertainty about the collectability of the consideration, rather than deferring revenue recognition until the consideration is collected.

- *Allocation of transaction price in proportion to the estimated stand-alone selling price*—If an entity does not sell a distinct good or service separately, it would be required to estimate the price at which it would sell that good or service in order to allocate some of the consideration to it. This proposal will affect some existing practices that currently result in the deferral of revenue if an entity does not have objective evidence of the selling price of a good or service to be provided.

- *Expensing of contract acquisition costs*—An entity would be required to recognize as an expense the costs of obtaining a contract. This proposal would affect companies that currently capitalize such costs—for example, commissions and other directly incremental costs—and amortize them over the contract period.

The new proposed revenue recognition model will also be applicable to construction contracts.

In June 2011, the IASB and FASB agreed to reexpose the above Exposure Draft on revenue recognition. It is anticipated that a new IFRS will be published in 2012.

US GAAP COMPARISON

The core principles of revenue recognition for US GAAP are identical to IFRS: A valid agreement with a customer must be in place that establishes the terms of the exchange, performance must have occurred, the risks and rewards of ownership must have passed, and collectability must be reasonably assured. The language used under US GAAP is, however, different: Persuasive evidence of an arrangement exists, delivery has occurred or services have been rendered, the seller's price to the buyer is fixed or determinable, and collectability is reasonably assured. Despite this similarity, US GAAP contains many exceptions to these principles that have the effect of deferring revenue that is otherwise earned.

US GAAP includes specialized accounting for multiple-deliverable arrangements which, in principle, are the same as IFRS but include clauses that delay recognition until reliability of measurement complies to a concept called Vendor-Specific Objective Evidence (VSOE). In summary, if VSOE is not available for any of the elements, the full revenue of the arrangement cannot be recognized.

Another departure from the core principles is called the Milestone Method. This method, used mainly for research and development arrangements, delays revenue recognition based on satisfying conditions agreed at the inception of the agreement. These milestones cannot be changed once work has begun. Additionally, entities are permitted to delay revenue recognition further, based on accounting policy decision.

US GAAP includes extensive guidance for recognition and presentation of customer incentive payments which are largely within the IFRS Framework, with some exceptions for measuring "breakage" or nonuse of incentives by customers.

US GAAP literature for revenue recognition for construction and production-type contracts contains much more guidance than IFRS. Separation and combination of contracts is different in some instances. The language in US GAAP is directed more in terms of options than prescription, although, in practice, the guidance is treated as mandatory.

Other detailed US GAAP guidance is available for the following industries: real estate, healthcare, entertainment, development stage, and nonprofit.

21 GOVERNMENT GRANTS

INTRODUCTION

Government grants or other types of assistance, where provided, are usually intended to encourage entities to embark on activities that they would not have otherwise undertaken. IAS 20 addresses selected accounting and reporting issues arising in connection with such grants. Government *assistance*, according to this standard, is action by the government aimed at providing economic benefits to some constituency by subsidizing entities that will provide them with jobs, services, or goods that might not otherwise be available, either at all or at the desired cost. A government *grant*, on the other hand, is government assistance that entails the transfer of resources in return for compliance, either past or future, with certain conditions relating to the enterprise's operating activities, such as for remediating an environmentally compromised plant site.

Accounting for grants as a deferred credit is considered to be inconsistent with the IASB's *Framework,* and reducing the carrying amount of assets by a grant is not accepted by some. The Board had taken the view that it should await finalization of a general standard on revenue recognition before undertaking an overhaul of IAS 20. However, the perceived need to deal with the grant of emission rights (which led to the promulgation of IFRIC 3, subsequently withdrawn) at first persuaded the Board to seek to make a short-term change by harmonizing IAS 20 with the government grant rules in IAS 41, but inadequacies of that approach were soon identified. An initial undertaking, as part of the IASB-FASB convergence program, has been superseded by a stand-alone project to revise, which effort would incorporate emission rights as well as other types of grants.

As originally issued, IAS 20 held that below-market interest on government loans was not government assistance, per se. As part of the *2007 Improvements Project*, the IASB issued in early 2008 an amendment to IAS 20 (effective 2009), under which the economic effect of below-market interest rates on government loans is to be measured and reported as a government grant. The economic effect is gauged by the difference between the face amount of the loan and the present value of the future payments discounted by a relevant (market) interest rate, as illustrated in this chapter.

A former gap in the literature, addressing the accounting for service concessions, which occur relatively frequently in Europe, where government assets may be operated by commercial entities, has recently been dealt with by the issuance of IFRIC 12, *Service Concession Arrangements,* which resolved a related series of three draft interpretations. IFRIC 12 is discussed later in this chapter.

Until it is revised, however, IAS 20 provides authoritative guidance on financial statement presentation for all entities enjoying government assistance, with additional guidance to be found in IAS 41, which is, however, at this time restricted to agriculture situations. IAS 20 deals with the accounting treatment and disclosure of government grants and the disclosure requirements of government assistance. Depending on the nature of the assistance given and the associated conditions, government assistance could be of many types, including grants, forgivable loans, and indirect or nonmonetary forms of assistance, such as technical advice.

Sources of IFRS	
IAS 20, 41	*SIC* 10, 29, *IFRIC* 12

SCOPE

IAS 20 deals with the accounting treatment and disclosure requirements of grants received by enterprises from a government. It also mandates disclosure requirements of other forms of government assistance.

The standard specifies certain exclusions. In addition to the four exclusions contained within the definitions of the terms "government grant" and "government assistance," IAS 20 *excludes* the following from the purview of the standard:

1. Special problems arising in reflecting the effects of changing prices on financial statements or similar supplementary information;
2. Government assistance provided in the form of tax benefits (including income tax holidays, investment tax credits, accelerated depreciation allowances and concessions in tax rates);
3. Government participation in the ownership of the enterprise; and
4. Government grants covered by IAS 41.

The rationale behind excluding items 1. and 2. above seems fairly obvious, as they are covered by other IFRS: IAS 29 addresses accounting in hyperinflationary conditions, while tax benefits are dealt with by IAS 12. Government participation in the ownership of the enterprise has been excluded from the scope of IAS 20 as participation in ownership of an enterprise is normally made in anticipation of a return on the investment, while government assistance is provided with a different economic objective in mind, for example, the public interest or public policy. Thus, when the government invests in the equity of an enterprise (with the intention, for example, of encouraging the enterprise to undertake a line of business that it would normally not have embarked upon), such government participation in ownership of the enterprise would *not qualify* as a government grant under this standard.

Government Grants

Government grants are assistance provided by government by means of a transfer of resources (either monetary or nonmonetary) to business or other types of entities. In order to qualify as a government grant, in strict technical terms, it is a prerequisite that the grant should be provided by the government to an enterprise in return for past or future compliance with conditions relating to the operating activities of the enterprise.

Prior to the issuance of SIC 10, it was unclear whether the provisions of IAS 20 would apply even to government assistance aimed at encouraging or supporting business activities in certain regions or industry sectors, since related conditions may not specifically relate to the operating activities of the enterprise. Examples of such grants are: government grants which involve transfer of resources to enterprises to operate in a particular area (e.g., an economically less developed area) or a particular industry (e.g., one that due to low profitability may not otherwise be attractive to entrepreneurs). SIC 10 clarified that "the general requirement to operate in certain regions or industry sectors in order to qualify for the government assistance constitutes such a condition in accordance with IAS 20." This confirms that such government assistance does fall within the definition of government grants, and thus the requirements of IAS 20 apply to them as well.

DEFINITIONS OF TERMS

Fair value. The amount for which an asset could be exchanged between a knowledgeable, willing buyer and a knowledgeable, willing seller in an arm's-length transaction.

Forgivable loans. Those loans which the lender undertakes to waive repayment of under certain prescribed conditions.

Government. For the purposes of IAS 20, the term government refers not only to a government (of a country), as is generally understood, but also to government agencies and similar bodies whether local, national, or international.

Government assistance. Government assistance is action taken by government designed to provide an economic benefit specific to an entity or range of entities qualifying under certain criteria. Government assistance for the purpose of this Standard does not include benefits provided only indirectly through action affecting general trading conditions, such as the provision of infrastructure in development areas or the imposition of trading constraints on competitors.

Government grants. A government grant is a form of a government assistance that involves the transfer of resources to an enterprise in return for past or future compliance (by the enterprise) of certain conditions relating to its operating activities. It excludes

- Those forms of government assistance that cannot reasonably be valued, and
- Transactions with governments that cannot be distinguished from the normal trading transactions of the enterprise.

Grants related to assets. Those government grants whose primary condition is that an enterprise qualifying for them should acquire (either purchase or construct) a long-term asset or assets are referred to as "grants related to assets." Subsidiary conditions may also be attached to such a grant. Examples of subsidiary conditions include specifying the type of long-term assets, location of long-term assets, or periods during which the long-term assets are to be acquired or held.

Grants related to income. Government grants, other than those related to assets, are grants related to income.

RECOGNITION OF GOVERNMENT GRANTS

Criteria for recognition. Government grants are provided in return for past or future compliance with certain defined conditions. Thus grants should not be recognized until there is *reasonable assurance* that both

1. The enterprise will comply with the conditions attaching to the grant; and
2. The grant(s) will be received.

Certain concerns affecting the application of IAS 20, relating to recognition and treatment of government grants, are addressed in the following paragraphs.

Firstly, the mere receipt of the grant does not provide any assurance that, in fact, the conditions attaching to the grant have been or will be complied with by the enterprise. Both of these conditions are equally important, and the reporting entity should have reasonable assurance with respect to these two conditions before a grant is to be recognized.

Secondly, the term "reasonable assurance" has not been defined by this standard. However, one of the recognition criteria for income under the IASB's *Framework* is the existence of "sufficient degree of certainty."

Thirdly, under IAS 20 a forgivable loan from a government is treated as a government grant when there is *reasonable assurance* that the enterprise will meet the terms of forgiveness set forth in the loan agreement. Thus, upon receiving a forgivable loan from a government and furthermore upon fulfilling the criterion of reasonable assurance with respect to meeting the terms of forgiveness of the loan, an enterprise would normally recognize the receipt of a government grant, rather than a loan. Some have suggested that the grant should be recognized when the loan is forgiven, not when the forgivable loan is received. Under IAS 20, however, it is quite apparent that delayed recognition is not prescribed, but that "a forgivable loan from the government is treated as a grant when there is reasonable assurance that the enterprise will meet the terms for forgiveness of the loan." In the authors' opinion, this unambiguously directs that the recognition of the grant is to be made at the point of time when the forgivable loan is granted, as opposed to the point of time when it is actually forgiven.

Once a grant has been recognized, IAS 20 clarifies that any related contingency would be accounted for in accordance with IAS 37.

Fourthly, a conflict between IAS 20 and IAS 39 has been resolved by the issuance of an amendment to IAS 20 effected by the *2007 Improvements Project*. Previously, IAS 20 did not take account of low-interest or interest-free loans, or of the effect of government guarantees, while IAS 39 states that liabilities should be measured at fair value, which implies recognition of market rates of interest. The IAS 20 exclusion has now been removed, and the principle set forth by IAS 39 became applicable beginning in 2009.

Example of application of amendment to IAS 20 for below-market loans

Maytag Corp. is encouraged to relocate to Springville Township on July 1, 2011, by an economic stimulus package that includes a €3,000,000 loan due in equal annual installments (inclusive of interest) through 2021. The local government provides this loan at a below-market rate of 3%, which differs markedly from Maytag's own marginal borrowing rate of 6.5%. The present value of the annual payments ($351,000 each), discounted at 6.5%, is only $2,528,251. Accordingly, the receipt of the loan on July 1, 2011, is recorded by the following journal entry:

Cash	3,000,000	
Loan payable		2,528,251
Income—government grants		471,749

The discount on the loan payable is amortized over the ten-year term, such that an effective rate of 6.5% on the loan balance will be reported as interest expense in Maytag's income statements. If the grant was unconditional, it would be taken into income immediately, as suggested by the above journal entry. However, if Maytag has ongoing obligations (such as to remain as an employer in the community throughout the term of the loan), then it should be amortized to income (straight-line) over the term of the obligation.

Recognition period. There are two broad approaches to the accounting treatment of government grants that have been discussed by the standard: the "capital approach" and the "income approach." IAS 20 does *not* support the capital approach, which advocates crediting a grant directly to shareholders' equity. Endorsing the income approach, the standard sets forth the rule for recognition of government grants as follows: Government grants should be recognized as income, on a systematic and rational basis, over the periods necessary to match them with the related costs. As a corollary, and by way of abundant precaution, the standard reiterates that government grants should *not* be credited directly to shareholders' interests.

The standard established rules for recognition of grants under different conditions. These are explained through numerical examples as follows:

1. Grants in recognition of specific costs are recognized as income over the same period as the relevant expense.

   To illustrate this, let us consider the following example:

   An enterprise receives a grant of €30 million to defray environmental costs over a period of five years. Environmental costs will be incurred by the enterprise as follows:

Year	Costs
1	€1 million
2	€2 million
3	€3 million
4	€4 million
5	€5 million

   Total environment costs will equal €15 million, whereas the grant received is €30 million.

   Applying the principle outlined in the standard for recognition of the grant, that is, recognizing the grant as income "over the period which matches the costs" and using a "systematic and rational basis" (in this case, a reverse sum-of-the-years' digits amortization), the total grant would be recognized as follows:

Year	Grant recognized
1	€30 * (1/15) = € 2 million
2	€30 * (2/15) = € 4 million
3	€30 * (3/15) = € 6 million
4	€30 * (4/15) = € 8 million
5	€30 * (5/15) = €10 million

2. Grants related to depreciable assets are usually recognized as income over the periods and in the proportions in which depreciation on those assets is charged.

   The following example will illustrate the above:

An enterprise receives a grant of €100 million to purchase a refinery in an economically backward area. The enterprise has estimated that such a refinery would cost €200 million. The secondary condition attached to the grant is that the enterprise should hire labor locally (i.e., from the economically backward area where the refinery is located) instead of employing workers from other parts of the country. It should maintain a ratio of 1:1 (local workers : workers from outside) in its labor force for the next five years. The refinery is to be depreciated using the straight-line method over a period of ten years.

The grant will be recognized over a period of ten years. In each of the ten years, the grant will be recognized in proportion to the annual depreciation on the refinery. Thus, €10 million will be recognized as income in each of the ten years. With regard to the secondary condition of maintenance of the ratio of 1:1 in the labor force, this contingency would need to be disclosed in the notes to the financial statements for the next five years (during which period the condition is in force) in accordance with disclosure requirements of IAS 37.

3. Grants related to nondepreciable assets may also require the fulfillment of certain obligations and would then be recognized as income over periods which bear the cost of meeting the obligations.

To understand this, let us consider the following case study:

ABN Inc. was granted 1000 acres of land, on the outskirts of the city, by a local government authority. The condition attached to this grant was that ABN Inc. should clean up this land and lay roads by employing laborers from the village in which the land is located. The government has fixed the minimum wage payable to the workers. The entire operation will take three years and is estimated to cost €60 million. This amount will be spent as follows: €10 million each in the first and second years and €40 million in the third year. The fair value of this land is presently €120 million.

ABN Inc. would need to recognize the fair value of the grant over the period of three years in proportion to the cost of meeting the obligation. Thus, €120 million will be recognized as follows:

Year	Grant recognized
1	€120 * (10/60) = €20 million
2	€120 * (10/60) = €20 million
3	€120 * (40/60) = €80 million

4. Grants are sometimes received as part of a package of financial or fiscal aids to which a number of conditions are attached.

When different conditions attach to different components of the grant, the terms of the grant would have to be evaluated in order to determine how the various elements of the grant would be earned by the enterprise. Based on that assessment, the total grant amount would then be apportioned.

For example:

An enterprise receives a consolidated grant of 120 million. Two-thirds of the grant is to be utilized to purchase a college building for students from third-world or developing countries. The balance of the grant is for subsidizing the tuition costs of those students for four years from the date of the grant.

The grant would first be apportioned as follows:

Grant related to assets (2/3) = €80 million, and
Grant related to income (1/3) = €40 million

The grant related to assets would be recognized in income over the useful life of the college building, for example, ten years, using a systematic and rational basis. Assuming the college building is depreciated using the straight-line method, this portion of the grant (i.e., €80 million) would be recognized as income over a period of ten years at €8 million per year.

The grant related to income would be recognized over a period of four years. Assuming that the tuition subsidy will be offered evenly over the period of four years, this portion of the grant (i.e., €40 million) would be taken to income over a period of four years at €10 million per year.

5. A government grant that becomes receivable as compensation for expenses or losses already incurred or for the purpose of giving immediate financial support to the enterprise with no future related costs should be recognized as income of the period in which it becomes receivable.

Sometimes grants are awarded for the purposes of giving immediate financial support an enterprise, for example, to revive a commercial insolvent business (referred to as "sick unit" in some less-developed countries). Such grants are not given as incentives to invest funds in specified areas or for a specified purpose from which the benefits will be derived over a period of time in the future. Instead such grants are awarded to compensate an enterprise for losses incurred in the past. Thus, they should be recognized as income in the period in which the enterprise becomes eligible to receive such grants.

Nonmonetary Grants

A government grant may not always be given in cash or cash equivalents. Sometimes a government grant may take the form of a transfer of a nonmonetary asset, such as grant of a plot of land or a building in a remote area. In these circumstances the standard prescribes the following optional accounting treatments:

1. To account for both the grant and the asset at the fair value of the nonmonetary asset, or
2. To record both the asset and the grant at a "nominal amount."

PRESENTATION AND DISCLOSURE

Presentation of Grants Related to Assets

Presentation on the statement of financial position. Government grants related to assets, including nonmonetary grants at fair value, should be presented in the statement of financial position in either of two ways:

1. By setting up the grant as deferred income, or
2. By deducting the grant in arriving at the carrying amount of the asset.

To understand this better, let us consider the following case study:

Natraj Corp. received a grant related to a factory building which it bought in 2010. The total amount of the grant was €3 million. Natraj Corp. purchased the building from an industrialist identified by the government. The factory building was located in the slums of the city and was to be repossessed by a government agency from the industrialist, in case Natraj Corp. had not purchased it from him. The factory building was purchased for €9 million by Natraj Corp. The useful life of the building is not considered to be more than three years mainly because it was not properly maintained by the industrialist.

Under Option 1: Set up the grant as deferred income.

- The grant of €3 million would be set up initially as deferred income in 2010.
- At the end of 2010, €1 million would be recognized as income and the balance of €2 million would be carried forward in the statement of financial position.
- At the end of 2011, €1 million would be taken to income and the balance of €1 million would be carried forward in the statement of financial position.
- At the end of 2012, €1 million would be taken to income.

Under Option 2: The grant will be deducted from the carrying amount.

The grant of €3 million is deducted from the gross carrying amount of the asset to arrive at the carrying amount of €6 million. The useful life being three years, annual depreciation of €2 million per year is charged to the income statement for the years 2010, 2011, and 2012.

The effect on the operating results is the same whether the first or the second option is chosen.

Under the second option, the grant is indirectly recognized in income through the reduced depreciation charge of €1 million per year, whereas under the first option, it is taken to income directly.

Presentation in the statement of cash flows. When grants related to assets are received in cash, there is an inflow of cash to be shown under the investing activities section of the statement of cash flows. Furthermore, there would also be an outflow resulting from the purchase of the asset. IAS 20 specifically requires that both these movements should be shown separately and not be netted. The standard further clarifies that such movements should be shown separately regardless of whether or not the grant is deducted from the related asset for the purposes of the statement of financial position presentation.

Presentation of Grants Related to Comprehensive Income

The standard allows a free choice between two presentations.

Option 1: Grant presented as a credit in the statement of profit or loss and comprehensive income, either separately or under a general heading other income

Option 2: Grant deducted in reporting the related expense

The standard does not show any bias towards any one option. It acknowledges the reasoning given in support of each approach by its supporters. The standard considers both methods as acceptable. However, it does recommend disclosure of the grant for a proper understanding of the financial statements. The standard recognizes that the disclosure of the effect of the grants on any item of income or expense may be appropriate.

Disclosures

The following disclosures are prescribed:

1. The accounting policy adopted for government grants, including the methods of presentation adopted in the financial statements;
2. The nature and extent of government grants recognized in the financial statements and an indication of other forms of government assistance from which the enterprise has directly benefited; and
3. Unfulfilled conditions and other contingencies attaching to government assistance that has been recognized.

OTHER ISSUES

Repayment of Government Grants

When a government grant becomes repayable—for example, due to nonfulfillment of a condition attaching to it—it should be treated as a change in estimate, under IAS 8, and accounted for prospectively (as opposed to retrospectively).

Repayment of a grant related to income should

1. First be applied against any unamortized deferred income (credit) set up in respect of the grant, and
2. To the extent the repayment exceeds any such deferred income (credit), or in case no deferred credit exists, the repayment should be recognized immediately as an expense.

Repayment of a grant related to an asset should be

1. Recorded by increasing the carrying amount of the asset or reducing the deferred income balance by the amount repayable, and
2. The cumulative additional depreciation that would have been recognized to date as an expense in the absence of the grant should be recognized immediately as an expense.

When a grant related to an asset becomes repayable, it would become incumbent upon the enterprise to assess whether any impairment in value of the asset (to which the repayable grant relates) has resulted. For example, a bridge is being constructed through funding from a government grant and during the construction period, because of nonfulfillment of the terms of the grant, the grant became repayable. Since the grant was provided to assist in the construction, it is possible that the enterprise may not be in a position to arrange funds to complete the project. In such a circumstance, the asset is impaired and may need to be written down to its recoverable value, in accordance with IAS 36.

Government Assistance

Under the provisions of IAS 20, government grants exclude government assistance. Government assistance is defined as action taken by government designed to provide an economic benefit specific to an entity or range of entities qualifying under certain criteria. IAS 20 deals with both accounting and disclosure of government grants and disclosure of government assistance. Thus government assistance comprises government grants and other forms of government assistance (i.e., those not involving transfer of resources).

Excluded from the government assistance are certain forms of government benefits that cannot reasonably have a value placed on them, such as free technical or other professional advice. Also excluded from government assistance are government benefits that cannot be distinguished from the normal trading transactions of the enterprise. The reason for the second exclusion is obvious: although the benefit cannot be disputed, any attempt to segregate it would necessarily be arbitrary.

SERVICE CONCESSIONS

Government involvement directly with business is much more common in Europe and elsewhere than in North America, and European adoption of IFRS has created a need to expand the IFRS literature to address a number of such circumstances. The *service concession*, particularly common in France, typically occurs when a commercial entity operates a commercial asset which is owned by, or has to be transferred to, a local, regional, or national government organization. More generally, these arrangements exist when the public is provided with access to major economic or social facilities. The most famous example of this is perhaps the Channel Tunnel, linking England and France. This was built by a commercial entity which has a concession to operate it for a period of years, at the end of which time the asset reverts to the British and French governments. A more mundane example would be companies that erect bus shelters free of charge in municipalities, in return for the right to advertise on them for a period of time.

SIC 29, issued in 2001 as an interpretation of IAS 1, addressed only disclosures to be made for service concession arrangements. Under SIC 29, both the concession operator and the concession provider are directed to make certain disclosures in the notes to financial statements that purport to conform with IFRS. These disclosures include

1. A description of the arrangement
2. The significant terms of the arrangement that might affect the nature, timing, or amounts of future cash flows, which could include terms and repricing dates and formulae.
3. The nature and the extent of rights to use specified assets; obligations to provide (or rights to expect) services; obligations to acquire or build property or equipment; options to deliver (or rights to receive) specific assets at the conclusion of the concession period; renewal and termination options; and other rights and obligations, such as for major overhauls of equipment.
4. Changes to the concession arrangement occurring during the reporting period.

In 2006, the IASB issued IFRIC 12 to deal with the accounting for service concession arrangements. IFRIC 12 sets forth two accounting models, and stipulates how revenue is to be recognized.

Service concession arrangements. Service concession arrangements are those whereby a government or other body grants contracts for the supply of public services (e.g., roads, energy distribution, prisons or hospitals) to private operators. The Interpretation draws a distinction between two types of service concession arrangements. In one, the operator receives a *financial asset,* specifically an unconditional contractual right to receive cash or another financial asset from the government in return for constructing or upgrading the public sector asset. In the other, the operator receives an *intangible asset*—a right to charge for use of the public sector asset that it constructs or upgrades. The right to charge users is not an unconditional right to receive cash, because the amounts that might be received are contingent on the extent to which the public uses the service.

IFRIC 12 allows for the possibility that both types of arrangement may exist within a single contract: to the extent that the government has given an unconditional guarantee of payment for the construction of the public sector asset, the operator has a financial asset; to the extent that the operator has to rely on the public using the service in order to obtain payment, the operator has an intangible asset. The accounting to be applied is governed by the extent to which one or both types of assets are received.

Accounting under the financial asset model. The operator recognizes a financial asset to the extent that it has an *unconditional* contractual right to receive cash or another financial asset from, or at the direction of, the grantor for the construction services. The operator has an unconditional right to receive cash if the grantor contractually guarantees to pay the operator

- Specified or determinable amounts or
- The shortfall, if any, between amounts received from users of the public service and specified or determinable amounts, even if payment is contingent on the operator ensuring that the infrastructure meets specified quality or efficiency requirements.

Under the provisions of IFRIC 12, the operator measures the financial asset at fair value.

Accounting under the intangible asset model. The operator recognizes an intangible asset to the extent that it receives a right (a license) to charge users of the public service. A right to charge users of the public service is not an unconditional right to receive cash because the amounts are contingent on the extent that the public uses the service.

Under the provisions of IFRIC 12, the operator measures the intangible asset at fair value.

Operating revenue. The operator of a service concession arrangement recognizes and measures revenue in accordance with IAS 11 or IAS 18 for the services it performs. No special revenue recognition principles are to be applied. Thus, the financial asset model would require the use of percentage of completion revenue recognition in most instances, while the intangible asset model would suggest that revenue be recognized as services are performed.

Accounting by the government (grantor). IFRIC 12 does not deal with the accounting to be applied by the government unit that grants service concession arrangements. That is because IFRS are not designed to apply to not-for-profit activities in the private sector or the public sector.

IFRIC 12 was made effective for annual periods beginning on or after January 1, 2008.

US GAAP COMPARISON

No specific US GAAP standard is issued regarding government grants.

22 LEASES

INTRODUCTION

Leasing has long been a popular financing option for the acquisition of business property. During the past few decades, however, the business of leasing has experienced staggering growth, and much of this volume is reported in the statements of financial position. The tremendous popularity of leasing is quite understandable, as it offers great flexibility, often coupled with a range of economic advantages over ownership. Thus, with leasing, a lessee (borrower) is typically able to obtain 100% financing, whereas under a traditional credit purchase arrangement the buyer would generally have to make an initial equity investment. In many jurisdictions, a leasing arrangement offers tax benefits compared to the purchase option. The lessee is protected to an extent from the risk of obsolescence, although the lease terms will vary based on the extent to which the lessor bears this risk. For the lessor, there will be a regular stream of lease payments, which include interest that often will be at rates above commercial lending rates, and, at the end of the lease term, usually some residual value.

The accounting for lease transactions involves a number of complexities, which derive partly from the range of alternative structures that are available to the parties. For example, in many cases leases can be configured to allow manipulation of the tax benefits, with other features such as lease term and implied interest rate adjusted to achieve the intended overall economics of the arrangement. Leases can be used to transfer ownership of the leased asset, and they can be used to transfer some or all of the risks normally associated with ownership. The financial reporting challenge is to have the economic substance of the transaction dictate the accounting treatment.

The accounting for lease transactions is one of the best examples of the application of the principle of substance over form, as set forth in the IASB's *Framework*. If the transaction effectively transfers ownership to the lessee, the substance of the transaction is that of a sale of the underlying property, which should be recognized as such even though the transaction takes the contractual form of a lease, which is only a right to use the property at issue.

The guidance on lease accounting under IFRS is not as fully elaborated as is that provided under certain national GAAP, consistent with the somewhat more "principles-based" approach of the international standards. Even applying such an approach, however, IFRS still does not result in the capitalization (treatment as assets and related debt) of all lease arrangements, and variations can be made to lease terms that can achieve operating (noncapitalization) treatment, which is often desired by lessees.

While almost any type of arrangement that satisfies the definition of a lease is covered by this standard, the following specialized types of lease agreements are specifically excluded:

1. Lease agreements to explore for or use natural resources, such as oil, gas, timber, metals, and other mineral rights
2. Licensing agreements for such items as motion picture films, video recordings, plays, manuscripts, patents, and copyrights

The accounting for rights to explore and develop natural resources has yet to be formally addressed by IFRS; IFRS 6, which deals with exploration and evaluation assets arising in the mineral exploration process, offers no accounting guidance for leases. Licensing agreements are addressed by IAS 38, which is discussed in Chapter 11.

Sources of IFRS		
IAS 17, 24, 36	*SIC* 15, 27	*IFRIC* 4

DEFINITIONS OF TERMS

Bargain purchase option (BPO). A provision in the lease agreement allowing the lessee the option of purchasing the leased property for an amount that is sufficiently lower than the fair value of the property at the date the option becomes exercisable. Exercise of the option must appear reasonably assured at the inception of the lease.

Contingent rentals. Those lease rentals that are not fixed in amount but are based on a factor other than simply the passage of time; for example, if based on percentage of sales, price indices, market rates of interest, or degree of use of the leased asset.

Economic life of leased property. Either the period over which the asset is expected to be economically usable by one or more users, or the number of production or similar units expected to be obtained from the leased asset by one or more users.

Executory costs. Costs such as insurance, maintenance, and taxes incurred for leased property, pertaining to the current period, whether paid by the lessor or lessee. If the obligation of the lessee, these are excluded from the minimum lease payments.

Fair value of leased property (FMV). The amount for which an asset could be exchanged between a knowledgeable, willing buyer and a knowledgeable, willing seller in an arm's-length transaction. When the lessor is a manufacturer or dealer, the fair value of the property at the inception of the lease will ordinarily be its normal selling price, net of any volume or trade discounts. When the lessor is not a manufacturer or dealer, the fair value of the property at the inception of the lease will ordinarily be its cost to the lessor, unless a significant amount of time has elapsed between the acquisition of the property by the lessor and the inception of the lease, in which case fair value should be determined in light of market conditions prevailing at the inception of the lease. Thus, fair value may be greater or less than the lessor's cost or the carrying amount of the property.

Finance lease. A lease that transfers substantially all the risks and rewards associated with the ownership of an asset. The risks related to ownership of an asset include the possibilities of losses from idle capacity or technological obsolescence, and that flowing from variations in return due to changing economic conditions; rewards incidental to ownership of an asset include an expectation of profitable operations over the asset's economic life and expectation of gain from appreciation in value or the ultimate realization of the residual value. Title may or may not eventually be transferred to the lessee under finance lease arrangements.

Gross investment in the lease. The sum total of (1) the minimum lease payments under a finance lease (from the standpoint of the lessor), plus (2) any unguaranteed residual value accruing to the lessor.

Inception of the lease. The date of the written lease agreement or, if earlier, the date of a commitment by the parties to the principal provisions of the lease.

Initial direct costs. Initial direct costs, such as commissions and legal fees, incurred by lessors in negotiating and arranging a lease. These generally include (1) costs to originate a lease incurred in transactions with independent third parties that (a) result directly from and are essential to acquire that lease and (b) would not have been incurred had that leasing transaction not occurred; and (2) certain costs directly related to specified activities performed by the lessor for that lease, such as evaluating the prospective lessee's financial condition; evaluating and recording guarantees, collateral, and other security arrangements; negotiating lease terms; preparing and processing lease documents; and closing the transaction.

Lease. An agreement whereby a lessor conveys to the lessee, in return for payment or series of payments, the right to use an asset (property, plant, equipment, or land) for an agreed-upon period of time. Other arrangements essentially similar to leases, such as hire-purchase contracts, installment sale agreements, bare-boat charters, and so on, are also considered leases for purposes of the standard.

Lease term. The initial noncancelable period for which the lessee has contracted to lease the asset together with any further periods for which the lessee has the option to extend the lease of the asset, with or without further payment, which option it is reasonably certain (at the inception of the lease) that the lessee will exercise.

Lessee's incremental borrowing rate. The interest rate that the lessee would have to pay on a similar lease, or, if that is not determinable, the rate that at the inception of the lease the lessee would have incurred to borrow over a similar term (i.e., a loan term equal to the lease term), and with a similar security, the funds necessary to purchase the leased asset.

Minimum lease payments (MLP).

1. *From the standpoint of the lessee.* The payments over the lease term that the lessee is or can be required to make in connection with the leased property. The lessee's obligation to pay executory costs (e.g., insurance, maintenance, or taxes) and contingent rents are excluded from minimum lease payments. If the lease contains a bargain purchase option, the minimum rental payments over the lease term plus the payment called for in the bargain purchase option are included in minimum lease payments.

   If no such provision regarding a bargain purchase option is included in the lease contract, the minimum lease payments include the following:

   a. The minimum rental payments called for by the lease over the lease contract over the term of the lease (excluding any executory costs), plus
   b. Any guarantee of residual value, at the expiration of the lease term, to be paid by the lessee or a party related to the lessee.

2. *From the standpoint of the lessor.* The payments described above plus any guarantee of the residual value of the leased asset by a third party unrelated to either the lessee or lessor (provided that the third party is financially capable of discharging the guaranteed obligation).

Net investment in the lease. The difference between the lessor's gross investment in the lease and the unearned finance income.

Noncancelable lease. A lease that is cancelable only

1. On occurrence of some remote contingency
2. With the concurrence (permission) of the lessor
3. If the lessee enters into a new lease for the same or an equivalent asset with the same lessor
4. On payment by the lessee of an additional amount such that at inception, continuation of the lease appears reasonably assured

Operating lease. A lease that does not meet the criteria prescribed for a finance lease.

Penalty. Any requirement that is imposed or can be imposed on the lessee by the lease agreement or by factors outside the lease agreement to pay cash, incur or assume a liability, perform services, surrender or transfer an asset or rights to an asset, or otherwise forego an economic benefit or suffer an economic detriment.

Rate implicit in the lease. The discount rate that at the inception of the lease, when applied to the minimum lease payments, and the unguaranteed residual value accruing to the benefit of the lessor, causes the aggregate present value to be equal to the fair value of the leased property to the lessor.

Related parties in leasing transactions. Entities that are in a relationship where one party has the ability to control the other party or exercise significant influence over the operating and financial policies of the related party. Examples include the following:

1. A parent company and its subsidiaries
2. An owner company and its joint ventures and partnerships
3. An investor and its investees

Renewal or extension of a lease. The continuation of a lease agreement beyond the original lease term, including a new lease where the lessee continues to use the same property.

Residual value of leased property. The fair value, estimated at the inception of the lease, that the enterprise expects to obtain from the leased property at the end of the lease term.

Sale and leaseback accounting. A method of accounting for a sale-leaseback transaction in which the seller-lessee records the sale, removes all property and related liabilities from its statement of financial position, recognizes gain or loss from the sale, and classifies the leaseback in accordance with IAS 17.

Unearned finance income. The excess of the lessor's gross investment in the lease over its present value.

Unguaranteed residual value. Part of the residual value of the leased asset (estimated at the inception of the lease) the realization of which by the lessor is not assured or is guaranteed by a party related to the lessor.

Useful life. The estimated period over which the economic benefits embodied by the asset are expected to be consumed, without being limited to the lease term.

CLASSIFICATION OF LEASES

Classification of Leases—Lessee

For accounting and reporting purposes a lessee has two alternatives in classifying a lease.

1. Operating
2. Finance

Finance leases (which are known as *capital* leases under the corresponding US GAAP, because such leased property is treated as owned, and accordingly, capitalized in the statement of financial position) are those that essentially are alternative means of financing the acquisition of property or of substantially all the service potential represented by the property.

The proper classification of a lease is determined by the circumstances surrounding the leasing transaction. According to IAS 17, whether a lease is a finance lease or not will have to be judged based on the *substance* of the transaction, rather than on its mere *form*. If substantially all of the benefits and risks of ownership have been transferred to the lessee, the lease should be classified as a finance lease; such a lease is normally noncancelable and the lessor is assured (subject to normal credit risk) of recovery of the capital invested plus a reasonable return on its investment. IAS 17 stipulates that substantially all of the risks or benefits of ownership are deemed to have been transferred if *any one* of the following five criteria has been met:

1. The lease transfers ownership to the lessee by the end of the lease term.
2. The lease contains a bargain purchase option (an option to purchase the leased asset at a price that is expected to be substantially lower than the fair value at the date the option becomes exercisable) and it is reasonably certain that the option will be exercisable.
3. The lease term is for the *major part* of the economic life of the leased asset.
4. The present value (PV), at the inception of the lease, of the minimum lease payments is at least equal to *substantially all* of the fair value of the leased asset, net of grants and tax credits to the lessor at that time; title may or may not eventually pass to the lessee.

5. The leased assets are of a specialized nature such that only the lessee can use them without major modifications being made.

Further indicators which suggest that a lease *might* be properly considered to be a finance lease are

6. If the lessee can cancel the lease, the lessor's losses that are associated with the cancellation are to be borne by the lessee.
7. Gains or losses resulting from the fluctuations in the fair value of the residual will accrue to the lessee.
8. The lessee has the ability to continue the lease for a supplemental term at a rent that is substantially lower than market rent (i.e., there is a bargain renewal option).

Thus, under IAS 17, an evaluation of all eight of the foregoing criteria would be required to properly assess whether there is sufficient evidence to conclude that a given arrangement should be accounted for as a finance lease. Of the eight criteria set forth in the standard, the first five are essentially determinative in nature; that is, meeting *any one* of these would normally result in concluding that a given arrangement is in fact a finance lease. The final three criteria, however, are more suggestive in nature, and the standard states that these could lead to classification as a finance lease.

The interest rate used to compute the present value should be the lessee's *incremental borrowing rate,* unless it is practicable to determine the rate *implicit* in the lease, in which case that implicit rate should be used.

The language used in the third and fourth lease accounting criteria, as set forth above, makes them rather subjective and somewhat difficult to apply in practice. Thus, given the same set of facts, it is possible for two reporting entities to reach different conclusions regarding the classification of a given lease.

The purpose of the third criterion is to define leases covering essentially all of the asset's useful life as being financing arrangements. Under the current US GAAP standard, a clearly defined threshold of 75% of the useful life has been specified for classifying a lease as a finance lease, which thus creates a "bright line" test that can be applied mechanically. The corresponding language under IAS 17 stipulates that capitalization results when the lease covers a "major part of the economic life" of the asset. Reasonable persons obviously can debate whether "major part" implies a proportion lower than 75% (say, as little as 51%), or implies a higher proportion (such as 90%). It should be noted that the previous version of IAS 17 had these "bright lines" in the standard, but these were removed in favor of a more principle-based approach.

The fourth criterion defines what are essentially arrangements to fully compensate the lessor for the entire value of the leased property as financing arrangements. In contrast to US GAAP, this quantitative threshold is not provided under IFRS. A threshold, "the present value of minimum lease payments equaling at least 90% of leased asset fair value," is set under the US standard, while the corresponding language, "substantially all of the fair value of the leased asset," is employed under IFRS. Again, there is room for debate over whether "substantially all" implies a threshold lower than 90% or, less likely, an even higher one. Once again, the IASB chose to remove the 90% from the previous IAS 17 standard.

IAS 17 addresses the issue of change in lease classification resulting from alterations in lease terms, stating that if the parties agree to revise the terms of the lease, other than by means of renewing the lease, in a manner that would have resulted in a different classification of the lease had the changed terms been in effect at inception of the lease, then the revised lease is to be considered a new lease agreement.

Leases Involving Land and Buildings

IAS 17 addresses leases involving both land and buildings. In general, the accounting treatment of such leases is the same as for simple leases of other types of assets. Prior to the most recent revisions to IAS 17, the standard required that leases for land and buildings be analyzed into their component parts, with each element separately accounted for, unless title to both elements is expected to pass to the lessee by the end of the lease term. It continued the operating lease treatment requirement for the land portion of the lease, unless title is expected to pass to the lessee by the end of the lease term, in which case finance lease treatment is warranted. The buildings element is to be classified as a finance or operating lease in accordance with IAS 17's provisions.

However, the *Improvements Project 2009* resulted in an amendment that revised IAS 17 regarding this issue. Under the revised standard, the above guidance was removed from IAS 17. This had the effect of requiring a lessee to analyze both the land and building components of the lease separately to determine whether each component was a finance or operating lease. The presumption that land was always an operating lease unless ownership passed was removed. The standard does, however, state that when analyzing a land lease under the IAS 17 requirements, the criteria requiring that the lease be for the majority of the useful life would probably not be met as land has an indefinite economic life.

Under IAS 17, the minimum lease payments at the inception of a lease of land and buildings (including any up front payments) are to be allocated between the land and the buildings elements in proportion to their relative fair values at the inception of the lease. In those circumstances where the lease payments cannot be allocated reliably between these two elements, the entire lease is to be classified as a finance lease, unless it is clear that both elements are operating leases.

Furthermore, IAS 17 specifies that for a lease of land and buildings in which the value of the land element at the inception of the lease is immaterial, the land and buildings may be treated as a single unit for the purpose of lease classification, in which case the criteria set forth in IAS 17 will govern the classification as a finance or operating lease. If this is done, the economic life of the buildings is regarded as the economic life of the entire leased asset.

Additional guidance, drawn from US GAAP, and an example of accounting for a combined land and building lease, are presented in Appendix A.

Classification of Leases—Lessor

The lessor has the following alternatives in classifying a lease:

1. Operating lease
2. Finance lease

Consistent accounting by lessee and lessor. Since the events or transactions that take place between the lessor and the lessee are based on an agreement (the lease) that is common to both the parties, it is normally appropriate that the lease be classified in a consistent manner by both parties. Thus, if the requirements listed above result in classification of a lease as a finance lease by the lessee, the lease should also be classified as a finance lease by the lessor. However, as the standard does require judgment to be applied when assessing lease classification, in practice the accounting treatment may differ between lessor and lessee. Of course, neither party to the lease can control whether the other applies proper accounting to the transaction.

Notwithstanding this general observation, IAS 17 alludes to an exception to this rule when it speaks about the "differing circumstances" sometimes resulting in the same lease being classified differently by the lessor and lessee. This could occur, for example, when the lessor benefits by having a third-party residual value guarantee in place. The standard does not elaborate on such circumstances.

Different Types of Finance Leases

Finance leases can have various forms. Some common examples are sales-type, direct financing, and leveraged leases.

A lease is classified as a sales-type lease when the criteria set forth above have been met and the lease transaction is structured such that the lessor (generally a manufacturer or dealer) recognizes a profit or loss on the transaction in addition to interest revenue. For this to occur, the fair value of the property, or if lower, the sum of the present values of the minimum lease payments and the estimated unguaranteed residual value, must differ from the cost (or carrying value, if different). The essential substance of this transaction is that of a sale, thus its name. Common examples of sales-type leases: (1) when an automobile dealership opts to lease a car to its customers in lieu of making an actual sale, and (2) the re-lease of equipment coming off an expiring lease.

A direct financing lease differs from a sales-type lease in that the lessor does not realize a profit or loss on the transaction other than the interest revenue to be earned over the lease term. In a direct financing lease, the fair value of the property at the inception of the lease is equal to the cost (or carrying value, if the property is not new). This type of lease transaction most often involves entities regularly engaged in financing operations. The lessor (usually a bank or other financial institution) purchases the asset and then leases the asset to the lessee. This mode of transaction is merely a replacement for the conventional lending transaction, where the borrower uses the borrowed funds to purchase the asset.

There are many economic reasons why a lease transaction may be considered. These include

1. The lessee (borrower) is often able to obtain 100% financing.
2. There may be tax benefits for the lessee, such as the ability to expense the asset over its lease term, instead of over a longer depreciable life.
3. The lessor receives the equivalent of interest as well as an asset with some remaining value at the end of the lease term (unless title transfers as a condition of the lease).
4. The lessee is protected from risk of obsolescence (although presumably this risk protection is priced into the lease terms).

In summary, it may help to visualize the following chart when considering the classification of a lease:

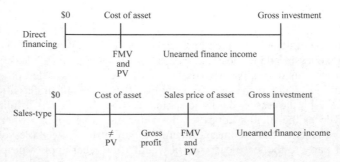

One specialized form of a direct financing lease is a *leveraged lease*. This type is mentioned separately both here and in the following section on how to account for leases because it is to receive a different accounting treatment by a lessor. A leveraged lease meets all the definitional criteria of a direct financing lease, but differs because it involves at least three parties: a lessee, a long-term creditor, and a lessor (commonly referred to as the equity participant). Other characteristics of a leveraged lease are as follows:

1. The financing provided by the long-term creditor must be without recourse as to the general credit of the lessor, although the creditor may hold recourse with respect to the leased property. The amount of the financing must provide the lessor with substantial leverage in the transaction.
2. The lessor's net investment declines during the early years and rises during the later years of the lease term before its elimination.

RECOGNITION AND MEASUREMENT

Accounting for Leases—Lessee

As discussed in the preceding section, there are two classifications under IAS 17 that apply to a lease transaction in the financial statements of the lessee. They are as follows:

1. Operating
2. Finance

Operating leases. The accounting treatment accorded an operating lease is relatively simple; rental expense should be charged to profit or loss as the payments are made or become payable. IAS 17 stipulates that rental expense be "recognized on a systematic basis that is representative of the time pattern of the user's benefits, even if the payments are not on that basis." In many cases, the lease payments are being made on a straight-line basis (i.e., equal payments per period over the lease term), and recognition of rental expense would normally also be on a straight-line basis.

However, even if the lease agreement calls for an alternative payment schedule or a scheduled rent increase over the lease term, the lease expense should still be recognized on a straight-line basis unless another systematic and rational basis is a better representation of actual physical use of the leased property. In such instances it will be necessary to create either a prepaid asset or a liability, depending on the structure of the payment schedule. In SIC 15, it has been held that all incentives relating to a new or renewed operating lease are to be considered in determining the total cost of the lease, to be recognized on a straight-line basis over the term of the lease. Thus, for example, a rent holiday for six months, offered as part of a five-year lease commitment, would not result in the reporting of only six months' rent expense during the first full year. Rather, four and one-half years' rent would be allocated over the full five-year term, such that monthly expense would equal 90% (=54 months' payments/60-month term) of the stated monthly rental payments that begin after the holiday ends. This accounting method would apply to both lessor and lessee.

The accounting would differ if rental increases were directly tied to expanded space utilization, however, but not if related merely to the extent that the property were being used. For example, if the lease agreement provides for a scheduled increase(s) in contemplation of the lessee's increased (i.e., more intensive) physical use of the leased property (e.g., more sustained usage of machinery after an initial set-up period), the total amount of rental payments, including the scheduled increase(s), should be charged to expense over the lease term on a straight-line basis; the increased rent should not impact the accounting. On the other hand, if the scheduled increase(s) is due to additional leased property (e.g., expanding to adjacent space after two years), recognition should be proportional to the amount of leased property, with the increased rents recognized over the years that the lessee has control over the use of the additional leased property. Scheduled increases could envision more than one of these events occurring, making the accounting more complex.

Notice that in the case of an operating lease there is no recognition in the statement of financial position of the leased asset because the substance of the lease is merely that of a rental. There is no reason to expect that the lessee will derive any future economic benefit from the leased asset beyond the lease term. There may, however, be a deferred charge or credit in the statement of financial position if the payment schedule under terms of the lease does not correspond with the expense recognition, as suggested in the preceding paragraph.

Example of straight lining of lease payments

Rockwood Limited has 2 leases:

Lease 1:

   3 year lease
   Lease payment $100,000 p.a. escalating at inflation
   Inflation for years 1 – 3 is 8%

Lease 2:

   3 year lease
   Lease payment $100,000 p.a. escalating at 8% p.a. to reflect inflation
   Inflation for years 1 – 3 is ±8%

Accounting for Lease 1:

Year 1
Statement of Comprehensive Income – Lease Expense	100,000	
Bank		100,000

Year 2
Statement of Comprehensive Income – Lease Expense	108,000	
Bank		108,000

Year 3
Statement of Comprehensive Income – Lease Expense	116,640	
Bank		116,640

Accounting for Lease 2:

As the escalation is a fixed percentage, and not a contingent amount as per Lease 1 (note that inflation is considered contingent), then the lease payments must be straight lined. Note that the difference between the amount charged to the statement of comprehensive income and the amount paid to the lessor should be recognized in the statement of financial provision as a liability.

Total lease payments over lease term:

Year 1	100,000
Year 2	108,000
Year 3	116,640
Total	324,640
Therefore the annual charge will be 324,640/3 =	108,213

Year 1
Statement of Comprehensive Income – Lease Expense	108,213	
Bank		100,000
Operating Lease Provision (SoFP)		8,213

Year 2

Statement of Comprehensive Income – Lease Expense	108,213	
Bank		108,000
Operating Lease Provision (SoFP)		213

Year 3

Statement of Comprehensive Income – Lease Expense	108,214	
Operating Lease Provision (SoFP)	8,426	
Bank		116,640

Finance leases. Assuming that the lease agreement satisfies the criteria set forth above for finance lease accounting, it must be accounted for as a finance lease.

According to IAS 17, the lessee is to record a finance lease as an asset and an obligation (liability) at an amount equal to the lesser of (1) the fair value of the leased property at the inception of the lease, net of grants and tax credits receivable by the lessors, or (2) the present value of the minimum lease payments.

For purposes of this computation, the minimum lease payments are considered to be the payments that the lessee is obligated to make or can be required to make, excluding contingent rent and executory costs such as insurance, maintenance, and taxes. The minimum lease payments generally include the minimum rental payments, and any guarantee of the residual value made by the lessee or a party related to the lessee. If the lease includes a bargain purchase option (BPO), the amount required to be paid under the BPO is included in the minimum lease payments. The present value shall be computed using the incremental borrowing rate of the lessee unless it is practicable for the lessee to determine the implicit rate computed by the lessor, in which case it is to be employed, whether higher or lower than the incremental borrowing rate.

The lease term to be used in the present value computation is the fixed, noncancelable term of the lease, plus any further terms for which the lessee has the option to continue to lease the asset, with or without further payment, provided that it is reasonably certain, as of the beginning of the lease, that lessee will exercise such a renewal option.

Depreciation of leased assets. The depreciation of the leased asset will depend on which criterion resulted in the lease being qualified as a finance lease. If the lease transaction met the criteria as either transferring ownership or containing a bargain purchase option, the asset arising from the transaction is to be depreciated over the estimated useful life of the leased property, which will, after all, be used by the lessee (most likely) after the lease term expires. If the transaction qualifies as a finance lease because it met either the criterion of encompassing the major part of the asset's economic life, or because the present value of the minimum lease payments represented substantially all of the fair value of the underlying asset, then it must be depreciated over the shorter of the lease term or the useful life of the leased property. The conceptual rationale for this differentiated treatment arises because of the substance of the transaction. Under the first two criteria, the asset actually becomes the property of the lessee at the end of the lease term (or on exercise of the BPO). In the latter situations, title to the property remains with the lessor.

Thus, the leased asset is to be depreciated (amortized) over the shorter of the lease term or its useful life if title does not transfer to the lessee, but when it is reasonably certain that the lessee will obtain ownership by the end of the lease term, the leased asset is to be depreciated over the asset's useful life. The manner in which depreciation is computed should be consistent with the lessee's normal depreciation policy for other depreciable assets owned by the lessee, recognizing depreciation on the basis set out in IAS 16. Therefore, the accounting treatment and method used to depreciate (amortize) the leased asset is very similar to that used for an owned asset.

In some instances when the property is to revert back to the lessor, there may be a guaranteed residual value. This is the value at lease termination that the lessee guarantees to the lessor. If the fair value of the asset at the end of the lease term is greater than or equal to the guaranteed residual amount, the lessee incurs no additional obligation. On the other hand, if the fair value of the leased asset is less than the guaranteed residual value, the lessee must make up the difference, usually with a cash payment. The guaranteed residual value is often used as a device to reduce the periodic payments by substituting the lump-sum amount at the end of the term that results from the guarantee. In any event the depreciation (amortization) must still be based on the estimated residual value. This results in a rational and systematic allocation of the expense through the periods and avoids having to recognize a disproportionately large expense (or loss) in the last period as a result of the guarantee.

The annual (periodic) rent payments made during the lease term are to be apportioned between the reduction in the obligation and the finance charge (interest expense) in a manner such that the finance charge (interest expense) represents a constant periodic rate of interest on the remaining balance of the lease obligation. This is commonly referred to as the *effective rate* interest method. However, it is to be noted that IAS 17 also recognizes that an approximation of this pattern can be made, as an alternative. The effective rate method, which is used in many other applications, such as mortgage amortization, is almost universally understood, and therefore should be applied in virtually all cases.

At the inception of the lease the asset and the liability relating to the future rental obligation are reported in the statement of financial position of the lessee at the same amounts. However, since the depreciation charge for use of the leased asset and the finance expense during the lease term differ due to different policies being used to recognize them, as explained above, it is likely that the asset and related liability balances would not be equal in amount after inception of the lease.

The following examples illustrate the treatment described in the foregoing paragraphs:

Example of accounting for a finance lease—asset returned to lessor at termination

Assume the following:

1. The lease is initiated on January 1, 2011, for equipment with an expected useful life of three years. The equipment reverts back to the lessor on expiration of the lease agreement.
2. The FMV of the equipment is €135,000.
3. Three payments are due to the lessor in the amount of €50,000 per year beginning December 31, 2011. An additional sum of €1,000 is to be paid annually by the lessee for insurance.
4. Lessee guarantees a €10,000 residual value on December 31, 2013, to the lessor.
5. Irrespective of the €10,000 residual value guarantee, the leased asset is expected to have only a €1,000 salvage value on December 31, 2013.
6. The lessee's incremental borrowing rate is 10% (implicit rate is unknown).
7. The present value of the lease obligation is as follows:

PV of guaranteed residual value	=	€10,000 × 0.7513*	=	€ 7,513
PV of annual payments	=	€50,000 × 2.4869**	=	124,345
				€131,858

  * *The present value of an amount of €1 due in three periods at 10% is 0.7513.*
 ** *The present value of an ordinary annuity of €1 for three periods at 10% is 2.4869.*

The first step in accounting for any lease transaction is to classify the lease. In this case, the lease term is for three years, which is equal to 100% of the expected useful life of the asset. Notice that the test of fair value versus present value is also fulfilled, as the PV of the minimum lease payments (€131,858) could easily be considered as being equal to substantially all the FMV (€135,000), being equal to 97.7% of the FMV. Thus, this lease should be accounted for as a finance lease.

In assumption 7 above, the present value of the lease obligation is computed. Note that the executory costs (insurance) are not included in the minimum lease payments and that the incremental borrowing rate of the lessee was used to determine the present value. This rate was used because the implicit rate was not determinable.

The entry necessary to record the lease on January 1, 2011, is

Leased equipment	131,858	
Lease obligation		131,858

Note that the lease is recorded at the present value of the minimum lease payments, which in this case is less than the fair value of the asset. If the present value of the minimum lease payments had exceeded the fair value, the lease would be recorded at the fair value.

The next step is to determine the proper allocation between interest and a reduction in the lease obligation for each lease payment. This is done using the effective interest method as illustrated below.

Year	Cash payment	Interest Expense	Reduction in lease obligation	Balance of lease obligation
Inception of lease				€131,858
1	€50,000	€13,186	€36,814	95,044
2	50,000	9,504	40,496	54,548
3	50,000	5,452	44,548	10,000

The interest is calculated at 10% (the incremental borrowing rate) of the balance of the lease obligation for each period, and the remainder of the €50,000 payment is allocated to a reduction in the lease obligation. The lessee is also required to pay €1,000 for insurance on an annual basis. The entries necessary to record all payments relative to the lease for each of the three years are shown below.

	December 31, 2011		December 31, 2012		December 31, 2013	
Insurance expense	1,000		1,000		1,000	
Interest expense	13,186		9,504		5,452	
Lease obligation	36,184		40,496		44,548	
Cash		51,000		51,000		51,000

The leased equipment recorded as an asset must also be amortized (depreciated). The balance of this account is €131,858; however, as with any other asset, it cannot be depreciated below the estimated residual value of €1,000 (note that it is depreciated down to the actual estimated residual value, *not* the guaranteed residual value). In this case, the straight-line depreciation method is applied over a period of three years. This three-year period represents the lease term, *not* the life of the asset, because the asset reverts back to the lessor at the end of the lease term. Therefore, the following entry will be made at the end of each year:

Depreciation expense	43,619	
Accumulated depreciation		43,619 [(€131,858 – €1,000) ÷ 3]

Finally, on December 31, 2013, we must recognize the fact that ownership of the property has reverted back to the owner (lessor). The lessee made a guarantee that the residual value would be €10,000 on December 31, 2013; as a result, the lessee must make up the difference between the guaranteed residual value and the actual residual value with a cash payment to the lessor. The following entry illustrates the removal of the leased asset and obligation from the books of the lessee:

Lease obligation	10,000	
Accumulated depreciation	130,858	
Cash		9,000
Leased equipment		131,858

The foregoing example illustrated a situation where the asset was to be returned to the lessor. Another situation exists (where there is a bargain purchase option or automatic transfer of title) where the asset is expected to remain with the lessee. Recall that, under IAS 17, leased assets are amortized over their useful life when title transfers or a bargain purchase option exists. In such a circumstance, the lease liability may not be amortized completely as of the termination date of the lease. At the end of the lease, the balance of the lease obligation should equal the guaranteed residual value, the bargain purchase option price, or a termination penalty.

Example of accounting for a finance lease—asset ownership transferred to lessee *and* fair market value of leased asset lower than present value of minimum lease payments

---

Assume the following:

1. A three-year lease is initiated on January 1, 2011, for equipment with an expected useful life of five years.
2. Three annual lease payments of €52,000 are required beginning on January 1, 2011, (note that the payment at the beginning of the year changes the PV computation). The lessor pays €2,000 per year for insurance on the equipment.
3. The lessee can exercise a bargain purchase option on December 31, 2013, for €10,000. The expected residual value at December 31, 2015, is €1,000.
4. The lessee's incremental borrowing rate is 10% (implicit rate is unknown).
5. The fair market value of the property leased is €140,000.

Once again, the classification of the lease must take place prior to the accounting for it. This lease is classified as a finance lease because it contains a bargain purchase option (BPO). Note that in this case, the PV versus FMV test is also clearly fulfilled.

The PV of the lease obligation is computed as follows:

PV of bargain purchase option	=	€10,000	×	0.7513*	=	€ 7,513
PV of annual payments	=	(€52,000 – €2,000)	×	2.7355**	=	136,755
						€144,288

* *The present value of an amount of €1 due in three periods at 10% is 0.7513.*
** *The present value of an annuity due of €1 for three periods at 10% is 2.7355.*

Notice that in the example above, the present value of the lease obligation is greater than the fair value of the asset. Also notice that since the lessor pays €2,000 a year for insurance, this payment is treated as executory costs and hence excluded from calculation of the present value of annual payments. Since the PV is greater than the fair value, the lease obligation (as well as the leased asset) must be recorded at the fair value of the asset leased (being the lower of the two). The entry on January 1, 2011, is as follows:

Leased equipment	140,000	
Obligation under finance lease		140,000

According to IAS 17, the apportionment between interest and principal is to be such that interest recognized reflects the use of a constant periodic rate of interest applied to the remaining balance of the obligation. When the PV exceeds the fair value of the leased asset, a new, effective rate must be computed which will be applied to the liability. (Note, however, that if an impairment were subsequently recognized on the asset as an expense in the period of the impairment, following the procedures set forth in IAS 36, this would not affect the recorded amount of the lease obligation (i.e., the liability) and thus would not alter the initially determined interest rate. In this example, the interest rate was determined to be 13.265%. The amortization of the lease takes place as follows:

Year	Cash payment	Interest Expense	Reduction in lease obligation	Balance of lease obligation
Inception of lease				€140,000
January 1, 2011	€50,000	€ --	€50,000	90,000
January 1, 2012	50,000	11,939	38,061	51,939
January 1, 2013	50,000	6,890	43,110	8,829
December 31, 2013	10,000	1,171	8,829	--

The following entries are required in years 2010 through 2012 to recognize the payment and depreciation (amortization).

		2011		2012		2013	
January 1	Operating expense	2,000		2,000		2,000	
	Obligation under finance lease	50,000		38,061		43,110	
	Accrued interest payable			11,939		6,890	
	Cash		52,000		52,000		52,000
December 31	Interest expense	11,939		6,890		1,171	
	Accrued interest payable		11,939		6,890		
	Obligation under finance lease						1,171
December 31	Depreciation expense	27,800		27,800		27,800	
	Accumulated depreciation		27,800		27,800		27,800
	(€139,000, five years)						
December 31	Obligation under finance lease					10,000	
	Cash						10,000

Impairment of leased asset. IAS 17 did not originally address the issue of how impairments of leased assets are to be assessed or, if determined to have occurred, how they would need to be accounted for. Subsequently, IAS 17 was revised to note that the provisions of IAS 36 should be applied to leased assets in the same manner as they would be applied to owned assets. Impairments to the leased asset (occurring after the inception of the lease) are recognized by charges to expense in the current reporting period. IAS 36 is discussed more fully in Chapter 9.

Accounting for Leases—Lessor

As illustrated above, there are two classifications of leases with which a lessor must be concerned.

1. Operating
2. Finance

Operating leases. As is the case for the lessee, the operating lease requires a less complex accounting treatment than does a finance lease. The payments received by the lessor are to be recorded as rental income in the period in which the payment is received or becomes receivable. As with the lessee, if the rentals vary from a straight-line basis, or if the lease agreement contains a scheduled rent increase over the lease term, the revenue is nonetheless to be recognized on a straight-line basis unless an alternative basis of systematic and rational allocation is more representative of the time pattern of earning process contained in the lease.

Additionally, if the lease agreement provides for a scheduled increase(s) in contemplation of the lessee's increased (i.e., more intensive) physical use of the leased property, the total amount of rental payments, including the scheduled increase(s), is allocated to revenue over the lease term on a straight-line basis. However, if the scheduled increase(s) is due to additional leased property (e.g., larger space, more machines), recognition should be proportional to the leased property, with the increased rents recognized over the years that the lessee has control over use of the additional leased property.

Under the leasing standard all initial direct costs incurred must be added to the carrying amount of the leased asset and recognized as an expense over the lease term on the same basis as the lease income. Initial direct costs are incurred by lessors in negotiating and arranging an operating lease, and may include commissions, legal fees, and those internal costs that are actually incremental (i.e., would not exist if the lease were not being negotiated) and directly attributable to negotiating and arranging the lease.

Although there is no guidance on this matter under IFRS, logically any incentives granted by the lessor to the lessee are to be treated as reductions of rent and recognized on a straight-line basis over the term of the lease.

Depreciation of leased assets should be on a basis consistent with the lessor's normal depreciation policy for similar assets, and the depreciation expense should be computed on the basis set out in IAS 16.

Example of straight lining of lease income

SandStone PLC leases 2 buildings to Rockwood Limited. The details are as follows:

Lease 1:

> 3 year lease
> Lease payment $100,000 p.a. escalating at inflation
> Inflation for years 1 – 3 is 8%

Lease 2:

> 3 year lease
> Lease payment $100,000 p.a. escalating at 8% p.a. to reflect inflation
> Inflation for years 1 – 3 is ±8%

Accounting for Lease 1:

Year 1

Bank	100,000	
Statement of Comprehensive Income – Lease Income		100,000

Year 2

Bank	108,000	
Statement of Comprehensive Income – Lease Income		108,000

Year 3

Bank	116,640	
Statement of Comprehensive Income – Lease Income		116,640

Accounting for Lease 2:

As the escalation is a fixed percentage, and not a contingent amount as per Lease 1 (note that inflation is considered contingent), then the lease income must be straight lined. Note that the difference between the amount charged to the statement of comprehensive income and the amount received from the lessee should be recognized in the statement of financial provision as an asset.

Total lease payments over lease term:

Year 1	100,000
Year 2	108,000
Year 3	<u>116,640</u>
Total	324,640

Therefore the annual charge will be 324,640/3 =   108,213

Year 1

Bank	100,000	
Operating Lease Provision (SoFP)	8,213	
Statement of Comprehensive Income – Lease Income		108,213

Year 2

Bank	108,000	
Operating Lease Provision (SoFP)	213	
Statement of Comprehensive Income – Lease Income		108,213

Year 3

Bank	116,640	
Operating Lease Provision (SoFP)		8,426
Statement of Comprehensive Income – Lease Income		108,214

Finance leases. The accounting by the lessor for finance leases depends on which variant of finance lease is at issue. In sales-type leases, an initial profit, analogous to that earned by a manufacturer or dealer, is recognized, whereas a direct financing lease does not give rise to an initial recognition of profit.

Sales-type leases. In the accounting for a sales-type lease, it is necessary for the lessor to determine the following amounts:

1. Gross investment
2. Fair value of the leased asset
3. Cost

From these amounts, the remainder of the computations necessary to record and account for the lease transaction can be made. The first objective is to determine the numbers necessary to complete the following entry:

Lease receivable	xx	
Cost of goods sold	xx	
Sales		xx
Inventory		xx
Unearned finance income		xx

The gross investment (lease receivable) of the lessor is equal to the sum of the minimum lease payments (excluding contingent rent and executory costs) from the standpoint of the lessor, plus the unguaranteed residual value accruing to the lessor. The difference between the gross investment and the present value of the two components of gross investment (i.e., minimum lease payments and unguaranteed residual value) is recorded as "unearned finance income" (also referred to as "unearned interest revenue"). The present value is to be computed using the lease term and implicit interest rate (both of which were discussed earlier).

IAS 17 stipulates that the resulting unearned finance income is to be amortized and recognized into income using the effective rate (or yield) interest method, which will result in a constant periodic rate of return on the "lessor's net investment" (which is computed as the "lessor's gross investment" less the "unearned finance income").

Recall that the fair value of the leased property is by definition equal to the normal selling price of the asset adjusted by any residual amount retained (including any unguaranteed residual value, investment credit, etc.). According to IAS 17, the selling price to be used for a sales-type lease is equal to the fair value of the leased asset, or if lower, the sum of the present values of the MLP and the estimated unguaranteed residual value accruing to the lessor, discounted at a commercial rate of interest. In other words, the normal selling price less the present value of the unguaranteed residual value is equal to the present value of the MLP. (Note that this relationship is sometimes used while computing the MLP when the normal selling price and the residual value are known; this is illustrated in a case study that follows.)

Under IAS 17, initial direct costs incurred in connection with a sales-type lease (i.e., where the lessor is a manufacturer or dealer) must be expensed as incurred. This is a reasonable requirement, since these costs offset some of the profit recognized at inception, as do other selling expenses. Thus, the costs recognized at the inception of such lease arrangements would include the carrying value of the equipment or other items being leased, as well as incidental costs of negotiating and executing the lease. The profit recognized at inception would be the gross profit on the sale of the leased asset, less all operating costs, including the initial direct costs of creating the lease arrangement.

The estimated unguaranteed residual values used in computing the lessor's gross investment in a lease should be reviewed regularly. In case of a permanent reduction (impairment) in the estimated unguaranteed residual value, the income allocation over the lease term is revised and any reduction with respect to amounts already accrued is recognized immediately.

To attract customers, manufacturer or dealer lessors sometimes quote artificially low rates of interest. This has a direct impact on the recognition of initial profit, which is an integral part of the transaction and is inversely proportional to the finance income to be generated by it. Thus, if finance income is artificially low, this results in recognition of excessive profit from the transaction at the time of the sale. Under such circumstances, the standard requires that the profit recognized at inception, analogous to a cash sale of the leased asset, be restricted to that which would have resulted had a commercial rate of interest been used in the deal. Thus, the substance, not the form, of the transaction should be reflected in the financial statements. The present value of the scheduled lease payments, discounted at the appropriate commercial rate, must be computed to derive the effective selling price of the leased asset under these circumstances.

The difference between the selling price and the amount computed as the cost of goods sold is the gross profit recognized by the lessor on the inception of the lease (sale). Manufacturer or dealer lessors often give an option to their customers of either leasing the asset (with financing provided by them) or buying the asset outright. Thus, a finance lease by a manufacturer or dealer lessor, also referred to as a sales-type lease, generates two types of revenue for the lessor.

1. The gross profit (or loss) on the sale, which is equivalent to the profit (or loss) that would have resulted from an outright sale at normal selling prices, adjusted if necessary for a noncommercial rate of interest.
2. The finance income or interest earned on the lease receivable to be spread over the lease term based on a pattern reflecting a constant periodic rate of return on either the lessor's net investment outstanding or the net cash investment outstanding in respect of the finance lease.

The application of these points is illustrated in the example below.

Example of accounting for a sales-type lease

XYZ Inc. is a manufacturer of specialized equipment. Many of its customers do not have the necessary funds or financing available for outright purchase. Because of this, XYZ offers a leasing alternative. The data relative to a typical lease are as follows:

1. The noncancelable fixed portion of the lease term is five years. The lessor has the option to renew the lease for an additional three years at the same rental. The estimated useful life of the asset is ten years. The lessee guarantees a residual value of €40,000 at the end of five years, but the guarantee lapses if the full three renewal periods are exercised.
2. The lessor is to receive equal annual payments over the term of the lease. The leased property reverts back to the lessor on termination of the lease.
3. The lease is initiated on January 1, 2011. Payments are due on December 31 for the duration of the lease term.
4. The cost of the equipment to XYZ Inc. is €100,000. The lessor incurs cost associated with the inception of the lease in the amount of €2,500.
5. The selling price of the equipment for an outright purchase is €150,000.
6. The equipment is expected to have a residual value of €15,000 at the end of five years and €10,000 at the end of eight years.
7. The lessor desires a return of 12% (the implicit rate).

The first step is to calculate the annual payment due to the lessor. Recall that the present value (PV) of the minimum lease payments is equal to the selling price adjusted for the present value of the residual amount. The present value is to be computed using the implicit interest rate and the lease term. In this case, the implicit rate is given as 12% and the lease term is 8 years (which includes the fixed noncancelable portion plus the renewal period, since the lessee guarantee terms make renewal virtually inevitable). Thus, the structure of the computation would be as follows:

$$\text{Normal selling price} - \text{PV of residual value} = \text{PV of minimum lease payment}$$

Or, in this case,

€150,000	–	(0.40388* × €10,000)	=	4.96764** × Minimum lease payment
€145,961.20	÷	4.96764	=	Minimum lease payment
		€29,382.40	=	Minimum lease payment

* *0.40388 is the present value of an amount of €1 due in eight periods at a 12% interest rate.*
** *4.96764 is the present value of an annuity of €1 for eight periods at a 12% interest rate.*

Prior to examining the accounting implications of a lease, we must determine the lease classification. In this example, the lease term is eight years (discussed above) while the estimated useful life of the asset is 10 years; thus this lease qualifies as something other than an operating lease. Note that the lease also meets the FMV versus PV criterion because the PV of the minimum lease payments of €145,961.20, which is 97% of the FMV [€150,000], could be considered to be equal to substantially all of the fair value of the leased asset. Now it must be determined if this is a sales-type or direct financing lease. To do this, examine the FMV or selling price of the asset and compare it to the cost. Because the two are not equal, we can determine this to be a sales-type lease.

Next, obtain the figures necessary to record the entry on the books of the lessor. The gross investment is the total minimum lease payments plus the unguaranteed residual value, or

$$(\text{€}29,382.40 \times 8) + \text{€}10,000 = \text{€}245,059.20$$

The cost of goods sold is the historical cost of the inventory (€100,000) plus any initial direct costs (€2,500) less the PV of the unguaranteed residual value (€10,000 × 0.40388). Thus, the cost of goods sold amount is €98,461.20 (€100,000 + €2,500 – €4,038.80). Note that the initial direct costs will require a credit entry to some account, usually accounts payable or cash. The inventory account is credited for the carrying value of the asset, in this case €100,000.

The adjusted selling price is equal to the PV of the minimum payments, or €145,961.20. Finally, the unearned finance income is equal to the gross investment (i.e., lease receivable) less the present value of the components making up the gross investment (the minimum lease payment of €29,382.40 and the unguaranteed residual of €10,000). The present value of these items is €150,000 [(€29,382.40 × 4.96764) + (€10,000 × 0.40388)]. Therefore, the entry necessary to record the lease is

Lease receivable	245,059.20	
Cost of goods sold	98,461.20	
Inventory		100,000.00
Sales		145,961.20
Unearned finance income		95,059.20
Accounts payable (initial direct costs)		2,500.00

The next step in accounting for a sales-type lease is to determine proper handling of the payment. Both principal and interest are included in each payment. According to IAS 17, interest is recognized on a basis such that a constant periodic rate of return is earned over the term of the lease. This will require setting up an amortization schedule as illustrated below.

Date or year ended	Cash payment	Interest	Reduction in principal	Balance of net investment
January 1, 2011				€150,000.00
December 31, 2012	€ 29,382.40	€18,000.00	€ 11,382.40	138,617.00
December 31, 2013	29,382.40	16,634.11	12,748.29	125,869.31
December 31, 2014	29,382.40	15,104.32	14,278.08	111,591.23
December 31, 2015	29,382.40	13,390.95	15,991.45	95,599.78
December 31, 2016	29,382.40	11,471.97	17,910.43	77,689.35
December 31, 2017	29,382.40	9,322.72	20,059.68	57,629.67
December 31, 2018	29,382.40	6,915.56	22,466.84	35,162.83
December 31, 2019	29,382.40	4,219.57	25,162.83	10,000.00
	€235,059.20	€95,059.20	€140,000.00	

A few of the columns need to be elaborated on. First, the net investment is the gross investment (lease receivable) less the unearned finance income. Notice that at the end of the lease term, the net investment is equal to the estimated residual value. Also note that the total interest earned over the lease term is equal to the unearned interest (unearned finance income) at the beginning of the lease term.

The entries below illustrate the proper treatment to record the receipt of the lease payment and the amortization of the unearned finance income in the year ended December 31, 2011.

Cash	29,382.40	
Lease receivable		29,382.40
Unearned finance income	18,000.00	
Interest revenue		18,000.00

Notice that there is no explicit entry to recognize the principal reduction. This is done automatically when the net investment is reduced by decreasing the lease receivable (gross investment) by €29,382.40 and the unearned finance income account by only €18,000. The €18,000 is 12% (implicit rate) of the net investment. These entries are to be made over the life of the lease.

At the end of the lease term, December 31, 2019, the asset is returned to the lessor and the following entry is required:

Asset	10,000	
Leased receivable		10,000

If the estimated residual value has changed during the lease term, the accounting computations would have also changed to reflect this.

Direct financing leases. Another form of finance lease is a direct financing lease. The accounting for a direct financing lease exhibits many similarities to that for a sales-type lease. Of particular importance is that the terminology used is much the same; however, the treatment accorded these items varies greatly. Again, it is best to preface the discussion by determining the objectives in the accounting for a direct financing lease. Once the lease has been classified, it must be recorded. To do this, the following amounts must be determined:

1. Gross investment
2. Cost
3. Residual value

As noted, a direct financing lease generally involves a leasing company or other financial institution and results in only interest revenue being earned by the lessor. This is because the FMV (selling price) and the cost are equal, and therefore no dealer profit is recognized on the actual lease transaction. Note how this is different from a sales-type lease, which involves both a profit on the transaction and interest revenue over the lease term. The reason for this difference is derived from the conceptual nature underlying the purpose of the lease transaction. In a sales-type lease, the manufacturer (distributor, dealer, etc.) is seeking an alternative means to finance the sale of his product, whereas a direct financing lease is a result of the consumer's need to finance an equipment purchase. Because the consumer is unable to obtain conventional financing, he or she turns to a leasing company that will purchase the desired asset and then lease it to the consumer. Here the profit on the transaction remains with the manufacturer while the interest revenue is earned by the leasing company.

Like a sales-type lease, the first objective is to determine the amounts necessary to complete the following entry:

Lease receivable	xxx	
Asset		xxx
Unearned finance income		xxx

The gross investment is still defined as the minimum amount of lease payments (from the standpoint of a lessor) exclusive of any executory costs, plus the unguaranteed residual value. The difference between the gross investment as determined above and the cost (carrying value) of the asset is to be recorded as the unearned finance income because there is no manufacturer's/dealer's profit earned on the transaction. The following entry would be made to record initial direct costs:

Initial direct costs	xx	
Cash		xx

Under IAS 17, the net investment in the lease is defined as the gross investment less the unearned income plus the unamortized initial direct costs related to the lease. Initial direct costs are incremental costs that are directly attributable to negotiating and arranging a lease, except for such costs incurred by manufacturer or dealer lessors. These are to be capitalized and allocated over the lease term.

Employing initial direct cost capitalization, the unearned lease (i.e., interest) income and the initial direct costs will be amortized to income over the lease term so that a constant periodic rate is earned either on the lessor's net investment outstanding or on the net cash investment outstanding in the finance lease (i.e., the balance of the cash outflows and inflows in respect of the lease, excluding any executory costs that are chargeable to the lessee).

Thus, the effect of the initial direct costs is to reduce the implicit interest rate or, yield, to the lessor over the life of the lease.

An example follows that illustrates the preceding principles.

Example of accounting for a direct financing lease

Emirates Refining needs new equipment to expand its manufacturing operation; however, it does not have sufficient capital to purchase the asset at this time. Because of this, Emirates Refining has employed Consolidated Leasing to purchase the asset. In turn, Emirates will lease the asset from Consolidated. The following information applies to the terms of the lease:

1. A three-year lease is initiated on January 1, 2011, for equipment costing €131,858, with an expected useful life of five years. FMV at January 1, 2011, of equipment is €131,858.
2. Three annual payments are due to the lessor beginning December 31, 2011. The property reverts back to the lessor on termination of the lease.
3. The unguaranteed residual value at the end of year three is estimated to be €10,000.
4. The annual payments are calculated to give the lessor a 10% return (the implicit rate).
5. The lease payments and unguaranteed residual value have a PV equal to €131,858 (FMV of asset) at the stipulated discount rate.
6. The annual payment to the lessor is computed as follows:

PV of residual value	=	€10,000 × .7513* = €7,513
PV of lease payments	=	Selling price – PV of residual value
	=	€131,858 – €7,513 = €124,345
Annual payment	=	€124,345 ÷ 2.4869** = €50,000

* *.7513 is the PV of an amount due in three periods at 10%.*
** *2.4869 is the PV of an ordinary annuity of €1 per period for three periods, at 10% interest.*

7. Initial direct costs of €7,500 are incurred by ABC in the lease transaction.

As with any lease transaction, the first step must be to classify the lease appropriately. In this case, the PV of the lease payments (€124,345) is equal to 94% of the FMV (€131,858), thus could be considered as equal to substantially all of the FMV of the leased asset. Next, the unearned interest and the net investment in lease are to be determined.

Gross investment in lease [(3 × €50,000) + €10,000]	€160,000
Cost of leased property	131,858
Unearned finance income	€ 28,142

The unamortized initial direct costs are to be added to the gross investment in the lease, and the unearned finance income is to be deducted to arrive at the net investment in the lease. The net investment in the lease for this example is determined as follows:

Gross investment in lease	€160,000
Add:	
Unamortized initial direct costs	7,500
Less:	
Unearned finance income	28,142
Net investment in lease	€139,358

The net investment in the lease (Gross investment – Unearned finance income) has been increased by the amount of initial direct costs. Therefore, the implicit rate is no longer 10%, and the implicit rate must be recomputed, which is the result of performing an internal rate of return calculation. The lease payments are to be €50,000 per annum and a residual value of €10,000 is available at the end of the lease term. In return for these payments (inflows), the lessor is giving up equipment (an outflow) and incurring initial direct costs (also an outflow), with a net investment of €139,358 (€131,858 + €7,500). The way to obtain the new implicit rate is to employ a calculator or computer routine that does this iterative computation automatically.

$$\frac{50,000}{(1+i)} \ 1 + \ \frac{50,000}{(1+i)} \ 2 + \ \frac{50,000}{(1+i)} \ 3 + \ \frac{10,000}{(1+i)} \ 3 = €139,358$$

Where: i = implicit rate of interest

In this case, the implicit rate is equal to 7.008%. Thus, the amortization table would be set up as follows:

	(a) *Lease* *payments*	*(b)* *Reduction in* *unearned* *Interest*	*(c)* *PV x* *Implicit rate* *(7.008%)*	*(d)* *Reduction in* *initial direct* *costs* *(b-c)*	*(e)* *Reduction in* *PVI net* *investment* *(a-b + d)*	*(f)* *PVI net investment* *in lease* *(f)(n+1) = (f)n − (e)*
At inception						€139,358
2011	€ 50,000	€13,186 (1)	€ 9,766	€3,420	€ 40,234	99,124
2012	50,000	9,504 (2)	6,947	2,557	43,053	56,071
2013	50,000	5,455 (3)	3,929	1,526	46,071	10,000
	€150,000	€28,145*	€20,642	€7,503	€129,358	

Rounded

(b.1) €131,858 × 10% = €13,186
(b.2) [€131,858 − (€50,000 − 13,186)] × 10% = €9,504
(b.3) [€95,044 − (€50,000 − 9,504)] × 10% = €5,455

Here the interest is computed as 7.008% of the net investment. Note again that the net investment at the end of the lease term is equal to the estimated residual value.

The entry made initially to record the lease is as follows:

Lease receivable** [(€50,000 × 3) + €10,000]	160,000	
Asset acquired for leasing		131,858
Unearned lease revenue		28,142

When the payment (or obligation to pay) of the initial direct costs occurs, the following entry must be made:

Initial direct costs	7,500	
Cash		7,500

Using the schedule above, the following entries would be made during each of the indicated years:

	2011		*2012*		*2013*	
Cash	50,000		50,000		50,000	
Lease receivable**		50,000		50,000		50,000
Unearned finance income	13,186		9,504		5,455	
Initial direct costs		3,420		2,557		1,526
Interest income		9,766		6,947		3,929

Finally, when the asset is returned to the lessor at the end of the lease term, it must be recorded on the books. The necessary entry is as follows:

Property, plant & equipment	10,000	
Lease receivable**		10,000

** *Also commonly referred to as the "gross investment in lease."*

Leveraged leases. Leveraged leases are discussed in detail in Appendix B of this chapter because of the complexity involved in the accounting treatment based on guidance available under US GAAP, where this topic has been given extensive coverage. Under IFRS, this concept has been defined, but with only a very brief outline of the treatment to be accorded to this kind of lease. A leveraged lease is defined as a finance lease which is structured such that there are at least three parties involved: the lessee, the lessor, and one or more long-term creditors who provide part of the acquisition finance for the leased asset, usually without any general recourse to the lessor. Succinctly, this type of a lease is given the following unique accounting treatment:

1. The lessor records his or her investment in the lease net of the nonrecourse debt and the related finance costs to the third-party creditor(s).
2. The recognition of the finance income is based on the lessor's net cash investment outstanding in respect of the lease.

Sale-Leaseback Transactions

Sale-leaseback describes a transaction where the owner of property (the seller-lessee) sells the property and then immediately leases all or part of it back from the new owner (the buyer-lessor). These transactions may occur when the seller-lessee is experiencing cash flow or financing problems or because there are tax advantages in such an arrangement in the lessee's tax jurisdiction. The important consideration in this type of transaction is recognition of two separate and distinct economic transactions. However, it is important to note that there is not a physical transfer of property. First, there is a sale of property, and second, there is a lease agreement for the same property in which the original seller is the lessee and the original buyer is the lessor. This is illustrated as follows:

A sale-leaseback transaction is usually structured such that the sales price of the asset is greater than or equal to the current market value. The higher sales price has the concomitant effect of a higher periodic rental payment over the lease term than would otherwise have been negotiated. The transaction is usually attractive because of the tax benefits associated with it, and because it provides financing to the lessee. The seller-lessee benefits from the higher price because of the increased gain on the sale of the property and the deductibility of the lease payments, which are usually larger than the depreciation that was previously being taken. The buyer-lessor benefits from both the higher rental payments and the larger depreciable basis.

Under IAS 17, the accounting treatment depends on whether the leaseback results in a finance lease or an operating lease. If it results in a finance lease, any excess of sale proceeds over previous carrying value may not be recognized immediately as income in the financial statements of the seller-lessee. Rather, it is to be deferred and amortized over the lease term.

Accounting for a sale-leaseback that involves the creation of an operating lease depends on whether the sale portion of the compound transaction was on arm's-length terms. If the leaseback results in an operating lease, and it is evident that the transaction is established at fair value, then any profit or loss should be recognized immediately. On the other hand, if the sale price is *not* established at fair value, then

1. If sale price is *below* fair value, any profit or loss should be recognized immediately, except that when a loss is to be compensated by below fair market future rentals, the loss should be deferred and amortized in proportion to the rental payments over the period the asset is expected to be used.
2. If the sale price is *above* fair value, the excess over fair value should be deferred and amortized over the period for which the asset is expected to be used.

IAS 17 stipulates that, in case of operating leasebacks, if at the date of the sale and lease-back transaction the fair value is less than the carrying amount of the leased asset, the difference between the fair value and the carrying amount should immediately be recognized. In other words, impairment is recognized first, before the actual sale-leaseback transaction is given recognition. This logically follows from the fact that impairments are essentially catch-up depreciation charges, belated recognition that the consumption of the utility of the assets had not been correctly recognized in earlier periods.

However, in case the sale and leaseback result in a finance lease, no such adjustment is considered necessary unless there has been an impairment in value, in which case the carrying value should be reduced to the recoverable amount in accordance with the provisions of IAS 36.

The guidance under IFRS pertaining to sale-leaseback transactions is limited, and many variations in terms and conditions are found in actual practice. To provide further insight, albeit not with the suggestion that this constitutes IFRS, selected guidance found under US GAAP is offered in Appendix A to this chapter.

Other leasing guidance. SIC 27 addresses arrangements between an enterprise and an investor that involve the legal form of a lease. SIC 27 establishes that the accounting for such arrangements is in all instances to reflect the substance of the relationship. All aspects of the arrangement are to be evaluated to determine its substance, with particular emphasis on those that have an economic effect. To assist in doing this, SIC 27 identifies certain indicators that may demonstrate that an arrangement might not involve a lease under IAS 17. For example, a series of linked transactions that in substance do not transfer control over the asset, and which keep the right to receive the benefits of ownership with the transferor, would not be a lease. Also, transactions arranged for specific objectives, such as the transfer of tax attributes, would generally not be accounted for as leases.

SIC 27 deals most specifically with those arrangements that have characteristics of leases coupled with corollary subleases, whereby the lessor is the sublessee and the lessee is the sublessor, which may also involve a purchase option. The financing party (the lessee-sublessor) is often guaranteed a certain economic return on such transactions, further revealing that the substance might in fact be that of a secured borrowing rather than a series of lease arrangements. Since nominal lease and sublease payments will net to zero, the exchange of funds is often limited to the fee given by the property owner to the party providing financing; tax advantages are often the principal objective of these transactions. Accounting questions arising from the transactions include recognition of fees received by the financing party; the presentation of separate investment and sublease payment obligation accounts as an asset and a liability, respectively; and the accounting for resulting obligations.

SIC 27 imposes a substance over form solution to this problem. Accordingly, when an arrangement is found to not meet the definition of a lease, a separate investment account and a lease payment obligation would not meet the definitions of an asset and a liability, and should not be recognized by the entity. It presents certain indicators which imply that a given arrangement is not a lease (e.g., when the right to use the property for a given term is not in fact transferred to the nominal lessee) and that lease accounting cannot be applied.

The interpretation provides that the fee paid to the financing provider should be recognized in accordance with IAS 18. Fees received in advance would generally be deferred and recognized over the lease term when future performance is required in order to retain the fee, when limitations are placed on the use of the underlying asset, or when the nonremote likelihood of early termination would necessitate some fee repayment.

Finally, SIC 27 identifies certain factors that would suggest that other obligations of an arrangement, including any guarantees provided and obligations incurred upon early termination, should be accounted for under either IAS 37 (contingent liabilities) or IAS 39 (financial obligations), depending on the terms.

IFRIC 4 describes arrangements, comprising transactions or series of related transactions, that do not take the legal form of a lease, but which convey rights to use assets in return for series of payments. Examples of such arrangements include

- Outsourcing arrangements (e.g., the outsourcing of the data processing functions of an entity).
- Various arrangements in the telecommunications industry, in which suppliers of network capacity enter into contracts to provide other entities with rights to capacity.
- "Take-or-pay" and similar contracts, in which purchasers must make specified payments regardless of whether they take delivery of the contracted products or services (these often are styled as capacity contracts, giving one party exclusive rights to the counterparty's output).

IFRIC 4 provides guidance for determining whether such arrangements are, or contain, leases that should be accounted for in accordance with IAS 17. It does not address how such arrangements, if determined to be leases, should be classified. In some of these arrangements, the underlying asset that is the subject of the lease is a portion of a larger asset. IFRIC 4 does not address how to ascertain if the portion of a larger asset is itself the underlying asset for the purposes of applying IAS 17. However, arrangements in which the underlying asset would represent a unit of account under either IAS 16 or IAS 38 are within the scope of this interpretation. Leases which would be excluded from IAS 17 (as noted earlier in this chapter) are not subject to the provisions of IFRIC 4.

Determining whether an arrangement is, or contains, a lease is required to be based on the substance of the arrangement. It requires an assessment of whether

1. Fulfillment of the arrangement is dependent on the use of a specific asset or assets; *and*
2. The arrangement conveys a right to use the asset.

An arrangement is not the subject of a lease if its fulfillment is not dependent on the use of the specified asset. Thus, if terms call for delivery of a specified quantity of goods or services, and the entity has the right and ability to provide those goods or services using other assets not specified in the arrangement, it is not subject to this interpretation. On the other hand, a warranty obligation that permits or requires the substitution of the same or similar assets when the specified asset is not operating properly, or a contractual provision (whether or not contingent) permitting or requiring the supplier to substitute other assets for any reason on or after a specified date, do not preclude lease treatment before the date of substitution.

IFRIC 4 states that an asset has been *implicitly specified* if, for example, the supplier owns or leases only one asset with which to fulfill the obligation, and it is not economically feasible to perform its obligation through the use of alternative assets.

An arrangement conveys the right to use the asset if the arrangement conveys to the purchaser (putatively, the lessee) the right to control the use of the underlying asset. This occurs if

1. The purchaser has the ability or right to operate the asset (or direct others to operate the asset) in a manner it determines while obtaining or controlling more than an insignificant amount of the output or other value of the asset;
2. The purchaser has the ability or right to control physical access to the underlying asset while obtaining or controlling more than an insignificant amount of the output or other utility of the asset; or
3. Fact and circumstances suggest that it is remote that one or more parties other than the purchaser will take more than an insignificant amount of the output of the asset, or other value that will be produced or generated by the asset during the term of the arrangement, and the price that the purchaser will pay for the output is neither contractually fixed per unit of output nor equal to the current market price per unit of output as of the time of delivery of the output.

According to IFRIC 4, the assessment of whether an arrangement contains a lease is to be made at the inception of the arrangement. This is defined as the earlier of the date of the arrangement or the date the parties commit to the principal terms of the arrangement, on the basis of all of the facts and circumstances. Once determined, a reassessment is permitted only if

1. There is a change in the contractual terms, unless the change only renews or extends the arrangement;
2. A renewal option is exercised or an extension is agreed to by the parties, unless the term of the renewal or extension had initially been included in the lease term in accordance with IAS 17 (a renewal or extension of the arrangement that does not include modification of any of the terms in the original arrangement before the end of the term of the original arrangement is to be evaluated only with respect to the renewal or extension period);
3. There is a change in the determination of whether fulfillment is dependent on a specified asset; or
4. There is a substantial change to the asset, (e.g., a substantial physical change to property, plant, or equipment).

Any reassessment of an arrangement is to be based on the facts and circumstances as of the date of reassessment, including the remaining term of the arrangement. Changes in estimate (e.g., as to the expected output to be delivered) may not be used to trigger a reassessment. If the reassessment concludes that the arrangement contains (or does not contain) a lease, lease accounting is to be applied (or cease to be applied) from when the change in circumstances giving rise to the reassessment occurs (if other than exercise of a renewal or extension), or the inception of the renewal or extension period.

If an arrangement is determined to contain a lease, both parties are to apply the requirements of IAS 17 to the lease element of the arrangement. Accordingly, the lease must be classified as a finance lease or an operating lease. Other elements of the arrangement, not within the scope of that standard, are to be accounted for as required by the relevant IFRS. For the purpose of applying IAS 17, payments and other consideration required must be separated, at inception or upon a reassessment of the arrangement, into that being made for the lease and that applicable to the other elements, on the basis of relative fair values. Minimum lease payments (per IAS 17) include only payments for the lease itself.

In some instances it will be necessary to make assumptions and estimates in order to separate the payments for the lease from payments for the other elements. IFRIC 4 suggests that a purchaser might estimate the lease payment portion by reference to a lease for a comparable asset that contains no other elements, or might estimate the payments for the other elements by reference to comparable agreements, deriving the payments for the other component by deduction. However, if a purchaser concludes that it is impracticable to separate the payments reliably, the procedure to be followed depends on whether the lease is operating or finance in nature.

If a finance lease, the purchaser/lessee is to recognize an asset and a liability at an amount equal to the fair value of the underlying asset that was identified as being the subject of the lease. As payments are later made, the liability will be reduced and an imputed finance charge on the liability will be recognized using the purchaser's incremental borrowing rate of interest (as described earlier in this chapter).

If an operating lease, the purchaser/lessee is to treat all payments as lease payments for the purposes of complying with the disclosure requirements of IAS 17, but (1) disclose those payments separately from minimum lease payments of other arrangements that do not include payments for nonlease elements, and (2) state that the disclosed payments also include payments for nonlease elements in the arrangement.

DISCLOSURE REQUIREMENTS UNDER IAS 17

Lessee Disclosures

1. **Finance Leases**

    IAS 17 mandates the following disclosures for lessees under finance leases, in addition to disclosures required under IFRS 7 for all financial instruments:

    a. For each class of asset, the net carrying amount at the end of the reporting period (the date of the statement of financial position)
    b. A reconciliation between the total of minimum lease payments at the end of the reporting period, and their present value. In addition, an enterprise should disclose the total of the minimum lease payments at the end of the reporting period, their present value, for each of the following periods:

       (1) Due in one year or less
       (2) Due in more than one but no more than five years
       (3) Due in more than five years

    c. Contingent rents included in profit or loss for the period
    d. The total of minimum sublease payments to be received in the future under noncancelable subleases at the end of the reporting period
    e. A general description of the lessee's significant leasing arrangements including, but not necessarily limited to the following:

       (1) The basis for determining contingent rentals
       (2) The existence and terms of renewal or purchase options and escalation clauses
       (3) Restrictions imposed by lease arrangements such as on dividends or assumptions of further debt or further leasing

2. Operating Leases

IAS 17 sets forth in greater detail the disclosure requirements that will be applicable to lessees under operating leases.

Lessees should, in addition to the requirements of IFRS 7, make the following disclosures for operating leases:

a. Total of the future minimum lease payments under noncancelable operating leases for each of the following periods:

    (1) Due in one year or less
    (2) Due in more than one year but no more than five years
    (3) Due in more than five years

b. The total of future minimum sublease payments expected to be received under noncancelable subleases at the end of the reporting period
c. Lease and sublease payments included in profit or loss for the period, with separate amounts of minimum lease payments, contingent rents, and sublease payments
d. A general description of the lessee's significant leasing arrangements including, but not necessarily limited to the following:

    (1) The basis for determining contingent rentals
    (2) The existence and terms of renewal or purchase options escalation clauses
    (3) Restrictions imposed by lease arrangements such as on dividends or assumption of further debt or on further leasing

Lessor Disclosures

1. Finance Leases

IAS 17 requires enhanced disclosures compared to the original standard. Lessors under finance leases are required to disclose, in addition to disclosures under IFRS 7, the following:

a. A reconciliation between the total gross investment in the lease at the end of the reporting period, and the present value of minimum lease payments receivable at the end of the reporting period, categorized into

    (1) Those due in one year or less
    (2) Those due in more than one year but not more than five years
    (3) Those due beyond five years

b. Unearned finance income
c. The unguaranteed residual values accruing to the benefit of the lessor
d. The accumulated allowance for uncollectible minimum lease payments receivable
e. Total contingent rentals included in income
f. A general description of the lessor's significant leasing arrangements

2. Operating Leases

For lessors under operating leases, IAS 17 has prescribed the following expanded disclosures:

a. The future minimum lease payments under noncancellable operating leases, in the aggregate and classified into

(1) Those due in no more than one year
(2) Those due in more than one but not more than five years
(3) Those due in more than five years

b. Total contingent rentals included in profit or loss for the period
c. A general description of leasing arrangements to which it is a party

In addition to the above, the disclosure requirements relating to the assets recognized by the lessor or lessee required in the respective standards governing the accounting for those assets, should be given. These include IAS 16, IAS 38, IAS 40 and IAS 41. These disclosure requirements are detailed in the respective chapters looking at each of these sections.

Examples of Financial Statement Disclosures

Nestlé SA
Year Ended December 31, 2010

Accounting Policy

Leased assets

Assets acquired under finance leases are capitalized and depreciated in accordance with the Group's policy on property, plant, and equipment unless the lease term is shorter. Land and building leases are recognized separately provided an allocation of the lease payments between these categories is reliable. The associated obligations are included under financial liabilities.

Rentals payable under operating leases are expensed.

The costs of the agreements that do not take the legal form of a lease but convey the right to use an asset are separated into lease payments and other payments if the entity has the control of the use or of the access to the asset or takes essentially all the output of the asset. Then the entity determines whether the lease component of the agreement is a finance or an operating lease.

Notes to the financial statements

19. Lease commitments

19.1 Operating leases

	2010	2009
In millions of CHF	*Minimum lease payments*	
	Future value	
Within one year	600	583
In the second year	467	460
In the third to the fifth year inclusive	939	834
After the fifth year	569	575
	2,575	2,452

Lease commitments refer mainly to buildings, industrial equipment, vehicles and IT equipment. Operating lease charge for the year 2010 amounts to CHF 701 million (2009: CHF 627 million).

19.2 Finance leases

In millions of CHF	*2010*		*2009*	
	Minimum lease payments			
	Present value	*Future value*	*Present value*	*Future value*
Within one year	68	74	71	75
In the second year	57	68	58	68
In the third to the fifth year inclusive	106	155	120	169
After the fifth year	69	145	80	182
	300	442	329	494

The difference between the future value of the minimum lease payments and their present value represents the discount on the lease obligations.

Vodafone PLC
Year ended March 31, 2010

Accounting Policy

Leasing

Leases are classified as finance leases whenever the terms of the lease transfer substantially all the risks and rewards of ownership of the asset to the lessee. All other leases are classified as operating leases.

Assets held under finance leases are recognized as assets of the Group at their fair value at the inception of the lease or, if lower, at the present value of the minimum lease payments as determined at the inception of the lease. The corresponding liability to the lessor is included in the statement of financial position as a finance lease obligation. Lease payments are apportioned between finance charges and reduction of the lease obligation so as to achieve a constant rate of interest on the remaining balance of the liability. Finance charges are recognized in the income statement.

Rentals payable under operating leases are charged to the income statement on a straight-line basis over the term of the relevant lease. Benefits received and receivable as an incentive to enter into an operating lease are also spread on a straight-line basis over the lease term.

Notes to the financial statements

28. Commitments

Operating lease commitments

The Group has entered into commercial leases on certain properties, network infrastructure, motor vehicles and items of equipment. The leases have various terms, escalation clauses, purchase options, and renewal rights, none of which are individually significant to the Group.

Future minimum lease payments under noncancelable operating leases comprise

	2010	*2009*
	€m	*€m*
Within one year	1,200	1,041
In more than one year but less than two years	906	812
In more than two years but less than three years	776	639
In more than three years but less than four years	614	539
In more than four years but less than five years	512	450
In more than five years	2,235	2,135
	6,243	**5,616**

The total of future minimum sublease payments expected to be received under noncancelable subleases is €246 million (2009: €197 million)

Capital commitments

	Company and subsidiaries		Share of joint ventures		Group	
	2010	2009	2010	2009	2010	2009
	€m	€m	€m	€m	€m	€m
Contracts placed for future capital expenditure not provided in the financial statements[1]	1,800	1,706	219	401	2,019	2,107

[1] *Commitment includes contracts placed for property, plant, and equipment, and intangible assets.*

Anglo Platinum
Year Ended December 31, 2009

Notes to the consolidated financial statements

30. Obligations due under finance leases

The Group previously financed certain housing requirements through finance leases. The Group held a call option to acquire legal title to the land and houses at the end of the lease term. The lessor, Group Five Limited, held a put option to put legal title of the remaining land and houses back to the Group. The implicit interest rate was linked to JIBAR (Johannesburg Interbank Agreed Rate) and an average rate of 13.8% was paid in the 2008 year. The lease was repaid in the current year. The current year's finance lease obligation relates to leases over other assets. The carrying amount of assets held under finance leases amounts to R4 million (2008: R313 million).

	2009 Rm	2008 Rm
Finance lease obligations	3	511
Less: Short-term portion transferred to trade and other payables (Note 35)	(1)	(2)
	2	509

Reconciliation of future minimum lease payments under finance leases

	Minimum lease payments		Present value of minimum lease payments	
	2009 Rm	2008 Rm	2009 Rm	2008 Rm
Within one year	1	71	1	2
In the second to fifth years	2	282	2	3
Six years and thereafter	--	787	--	506
	3	1,140	3	511
Less: Future finance charges	--	(629)	--	--
Present value of leasing obligations	3	511	3	511

43. Commitments

Operating lease rentals–buildings	552	647
Due within one year	98	95
Due within two to five years	256	238
More than five years	198	314

FUTURE DEVELOPMENTS

Because of the significance of this area of practice in all economies, and the remaining divergence of requirements under alternative sets of standards, the IASB and the FASB have undertaken a project to reconsider lease accounting. In March 2009, the IASB published a Discussion Paper proposing changes to lease accounting. This was followed up by an Exposure Draft in August 2010. The aim of the project is to develop a new single approach to lease accounting that would ensure that all assets and liabilities arising under lease contracts are recognized in the statement of financial position. This would do away with the arbitrary distinction between finance and operating leases under the current IAS 17, and replace it with the recognition of a lease liability and the right to use an asset.

Some of the key issues the exposure draft addressed are as follows:

- Lessees would recognize assets and liabilities for all leases—operating leases that currently exist under IAS 17 would cease to exist.
- For entities currently accounting for operating leases, rent expense would be replaced with amortization expense and interest expense, with total expense being recognized earlier in the lease term.
- Estimates of contingent rentals, residual value guarantees and term option penalties would be included as part of the lease liability using an expected outcome approach.
- Rentals during renewal periods would be included as part of the lease liability on the basis of the longest possible lease term that is more-likely-than-not to occur.
- A reassessment of the estimates of lease payments and renewal periods would be required if facts or circumstances indicate that there would be a significant change.
- Lessors would apply one of two models—the performance obligation approach or derecognition approach—depending on whether control and the extent to which the risks and benefits of the entire underlying asset are transferred to the lessee.
- The proposed transition requirements would not grandfather existing leases and would require adjustment of comparative periods.

The IASB had initially anticipated completing this project and issuing a new IFRS to replace IAS 17 by June 2011. However, in July 2011 the IASB and the FASB discussed reexposure of the proposed standard, lessor accounting, the accounting for lease payments that depend on an index or a rate, the accounting for embedded derivatives in lease contracts, lessee presentation and disclosure, presentation: lessee statement of financial position and lessee statement of cash flows. As a result the standard will most likely be issued in early 2012.

US GAAP COMPARISON

US GAAP accounting and criteria for leases is very similar. See Appendix A attached to this chapter for specific US interpretations. However, US GAAP uses quantitative criteria to classify a lease as either operating or capital. IFRS is based on the substance of the transaction to assess whether a substantial amount of the value or useful life of the asset is conveyed to the lessee.

Third-party guarantees are not included in the minimum lease payments (nor measurement of the obligation and asset). Leases of land and buildings are accounted for together unless land is greater than 25% of the property value.

US GAAP does not contain the direct guidance about identifying an embedded derivative in the lease if the lessee has a stake in the market value of the asset.

APPENDIX A:

SPECIAL SITUATIONS NOT ADDRESSED BY IAS 17 BUT WHICH HAVE BEEN INTERPRETED UNDER US GAAP

In the following section, a number of interesting and common problem areas that have not yet been addressed by IFRS are briefly considered. The guidance found in US GAAP is referenced, as this is likely to represent the most comprehensive source of insight into these matters. However, it should be understood that this constitutes only *possible* approaches to selected fact situations, and is not authoritative guidance. Some of these matters may be more fully addressed by IFRS if the proposed amendments to IAS 17 are brought to fruition.

Sale-Leaseback Transactions

The accounting treatment from the seller-lessee's perspective will depend on the degree of rights to use retained by the seller-lessee. The degree of rights to use retained may be categorized as follows:

1. Substantially all
2. Minor
3. More than minor but less than substantially all

The guideline for the determination substantially all is based on the classification criteria presented for the lease transaction. For example, a test based on the 90% recovery criterion seems appropriate. That is, if the present value of fair rental payments is equal to 90% or more of the fair value of the sold asset, the seller-lessee is presumed to have retained substantially all the rights to use the sold property. The test for retaining minor rights would be to substitute 10% or less for 90% or more in the preceding sentence.

If substantially all the rights to use the property are retained by the seller-lessee and the agreement meets at least one of the criteria for capital lease treatment, the seller-lessee should account for the leaseback as a capital lease, and any profit on the sale should be deferred and either amortized over the life of the property or treated as a reduction of depreciation expense. If the leaseback is classified as an operating lease, it should be accounted for as one, and any profit or loss on the sale should be deferred and amortized over the lease term. Any loss on the sale would also be deferred unless the loss were perceived to be a real economic loss, in which case the loss would be recognized immediately and not deferred.

If only a minor portion of the rights to use are retained by the seller-lessee, the sale and the leaseback should be accounted for separately. However, if the rental payments appear unreasonable based on the existing market conditions at the inception of the lease, the profit or loss should be adjusted so that the rentals are at a reasonable amount. The amount created by the adjustment should be deferred and amortized over the life of the property if a capital lease is involved or over the lease term if an operating lease is involved.

If the seller-lessee retains more than a minor portion but less than substantially all the rights to use the property, any excess profit on the sale should be recognized on the date of the sale. For purposes of this paragraph, excess profit is derived as follows:

1. If the leaseback is classified as an operating lease, the excess profit is the profit that exceeds the present value of the minimum lease payments over the lease term. The seller-lessee should use its incremental borrowing rate to compute the present value of the minimum lease payments. If the implicit rate of interest in the lease is known, it should be used to compute the present value of the minimum lease payments.
2. If the leaseback is classified as a capital (i.e., finance) lease, the excess profit is the amount greater than the recorded amount of the leased asset.

When the fair value of the property at the time of the leaseback is less than its undepreciated cost, the seller-lessee should immediately recognize a loss for the difference. In the example below, the sales price is less than the book value of the property. However, there is no economic loss because the FMV is greater than the book value.

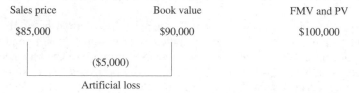

Sales price	Book value	FMV and PV
$85,000	$90,000	$100,000

($5,000)

Artificial loss

The artificial loss must be deferred and amortized as an addition to depreciation.

The following diagram summarizes the accounting for sale-leaseback transactions.

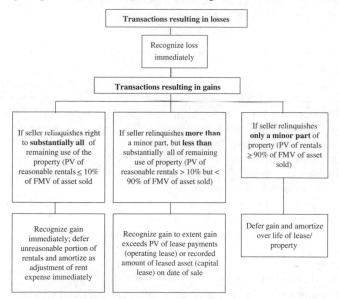

In the foregoing circumstances, when the leased asset is land only, any amortization should be on a straight-line basis over the lease term, regardless of whether the lease is classified as a capital or an operating lease.

Executory costs are not to be included in the calculation of profit to be deferred in a sale-leaseback transaction. The buyer-lessor should account for the transaction as a purchase and a direct financing lease if the agreement meets the criteria of *either* a direct financing lease **or** a sales-type lease. Otherwise, the agreement should be accounted for as a purchase and an operating lease.

Sale-leaseback involving real estate. Under US GAAP, three requirements are necessary for a sale-leaseback involving real estate (including real estate with equipment) to qualify for sale-leaseback accounting treatment. Those sale-leaseback transactions not meeting the three requirements should be accounted for as a deposit or as a financing. The three requirements are

1. The lease must be a normal leaseback.
2. Payment terms and provisions must adequately demonstrate the buyer-lessor's initial and continuing investment in the property.
3. Payment terms and provisions must transfer all the risks and rewards of ownership as demonstrated by a lack of continuing involvement by the seller-lessee.

A normal leaseback involves active use of the leased property in the seller-lessee's trade or business during the lease term.

The buyer-lessor's initial investment is adequate if it demonstrates the buyer-lessor's commitment to pay for the property and indicates a reasonable likelihood that the seller-lessee will collect any receivable related to the leased property. The buyer-lessor's continuing investment is adequate if the buyer is contractually obligated to pay an annual amount at least equal to the level of annual payment needed to pay that debt and interest over no more than (1) twenty years for land and (2) the customary term of a first mortgage loan for other real estate.

Any continuing involvement by the seller-lessee other than normal leaseback disqualifies the lease from sale-leaseback accounting treatment. Some examples of continuing involvement other than normal leaseback include

1. The seller-lessee has an obligation or option (excluding the right of first refusal) to repurchase the property.
2. The seller-lessee (or party related to the seller-lessee) guarantees the buyer-lessor's investment or debt related to that investment or a return on that investment.
3. The seller-lessee is required to reimburse the buyer-lessor for a decline in the fair value of the property below estimated residual value at the end of the lease term based on other than excess wear and tear.
4. The seller-lessee remains liable for an existing debt related to the property.
5. The seller-lessee's rental payments are contingent on some predetermined level of future operations of the buyer-lessor.
6. The seller-lessee provides collateral on behalf of the buyer-lessor other than the property directly involved in the sale-leaseback.
7. The seller-lessee provides nonrecourse financing to the buyer-lessor for any portion of the sales proceeds or provides recourse financing in which the only recourse is the leased asset.
8. The seller-lessee enters into a sale-leaseback involving property improvements or integral equipment without leasing the underlying land to the buyer-lessor.
9. The buyer-lessor is obligated to share any portion of the appreciation of the property with the seller-lessee.
10. Any other provision or circumstance that allows the seller-lessee to participate in any future profits of the buyer-lessor or appreciation of the leased property.

Example of accounting for a sale-leaseback transaction

To illustrate the accounting treatment in a sale-leaseback transaction, suppose that Lessee Corporation sells equipment that has a book value of €80,000 and a fair value of €100,000 to Lessor Corporation, and then immediately leases it back under the following conditions:

1. The sale date is January 1, 2010, and the equipment has a fair value of €100,000 on that date and an estimated useful life of 15 years.
2. The lease term is 15 years, noncancelable, and requires equal rental payments of €13,109 at the beginning of each year.
3. Lessee Corp. has the option annually to renew the lease at the same rental payments on expiration of the original lease.
4. Lessee Corp. has the obligation to pay all executory costs.
5. The annual rental payments provide the lessor with a 12% return on investment.
6. The incremental borrowing rate of Lessee Corp. is 12%.
7. Lessee Corp. depreciates similar equipment on a straight-line basis.

Lessee Corp. should classify the agreement as a capital lease since the lease term exceeds 75% (which is deemed to be a major part) of the estimated economic life of the equipment, and because the present value of the lease payments is greater than 90% (deemed to be substantially all) of the fair value of the equipment. Assuming that collectibility of the lease payments is reasonably predictable and that no important uncertainties exist concerning the amount of nonreimbursable costs yet to be incurred by the lessor, Lessor Corp. should classify the transaction as a direct financing lease because the present value of the minimum lease payments is equal to the fair market value of €100,000 (€13,109 × 7.62817).

Lessee Corp. and Lessor Corp. would normally make the following journal entries during the first year:

Upon Sale of Equipment on January 1, 2010

Lessee Corp.			*Lessor Corp.*		
Cash	100,000		Equipment	100,000	
Equipment*		80,000	Cash		100,000
Unearned profit on					
sale-leaseback		20,000			
Leased equipment	100,000		Lease receivable		
Lease obligations		100,000	(€13,109 × 15)	196,635	
			Equipment		100,000
			Unearned interest		96,635

* *Assumes new equipment*

To Record First Payment on January 1, 2010

Lessee Corp.			*Lessor Corp.*		
Lease obligations	13,109		Cash	13,109	
Cash		13,109	Lease receivable		13,109

To Record Incurrence and Payment of Executory Costs

Lessee Corp.			*Lessor Corp.*	
Insurance, taxes, etc.	xxx		(No entry)	
Cash (accounts payable)		xxx		

To Record Depreciation Expense on the Equipment, December 31, 2010

Lessee Corp.			*Lessor Corp.*	
Depreciation expense	6,667		(No entry)	
Accum. depr.— capital				
leases (€100,000 ÷ 15)		6,667		

To Amortize Profit on Sale-Leaseback by Lessee Corp., December 31, 2010

Lessee Corp.		*Lessor Corp.*	
Unearned profit on sale-leaseback	1,333	(No entry)	
Depr. expense (€20,000 ÷ 15)		1,333	

To Record Interest for December 31, 2010

Lessee Corp.		*Lessor Corp.*	
Interest expense	10,427	Unearned interest income	10,427
Accrued interest payable	10,427	Interest income	10,427

Partial Lease Amortization Schedule

Date	Cash payment	Interest expense	Reduction of obligation	Lease obligation
Inception of lease				€100,000
January 1, 2010	€13,109	€ --	€13,109	86,891
January 1, 2011	13,109	10,427	2,682	84,209

Leases Involving Real Estate—Guidance under US GAAP

While required practice regarding lease accounting is rather clearly set forth under IAS 17, as is typical under IFRS this is presented in rather general terms. US GAAP, by contrast, offers a great deal of very specific guidance on this topic. It is instructive to at least consider the US GAAP rules for lease accounting, which may provide some further insight and, in some circumstances, offer operational guidance to those attempting to apply IAS 17 to particular fact situations. Under US GAAP (which consists of many discrete standards and a large volume of interpretive literature), leases involving real estate are categorized into four groups:

1. Leases involving land only
2. Leases involving land and building(s)
3. Leases involving real estate and equipment
4. Leases involving only part of a building

Leases Involving Land Only

Lessee accounting. If the lease agreement transfers ownership or contains a bargain purchase option, the lessee should account for the lease as a capital lease and record an asset and related liability in an amount equal to the present value of the minimum lease payments. If the lease agreement does not transfer ownership or contain a bargain purchase option, the lessee should account for the lease as an operating lease.

Lessor accounting. If the lease gives rise to dealer's profit (or loss) and transfers ownership (i.e., title), the standards require that the lease shall be classified as a sales-type lease and accounted for under the provisions of the US standard dealing with sales of real estate, in the same manner as would a seller of the same property. If the lease transfers ownership, both the collectibility and the no material uncertainties criteria are met, but if it does not give rise to dealer's profit (or loss), the lease should be accounted for as a direct financing or leveraged lease, as appropriate. If the lease contains a bargain purchase option and both the collectibility and no material uncertainties criteria are met, the lease should be accounted for as a direct financing, leveraged, or operating lease as appropriate. If the lease does not meet the collectibility and/or no material uncertainties criteria, the lease should be accounted for as an operating lease.

Leases Involving Land and Building

Lessee accounting. Under US GAAP, if the agreement transfers title or contains a bargain purchase option, the lessee should account for the agreement by separating the land and building components and capitalize each separately. The land and building elements should be allocated on the basis of their relative fair market values measured at the inception of the lease. The land and building components are accounted for separately because the lessee is expected to own the real estate by the end of the lease term. The building should be depreciated over its estimated useful life without regard to the lease term.

When the lease agreement neither transfers title nor contains a bargain purchase option, the fair value of the land must be determined in relation to the fair value of the aggregate properties included in the lease agreement. If the fair value of the land is less than 25% of the fair value of the leased properties in aggregate, the land is considered immaterial. Conversely, if the fair value of the land is 25% or greater of the fair value of the leased properties in aggregate, the land is considered material.

When the land component of the lease agreement is considered immaterial (FMV land < 25% total FMV), the lease should be accounted for as a single lease unit. The lessee should capitalize the lease if one of the following occurs:

1. The term of the lease is 75% or more of the economic useful life of the real estate
2. The present value of the minimum lease payments equals 90% or more of the fair market value of the leased real estate less any lessor tax credits

If neither of the two criteria above is met, the lessee should account for the lease agreement as a single operating lease.

When the land component of the lease agreement is considered material (FMV land ≥ 25% total FMV), the land and building components should be separated. By applying the lessee's incremental borrowing rate to the fair market value of the land, the annual minimum lease payment attributed to land is computed. The remaining payments are attributed to the building. The division of minimum lease payments between land and building is essential for both the lessee and lessor. The lease involving the land should *always* be accounted for as an operating lease. Under US GAAP, the lease involving the building(s) must meet either the 75% (of useful life) or 90% (of fair value) test to be treated as a capital lease. If neither of the two criteria is met, the building(s) will also be accounted for as an operating lease.

Lessor accounting. The lessor's accounting depends on whether the lease transfers ownership, contains a bargain purchase option, or does neither of the two. If the lease transfers ownership and gives rise to dealer's profit (or loss), US GAAP requires that the lessor classify the lease as a sales-type lease and account for the lease as a single unit under the provisions of FAS 66 in the same manner as a seller of the same property. If the lease transfers ownership, meets both the collectibility and no important uncertainties criteria, but does not give rise to dealer's profit (or loss), the lease should be accounted for as a direct financing or leveraged lease as appropriate.

If the lease contains a bargain purchase option and gives rise to dealer's profit (or loss), the lease should be classified as an operating lease. If the lease contains a bargain purchase option, meets both the collectibility and no material uncertainties criteria, but does not give rise to dealer's profit (or loss), the lease should be accounted for as a direct financing lease or a leveraged lease, as appropriate.

If the lease agreement neither transfers ownership nor contains a bargain purchase option, the lessor should follow the same rules as the lessee in accounting for real estate leases involving land and building(s).

However, the collectibility and the no material uncertainties criteria must be met before the lessor can account for the agreement as a direct financing lease, and in no such case may the lease be classified as a sales-type lease (i.e., ownership must be transferred).

The treatment of a lease involving both land and building can be illustrated in the following examples.

Example of accounting for land and building lease containing transfer of title

Assume the following:

1. The lessee enters into a ten-year noncancelable lease for a parcel of land and a building for use in its operations. The building has an estimated useful life of 12 years.
2. The FMV of the land is €75,000, while the FMV of the building is €310,000.
3. A payment of €50,000 is due to the lessor at the beginning of each of the 10 years of the lease.
4. The lessee's incremental borrowing rate is 10%. (Lessor's implicit rate is unknown.)
5. Ownership will transfer to the lessee at the end of the lease.

The present value of the minimum lease payments is €337,951 (€50,000 × 6.75902*). The portion of the present value of the minimum lease payments that should be capitalized for each of the two components of the lease is computed as follows:

FMV of land		€ 75,000
FMV of building		310,000
Total FMV of leased property		€385,000
Portion of PV allocated to land	€337,951 × $\frac{75,000}{385,000}$ =	€ 65,835
Portion of PV allocated to building	€337,951 × $\frac{310,000}{385,000}$ =	272,116
Total PV to be capitalized		€337,951

The entry made to record the lease initially is as follows:

Leased land	65,835	
Leased building	272,116	
Lease obligation		337,951

* *6.75902 is the PV of an annuity due for ten periods at 10%.*

Subsequently, the obligation will be decreased in accordance with the effective interest method. The leased building will be amortized over its expected useful life.

Example of accounting for land and building lease without transfer of title or bargain purchase option

Assume the same facts as in the previous example except that title does not transfer at the end of the lease.

The lease is still a capital lease because the lease term is more than 75% of the useful life. Since the FMV of the land is less than 25% of the leased properties in aggregate, (€75,000/€385,000 = 19%), the land component is considered immaterial and the lease will be accounted for as a single lease. The entry to record the lease is as follows:

Leased property	337,951	
Lease obligation		337,951

Assume the same facts as in the previous example except that the FMV of the land is €110,000 and the FMV of the building is €275,000. Once again, title does not transfer.

Because the FMV of the land exceeds 25% of the leased properties in aggregate (€110,000/€385,000 = 28%), the land component is considered material and the lease would be separated into two components. The annual minimum lease payment attributed to the land is computed as follows:

$$\frac{\text{FMV of land}}{\text{PV factor}} \qquad \frac{€100,000}{6.75902^*} = €16,275$$

The remaining portion of the annual payment is attributed to the building.

Annual payment	€ 50,000
Less amount attributed to land	(16,275)
Annual payment attributed to building	€33,725

The present value of the minimum annual lease payments attributed to the building is then computed as follows:

Minimum annual lease payment attributed to building	€ 33,725
PV factor	× 6.75902*
PV of minimum annual lease payments attributed to building	€227,948

The entry to record the capital portion of the lease is as follows:

Leased building	227,948	
Lease obligation		227,948

* *6.75902 is the PV of an annuity due for ten periods at 10%.*

There would be no computation of the present value of the minimum annual lease payment attributed to the land since the land component of the lease will be treated as an operating lease. For this reason, each year, €16,275 of the €50,000 lease payment will be recorded as land rental expense. The remainder of the annual payment (€33,725) will be applied against the lease obligation using the effective interest method.

Leases involving real estate and equipment. When real estate leases also involve equipment or machinery, the equipment component should be separated and accounted for as a separate lease agreement by both lessees and lessors. According to US GAAP, "the portion of the minimum lease payments applicable to the equipment element of the lease shall be estimated by whatever means are appropriate in the circumstances." The lessee and lessor should apply the capitalization requirements to the equipment lease independently of accounting for the real estate lease(s). The real estate leases should be handled as discussed in the preceding two sections. In a sale-leaseback transaction involving real estate with equipment, the equipment and land are not separated.

Leases involving only part of a building. It is common to find lease agreements that involve only part of a building, as, for example, when a floor of an office building is leased or when a store in a shopping mall is leased. A difficulty that arises in this situation is that the cost and/or fair market value of the leased portion of the whole may not be determinable objectively.

TREATMENT OF SELECTED ITEMS IN ACCOUNTING FOR LEASES UNDER US GAAP

	Lessor		Lessee	
	Operating	*Direct financing and sales-type*	*Operating*	*Capital*
Initial direct costs	Capitalize and amortize over lease term in proportion to rent revenue recognized (normally SL basis)	Direct financing: Record in separate account Add to net investment in lease Compute new effective rate that equates gross amt. of min. lease payments and unguar. residual value with net invest. Amortize so as to produce constant rate of return over lease term Sales-type: Expense in period incurred	N/A	N/A
Investment tax credit retained by lessor	N/A	Reduces FMV of leased asset for 90% test	N/A	Reduces FMV of leased asset for 90% test
Bargain purchase option	N/A	Include in: Minimum lease payments 90% test	N/A	Include in: Minimum lease payments 90% test
Guaranteed residual value	N/A	Include in: Minimum lease payments 90% test Sales-type: Include PV in sales revenues	N/A	Include in: Minimum lease payments 90% test
Unguaranteed residual value	N/A	Include in: "Gross Investment in Lease" Not included in: 90% test Sales-type: Exclude from sales revenue Deduct PV from cost of sales	N/A	Include in: Minimum lease payments 90% test
Contingent rentals	Revenue in period earned	Not part of minimum lease payments; revenue in period earned	Expense in period incurred	Not part of minimum lease payments; expense in period incurred
Amortization period	Amortize down to estimated residual value over estimated economic life of asset	N/A	N/A	Amortize down to estimated residual value over lease term or estimated economic life[c]
Revenue (expense)[a]	Rent revenue (normally SL basis) Amortization (depreciation expense)	Direct financing: Interest revenue on net investment in lease (gross investment less unearned interest income) Sales-type: Dealer profit in period of sale (sales revenue less cost of leased asset) Interest revenue on net investment in lease	Rent expense (normally SL basis)[b]	Interest expense and depreciation expense

[a] Elements of revenue (expense) listed for the items above are not repeated here (e.g., treatment of initial direct costs).

[b] If payments are not on a SL basis, recognize rent expense on a SL basis unless another systematic and rational method is more representative of use benefit obtained from the property, in which case, the other method should be used.

[c] If lease has automatic passage of title or bargain purchase option, use estimated economic life; otherwise, use the lease term.

For the lessee, if the fair value of the leased property is objectively determinable, the lessee should follow the rules and account for the lease as described in "leases involving land and building." If the fair value of the leased property cannot be determined objectively but the agreement satisfies the 75% test, the estimated economic life of the building in which the leased premises are located should be used. If this test is not met, the lessee should account for the agreement as an operating lease.

From the lessor's position, both the cost and fair value of the leased property must be objectively determinable before the procedures described under "leases involving land and building" will apply. If either the cost or the fair value cannot be determined objectively, the lessor should account for the agreement as an operating lease.

Termination of a Lease

The lessor shall remove the remaining net investment from his or her books and record the leased equipment as an asset at the lower of its original cost, present fair value, or current carrying value. The net adjustment is reflected in income of the current period.

The lessee is also affected by the terminated agreement because he or she has been relieved of the obligation. If the lease is a capital lease, the lessee should remove both the obligation and the asset from his or her accounts and charge any adjustment to the current period income. If accounted for as an operating lease, no accounting adjustment is required.

Renewal or Extension of an Existing Lease

The renewal or extension of an existing lease agreement affects the accounting of both the lessee and the lessor. US GAAP specifies two basic situations in this regard: (1) the renewal occurs and makes a residual guarantee or penalty provision inoperative or (2) the renewal agreement does not do the foregoing and the renewal is to be treated as a new agreement. The accounting treatment prescribed under the latter situation for a lessee is as follows:

1. If the renewal or extension is classified as a capital lease, the (present) current balances of the asset and related obligation should be adjusted by an amount equal to the difference between the present value of the future minimum lease payments under the revised agreement and the (present) current balance of the obligation. The present value of the minimum lease payments under the revised agreement should be computed using the interest rate that was in effect at the inception of the original lease.
2. If the renewal or extension is classified as an operating lease, the current balances in the asset and liability accounts are removed from the books and a gain (loss) recognized for the difference. The new lease agreement resulting from a renewal or extension is accounted for in the same manner as other operating leases.

Under the same circumstances, US GAAP prescribes the following treatment to be followed by the lessor:

1. If the renewal or extension is classified as a direct financing lease, then the existing balances of the lease receivable and the estimated residual value accounts should be adjusted for the changes resulting from the revised agreement.

NOTE: Remember that an upward adjustment of the estimated residual value is not allowed.

The net adjustment should be charged or credited to an unearned income account.

2. If the renewal or extension is classified as an operating lease, the remaining net investment under the existing sales-type lease or direct financing lease is removed from the books and the leased asset recorded as an asset at the lower of its original cost, present fair value, or current carrying amount. The difference between the net investment and the amount recorded for the leased asset is charged to profit or loss of the period. The renewal or extension is then accounted for as for any other operating lease.

3. If the renewal or extension is classified as a sales-type lease *and* it occurs at or near the end of the existing lease term, the renewal or extension should be accounted for as a sales-type lease.

NOTE: A renewal or extension that occurs in the last few months of an existing lease is considered to have occurred at or near the end of the existing lease term.

If the renewal or extension causes the guarantee or penalty provision to be inoperative, the lessee adjusts the current balance of the leased asset and the lease obligation to the present value of the future minimum lease payments (according to the relevant standard, "by an amount equal to the difference between the PV of future minimum lease payments under the revised agreement and the present balance of the obligation"). The PV of the future minimum lease payments is computed using the implicit rate used in the original lease agreement.

Given the same circumstances, the lessor adjusts the existing balance of the lease receivable and estimated residual value accounts to reflect the changes of the revised agreement (remember, no upward adjustments to the residual value). The net adjustment is charged (or credited) to unearned income.

Leases between Related Parties

Leases between related parties are classified and accounted for as though the parties are unrelated, except in cases where it is clear that the terms and conditions of the agreement have been influenced significantly by the fact of the relationship. When this is the case, the classification and/or accounting is modified to reflect the true economic substance of the transaction rather than the legal form.

If a subsidiary's principal business activity is leasing property to its parent or other affiliated companies, consolidated financial statements are presented. The US GAAP standard on related parties requires that the nature and extent of leasing activities between related parties be disclosed.

Accounting for Leases in a Business Combination

A business combination, in and of itself, has no effect on the classification of a lease. However, if, in connection with a business combination, the lease agreement is modified to change the original classification of the lease, it should be considered a new agreement and reclassified according to the revised provisions.

In most cases, a business combination that is accounted for by the pooling-of-interest method or by the purchase method will not affect the previous classification of a lease unless the provisions have been modified as indicated in the preceding paragraph.

The acquiring company should apply the following procedures to account for a leveraged lease in a business combination accounted for by the purchase method:

1. The classification of leveraged lease should be kept.
2. The net investment in the leveraged lease should be given a fair market value (present value, net of tax) based on the remaining future cash flows. Also, the estimated tax effects of the cash flows should be given recognition.
3. The net investment should be broken down into three components: net rentals receivable, estimated residual value, and unearned income.
4. Thereafter, the leveraged lease should be accounted for as described above in the section on leveraged leases.

Sale or Assignment to Third Parties—Nonrecourse Financing

The sale or assignment of a lease or of property subject to a lease that was originally accounted for as a sales-type lease or a direct financing lease will not affect the original accounting treatment of the lease. Any profit or loss on the sale or assignment should be recognized at the time of transaction except under the following two circumstances:

1. When the sale or assignment is between related parties, apply the provisions presented above under "Leases between Related Parties."
2. When the sale or assignment is with recourse, it should be accounted for using the provisions of the US GAAP standard on sale of receivables with recourse.

The sale of property subject to an operating lease should not be treated as a sale if the seller (or any related party to the seller) retains substantial risks of ownership in the leased property. A seller may retain substantial risks of ownership by various arrangements. For example, if the lessee defaults on the lease agreement or if the lease terminates, the seller may arrange to do one of the following:

1. Acquire the property or the lease
2. Substitute an existing lease
3. Secure a replacement lessee or a buyer for the property under a remarketing agreement

A seller will not retain substantial risks of ownership by arrangements where one of the following occurs:

1. A remarketing agreement includes a reasonable fee to be paid to the seller
2. The seller is not required to give priority to the releasing or disposition of the property owned by the third party over similar property owned by the seller

When the sale of property subject to an operating lease is not accounted for as a sale because the substantial risk factor is present, it should be accounted for as a borrowing. The proceeds from the sale should be recorded as an obligation on the seller's books. Rental payments made by the lessee under the operating lease should be recorded as revenue by the seller even if the payments are paid to the third-party purchaser. The seller shall account for each rental payment by allocating a portion to interest expense (to be imputed in accordance with the provisions of APB 21), and the remainder will reduce the existing obligation. Other normal accounting procedures for operating leases should be applied except that the depreciation term for the leased asset is limited to the amortization period of the obligation.

The sale or assignment of lease payments under an operating lease by the lessor should be accounted for as a borrowing as described above.

Nonrecourse financing is a common occurrence in the leasing industry whereby the stream of lease payments on a lease is discounted on a nonrecourse basis at a financial institution with the lease payments collateralizing the debt. The proceeds are then used to finance future leasing transactions. Even though the discounting is on a nonrecourse basis, US GAAP prohibits the offsetting of the debt against the related lease receivable unless a legal right of offset exists or the lease qualified as a leveraged lease at its inception.

Money-Over-Money Lease Transactions

In cases where a lessor obtains nonrecourse financing in excess of the leased asset's cost, a technical bulletin states that the borrowing and leasing are separate transactions and should not be offset against each other unless a right of offset exists. Only dealer profit in sales-type leases may be recognized at the beginning of the lease term.

Acquisition of Interest in Residual Value

Recently, there has been an increase in the acquisition of interests in residual values of leased assets by companies whose primary business is other than leasing or financing. This generally occurs through the outright purchase of the right to own the leased asset or the right to receive the proceeds from the sale of a leased asset at the end of its lease term.

In instances such as these, the rights should be recorded by the purchaser at the fair value of the assets surrendered. Recognition of increases in the value of the interest in the residual (i.e., residual value accretion) to the end of the lease term are prohibited. However, a nontemporary write-down of the residual value interest should be recognized as a loss. This guidance also applies to lessors who sell the related minimum lease payments but retain the interest in the residual value. Guaranteed residual values also have no effect on this guidance.

Accounting for a Sublease

A sublease is used to describe the situation where the original lessee re-leases the leased property to a third party (the sublessee), and the original lessee acts as a sublessor. Normally, the nature of a sublease agreement does not affect the original lease agreement, and the original lessee/sublessor retains primary liability.

The original lease remains in effect, and the original lessor continues to account for the lease as before. The original lessee/sublessor accounts for the lease as follows:

1. If the original lease agreement transfers ownership or contains a bargain purchase option and if the new lease meets any one of the four criteria specified in US GAAP (i.e., transfers ownership, BPO, the 75% test, or the 90% test) and both the collectibility and uncertainties criteria, the sublessor should classify the new lease as a sales-type or direct financing lease; otherwise, as an operating lease. In either situation, the original lessee/sublessor should continue accounting for the original lease obligation as before.

2. If the original lease agreement does not transfer ownership or contain a bargain purchase option, but it still qualified as a capital lease, the original lessee/sublessor should (with one exception) apply the usual criteria set by US GAAP in classifying the new agreement as a capital or operating lease. If the new lease qualifies for capital treatment, the original lessee/sublessor should account for it as a direct financing lease, with the unamortized balance of the asset under the original lease being treated as the cost of the leased property. The one exception arises when the circumstances surrounding the sublease suggest that the sublease agreement was an important part of a predetermined plan in which the original lessee played only an intermediate role between the original lessor and the sublessee. In this situation, the sublease should be classified by the 75% and 90% criteria as well as collectibility and uncertainties criteria. In applying the 90% criterion, the fair value for the leased property will be

the fair value to the original lessor at the inception of the original lease. Under all circumstances, the original lessee should continue accounting for the original lease obligation as before. If the new lease agreement (sublease) does not meet the capitalization requirements imposed for subleases, the new lease should be accounted for as an operating lease.

3. If the original lease is an operating lease, the original lessee/sublessor should account for the new lease as an operating lease and account for the original operating lease as before.

APPENDIX B:
LEVERAGED LEASES UNDER US GAAP

One of the most complex accounting subjects regarding leases is the accounting for a leveraged lease. Once again, as with both sales-type and direct financing, the classification of the lease by the lessor has no effect on the accounting treatment accorded the lease by the lessee. The lessee simply treats it as any other lease and thus is interested only in whether the lease qualifies as an operating or a capital lease. The lessor's accounting problem is substantially more complex than that of the lessee.

Leveraged leases are not directly addressed under IFRS. However, such three-party leasing transactions may be encountered occasionally. This guidance under US GAAP is therefore offered to fill a void in IFRS literature.

To qualify as a leveraged lease, a lease agreement must meet the following requirements, and the lessor must account for the investment tax credit (when in effect) in the manner described below.

NOTE: Failure to do so will result in the lease being classified as a direct financing lease.

---

1. The lease must meet the definition of a direct financing lease. (The 90% of FMV criterion does not apply.)[1]
2. The lease must involve at least three parties.

   a. An owner-lessor (equity participant)
   b. A lessee
   c. A long-term creditor (debt participant)

3. The financing provided by the creditor is nonrecourse as to the general credit of the lessor and is sufficient to provide the lessor with substantial leverage.
4. The lessor's net investment (defined below) decreases in the early years and increases in the later years until it is eliminated.

The last characteristic (item 4) poses the accounting problem.

The leveraged lease arose as a result of an effort to maximize the tax benefits associated with a lease transaction. To accomplish this, it was necessary to involve a third party to the lease transaction (in addition to the lessor and lessee), a long-term creditor. The following diagram illustrates the existing relationships in a leveraged lease agreement:

---

[1] *A direct financing lease must have its cost or carrying value equal to the fair value of the asset at the inception of the lease. Thus, even if the amounts are not significantly different, leveraged lease accounting should not be used.*

The leveraged lease arrangement*

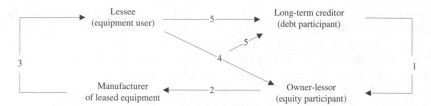

* *Adapted from "A Straightforward Approach to Leveraged Leasing" by Pierce R. Smith,* **The Journal of Commercial Bank Lending***, July 1973, pp. 40-47.*

1. The owner-lessor secures long-term financing from the creditor, generally in excess of 50% of the purchase price. US GAAP indicates that the lessor must be provided with sufficient leverage in the transaction; thus the 50%.
2. The owner then uses this financing along with his or her own funds to purchase the asset from the manufacturer.
3. The manufacturer delivers the asset to the lessee.
4. The lessee remits the periodic rent to the lessor.
5. The debt is guaranteed by either using the equipment as collateral, the assignment of the lease payments, or both, depending on the demands established by the creditor.

The FASB concluded that the entire lease agreement be accounted for as a single transaction and not a direct financing lease plus a debt transaction. The feeling was that the latter did not readily convey the net investment in the lease to the user of the financial statements. Thus, the lessor is to record the investment as a net amount. The gross investment is calculated as a combination of the following amounts:

1. The rentals receivable from the lessee, net of the principal and interest payments due to the long-term creditor
2. A receivable for the amount of the investment tax credit (ITC) to be realized on the transaction (repealed in the United States but may yet exist in other jurisdictions)
3. The estimated residual value of the leased asset
4. The unearned and deferred income, consisting of

   a. The estimated pretax lease income (or loss), after deducting initial direct costs, remaining to be allocated to income
   b. The ITC remaining to be allocated to profit or loss over the remaining term of the lease

The first three amounts described above are readily obtainable; however, the last amount, the unearned and deferred income, requires additional computations. To derive this amount, it is necessary to create a cash flow (income) analysis by year for the entire lease term. As described in item 4 above, the unearned and deferred income consists of the pretax lease income (Gross lease rentals – Depreciation – Loan interest) and the unamortized investment tax credit. The total of these two amounts for all the periods in the lease term represents the unearned and deferred income at the inception of the lease.

The amount computed as the gross investment in the lease (foregoing paragraphs) less the deferred taxes relative to the difference between pretax lease income and taxable lease income is the net investment for purposes of computing profit or loss for the period. To compute the periodic profit or loss, another schedule must be completed that uses the cash flows derived in the first schedule and allocates them between income and a reduction in the net investment.

The amount of profit or loss is first determined by applying a rate to the net investment. The rate to be used is the rate that will allocate the entire amount of cash flow (income) when applied in the years in which the net investment is positive. In other words, the rate is derived in much the same way as the implicit rate (trial and error), except that only the years in which there is a positive net investment are considered. Thus, income is recognized only in the years in which there is a positive net investment.

The profit or loss recognized is divided among the following three elements:

1. Pretax accounting income
2. Amortization of investment tax credit
3. The tax effect of the pretax accounting income

The first two are allocated in proportionate amounts from the unearned and deferred income included in calculation of the net investment. In other words, the unearned and deferred income consists of pretax lease accounting income and any investment tax credit. Each of these is recognized during the period in the proportion that the current period's allocated income is to the total income (cash flow). The last item, the tax effect, is recognized in the tax expense for the year. The tax effect of any difference between pretax lease accounting income and taxable lease income is charged (or credited) to deferred taxes.

When tax rates change, all components of a leveraged lease must be recalculated from the inception of the lease, using the revised after-tax cash flows arising from the revised tax rates.

If, in any case, the projected cash receipts (income) are less than the initial investment, the deficiency is to be recognized as a loss at the inception of the lease. Similarly, if at any time during the lease period the aforementioned method of recognizing income would result in a future period loss, the loss shall be recognized immediately.

This situation may arise as a result of the circumstances surrounding the lease changing. Therefore, any estimated residual value and other important assumptions must be reviewed on a periodic basis (at least annually). Any change is to be incorporated into the income computations; however, there is to be no upward revision of the estimated residual value.

The following example illustrates the application of these principles to a leveraged lease.

Example of simplified leveraged lease

Assume the following:

1. A lessor acquires an asset for €100,000 with an estimated useful life of 3 years in exchange for a €25,000 down payment and a €75,000 3-year note with equal payments due on December 31 each year. The interest rate is 18%.
2. The asset has no residual value.
3. The PV of an ordinary annuity of €1 for three years at 18% is 2.17427.
4. The asset is leased for 3 years with annual payments due to the lessor on December 31 in the amount of €45,000.
5. The lessor uses the ACRS method of depreciation for tax purposes and elects to reduce the ITC rate to 4%, as opposed to reducing the depreciable basis.
6. Assume a constant tax rate throughout the life of the lease of 40%.

Chart 1 analyzes the cash flows generated by the leveraged leasing activities. Chart 2 allocates the cash flows between the investment in leveraged leased assets and income from leveraged leasing activities. The allocation requires finding that rate of return which, when applied to the investment balance at the beginning of each year that the investment amount is positive, will allocate the net cash flow fully to net income over the term of the lease. This rate can be found only by a computer program or by an iterative trial-and-error process. The example that follows has a positive investment value in each of the three years, and thus the allocation takes place in each time period. Leveraged leases usually have periods where the investment account turns negative and is below zero.

Allocating principal and interest on the loan payments is as follows:

$$€75,000 \div 2.17427 = €34,494$$

Year	Payment	Interest 18%	Principal	Balance
Inception of lease	€ --	€ --	€ --	€75,000
1	34,494	13,500	20,994	54,006
2	34,494	9,721	24,773	29,233
3	34,494	5,261	29,233	--

Chart 1

	A	B	C	D	E	F	G	H	I
					Income tax			Cash	
				Taxable	payable	Loan		flow	Cumulative
			Interest	income	(rcvbl.)	principal		(A+G-C	cash
	Rent	Depr.	on loan	(A-B-C)	Dx40%	payments	ITC	-E-F)	flow
Initial	€ --	€ --	€ --	€ --	€ --	€ --	€ --	€(25,000)	€(25,000)
Year 1	45,000	25,000	13,500	6,500	2,600	20,994	4,000	11,906	(13,094)
Year 2	45,000	38,000	9,721	(2,721)	(1,088)	24,773	--	11,594	(1,500)
Year 3	45,000	37,000	5,261	2,739	1,096	29,233	--	9,410	7,910
Total	€135,000	€100,000	€28,482	€ 6,518	€ 2,608	€75,000	€4,000	€ 7,910	

The chart below allocates the cash flows determined above between the net investment in the lease and income. Recall that the income is then allocated between pretax accounting income and the amortization of the investment for credit. The income tax expense for the period is a result of applying the tax rate to the current periodic pretax accounting income.

The amount to be allocated in total in each period is the net cash flow determined in column H above. The investment at the beginning of year 1 is the initial down payment of €25,000. This investment is then reduced on an annual basis by the amount of the cash flow not allocated to income.

Chart 2

	1	2	3	4	5	6	7
		Cash Flow Assumption				Income Analysis	
	Investment		Allocated	Allocated		Income	Investment
	beginning	Cash	to	to	Pretax	tax	tax
	of year	flow	investment	income	income	expense	credit
Year 1	€25,000	€11,906	€ 7,964	€ 3,942	€3,248	€1,300	€1,994
Year 2	17,036	11,594	8,908	2,686	2,213	885	1,358
Year 3	8,128	9,410	8,128	1,282	1,057	423	648
		€32,910	€25,000	€7,910	€6,518	€2,608	€4,000
		Rate of return = 15.77%					

1. Column 2 is the net cash flow after the initial investment, and Columns 3 and 4 are the allocation based on the 15.77% rate of return. The total of Column 4 is the same as the total of Column H in Chart 1.
2. Column 5 allocates Column D in Chart 1 based on the allocations in Column 4. Column 6 allocates Column E in Chart 1, and Column 7 allocates Column G in Chart 1 in the same basis.

The journal entries below illustrate the proper recording and accounting for the leveraged lease transaction. The initial entry represents the cash down payment, investment tax credit receivable, the unearned and deferred revenue, and the net cash to be received over the term of the lease.

The remaining journal entries recognize the annual transactions that include the net receipt of cash and the amortization of income.

	Year 1	Year 2	Year 3
Rents receivable [Chart 1 (A-C-F)]	31,518		
Investment tax credit receivable	4,000		
Cash		25,000	
Unearned and deferred income		10,518	
[Initial investment, Chart 2 (5+7) totals]			
Cash	10,506	10,506	10,506
Rent receivable		10,506	10,506	10,506
[Net for all cash transactions, Chart 1 (A-C-F) line by line for each year]			
Income tax receivable (cash)	4,000		
Investment tax credit receivable		4,000	
Unearned and deferred income	5,242	3,571	1,705
Income from leveraged leases		5,242	3,571	1,705
[Amortization of unearned income, Chart 2 (5+7) line by line for each year]			

The following schedules illustrate the computation of deferred income tax amount. The annual amount is a result of the temporary difference created due to the difference in the timing of the recognition of income for book and tax purposes. The income for tax purposes can be found in Column D in Chart 1, while the income for book purposes is found in Column 5 of Chart 2. The actual amount of deferred tax is the difference between the tax computed with the temporary difference and the tax computed without the temporary difference. These amounts are represented by the income tax payable or receivable as shown in Column E of Chart 1 and the income tax expense as shown in Column 6 of Chart 2. A check of this figure is provided by multiplying the difference between book and tax income by the annual rate.

Year 1

Income tax payable	€ 2,600	
Income tax expense	(1,300)	
Deferred income tax (Dr)		€1,300
Taxable income	€ 6,500	
Pretax accounting income	(3,248)	
Difference	€ 3,252	

$€3,252 \times 40\% = €1,300$

Year 2

Income tax receivable	€ 1,088	
Income tax expense	885	
Deferred income tax (Cr)		€1,973
Taxable loss	€ 2,721	
Pretax accounting income	2,213	
Difference	€ 4,934	

$€4,934 \times 40\% = €1,973$

Year 3

Income tax payable	€ 1,096	
Income tax expense	(423)	
Deferred income tax (Dr)		€ 673
Taxable income	€ 2,739	
Pretax accounting income	(1,057)	
Difference	€ 1,682	

$€1,682 \times 40\% = €673$

23 FOREIGN CURRENCY

INTRODUCTION

International trade continues to become more prevalent, and "multinational corporations" (MNC), now comprised not only of the international giants which are household names, but also many midtier companies. Corporations worldwide are reaching beyond national boundaries and engaging in international trade. Global economic restructuring is rampant: trade pacts such as GATT, NAFTA, and the World Trade Organization (WTO) have lent further impetus to the process of internationalization. International activity by most domestic corporations has increased significantly, which means that transactions are consummated not only with independent foreign entities but also with foreign subsidiaries.

Foreign subsidiaries, associates, and branches often handle their accounts and prepare financial statements in the respective currencies of the countries in which they are located. Thus, it is more than likely that a MNC ends up receiving, at year-end, financial statements from various foreign subsidiaries expressed in a number of foreign currencies, such as dollars, euros, pounds, lira, dinars, won, rubles, rands, and yen. However, for users of these financial statements to analyze the MNC's foreign involvement and overall financial position and results of operations properly, foreign-currency-denominated financial statements must first be expressed in terms that the users can understand. This means that the foreign currency financial statements of the various subsidiaries will have to be translated into the currency of the country where the MNC is registered or has its major operations.

In addition to foreign operations, an entity may have foreign currency transactions (e.g., export and import transactions denominated in the foreign currency). These give rise to other financial reporting implications, which are also addressed in this chapter. Note that even a purely domestic company may have transactions (e.g., with foreign suppliers or customer) denominated in foreign currencies, and these same guidelines will apply in those circumstances, as well.

IFRS governing the translation of foreign currency financial statements and the accounting for foreign currency transactions are found primarily in IAS 21, *The Effects of Changes in Foreign Exchange Rates*. IAS 21 applies to

1. Accounting for foreign currency transactions (e.g., exports, imports, and loans) which are denominated in other than the reporting entity's functional currency
2. Translation of foreign currency financial statements of branches, divisions, subsidiaries, and other investees that are incorporated in the financial statements of an entity by consolidation, proportionate consolidation, or the equity method of accounting

AMENDMENTS EFFECTIVE IN THE CURRENT PERIOD

As part of the *Improvements to IFRS* published in May 2010, the IASB amended the effective date relating to the accounting for disposals or partial disposals of foreign operations from July 1, 2009, to July 1, 2010.

DEFINITIONS OF TERMS

Closing rate. This refers to the spot exchange rate (defined below) at the end of the reporting period.

Conversion. The exchange of one currency for another.

Exchange difference. The difference resulting from reporting the same number of units of a foreign currency in the presentation currency at different exchange rates.

Exchange rate. This refers to the ratio for exchange between two currencies.

Fair value. The amount for which an asset could be exchanged, or a liability could be settled, between knowledgeable willing parties in an arm's-length transaction.

Foreign currency. A currency other than the functional currency of the reporting entity (e.g., the Japanese yen is a foreign currency for a Euro-reporting entity).

Foreign currency financial statements. Financial statements that employ as the unit of measure a foreign currency that is not the presentation currency of the entity.

Foreign currency transactions. Transactions whose terms are denominated in a foreign currency or require settlement in a foreign currency. Foreign currency transactions arise when an entity

1. Buys or sells goods or services whose prices are denominated in foreign currency,
2. Borrows or lends funds and the amounts payable or receivable are denominated in foreign currency,
3. Is a party to an unperformed foreign exchange contract, or
4. For other reasons acquires or disposes of assets or incurs or settles liabilities denominated in foreign currency.

Foreign currency translation. The process of expressing in the presentation currency of the entity amounts that are denominated or measured in a different currency.

Foreign entity. When the activities of a foreign operation are not an integral part of those of the reporting entity, such a foreign operation is referred to as a foreign entity.

Foreign operation. A foreign subsidiary, associate, joint venture, or branch of the reporting entity whose activities are based or conducted in a country other than the country where the reporting entity is domiciled.

Functional currency. The currency of the primary economic environment in which the entity operates, which thus is the currency in which the reporting entity measures the items in its financial statements, and which may differ from the presentation currency in some instances.

Group. A parent company and all of its subsidiaries.

Monetary items. Money held and assets and liabilities to be received or paid in fixed or determinable amounts of money.

Net investment in a foreign operation. The amount refers to the reporting entity's interest in the net assets of that foreign operation.

Nonmonetary items. All items presented in the statement of financial position other than cash, claims to cash, and cash obligations.

Presentation currency. The currency in which the reporting entity's financial statements are presented. There is no limitation on the selection of a presentation currency by a reporting entity.

Reporting entity. An entity or group whose financial statements are being referred to. Under this standard, those financial statements reflect (1) the financial statements of one or more foreign operations by consolidation, proportionate consolidation, or equity accounting; (2) foreign currency transactions; or (3) both of the foregoing.

Spot exchange rate. The exchange rate for immediate delivery of currencies exchanged.

Transaction date. In the context of recognition of exchange differences from settlement of monetary items arising from foreign currency transactions, transaction date refers to the date at which a foreign currency transaction (e.g., a sale or purchase of merchandise or services the settlement for which will be in a foreign currency) occurs and is recorded in the accounting records.

SCOPE, OBJECTIVES, AND DISCUSSION OF DEFINITIONS

The objective of IAS 21 is to prescribe (1) how to include foreign currency transactions and foreign operations in the financial statements of an entity, and (2) how to translate financial statements into a presentation currency. The scope of IAS 21 applies to

1. Accounting for transactions and balances in foreign currencies, except for those derivative transactions and balances that are within the scope of IAS 39, *Financial Instruments: Recognition and Measurement.* However, those foreign currency derivatives that are not within the scope of IAS 39 (e.g., some foreign currency derivatives that are embedded in other contracts), and the translation of amounts relating to derivatives from its functional currency to its presentation currency are within the scope of this standard;
2. Translating the financial position and financial results of *foreign operations* that are included in the financial statements of the reporting entity as a result of consolidation, proportionate consolidation or the equity method; and

3. Translating an entity's financial statements into a *presentation currency*.

IAS 21 does not apply to the presentation, in the statement of cash flows, of cash flows arising from transactions in a foreign currency, or to the translation of cash flows of a foreign operation, which are within the scope of IAS 7, *Statement of Cash Flows*.

Functional Currency

The concept of *functional currency* is key to understanding translation of foreign currency financial statements. Functional currency is defined as being the currency of the primary economic environment in which an entity operates. This is normally, but not necessarily, the currency in which that entity principally generates and expends cash.

In determining the relevant functional currency, an entity would give primary consideration to the following factors:

1. The currency that mainly influences sales prices for goods and services, as well as the currency of the country whose competitive forces and regulations mainly determine the sales prices of the entity's goods and services, and
2. The currency that primarily influences labor, material, and other costs of providing those goods or services.

Note that the currency which influences selling prices is often that currency in which sales prices are denominated and settled, while the currency that most influences the various input costs is normally that in which input costs are denominated and settled. There are many situations in which input costs and output prices will be denominated in or influenced by differing currencies (e.g., an entity which manufactures all of its goods in Mexico, using locally sourced labor and materials, but sells all or most of its output in Europe in euro-denominated transactions).

In addition to the foregoing, IAS 21 notes other factors which may provide additional evidence of an entity's functional currency. These may be deemed secondary considerations, and these are

1. The currency in which funds from financing activities (i.e., from the issuance of debt and equity instruments) are generated, and
2. The currency in which receipts from operating activities are usually retained.

In making a determination of whether the functional currency of a foreign operation (e.g., a subsidiary, branch, associate, or joint venture) is the same as that of the reporting entity (parent, investor, etc.), certain additional considerations may also be relevant. These include

1. Whether the activities of the foreign operation are carried out as an extension of the reporting entity, rather than being executed more or less autonomously;
2. What proportion of the foreign operation's activities is comprised of transactions with the reporting entity;
3. Whether the foreign operation's cash flows directly impact upon the cash flows of the reporting entity, and are available for prompt remittance to the reporting entity; and
4. Whether the foreign operation is largely cash flow independent (i.e., if its own cash flows are sufficient to service its existing and reasonably anticipated debts without the injection of funds by the reporting entity).

Foreign operations are characterized as being adjuncts of the operations of the reporting entity when, for example, the foreign operation only serves to sell goods imported from the reporting entity and in turn remits all sales proceeds to the reporting entity. On the other hand, the foreign operation is seen as being essentially autonomous when it accumulates cash and other monetary items, incurs expenses, generates income and arranges borrowings, all done substantially in its local currency.

In practice, there are many gradations along the continuum between full autonomy and the state of being a mere adjunct to the reporting entity's operations. When there are mixed indications, and thus the identity of the functional currency is not obvious, judgment is required to make this determination. The selection of the functional currency should most faithfully represent the economic effects of the underlying transactions, events and conditions. According to IAS 21, however, priority attention is to be given to the identity of the currency (or currencies) that impact selling prices for outputs of goods and services, and inputs for labor and materials and other costs. The other factors noted above are to be referred to secondarily, when a clear conclusion is not apparent from considering the two primary factors.

Example

    A US-based company, Majordomo, Inc., has a major subsidiary located in the UK, John Bull Co., which produces and sells goods to customers almost exclusively in EU member states. Transactions are effected primarily in euros, both for sales and, to a lesser extent, for raw materials purchases. The functional currency is determined to be euros in this instance, given the facts noted. Transactions are to be measured in euros, accordingly. For purposes of the John Bull Co.'s stand-alone financial reporting, euro-based financial data will be translated into pounds Sterling, using the translation rules set forth in revised IAS 21. For consolidation of the UK subsidiary into the financial statements of parent entity Majordomo, Inc., translation into US dollars will be required, again using the procedures defined in the standard.

In some cases the determination of functional currency can be complex and time-consuming. The process is difficult especially if the foreign operation acts as an investment company or holding company within a group and has few external transactions. Management must document the approach followed in the determination of the functional currency for each entity within a group— particularly when factors are mixed and judgment is required.

Once determined, an entity's functional currency will rarely be altered. However, since the entity's functional currency is expected to reflect its most significant underlying transactions, events and conditions, there obviously can be a change in functional currency if there are fundamental changes in those circumstances. For example, if the entity's manufacturing and sales operations are relocated to another country, and inputs are thereafter sourced from that new location, this may justify changing the functional currency for that operation. When there is a change in an entity's functional currency, the entity should apply the translation procedures applicable to the new functional currency *prospectively* from the date of the change.

If the functional currency is the currency of a hyperinflationary economy, as that term is defined under IAS 29, *Financial Reporting in Hyperinflationary Economies*, the entity's financial statements are restated in accordance with the provisions of that standard. IAS 21 stresses that an entity cannot avert such restatement by employing tactics such as adopting an alternate functional currency, such as that of its parent entity. There are currently very few such economies in the world, but this situation of course may change in the future. There are also instances that have been noted where economies have experienced severe hyperinflation and have been unable to restate their financial statements in terms of the procedures required by IAS 29 due to the unavailability of reliable information on restatement factors. The difficulties experienced by reporters in such jurisdictions have been noted by the IASB, and a project is currently underway to address the accounting that should be followed in such scenarios.

Monetary and Nonmonetary Items

For purposes of applying IAS 21, it is important to understand the distinction between monetary and nonmonetary items. Monetary items are those granting or imposing "a right to receive, or an obligation to deliver, a fixed or determinable number of units of currency." In contrast, nonmonetary items are those exhibiting "the absence of a right to receive, or an obligation to deliver, a fixed or determinable number of units of currency." Examples of monetary items include accounts and notes receivable; pensions and other employee benefits to be paid in cash; provisions that are to be settled in cash; and cash dividends that are properly recognized as a liability. Examples of nonmonetary items include inventories; amounts prepaid for goods and services (e.g., prepaid insurance); property, plant, and equipment; goodwill; other intangible assets; and provisions that are to be settled by the delivery of a nonmonetary asset.

FOREIGN CURRENCY TRANSACTIONS

Foreign Currency Transactions

Foreign currency transactions are those denominated in, or requiring settlement in, a foreign currency. These can include such common transactions as those arising from

1. The purchase or sale of goods or services in transactions where the price is denominated in a foreign currency.
2. The borrowing or lending of funds, where the amounts owed or to be received are denominated in a foreign currency; or
3. Other routine activities such as the acquisition or disposal of assets, or the incurring or settlement of liabilities, if denominated in a foreign currency.

Under the provisions of IAS 21, foreign currency transactions are to be initially recorded in the functional currency by applying to the foreign-currency-denominated amounts the spot exchange rate between the functional currency and the foreign currency at the date of the transaction. However, when there are numerous, relatively homogeneous transactions over the course of the reporting period (e.g., year), it is acceptable, and much more practical, to apply an appropriate average exchange rate provided such an average would approximate the spot rates applicable. In the simplest scenario, the simple numerical average (i.e., the midpoint between the beginning and ending exchange rates) could be used. Care must be exercised to ensure that such a simplistic approach is actually meaningful, however.

If exchange rate movements do not smoothly occur throughout the reporting period, or if rates move alternately up and down over the reporting interval, rather than monotonically up or down, then a more carefully constructed, weighted-average exchange rate should be used. Also, if transactions occur in other than a smooth pattern over the period—as might be the case for products characterized by seasonal sales—then a weighted-average exchange rate might be needed if exchange rates have moved materially over the course of the reporting period. For example, if the bulk of revenues is generated in the fourth quarter, the annual average exchange rate would probably not result in an accurately translated statement of comprehensive income.

Example

Continuing the preceding example, the UK-based subsidiary, John Bull, which produces and sells goods to customers almost exclusively in EU member states, also had sizeable sales to a Swiss company in 2010, denominated in Swiss francs. These occurred primarily in the fourth quarter of the year, when the Swiss franc-euro exchange rate was atypically strong. In converting these sales to the functional currency (euros), the average exchange rate in the fourth quarter was deemed to be most relevant.

Subsequent to the date of the underlying transaction, there may be a continuing need to translate the foreign-currency-denominated event into the entity's functional currency. For example, a purchase or sale transaction may have given rise to an account payable or an account receivable, which remains unsettled at the next financial reporting date (e.g., the following month-end). According to IAS 21, at each end of the reporting period the foreign currency *monetary* items (such as payables and receivables) are to be translated using the closing rate (i.e., the exchange rate at the date of the statement of financial position).

Example

If John Bull Co. (from the preceding examples) acquires receivables denominated in a foreign currency, Swiss francs (CHF), in 2010, these are translated into the functional currency, euros, at the date of the transaction. If the CHF-denominated receivables are still outstanding at year-end, the company will translate those (ignoring any allowance for uncollectibles) into euros at the year-end exchange rate. If these remain outstanding at the end of 2011 (again ignoring collectibility concerns), these will be translated into euros using the *year-end 2011* exchange rate.

To the extent that exchange rates have changed since the transaction occurred (which will likely happen), exchange differences will have to be recognized by the reporting entity, since the amount due to or from a vendor or customer, denominated in a foreign currency, is now more or less valuable than when the transaction occurred.

Example

Assume now that John Bull Co. acquired the above-noted receivables denominated in Swiss francs in 2010, when the exchange rate of the Swiss franc versus the euro was CHF 1 = €.65. At year-end 2010, the rate is CHF 1 = €.61, and by year-end 2011, the euro has further strengthened to CHF 1 = €.58. Assume that John Bull acquired CHF 10,000 of receivables in mid-2010, and all remain outstanding at year-end 2011. (Again, for purposes of this example only, ignore collectibility concerns).

At the date of initial recognition, John Bull records accounts receivable denominated in CHF in the euro equivalent value of €6,500, since the euro is the functional currency (translation to British pounds or US dollars—a presentation currency—will be dealt with later). At year-end 2010 these receivables are the equivalent of only €6,100, and as a result a loss of €400, which must be recognized in the company's 2010 profit and loss statement. In effect, by holding CHF-denominated receivables while the Swiss franc declined in value against the euro, John Bull suffered a loss. The Swiss franc further weakens over 2011, so that by year-end the CHF 10,000 of receivables will be worth only €5,800, for a further loss of €300 in 2011, which again is to be recognized currently in John Bull's profit and loss statement.

Nonmonetary items (such as property purchased for the company's foreign operation), on the other hand, are to be translated at historical exchange rates. The actual historical exchange rate to be used, however, depends on whether the nonmonetary item is being reported on the historical cost basis, or on a revalued basis, in those instances where the latter method of reporting is permitted under IFRS. If the nonmonetary items are measured in terms of historical cost in a foreign currency, then these are to be translated by using the exchange rate at the actual historical date of the transaction. If the item has been restated to a fair value measurement, then it must be translated into the functional currency by applying the exchange rate at the date when the fair value was determined.

Example—historical cost accounting employed by reporting entity

Assume that John Bull Co. acquired machinery from a Swiss manufacturer, in a transaction denominated in Swiss francs in 2010, when the CHF-euro exchange rate was CHF 1 = €.65. The price paid was CHF 250,000. For purposes of this example, ignore depreciation. At the transaction date, John Bull Co. records the machinery at €162,500. This same amount will be presented in the year-end 2010 and 2011 statements of financial position. The change in exchange rates subsequent to the transaction date will not be considered, since machinery is a nonmonetary asset.

Example—revaluation accounting employed by reporting entity

Assume again that John Bull Co. acquired machinery from a Swiss manufacturer, in a transaction denominated in Swiss francs in 2010, when the CHF-euro exchange rate was CHF 1 = €.65. The price paid was CHF 250,000. For purposes of this example, ignore depreciation. At year-end 2010, John Bull Co. elects to use the allowed alternative method of accounting under IAS 16, and determines that the fair value of the machinery is CHF 285,000. In the entity's year-end statement of financial position, this is reported at the euro equivalent of the revalued amount, using the exchange rate at the revaluation date, or €173,850 (= CHF 285,000 × €.61). This same amount will appear in the 2011 statement of financial position (assuming no further revaluation is undertaken post-2010).

If a nonmonetary asset was acquired in a foreign currency transaction by incurring debt which is to be repaid in the foreign currency (e.g., when a building for the foreign operation was financed locally by commercial debt), subsequent to the actual transaction date the translation of the asset and the related debt will be at differing exchange rates (unless rates remain unchanged, which is not likely to happen.) The result will be either a gain or a loss, which reflects the fact that a nonmonetary asset was purchased but the burden of the related obligation for future payment will vary as the exchange rates fluctuate over time, until the debt is ultimately settled—in other words, the reporting entity has assumed exchange rate risk. On the other hand, if the debt were obtained in the reporting (parent) entity's home country or were otherwise denominated in the buyer's functional currency, there would be no exchange rate risk and no subsequent gain or loss resulting from such an exposure.

Example

Assume now that John Bull Co. acquired machinery from a Swiss manufacturer, in a transaction denominated in Swiss francs in 2010, when the CHF-euro exchange rate was CHF 1 = €.65. The price paid was CHF 250,000. For purposes of this example, ignore depreciation. At the transaction date, John Bull Co. records the machinery at €162,500. This same amount will be presented in the year-end 2010 and 2011 statements of financial position. The change in exchange rates subsequent to the transaction date will not be considered, since machinery is a nonmonetary asset.

However, the purchase of the machinery was effected by signing a 5-year note, payable in Swiss francs. Assume for simplicity the note is not subject to amortization (i.e., due in full at maturity). The note is recorded, at transaction date, as a liability of €162,500. However, at year-end 2010, since the euro has strengthened, the obligation is the equivalent of €152,500. As a result an exchange gain of €10,000 is reported in profit or loss in the current period.

At year-end 2011, this obligation has the euro-equivalent value of €145,000, and thus a further gain of €7,500 is recognized by John Bull Co. for financial reporting purposes.

Had the machinery been acquired for a euro-denominated obligation of €162,500, this valuation would remain in the financial statements until ultimately retired. In this case, the Swiss machinery manufacturer, not the British customer (whose functional currency is the euro), accepted exchange rate risk, and John Bull Co. will report no gain or loss arising from exchange differences.

Other complications can arise when accounting for transactions executed in a foreign currency. IAS 21 identifies circumstances where the carrying amount of an item is determined by comparing two or more amounts, for example when inventory is to be presented at the lower of cost or net realizable value, consistent with the requirements of IAS 2, *Inventories*. Another cited example pertains to long-lived assets, which must be reviewed for impairment, per IAS 36, *Impairments of Assets*. In situations such as these (i.e., where the asset is nonmonetary and is measured in a foreign currency) the carrying amount in terms of functional currency is determined by comparing

1. The cost or carrying amount, as appropriate, translated at the exchange rate at the date when that amount was determined (i.e., the rate at the date of the transaction for an item measured in terms of historical cost, or the date of revaluation if the item were restated under relevant IFRS); and

2. The net realizable value or recoverable amount, as appropriate, translated at the exchange rate at the date when *that* value was determined (which would normally be the closing rate at the end of the reporting period).

Note that by comparing translated amounts that are determined using exchange rate ratios as of differing dates, the actual effect of performing the translation will reflect two economic phenomena; namely, the IFRS-driven lower of cost or fair value comparison (or equivalent), and the changing exchange rates. The effect may be that an impairment loss is to be recognized in the functional currency when it would not have been recognized in the foreign currency, or the opposite relationship may hold (and, of course, there could be impairments in either case, albeit for differing amounts).

Example

John Bull Co. acquired raw materials inventory from a Swiss manufacturer, in a transaction denominated in Swiss francs in 2010, when the CHF-euro exchange rate was CHF 1 = €.65. The price paid was CHF 34,000. At year-end, when the exchange rate was CHF 1 = €.61, the net realizable value of the inventory, which was still on hand, was CHF 32,000. Applying the IAS 21 requirements, it is determined that (1) the purchase price in euros was €22,100 (= CHF 34,000 × €.65); and (2) NRV at the end of the reporting period is €19,520 (= CHF 32,000 × €.61). A lower of cost or realizable value impairment adjustment is reported equal to €2,580. (= €22,100 − €19,520).

See below for another example, where a NRV loss is called for even though NRV in the foreign currency is greater than cost, due to the interaction of exchange rate changes and NRV movements.

TRANSLATION OF FOREIGN CURRENCY FINANCIAL STATEMENTS

IAS 21 adopted the functional currency approach that requires the foreign entity to present all of its transactions in its functional currency. Translation is the process of converting transactions denominated in its functional currency into the investor's presentation currency. If an entity's transactions are denominated in other than its functional currency, the foreign transactions must be first adjusted to their equivalent functional currency value before translating to the presentation currency (if different than the functional currency). Three different situations that can arise in translating foreign currency financial statements are illustrated in the following example:

Foreign entity's local currency	Foreign entity's functional currency	Investor's presentation currency	Translation method	Exchange differences
Euro	Euro	Canadian dollar	Translation to the presentation currency at the closing rate for all assets and liabilities	Other comprehensive income (OCI) and equity
Euro	Canadian dollar	Canadian dollar	Translation to the functional currency (which is also the presentation currency) at the closing rate for all monetary items	Gain (or loss) in profit or loss
Swiss franc	Euro	Canadian dollar	1.Translation to the functional currency (€) 2. Translation to the presentation currency (Can $)	Gain (or loss) in profit or loss OCI and equity

IAS 21 prescribes two sets of requirements when translating foreign currency financial statements. The first of these deals with reporting foreign currency *transactions* by each individual entity, which may also be part of reporting group (e.g., consolidated parent and subsidiaries) in the individual entities' functional currencies or remeasuring the foreign currency financial statements into the functional currency. The second set of requirements is for the translation of entities' financial statements (e.g., those of subsidiaries) from the functional currency into presentation currency (e.g., of the parent). These matters are addressed in the following paragraphs.

Translation of functional currency financial statements into a presentation currency. If the investor's presentation currency (e.g., Canadian dollar) differs from the foreign entity's functional currency (e.g., euro), the foreign entity's financial statements have to be translated into the presentation currency when preparing consolidated financial statements. In accordance with IAS 21, the method used for translation of the foreign currency financial statements from the functional currency into the presentation currency is essentially what is commonly called the *current (closing) rate* method under US GAAP. In general, the translation method under both IFRS and US GAAP are the same, except for the translation of financial statements in hyperinflationary economies (See Chapter 35).

Under the translation to the presentation currency approach, all assets and liabilities, both monetary and nonmonetary, are translated at the closing (end of the reporting period) rate, which simplifies the process compared to all other historically advocated methods. More importantly, this more closely corresponds to the viewpoint of financial statement users, who tend to relate to currency exchange rates in existence at the end of the reporting period rather than to the various specific exchange rates that may have applied in prior months or years.

However, financial statements of preceding years should be translated at the rate(s) appropriately applied when these translations were first performed, (i.e., these are *not* to be updated to current closing or average rates). This rule applies because it would cause great confusion to users of financial statements if amounts once reported (when current) were now all restated even though no changes were being made to the underlying data, and of course the underlying economic phenomena, now one or more years in the past, cannot have changes since initially reported upon.

The theoretical basis for this translation approach is the "net investment concept," wherein the foreign entity is viewed as a separate entity that the parent invested into, rather than being considered as part of the parent's operations. Information provided about the foreign entity retains the internal relationships and results created in the foreign environments (economic, legal, and political) in which the entity operates. This approach works best, of course, when foreign-denominated debt is used to purchase the assets that create foreign-denominated revenues; these assets thus serve as a hedge against the effects caused by changes in the exchange rate on the debt. Any excess (i.e., net) assets will be affected by this foreign exchange risk, and this is the effect that is recognized in the parent company's statement of financial position, as described below.

The following rules should be used in translating the financial statements of a foreign entity:

1. All assets and liabilities in the current year-end statement of financial position, whether monetary or nonmonetary, should be translated at the closing rate in effect at the date of that statement of financial position.
2. Income and expense items in each statement of comprehensive income should be translated at the exchange rates at the dates of the transactions, except when the foreign entity reports in a currency of a hyperinflationary economy (as defined in IAS 29), in which case they should be translated at the closing rates.
3. All resulting exchange differences should be recognized in other comprehensive income and reclassified from equity to profit or loss on the disposal of the net investment in a foreign entity.
4. All assets and liabilities in *prior period* statements of financial position, being presented currently (e.g., as comparative information) whether monetary or nonmonetary, are translated at the exchange rates (closing rates) in effect at the date of each of the statements of financial position.
5. Income and expense items in *prior period* statements of income, being presented currently (e.g., as comparative information), are translated at the exchange rates as of the dates of the original transactions (or averages, where appropriate).

Under the translation to the presentation currency approach, all assets and liabilities are valued (1) higher, as a result of a direct exchange rate increase, or (2) lower, as a result of a direct rate decrease. Since the liabilities offset a portion of the assets, constituting a natural hedge, only the subsidiary's net assets (assets in excess of liabilities) are exposed to the risk of fluctuations in the currency exchange rates. As a result, the effect of the exchange rate change can be calculated by multiplying the foreign entity's average net assets by the change in the exchange rate.

On the books of the parent, the foreign entity's net asset position is reflected in the parent's investment account. If the equity method is applied, the investment account should be adjusted upward or downward to reflect changes in the exchange rate; if a foreign entity is included in the consolidated financial statements, the investment account is eliminated. (See *Comprehensive example: Translation into the presentation currency* later in this chapter).

Translation (remeasurement) of financial statements into a functional currency. When a foreign entity keeps its books and records in a currency other than its functional currency, translation of foreign currency items presented in the statement of financial position into functional currency (remeasurement) is driven by the distinction between monetary and nonmonetary items. Foreign currency monetary items are translated using the closing rate (the spot exchange rate at the end of the reporting period). Foreign currency nonmonetary items are translated using the historical exchange rates. There is a presumption that the effect of exchange rate changes on the foreign operation's net assets will directly affect the parent's cash flows, so the exchange rate adjustments are reported in the parent's profit or loss.

For example, branch sales offices or production facilities of a large, integrated operation (e.g., the European field operation of a US corporation, which is principally supplied by the home office but which occasionally also enters into local currency transactions) would qualify for this treatment. Since the US dollar influences sales prices, most (but not all) of its sales are US dollar denominated, and most of its costs, including merchandise, are the result of US transactions, the application of the previously mentioned criteria would conclude that the functional currency of the European sales office is the US dollar, and translation of foreign-currency-denominated assets and liabilities, and transactions would follow the monetary/nonmonetary distinction noted above with the effect of exchange rate differences reported in profit or loss.

In general, translation of nonmonetary items (inventory, plant assets, etc.) is done by applying the historical exchange rates. The historical rates usually are those in effect when the asset was acquired or (less often) when the nonmonetary liability was incurred, but if there was a subsequent revaluation, if this is permitted under IFRS, then using the exchange rate at the date when the fair value was determined.

When a gain or loss on a nonmonetary item is recognized in profit or loss (e.g., from applying lower of cost or realizable value for inventory), any exchange component of that gain or loss should be recognized in profit or loss. When, on the other hand, a gain or loss on a nonmonetary item is recognized under IFRS in other comprehensive income (e.g., from revaluation of plant assets, or from fair value adjustments made to available-for-sale-securities investments), any exchange component of that gain or loss should also be recognized in other comprehensive income.

As a result of conversion into functional currency, if a foreign unit is in a net monetary asset position (monetary assets in excess of monetary liabilities), an increase in the direct exchange rate causes a favorable result (gain) to be reported in profit or loss; if it is in a net monetary liability position (monetary liabilities in excess of monetary assets), it reports an unfavorable result (loss). If a foreign unit is in a net monetary asset position, a decrease in the direct exchange rate causes an unfavorable result (loss) to report, but if it is in a net monetary liability position, a favorable result (gain) is reported.

In cases when an entity keeps its books and records in a currency (e.g., Swiss franc) other than its functional currency (e.g., euro), and other than the presentation currency of the parent (e.g., Canadian dollar), the two-step translation process would be required: (1) translation of the financial statements (e.g., from Swiss franc) into functional currency (e.g., euro) and (2) translation of functional currency (e.g., euro) into the reporting currency (e.g., Canadian dollar).

Net investment in a foreign operation. A special rule applies to a net investment in a foreign operation. According to IAS 21, when the reporting entity has a monetary item that is receivable from or payable to a foreign operation for which settlement is neither planned nor likely to occur in the foreseeable future, this is, in substance, a part of the entity's net investment in its foreign operation. This item should be accounted for as follows:

1. Exchange differences arising from translation of monetary items forming part of the net investment in the foreign operation should be reflected in profit or loss in the *separate* financial statements of the reporting entity (investor/parent) and in the separate financial statements of the foreign operation, *but*

2. In the consolidated financial statements which include the investor/parent and the foreign operation, the exchange difference should be recognized initially in other comprehensive income and reclassified from equity to profit or loss upon disposal of the foreign operation.

Note that when a monetary item is a component of a reporting entity's net investment in a foreign operation and it is denominated in the functional currency of the reporting entity, an exchange difference arises only in the foreign operation's individual financial statements. Conversely, if the item is denominated in the functional currency of the foreign operation, an exchange difference arises only in the reporting entity's separate financial statements.

Consolidation of foreign operations. The most commonly encountered need for translating foreign currency financial statements into the investor entity reporting currency is when the parent entity is preparing consolidated financial statements, and one or more of the subsidiaries have reported in their respective (local) currencies. The same need presents itself if an investee or joint venture's financial information is to be incorporated via the proportionate consolidation or the equity methods of accounting. When consolidating the assets, liabilities, income, and expenses of a foreign operation with those of the reporting entity, the general consolidation processes apply, including the elimination of intragroup balances and intragroup transactions. Goodwill and any adjustments to the carrying amounts of foreign operation's assets and liabilities should be expressed in the functional currency and translated using the closing rate.

Comprehensive example: Translation into the presentation currency

Assume that a US company has a 100%-owned subsidiary in Germany that began operations in 2010. The subsidiary's operations consist of utilizing company-owned space in an office building. This building, which cost five million euros, was financed primarily by German banks, although the parent did invest two million euros in the German operation. All revenues and cash expenses are received and paid in euros. The subsidiary also maintains its books and records in euros, its functional currency.

The financial statements of the German subsidiary are to be translated (from the functional currency euros to the presentation currency US dollars) for incorporation into the US parent's financial statements. The subsidiary's statement of financial position at December 31, 2011, and its combined statement of income and retained earnings for the year ended December 31, 2011, are presented below in euros.

German Company
Statement of Financial Position
December 31, 2011
(in thousands of €)

Assets		*Liabilities and shareholders' equity*	
Cash	€ 500	Accounts payable	€ 300
Note receivable	200	Unearned rent	100
Land	1,000	Mortgage payable	4,000
Building	5,000	Ordinary shares	400
Accumulated depreciation	(100)	Additional paid-in capital	1,600
		Retained earnings	200
		Total liabilities and	
Total assets	€6,600	shareholders' equity	€6,600

German Company
Combined Statement of Profit or Loss and Retained Earnings
For the Year Ended December 31, 2011
(in thousands of €)

Revenues	€2,000
Operating expenses (including depreciation expense of €100)	1,700
Profit for the year	300
Add retained earnings, January 1, 2011	--
Deduct dividends	(100)
Retained earnings, December 31, 2011	€ 200

Various *assumed* exchange rates for 2011 are as follows:

€1 = $0.90 at the beginning of 2011 (when the ordinary shares were issued and the land and building were financed through the mortgage)
    €1 = $1.05 weighted-average for 2011
    €1 = $1.10 at the date the dividends were declared and the unearned rent was received
    €1 = $1.20 closing (December 31, 2011)

The German company's financial statements must be translated into US dollars in terms of the provisions of IAS 21 (i.e., by the current rate method). This translation process is illustrated below.

German Company
Statement of Financial Position Translation
December 31, 2011
(in thousands of €)

	Euros	*Exchange rates*	*US dollars*
Assets			
Cash	€ 500	1.20	$ 600
Accounts receivable	200	1.20	240
Land	1,000	1.20	1,200
Building (net)	4,900	1.20	5,880
Total assets	€6,600		$7,920
Liabilities and shareholders' equity			
Accounts payable	€ 300	1.20	$ 360
Unearned rent	100	1.20	120
Mortgage payable	4,000	1.20	4,800
Ordinary shares	400	0.90	360
Additional paid-in capital	1,600	0.90	1,440
Retained earnings	200	(see combined income and retained earnings statement translation)	205
Cumulative exchange difference (translation adjustments)	--	--	635
Total liabilities and shareholders' equity	€6,600		$7,920

German Company
Combined Statement of Profit or Loss and Retained Earnings Translation
For the Year Ended December 31, 2011
(in thousands of €)

	Euros	Exchange rates	US dollars
Revenues	€2,000	1.05	$2,100
Expenses (including €100 depreciation expense)	1,700	1.05	1,785
Profit for the year	300		315
Add retained earnings, January 1	--	--	--
Deduct dividends	(100)	1.10	(110)
Retained earnings, December 31	€ 200		$ 205

German Company
Statement of Cash Flows Translation
For the Year Ended December 31, 2011
(in thousands of €)

	Euros	Exchange rates	US dollars
Operating activities			
Profit for the year	€ 300	1.05	$ 315
Adjustments to reconcile net income to net cash provided by operating activities:			
Depreciation	100	1.05	105
Increase in accounts receivable	(200)	1.05	(210)
Increase in accounts payable	300	1.05	315
Increase in unearned rent	100	1.10	110
Net cash provided by operating activities	600		635
Investing activities			
Purchase of land	(1,000)	0.90	(900)
Purchase of building	(5,000)	0.90	(4,500)
Net cash used by investing activities	(6,000)		(5,400)
Financing activities			
Ordinary shares issue	2,000	0.90	1,800
Mortgage payable	4,000	0.90	3,600
Dividends paid	(100)	1.10	(110)
Net cash provided by financing	5,900		5,290
Effect on exchange rate changes on cash	N/A		75
Increase in cash and equivalents	500		600
Cash at beginning of year	--		--
Cash at end of year	€ 500	1.20	$ 600

The following points should be noted concerning the translation into the presentation currency:

1. All assets and liabilities are translated using the closing rate at the end of the reporting period (€1 = $1.20). All revenues and expenses should be translated at the rates in effect when these items are recognized during the period. Due to practical considerations, however, weighted-average rates can be used to translate revenues and expenses (€1 = $1.05) only if such weighted-average rates approximate actual rates that were ruling at the time of the transactions.
2. Shareholders' equity accounts are translated by using historical exchange rates. Ordinary shares were issued at the beginning of 2011 when the exchange rate was €1 = $0.90. The translated balance of retained earnings is the result of the weighted-average rate applied

to revenues and expenses and the specific rate in effect when the dividends were declared (€1 = $1.10).

3. Cumulative exchange differences (translation adjustments) result from translating all assets and liabilities at the closing (current) rate, while shareholders' equity is translated by using historical and weighted-average rates. The adjustments have no direct effect on cash flows; however, changes in exchange rate will have an indirect effect on sale or liquidation. Prior to this time, the effect is uncertain and remote. Also, the effect is due to the net investment rather than the subsidiary's operations. For these reasons the translation adjustments balance is reported as "an other comprehensive income item" in the statement of comprehensive income and as a separate component in the shareholders' equity section of the US company's consolidated statement of financial position. This balance essentially equates the total debits of the subsidiary (now expressed in US dollars) with the total credits (also in dollars). It may also be determined directly, as shown next, to verify the translation process.

4. The cumulative exchange differences (translation adjustments) credit of $635 is calculated as follows:

Net assets at the beginning of 2011 (after ordinary shares were issued and the land and building were acquired through mortgage financing)	€2,000 (1.20 – 0.90)	= $600	credit
Profit for the year	€ 300 (1.20 – 1.05)	= 45	credit
Dividends	€ 100 (1.20 – 1.10)	= 10	debit
Exchange difference (translation adjustment)		$635	credit

5. Since the net exchange differences (translation adjustment) balance that appears as a separate component of shareholders' equity is cumulative in nature, the change in this balance during the year should be disclosed in the financial statements. In the illustration, this balance went from zero to $635 at the end of 2011. The analysis of this change was presented previously. The translation adjustment has a credit balance because the German entity was in a net asset position during the period (assets in excess of liabilities) and the spot exchange rate at the end of the period is higher than the exchange rate at the beginning of the period or the average for the period.

In addition to the foregoing transactions, assume that the following occurred during 2012:

German Company
Statement of Financial Position
December 31, 2012
(in thousands of €)

	2012	2011	Increase/(decrease)
Assets			
Cash	€1,000	€ 500	€500
Accounts receivable	--	200	(200)
Land	1,500	1,000	500
Building (net)	4,800	4,900	(100)
Total assets	€7,300	€6,600	€700
Liabilities and shareholders' equity			
Accounts payable	€ 500	€ 300	€200
Unearned rent	--	100	(100)
Mortgage payable	4,500	4,000	500
Ordinary shares	400	400	--
Additional paid-in capital	1,600	1,600	--
Retained earnings	300	200	100
Total liabilities and shareholders' equity	€7,300	€6,600	€700

German Company
Combined Statement of Profit or Loss and Retained Earnings
For the Year Ended December 31, 2012
(in thousands of €)

Revenues	€2,200
Operating expenses (including depreciation expense of €100)	1,700
Profit for the year	500
Add: Retained earnings, Jan. 1, 2012	200
Deduct dividends	(400)
Retained earnings, Dec. 31, 2012	€ 300

Exchange rates were

€1 = $1.20 at the beginning of 2012
€1 = $1.16 weighted-average for 2012
€1 = $1.08 closing (December 31, 2012)
€1 = $1.10 when dividends were paid in 2012 and land bought by incurring mortgage

The translation process for 2012 is illustrated below.

German Company
Statement of Financial Position Translation
December 31, 2012
(in thousands of €)

	Euros	Exchange rates	US dollars
Assets			
Cash	€1,000	1.08	$1,080
Land	1,500	1.08	1,620
Building	4,800	1.08	5,184
Total assets	€7,300		$7,884
Liabilities and shareholders' equity			
Accounts payable	€ 500	1.08	$ 540
Mortgage payable	4,500	1.08	4,860
Ordinary shares	400	0.90	360
Addl. paid-in capital	1,600	0.90	1,440
		(see combined income and retained	
Retained earnings	300	earnings statement translation)	345
Cumulative translation adjustments	--		339
Total liabilities and shareholders' equity	€7,300		$7,884

German Company
Combined Statement of Profit or Loss and Retained Earnings Translation
For the Year Ended December 31, 2012
(in thousands of €)

	Euros	Exchange rates	US dollars
Revenues	€2,200	1.16	$2,552
Operating expenses (including depreciation of €100)	1,700	1.16	1,972
Profit for the year	500	1.16	580
Add: Retained earnings 1/1/11	200	--	205
Less: Dividends	(400)	1.10	(440)
Retained earnings 12/31/11	€ 300		$ 345

German Company
Statement of Cash Flows Translation
For the Year Ended December 31, 2012
(in thousands of €)

	Euros	Exchange rates	US dollars
Operating activities			
Profit for the year	€ 500	1.16	$ 580
Adjustments to reconcile net income to net cash provided by operating activities:			
Depreciation	100	1.16	116
Decrease in accounts receivable	200	1.16	232
Increase in accounts payable	200	1.16	232
Decrease in unearned rent	(100)	1.16	(116)
Net cash provided by operating activities	900		1,044
Investing activities			
Purchase of land	(500)	1.10	(550)
Net cash used in investing activities	(500)		(550)
Financing activities			
Mortgage payable	500	1.10	550
Dividends	(400)	1.10	(440)
Net cash provided by financing activities	100		110
Effect of exchange rate changes on cash	N/A		(124)
Increase in cash and equivalents	500		480
Cash at beginning of year	500		600
Cash at end of year	€1,000	1.08	$1,080

Using the same mode of analysis that was presented before, the total exchange differences (translation adjustment) attributable to 2012 would be computed as follows:

Net assets at January 1, 2012	€2,200 (1.08 – 1.20)	=	$264	credit
Net income for 2012	€500 (1.08 – 1.16)	=	40	credit
Dividends for 2012	€400 (1.08 – 1.10)	=	8	debit
Total			$296	credit

The balance in the exchange differences (translation adjustment) account at the end of 2012 would be $339 ($635 from 2011 less $296 from 2012). The balance in this account decreased during 2012 since the German entity was in a net asset position during the period and the spot exchange rate at the end of the period (closing rate) is lower than the exchange rate at the beginning of the period or the average for the period.

6. Use of the equity method by the US company in accounting for the subsidiary would result in the following journal entries based on the information presented above:

	2011	2012
Original investment		
Investment in German subsidiary	1,800*	--
Cash	1,800	--

* *[$0.90 × common share of €400 plus additional paid-in capital of €1,600]*

Earnings pickup		
Investment in German subsidiary	315*	580**
Equity in subsidiary income	315	580

* *[$1.05 × net income of €300]*
** *[$1.16 × net income of €500]*

	2011		*2012*	
Dividends received				
Cash	110*		440**	
Investment in German subsidiary		110		440
Exchange difference (translation adjustments)				
Investment in German subsidiary	635			
OCI (Translation adjustments)		635		
OCI (Translation adjustments)			296	
Investment in German subsidiary				296

* *[$1.10 × dividend of €100]*
** *[$1.10 × dividend of €400]*

Note that the shareholders' equity of the US company should be the same whether or not the German subsidiary is consolidated (per IAS 28). Since the subsidiary does not report the translation adjustments on its financial statements, care should be exercised so that it is not forgotten in application of the equity method.

7. If the US company disposes of its investment in the German subsidiary, the translation adjustments balance becomes part of the gain or loss that results from the transaction and must be eliminated. For example, assume that on January 2, 2012, the US company sells its entire investment for €3,000. The exchange rate at this date is €1 = $1.08. The balance in the investment account at December 31, 2012, is $2,484 as a result of the entries made previously.

Investment in German Subsidiary

1/1/11	1,800	
	315	110
	635	
1/1/12	2,640	
	580	440
		296
12/31/12	2,484	

The following entries would be made to reflect the sale of the investment:

Cash (€3,000 × $1.08)	3,240	
Investment in German subsidiary		2,484
Gain from sale of subsidiary		756
Translation adjustments	339	
Gain from sale of subsidiary		339

If the US company had sold a portion of its investment in the German subsidiary, only a proportionate share of the translation adjustments balance (cumulative amount of exchange differences) would have become part of the gain or loss from the transaction. To illustrate, if 80% of the German subsidiary was sold for €2,500 on January 2, 2012, the following journal entries would be made:

Cash (€2,500 × $1.08)	2,700.00	
Investment in German subsidiary (0.8 × $2,484)		1,987.20
Gain from sale of subsidiary		712.80
Cumulative exchange difference (translation adjustments)		
(0.8 × $339)	271.20	
Gain from sale of subsidiary		271.20

GUIDANCE APPLICABLE TO SPECIAL SITUATIONS

Noncontrolling interests. When a foreign entity is consolidated, but it is not wholly owned by the reporting entity, there will be noncontrolling interest reported in the consolidated statement of financial position. IAS 21 requires that the accumulated exchange differences resulting from translation and attributable to the noncontrolling interest be allocated to and reported as noncontrolling interest in net assets.

Goodwill and fair value adjustments. Any goodwill arising on the acquisition of a foreign entity and any fair value adjustments to the carrying amounts of assets and liabilities arising on the acquisition of that foreign operation should be treated as assets and liabilities of the foreign operation. Thus they should be expressed in the functional currency of the foreign operation and translated at the closing rate in accordance with IAS 21.

Exchange differences arising from elimination of intragroup balances. While incorporating the financial statements of a foreign entity into those of the reporting entity, normal consolidation procedures such as elimination of intragroup balances and transactions are undertaken as required by IAS 27, IAS 28, and IAS 31.

Different reporting dates. When reporting dates for the financial statements of a foreign entity and those of the reporting entity differ, the foreign entity normally switches and prepares financial statements with reporting dates coinciding with those of the reporting entity. However, sometimes this may not be practicable to do. Under such circumstances IAS 27 allows the use of financial statements prepared as of different dates, provided that the difference is no more than three months. In such a case, the assets and liabilities of the foreign entity should be translated at the exchange rates prevailing at the end of the reporting period of the foreign entity. Adjustments should be made for any significant movements in exchange rates between the end of the reporting period of the foreign entity and that of the reporting entity in accordance with the provisions of IAS 27, IAS 28, and IAS 31 relating to this matter.

Disposal of a foreign entity. Any cumulative exchange differences are to be recognized in other comprehensive income and accumulated in a separate component of equity until the disposal of the foreign entity. The standard prescribes the treatment of the cumulative exchange differences account on the disposal of the foreign entity. This balance, which has been deferred, should be reclassified from equity to profit or loss in the same period in which the gain or loss on disposal is recognized.

Disposal has been defined to include a sale, liquidation, repayment of share capital, or abandonment of all or part of the entity. Normally, payment of dividends would not constitute a repayment of capital. However, in rare circumstances, it does; for instance, when an entity pays dividends out of capital instead of accumulated profits, as defined in the companies' acts of certain countries, such as the United Kingdom, this would constitute repayment of capital. In such circumstances, obviously, dividends paid would constitute a disposal for the purposes of this standard.

IAS 21 further stipulates that in the case of a partial disposal of an interest in a foreign entity, only a proportionate share of the related accumulated exchange differences is recognized as a gain or a loss. A write-down of the carrying amount of the foreign entity does not constitute a partial disposal, and thus the deferred exchange differences carried forward as part of equity would not be affected by such a write-down.

Change in functional currency. If there is a change in the functional currency, an entity should apply the translation procedures applicable to the new functional currency prospectively from the date of this change.

Reporting a Foreign Operation's Inventory

Under IAS 21, only a single method can be used for translating functional currency financial statements into the presentation currency. Specifically, the reporting entity is required to translate the assets and liabilities of its foreign operations and foreign entities at the closing (end of the reporting period) rate, and required to translate income and expenses at the exchange rates at the dates of the transactions (or at the average rate for the period, if this offers a reasonable approximation of actual transaction date rates).

As noted previously, sometimes an adjustment may be required to reduce the carrying amount of an asset in the financial statements of the reporting entity even though such an adjustment was not necessary in the separate, foreign-currency-based financial statements of the foreign operation. This stipulation of IAS 21 can best be illustrated by the following case study.

Example

Inventory of merchandise owned by a foreign operation of the reporting entity is being carried by the foreign operation at 3,750,000 SR (Saudi riyals) in its statement of financial position. Suppose that the indirect exchange rate fluctuated from 3.75 SR = 1 US dollar at September 15, 2011, when the merchandise was bought, to 4.25 SR = 1 US dollar at December 31, 2011 (i.e., the end of the reporting period). The translation of this item into the functional currency will necessitate an adjustment to reduce the carrying amount of the inventory to its net realizable value if this value when translated into the functional currency is lower than the carrying amount translated at the rate prevailing on the date of purchase of the merchandise.

Although the net realizable value, which in terms of Saudi riyals is 4,000,000 (SR), is higher than the carrying amount in Saudi riyals (i.e., 3,750,000 SR) when translated into the functional currency (i.e., US dollars) at the end of the reporting period, the net realizable value is lower than the carrying amount (translated into the functional currency at the exchange rate prevailing on the date of acquisition of the merchandise). Thus, on the financial statements of the foreign operation the inventory would not have to be adjusted. However, when the net realizable value is translated at the closing rate (which is 4.25 SR = 1 US dollar) into the functional currency, it will require the following adjustment:

1. Carrying amount translated at the exchange rate on September 15, 2011 (i.e., the date of acquisition) = SR 3,750,000 ÷ 3.75 = $1,000,000
2. Net realizable value translated at the closing rate = SR 4,000,000 ÷ 4.25 = $941,176
3. Adjustment needed = $1,000,000 – $941,176 = $58,824

Conversely, IAS 21 further stipulates that an adjustment that already exists on the financial statements of the foreign operation may need to be reversed in the financial statements of the reporting entity. To illustrate this point, the facts of the example above are repeated, with some variation, below.

Example

All other factual details remaining the same as the preceding example, it is now assumed that the inventory, which is carried on the books of the foreign operation at Saudi riyals (SR) 3,750,000, instead has a net realizable value of SR 3,250,000 at year-end. Also assume that the indirect exchange rate fluctuated from SR 3.75 = 1 US dollar at the date of acquisition of the merchandise to SR 3.00 = 1 US dollar at the end of the reporting period.

Since in terms of Saudi riyals, the net realizable value at the end of the reporting period was lower than the carrying value of the inventory, an adjustment must have been made in the statement of financial position of the foreign operation (in Saudi riyals) to reduce the carrying amount to the lower of cost or net realizable value. In other words, a contra asset account (i.e., a lower of cost or NRV) representing the difference between the carrying amount (SR 3,750,000) and the net realizable value (SR 3,250,000) must have been created on the books of the foreign operation.

On translating the financial statements of the foreign operation into the functional currency, however, it is noted that due to the fluctuation of the exchange rates the net realizable value when converted to the functional currency (SR 3,250,000 ÷ 3.00 = $1,083,333) is no longer lower than the translated carrying value which is to be converted at the exchange rate prevailing on the date of acquisition of the merchandise (SR 3,750,000 ÷ 3.75 = $1,000,000).

Thus, a reversal of the adjustment (for lower of cost or NRV) is required on the financial statements of the reporting entity, upon translation of the financial statements of the foreign operation.

Translation of Foreign Currency Transactions in Further Detail

According to IAS 21, a foreign currency transaction is a transaction that is "denominated in or requires settlement in a foreign currency." Denominated means that the amount to be received or paid is fixed in terms of the number of units of a particular foreign currency, regardless of changes in the exchange rate.

From the viewpoint of a US company, for instance, a foreign currency transaction results when it imports or exports goods or services to a foreign entity or makes a loan involving a foreign entity and agrees to settle the transaction in currency other than the US dollar (the presentation currency of the US company). In these situations, the US company has "crossed currencies" and directly assumes the risk of fluctuating exchange rates of the foreign currency in which the transaction is denominated. This risk may lead to recognition of foreign exchange differences in the profit or loss of the US company. Note that exchange differences can result only when the foreign currency transactions are denominated in a foreign currency.

When a US company imports or exports goods or services and the transaction is to be settled in US dollars, the US company will incur neither a gain nor loss because it bears no risk due to exchange rate fluctuations. The following example illustrates the terminology and procedures applicable to the translation of foreign currency transactions.

Assume that a US company, an exporter, sells merchandise to a customer in Germany on December 1, 2011, for €10,000. Receipt is due on January 31, 2012, and the US company prepares financial statements on December 31, 2011. At the transaction date (December 1, 2011), the spot rate for immediate exchange of foreign currencies indicates that €1 is equivalent to $1.18.

To find the US dollar equivalent of this transaction, the foreign currency amount, €10,000, is multiplied by $1.18 to get $11,800. At December 1, 2011, the foreign currency transaction should be recorded by the US company in the following manner:

Accounts receivable—Germany	11,800	
Sales		11,800

The accounts receivable and sales are measured in US dollars at the transaction date using the spot rate at the time of the transaction. While the accounts receivable is measured and reported in US dollars, the receivable is denominated or fixed in euros.

Foreign exchange gains or losses may occur if the spot rate for euros changes between the transaction date and the date of settlement (January 31, 2012). If financial statements are prepared between the transaction date and the settlement date, all receivables and payables that are denominated in a currency different than that in which payment will ultimately be received or paid (the euro) must be restated to reflect the spot rates in existence at the end of the reporting period.

Assume that on December 31, 2011, the spot rate for euros is €1 = $1.20. This means that the €10,000 is now worth $12,000 and that the accounts receivable denominated in euros should be increased by $200. The following journal entry would be recorded as of December 31, 2011:

Accounts receivable—Germany	200	
Foreign currency exchange difference		200

Note that the sales account, which was credited on the transaction date for $11,800, is not affected by changes in the spot rate. This treatment exemplifies what may be called a two-transaction viewpoint. In other words, making the sale is the result of an operating decision, while bearing the risk of fluctuating spot rates is the result of a financing decision. Therefore, the amount determined as sales revenue at the transaction date should not be altered because of a financing decision to wait until January 31, 2012, for payment of the account.

The risk of a foreign exchange transaction loss can be avoided either by demanding immediate payment on December 1 or by entering into a forward exchange contract to hedge the exposed asset (accounts receivable). The fact that the US company in the example did not act in either of these two ways is reflected by requiring the recognition of foreign currency exchange differences (transaction gains or losses) in its profit or loss (reported as financial or nonoperating items) in the period during which the exchange rates changed.

On the settlement date (January 31, 2012), assume that the spot rate is €1 = $1.17. The receipt of €10,000 and their conversion into US dollars would be journalized in the following manner:

Foreign currency	11,700	
Foreign currency transaction loss	300	
Accounts receivable—Germany		12,000
Cash	5,100	
Foreign currency		5,100

The net effect of this foreign currency transaction was to receive $11,700 from a sale that was measured originally at $11,800. This realized net foreign currency transaction loss of $100 is reported on two income statements: a $200 gain in 2011 and a $300 loss in 2012. The reporting of the gain or loss in two income statements causes a temporary difference between pretax accounting and taxable income. This results because the transaction loss of $100 is not deductible until 2012, the year the transaction was completed or settled. Accordingly, interperiod tax allocation is required for foreign currency transaction gains or losses.

DISCLOSURE

A number of disclosure requirements have been prescribed by IAS 21. Primarily, disclosure is required of the amounts of exchange differences included in profit or loss for the period, exchange differences that are included in the carrying amount of an asset, and those that are recognized in other comprehensive income.

When there is a change in classification of a foreign operation, disclosure is required as to the nature of the change, reason for the change, and the impact of the change on the current and each of the prior years presented. When the presentation currency is different from the currency of the country of domicile, the reason for this should be disclosed, and in case of any subsequent change in the presentation currency, the reason for making this change should also be disclosed. An entity should also disclose the method selected to translate goodwill and fair value adjustments arising on the acquisition of a foreign entity. Disclosure is encouraged of an entity's foreign currency risk management policy.

The following additional disclosures are required:

- When the functional currency is different from the currency of the country in which the entity is domiciled, the reason for using a different currency;
- The reason for any change in functional currency or presentation currency;
- When financial statements are presented in a currency other than the entity's functional currency, the reason for using a different presentation currency, and a description of the method used in the translation process;
- When financial statements are presented in a currency other than the functional currency, an entity should state the fact that the functional currency reflects the economic substance of underlying events and circumstances;
- When financial statements are presented in a currency other than the functional currency, and the functional currency is the currency of a hyperinflationary economy, an entity should disclose the closing exchange rates between functional currency and presentation currency existing at the end of each reporting period presented;
- When additional information not required by IAS is displayed in financial statements and in a currency other than presentation currency, as a matter of convenience to certain users, an entity should

  - Clearly identify such information as supplementary information;
  - Disclose the functional currency used to prepare the financial statements and the method of translation used to determine the supplementary information displayed;
  - Disclose the fact that the functional currency reflects the economic substance of the underlying events and circumstances of the entity and the supplementary information is displayed in another currency for convenience purposes only; and
  - Disclose the currency in which supplementary information is displayed.

HEDGING

Hedging a Net Investment in a Foreign Operation or Foreign Currency Transaction

Hedges of a net investment in a foreign operation. While IAS 21 did not address hedge accounting for foreign currency items other than classification of exchange differences arising on a foreign currency liability accounted for as a hedge of a net investment in a foreign entity, IAS 39 has established accounting requirements which largely parallel those for cash flow hedges. (Cash flow hedging is discussed in Chapter 24.) Specifically, IAS 39 states that the portion of the gain or loss on the hedging instrument that is determined to be an effective hedge is to be recognized in other comprehensive income, whereas the ineffective portion of the hedge is to be either recognized immediately in results of operations if the hedging instrument is a derivative instrument, or else reported in other comprehensive income if the instrument is not a derivative.

The gain or loss associated with an effective hedge is reported in other comprehensive income, similar to foreign currency translation gain or loss. In fact, if the hedge is fully effective (which is rarely achieved in practice, however) the hedging gain or loss will be equal in amount and opposite in sign to the translation loss or gain.

In the examples set forth earlier in this chapter which illustrated the accounting for a foreign (German) operation of a US company, the cumulative translation gain as of year-end 2011 was reported as $635,000. If the US entity had been able to enter into a hedging transaction that was perfectly effective (which would most likely have involved a series of currency forward contracts), the net loss position on the hedging instrument as of that date would have been $635,000. If this were reported in other comprehensive income and accumulated in shareholders' equity, as required under IAS 39 and revised IAS 1, it would have served to exactly offset the cumulative translation gain at that point in time.

It should be noted that under the translation methodology prescribed by IAS 21 the ability to precisely hedge the net (accounting) investment in the German subsidiary would have been very remote, since the cumulative translation gain or loss is determined by both the changes in exchange rates since the common share issuances of the subsidiary (which occurred at discrete points in time and thus could conceivably have been hedged), as well as the changes in the various periodic increments or decrements to retained earnings (which having occurred throughout the years of past operations, would involve a complex array of exchange rates, making hedging very difficult to achieve). As a practical matter, hedging the net investment in a foreign subsidiary would serve a very limited economic purpose at best. Such hedging is more often done to avoid the potentially embarrassing impact of changing exchange rates on the reported financial position and financial results of the parent company, which may be important to management, but rarely connotes real economic performance over a longer time horizon.

Notwithstanding the foregoing comments, it is possible for a foreign currency transaction to act as an economic hedge against a parent's net investment in a foreign entity if

1. The transaction is designated as a hedge.
2. It is effective as a hedge.

To illustrate, assume that a US parent has a wholly owned British subsidiary which has net assets of £2 million. The US parent can borrow £2 million to hedge its net investment in the British subsidiary. Assume further that the British pound is the functional currency and that the £2 million liability is denominated in pounds. Fluctuations in the exchange rate for pounds will have no net effect on the parent company's consolidated statement of financial position because increases (decreases) in the translation adjustments balance due to the translation of the net investment will be offset by decreases (increases) in this balance due to the adjustment of the liability denominated in pounds.

In 2008, the IFRS Interpretations Committee issued IFRIC Interpretation 16, *Hedges of a Net Investment in a Foreign Operation*, which came into effect for annual periods beginning on or after October 1, 2008, with earlier application permitted.

IFRIC 16 clarifies that an entity can hedge (the hedge item) up to 100% of the carrying amount of the net assets (net investment) of the foreign operation in the consolidated financial statements of the parent. In addition, as with other hedge relationships, an exposure to foreign currency risk cannot be hedged twice. This means that if the same foreign currency risk is nominally hedged by more than one parent entity within the group (a direct and an indirect parent entity), only one hedge relationship can qualify for hedge accounting.

IAS 39 does not require that the operating unit that is exposed to the risk being hedged hold the hedging instrument. IFRIC 16 clarifies that this requirement also applies to the hedge of the net investment in a foreign operation. The functional currency of the entity holding the instrument is irrelevant in determining effectiveness, and any entity within the group, regardless of its functional currency, can hold the hedging instrument.

IFRIC 16 originally had a statement that the hedging instrument could not be held by the foreign operation whose net investment was being hedged. *2009 Improvements to IFRS* removed restriction on the entity that holds the hedging instruments, effective for annual periods beginning on or after July 1, 2009, which basically means that even the hedged entity can hold the hedging instrument itself as long as the designation, documentation, and effectiveness requirements of IAS 39, paragraph 88, that relate to a net investment hedge are satisfied.

Hedges of foreign currency transactions. It may be more important for managers to hedge specific foreign currency denominated transactions, such as merchandise sales or purchases which involve exposure for the time horizon over which the foreign currency denominated receivable or payable remains outstanding. For example, consider the illustration set forth earlier in this chapter which discussed the sale of merchandise by a US entity to a German customer, denominated in euros, with the receivable being due sometime after the sale. During the period the receivable remains pending, the creditor is at risk for currency exchange rate changes that might occur, leading to exchange rate gains or losses, depending on the direction the rates move. The following discussion sets forth the possible approach that could have been taken (and the accounting therefor) to reduce or eliminate this risk.

In the example, the US company could have entered into a forward exchange contract on December 1, 2010, to sell €10,000 for a negotiated amount to a foreign exchange broker for future delivery on January 31, 2011. Such a forward contract would be a hedge against the exposed asset position created by having an account receivable denominated in euros. The negotiated rate referred to above is called a futures or forward rate. This instrument would qualify as a derivative under IAS 39.

In most cases, this futures rate is not identical to the spot rate at the date of the forward contract. The difference between the futures rate and the spot rate at the date of the forward contract is referred to as a discount or premium. Any discount or premium must be amortized over the term of the forward contract, generally on a straight-line basis. The amortization of discount or premium is reflected in a separate revenue or expense account, not as an addition or subtraction to the foreign currency transaction gain or loss amount. It is important to observe that under this treatment, no net foreign currency transaction gains or losses result if assets and liabilities denominated in foreign currency are completely hedged at the transaction date.

To illustrate a hedge of an exposed asset, consider the following additional information for the German transaction.

On December 1, 2010, the US company entered into a forward exchange contract to sell €10,000 on January 31, 2011, at $1.14 per euro. The spot rate on December 1 is $1.12 per euro. The journal entries that reflect the sale of goods and the forward exchange contract appear as follows:

Sale transaction entries			*Forward exchange contract entries (futures rate €1 = $1.14)*		
12/1/10 (spot rate €1 = $1.12)			Due from exchange broker ($)	11,400	
Accounts receivable (€)—Germany	11,200		Due to exchange broker (€)		11,200
Sales		11,200	Premium on forward contract		200
12/31/10 (spot rate €1 = $1.15)			Foreign currency transaction loss	300	
Accounts receivable (€)—Germany	300		Due to exchange broker (€)		300
Foreign currency transaction gain		300	Premium on forward contract	100	
			Financial revenue		
			($100 = $200/2 months)		100

Sale transaction entries			*Forward exchange contract entries* *(futures rate €1 = $1.14)*		
1/31/11 (spot rate €1 = $1.17)					
Foreign currency	11,700		Due to exchange broker	11,500	
Accounts receivable (€)—			Foreign currency transaction loss	200	
Germany		11,500	Foreign currency		11,700
Foreign currency transaction gain		200			
			Cash	11,400	
			Due from exchange broker		11,400
			Premium on forward contract	100	
			Financial revenue		100

The following points should be noted from the entries above:

1. The net foreign currency transaction gain or loss is zero. The account "Due from exchange broker" is fixed in terms of US dollars, and this amount is not affected by changes in spot rates between the transaction and settlement dates. The account "Due to exchange broker" is fixed or denominated in euros. The US company owes the exchange broker €10,000, and these must be delivered on January 31, 2011. Because this liability is denominated in euros, its amount is determined by spot rates. Since spot rates change, this liability changes in amount equal to the changes in accounts receivable because both of the amounts are based on the same spot rates. These changes are reflected as foreign currency transaction gains and losses that net out to zero.
2. The premium on forward contract is fixed in terms of US dollars. This amount is amortized to a financial revenue account over the life of the forward contract on a straight-line basis.
3. The net effect of this transaction is that $11,400 was received on January 31, 2011, for a sale originally recorded at $11,200. The $200 difference was taken into income via amortization.

Currency of Monetary Items Comprising Net Investment in Foreign Operations

Amendments made to IAS 21 in December 2005 clarified that monetary items (whether receivable or payable) between any subsidiary of the group and a foreign operation may form part of the group's investment in that foreign operation. Thus, these monetary items can be denominated in a currency other than the functional currency of either the parent or the foreign operation itself, for exchange differences on these monetary items to be recognized in other comprehensive income and accumulated in a separate component of equity until the disposal of the foreign operation.

Example

Assume the following group structure: Parent, a French company, Eiffel SARL (Group Eiffel), has a functional currency of the euro. Parent company has a 100% direct interest in a US investment company, Freedom, Inc., which has a functional currency of the US dollar. Freedom, in turn, owns a British subsidiary, Royal Ltd. (100% ownership), which has a functional currency of the pound sterling. Freedom lends $100,000 to Royal. The question is whether the loan can be accounted for as part of Group Eiffel's net investment in Royal with any exchange differences recognized in other comprehensive income.

Examples of Financial Statement Disclosures

Roche Group
Annual Report 2010

Notes to the consolidated financial statements

Foreign currency translation

Most Group companies use their local currency as their functional currency. Certain Group companies use other currencies (such as US dollars, Swiss francs, or euros) as their functional currency where this is the currency of the primary economic environment in which the entity operates. Local transactions in other currencies are initially reported using the exchange rate at the date of the transaction. Gains and losses from the settlement of such transactions and gains and losses on translation of monetary assets and liabilities denominated in other currencies are included in income, except when they are qualifying cash flow hedges or arise on monetary items that, in substance, form part of the Group's net investment in a foreign entity. In such cases the gains and losses are deferred into equity.

Upon consolidation, assets and liabilities of Group companies using functional currencies other than Swiss francs (foreign entities) are translated into Swiss francs using year-end rates of exchange. Sales, costs, expenses, net income, and cash flows are translated at the average rates of exchange for the year. Translation differences due to the changes in exchange rates between the beginning and the end of the year and the difference between net income translated at the average and year-end exchange rates are taken directly to equity. On disposal of a foreign entity, the identified cumulative currency translation differences within equity relating to that foreign entity are recognized in income as part of the gain or loss on divestment.

Foreign exchange risk

The Group operates across the world and is exposed to movements in foreign currencies affecting the Group financial result and the value of Group's equity. Foreign exchange risk arises because the amount of local currency paid or received for transactions denominated in foreign currencies may vary due to changes in exchange rates ("transaction exposures") and because the foreign currency denominated financial statements of the Group's foreign subsidiaries may vary upon consolidation into the Swiss franc-denominated Group Financial Statements ("translation exposures").

The objective of the Group's foreign exchange risk management activities is to preserve the economic value of its current and future assets and to minimise the volatility of the Group's financial result. The primary focus of the Group's foreign exchange risk management activities is on hedging transaction exposures arising through foreign currency flows or monetary positions held in foreign currencies. The Group does not currently hedge translation exposures using financial instruments.

The Group monitors transaction exposures on a daily basis. The net foreign exchange result and the corresponding VaR parameters are reported on a monthly basis. The Group uses forward contracts, foreign exchange options, and cross-currency swaps to hedge transaction exposures. Application of these instruments intends to continuously lock in favorable developments of foreign exchange rates, thereby reducing the exposure to potential future movements in such rates.

Nokia
Annual Report 2010

Notes to the consolidated financial statements

Foreign currency translation

Functional and presentation currency

The financial statements of all Group entities are measured using the currency of the primary economic environment in which the entity operates (functional currency). The consolidated financial statements are presented in Euro, which is the functional and presentation currency of the Parent Company.

Transactions in foreign currencies

Transactions in foreign currencies are recorded at the rates of exchange prevailing at the dates of the individual transactions. For practical reasons, a rate that approximates the actual rate at the date of the transaction is often used. At the end of the accounting period, the unsettled balances on foreign currency assets and liabilities are valued at the rates of exchange prevailing at the end of the accounting period. Foreign exchange gains and losses arising from statement of financial position items, as well as changes in fair value in the related hedging instruments, are reported in financial income and expenses. For nonmonetary items, such as shares, the unrealized foreign exchange gains and losses are recognized in other comprehensive income.

Foreign Group companies

In the consolidated accounts, all income and expenses of foreign subsidiaries are translated into Euro at the average foreign exchange rates for the accounting period. All assets and liabilities of Group companies, where the functional currency is other than euro, are translated into euro at the year-end foreign exchange rates. Differences resulting from the translation of income and expenses at the average rate and assets and liabilities at the closing rate are recognized in other comprehensive income as translation differences within consolidated shareholder's equity. On the disposal of all or part of a foreign Group company by sale, liquidation, repayment of share capital or abandonment, the cumulative amount or proportionate share of the translation difference is recognized as income or as expense in the same period in which the gain or loss on disposal is recognized.

US GAAP COMPARISON

US GAAP, similar to IFRS, requires translation of the financial positions and income of a subsidiary with a functional currency different from the reporting currency to be translated before consolidation using, as appropriate, end-of-period or transaction-date conversion rates for balance sheet and income statement amounts.

Translation adjustments into the reporting currency (termed the presentation currency in IFRS) are recognized in other comprehensive income. Transactions or balances denominated in a currency other than the functional currency must be remeasured into the functional currency. The remeasurement difference is included in profit and loss for the period.

Under US GAAP if the cumulative inflation rate for three years exceeds 100%, the entity is deemed to be using a functional currency of a highly inflationary economy. No such bright-line exists in IFRS, although a 100% cumulative inflation rate is an indicator that must be considered. For subsidiaries, both consolidated and equity-method accounted, that are using highly inflationary currencies must substitute the reporting currency for the functional currency. Accordingly, remeasurement effect from the transaction currency into the reporting currency is recognized in profit and loss. If the currency of a subsidiary ceases to be highly inflationary, the reporting currency amounts at the date of change shall be translated into the local currency at current exchange rates and become the new basis.

Upon partial or full disposal of a subsidiary, the pro rata or full amount, respectively, is removed from other comprehensive income and included in the gain or loss on disposal.

24 FINANCIAL INSTRUMENTS

INTRODUCTION

The accounting for financial instruments received a great deal of attention from the IFRS Foundation—being the subject of its two most voluminous and controversial standards—and continued attention is a certainty. The original intent, which was to address all matters of recognition, measurement, derecognition, presentation, and disclosure in a single comprehensive standard, proved to be unworkable (as was also the case under US GAAP), and thus matters have been dealt with piecemeal. The first standard, IAS 32, which first became effective in 1996, has subsequently been revised and/or amended intermittently since then. It addressed only the presentation and disclosure requirements for financial instruments. The disclosure requirements set forth in IAS 32 were removed from that standard, effective 2007, and are now incorporated into IFRS 7, which also includes the financial institution disclosure requirements previously set forth by IAS 30. IFRS 7 is discussed in detail in this chapter.

The more intractable problems of recognition, measurement, and derecognition were dealt with by IAS 39, which became mandatory in 2001. IAS 39 has been amended several times in the past few years, initially due to efforts by the IASB as it struggled to gain EU acceptance for IFRS and more recently to respond to the challenges of the global financial crisis. IAS 39 was intended as only an interim standard, since it failed to comprehensively embrace fair value accounting for all financial assets and liabilities, which had been held out as the goal to which the IFRS Foundation was committed at the time. Fair value accounting, particularly for liabilities, was and remains a controversial topic. Subsequent to IAS 39's promulgation, IASB has indicated that any decision to impose comprehensive fair value accounting for financial assets and liabilities is likely to be several years in the future, at best, and must be viewed as a longer-term objective. The global financial crisis also highlighted some potential weaknesses in the application of fair value accounting to financial liabilities, and the objective of comprehensive fair value accounting may take even longer to achieve than initially considered.

Because of the complexity of IAS 39, a number of difficult implementation issues needed to be addressed, and in response the IFRS Foundation constituted an IAS 39 Implementation Guidance Committee (IGC). Several hundred questions and answers were published by this committee, and a compendium of guidance was produced in connection with the 2003 revisions to IAS 39 as well as incorporated into revised IAS 32 and IAS 39.

The recent (2008-2009) global financial crisis has underscored how closely the financial markets and the wider economy are interconnected, and the need for a commonly accepted high-quality set of accounting standards, particularly standards relating to financial instruments. Also it has shown how a lack of transparency can threaten the financial system as a whole, and therefore companies, especially financial institutions, need to provide more useful information to better communicate the risks flowing from transactions relating to financial instruments. The IASB has realized that there is an urgent need to improve the accounting for financial instruments, since the current accounting rules have permitted numerous options and added what is now seen as having been unnecessary (or, at least, unwelcomed) complexity. In response to the global financial crisis, the IASB has embarked upon a number of projects that will ultimately amend the existing accounting standards on financial instruments. The IASB's major ongoing projects relating to financial instruments are discussed at the end of this chapter.

In this chapter, the overall requirements of IAS 32 and 39, and IFRS 7 will be set forth. In addition, this chapter will present detailed examples on a range of topics involving cash and receivables (e.g., the accounting for factored receivables) that are derived from the most widespread and venerable practices in these areas, even if not codified in the IAS.

Sources of IFRS		
IAS 1, 32, 39	*IFRS* 7	*IFRIC* 2, 9, 10, 16,19

FUTURE DEVELOPMENTS AND IFRS 9

The IASB published the ED *Derecognition: Proposed Amendments to IAS 39 and IFRS 7* in March 2009, proposing to replace the existing guidance on derecognition of financial assets and financial liabilities and the related disclosures. This ED proposed a single approach to derecognition based on "control," as opposed to the complex current requirements set forth under IAS 39, which combine elements of several derecognition concepts (e.g., risks and rewards, control, and continuing involvement). The IASB decided to stop this project and only develop a standard on disclosure regarding derecognition; this project was completed in October 2010.

The project to replace IAS 39 is being conducted in three phases, which are (1) classification and measurement; (2) impairment of financial assets; and (3) hedge accounting. Phase I has been completed and the IASB issued IFRS 9, *Financial Instruments,* in November 2009, dealing solely with the measurement and classification of financial assets and effective from January 2013. It will eventually replace IAS 39; however, this version deals only with the measurement and classification of financial assets and is the result of Phase I of the project to replace IAS 39. The IASB has indicated that some changes may yet be made to IFRS 9 with respect to conclusions reached in Phase I when Phases II and III are incorporated into IFRS 9, as the project has many "moving parts" and consistency within and between the different phases may necessitate such changes. The IASB has extended its initial timeline for the completion of the IFRS 9 project, and in July 2011 signaled that it expects only to complete it in 2012 and consequently is seeking comments on a proposal to move out the effective date of all phases of IFRS 9 (completed and in progress) from January 1, 2013 to January 1, 2015. We expect that this proposal will meet with the support of most stakeholders.

IFRS 9 maintains the recognition and derecognition requirements of IAS 39 as well as the impairment model. As each phase is completed, IFRS 9 will be expanded accordingly to incorporate the various elements of each one.

Simplifying the requirements of IAS 39 was one of the objectives of the IASB when it embarked on the financial instruments project and it set out as one of its aims the requirement to reduce the number of categories of financial assets. As a result, IFRS 9 categorizes financial assets into just two categories, amortized cost and fair value.

For a financial asset to be classified as amortized cost, both of the following requirements must be applicable: (1) it must be held within a business model whose objective is to hold assets in order to collect contractual cash flows and (2) the contractual terms of the financial asset give rise on specified dates to cash flows that are solely payments of principal and interest on the principal amount outstanding. All other financial assets are classified at fair value.

An entity may, however, elect to designate on initial recognition a financial asset at fair value if that would eliminate an accounting mismatch (the same option exists in terms of IAS 39 and was carried forward from there) that would otherwise arise from measuring assets or liabilities or recognizing the gains and losses on them on different bases.

Within the fair value classification, fair value adjustments are recognized in profit or loss with the following exception: if an entity makes an irrevocable election upon initial recognition to recognize all gains or losses in other comprehensive income with the exception of dividends which shall be recognized in profit or loss.

Subsequent to initial recognition an entity may only reclassify a financial asset if the business model within which it holds that asset changes. Any reclassification shall be applied prospectively from the date of reclassification, and the entity shall not restate any amounts with respect to the previous accounting. If an item is reclassified from amortized cost to fair value, any gain or loss or remeasurement to fair value shall be recognized in profit or loss. If an item is reclassified from fair value to amortized cost, its fair value at the date of reclassification shall become its new carrying amount.

IFRS 9 differs in its treatment of embedded derivatives that have a financial asset host compared to IAS 39. IFRS 9 requires that where the host contract itself is within the scope of it, then the classification and measurement requirements shall be applied to the entire contract and not to the separate components of it; in other words the contract may not be bifurcated between the host and the embedded derivative.

In October 2010 the IASB issued additions to IFRS 9, *Financial Instruments*, in relation to financial liabilities that an entity has elected to measure at fair value. These improvements have an effective date of January 1, 2013, with earlier application permitted. Most of the requirements related to financial liabilities were carried forward unchanged from IAS 39. However, the requirements related to the fair value option for financial liabilities were changed to address the issue of own credit risk in response to consistent feedback from users of financial statements and others that the effects of changes in a liability's credit risk ought not to affect profit or loss unless the liability is held for trading. Therefore the portion of the fair value of nontrading liabilities recognized at fair value attributable to credit risk should be recognized in other comprehensive income.

The ED regarding Phase II of financial instruments—*Amortized Cost and Impairment of Financial Assets*—was published November 5, 2009. The IASB is proposing to move from the current incurred loss impairment model to an expected losses model. Such a model proposes

- To determine expected credit losses when financial assets are recognized for the first time

- To recognize contractual interest revenue, less the initial expected credit losses, over the life of the instrument
- To build up a provision over the life of the instrument for the expected credit losses
- To reassess the expected credit loss each period and recognize the effects of any changes in credit loss expectations immediately.

On January 31, 2011, the IASB published a supplementary document to the Exposure Draft *Financial Instruments: Amortized Cost and Impairment* that proposes the separation of the calculation of interest and the recognition of expected losses (impairment) to simplify the practical application of the model. The supplement document also proposes separating the good book from the bad book. Expected losses on the good book are recognized over time while the expected losses on the bad book are recognized immediately.

In December 2010 the ED regarding Phase III, *Hedge Accounting*, was issued. The ED only deals with general hedge accounting and not macro hedge accounting, which will be issued separately. The IASB also issued in January 2010 an ED on asset and liability offsetting.

The remainder of the information in this chapter as it refers to financial instruments is based on IAS 39 and not IFRS 9.

Due to the strong indications of the extension for the completion of the IFRS 9 project, as well as possible changes to already completed phases due to ongoing interactions with stakeholders making amendments probable, we have elected not to include significant detail on this work-in-progress in this edition. The IASB has in fact already committed to re-exposing the draft proposals relating to impairment as well and hedge accounting.

DEFINITIONS OF TERMS

Accounts receivable. Amounts due from customers for goods or services provided in the normal course of business operations.

Aging the accounts. Procedure for the computation of the adjustment for uncollectible accounts receivable based on the length of time the end-of-period outstanding accounts have been unpaid.

Amortized cost of financial asset or financial liability. The amount at which the asset or liability was measured upon initial recognition, minus principal repayments, plus or minus the cumulative amortization of any premium or discount, and minus any write-down for impairment or uncollectibility.

Assignment. Formal procedure for collateralization of borrowings through the use of accounts receivable. It normally does not involve debtor notification.

Available-for-sale financial assets. Those nonderivative financial assets that are designated as available-for-sale or are not classified as (1) loans and receivables, (2) held-to-maturity investments, or (3) financial assets at fair value through profit or loss.

Carrying amount (value). The amount at which an asset is presented in the statement of financial position.

Cash. Cash on hand and demand deposits with banks or other financial institutions.

Cash equivalents. Short-term, highly liquid investments that are readily convertible to known amounts of cash which are subject to an insignificant risk of changes in value. Examples include Treasury bills, commercial paper, and money market funds.

Compound instrument. An issued single financial instrument that contains both liability and equity features (e.g., convertible bond). In terms of IAS 32, "split accounting" is required for such instruments.

Control. The ability to direct the strategic financial and operating policies of an entity so as to obtain benefits from its activities.

Credit risk. The risk that a loss may occur from the failure of one party to a financial instrument to discharge an obligation according to the terms of a contract.

Current assets. An asset should be classified as current when it satisfies any of the following criteria: (1) it is expected to be realized in, or is intended for sale or consumption in, the entity's normal operating cycle; (2) it is held primarily for the purpose of being traded; (3) it is expected to be realized within twelve months after the reporting period; or (4) it is cash or cash equivalent unless it is restricted from being exchanged or used to settle a liability for at least twelve months after the reporting period.

Derecognition. Removal of a previously recognized financial asset or liability from an entity's statement of financial position.

Derivative. A financial instrument or other contract with all three of the following characteristics: (1) its value changes in response to changes in a specified interest rate, security price, commodity price, foreign exchange rate, index of prices or rates, a credit rating or credit index, or other variable, provided in the case of a nonfinancial variable that the variable is not specific to a party to the contract (sometimes called the "underlying" or "cash" position), (2) it requires little or no initial net investment relative to other types of contracts that have a similar response to changes in market conditions, and (3) it is settled at a future date.

Effective interest method. A method of calculating the amortized cost of a financial asset or a financial liability (or group of financial instruments) and of allocating the interest income or interest expense over the relevant period.

Effective interest rate. The rate that exactly discounts estimated future cash flows (receipts or payments) to the net carrying amount of the financial instrument through the expected life of this instrument (or a shorter period, when appropriate). In calculating the effective interest rate, an entity should estimate future cash flows after considering all contractual terms of the financial instrument (e.g., prepayment, call and similar options), but without considering future credit losses. All fees and points paid or received between parties to the contract, transaction costs and other premium and discounts must also be included.

Embedded derivative. A component of a hybrid (combined) financial instrument that also includes a nonderivative host contract—with the effect that some of the cash flows of the combined instrument vary in a way similar to a stand-alone derivative.

Equity instrument. Any contract that evidences a residual interest in the assets of an entity after deducting all its liabilities.

Factoring. Outright sale of accounts receivable to a third-party financing entity. The sale may be with or without recourse.

Fair value. Amount for which an asset could be exchanged, or a liability settled, between knowledgeable willing parties in an arm's-length transaction.

Fair value through profit or loss. An option in IAS 39 that permits an entity to irrevocably designate any financial asset or financial liability, but only upon its initial recognition, as one to be measured at fair value, with changes in fair value recognized in profit or loss.

Financial asset. Any asset that is

1. Cash
2. An equity instrument of another entity
3. A contractual right

    a. To receive cash or another financial asset from another entity, or

b. To exchange financial instruments with another entity under conditions that are potentially favorable

4. A contract that will be settled in the reporting entity's own equity instruments and is

a. A nonderivative for which the entity is or may be obligated to receive a variable number of its own equity instruments, or

b. A derivative that will or may be settled other than by the exchange of a fixed amount of cash or another financial asset for a fixed number of the entity's own equity instruments (which excludes puttable financial instruments classified as equity and instruments that are themselves contracts for the future receipt or delivery of the entity's equity instruments)

Financial assets (categories). Include the following four principal categories (1) at fair value through profit or loss (held for trading, and those designated as at fair value through profit or loss [FVTPL] upon initial recognition); (2) available-for-sale; (3) held-to-maturity; and (4) loans and receivables.

Financial asset or liability reported at fair value through profit or loss. One which *either* is acquired or incurred for trading (i.e., is principally for the purpose of generating a profit from short-term fluctuations in price or dealer's margin, or which is part of identified commonly managed financial instruments and for which there is a pattern of short-term profit-taking by the entity, or which is a derivative unless designated for, and effective as, a hedging instrument) or upon initial recognition is designated for carrying at fair value through profit or loss.

Fair value through profit or loss designation. IAS 39 permits an entity to irrevocably designate any financial asset or financial liability, upon its initial recognition, as one to be measured at fair value, with changes in fair value recognized in profit or loss.

Financial guarantee contract. A contract that requires the issuer to make specified payments to reimburse the holder for losses incurred because a specified debtor failed to make payment when due based on the original or modified terms of a debt instrument.

Financial instrument. Any contract that gives rise to both a financial asset of one entity and a financial liability or equity instrument of another entity.

Financial liability. Any liability that is

1. A contractual obligation

a. To deliver cash or another financial asset to another entity

b. To exchange financial instruments with another entity under conditions that are potentially unfavorable to the entity

2. A contract that will or may be settled in the entity's own equity instruments and is

a. A nonderivative for which the entity is or may be obligated to deliver a variable number of its own equity instruments, or

b. A derivative that will or may be settled other than by the exchange of a fixed amount of cash or another financial asset for a fixed number of the entity's own equity instruments (which excludes puttable financial instruments classified as equity and instruments that are themselves contracts for the future receipt or delivery of the entity's equity instruments)

Firm commitment. A binding agreement for the exchange of a specified quantity of resources at a specified price on a specified future date or dates.

Hedge effectiveness. The degree to which changes in the fair value or cash flows of the hedged item that are attributable to a hedged risk are offset by changes in the fair value or cash flows of the hedging instrument.

Hedged item. An asset, liability, firm commitment, highly probable forecast transaction or net investment in a foreign operation that (1) exposes the entity to risk of changes in fair value or future cash flows, and (2) is designated as being hedged.

Hedging. Designating one or more hedging instruments such that the change in fair value or cash flows of the hedging instrument is an offset, in whole or part, to the change in fair value or cash flows of the hedged item. The objective is to ensure that the gain or loss on the hedging instrument is recognized in profit or loss in the same period that the hedged item affects profit or loss. Types of hedges are (1) fair value, (2) cash flow, and (3) net investment in a foreign operation.

Hedging instrument. For hedge accounting purposes, a designated derivative or (for a hedge of the risk of changes in foreign currency exchange rates only) a designated nonderivative financial asset or nonderivative financial liability whose fair value or cash flows are expected to offset changes in the fair value or cash flows of a designated hedged item.

Held-to-maturity investments. Nonderivative financial assets with fixed or determinable payments and fixed maturities, that the entity has the positive intent and ability to hold to maturity, except for (1) those at fair value through profit or loss, (2) those designated as available-for-sale, and (3) loans and receivables. An entity should not classify any financial assets as held-to-maturity if the entity has, during the current financial year or during the two preceding financial years, sold or reclassified more than an insignificant amount (in relation to the total amount of held-to-maturity investments) of held-to-maturity investments before maturity (the so-called "tainting" rules).

Liquidity risk. The risk that an entity may encounter difficulty in meeting obligations associated with financial liabilities.

Loans and receivables. Nonderivative financial assets with fixed or determinable payments that are not quoted in an active market, other than (1) those at fair value through profit or loss, (2) those designated as available-for-sale, and (3) those which the holder may not recover substantially all of its initial investment (other than because of credit deterioration), which should be classified as available-for-sale.

Market risk. The risk that the fair value or future cash flows of a financial instrument will fluctuate because of changes in market prices; it comprised three types of risk: currency risk, interest rate risk, and other price risk.

Market value. Amount obtainable from a sale, or payable on acquisition, of a financial instrument in an active market.

Marketable equity instruments. Instruments representing actual ownership interest, or the rights to buy or sell such interests, that are actively traded or listed on a national securities exchange.

Monetary financial assets and financial liabilities. Financial assets and financial liabilities to be received or paid in fixed or determinable amounts of currency.

Net realizable value. The estimated selling price in the ordinary course of business less the estimated costs of completion and the estimated costs necessary to make the sale.

Operating cycle. Average time between the acquisition of materials or services and the final cash realization from the sale of products or services.

Other price risk. The risk that the fair value or future cash flows of a financial instrument will fluctuate because of changes in market prices (other than those arising from interest rate risk or currency risk), whether those changes are caused by factors specific to the individual financial instrument or its issuer, or factors affecting all similar financial instruments traded in the market.

Percentage-of-sales method. Procedure for computing the adjustment for uncollectible accounts receivable based on the historical relationship between bad debts and gross credit sales.

Pledging. Process of using an asset as collateral for borrowings. It generally refers to borrowings secured by accounts receivable.

Puttable instrument. A financial instrument that gives the holder the right to put the instrument back to the issuer for cash or another financial asset. It can also be automatically put back to the issuer on the occurrence of an uncertain future event or the death or retirement of the instrument holder.

Realized gain (loss). Difference between the cost or adjusted cost of a marketable security and the net selling price realized by the seller, which is to be included in the determination of profit or loss in the period of the sale.

Recourse. Right of the transferee (factor) of accounts receivable to seek recovery for an uncollectible account from the transferor. It is often limited to specific conditions.

Repurchase agreement. An agreement to transfer a financial asset to another party in exchange for cash or other considerations, with a concurrent obligation to reacquire the asset at a future date.

Securitization. The process whereby financial assets are transformed into securities.

Short-term investments. Financial instruments or other assets acquired with excess cash, having ready marketability and intended by management to be liquidated, if necessary, within the current operating cycle.

Transaction costs. Incremental costs directly attributable to the acquisition or disposal of a financial asset or liability.

DISCUSSION OF CERTAIN CONCEPTS

Cash

The only actual guidance to the accounting for cash offered by IFRS is that found in IAS 1. Common practice is to define cash as including currency on hand, as well as current and other accounts maintained with banks. However, cash that is not available for immediate use is normally given separate disclosure to prevent misleading implications. IAS 1 (as revised effective 2005) generally requires that statements of financial position be *classified* (i.e., that current and noncurrent assets and liabilities be grouped separately), unless presentation in the order of liquidity is deemed more reliable and relevant. If a classified statement of financial position is presented, cash which is restricted and not available for use within one year of the reporting period should be included in noncurrent assets. This guidance is not altered by the latest revision to IAS 1, which became effective in 2009 (see Chapter 3).

For a current asset classification to be warranted, it must furthermore be management's intention that the cash be available for current purposes. For example, cash in a demand deposit account, being held specifically for the retirement of long-term debts not maturing currently, should be excluded from current assets and shown as a noncurrent investment. This would apply only if management's intention was clear; otherwise it would not be necessary to segregate from the general cash account the funds that presumably will be needed for a scheduled debt retirement, as those funds could presumably be obtained from alternative sources, including new borrowings.

It has become common for the caption "cash and cash equivalents" to appear in the statement of financial position. This term includes other forms of near-cash items as well as demand deposits and liquid, short-term instruments.

IAS 7 defines cash equivalents as short-term, highly liquid investments, readily convertible into known amounts of cash that are subject to an insignificant risk of changes in value. The reasonable, albeit arbitrary, limit of three months is placed on the maturity dates of any instruments acquired to be part of cash equivalents. (This is, not coincidentally, the same limit applied by the US standard on cash flow statements, FAS 95, promulgation of which preceded the revision of IAS 7 by several years.)

Compensating balances are cash amounts that are not immediately accessible by the owner. Pursuant to borrowing arrangements with lenders, an entity will often be required to maintain a minimum amount of cash on deposit (as a "compensating balance"). While stated to provide greater security for the loan, the actual purpose of this balance is to increase the yield on the loan to the lender. Since most organizations will need to maintain a certain working balance in their cash accounts simply to handle routine transactions and to cushion against unforeseen fluctuations in the demand for cash, borrowers often find compensating balance arrangements not objectionable and may well have sufficient liquidity to maintain these with little hardship being incurred. They may even be viewed as comprising "rotating" normal cash balances that are flowing into and out of the bank on a regular basis.

Notwithstanding how these are viewed by the debtor, however, the fact is that compensating balances are not available for unrestricted use, and penalties will result if they are withdrawn rather than being left intact, as called for under the arrangement. Therefore, the portion of an entity's cash account that is held as a compensating balance must be segregated and shown as a noncurrent asset if the related borrowings are noncurrent liabilities. If the borrowings are current liabilities, it is acceptable to show the compensating balance as a separately captioned current asset, but under no circumstances should these be included in the caption "cash."

In some jurisdictions, certain cash deposits held by banks, such as savings accounts or corporate time deposits, are subject to terms and conditions that might prevent immediate withdrawals. While not always exercised, these rights permit a delay in honoring withdrawal requests for a stated period of time, such as seven days or one month. These rules were instituted to discourage panic withdrawals and to give the depository institution adequate time to liquidate investments in an orderly fashion. Cash in savings accounts subject to a statutory notification requirement and cash in certificates of deposit maturing during the current operating cycle or within one year may be included as current assets, but as with compensating balances, should be separately captioned in the statement of financial position to avoid the misleading implication that these funds are available immediately upon demand. Typically, such items will be included in the short-term investments caption, but these could be separately labeled as time deposits or restricted cash deposits.

Petty cash and other imprest cash accounts are usually presented in financial statements with other cash accounts. Due to materiality considerations, under current rules these need not be set forth in a separate caption unless so desired.

Receivables

Receivables include trade receivables, which are amounts due from customers for goods sold or services performed in the normal course of business, as well as such other categories of receivables as notes receivable, trade acceptances, third-party instruments, and amounts due from officers, shareholders, employees, or affiliated companies.

Notes receivable are formalized obligations evidenced by written promissory notes. The latter categories of receivables generally arise from cash advances but could develop from sales of merchandise or the provision of services. The basic nature of amounts due from trade customers is often different from that of balances receivable from related parties, such as employees or shareholders. Thus, the general practice is to insist that the various classes of receivables be identified separately either on the face of the statement of financial position or in the notes. Revised IAS 1 does not explicitly require such presentation.

IAS 39 addresses recognition and measurement of receivables. In addition, a number of international standards allude to the accounting for receivables. For example, IAS 18, *Revenue Recognition*, addresses the timing of revenue recognition, which implicitly addresses the timing of recognition of the resulting receivables.

IAS 39 requires that at reporting dates receivables be measured at amortized costs including the effect of impairment. Entities use a variety of techniques to estimate the possible level of write-offs, all of which should aim to measure receivables at an amount that takes due consideration of credit losses that have occurred at reporting date. This requires significant elements of estimation including estimating expected losses rates, as well as when any expected cash inflows will occur, which may have a significant impact as the expected cash flows are discounted to present value at the original effective interest rate.

Pledging, Assigning, and Factoring Receivables

An organization can alter the timing of cash flows resulting from sales to its customers by using its accounts receivable as collateral for borrowings or by selling the receivables outright. A wide variety of arrangements can be structured by the borrower and lender, but the most common are pledging, assignment, and factoring. The IFRS do not offer specific accounting guidance on these assorted types of arrangements, although the derecognition rules of IAS 39 generally apply to these as well as other financial instruments of the reporting entity.

Pledging of receivables. Pledging is an agreement whereby accounts receivable are used as collateral for loans. Generally, the lender has limited rights to inspect the borrower's records to achieve assurance that the receivables do exist. The customers whose accounts have been pledged are not aware of this event, and their payments are still remitted to the original obligee. The pledged accounts merely serve as security to the lender, giving comfort that sufficient assets exist that will generate cash flows adequate in amount and timing to repay the debt. However, the debt is paid by the borrower whether or not the pledged receivables are collected and whether or not the pattern of such collections matches the payments due on the debt.

The only accounting issue relating to pledging is that of adequate disclosure. The accounts receivable, which remain assets of the borrowing entity, continue to be shown as current assets in its financial statements but must be identified as having been pledged.

It is common practice to include the disclosure regarding the pledging of receivables in the notes to the financial statements and is required in terms of IFRS 7.

Assignment of receivables. The assignment of accounts receivable is a more formalized transfer of the asset to the lending institution. The lender will make an investigation of the specific receivables that are being proposed for assignment and will approve those that are deemed to be worthy as collateral. Customers are not usually aware that their accounts have been assigned and they continue to forward their payments to the original obligee. In some cases, the assignment agreement requires that collection proceeds be delivered to the lender immediately. The borrower is, however, the primary obligor and is required to make timely payment on the debt whether or not the receivables are collected as anticipated. The borrowing is with recourse, and the general credit of the borrower is pledged to the payment of the debt.

Since the lender knows that not all the receivables will be collected on a timely basis by the borrower, only a fraction of the face value of the receivables will be advanced as a loan to the borrower. Typically, this amount ranges from 70% to 90%, depending on the credit history and collection experience of the borrower.

Assigned accounts receivable remain the assets of the borrower and continue to be presented in its financial statements, with appropriate disclosure of the assignment similar to that for pledged receivables. Prepaid finance charges would be debited to a prepaid expense account and amortized to expense over the period to which the charges apply.

Factoring of receivables. This category of financing is the most significant in terms of accounting implications. Factoring traditionally has involved the outright sale of receivables to a financing institution known as a factor. These arrangements involved (1) notification to the customer to forward future payments to the factor, and (2) the transfer of receivables without recourse. The factor assumes the risk of an inability to collect. Thus, once a factoring arrangement was completed, the entity had no further involvement with the accounts except for a return of merchandise.

The classical variety of factoring provides two financial services to the business: (1) it permits the entity to obtain cash earlier, and (2) the risk of bad debts is transferred to the factor. The factor is compensated for each of the services. Interest is charged based on the anticipated length of time between the date the factoring is consummated and the expected collection date of the receivables sold, and a fee is charged based on the factor's anticipated bad debt losses.

Some companies continue to factor receivables as a means of transferring the risk of bad debts but leave the cash on deposit with the factor until the weighted-average due date of the receivables, thereby avoiding interest payments. This arrangement is still referred to as factoring, since the customer receivables have been sold. However, the borrowing entity does not receive cash but instead has created a new receivable, usually captioned "due from factor." In contrast to the original customer receivables, this receivable is essentially riskless and will be presented in the statement of financial position without a deduction for an estimated uncollectible amount.

Merchandise returns will normally be the responsibility of the original vendor, who must then make the appropriate settlement with the factor. To protect against the possibility of merchandise returns that diminish the total of receivables to be collected, very often a factoring arrangement will not advance the full amount of the factored receivables (less any interest and factoring fee deductions). Rather, the factor will retain a certain fraction of the total proceeds relating to the portion of sales that are anticipated to be returned by customers. This sum is known as the factor's *holdback*. When merchandise is returned to the borrower, an entry is made offsetting the receivable from the factor. At the end of the return privilege period, any remaining holdback will become due and payable to the borrower.

Examples of journal entries to be made by the borrower in a factoring situation

1. Thirsty Corp. on July 1, 2012, enters into an agreement with Rich Company to sell a group of its receivables without recourse. A total face value of €200,000 accounts receivable (against which a 5% allowance had been recorded) is involved. The factor will charge 20% interest computed on the (weighted) average time to maturity of the receivables of 36 days plus a 3% fee. A 5% holdback will also be retained.
2. Thirsty's customers return for credit €4,800 of merchandise.

3. The customer return privilege period expires and the remaining holdback is paid to the transferor.

The entries required are as follows:

1. Cash	180,055	
Allowance for bad debts (€200,000 × .05)	10,000	
Interest expense (or prepaid) (€200,000 × .20 × 36/365)	3,945	
Factoring fee (€200,000 × .03)	6,000	
Factor's holdback receivable (€200,000 × .05)	10,000	
Bad debts expense		10,000
Accounts receivable		200,000

(Alternatively, the interest and factor's fee can be combined into a €9,945 charge to loss on sale of receivables.)

2. Sales returns and allowances	4,800	
Factor's holdback receivable		4,800
3. Cash	5,200	
Factor's holdback receivable		5,200

Transfers of Receivables with Recourse

In recent decades, a variant on traditional receivables factoring has become popular. This variation has been called factoring with recourse, the terms of which suggest somewhat of a compromise between true factoring and the assignment of receivables. Accounting practice has varied considerably because of the hybrid nature of these transactions, and a strong argument can be made, in fact, that the factoring with recourse is nothing more than the assignment of receivables, and that the proper accounting (as discussed above) is to present this as a secured borrowing, not as a sale of the receivables. While "factoring with recourse" was previously held to qualify for derecognition by the transferor, this is now seen to be consistent with the derecognition rules of IAS 39, due to the nominal transferor's continuing involvement and retention of risk.

IAS 32: FINANCIAL INSTRUMENTS—PRESENTATION

When first issued in 1995, IAS 32 was an important achievement for several reasons. It represented a commitment to a strict "substance over form" approach. The substance of a financial instrument, rather than its legal form, governs its classification on the statement of financial position. The most signal accomplishment, perhaps, was the requirement that disparate elements of compound financial instruments be separately presented in the statement of financial position.

The objective of IAS 32 is to provide principles for

- Presenting financial instruments as liabilities or equity
- Offsetting financial assets and financial liabilities
- Classifying financial instruments, from the perspective of the issuer, into financial assets, financial liabilities, and equity instruments (and classification of related interest, dividends, losses and gains)

Scope exceptions in IAS 32, IAS 39, and IFRS 7 include

- Interests in subsidiaries, associates, and joint ventures (IAS 27, IAS 28, and IAS 31)
- Employers' rights and obligations under employee benefit plans (IAS 19)

- Insurance contracts, except for certain financial guarantee contracts (IFRS 4)
- Acquirer accounting for contingent consideration contracts in a business combination (IFRS 3)
- Financial instruments, contracts, and obligations under share-based payment transactions (IFRS 2)

Issues Addressed by IAS 32

Distinguishing liabilities from equity. It sometimes happens that financial instruments of a given issuer may have attributes of both liabilities and equity. A compound instrument is an issued single financial instrument that contains both a liability and an equity element (e.g., convertible bond). From a financial reporting perspective, the central issue is whether to account for these "compound" instruments in total as *either* liabilities or equity, *in toto*, or to disaggregate them into both liabilities and equity instruments. In 2003 the FASB adopted FAS 150, which requires debt-like instruments to be classified as liabilities. However, due to strong opposition, implementation of certain aspects of that standard have been delayed, some indefinitely. The IFRS Foundation, however, resolutely dealt with this matter.

Under the provisions of IAS 32, the issuer of a financial instrument must classify it, or its component parts, in accordance with the substance of the respective contractual arrangement. Thus it is quite clear that under IFRS, when the instrument gives rise to an obligation on the part of the issuer to deliver cash or another financial asset or to exchange financial instruments on potentially unfavorable terms, it is to be classified as a liability, not as equity. Mandatorily redeemable preference share and preference share issued with put options (options that can be exercised by the holder, potentially requiring the issuer to redeem the shares at agreed-upon prices) must, under this definition, be presented as liabilities.

The presentation of ordinary shares subject to a buyout agreement with the entity's shareholders is less clear. Closely held entities frequently structure *buy-sell agreements* with each shareholder, which require that upon the occurrence of defined events, such as a shareholder's retirement or death, the entity will be required to redeem the former shareholder's ownership interest at a defined or determinable price, such as fair or book value. The practical effect of buy-sell agreements is that all but the final shareholder will eventually become creditors; the last to retire or die will be, by default, the residual owner of the business, since the entity will be unable to redeem that holder's shares unless a new investor enters the picture. IAS 32 does not address this type of situation explicitly, although circumstances of this sort are clearly alluded to by the standard, which notes that "if a financial instrument labeled as a share gives the holder an option to require redemption upon the occurrence of a future event that is highly likely to occur, classification as a financial liability on initial recognition reflects the substance of the instrument." Notwithstanding this guidance, entities can be expected to be quite reluctant to reclassify the majority of shareholders' equity as debt in cases such as that described above.

IAS 32 goes beyond the formal terms of a financial instrument in seeking to determine whether it might be a liability. Thus, for example, under IAS 32, prior to amendments made in 2008 (see immediately following paragraphs), a preference share which has mandatory redemption provisions, or which is "puttable" by the holder, was to be classified and accounted for as a liability upon its original issuance.

According to IAS 32, before revision, if an issuer was subject to a requirement that it pay cash or deliver another financial asset in return for redeeming or repurchasing a financial instrument, the instrument was to be classified as a financial liability. This was consistent with the long-held definition of a liability as an obligation to make a future payment as a consequence of a past action. As interpreted, this held even if the amount payable was equal to the holder's interest in the net assets of the issuer, or if the amount would only become payable at liquidation and liquidation was deemed to be certain because, for example, a fixed liquidation date for the entity was defined.

Some believed that this mandate resulted in liability treatment even where it might be unwarranted, with the result that otherwise financially healthy entities could be forced to report negative equity. This would occur, for example, where the total amount payable would equal the *market value* of the whole entity, which could well exceed the *accounting net assets* of the entity. Alternatively, where liquidation is certain or is at the option of the holder, instruments that represent the last residual interest in the entity may be recognized as financial liabilities even when the instruments have characteristics similar to equity, since not all equity can be redeemed if the entity is to be considered a going concern.

To deal with these perceived anomalies, in February 2008, amendments to IAS 32 were adopted, to provide a "short-term, limited scope amendment" to obviate these unwelcome outcomes. IASB concluded that some puttable financial instruments and financial instruments that impose on the issuer an obligation to deliver a pro rata share of net assets of the entity only on liquidation are equity, and thus should not be presented as liabilities. The amendments are very particularized and cannot be analogized to any other fact patterns, and very extensive detailed criteria need to be met in order to present these instruments as equity.

The revised IAS 32 clarifies that an issuer can classify a financial instrument as equity only if both conditions are met

1. Instrument includes no contractual obligations (a) to deliver cash or another financial asset or (b) to exchange financial assets or financial liabilities with another entity under potentially unfavorable conditions to the issuer.
2. If the instrument will or may be settled in the issuer's own shares (equity instruments), it is a nonderivative that includes no contractual obligation for the issuer to deliver a variable number of its own shares, or a derivative that will be settled by the issuer exchanging a fixed amount of cash or another financial asset for a fixed number or its own shares. (For this purpose, the issuer's own shares do not include instruments that are themselves contracts for the future receipt or delivery of the issuer's own shares.)

Example of classification of contracts settled in an entity's own equity instruments (IAS 32)			
Derivative contract	*Gross physical settlement**	*Net settlement (net cash or net shares)*	*Issuer/counterparty right of gross or net settlement*
Purchased or written call	Equity	Derivative	Derivative
Purchased put	Equity	Derivative	Derivative
Written put	Liability	Derivative	Derivative/Liability
Forward to buy	Liability	Derivative	Derivative/Liability
Forward to sell	Liability	Derivative	Derivative

* *Fixed number of shares for fixed amount of cash/financial asset*

Puttable financial instruments. Under revised IAS 32, puttable financial instruments are now to be presented as equity, but only if *all* of the following criteria are met:

1. The holder is entitled to a pro rata share of the entity's net assets on liquidation;
2. The instruments is in the class of instruments that is the most subordinate and all instruments in that class have identical features;
3. The instrument has no other characteristics that would meet the definition of a financial liability; and

4. The total expected cash flows attributable to the instrument over its life are based substantially on either (1) profit or loss, (2) the change in the recognized net assets, or (3) the change in the fair value of the recognized and unrecognized net assets of the entity (excluding any effects of the instrument itself). Profit or loss or change in recognized net assets for this purpose is as measured in accordance with relevant IFRS.

In addition to the above criteria, the reporting entity is permitted to have no other instrument with terms equivalent to 4. above that has the effect of substantially restricting or fixing the residual return to the holders of the puttable financial instruments. A financial instrument that imposes an obligation to deliver a pro rata share of the net assets of an entity on liquidation should meet the first two criteria above to be classified as equity.

Based on these new requirements, it is clear that certain classifications of financial instruments issued by the reporting entity will now have to be changed. Shares that are puttable throughout their lives at fair value, that are also the most subordinate of the instruments issued by the reporting entity, and which do not contain any other obligation, and which have only discretionary (i.e., nonfixed) dividends based on profits of the issuer, will now be deemed equity, although classed as liabilities under IAS 32 prior to this amendment.

By contrast, shares that are puttable at fair value, but which are *not* the most subordinate class of instrument issued, must still be classified as liabilities under revised IAS 32.

Shares that are puttable at fair value only on liquidation, and that are also the most subordinate class of instrument, but which specify a fixed nondiscretionary dividend obligation, will now be treated as compound financial instruments (that is, as being part equity, part liability). Rules governing the allocation of proceeds among elements of compound instruments are discussed in a subsequent section of this chapter and also later in this publication.

Finally, shares that are puttable at fair value only on liquidation, and that are also part of the most subordinate class of instruments issued, but are entitled to fixed, discretionary dividends, and do not contain any other obligation, are now to be deemed part of equity, and not liabilities.

If any of these instruments have been issued by a subsidiary (rather than by the reporting parent entity), and are held by noncontrolling parties, these must be reported as liabilities in the consolidated financial statements. Thus, certain equity of the subsidiary, in its separate financial statements, to the extent held by noncontrolling interests, would have to be reclassified to liabilities in the consolidation process.

IAS 32—Presentation examples

Financial instrument	*Presentation*
Common shares	Equity
Mandatorily redeemable instruments	Liabilities*
Instruments redeemable at the option of the holder	Liabilities*
Puttable instruments	Liabilities*
Obligation to issue shares worth a fixed or determinable amount	Liabilities
Perpetual debt	Liabilities
Instruments with contingent settlement provisions	Liabilities (unless nonsubstantive provision)
Convertible debt	Potentially compound instrument

*With certain exceptions

Interests in cooperatives. IFRIC 2, *Members' Shares in Cooperative Entities and Similar Instruments*, states that the contractual right of the holder of a financial instrument (including members' shares in cooperative entities) to request redemption does not, in itself, require that financial instrument to be classified as a financial liability. Rather, the entity must consider all of the terms and conditions of the financial instrument in determining its classification as a financial liability or equity, including relevant local laws, regulations, and the entity's governing charter in effect at the date of classification.

Members' shares are equity if the entity has an unconditional right to refuse redemption of the members' shares or if redemption is unconditionally prohibited by local law, regulation, or the entity's governing charter. However, if redemption is prohibited only if defined conditions—such as liquidity constraints—are met (or are not met), members' shares are not equity.

Convertible Debt Instruments

Bonds are frequently issued with the right to convert them into ordinary shares of the company at the holder's option when certain terms and conditions are met (i.e., a target market price is reached). Convertible debt is used for two reasons. First, when a specific amount of funds is needed, convertible debt often allows fewer shares to be issued (assuming that conversion ultimately occurs) than if the funds were raised by directly issuing the shares. Thus, less dilution is suffered by the other shareholders. Second, the conversion feature allows debt to be issued at a lower interest rate and with fewer restrictive covenants than if the debt were issued without it. That is because the bondholders are receiving the benefit of the conversion feature in lieu of higher current interest returns.

This dual nature of debt and equity, however, creates a question as to whether the equity element should receive separate recognition. Support for separate treatment is based on the assumption that this equity element has economic value. Since the convertible feature tends to lower the rate of interest, it can easily be argued that a portion of the proceeds should be allocated to this equity feature. On the other hand, a case can be made that the debt and equity elements are inseparable, and thus that the instrument is either all debt or all equity. IFRS had not previously addressed this matter directly, although the focus of the IASB *Framework* on "true and fair presentation" could be said to support the notion that the proceeds of a convertible debt offering be allocated between debt and equity accounts. The promulgation of IAS 32 resulted in the defining of convertible bonds (among other instruments) as being compound financial instruments, the component parts of which must be classified according to their separate characteristics.

Features of convertible debt instruments. Revised IAS 32 addresses the accounting for compound financial instruments from the perspective of issuers. Convertible debt probably accounts for most of the compound instruments that will be of concern to those responsible for financial reporting. IAS 32 requires the issuer of such a financial instrument to present the liability component and the equity component separately in the statement of financial position. Allocation of proceeds between liability and equity proceeds as follows:

1. Upon initial recognition, the fair value of the liability component of compound (convertible) debt instruments is computed as the present value of the contractual stream of future cash flows, discounted at the rate of interest applied at inception by the market to instruments of comparable credit status and providing substantially the same cash flows, on the same terms, but absent the conversion option. For example, if a 5% interest-bearing convertible bond would have commanded an 8% yield if issued without the conversion feature, the contractual cash flows are to be discounted at 8% in order to calculate the fair value of the unconditional debt component of the compound instrument.

2. The equity portion of the compound instrument is actually an embedded option to convert the liability into equity of the issuer. The fair value of the option is deter-

mined by time value and by the intrinsic value, if there is any. This option has value on initial recognition even when it is out of the money.

The issuance proceeds from convertible debt should be assigned to the components as described below.

Convertible debt also has its disadvantages. If the share price increases significantly after the debt is issued, the issuer would have been better off simply by issuing the share. Additionally, if the price of the share does not reach the conversion price, the debt will never be converted (a condition known as overhanging debt).

Classification of compound instruments. Compound instruments are those which are sold or acquired jointly, but which provide the holder with more than a single economic interest in the issuing entity. For example, a bond sold with share purchase warrants provides the holder with an unconditional promise to pay (the bond, which carries a rate of interest and a fixed maturity date) plus a right to acquire the issuer's shares (the warrant, which may be for common or preferred shares, at either a fixed price per share or a price based on some formula, such as a price that increases over time). In some cases, one or more of the component parts of the compound instrument may be financial derivatives, as a share purchase warrant would be. In other instances, each element might be a traditional, nonderivative instrument, as would be the case when a debenture is issued with common shares as a unit offering.

The accounting issue that is most obviously associated with compound instruments is how to allocate price or proceeds to the constituent elements. This becomes most important when the compound instrument consists of parts that are both liabilities and equity items. Proper classification of the elements is vital to accurate financial reporting, affecting potentially such matters as debt covenant compliance (if the debt-to-equity ratio, for example, is a covenant to be met by the debtor entity). Under IFRS, there is no mezzanine equity section as is sometimes observed under US GAAP and, for example, redeemable shares, including contingently redeemable shares, are classified as liabilities (exceptions: redeemable only at liquidation, redemption option not genuine or certain puttable instruments representing the most residual interest in the entity).

IAS 32, revised, requires that fair value be ascertained and then allocated to the liability components, with only the residual amount being assigned to equity. This position has been taken in order to be fully consistent with the definition of equity as instruments that evidence only a residual interest in the assets of an entity, after satisfying all of its liabilities.

If the compound instruments include a derivative element (e.g., a put option), the value of those features, to the extent they are embedded in the compound financial instrument other than the equity component, is to be included in the liability component.

The sum of the carrying amounts assigned to the liability and equity components on initial recognition its always equal to the fair value that would be ascribed to the instrument as a whole. In other words, there can be no "day one" gains from issuing financial instruments.

Example of accounting by issuer of compound instrument

To illustrate the allocation of proceeds in a compound instrument situation, assume these facts.

1. 5,000 convertible bonds are sold by Needy Company on January 1, 2012. The bonds are due December 31, 2015.
2. Issuance price is par (€1,000 per bond); total issuance proceeds are €5,000,000.
3. Interest is due in arrears, semiannually, at a nominal rate of 5%.

4. Each (€1,000 face amount) bond is convertible into 150 ordinary shares of Needy Company.

5. At issuance date, similar, nonconvertible debt must yield 8%.

Required residual value method. Under the provisions of revised IAS 32, the issuer of compound financial instruments must assign full fair value to the portion that is to be classified as a liability, with only the residual value being allocated to the equity component. The computation for the above fact situation would be as follows:

1. Use the reference discount rate, 8%, to compute the market value of straight debt carrying a 5% yield:

PV of €5,000,000 due in 4 years, discounted at 8%	€3,653,451
PV of semiannual payments of €125,000 for 8 periods, discounted at 8%	841,593
Total	€4,495,044

2. Compute the amount allocable to the conversion feature

Total proceeds from issuance of compound instrument	€5,000,000
Value allocable to debt	4,495,044
Residual value allocable to equity component	€ 504,956

Thus, Needy Company received €4,495,044 in consideration of the actual debt being issued, plus a further €504,956 for the conversion feature, which is a call option on the underlying ordinary share of the issuer. The entry to record this would be

Cash	5,000,000	
Discount on bonds payable	504,956	
Bonds payable		5,000,000
Paid-in capital—bond conversion option		504,956

The bond discount would be amortized as additional interest over the term of the debt.

Example of accounting by acquirer of compound instrument

From the perspective of the acquirer, compound financial instruments will often be seen as containing an embedded derivative—for example, a put option or a conversion feature of a debt instrument being held for an investment. This may be required to be valued and accounted for separately (which does not necessarily imply separate presentation in the financial statements, however). In terms of IAS 39, separate accounting is necessary if, and only if, the economic characteristics and risks of the embedded derivative are not closely related to the host contract; a separate instrument with the same terms would meet the definition of a derivative; and the combined instrument is not to be measured at fair value with changes included in profit or loss (i.e., it is neither held for trading nor subject to the "fair value option" election).

To illustrate the allocation of purchase cost in a compound financial asset situation, assume these facts.

1. 500 convertible Needy Company bonds are acquired by Investor Corp. January 1, 2012. The bonds are due December 31, 2015.
2. The purchase price is par (€1,000 per bond); total cost is thus €500,000.
3. Interest is due in arrears, semiannually, at a nominal rate of 5%.
4. Each bond is convertible into 150 ordinary shares of the issuer.
5. At purchase date, similar, nonconvertible debt issued by borrowers having the same credit rating as Needy Company yield 8%.
6. At purchase date, Needy Company common shares are trading at €5, and dividends over the next 4 years are expected to be €0.20 per share per year.
7. The relevant risk-free rate on 4-year obligations is 4%.
8. The historic variability of Needy Company's share price can be indicated by a standard deviation of annual returns of 25%.

In terms of IAS 32, the fair value of the conversion feature should be determined, if possible, and assigned to that embedded derivative. In this example, the popular Black-Scholes-Merton model will be used (but other approaches are also acceptable).

1. Compute the standard deviation of proportionate changes in the fair value of the asset underlying the option multiplied by the square root of the time to expiration of the option.

$$.25 \times \sqrt{4} = .25 \times 2 = .50$$

2. Compute the ratio of the fair value of the asset underlying the option to the present value of the option exercise price.

   a. Since the expected dividend per share is €0.20 per year, the present value of this stream over 4 years would (at the risk-free rate) be €0.726.
   b. The shares are trading at €5.00.
   c. Therefore, the value of the underlying optioned asset, stripped of the stream of dividends that a holder of an unexercised option would obviously not receive, is

   $$€5.00 - .726 = €4.274 \text{ per share}$$

   d. The implicit exercise price is €1,000 ÷ 150 shares = €6.667 per share. This must be discounted at the risk-free rate, 4%, over 4 years, assuming that conversion takes place at the expiration of the conversion period, as follows:

   $$€6.667 \div 1.04^4 = 6.667 \div 1.170 = €5.699$$

   e. Therefore, the ratio of the underlying asset, €4.274, to the present value of the exercise price, €5.699, is .750.

3. Reference must now be made to a call option valuation table to assign a fair value to these two computed amounts (the standard deviation of proportionate changes in the fair value of the asset underlying the option multiplied by the square root of the time to expiration of the option, .50, and the ratio of the fair value of the asset underlying the option to the present value of the option exercise price, .750). For this example, assume that the table value is 13.44% (meaning that the fair value of the option is 13.44%) of the fair value of the underlying asset.

4. The valuation of the conversion option, then, is given as

   $$.1344 \times €4.274 \text{ per share} \times 150 \text{ shares/bond} \times 500 \text{ bonds} = €43,082$$

5. Since the fair value of the options (€43,082) has been determined, this is assigned to the conversion option. The difference between the cost of the hybrid investment, €500,000, and the amount allocated to the conversion feature, €43,082, or €456,918, should be attributed to the debt instrument.

6. The discount on the debt should be amortized, using the effective yield method, over the projected four-year holding period. The effective yield, taking into account the semiannual interest payments to be received, will be about 7.54%.

If, for some reason, the value of the derivative (the conversion feature, in this case) could not be ascertained, the fair value of the debt portion would be computed, and the residual allocated to the derivative. This is illustrated as follows:

1. Use the reference discount rate, 8%, to compute the market value of straight debt carrying a 5% yield.

PV of €500,000 due in 4 years, discounted at 8%	€365,345
PV of semiannual payments of €12,500 for 8 periods, discounted at 8%	84,159
Total	€449,504

2. Compute the residual amount allocable to the conversion feature.

Total proceeds from issuance of compound instrument	€500,000
Value allocable to debt	449,504
Residual value allocable to embedded derivative	€ 50,496

Induced conversion of debt instruments. A special situation may occur in that the conversion privileges of convertible debt are modified after issuance of the debt. These modifications may take the form of reduced conversion prices or additional consideration paid to the convertible debt holder. The debtor offers these modifications or "sweeteners" to induce prompt conversion of the outstanding debt. This is in addition to the normal strategy of calling the convertible debt to induce the holders to convert, assuming the underlying economic values make this attractive (debtors often do this when only a small fraction of the originally issued convertible debt remains outstanding). The issuance of these "sweeteners" should be accounted for as a reduction in the proceeds of the share offering, thereby reducing contributed capital from the transaction.

A previously acceptable alternative accounting treatment, recording the sweetener payments as an expense in the period of conversion, is no longer deemed appropriate given the proceeds allocation scheme mandated by revised IAS 32. That latter approach derived from a recognition that if it had been part of the original arrangement, a change in the exchange ratio or other adjustment would have affected the allocation of the original proceeds between debt and equity, and the discount or premium originally recognized would have been different in amount, and hence periodic amortization would have differed as well.

Debt instruments issued with share warrants. Warrants are certificates enabling the holder to purchase a stated number of shares at a certain price within a certain period. They are often issued with bonds to enhance the marketability of the bonds and to lower the bond's interest rate.

Detachable warrants are similar to other features, such as the conversion feature discussed earlier, which under IAS 32 make the debt a compound financial instrument and which necessitates that there is an allocation of the original proceeds among the constituent elements. Since warrants, which will often be traded in the market, are easier to value than are conversion features, prior to the most recent revision to IAS 32 it was logical to employ pro rata allocation based on relative market values. However, since revised IAS 32 requires allocation of only residual value to the equity element of compound instruments consisting of both liability and equity components, that approach is no longer acceptable

Instruments having contingent settlement provisions. Some financial instruments are issued which have contingent settlement provisions—that is, which may or may not require the issuer/obligor to utilize its resources in subsequent settlement. For example, a note can be issued that will be payable either in cash or in the issuer's shares, depending on whether certain contingent events, such as the share price exceeding a defined target over a defined number of days immediately preceding the maturity date of the note, are met or not. This situation differs from convertible debt, which is exchangeable into the shares of the borrower, at the holder's option.

Revised IAS 32 incorporates the conclusion previously set forth separately in SIC 5, *Classification of Financial Instruments—Contingent Settlement Provisions*, that a financial instrument is a financial liability when the manner of settlement depends on the occurrence or nonoccurrence of uncertain future events or on the outcome of uncertain circumstances that are beyond the control of *both* the issuer and the holder. Contingent settlement provisions are ignored when they apply only in the event of liquidation of the issuer or are not genuine.

Examples of such contingent conditions would be changes in a stock market index, the consumer price index, a reference interest rate or taxation requirements, or the issuer's future revenues, profit or loss or debt to equity ratio. The issuer cannot impact these factors and thus cannot unilaterally avoid settlement as a liability, delivering cash or other assets to resolve the obligation.

Under revised IAS 32, certain exceptions to the foregoing rule have been established. These exist when

1. The part of the contingent settlement provision that could require settlement in cash or another financial asset (or otherwise in such a way that it would be a financial liability) is not genuine; or
2. The issuer can be required to settle the obligation in cash or another financial asset (or otherwise to settle it in such a way that it would be a financial liability) only in the event of liquidation of the issuer.

By "not genuine," IAS 32 means that there is no reasonable expectation that settlement in cash or other asset will be triggered. Thus, a contract that requires settlement in cash or a variable number of the entity's own shares only on the occurrence of an event that is extremely rare, highly abnormal and very unlikely to occur is an equity instrument. Similarly, settlement in a fixed number of the entity's own shares may be contractually precluded in circumstances that are outside the control of the entity, but if these circumstances have no genuine possibility of occurring, classification as an equity instrument is appropriate.

If the settlement option is only triggered upon liquidation, this possibility is ignored in classifying the instrument, since the going concern assumption, underlying IFRS-basis financial reporting, presumes ongoing existence rather than liquidation.

In other instances the instrument includes a "put" option (i.e., an option that gives the holder the right, but not the obligation, to cause the issuer to redeem it at a fixed or determinable price). Notwithstanding certain prominent features suggesting an equity ownership, under the provisions of the revised IAS 32, any such instruments would have to be classified as liabilities. Again, this is because the issuer does not retain an unconditional right to avoid settlement using cash or other resources of the entity.

It also happens that entities will enter into contractual obligations of a fixed amount or of an amount that fluctuates in part or in full in response to changes in a variable other than the market price of the entity's own equity instruments, but which the entity must or can settle by delivery of its own equity instruments, the number of which depends on the amount of the obligation. Under revised IAS 32, such an obligation must be reported as a financial liability of the entity, unless the terms are such that this is deemed "not genuine." The reasoning is that if the number of an entity's own shares or other own equity instruments required to settle an obligation varies with changes in their fair value so that the total fair value of the entity's own equity instruments to be delivered always equals the amount of the contractual obligation, then the counterparty does not hold a true residual interest in the entity. Furthermore, settlement in shares could require the issuing entity to deliver more or fewer of its own equity instruments than would be the case at the date of entering into the contractual arrangement. This leads the IASB to conclude that such an obligation is a financial liability of the entity even though the entity must or can settle it by delivering shares

Treasury shares. When an entity reacquires its own equity instruments ("treasury shares"), the consideration paid is deducted from equity. Treasury shares are not treated as assets, but are to be deducted from equity. No gain or loss should be recognized in profit or loss on the purchase, sale, issue or cancellation of an entity's own equity instruments since transactions with shareholders do not affect profit or loss. Treasury shares may be acquired and held by the entity or by other members of the consolidated group. Consideration paid or received from transactions with treasury shares should be recognized directly in equity. An entity must disclose the number of treasury shares held either in the statement of financial position or in the notes, in accordance with IAS 1. In addition, disclosures under IAS 24 must be provided if an entity reacquires its own shares from related parties.

Reporting interest, dividends, losses, and gains. IAS 32 establishes that interest, dividends, losses and gains relating to a financial instrument or a component that is a financial *liability* should be recognized as income or expense in profit or loss in the statement of comprehensive income or in the income statement, if it is presented separately. Distributions (dividends) paid on *equity* instruments issued should be charged directly to equity, net of any related income tax benefit. (These will be reported in the statement of changes in equity.) Transaction costs of an equity transaction should be accounted for as a deduction from equity, net of any related income tax benefit. The statement of financial position classification of the instrument drives the statement of comprehensive income classification of the related interest or dividends. For example, if mandatorily redeemable preferred shares have been categorized as debt in the issuer's statement of financial position, dividend payments on those shares must be recognized in profit or loss in the same manner as interest expense. Similarly, gains or losses associated with redemptions or refinancing of financial instruments classed as liabilities would be recognized in profit or loss, while gains or losses on equity are credited or charged to equity directly.

Offsetting financial assets and liabilities. Under the provisions of IAS 32, offsetting financial assets and liabilities is permitted only when the entity *both* (1) has the legally enforceable right to set off the recognized amounts, and (2) intends either to settle on a net basis, or to realize the asset and settle the liability simultaneously. Simultaneous settlement of a financial asset and a financial liability can be presumed only under defined circumstances. The most typical of such cases is when both instruments will be settled through a clearinghouse functioning for an organized exchange. Other situations may superficially appear to warrant the same accounting treatment but in fact do not give rise to legitimate offsetting. For example, if the entity will exchange checks with a single counterparty for the settlement of both instruments, it becomes exposed to credit risk for a time, however brief, when it has paid the other party for the amount of the obligation owed to it but has yet to receive the counterparty's funds to settle the amount it is owed by the counterparty. Offsetting would not be warranted in such a context.

The standard sets forth a number of other circumstances in which offsetting would *not* be justified. These include

1. When several different instruments are used to synthesize the features of another type of instrument (which typically would involve a number of different counterparties, thus violating a basic principle of offsetting).
2. When financial assets and financial liabilities arise from instruments having the same primary risk exposure (such as when both are forward contracts) but with different counterparties.
3. When financial assets are pledged as collateral for nonrecourse financial liabilities (as the intention is not typically to effect offsetting, but rather, to settle the obligation and gain release of the collateral).
4. When financial assets are set aside in a trust for the purpose of discharging a financial obligation but the assets have not been formally accepted by the creditor (as when a sinking fund is established, or when in-substance defeasance of debt is arranged).

5. When obligations incurred as a consequence of events giving rise to losses are expected to be recovered from a third party by virtue of an insurance claim (again, different counterparties means that the entity is exposed to credit risk, however slight).

Even the existence of a master netting agreement does not automatically justify the off-setting of financial assets and financial liabilities. Only if both the stipulated conditions (both the right to offset and the intention to do so) are met can this accounting treatment be employed.

Disclosure requirements under IAS 32. The disclosure requirements established by IAS 32 were later largely subsumed under those established by IAS 39. Per another revision in 2003, however, the disclosure requirements were again situated in IAS 32. In August 2005, all disclosure requirements were removed from IAS 32 (which continues as the authoritative source of presentation requirements) and placed in new IFRS 7. Disclosure requirements in accordance with IFRS 7 are discussed later in this chapter.

IAS 39: FINANCIAL INSTRUMENTS—RECOGNITION AND MEASUREMENT

Applicability

IAS 39 is applicable to all financial instruments *except* interests in subsidiaries, associates and joint ventures that are accounted for in accordance with IAS 27, 28, and 31, respectively; rights and obligations under operating leases, to which IAS 17 applies; most rights and obligations under insurance contracts; employers' assets and liabilities under employee benefit plans and employee equity compensation plans, to which IAS 19 applies; and equity instruments issued by the reporting entity.

IAS 39 as originally promulgated was not applicable to financial guarantee contracts, such as letters of credit, when such contracts call for payments that would have to be made only if the primary debtor fails to perform; accounting for these types of arrangements was specified by IAS 37. However, amendments to IAS 39 and IFRS 4 made in 2005 have prescribed the accounting for guarantee contracts by the guarantor. It states that financial guarantees are initially to be measured at fair value, with subsequent measurement at the greater of the initial measurement and the best estimate as defined in IAS 37. The effect of this amendment was to bring the *recognition* decision under IAS 39, while leaving *measurement* guidance under IAS 37.

IAS 39 criteria apply where the guarantor will have to make payments when a defined change in credit rating, commodity prices, interest rates, security price, foreign exchange rate, an index of rates or prices, or other underlying indicator occurs. Also, if a guarantee arises from an event leading to the derecognition of a financial instrument, the guarantee must be recognized as set forth in this standard.

IAS 39 does not apply to contingent consideration arrangements pursuant to a business combination for business combinations concluded before the effective date of IFRS 3, *Business Combinations* (revised 2008).

The standard does not apply to contracts that require payments dependent upon climatic, geological, or other physical factors or events, although if other types of derivatives are embedded therein, IAS 39 would set the requirements for recognition, measurement, disclosure, and derecognition.

IAS 39 must be applied to commodity-based contracts that give either party the right to settle by cash or some other financial instrument, with the exception of commodity contracts that were entered into and continue to meet the entity's expected purchase, sale, or usage requirements and were designated for that purpose at their inception. With regard to embedded derivatives, if their economic characteristics and risks are not closely related to the economic characteristics and risks of the host contract, and if a separate instrument with the same terms as the embedded derivative would meet the definition of a derivative, they are to be separated from the host contract and accounted for as a derivative in accordance with the standard. IFRIC 9, *Reassessment of Embedded Derivatives*, provides additional interpretation concerning this matter. An entity should assess whether an embedded derivative is required to be separated from the host contract and accounted for as a derivative when the entity first becomes a party to the contract. Subsequent reassessment is *prohibited* unless there is a change in the terms of the contract that significantly modifies the cash flows that otherwise would be required under the contract; in this case reassessment is required.

A first-time IFRS adopter should assess whether an embedded derivative is required to be separated from the host contract and accounted for as a derivative on the basis of conditions existing at the later of the date it first becomes a party to the contract and the date a reassessment is required because a change in the terms of the arrangement significantly alters the cash flows otherwise mandated under the contract.

Initial Recognition and Measurement

An entity should recognize a financial asset or a financial liability in its statement of financial position only when the entity becomes a party to the contractual provisions of that instrument. Debt and equity instruments held as financial assets (investments) are initially measured at fair value (cost), including transactions costs directly attributable to the acquisition (e.g., fees, commissions, transfer taxes, etc.), as of the date when the investor entity becomes a party to the contractual provisions of the instrument. In general this date is readily determinable and unambiguous. Transaction costs are *not* included in initial measurement of instruments classified as at fair value through profit or loss (FVTPL).

For instruments purchased "regular way" (when settlement date follows the trade date by several days), however, recognition may be on either the trade or the settlement date. In "regular-way purchase or sale" delivery must be within the time frame generally established by regulation or convention in the market concerned (e.g., settlement on T + 3 days). An entity has a choice between the trade date or settlement date accounting rather than derivatives accounting, but a policy should be applied consistently for each category of financial assets. Any change in fair value between these dates must be recognized (strictly speaking, regular-way trades involve a forward contract, which is a derivative financial instrument, but IAS 39 does not require that these be actually accounted for as derivatives). If a transaction is considered "regular-way," a derivative is not recognized for the time period between the trade and the settlement date.

If an entity recognizes financial assets using the settlement date, any change in fair value of assets received between the trade date and the settlement date is recognized in profit or loss (if assets classified as at FVTPL) or equity (if assets classified as available-for-sale); changes in fair value during this period are not recognized for assets carried at cost or amortized cost.

Derecognition

Derecognition of financial assets. IAS 39 prescribes the accounting treatment for derecognition of a financial asset. Revisions to the standard effective in 2005 altered somewhat the criteria for derecognition of investments in financial instruments. A guiding principle has become the "continuing involvement approach," which prohibits derecognition to the extent to which the transferor has continuing involvement in an asset or a portion of an asset it has transferred.

In accordance with IAS 39 there are two main concepts—risks and rewards, and control—that govern derecognition decisions. The standard makes it clear that evaluation of the transfer of risks and rewards of ownership must in all instances precede the evaluation of the transfer of control.

Appendix A to IAS 39 provides the following flowchart illustrating the evaluation of whether and to what extent a financial asset should be derecognized:

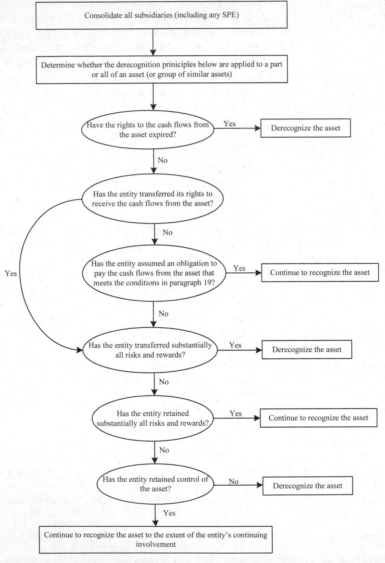

The derecognition approach should be considered at the consolidated group level after applying IAS 27 and SIC 12 prior to derecognition assessment. In accordance with IAS 27 all controlled entities should be included in the consolidated financial statements. In addition,

SIC 12 requires that a special-purpose entity (SPE) be consolidated if the substance of the relationship indicates that the SPE is controlled by the reporting entity.

The term "financial asset" refers to either a part of a financial asset or a part of a group of similar assets. An entity needs to determine whether derecognition principles are applied to a part or all of a financial asset (or group of similar assets). Derecognition is applied to a part of an asset transferred only if the part comprises

- Specifically identified cash flows (e.g., an interest-only strip) when the counterparty obtains the right to interest cash flows but not the principal cash flows from a debt instrument;
- A fully proportionate (pro rata) share of cash flows (e.g., 90 % of all cash flows); and
- A fully proportionate share of specifically identified cash flows (e.g., 90% of interest cash flows from a financial asset).

Unless one of the foregoing criteria is satisfied, derecognition of a portion of a financial asset is not permitted. In that case, the financial asset must be considered for derecognition in its entirety.

An entity should remove (derecognize) a previously recognized financial asset from its statement of financial position *only* when (1) the contractual rights to the cash flows from the financial asset expire (e.g., expired option) or (2) it transfers the financial asset and the transfer qualifies for derecognition.

An entity transfers a financial asset only if

1. It transfers the contractual rights to receive the cash flows of the financial asset; or
2. It retains the contractual rights to receive the cash flows of the financial asset, but assumes an obligation to pay the cash flows to one or more recipients in a "pass-through arrangement."

If the entity has transferred its rights to receive the cash from the financial asset, the next step would be to consider whether risks and rewards of ownership are transferred. If rights to the cash flows are retained, an entity should consider whether a "pass-through arrangement" exists. The entity treats the transaction as a transfer of a financial asset when all of the following three conditions are met for the transaction to be a "pass-through arrangement":

1. The entity has no obligation to pay amounts not collected; short-term advances by the entity with the right of full recovery of the amount lent plus accrued interest at market rates do not violate this condition.
2. The entity is prohibited from selling or pledging the original asset other than as security to the eventual recipients for the obligation to pay them cash flows.
3. The entity has an obligation to remit any cash flows collected on behalf of the eventual recipients without material delay. In addition, the entity must not be entitled to reinvest the cash flows, except for investments in cash or cash equivalents; and interest earned (if any) on such investments must be passed on to the eventual recipients.

When an entity transfers a financial asset, the next step in applying derecognition principles is to evaluate the extent to which it retains the risks and rewards of ownership of the financial asset.

If the entity has transferred substantially all the risks and rewards of ownership of the financial asset, the entity should derecognize the financial asset and recognize separately as assets or liabilities any rights and obligations created or retained in the transfer. The entity's exposure before and after the transfer should be evaluated; risks and rewards are retained if exposure to variability in cash flows does not change significantly as a result of the transfer.

Examples of transactions when the entity transfers substantially all of the risks and rewards of ownership include (1) unconditional sale of a financial asset, and (2) sale of a financial asset with an option to repurchase at fair value at the time of repurchase.

If the entity retains substantially all the risks and rewards of ownership of the financial asset, the entity should not remove this asset from its statement of financial position and continue to recognize the financial asset. Examples of transactions when substantially all risks and rewards are retained include (1) sale and repurchase transaction with repurchase price being fixed; (2) sale of a financial asset with a total return swap; (3) sale of a financial asset with a deep-in-the-money option (and it is highly unlikely to go out of the money before expiry); and (4) sale of short-term receivables with a guarantee to compensate for likely-to-occur credit losses.

If the entity *neither* transfers *nor* retains substantially all the risks and rewards of ownership of the financial asset, the next step is to determine whether it has retained *control* of the financial asset.

- If control has not been retained, the entity derecognizes the financial asset and recognizes separately as assets or liabilities any rights and obligations created or retained in the transfer.
- If the entity has retained control, it continues to recognize the financial asset to the extent of its continuing involvement in the financial asset.

In accordance with IAS 39, whether the entity has retained control of the transferred asset depends on the transferee's ability to sell the assets to an unrelated third party; to exercise that ability unilaterally; and without needing to impose additional restrictions on the transfer. In all other cases, the entity has retained control and continues recognizing the financial asset to the extent of continuing involvement and recognizing an associated liability. Examples of continuing involvements and the requisite measurement approaches include

1. Guarantee—the transferred asset continues to be recognized at the lower of (a) the amount of the asset and (b) the maximum amount of consideration that the entity could be required to repay.
2. Written put option on asset measured at fair value—the transferred asset continues to be recognized at the lower of the fair value of the asset or the option exercise price.
3. Purchased call option—the transferred asset continues to be recognized at the amount of the transferred asset that the transferor could repurchase.

If an entity has retained control of a financial instrument, measurement of the financial asset and financial liability is on the basis that reflects rights and obligations that the entity has retained. The entity continues to recognize an asset to the extent of its continuing involvement, and also recognizes the associated liability, measured so that net carrying amount of the transferred asset and associated liability is

- Amortized cost of the rights and obligations retained by the entity, if the transferred asset is measured at amortized cost; or
- Equal to the fair value of the rights and obligations retained by the entity, if the transferred asset is measured at fair value.

Derecognition of financial liabilities. According to IAS 39, removing a financial liability (or part of a financial liability) from the reporting entity's statement of financial position is warranted only when the obligation is *extinguished*. This will be deemed to have occurred when the obligation specified in the contract is discharged or canceled or expires.

In some instances, the debt issuer exchanges newly issued debt carrying different terms (as to maturities, interest rates, etc.) for outstanding debt. Under IAS 39, under such circumstances the original debt will be deemed extinguished, and a new liability will be deemed to have been incurred. Likewise, substantial modifications to the terms of existing financial liabilities, or to a part of that debt, whether this is attributable to financial exigencies or not, are now to be accounted for as extinguishments.

If there is a difference between the carrying amount (i.e., book value) of a financial liability extinguished or transferred (or relevant portion thereof) and the consideration paid to accomplish this, including the fair value of noncash assets transferred or liabilities assumed, this gain or loss will be recognized in profit or loss.

When only a part of an existing liability is repurchased, the carrying value is allocated pro rata between the part extinguished and the part that remains outstanding. This allocation is to be based upon relative fair values. Gain on loss is recognized as the difference between the carrying value allocated to the portion extinguished and the consideration paid to accomplish this extinguishment, using the same approach as described above.

If the extinguishment of debt does not occur on the interest date, the interest payable accruing between the last interest date and the acquisition date must also be recorded.

Example of accounting for the extinguishment of debt

1. A 10%, ten-year, €200,000 bond is dated and issued on 1/1/11 at €98, with the interest payable semiannually.
2. Associated bond issue costs of €14,000 are incurred.
3. Four years later, on 1/1/15 the entire bond issue is repurchased at €102 per €100 face value and is retired.
4. The straight-line method of amortization is used since the result is not materially different from that when the effective interest method is used.

The gain or loss on the repurchase is computed as follows:

Reacquisition price [(102/100) × €200,000]	€204,000	
Net carrying amount:		
Face value	€200,000	
Unamortized discount [2% × €200,000 × (6/10)]	(2,400)	
Unamortized issue costs [€14,000 × (6/10)]	(8,400)	189,200
Loss on bond repurchase		€ 14,800

Gain or loss on derecognition of financial liabilities. The difference between the net carrying value and the consideration paid, including any noncash assets transferred or liabilities assumed, is recorded as a gain or loss. If the acquisition price is greater than the carrying value, a loss is incurred and must be accounted for. A gain is generated if the acquisition price is less than the carrying value. These gains or losses are to be recognized in the period in which the extinguishment takes place. These should be reported as "other" income or expense, because this is the same profit or loss category where interest expense is normally reported. It would not be appropriate, however, to include any gain or loss in the interest pool from which capitalized interest is computed under IAS 23 (discussed in Chapter 10).

Subsequent Measurement

Subsequent measurement of financial assets. The accounting of financial instruments is dependent upon whether instruments are classified as (1) at fair value through profit or loss (those held for trading and those designated as at fair value through profit or loss upon initial recognition), (2) available-for-sale, or (3) held-to-maturity.

Debt and equity instruments held as investments are to be accounted for at fair value, if classified as at fair value through profit or loss (FVTPL), or available for sale. For instruments subsequently measured at fair value through profit or loss, transaction costs may not be capitalized.

In the case of investments carried at FVTPL (those held for trading purposes or those otherwise designated as held at FVTPL), gains and losses arising from changes in fair value from period to period are included in profit or loss. Given the explicit presumption that these financial instruments will be disposed of in the near term, as market conditions may warrant, marking these to fair value through profit and loss is entirely logical, and mandatory.

Gains and losses arising from changes in fair value of investments classified as available-for-sale are recognized in other comprehensive income and accumulated in equity, under the caption "Available-for-Sale Financial Assets," except for impairment losses and foreign exchange gains and losses, which must be reflected in current profit or loss, until the financial asset is derecognized. Under provisions of the original IAS 39, the changes in fair value could either be included in profit or loss, or recognized in other comprehensive income, although each reporting entity had been required to make a onetime election as to which of these alternatives it would conform to thereafter. However, revised IAS 39 (effective 2005) eliminated this option, so optional recognition in profit or loss is not permitted, although the "fair value (FVTPL) option" is available and accomplishes the same objective (see discussion below).

Exceptions to the general principle of measuring financial assets at their fair values include

- Held-to-maturity investments measured at amortized cost using the effective interest method
- Loans and receivables measured at amortized cost using the effective interest method
- Investments in equity instruments that do not have a quoted market price in an active market and whose fair value cannot be reliably measured (and derivatives that must be settled by delivery of such unquoted equity instruments) measured at cost.

Debt instruments to be held to maturity are maintained at amortized cost, unless objective evidence of impairment exists. Of course, this assumes that the conditions for classification as held-to-maturity as set forth by IAS 39 are met; namely, that management has demonstrated both the intent and the ability to hold the instruments until the maturity date.

When an investment in bonds is classified as available-for-sale, so that fair value changes are reported in other comprehensive income and accumulated in equity until the investment is sold, the amortization of premium or discount on such an investment should nonetheless be reported in profit or loss as part of interest income or expense. Amortization cannot be included as part of the change in fair value and included in other comprehensive income. Under provisions of IAS 39, as well as under provisions of IAS 18 and IAS 32, these amounts are measured using the effective interest method, which means that the amortization of premium or discount is part of interest income or interest expense and therefore included in determining net profit or loss.

A summary of subsequent measurement of financial assets is presented in Table 1 below.

Table 1. Subsequent Measurement of Financial Assets: Summary

Category	*Measurement*
Fair value through profit and loss (FVTPL)	Fair value—through profit or loss (P&L)
Held-to-maturity (HTM)	Amortized cost—effective interest method
Loans and receivables (L&R)	Amortized cost—effective interest method
Available-for-sale (AFS)	Fair value—through other comprehensive income (OCI) and equity

The transaction costs included in the originally recorded basis of held-to-maturity financial assets are included in the calculation of effective interest rate and amortized to the P&L over the expected life of the investment, as part of any premium or discount. Transaction costs included in the carrying value of financial assets classified as available-for-sale are recognized as part of changes in fair value. If available-for-sale instruments have fixed or determinable payments, transaction costs are amortized to the P&L using the effective interest method. For those instruments listed as available-for-sale without fixed or determinable payments, costs are recognized in the P&L when the assets are derecognized or impaired.

Subsequent measurement of liabilities. After initial recognition, financial liabilities are subsequently measured at amortized cost, using the effective interest method. Exceptions to the general rule of measuring financial liabilities at amortized cost include

- Financial liabilities classified as at fair value through profit or loss, including derivatives that are liabilities, are accounted for at fair value, with changes in fair value recognized in profit or loss in the current period (except for a derivative liability, measured at cost, that is linked and must be settled by delivery of an unquoted equity instrument whose fair value cannot be reliably determined).
- Financial liabilities recognized when a transfer of a financial asset does not qualify for derecognition or when the continuing involvement approach applies.
- Financial guarantee contracts measured at the higher of (1) the amount determined in accordance with IAS 37 and (2) the amount initially recognized less cumulative amortization (IAS 18).
- Commitments to provide a loan at a below-market interest rate measured at the higher of (1) the amount determined in accordance with IAS 37 and (2) the amount initially recognized less cumulative amortization (IAS 18).

In addition, financial liabilities designated as hedge items are accounted for in accordance with the hedge accounting requirements.

Substantial modification of the terms of existing debt instruments. When an existing borrower and lender of debt exchange instruments with substantially different terms, this represents an extinguishment of the old debt and results in derecognition of that debt and recognition of a new debt instrument. IAS 39 defines "substantial modification of the terms" of an existing debt instrument and the standard requires that those modifications should be accounted for as extinguishments, provided that the discounted present value of cash flows under the terms of the new debt differs by at least 10% from the discounted present value of the remaining cash flows of the original debt instrument.

In computing the discounted present values for determining whether the 10% limit has been exceeded, the effective interest rate of the (old) debt being modified or exchanged is to be used. If the difference in present values is at least 10% the transaction is to be accounted for as an extinguishment of the old debt. In such case, the new, modified debt is initially recognized at fair value. On the other hand, a difference of less than 10%, is to be amortized over the remaining term of the debt instrument. In this instance, the debt is not to be remeasured at fair value and any costs or fees incurred adjust the carrying value of the debt and will be amortized by the effective interest method.

If an exchange of debt instruments, or if a modification of terms is accounted for under IAS 39 as an extinguishment, costs or fees incurred are to be recognized as part of the gain or loss incurred in the extinguishment. In nonextinguishment instances, any costs or fees incurred in the transaction are to be accounted for as adjustments to the carrying amount of the liability, to be amortized over the remaining term of the modified loan.

Under IAS 39, the reasons for the debt modification or exchange are irrelevant to the determination of the accounting to be applied. In this regard, IFRS contrasts with US GAAP, which historically had applied different accounting to those debt modifications which were identified as "troubled debt restructurings."

Example of accounting for debt exchange or restructuring with gain recognition

Assume that Debtor Corp. owes Friendly Bank €90,000 on a 5% interest-bearing nonamortizing note payable in five years, plus accrued and unpaid interest, due immediately, of €4,500. Friendly Bank agrees to a restructuring to assist Debtor Corp., which is suffering losses and is threatening to declare bankruptcy. The interest rate is reduced to 4%, the principal is reduced to €72,500, and the accrued interest is forgiven outright. Future payments will be on normal terms.

Whether there is recognition of a gain on the restructuring depends on the 10% threshold. The relevant discount rate to be used to compare the present values of the old and the new debt obligations is 5%. The present value of the old debt is simply the principal amount, €90,000, plus the interest due at present, €4,500, for a total of €94,500.

The present value of the replacement debt is the discounted present value of the reduced principal and the reduced future interest payments; the forgiven interest does not affect this. The new principal, €72,500, discounted at 5%, equals €56,806. The stream of future interest payments (€72,500 × .04 = €2,900 annually in arrears), discounted at 5%, equals €12,555. The total present value, therefore, is €69,361, which is about 27% below the present value of the old debt obligation. Thus, the 10% threshold is exceeded, and a gain will be recognized at the date of the restructuring.

However, given Debtor's current condition, the market rate of interest for its debt would actually be 12%, and since the new obligation must be recorded at fair value, this must be computed. The present value of the reduced principal, €72,500, discounted at 12%, has a present value of €41,138. The stream of future interest payments (€72,500 × .04 = €2,900 annually, in arrears), discounted at 12%, has a present value of €10,454. The total obligation thus has a fair value of €51,592.

The entry to record this event would be

Debt obligation (old) payable	90,000	
Interest payable	4,500	
Discount on debt obligation (new)	20,908	
Debt obligation (new) payable		72,500
Gain on debt restructuring		42,908

Note that the new debt obligation is recorded at a net of €51,592, not at the face value of €72,500. The difference, €20,908, is a discount to be amortized to interest expense over the next five years, in order to reflect the actual market rate of 12%, rather than the nominal 4% being charged. Amortization should be accomplished on the effective yield method.

Example of accounting for debt exchange or restructuring with gain deferral

Assume now that Hopeless Corp. owes Callous Bank €90,000 on a 5% interest-bearing non-amortizing note payable in five years, plus accrued and unpaid interest, due immediately, of €4,500. Callous Bank agrees to a restructuring to assist Hopeless Corp., which is also suffering losses and is threatening to declare bankruptcy. However, Callous is only willing to reduce the principal amount from €90,000 to €85,000, and reduce interest to 4.5% from 5%. It is not willing to forego the currently owed €4,500 interest payment, and furthermore requires that the loan maturity be shortened to three years, from five, in order to limit its risk. Hopeless agrees to the new terms.

In order to comply with IAS 39, the present value of the new debt must be compared to the present value of the old, existing obligation. As in the preceding example, the present value of the old debt is simply the principal amount, €90,000, plus the interest due at present, €4,500, for a total of €94,500.

The present value of the replacement debt is the discounted present value of the reduced principal and the reduced future interest payments, plus the interest using a 5% discount factor (= .86384 for the new three-year term), has a present value of €73,426. The stream of future interest payments (€85,000 × .045 = €3,825 annually in arrears), discounted at 5% (= 2.7231 annuity factor), has a present value of €10,416. The total present value, therefore, is (€73,426 + €10,416 + €4,500 =) €88,342, which is about 7% below the present value of the old debt obligation. Accordingly, since the 10% threshold is not exceeded, the difference of (€94,500 – €88,342 =) €6,158 is not recognized as a gain at the date of the restructuring, but rather is deferred and amortized over the new three-year term of the restructured loan.

The entry to record this event would be

Debt obligation (old) payable	90,000	
Discount on debt obligation (new)	1,158	
Debt obligation (new) payable		85,000
Deferred gain on debt restructuring		6,158

Note that the new debt obligation is recorded at a net of €83,842, not at the face value of €85,000. The difference of €1,158 represents a discount to be amortized to interest expense over the subsequent three years; this will result in an interest expense at the actual market rate of 5%, rather than at the nominal 4.5% rate. Amortization should be computed on the effective yield method, although if the discrepancy is not material the straight-line method may be employed. The deferred gain, €6,158, will be amortized over the three-year revised term. While the discount amortization will be added to interest expense. IAS 39 is silent as to how the amortization of the deferred gain should be handled. However, by reference to how a gain in excess of the 10% threshold (and thus been subject to immediate recognition) would have been reported, it is thought likely that this amortization should be included in "other income," and should not be offset against interest expense.

Presentation of the gain or loss from debt restructurings is not explicitly dealt with under IFRS. However, since IAS 8 has been revised, as part of the IASB's *Improvements Project* to eliminate the presentation of extraordinary items in profit or loss, there is no difficulty in making the appropriate decision. Gain or loss on debt extinguishments should, in the authors' opinion, be displayed as items of "other" income or expense in profit or loss

Determining fair value. In accordance with IAS 39, fair value is the amount for which an asset could be exchanged, or a liability settled, between knowledgeable, willing parties in an arm's-length transaction, which generally equals transaction price. The best evidence of fair values is provided by quoted prices in active markets. A financial instrument is regarded as quoted in an active market if quoted prices are readily and regularly available from an exchange, dealer, broker, industry group, pricing service or regulatory agency, and those prices represent actual and regularly occurring market transactions on an arm's-length basis.

If no active market exists, valuation techniques must be used which would maximize market inputs and minimize entity-specific inputs. Valuation techniques include using recent quoted prices in active markets for similar instruments, discounted cash flow analysis and option pricing models. Chapter 25 discusses in further detail the IASB project, *Fair Value Measurement.*

The financial crisis has arguably made it difficult for many entities to determine the fair value of certain financial instruments, because the markets for many financial instruments have become relatively inactive. In April 2008, the IASB established an expert advisory panel to identify best practices and establish guidance on measuring and disclosing the fair value of financial instruments. In October 2008, the IASB released its final report, *Measuring and Disclosing the Fair Value of Financial Instruments in Markets That Are No Longer Active,* summarizing the discussions held by the panel. An *IASB Staff Summary* was also released, providing educational guidance on using judgment to measure the fair value of financial instruments when markets are no longer active. In response to the financial crisis, the IASB has also announced that it has accelerated its project on Fair Value Measurement Guidance, which is discussed in Chapter 25.

The objective of fair value measurement in IAS 39 is to determine the price at which an orderly transaction (excluding forced liquidation or a distress transaction) would take place between market participants at the measurement date. An entity should consider all relevant market information that is available when measuring fair value, and when using a valuation technique, should maximize the use of relevant observable inputs and minimize the use of unobservable inputs. Determining fair value in a market that has become inactive may require the use of significant judgment and include appropriate risk adjustments that market participants would make, such as for credit quality and liquidity.

In some cases, when significant adjustments are required to available observable inputs, it might be appropriate to use a valuation technique based primarily on unobservable inputs (commonly referred to as "mark-to-model"). Multiple inputs from different sources (including broker or pricing service) might provide the best evidence of fair value, and the weighting of those inputs based on the extent to which they provide relevant information about the fair value is required. In weighing a broker quote as an input to a fair value measurement, an entity should place less reliance on quotes that do not reflect the result of market transactions and consider the nature of the quote (for example, whether the quote is an indicative price or a binding offer).

IAS 39 provides guidance about how to determine fair values using valuation techniques. A valuation technique that would be acceptable for use would (1) incorporate all factors that market participants would consider in setting a price and (2) be consistent with accepted economic methodologies for pricing financial instruments. In applying valuation techniques, the reporting entity is to use estimates and assumptions that are consistent with available information about the estimates and assumptions that market participants would use in setting a price for the financial instrument.

Fair value through profit and loss (FVTPL) option. Under the provisions of IAS 39, an entity can designate any financial asset or financial liability as one to be measured at fair value, with changes in fair value recognized in current profit or loss. However, this election can only be made upon initial recognition. To preclude the obvious temptation to selectively determine which assets to treat this way from one period to the next, the reporting entity is prohibited from reclassifying financial instruments into or out of this category. Thus, the election is irrevocable upon initial recognition. Since it will not be known at the date of initial recognition whether the fair value of the instrument will increase or decrease in subsequent periods, manipulation of financial results cannot easily occur.

The fair value option can be employed in connection with either available-for-sale or held-to-maturity investments. Designation is made on an instrument-by-instrument basis and the whole instrument approach, so a portion (e.g., 80%) of a financial instrument or a component (e.g., interest rate risk only) cannot be designated. Investments in equity instruments that do not have quoted prices in active markets and whose fair value cannot be reliably measured are *not* eligible for designation as FVTPL.

Constraints on use of held-to-maturity classification. Under IAS 39, held-to-maturity investments are nonderivative financial assets having fixed or determinable payments and fixed maturity, that an entity has the positive intention and ability to hold to maturity other than those that

1. The entity designates as being carried at fair value through profit or loss at the time of initial recognition;
2. The entity designates as available for sale; or
3. Meet the definition of loans and receivables.

Importantly, an entity is not permitted to classify any financial assets as held-to-maturity if it has, during the current financial reporting year or during the two preceding financial reporting years, sold or reclassified more than an insignificant amount of held-to-maturity investments before maturity other than sales or reclassifications that

1. Are so close to maturity or to the asset's call date (e.g., less than three months before maturity) that changes in the market rate of interest would not have a significant effect on the financial asset's fair value over that time interval;
2. Occur after the entity has collected substantially all of the financial asset's original principal through scheduled payments (e.g., from payments on serial bonds) or prepayments; or
3. Are attributable to an isolated event that is beyond the entity's control, is nonrecurring and could not have been reasonably anticipated by the entity.

In applying the foregoing rule, *more than insignificant* is evaluated in relation to the total amount of held-to-maturity investments.

It is clear that an entity cannot have a demonstrated ability to hold an investment to maturity if it is subject to a constraint that could frustrate its intention to hold the financial asset to maturity. One question that arises is whether a debt security that has been pledged as collateral or transferred to another party under a repurchase agreement ("repo") or instruments lending transaction and continues to be recognized by the reporting entity, can still be classified as a held-to-maturity investment. Accordingly to the IGC (IASB's Implementation Guidance Committee), an entity's intent and ability to hold debt instruments to maturity is not necessarily constrained if those instruments have been pledged as collateral or are subject to a repurchase agreement or instruments lending agreement. However, an entity does not have the positive intent and ability to hold the debt instruments until maturity if it does not expect to be able to maintain or recover access to the instruments. Thus, the specific facts and circumstances of the repo arrangement must be given careful consideration in concluding on the classification of the instruments.

The strictures against early sales of instruments that had been classified as held-to-maturity are quite severe. For example, if an investor sells a significant amount of financial assets classified as held-to-maturity, and does not thereafter classify any financial assets acquired subsequently as held-to-maturity, but maintains that it still intends to hold the remaining investments originally categorized as held-to-maturity to their respective maturities and accordingly does not reclassify them, the reporting entity will be deemed to be not in compliance with IAS 39. Thus, whenever a sale or transfer of more than an insignificant amount of financial assets classified as held-to-maturity results in the conditions in IAS 39 not being satisfied, no instruments should continue to be classified in that category. Any remaining held-to-maturity assets must be reclassified as available-for-sale. The reclassification is recorded in the reporting period in which the sales or transfers occurred and is accounted for as a change in classification as prescribed by the standard. Once this violation has occurred, at least two full years must pass before an entity can again classify financial assets as held-to-maturity.

Another question concerning continuing classification of investments as held-to-maturity relates to sales that are triggered by a change in the management of the investor entity. According to the IGC, such sales would definitely compromise the classification of other financial assets as held-to-maturity. A change in management is not identified under IAS 39 as an instance where sales or transfers from held-to-maturity do not compromise the classification as held-to-maturity. Sales that are made in response to such a change in management would, therefore, call into question the entity's intent to hold any of its investments to maturity.

The IGC cited an example similar to the following: A company held a portfolio of financial assets that was classified as held-to-maturity. In the current period, at the direction of the board of directors, the entire senior management team was replaced. The new management wishes to sell a portion of the held-to-maturity financial assets in order to carry out an expansion strategy designated and approved by the board, as part of its recovery strategy. Although the previous management team had been in place since the entity's inception and the company had never before undergone a major restructuring, the sale will nevertheless call into question this entity's intent to hold remaining held-to-maturity financial assets to maturity. If the sale goes forward, all held-to-maturity instruments would have to be reclassified, and the entity will be precluded from using that classification for investments for another two years (the "tainting" rule).

Another indication of the stringency of the requirements for classifying instruments as held-to-maturity is suggested by an IGC position on sales made to satisfy regulatory authorities. In some countries, regulators of banks or other industries may set capital requirements on an entity-specific basis based on an assessment of the risk in that particular entity. IAS 39 indicates that an entity that sells held-to-maturity investments in response to an unanticipated significant increase by the regulator of the industry's capital requirements may do so under that standard without necessarily raising a question about its intention to hold other investments to maturity. The IGC has ruled, however, that sales of held-to-maturity investments that are due to a significant increase in *entity-specific* capital requirements imposed by regulators will indeed "taint" the entity's intent to hold other financial assets as held-to-maturity. Thus, unless it can be demonstrated that the sales fulfill the condition in IAS 39 in that the sales were the result of an increase in capital requirements which was an isolated event that was beyond the entity's control and that is nonrecurring and could not have been reasonably anticipated by the entity.

Held-to-maturity investments disposed of before maturity. As noted above, an entity may not classify any financial asset as held-to-maturity unless it has both the positive intent and ability to hold it to maturity. To put teeth into this threshold criterion, IAS 39 stipulates that, if a sale of a held-to-maturity financial asset occurs, it calls into question the entity's intent to hold all other held-to-maturity financial assets to maturity. However, IAS 39 provides exceptions for held-to-maturity investments that can be disposed of before maturity under certain conditions: for sales "close enough to maturity," and after collection of "substantially all" of the original principal.

Questions have arisen in practice on how these conditions should be interpreted. The IGC has offered certain insights into the application of these exception criteria. As interpreted, these conditions relate to situations in which an entity can be expected to be indifferent whether to hold or sell a financial asset because movements in interest rates—occurring after substantially all of the original principal has been collected or when the instrument is close to maturity—will not have a significant impact on its fair value. In such situations, a sale would not affect reported net profit or loss and no price volatility would be expected during the remaining period to maturity.

More specifically, the condition "close enough to maturity" addresses the extent to which interest rate risk is substantially eliminated as a pricing factor. According to the IGC, if an entity sells a financial asset less than three months before its scheduled maturity, the application of the held-to-maturity classification can still be used. The impact on the fair value of the instrument for a difference between the stated interest rate and the market rate generally would be small for an instrument that matures in three months, in contrast to an instrument that matures in several years, for example.

The condition of having collected "substantially all" of the original principal provides guidance as to when a sale is for not more than an insignificant amount. Thus, if an entity sells a financial asset after it has collected 90% or more of the financial asset's original principal through scheduled payments or prepayments, the requirements of IAS 39 would probably not be deemed to have been violated. However, if the entity has collected only 10% of the original principal, then that condition clearly is not met. The 90% threshold is apparently not meant to be absolute, so some judgment is still needed to operationalize this exception.

In some cases a debt instrument will have a put option associated with it; this gives the holder (the investor) the right, but not the obligation, to require that the issuer redeem the debt, under defined conditions. The existence of the put option need not be an impediment to held-to-maturity classification. IAS 39 permits an entity to classify a puttable debt instrument as held-to-maturity, provided that the investor has the positive intent and ability to hold the investment until maturity and does not intend to exercise the put option. However, if an entity has sold, transferred, or exercised a put option on more than an insignificant amount of other held-to-maturity investments, the continued use of the held-to-maturity classification would be prohibited, subject to exceptions for certain sales (very close to maturity, after substantially all principal has been recovered, and due to certain isolated events). The IGC has stated that these same exceptions apply to transfers and exercises (rather than outright sales) of put options in similar circumstances. The IGC cautions, however, that classification of puttable debt as held-to-maturity requires great care, as it seems inconsistent with the likely intent when purchasing a puttable debt instrument. Given that the investor presumably would have paid extra for the put option, it would seem counterintuitive that the investor would be willing to represent that it does not intend to exercise that option.

In addition to debt instruments being held to maturity, any financial asset that does not have a quoted market price in an active market, fair value of which cannot be reliably measured, will of necessity also be maintained at cost, unless there is evidence of impairment in value. Furthermore, loans or receivables which are originated by the reporting entity, and which are *not* held for trading purposes, are also to be maintained at cost, per IAS 39. Loans or receivables that are acquired from others, however, are accounted for in the same manner as other debt instruments (i.e., they must be classified as at fair value through profit or loss, available-for-sale, or held-to-maturity, and accounted for accordingly).

Under IAS 39, held-to-maturity financial assets (i.e., debt instruments held for long-term investment) and originated loans are measured at amortized cost, using the effective interest method. This requires that any premium or discount be amortized not on the straight-line basis, but rather by the effective interest method, in order to achieve a constant yield on the amortized carrying value. One question that arises is how discount or premium arising in connection with the purchase of a variable-rate debt instrument should be amortized (i.e., whether it should be amortized to maturity or to the next repricing date.)

The IGC has ruled that this depends generally on whether, at the next repricing date, the fair value of the financial asset will be its par value. In theory, of course, a constantly repricing variable-rate instrument will sell at or very close to par value, since it offers a current yield fully reflective of market rates and the issuer's credit risk. Accordingly, the IGC notes that there are two potential reasons for the discount or premium: it either (1) could reflect the timing of interest payments—for instance, because interest payments are in arrears or have otherwise accrued since the most recent interest payment date or market rates of interest have changed since the debt instrument was most recently repriced to par—or (2) the market's required yield differs from the stated variable rate, for instance, because the credit spread required by the market for the specific instrument is higher or lower than the credit spread that is implicit in the variable rate.

Thus, a discount or premium that reflects interest that has accrued on the instrument since interest was last paid or changes in market rates of interest since the debt instrument was most recently repriced to par is to be amortized to the date that the accrued interest will be paid and the variable interest rate will be reset to the market rate. On the other hand, to the extent the discount or premium results from a change in the credit spread over the variable rate specified in the instrument, it is to be amortized over the remaining term to maturity of the instrument. In this case, the date the interest rate is next reset is not a market-based repricing date of the entire instrument, since the variable rate is not adjusted for changes in the credit spread for the specific issue.

Example

To illustrate, a twenty-year bond is issued at €10,000,000, which is the principal (i.e., par) amount. The debt requires quarterly interest payments equal to current three-month LIBOR plus 1% over the life of the instrument. The interest rate reflects the market-based required rate of return associated with the bond issue at issuance. Subsequent to issuance, the credit quality of the issuer deteriorates, resulting in a bond rating downgrade. Thereafter, the bond trades at a significant discount. Columbia Co. purchases the bond for €9,500,000 and classifies it as held-to-maturity. In this case, the discount of €500,000 is amortized to profit or loss over the period to the maturity of the bond. The discount is not amortized to the next date interest rate payments are reset. At each reporting date, Columbia assesses the likelihood that it will not be able to collect all amounts due (principal and interest) according to the contractual terms of the instrument, to determine the need for recognizing an impairment loss as a charge against profit or loss.

With the foregoing principles in mind, a basic example of the accounting for investments in equity instruments is next presented.

Example of accounting for investments in equity instruments

Assume that Raphael Corporation acquires the following equity instruments for investment purposes during 2010:

Security description	Acquisition cost	Fair value at year-end
1,000 shares Belarus Steel common stock	€ 34,500	€ 37,000
2,000 shares Wimbledon pfd. "A" share	125,000	109,500
1,000 shares Hillcrest common stock	74,250	88,750

Assume that, at the respective dates of acquisition, management of Raphael Corporation designated the Belarus Steel and Hillcrest common stock investments as being for trading purposes, while the Wimbledon preferred shares were designated as having been purchased for long-term investment purposes (and will thus be categorized as available-for-sale rather than trading). Accordingly, the entries to record the purchases were as follows:

Investment in equity instruments—held-for-trading	108,750	
Cash		108,750
Investment in equity instruments—available-for-sale	125,000	
Cash		125,000

At year-end, both portfolios are adjusted to fair value; the decline in Wimbledon preferred share, series A, is judged to be a temporary market fluctuation because there is no objective evidence of impairment. The entries to adjust the investment accounts at December 31, 2010, are as follows:

Investment in equity instruments—held-for-trading	17,000	
Gain on holding equity instruments		17,000
Unrealized loss on equity instruments (OCI)—available-for-sale (other comprehensive income account)	15,500	
Investment in equity instruments—available-for-sale		15,500

Thus, the change in value of the portfolio of trading financial assets is recognized in profit or loss, whereas the change in the value of the available-for-sale financial assets is reflected in other comprehensive income and accumulated in equity.

Notes and Bonds

Noncurrent liabilities generally take one of two forms: notes or bonds. *Notes* generally represent debt issued to a single investor without intending for the debt to be broken up among many investors. Their maturity, usually lasting one to seven years, tends to be shorter than that of a bond. *Bonds* also result from a single agreement. However, a bond is intended to be broken up into various subunits, for example, 1,000 (or equivalent) each, which can be issued to a variety of investors.

Notes and bonds share common characteristics: a written agreement stating the amount of the principal, the interest rate, when the interest and principal are to be paid, and the restrictive covenants, if any, that must be met. The interest rate is affected by many factors including the cost of money, the business risk factors, and the inflationary expectations associated with the business.

Nominal vs. effective rates. The stated rate on a note or bond often differs from the market rate at the time of issuance. When this occurs, the present value of the interest and principal payments will differ from the maturity, or face value. If the market rate exceeds the stated rate, the cash proceeds will be less than the face value of the debt because the present value of the total interest and principal payments discounted back to the present yields an amount that is less than the face value. Because an investor is rarely willing to pay more than the present value, the bonds must be issued at a discount. The discount is the difference between the issuance price (present value) and the face, or stated, value of the bonds. This discount is then amortized over the life of the bonds to increase the recognized interest expense so that the total amount of the expense represents the actual bond yield.

When the stated rate exceeds the market rate, the bond will sell for more than its face value (at a premium) to bring the effective rate to the market rate and will decrease the total interest expense. When the market and stated rates are equivalent at the time of issuance, no discount or premium exists and the instrument will sell at its face value. Changes in the market rate subsequent to issuance are irrelevant in determining the discount or premium or the amount of periodic amortization.

Notes are a common form of exchange in business transactions for cash, property, goods, and services. Most notes carry a stated rate of interest, but it is not uncommon for noninterest-bearing notes or notes bearing an unrealistic rate of interest to be exchanged. Notes such as these, which are long-term in nature, do not reflect the economic substance of the transaction since the face value of the note does not represent the present value of the consideration involved. Not recording the note at its present value will misstate the cost of the asset or services to the buyer, as well as the selling price and profit to the seller. In subsequent periods, both the interest expense and revenue will be misstated.

In general, the transaction price (cash, or the fair value of any noncash consideration) will define the fair value of a financial instrument, including liabilities, at initial recognition. For most liabilities, this will be equivalent to the present value of all associated contractual cash flows, discounted at the relevant interest rate. However, when part of the consideration is other than the instrument, fair value may be estimated using a valuation technique (e.g., option pricing models). When a long-term loan is received which bears no interest or a nonmarket rate of interest, the present value must be computed with reference to contractual cash flows and current market rates. Any extra amount given is reflected in current earnings unless some other asset has been obtained.

Accordingly, it is suggested that all commitments to pay (and receive) money at a determinable future date be subjected to present value calculations and, if necessary, interest imputation, with the exceptions of the following:

1. Normal accounts payable due within one year
2. Amounts to be applied to purchase price of goods or services or that provide security to an agreement (e.g., advances, progress payments, security deposits, and retainages)
3. Obligations payable at some indeterminable future date (warranties)
4. Lending and depositor savings activities of financial institutions whose primary business is lending money
5. Transactions where interest rates are affected by prescriptions of a governmental agency (e.g., revenue bonds, tax exempt obligations, etc.)

Notes issued solely for cash. When a note is issued solely for cash, its present value is assumed to be equal to the cash proceeds. The interest rate is that rate which equates the cash proceeds to the amounts to be paid in the future (i.e., *no* interest rate is to be imputed). For example, a €1,000 note due in three years that sells for €889 has an implicit rate of 4% (€1,000 × .889, where .889 is the present value factor of a lump sum at 4% for three years). This rate is to be used when amortizing the discount.

Noncash transactions. When a note is issued for consideration such as property, goods, or services, and the transaction is entered into at arm's length, the stated interest rate is presumed to be fair unless (1) no interest rate is stated, (2) the stated rate is unreasonable, or (3) the face value of the debt is materially different from the consideration involved or the current market value of the note at the date of the transaction. As discussed above, it is recommended that when the rate on the note is not considered fair, the note is to be recorded at the fair market value of the property, goods, or services received or at an amount that reasonably approximates the market value of the note, whichever is the more clearly determinable. When this amount differs from the face value of the note, the difference is to be recorded as a discount or premium and amortized to interest expense.

Example of accounting for a note exchanged for property

1. Alpha sells Beta a machine that has a fair market value of €7,510.
2. Alpha receives a 3-year noninterest-bearing note having a face value of €10,000.

In this situation, the fair market value of the consideration is readily determinable and thus represents the amount at which the note is to be recorded. The following entry is necessary:

Machine	7,510	
Discount on notes payable	2,490	
Notes payable		10,000

The discount will be amortized to interest expense over the 3-year period using the interest rate implied in the transaction.

If the fair market value of the consideration or note is not determinable, the present value of the note must be determined using an *imputed* interest rate. This rate will then be used to establish the present value of the note by discounting all future payments on the note at this rate. General guidelines for imputing the interest rate include the prevailing rates of similar instruments from creditors with similar credit ratings and the rate the debtor could obtain for similar financing from other sources. Other determining factors include any collateral or restrictive covenants involved, the current and expected prime rate, and other terms pertaining to the instrument. The objective is to approximate the rate of interest that would have resulted if an independent borrower and lender had negotiated a similar transaction under comparable terms and conditions. This determination is as of the issuance date, and any subsequent changes in interest rates would be irrelevant.

Bonds represent a promise to pay a sum of money at a designated maturity date plus periodic interest payments at a stated rate. Bonds are used primarily to borrow funds from the general public or institutional investors when a contract for a single amount (a note) is too large for one lender to supply. Dividing up the amount needed into €1,000 or €10,000 units makes it easier to sell the bonds.

In most situations, a bond is issued at a price other than its face value. The amount of the cash exchanged is equal to the total of the present value of the interest and principal payments. The difference between the cash proceeds and the face value is recorded as a premium if the cash proceeds are greater or a discount if they are less. The journal entry to record a bond issued at a premium follows:

Cash	(proceeds)	
Premium on bonds payable		(difference)
Bonds payable		(face value)

The premium will be recognized over the life of the bond issue. If issued at a discount, "Discount on bonds payable" would be debited for the difference. As the premium is amortized, it will reduce interest expense on the books of the issuer (a discount will increase interest expense). The premium (discount) would be added to (deducted from) the related liability when a statement of financial position is prepared.

The *effective interest method* is the prescribed method of accounting for a discount or premium arising from a note or bond, although some other method may be used (e.g., straight-line) if the results are not materially different. Under the effective interest method, the discount or premium is to be amortized over the life of the debt so as to produce a constant rate of interest when applied to the amount outstanding at the beginning of any given period. Therefore, interest expense is equal to the market rate of interest at the time of issuance multiplied by this beginning figure. The difference between the interest expense and the cash paid represents the amortization of the discount or premium. The effective rate is a required disclosure under IAS 32.

As with other aspects of financial reporting requirements, if alternative methods do not result in material disparities versus the prescribed approaches to measurement, they may also be used. Interest expense under the *straight-line method* is equal to the cash interest paid plus the amortized portion of the discount or minus the amortized portion of the premium. The amortized portion is equal to the total amount of the discount or premium divided by the life of the debt from issuance in months multiplied by the number of months the debt has been outstanding that year.

Example of applying the effective interest method

1. A three-year, 12%, €10,000 bond is issued at 1/1/11 with interest payments due semiannually.
2. The market rate is 10%.

The amortization table would appear as follows:

Date	Credit cash	Debit int. exp.	Debit premium	Unamortized prem. bal.	Carrying Value
1/1/11				€507.61	€10,507.61[(a)]
7/1/11	€ 600.00[(b)]	€ 525.38[(c)]	€ 74.62[(d)]	432.99[(e)]	10,432.99[(f)]
1/1/12	600.00	521.65	78.35	354.64	10,354.64
7/1/12	600.00	517.73	82.27	272.37	10,272.37
1/1/13	600.00	513.62	86.38	185.99	10,185.99
7/1/13	600.00	509.30	90.70	95.29	10,095.29
1/1/14	600.00	504.71[(g)]	95.29	--	€10,000.00
	€3,600.00	€3,092.39	€507.61		

[(a)] PV of principal and interest payments

€10,000(.74622) = € 7,462.20

€   600(5.07569) = 3,045.41

€10,507.61

[(b)] €10,000.00 × .06

[(c)] €10,507.61 × .05

[(d)] €600.00 – €525.38

[(e)] €507.61 – €74.62

[(f)] €10,507.61 – €74.62 (or €10,000 + €432.99)

[(g)] Rounding error = €.05

When the interest date does not coincide with the year-end, an adjusting entry must be made. The proportional share of interest payable should be recognized along with the amortization of the discount or premium. Within the amortization period, the discount or premium can be amortized using the straight-line method, as a practical matter, or can be computed more precisely as described above.

If the bonds are issued between interest dates, discount or premium amortization must be computed for the period between the sale date and the next interest date. This is accomplished by "straight-lining" the period's amount calculated using the usual method of amortization. In addition, the purchaser prepays the seller the amount of interest that has accrued since the last interest date. This interest is recorded as a payable by the seller. At the next interest date, the buyer then receives the full amount of interest regardless of how long the bond has been held. This procedure results in interest being paid equivalent to the time the bond has been outstanding.

Various costs may be incurred in connection with issuing bonds. Examples include legal, accounting, and underwriting fees; commissions; and engraving, printing, and registration costs. These costs should be deducted from the initial carrying amount of the bonds and amortized using the effective interest method; generally the amount involved is insignificant enough that use of the simpler straight-line method would not result in a material difference. These costs do not provide any future economic benefit and therefore should not be considered an asset. Since these costs reduce the amount of cash proceeds, they in effect increase the effective interest rate and probably should be accounted for the same as an unamortized discount. Current liabilities that are expected to be refinanced on a long-term basis, and that accordingly are classified as noncurrent liabilities according to IAS 1, are discussed in Chapter 18.

Reclassifications

2008 relaxation of rules against reclassifications from the held-for-trading category. There is only a limited ability to revise the classification of investments in financial instruments under IAS 39. This limitation was imposed to preclude manipulation of profit or loss by, for example, deciding on a period-by-period basis which value changes will be reflected in profit or loss and which will be reported in other comprehensive income (and thus accumulated directly in equity). Entities cannot reclassify instruments that were designated as at fair value through profit or loss using the fair value option, nor derivatives.

In October 2008, the IASB published amendments to IAS 39 and IFRS 7 to allow reclassification of certain financial instruments from held-for-trading to either held-to-maturity, loans and receivables, or available-for-sale categories under certain circumstances. The amendments were made in response to requests by regulators to allow banks to measure instruments which are no longer traded in an active market at amortized cost, and consequently reducing reported profit or loss volatility. Under US GAAP, transfers from those categories are restricted but still possible, whereas under IAS 39 no such reclassifications were previously permitted. This change to IFRS thus moves practice somewhat closer to that under US GAAP, at least in this limited domain.

Entities are allowed to reclassify certain financial instruments out of the held-for-trading category if the original intent has changed and they are no longer held for sale in the near future. The amended IAS 39 distinguishes between those financial assets which are eligible for classification as loans and receivables and those which are not. Financial assets are eligible for classification as loans and receivables if they are held for trading and, in addition, have fixed or determinable payments, are not quoted in an active market, and are those for which the holder should recover substantially all of its initial investment, other than as might be impacted by credit deterioration.

Financial assets that are not eligible for classification as loans and receivables can be transferred from the held-for-trading category to held-to-maturity or to available-for-sale only in "rare" circumstances. The Basis for Conclusions to IAS 39 states that "rare" circumstances arise from a single event that is "unusual and highly unlikely to recur in the near term." On its Web site, the IASB has confirmed that the deterioration of world markets that occurred during the third quarter of 2008 is a possible example of rare circumstances. It is thus clear that the unusual occurrences of mid-to-late 2008, which continued through at least the first part of 2009, provided the impetus for this significant change to IFRS, which was (and will continue to be) rather controversial.

In addition, concerning loans and receivables, if an entity has the intention and the ability to hold the asset for the "foreseeable future" or until maturity, then

- Financial assets that would *not* meet the criteria to be classified as loans and receivables may be transferred from held-for-trading to loans and receivables, and
- Financial assets that would now meet the criteria to be classified as loans and receivables may be reclassified out of the available-for-sale category to loans and receivables.

The reclassification should be based on the fair value on the date of reclassification, which becomes the new cost (or amortized cost) basis. For example, an instrument that was acquired at its par value of €1,000 had declined in fair value to €700, and is now reclassified as held-to-maturity, should be measured at amortized cost of €700. Any difference between the new amortized cost and the instrument's expected recoverable amount is amortized using the new effective interest rate over the expected remaining life, similar to the amortization of a premium or discount. Gain or loss that has already been recognized in profit or loss should not be reversed. Therefore, in the above example, the loss of €300 recognized previously, would not be reversed through profit or loss, either on reclassification or in future, except through adjustments to interest income.

Any reclassified instruments are subsequently tested for impairments in accordance with the IAS 39 impairment requirements for the categories into which they are reclassified. For example, any subsequent changes in fair value of an instrument reclassified into the available-for-sale category (other than amortization of interest using the new effective interest rate) from the date of reclassification will be recorded in other comprehensive income and accumulated in equity as revaluation surplus until the instrument is derecognized or impaired.

The effective date of the amended IAS 39 was July 1, 2008, several months earlier than the October 2008 date on which the amendment was finalized. Reclassifications before this date were not permitted; so with the first application of the amended standard, entities were able to reclassify instruments as of July 1, 2008.

Reclassifications from the held-to-maturity to available-for-sale category. IAS 39 requires that a held-to-maturity investment must be reclassified as available-for-sale and re-measured at fair value as of the date of transfer if there is a change of intent or ability. Note that this may well be at an interim date, and fair value as of the next reporting date would not necessarily suffice to gauge the gain or loss to be recognized. Transfers from the held-to-maturity category to available-for-sale are measured at fair value at the date of transfer with the difference between the financial instrument's carrying amount and fair value recognized in other comprehensive income (and accumulated in equity)

Reclassifications out of the held-to-maturity category may jeopardize all other similar classifications. The IGC has addressed the issue of whether such a reclassification might call into question the classification of other held-to-maturity investments. It finds that such reclassifications could well raise the specter of having to reclassify all similarly categorized investments. IAS 39's requirements concerning early sales of some held-to-maturity investments apply not only to sales, but also to transfers of such investments. The term "transfer" comprises any reclassification out of the held-to-maturity category. Thus, the transfer of more than an insignificant portion of held-to-maturity investments into the available-for-sale category would not be consistent with an intention to hold other held-to-maturity investments to maturity.

Consequently, investments classified as held-to-maturity may be mandatorily reclassified to available-for-sale if the entity, during the current year or the two prior years, has sold, transferred, or exercised a put option on more than an insignificant amount of similarly classified instruments before maturity date. However, sales very close to the maturity dates (or exercised call dates) will not "taint" the classification of other held-to-maturity financial assets, nor will sales occurring after substantially all of the asset's principal has been collected (e.g., in the case of serial bonds or mortgage instruments), or when made in response to isolated events beyond the entity's control (e.g., the debtor's impending financial collapse) when nonrecurring in nature and not subject to having been forecast by the entity.

Reclassification from the available-for-sale to held-to-maturity category. An entity is permitted, as a result of a change in intention or ability and because the two-year "tainting period" has passed, to reclassify any financial assets from the available-for-sale category to the held-to-maturity category. Transfers from the available-for-sale to the held-to-maturity category are measured at fair value at the date of transfer with the fair value on the date of reclassification becoming the amortized cost.

Reclassifications from the available-for-sale category to cost. Any financial asset classified as available-for-sale that does not have a quoted market price in an active market or has fair value which cannot be reliably measured, will of necessity be carried at cost, unless there is evidence of impairment in value. Furthermore, on the date when a quoted price in active markets becomes available or its fair value can be reliably measured, the financial asset must be reclassified to the available-for-sale category, with changes in fair value recognized in other comprehensive income and accumulated in equity.

Impairments and Uncollectibility

Accounting for impairments—general concerns. A financial asset or group of financial assets (except those carried at FVTPL) need to be assessed at the end of each reporting period, whether there is any objective evidence that the assets are impaired. This is to be assessed as a result of one or more events that occurred after the initial recognition of the asset (a "loss event") and that loss event (or events) impacts the estimated future cash flows of the financial asset(s) that can be reliably estimated. Loss events include any significant financial difficulties of the issuer, a contractual breach (default or delinquency) by the issuer, the probability of a bankruptcy or financial reorganization, or the disappearance of an active market for the issuer's instruments (although the fact that an entity has "gone private" does not create the presumption of impairment).

If there is an objective evidence of impairment, measurement of impairment losses presented in Table 2 is as follows:

Table 2. Measurement of Impairment Losses

Financial assets carried at	*Measurement of impairment loss*
Amortized cost (Loans & receivables; Held to maturity)	Difference between the carrying amount and the present value of expected future cash flows, discounted using the instrument's original discount rate
Fair value (Available for sale)	Difference between the acquisition cost (net of any principal repayment and amortization) and current fair value, less any impairment loss previously recognized in profit or loss
Cost (Fair value cannot be reliably measured)	Difference between the carrying amount of the financial asset and the present value of estimated future cash flows discounted at the current market rate of return for similar financial asset

For financial assets being reported at amortized cost (those held to maturity, plus loans or receivables originated by the entity), the amount of the impairment to be recognized is the difference between the carrying amount and the present value of expected future cash flows, discounted using the instrument's original discount rate. Unquoted equity instruments carried at cost (because its fair value cannot be reliably measured) are also tested for impairment and the amount of impairment loss is calculated as the difference between the carrying amount of the financial asset and the present value of estimated future cash flows discounted at the current market rate of return for similar financial asset. If a decline in the fair value of an available-for-sale financial asset has been recognized in other comprehensive income and there is objective evidence that the asset is impaired, the cumulative impairment loss should be reclassified from equity to profit or loss.

Evidence of impairment. A financial asset (or a group of assets) is impaired only if there is objective evidence of impairments as a result of one or more events that occurred after the initial recognition of the asset (which IAS 39 calls a "loss event") and that loss event (or events) has an impact on the estimated future cash flows of the financial asset (or group of assets) that can be reliably estimated. Losses that are anticipated to occur as a result of future events, no matter how likely this may appear to be, cannot be given current recognition. (This is consistent with guidance on provisions and contingencies under IAS 37.)

In practice, it may not be possible to identify a single, specific event that causes an impairment. Rather, the combined effect of several events may be the cause. Revised IAS 39 does offer a useful tabulation of such factors, however. These include the following matters:

1. Significant financial difficulty of the issuer or obligor;
2. A default or delinquency in interest or principal payments, or other breach of contract by the borrower;
3. The lender, for economic or legal reasons relating to the borrower's financial difficulty, granting an otherwise unlikely concession to the borrower;
4. A growing likelihood that the borrower will enter bankruptcy or reorganize;
5. The elimination of an active market for the asset because of financial difficulties; or
6. Observable data about a measurable decrease in the estimated future cash flows from a *group* of financial assets since their initial recognition, although the decrease cannot yet be identified with the individual financial assets in the group, including

   a. Adverse changes in the payment status of borrowers in the group (e.g., an increased number of late payments; increased frequency of credit card borrowers reaching their credit limits and that are paying monthly minimums); or
   b. National or local economic indicators that correlate with defaults on the assets in the group (e.g., increased unemployment rate in the geographical area of the borrowers; decreased property prices (for mortgage assets); decreased commodity prices (for loans to commodity producers); adverse changes in other industry conditions).

In addition to the above loss events, objective evidence of impairment for an investment in an equity instrument includes information about changes in technological, economic, and legal environments. A significant or prolonged decline in the fair value of an investment in equity instruments below its cost may also constitute objective evidence of impairment.

The disappearance of an active market because an entity's financial instruments are no longer publicly traded, and a decline in the fair value of a financial asset below its cost or amortized cost, is not necessarily evidence of impairment, although it may be evidence of impairment when considered with other available information. In some cases experienced professional judgment must be used to estimate the amount of impairment losses, for example when a borrower is in financial difficulties and there are few available historical data relating to similar borrowers.

Impairments of financial assets is one of the issues that the IASB is addressing in the second phase of its project to replace IAS 39. The current impairment approach under the *incurred loss* model could be replaced by another model, such as *expected loss* model.

Impairment of financial assets carried at amortized cost. IAS 39 requires that impairment be recognized for financial assets carried at amortized cost (loans and receivables or held-to-maturity investments) if there is objective evidence that an impairment has been incurred. That impairment may be measured and recognized individually or, for a group of similar financial assets, on a portfolio basis. As noted above, the amount of the loss is measured as the difference between the asset's carrying amount and the present value of estimated future cash flows discounted at the financial asset's original effective interest rate. Future credit losses that have not been incurred cannot be included in this computation (again, the concepts underlying IAS 37 must be observed). The original effective rate is not the nominal or contractual rate of the debt, but rather is the effective interest rate computed at the date of initial recognition of the investment. If an impairment is determined to exist, the carrying amount of the asset may either be reduced directly or via the use of an allowance account. Any loss is to be recognized currently in profit or loss.

Where there is no ability to individually assess financial assets accounted for at amortized cost for impairment, IAS 39 directs that these assets be grouped and assessed on a portfolio basis. The following additional guidance is provided to evaluate impairment inherent in a group of loans, receivables or held-to-maturity investments that cannot be identified with any individual financial asset in the group:

- Assets individually assessed for impairment and found to be impaired should not be included in a group of assets that are collectively assessed for impairment
- Assets individually assessed for impairment and found *not* to be individually impaired should be included in a collective assessment of impairment
- When performing a collective assessment of impairment, an entity groups assets by similar credit risk characteristics
- Expected cash flows are estimated based on contractual cash flows and historical loss experience (adjusted on the basis of relevant observable data reflecting current economic conditions)
- Impairment loss should not be recognized on the initial recognition of an asset.

A reversal of a previously recognized impairment is permitted when there is clear evidence that the reversal occurred subsequent to the initial impairment recognition and is the result of a discrete event, such as the improved credit rating of the debtor. This reversal is accounted for consistent with the impairment—that is, it is recognized in current period profit or loss. However, the amount of recovery recognition is limited, so that the new carrying value of the asset is no greater than what its carrying value would have been had the impairment not occurred, adjusted for any amortization over the intervening period.

For example, consider an asset that was carried at €8,000 and being accreted, at €500 per year, to a maturity value of €10,000 at the time it was found to be impaired and written down to €5,000. Two years later the credit-related problem was resolved and the fair value was assessed as €9,500. However, it can only be restored to a carrying value of €9,000, which is what would have been the carrying value had two further years' amortization (at €500 per year) been accreted.

If an asset has been individually assessed for impairment and was found not be individually impaired, according to IAS 39 it should be included in the collective assessment of impairment. According to the standard, this is to reflect that, in the light of the law of large numbers, impairment may be evident in a group of assets, but not yet meet the threshold for recognition when any individual asset in that group is assessed.

However, it is not permissible to avoid addressing impairment on an individual asset basis in order to use group assessment, in a deliberate effort to benefit from the implicit offsetting described above. If one asset in the group is impaired but the fair value of another asset in the group is above its amortized cost, nonrecognition of the impairment of the first asset is not permitted. If it is known that an individual financial asset carried at amortized cost is impaired, IAS 39 requires that the impairment of that asset be recognized. Measurement of impairment on a portfolio basis under IAS 39 is applicable *only* when there is indication of impairment in a group of similar assets, and impairment cannot be identified with an individual asset in that group.

In actually assessing impairment on a portfolio basis (a "collective assessment of impairment"), care should be taken to include only assets having similar credit risk characteristics, indicative of the debtors' ability to pay all amounts due according to the contractual terms. While contractual cash flows and historical loss experience will provide a basis for estimating *expected* cash flows, these historical data must be adjusted for relevant observable data reflecting current (i.e., as of the end of the reporting period) economic conditions.

IAS 39 further cautions that whatever methodology is used to measure impairment, it should ensure that an impairment loss is not recognized at the initial recognition of an asset. Put another way, the imputed interest rate on a newly acquired debt instrument should be the rate that equates the net carrying amount of the financial instrument and the present value of future cash flows, and this rate is used consistently thereafter in valuing the asset as future cash flow expectations change. An impairment on "day one" thus cannot exist, and would indicate an error in methodology should it occur.

Assessment and recognition of loan impairment. If an originated loan with fixed interest rate payments is hedged against the exposure to interest rate risk by a "receive-variable, pay-fixed" interest rate swap, the hedge relationship qualifies for fair value hedge accounting and is reported as a fair value hedge. Thus, the carrying amount of the loan includes an adjustment for fair value changes attributable to movements in interest rates. According to an interpretive finding by the IGC, an assessment of impairment in the loan should take into account the fair value adjustment for interest rate risk. Since the loan's original effective interest rate prior to the hedge is made irrelevant once the carrying amount of the loan is adjusted for any changes in its fair value attributable to interest rate movements, the original effective interest rate and amortized cost of the loan are adjusted to take into account recognized fair value changes. The adjusted effective interest rate is calculated using the adjusted carrying amount of the loan. An impairment loss on the hedged loan should therefore be calculated as the difference between its carrying amount after adjustment for fair value changes attributable to the risk being hedged and the expected future cash flows of the loan discounted at the adjusted effective interest rate.

Assume that, due to financial difficulties of Knapsack Co., one of its customers, the Galactic Bank, becomes concerned that Knapsack will not be able to make all principal and interest payments due on an originated loan when they become due. Galactic negotiates a restructuring of the loan, and it now expects that Knapsack will be able to meet its obligations under the restructured terms. Whether Galactic Bank will recognize an impairment loss—and in what magnitude—will depend, according to the IGC, on the specifics of the restructured terms. The IGC offers the following guidelines.

If, under the terms of the restructuring, Knapsack Co. will pay the full principal amount of the original loan five years after the original due date, but none of the interest due under the original terms, an impairment must be recognized, since the present value of the future principal and interest payments discounted at the loan's original effective interest rate (i.e., the recoverable amount) will be lower than the carrying amount of the loan.

If, on the other hand, Knapsack Co.'s restructuring agreement calls for it to pay the full principal amount of the original loan on the original due date, but none of the interest due under the original terms, the same result as the foregoing will again hold. The impairment will be measured as the difference between the former carrying amount and the present value of the future principal and interest payments discounted at the loan's original effective interest rate.

As yet another variation on the restructuring theme, if Knapsack will pay the full principal amount on the original due date with interest, only at a lower interest rate than the interest rate inherent in the original loan, again the same guidance is offered by the IGC, so that an impairment must be recognized.

This same outcome prevails if Knapsack agrees to pay the full principal amount five years after the original due date and all interest accrued during the original loan term, but no interest for the extended term. Since the present value of future cash flows is lower than the loan's carrying amount, impairment is to be recognized.

As a final option, the IGC offers the loan restructuring situation whereby Knapsack is to pay the full principal amount five years after the original due date and all interest, including interest for both the original term of the loan and the extended term. In this scenario, even though the amount and timing of payments has changed, Galactic Bank will nonetheless receive interest on interest, so that the present value of the future principal and interest payments discounted at the loan's original effective interest rate will equal the carrying amount of the loan. Therefore, there is no impairment loss.

Impairment of financial assets carried at cost. Impairment losses on unquoted equity instruments that are not carried at fair value because the fair value cannot be reliably measured, or on a derivative asset that is linked to and must be settled by delivery of such an unquoted equity instrument, are recognized if there is objective evidence that impairment losses have occurred. These are measured as the difference between the carrying amount of the financial asset and the present value of estimated future cash flows discounted at the current market rate of return for a similar financial asset. Note that current rates, not the original effective rate, are the relevant reference, since these investments were being maintained at cost by default (i.e., due to the absence of reliable fair value data), not because they qualified for amortized cost due to being held to maturity. Accordingly, the application of fair value accounting, or a reasonable surrogate for it, is valid in such instances. No reversals of prior impairment losses are allowed for financial assets measured at cost.

Impairment of financial assets carried at fair value. The fair value of an equity security that is classified as available-for-sale may fall below its carrying amount and that is not necessarily evidence of impairment. When an entity reports fair value changes on available-for-sale financial assets in other comprehensive income and equity in accordance with IAS 39, it continues to do so until there is objective evidence of impairment, such as the circumstances identified in the standard. If objective evidence of impairment exists, any cumulative impairment loss that has been recognized in other comprehensive income should be reclassified from equity to profit or loss for the period.

The amount of the cumulative impairment loss that is reclassified from equity to profit or loss is the difference between the acquisition cost (net of any principal repayment and amortization) and current fair value, less any impairment loss previously recognized in profit or loss.

Reversals of impairment losses recognized in profit or loss for an investment in *equity* instruments are *not* allowed. Since no reversal of the impairment loss is allowed for equity instruments, so that, if subsequent to impairment recognition there is an increase in the fair value of the available-for-sale investment, that increase is recognized in other comprehensive income and not in profit or loss.

Reversals of impairment losses recognized in profit or loss for an investment in *debt* instruments should be reversed, with the amount of the reversal recognized in profit or loss if the increase in the fair value is objectively linked to an event occurring after the impairment loss was recognized.

No assessment of impairment is conducted for investments in debt and equity instruments classified as at FVTPL since these instruments are valued at fair value with mark-to-market adjustments recognized in profit or loss.

IFRIC 10, *Interim Financial Reporting and Impairment*, addressing conflicts between the requirements of IAS 34, *Interim Financial Reporting*, and those in other standards on the recognition and reversal in the financial statements of impairment losses in respect of goodwill or an investment in either an equity instrument or a financial asset carried at cost under

IAS 39, states that any impairment losses recognized in an interim financial statement must not be reversed in subsequent interim or annual financial statements.

Example of impairment of investments

Given the foregoing, assume now, with reference again to the Raphael Corporation example first presented earlier in this chapter, that in January 2011 new information comes to Raphael Corporation management regarding the viability of Wimbledon Corp. Based on this information, it is determined that the decline in Wimbledon preferred share is probably not a temporary one, but rather is an impairment of the asset as that term is used in IAS 39. The standard prescribes that such a decline be reflected in profit or loss. The share's fair value has remained at the amount last reported, €109,500, but this value is no longer viewed as being only a market fluctuation. Accordingly, the entry to recognize the fact of the investment's permanent impairment is as follows:

Impairment loss on holding equity instruments	15,500	
Unrealized loss on equity instruments—available-for-sale		
(other comprehensive income)		15,500

Any later recovery of impairment losses on available-for-sale equity instruments cannot be reversed. Later market fluctuations will be reported in other comprehensive income.

To illustrate this point, assume that in March 2011 new information comes to management's attention, which suggests that the decline in Wimbledon preferred had indeed been only a temporary decline; in fact, the value of Wimbledon now rises to €112,000. It would not be permitted under revised IAS 39 to reverse the impairment loss that had been included in profit or loss. The carrying value after the recognition of the impairment was €109,500, and the current period increase to €112,000 will have to be accounted for as an increase to be reflected in other comprehensive income, rather than in profit or loss. The entry required to reflect this is

Investment in equity instruments—available-for-sale	2,500	
Unrealized gain on equity instruments—available-for-sale		
(other comprehensive income)		2,500

However, if this investment is a debt instrument classified as available-for-sale, evidence of any specific event occurring after the date of the impairment loss recognized in profit or loss that is responsible for this recovery in value can be reversed through profit or loss. Any increases in value above the original cost basis would not be taken into profit or loss, but rather recognized in other comprehensive income, since the investment is classified as available-for-sale.

Structured notes as held-to-maturity investments. Among the more complex of what are commonly referred to as "engineered" financial products, which have become commonplace over the last decade, are "structured notes." Structured notes and related products are privately negotiated and not easily marketable once acquired. These instruments often appear to be straightforward debt investments, but in fact contain provisions which have the potential to greatly increase or decrease the return to the investor, based on (typically) the movement of some index related to currency exchange rates, interest rates, or, in some cases, share price indices. The IGC has addressed the question of whether these assets can be considered as held-to-maturity investments. The IGC offers as an example a structured note tied to an equity price index, upon which the following illustration is based.

Example of structured debt instrument

Cartegena Co. purchases a five-year "equity-index-linked note" with an original issue price of €1,000,000 at its market price of €1,200,000 at the time of purchase. The note requires no interest payments prior to maturity. At maturity, the note requires payment of the original issue price of €1,000,000 plus a supplemental redemption amount that depends on whether a specified share price index (e.g. the Dow Jones Industrial Average) exceeds a predetermined level at the maturity date. If the share index does not exceed or is equal to the predetermined level, no supplemental redemption amount is paid. If the share index exceeds the predetermined level, the supplemental redemption amount will equal 115% of the difference between the level of the share index at maturity and the level of the share index at original issuance of the note divided by the level of the share index at original issuance.

Obviously, the investment is largely a gamble on an increase in the Dow Jones average over the five-year term, since Cartegena is paying a substantial premium and, as a worst-case scenario, could lose its entire premium plus the opportunity cost of lost interest over the five years. Structured notes such as this are very difficult to dispose of on the secondary (i.e., resale) market, having been created (structured) to fit the unique needs or desires of the issuer and investor. Determining a fair value at any intermediate point in the five-year holding period would be difficult or impossible, absent arm's-length bids, particularly if the underlying index has yet to advance to a level at which a gain will be reaped by the investor.

In the present example, assume that Cartegena has the positive intent and ability to hold the note to maturity. According to guidance issued by the IGC, it can indeed classify this note as a held-to-maturity investment, because it has a fixed payment of €1,000,000 and a fixed maturity, and because Cartegena Co. has the positive intent and ability to hold it to maturity. However, the equity index feature is a call option not closely related to the debt host, and accordingly, it must be separated as an embedded derivative under IAS 39. The purchase price of €1,200,000 must be allocated between the host debt instrument and the embedded derivative. For instance, if the fair value of the embedded option at acquisition is €400,000, the host debt instrument is measured at €800,000 on initial recognition. In this case, the discount of €200,000 that is implicit in the host bond is amortized to net profit or loss over the term to maturity of the note using the effective interest method.

A similar situation arises if the investment is a bond with a fixed payment at maturity and a fixed maturity date, but with variable interest payments indexed to the price of a commodity or equity (commodity-indexed or equity-indexed bonds). If the entity has the positive intent and ability to hold the bond to maturity, it can be classified as held-to-maturity. However, as confirmed in an interpretation offered by the IGC, the commodity-indexed or equity-indexed interest payments result in an embedded derivative that is separated and accounted for as a derivative at fair value. The special exception in IAS 39, under which, if the two components cannot be reasonably separated the entire financial asset is classified as held for trading purposes, is found not to be applicable. According to the IGC, it should be straightforward to separate the host debt investment (the fixed payment at maturity) from the embedded derivative (the index-linked interest payments).

Accounting for sales of investments in financial instruments. In general, sales of investments are accounted for by eliminating the carrying value and recognizing a gain or loss for the difference between carrying amount and sales proceeds. Derecognition will occur only when the entity transfers control over the contractual rights which comprise the financial asset, or a portion thereof. IAS 39 sets forth certain conditions to define an actual transfer of control. Thus, for example, in most cases if the transferor has the right to reacquire the transferred asset, derecognition will not be warranted, unless the asset is readily obtainable in the market or reacquisition is to be at then-fair value. Arrangements which are essentially repurchase (repo) arrangements are similarly not sales and do not result in derecognition. In general, the transferee must obtain the benefits of the transferred asset in order to warrant derecognition by the transferor.

In accordance with IAS 39 there are two main concepts—risks and rewards, and control—that govern derecognition decisions. However, the standard clarifies that evaluation of the transfer of risks and rewards of ownership must in all instances precede the evaluation of the transfer of control (see discussion in the paragraph, "Derecognition of Financial Asset" earlier in this chapter).

In some instances, the asset will be sold as part of a compound transaction in which the transferor either retains part of the asset, obtains another financial instrument, or incurs a financial liability. If the fair values of all components of the transaction (asset retained, new asset acquired, etc.) are known, computing the gain or loss will be no problem. However, if one or more elements are not subject to an objective assessment, special requirement apply. In the unlikely event that the fair value of the component retained cannot be determined, it should be recorded at zero, thereby conservatively measuring the gain (or loss) on the transaction. Similarly, if a new financial asset is obtained and it cannot be objectively valued, it must be recorded at zero value.

On the other hand, if a financial liability is assumed (e.g., a guarantee) and it cannot be measured at fair value, then the initial carrying amount should be such (i.e., large enough) that no gain is recognized on the transaction. If necessitated by IAS 39's provisions, a loss should be recognized on the transaction. For example, if an asset carried at €4,000 is sold for €4,200 in cash, with the transferor assuming a guarantee obligation which cannot be valued (admittedly, such a situation is unlikely to occur in the context of a truly "arm's-length" transaction), no gain would be recognized and the financial liability would accordingly be initially recorded at €200. On the other hand, if the selling price were instead only €3,800, a loss of €200 would be immediately recognized, and the guarantee obligation would be given no value (but would be disclosed).

Accounting for Hedging Activities

The topic of hedging is almost inextricably intertwined with the subject of financial derivatives, since most (but not all) hedging is accomplished using derivatives. Revised IAS 39 addresses both of these matters extensively, and the IGC has provided yet more instructional materials on these issues. In the following sections, a basic review of, first, derivative financial instruments, and second, hedging activities, will be presented.

Derivatives. As defined by IAS 39, a derivative is a financial instrument with all the following characteristics:

1. Its value changes in response to the change in a specified interest rate, security price, commodity price, foreign exchange rate, index of prices or rates, a credit rating or credit index, or similar variable (sometimes called the underlying);
2. It requires no initial net investment or little initial net investment relative to other types of contracts that have a similar response to changes in market conditions; and
3. It is settled at a future date.

Examples of financial instruments that meet the foregoing definition include the following, along with the underlying variable which affects the derivative's value.

Type of contract	*Main pricing—settlement variable (underlying variable)*
Interest rate swap	Interest rates
Currency swap (foreign exchange swap)	Currency rates
Commodity swap	Commodity prices
Equity swap (equity of another entity)	Equity prices
Credit swap	Credit rating, credit index, or credit price
Total return swap	Total fair value of the reference asset and interest rates
Purchased or written treasury bond option (call or put)	Interest rates
Purchased or written currency option (call or put)	Currency rates
Purchased or written commodity option (call or put)	Commodity prices

Type of contract	*Main pricing—settlement variable (underlying variable)*
Purchased or written share option (call or put)	Equity prices (equity of another entity)
Interest rate futures linked to government debt (treasury futures)	Interest rates
Currency futures	Currency rates
Commodity futures	Commodity prices
Interest rate forward linked to government debt (treasury forward)	Interest rates
Currency forward	Currency rates
Commodity forward	Commodity prices
Equity forward	Equity prices (equity of another entity)

The issue of what is meant by "little or no net investment" has been explored by the IGC. According to the IGC, professional judgment will be required in determining what constitutes little or no initial net investment, and is to be interpreted on a relative basis—the initial net investment is less than that needed to acquire a primary financial instrument with a similar response to changes in market conditions. This reflects the inherent leverage features typical of derivative agreements compared to the underlying instruments. If, for example, a "deep in the money" call option is purchased (that is, the option's value consists mostly of intrinsic value), a significant premium is paid. If the premium is equal or close to the amount required to invest in the underlying instrument, this would fail the "little initial net investment" criterion.

A margin account is not part of the initial net investment in a derivative instrument. Margin accounts are a form of collateral for the counterparty or clearinghouse and may take the form of cash, instruments, or other specified assets, typically liquid ones. Margin accounts are separate assets that are to be accounted for separately. Accordingly, in determining whether an arrangement qualifies as a derivative, the margin deposit is not a factor in assessing whether the "little or no net investment" criterion has been met.

A financial instrument can qualify as a derivative even if the settlement amount does not vary proportionately. An example of this phenomenon was provided by the IGC.

Example of derivative transaction

Accurate Corp. enters into a contract that requires it to pay Aimless Co. €2 million if the share of Reference Corp. rises by €5 per share or more during a six-month period. Conversely, Accurate Corp. will receive from Aimless Co. a payment of €2 million if the share of Reference Corp. declines by €5 or more during that same six-month period. If price changes are within the ± €5 collar range, no payments will be made or received by the parties. This arrangement would qualify as a derivative instrument, the underlying being the price of Reference Corp. common share. IAS 39 provides that "a derivative could require a fixed payment as a result of some future event that is unrelated to a notional amount."

In some instances what might first appear to be normal financial instruments are actually derivative transactions. The IGC offers the example of offsetting loans, which serve the same purpose and should be accounted for as an interest rate swap. The example is as follows:

Example of apparent loans that qualify as derivative transaction

Aguilar S.A. makes a five-year *fixed-rate* loan to Battapaglia Spa, while Battapaglia at the same time makes a five-year *variable-rate* loan for the same amount to Aguilar. There are no transfers of principal at inception of the two loans, since Aguilar and Battapaglia have a netting agreement. While superficially these appear to be two unconditional debt obligations, in fact this meets the definition of a derivative. Note that there is an underlying variable, no or little initial net investment, and future settlement, such that the contractual effect of the loans is the equivalent of an interest rate swap arrangement with no initial net investment. Nonderivative transactions are aggregated and treated as a derivative when the transactions result, in substance, in a derivative.

Indicators of this situation would include (1) the transactions are entered into at the same time and in contemplation of one another, (2) they have the same counterparty, (3) they relate to the same risk, and (4) there is no apparent economic need or substantive business purpose for structuring the transactions separately that could not also have been accomplished in a single transaction. Note that even in the absence of a netting agreement, the foregoing arrangement would have been deemed to be a derivative.

Difficulty of identifying whether certain transactions involve derivatives. The definition of derivatives has already been addressed. While seemingly straightforward, the almost limitless and still expanding variety of "engineered" financial products often makes definitive categorization more difficult than this at first would appear to be. The IGC illustrates this with examples of two variants on interest rate swaps, both of which involve prepayments. The first of these, a prepaid interest rate swap (fixed-rate payment obligation prepaid at inception or subsequently) qualifies as a derivative; the second, a variable-rate payment obligation prepaid at inception or subsequently) would not be a derivative. The reasoning is set forth in the next paragraphs, which are adapted from the IGC guidance.

Example of interest rate swap to be accounted for as a derivative

First consider the "pay-fixed, receive-variable" interest rate swap that the party prepays at inception. Assume Agememnon Corp. enters into a €100 million notional amount five-year pay-fixed, receive-variable interest rate swap with Baltic Metals, Inc. The interest rate of the variable part of the swap resets on a quarterly basis to the three-month LIBOR. The interest rate of the fixed part of the swap is 10% per year. Agememnon Corp. prepays its fixed obligation under the swap of €50 million (= €100 million × 10% × 5 years) at inception, discounted using market interest rates, while retaining the right to receive interest payments on the €100 million reset quarterly based on three-month LIBOR over the life of the swap.

The initial net investment in the interest rate swap is significantly less than the notional amount on which the variable payments under the variable leg will be calculated. The contract requires little initial net investment relative to other types of contracts that have a similar response to changes in market conditions, such as a variable-rate bond. Therefore, the contract fulfills the "no or little initial net investment" provision of IAS 39. Even though Agememnon Corp. has no future performance obligation, the ultimate settlement of the contract is at a future date and the value of the contract changes in response to changes in the LIBOR index. Accordingly, the contract is considered to be a derivative contract. The IGC further notes that if the fixed-rate payment obligation is prepaid subsequent to initial recognition, which would be considered a termination of the old swap and an origination of a new instrument, which would have to be evaluated under IAS 39.

Now consider the opposite situation, a prepaid pay-variable, receive-fixed interest rate swap, which the IGC concludes is *not* a derivative. This result obtains because it provides a return on the prepaid (invested) amount comparable to the return on a debt instrument with fixed cash flows.

Example of interest rate swap *not* to be accounted for as a derivative

Assume that Synchronous Ltd. enters into a €100 million notional amount five-year "pay-variable, receive-fixed" interest rate swap with counterparty Cabot Corp. The variable leg of the swap resets on a quarterly basis to the three-month LIBOR. The fixed interest payments under the swap are calculated as 10% times the swap's notional amount, or €10 million per year. Synchronous Ltd. prepays its obligation under the variable leg of the swap at inception at current market rates, while retaining the right to receive fixed interest payments of 10% on €100 million per year.

The cash inflows under the contract are equivalent to those of a financial instrument with a fixed annuity stream, since Synchronous Ltd. knows it will receive €10 million per year over the life of the swap. Therefore, all else being equal, the initial investment in the contract should equal that of other financial instruments that consist of fixed annuities. Thus, the initial net investment in the pay-variable, receive-fixed interest rate swap is equal to the investment required in a nonderivative contract that has a similar response to changes in market conditions. For this reason, the instrument fails the "no or little net investment" criterion of IAS 39. Therefore, the contract is *not* to be accounted for as a derivative under IAS 39. By discharging the obligation to pay variable interest rate payments, Synchronous Ltd. effectively extends an annuity loan to Cabot Corp. In this situation, the instrument is accounted for as a loan originated by the entity unless Synchronous Ltd. has the intent to sell it immediately or in the short term.

In yet other instances arrangements that technically meet the definition of derivatives are not to be accounted for as such.

Example of derivative not to be settled for cash

Assume National Wire Products Corp. enters into a fixed-price forward contract to purchase two million kilograms of copper. The contract permits National Wire to take physical delivery of the copper at the end of twelve months or to pay or receive a net settlement in cash, based on the change in fair value of copper. While such a contract meets the definition of a derivative, it is not necessarily accounted for as a derivative. The contract is a derivative instrument because there is no initial net investment, the contract is based on the price of an underlying, copper, and it is to be settled at a future date. However, if National Wire intends to settle the contract by taking delivery and has no history of settling in cash, the contract is not accounted for as a derivative under IAS 39. Instead, it is accounted for as an executory contract for the purchase of inventory.

Just as some seemingly derivative transactions may be accounted for as not involving a derivative instrument, the opposite situation can also occur, where some seemingly nonderivative transactions would be accounted for as being derivatives.

Example of nonfinancial derivative to be settled for cash

Argyle Corp. enters into a forward contract to purchase a commodity or other nonfinancial asset that contractually is to be settled by taking delivery. Argyle has an established pattern of settling such contracts prior to delivery by contracting with a third party. Argyle settles any market value difference for the contract price directly with the third party. This pattern of settlement prohibits Argyle Corp. from qualifying for the exemption based on normal delivery; the contract is accounted for as a derivative. IAS 39 applies to a contract to purchase a nonfinancial asset if the contract meets the definition of a derivative and the contract does not qualify for the exemption for delivery in the normal course of business. In this case, Argyle does not expect to take delivery. Under the standard, a pattern of entering into offsetting contracts that effectively accomplishes settlement on a net basis does not qualify for the exemption on the grounds of delivery in the normal course of business.

Forward contracts. Forward contracts to purchase, for example, fixed-rate debt instruments (such as mortgages) at fixed prices are to be accounted for as derivatives. They meet the definition of a derivative because there is no or little initial net investment, there is an underlying variable (interest rates), and they will be settled in the future. However, such transactions are to be accounted for as a regular-way transaction, if regular-way delivery is required. "Regular-way" delivery is defined by IAS 39 to include contracts for purchases or sales of financial instruments that require delivery in the time frame generally established by regulation or convention in the marketplace concerned. Regular-way contracts are explicitly defined as *not* being derivatives.

Future contracts. Future contracts are financial instruments that require delivery of a commodity, for example an equity instrument or currency, at a specified price agreed to on the contract inception date (exercise price), on a specified future date. Futures are similar to forward contracts except futures have standardized contract terms and are traded on organized exchanges.

Options. Options are contracts that give the buyer (option holder) the right, but not the obligation, to acquire from or sell to the option seller (option writer) a certain quantity of an underlying financial instrument or other commodity, at a specified price (the strike price) and up to a specified date (the expiration date). An option to buy is referred to as a "call"; an option to sell is referred to as a "put."

Swaps. Interest rate (and currency) swaps have become widely used financial arrangements. Swaps are to be accounted for as derivatives whether an interest rate swap settles gross or net. Regardless of how the arrangement is to be settled, the three key defining characteristics are present in all interest rate swaps—namely, that value changes are in response to changes in an underlying variable (interest rates or an index of rates), that there is little or no initial net investment, and that settlements will occur at future dates. Thus, swaps are always derivatives.

Derivatives that are not based on financial instruments. Not all derivatives involve financial instruments. Consider Corboy Co., which owns an office building and enters into a put option, with a term of five years, with an investor that permits it to put the building to the investor for €15 million. The current value of the building is €17.5 million. The option, if exercised, may be settled through physical delivery or net cash, at Corboy's option. Corboy's accounting depends on Corboy's intent and past practice for settlement. Although the contract meets the definition of a derivative, Corboy does not account for it as a derivative if it intends to settle the contract by delivering the building if it exercises its option, and there is no past practice of settling net.

The investor, however, cannot conclude that the option was entered into to meet the investor's expected purchase, sale, or usage requirements because the investor does not have the ability to require delivery. Therefore, the investor has to account for the contract as a derivative. Regardless of past practices, the investor's intention does not affect whether settlement is by delivery or in cash. The investor has written an option, and a written option in which the holder has the choice of physical delivery or net cash settlement can never satisfy the normal delivery requirement for the exemption from IAS 39 for the investor. However, if the contract required physical delivery and the reporting entity had no past practice of settling net in cash, the contract would not be accounted for as a derivative.

Embedded derivatives. In certain cases, IAS 39 requires that an embedded derivative be separated from a host contract. The embedded derivative must then be accounted for separately as a derivative, at fair value. That does not, however, require separating them in the statement of financial position; IAS 39 does not address the presentation in the statement of financial position of embedded derivatives. However, IFRS 7 requires separate disclosure of financial assets carried at cost and financial assets carried at fair value, although this could be in the notes rather than in the statement of financial position.

IFRIC 9, *Reassessment of Embedded Derivatives*, states that an entity should assess whether an embedded derivative is required to be separated from the host contract and accounted for as a derivative when the entity first becomes a party to the contract. Subsequent reassessment is prohibited unless there is a change in the terms of the contract that significantly modifies the cash flows that otherwise would be required under the contract; in this case reassessment is required.

The concept of embedded derivatives embraces such elements as conversion features, such as are found in convertible debts. For example, an investment in a bond (a financial asset) may be convertible into shares of the issuing entity or another entity at any time prior to the bond's maturity, at the option of the holder. The existence of the conversion feature in such a situation generally precludes classification as a held-to-maturity investment because that would be inconsistent with paying for the conversion feature—the right to convert into equity shares before maturity.

An investment in a convertible bond can be classified as an available-for-sale financial asset provided it is not purchased for trading purposes. The equity conversion option is an embedded derivative. If the bond is classified as available-for-sale with fair value changes recognized in other comprehensive income until the bond is sold, the equity conversion option (the embedded derivative) is generally separated. The amount paid for the bond is split between the debt security without the conversion option and the equity conversion option itself. Changes in the fair value of the equity conversion option are recognized in profit or loss unless the option is part of a cash flow hedging relationship. If the convertible bond is carried at fair value with changes in fair value reported in profit or loss, separating the embedded derivative from the host bond is not permitted.

When an evaluation made using the criteria in IAS 39 leads to a conclusion that the embedded derivative must be separately accounted for, the initial carrying amounts of a host and the embedded derivative must be determined. Since the embedded derivative must be recorded at fair value with changes in fair value reported in profit or loss, the initial carrying amount assigned to the host contract on separation is determined as the difference between the cost (i.e., the fair value of the consideration given) for the hybrid (combined) instrument and the fair value of the embedded derivative.

IAS 32, as revised and effective 2005, requires that in separating the liability and equity components contained in a compound financial instrument, the issuer must first allocate fair value to the liability component, leaving only the residual (the difference between aggregate fair value and that allocated to liabilities) to be assigned to the equity component. However, IAS 32 is not applicable to the separation of a derivative from a hybrid instrument under IAS 39. It would be inappropriate to allocate the basis in the hybrid instrument under IAS 39 to the derivative and nonderivative components based on their relative fair values, since that might result in an immediate gain or loss being recognized in profit or loss on the subsequent measurement of the derivative at fair value.

Example of separate contracts that cannot be deemed an embedded derivative

Erehwon AG acquires a five-year floating-rate debt instrument issued by Spacemaker Co. At the same time, it enters into a five-year "pay-variable, receive-fixed" interest rate swap with the St. Helena Bank. Erehwon argues that the combination of the debt instrument and swap is a "synthetic fixed-rate instrument" and accordingly classifies the instrument as a held-to-maturity investment, since it has the positive intent and ability to hold it to maturity. Erehwon contends that separate accounting for the swap is inappropriate, since IAS 39 requires an embedded derivative to be classified together with its host instrument if the derivative is linked to an interest rate that can change the amount of interest that would otherwise be paid or received on the host debt contract.

The company's analysis is not correct. Embedded derivative instruments are terms and conditions that are included in nonderivative host contracts. It is generally inappropriate to treat two or more separate financial instruments as a single combined instrument (synthetic instrument accounting) for the purposes of applying IAS 39. Each of the financial instruments has its own terms and conditions and each may be transferred or settled separately. Therefore, the debt instrument and the swap are classified separately.

Hedging Accounting under IAS 39

When there is a hedging relationship between a hedging instrument and another item (the underlying), and certain conditions are met, then special "hedging accounting" will be applied. The objective is to ensure that the gain or loss on the hedging instrument is recognized in profit or loss in the same period that the hedged item affects profit or loss. Hedge accounting recognizes the offsetting effects on profit or loss of changes in the fair values of the hedging instrument and the hedged item. Hedging instruments are often financial derivatives, such as forwards, options, swaps or futures, but this is not a necessary condition. Hedging may be engaged in to protect against changes in fair values, changes in expected cash flows, or changes in the value of an investment in a foreign operation, such as a subsidiary, due to currency rate movements. There is no requirement that entities engage in hedging, but the principles of good management will often dictate that this be done.

For a simplistic example of the need for, and means of, hedging, consider an entity that holds US Treasury bonds as an investment. The bonds have a maturity some ten years in the future, but the entity actually intends to dispose of these in the intermediate term, for example, within four years to partially finance a plant expansion currently being planned. Obviously, an unexpected increase in general interest rates during the projected four-year holding period would be an unwelcome development, since it would cause a decline in the market value of the bonds and could accordingly result in an unanticipated loss of principal. One means of guarding against this would be to purchase a put option on these bonds, permitting the entity to sell them at an agreed-upon price, which would be most valuable should there be a price decline. If interest rates do indeed rise, the increasing value of the "put" will (if properly structured) offset the declining value of the bonds themselves, thus providing an effective fair value hedge. (Other hedging strategies are also available, including selling short Treasury bond futures, and the entity of course could have reduced or eliminated the need to hedge entirely by having invested in Treasury bonds having a maturity more closely matched to its anticipated cash need.)

Special hedge accounting is necessitated by the fact that fair value changes in not all financial instruments are reported in current profit or loss. Thus, if the entity in the foregoing example holding the Treasuries has elected to report changes in available-for-sale investments (which would include the Treasury bonds in this instance) in other comprehensive income, but the changes in the hedging instrument's fair value were to be reported in profit or loss, there would be a fundamental mismatching which would distort the real hedging relationship that had been established. To avoid this result, the entity may elect to apply special hedge accounting as prescribed by IAS 39. It should be noted, though, that hedge accounting is optional. An entity that carries out hedging activities for risk management purposes may well decide not to apply hedge accounting for some hedging transactions if it wishes to reduce the cost and burden of complying with the hedge accounting requirements in IAS 39.

Accounting for gains and losses from fair value hedges. The accounting for qualifying gains and losses on fair value hedges is as follows:

1. On the hedging instrument, they are recognized in profit or loss.
2. On the hedged item, they are recognized in profit or loss even if the gains or losses would normally have been recognized in other comprehensive income if not hedged.

The foregoing rule applies even in the case of investments (classified as available-for-sale) for which unrealized gains and losses are being recognized in other comprehensive income, if that method was appropriately elected by the reporting entity, as permitted by IAS 39. In all instances, to the extent that there are differences between the amounts of gain or loss on hedging and hedged items, these will be due either to amounts excluded from assessment effectiveness, or to hedge ineffectiveness; in either event, these are recognized currently in profit or loss.

As an example, consider an available-for-sale (AFS) financial asset, the carrying amount of which is adjusted by the amount of gain or loss resulting from the hedged risk, a fair value hedge. It is assumed that the entire investment was hedged, but it is also possible to hedge merely a portion of the investment. The facts are as follows:

Hedged item:	Available-for-sale financial asset
Hedging instrument:	Put option
Underlying:	Price of the security
Notional amount:	100 shares of the financial asset

Example 1

On July 1, 2011, Gardiner Company purchased 100 shares of Dizzy Co. ordinary shares at €15 per share and classified it as an available-for-sale financial asset. On October 1, Gardiner Company purchased an at-the-money put on Dizzy with an exercise price of €25 and an expiration date of April 2012. This put purchase locks in a profit of €650, as long as the price is equal to €25 or lower, but allows continued profitability if the price of the Dizzy share goes above €25. (In other words, the put cost a premium of €350, which if deducted from the locked-in gain [= €2,500 market value less €1,500 cost] leaves a net gain of €650 to be realized.)

The premium paid for an at-the-money option (i.e., where the exercise price is current fair value of the underlying) is the price paid for the right to have the entire remaining option period in which to exercise the option. In the present example, Gardiner Company specifies that only the intrinsic value of the option is to be used to measure effectiveness. Thus, the time value decreases of the put will be charged against profit or loss of the period, and not offset against the change in value of the underlying, hedged item. Gardiner Company then documents the hedge's strategy, objectives, hedging relationships, and method of measuring effectiveness. The following table shows the fair value of the hedged item and the hedging instrument.

Case One

	10/1/11	*12/31/11*	*3/31/12*	*4/17/12*
Hedged item:				
Dizzy share price	€ 25	€ 22	€ 20	€ 20
Number of shares	100	100	100	100
Total value of shares	€2,500	€2,200	€2,000	€2,000
Hedging instrument:				
Put option (100 shares)				
Intrinsic value	€ 0	€ 300	€ 500	€ 500
Time value	350	215	53	0
Total	€ 350	€ 515	€ 553	€ 500
Intrinsic value				
Gain (loss) on put from last measurement date	€ 0	€ 300	€ 200	€ 0

Entries to record the foregoing changes in value, ignoring tax effects and transaction costs, are as follows:

7/1/11	Purchase:	Available-for-sale investment	1,500	
		Cash		1,500
9/30/11	End of quarter:	Valuation allowance—available-for-sale investment	1,000	
		Other comprehensive income		1,000
10/1/11	Put purchase:	Put option	350	
		Cash		350
12/31/11	End of year:	Put option	300	
		Hedge gain/loss (intrinsic value gain)		300
		Gain/loss	162	
		Put option (time value loss)		162
		Hedge gain/loss	300	
		Available-for-sale investment (market value loss)		300
3/31/12	End of quarter:	Put option	200	
		Hedge gain/loss (intrinsic value changes)		200
		Gain/loss	162	
		Put option (time value loss)		162
		Hedge gain/loss	200	
		Available-for-sale investment (market value loss)		200
4/17/12	Put expires:	Put option	0	
		Hedge gain/loss (intrinsic value changes)		0
		Gain/loss	53	
		Put option (time value changes)		53
		Hedge gain/loss	0	
		Available-for-sale investment (market value changes)		0

An option is said to be "in-the-money" if the exercise price is above the market value (for a put option) or below the market value (for a call option). At or before expiration, an in-the-money put should be sold or exercised (to let it simply expire would be to effectively discard a valuable asset). It should be stressed that this applies to so-called "American options," which may be exercised at any time prior to expiration; so-called "European options" can only be exercised at the expiration date. Assuming that the put option is sold immediately before its expiration date, the entry would be

4/17/12	Put sold:	Cash	500	
		Put option		500

On the other hand, if the put is exercised (i.e., the underlying instrument is delivered to the counterparty, which is obligated to pay €25 per share), the entry would be

4/17/11	Cash	2,500	
	Other comprehensive income	1,000	
	Valuation allowance—available-for-sale investment		1,000
	Available-for-sale investment		1,000
	Put option		500
	Gain on sale of investment		1,000

The cumulative effect on retained earnings of the hedge and sale is a net gain of €650 (= €1,000 – €350).

Example 2

To further illustrate fair value hedge accounting, the facts in the preceding example will now be slightly modified. Now, the share price increases after the put option is purchased, thus making the put worthless, since the shares could be sold for a more advantageous price on the open market.

Case Two

	10/1/11	*12/31/11*	*3/31/12*	*4/17/12*
Hedged item:				
Dizzy share price	€ 25	€ 28	€ 30	€ 31
Number of shares	100	100	100	100
Total value of shares	€2,500	€2,800	€3,000	€3,100
Hedging instrument:				
Put option (100 shares)				
Intrinsic value	€ 0	€ 0	€ 0	€ 0
Time value	350	100	25	0
Total	€ 350	€ 100	€ 25	€ 0
Intrinsic value				
Gain (loss) on put from last measurement date	€ 0	€ 0	€ 0	€ 0

Entries to record the foregoing changes in value, ignoring tax effects and transaction costs, are as follows:

7/1/11	Purchase:	Available-for-sale investment	1,500	
		Cash		1,500
9/30/11	End of quarter:	Valuation allowance—available-for-sale investment	1,000	
		Other comprehensive income		1,000
10/1/11	Put purchase:	Put option	350	
		Cash		350
12/31/11	End of year:	Put option	0	
		Hedge gain/loss (intrinsic value gain)		0
		Hedge gain/loss	250	
		Put option (time value loss)		250
		Available-for-sale investment	300	
		Other comprehensive income		300
3/31/12	End of quarter:	Put option	0	
		Hedge gain/loss (intrinsic value change)		0
		Hedge gain/loss	75	
		Put option (time value loss)		75
		Available-for-sale investment	200	
		Other comprehensive income		200
4/17/12	Put expires:	Put option	0	
		Hedge gain/loss (intrinsic value change)		0
		Hedge gain/loss	25	
		Put option (time value change)		25
		Available-for-sale investment	100	
		Other comprehensive income		100

The put expired unexercised and Gardiner Company must decide whether to sell the investment. If it continues to hold, normal IAS 39 accounting would apply. In this example, since it was hypothesized that Gardiner had elected to record the effects of value changes (apart from those which were hedging related) in other comprehensive income, it would continue to apply this accounting after the expiration of the put option. Assuming, however, that the investment is instead sold, the entry would be

4/17/12	Cash	3,100	
	Other comprehensive income	1,600	
	Available-for-sale investment		1,500
	Valuation allowance—available-for-sale investment		1,600
	Gain on sale of investment		1,600

Accounting for gains and losses from cash flow hedges. Cash flow hedges generally involve forecasted transactions or events. The intention is to defer the recognition of gains or losses arising from the hedging activity itself until the forecasted transaction takes place, and then to have the formerly deferred gain or loss affect profit or loss when the forecasted transaction affects profit or loss. While overwhelmingly it will be derivative financial instruments that are used to hedge cash flows relating to forecasted transactions, IAS 39 contemplates the use of nonderivatives for this purpose as well in the case of hedges of foreign currency risk. Forecasted transactions may include future cash flows arising from presently existing, recognized assets or liabilities—for example, future interest rate payments to be made on debt carrying floating interest rates are subject to cash flow hedging.

The accounting for qualifying gains and losses on cash flow hedges is as follows:

1. On the hedging instrument, the portion of the gain or loss that is determined to be an effective hedge will be recognized in other comprehensive income.
2. Also on the hedging instrument, the ineffective portion should be reported in profit or loss, if the instrument is a derivative; otherwise, it should be reported in a manner consistent with the accounting for other financial assets or liabilities as set forth in IAS 39. Thus, if an available-for-sale financial asset has been used as the hedging instrument in a particular cash flow hedging situation, and the entity has elected to report value changes in other comprehensive income, then any ineffective portion of the hedge should continue to be recorded in other comprehensive income.

According to IAS 39, the separate component of equity associated with the hedged item should be adjusted to the lesser (in absolute terms) of either the cumulative gain or loss on the hedging instrument necessary to offset the cumulative change in expected future cash flows on the hedged item from hedge inception, excluding the ineffective portion, or the fair value of the cumulative change in expected future cash flows on the hedged item from inception of the hedge. Furthermore, any remaining gain or loss on the hedging instrument (i.e., the ineffective portion) must be recognized currently in profit or loss or in other comprehensive income, as dictated by the nature of the instrument and entity's accounting policy (for available-for-sale instruments, where there is a choice of reporting in other comprehensive income or in profit or loss). If the entity's policy regarding the hedge is to exclude a portion from the measure of hedge effectiveness (e.g., time value of options in the preceding example in this section), then any related gain or loss must be recognized in either profit or loss or other comprehensive income based on the nature of the item and the elected policy.

Example of "plain vanilla" interest rate swap

On July 1, 2011, Abbott Corp. borrows €5 million with a fixed maturity (no prepayment option) of June 30, 2015, carrying interest at the US prime interest rate + 1/2%. Interest payments are due semiannually; the entire principal is due at maturity. At the same date, Abbott Corp. enters into a "plain-vanilla-type" swap arrangement, calling for fixed payments at 8% and the receipt of prime + 1/2%, on a notional amount of €5 million. At that date prime is 7.5%, and there is no premium due on the swap arrangement since the fixed and variable payments are equal. (Note that swaps are privately negotiated and, accordingly, a wide range of terms will be encountered in practice; this is simply intended as an example, albeit a very typical one.)

The foregoing swap qualifies as a cash flow hedge under IAS 39. Given the nature of this swap, it is reasonable to assume no ineffectiveness, but in real world situations this must be carefully evaluated with reference to the specific circumstances of each case; IAS 39 does not provide a short-cut method (which contrasts with the corresponding US GAAP standard). IAS 39 defines effectiveness in terms of results: if at inception and throughout the life of the hedge, the entity can expect an almost complete offset of cash flow variations, and in fact (retrospectively) actual results are within a range of 80 to 125%, the hedge will be judged highly effective.

In the present example, assume that in fact the hedge proves to be highly effective. Also, assume that the prime rate over the four-year term of the loan, as of each interest payment date, is as follows, along with the fair value of the remaining term of the interest swap at those dates:

Date	Prime rate (%)	Fair value of swap*
December 31, 2011	6.5	€(150,051)
June 30, 2012	6.0	(196,580)
December 31, 2012	6.5	(111,296)
June 30, 2013	7.0	(45,374)
December 31, 2013	7.5	0
June 30, 2014	8.0	23,576
December 31, 2014	8.5	24,038
June 30, 2015	8.0	0

* *Fair values are determined as the present values of future cash flows resulting from expected interest rate differentials, based on current prime rate, discounted at 8%.*

Regarding the fair values presented in the foregoing table, it should be assumed that the fair values of the swap contract are precisely equal to the present value, at each valuation date (assumed to be the interest payment dates), of the differential future cash flows resulting from utilization of the swap. Future variable interest rates (prime + 1/2%) are assumed to be the same as the existing rates at each valuation date (i.e., the yield curve is flat and there is no basis for any expectation of rate changes, and therefore, the best estimate at any given moment is that the current rate will persist over time). The discount rate, 8%, is assumed to be constant over time.

Thus, for example, the fair value of the swap at December 31, 2011, would be the present value of an annuity of seven payments (the number of remaining semiannual interest payments due) of €25,000 each (pay 8%, receive 7%, based on then-existing prime rate of 6.5%) to be made to the swap counterparty, discounted at an annual rate of 8%. (Consistent with the convention for quoting interest rates as bond-equivalent yields, 4% is used for the semiannual discounting, rather than the rate that would compound to 8% annually.) The present value of a stream of seven €25,000 payments to the swap counterparty amounts to €150,051 at December 31, 2011, which is the swap liability to be reported by Abbott Corp. at that date. The offset is a debit to other comprehensive income, since the hedge is continually judged to be 100% effective in this case.

The semiannual accounting entries will be as follows:

December 31, 2011

Interest expense	175,000	
Accrued interest (or cash)		175,000

To accrue or pay interest on the debt at the variable rate of prime + 1/2% (7.0%)

Interest expense	25,000	
Accrued interest (or cash)		25,000

To record net settle-up on swap arrangement [8.0 – 7.0%]

| Other comprehensive income | 150,051 | |
| Obligation under swap contract | | 150,051 |

To record the fair value of the swap contract as of this date (a net liability because fixed rate payable is below expected variable rate based on current prime rate)

June 30, 2012

| Interest expense | 162,500 | |
| Accrued interest (or cash) | | 162,500 |

To accrue or pay interest on the debt at the variable rate of prime + 1/2% (6.5%)

| Interest expense | 37,500 | |
| Accrued interest (or cash) | | 37,500 |

To record net settle-up on swap arrangement [8.0 – 6.5%]

| Other comprehensive income | 46,529 | |
| Obligation under swap contract | | 46,529 |

To record the fair value of the swap contract as of this date (increase in obligation because of further decline in prime rate)

December 31, 2012

| Interest expense | 175,000 | |
| Accrued interest (or cash) | | 175,000 |

To accrue or pay interest on the debt at the variable rate of prime + 1/2% (7.0%)

| Interest expense | 25,000 | |
| Accrued interest (or cash) | | 25,000 |

To record net settle-up on swap arrangement [8.0 – 7.0%]

| Obligation under swap contract | 85,284 | |
| Other comprehensive income | | 85,284 |

To record the fair value of the swap contract as of this date (decrease in obligation due to increase in prime rate)

June 30, 2013

| Interest expense | 187,500 | |
| Accrued interest (or cash) | | 187,500 |

To accrue or pay interest on the debt at the variable rate of prime + 1/2% (7.5%)

| Interest expense | 12,500 | |
| Accrued interest (or cash) | | 12,500 |

To record net settle-up on swap arrangement [8.0 – 7.5%]

| Obligation under swap contract | 65,922 | |
| Other comprehensive income | | 65,922 |

To record the fair value of the swap contract as of this date (further increase in prime rate reduces fair value of derivative)

December 31, 2013

| Interest expense | 200,000 | |
| Accrued interest (or cash) | | 200,000 |

To accrue or pay interest on the debt at the variable rate of prime + 1/2% (8.0%)

| Interest expense | 0 | |
| Accrued interest (or cash) | | 0 |

To record net settle-up on swap arrangement [8.0 – 8.0%]

| Obligation under swap contract | 45,374 | |
| Other comprehensive income | | 45,374 |

To record the fair value of the swap contract as of this date (further increase in prime rate eliminates fair value of the derivative)

June 30, 2014

| Interest expense | 212,500 | |
| Accrued interest (or cash) | | 212,500 |

To accrue or pay interest on the debt at the variable rate of prime + 1/2% (8.5%)

| Accrued interest (or cash) | 12,500 | |
| Interest expense | | 12,500 |

To record net settle-up on swap arrangement [8.0 – 8.5%]

| Receivable under swap contract | 23,576 | |
| Other comprehensive income | | 23,576 |

To record the fair value of the swap contract as of this date (increase in prime rate creates net asset position for derivative)

December 31, 2014

| Interest expense | 225,000 | |
| Accrued interest (or cash) | | 225,000 |

To accrue or pay interest on the debt at the variable rate of prime + 1/2% (9.0%)

| Accrued interest (or cash) | 25,000 | |
| Interest expense | | 25,000 |

To record net settle-up on swap arrangement [8.0 – 9.0%]

| Receivable under swap contract | 462 | |
| Other comprehensive income | | 462 |

To record the fair value of the swap contract as of this date (increase in asset value due to further rise in prime rate)

June 30, 2015

| Interest expense | 212,500 | |
| Accrued interest (or cash) | | 212,500 |

To accrue or pay interest on the debt at the variable rate of prime + 1/2% (8.5%)

| Accrued interest (or cash) | 12,500 | |
| Interest expense | | 12,500 |

To record net settle-up on swap arrangement [8.0 – 8.5%]

| Other comprehensive income | 24,038 | |
| Receivable under swap contract | | 24,038 |

To record the fair value of the swap contract as of this date (value declines to zero as expiration date approaches)

Example of option on an interest rate swap

The facts of this example are a further variation on the previous one (the "plain vanilla" swap). Abbott Corp. anticipates that as of June 30, 2013, it will become a borrower of €5 million with a fixed maturity four years hence (i.e., at June 30, 2017). Based on its current credit rating, it will be able to borrow at the US prime interest rate + 1/2%. As of June 30, 2011, it is able to purchase a "swaption" (an option on an interest rate swap, calling for fixed pay at 8% and variable receipt at prime + 1/2%, on a notional amount of €5 million, for a term of four years) for a single payment of €25,000. The option will expire in two years. At June 30, 2011, the prime is 7.5%.

NOTE: *The interest rate behavior in this example differs somewhat from the prior example, to better illustrate the "one-sidedness" of options, versus the obligation under a plain vanilla swap arrangement or of other nonoption contracts, such as futures and forwards.*

It will be assumed that the time value of the swaption expires ratably over the two years.

This swaption qualifies as a cash flow hedge under IAS 39. However, while the change in fair value of the contract is an effective hedge of the cash flow variability of the prospective debt issuance, the premium paid is a reflection of the time value of money and would not be an effective part of the hedge. Accordingly, it is to be expensed as incurred, rather than being deferred.

The table below gives the prime rate at semiannual intervals including the two-year period prior to the debt issuance, plus the four years during which the debt (and the swap, if the option is exercised) will be outstanding, as well as the fair value of the swaption (and later, the swap itself) at these points in time.

Date	Prime rate (%)	Fair value of swaption/swap*
December 31, 2011	7.5	€ 0
June 30, 2012	8.0	77,925
December 31, 2012	6.5	0
June 30, 2013	7.0	(84,159)
December 31, 2013	7.5	0
June 30, 2014	8.0	65,527
December 31, 2014	8.5	111,296
June 30, 2015	8.0	45,374
December 31, 2015	8.0	34,689
June 30, 2016	7.5	0
December 31, 2016	7.5	0
June 30, 2017	7.0	0

* *Fair value is determined as the present value of future expected interest rate differentials, based on current prime rate, discounted at 8%. An "out-of-the-money" swaption is valued at zero, since the option does not have to be exercised. Since the option is exercised on June 30, 2011, the value at that date is recorded, although negative.*

The value of the swaption contract is only recorded (unless and until exercised, of course, at which point it becomes a contractually binding swap) if it is positive, since if "out-of-the-money," the holder would forego exercise in most instances and thus there is no liability by the holder to be reported. This illustrates the asymmetrical nature of options, where the most that can be lost by the option holder is the premium paid, since exercise by the holder is never required, unlike the case with futures and forwards, in which both parties are obligated to perform.

The present example is an illustration of counterintuitive (but not really illogical) behavior by the holder of an out-of-the-money option. Despite having a negative value, the option holder determines that exercise is advisable, presumably because it expects that over the term of the debt unfavorable movements in interest rates will occur.

At June 30, 2011, the swaption is an asset, since the reference variable rate (prime + 1/2%) is greater than the fixed swap rate, and thus the expectation is that the option will be exercised at expiration. This would (if present rates hold steady, which is the naïve assumption) result in a series of eight semiannual payments from the swap counterparty in the amount of €12,500. Discounting this at a nominal 8%, the present value as of the debt origination date (to be June 30, 2013) would be €84,159, which, when further discounted to June 30, 2012, yields a fair value of €77,925.

Note that the following period (at December 31, 2012) prime drops to such an extent that the value of the swaption evaporates entirely. Actually, the value becomes negative, which will not be reported since the holder is under no obligation to exercise the option under unfavorable conditions; the carrying value is therefore eliminated as of that date.

At the expiration of the swaption contract, the holder does (for this example) exercise, notwithstanding a negative fair value, and from that point forward the fair value of the swap will be reported, whether positive (an asset) or negative (a liability). Once exercised, the swap represents a series of forward contracts, the fair value of which must be fully recognized under IAS 39. (Note that, in the real world, the holder would have likely had another choice: to let the unfavorable swaption expire unexercised, but to negotiate a new interest rate swap, presumably at more favorable terms given that prime is only 7% at that date; for example, a swap of 7.5% fixed versus prime + 1/2% would likely be available at little or no cost.)

As noted above, assume that, at the option expiration date, despite the fact that prime + 1/2% is below the fixed pay rate on the swap, the management is convinced that rates will climb over the four-year term of the loan, and thus it does exercise the swaption at that date. Given this, the accounting journal entries over the entire six years are as follows:

June 30, 2011

Swaption contract	25,000	
Cash		25,000

To record purchase premium on swaption contract

December 31, 2011

Gain/loss on hedging arrangement	6,250	
Swaption contract		6,250

To record change in time value of swaption contract—charge premium to income since this represents payment for time value of money, which expires ratably over two-year term

June 30, 2012

Swaption contract	77,925	
Other comprehensive income		77,925

To record the fair value of the swaption contract as of this date

Gain/loss on hedging arrangement	6,250	
Swaption contract		6,250

To record change in time value of swaption contract—charge premium to profit or loss since this represents payment for time value of money, which expires ratably over two-year term

December 31, 2012

Other comprehensive income	77,925	
Swaption contract		77,925

To record the change in fair value of the swaption contract as of this date; since contract is out-of-the-money, it is not written down below zero (i.e., a net liability is not reported)

Gain/loss on hedging arrangement	6,250	
Swaption contract		6,250

To record change in time value of swaption contract—charge premium to profit or loss since this represents payment for time value of money, which expires ratably over two-year term

June 30, 2013

Other comprehensive income	84,159	
Swaption contract		84,159

To record the fair value of the swaption contract as of this date—a net liability is reported since swap option was exercised

| Gain/loss on hedging arrangement | 6,250 | |
| Swaption contract | | 6,250 |

To record change in time value of swaption contract—charge premium to profit or loss since this represents payment for time value of money, which expires ratably over two-year term

December 31, 2013

| Interest expense | 200,000 | |
| Accrued interest (or cash) | | 200,000 |

To accrue or pay interest on the debt at the variable rate of prime + 1/2% (8.0%)

| Interest expense | 0 | |
| Accrued interest (or cash) | | 0 |

To record net settle-up on swap arrangement [8.0 – 8.0%]

| Swap contract | 84,159 | |
| Other comprehensive income | | 84,159 |

To record the change in the fair value of the swap contract as of this date

June 30, 2014

| Interest expense | 212,500 | |
| Accrued interest (or cash) | | 212,500 |

To accrue or pay interest on the debt at the variable rate of prime + 1/2% (8.5%)

| Accrued interest (or cash) | 12,500 | |
| Interest expense | | 12,500 |

To record net settle-up on swap arrangement [8.0 – 8.5%]

| Swap contract | 65,527 | |
| Other comprehensive income | | 65,527 |

To record the fair value of the swap contract as of this date

December 31, 2014

| Interest expense | 225,000 | |
| Accrued interest (or cash) | | 225,000 |

To accrue or pay interest on the debt at the variable rate of prime + 1/2% (9.0%)

| Accrued interest (or cash) | 25,000 | |
| Interest expense | | 25,000 |

To record net settle-up on swap arrangement [8.0 – 9.0%]

| Swap contract | 45,769 | |
| Other comprehensive income | | 45,769 |

To record the fair value of the swap contract as of this date

June 30, 2015

| Interest expense | 212,500 | |
| Accrued interest (or cash) | | 212,500 |

To accrue or pay interest on the debt at the variable rate of prime + 1/2% (8.5%)

| Accrued interest (cash) | 12,500 | |
| Interest expense | | 12,500 |

To record net settle-up on swap arrangement [8.0 – 8.5%]

| Other comprehensive income | 65,922 | |
| Swap contract | | 65,922 |

To record the change in the fair value of the swap contract as of this date (declining prime rate causes swap to lose value)

December 31, 2015

Interest expense	212,500	
Accrued interest (or cash)		212,000

To accrue or pay interest on the debt at the variable rate of prime + 1/2% (8.5%)

Accrued interest (or cash)	12,500	
Interest expense		12,500

To record net settle-up on swap arrangement [8.0 – 8.5%]

Other comprehensive income	10,685	
Swap contract		10,685

To record the fair value of the swap contract as of this date (decline is due to passage of time, as the prime rate expectations have not changed from the earlier period)

June 30, 2016

Interest expense	200,000	
Accrued interest (or cash)		200,000

To accrue or pay interest on the debt at the variable rate of prime + 1/2% (8.0%)

Accrued interest (or cash)	0	
Interest expense		0

To record net settle-up on swap arrangement [8.0 – 8.5%]

Other comprehensive income	34,689	
Swap contract		34,689

To record the fair value of the swap contract as of this date

December 31, 2016

Interest expense	200,000	
Accrued interest (or cash)		200,000

To accrue or pay interest on the debt at the variable rate of prime + 1/2% (8.0%)

Accrued interest (or cash)	0	
Interest expense		0

To record net settle-up on swap arrangement [8.0 – 8.0%]

Swap contract	0	
Other comprehensive income		0

No change to the fair value of the swap contract as of this date

June 30, 2017

Interest expense	187,500	
Accrued interest (or cash)		187,500

To accrue or pay interest on the debt at the variable rate of prime + 1/2% (7.5%)

Interest expense	12,500	
Accrued interest (or cash)		12,500

To record net settle-up on swap arrangement [8.0 – 7.5%]

Other comprehensive income	0	
Swap contract		0

No change to the fair value of the swap contract, which expires as of this date

Example of using options to hedge a future purchase of inventory

Friendly Chemicals Corp. uses petroleum as a feedstock from which it produces a range of chemicals for sale to producers of synthetic fabrics and other consumer goods. It is concerned about the rising price of oil and decides to hedge a major purchase it plans to make in mid-2010. Oil futures and options are traded on the New York Mercantile Exchange and in other markets; Friendly decides to use options rather than futures because it is only interested in protecting itself from a price increase; if prices decline, it wishes to reap that benefit rather than suffer the loss which would result from holding a futures contract in a declining market environment.

At December 31, 2011, Friendly projects a need for 10 million barrels of crude oil of a defined grade to be purchased by mid-2012; this will suffice for production through mid-2012. The current world price for this grade of crude is €64.50 per barrel, but prices have been rising recently. Management desires to limit its crude oil costs to no higher than €65.75 per barrel, and accordingly purchases, at a cost of €2 million, an option to purchase up to 10 million barrels at a cost of €65.55 per barrel, at any time through December 2010. When the option premium is added to this €65.55 per barrel cost, it would make the total cost €65.75 per barrel if the full 10 million barrels are acquired.

Management has studied the behavior of option prices and has concluded that changes in option prices that relate to time value are not correlated to price changes and hence are ineffective in hedging price changes. On the other hand, changes in option prices that pertain to pricing changes (intrinsic value changes) are highly effective as hedging vehicles. The table below reports the value of these options, analyzed in terms of time value and intrinsic value, over the period from December 2011 through December 2012.

Date	Price of oil/barrel	Fair value of option relating to Time value*	Intrinsic value
December 31, 2011	€64.50	€2,000,000	€ 0
January 31, 2012	64.90	1,900,000	0
February 28, 2012	65.30	1,800,000	0
March 31, 2012	65.80	1,700,000	2,500,000
April 30, 2012	66.00	1,600,000	4,500,000
May 31, 2012	65.85	1,500,000	3,000,000
June 30, 2012**	66.00	700,000	2,250,000
July 31, 2012	65.60	650,000	250,000
August 31, 2012	65.50	600,000	0
September 30, 2012	65.75	550,000	1,000,000
October 31, 2012	65.80	500,000	1,250,000
November 30, 2012	65.85	450,000	1,500,000
December 31, 2012***	65.90	400,000	1,750,000

*   *This example does not address how the time value of options would be computed in practice.*
**   *Options for five million barrels exercised; remainder held until end of December, then sold.*
***   *Values cited are immediately prior to sale of remaining options.*

At the end of June 2012, Friendly Chemicals exercises options for five million barrels, paying €65.55 per barrel for oil that is then selling on world markets for €66.00 each. It holds the remaining options until December, when it sells these for an aggregate price of €2.1 million, a slight discount to the nominal fair value at that date.

The inventory acquired in mid-2012 is processed and included in goods available for sale. Sales of these goods, in terms of the five million barrels of crude oil which were consumed in their production, are as follows:

Date	Equivalent barrels sold in month	Equivalent barrels on hand at month-end
June 30, 2012	300,000	4,700,000
July 31, 2012	250,000	4,450,000

Date	Equivalent barrels sold in month	Equivalent barrels on hand at month-end
August 31, 2012	400,000	4,050,000
September 30, 2012	350,000	3,700,000
October 31, 2012	550,000	3,150,000
November 30, 2012	500,000	2,650,000
December 31, 2012	650,000	2,000,000

Based on the foregoing facts, the journal entries prepared on a *monthly* basis (for illustrative purposes) for the period December 2011 through December 2012 are as follows:

December 31, 2011

Option contract	2,000,000	
Cash		2,000,000

To record purchase premium on option contract for up to 10 million barrels of oil at price of €65.55 per barrel

January 31, 2012

Gain/loss on hedging transaction	100,000	
Option contract		100,000

To record change in time value of option contract—charge premium to profit or loss since this represents payment for time value of money, which expires ratably over two-year term and does not qualify for hedge accounting treatment

Option contract	0	
Other comprehensive income		0

To reflect change in intrinsic value of option contracts (no value at this date)

February 28, 2012

Gain/loss on hedging transaction	100,000	
Option contract		100,000

To record change in time value of option contract—charge premium to profit or loss since this represents payment for time value of money, which expires ratably over two-year term and does not qualify for hedge accounting treatment

Option contract	0	
Other comprehensive profit or loss		0

To reflect change in intrinsic value of option contracts (no value at this date)

March 31, 2012

Gain/loss on hedging transaction	100,000	
Option contract		100,000

To record change in time value of option contract—charge premium to profit or loss since this represents payment for time value of money, which expires ratably over two-year term and does not qualify for hedge accounting treatment

Option contract	2,500,000	
Other comprehensive profit or loss		2,500,000

To reflect change in intrinsic value of option contracts

April 30, 2012

Gain/loss on hedging transaction	100,000	
Option contract		100,000

To record change in time value of option contract—charge premium to profit or loss since this represents payment for time value of money, which expires ratably over two-year term and does not qualify for hedge accounting treatment

Option contract	2,000,000	
Other comprehensive profit or loss		2,000,000

To reflect change in intrinsic value of option contracts (further increase in value)

May 31, 2012

Gain/loss on hedging transaction	100,000	
Option contract		100,000

To record change in time value of option contract—charge premium to profit or loss since this represents payment for time value of money, which expires ratably over two-year term and does not qualify for hedge accounting treatment

Other comprehensive profit or loss	1,500,000	
Option contract		1,500,000

To reflect change in intrinsic value of option contracts (decline in value)

June 30, 2012

Gain/loss on hedging transaction	800,000	
Option contract		800,000

To record change in time value of option contract—charge premium to profit or loss since this represents payment for time value of money, which expires ratably over two-year term and does not qualify for hedge accounting treatment; since one-half the options were exercised in June, the remaining unexpensed time value of that portion is also entirely written off at this time

Option contracts	1,500,000	
Other comprehensive income		1,500,000

To reflect change in intrinsic value of option contracts (further increase in value) before accounting for exercise of options on five million barrels

June 30 value of options before exercise	4,500,000
Allocation to oil purchased at €65.55	2,250,000
Remaining option valuation	2,250,000

The allocation to exercised options will be used to adjust the carrying value of the inventory, and ultimately will be transferred to cost of goods sold as a contra cost, as the five million barrels are sold, at the rate of 45¢ per equivalent barrel.

Inventory	327,750,000	
Cash		327,750,000

To record purchase of five million barrels of oil at option price of €65.55/barrel

Inventory	2,250,000	
Option contract		2,250,000

To increase the recorded value of the inventory to include the fair value of options given up in acquiring the oil (taken together, the cash purchase price and the fair value of options surrendered add to €66.00 per barrel, the world market price at date of purchase)

Other comprehensive income	2,250,000	
Inventory		2,250,000

To reclassify deferred gain from equity and include in initial measurement of inventory

Cost of goods sold	19,665,000	
Inventory		19,665,000

To record cost of goods sold

July 31, 2012

Gain/loss on hedging transaction	50,000	
Option contract		50,000

To record change in time value of option contract—charge premium to profit or loss since this represents payment for time value of money, which expires ratably over two-year term, and does not qualify for hedge accounting treatment

Other comprehensive income	2,000,000	
Option contract		2,000,000

To reflect change in intrinsic value of remaining option contracts (decline in value)

Cost of goods sold	16,387,500	
Inventory		16,387,500

To record cost of goods sold

August 31, 2012

Loss on hedging transaction	50,000	
Option contract		50,000

To record change in time value of option contract—charge premium to profit or loss since this represents payment for time value of money, which expires ratably over two-year term, and does not qualify for hedge accounting treatment

Other comprehensive income	250,000	
Option contract		250,000

To reflect change in intrinsic value of remaining option contracts (decline in value)

Cost of goods sold	26,220,000	
Inventory		26,220,000

To record cost of goods sold

September 30, 2012

Gain/loss on hedging transaction	50,000	
Option contract		50,000

To record change in time value of option contract—charge premium to profit or loss since this represents payment for time value of money, which expires ratably over two-year term, and does not qualify for hedge accounting treatment

Option contract	1,000,000	
Other comprehensive income		1,000,000

To reflect change in intrinsic value of remaining option contracts (increase in value)

Cost of goods sold	22,942,500	
Inventory		22,942,500

To record cost of goods sold

October 31, 2012

Gain/loss on hedging transaction	50,000	
Option contract		50,000

To record change in time value of option contract—charge premium to profit or loss since this represents payment for time value of money, which expires ratably over two-year term, and does not qualify for hedge accounting treatment

Option contract	250,000	
Other comprehensive income		250,000

To reflect change in intrinsic value of remaining option contracts (further increase in value)

Cost of goods sold	36,052,500	
Inventory		36,052,500

To record cost of goods sold

November 30, 2012

Gain/loss on hedging transaction	50,000	
Option contract		50,000

To record change in time value of option contract—charge premium to profit or loss since this represents payment for time value of money, which expires ratably over two-year term, and does not qualify for hedge accounting treatment

Option contract	250,000	
Other comprehensive income		250,000

To reflect change in intrinsic value of remaining option contracts (further increase in value)

Cost of goods sold	32,775,000	
Inventory		32,775,000

To record cost of goods sold

December 31, 2012

Gain/loss on hedging transaction	50,000	
Option contract		50,000

To record change in time value of option contract—charge premium to profit or loss since this represents payment for time value of money, which expires ratably over two-year term, and does not qualify for hedge accounting treatment

Option contract	250,000	
Other comprehensive income		250,000

To reflect change in intrinsic value of remaining option contracts (further increase in value) before sale of options

Cost of goods sold	42,607,500	
Inventory		42,607,500

To record cost of goods sold

Cash	2,100,000	
Loss on sale of options	50,000	
Option contract		2,150,000
Other comprehensive income	1,750,000	
Gain on sale of options		1,750,000

To record sale of remaining option contracts; the cash price was €50,000 lower than carrying value of asset sold (options having unexpired time value of €400,000 plus intrinsic value of €1,750,000), but reclassification from equity to profit or loss recognizes formerly deferred gain; since no further inventory purchases are planned in connection with this hedging activity, the unrealized gain is recognized in profit or loss

Example of hedging of a net investment in a foreign subsidiary

IAS 39 permits hedging of a net investment in foreign subsidiaries ("net investment hedge"). For example, Swartzwald GmbH has a net investment of $100,000 in its US subsidiary, Simpsons

Inc., for which it paid €110,000 on January 1, 2012. Swartzwald could hedge its net asset investment by entering, for example, into a forward exchange contract to sell US dollars, or the company could incur a US dollar-based liability. IAS 39 states that the gain or loss on the effective portion of a hedge of a net investment is reported in other comprehensive income and accumulated in equity as part of the foreign currency translation adjustment. However, the amount of offset to other comprehensive income is limited to the translation adjustment for the net investment. For example, if the forward exchange rate is used to measure hedge effectiveness, the amount of offset is limited to the change in spot rates during the period. Any excess of the ineffective portion of the hedge must be recognized currently in profit or loss.

On January 1, 2012, Swartzwald decided to hedge its investment in Simpsons for the amount equal to the book value of the US company's net investment (net assets). Swartzwald is unsure whether the exchange rate for the dollar will increase or decrease for the year and wants to hedge its net asset investment. On January 1, 2012, Swartzwald's ownership share of Simpson's net assets is equal to $100,000 ($80,000 share capital and $20,000 retained earnings). On that day Swartzwald borrows $100,000, at a 5% rate of interest, to hedge its equity investment in the US company, and the principal and interest are due and payable on January 1, 2013.

The spot exchange rates are	January 1, 2012	$1 = €.90
	December 31, 2012	$1 = €.80
The average exchange rate for the year 2012 is		$1 = €.85

The journal entries on Swartzwald's Euro-denominated books to account for this hedge of a net investment are as follows:

January 1, 2012

| Cash | 90,000 | |
| Loan payable ($ denominated debt) | | 90,000 |

To record a dollar-denominated loan to hedge net investment in US subsidiary €90,000 = $100,000 × €.90 spot rate

December 31, 2012

| Loan payable ($ denominated debt) | 10,000 | |
| Other comprehensive income (OCI) | | 10,000 |

To revalue foreign currency-denominated payable to end-of-period spot rate €10,000 = $100,000 × (€.90 – €.80)

Interest expense	4,250	
Foreign currency exchange gain		250
Interest payable		4,000

To accrue interest expense and payable on dollar loan €4,250 = $100,000 × 0.05 interest × €.85 average exchange rate €4,000 = $100,000 × 0.05 interest × €.80 ending spot rate

Other comprehensive income (OCI)	10,000	
Foreign currency exchange gain	250	
Profit or loss summary (retained earnings)		250
Translation adjustment—accumulated OCI		10,000

To record closing of nominal accounts related to hedge of net investment in foreign subsidiary

January 1, 2013

Interest payable ($ denominated debt)	4,000	
Loan payable ($ denominated debt)	80,000	
Cash		84,000

To record repayment of principal and interest. €80,000 = €90,000 – €10,000

During 2012 the euro has strengthened relative to the dollar (the direct exchange rate has decreased from €.90 to €.80) and Swartzwald would recognize a loss on a net asset investment in dollars and gain on a liability payable in dollars. Without this hedge of the net investment, Swartzwald would report a €10,850 debit balance in other comprehensive income (the cumulative translation adjustment portion of accumulated other comprehensive income equals €10,000 + €850 differential adjustment). With the hedge of its net investment, Swartzwald will report only €850 (€10,850 – €10,000 effect of hedge) as the change in the cumulative translation adjustment for 2012. Note also that the amount of the offset to other income is limited to the effective portion of the hedge based on the revaluation of the net assets. Any excess, in this case the €250 gain on the revaluation of the interest payable, is reported currently in the profit or loss.

Hedging on a "net" basis and "macrohedging." The IGC has addressed the issue of whether a reporting entity can group financial assets together with financial liabilities for the purpose of determining the net cash flow exposure to be hedged for hedge accounting purposes. It ruled that while an entity's hedging strategy and risk management practices may assess cash flow risk on a net basis, IAS 39 does not permit designating a net cash flow exposure as a hedged item for hedge accounting purposes. IAS 39 provides an example of how a bank might assess its risk on a net basis (with similar assets and liabilities grouped together) and then qualify for hedge accounting by hedging on a gross basis.

In 2004 IASB amended IAS 39 to permit "macrohedging" (more formally, hedging a portfolio hedge of interest rate risk). This permits an entity to apply *fair value* hedging (but not cash flow hedging) to a grouping of assets and/or liabilities, which essentially means that the net exposure can be hedged, without a need to separately put hedge positions on for each of the individual assets and/or liabilities.

Partial term hedging. IAS 39 indicates that a hedging relationship may not be designated for only a portion of the time period in which a hedging instrument is outstanding. On the other hand, it is permitted to designate a derivative as hedging only a portion of the time period to maturity of a hedged item. For example, if Aquarian Corp. acquires a 10% fixed-rate government bond with a remaining term to maturity of ten years, and classifies the bond as available-for-sale, it may hedge itself against fair value exposure on the bond associated with the present value of the interest rate payments until year five by acquiring a five-year "pay-fixed, receive-floating" swap. The swap may be designated as hedging the fair value exposure of the interest rate payments on the government bond until year five and the change in value of the principal payment due at maturity to the extent affected by changes in the yield curve relating to the five years of the swap.

Interest rate risk managed on a net basis should be designated as hedge of gross exposure. If an entity manages its exposure to interest rate risk on a net basis, a number of complex financial reporting issues must be addressed, regarding the ability to use hedge accounting. The IGC has offered substantial guidance on a number of matters, the more generally applicable of which are summarized in the following paragraphs.

The IGC has concluded that a derivative that is used to manage interest rate risk on a net basis be designated as a hedging instrument in a fair value hedge or a cash flow hedge of a gross exposure under IAS 39. An entity may designate the derivative used in interest rate risk management activities either as a fair value hedge of assets or liabilities or as a cash flow hedge of forecasted transactions, such as the anticipated reinvestment of cash inflows, the anticipated refinancing or rollover of a financial liability, and the cash flow consequences of the resetting of interest rates for an asset or a liability.

The IGC also notes that firm commitments to purchase or sell assets at fixed prices create fair value exposures, but are accounted for as cash flow hedges. (Note, however, the IASB has proposed to reverse the former rule, such that hedges of firm commitments will henceforth be accounted for as fair value hedges.) In economic terms, it does not matter whether the derivative instrument is considered a fair value hedge or a cash flow hedge. Under either perspective of the exposure, the derivative has the same economic effect of reducing the net exposure. For example, a receive-fixed, pay-variable interest rate swap can be considered to be a cash flow hedge of a variable-rate asset or a fair value hedge of a fixed-rate liability. Under either perspective, the fair value or cash flows of the interest rate swap offsets the exposure to interest rate changes. However, accounting consequences differ depending on whether the derivative is designated as a fair value hedge or a cash flow hedge, as discussed below.

Consider the following illustration. Among its financial resources and obligations, a bank has the following assets and liabilities having maturities of two years:

	Variable interest	*Fixed interest*
Assets	60,000	100,000
Liabilities	(100,000)	(60,000)
Net	(40,000)	40,000

The bank enters into a two-year interest rate swap with a notional principal of €40,000 to receive a variable interest rate and pay a fixed interest rate, in order to hedge the net exposure of the two-year maturity financial assets and liabilities. According to the IGC, this may be designated either as a fair value hedge of €40,000 of the fixed-rate assets or as a cash flow hedge of €40,000 of the variable-rate liabilities. It cannot be designated as a hedge of the net exposure, however.

Determining whether a derivative that is used to manage interest rate risk on a net basis should be designated as a hedging instrument in a fair value hedge or a cash flow hedge of a gross exposure is based on a number of critical considerations. These include the assessment of hedge effectiveness in the presence of prepayment risk, and the ability of the information systems to attribute fair value or cash flow changes of hedging instruments to fair value or cash flow changes, respectively, of hedged items. For accounting purposes, the designation of the derivative as hedging a fair value exposure or a cash flow exposure is important because both the qualification requirements for hedge accounting and the recognition of hedging gains and losses differ for each of these categories. The IGC has observed that it will often be easier to demonstrate high effectiveness for a cash flow hedge than for a fair value hedge.

Another important issue involves the effects of prepayments on the fair value of an instrument and the timing of its cash flows, as well as the impacts on the effectiveness test for fair value hedges and the probability test for cash flow hedges, respectively. Effectiveness is often more difficult to achieve for fair value hedges than for cash flow hedges when the instrument being hedged is subject to prepayment risk. For a fair value hedge to qualify for hedge accounting, the changes in the fair value of the derivative hedging instrument must be expected to be highly effective in offsetting the changes in the fair value of the hedged item. This test may be difficult to meet if, for example, the derivative hedging instrument is a forward contract having a fixed term, and the financial assets being hedged are subject to prepayment by the borrower.

Also, it may be difficult to conclude that, for a portfolio of fixed-rate assets that are subject to prepayment, the changes in the fair value for each individual item in the group will be expected to be approximately proportional to the overall changes in fair value attributable to the hedged risk of the group. Even if the risk being hedged is a benchmark interest rate, to be able to conclude that fair value changes will be proportional for each item in the portfolio, it may be necessary to disaggregate the asset portfolio into categories based on term, coupon, credit, type of loan, and other characteristics.

In economic terms, a forward derivative instrument could be used to hedge assets that are subject to prepayment, but it would be effective only for small movements in interest rates. A reasonable estimate of prepayments can be made for a given interest rate environment and the derivative position can be adjusted as the interest rate environment changes. However, for accounting purposes, the expectation of effectiveness has to be based on existing fair value exposures and the potential for interest rate movements, without consideration of future adjustments to those positions. The fair value exposure attributable to prepayment risk can generally be hedged with options.

For a cash flow hedge to qualify for hedge accounting, the forecasted cash flows, including the reinvestment of cash inflows or the refinancing of cash outflows, must be highly probable, and the hedge expected to be highly effective in achieving offsetting changes in the cash flows of the hedged item and hedging instrument. Prepayments affect the timing of cash flows and, therefore, the probability of occurrence of the forecasted transaction. If the hedge is established for risk management purposes on a net basis, an entity may have sufficient levels of highly probable cash flows on a gross basis to support the designation for accounting purposes of forecasted transactions associated with a portion of the gross cash flows as the hedged item. In this case, the portion of the gross cash flows designated as being hedged may be chosen to be equal to the amount of net cash flows being hedged for risk management purposes.

The IAS 39 Implementation Guidance Committee has also emphasized that there are important systems considerations relating to the use of hedge accounting. It notes that the accounting differs for fair value hedges and cash flow hedges. It is usually easier to use existing information systems to manage and track cash flow hedges than it is for fair value hedges.

Under fair value hedge accounting, the assets or liabilities that are designated as being hedged are remeasured for those changes in fair values during the hedge period that are attributable to the risk being hedged. Such changes adjust the carrying amount of the hedged items and, for interest-sensitive assets and liabilities, may result in an adjustment of the effective yield of the hedged item. As a consequence of fair value hedging activities, the changes in fair value have to be allocated to the hedged assets or liabilities being hedged in order to be able to recompute their effective yield, determine the subsequent amortization of the fair value adjustment to net profit or loss, and determine the amount that should be recognized in net profit or loss when assets are sold or liabilities extinguished. To comply with the requirements for fair value hedge accounting, it generally will be necessary to establish a system to track the changes in the fair value attributable to the hedged risk, associate those changes with individual hedged items, recompute the effective yield of the hedged items, and amortize the changes to net profit or loss over the life of the respective hedged item.

Under cash flow hedge accounting, the cash flows relating to the forecasted transactions that are designated as being hedged reflect changes in interest rates. The adjustment for changes in the fair value of a hedging derivative instrument is initially recognized in other comprehensive income. To comply with the requirements for cash flow hedge accounting, it is necessary to determine when the adjustments from changes in the fair value of a hedging instrument should be recognized in profit or loss. For cash flow hedges, it is not necessary to create a separate system to make this determination. The system used to determine the extent of the net exposure provides the basis for scheduling out the changes in the cash flows of the derivative and the recognition of such changes in profit or loss. The timing of the recognition in profit or loss can be predetermined when the hedge is associated with the exposure to changes in cash flows.

The forecasted transactions that are being hedged can be associated with a specific principal amount in specific future periods, composed of variable-rate assets and cash inflows being reinvested or variable-rate liabilities and cash outflows being refinanced, each of which create a cash flow exposure to changes in interest rates. The specific principal amounts in specific future periods are equal to the notional amount of the derivative hedging instruments and are hedged only for the period that corresponds to the repricing or maturity of the derivative hedging instruments so that the cash flow changes resulting from changes in interest rate are matched with the derivative hedging instrument. IAS 39 specifies that the amounts recognized in other comprehensive income should be included in profit or loss in the same period or periods during which the hedged item affects profit or loss.

If a hedging relationship is designated as a cash flow hedge relating to changes in cash flows resulting from interest rate changes, the documentation required by IAS 39 would include information about the hedging relationship; the entity's risk management objective and strategy for undertaking the hedge; the type of hedge; the hedged item; the hedged risk; the hedging instrument; and the method of assessing effectiveness.

Information about the hedging relationship would include the maturity schedule of cash flows used for risk management purposes; to determine exposures to cash flow mismatches on a net basis would provide part of the documentation of the hedging relationship. The entity's risk management objective and strategy for undertaking the hedge would be addressed in terms of the entity's overall risk management objective, and strategy for hedging exposures to interest rate risk would provide part of the documentation of the hedging objective and strategy. The fact that the hedge is a cash flow hedge would also be noted.

The hedged item will be documented as a group of forecasted transactions (interest cash flows) that are expected to occur with a high degree of probability in specified future periods, for instance, scheduled on a monthly basis. The hedged item may include interest cash flows resulting from the reinvestment of cash inflows, including the resetting of interest rates on assets, or from the refinancing of cash outflows, including the resetting of interest rates on liabilities and rollovers of financial liabilities. The forecasted transactions meet the probability test if there are sufficient levels of highly probable cash flows in the specified future periods to encompass the amounts designated as being hedged on a gross basis.

The risk designated as being hedged is documented as a portion of the overall exposure to changes in a specified market interest rate, often the risk-free interest rate or an interbank offered rate, common to all items in the group. To help ensure that the hedge effectiveness test is met at inception of the hedge and subsequently, the designated hedged portion of the interest rate risk could be documented as being based off the same yield curve as the derivative hedging instrument.

Each derivative hedging instrument is documented as a hedge of specified amounts in specified future time periods corresponding with the forecasted transactions occurring in the specified future periods designated as being hedged.

The method of assessing effectiveness is documented by comparing the changes in the cash flows of the derivatives allocated to the applicable periods in which they are designated as a hedge to the changes in the cash flows of the forecasted transactions being hedged. Measurement of the cash flow changes is based on the applicable yield curves of the derivatives and hedged items.

When a hedging relationship is designated as a cash flow hedge, the entity might satisfy the requirement for an expectation of high effectiveness in achieving offsetting changes by preparing an analysis demonstrating high historical and expected future correlation between the interest rate risk designated as being hedged and the interest rate risk of the hedging instrument. Existing documentation of the hedge ratio used in establishing the derivative contracts may also serve to demonstrate an expectation of effectiveness.

If the hedging relationship is designated as a cash flow hedge, an entity may demonstrate a high probability of the forecasted transactions occurring by preparing a cash flow maturity schedule showing that there exist sufficient aggregate gross levels of expected cash flows, including the effects of the resetting of interest rates for assets or liabilities, to establish that the forecasted transactions that are designated as being hedged are highly probable of occurring. Such a schedule should be supported by management's stated intent and past practice of reinvesting cash inflows and refinancing cash outflows.

For instance, an entity may forecast aggregate gross cash inflows of €10,000 and aggregate gross cash outflows of €9,000 in a particular time period in the near future. In this case, it may wish to designate the forecasted reinvestment of gross cash inflows of €1,000 as the hedged item in the future time period. If more than €1,000 of the forecasted cash inflows are contractually specified and have low credit risk, the entity has very strong evidence to support an assertion that gross cash inflows of €1,000 are highly probable of occurring and support the designation of the forecasted reinvestment of those cash flows as being hedged for a particular portion of the reinvestment period. A high probability of the forecasted transactions occurring may also be demonstrated under other circumstances.

If the hedging relationship is designated as a cash flow hedge, an entity will assess and measure effectiveness under IAS 39, at a minimum, at the time an entity prepares its annual or interim financial reports. However, an entity may wish to measure it more frequently on a specified periodic basis, at the end of each month or other applicable reporting period. It is also measured whenever derivative positions designated as hedging instruments are changed or hedges are terminated, to ensure that the recognition in net profit or loss of the changes in the fair value amounts on assets and liabilities and the recognition of changes in the fair value of derivative instruments designated as cash flow hedges are appropriate.

Changes in the cash flows of the derivative are computed and allocated to the applicable periods in which the derivative is designated as a hedge and are compared with computations of changes in the cash flows of the forecasted transactions. Computations are based on yield curves applicable to the hedged items and the derivative hedging instruments and applicable interest rates for the specified periods being hedged. The schedule used to determine effectiveness could be maintained and used as the basis for determining the period in which the hedging gains and losses recognized initially in other comprehensive income are reclassified out of equity and recognized in profit or loss.

If the hedging relationship is designated as a cash flow hedge, an entity will account for the hedge as follows: (1) the portion of gains and losses on hedging derivatives determined to result from effective hedges is recognized in other comprehensive income whenever effectiveness is measured and (2) the ineffective portion of gains and losses resulting from hedging derivatives is recognized in net profit or loss.

The amounts recognized in other comprehensive income should be included in net profit or loss in the same period or periods during which the hedged item affects net profit or loss. Accordingly, when the forecasted transactions occur, the amounts previously recognized in other comprehensive income are reclassified from equity to profit or loss. For instance, if an interest rate swap is designated as a hedging instrument of a series of forecasted cash flows, the changes in the cash flows of the swap are recognized in net profit or loss in the periods when the forecasted cash flows and the cash flows of the swap offset each other.

If the hedging relationship is designated as a cash flow hedge, the treatment of any net cumulative gains and losses recognized in other comprehensive income if the hedging instrument is terminated prematurely, the hedge accounting criteria are no longer met, or the hedged forecasted transactions are no longer expected to take place, will be as described in the following. If the hedging instrument is terminated prematurely or the hedge no longer meets the criteria for qualification for hedge accounting (for instance, the forecasted transactions are no longer highly probable), the net cumulative gain or loss reported in other comprehensive income remains in equity until the forecasted transaction occurs. If the hedged forecasted transactions are no longer expected to occur, the net cumulative gain or loss is reclassified from equity to profit or loss for the period.

IAS 39 states that a hedging relationship may not be designated for only a portion of the time period in which a hedging instrument is outstanding. If the hedging relationship is designated as a cash flow hedge, and the hedge subsequently fails the test for being highly effective, IAS 39 does not preclude redesignating the hedging instrument. The standard indicates that a derivative instrument may not be designated as a hedging instrument for only a portion of its remaining period to maturity but does not refer to the derivative instrument's original period to maturity. If there is a hedge effectiveness failure, the ineffective portion of the gain or loss on the derivative instrument is recognized immediately in net profit or loss and hedge accounting based on the previous designation of the hedge relationship cannot be continued. In this case, the derivative instrument may be redesignated prospectively as a hedging instrument in a new hedging relationship, provided this hedging relationship satisfies the necessary conditions. The derivative instrument must be redesignated as a hedge for the entire time period it remains outstanding.

For cash flow hedges, IAS 39 states that "if the hedged firm commitment or forecasted transaction results in the recognition of an asset or liability, then at the time the asset or liability is recognized the associated gains or losses that were recognized in other comprehensive income should enter into the initial measurement of the carrying amount of the asset or liability" (basis adjustment). If a derivative is used to manage a net exposure to interest rate risk and the derivative is designated as a cash flow hedge of forecasted interest cash flows or portions thereof on a gross basis, there will be no basis adjustment when the forecasted cash flow occurs. There is no basis adjustment because the hedged forecasted transactions do not result in the recognition of assets or liabilities and the effect of interest rate changes that are designated as being hedged is recognized in net profit or loss in the period in which the forecasted transactions occur. Although the types of hedges described herein would not result in basis adjustment if instead the derivative is designated as a hedge of a forecasted purchase of a financial asset or issuance of a liability, the derivative gain or loss would be an adjustment to the basis of the asset or liability upon the occurrence of the transaction.

IAS 39 permits a portion of a cash flow exposure to be designated as a hedged item. While IAS 39 does not specifically address a hedge of a portion of a cash flow exposure for a forecasted transaction, it specifies that a financial asset or liability may be a hedged item with respect to the risks associated with only a portion of its cash flows or fair value, if effectiveness can be measured. The ability to hedge a portion of a cash flow exposure resulting from the resetting of interest rates for assets and liabilities suggests that a portion of a cash flow exposure resulting from the forecasted reinvestment of cash inflows or the refinancing or rollover of financial liabilities can also be hedged. The basis for qualification as a hedged item of a portion of an exposure is the ability to measure effectiveness.

Furthermore, IAS 39 specifies that a nonfinancial asset or liability can be hedged only in its entirety or for foreign currency risk but not for a portion of other risks because of the difficulty of isolating and measuring the risks attributable to a specific risk. Accordingly, assuming effectiveness can be measured, a portion of a cash flow exposure of forecasted transactions associated with, for example, the resetting of interest rates for a variable-rate asset or liability can be designated as a hedged item.

Since forecasted transactions will have different terms when they occur, including credit exposures, maturities, and option features, there may be an issue over how an entity can satisfy the tests in IAS 39 requiring that the hedged group have similar risk characteristics. According to the IGC, the standard provides for hedging a group of assets, liabilities, firm commitments, or forecasted transactions with similar risk characteristics. IAS 39 provides additional guidance and specifies that portfolio hedging is permitted if two conditions are met, namely: the individual items in the portfolio share the same risk for which they are designated and the change in the fair value attributable to the hedged risk for each individual item in the group will be expected to be approximately proportional to the overall change in fair value.

When an entity associates a derivative hedging instrument with a gross exposure, the hedged item typically is a group of forecasted transactions. For hedges of cash flow exposures relating to a group of forecasted transactions, the overall exposure of the forecasted transactions and the assets or liabilities that are repricing may have very different risks. The exposure from forecasted transactions may differ based on the terms that are expected as they relate to credit exposures, maturities, option, and other features. Although the overall risk exposures may be different for the individual items in the group, a specific risk inherent in each of the items in the group can be designated as being hedged.

The items in the portfolio do not necessarily have to have the same overall exposure to risk, providing they share the same risk for which they are designated as being hedged. A common risk typically shared by a portfolio of financial instruments is exposure to changes in the risk-free interest rate or to changes in a specified rate that has a credit exposure equal to the highest credit-rated instrument in the portfolio (that is, the instrument with the lowest credit risk). If the instruments that are grouped into a portfolio have different credit exposures, they may be hedged as a group for a portion of the exposure. The risk they have in common that is designated as being hedged is the exposure to interest rate changes from the highest credit-rated instrument in the portfolio. This ensures that the change in fair value attributable to the hedged risk for each individual item in the group is expected to be approximately proportional to the overall change in fair value attributable to the hedged risk of the group. It is likely there will be some ineffectiveness if the hedging instrument has a credit quality that is inferior to the credit quality of the highest credit-rated instrument being hedged, since a hedging relationship is designated for a hedging instrument in its entirety.

For example, if a portfolio of assets consists of assets rated A, BB, and B, and the current market interest rates for these assets are LIBOR + 20 basis points, LIBOR + 40 basis points, and LIBOR + 60 basis points, respectively, an entity may use a swap that pays fixed interest rate and for which variable interest payments are made based on LIBOR to hedge the exposure to variable interest rates. If LIBOR is designated as the risk being hedged, credit spreads above LIBOR on the hedged items are excluded from the designated hedge relationship and the assessment of hedge effectiveness.

DISCLOSURE

Disclosures Required under IFRS 7

IAS 32 established an expansive set of disclosure requirements. IAS 39 carried forward these requirements with only minor changes and added further informational disclosure requirements. Both IAS 32 and IAS 39 were revised as part of the IASB's *Improvements Project* in 2003, and at that time all disclosure requirements were relocated to IAS 32. In mid-2005, IFRS 7 was promulgated, which set forth all financial instruments disclosure requirements, superseding (but not changing) the disclosure requirements previously found in both IAS 30 and IAS 32.

IFRS 7 sets out the requirements for the disclosure of financial instruments under two broad categories, quantitative disclosures and qualitative disclosures. The quantitative disclosures provide information about the effect of financial instruments on the financial position and financial performance of the entity, whereas the qualitative disclosures provide useful information about how risks relating to financial instruments arise in the entity and how these risks are being managed. The nature of the reporting entity's business and the extent to which it holds financial assets or is obligated by financial liabilities will affect the manner in which such disclosures are presented, and no single method of making such disclosures will be suitable for every entity. The standard therefore adopts an approach that requires the entity to disclosure the information required in the form that it is presented internally for use by management and in those areas where management does not prepare the required information it must develop the appropriate disclosures. This approach means that financial instrument disclosures may not be easily comparable between entities.

The risks arising from financial instruments are categorized as follows:

1. **Market risk,** which implies not merely the risk of loss but also the potential for gain, and which is in turn comprised of

    a. **Currency risk**—The risk that the value of an instrument will vary due to changes in currency exchange rates.
    b. **Interest rate risk**—The risk that the value of the instrument will fluctuate due to changes in market interest rates.
    c. **Other price risk**—A broader concept that subsumes interest rate risk, this is, the risk that the fair value or future cash flows of a financial instrument will fluctuate due to factors specific to the financial instrument or due to factors that are generally affecting all similar instruments traded in the same markets.

2. **Credit risk** is related to a loss that may occur from the failure of another party to a financial instrument to discharge an obligation according to the terms of a contract.

3. **Liquidity risk** is the risk that an entity may encounter difficulty in meeting obligations associated with financial liabilities.

Interest rate risk. Interest rate risk is the risk associated with holding fixed-rate instruments in a changing interest-rate environment. As market rates rise, the price of fixed-interest-rate instruments will decline, and vice versa. This relationship holds in all cases, irrespective of other specific factors, such as changes in perceived creditworthiness of the borrower. However, with certain complex instruments such as mortgage-backed bonds (a popular form of derivative instrument), where the behavior of the underlying debtors can be expected to be altered by changes in the interest rate environment (i.e., as market interest rates decline, prepayments by mortgagors increase in frequency, raising reinvestment rate risk to the bondholders and accordingly tempering the otherwise expected upward movement of the bond prices), the inverse relationship will become distorted.

Credit risk. For each class of financial asset, both recognized (i.e., on-balance-sheet) and unrecognized (off-balance-sheet), information is to be provided about exposure to credit risk. Specifically, the maximum amount of credit risk exposure as of the date of the statement of financial position, without considering possible recoveries from any collateral that may have been provided, should be stated and any significant concentrations of credit risk should be discussed.

Disclosure Requirements Added by IFRS 7

IFRS 7 has superseded the disclosure requirements previously found in IAS 32, as well as the financial institution-specific disclosure requirements of IAS 30, which were accordingly withdrawn. Presentation requirements set forth in IAS 32 continue in effect under that standard. IFRS 7 became effective for years beginning in 2007.

IFRS 7 was made necessary by the increasingly sophisticated (but opaque) methods that reporting entities have begun using to measure and manage their exposure to risks arising from financial instruments. At the same time, new risk management concepts and approaches have gained acceptance. IASB concluded that users of financial statements need information about the reporting entities' exposures to risks and how those risks are being managed.

Risk management information can influence the users' assessments of the financial position and performance of reporting entities, as well as of the amount, timing, and uncertainty of the respective entity's future cash flows. In short, greater transparency regarding those risks allows users to make more informed judgments about risk and return. This is entirely consistent with the fundamental objective of financial reporting and is consistent with the widely accepted efficient markets hypothesis.

IFRS 7 applies to all risks arising from all financial instruments, with limited exceptions. It furthermore applies to all entities, including those that have few financial instruments (e.g., an entity whose only financial instruments are accounts receivable and payable), as well as those that have many financial instruments (e.g., a financial institution, most assets and liabilities of which are financial instruments). Under IFRS 7, the extent of disclosure required depends on the extent of the entity's use of financial instruments and of its exposure to risk.

IFRS 7 requires disclosure of

1. The significance of financial instruments for an entity's financial position and performance (which incorporates many of the requirements previously set forth by IAS 32); and
2. Qualitative and quantitative information about exposure to risks arising from financial instruments, including specified minimum disclosures about credit risk, liquidity risk, and market risk. The *qualitative* disclosures describe managements' objectives, policies, and processes for managing those risks. The *quantitative* disclosures provide information about the extent to which the entity is exposed to risk, based on information provided internally to the entity's key management personnel. Together, these disclosures are expected to provide an overview of the reporting entity's use of financial instruments and the exposures to risks they create.

Exceptions to applicability. IFRS 7 identifies the following types of financial instruments to which the requirements do not apply:

1. Interests in subsidiaries, associates, and joint ventures accounted for in accordance with IAS 27, IAS 28, or IAS 31, respectively. However, given that in some cases those standards permit an entity to account for an interest in a subsidiary, associate, or joint venture using IAS 39, in those cases the reporting entities are to apply the disclosure requirements in those other standards as well as those in IFRS 7. Entities are also to apply IFRS 7 to all derivatives linked to interests in subsidiaries, associates, or joint ventures, unless the derivative meets the definition of an equity instrument first established by IAS 32.
2. Employers' rights and obligations arising from employee benefit plans, to which IAS 19 applies.
3. Contracts for contingent consideration in a business combination, per IFRS 3, in financial reporting by the acquirer.
4. Insurance contracts as defined in IFRS 4. However, IFRS 7 applies to derivatives that are embedded in insurance contracts if IAS 39 requires the entity to account for them separately.

5. Financial instruments, contracts, and obligations under share-based payment transactions to which IFRS 2 applies, except that IFRS 7 applies to certain contracts that are within the scope of IAS 39.

Applicability. IFRS 7 applies to both recognized and unrecognized financial instruments. *Recognized* financial instruments include financial assets and financial liabilities that are within the scope of IAS 39. *Unrecognized* financial instruments include some financial instruments that, although outside the scope of IAS 39, are within the scope of this IFRS (such as some loan commitments). The requirements also extend to contracts involving non-financial items if they are subject to IAS 39.

Classes of financial instruments and level of disclosure. Many of the IFRS 7 requirements pertain to grouped data. In such cases, the grouping into classes is to be effected in the manner that is appropriate to the nature of the information disclosed and that takes into account the characteristics of the financial instruments. Importantly, sufficient information must be provided so as to permit reconciliation to the line items presented in the statement of financial position. Enough detail is required so that users are able to assess the significance of financial instruments to the reporting entity's financial position and results of operations.

IFRS 7 requires that carrying amounts of each of the following categories, as defined in IAS 39, is to be disclosed either on the face of the statement of financial position or in the notes:

1. Financial assets at fair value through profit or loss, showing separately

   a. Those designated as such upon initial recognition via the "fair value option" and
   b. Those classified as held-for-trading in accordance with IAS 39;

2. Held-to-maturity investments;
3. Loans and receivables;
4. Available-for-sale financial assets;
5. Financial liabilities at fair value through profit or loss, showing separately,

   a. Those designated as such upon initial recognition via the "fair value option" and
   b. Those classified as held-for-trading in accordance with IAS 39; and

6. Financial liabilities carried at amortized cost.

Special disclosures apply to those financial assets and liabilities accounted for by the "fair value option." If the reporting entity designated a loan or receivable (or groups thereof) to be reported at fair value through profit or loss, it is required to disclose

1. The maximum exposure to *credit risk* of the loan or receivable (or group thereof) at the reporting date.
2. The amount by which any related credit derivatives or similar instruments mitigate that maximum exposure to credit risk.
3. The amount of change, both during the reporting period *and* cumulatively, in the fair value of the loan or receivable (or group thereof) that is attributable to *changes in the credit risk* of the financial asset determined either

   a. As the amount of change in its fair value that is not attributable to changes in market conditions that give rise to market risk; or
   b. Using an alternative method the entity believes more faithfully represents the amount of change in its fair value that is attributable to changes in the credit risk of the asset.

Changes in market conditions that give rise to market risk include changes in an observed (benchmark) interest rate, commodity price, foreign exchange rate, or index of prices or rates.

4. The amount of the change in the fair value of any related derivatives or similar instruments that has occurred during the period and cumulatively since the loan or receivable was designated.

If the reporting entity has designated a financial liability to be reported at fair value through profit or loss, it is to disclose

1. The amount of change, both during the period *and* cumulatively, in the fair value of the financial liability that is attributable to *changes in the credit risk* of that liability determined either

   a. As the amount of change in its fair value that is not attributable to changes in market conditions that give rise to market risk; or
   b. Using an alternative method the entity believes more faithfully represents the amount of change in its fair value that is attributable to changes in the credit risk of the liability.

   Changes in market conditions that give rise to market risk include changes in a benchmark interest rate, the price of another entity's financial instrument, a commodity price, a foreign exchange rate, or an index of prices or rates. For contracts that include a unit-linking feature, changes in market conditions include changes in the performance of the related internal or external investment fund.

2. The difference between the financial liability's carrying amount and the amount the entity would be contractually required to pay at maturity to the holder of the obligation.

Reclassifications. If a financial asset has been reclassified to one that is measured: (1) at cost or amortized cost, rather than at fair value; or (2) at fair value, rather than at cost or amortized cost, the amount reclassified into and out of each category and the reason for that reclassification are to be disclosed.

Certain derecognition matters. If financial assets were transferred in such a way that part or all of those assets did not qualify for derecognition under IAS 39, the following disclosures are required for each class of such financial assets:

1. The nature of the assets;
2. The nature of the risks and rewards of ownership to which the entity remains exposed;
3. When the entity continues to recognize all of the assets, the carrying amounts of the assets and of the associated liabilities; and
4. When the entity continues to recognize the assets to the extent of its continuing involvement, the total carrying amount of the original assets, the amount of the assets that the entity continues to recognize, and the carrying amount of the associated liabilities.

Collateral. The reporting entity must disclose the carrying amount of financial assets it has pledged as collateral for liabilities or contingent liabilities, including amounts that have been reclassified in accordance with the provision of IAS 39 pertaining to rights to repledge; and the terms and conditions relating to its pledge.

Conversely, if the reporting entity holds collateral (of either financial or nonfinancial assets) and is permitted to sell or repledge the collateral in the absence of default by the owner of the collateral, it must now disclose the fair value of the collateral held and the fair value of any such collateral sold or repledged, and whether it has an obligation to return it; and the terms and conditions associated with its use of the collateral.

Allowances for bad debts or other credit losses. When financial assets are impaired by credit losses and the entity records the impairment in a separate account (whether associated with a specific asset or for the collective impairment of assets), rather than directly reducing the carrying amount of the asset, it is to disclose a reconciliation of changes in that account during the period, for each class of financial assets.

Certain compound instruments. If the reporting entity is the *issuer* of compound instruments, such as convertible debt, having multiple embedded derivatives having interdependent values (such as the conversion feature and a call feature, such that the issuer can effectively force conversion), these matters must be disclosed.

Defaults and breaches. If the reporting entity is the obligor under loans payable at the date of the statement of financial position, it must disclose

1. The details of any defaults during the period, involving payment of principal or interest, or into a sinking fund, or of the redemption terms of those loans payable;
2. The carrying amount of the loans payable in default at the reporting date; and
3. Whether the default was remedied, or the terms of the loans payable were renegotiated, before the financial statements were authorized for issue.

Similar disclosures are required for any other breaches of loan agreement terms, if such breaches gave the lender the right to accelerate payment, unless these were remedied or terms were renegotiated before the reporting date.

Disclosures in the statements of comprehensive income and changes in equity. The reporting entity is to disclose the following items of revenue, expense, gains, or losses, either on the face of the financial statements or in the notes thereto:

1. Net gain or net losses on

   a. Financial assets or financial liabilities carried at fair value through profit or loss, showing separately those incurred on financial assets or financial liabilities designated as such upon initial recognition, and those on financial assets or financial liabilities that are classified as held-for-trading in accordance with IAS 39;
   b. Available-for-sale financial assets, showing separately the amount of gain or loss recognized in other comprehensive income during the period and the amount reclassified from equity and recognized in profit or loss for the period;
   c. Held-to-maturity investments;
   d. Loans and receivables; and
   e. Financial liabilities carried at amortized cost;

2. Total interest income and total interest expense (calculated using the effective interest method) for financial assets or financial liabilities that are not carried at fair value through profit or loss;
3. Fee income and expense (other than amounts included in determining the effective interest rate) arising from

   a. Financial assets or financial liabilities that are not carried at fair value through profit or loss; and
   b. Trust and other fiduciary activities that result in the holding or investing of assets on behalf of individuals, trusts, retirement benefit plans, and other institutions

4. Interest income on impaired financial assets accrued in accordance with the provision of IAS 39 that stipulates that, once written down for impairment, interest income thereafter is to be recognized at the rate used to discount cash flows in order to compute impairment; and
5. The amount of any impairment loss for each class of financial asset.

Accounting policies disclosure. The reporting entity is to disclose the measurement basis (or bases) used in preparing the financial statements and the other accounting policies used that are relevant to an understanding of the financial statements.

Hedging disclosures. Hedge accounting is one of the more complex aspects of financial instruments accounting under IAS 39. IFRS 7 specifies that an entity engaged in hedging must disclose, separately for each type of hedge described in IAS 39 (i.e., fair value hedges, cash flow hedges, and hedges of net investments in foreign operations)

1. A description of each type of hedge;
2. A description of the financial instruments designated as hedging instruments and their fair values at the reporting date; and
3. The nature of the risks being hedged.

In the case of cash flow hedges, the reporting entity is to disclose

1. The periods when the cash flows are expected to occur and when they are expected to affect profit or loss;
2. A description of any forecasted transaction for which hedge accounting had previously been used, but which is no longer expected to occur;
3. The amount that was recognized in other comprehensive income during the period;
4. The amount that was reclassified from equity and included in profit or loss for the period, showing the amount included in each line item in the statement of comprehensive income; and
5. The amount that was reclassified from equity during the period and included in the initial cost or other carrying amount of a nonfinancial asset or nonfinancial liability whose acquisition or incurrence was a hedged highly probable forecast transaction.

The reporting entity is to disclose separately

1. For fair value hedges, gains, or losses

    a. From the hedging instrument; and
    b. From the hedge item attributable to the hedged risk.

2. The ineffectiveness recognized in profit or loss that arises from cash flow hedges; and
3. The ineffectiveness recognized in profit or loss that arises from hedges of net investments in foreign operations.

Fair value disclosures. IFRS 7 requires that for each class of financial assets and financial liabilities, the reporting entity is to disclose the fair value of that class of assets and liabilities in a way that permits it to be compared with its carrying amount. Grouping by class is required, but offsetting assets and liabilities is generally not permitted (but will conform with statement of financial position presentation). To be disclosed are

1. The methods and, if a valuation technique is used, the assumptions applied in determining fair values of each class of financial assets or financial liabilities (e.g., as to

prepayment rates, rates of estimated credit losses, and interest rates or discount rates).
2. Whether fair values are determined, in whole or in part, directly by reference to published price quotations in an active market or are estimated using a valuation technique.
3. Whether the fair values recognized or disclosed in the financial statements are determined in whole or in part using a valuation technique based on assumptions that are *not* supported by prices from observable current market transactions in the same instrument (that is, without modification or repackaging) and *not* based on available observable market data. If fair values are recognized in the financial statements, and if changing one or more of those assumptions to reasonably possible alternative assumptions would change fair value significantly, then this fact must be stated, and the effect of those changes must be disclosed. Significance is to be assessed in light of the entity's profit or loss, and total assets or total liabilities, or, total comprehensive income and equity, when changes in fair value are recognized in other comprehensive income.
4. If 3. applies, the total amount of the change in fair value estimated using such a valuation technique that was recognized in profit or loss during the period.

In instances where the market for a financial instrument is not active, the reporting entity establishes the fair value using a valuation technique. The best evidence of fair value at initial recognition is the transaction price, so there could be a difference between the fair value at initial recognition and the amount that would be determined at that date using the valuation technique. In such a case, disclosure is required, by the class of financial instrument of

1. The entity's accounting policy for recognizing that difference in profit or loss to reflect a change in factors (including time) that market participants would consider in setting a price; and
2. The aggregate difference yet to be recognized in profit or loss at the beginning and end of the period and a reconciliation of changes in the balance of this difference.

Disclosures of fair value are not required in these circumstances.

1. When the carrying amount is a reasonable approximation of fair value, (e.g., for short-term trade receivables and payables);
2. For an investment in equity instruments that do not have a quoted market price in an active market, or derivatives linked to such equity instruments, that is measured at cost in accordance with IAS 39 because its fair value cannot be measured reliably; or
3. For an insurance contract containing a discretionary participation feature if the fair value of that feature cannot be measured reliably.

In instances identified in 2. and 3. immediately above, the reporting entity must disclose information to help users of the financial statements make their own judgments about the extent of possible differences between the carrying amount of those financial assets or financial liabilities and their fair value, including

1. The fact that fair value information has not been disclosed for these instruments because their fair value cannot be measured reliably;
2. A description of the financial instruments, their carrying amount, and an explanation of why fair value cannot be measured reliably;
3. Information about the market for the instruments;

4. Information about whether and how the entity intends to dispose of the financial instruments; and
5. If financial instruments whose fair value previously could not be reliably measured
are derecognized, that fact, their carrying amount at the time of derecognition, and
the amount of gain or loss recognized.

In January 2009 the IASB issued amendments to IFRS 7 requiring additional information to be disclosed with respect to the fair value of financial instruments. The amendments
required financial instruments measured at fair value to be categorized within a hierarchy of
"fair values" much in line with the requirements under US GAAP Statement SFAS 157, *Fair
Value Measurements*.

1. Level 1. Fair values determined from observable prices quoted in an active market.
2. Level 2. Fair values evidenced by comparison to other observable current market
transactions in the same instrument (without modification) or based on a valuation
technique whose variables include only data from observable markets
3. Level 3. Financial instruments whose fair value is determined in whole or in part using a valuation technique based on assumptions that are not supported by prices from
observable current market transactions in the same instrument (without modification)
and not based on available observable market data.

An entity is also required to disclose the movement of financial instruments in between
these levels as well as disclosure of gains or losses recognized in profit or loss or other comprehensive income relating in particular to financial instruments in Level 3. These disclosure
amendments above did not amend any of the recognition and measurement requirements of
IAS 39.

**Disclosures about the nature and extent of risks flowing from financial instru-
ments.** Reporting entities are required to disclose various information that will enable the
users to evaluate the nature and extent of risks the reporting entity is faced with as a consequence of financial instruments it is exposed to at the date of the statement of financial position. Both qualitative and quantitative disclosures are required under IFRS 7, as described in
the following paragraphs.

Qualitative disclosures. For each type of risk arising from financial instruments, the reporting entity is expected to disclose

1. The exposures to risk and how they arise;
2. Its objectives, policies and processes for managing the risk and the methods used to
measure the risk; and
3. Any changes in 1. or 2. from the previous period.

Quantitative disclosures. For each type of risk arising from financial instruments, the
entity must present

1. Summary quantitative data about its exposure to that risk at the reporting date. This
is to be based on the information provided internally to key management personnel
of the entity.
2. The disclosures required as set forth below (credit risk, et al.), to the extent not provided in 1., unless the risk is not material.
3. Concentrations of risk, if not apparent from 1. and 2.

If the quantitative data disclosed as of the date of the statement of financial position are
not representative of the reporting entity's exposure to risk during the period, it must provide
further information that is representative.

Specific disclosures are mandated, concerning credit risk, liquidity risk, and market risk. These are set forth as follows in IFRS 7:

Credit risk disclosures. To be disclosed, by class of financial instrument, are

1. The amount that best represents the entity's maximum exposure to credit risk at the reporting date, before taking into account any collateral held or other credit enhancements;
2. In respect of the amount disclosed in a., a description of collateral held as security and other credit enhancements;
3. Information about the credit quality of financial assets that are *neither* past due *nor* impaired; and
4. The carrying amount of financial assets that would otherwise be past due or impaired whose terms have been renegotiated.

Regarding financial assets that are either past due or impaired, the entity must disclose, again by class of financial asset

1. An analysis of the age of financial assets that are past due as of the date of the statement of financial position but which are not judged to be impaired;
2. An analysis of financial assets that are individually determined to be impaired as at the reporting date, including the factors that the entity considered in determining that they are impaired; and
3. For the amounts disclosed in 1. and 2., a description of collateral held by the entity as security and other credit enhancements and, unless impracticable, an estimate of their fair value.

Regarding any collateral and other credit enhancements obtained, if these meet recognition criteria in the relevant IFRS, the reporting entity is to disclose

1. The nature and carrying amount of the assets obtained; and
2. If the assets are not readily convertible into cash, its policies for disposing of such assets or for using them in its operations.

Liquidity risk. The entity is to disclose

1. A maturity analysis for financial liabilities that shows the remaining contractual maturities; and
2. A description of how the entity manages the liquidity risk inherent in 1.

Market risk. A number of informative disclosures are mandated, as described in the following paragraphs.

Sensitivity analysis is generally required, as follows:

1. A sensitivity analysis for each type of market risk to which the entity is exposed at the reporting date, showing how profit or loss and equity would have been affected by changes in the relevant risk variable that were reasonably possible at that date;
2. The methods and assumptions used in preparing the sensitivity analysis; and
3. Changes from the previous period in the methods and assumptions used, and the reasons for such changes.

If the reporting entity prepares a sensitivity analysis, such as value-at-risk, that reflects interdependencies between risk variables (e.g., between interest rates and exchange rates) and uses it to manage financial risks, it may use that sensitivity analysis in place of the analysis specified in the preceding paragraph. The entity would also have to disclose

1. An explanation of the method used in preparing such a sensitivity analysis, and of the main parameters and assumptions underlying the data provided; and
2. An explanation of the objective of the method used and of limitations that may result in the information not fully reflecting the fair value of the assets and liabilities involved.

Other market risk disclosures may also be necessary to fully inform financial statement users. When the sensitivity analyses are unrepresentative of a risk inherent in a financial instrument (e.g., because the year-end exposure does not reflect the actual exposure during the year), the entity is to disclose that fact, together with the reason it believes the sensitivity analyses are unrepresentative.

Amendments to IAS 39 Adopted in 2008

Reclassifications of financial instruments. The global financial crisis led to massive impairments of financial instruments by financial institutions and other investors. One question arising from the crisis is whether reclassifications of investments, particularly to a classification in the statement of financial position for which fair value accounting would not be mandatory, would be acceptable, especially in light of volatile market conditions that cast doubt on the validity of fair value determinations.

Suspension or modification of fair value accounting rules had been proposed by financial institutions and others. In response to the debate the IASB, under some pressure from the G20, set up a Financial Crisis Advisory Group (FCAG) which was to look into the role of financial reporting in contributing to the crisis and how IFRS could be useful in avoiding or limiting the impact of future crises.

The IASB adopted (with little debate) a change to IAS 39 that permits nonderivative financial assets held for trading and available-for-sale financial assets to be reclassified in particular situations. The IASB received some criticism from some quarters for the perceived lack of due process in formulating and approving these amendments; however, there were others that felt that the promptness of its response was positive.

The proximate reason for adopting this amendment was the distinction between US GAAP and IFRS relative to transfers from the trading category (for most investments) and from the held-for-sale category (for mortgage loans). Under US GAAP transfers from those categories are restricted but still possible, whereas under IAS 39 no such reclassifications were previously permitted. IASB was asked to grant users of IFRS the same (limited) flexibility as that allowed under US GAAP.

IFRS 7 was consequently amended to expand the disclosures required whenever these amended provisions of IAS 39 are invoked. Specifically, if the reporting entity has reclassified a financial asset (in accordance with the above-described amended provisions of IAS 39) as one measured either at (1) cost or amortized cost, rather than fair value; or (2) fair value, rather than at cost or amortized cost; then it must disclose the amount reclassified into and out of each category and the reason for that reclassification. If the entity has reclassified a financial out of the fair value through current earnings category in accordance with the amended provisions of IAS 39, it must disclose

1. The amount reclassified into and out of each category;
2. For each reporting period until derecognition, the carrying amounts and fair values of all financial assets that have been reclassified in the current and previous reporting periods;

3. If a financial asset was reclassified in accordance with the amendment restricting such transfers to rare situations, the rare situation, and the facts and circumstances indicating that the situation was rare;

4. For the reporting period when the financial asset was reclassified, the fair value gain or loss on the financial asset recognized in profit or loss or other comprehensive income in that reporting period and in the previous reporting period;

5. For each reporting period following the reclassification (including the reporting period in which the financial asset was reclassified) until derecognition of the financial asset, the fair value gain or loss that would have been recognized in profit or loss or other comprehensive income if the financial asset had not been reclassified, and the gain, loss, income and expense recognized in profit or loss; and

6. The effective interest rate and estimated amounts of cash flows the entity expects to recover, as at the date of reclassification of the financial asset.

US GAAP COMPARISON

The guidance for financial instruments for both US GAAP and IFRS is undergoing significant changes under a joint project between the IASB and FASB as a result of a study issued by the Financial Crisis Advisory Group (FCAG) after the 2008 financial crises. However, while IFRS 9 is partially formed, it is not effective until possibly 2015.

Currently effective US GAAP and IFRS guidance contains many similarities, but also many differences, particularly with regard to hedging. Both standards segregate financial instruments into held-to-maturity, available-for-sale, and trading. Similar to IFRS, held-to-maturity assets are maintained at amortized costs. Available-for-sale instruments are marked to market with changes offset to other comprehensive income. Trading instruments are marked to fair value and reflected in profit and loss.

Differences include

- US GAAP does not allow designation of a financial instrument through profit and loss. Presentation in profit and loss or other comprehensive income is determined by the classification as trading or available-for-sale.

- The hedging of a portfolio of assets and liabilities is much more difficult to achieve under US GAAP. Instruments must be almost perfectly correlated. US GAAP allows a "short-cut" method for hedging of interest rates when specific conditions are met. This allows simpler testing to prove effectiveness of a hedge. There is no specified range of loss or gain offset to determine hedge effectiveness for decision on whether hedge accounting is still permitted (IFRS employs a range of 80 to 125%). Also, guidance of documentation of hedging strategy is more prescriptive.

- Impairments of financial instruments cannot be reversed under US GAAP.

- US GAAP contains more detailed guidance as to when a transfer of a financial instrument is a sale rather than a financing.

25 FAIR VALUE

INTRODUCTION

The Debate over the Use of Fair Value Measurements

Financial statement preparers, users, auditors, standard setters, and regulators have long engaged in a debate regarding the relevance, transparency, and decision-usefulness of financial statements prepared under IFRS, which is one among the various families of comprehensive financial reporting standards that rely on what has been called the "mixed attribute" model for measuring assets and liabilities. That is, existing IFRS imposes a range of measurement requirements, including both historical (i.e., transaction-based) cost and a variety of approximations to current economic values, for the initial and subsequent reporting of the assets and liabilities that define the reporting entity's financial position and, indirectly, for the periodic determination of its results of operations.

While current fair or market value data has become more readily obtainable, some of these measures do exhibit some degree of volatility, albeit this is typically only a reflection of the turbulence in the markets themselves, and is not an artifact of the measurement process. Nonetheless, the ever-expanding use of fair value for accounting measurements, under various national GAAP as well as under IFRS, has attracted its share of critical commentary. The debate has become even more heated due to the recent economic turmoil in credit markets, which more than a few observers have cited as having been exacerbated by required financial reporting of current value-based measures of financial performance.

Although the evidence will ultimately demonstrate that fundamental economic and financial behaviors (such as bank lending decisions) were not, in the main, caused by the mandatory reporting of value changes, the chorus of complaints have caused the standard setters to take certain steps to mollify their critics, including revisiting some of the mechanisms by which fair values have heretofore been assessed. Notwithstanding, both the IASB and FASB have reaffirmed their commitment to the continued use of fair values in financial reporting in appropriate circumstances, while acknowledging the need for more guidance with respect to the determination of fair values.

The majority of investors and creditors that use financial statements for decision-making purposes argue that reporting financial instruments at historical cost or amortized cost deprives them of important information about the economic impact on the reporting entity of real economic gains and losses associated with changes in the fair values of assets and liabilities that it owns or owes. Many assert that, had they been provided timely fair value information, they might well have made different decisions regarding investing in, lending to, or entering into business transactions with the reporting entities.

Others, however, argue that transparent reporting of fair values creates "procyclicality," whereby the reporting of fair values has the effect of directly influencing the economy and potentially causing great harm. These arguments are countered by fair value advocates, who state their belief that the "Lost Decade"—the extended economic malaise that afflicted Japan from 1991 to 2000—was exacerbated by the lack of transparency in its commercial banking system, which allowed its banks to avoid recognizing losses on loans of questionable credit quality and diminished, but concealed, values.

IASB has been on record for many years regarding its long-term goal of having all financial assets and liabilities reported at fair value. That said, it has taken a cautious, incremental approach towards attaining this goal, not unlike the experience of the FASB in setting US GAAP. After addressing a number of matters that had been assigned higher priority, however, IASB dedicated significant attention to the fair value project beginning in 2005, as part of its announced convergence efforts with FASB. It was decided early in this process that FASB's monumental standard, FAS 157, *Fair Value Measurements* (now codified as ASC 820), issued in 2006, would serve as the basis for IASB's intended standard. IASB issued a Discussion Paper to that effect in late 2006, followed by an Exposure Draft (ED) in mid-2009.

In June 2011 the IASB completed its project and issued IFRS 13, *Fair Value Measurement*, on which the balance of this chapter is based. IFRS 13 is effective for annual periods beginning on or after 1 January 2013. Earlier application is permitted. This chapter was previously based on the IASB's Exposure Draft and is updated fully with IFRS 13 although IFRS 13 is not effective in 2012.

Sources of IFRS
IFRS 13

SCOPE

IFRS 13, *Fair Value Measurement* applies when another IFRS requires or permits the use of fair value measurements or disclosures about fair value measurements. To that extent the IFRS does not extend the use of fair value measures in financial reporting but does bring about a more cohesive and comprehensive within which the concept of fair values is applied. This could be seen as an important building block in the extended use of fair values in the future, although that is not an objective the IASB has stated categorically at this time.

Excluded from the scope of the IFRS however is some "fair value based" transactions such as

- Share based payments within the scope of IFRS 2, *Share-Based Payments*
- Leasing transactions within the scope of IAS 17, *Leases*
- And other measurements with similarities to fair value such as net realizable value as it relates to IAS 2, *Inventory,* or value in use in terms of IAS 36, *Impairment of Assets*

In addition the disclosure requirements of the IFRS do not apply to disclosures relating to

- Fair value of plan assets in terms of IAS 19, *Employee Benefits*
- Retirement benefit plan investments in terms of IAS 26, *Accounting and Reporting by Retirement Benefit Plans*
- Assets for which the recoverable amount is fair value less costs to sell in terms of IAS 36, *Impairment of Assets*

DEFINITIONS OF TERMS

Active market. A market in which transactions occur with sufficient frequency and volume to provide pricing information on an ongoing basis.

Cost approach. A valuation technique that reflects the amount that would be required currently replace the service capacity of an asset (sometimes referred to as current replacement cost).

Entry price. The price paid to acquire an asset or received to assume a liability in an exchange transaction.

Exit price. The price that would be received to sell an asset or paid to transfer a liability.

Expected cash flow. The probability-weighted average (i.e. mean of the distribution) of possible future cash flows.

Fair value. The price that would be received to sell an asset or paid to transfer a liability in an orderly transaction between market participants at the measurement date.

Highest and best use. The use of a nonfinancial asset by market participants that would maximize the value of the group of assets and liabilities (e.g. a business) within which the asset would be used.

Income approach. Valuation techniques that convert future amounts (e.g. cash flows or income and expenses) to a single current amount.

Inputs. The assumptions that market particicpants would use when pricing the asset or liability, including assumptions about risk, such as the risk inherent in a particular valuation technique used to measure fair value and the risk inherent in the inputs to the valuation technique. Inputs may be observable or unobservable.

Level 1 inputs. Quoted prices (unadjusted) in active markets for identical assets or liabilities that the entity can access at the measurement date.

Level 2 inputs. Inputs other than quoted prices included within Level 1 that are observable for the asset or liability, either directly (i.e., as prices) or indirectly (i.e., derived from prices).

Level 3 inputs. Unobservable inputs for the asset or liability.

Market approach. A valuation approach that uses prices and other relevant information generated by market transactions involving identical or comparable assets, liabilities or a group of assets and liabilities (i.e. a business)

Market participants. Buyers and sellers in the principal (or most advantageous) market for an asset or liability with all of the following characteristics:

1. Independent of each other, not related parties as defined in IAS 24, *Related Parties*
2. Knowledgeable and have a reasonable understanding about the asset or liability and the transaction using all available information, including information that might be obtained through due diligence efforts that are usual and customary

3. Able to enter into a transaction for the asset or liability
4. Willing to enter into a transaction for the asset or liability (i.e., they are not under duress that would force or compel them to enter into the transaction)

Most advantageous market. The market that maximizes the amount that would be received from the sale of the asset or that minimizes the amount that would be paid to transfer the liability, after consideration of transaction and transport costs. (Although transaction costs are considered in making a determination of the market that is most advantageous, such costs are not to be factored into the fair value valuation determined by reference to that market).

Nonperformance risk. The risk that the entity will not fulfill an obligation. This includes, but is not limited to, the entity's own credit risk.

Observable inputs. Inputs that are developed on the basis of available market data, such as publicly available information about actual events or transactions, and that reflect the assumptions that market participants would use when pricing the asset or liability.

Orderly transaction. A transaction that assumes exposure to the market for a period before the measurement date to allow for marketing activities that are usual and customary for transactions involving such assets or liabilities; it is not a forced transaction (e.g., a forced liquidation or distress sale).

Principal market. The market with the greatest volume and level of activity for the asset or the liability.

Risk premium. Compensation sought by risk-averse market participants for bearing the uncertainty inherent in the cash flows of an asset or a liability, sometime referred to as a "risk adjustment."

Transaction costs. The costs to sell an asset or transfer a liability in the principal (or most advantageous) market for the asset or liability that are directly attributable to the disposal of the asset or the transfer of the liability and result directly from and are essential to the transaction, and would not have been incurred had the transaction not occurred (similar to the 'costs to sell' in terms of IFRS 5, *Noncurrent Assets Held for Sale and Discontinued Operations*).

Transport costs. The costs that would be incurred to transport an asset from its current location to its principal or most advantageous market.

Unit of account. The level at which an asset or liability is aggregated or disaggregated in an IFRS for recognition purposes.

Unobservable inputs. Inputs for which market data are not available and that are developed using the best information available about the assumptions that market participants would use when pricing the asset or liability.

FAIR VALUE MEASUREMENT PRINCIPLES AND METHODOLOGIES

In its objectives the IFRS clearly sets out that fair value is a market-based measurement and not an entity specific measurement. This premise permeates the entire approach to the determination of fair value for assets and liabilities, and makes the asset or the liability and the related markets the center of the approach and not the entity's circumstances at the measurement date. Consequently fair value is based on the presumption of an orderly transaction between market participants (as defined) at measurement date under current market conditions, from the perspective of the participant that holds the asset or owes the liability, in other words it is an exit price.

To the extent possible, fair value should be based on an observable price. However, in many instances such a price may be available and the determination of fair value will rely on the use of valuation techniques. Such valuation techniques should have a strong bias towards the use of observable rather than unobservable inputs, as these are considered more objective and more likely to be taken into consideration by market participants that unobservable inputs.

Although the IFRS has a focus on assets and liabilities, the requirements of the IFRS are equally applicable to the determination of the fair value of an entity's own equity instrument, where required.

IASB has explicitly addressed the logic of requiring an exit price definition. It has stated that it is the exit price of an asset or liability that embodies expectations about the future cash inflows and outflows associated with the asset or liability from the perspective of market participants at the measurement date. Since an entity generates cash inflows from an asset either by using it or by selling it, even if an entity intends to generate cash inflows from an asset by using it rather than by selling it, an exit price embodies expectations of the cash flows that would arise for a market participant holding the asset. For this reason, IASB concluded that an exit price is always a relevant definition of fair value for assets, regardless of whether an entity intends to use an asset or to sell it.

For a similar reason, IASB found that a liability gives rise to outflows of cash (or other economic resources) as an entity fulfills the liability over time or when it transfers the liability to another party. Even if an entity intends to fulfill the liability over time, an exit price embodies expectations about cash outflows because a market participant transferee would ultimately be required to fulfill the liability. Accordingly, IASB concluded that an exit price is always a relevant definition of fair value for liabilities, regardless of whether an entity intends to fulfill the liability over time or to transfer it to another party that will fulfill it over time.

The level at which this IFRS is to be applied is determined by the unit of account in terms of the relevant IFRS that requires or permits the use of fair value in the first instance, and therefore the level of application is not specifically addressed by this IFRS unless otherwise specified.

It is helpful to break down the measurement process of determining fair value measurement into a series of steps. Although not necessarily performed in a linear manner, the following procedures and decisions need to be applied and made, in order to value an asset or liability at fair value. Each of the steps will be discussed in greater detail.

1. *Identify the item to be valued and the unit of account.* Identify the asset or liability, including the unit of account to be used for the measurement. One needs to refer to other IFRS for directions regarding unit of account, since the proposed standard on fair value measurement does not provide these.
2. *Determine the most advantageous market and the relevant market participants.* From the reporting entity's perspective, determine the most advantageous market in which it would sell the asset or transfer the liability. In the absence of evidence to the contrary, the most advantageous market can be considered to be the principal market for the asset or the liability, which is the market with the greatest volume of transactions and level of activity. Once the most advantageous market is identified, determine the characteristics of the market participants. It is not necessary that specifically named individuals or enterprises be identified for this purpose.
3. *Select the valuation premise to be used for asset measurements.* If the item being measured is a nonfinancial asset, determine the valuation premise to be used by evaluating how market participants would apply the "highest and best use," for ex-

ample, considering the value of the asset on a stand-alone basis or its fair value in conjunction with other related assets and liabilities.

4. *Consider the risk assumptions applicable to liability measurements.* If the item being measured is a liability, identify the key assumptions that market participants would make regarding nonperformance risk including, but not limited to, the reporting entity's own credit risk (credit standing).

5. *Identify available inputs.* Identify the key assumptions that market participants would use in pricing the asset or liability, including assumptions about risk. In identifying these assumptions, referred to as "inputs," maximize the inputs that are relevant and observable (i.e., that are based on market data available from sources independent of the reporting entity). In so doing, assess the availability of relevant, reliable market data for each input that significantly affects the valuation, and identify the level of the new fair value input hierarchy in which it is to be categorized.

6. *Select the appropriate valuation technique(s).* Based on the nature of the asset or liability being valued, and the types and reliability of inputs available, determine the appropriate valuation technique or combination of techniques to use in valuing the asset or liability. The three broad categories of techniques are the market approach, the income approach, and the cost approach.

7. *Make the measurement.* Measure the asset or liability.

8. *Determine amounts to be recognized and information to be disclosed.* Determine the amounts and information to be recorded, classified, and disclosed in interim and annual financial statements

Item identification and unit of account. In general, the same unit of account at which the asset or liability is aggregated or disaggregated by applying other applicable IFRS pronouncements is to be used for fair value measurement purposes. No adjustment may be made to the valuation for a "blockage factor." A blockage factor is an adjustment made to a valuation that takes into account the fact that the investor holds a large quantity (block) of shares relative to the market trading volume in those shares. The prohibition applies even if the quantity held by the reporting entity exceeds the market's normal trading volume—and that, if the reporting entity were, hypothetically, to place an order to sell its entire position in a single transaction, that transaction could affect the quoted price.

The principal or most advantageous market. The IFRS requires the entity performing the valuation to maximize the use of relevant assumptions (inputs) that are observable from market data obtained from sources independent of the reporting entity. In making a fair value measurement, management is to assume that the asset or liability is exchanged in a hypothetical, orderly transaction between market participants at the measurement date.

To characterize the exchange as orderly, it is assumed that the asset or liability will have been exposed to the market for a sufficient period of time prior to the measurement date to enable marketing activities to occur that are usual and customary with respect to transactions involving such assets or liabilities. It is also to be assumed that the transaction is not a forced transaction (e.g., a forced liquidation or distress sale).

The fair value is to be measured by reference to the principal market, or in the absence of a principal market, the most advantageous market. Unless otherwise apparent it is assumed that the principal market is the market in which the entity would normally transact to sell the asset or transfer the liability. An entity, therefore, need not engage in elaborate efforts to identify the principal market. This approach is deemed appropriate and broadly consistent with the concept of the most advantageous market, as it is reasonable that an entity would normally transact in the most advantageous market to which it is has access, taking into consideration *transaction and transport costs.*

Note that the determination of the most advantageous market is made from the perspective of the reporting entity. Thus, different reporting entities engaging in different specialized industries, or with access to different markets, might not have the same most advantageous market for an identical asset or liability. The IFRS provides a typology of markets that potentially exist for assets or liabilities.

1. *Exchange markets.* A market in which closing prices are readily available and generally representative of fair value. Examples of such markets include NYSE, Euronext, Toronto Stock Exchange, London Stock Exchange, Hong Kong Stock Exchange, and Johannesburg Securities Exchange amongst others.
2. *Dealer markets.* A market in which parties (dealers referred to as market makers) stand ready to buy or sell a particular investment for their own account at bid and ask prices that they quote. The bid price is the price the dealer is willing to pay to purchase the investment and the ask price is the price at which the dealer is willing to sell the investment. In these markets, these bid and ask prices are typically more readily available than are closing prices characteristic of active exchange markets. By using their own capital to finance and hold an inventory of the items for which they "make a market," these dealers provide the market with liquidity. Dealer markets include over-the-counter markets for which the prices at which transactions have been concluded could be publicly available. Dealer markets exist for financial instruments and nonfinancial assets such as commodities, equipment and such items.
3. *Brokered market.* These markets use "brokers" or intermediaries to match buyers with sellers. Brokers do not trade for their own account and do not hold an inventory in the security. The broker knows the bid and asked prices of the potential counterparties to the transaction but the counterparties are unaware of each other's price requirements. Prices of consummated transactions are sometimes available privately or as a matter of public record. Brokered markets include electronic communication networks that match buy and sell orders, as well as commercial and residential real estate markets. In some cases, each of the counterparties is aware of the other's identity, while in other cases, their identities are not disclosed by the broker.
4. *Principal-to-principal market.* A market in which the counterparties negotiate directly and independently without an intermediary. Because no intermediary or exchange is involved, little if any information about these transactions is released to the public.

Market participants. Fair value will be measured using the assumptions that a market participant would take into consideration assuming that the market participant would behave in his best economic interests. it is not necessary for an entity to identify an actual market participant for this purpose as this is a hypothetical construct. Instead the entity will develop a "picture" of the market participant by taking into consideration factors such as the nature of the asset or liability, the principal (or most advantageous) market and the market participants with whom the entity would enter into a transaction with in that market.

The hypothetical market participants can be summarized as

1. Independent of each other (i.e., are unrelated third parties)
2. Knowledgeable (i.e., are sufficiently informed to make an investment decision and are presumed to be as knowledgeable as the reporting entity about the asset or liability)
3. Able to enter into a transaction for the asset or liability
4. Willing to enter into a transaction for the asset or liability (i.e., they are motivated but not forced or otherwise compelled to do so)

Measurement considerations when transactions are not orderly. In recent years, there have been heightened concerns about the effects of tumultuous or illiquid credit markets in the US and abroad. The previously active markets for certain types of securities have become illiquid or less liquid. Questions have arisen regarding whether transactions occurring in less liquid markets with less frequent trades might cause those market transactions to be considered forced or distress sales, thus rendering valuations made using those prices not indicative of the actual fair value of the securities.

The presence of the following factors may indicate that a quoted price is not obtained from a transaction that could be considered orderly and therefore may not be indicative of fair value:

1. There has been a significant decrease in the volume and level of activity for the asset or liability when compared with normal market activity for the asset or liability (or for similar assets or liabilities).
2. There have been few recent transactions.
3. Price quotations are not based on current information about the fair value of an asset or liability
5. Indices that previously were highly correlated with the fair values of the asset or liability are demonstrably uncorrelated with recent indications of fair value for that asset or liability.
6. There has been a significant increase in implied liquidity risk premiums, yields or performance indicators (such as delinquency rates or loss severities) for observed transactions or quoted prices when compared with the entity's estimate of expected cash flows, considering all available market data about credit and other nonperformance risk for the asset or liability.
7. There has been a wide bid-ask spread or significant increase in the bid-ask spread.
8. There has been a significant decline or absence of a market for new issues (i.e., in the primary market) for the asset or liability (or similar assets or liabilities).
9. Little information has been released publicly (e.g., as occurs in a principal-to-principal market).

An entity should evaluate the significance and relevance of the foregoing indicators (together with other pertinent factors) to determine whether, on the basis of the evidence available, a market is not active. If it concludes that a market is not active, it may then also deduce that transactions or quoted prices in that market are not determinative of fair value (e.g., because there may be transactions that are not orderly). Further analysis of the transactions or quoted prices may therefore be needed, and a significant adjustment to the transactions or quoted prices may be necessary to measure fair value.

The IFRS does not prescribe a methodology for making significant adjustments to transactions or quoted prices in such circumstances, however the typology of valuation techniques—the market, income, and cost approaches, respectively—apply to these situations equally. Regardless of the valuation technique used, an entity must include any appropriate risk adjustments, including a risk premium reflecting the amount market participants would demand because of the risk (uncertainty) inherent in the cash flows of an asset or liability. Absent this, the measurement would not faithfully represent fair value. The risk premium should be reflective of an orderly transaction between market participants at the measurement date under current market conditions.

Of utmost importance, even when a market is not active, the objective of a fair value measurement remains the same—to identify the price that would be received to sell an asset or paid to transfer a liability in a transaction that is orderly and not a forced liquidation or distress sale, between market participants at the measurement date under current market conditions.

Even if a market is not active, it would be inappropriate to conclude that all transactions in that market are not orderly (i.e., that they are forced or distress sales). Circumstances that may suggest that a transaction is not orderly, however, include, *inter alia*, the following:

1. There was not adequate exposure to the market for a period before the measurement date to allow for marketing activities that are usual and customary for transactions involving such assets or liabilities under current market conditions.
2. There was a usual and customary marketing period, but the seller marketed the asset or liability to a single market participant.
3. The seller is in or near bankruptcy or receivership (i.e., distressed) or the seller was required to sell to meet regulatory or legal requirements (i.e., forced).
4. The transaction price is an outlier when compared with other recent transactions for the same or similar asset or liability.

The reporting entity is required to evaluate the circumstances to determine, based on the weight of the evidence then available, whether the transaction is orderly. If it indicates that a transaction is indeed *not* orderly, the reporting entity places little, if any, weight (in comparison with other indications of fair value) on that transaction price when measuring fair value or estimating market risk premiums.

On the other hand, if the evidence indicates that a transaction is in fact orderly, the reporting entity is to consider that transaction price when measuring fair value or estimating market risk premiums. The weight to be placed on that transaction price when compared with other indications of fair value will depend on the facts and circumstances—such as the size of the transaction, the comparability of the transaction to the asset or liability being measured, and the proximity of the transaction to the measurement date.

The IFRS does not preclude the use of quoted prices provided by third parties—such as pricing services or brokers—when the entity has determined that the quoted prices provided by those parties are determined in accordance with the standard. If a market is not active, however, the entity must evaluate whether the quoted prices are based on current information that reflects orderly transactions or a valuation technique that reflects market participant assumptions (including assumptions about risks). In weighting a quoted price as an input to a fair value measurement, however, the entity should place less weight on quotes that do not reflect the result of transactions.

Selection of the valuation premise for asset measurements. The measurement of the fair value of a nonfinancial asset is to assume the highest and best use of that asset by market participants. Generally, the highest and best use is the way that market participants would be expected to deploy the asset (or a group of assets and liabilities within which they would use the asset) that would maximize the value of the asset (or group). This highest and best use assumption might differ from the way that the reporting entity is currently using the asset or group of assets or its future plans for using it (them).

At the measurement date, the highest and best use must be physically possible, legally permissible, and financially feasible. In this context, *physically possible* takes into account the physical characteristics of the asset that market participants would consider when pricing the asset (e.g., the location or size of a property). *Legally permissible* takes into account any legal restrictions on the use of the asset that market participants would consider when pricing the asset (e.g., the zoning regulations applicable to a property). *Financially feasible* takes into account whether a use of the asset that is physically possible and legally permissible generates adequate income or cash flows (taking into consideration the costs of converting the asset to that use) to produce an investment return that market participants would require from an investment in that asset put to that use.

In all cases, the highest and best use is determined from the perspective of market participants, even if the reporting entity intends a different use. The highest and best use of an asset acquired in a business combination might differ from the intended use of the asset by the acquirer. The highest and best use is normally the use for which an asset is currently engaged unless market or other factors indicate otherwise. For example, for competitive or other reasons, the acquirer may intend not to use an acquired asset actively or it may not intend to use the asset in the same way as other market participants. This may particularly be the case for certain acquired intangible assets, for example, an acquired trademark that competes with an entity's own trademark. Nevertheless, the reporting entity is to measure the fair value of the asset assuming its highest and best use by market participants.

Where the highest and best use of an asset is determined by its use in conjunction with other assets and liabilities, fair value should be determined on that basis. Consequently the fair value of all other assets in that group of associated should be determined on the same basis.

Risk assumptions when valuing a liability. Many accountants, analysts, and others find the concept of computing fair value of liabilities and recognizing changes in the fair value thereof to be counterintuitive. Consider the case when a reporting entity's own credit standing declines (universally acknowledged as a "bad thing"). A fair value measurement that incorporates the effect of this decline in credit rating would result in a decline in the fair value of the liability and a resultant increase in stockholders' equity (which would be seen as a "good thing"). Nonetheless, the logic of measuring the fair value of liabilities is as valid, and as useful, as it is for assets. The IFRS does not expand the applicability of fair value measures from what currently exists, however.

Liabilities and equity instruments with no observable fair values from quoted price. Fair value measurements of liabilities assume that a hypothetical transfer to a market participant occurs on the measurement date. In measuring the fair value of a liability, the evaluator is to assume that the reporting entity's obligation to its creditor (i.e., the counterparty to the obligation) will continue at and after the measurement date (i.e., the obligation will not be repaid or settled prior to its contractual maturity). This being the case, this hypothetical transfer price would most likely represent the price that the current creditor (holder of the debt instrument) could obtain from a marketplace participant willing to purchase the debt instrument in a transaction involving the original creditor assigning its rights to the purchaser. In effect, the hypothetical market participant that purchased the instrument would be in the same position as the current creditor with respect to expected future cash flows (or expected future performance, if the liability is not able to be settled in cash) from the reporting entity.

The evaluator is to further assume that the nonperformance risk related to the obligation would be the same before and after the hypothetical transfer occurs. Nonperformance risk is the risk that the obligation will not be fulfilled. It is an all-encompassing concept that includes the reporting entity's own credit standing but also includes other risks associated with the nonfulfillment of the obligation. For example, a liability to deliver goods and/or perform services may bear nonperformance risk associated with the ability of the debtor to fulfill the obligation in accordance with the timing and specifications of the contract. Further, nonperformance risk increases or decreases as a result of changes in the fair value of credit enhancements associated with the liability (e.g., collateral, credit insurance, and/or guarantees).

Liabilities and equity instruments with observable fair values from quoted price. While it is fair to say that there will often not be any observable market prices applicable to the assignment of fair values to liabilities, in cases where such prices are available the reporting entity is to measure the fair value of a liability using the same methodology that the counterparty would use to measure the fair value of the corresponding asset (i.e., the receivable it would be acquiring). It provides that, in those instances (a likely minority of cases) when there is an active market for transactions between parties who hold debt securities as an asset, the observed price in that market also represents the fair value of the issuer's liability. If so, the entity should adjust the observed price for the asset for features that are present in the asset but not present in the liability, or vice versa. For example, in some instances the observed price for an asset reflects both the amounts due from the issuer and a third-party credit enhancement. Since the objective is to estimate the fair value of the issuer's liability, and not the price of the combined package, the entity should adjust the observed price for the asset to exclude the effect of the third-party credit enhancement, which is not present in the liability.

Where this is no corresponding asset for the liability. If there is no corresponding asset for a liability (e.g., for a decommissioning liability assumed in a business combination, for warranty obligations, and for many other performance commitments). The IFRS states that the reporting entity would have to estimate the price that market participants would demand to assume the liability. This could be accomplished by using present value techniques or other (market, income or cost) valuation techniques. When using a present value technique, the entity would, among other things, have to estimate the future cash outflows that market participants would incur in fulfilling the obligation. An entity may estimate those future cash outflows by

1. Estimating the cash flows the entity would incur in fulfilling the obligation;
2. Excluding cash flows, if any, that other market participants would not incur; and
3. Including cash flows, if any, that other market participants would incur but the entity would not incur.

Nonperformance risk in valuing liabilities. The fair value of a liability reflects the effect of *nonperformance risk*, which is the risk that an entity will not fulfill an obligation. For valuation purposes, nonperformance risk is assumed to be the same before and after the transfer of the liability. This assumption is rational, because market participants would not enter into a transaction that changes the nonperformance risk associated with the liability without reflecting that change in the price.

Nonperformance risk includes credit risk, the effect of which may differ depending on the nature of the liability. For example, an obligation to deliver cash (a financial liability) is distinct from an obligation to deliver goods or services (a nonfinancial liability). Also, the terms of credit enhancements related to the liability, if any, would impact valuation.

Liabilities with inseparable third-party credit enhancements. Creditors often impose a requirement, in connection with granting credit to a debtor, that the debtor obtain a guarantee of the indebtedness from a creditworthy third party. Under such an arrangement, should the debtor default on its obligation, the third-party guarantor would become obligated to repay the obligation on behalf of the defaulting debtor and, of course, the debtor would be obligated to repay the guarantor for having satisfied the debt on its behalf.

The issuer of a liability issued with an inseparable third party credit enhancement that is accounted for separately from the liability shall not include the effect of the credit enhancement in the fair value measurement of the liability. If the credit enhanced is accounted for separately from the liability, the issuer should take into account its own credit standing and not that of the third party guarantor.

Restriction preventing the transfer of a liability or an entity's own equity instrument. If there are restrictions on the transfer of a liability or equity instrument, which is not an uncommon feature in certain circumstances, that should not be a consideration when measuring the fair value of such an instrument. The IFRS takes the view that the effect of such a feature is already included in other inputs to the fair value measurement of such instruments.

Financial liability with a demand feature. The fair value of financial liability with a demand feature is not less than the amount payable on demand, discounted from the first date that the amount could be required to be paid.

Fair value for net exposures. Where an entity manages and portfolio of financial assets and liabilities with a view to managing net exposures to counterparty risk including credit and market risks, the standard permits that fair value may be determined for the net long (asset) or short (liability) position. This exception is available only if the entity qualifies for that exception by demonstrating that the net exposure is consistent with how it manages risk and it has elected to measure the financial assets and liabilities at fair value. Fair value would therefore be determined on the basis on what market participants would take into consideration when considering a transaction on the net exposure risks.

The exception does not however extend to the presentation of such net exposures in the financial statements, unless otherwise permitted by another IFRS.

Inputs. For the purpose of fair value measurements, inputs are the assumptions that market participants would use in pricing an asset or liability, including assumptions regarding risk. An input is either observable or unobservable. Observable inputs are either directly observable or indirectly observable. The IFRS requires the entity to maximize the use of relevant observable inputs and minimize the use of unobservable inputs.

An observable input is based on market data obtainable from sources independent of the reporting entity. For an input to be considered relevant, it must be considered determinative of fair value.

An unobservable input reflects assumptions made by management of the reporting entity with respect to assumptions it believes market participants would use to price an asset or liability based on the best information available under the circumstances.

The standard provides a fair value input hierarchy (see diagram below) to serve as a framework for classifying inputs based on the extent to which they are based on observable data. In some instances that inputs used in a valuation technique may be categorized at different levels across the hierarchy, in such instances the fair value measurement is categorized in the same level as the lowest level of input significant to the measurement of fair value. Determining significance in this context requires the use of judgment.

Hierarchy of Fair Value Inputs

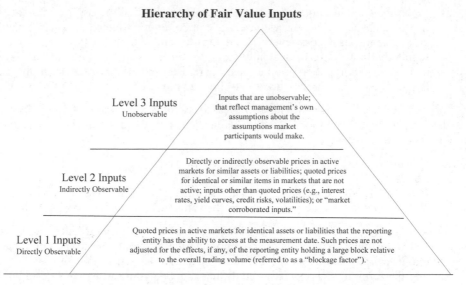

Level 3 Inputs
Unobservable

Inputs that are unobservable; that reflect management's own assumptions about the assumptions market participants would make.

Level 2 Inputs
Indirectly Observable

Directly or indirectly observable prices in active markets for similar assets or liabilities; quoted prices for identical or similar items in markets that are not active; inputs other than quoted prices (e.g., interest rates, yield curves, credit risks, volatilities); or "market corroborated inputs."

Level 1 Inputs
Directly Observable

Quoted prices in active markets for identical assets or liabilities that the reporting entity has the ability to access at the measurement date. Such prices are not adjusted for the effects, if any, of the reporting entity holding a large block relative to the overall trading volume (referred to as a "blockage factor").

Level 1 inputs. Level 1 inputs are considered the most reliable evidence of fair value and are to be used whenever they are available. These inputs consist of quoted prices in active markets for identical assets or liabilities. The active market must be one in which the reporting entity has the ability to access the quoted price at the measurement date. A quoted price in an active market is the most reliable evidence of fair value and should be used without adjustment except in the following circumstances:

1. As a practical expedient where and entity holds a large number of similar but non-identical assets and liabilities that are measured at fair value and a quoted price is available but not readily accessible for each of those assets without difficulty. The entity may use a pricing alternative (e.g. pricing matrix) but the resultant fair value is will be categorized as lower than Level 1.
2. When a quoted price does not reflect fair value at measurement, for example when there is a significant after-market transaction. If an adjustment is made in this regard the resultant fair value will be categorized as lower than Level 1
3. Where the fair value of a liability is determined using the quoted price for the identical asset adjusted for features present in the asset but not the liability. The resultant fair value is categorized as lower than Level 1.

Under no circumstances, however, is management to adjust the quoted price for blockage factors. Blockage adjustments arise when an entity holds a position in a single financial instrument that is traded on an active market that is relatively large in relation to the market's daily trading volume.

Level 2 inputs. Level 2 inputs are quoted prices for the asset or liability (other than those included in Level 1) that are either directly or indirectly observable. Level 2 inputs are to be considered when quoted prices for the identical asset or liability are not available. If the asset or liability being measured has a contractual term, a Level 2 input must be observable for substantially the entire term. These inputs include

1. Quoted prices for *similar* assets or liabilities in active markets
2. Quoted prices for identical or similar assets or liabilities in markets that are *not active*.

3. Inputs other than quoted prices that are observable for the asset or liability (e.g., interest rates and yield curves observable at commonly quoted intervals; volatilities; prepayment speeds; loss severities; credit risks; and default rates)
4. Inputs that are derived principally from or corroborated by observable market data that, through correlation or other means, are determined to be relevant to the asset or liability being measured (market-corroborated inputs)

Adjustments made to Level 2 inputs necessary to reflect fair value, if any, will vary depending on an analysis of specific factors associated with the asset or liability being measured. These factors include

1. Condition
2. Location
3. Extent to which the inputs relate to items comparable to the asset or liability
4. Volume and level of activity in the markets in which the inputs are observed

Depending on the level of the fair value input hierarchy in which the inputs used to measure the adjustment are classified, an adjustment that is significant to the fair value measurement in its entirety could render the measurement a Level 3 measurement.

During the turmoil experienced in credit markets beginning in early 2008, a holder of collateralized mortgage obligations (CMOs) backed by a pool of subprime mortgages might determine that no active market exists for the CMOs. Management might use an appropriate ABX credit default swap index for subprime mortgage bonds to provide a Level 2 fair value measurement input in measuring the fair value of the CMOs.

Level 3 inputs. Level 3 inputs are unobservable inputs. These are necessary when little, if any, market activity occurs for the asset or liability. Level 3 inputs are to reflect management's own assumptions about the assumptions regarding an exit price that a market participant holding the asset or owing the liability would make including assumptions about risk. The best information available in the circumstances is to be used to develop the Level 3 inputs. This information might include internal data of the reporting entity. Cost-benefit considerations apply in that management is not required to "undertake all possible efforts" to obtain information about the assumptions that would be made by market participants. Attention is to be paid, however, to information available to management without undue cost and effort and, consequently, management's internal assumptions used to develop unobservable inputs are to be adjusted if such information contradicts those assumptions.

Inputs based on bid and ask prices. Quoted bid prices represent the maximum price at which market participants are willing to buy an asset; quoted ask prices represent the minimum price at which market participants are willing to sell an asset. If available market prices are expressed in terms of bid and ask prices, management is to use the price within the bid-ask spread (the range of values between bid and ask prices) that is most representative of fair value irrespective of where in the fair value hierarchy the input would be classified. The standard permits the use of pricing conventions such as midmarket pricing as a practical alternative for determining fair value measurements within a bid-ask spread.

Valuation techniques. In measuring fair value, management may employ one or more valuation techniques consistent with the market approach, the income approach, and/or the cost approach. As previously discussed, the selection of a particular technique (or techniques) to measure fair value is to be based on its appropriateness to the asset or liability being measured as well as the sufficiency and observability of inputs available.

In certain situations, such as when using Level 1 inputs, use of a single valuation technique will be sufficient. In other situations, such as when valuing a reporting unit, management may need to use multiple valuation techniques. When doing so, the results yielded by applying the various techniques are to be evaluated and appropriately weighted based on judgment as to the reasonableness of the range of results. The objective of the weighting is to determine the point within the range that is most representative of fair value.

Management is required to consistently apply the valuation techniques it elects to use to measure fair value. It would be appropriate to change valuation techniques or how they are applied if the change results in fair value measurements that are equally or more representative of fair value. Situations that might give rise to such a change would be when new markets develop, new information becomes available, previously available information ceases to be available, or improved techniques are developed. Revisions that result from either a change in valuation technique or a change in the application of a valuation technique are to be accounted for as changes in accounting estimate under IAS 8.

Market approaches. Market approaches to valuation use information generated by actual market transactions for identical or comparable assets or liabilities (including a business in its entirety). Market approach techniques often will use market multiples derived from a set of comparable transactions for the asset or liability or similar items. The entity will need to consider both qualitative and quantitative factors in determining the point within the range that is most representative of fair value. An example of a market approach is matrix pricing. This is a mathematical technique used primarily for the purpose of valuing debt securities without relying solely on quoted prices for the specific securities. Matrix pricing uses factors such as the stated interest rate, maturity, credit rating, and quoted prices of similar issues to develop the issue's current market yield.

Income approaches. Techniques classified as income approaches measure fair value based on current market expectations about future amounts (such as cash flows or net income) and discount them to an amount in measurement date dollars. Valuation techniques that follow an income approach include the Black-Scholes-Merton model (a closed-form model) and binomial or lattice models (an open-form model), which use present value techniques, as well as the multi-period excess earnings method that is used in fair value measurements of certain intangible assets such as in-process research and development.

Cost approaches. Cost approaches are based on quantifying the amount required to replace an asset's remaining service capacity (i.e., the asset's current replacement cost). A valuation technique classified as a cost approach would measure the cost to a market participant (buyer) to acquire or construct a substitute asset of comparable utility, adjusted for obsolescence. Obsolescence adjustments include factors for physical wear and tear, improvements to technology, and economic (external) obsolescence. Thus, obsolescence is a broader concept than financial statement depreciation, which simply represents a cost allocation convention and is not intended to be a valuation technique.

Measurement Considerations

Initial recognition. When the reporting entity first acquires an asset or incurs (or assumes) a liability in an exchange transaction, the transaction price represents an entry price, the price paid to acquire the asset and the price received to assume the liability. Fair value measurements are based not on entry prices, but rather on exit prices; the price that would be received to sell the asset or paid to transfer the liability. In some cases (e.g., in a business combination) there is not a transaction price for each individual asset or liability. Likewise, sometimes there is not an exchange transaction for the asset or liability (e.g. when biological assets regenerate).

While entry and exit prices differ conceptually, in many cases they may be nearly identical and can be considered to represent fair value of the asset or liability at initial recognition. This is not always the case, however, and in assessing fair value at initial recognition, management is to consider transaction-specific factors and factors specific to the assets and/or liabilities that are being initially recognized.

Examples of situations where transaction price is not representative of fair value at initial recognition include

1. Related-party transactions
2. Transactions taking place under duress such as a forced or liquidation transaction. Such transactions do not meet the criterion in the definition of fair value that they be representative of an "orderly transaction."
3. Different units of account that apply to the transaction price and the assets/liabilities being measured. This can occur, for example, where the transaction price includes other elements besides the assets/liabilities that are being measured such as unstated rights and privileges that are subject to separate measurement or when the transaction price includes transaction costs (see discussion below).
4. The exchange transaction takes place in a market different from the principal (or most advantageous) market in which the reporting entity would sell the asset or transfer the liability. An example of this situation is when the reporting entity is a securities dealer that enters into transactions in different markets depending on whether the counterparty is a retail customer or another securities dealer.

Transaction costs. Transaction costs are the incremental direct costs that would be incurred to sell an asset or transfer a liability. While, as previously discussed, transaction costs are considered in determining the market that is most advantageous, they are not used to adjust the fair value measurement of the asset or liability being measured. IASB excluded them from the measurement because they do not represent an attribute of the asset or liability being measured.

Transport costs. If an attribute of the asset or liability being measured is its location, the price determined in the principal (or most advantageous) market is to be adjusted for the costs that would be incurred by the reporting entity to transport it to or from that market.

The possible discrepancies between entry and exit values may create so-called "day one gains or losses." If an IFRS requires or permits an entity to measure an asset or liability initially at fair value and the transaction price differs from fair value, the entity recognizes the resulting gain or loss in profit or loss unless the IFRS requires otherwise.

FAIR VALUE DISCLOSURE

The IFRS on fair value measurement provides that, for assets and liabilities that are measured at fair value, the reporting entity is to disclose information that enables users of its financial statements to assess the methods and inputs used to develop those measurements and, for fair value measurements using significant unobservable inputs (Level 3), the effect of the measurements on profit or loss or other comprehensive income for the period. To accomplish these objectives, it must (except as noted below) determine how much detail to disclose, how much emphasis to place on different aspects of the disclosure requirements, the extent of aggregation or disaggregation, and whether users need any additional (qualitative) information to evaluate the quantitative information disclosed.

At a minimum, the entity is to disclose the following information for each class of assets and liabilities:

1. The fair value measurement at the end of the reporting period.
2. The level of the fair value hierarchy within which the fair value measurements are categorized in their entirety (Level 1, 2 or 3).
3. For assets and liabilities held at the reporting date, any significant transfers between Level 1 and Level 2 of the fair value hierarchy and the reasons for those transfers. Transfers into each level are to be disclosed and discussed separately from transfers out of each level. For this purpose, significance is to be judged with respect to profit or loss, and total assets or total liabilities.
4. The methods and the inputs used in the fair value measurement and the information used to develop those inputs. If there has been a change in valuation technique (e.g., changing from a market approach to an income approach), the entity must disclose that change, the reasons for making it, and its effect on the fair value measurement.
5. For fair value measurements categorized within Level 3 of the fair value hierarchy, a reconciliation from the opening balances to the closing balances, disclosing separately changes during the period attributable to the following:

   a. Total gains or losses for the period recognized in profit or loss, and a description of where they are presented in the statement of comprehensive income or the separate income statement (if presented).
   b. Total gains or losses for the period recognized in other comprehensive income.
   c. Purchases, sales, issues and settlements (each of those types of change disclosed separately).
   d. Transfers into or out of Level 3 (e.g., transfers attributable to changes in the observability of market data) and the reasons for those transfers. For significant transfers, transfers into Level 3 shall be disclosed and discussed separately from transfers out of Level 3. For this purpose, significance shall be judged with respect to profit or loss, and total assets or total liabilities.

6. The amount of the total gains or losses for the period in 5a above included in profit or loss that are attributable to gains or losses relating to those assets and liabilities held at the reporting date, and a description of where those gains or losses are presented in the statement of comprehensive income or separate income statement (if presented).
7. For fair value measurements categorized within Level 3 of the fair value hierarchy, if changing one or more of the inputs to reasonably possible alternative assumptions would change fair value significantly, the entity is to state that fact and disclose the effect of those changes. An entity is to disclose how it calculated those changes. For this purpose, significance is to be judged with respect to profit or loss, and total assets or total liabilities.

In addition to the foregoing, for each class of assets and liabilities *not* measured at fair value in the statement of financial position, but for which the fair value is disclosed, the reporting entity is to disclose the fair value by the level of the fair value hierarchy.

26 INCOME TAXES

INTRODUCTION

Income taxes are an expense incurred in operating most businesses, and as such are to be reflected in the entity's operating results. However, accounting for income taxes is complicated by the fact that, in most jurisdictions, the amounts of revenues and expenses recognized in a given period for taxation purposes will not fully correspond to what is reported in the financial statements (whether prepared in accordance with various national GAAP or IFRS). The venerable matching principle (still having some relevance, although it is no longer a central concept underlying financial reporting rules) implies that for financial reporting purposes the amount presented as current period tax expense should bear an appropriate relationship to the amount of pretax accounting income being reported. That expense will normally not equal—and may differ markedly from—the amount of the current period's tax payment obligation. The upshot is that deferred income tax assets and/or liabilities must be recognized. These are measured, approximately, as the difference between the amounts currently owed and the amounts recognizable for financial reporting purposes.

Various theories of interperiod income tax allocation have been proposed and mandated over the years, both by various national GAAP and by IFRS. Under the current provisions of IAS 12, which was substantially revised effective in 1998, the *liability method* of computing interperiod income tax allocation is required. This method is oriented toward the statement of financial position, rather than the statement of comprehensive income, and has as its highest objective the accurate, appropriate measurement of assets and liabilities, so that the statement of financial position representation of deferred tax benefits and obligations will comply with the definitions of assets and liabilities set forth by the IASB's *Framework*. In order to achieve this, at each statement of financial position date the amounts in the deferred tax asset and/or liability accounts must be assessed, with whatever adjustment(s) are needed to achieve the correct balance(s) being reported in the tax provisions for the period. In other words, tax expense is a residual, with the primary objective being achieving the correct balances in the deferred tax asset and liability accounts.

The statement of financial position liability method applied in IAS 12 focuses on temporary differences, which are the difference between the carrying value and tax base of all assets and liabilities. The income statement liability method applied previously focuses on timing differences, which was the difference between the amounts recognized in the accounting profit or loss and the taxable income for a reporting period.

Under IAS 12, deferred tax assets and liabilities are to be presented at the amounts that are expected to flow to or from the reporting entity when the tax benefits are ultimately realized or the tax obligations are settled. IAS 12 does not distinguish operating losses from other types of deductible temporary differences, and requires that both be given recognition, when realization is deemed to be *probable*. Discounting of these amounts to present values is not permitted, as debate continues about the role of discounting in the presentation of assets and liabilities on the statement of financial position. (Uncertainty about the timing of deferred tax realization or settlement makes discounting a practical challenge, also).

Both deferred tax assets and liabilities are measured by reference to expected tax rates, which in general are the enacted, effective rates as of the date of the statement of financial position. IAS 12 has particular criteria to be used for the recognition of the tax effects of temporary differences arising from ownership interests in investees and subsidiaries, and for the accounting related to goodwill arising from business acquisitions. Presentation of deferred tax assets or liabilities as current assets or liabilities is prohibited by the standard, which also establishes extensive financial statement disclosures.

Sources of IFRS
IAS 12, 25

AMENDMENTS EFFECTIVE DURING 2012

The amendment *Defered Tax: Recovery of Underlying Assets* issued December 2011 is effective from 1 January 2012. This amendment provides a practical approach when it is difficult and subjective to determine the manner of recovery of an investment property. This amendment also incorporates SIC 21 *Income Tax – Recovery of Revalued Nondepreciable Assets*. Refer to the discussion under the measurement of deferred tax for these amendments.

SCOPE

IAS 12 is applied in the accounting for income taxes. Income taxes include all domestic and foreign taxes which are based on taxable profit, including withholding taxes payable on distributions by the reporting entity. Although IAS 12 does not deal with the accounting of government grants and investment tax credits, it deals with the accounting of temporary differences on such transactions.

DEFINITIONS OF TERMS

Accounting profit. Net profit or loss for the reporting period before deducting income tax expense.

Current tax expense (benefit). The amount of income taxes payable (recoverable) in respect of the taxable profit (tax loss) for a period.

Deductible temporary differences. Temporary differences that result in amounts that are deductible in determining future taxable profit (tax loss) when the carrying amount of the asset or liability is recovered or settled.

Deferred tax asset. The amounts of income taxes recoverable in future periods in respect of deductible temporary differences, the carryforward of unused tax losses, and the carryforward of unused tax credits.

Deferred tax expense (benefit). The change during a reporting period in the deferred tax liabilities and deferred tax assets of an entity.

Deferred tax liability. The amounts of income taxes payable in future periods in respect of taxable temporary differences.

Tax basis. The amount attributable to an asset or liability for the tax purposes.

Tax credits. Reductions in the tax liability as a result of certain expenditures accorded special treatment under the tax regulations.

Tax expense (tax income). The aggregate amount included in the determination of profit or loss for the period in respect of current tax and deferred tax

Taxable profit (loss). The profit (loss) for a taxable period, determined in accordance with the rules established by the taxation authorities, upon which income taxes are payable (recoverable).

Taxable temporary differences. Temporary differences that result in taxable amounts in determining taxable profit (tax loss) of future periods when the carrying amount of the asset or liability is recovered or settled.

Temporary differences. Differences between the carrying amount of an asset or liability in the statement of financial position and its tax base.

IDENTIFICATION

Tax expense. Tax expense (income) comprises two components: current tax expense and deferred tax expense. Either of these can be an income (i.e., a credit amount in the statement of comprehensive income), rather than an expense (a debit), depending on whether there is taxable profit or loss for the period. For convenience, the term "tax expense" will be used to denote either an expense or an income. Current tax expense is easily understood as the tax effect of the entity's reported taxable income or loss for the period, as determined by relevant rules of the various taxing authorities to which it is subject. Deferred tax expense, in general terms, arises as the tax effect of temporary differences occurring during the reporting period.

Using the liability method, the reporting entity's current period total income tax expense cannot be computed directly (except when there are no temporary differences). Rather, it must be calculated as the sum of the two components: current tax expense and deferred tax expense. This total will not, in general, equal the amount that would be derived by applying the current tax rate to pretax accounting profit. The reason is that deferred tax expense is defined as the change in the deferred tax asset and liability accounts occurring in the current period, and this change may encompass more than the mere effect of the current tax rate times the net temporary differences arising or being reversed in the present reporting period.

Although the primary objective of income tax accounting is no longer the proper matching of current period revenue and expenses, the once-critical matching principle retains some importance in financial reporting theory. Therefore, the tax effects of items excluded from profit and loss are also excluded from the profit and loss section of the statement of comprehensive income. For example, the tax effects of items reported in other comprehensive income are likewise reported in other comprehensive income.

The recognition of income tax is based on the liability method. The liability method is statement of financial position–oriented to understand the application of the liability method as incorporated in IAS 12, the basic recognition and measurement principles in IAS 12 must be understood, including how these recognition and measurement principles are applied to determine the current and deferred tax amounts.

RECOGNITION AND MEASUREMENT OF CURRENT TAX

Recognition of Current Tax

The primary goal of the liability method is to present the estimated actual taxes to be payable in current and future periods as the income tax liability on the statement of financial position. Based on this goal, current tax for the current and prior periods is recognized as a liability to the extent it is unpaid at the end of the reporting period. If the amount paid exceeds the respective current tax recorded, an asset is recognized. The benefit of a tax loss that can be carried back to recover current tax of previous periods must also be recognized as an asset.

Measurement of Current Tax

Current tax liabilities are measured at the amount expected to be paid to the taxation authorities, using the tax rates (and tax laws) that have been enacted or substantially enacted by the end of the reporting period. Current tax assets are similarly measured at the amount expected to be recovered from the taxation authorities.

RECOGNITION AND MEASUREMENT OF DEFERRED TAX

Recognition of Deferred Tax

The recognition of deferred tax is based on a statement of financial position orientation. Based on this orientation, deferred tax liabilities are recognized for taxable temporary differences and deferred tax assets are recognized for deductible temporary differences, the carry forward of unused tax losses and the carry forward of unused tax credits.

The general principle is that a deferred tax liability is recognized for all taxable temporary differences. Two exceptions are, however, applicable. The first is temporary differences arising from the initial recognition of goodwill and the second is temporary differences arising from the initial recognition of an asset or liability in a transaction which is not a business combination and at the time of the transaction, affects neither accounting profit nor taxable profit (tax loss).

Deferred tax assets recognized for deductible temporary difference, the carry forward of unused tax losses and the carry forward of unused tax credits are subject to a probability limitation. Deferred tax is only recognized to the extent that is probable that taxable profits are available against which the deductible temporary difference could be utilized. An exception is also, similar to a deferred tax liability, applicable to deductible temporary differences arising from the initial recognition of an asset or liability in a transaction which is not a business combination and at the time of the transaction, affects neither accounting profit nor taxable profit (tax loss).

Special principles are applicable to the recognition of temporary differences associated with investments in subsidiaries, branches and interest in joint ventures, which is discussed under special transactions.

Measurement of Deferred Tax Assets

Deferred tax assets and deferred tax liabilities are measure at the tax rates that are expected to apply to the period when the assets is realized or the liabilities is settled. The applicable tax rate is based on the tax rate (and tax laws) that have been enacted or substantively enacted by the end of the reporting period.

The computation of the amount of deferred taxes is based on the rate expected to be in effect when the temporary differences reverse. The annual computation is considered a tentative estimate of the liability (or asset) that is subject to change as the statutory tax rate changes or as the taxpayer moves into other tax rate brackets. The measurement of deferred tax liabilities and deferred tax assets reflects the tax consequences that would follow the manner in which management expects, at the end of the reporting period, to recover or settle the carrying amount of its assets and liabilities.

The issue is that both the tax rate and the tax base of an asset or liability can be dependent on the manner in which the entity recovers or settle the asset or liability. An asset can either be recovered through usage or sale, or a combination. IAS 12 clarifies that the tax rate and tax base consistent with the expected manner of recovery or settlement must be used.

Special guidance is applicable to nondepreciable assets measured under the revaluation model and investment properties measured under the fair value model:

- Revalued nondepreciable assets are regarded to be recovered only through sale, since these assets are not depreciated. The tax rate and tax base that should be used is the one that would be applicable if the asset were sold at the end of the reporting period.
- A rebuttable presumption exists that investment properties carried at fair value will be recovered through sale. Deferred tax is thus created as if the entire investment property is recovered through sale at the end of the reporting period.

The presumption regarding investment properties is rebutted if the investment property is depreciated (for example buildings and leasehold land) and held within a business model whose objective is to consume substantially all the economic benefits embodied in the investment property over time, rather than through sale. The presumption can not be rebutted for freehold land, which is not depreciable. The rebuttable presumption is also applicable to investment properties measured at fair value in a business combination.

RECOGNITION IN PROFIT OR LOSS

The general principle is that all changes in current and deferred tax are recognized in profit or loss. Two exceptions are applicable. The first relates to transactions recognized in other comprehensive income. The current and deferred tax related to items recognized in other comprehensive income and equity should also be recognized in other comprehensive income and equity.

Secondly the initial deferred tax recognized on assets and liabilities acquired in a business combination are recognized as an adjustment to goodwill or any gain on a bargain purchase.

CALCULATION OF DEFERRED TAX ASSET OR LIABILITY

While conceptually the application of the liability method is straightforward, in the application of IAS 12 a number of complexities need to be addressed. The following process needs to be followed to calculate and measure deferred tax assets and liabilities.

1. Identification of temporary differences
2. Identification of exceptions
3. Identification of unused tax losses or tax credits
4. Calculation and measurement of deferred tax assets or deferred tax liabilities
5. Limitations on the recognition of deferred tax assets

Identification of Temporary Differences

The preponderance of the typical reporting entity's revenue and expense transactions are treated identically for tax and financial reporting purposes. Some transactions and events, however, will have different tax and accounting implications. In many of these cases, the difference relates to the period in which the income or expense will be recognized. Under earlier iterations of IAS 12, the latter differences were referred to as *timing differences* and were said to originate in one period and to reverse in a later period.

The current IAS 12 introduced the concept of *temporary differences*, which is a somewhat more comprehensive concept than that of timing differences. Temporary differences include all the categories of items defined under the earlier concept, and add a number of additional items, as well. Temporary differences are defined to include *all* differences between the carrying amount and the tax base of assets and liabilities. The tax base of an asset or liability is defined as the amount attributable to that asset or liability for tax purposes. The following principles are included in IAS 12 to determine the tax base of assets and liabilities:

Element	Tax base
Asset	The amount that would be deductible for tax purposes when the carrying amount of the asset is recovered. If the economic benefits recovered from the asset is not taxable, the tax base of the asset is equal to its carrying amount.
Liability	The carrying amount less any amount that will be deductible for tax purposes in respect of the liability in future periods. In the case of revenue received in advance, the tax base is the carrying amount less any amount of the revenue that will not be taxed in future periods.

The tax base can also be determined for transactions not recognized in the statement of financial position. For example if an amount is expensed, but the amount is only deductible for tax purposes in the future, the tax base will be equal to the amount deductible in the future. When the tax base of an item is not immediate apparent, the following general principle of IAS 12 must be followed to determine the tax base:

> Recognize a deferred tax asset when recovery or settlement of the carrying amount will reduce future taxable income and a deferred tax liability when the recovery or settlement of the carrying amount will increase future taxable income.

Once the tax base is determined the related temporary difference is calculated as the difference between carrying value and the tax base. Temporary differences are divided into taxable and deductible temporary differences. Taxable temporary differences represents a liability and are defined as temporary differences that will result in taxable amounts in determining taxable profits of future periods when the carrying amount of the asset or liability is recovered or settled. Deductible temporary differences represent an asset and are defined as temporary differences that will result in amounts that will be deductible in determining the taxable profits of future periods when the carrying amount of the asset or liability is recovered or settled.

Deductible and taxable temporary differences are thus based on the future taxable effect explained in the following examples:

1. **Revenue recognized for financial reporting purposes before being recognized for tax purposes.** Examples include revenue accounted for by the installment method for tax purposes, but reflected in income currently; certain construction-related revenue recognized on a completed-contract method for tax purposes, but on a percentage-of-completion basis for financial reporting; earnings from investees recognized by the equity method for accounting purposes but taxed only when later distributed as dividends to the investor. These are taxable temporary differences because the amounts are taxable in future periods, which give rise to deferred tax liabilities.

2. **Revenue recognized for tax purposes prior to recognition in the financial statements.** These include certain types of revenue received in advance, such as prepaid rental income and service contract revenue that is taxable when received. Referred to as deductible temporary differences, these items give rise to deferred tax assets.

3. **Expenses that are deductible for tax purposes prior to recognition in the financial statements.** This results when accelerated depreciation methods or shorter useful lives are used for tax purposes, while straight-line depreciation or longer useful economic lives are used for financial reporting; and when there are certain preoperating costs and certain capitalized interest costs that are deductible currently for tax purposes. These items are taxable temporary differences and give rise to deferred tax liabilities.

4. **Expenses that are reported in the financial statements prior to becoming deductible for tax purposes.** Certain estimated expenses, such as warranty costs, as well as such contingent losses as accruals of litigation expenses, are not tax deductible until the obligation becomes fixed. These are deductible temporary differences, and accordingly give rise to deferred tax assets.

Other examples of temporary differences include

1. **Reductions in tax-deductible asset bases arising in connection with tax credits.** Under tax provisions in certain jurisdictions, credits are available for certain quali-

fying investments in plant assets. In some cases, taxpayers are permitted a choice of either full accelerated depreciation coupled with a reduced investment tax credit, or a full investment tax credit coupled with reduced depreciation allowances. If the taxpayer chose the latter option, the asset basis is reduced for tax depreciation, but would still be fully depreciable for financial reporting purposes. Accordingly, this election would be accounted for as a taxable timing difference, and give rise to a deferred tax liability.

2. **Increases in the tax bases of assets resulting from the indexing of asset costs for the effects of inflation.** Occasionally, proposed and sometimes enacted by taxing jurisdictions, such a tax law provision allows taxpaying entities to finance the replacement of depreciable assets through depreciation based on current costs, as computed by the application of indices to the historical costs of the assets being remeasured. This reevaluation of asset costs gives rise to deductible temporary differences that would be associated with deferred tax benefits.

3. **Certain business combinations accounted for by the acquisition method.** Under certain circumstances, the costs assignable to assets or liabilities acquired in purchase business combinations will differ from their tax bases. The usual scenario under which this arises is when the acquirer must continue to report the predecessor's tax bases for tax purposes, although the price paid was more or less than book value. Such differences may be either taxable or deductible and, accordingly, may give rise to deferred tax liabilities or assets. These are recognized as temporary differences by IAS 12.

4. **Assets that are revalued for financial reporting purposes although the tax bases are not affected.** This is analogous to the matter discussed in the preceding paragraph. Under certain IFRS (such as IAS 16 and IAS 40), assets may be upwardly adjusted to current fair values (revaluation amounts), although for tax purposes these adjustments are ignored until and unless the assets are disposed of. The discrepancies between the adjusted book carrying values and the tax bases are temporary differences under IAS 12, and deferred taxes are to be provided on these variations. This is required even if there is no intention to dispose of the assets in question, or if, under the salient tax laws, exchanges for other similar assets (or reinvestment of proceeds of sales in similar assets) would effect a postponement of the tax obligation.

Identification of Exemptions

Two exemptions are applicable to the recognition of deferred tax, namely goodwill and initial recognition exception.

Goodwill. No deferred tax liability should be recognized on the initial recognition of goodwill. Although goodwill represents an asset, no deferred tax is considered to arise since goodwill is measured as a residual of the value of net assets acquired in a business combination. The deferred tax recognized on the acquired net assets of the business combination, however, affects the value of goodwill as the residual. IAS 12 also clarifies that no deferred tax effects are applicable to the later impairment of goodwill.

If goodwill or a gain on a bargain purchase is not deductible or taxable, respectively, in a given tax jurisdiction (that is, it is a permanent difference), in theory its tax base is zero, and thus there is a difference between tax and financial reporting bases, to which one would logically expect deferred taxes would be attributed. However, given the residual nature of goodwill or a gain on a bargain purchase, recognition of deferred taxes would in turn create yet more goodwill, and thus more deferred tax, etc. There would be little purpose achieved by loading up the statement of financial position with goodwill and related deferred tax in such circumstances, and the computation itself would be quite challenging. Accordingly, IAS 12 prohibits grossing up goodwill in such a fashion. Similarly, no deferred tax benefit will be computed and presented in connection with the financial reporting recognition of a gain on a bargain purchase.

However, IAS 12 states that if the carrying amount of goodwill under a business combination is less than its tax base, a deferred tax asset should be recognized. This will be in jurisdictions where future tax deductions are available for goodwill. The deferred tax assets will only be recognized to the extent that it is probable that future taxable profits will be available to utilize the deduction.

Initial recognition exemption. No deferred tax liability or asset is recognized on the initial recognition of an asset or liability that is not part of a business combination, and at the time of the transaction, affects neither accounting profit nor taxable profits. IAS 12, for example, states that an asset which is not depreciated for tax purposes, will be exempt under this initial recognition exemption, provided that any capital gain or loss on the disposal of the asset will also be exempt for tax purposes.

In some tax jurisdictions, the costs of certain assets are never deductible in computing taxable profit. For accounting purposes such assets may be subjected to depreciation or amortization. Thus, the asset in question has a differing accounting base than tax base, and this results in a temporary difference. Similarly, certain liabilities may not be recognized for tax purposes resulting in a temporary difference. While IAS 12 accepts that these represent temporary differences a decision was made to not permit recognition of deferred tax on these. The reason given is that the new result would be to "gross up" the recorded amount of the asset or liability to offset the recorded deferred tax liability or benefit, and this would make the financial statements "less transparent." It could also be argued that when an asset has, as one of its attributes, nondeductibility for tax purposes, the price paid for this asset would have been affected accordingly, so that any such "gross-up" would cause the asset to be reported at an amount in excess of fair value.

Basic example of initial recognition example

Johnson PLC purchases an intangible asset from Peters PLC. Johnson will not be entitled to any tax deductions on the intangible asset. The asset was purchased for $1,000,000.

On day 1, the temporary difference would be as follows:

Carrying value	1,000,000
Tax base	0
Temporary difference	1,000,000
Tax rate	20%
Deferred tax	200,000

Without this exemption, the journal entries on day 1 would be as follows:

Intangible asset	1,200,000	
Bank		1,000,000
Deferred tax liability		200,000

As a result, the carrying value of the asset would also now be 1,200,000 and deferred tax would again be calculated to incorporate the increase in the assets carrying value. This is a circular calculation which would eventually result in a carrying amount much higher than the purchase price. The initial recognition exemption criterion, therefore, requires no deferred tax to be recognized in this example.

Identification of Unused Tax Losses or Tax Credits

Unused tax losses or unused tax credits must be identified to determine whether deferred tax assets should be recognized in such transactions.

Calculation and Measurement of Deferred Tax Assets and Liabilities

The procedure to compute the gross deferred tax provision (i.e., before addressing whether the deferred tax asset is probable of being realized and therefore should be recognized) after exempt temporary differences and unused tax losses and tax credits are identified is as follows:

1. Segregate the temporary differences into those that are taxable and those that are deductible. This step is necessary because under IAS 12 only those deferred tax assets that are probable of being realized are recognized, whereas all deferred tax liabilities are given full recognition.
2. Accumulate information about the *deductible* temporary differences, particularly the net operating loss and credit carryforwards that have expiration dates or other types of limitations.
3. Measure the tax effect of aggregate *taxable* temporary differences by applying the appropriate expected tax rates (federal plus any state, local, and foreign rates that are applicable under the circumstances).
4. Similarly, measure the tax effects of *deductible* temporary differences, including net operating loss carryforwards.

It should be emphasized that separate computations should be made for each tax jurisdiction, since in assessing the propriety of recording the tax effects of deductible temporary differences it is necessary to consider the entity's ability to absorb deferred tax assets against tax liabilities. Inasmuch as assets receivable from one tax jurisdiction will not reduce taxes payable to another jurisdiction, separate calculations will be needed. Also, for purposes of statement of financial position presentation (discussed below in detail), the offsetting of deferred tax assets and liabilities may be permissible only within jurisdictions, since there may not be a legal right to offset obligations due to and from different taxing authorities. Similarly, separate computations should be made for each taxpaying component of the business. Thus, if a parent company and its subsidiaries are consolidated for financial reporting purposes but file separate tax returns, the reporting entity comprises a number of components, and the tax benefits of any one will be unavailable to reduce the tax obligations of the others.

The principles set forth above are illustrated by the following examples.

Basic example of the computation of deferred tax liability and asset

Assume that Noori Company has pretax financial income of €250,000 in 2011, a total of €28,000 of taxable temporary differences, and a total of €8,000 of deductible temporary differences. Noori has no operating loss or tax credit carryforwards. The tax rate is a flat (i.e., not graduated) 40%. Also assume that there were no deferred tax liabilities or assets in prior years.

Taxable income is computed as follows:

Pretax financial income	€250,000
Taxable temporary differences	(28,000)
Deductible temporary differences	8,000
Taxable income	€230,000

The journal entry to record required amounts is

Current income tax expense	92,000	
Deferred tax asset	3,200	
Income tax expense—deferred	8,000	
Deferred tax liability		11,200
Income taxes currently payable		92,000

Current income tax expense and income taxes currently payable are each computed as taxable income times the current rate (€230,000 × 40%). The deferred tax asset of €3,200 represents 40% of deductible temporary differences of €8,000. The deferred tax liability of €11,200 is calculated as 40% of taxable temporary differences of €28,000. The deferred tax expense of €8,000 is the *net* of the deferred tax liability of €11,200 and the deferred tax asset of €3,200.

In 2012, Noori Company has pretax financial income of €450,000, aggregate taxable and deductible temporary differences are €75,000 and €36,000, respectively, and the tax rate remains a flat 40%. Taxable income is €411,000, computed as pretax financial income of €450,000 minus taxable differences of €75,000 plus deductible differences of €36,000. Current income tax expense and income taxes currently payable each are €164,400 (€411,000 × 40%).

Deferred amounts are calculated as follows:

	Deferred tax liability	*Deferred tax asset*	*Deferred tax expense*
Required balance at 12/31/12			
€75,000 × 40%	€30,000		--
€36,000 × 40%		€14,400	--
Balances at 12/31/11	11,200	3,200	--
Adjustment required	€18,800	€11,200	€7,600

The journal entry to record the deferred amounts is

Deferred tax asset	11,200	
Income tax expense—deferred	7,600	
Deferred tax liability		18,800

Because the *increase* in the liability in 2012 is larger (by €7,600) than the increase in the asset for that year, the result is a deferred tax *expense* for 2012.

Limitation on the Recognition of Deferred Tax Assets

Although the case for presentation in the financial statements of any amount computed for deferred tax liabilities is clear, it can be argued that deferred tax assets should be included in the statement of financial position only if they are, in fact, very likely to be realized in future periods. Since realization will almost certainly be dependent on the future profitability of the reporting entity, it may become necessary to ascertain the likelihood that the enterprise will be profitable. Absent convincing evidence of that, the concepts of conservatism and realization would suggest that the asset be treated as a contingent gain, and not accorded recognition until and unless ultimately realized.

Under IAS 12, deferred tax assets resulting from temporary differences and from tax loss carryforwards are to be given recognition only if realization is deemed to be *probable*. To operationalize this concept, the standard sets forth several criteria, which variously apply to deferred tax assets arising from temporary differences and from tax loss carryforwards. The standard establishes that

1. It is *probable* that future taxable profit will be available against which a deferred tax asset arising from a deductible temporary difference can be utilized when there are sufficient taxable temporary differences relating to the same taxation authority which will reverse either

    a. In the same period as the reversal of the deductible temporary difference, or

    b. In periods into which the deferred tax asset can be carried back or forward; or

2. If there are insufficient taxable temporary differences relating to the same taxation authority, it is probable that the enterprise will have taxable profits in the same period as the reversal of the deductible temporary difference or in periods to which the deferred tax can be carried back or forward, or there are tax-planning opportunities available to the enterprise that will create taxable profit in appropriate periods.

Thus, there necessarily will be an element of judgment in making an assessment about how probable the realization of the deferred tax asset is, for those circumstances in which there is not an existing balance of deferred tax liability equal to or greater than the amount of the deferred tax asset. If it cannot be concluded that realization is probable, the deferred tax asset is not given recognition.

As a practical matter, there are a number of positive and negative factors which may be evaluated in reaching a conclusion as to amount of the deferred tax asset to be recognized. Positive factors (those suggesting that the full amount of the deferred tax asset associated with the gross temporary difference should be recorded) might include

1. Evidence of sufficient future taxable income, exclusive of reversing temporary differences and carryforwards, to realize the benefit of the deferred tax asset.

2. Evidence of sufficient future taxable income arising from the reversals of existing taxable temporary differences (deferred tax liabilities) to realize the benefit of the tax asset.

3. Evidence of sufficient taxable income in prior year(s) available for realization of an operating loss carryback under existing statutory limitations.

4. Evidence of the existence of prudent, feasible tax planning strategies under management control that, if implemented, would permit the realization of the tax asset. These are discussed in greater detail below.

5. An excess of appreciated asset values over their tax bases, in an amount sufficient to realize the deferred tax asset. This can be thought of as a subset of the tax strategies idea, since a sale or sale/leaseback of appreciated property is one rather obvious tax-planning strategy to salvage a deferred tax benefit that might otherwise expire unused.

6. A strong earnings history exclusive of the loss that created the deferred tax asset. This would, under many circumstances, suggest that future profitability is likely and therefore that realization of deferred tax assets is probable.

Although the foregoing may suggest that the reporting entity will be able to realize the benefits of the deductible temporary differences outstanding as of the date of the statement of financial position, certain negative factors should also be considered in determining whether realization of the full amount of the deferred tax benefit is probable under the circumstances. These factors could include

1. A cumulative recent history of accounting losses. Depending on extent and length of time over which losses were experienced, this could reduce the assessment of likelihood of realization below the important "probable" threshold.

2. A history of operating losses or of tax operating loss or credit carryforwards that have expired unused.

3. Losses that are anticipated in the near future years, despite a history of profitable operations.

Thus, the process of determining how much of the computed gross deferred tax benefit should be recognized involves the weighing of both positive and negative factors to determine whether, based on the preponderance of available evidence, it is probable that the deferred tax asset will be realized. IAS 12 notes that a history of unused tax losses should be considered "strong evidence" that future taxable profits might prove elusive. In such cases, it would be expected that primary reliance would be placed on the existence of taxable temporary differences that, upon reversal, would provide taxable income to absorb the deferred tax benefits that are candidates for recognition in the financial statements. In the absence of those taxable temporary differences, recognition would be much more difficult.

Example

To illustrate this computation in a more specific fact situation, assume the following facts:

1. Malpasa Corporation reports deferred tax under IAS 12. As of the December 31, 2012 statement of financial position, Malpasa has taxable temporary differences of €85,000 relating to depreciation, deductible temporary differences of €12,000 relating to deferred compensation arrangements, a net operating loss carryforward (which arose in 2011) of €40,000, and a capital loss carryover of €10,000. Note that capital losses can only be offset against capital gains (not ordinary income), but may be carried forward until used.
3. Malpasa's expected tax rate for future years is 40% for ordinary income, and 25% for net long-term capital gains.

The first steps are to compute the required balances of the deferred tax asset and liability accounts, without consideration of whether the tax asset would be probable of realization. The computations would proceed as follows:

Deferred tax liability	
Taxable temporary difference (depreciation)	€85,000
Effective tax rate	× 40%
Required balance	€34,000
Deferred tax asset	
Deductible temporary differences	€12,000
Deferred compensation	40,000
Net operating loss	€52,000
Effective tax rate	× 40%
Required balance (a)	€20,800
Capital loss	€10,000
Effective tax rate	× 25%
Required balance (b)	€ 2,500
Total deferred tax asset	
Ordinary (a)	€20,800
Capital (b)	2,500
Total required balance	€23,300

The next step would be to consider whether realization of the deferred tax asset is probable. Malpasa management must evaluate both positive and negative evidence to determine this matter. Assume now that management identifies the following factors that may be relevant:

1. Before the net operating loss deduction, Malpasa reported taxable income of €5,000 in 2012. Management believes that taxable income in future years, apart from NOL deductions, should continue at about the same level experienced in 2012.
2. The taxable temporary differences are not expected to reverse in the foreseeable future.

3. The capital loss arose in connection with a transaction of a type that is unlikely to recur. The company does not generally engage in activities that have the potential to result in capital gains or losses.

4. Management estimates that certain productive assets have a fair value exceeding their respective tax bases by about €30,000. The entire gain, if realized for tax purposes, would be a recapture of depreciation previously taken. Since the current plans call for a substantial upgrading of the company's plant assets, management feels that it could easily accelerate those actions to realize taxable gains, should it be desirable to do so for tax-planning purposes.

Based on the foregoing information, Malpasa Corporation management concludes that a €2,500 adjustment to deferred tax assets is required. The reasoning is as follows:

1. There will be some taxable operating income generated in future years (€5,000 annually, based on the earnings experienced in 2012), which will absorb a modest portion of the reversal of the deductible temporary difference (€12,000) and net operating loss carry-forward (€40,000) existing at year-end 2012.

2. More important, the feasible tax planning strategy of accelerating the taxable gain relating to appreciated assets (€30,000) would certainly be sufficient, in conjunction with operating income over several years, to permit Malpasa to realize the tax benefits of the deductible temporary difference and NOL carryover.

3. However, since capital loss carryovers are only usable to offset future capital gains and Malpasa management is unable to project future realization of capital gains, the associated tax benefit accrued (€2,500) will probably not be realized, and thus cannot be recognized.

Based on this analysis, deferred tax benefits in the amount of €20,800 should be recognized.

Future temporary differences as a source for taxable profit to offset deductible differences. In some instances, an entity may have deferred tax assets that will be realizable when future tax deductions are taken, but it cannot be concluded that there will be sufficient taxable profits to absorb these future deductions. However, the enterprise can reasonably predict that if it continues as a going concern, it will generate other temporary differences such that taxable (if not book) profits will be created. It has indeed been argued that the going concern assumption underlying much of accounting theory is sufficient rationale for the recognition of deferred tax assets in such circumstances.

However, IAS 12 makes it clear that this is not valid reasoning. The new taxable temporary differences anticipated for future periods will themselves reverse in even later periods; these cannot do "double duty" by also being projected to be available to absorb currently existing deductible temporary differences. Thus, in evaluating whether realization of currently outstanding deferred tax benefits is probable, it is appropriate to consider the currently outstanding taxable temporary differences, but not taxable temporary differences that are projected to be created in later periods.

Tax-planning opportunities that will help realize deferred tax assets. When an entity has deductible temporary differences and taxable temporary differences pertaining to the same tax jurisdiction, there is a presumption that realization of the relevant deferred tax assets is probable, since the relevant deferred tax liabilities should be available to offset these. However, before concluding that this is valid, it will be necessary to consider further the *timing* of the two sets of reversals. If the deductible temporary differences will reverse, say, in the very near term, and the taxable differences will not reverse for many years, it is a matter for concern that the tax benefits created by the former occurrence may expire unused prior to the latter event occurring. Thus, when the existence of deferred tax obligations serves as the logical basis for the recognition of deferred tax assets, it is also necessary to consider whether, under pertinent tax regulations, the benefit carryforward period is sufficient to assure that the benefit will not be lost to the reporting enterprise.

For example, if the deductible temporary difference is projected to reverse in two years but the taxable temporary difference is not anticipated to occur for another ten years, and the tax jurisdiction in question offers only a five-year tax loss carryforward, then (absent other facts suggesting that the tax benefit is probable of realization) the deferred tax benefit could not be given recognition under IAS 12.

However, the entity might have certain tax-planning opportunities available to it, such that the pattern of taxable profits could be altered to make the deferred tax benefit, which might otherwise be lost, probable of realization. For example, again depending on the rules of the salient tax jurisdiction, an election might be made to tax interest income on an accrual rather than on a cash received basis, which might accelerate income recognition such that it would be available to offset or absorb the deductible temporary differences. Also, claimed tax deductions might be deferred to later periods, similarly boosting taxable profits in the short term.

More subtly, a reporting entity may have certain assets, such as buildings, which have appreciated in value. It is entirely feasible, in many situations, for an enterprise to take certain steps, such as selling the building to realize the taxable gain thereon and then either leasing back the premises or acquiring another suitable building, to salvage the tax deduction that would otherwise be lost to it due to the expiration of a loss carryforward period. If such a strategy is deemed to be reasonably available, even if the entity does not expect to have to implement it (for example, because it expects other taxable temporary differences to be originated in the interim), it may be used to justify recognition of the deferred tax benefits.

Consider the following example of how an available tax planning strategy might be used to support recognition of a deferred tax asset that otherwise might have to go unrecognized.

Example of the impact of a qualifying tax strategy

Assume that Kirloski Company has a €180,000 operating loss carryforward as of 12/31/11, scheduled to expire at the end of the following year. Taxable temporary differences of €240,000 exist that are expected to reverse in approximately equal amounts of €80,000 in 2011, 2012, and 2013. Kirloski Company estimates that taxable income for 2012 (exclusive of the reversal of existing temporary differences and the operating loss carryforward) will be €20,000. Kirloski Company expects to implement a qualifying tax planning strategy that will accelerate the total of €240,000 of taxable temporary differences to 2012. Expenses to implement the strategy are estimated to approximate €30,000. The applicable expected tax rate is 40%.

In the absence of the tax planning strategy, €100,000 of the operating loss carryforward could be realized in 2012 based on estimated taxable income of €20,000 plus €80,000 of the reversal of taxable temporary differences. Thus, €80,000 would expire unused at the end of 2012 and the net amount of the deferred tax asset at 12/31/12 would be recognized at €40,000, computed as €72,000 (= €180,000 × 40%) minus the valuation allowance of €32,000 (€80,000 × 40%).

However, by implementing the tax planning strategy, the deferred tax asset is calculated as follows:

Taxable income for 2012

Expected amount without reversal of taxable temporary differences	€ 20,000
Reversal of taxable temporary differences due to tax planning strategy, net of costs	210,000
	230,000
Operating loss to be carried forward	(180,000)
Operating loss expiring unused at 12/31/12	€ 0

The deferred tax asset to be recorded at 12/31/12 is €54,000. This is computed as follows:

Full benefit of tax loss carryforward	
€180,000 × 40% =	€72,000
Less: Net-of-tax effect of anticipated expenses related to implementation of the strategy	
€30,000 – (€30,000 × 40%) =	18,000
Net	€54,000

Kirloski Company will also recognize a deferred tax liability of €96,000 at the end of 2012 (40% of the taxable temporary differences of €240,000).

Subsequently revised expectations that a deferred tax benefit is realizable. It may happen that, in a given reporting period, a deferred tax asset is deemed not probable of being realized and accordingly is not recognized, but in a later reporting period the judgment is made that the amount is in fact realizable. If this change in expectation occurs, the deferred tax asset previously not recognized will now be recorded. This does not constitute a prior period adjustment because no accounting error occurred. Rather, this is a change in estimate and is to be included in current earnings. Thus, the tax provision in the period when the estimate is revised will be affected.

Similarly, if a deferred tax benefit provision is made in a given reporting period, but later events suggest that the amount is, in whole or in part, not probable of being realized, the provision should be partially or completely reversed. Again, this adjustment will be included in the tax provision in the period in which the estimate is altered, since it is a change in an accounting estimate. Under either scenario the footnotes to the financial statements will need to provide sufficient information for the users to make meaningful interpretations, since the amount reported as tax expense will seemingly bear an unusual relationship to the reported pretax accounting profit for the period.

If the deferred tax provision in a given period is misstated due to a clerical error, such as miscalculation of the effective expected tax rate, this would constitute an accounting error, and this must be accounted for according to IAS 8's provisions; as revised, this standard requires restatement of prior period financial statements and does not permit adjusting opening retained earnings for the effect of the error. Errors are thus distinguished from changes in accounting estimate, as the latter are accounted for prospectively, without restatement of prior period financial statements. Correction of accounting errors is discussed in Chapter 7.

Example of determining the extent to which the deferred tax asset is realizable

Assume that Zacharias Corporation has a deductible temporary difference of €60,000 at December 31, 2012. The applicable tax rate is a flat 40%. Based on available evidence, management of Zacharias Corporation concludes that it is probable that all sources will not result in future taxable income sufficient to realize more than €15,000 (i.e., 25%) of the deductible temporary difference. Also, assume that there were no deferred tax assets in previous years and that prior years' taxable income was inconsequential.

At 12/31/12 Zacharias Corporation records a deferred tax asset in the amount of €6,000 (= €60,000 × 25% × 40%). The journal entry at 12/31/12 is

Deferred tax asset	6,000	
Income tax benefit—deferred		6,000

The deferred income tax benefit of €6,000 represents the tax effect of that portion of the deferred tax asset (25%) that is probable of being realized.

EFFECT OF CHANGED CIRCUMSTANCES

The carrying amount of deferred tax assets or liabilities may change when there is no change in the amount of the related temporary differences. Examples are tax rate or tax law changes, reassessment of the recoverability of deferred tax assets and changes in the expected manner of recovery of an asset. These changes are normally recognized in profit or loss as discussed below.

Effect of Tax Law Changes on Previously Recorded Deferred Tax Assets and Liabilities

The statement of financial position oriented measurement approach of IAS 12 necessitates the reevaluation of the deferred tax asset and liability balances at each year-end. Although IAS 12 does not directly address the question of changes to tax rates or other provisions of the tax law (e.g., deductibility of items) which may be enacted that will affect the realization of future deferred tax assets or liabilities, the effect of these changes should be reflected in the year-end deferred tax accounts in the period the changes are enacted. The offsetting adjustments should be made through the current period tax provision.

When revised tax rates are enacted, they may affect not only the unreversed effects of items which were originally reported in the continuing operations section of the statement of income (under revised IAS 1, the income statement section of a combined statement of comprehensive income), but also the unreversed effects of items first presented as other comprehensive income. Although it might be conceptually superior to report the effects of tax law changes on such unreversed temporary differences in these same statement of comprehensive income captions, as a practical matter the complexities of identifying the diverse treatments of these originating transactions or events would make such an approach unworkable. Accordingly, remeasurements of the effects of tax law changes should generally be reported in the tax provision associated with continuing operations.

Example of the computation of a deferred tax asset with a change in rates

Assume that the Fanuzzi Company has €80,000 of deductible temporary differences at the end of 2012, which are expected to result in tax deductions of approximately €40,000 each on tax returns for 2013-2014. Enacted tax rates are 50% for the years 2008-2012, and 40% for 2013 and thereafter.

The deferred tax asset is computed at December 31, 2012, under each of the following independent assumptions:

1. If Fanuzzi Company expects to offset the deductible temporary differences against taxable income in the years 2013-2014, the deferred tax asset is €32,000 (€80,000 × 40%).
2. If Fanuzzi Company expects to realize a tax benefit for the deductible temporary differences by loss carryback refund, the deferred tax asset is €40,000 (= €80,000 × 50%).

Changes in tax law may affect rates, and may also affect the taxability or deductibility of income or expense items. While the latter type of change occurs infrequently, the impact is similar to the more common tax rate changes.

Example of effect of change in tax law

Leipzig Corporation has, at December 31, 2011, gross receivables of €12,000,000 and an allowance for bad debts in the amount of €600,000. Also assume that expected future taxes will be at a 40% rate. Effective January 1, 2012, the tax law is revised to eliminate deductions for accrued bad debts, with existing allowances required to be taken into income over three years (a three-year spread). A statement of financial position of Leipzig Corporation prepared on January 1, 2012, would report a deferred tax benefit in the amount of €240,000 (i.e., €600,000 × 40%, which is the tax effect of future deductions to be taken when specific receivables are written off and bad debts are incurred for tax purposes); a current tax liability of €80,000 (one-third of the tax obligation); and a noncurrent tax liability of €160,000 (two-thirds of the tax obligation). Under the requirements of IAS 12, the deferred tax benefit must be entirely reported as noncurrent in classified statements of financial position, inasmuch as no deferred tax benefits or obligations can be shown as current.

Reporting the Effect of Tax Status Changes

Changes in the tax status of the reporting entity should be reported in a manner that is entirely analogous to the reporting of enacted tax law changes. When the tax status change becomes effective, the consequent adjustments to deferred tax assets and liabilities are reported in current tax expense as part of the tax provision relating to continuing operations.

The most commonly encountered changes in status are those attendant to an election, where permitted, to be taxed as a partnership or other flow-through enterprise. (This means that the corporation will not be treated as a taxable entity but rather as an enterprise that "flows through" its taxable income to the owners on a current basis. This favorable tax treatment is available to encourage small businesses, and often will be limited to entities having sales revenue under a particular threshold level, or to entities having no more than a maximum number of shareholders.) Enterprises subject to such optional tax treatment may also request that a previous election be terminated. When a previously taxable corporation becomes a nontaxed corporation, the stockholders become personally liable for taxes on the company's earnings, whether the earnings are distributed to them or not (similar to the relationship among a partnership and its partners).

As issued, IAS 12 did not explicitly address the matter of reporting the effects of a change in tax status, although the appropriate treatment was quite obvious given the underlying concepts of that standard. This ambiguity was subsequently resolved by the issuance of SIC 25, which stipulates that in most cases the current and deferred tax consequences of the change in tax status should be included in net profit or loss for the period in which the change in status occurs. The tax effects of a change in status are included in results of operations because a change in a reporting entity's tax status (or that of its shareholders) does not give rise to increases or decreases in the pretax amounts recognized directly in equity.

The exception to the foregoing general rule arises in connection with those tax consequences which relate to transactions and events that result, in the same or a different period, in a direct credit or charge to the recognized amount of equity. For example, an event that is recognized directly in equity is a change in the carrying amount of property, plant, or equipment revalued under IAS 16. Those tax consequences that relate to change in the recognized amount of equity, in the same or a different period (not included in net profit or loss) should be charged or credited directly to equity.

The most common situation giving rise to a change in tax status would be the election by a corporation, in those jurisdictions where it is permitted to do so, to be taxed as a partnership, trust, or other flow-through entity. If a corporation having a net deferred tax liability elects nontaxed status, the deferred taxes will be eliminated through a credit to current period earnings. That is because what had been an obligation of the corporation has been eliminated (by being accepted directly by the shareholders, typically); a debt thus removed constitutes earnings for the formerly obligated party.

Similarly, if a previously nontaxed corporation becomes a taxable entity, the effect is to assume a net tax benefit or obligation for unreversed temporary differences existing at the date the change becomes effective. Accordingly, the financial statements for the period of such a change will report the effects of the event in the current tax provision. If the entity had at that date many taxable temporary differences as yet unreversed, it would report a large tax expense in that period. Conversely, if it had a large quantity of unreversed deductible temporary differences, a substantial deferred tax benefit (if probable of realization) would need to be recorded, with a concomitant credit to the current period's tax provision in the statement of comprehensive income. Whether eliminating an existing deferred tax balance or recording an initial deferred tax asset or liability, the income tax note to the financial statements will need to fully explain the nature of the events that transpired.

In some jurisdictions, nontaxed corporation elections are automatically effective when filed. In such a case, if a reporting entity makes an election before the end of the current fiscal year, it is logical that the effects be reported in current year income to become effective at the start of the following period. For example, an election filed in December 2011 would be reported in the 2011 financial statements to become effective at the beginning of the company's next fiscal year, January 1, 2012. No deferred tax assets or liabilities would appear on the December 31, 2010 statement of financial position, and the tax provision for the year then ended would include the effects of any reversals that had previously been recorded. Practice varies, however, and in some instances the effect of the elimination of the deferred tax assets and liabilities would be reported in the year the election actually becomes effective.

Reporting the Effect of Accounting Changes Made for Tax Purposes

Occasionally, an entity will initiate or be required to adopt changes in accounting that affect income tax reporting, but that will not impact on financial reporting. For example, in certain jurisdictions at varying times, the following changes have been mandated: use of the direct write-off method of bad debt recognition instead of providing an allowance for bad debts, while continuing to use the reserve method as required by GAAP for financial reporting; the "full costing" method of computing inventory valuations for tax purposes (adding some items that are administrative costs to overhead), while continuing to expense currently those costs not inventoriable under GAAP; and use of accelerated capital recovery (depreciation) methods for tax reporting while continuing to use normal methods for financial reporting. Often, these changes really involve two distinct temporary differences. The first of these is the onetime, catch-up adjustment which either immediately or over a prescribed time period affects the tax basis of the asset or liability in question (net receivables or inventory, in the examples above), and which then reverses as these assets or liabilities are later realized or settled and are eliminated from the statement of financial position. The second change is the ongoing differential in the amount of newly acquired assets or incurred liabilities being recognized for tax and accounting purposes; these differences also eventually reverse. This second type of change is the normal temporary difference which has already been discussed. It is the first change that differs from those previously discussed earlier in the chapter.

Implications of Changes in Tax Rates and Status Made in Interim Periods

Tax rate changes may occur during an interim reporting period, either because a tax law change mandated a midyear effective date, or because tax law changes were effective at year-end but the reporting entity has adopted a fiscal year-end other than the natural year (December 31). The IFRS on interim reporting, IAS 34 (addressed in detail in Chapter 34), has essentially embraced a mixed view on interim reporting—with many aspects conforming to a "discrete" approach (each interim period standing on its own) but others, including accounting for income taxes, conforming to the "integral" manner of reporting. Whatever the philosophical strengths and weaknesses of the discrete and integral approaches in general, the integral approach was clearly warranted in the matter of accounting for income taxes.

The fact that income taxes are assessed annually is the primary reason for concluding that taxes are to be accrued based on an entity's estimated average annual effective tax rate for the full fiscal year. If rate changes have been enacted to take effect later in the fiscal year, the expected effective rate should take into account the rate changes as well as the anticipated pattern of earnings to be experienced over the course of the year. Thus, the rate to be applied to interim period earnings (or losses, as discussed further below) will take into account the expected level of earnings for the entire forthcoming year, as well as the effect of enacted (or substantially enacted) changes in the tax rates to become operative later in the fiscal year. In other words, and as expressed by IAS 34, the estimated average annual rate would "reflect a blend of the progressive tax rate structure expected to be applicable to the full year's earnings enacted or substantially enacted changes in the income tax rates scheduled to take effect later in the financial year."

While the principle espoused by IAS 34 is both clear and logical, a number of practical issues can arise. The standard does address in detail the various computational aspects of an effective interim period tax rate, some of which are summarized in the following paragraphs.

Many modern business entities operate in numerous nations or states and therefore are subject to a multiplicity of taxing jurisdictions. In some instances the amount of income subject to tax will vary from one jurisdiction to the next, since the tax laws in different jurisdictions will include and exclude disparate items of income or expense from the tax base. For example, interest earned on government-issued bonds may be exempted from tax by the jurisdiction that issued them, but be defined as fully taxable by other tax jurisdictions the entity is subject to. To the extent feasible, the appropriate estimated average annual effective tax rate should be separately ascertained for each taxing jurisdiction and applied individually to the interim period pretax income of each jurisdiction, so that the most accurate estimate of income taxes can be developed at each interim reporting date. In general, an overall estimated effective tax rate will not be as satisfactory for this purpose as would a more carefully constructed set of estimated rates, since the pattern of taxable and deductible items will fluctuate from one period to the next.

Similarly, if the tax law prescribes different income tax rates for different categories of income, then to the extent practicable, a separate effective tax rate should be applied to each category of interim period pretax income. IAS 34, while mandating such detailed rules of computing and applying tax rates across jurisdiction or across categories of income, nonetheless recognized that such a degree of precision may not be achievable in all cases. Thus, IAS 34 allows usage of a weighted-average of rates across jurisdictions or across categories of income provided it is a reasonable approximation of the effect of using more specific rates.

In computing an expected effective tax rate given for a tax jurisdiction, all relevant features of the tax regulations should be taken into account. Jurisdictions may provide for tax credits based on new investment in plant and machinery, relocation of facilities to backward or underdeveloped areas, research and development expenditures, levels of export sales, and so forth, and the expected credits against the tax for the full year should be given consideration in the determination of an expected effective tax rate. Thus, the tax effect of new investment in plant and machinery, when the local taxing body offers an investment credit for qualifying investment in tangible productive assets, will be reflected in those interim periods of the fiscal year in which the new investment occurs (assuming it can be forecast to occur later in a given fiscal year), and not merely in the period in which the new investment occurs. This is consistent with the underlying concept that taxes are strictly an annual phenomenon, but it is at variance with the purely discrete view of interim financial reporting.

IAS 34 notes that, although tax credits and similar modifying elements are to be taken into account in developing the expected effective tax rate to apply to interim earnings, tax benefits that will relate to onetime events are to be reflected from the interim period when those events take place. This is perhaps most likely to be encountered in the context of capital gains taxes incurred in connection with occasional dispositions of investments and other capital assets; since it is not feasible to project the timing of such transactions over the course of a year, the tax effects should be recognized only as the underlying events actually do transpire.

While in most cases tax credits are to be handled as suggested in the foregoing paragraphs, in some jurisdictions tax credits, particularly those that relate to export revenue or capital expenditures, are in effect government grants. Accounting for government grants is set forth in IAS 20; in brief, grants are recognized in income over the period necessary to properly match them to the costs which the grants are intended to offset or defray. Thus, compliance with both IAS 20 and IAS 34 would require that tax credits be carefully analyzed to identify those which are in substance grants, and that credits be accounted for consistent with their true natures.

When an interim period loss gives rise to a tax loss carryback, it should be fully reflected in that interim period. Similarly, if a loss in an interim period produces a tax loss carryforward, it should be recognized immediately, but only if the criteria set forth in IAS 12 are met. Specifically, it must be deemed probable that the benefits will be realizable before the loss benefits can be given formal recognition in the financial statements. In the case of interim period losses, it may be necessary to assess not only whether the enterprise will be profitable enough in future fiscal years to utilize the tax benefits associated with the loss, but furthermore, whether interim periods later in the same year will provide earnings of sufficient magnitude to absorb the losses of the current period.

IAS 12 provides that changes in expectations regarding the realizability of benefits related to net operating loss carryforwards should be reflected currently in tax expense. Similarly, if a net operating loss carryforward benefit is not deemed probable of being realized until the interim (or annual) period when it in fact becomes realized, the tax effect will be included in tax expense of that period. Appropriate explanatory material must be included in the notes to the financial statements, even on an interim basis, to provide users with an understanding of the unusual relationship reported between pretax accounting income and the provision for income taxes.

SPECIFIC TRANSACTIONS

Income Tax Consequences of Dividends Paid

Historically, some taxing jurisdictions have levied income tax rates on corporate earnings at differential rates, depending on whether the earnings are retained by the entity or are distributed to shareholders. Typically, the rationale for this disparate treatment is that it motivates business entities to make distributions to shareholders, which is deemed a socially worthwhile goal by some (although it doesn't really alter wealth accumulation unless distortions are introduced by fiscal policy). A secondary reason for such rules is that this partially ameliorates the impact of the double taxation of corporate profits (which are typically first taxed at the corporate level, then taxed again as distributed to shareholders as taxable dividends).

Under the provisions of IAS 12, tax effects are to be provided for current taxable earnings without making any assumptions about future dividend declarations. In other words, the tax provision is to be computed using the tax rate applicable to undistributed earnings, even if the enterprise has a long history of making earnings distributions subsequent to year-end, which when made will generate tax savings. If dividends are later declared, the tax effect of this event will be accounted for in the period in which the proposed dividend is paid or becomes accruable as a liability by the enterprise, if earlier. Since there is typically no legal requirement to declare distributions to shareholders, this approach is clearly appropriate because to recognize tax benefits associated with dividend payments before declaration would be to anticipate income (in the form of tax benefits) before it is earned.

The standard holds that the tax effect of the dividend declaration (or payment) is to be included in the current period's tax provision, not as an adjustment to the earlier period's earnings, taken through the retained earnings account. This is true even when it is clear that the dividend is a distribution being made out of the earlier period's profits. The logic of this requirement is that the tax benefits are more closely linked to events reported in the statement of comprehensive income (i.e., the past or current transactions producing net income) than they are to the dividend distribution. In other words, it is the transactions and events resulting in earnings and not the act of distributing some of these earnings to shareholders that is of the greatest pertinence to financial statement users.

If dividends are declared before the end of the year, but are payable after year-end, the dividends become a legal liability of the reporting entity and taxes should be computed at the appropriate rate on the amount thus declared. If the dividend is declared after year-end but before the financial statements are issued, under IAS 10 a liability cannot be recognized on the statement of financial position at year-end, and thus the tax effect related thereto also cannot be given recognition. Disclosure would be made, however, of this post-year-end event.

To illustrate the foregoing, consider the following example:

> Amir Corporation operates in a jurisdiction where income taxes are payable at a higher rate on undistributed profits than on distributed earnings. For the year 2012, the company's taxable income is €150,000. Amir also has net taxable temporary differences amounting to €50,000 for the year, thus creating the need for a deferred tax provision. The tax rate on distributed profits is 25%, and the rate on undistributed profits is 40%; the difference is refundable if profits are later distributed. As of the date of the statement of financial position no liability for dividends proposed or declared has been reflected on the statement of financial position. March 31, 2013, however, the company distributes dividends of €50,000.

> The tax consequences of dividends on undistributed profits, current and deferred taxes for the year 2012, and the recovery of 2012 income taxes when dividends are subsequently declared would be as follows:

> 1. Amir Corporation recognizes a current tax liability and a current tax expense for 2012 of €150,000 × 40% = €160,000;
> 2. No asset is recognized for the amount that will be (potentially) recoverable when dividends are distributed;
> 3. Deferred tax liability and deferred tax expense for 2012 would be €50,000 × 40% = €20,000, and
> 4. In the following year (2013) when the company recognizes dividends of €50,000, the company will also recognize the recovery of income taxes of €50,000 × (40% − 25%) = €7,500 as a current tax asset and a reduction of the current income tax expense.

The only exception to the foregoing accounting for tax effects of dividends that are subject to differential tax rates arises in the situation of a dividend-paying corporation which is required to withhold taxes on the distribution and remit these to the taxing authorities. In general, withholding tax is offset against the amounts distributed to shareholders, and is later forwarded to the taxing bodies rather than to the shareholders, so that the total amount of the dividend declaration is not altered. However, if the corporation pays the tax in addition to the full amount of the dividend payments to shareholders, some might view this as a tax falling on the corporation and, accordingly, add this to the tax provision reported on the statement of comprehensive income. IAS 12, however, makes it clear that such an amount, if paid or payable to the taxing authorities, is to be charged to equity as part of the dividend declaration if it does not affect income taxes payable or recoverable by the enterprise in the same or a different period.

Finally, IAS 12 provides that disclosure will be required of the potential income tax consequences of dividends. The reporting enterprise should disclose the amounts of the potential income tax consequences that are practically determinable, and whether there are any potential income tax consequences not practically determinable.

Accounting for Business Combinations at the Acquisition Date

When assets and liabilities are valued at fair value, as required under IFRS 3, but the tax base is not adjusted (i.e., there is a carryforward basis for tax purposes), there will be differences between the tax and financial reporting bases of these assets and liabilities, which will constitute temporary differences. Deferred tax assets and liabilities need to be recognized for these differences as an adjustment to goodwill or the bargain purchase gain. The most common example of this is where taxes are calculated at a subsidiary level in a group, and when these items are consolidated into the group accounts, there are consolidation adjustments to the carrying amounts of the assets which result in additional temporary differences at group level.

The limitation on the recognition of deferred tax assets is also applicable to business combinations.

Example of temporary differences in business acquisition

An example, in the context of the business acquisition of Windlass Corp., follows:

1. The income tax rate is a flat 40%.
2. The acquisition of a business is effected at a cost of €500,000.
3. The fair values of assets acquired total €750,000.
4. The carryforward tax bases of assets acquired total €600,000.
5. The fair and carryforward tax bases of the liabilities assumed in the purchase are €250,000.
6. The difference between the tax and fair values of the assets acquired, €150,000, consists of taxable temporary differences of €200,000 and deductible temporary differences of €50,000.
7. There is no doubt as to the realizability of the deductible temporary differences in this case.

Based on the foregoing facts, allocation of the purchase price is as follows:

Gross purchase price	€ 500,000
Allocation to identifiable assets and (liabilities):	
Assets acquired	750,000
Deferred tax asset (€50,000 * 40%).	20,000
Liabilities acquired,	(250,000)
Deferred tax liability (€200,000 * 40%)	(80,000)
Net of the above allocations	440,000
Goodwill	€ 60,000

Accounting for Purchase Business Combinations After the Acquisition

Under the provisions of IAS 12, net deferred tax benefits are not to be carried forward as assets unless the deferred tax assets are deemed *probable* of being realized. The assessment of this probability was discussed earlier in the chapter.

In the above example (Windlass), it was specified that all deductible temporary differences were fully realizable, and therefore the deferred tax benefits associated with those temporary differences were recorded as of the acquisition date. In other situations there may be substantial doubt concerning realizability; that is, it may not be probable that the benefits will be realized. Accordingly, under IAS 12, the deferred tax asset would not be recognized at the date of the business acquisition. If so, the allocation of the purchase price would have to reflect that fact, and more of the purchase cost would be allocated to goodwill than would otherwise be the case.

If, at a later date, it is determined that some or all of the deferred tax asset that was not recognized at the date of the acquisition is, in fact, probable of being ultimately realized, the effect of that re-evaluation will reduce the carrying amount of goodwill. If the carrying amount of goodwill is reduced to nil, any remaining deferred tax asset will be recognized in the tax expense in profit or loss. If a bargain purchase price gain was recognized initially, the deferred tax asset adjustment must be recorded in profit or loss.

Example of revising estimate of tax benefit realizability in business combination

To illustrate this last concept, assume that a business acquisition occurs on January 1, 2010, and that deferred tax assets of €100,000 are *not* recognized at that time, due to an assessment that realization is not probable. The unrecognized tax asset is implicitly allocated to goodwill during the purchase price assignment process. On January 1, 2012, the likelihood of ultimately realizing the tax benefit is reassessed as being probable, with realization projected for later years. The balance of goodwill on January 1, 2012, was €80,000. The entries at that date are as follows:

Deferred tax asset	100,000	
Goodwill		80,000
Profit and loss		20,000

A related issue is that the probability of realizing a pre-acquisition deferred tax asset of the acquirer could change due to the business combination. For instance the acquirer has an unrecognized deferred tax loss that would in the future be recoverable from income receivable from the acquired subsidiary. The acquirer recognizes the change in the deferred tax asset in the period of the acquisition, but cannot include it in the accounting of the business combination, and therefore in the determining of the goodwill or bargain purchase gain of the business combination. This is because the unrecognized deferred tax is not a transaction of the acquiree.

Temporary Differences in Consolidated Financial Statements

Temporary differences in consolidated financial statements are determined by comparing the consolidated carrying values of assets and liabilities with the relevant tax base. The tax base is determined by reference to the applicable tax regime. If the entity is taxed on a group base the tax base is the group tax base. However, if each entity in the group is tax separately, the tax base is determined with reference to each individual entity.

Assets Carried at Fair Value

IFRS allows certain assets to be recognized at fair value or at revalued amounts. If the revaluation or adjustment to the fair value affects the taxable profit immediately, the tax base is also adjusted and no deferred tax would be recognized. Examples include derivatives recognized at fair value for both accounting and tax purposes. However, if the revaluation or restatement to fair value does not affect the taxable profit immediately, deferred tax must be created on the revaluation. The tax base of the asset is not adjusted. The difference between the adjusted carrying value and the tax base is a temporary difference. The normal principles regarding the recovery of the assets through use or sale will be applicable to determine the amount of the related deferred tax.

Tax on Investments in Subsidiaries, Associates, and Joint Ventures

In terms of the general rule deferred tax should also be recognized on investments in subsidiaries, associates and joint ventures similar to other assets. In an important exception to the general rule, IAS 12 provides that when the parent, investor, or joint venturer can prevent the taxable event from occurring, deferred taxes are not recognized. Specifically, under IAS 12, two conditions must *both* be satisfied to justify *not* reflecting deferred taxes in connection with the earnings of a subsidiary (a control situation), branches and associates (significant influence), and joint ventures. These are (1) that the parent, investor, or venturer is able to control the timing of the reversal of the temporary difference and (2) it is probable that the difference will not reverse in the foreseeable future. Unless *both* conditions are met, the tax effects of these temporary differences must be given recognition.

When a parent company that has the ability to control the dividend and other policies of its subsidiary determines that dividends will not be declared, and thus that the undistributed profit of the subsidiary will not be taxed at the parent company level, no deferred tax liability is to be recognized. If this intention is later altered, the tax effect of this change in estimate would be reflected in the current period's tax provision.

On the other hand, an investor, even one having significant influence, cannot absolutely determine the associate's dividend policy. Accordingly, it has to be presumed that earnings will eventually be distributed and that these will create taxable income at the investor company level. Therefore, deferred tax liability must be provided for the reporting entity's share of all undistributed earnings of its associates for which it is accounting by the equity method, unless there is a binding agreement for the earnings of the investee to not be distributed within the foreseeable future.

In the case of joint ventures there are a wide range of possible relationships between the venturers, and in some cases the reporting entity has the ability to control the payment of dividends. As in the foregoing, if the reporting entity has the ability to exercise this level of control and it is probable that distributions will not be made within the foreseeable future, no deferred tax liability will be reported.

In all these various circumstances, it will be necessary to assess whether distributions within the foreseeable future are probable. The standard does not define "foreseeable future" and thus this will remain a matter of subjective judgment. The criteria of IAS 12, while subjective, are less ambiguous than under the original standard, which permitted nonrecognition of deferred tax liability when it was "reasonable to assume that (the associate's) profits will not be distributed."

Example of tax allocation for investee and subsidiary income

To illustrate the application of these concepts, assume that Parent Company owns 30% of the outstanding ordinary shares of an Associate Company and 70% of the ordinary shares of a Subsidiary Company. Additional data for the year 2012 are as follows:

	Associate Company	*Subsidiary Company*
Net income	€50,000	€100,000
Dividends paid	20,000	60,000

How the foregoing data are used to recognize the tax effects of the stated events is discussed below.

Investment in associate company. The investment in the associate company will be equity accounted. The equity income capitalized will be after the dividend received. The investments in the associate will thus increase with €9,000 (30% x (€50,000 – €20,000)). Deferred tax needs to be created on the increase of the investment of €9,000. The increase in the carrying amount could be recovered through dividends or through the ultimate sale of the associate. Dividend income might be taxed at a different rate than the capital gains on the sale of the associate. Assume that only 20% of the dividend is subject to tax of 34% and the capital gains tax rate is also 34%. Based on recovery through dividends the deferred tax will be €612 (20% x 34% x €9,000). Based on the recovery through sale the deferred tax will be €3,060 (34% x €9,000).

Investment in subsidiary company. Normally an investment in a subsidiary company will be recorded at cost in the records of the parent company. No deferred tax will therefore be recognized. However, if the option is followed to fair value the investment, deferred tax must be created using the appropriate rate of recovery of the investment, unless the exception to the general rule applies.

However, in the consolidated financial statements the investment in the subsidiary will be replaced by the assets and liabilities. Therefore any deferred tax created on the investment in the subsidiary company in the parents' own financial statements should also be reversed.

Tax Effects of Compound Financial Instruments

IAS 32 established the important notion that when financial instruments are compound, the separately identifiable components are to be accounted for according to their distinct natures. For example, when an entity issues convertible debt instruments, those instruments may have characteristics of both debt and equity securities, and accordingly, the issuance proceeds should be allocated among those components. (IAS 32 requires that the full fair value of the liability component be recognized, with only the residual allocated to equity, consistent with the concept that equity is only the residual interest in an entity.) A problem arises when the taxing authorities do not agree that a portion of the proceeds should be allocated to a secondary instrument. IAS 12 requires that deferred tax must be created on both the liability and equity component. The deferred tax on the equity component should be recognized direct in equity.

Example of tax effects of compound financial instrument at issuance

Consider the following scenario. Tamara Corp. issues 6% convertible bonds with a face value of €3,000,000, due in ten years, with the bonds being convertible into Tamara ordinary shares at the holders' option. Proceeds of the offering amount to €3,200,000, for an effective yield of approximately 5.13% at a time when "straight" debt with similar risks and time to maturity is yielding just under 6.95% in the market. Since the fair value of the debt component is thus €2.8 million out of the actual proceeds of €3.2 million, the convertibility feature is seemingly worth €400,000 in the financial marketplace. Under revised IAS 32, the full fair value of the liability component must be allocated to it, with only the residual value being attributed to equity.

The entry to record the issuance of the bonds follows:

Cash	3,200,000	
Unamortized debt discount	200,000	
Debt payable		3,000,000
Equity portion of bond		400,000

Deferred tax is created on both the carrying amount of the equity and liability component.

Example of tax effects of compound financial instrument in subsequent periods

To illustrate, continue the preceding example and assume that the tax rate is 30%, and for simplicity, also assume that the debt discount will be amortized on a straight-line basis over the ten-year term (€200,000 ÷ 10 = €20,000 per year), although in theory amortization using the "effective yield" method is preferred. The tax effect of the total debt discount is €200,000 × 30% = €60,000. Annual interest expense is €20,000 + (€3,000,000 × 6%) = €200,000. The entries to establish deferred tax liability accounting at inception, and to reflect interest accrual and reversal of the deferred tax account are as follows:

At inception (in addition to the entry shown above)

Equity portion of bond	60,000	
Deferred tax liability		60,000

Each year thereafter

Interest expense	200,000	
Interest payable		180,000
Unamortized debt discount		20,000
Deferred tax liability	6,000	
Tax expense—deferred		6,000

Note that the offset to deferred tax liability at inception is a charge to equity, in effect reducing the credit to the portion of the bond recognized in equity of the compound financial instrument to a net-of-tax basis, since allocating a portion of the proceeds to the equity component caused the creation of a nondeductible deferred charge, debt discount. When the deferred charge is later amortized, however, the reversing of the temporary difference leads to a reduction in tax expense to better "match" the higher interest expense reported in the financial statements than on the tax return.

Share-Based Payment Transactions

Share-based payment transactions are similar to other transactions subject to deferred tax if the carrying amount differs from the tax base. For example, the expense for the share options granted as compensations are recognized over the vesting period of the share options. For tax purposes assume the amount is only deducted when the options are granted, The tax base will be the expense recognized in equity that is only deducted for tax in future periods. A deferred tax asset is created for the amount that is deducted in the future.

PRESENTATION AND DISCLOSURE

Presentation

Somewhat surprisingly, IAS 12 stated that should the reporting entity classify its statement of financial position (into current and noncurrent assets and liabilities), deferred tax assets and liabilities should never be included in the current category. All deferred tax balances are always classified as noncurrent.

Current tax and deferred tax assets and liabilities may only be offset if specific criteria is met. Current tax assets and current tax liabilities may only be offset if

- The entity has a legally enforceable right to offset the recognized amounts, and
- The entity intends either to settle on a net basis, or to realize the asset and settle the liability simultaneously.

Current tax assets and current tax liabilities of different entities can also only be offset if the above offsetting rules apply, which would be rare, except if the group is taxed on a consolidated basis.

Deferred tax assets and deferred tax liabilities are only offset if

- The entity has a legal enforceable right to set off current tax assets and current tax liabilities; and
- The deferred tax asset and deferred tax liabilities relate to income levied by the same tax authority on the same tax entity or different entities which intend either to settle current tax assets and liabilities on a net basis or simultaneously, in each future period when significant deferred tax asset or liabilities are expected to be recovered or settled.

Disclosures

Revised IAS 12 mandated a number of disclosures, including some that had not been required under earlier practice. The purpose of these disclosures is to provide the user with an understanding of the relationship between pretax accounting profit and the related tax effects, as well as to aid in predicting future cash inflows or outflows related to tax effects of assets and liabilities already reflected in the statement of financial position. The more recently imposed disclosures were intended to provide greater insight into the relationship between deferred tax assets and liabilities recognized, the related tax expense or benefit recognized in earnings, and the underlying natures of the related temporary differences resulting in those items. There is also enhanced disclosure for discontinued operations under IAS 12. Finally, when deferred tax assets are given recognition under defined conditions, there will be disclosure of the nature of the evidence supporting recognition. The specific disclosures are presented in greater detail in the following paragraphs.

Statement of financial position disclosures. A reporting entity is required to disclose the amount of a deferred tax asset and the nature of evidence supporting its recognition, when

1. Utilization of the deferred tax asset is dependent on future taxable profits in excess of the profits arising from the reversal of the existing taxable temporary differences; *and*
2. The enterprise has suffered a loss in the same tax jurisdiction to which the deferred tax assets relate in either the current or preceding period.

Statement of comprehensive income disclosures. IAS 12 places primary emphasis on disclosure of the components of income tax expense or benefit. The following information must be disclosed about the components of tax expense for each year for which a statement of comprehensive income is presented.

The components of tax expense or benefit, which may include some or all of the following:

1. Current tax expense or benefit
2. Any adjustments recognized in the current period for taxes of prior periods

3. The amount of deferred tax expense or benefit relating to the origination and reversal of temporary differences

4. The amount of deferred tax expense or benefit relating to changes in tax rates or the imposition of new taxes

5. The amount of the tax benefit arising from a previously unrecognized tax loss, tax credit, or temporary difference of a prior period that is used to reduce current period tax expense

6. The amount of the tax benefit from a previously unrecognized tax loss, tax credit, or temporary difference of a prior period that is used to reduce deferred tax expense

7. Deferred tax expense arising from the write-down of a deferred tax asset because it is no longer deemed probable of realization

8. The amount of tax expense relating to changes in accounting policies and errors that cannot be accounted for retrospectively

In addition to the foregoing, IAS 12 also requires that disclosures be made of the following items which are to be separately stated:

1. The aggregate current and deferred tax relating to items that are charged or credited to equity

2. The amount of income tax related to each component of other comprehensive income

3. The relationship between tax expense or benefit and accounting profit or loss either (or both) as

    a. A numerical reconciliation between tax expense or benefit and the product of accounting profit or loss times the applicable tax rate(s), with disclosure of how the rate(s) was determined; or

    b. A numerical reconciliation between the average effective tax rate and applicable rate, also with disclosure of how the applicable rate was determined.

4. An explanation of changes in the applicable rate vs. the prior reporting period

5. The amount and date of expiration of unrecognized tax assets relating to deductible temporary differences, tax losses and tax credits

6. The aggregate amount of any temporary differences relating to investments in subsidiaries, branches, and associates and interests in joint ventures for which deferred liabilities have not been recognized

7. For each type of temporary difference, including unused tax losses and credits, disclosure of

    a. The amount of the deferred tax assets and liabilities included in each statement of financial position presented; and

    b. The amount of deferred income or expense recognized in the statement of comprehensive income, if not otherwise apparent from changes in the statements of financial position.

7. Disclosure of the tax expense or benefit related to discontinued operations

8. Amount of income tax consequences of dividends proposed or declared before the authorization of the financial statement not recognized as a liability

9. Changes in the preacquisition deferred tax assets of the acquirer of a business combination due to the incorporation of the business acquired

10. Deferred tax assets of a business combination recognized after the acquisition date with a description of the event or change in circumstances

Disclosure must be made of the amount of deferred tax asset and the evidence supporting its presentation in the statement of financial position, when both these conditions exist: utilization is dependent upon future profitability beyond that assured by the future reversal of taxable temporary differences, *and* the entity has suffered a loss in either the current period or the preceding period in the jurisdiction to which the deferred tax asset relates.

The nature of potential income tax consequences related to the payments of dividends must also be disclosed.

Examples of informative disclosures about income tax expense

The disclosure requirements imposed by IAS 12 are extensive and in some instances complicated. The following examples have been adapted from the standard itself, with some modifications.

Note: Income tax expense

Major components of the provisions for income taxes are as follows:

	2011	2012
Current tax expense	€75,500	€82,450
Deferred tax expense (benefit), relating to the origination and reversal of temporary differences	12,300	(16,275)
Effect on previously provided deferred tax assets and liabilities resulting from increase in statutory tax rates	--	7,600
Total tax provision for the period	€87,800	€73,775

The aggregate current and deferred income tax expense (benefit) that was charged (credited) to stockholders' equity for the periods

	2011	2012
Current tax, related to correction of error	€(5,200)	€ --
Deferred tax, related to revaluation of investments	--	45,000
Total	€(5,200)	€45,000

The relationship between tax expense and accounting profit is explained by the following reconciliations:

NOTE: Only one required.

	2011	2012
Accounting profit	€167,907	€132,398
Tax at statutory rate (43% in 2010; 49% in 2011)	€ 72,200	€ 64,875
Tax effect of expenses which are not deductible:		
Charitable contributions	600	1,300
Civil fines imposed on the entity	15,000	
Effect on previously provided deferred tax assets and liabilities resulting from increase in statutory rates	--	7,600
Total tax provision for the period	€ 87,800	€ 73,775
Statutory tax rate	43.0%	49.0%
Tax effect of expenses which are not deductible:		
Charitable contributions	0.4	1.0
Civil fines imposed on the entity	8.9	--
Effect on previously provided deferred tax assets and liabilities resulting from increase in statutory rates	--	5.7
Total tax provision for the period	52.3%	55.7%

In 2012, the government imposed a 14% surcharge on the income tax, which has affected 2012 current tax expense as well as the recorded amounts of deferred tax assets and liabilities, since when these benefits are ultimately received or settled, the new higher tax rates will be applicable.

Deferred tax assets and liabilities included in the accompanying statements of financial position as of December 31, 2011 and 2012 are as follows, as classified by categories of temporary differences:

	2011	2012
Accelerated depreciation for tax purposes	€26,890	€22,300
Liabilities for postretirement health care that are deductible only when paid	(15,675)	(19,420)
Product development costs deducted from taxable profits in prior years	2,500	--
Revaluation of fixed assets, net of accumulated depreciation	--	2,160
Deferred tax liability, net	€13,715	€5,040

Examples of Financial Statement Disclosures

Clariant Group
Period ending December 2010

1.18 Current income tax

The taxable profit (loss) of Group companies, on which the reporting period's income tax payable (recoverable) is calculated using applicable local tax rates and is determined in accordance with the rules established by the taxation authorities of the countries in which they operate. Current income taxes for current and prior periods, to the extent they are unpaid, are recognized as liabilities.

In case income taxes already paid in respect of current and prior periods exceed the income tax liability amount of those periods, the exceeding amounts are recognized as assets. Current income tax receivables and current income tax liabilities are offset if there is a legally enforceable right to set off the recognized amounts and if there is the intention to settle on a net basis or to realize the asset and settle the liability simultaneously.

1.19 Deferred income tax

Deferred income tax is calculated using the comprehensive liability method. This method calculates a deferred tax asset or liability on the temporary differences that arise between the recognition of items in the balance sheets of the Group companies used for tax purposes and the one prepared for consolidation purposes. An exception is that no deferred income tax is calculated for the temporary differences in investments in Group companies, provided that the investor (parent company) is able to control the timing of the reversal of the temporary difference and it is probable that the temporary differences will not reverse in the foreseeable future. Furthermore, withholding taxes or other taxes on the eventual distribution of retained earnings of Group companies are only taken into account when a dividend has been planned, since generally the retained earnings are reinvested.

Deferred taxes, calculated using applicable local tax rates, are included in noncurrent assets and noncurrent liabilities, with any changes during the year recorded in the income statement. Changes in deferred taxes on items that are recognized in "Other comprehensive income" are recorded in "Other comprehensive income."

Deferred income tax is determined using tax rates (and laws) that have been enacted or substantively enacted by the balance sheet date and are expected to apply when the related deferred income tax asset is realized or the deferred income tax liability is settled.

Deferred income tax assets are recognized to the extent that it is probable that future taxable profits will be available against which the temporary differences or the tax losses carried forward can be utilized.

Deferred income tax assets and liabilities are offset when there is a legally enforceable right to offset current tax assets against current tax liabilities and when the deferred income taxes relate to the same taxation authority.

9. Taxes

CHF mn	2010	2009
Current income taxes	(123)	(102)
Deferred income taxes	71	29
	(52)	(73)

The main elements contributing to the difference between the Group's overall expected tax expense/rate and the effective tax expense/rate for continuing operations are

	2010		2009	
	CHF mn	%	CHF mn	%
Income/loss before tax	243		(121)	
Expected tax expense/rate[1]	(81)	33.3	(13)	(10.7)
Effect of taxes on items not tax-deductible	(88)	36.2	(69)	(57.1)
Effect of utilization and changes in recognition of tax losses and tax credits	98	(40.3)	22	18.2
Effect of tax losses and tax credits of current year not recognized	(13)	5.4	(23)	(19.9)
Effect of adjustments to current taxes of prior periods	5	(2.1)	2	1.7
Effect of tax-exempt income	31	(12.7)	10	8.3
Effect of other items	(4)	1.6)	(2)	(1.7)
Effective tax expense/rate	(52)	21.4	(73)	60.3

The deviation in the expected tax rate from 2010 to 2009 is explained by the fact that in 2010 a pretax profit was reported, whereas in 2009 there was a pretax loss. In 2010 a number of companies operating in high-tax countries reported a higher profit as compared to a lower profit or a loss in 2009. In 2011, Clariant expects the expected tax rate to be similar to that of 2010. Operations in Germany, Italy, Brazil, Japan, India, and the United States are expected to contribute most importantly to the pretax income.

The movement of the net deferred tax balance is as follows:

CHF mn	PPE and intangible assets	Retirement benefit obligations	Tax losses and tax credits	Other accruals and provisions	Total	Thereof offset with deferred tax assets within the same jurisdiction	Total
Deferred tax assets at January 1, 2009	32	55	41	91	219	(152)	67
Deferred tax liabilities at January 1, 2009	(221)	(1)	--	(64)	(286)	152	(134)
Net deferred tax balance at January 1, 2009	**(189)**	**54**	**41**	**27**	**(67)**	**--**	**(67)**
Charged/credited to income		(4)	(3)	36	29		
Exchange rate differences	(8)	1	(2)	10	1		

---

[1] *Calculated based on the income before tax of each subsidiary (weighted-average).*

CHF mn	PPE and intangible assets	Retirement benefit obligations	Tax losses and tax credits	Other accruals and provisions	Total	Thereof offset with deferred tax assets within the same jurisdiction	Total
Net deferred tax balance at December 31, 2009	**(197)**	**51**	**36**	**73**	**(37)**		
Deferred tax assets at December 31, 2009	31	55	36	106	225	(150)	75
Deferred tax liabilities at December 31, 2009	(228)	(1)	--	(33)	(262)	150	(112)
Net deferred tax balance at January 1, 2010	**(197)**	**51**	**36**	**73**	**(37)**	**--**	**(37)**
Charged/credited to income	8	4	77	(18)	71		
Exchange rate differences	21	(6)	(13)	(2)	-		
Net deferred tax balance at December 31, 2010	**(168)**	**49**	**100**	**53**	**34**		
Deferred tax assets at December 31, 2010	35	50	1001	97	282	(163)	119
Deferred tax liabilities at December 31, 2010	(203)	(1)	--	(44)	(248)	152	(84)

Of the deferred tax assets capitalized on tax losses, CHF 22 million refer to tax losses of the French subsidiaries (2009: CHF 17 million), CHF 16 million to tax losses of the Italian subsidiaries (2009: CHF 8 million) and CHF 26 million to tax losses of the US subsidiaries (2009: CHF 0). Clariant considers it highly probable that these tax losses can be recovered.

The total of temporary differences on investments in subsidiaries, for which no deferred taxes were calculated, was CHF 390 million at December 31, 2010 (CHF 643 million at December 31, 2009).

Deferred income tax liabilities have not been established for the withholding tax and other taxes that would be payable on the unremitted earnings of certain foreign subsidiaries, as such amounts are currently regarded as permanently reinvested. These unremitted earnings totalled CHF 1,599 million at the end of 2010 (2009: CHF 1,782 million).

The tax losses on which no deferred tax assets are recognized are reviewed for recoverability at each balance sheet date. The largest part of these tax losses arose in Switzerland (with a weighted-average tax rate of 19.1 percent) and in the United States (with a tax rate of 40.1%) and is not deemed to be recoverable before they expire.

Tax losses on which no deferred tax assets were recognized are as follows:

CHF mn	12/31/2010	12/31/2009
Expiry by: 2010		1
2011	6	53
2012	4	5
2013	1	16
2014	5	
after 2014 (2009: after 2013)	687	1,192
Total	703	1,267
Unrecognized tax credits	47	43

The tax credits in the amount of CHF 12 million expire between 2011 and 2014. The remaining tax credits of CHF 35 million expire in and after 2015.

US GAAP COMPARISON

Accounting for income taxes under US GAAP is very similar to IFRS. Both standards use an asset and liability approach to calculating deferred taxes where temporary differences between tax and book basis result in deferred tax assets or liabilities, with some exceptions.

Under US GAAP, deferred taxes are not recognized on foreign earnings if an entity does not intend to remit the earning for an indefinite period of time.

US GAAP contains specific, prescriptive guidance on how to calculate and report liabilities for unrecognized tax positions (that is, potential tax in excess of what was claimed on a tax return). This is a two-step process. First, the entity must determine if it the tax position is more likely than not to be sustained upon examination by the tax authority. The assumptions underlying the judgment of more-likely-than-not are twofold (1) the tax authority has all the information that the company has, and (2) will have taken the resolution to the mechanism of last resort (e.g., superior tax court). If it is more likely than not, the second step calculates the position. An entity must take an inventory of all their uncertain tax positions and assign probabilities to settlement outcomes. The amount to recognize is the amount with the cumulative probably greater than 50%. In other words, the amounts that accompany the probabilities are summed from lowest probability to highest until the cumulative probability exceeds 50%. This sum is then recorded as a liability.

Other areas of differences include that, under US GAAP, deferred tax assets are recognized in full and are then subject to an allowance based on the amount that is realizable. This valuation allowance is disclosed. The tax rate used can only be what the currently enacted law prescribes. Anticipated rates, no matter how probable, are not applied until the law has been signed into effect by the relevant authority.

27 EARNINGS PER SHARE

INTRODUCTION

Many investors and other consumers of corporate financial information find comfort in identifying a "shorthand" means of measuring an entity's performance, notwithstanding oft-voiced concerns that any condensed gauge of earnings inevitably risks being incomplete, and even misleading, as a picture of the entity's results for the period. Investors in particular are devoted users of earning per share data, which is taken by many to be the single best predictor of the entity's future performance. Ultimately, recognizing that such statistics were being computed in widely varying ways and then broadly disseminated, the accounting standard setters decided to at least impose uniform practices.

The IFRS governing the calculation and disclosure of earnings per share (EPS) is IAS 33. It requires that one measure—or two measures in the case of those reporting entities having complex capital structures—be presented for each period for which a statement of profit or loss and other comprehensive income is being reported. According to IAS 1, if an entity presents the components of profit or loss in a separate statement of profit or loss, it should present basic and fully diluted earnings per share (or one earnings per share measure, if applicable) in that separate statement. The principal goal in these measures is to ensure that the number of shares used in the computation(s) fully reflects the impact of dilutive securities, including those which may not be outstanding during the period, but which, if they were to become outstanding, would impact the actual future earnings available for allocation to current shareholders.

When the entity's capital structure is simple, EPS is computed by simply dividing profit or loss by the average number of outstanding equity shares. The computation becomes more complicated with the existence of securities that, while not presently equity shares, have the potential of causing additional equity shares to be issued in future, thereby diluting each currently outstanding share's claim to future earnings. Examples of such dilutive securities include convertible preference shares and convertible debt, as well as various options and warrants. It was long recognized that if calculated earnings per share were to ignore these potentially dilutive securities, there would be a great risk of misleading current shareholders regarding their claim to future earnings of the reporting entity.

Sources of IFRS
IAS 33

SCOPE

IAS 33 states that the standard's applicability is both to entities whose ordinary shares or potential ordinary shares are publicly traded, and those entities that are in the process of issuing ordinary shares or potential ordinary shares in public securities markets. While IAS 33 does not define the point in the share issuance process when these requirements become effective, in practice this ambiguity has not been a source of difficulty.

Some private entities wish to report a statistical measure of performance, and often choose to use EPS as the well-understood yardstick to employ. While these entities are not required to issue EPS data, when they elect to do so they must also comply with the requirements of IAS 33.

In situations when both parent company and consolidated financial statements are presented, IAS 33 stipulates that the information called for by this standard need only be presented for consolidated information. The reason for this rule is that users of financial statements of a parent company are interested in the results of operations of the group as a whole, as opposed to the parent company on a stand-alone basis. Of course, nothing prevents the entity from also presenting the parent-only information, including EPS, should it choose to do so. Again, the requirements of IAS 33 would have to be met by those making such an election.

DEFINITIONS OF TERMS

A number of terms used in a discussion of earnings per share have special meanings in that context. When used, they are intended to have the meanings given in the following definitions.

Antidilution. An increase in earnings per share or reduction in loss per share, resulting from the inclusion of potentially dilutive securities, in EPS calculations. The assumption is that convertible securities are converted, options or warrants are exercised, or that ordinary shares are issued upon the satisfaction of specified conditions.

Basic earnings per share. The amount of profit or loss for the period that is attributable to each ordinary share that is outstanding during all or part of the period.

Call price. The amount at which a security may be redeemed by the issuer at the issuer's option.

Contingently issuable ordinary shares issuance. A possible issuance of ordinary shares, for little or no cash or other consideration, that is dependent on the satisfaction of certain conditions set forth in a contingent share agreement.

Conversion price. The price that determines the number of ordinary shares into which a security is convertible. For example, €100 face value of debt convertible into five ordinary shares would be stated to have a conversion price of €20.

Conversion rate. The ratio of the number of ordinary shares issuable on conversion to a unit of convertible security. For example, a preference share may be convertible at the rate of three ordinary shares for each preference share.

Conversion value. The current market value of the ordinary shares obtainable on conversion of a convertible security, after deducting any cash payment required on conversion.

Diluted earnings per share. The amount of net profit for the period per share, reflecting the maximum dilutions that would have resulted from conversions, exercises, and other contingent issuances that individually would have decreased earnings per share and in the aggregate would have had a dilutive effect.

Dilution. A reduction in earnings per share or an increase in net loss per share, resulting from the assumption that convertible securities have been converted and/or that options and warrants have been exercised, or other contingent shares have been issued on the fulfillment of certain conditions. Securities that would cause such earnings dilution are referred to as dilutive securities.

Dual presentation. The presentation with equal prominence of two different earnings per share amounts in the statement of profit or loss and comprehensive income: One is basic earnings per share; the other is diluted earnings per share.

Earnings per share. The amount of earnings (profit or loss) for a period attributable to each ordinary share (common share). It should be used without qualifying language (e.g., diluted) only when no potentially dilutive convertible securities, options, warrants, or other agreements providing for contingent issuances of ordinary shares are outstanding.

Exercise price. The amount that must be paid for an ordinary share on exercise of a share option or warrant.

If-converted method. A method of computing earnings per share data that assumes conversion of convertible securities as of the beginning of the earliest period reported (or at time of issuance, if later). This method was mandated under US GAAP and can be analogized to IFRS when appropriate.

Option. The right to purchase ordinary shares in accordance with an agreement upon payment of a specified amount including, but not limited to, options granted to and share purchase agreements entered into with employees.

Ordinary shares. Those shares that are subordinate to all other shares of the issuer. Also known as common shares. Ordinary shares participate in profit for the period only after other types of shares such as preference shares have participated. An entity may have more than one class of ordinary shares; ordinary shares of the same class have the same rights as to dividends.

Potential ordinary shares. A financial instrument or other contract which could result in the issuance of ordinary shares to the holder. Examples include convertible debt or preferred shares, warrants, options, and employee share purchase plans.

Put option (on ordinary shares). Contract which gives the holder the right to sell ordinary shares held, at a specified price, usually for a limited stipulated time period.

Redemption price. The amount at which a security is required to be redeemed at maturity or under a sinking-fund arrangement.

Time of issuance. In general, the date when agreement as to terms of share issuance has been reached and announced, even though such agreement is subject to certain further actions, such as directors' or shareholders' approval.

Treasury share method. A method of recognizing the use of proceeds that would be obtained on exercise of options and warrants in computing earnings per share. It assumes that any proceeds would be used to purchase ordinary shares at the average market price.

Warrant. A security giving the holder the right to purchase ordinary shares in accordance with the terms of the instrument, usually on payment of a specified amount.

Weighted-average number of shares. The number of shares determined by relating the portion of time within a reporting period that a particular number of shares of a certain security has been outstanding to the total time in that period. For example, if 100 shares of a certain security were outstanding during the first quarter of a fiscal year and 300 shares were outstanding during the balance of the year, the weighted-average number of outstanding shares would be 250 [= $(100 \times 1/4) + (300 \times 3/4)$].

CONCEPTS, RULES, AND EXAMPLES

Simple Capital Structure

A simple capital structure may be said to exist either when the capital structure consists solely of ordinary shares or when it includes no potential ordinary shares, which could be in the form of options, warrants, or other rights, that on conversion or exercise could, in the aggregate, dilute earnings per share. Dilutive securities are essentially those that exhibit the rights of debt or other senior security holders (including warrants and options) and which have the potential on their issuance to reduce the earnings per share.

Computational guidelines. In its simplest form, the EPS calculation is profit or loss divided by the weighted-average number of ordinary shares outstanding. The objective of the EPS calculation is to determine the amount of earnings attributable to each ordinary share. Complexities arise because profit or loss does not necessarily represent the earnings available to the ordinary equity holder, and a simple weighted-average of ordinary shares outstanding does not necessarily reflect the true nature of the situation. Adjustments can take the form of manipulations of the numerator or of the denominator of the formula used to compute EPS, as discussed in the following paragraphs.

Numerator. The profit or loss figure used as the numerator in any of the EPS computations must reflect any claims against it by holders of senior securities. The justification for this reduction is that the claims of the senior securities must be satisfied before any income is available to the ordinary shareholder. These senior securities are usually in the form of preference shares, and the deduction from profit or loss is the amount of the dividend declared during the year on the preference shares. If the preference shares are cumulative, the dividend is to be deducted from profit (or added to the loss), whether it is declared or not. If preference shares do not have a cumulative right to dividends and current period dividends have been omitted, such dividends should not be deducted in computing EPS. Cumulative dividends in arrears that are paid currently do not affect the calculation of EPS in the current period, since such dividends have already been considered in prior periods' EPS computations. However, the amount in arrears should be disclosed, as should all of the other effects of the rights given to senior securities on the EPS calculation.

Denominator. The weighted-average number of ordinary shares outstanding is used so that the effect of increases or decreases in outstanding shares on EPS data is related to the portion of the period during which the related consideration affected operations. The difficulty in computing the weighted-average exists because of the effect that various transactions have on the computation of ordinary shares outstanding. Although it is impossible to analyze all the possibilities, the following discussion presents some of the more common transactions affecting the number of ordinary shares outstanding. The theoretical construct set forth in these relatively simple examples can be followed in all other situations.

If a company reacquires its own shares in countries where it is legally permissible to do so, the number of shares reacquired (referred to as treasury shares) should be excluded from EPS calculations from the date of acquisition. The same computational approach holds for the issuance of ordinary shares during the period. The number of shares newly issued is included in the computation only for the period after their issuance date. The logic for this treatment is that since the consideration for the shares was not available to the reporting entity, and hence could not contribute to the generation of earnings, until the shares were issued, the shares should not be included in the EPS computation prior to issuance. This same logic applies to the reacquired shares because the consideration expended in the repurchase of those shares was no longer available to generate earnings after the reacquisition date.

A share dividend (bonus issue) or a share split does not generate additional resources or consideration, but it does increase the number of shares outstanding. The increase in shares as a result of a share split or dividend, or the decrease in shares as a result of a reverse split, should be given retroactive recognition for all periods presented. Thus, even if a share dividend or split occurs at the end of the period, it is considered effective for the entire period of each (i.e., current and historical) period presented. The reasoning is that a share dividend or split has no effect on the ownership percentage of ordinary shares, and likewise has no impact on the resources available for productive investment by the reporting entity. As such, to show a dilution in the EPS in the period of the split or dividend would erroneously give the impression of a decline in profitability when in fact it was merely an increase in the shares outstanding due to the share dividend or split. Furthermore, financial statement users' frame of reference is the number of shares outstanding at the end of the reporting period, including shares resulting from the split or dividend, and using this in computing all periods' EPS serves to most effectively communicate to them.

IAS 33 carries this logic one step further by requiring the disclosure of pro forma (adjusted) amounts of basic and diluted earnings per share for the period in case of issue of shares with no corresponding change in resources (e.g., share dividends or splits) occurring *after* the end of the reporting period, *but before* the issuance of the financial statements. The reason given is that the nondisclosure of such transactions would affect the ability of the users of the financial statements to make proper evaluations and decisions. It is to be noted, however, that the EPS numbers as presented in the statement of profit or loss and other comprehensive income are not required by IAS 33 to be retroactively adjusted because such transactions do not reflect the amount of capital used to produce the net profit or loss for the period.

Complications also arise when a business combination occurs during the period. In a combination accounted for as an acquisition (the only method allowable since IFRS 3 eliminated the pooling of interests method), the shares issued in connection with a business combination are considered issued and outstanding as of the date of acquisition and the income of the acquired company is included only for the period after acquisition.

IAS 33 recognizes that in certain countries it is permissible for ordinary shares to be issued in partly paid form, and the standard accordingly stipulates that partly paid instruments should be included as ordinary share equivalents to the extent to which they carry rights (during the financial reporting year) to participate in dividends in the same manner as fully paid shares. Further, in the case of contingently issuable shares (i.e., ordinary shares issuable on fulfillment of certain conditions, such as achieving a certain level of profits or sales), IAS 33 requires that such shares be considered outstanding and included in the computation of basic earnings per share only when all the required conditions have been satisfied.

IAS 33 gives examples of situations where ordinary shares may be issued, or the number of shares outstanding may be reduced, without causing corresponding changes in resources of the corporation. Such examples include bonus issues, a bonus element in other issues such as a rights issue (to existing shareholders), a share split, a reverse share split, and a capital reduction without a corresponding refund of capital. In all such cases the number of ordinary shares outstanding before the event is adjusted, as if the event had occurred at the beginning of the earliest period reported. For instance, in a "5-for-4 bonus issue" the number of shares outstanding prior to the issue is multiplied by a factor of 1.25. These and other situations are summarized in the tabular list that follows.

Weighted-Average (W/A) Computation	
Transaction	*Effect on W/A computation*
Ordinary shares outstanding at the beginning of the period	Increase number of shares outstanding by the number of shares
Issuance of ordinary shares during the period	Increase number of shares outstanding by the number of shares issued weighted by the portion of the year the ordinary shares are outstanding
Conversion into ordinary shares	Increase number of shares outstanding by the number of shares converted weighted by the portion of the year shares are outstanding
Company reacquires its shares	Decrease number of shares outstanding by number of shares reacquired times portion of the year outstanding
Share dividend or split	Increase number of shares outstanding by number of shares issued or increased due to the split
Reverse split	Decrease number of shares outstanding by decrease in shares
Pooling of interest	Increase number of shares outstanding by number of shares issued
Acquisition	Increase number of shares outstanding by number of shares issued weighted by the portion of year since the date of acquisition

Rights offerings are used to raise additional capital from existing shareholders. These involve the granting of rights in proportion to the number of shares owned by each shareholder (e.g., one right for each 100 shares held). The right gives the holder the opportunity to purchase a share at a discounted value, as an inducement to invest further in the entity, and in recognition of the fact that, generally, rights offerings are less costly as a means of floating more shares, versus open market transactions which involve fees to brokers. In the case of rights shares, the number of ordinary shares to be used in calculating basic EPS is the number of ordinary shares outstanding prior to the issue, multiplied by the following factor:

$$\frac{\text{Fair value immediately prior to the exercise of the rights}}{\text{Theoretical ex-rights fair value}}$$

There are several ways to compute the theoretical value of the shares on an ex-rights basis. IAS 33 suggests that this be derived by adding the aggregate fair value of the shares immediately prior to exercise of the rights to the proceeds from the exercise, and dividing the total by the number of shares outstanding after exercise.

To illustrate, consider that the entity currently has 10,000 shares outstanding, with a market value of €15 per share, when it offers each holder rights to acquire one new share at €10 for each four shares held. The theoretical value ex-rights would be given as follows:

$$\frac{(10,000 \times €15) + (2,500 \times €10)}{12,500} = \frac{€175,000}{12,500} = €14$$

Thus, the ex-rights value of the ordinary shares is €14 each.

The foregoing do not characterize all possible complexities arising in the EPS computation; however, most of the others occur under a complex structure which is considered in the following section of this chapter. The illustration below applies the foregoing concepts to a simple capital structure.

Example of EPS computation—Simple capital structure

Assume the following information:

Numerator information			*Denominator information*	
a. Profit from continuing operations	€130,000	a. Ordinary shares outstanding January 1, 2011	100,000
b. Loss on discontinued operations	30,000	b. Shares issued for cash April 1, 2011	20,000
c. Profit for the year	100,000	c. Shares issued in 10% share dividend declared in July 2011	12,000
d. 6% cumulative preference shares, €100 par, 1,000 shares issued and outstanding	100,000	d. Treasury shares purchased October 1, 2011	10,000

When calculating the numerator, the claims of senior securities (i.e., preference shares) should be deducted to arrive at the earnings attributable to ordinary equity holders. In this example the preference shares are cumulative. Thus, regardless of whether or not the board of directors declares a preference dividend, holders of the preference shares have a claim of €6,000 (1,000 shares × €100 × 6%) against 2011 earnings. Therefore, €6,000 must be deducted from the numerator to arrive at profit or loss attributable to the owners of ordinary shares.

Note that any cumulative preference dividends in arrears are ignored in computing this period's EPS since they would have been incorporated into previous periods' EPS calculations. Also note that this €6,000 would have been deducted for noncumulative preferred only if a dividend of this amount had been declared during the period.

There may be various complications resulting from the existence, issuance, or redemption of preferred shares. Thus, if "increasing rate" preferred shares are outstanding—where contractually the dividend rate is lower in early years and higher in later years—the amount of preferred dividends in the early years must be adjusted in order to accrete the value of later, increased dividends, using an effective yield method akin to that used to amortize bond discount. If a premium is paid to preferred shareholders to retire the shares during the reporting period, this payment is treated as additional preferred dividends paid for purposes of EPS computations. Similarly, if a premium is paid (in cash or in terms of improved conversion terms) to encourage the conversion of convertible preferred shares, that payment (including the fair value of additional ordinary shares granted as an inducement) is included in the preferred dividends paid in the reporting period, thereby reducing earnings allocable to ordinary shares for EPS calculation purposes. Contrariwise, if preferred shares are redeemed at a value lower than carrying (book) amount—admittedly, not a very likely occurrence—that amount is used to reduce earnings available for ordinary equity holders in the period, thereby increasing EPS.

The EPS calculations for the foregoing fact pattern follow.

Earnings per ordinary share

On profit from continuing operations = (€130,000 – €6,000 preference dividends) ÷ Weighted number of ordinary shares outstanding (see below) = €1.00

On profit for the year = (€130,000 – €30,000 – €6,000) ÷ Weighted number of ordinary shares outstanding (see below) = €0.76

Only the EPS amounts relating to the parent company, in the case of consolidated (group) financial statements, must be provided.

The computation of the denominator is based on the weighted-average number of ordinary shares outstanding. Recall that use of a simple average (e.g., the sum of year-beginning and year-end outstanding shares, divided by two) is not considered appropriate because it fails to accurately give effect to various complexities. The table below illustrates one way of computing the weighted-average number of shares outstanding. Note that, had share issuances occurred mid-month, the weighted-average number of shares would have been based on the number of days elapsing between events.

Item	*Number of shares actually outstanding*	*Fraction of the year outstanding*	*Shares times fraction of the year*
Number of shares as of beginning of the year January 1, 2011	110,000 [100,000 + 10%(100,000)]	12/12	110,000
Shares issued April 1, 2011	22,000 [20,000 + 10%(20,000)]	9/12	16,500
Treasury shares purchased October 1, 2011	(10,000)	3/12	(2,500)
Weighted-average number of ordinary shares outstanding			124,000

Recall that the share dividend declared in July is considered to be retroactive to the beginning of the year. Thus, for the period January 1, 2011 through April 1, 2011, 110,000 shares are considered to be outstanding. When shares are issued, they are included in the weighted-average beginning with the date of issuance. The share dividend applicable to these newly issued shares is also assumed to have existed for the same period. Thus, we can see that of the 12,000 share dividend, 10,000 shares relate to the beginning balance and 2,000 shares to the new issuance (10% of 100,000 and 20,000, respectively). The purchase of the treasury shares requires that these shares be excluded from the calculation for the remainder of the period after their acquisition date. The figure is subtracted from the calculation because the shares were purchased from those outstanding prior to acquisition. To complete the example, we divided the previously derived numerator by the weighted-average number of ordinary shares outstanding to arrive at EPS, which is [(€100,000 − €6,000) ÷ 124,000 =] €0.76.

Reporting a €0.24 loss per share (€30,000 ÷ 124,000) due to the discontinued operations is optional. The numbers computed above for the EPS based on profit for the year are the only presentation required in the statement of profit or loss and other comprehensive income (or separate statement of profit or loss, if presented).

Complex Capital Structure

The computation of EPS under a complex capital structure involves all of the complexities discussed under the simple structure and many more. By definition, a complex capital structure is one that has dilutive potential ordinary shares, which are shares or other instruments that have the potential to be converted or exercised and thereby reduce EPS. The effects of any antidilutive potential ordinary shares (those that would increase EPS) is not to be included in the computation of diluted earnings per share. Thus, diluted EPS can never provide a more favorable impression of financial performance than does the basic EPS.

Note that a complex structure requires dual presentation of both basic EPS and diluted EPS even when the basic earnings per share is a loss per share. Under the current standard, both basic and diluted EPS must be presented, unless diluted EPS would be antidilutive.

For the purposes of calculating diluted EPS, the profit or loss attributable to ordinary equity holders and the weighted-average number of ordinary shares outstanding should be adjusted for the effects of the dilutive potential ordinary shares. That is, the presumption is that the dilutive securities have been converted or exercised, with ordinary shares being outstanding for the entire period, and with the effects of the dilution removed from earnings (e.g., interest or dividends). In removing the effects of dilutive securities that in fact were outstanding during the period, the associated tax effects must also be eliminated, and all consequent changes—such as employee profit-sharing contributions that are based on reported profit or loss—must similarly be adjusted.

According to IAS 33, the numerator, representing the profit or loss attributable to the ordinary equity holders for the period, should be adjusted by the after-tax effect, if any, of the following items:

1. Interest recognized in the period for the convertible debt which constitutes dilutive potential ordinary shares;
2. Any dividends recognized in the period for the convertible preferred shares which constitute dilutive potential ordinary shares, where those dividends have been deducted in arriving at net profit attributable to ordinary equity holders; and
3. Any other, consequential changes in profit or loss that would result from the conversion of the dilutive potential ordinary shares.

For example, the conversion of debentures into ordinary shares will reduce interest expense which in turn will cause an increase in the profit for the period. This will have a consequential effect on contributions based on the profit figure, for example, the employer's contribution to an employee profit-sharing plan. The effect of such consequential changes on profit or loss available for ordinary equity holders should be considered in the computation of the numerator of the diluted EPS ratio.

The denominator, which has the weighted number of ordinary shares, should be adjusted (increased) by the weighted-average number of ordinary shares that would have been outstanding assuming the conversion of all dilutive potential ordinary shares.

Example

To illustrate, consider Chelsea Corporation, which has 100,000 shares of ordinary shares outstanding the entire period. It also has convertible debentures outstanding, on which interest of €30,000 was paid during the year. The debentures are convertible into 100,000 shares. Profit after tax (effective rate is 30%) amounts to €15,000, which is net of an employee profit-sharing contribution of €10,000, determined as 40% of after-tax income. Basic EPS is €15,000 ÷ 100,000 shares = €0.15. Diluted EPS assumes that the debentures were converted at the beginning of the year, thereby averting €30,000 of interest which, after tax effect, would add €21,000 to net results for the year. Conversion also would add 50,000 shares, for a total of 200,000 shares outstanding. Furthermore, had operating results been boosted by the €21,000 of avoided after-tax interest cost, the employee profit sharing would have increased by €21,000 × 40% = €8,400, producing net results for the year of €15,000 + €21,000 − €8,400 = €27,600. Diluted EPS is thus €27,600 ÷ 200,000 = €0.138. Since this is truly dilutive, IFRS requires presentation of this amount.

Determining Dilution Effects

In the foregoing example, the assumed conversion of the convertible debentures proved to be dilutive. If it had been *antidilutive,* presentation of the (more favorable) diluted EPS would not be permitted under IFRS. To ascertain whether the effect would be dilutive or antidilutive, each potential ordinary share issue (i.e., each convertible debenture, convertible preferred, or other issuance outstanding having distinct terms) must be evaluated separately from other potential ordinary share issuances. Since the interactions among potential ordinary share issues might cause diluted EPS to be moderated under certain circumstances, it is important that each issue be considered in the order of decreasing effect on dilution. In other words, the most dilutive of the potential ordinary share issues must be dealt with first, then the next most dilutive, and so on.

Potential ordinary shares are generally deemed to have been outstanding ordinary shares for the entire reporting period. However, if the potential shares were only first issued, or became expired or were otherwise cancelled during the reporting period, then the related ordinary shares are deemed to have been outstanding for only a portion of the reporting period. Similarly, if potential share are exercised during the period, then for that part of the year the actual shares outstanding are included for purposes of determining basic EPS, and the potential (i.e., unexercised) shares are used in the determination of diluted EPS by deeming these to have been exercised or converted for only that fraction of the year before the exercise occurred.

To determine the sequencing of the dilution analysis, it is necessary to use a "trial and error" approach. However, options and warrants should be dealt with first, since these will not affect the numerator of the EPS equation, and thus are most dilutive in their impact. Convertible securities are dealt with subsequently, and these issues will affect both numerator and denominator, with varying dilutive effects.

Options and warrants. The exercise of options and warrants results in proceeds being received by the reporting entity. If actual exercise occurs, of course, the entity has resources which it will, logically, put to productive use, thereby increasing earnings to be enjoyed by ordinary equity holders (both those previously existing and those resulting from exercising their options and warrants). However, the presumed exercise for purposes of diluted EPS computations does not invoke actual resources being received, and earnings are not enhanced as they might have been in the case of actual exercise. If this fact were not dealt with, diluted EPS would be unrealistically depressed since the number of assumed shares would be increased but earnings would reflect the lower, actual level of investment being utilized by the entity.

IFRS prescribes the use of the "treasury share method" to deal with the hypothetical proceeds from the presumed option and warrant exercises. This method assumes that the proceeds from the option and warrant exercises would have been used to repurchase outstanding shares, at the average prevailing market price during the reporting period. This assumed repurchase of shares eliminates the need to speculate as to what productive use the hypothetical proceeds from option and warrant exercise would be put, and also reduces the assumed number of outstanding shares for diluted EPS calculation.

Treasury Share (Stock) Method

Denominator must be increased by net dilution, as follows:

Net dilution = Shares issued – Shares repurchased

where

Shares issued = Proceeds received/Exercise price

Shares repurchased = Proceeds received/Average market price per share

---

IAS 33's "shortcut" way of expressing the required use of the "treasury share/stock method" is as follows: "The difference between the number of ordinary shares issued and the number of ordinary shares that would have been issued at the average market price of ordinary shares during the period shall be treated as an issue of ordinary shares for no consideration."

Example

Assume the reporting entity issued 1,000 ordinary shares to option holders who exercised their rights and paid €15,000 to the entity. During the reporting period, the average price of ordinary shares was €25. Using the proceeds of €15,000 to acquire shares at a per share cost of €25 would have resulted in the purchase of 600 shares. Thus, a net of 400 additional shares would be assumed outstanding for the year, at no net consideration to or from the entity.

In all cases where the exercise price is lower than the market price, assumed exercise will be dilutive and some portion of the shares will be deemed issued for no consideration. If the exercise price is greater than the average market price, the exercise should not be assumed since the result of this would be antidilutive.

Convertible instruments. Convertible instruments are assumed to be converted when the effect is dilutive. Convertible preferred shares will be dilutive if the preferred dividend declared (or, if cumulative, accumulated) in the current period is lower than the computed basic EPS. If the contrary situation exists, the impact of assumed conversion would be antidilutive, which is not permitted by IFRS.

Similarly, convertible debt is dilutive, and thus assumed to have been converted, if the after-tax interest, including any discount or premium amortization, is lower than the computed basic EPS. If the contrary situation exists, the assumption of conversion would be antidilutive, and thus not to be taken into account for diluted EPS computations.

While the term "if converted" is not explicitly employed by IAS 33, the methodology of the if-converted method is used for those securities that are currently sharing in the earnings of the company through the receipt of interest or dividends as senior securities but have the potential for sharing in the earnings as ordinary shares. The if-converted method logically recognizes that the convertible security can only share in the earnings of the company as one or the other, not as both. Thus, the dividends or interest less tax effects applicable to the convertible security as a senior security are not recognized in the profit or loss figure used to compute EPS, and the weighted-average number of shares is adjusted to reflect the conversion as of the beginning of the year (or date of issuance, if later). See the example of the if-converted method for illustration of treatment of convertible securities when they are issued during the period and therefore were not outstanding for the entire year.

Example of the if-converted method

Assume a net profit for the year of €50,000 and a weighted-average number of ordinary shares outstanding of 10,000. The following information is provided regarding the capital structure.

1. 7% convertible debt, 200 bonds each convertible into 40 ordinary shares. The bonds were outstanding the entire year. The income tax rate is 40%. The bonds were issued at par (€1,000 per bond). No bonds were converted during the year.
2. 4% convertible, cumulative preferred shares, par €100, 1,000 shares issued and outstanding. Each preferred share is convertible into 2 ordinary shares. The preferred shares were issued at par and were outstanding the entire year. No shares were converted during the year.

The first step is to compute the basic EPS, that is, assuming only the issued and outstanding ordinary shares. This figure is simply computed as €4.60 (€50,000 – €4,000 preferred dividends) ÷ (10,000 ordinary shares outstanding). The diluted EPS must be less than this amount for the capital structure to be considered complex and for a dual presentation of EPS to be necessary.

To determine the dilutive effect of the preferred shares an assumption (generally referred to as the if-converted method) is made that all of the preferred shares are converted at the earliest date that it could have been during the year. In this example, the date would be January 1. (If the preferred had been first issued during the year, the earliest date conversion could have occurred would have been the issuance date.) The effects of this assumption are twofold: (1) if the preferred is converted, there will be no preferred dividends of €4,000 for the year; and (2) there will be an additional 2,000 ordinary shares outstanding during the year (the conversion rate is 2 for 1 on 1,000 shares of preferred). Diluted EPS is computed, as follows, reflecting these two assumptions:

$$\frac{\text{Net profit for the year}}{\begin{array}{c}\text{Weighted-average of ordinary shares outstanding}\\ + \text{Shares issued upon conversion of preferred}\end{array}} = \frac{€50,000}{12,000 \text{ shares}} = €4.17$$

The convertible preferred is dilutive because it reduced EPS from €4.60 to €4.17. Accordingly, a dual presentation of EPS is required.

In the example, the convertible bonds are also assumed to have been converted at the beginning of the year. Again, the effects of the assumption are twofold: (1) if the bonds are converted, there will be no interest expense of €14,000 (7% × €200,000 face value), and (2) there will be an additional 8,000 shares (200 bonds × 40 shares) of ordinary shares outstanding during the year. One note of caution, however, must be mentioned; namely, the effect of not having €14,000 of interest expense will increase income, but it will also increase tax expense. Consequently, the net effect of not having interest expense of €14,000 is €8,400 [(1 − 0.40) × €14,000]. Diluted EPS is computed as follows, reflecting the dilutive preferred and the effects noted above for the convertible bonds.

$$\frac{\text{Net profit for the year} + \text{Interest expense (net of tax)}}{\begin{array}{c}\text{Weighted-average of ordinary shares outstanding} + \text{Shares issued}\\ \text{upon conversion of preferred shares and conversion of bonds}\end{array}} = \frac{€50,000 + €8,400}{20,000 \text{ shares}} = €2.92$$

The convertible debt is also dilutive, as it reduces EPS from €4.17 to €2.92. Together the convertible bonds and preferred reduced EPS from €4.60 to €2.92.

Contingent Issuances of Ordinary Shares

As for the computation of basic EPS, shares whose issuance is contingent on the occurrence of certain events are considered outstanding and included in the computation of diluted EPS only if the stipulated conditions have been met (i.e., the event has occurred). If at the end of the reporting period the triggering event has not occurred, issuance of the contingently issuable shares is not to be assumed.

Issuances that are dependent on certain conditions being met can be illustrated as follows. Assume that a condition or requirement exists in a contract to increase earnings over a period of time to a certain stipulated level and that, upon attainment of this targeted level of earnings, the issuance of shares is to take place. This is regarded as a contingent issuance of shares for purposes of applying IAS 33. If the condition is met at the end of the reporting period, the effect is included in basic EPS, even if the actual issuance takes place after year end (e.g., upon delivery of the audited financial statements, per terms of the contingency agreement).

If the condition must be met and then maintained for a subsequent period, such as for a two-year period, then the effect of the contingent issuance is excluded from basic EPS, but is included in diluted EPS. In other words, the contingent shares, which will not be issued until the defined condition is met for two consecutive years, are assumed to be met for diluted EPS computation if the condition is met at the end of the reporting period. Meeting the terms of the contingency for the current period forms the basis for the expectation that the terms may again be met in the subsequent period, which would trigger the issuance of the added shares, causing dilution of EPS.

In some instances the terms of the contingent issuance arrangement make reference to share prices over a period of time extending beyond the end of the reporting period. In such instances, if issuance is to be assumed for purposes of computing diluted EPS, only the prices or other data through the end of the reporting period should be deemed pertinent to the computation of diluted EPS. Basic EPS is not affected, of course, since the contingent condition is not met at the end of the reporting period.

IAS 33 identifies circumstances in which the issuance of contingent shares is dependent upon meeting both future earnings and future share price threshold levels. Reference must be made to both these conditions, as they exist at the end of the reporting period. If both threshold conditions are met, the effect of the contingently issuable shares is included in the computation of diluted EPS.

The standard also cites circumstances where the contingency does not pertain to market price of ordinary shares or to earnings of the reporting entity. One such example is the achievement of a defined business expansion goal, such as the opening of a targeted number of retail outlets; other examples could be the achievement of defined level of gross revenues, or development of a certain number of commercial contracts. For purposes of computing diluted EPS, the number of retail outlets, level of revenue, etc., at the end of the reporting period are to be presumed to remain constant until the expiration of the contingency period.

> **Example**
>
> Contingent shares will be issued at year-end 2012, with 1,000 shares issued for each retail outlet in excess of the number of outlets at the base date, year-end 2010. At year-end 2011, seven new outlets are open. Diluted EPS should include the assumed issuance of 7,000 additional shares. Basic EPS would not include this, since the contingency period has not ended and no new shares are yet required to be issued.

Contracts Which May Be Settled in Shares or for Cash

Increasingly complex financial instruments have been issued by entities in recent decades. Among these are obligations that can be settled in cash or by the issuance of shares, at the option of the debtor (the reporting entity). Thus, debt may be incurred and later settled, at the entity's option, by increasing the number of its ordinary shares outstanding, thereby diluting EPS but averting the need to disperse its resources for purposes of debt retirement.

Note that this situation differs from convertible debt, discussed above, inasmuch as it is the debtor, not the debt holder, which has the right to trigger the issuance of shares.

Per revised IAS 33, it is to be presumed that the debtor will elect to issue shares to retire this debt, if making that assumption results in a dilution of EPS. This is assumed for the calculation of diluted EPS, but is not included in basic EPS.

A similar result obtains when the reporting entity has written (i.e., issued) a call option to creditors, giving them the right to demand shares instead of cash in settlement of an obligation. Again, if dilutive, share issuance is to be presumed for diluted EPS computation purposes.

Written put options. The entity may also write put options giving shareholders the right to demand that the entity repurchase certain outstanding shares. Exercise is to be presumed if the effect is dilutive. According to IAS 33, the effect of this assumed exercise is to be calculated by assuming that the entity will issue enough new shares, at average market price, to raise the proceeds needed to honor the put option terms.

> **Example**
>
> If the entity is potentially required to buy back 25,000 of its currently outstanding shares at €40 each, it must assume that it will raise the required €1,000,000 cash by selling new ordinary shares into the market. If the average market price was €35 during the reporting period, it must be assumed that €1,000,000 ÷ €35 = 28,572 shares would be issued, for a net dilution of about 3,572 net ordinary shares, which is used to compute diluted EPS.

The foregoing guidance does not apply, however, to the situation where the reporting entity holds options, such as call options on its own shares, since it is presumed that the options would only be exercised under conditions where the impact would be antidilutive. That is, the entity only would choose to repurchase its optioned shares if the option price were below market price. Similarly, if the entity held a put contract (giving it the right to sell shares to the option writer) on its own shares, it would only exercise this option if the option price were above market price. In either instance, the effect of assumed exercise would likely be antidilutive.

Computations of Basic and Diluted Earnings Per Share

Using the data presented earlier in this chapter, the complete computation of basic and diluted EPS under IAS 33 is shown in the following table:

Items	EPS on outstanding ordinary shares (the "benchmark" EPS)		Basic		Diluted	
	Numerator	Denominator	Numerator	Denominator	Numerator	Denominator
Profit for the year	€50,000		€50,000		€50,000	
Preferred dividend	(4,000)					
Ordinary shs. outstanding		10,000 shs.		10,000 shs.		10,000 shs.
Conversion of preferred				2,000		2,000
Conversion of bonds					8,400	8,000
Totals	€46,000 ÷	10,000 shs.	€50,000 ÷	12,000 shs.	€58,400 ÷	20,000 shs.
EPS		€4.60		€4.17		€2.92

The preceding example was simplified to the extent that none of the convertible securities were, in fact, converted during the year. In most real situations, some or all of the securities may have been converted, and thus actual reported earnings (and basic EPS) would already have reflected the fact that preferred dividends were paid for only part of the year and/or that interest on convertible debt was accrued for only part of the year. These factors would need to be taken into consideration in developing a time-weighted numerator and denominator for the EPS equations.

Furthermore, the sequence followed in testing the dilution effects of each of several series of convertible securities may affect the outcome, although this is not always true. It is best to perform the sequential procedures illustrated above by computing the impact of each issue of potential ordinary shares from the most dilutive to the least dilutive. This rule also applies if convertible securities (for which the if-converted method will be applied) and options (for which the treasury stock approach will be applied) are outstanding simultaneously.

Finally, if some potential ordinary shares are only issuable on the occurrence of a contingency, conversion should be assumed for EPS computation purposes only to the extent that the conditions were met by the end of the reporting period. In effect, the end of the reporting period should be treated as if it were also the end of the contingency period.

No antidilution. No assumptions of conversion should be made if the effect would be antidilutive. As in the discussion above, it may be that the sequence in which the different issues or series of convertible or other instruments that are potentially ordinary shares are considered will affect the ultimate computation. The goal in computing diluted EPS is to calculate the maximum dilutive effect. The individual issues of convertible securities, options, and other items should be dealt with from the most dilutive to the least dilutive to effect this result.

Presentation and Disclosure Requirements under IAS 33

1. Entities should present both basic EPS and diluted EPS in the statement of profit or loss and other comprehensive income or in the statement of profit or loss, if presented separately, for each class of ordinary shares that has a different right to share in profit or loss for the period. Equal prominence should be given to both the basic EPS and diluted EPS figures for all periods presented.
2. An entity that reports a discontinued operation shall disclose the basic EPS and diluted EPS for the discontinued operation either in the statement of profit or loss and other comprehensive income or in the notes.
3. Entities should present basic EPS and diluted EPS even if the amounts disclosed are negative. In other words, the standard mandates disclosure of not just *earnings per share,* but even *loss per share* figures.
4. Entities should disclose amounts used as the numerator in calculating basic EPS and diluted EPS along with a reconciliation of those amounts to profit or loss for the period. Disclosure is also required of the weighted-average number of ordinary shares used as the denominator in calculating basic EPS and diluted EPS along with a reconciliation of these denominators to each other, including instruments (i.e. contingently issuable shares) that could potentially dilute basic EPS in the future, but were not included in the calculation of diluted EPS because they were antidilutive for the period(s) presented.

5. a. In addition to the disclosure of the figures for basic EPS and diluted EPS, as required above, if an entity chooses to disclose per share amounts using a reported component of the separate statement of profit or loss other than profit or loss for the period attributable to ordinary equity holders, such amounts should be calculated using the weighted-average number of ordinary shares determined in accordance with the requirements of IAS 33; this will ensure comparability of the per share amounts disclosed;
   b. In cases where an entity chooses to disclose the above per share amounts using a reported component of the separate statement of profit or loss, other than profit or loss for the year, a reconciliation is mandated by the standard, which should reconcile the difference between the reported component of profit or loss and profit or loss reported in the statement of profit or loss and comprehensive income or separate statement of profit or loss presented; and
   c. When additional disclosure is made by an entity of the above per share amounts, basic and diluted per share amounts should be disclosed with equal prominence (just as basic EPS and diluted EPS figures are given equal prominence).

6. Entities are encouraged to disclose the terms and conditions of financial instruments or contracts generating potential ordinary shares since such terms and conditions may determine whether or not any potential ordinary shares are dilutive and, if so, the effect on the weighted-average number of shares outstanding and any consequent adjustments to profit or loss attributable to the ordinary equity holders.
7. If changes (resulting from a bonus issue or share split, etc.) in the number of ordinary or potential ordinary shares occur after the end of the reporting period but before issuance of the financial statements, and the per share calculations reflect such changes in the number of shares, such a fact should be disclosed.

8. Entities are also encouraged to disclose a description of ordinary share transactions or potential ordinary share transactions other than capitalization issues and share splits, occurring after the end of the reporting period that are of such importance that nondisclosure would affect the ability of the users of the financial statements to make proper evaluations and decisions.

Examples of Financial Statement Disclosures

Nestlé Group.
Period Ending December 2010

16. Earnings per share

	2010	*2009*
Basic earnings per share (in CHF)	10.16	2.92
Net profit (in millions of CHF)	34,233	10,428
Weighted-average number of shares outstanding (in millions of units)	3,371	3.572
Fully diluted earnings per share (in CHF)	10.12	2.91
Net profit, net of effects of dilutive potential ordinary shares (in millions of CHF)	34,233	10,428
Weighted-average number of shares outstanding net of effects of dilutive potential ordinary shares (in millions of units)	3,382	3,584
Reconciliation of weighted-average numbers of shares outstanding (in millions of units)		
Weighted-average number of shares outstanding used to calculate basic earnings per share	3,371	3,572
Adjustment for share-based payment schemes, where dilutive	11	12
Weighted-average number of shares outstanding used to calculate diluted earnings per share	3,382	3,584

US GAAP COMPARISON

The accounting and presentation under US GAAP for EPS is very similar to IFRS. Entities with simple capital structures, which are entities that have only one class of shares and no other potential equity instruments outstanding, present only basic EPS. Basic EPS is calculated by dividing the earnings available to ordinary shareholders by the average shares outstanding for the period (each quarter). This is done for operating results, net income, discontinued operations, and extraordinary effect. Since IFRS does not have extraordinary classification (items that are both infrequent and unusual), this is a consequential difference from IFRS. The earnings available to ordinary shareholders for entity with a simple capital structure can differ if the entity has noncontrolling interests.

Entities that have *potentially* issued shares must also present diluted earnings per share. The diluted EPS calculation includes the shares that would have been issued if events necessary to issue those shares had occurred. Potential shares include contingent share agreements, convertible debt, convertible preferred stock, options, and warrants. For all potentially issued shares, it is assumed in the calculation that the shares were outstanding from either the beginning of the period or the date at which the instruments or agreements were issued.

The number of potentially issued shares that require the holder to convey to the issuer assets in exchange (i.e. options with a strike price) are adjusted for the assumption that the issuer will use those proceeds to purchase outstanding shares (referred to as the *Treasury Stock Method*). This has the effect of always reducing the number of shares in the calculation. The theoretical number of shares purchased is calculated by dividing the total theoretical proceeds by the average price per share of the securities in the period. Potentially issued shares that require the holder to convey assets to the issuer are only included in the calculation of diluted EPS if the average price per share is above the strike price. This is because it is assumed that a holder would not exercise the option or warrant if it is "out-of-the-money."

Potentially issued shares are only included in diluted EPS if the effect is to reduce EPS (or decrease loss per share) below basic EPS. These shares are called *antidilutive*. To maximize the dilution, each series or set of potential shares are added to outstanding shares in order of most dilutive to least dilutive. Shares that would be issued that do not require the conveyance of assets would be the most dilutive.

Dividends on preference shares are deducted from earnings to calculate earnings available to ordinary shares.

If an entity has participating shares outstanding, that is separate classes of shares that are entitled to different dividends, both the basic and diluted EPS must reflect this. This is referred to in US GAAP as a *two-tiered* calculation.

28 OPERATING SEGMENTS

INTRODUCTION

As of January 1, 2009, IAS 14 was superseded by IFRS 8, which substantially changes the requirements for segment determinations and converges with US GAAP. As part of its *2009 Improvements*, IASB made a minor change to the segment assets disclosure requirement under IFRS 8, in order to eliminate an unintended divergence from the corresponding mandate under the US GAAP standard, FAS 131.

Sources of IFRS
IFRS 8

SCOPE

IFRS 8 applies to

a. The separate or individual financial statements of an entity

    (1) Whose debt or equity instruments are traded in a public market (a domestic or foreign stock exchange or an over-the-counter market, including local and regional markets), or

    (2) That files, or is in the process of filing, its financial statements with a securities commission or other regulatory organization for the purpose of issuing any class of instruments in a public market; and

b. The consolidated financial statements of a group with a parent

    (1) Whose debt or equity instruments are traded in a public market (a domestic or foreign stock exchange or an over-the-counter market, including local and regional markets), or

    (2) That files, or is in the process of filing, the consolidated financial statements with a securities commission or other regulatory organization for the purpose of issuing any class of instruments in a public market.

If an entity that is not required to apply this IFRS chooses to disclose information about segments that does not comply with this IFRS, it shall not describe the information as segment information.

If a financial report contains both the consolidated financial statements of a parent that is within the scope of this IFRS as well as the parent's separate financial statements, segment information is required only in the consolidated financial statements.

DEFINITIONS OF TERMS

Chief operating decision maker. The term "chief operating decision maker" identifies a function, not necessarily a manager with a specific title. That function is to allocate resources to and assess the performance of the operating segments of an entity. Often the chief operating decision maker of an entity is its chief executive officer or chief operating officer but, for example, it may be a group of executive directors or others.

Common costs. Operating expenses incurred by the enterprise for the benefit of more than one business segment.

Corporate assets. Assets maintained for general corporate purposes and not used in the operations of any business segment.

General corporate expenses. Expenses incurred for the benefit of the corporation as a whole, which cannot be reasonably allocated to any segment.

Identifiable assets. Those tangible and intangible assets used by a business segment, including those the segment uses exclusively, and an allocated portion of assets used jointly by more than one segment.

Intersegment sales. Transfers of products or services, similar to those sold to unaffiliated customers, between business segments or geographic areas of the entity.

Intrasegment sales. Transfers within a business segment or geographic area.

Operating activities. The principal revenue producing activities of an entity and other activities that are not investing or financing activities.

Operating profit or loss. A business segment's revenue minus all operating expenses, including an allocated portion of common costs.

Operating segment. A component of an entity

- That engages in business activities from which it may earn revenues and incur expenses (including revenues and expenses relating to transactions with other components of the same entity),
- Whose operating results are regularly reviewed by the entity's chief operating decision maker to make decisions about resources to be allocated to the segments and assess its performance, and
- For which discrete financial information is available.

Reportable segment. Operating segments that

- Have been identified in accordance to above or result from aggregating two or more of those segments in accordance with aggregation criteria, and
- Exceed the quantitative thresholds.

Segment accounting policies. The policies adopted for reporting the consolidated financial statements of the entity, as well as for segment reporting.

Segment assets. Operating assets employed by a segment in operating activities, whether directly attributable or reasonably allocable to the segment; these should exclude those generating revenues or expenses which are excluded from the definitions of segment revenue and segment expense.

Segment expense. Expense that is directly attributable to a segment, or the relevant portion of expense that can be allocated on a reasonable basis to a segment; it excludes interest expense, losses on sales of investments or extinguishment of debt, equity method losses of associates and joint ventures, income taxes, and corporate expenses not identified with specific segments.

Segment revenue. Revenue that is directly attributable to a segment, or the relevant portion of revenue that can be allocated on a reasonable basis to a segment, and that is derived from transactions with parties outside the enterprise and from other segments of the same entity; it excludes interest and dividend income, and gains on sales of investments or extinguishment of debt.

Transfer pricing. The pricing of products or services between business segments or geographic areas.

IDENTIFICATION

Identification of operating segments within business organizations has grown in complexity over the years, and the conglomerate form of organization (where unrelated or dissimilar operations are united within one reporting entity, sometimes to provide the overall entity with benefits of countercyclicality among the constituent operations) has become normal practice, and it consequently has become necessary to concede that financial statements which present the full scope of an entity's operations on an aggregated basis declined markedly in usefulness without further relevant detail. While it is certainly possible to assess the overall financial health of the reporting entity using such financial reports, it is much more difficult to evaluate management's operating and financial strategies, particularly with regard to its emphases on specific lines of business or geographic spheres of operation. For example, the extent to which operating results for a given period are the consequence of the development of new products having greater potential for future growth, compared to more mature product lines which nonetheless still account for a majority of the entity's total sales, would tend to be masked in financial statements which did not present results by business segment.

IFRS 8 does not define, but requires an explanation of how segment profit or loss, segment assets and segment liabilities are determined and measured for each reportable segment. This Standard also requires general and entity-wide disclosures, including information about products and services, geographical areas, major customers and important factors used to identify an entity's reportable segments.

Therefore the core principle of IFRS 8 is the disclosure of information to enable users of an entity's financial statements to evaluate the nature and financial effects of the business activities in which it engages and the economic environment in which it operates. This should be considered when an entity forms its judgments about how and what information should be disclosed.

CONCEPTS AND REQUIREMENTS UNDER IFRS 8

IFRS 8 establishes how an entity is to report information about its operating segments in *annual* financial statements. Additionally, due to a consequential amendment made to IAS 34, entities are required to report selected information about their operating segments in *interim* financial reports, when interim reports are issued. IFRS 8 also sets out requirements for related disclosures about products and services, geographical areas, and major customers.

IFRS 8 requires that an entity report financial and descriptive information about its *reportable segments.* Reportable segments are defined as *operating segments* or aggregations thereof that meet certain defined criteria. Operating segments are components of an entity about which separate financial information is available that is evaluated regularly by the chief operating decision maker in deciding how to allocate resources and in assessing performance. Generally, segment financial information is required to be reported on the same basis as is used internally for evaluating operating segment performance and deciding how to allocate resources to operating segments. This conforms to the objective of putting users in the "shoes of management" in their ability to evaluate management performance.

In the past, there had been debate over the value and validity of disclosing results of operations on a segmental basis. IFRS 8 requires an entity to report a measure of operating segment profit or loss and of segment assets. It also requires the reporting entity to report a measure of segment liabilities and particular income and expense items if such measures are regularly provided to the chief operating decision maker. It requires reconciliations of total reportable segment revenues, total profit or loss, total assets, liabilities, and other amounts disclosed for reportable segments to corresponding amounts in the entity's financial statements.

IFRS 8 also generally requires certain informational disclosures apart from any correspondence to information used in making management operating decisions. This includes information about the revenues derived from its products or services (or groups of similar products and services), about the countries in which it earns revenues and holds assets, and about major customers. However, information that is not prepared for internal use need not be reported if the necessary information is not available and the cost to develop it would be excessive.

Descriptive information about the way the operating segments were determined, the products and services provided by the segments, differences between the measurements used in reporting segment information and those used in the entity's financial statements, and changes in the measurement of segment amounts from period to period must also be provided in the notes to the financial statements. This information is necessary for users to meaningfully interpret the operating segment financial data, including making comparisons to prior periods.

Key principles of IFRS 8. The key changes from reporting under the immediate predecessor standard, revised IAS 14, are set forth in the following paragraphs.

1. IFRS 8 imposes a "management approach" to the identification of operating segments, which is to be based on internal reports that are regularly reviewed by the entity's chief operating decision maker in order to allocate resources to the segment and assess its performance. For purposes of this standard, an operating segment is a component of an entity:

    a. That engages in business activities from which it may earn revenues and incur expenses (including revenues and expenses relating to transactions with other components of the same entity),

    b. Whose operating results are regularly reviewed by the entity's chief operating decision maker to make decisions about resources to be allocated to the segment and assess its performance, and

      c. For which discrete financial information is available. The "chief operating decision maker" designation does not necessarily refer to a single individual, but to a function within the reporting entity.

2. IFRS 8 allows for the discrete reporting of a component of an entity that sells primarily or exclusively to other operating segments of the entity, if the entity is managed that way under the predecessor standard.

3. The standard requires that the amount of each operating segment item (revenue, assets, etc.) that is reported be the same measure that is reported to the chief operating decision maker for the purposes of allocating resources to the segment and assessing its performance. This requirement can prove to be controversial, since it may well be the case, for many reporting entities, that internal measures will diverge from IFRS-compliant ones. (Note that IFRS do not control or even instruct on management reporting practices, but only govern external reporting.)

4. IFRS 8 requires reconciliations of total reportable segment revenues, total profit or loss, total assets, and other total amounts disclosed for reportable segments to corresponding amounts in the entity's financial statements.

5. The standard requires an explanation of how segment profit or loss and segment assets are measured for each reportable segment. This is necessitated by the fact that the proposed standard does not define these terms in the abstract.

6. It also requires that the entity report information about the revenues derived from its products or services (or groups of similar products and services), about the countries in which it earns revenues and holds assets, and about major customers, regardless of whether that information is used by management in making operating decisions.

7. IFRS 8 requires the reporting entity to provide descriptive information about the way that the operating segments were determined, the products and services provided by the segments, differences between the measurements used in reporting segment information and those used in the entity's financial statements, and changes in the measurement of segment amounts from period to period.

8. Finally, it requires the reporting entity to report interest revenue separately from interest expense for each reportable segment, unless (principally for financial institutions) a majority of the segment's revenues are from interest and the chief operating decision maker relies primarily on net interest revenue to assess the performance of the segment and to make decisions about resources to be allocated to the segment.

IFRS 8 also expands disclosures of both segment and entity-wide information, which now must include the following:

1. General information, which includes the factors used to identify the entity's operating segments, including the basis of organization and the types of products and services from which each reportable segment derives its revenues.

2. Information about profit, including a measure (unspecified) of profit or loss and total assets and liabilities for each reportable segment; a number of specified income statement headings for each reportable segment—if the amounts are included in the measure of segment profit or loss reviewed by the chief operating decision maker (or are otherwise regularly provided to the chief operating decision maker); and, for each reportable segment (if the amounts are included in the determination of segment assets, or otherwise are also reviewed by the chief operating decision maker), the amount of investment in associates and joint ventures accounted for by the equity method; and the total expenditures for additions to noncurrent assets other than fi-

Wiley IFRS 2012

nancial instruments, deferred tax assets, postemployment benefit assets and rights arising under insurance contracts. The standard refers to noncurrent assets but the IASB annotated this statement to clarify that for assets classified according to a liquidity presentation, the term noncurrent assets refers to assets that are expected to be recovered more than twelve months after the reporting period. Also to be disclosed would be all measurements of segment profit or loss and segment assets to be explained, including an explanation of the nature of any differences between amounts reported for segment purposes and those for the entity as a whole; the nature and effect of any changes from prior periods in the measurements used; and the nature and effect of any asymmetrical allocations to reportable segments.

3. Reconciliations—These are required in respect of the total of the reportable segments' revenues to the entity's revenue, with all material reconciling items separately identified and described; of the total of the reportable segments' measures of profit or loss to the entity's profit or loss before income tax expense or income and discounted operations; of the total of the reportable segments' assets to the (continued) entity's assets; and of the total of the reportable segments' amounts for every other material item of information disclosed to the corresponding amount for the entity.

4. Entity-wide disclosures for all entities (including those having only a single reportable business segment), of information about its products and services, geographical areas, and major customers. This requirement applies, regardless of the entity's organization, if the information is not included as part of the disclosures about segments.

IFRS 8 requires the expanded application of segment reporting requirements to interim financial statements. While previously this was seen as an onerous burden, the embrace of the "management approach" and the countenancing (at least implicitly) of non-IFRS measures in segment data, means that the burden would be lightened, making inclusion in interim reports more feasible. Of course, there is no absolute requirement under IFRS to publish interim reports, nor is there a requirement to have interim financial statements comply with IFRS. However, if such IFRS-compliant interim financial reports are prepared, they will now have to include certain operating segment information (for qualifying reporting entities).

Operating Segments and Reportable Segments

IFRS 8 defines reportable segments as being a subset of operating segments. In other words, there may be certain operating segments that fail to meet the threshold test for being reportable under this standard. Therefore, an understanding of these key concepts is vital to the proper application of the standard.

Operating segments. An operating segment is a component of an entity

1. That engages in business activities from which it may earn revenues and incur expenses (including revenues and expenses relating to transactions with other components of the same entity),

2. Whose operating results are regularly reviewed by the entity's chief operating decision maker to make decisions about resources to be allocated to the segment and assess its performance, and

3. For which discrete financial information is available.

Revenue generation is not an absolute threshold test for an operating segment. An operating segment may engage in business activities for which it has yet to earn revenues; for example, start-up operations may be operating segments before earning revenues.

By the same token, not every part of an entity is necessarily an operating segment or part of an operating segment. Thus, a corporate headquarters, as well as certain functional departments, may earn no revenues, or may generate revenues that are merely incidental to the activities of the entity as a whole. These would not be deemed to be operating segments under the definitions set forth under IFRS 8. For the purposes of the new standard, an entity's postemployment benefit plans are not operating segments, either.

For many entities, the three characteristics of operating segments set forth above will serve to clearly identify its operating segments. In other situations, an entity may produce reports in which its business activities are presented in a variety of ways (particularly in so-called "matrix organization" structures, where there are multiple and overlapping lines of reporting responsibilities. If the chief operating decision maker uses more than one set of segment information, other factors may be necessary to identify a single set of components as constituting an entity's operating segments, including the nature of the business activities of each component, the existence of managers responsible for them, and information presented to the board of directors. Of course, any such decision should be documented, and should be maintained over time, to the extent possible, in order to ensure comparability of disclosures. The chief operating decision maker should review segment definitions to ensure accuracy and consistency.

Reportable segments. Only reportable segments give rise to the financial statement disclosures set forth by IFRS 8. Reportable segments are operating segments as defined above, or *aggregations* of two or more such operating segments, that exceed the quantitative thresholds described below.

Operating segments often exhibit similar long-term financial performance if they have similar economic characteristics. For example, similar long-term average gross margins for two operating segments would be expected if their economic characteristics were similar. Two or more operating segments may *optionally* be aggregated into a single operating segment if aggregation is consistent with the core principle of IFRS 8, the segments have similar economic characteristics, and segments are similar in each of the following respects:

1. The nature of the products and services;
2. The nature of the production processes;
3. The type or class of customer for their products and services;
4. The methods used to distribute their products or provide their services; and
5. If applicable, the nature of the regulatory environment, for example, banking, insurance or public utilities.

An operating segment (or aggregation thereof) becomes a mandatorily reportable segment if one of the defined quantitative thresholds is met. These are that

1. The segment's reported revenue, including both sales to external customers and intersegment sales or transfers, is 10% or more of the combined revenue, internal and external, of all operating segments.
2. The absolute amount of its reported profit or loss is 10% or more of the greater, in absolute amount, of (1) the combined reported profit of all operating segments that did not report a loss and (2) the combined reported loss of all operating segments that reported a loss.
3. Its assets are 10% or more of the combined assets of all operating segments.

Furthermore, if the total external revenue reported by operating segments constitutes less than 75% of the entity's revenue, additional operating segments must be identified as reportable segments, even if they do not meet the criteria established under IFRS 8, until at least 75% of the entity's revenue is included in reportable segments.

A reporting entity may combine information about operating segments that do not meet the quantitative thresholds with information about other operating segments that do not meet the quantitative thresholds to produce a reportable segment only if the operating segments have similar economic characteristics and share a majority of the aggregation criteria set forth above. Thus, a catch-all ("all other segments") category should not be used, unless truly immaterial. The sources of the revenue included in the all other segments category must be described.

More segments may be optionally defined by management as being reportable, even if the foregoing criteria are not met. Operating segments that do not meet any of the quantitative thresholds may be considered reportable, and separately disclosed, if management believes that information about the segment would be useful to users of the financial statements.

This may be particularly relevant if, for various reasons, an operating segment traditionally meeting the test as a reportable segment falls below each threshold in the current year, but management expects the segment to regain its former prominence within a relatively brief time. To ensure interperiod comparability, it may be maintained as a reportable segment notwithstanding its current diminished significance. If management judges that an operating segment identified as a reportable segment in the immediately preceding periods is of continuing significance, information about that segment must, per IFRS 8, continue to be reported separately in the current period even if it no longer meets the criteria for reportability.

If an operating segment is identified as a reportable segment in the current period in accordance with the above-stated quantitative thresholds, segment data for a prior period presented for comparative purposes is to be restated to reflect the newly reportable segment as a separate segment, even if that segment did not satisfy the criteria for reportability in the prior period, unless the necessary information is not available and the cost to develop it would be excessive.

The standard notes that there may be a practical limit to the number of reportable segments that an entity separately discloses beyond which segment information may become too detailed (the so-called information overload situation). Although no precise limit has been determined, as the number of segments that are reportable increases above ten, the entity should consider whether a practical limit has been reached. There is no absolute requirement to limit the number of segments, however.

DISCLOSURE REQUIREMENTS

A reporting entity is required to disclose information to enable users of its financial statements to evaluate the nature and financial effects of the business activities in which it engages and the economic environments in which it operates.

To operationalize this principle, the reporting entity is required to disclose the following *for each period for which a statement of comprehensive income* is presented:

1. General information, as follows:

    a. Factors used to identify the entity's reportable segments, including the basis of organization (for example, whether management has chosen to organize the entity around differences in products and services, geographical areas, regulatory environments, or a combination of factors, and whether operating segments have been aggregated), *and*

b. Types of products and services from which each reportable segment derives its revenues.

2. *Information about reported segment profit or loss,* including specified revenues and expenses included in reported segment profit or loss, *segment assets, segment liabilities* and the basis of measurement, as follows:

a. The reporting entity is to report a measure of profit or loss for each reportable segment.

b. It is to report a measure of total assets and liabilities for each reportable segment if such amounts are regularly provided to the chief operating decision maker.

c. It also is to disclose the following about each reportable segment if the specified amounts are included in the measure of segment profit or loss reviewed by the chief operating decision maker or are otherwise regularly provided to the chief operating decision maker even if not included in that measure of segment profit or loss:

(1) Revenues from external customers;
(2) Revenues from transactions with other operating segments of the same entity;
(3) Interest revenue;
(4) Interest expense;
(5) Depreciation and amortization;
(6) Material items of income and expense disclosed in accordance with IAS 1;
(7) The entity's interest in the profit or loss of associates and joint ventures accounted for by the equity method;
(8) Income tax expense or income; and
(9) Material noncash items other than depreciation and amortization.

An entity is to report interest revenue separately from interest expense for each reportable segment unless a majority of the segment's revenues are from interest and the chief operating decision maker relies primarily on net interest revenue to assess the performance of the segment and make decisions about resources to be allocated to the segment. In that situation, an entity may report that segment's interest revenue net of its interest expense and disclose that it has done so.

d. The reporting entity is to disclose the following about each reportable segment if the specified amounts are included in the measure of segment assets reviewed by the chief operating decision maker or are otherwise regularly provided to the chief operating decision maker, even if not included in the measure of segment assets:

(1) The amount of investment in associates and joint ventures accounted for by the equity method, and
(2) The amounts of additions to noncurrent assets other than financial instruments, deferred tax assets, postemployment benefit assets and rights arising under insurance contracts. If the entity does not present a classified statement of financial position, noncurrent assets are to be deemed those that include amounts expected to be recovered more than twelve months after the date of the statement of financial position.

(3) Reconciliations of the totals of segment revenues, reported segment profit or loss, segment assets, segment liabilities and other material segment items to corresponding entity amounts as follows:

(a) The total of the reportable segments' revenues to the entity's revenue.

(b) The total of the reportable segments' measures of profit or loss to the entity's profit or loss before tax expense (tax income) and discontinued operations. However, if an entity allocates to reportable segments items such as tax expense (tax income), the entity may reconcile the total of the segments' measures of profit or loss to the entity's profit or loss after those items.

(c) The total of the reportable segments' assets to the entity's assets.

(d) The total of the reportable segments' liabilities to the entity's liabilities if segment liabilities are reported to the entity's chief operating decision maker.

(e) The total of the reportable segments' amounts for every other material item of information disclosed to the corresponding amount for the entity.

IFRS 8 dictates that all material reconciling items are to be separately identified and described. For example, the amount of each material adjustment needed to reconcile reportable segment profit or loss to the entity's profit or loss arising from different accounting policies is required to be separately identified and described.

IFRS 8 also mandates that reconciliations of statements of financial position amounts for reportable segments to the entity's statement of financial position amounts be presented for *each date* at which a *statement of financial position* is presented. If, as is typical, comparative statements of financial position are presented, information for prior periods is to be restated.

If the reporting entity changes the structure of its internal organization in a manner that causes the composition of its reportable segments to change, the corresponding information for earlier periods, including interim periods, is to be restated, unless the information is not available and the cost to develop it would be excessive. The determination of whether the information is not available and the cost to develop it would be excessive must be made separately for each individual item of disclosure—thus a blanket conclusion regarding impracticability would normally not be appropriate. The standard demands that, following a change in the composition of its reportable segments, the entity disclose whether it has restated the corresponding items of segment information for earlier periods.

Furthermore, if the reporting entity has changed the structure of its internal organization in a manner that causes the composition of its reportable segments to change, and if segment information for earlier periods, including interim periods, is *not* restated to reflect the change, it must disclose in the year in which the change occurs segment information for the current period on both the old basis and the new basis of segmentation, unless the necessary information is not available and the cost to develop it would be excessive. This requirement is expected to discourage frequent changes in structure affecting segment reporting.

Entity-wide disclosure requirements. IFRS 8 also mandates disclosures of certain entity-wide data. These disclosures are required regardless of whether the entity has reportable segment disclosures to be made under this standard. These disclosures need not be provided, however, if they are redundant with information contained in the reportable segment disclosures.

1. *Information about products and services.* Revenues from external customers for each product and service, or each group of similar products and services, are to be

identified, unless the necessary information is not available and the cost to develop it would be excessive, in which case that fact shall disclosed. The amounts of revenues reported are to be based on the financial information used to produce the entity's financial statements.

2. *Information about geographical areas.* The reporting entity is to disclose the following geographical information, unless the necessary information is not available and the cost to develop it would be excessive:

   a. Revenues from external customers (1) attributed to the entity's country of domicile and (2) attributed to all foreign countries in total from which the entity derives revenues. If revenues from external customers attributed to an individual foreign country are material, those revenues are to be disclosed separately. An entity is required to disclose the basis for attributing revenues from external customers to individual countries.

   b. Noncurrent assets other than financial instruments, deferred tax assets, post-employment benefit assets, and rights arising under insurance contracts (1) located in the entity's country of domicile and (2) located in all foreign countries in total in which the entity holds assets. If assets in an individual foreign country are material, those assets shall be disclosed separately. If a classified statement of financial position is not presented (i.e., if liquidity ordering is utilized), noncurrent assets are to be defined as assets that include amounts expected to be recovered more than twelve months after the reporting date.

   The amounts reported are to be based on the financial information that is used to produce the entity's financial statements. If the necessary information is not available and the cost to develop it would be excessive, that fact shall be disclosed. An entity may provide, in addition to the information required by this paragraph, subtotals of geographical information about groups of countries.

3. *Information about major customers.* Information about the extent of the reporting entity's reliance on its major customers must be provided. If revenues from transactions with a single external customer amount to 10% or more of the entity's revenues, it is to disclose that fact, the total amount of revenues from each such customer, and the identity of segment or segments reporting the revenues. The entity need not disclose the identity of a major customer or amount of revenues that each segment reports from that customer. Originally, IFRS 8 explained that for the purposes of this requirement, a group of entities known to be under common control is to be considered a single customer, and a government (national, state, provincial, territorial, local or foreign) and entities known to be under the control of that government are to be considered a single customer. IAS 24, *Related Parties,* was revised during November 2009, and a key change arising from this revision was that transactions between components of a government and entities under the control of that government are no longer necessarily disclosable related-party transactions solely by virtue of the fact that they relate to the same government. As a result of the revision to IAS 24, IFRS 8 was consequently amended to reflect this thinking, and IFRS 8 now requires the application of judgment to assess whether a government (including government agencies and similar bodies whether local, national or international) and entities known to the reporting entity to be under the control of that government are considered a single customer. In assessing this, the reporting entity should consider the extent of economic integration between those entities. This consequential amendment to IFRS 8 is effective for annual periods beginning on or after January 1, 2011

(the effective date of revised IAS 24). If an entity applies IAS 24 (revised 2009) for an earlier period, it shall apply the amendment to IFRS 8 for that earlier period as well.

Example of Financial Statement Disclosures under IFRS 8

Roche Group
Consolidated Financial Statements 2008

Notes to the Roche Group Consolidated Financial Statements

1. Summary of significant accounting policies

Segment reporting

The determination of the Group's operating segments is based on the organization units for which information is reported to the Group's management. The Group has two divisions, Pharmaceuticals and Diagnostics. Revenues are primarily generated from the sale of prescription pharmaceutical products and diagnostic instruments, reagents and consumables, respectively. Both divisions also derive revenue from the sale or licensing of products or technology to third parties. Certain headquarter activities are reported as "Corporate." These consist of corporate headquarters, including the Corporate Executive Committee, corporate communications, corporate human resources, corporate finance, including treasury, taxes and pension fund management, corporate legal and corporate safety and environmental services. Subdivisional information for Roche Pharmaceuticals and Chugai, the previously aggregated operating segments within the Pharmaceuticals Division, is also presented.

Transfer prices between operating segments are set on an arm's-length basis. Operating assets and liabilities consist of property, plant, and equipment, goodwill and intangible assets, trade receivables/payables, inventories and other assets and liabilities, such as provisions, which can be reasonably attributed to the reported operating segments. Nonoperating assets and liabilities mainly include current and deferred income tax balances, postemployment benefit assets/liabilities and financial assets/liabilities such as cash, marketable securities, investments, and debt.

2. Operating segment information

Divisional information (in millions of CHF)

	Pharmaceuticals		*Diagnostics*		*Corporate*		*Group*	
	2010	*2009*	*2010*	*2009*	*2010*	*2009*	*2010*	*2009*
Revenues from external customers								
Sales	37,058	38,996	10,415	10,055	--	--	47,473	49,051
Royalties and other operating income	1,537	1,948	157	152	--	--	1,694	2,100
Total	**38,595**	**40,944**	**10,572**	**10,207**	**--**	**--**	**49,167**	**51,151**
Revenues from other operating segments								
Sales	3	7	14	10	--	--	17	17
Royalties and other operating income	--	--	--	--	--	--	--	--
Elimination of interdivisional revenue							(17)	(17)
Total	**3**	**7**	**14**	**10**	**--**	**--**	**--**	**--**
Segment results								
Operating profit	**12,301**	**11,419**	**1,579**	**1,198**	**(394)**	**(340)**	**13,486**	**12,277**

	Pharmaceuticals		Diagnostics		Corporate		Group	
	2010	*2009*	*2010*	*2009*	*2010*	*2009*	*2010*	*2009*
Capital expenditure								
Business combinations	430	57	372	50	--	--	802	107
Additions to property, plant and equipment	1,464	1,644	1,150	1,191	49	2	2,663	2,837
Additions to intangible assets	288	228	50	8	--	--	338	236
Total capital expenditure	**2,182**	**1,929**	**1,572**	**1,249**	**49**	**2**	**3,803**	**3,180**
Research and development								
Research and development costs	9,090	8,896	836	978	--	--	10,026	9,974
Other segment information								
Depreciation of property, plant and equipment	1,151	1,255	775	721	7	5	1,933	1,981
Amortization of intangible assets	175	253	444	459	--	--	619	712
Impairment of property, plant and equipment	109	1,118	29	9	--	--	138	1,127
Impairment of goodwill	--	--	--	--	--	--	--	--
Impairment of intangible assets	634	598	33	80	--	--	667	668
Equity compensation plan expenses	241	522	38	45	13	28	292	595

Pharmaceuticals subdivisional information (in millions of CHF)

	Roche Pharmaceuticals		Chugal		Pharmaceuticals Division	
	2010	*2009*	*2010*	*2009*	*2010*	*2009*
Revenues from external customers						
Sales	32,739	34,231	4,319	4,765	37,058	38,996
Royalties and other operating income	1,530	1,861	7	87	1,537	1,948
Total	**34,269**	**36,092**	**4,326**	**4,852**	**38,595**	**40,944**
Revenues from other operating segments						
Sales	1,050	1,398	151	103	1,201	1,501
Royalties and other operating income	20	88	43	30	63	68
Elimination of income within division					(1,261)	(1,562)
Total	**1,070**	**1,436**	**194**	**133**	**3**	**7**
Segment results						
Subdivisional profit	11,641	10,529	788	890	12,429	11,519
Elimination of interdivisional profit					(128)	(100)
Operating profit	**11,641**	**10,529**	**788**	**890**	**12,301**	**11,419**
Capital expenditure						
Business combinations	430	57	--	--	430	57
Additions to property, plant, and equipment	1,234	1,426	230	218	1,464	1,644
Additions to intangible assets	288	228	--	--	288	228
Total capital expenditure	**1,952**	**1,711**	**230**	**218**	**2,182**	**1,929**
Research and development						
Research and development costs	8,332	8,188	786	765	9,118	8,953
Elimination of costs within division					(28)	(57)
Total	**8,332**	**8,188**	**786**	**765**	**9,090**	**8,896**
Other segment information						
Depreciation of property, plant, and equipment	994	1,097	157	158	1,151	1,255
Amortization of intangible assets	102	183	73	70	175	259
Impairment of property, plant, and equipment	107	1,118	2	--	109	1,118
Impairment of goodwill	--	--	--	--	--	--
Impairment of intangible assets	694	588	--	--	634	588
Equity compensation plan expenses	238	520	3	2	241	522

Net operating assets (in millions of CHF)

	Assets			Liabilities			Net assets		
	2010	*2009*	*2008*	*2010*	*2009*	*2008*	*2010*	*2009*	*2008*
Pharmaceuticals	28,546	31,483	32,483	(8,185)	(8,885)	(7,213)	20,361	22,183	25,270
Diagnostics	17,454	19,027	18,750	(2,404)	(2,340)	(2,141)	15,050	16,687	16,609
Corporate	172	152	156	(214)	(199)	(248)	(42)	(47)	(92)
Total operating	**46,172**	**50,247**	**51,389**	**(10,803)**	**(11,424)**	**(9,602)**	**35,369**	**38,823**	**41,787**
Nonoperating	14,848	24,318	24,700	(38,555)	(53,727)	(12,665)	(23,707)	(29,409)	12,035
Group	61,020	74,565	76,089	(49,358)	(65,151)	(22,267)	11,662	9,414	53,822

Information by geographical area (in millions of CHF)

	Revenues from external customers		Noncurrent assets	
	Sales	Royalties and other operating income	Property, plant, and equipment	Goodwill and intangible assets
2010				
Switzerland	464	221	3,032	1,923
European Union	14,596	59	4,261	1,785
of which Germany	2,970	59	3,097	1,740
Rest of Europe	1,630	2	42	1
Europe	**16,690**	**282**	**7,335**	**3,709**
United States	16,446	1,372	5,849	8,394
Rest of North America	1,051	16	118	88
North America	**17,497**	**1,388**	**5,967**	**8,482**
Latin America	3,397	12	476	17
Japan	4,718	7	1,848	427
Rest of Asia	3,591	5	991	218
Asia	**8,309**	**12**	**2,839**	**645**
Africa, Australia and Oceania	1,580	--	112	2
Total	**47,473**	**1,694**	**16,729**	**12,955**
2009				
Switzerland	499	427	2,744	2,326
European Union	16,219	59	4,902	2,265
of which Germany	3,320	57	3,481	2,210
Rest of Europe	1,568	--	45	2
Europe	**18,286**	**486**	**7,691**	**4,593**
United States	17,208	1,499	6,554	9,074
Rest of North America	948	2	123	93
North America	**18,156**	**1,501**	**6,677**	**9,167**
Latin America	2,940	22	485	18
Japan	5,036	87	1,776	486
Rest of Asia	3,166	4	959	--
Asia	**8,202**	**91**	**2,735**	**486**
Africa, Australia and Oceania	1,467	--	109	2
Total	**49,051**	**2,100**	**17,697**	**14,266**

Supplementary unaudited information on sales by therapeutic areas in the Pharmaceuticals Division and by business areas in the Diagnostics Division are given on pages 6 to 10 and 14 to 16 respectively. Sales are allocated to geographical areas by destination according to the location of the customer. Royalties and other operating income are allocated according to the location of the Group company that receives the revenue. European Union information is based on members of the EU as at December 31, 2010.

Major customers

The US national wholesale distributor, AmerisourceBergen Corp., represented approximately 6 billion Swiss francs (2009: 6 billion Swiss francs) of the Group's revenues. Approximately 99% of these revenues were in the Pharmaceuticals operating segment, with the residual in the Diagnostics segment. The Group also reported substantial revenues from the US national wholesale distributors, Cardinal Health, Inc. and McKesson Corp. and in total these three customers represented approximately a quarter of the Group's revenues.

US GAAP COMPARISON

The IASB and FASB converged their segment reporting guidance in 2009. Consequently, the standards are nearly identical, with the following exceptions:

- Similar to IFRS, US GAAP requires an entity to provide a measure of assets that the chief operating decision maker uses in evaluating the performance of the segments. This includes expenditures on long-lived assets (some are excluded). US GAAP excludes goodwill. IFRS does not.
- US GAAP does not require disclosure of a measure of segment liabilities. IAS 8 requires disclosure of segment liabilities if such a measure is regularly provided to the chief operating decision maker.
- A matrix organization employs multiple management reporting relationships for the functions of people. US GAAP requires that an entity with a matrix form of organization to determine operating segments based on products and services. IFRS requires such an entity to determine operating segments by reference to the core principle of the IFRS.

29 RELATED-PARTY DISCLOSURES

INTRODUCTION

Transactions between entities that are considered *related parties,* as defined by IAS 24, *Related-Party Disclosures*, must be adequately disclosed in financial statements of the reporting entity. Such disclosures have long been a common feature of financial reporting, and most national accounting standard-setting bodies have imposed similar mandates. The rationale for compelling such disclosures is the concern that entities which are related to each other, whether by virtue of an ability to control or to exercise significant influence (both as defined under IFRS) usually have leverage in the setting of prices to be charged and on other transaction terms. If these events and transactions were simply mingled with transactions conducted with customers or vendors on normal arm's-length terms, the users of the financial statements would likely be impeded in their ability to project future earnings and cash flows for the reporting entity, given that related-party transaction terms could be arbitrarily altered at any time. Thus, in order to ensure transparency, reporting entities are required to disclose the nature, type, and components of transactions with related parties.

An amendment to IAS 24 in November 2009 (retrospectively effective for annual periods beginning on or after January 1, 2011) simplified the definition of related party, clarified its intended meaning, eliminated certain inconsistencies in the definition, and provided a partial exemption from the disclosure requirements for government-related entities.

Although IAS 24 states "related-party relationships are a normal feature of commerce and business," it nevertheless recognizes that a related-party relationship could have an effect on the financial position and operating results of the reporting entity, due to the possibility that transactions with related parties may not be effected at the same amounts as are those between unrelated parties. For that reason, extensive disclosure of such transactions is deemed necessary to convey a full picture of the entity's position and results of operations.

While IAS 24 has been operative for over two decades, it is commonly observed that related-party transactions are not being properly disclosed in all instances. This is due in part, perhaps, to the perceived sensitive nature of such disclosures. As a consequence, even when a note to financial statements that is captioned "related-party transactions" is presented, it is often fairly evident that the gamut of disclosures required by IAS 24 have not been included. There seems to be particular resistance to reporting certain types of related-party transactions, such as loans to directors, key management personnel, or close members of the executives' families. Presumably, these deficiencies will occur less frequently over time, and as independent auditors become more familiar with IFRS requirements.

IAS 1 demands, as a prerequisite to asserting that financial statements have been prepared in conformity with IFRS, that there be *full compliance* with all IFRS. This requirement pertains to all recognition and measurement standards, and extends to the disclosures to be made as well. As a practical matter, it becomes incumbent upon the auditors to ascertain whether disclosures, including related-party disclosures, comply with IFRS when the financial statements represent such to be the case.

Sources of IFRS
IAS 1, 8, 24, 27, 28, 31

DEFINITIONS OF TERMS

Close members of the family of an individual. For the purpose of IAS 24, close members of the family of an individual are defined as "those family members that may be expected to influence, or be influenced by, that person in their dealings with the entity." The following may be considered close members of the family: an individual's domestic partner, spouse and children, children of the individual's spouse or domestic partner, and dependents of the individual or the individual's spouse or domestic partner.

Compensation. Compensation encompasses all employee benefits (as defined in IAS 19) and also includes share-based payments as envisaged in IFRS 2. Employee benefits include all forms of consideration paid, payable, or provided by the entity, or on behalf of the entity, in exchange for services rendered to the entity. It also includes such consideration paid on behalf of a parent of the entity in respect to activities of the entity. Compensation thus includes short-term employee benefits (such as wages, salaries, paid annual leave), post-employment benefits (such as pensions), other long-term benefits (such as long-term disability benefits), termination benefits, and share-based payments.

Control. Is the power to govern the financial and operating policies of the other entity so as to obtain benefits from its activities.

Government. Government, government agencies, and similar bodies whether local, national, or international.

Government-related entity. An entity that is controlled, jointly controlled, or significantly influenced by a government.

Joint control. An entity is considered to be jointly in control with another entity if they contractually agree to share control over an economic activity.

Key management personnel. IAS 24 defines key management personnel as "those persons having authority and responsibility for planning, directing, and controlling the activities of the reporting entity, including directors (whether executive or otherwise) of the entity."

Related party. A person or a close member of that person's family is related to a reporting entity if that person

1. Has control or joint control over the reporting entity.
2. Has significant influence over the reporting entity.

3. Is a member of the key management personnel of the reporting entity or of a parent of the reporting entity.

An entity is related to a reporting entity if any of the following conditions apply:

1. The entity and the reporting entity are members of the same group (which means that each parent, subsidiary and fellow subsidiary is related to the others).
2. One entity is an associate or joint venture of the other entity (or an associate or joint venture of a member of a group of which the other entity is a member).
3. Both entities are joint ventures of the same third party.
4. One entity is a joint venture of a third entity and the other entity is an associate of the third entity.
5. The entity is a postemployment benefit plan for the benefit of employees of either the reporting entity or an entity related to the reporting entity. If the reporting entity is itself such a plan, the sponsoring employers are also related to the reporting entity.
6. The entity is controlled or jointly controlled by a person identified above.
7. A person identified in 1. above has significant influence over the entity or is a member of the key management personnel of the entity (or of a parent of the entity).

Related-party transactions. Related-party transactions are dealings between related parties involving the transfer of resources or obligations between them, regardless of whether a price is charged for the transactions.

Significant influence. The power to participate in the financial and operating policy decisions of that other entity, as opposed to control. Significant influence may be gained by share ownership, statute, or agreement.

IDENTIFICATION

The Need for Related-Party Disclosures

For strategic or other reasons, entities will sometimes carry out certain aspects of their business activities through associates or subsidiaries. For example, in order to ensure that it has a guaranteed supply of raw materials, an entity may decide to purchase a portion of its requirements (of raw materials) through a subsidiary or, alternatively, will make a direct investment in its vendor, to assure continuity of supply. In this way, the entity might be able to control or exercise significant influence over the financial and operating decisions of its major supplier (the investee), including insuring a source of supply and, perhaps, affecting the prices charged. Such related-party relationships and transactions are thus a normal feature of commerce and business, and need not suggest any untoward behavior.

A related-party relationship could have an impact on the financial position and operating results of the reporting entity because

1. Related parties may enter into certain transactions with each other which unrelated parties may not normally want to enter into (e.g., uneconomic transactions).
2. Amounts charged for transactions between related parties may not be comparable to amounts charged for similar transactions between unrelated parties (either higher or lower prices than arm's-length).
3. The mere existence of the relationship may sometimes be sufficient to affect the dealings of the reporting entity with other (unrelated) parties. (For instance, an entity may cease purchasing from its former major supplier upon acquiring a subsidiary which is the other supplier's competitor.)

4. Transactions between entities would not have taken place if the related-party relationship had not existed. For example, a company sells its entire output to an associate at cost. The producing entity might not have survived but for these related-party sales to the associate, if it did not have enough business with arm's-length customers for the kind of goods it manufactures.

5. The existence of related-party relationships may result in certain transactions *not* taking place, which otherwise would have occurred. Thus, even in the absence of actual transactions with related entities, the mere fact that these relationships exist could constitute material information from the viewpoints of various users of financial statements, including current and potential vendors, customers, and employees. Related-party information is thus unique, in that even an absence of transactions might be deemed a material disclosure matter.

Because of peculiarities such as these, which often distinguish related-party transactions from those with unrelated entities, accounting standards (including IFRS) have almost universally mandated financial statement disclosure of such transactions. Disclosures of related-party transactions in financial statements is a means of conveying to users of financial statements the messages that certain related-party relationships exist as of the date of the financial statements, and that certain transactions were consummated with related parties during the period which the financial statements cover, together with the financial impacts of these related-party transactions have been incorporated in the financial statements being presented. Since related-party transactions could have an effect on the financial position and operating results of the reporting entity, disclosure of such transactions would be prudent based on the increasingly cited principle of transparency (in financial reporting). Only if such information is disclosed to the users of financial statements will they be able to make informed decisions.

Scope of the Standard

IAS 24 is to be applied in dealing with related parties and transactions between a reporting entity and its related parties. The requirements of this standard apply to the financial statements of each reporting entity. IAS 24 sets forth disclosure requirements only; it does not prescribe the accounting for related-party transactions, nor does it address the measurements to be applied in the instance of such transactions. Thus, related-party transactions are reported at the nominal values ascribed to them, and are not subject to further interpretation for financial reporting purposes, since there is generally no basis upon which to conclude, or even speculate, about the extent to which related-party transactions might approximate or vary from those between unrelated parties with regard to prices or other terms of sale.

IAS 24 is to be employed in determining the existence of related-party transactions; identifying the outstanding balances between related parties; concluding on whether disclosures are required under the circumstances; and determining the content of such disclosures.

Related-party disclosures are required not only in the consolidated (group) financial statements, but also in the separate financial statements of the parent entity or a venturer or investor. In separate statements any intragroup transactions and balances must be disclosed in the related-party note, although these will be eliminated in consolidated financial reports.

Applicability

The requirements of the standard should be applied to related parties as identified in the definition of a related party.

Substance over Form

The standard clarifies that in applying the provisions of IAS 24 to each possible related-party relationship, consideration should be given to the substance of the relationship and not merely to its legal form. Thus, certain relationships might not rise to the level of related parties for purpose of necessitating disclosure under the provisions of IAS 24. Examples of such situations follow:

1. Two entities having only a common director or other key management personnel, notwithstanding the specific requirements of IAS 24 above.
2. Agencies and entities such as

   a. Providers of finance (e.g., banks and creditors)
   b. Trade unions
   c. Public utilities
   d. Government departments and agencies

3. Entities upon which the reporting entity may be economically dependent, due to the volume of business the entity transacts with them. For example

   a. A single customer;
   b. A major supplier;
   c. A franchisor;
   d. A distributor; or
   e. A general agent.

4. Two venturers, simply because they share joint control over a joint venture.

Significant Influence

The existence of the ability to exercise significant influence is an important concept in relation to this standard. It is one of the two criteria stipulated in the definition of a related party, which when present would, for the purposes of this standard, make one party related to another. In other words, for the purposes of this standard, if one party is considered to have the ability to exercise significant influence over another, then the two parties are considered to be related.

The existence of the ability to exercise significant influence may be evidenced in one or more of the following ways:

1. By representation on the board of directors of the other entity;
2. By participation in the policy-making process of the other entity;
3. By having material intercompany transactions between two entities;
4. By interchange of managerial personnel between two entities; or
5. By dependence on another entity for technical information.

Significant influence may be gained through agreement, by statute, or by means of share ownership. Under the provisions of IAS 24, similar to the presumption of significant influence under IAS 28, an entity is deemed to possess the ability to exercise significant influence if it directly or indirectly through subsidiaries holds 20% or more of the voting power of another entity (unless it can be clearly demonstrated that despite holding such voting power the investor does not have the ability to exercise significant influence over the investee). Conversely, if an entity, directly or indirectly through subsidiaries, owns less than 20% of the voting power of another entity, it is presumed that the investor does not possess the ability to exercise significant influence (unless it can be clearly demonstrated that the investor does have such an ability despite holding less than 20% of the voting power). Further, while explaining the concept of significant influence, IAS 28 also clarifies that "a substantial or majority ownership by another investor does not *necessarily* preclude an investor from having significant influence" (emphasis added).

In the authors' opinion, by defining the term "related-party" to include the concepts of control and significant influence, and by further broadening the definition to cover not just direct related-party relationships, but even indirect ones such as those with "close members of the family of an individual," the IASB intended to cast a wide net, in order to cover related-party transactions which would sometimes not be considered such. This creates some ambiguity relative to disclosures made under this standard, and thus makes the related-party issue itself a more contentious one, since it lends itself to aggressive interpretations by the reporting entity. This obviously could have a significant bearing on the related-party disclosures flowing from these interpretations. Experience suggests this is often a matter of some contention between reporting entities and their independent auditors.

DISCLOSURES

Financial Statement Disclosures

IAS 24 recognizes that in many countries certain related-party disclosures are prescribed by law. In particular, transactions with directors, because of the fiduciary nature of their relationship with the entity, are mandated financial statement disclosures in some jurisdictions. In fact, corporate legislation in some countries goes further and requires certain disclosures which are even more stringent than the disclosure requirements under IAS 24, or under most national GAAP.

For example, under one regulation, in addition to the usual disclosures pertaining to related-party transactions, companies are required to disclose not just year-end balances that are due to or due from directors or certain other related parties, but are also required to disclose the highest balances for the period (for which financial statements are presented) which were due to or due from them to the corporate entity. In the authors' opinion, such a requirement is appropriate, since in the absence of this disclosure, balances at year-end can be "cleaned up" (e.g., via short-term bank borrowings) and the artificially low amounts reported can provide a misleading picture to financial statement users regarding the real magnitude of such transactions and balances.

For example, a reporting entity which has advanced large sums of money to its directors could make arrangements for the directors to repay the loans to the entity a few days before the end of the reporting period, agreeing to reestablish the loans shortly after the first day of the new reporting period. This type of practice, which is often referred to as "window dressing," can cause the financial statements and associated notes to be somewhat misleading while nonetheless nominally compliant with the pertinent financial reporting requirements. Under IAS 24, it does not appear that the amounts of loans to directors outstanding *during* the year (despite being material) would need to be disclosed, since none were actually outstanding on the date of the statement of financial position. In such a situation, disclosure of not just outstanding balances at the end of the reporting period, but also the highest balance(s) due to or due from related parties during the period (or the time-weighted average balance), would improve the quality of information disclosed.

There is nothing in IAS 24 that prohibits supplemental disclosures such as those identified in the preceding paragraph. Commitment to a "substance over form" approach, with the goal of maximizing representational faithfulness and ensuring transparency of the financial reporting process would, indeed, make expanded disclosures such as this appear all but mandatory. While many do seek to satisfy the mere letter of the requirements under IFRS, the "principles-based" approach of these standards would, it could easily be argued, demand that preparers (and their auditors) undertake to comply with the spirit of the rules as well.

IAS 24 provides examples of situations where related-party transactions may lead to disclosures by a reporting entity in the period that they affect.

- Purchases or sales of goods (finished or unfinished, meaning work in progress)
- Purchases or sales of property and other assets
- Rendering or receiving of services
- Agency arrangements
- Leasing arrangement
- Transfer of research and development
- License agreements
- Finance (including loans and equity participation in cash or in kind)
- Guarantees and collaterals
- Commitments linked to the occurrence or nonoccurrence of particular events, including executory contracts (recognized and unrecognized)
- Settlement of liabilities on behalf of the entity or by the entity on behalf of another party.

The foregoing should not be considered an exhaustive list of situations requiring disclosure. As very clearly stated in the standard, these are only "examples of situations . . . which may lead to disclosures." In practice, many other situations are encountered which would warrant disclosure. For example, a contract for maintaining and servicing computers, entered into with a subsidiary company, would need to be disclosed by the reporting entity in parent company financial statements.

Disclosure of Parent-Subsidiary Relationships

IAS 24 requires disclosure of relationships between parent and subsidiaries irrespective of whether there have been transactions between the related parties. The name of the parent entity must be provided in the subsidiary's financial statement disclosures; if the ultimate controlling party is a different entity, its name must be disclosed. One reason for this requirement is to enable users of the reporting entity's financial statements to seek out the financial statements of the parent or ultimate controlling party for possible review. If neither of these produces consolidated financial statements available for public use, IAS 24 provides that the name of the "next most senior parent" that produces financial statements must be stated, in addition. These requirements are in addition to those set forth by IAS 27, IAS 28, and IAS 31.

To illustrate this point, consider the following example:

> Apex owns 25% of Bellweather, and by virtue of share ownership of more than 20% of the voting power, would be considered to possess the ability to exercise significant influence over Bellweather. During the year, Apex entered into an agency agreement with Bellweather; however, no transactions took place during the year between the two companies based on the agency contract. Since Apex is considered a related party to Bellweather by virtue of the ability to exercise significant influence, rather than control (i.e., there is not a parent-subsidiary relationship), no disclosure of this related-party relationship would be needed under IAS 24. In case, however, Apex owned 51% or more of the voting power of Bellweather and thereby would be considered related to Bellweather on the basis of control, disclosure of this relationship would be needed, irrespective of whether any transactions actually took place between them.

Disclosures to Be Provided

Per IAS 24, if there have been transactions between related parties, the reporting entity should disclose

1. The nature of the related-party transaction, and
2. Information about transactions and outstanding balances necessary to understand the potential effect of the relationship on the financial statements. At a minimum the following disclosure shall be made:

    a. The amount of the transaction;
    b. Amount of outstanding balances and their terms and conditions, including whether they are secured and details of any guarantees given or received;
    c. Provision for doubtful debts related to the amount of the outstanding balances;
    d. Any expense recognized during the period in respect of bad or doubtful debts due from the related parties.

The disclosures required are to be made *separately* for each of the following categories:

1. The parent;
2. Entities with joint control or significant influence over the entity;
3. Subsidiaries;
4. Associates;
5. Joint venture in which the entity is a venturer;
6. Key management personnel of the entity or its parent; and
7. Other related parties.

Arm's-length transaction price assertions. The assertion that related-party transactions were made at terms that are normal or that the related-party transactions are at arm's-length can be made only if it can be supported. It is presumed that it would rarely be prudent to make such an assertion. The default presumption is that related-party transactions are not *necessarily* conducted on arm's-length terms, which is not taken to imply that transactions were conducted on other bases, either.

Thus, for example, when an entity purchases raw materials amounting to €5 million from an associated company, these are at normal commercial terms (which can be supported, e.g., by competitive bids), and these purchases account for 75% of its total purchases for the year, the following disclosures would seem appropriate:

> During the year, purchases amounting to €5 million were made from an associated company. These purchases were made at normal commercial terms, at prices equivalent to those offered by competitive unrelated vendors. At December 31, 2011, the balance remaining outstanding and owed to this associated company amounted to €2.3 million.

Note that the obtaining of sufficient competent evidence to support an assertion that terms, including prices, for related-party transactions were equivalent to those which would have prevailed for transactions with unrelated parties may be difficult. For example, if the reporting entity formerly purchased from multiple unrelated vendors but, after acquiring a captive source of supply, moves a large portion of its purchases to that vendor, even if prices are the same as had been formerly negotiated with the many unrelated suppliers, this might not warrant an assertion such as the above. The reason is that, with 75% of all purchases being made with this single, related-party supplier, it might not be valid to compare those prices with the process previously negotiated with multiple vendors each providing only a smaller fraction of the reporting entity's needs. Had a large (almost single-source) supply arrangement been executed with any one of the previous suppliers, it might have been possible to negotiate a lower schedule of prices, making comparison of former prices paid for small purchases inapplicable to support this assertion.

Aggregation of disclosures. IAS 24 requires that items of a similar nature may be disclosed in the aggregate. However, when separate disclosure is necessary for an understanding of the effects of the related-party transactions on the financial statements of the reporting entity, aggregation would not be appropriate.

A good example of the foregoing is an aggregated disclosure of total sales made during the year to a number of associated companies, instead of separately disclosing sales made to each associated company. On the other hand, an example of separate disclosure (as opposed to aggregated disclosure) is the disclosure of year-end balances due from various related parties disclosed by category (e.g., advances to directors, associated companies, etc.). In the latter case, it makes sense to disclose separately by categories of related parties, instead of aggregating all balances from various related parties together and disclosing, say, the total amount due from all related parties as one amount, since the character of the transactions could well be at variance, as might be the likelihood of timely collection. In fact, separate disclosure in this case seems necessary for an understanding of the effects of related-party transactions on the financial statements of the reporting entity.

IAS 24 specifically cites other IFRS which also establish requirements for disclosures of related-party transactions. These include

- IAS 27, which requires disclosure of a listing of significant subsidiaries
- IAS 28, which requires disclosure of a listing of significant associates
- IAS 31, which requires disclosure of a listing of interests in significant joint ventures and the proportion of ownership interest held in jointly controlled entities

Compensation. A controversial topic is the disclosure of details regarding management compensation. In some jurisdictions, such disclosures (at least for the upper echelon of management) are required, but in other instances these are secrets closely kept by the reporting entities. The IASB considered deleting these disclosures, given privacy and other concerns, and the belief that other "approval processes" (i.e., internal controls) regulated these arrangements, which therefore would not be subject to frequent abuse. However, these disclosures were maintained in the revised standard because these are deemed relevant for decision making by statement users and are clearly related-party transactions.

The reporting entity is required to disclose key management personnel compensation in total and for each of the following categories:

- Short-term employee benefits,
- Postemployment benefits,
- Other long-term benefits,
- Terminal benefits, and
- Share-based payment.

Government-Related Entities

The reporting entity is exempt from the disclosure requirements for related-party transactions and outstanding balances, including commitments for the following entities:

1. A government that has control, joint control, or significant influence over the reporting entity; and
2. Another entity that is a related party because the same government has control, joint control, or significant influence over both the reporting entity and the other entity.

If the exemption is applicable, the reporting entity must disclose the following:

1. The name of the government and the nature of its relationship with the reporting entity (i.e., control, joint control, or significant influence).
2. The following information in sufficient detail to enable users of the entity's financial statements to understand the effect of related-party transactions on its financial statements

   a. The nature and amount of each individually significant transaction; and
   b. For other transactions that are collectively, but not individually, significant, a qualitative or quantitative indication of their extent

Judgment is used to determine the level of detail to be disclosed for significant transactions. The reporting entity should consider the closeness of the related-party relationship and the following factors in establishing the level of significance of the transaction:

1. Significance in terms of size.
2. Whether or not the transaction was carried out on non-market-related terms.
3. Whether or not the transaction was outside the entity's normal day-to-day business operations, such as the purchase and sale of businesses.
4. Whether or not the transaction was disclosed to regulatory or supervisory authorities.
5. Whether or not the transaction was reported to senior management.
6. Whether or not the transaction was subject to shareholder approval.

Examples of Financial Statement Disclosures

Anglo American
For the year ended December 31, 2010

Related-Party Transactions

The Group has a related-party relationship with its subsidiaries, joint ventures, and associates (see note 37).

The Company and its subsidiaries, in the ordinary course of business, enter into various sales, purchase and service transactions with joint ventures and associates, and others in which the Group has a material interest. These transactions are under terms that are no less favorable to the Group than those arranged with third parties. These transactions are not considered to be significant.

Dividends received from associates during the year totaled $225 million (2009: $616 million), as disclosed in the consolidated cash flow statement.

At December 31, 2010, the Group had provided loans to joint ventures of $319 million (2009; $262 million). These loans are included in financial asset investments. Amounts payable to joint ventures at December 31, 2010, were $59 million (2009: nil).

At December 31, 2010, the directors of the Company and their immediate relatives controlled 2% (2009: 3%) of the voting shares of the Company.

Remuneration and benefits received by directors are disclosed in the directors' remuneration report. Remuneration and benefits of key management personnel including directors are disclosed in note 8.

Information relating to pension fund arrangements is disclosed in note 28.

Related-Party Transactions with De Beers

During the year, the Group has entered into various transactions with DB Investments SA and De Beers SA (together De Beers). These transactions are considered to be related-party transactions for the purposes of the United Kingdom Listing Authority Listing Rules as a result of the interest in De Beers held by Central Holdings Limited and certain of its subsidiaries (together CHL) in which Mr. N.F. Oppenheimer, a director of the Company, has a relevant interest for the purpose of the rules.

In February 2010, the shareholders of De Beers agreed, as part of the refinancing of the De Beers group (the Refinancing), that additional equity was required by De Beers. As a result, such shareholders (including CHL) subscribed, in proportion to their shareholding, for $1 billion of additional equity in De Beers. The Group's share of this equity was $450 million and CHL's share was $400 million.

Pursuant to the Refinancing, and to satisfy the requirements of the lenders to De Beers, the shareholders agreed to certain restrictions until specified financial tests (Normalization) were met. De Beers has confirmed that Normalization occurred during November 2010 and accordingly such restrictions (other than certain subordination obligations) have fallen away. As part of the agreed equity subscription a temporary re-ranking of distribution rights, to be implemented following Normalization, was agreed. In pursuance of that agreement, in November 2010 a $20 million repayment of shareholders loans was made by De Beers (including to the Group and CHL) pro rata to their individual equity subscriptions and in priority to existing preferences under the terms of outstanding preference shares. However, during the period, De Beers also redeemed the remaining $88 million 10% noncumulative redeemable preferences shares held by the Group in De Beers, and settled all accrued dividends and interest, in an aggregate amount of $18 million, relating to such shares.

At December 31, 2010, the amount of outstanding loans owed by De Beers to the Group and included in financial asset investments accounted to $358 million (2009: $367 million). These loans are subordinated in favor of third-party lenders and include

- Dividend reinvestment loans of $133 million (2009: $142 million) advanced during 2008 and 2009. These loans are interest free for two years from the date of advance and subsequently interest bearing in line with market rates at the date of the initial reinvestment; and
- A further shareholder loan of $225 million advance in 2009. This loan is interest free for two years after which it reverts to a rate of interest equal to LIBOR plus 700 basis points until April 2016 and then, provided all interest payments are up to date, reduces to LIBOR plus 300 basis points.

US GAAP COMPARISON

Similar to IFRS, US GAAP requires disclosure of related-party transactions and relationships so users can assess the impact of such arrangements on the financial statements. However, unlike IFRS, disclosures about relationships with government bodies are subject to the general disclosures of other topics.

Transactions between related parties, with some exceptions, whether reflected in the financial statements or not (e.g., exchange of the services between subsidiaries under common control of a parent that are not reflected in the books of record) are disclosed. Exceptions are compensation, expense allowances, or similar items in the ordinary course of business. However, receivables from employees, officers, and affiliated entities must be presented separately from others.

The disclosures for related-party transactions are the nature of the relationships involved, description of the transactions, the dollar amount of such transactions, amounts due to or from related-parties, and the terms. Additionally, if an entity is a member of a group that is consolidated for income tax return purposes, the disclosures must include the aggregate amount of the current and deferred tax expense and the amount of any tax-related balances, as well as the method of allocating taxes to the entity from the tax parent.

Amounts disclosed can be aggregated by type provided that doing so does not obscure the nature or amount with a significant related party. General disclosures cannot imply that transactions with related parties are made on an arm's-length basis unless it can be substantiated.

30 ACCOUNTING AND REPORTING BY RETIREMENT BENEFIT PLANS

INTRODUCTION

IAS 26 sets out the form and content of the general-purpose financial reports of retirement benefit plans. This standard deals with accounting and reporting to all participants of a plan as a group, and not with reports which might be made to individuals about their particular retirement benefits. The standard applies to

- Defined contribution plans where benefits are determined by contributions to the plan together with investment earnings thereon; and
- Defined benefit plans where benefits are determined by a formula based on employees' earnings and/or years of service.

IAS 26 may be compared to IAS 19. The former addresses the financial reporting considerations for the benefit plan itself, as the reporting entity, while the latter deals with employers' accounting for the cost of such benefits as they are earned by the employees. While these standards are thus somewhat related, there will not be any direct interrelationship between amounts reported in benefit plan financial statements and amounts reported under IAS 19 by employers.

Sources of IFRS
IAS 26

DEFINITIONS OF TERMS

Actuarial present value of promised retirement benefits. The present value of the expected future payments by a retirement benefit plan to existing and past employees, attributable to the service already rendered.

Defined benefit plans. Retirement benefit plans whereby retirement benefits to be paid to plan participants are determined by reference to a formula usually based on employees' earnings and/or years of service.

Defined contribution plans. Retirement benefit plans whereby retirement benefits to be paid to plan participants are determined by contributions to a fund together with investment earnings thereon.

Funding. The transfer of assets to a separate entity (distinct from the employer's entity), the "fund," to meet future obligations for the payment of retirement benefits.

Net assets available for benefits. The assets of a retirement benefit plan less its liabilities other than the actuarial present value of promised retirement benefits.

Participants. The members of a retirement benefit plan and others who are entitled to benefits under the plan.

Retirement benefit plans. Formal or informal arrangements based upon which an entity provides benefits for its employees on or after termination of service, which are usually referred to as "termination benefits." These could take the form of annual pension payments or lump-sum payments. Such benefits, or the employer's contributions towards them, should however be determinable or possible of estimation in advance of retirement, from the provisions of a document (i.e., based on a formal arrangement) or from the entity's practices (which is referred to as an informal arrangement).

Vested benefits. Entitlements, the rights to which, under the terms of a retirement benefit plan, are not conditional on continued employment.

SCOPE

IAS 26 should be applied in accounting and reporting by retirement benefit plans. The terms of a retirement plan may require that the plan present an annual report; in some jurisdictions this may be a statutory requirement. IAS 26 does not establish a mandate for the publication of such reports by retirement plans. However, if such reports are prepared by a retirement plan, then the requirements of this standard should be applied to them.

IAS 26 regards a retirement benefit plan as a separate entity, distinct from the employer of the plan's participants. It is noteworthy that this standard also applies to retirement benefit plans that have sponsors other than the employer (e.g., trade associations or groups of employers). Furthermore, this standard deals with accounting and reporting by retirement benefit plans to all participants as a group; it does not deal with reports to individual participants with respect to their retirement benefit entitlements.

The standard applies the same basis of accounting and reporting to informal retirement benefit arrangements as it applies to formal retirement benefit plans. It is also worthy of mention that this standard applies whether or not a separate fund is created and regardless of whether there are trustees. The requirements of this standard also apply to retirement benefit plans with assets invested with an insurance company, unless the contract with the insurance company is in the name of a specified participant or a group of participants and the responsibility is solely of the insurance company. This standard does not deal with other forms of employment benefits such as employment termination indemnities, deferred compensation arrangements, long-service leave benefits, special early retirement or redundancy plans, health and welfare plans or bonus plans. Government social security-type arrangements are also excluded from the scope of this standard.

DEFINED CONTRIBUTION PLANS

Retirement benefit plans are usually described as being either defined contribution or defined benefit plans. When the quantum of the future benefits payable to the retirement benefit plan participants is determined by the contributions paid by the participants' employer, the participants, or both, together with investment earnings thereon, such plans are defined contribution plans. Defined benefit plans, by contrast, promise certain benefits, often determined by formulae which involve factors such as years of service and salary level at the time of retirement, without regard to whether the plan has sufficient assets; thus the ultimate responsibility for payment (which may be guaranteed by an insurance company, the government or some other entity, depending on local law and custom) remains with the employer. In rare circumstances, a retirement benefit plan may contain characteristics of both defined contribution and defined benefit plans; such a hybrid plan is deemed to be a defined benefit plan for the purposes of this standard.

IAS 26 requires that the report of a defined contribution plan contain a statement of the net assets available for benefits and a description of the funding policy. In preparing the statement of the net assets available for benefits, the plan investments should be carried at fair value, which for marketable securities would be market value. In case an estimate of fair value is not possible, disclosure is required of the reason as to why fair value has not been used. As a practical matter, most plan assets will have determinable market values, since the plans' trustees' discharge of their fiduciary responsibilities will generally mandate that only marketable investments be held.

An example of a statement of net assets available for plan benefits, for a defined contribution plan, is set forth below.

XYZ Defined Contribution Plan
Statement of Net Assets Available for Benefits
December 31, 2011
(€000)

Assets	
Investments at fair value	
Government securities	€ 5,000
Municipal bonds	3,000
Local equity securities	3,000
Foreign equity securities	3,000
Local debt securities	2,000
Foreign corporate bonds	2,000
Other	1,000
Total investments	19,000
Receivables	
Amounts due from stockbrokers on sale of securities	15,000
Accrued interest	5,000
Dividends receivable	2,000
Total receivables	22,000
Cash	5,000
Total assets	€46,000
Liabilities	
Accounts payable	
Amounts due to stockbrokers on purchase of securities	€10,000
Benefits payable to participants—due and unpaid	11,000
Total accounts payable	21,000
Accrued expenses	11,000
Total liabilities	€32,000
Net assets available for benefits	€14,000

DEFINED BENEFIT PLANS

When amounts to be paid as retirement benefits are determined by reference to a formula, usually based on employees' earnings and/or years of service, such retirement benefit plans are defined benefit plans. The key factor is that the benefits are fixed or determinable, without regard to the adequacy of assets which may have been set aside for payment of the benefits. This contrasts to the defined contribution plans approach, which is to provide the workers, upon retirement, with the amounts which have been set aside, plus or minus investment earnings or losses which have been accumulated thereon, however great or small that amount may be.

The standard requires that the report of a defined benefit plan should contain *either*

1. A statement that shows

    a. The net assets available for benefits;
    b. The actuarial present value of promised retirement benefits, distinguishing between vested and nonvested benefits; and
    c. The resulting excess or deficit;

or

2. A statement of net assets available for benefits including *either*

    a. A note disclosing the actuarial present value of promised retirement benefits, distinguishing between vested and nonvested benefits; or
    b. A reference to this information in an accompanying actuarial report.

IAS 26 recommends, but does not mandate, that in each of the three formats described above, a trustees' report in the nature of a management or directors' report and an investment report may also accompany the statements.

The standard does not make it incumbent upon the plan to obtain annual actuarial valuations. If an actuarial valuation has not been prepared on the date of the report, the most recent valuation should be used as the basis for preparing the financial statement. The date of the valuation used should be disclosed. Actuarial present values of promised benefits should be based either on current or projected salary levels; whichever basis is used should be disclosed. The effect of any changes in actuarial assumptions that had a material impact on the actuarial present value of promised retirement benefits should also be disclosed. The report should explain the relationship between actuarial present values of promised benefits, the net assets available for benefits and the policy for funding the promised benefits.

As in the case of defined contribution plans, investments of a defined benefit plan should be carried at fair value, which for marketable securities, would be market value.

The following are examples of the alternative types of reports prescribed for a defined benefit plan:

ABC Defined Benefit Plan
Statement of Net Assets Available for Benefits, Actuarial Present Value of Accumulated
Retirement Benefits and Plan Excess or Deficit
December 31, 2011
(€000)

1. Statement of net assets available for benefits

   Assets
   Investments at fair value

Government securities	€ 50,000
Municipal bonds	30,000
Local equity securities	30,000
Foreign equity securities	30,000
Local debt securities	20,000
Foreign corporate bonds	20,000
Other	10,000
Total investments	€190,000

   Receivables

Amounts due from stockbrokers on sale of securities	150,000
Accrued interest	50,000
Dividends receivable	20,000
Total receivables	220,000
Cash	50,000
Total assets	460,000

   Liabilities
   Accounts payable

Amounts due to stockbrokers on purchase of securities	100,000
Benefits payable to participants–due and unpaid	110,000
Total accounts payable	210,000
Accrued expenses	110,000
Total liabilities	320,000
Net assets available for benefits	€140,000

2. Actuarial present value of accumulated plan benefits

Vested benefits	€100,000
Nonvested benefits	20,000
Total	€120,000

3. Excess of net assets available for benefits over actuarial present value of accumulated plan benefits .... € 20,000

ABC Defined Benefit Plan
Statement of Changes in Net Assets Available for Benefits
December 31, 2011
(€000)

Investment income

Interest income	€ 40,000
Dividend income	10,000
Net appreciation (unrealized gain) in fair value of investments	10,000
Total investment income	60,000

Plan contributions

Employer contributions	50,000
Employee contributions	50,000
Total plan contributions	100,000
Total additions to net asset value	160,000

Plan benefit payments	
Pensions (annual)	30,000
Lump sum payments on retirement	30,000
Severance pay	10,000
Commutation of superannuation benefits	15,000
Total plan benefit payments	85,000
Total deductions from net asset value	85,000
Net increase in asset value	75,000
Net assets available for benefits	
Beginning of year	65,000
End of year	€140,000

DISCLOSURES

IAS 26 requires that the reports of a retirement benefit plan, both defined benefit plans and defined contribution plans, should also contain the following information:

1. A statement of changes in net assets available for benefits;
2. A summary of significant accounting policies; and
3. A description of the plan and the effect of any changes in the plan during the period.

Reports provided by retirement benefits plans may include the following, if applicable:

1. A statement of net assets available for benefits disclosing

    a. Assets at the end of the period suitably classified;
    b. The basis of valuation of assets;
    c. Details of any single investment exceeding either 5% of the net assets available for benefits or 5% of any class or type of security;
    d. Details of any investment in the employer; and
    e. Liabilities other than the actuarial present value of promised retirement benefits;

2. A statement of changes in net assets available for benefits showing the following:

    a. Employer contributions;
    b. Employee contributions;
    c. Investment income such as interest and dividends;
    d. Other income;
    e. Benefits paid or payable (analyzed, for example, as retirement, death and disability benefits, and lump-sum payments);
    f. Administrative expenses;
    g. Other expenses;
    h. Taxes on income;
    i. Profits and losses on disposal of investments and changes in value of investments; and
    j. Transfers from and to other plans;

3. A description of the funding policy;
4. For defined benefit plans, the actuarial present value of promised retirement benefits (which may distinguish between vested benefits and nonvested benefits) based on the benefits promised under the terms of the plan, on service rendered to date and using either current salary levels or projected salary levels. This information may be included in an accompanying actuarial report to be read in conjunction with the related information; and

5. For defined benefit plans, a description of the significant actuarial assumptions made and the method used to calculate the actuarial present value of promised retirement benefits.

According to the standard, since the report of a retirement benefit plan contains a description of the plan, either as part of the financial information or in a separate report, it may contain the following:

1. The names of the employers and the employee groups covered;
2. The number of participants receiving benefits and the number of other participants, classified as appropriate;
3. The type of plan—defined contribution or defined benefit;
4. A note as to whether participants contribute to the plan;
5. A description of the retirement benefits promised to participants;
6. A description of any plan termination terms; and
7. Changes in items 1. through 6. during the period covered by the report.

Furthermore, it is not uncommon to refer to other documents that are readily available to users and in which the plan is described, and to include only information on subsequent changes in the report.

31 AGRICULTURE

INTRODUCTION

Historically, agricultural activities received scant, if any, attention from the world's accounting standard setters. This may have been due to the fact that the major national and international accounting standard setters have been those of the US and the UK, whose economies are far less dependent upon agriculture than those of many lesser-developed nations of the world. For developing nations, agriculture is indeed disproportionately significant, and given the IASC's role in establishing financial reporting standards for those nations, this focus on agriculture was perhaps to be expected. The culmination of this lengthy project, IAS 41, is by far the most comprehensive addressing of this financial reporting topic ever undertaken.

The earlier exclusion of agriculture from most established accounting and financial reporting rules can best be understood in the context of certain unique features of the industry. These include biological transformations (growth, procreation, production, degeneration) which alter the very substance of the biological assets; the wide variety of characteristics of the living assets which challenge traditional classification schemes; the nature of management functions in the industry; and the predominance of small, closely held ownership. On the other hand, since in many nations agriculture is a major industry, in some cases accounting for over 50% of gross national product, logic would suggest that comprehensive systems of financial reporting for business entities cannot be deemed complete while excluding so large a segment of the economy.

In the realm of previously established international accounting standards, most of the rules which logically could have addressed agricultural issues (IAS 2 on inventories; IAS 16 on property, plant and equipment; and IAS 18 on revenue recognition) deliberately excluded most or all agriculture-related applications. A review of published financial statements for agriculture-related entities would have revealed the consequences of this neglect: a wide range of methods and principles have been applied to such businesses as forest products, livestock, and grain production.

For example, some forest products companies have accounted for timberlands at original cost, charging depreciation only to the extent of net harvesting, with reforestation costs charged to expense as incurred. Others in the same industry capitalized reforestation costs and even carrying costs, and charged depletion on a units-of-production basis. Still others have been valuing forest lands at the net present value of expected future cash flows. This wide disparity obviously has impaired users' ability to gauge the relative performance of entities operating within a single industry group, hindering investment and other decision making by them.

Sources of IFRS
IAS 41

SCOPE

IAS 41 applies only to biological assets, as those are the aspects of agriculture that have unique characteristics; the accounting for assets such as inventories and plant and equipment will be guided by such existing standards as IAS 2 and 16. In other words, once the biological transformation process is complete (e.g., when grain is harvested, animals are slaughtered, or trees are cut down), the specialized accounting principles imposed on agriculture will cease to apply.

DEFINITIONS OF TERMS

Active market. Market for which all these conditions exist: the items traded within the market are homogeneous; willing buyers and sellers can normally be found at any time; and prices are available to the public.

Agricultural activity. Managed biological transformation of biological assets into agricultural produce for sale, consumption, further processing, or into other biological assets.

Agricultural land. Land used directly to support and sustain biological assets in agricultural activity; the land itself is not a biological asset, however.

Agricultural produce. The harvested product of the entity's biological assets awaiting sale, processing, or consumption.

Bearer biological assets. Those which bear agricultural produce for harvest. The biological assets themselves are not the primary agricultural produce, but rather are self-regenerating (such as sheep raised for wool production; fruit trees).

Biological assets. Living plants and animals controlled by the entity as a result of past events. Control may be through ownership or through another type of legal arrangement.

Biological transformation. The processes of growth, degeneration, production and procreation, which cause qualitative and quantitative changes in living organisms and the generation of new assets in the form of agricultural produce or additional biological assets of the same class.

Carrying amount. Amount at which an asset is recognized in the statement of financial position after deducting any accumulated depreciation or amortization and accumulated impairment losses thereon.

Consumable biological assets. Those which are to be harvested as the primary agricultural produce, such as livestock intended for meat production, annual crops, and trees to be felled for pulp.

Fair value. The amount for which an asset could be exchanged or a liability settled between knowledgeable, willing parties in an arm's-length transaction.

Group of biological assets. A herd, flock, etc., that is managed jointly to ensure that the group is sustainable on an ongoing basis, and is homogeneous as to both type of animal or plant and activity for which the group is deployed.

Harvest. The detachment of agricultural produce from the biological asset, the removal of a living plant from agricultural land for sale and replanting, or the cessation of a biological asset's life processes.

Immature biological assets. Those that are not yet harvestable or able to sustain regular harvests.

Mature biological assets. Those that are harvestable or able to sustain regular harvest. Consumable biological assets are mature when they have attained harvestable specifications; bearer biological assets are mature when they are able to sustain regular harvests.

Net realizable value. Estimated selling price in the ordinary course of business, less the estimated costs of completion and the estimated costs necessary to make the sale.

IDENTIFICATION

Agriculture is defined as essentially the management of the biological transformation of plants and animals to yield produce for consumption or further processing. The term agriculture encompasses livestock, forestry, annual and perennial cropping, orchards, plantations, and aquiculture. Agriculture is distinguished from "pure exploitation," where resources are simply removed from the environment (e.g., by fishing or deforestation) without management initiatives such as operation of hatcheries, reforestation, or other attempts to manage their regeneration. IAS 41 does not apply to pure exploitation activities, nor does it apply to agricultural produce, which is harvested and is thus a nonliving product of the biological assets. The standard furthermore does not govern accounting for agriculture produce which is incorporated in further processing, as occurs in integrated agribusiness entities that involve activities which are not unique to agriculture.

IAS 41 sets forth a three-part test or set of criteria for agricultural activities. First, the plants or animals which are the object of the activities must be alive and capable of transformation. Second, the change must be managed, which implies a range of activities (e.g., fertilizing the soil and weeding in the case of crop growing; feeding and providing health care in the instance of animal husbandry; etc.). Third, there must be a basis for the measurement of change, such as the ripeness of vegetables, the weight of animals, circumference of trees, and so forth. If these three criteria are all satisfied, the activity will be impacted by the financial reporting requirements imposed by IAS 41.

Biological assets are the principal assets of agricultural activities, and they are held for their transformative potential. This results in two major types of outcomes: the first may involve asset changes—as through growth or quality improvement, degeneration, or procreation. The second involves the creation of separable products initially qualifying as agricultural produce. The management of the biological transformation process is the distinguishing characteristic of agricultural activities.

Biological assets often are managed in groups, as exemplified by herds of animals, groves of trees, and fields of crops. To be considered a group, however, the components must be homogeneous in nature and there must further be homogeneity in the activity for which the group is deployed. For example, cherry trees maintained for their production of fruit are not in the same group as cherry trees grown for lumber.

IAS 41 applies to forests and similar regenerative resources excluded from IAS 16; producers' inventories of livestock, agriculture, and forest products, including those excluded from IAS 2, to the extent they are to be measured at net realizable value; and natural increases in herds and agricultural and forest products excluded from IAS 18.

RECOGNITION AND MEASUREMENT

Basic Principles of IAS 41

IAS 41 applies to all entities which undertake agricultural activities. Animals or plants are to be recognized as assets when it is probable that the future economic benefits associated with the asset will flow to the reporting entity, and when the cost or value to the entity can be measured reliably. The standard also governs the initial measurement of agricultural produce, which is the end product of the biological transformation process; it furthermore guides the accounting for government grants pertaining to agricultural assets.

The most important feature of the standard is the requirement that biological assets are to be measured at their respective fair values as of each date of the statements of financial position. The imperative to deploy fair value accounting springs from the fact that there are long production periods for many crops (an extreme being forests under management for as long as thirty years before being harvested) and, even more typically, for livestock. In the absence of fair value accounting with changes in value being reported in operating results, the entire earnings of a long-term production process might only be reported at lengthy intervals, which would not faithfully represent the underlying economic activities being carried out. This is entirely analogous to long-term construction projects, for which percentage-of-completion accounting is commonly prescribed, for very similar reasons.

Historical cost based accounting, with revenue to be recognized only upon ultimate sale of the assets, would often result in a gross distortion of reported results of operations, with little or no earnings being reflected in some periods, or even losses being reported to the extent that production expenses are not inventoried. Other periods—when trees are harvested, for example—would reflect substantial reported profits. Thus, the use of historical costs based on completed transactions is no longer deemed meaningful in the case of agricultural activities.

Not only are such periodic distortions seen as being misleading, but it also has been concluded that each stage of the biological transformation process has significance. Each stage (growth, degeneration, procreation, and production) is now seen as contributing to the expected economic benefits to be derived from the biological assets. Unless a fair value model were employed for financial reporting, there would be a lack of explicit recognition (in effect, no matching) of the benefits associated with each of these discrete events. Furthermore, this recognition underlines the need to apply the same measurement concept to each stage in the life cycle of the biological assets; for example, for live weight change, fleece weight change, aging, deaths, lambs born, and wool shorn, in the case of a flock of sheep.

The obvious argument in favor of historical cost–based measures derives from the superior reliability of that mode of measurement. With completed transactions, there is no imprecision due to the inherently subjective process of making or obtaining fair value assessments. By contrast, superior relevance is the strongest argument for current value measurement schemes. The IASC ultimately identified fair value as having the best combination of attributes for the determination of agriculture-related earnings. The IASC was particularly influenced by the market context in which agriculture takes place and the transformative characteristics of biological assets, and it concluded that fair value would offer the best balance of relevance, reliability, comparability, and understandability.

The IASC also concluded that annual determinations of fair value would be necessary to properly portray the combined impact of nature and financial transactions for any given reporting period. Less frequent measurements were rejected because of the continuous nature of biological transformations, the lack of direct correlation between financial transactions and the different outcomes arising from biological transformation (thus, the former could not serve as surrogate indicators of the latter during off periods), the volatilities which often characterize natural and market environments affecting agriculture, and the fact that market-based measures are in fact readily available.

Notwithstanding the fact that historical cost is rejected as being meaningful in this context, the IASC agreed that an exception should exist for those circumstances when fair value cannot be reliably estimated. In such instances, historical costs will continue to be employed instead.

Determining Fair Values

The primary determinant of fair value is observable market prices, just as it is for financial instruments having active markets (as defined in IAS 32, discussed at length in Chapter 24). Chapter 25 discusses fair value measurements in more depth. The required use of "farm gate" market prices will reflect both the "as is" and "where is" attributes of the biological assets. That is, the value is meant to pertain to the assets as they exist, where they are located, in the condition they are in as of the measurement (statement of financial position) date. They are not hypothetical values, as for instance hogs when delivered to the slaughterhouse. Where these "farm gate" prices are not available, market values will have to be reduced by transaction costs, including transport, to arrive at net market values which would equate to fair values as intended by IAS 41.

In the case of products for which market values might not be readily available, other approaches to fair value determination will have to be employed. This is most likely to become an issue where market values exist but, due to market imperfections, are not deemed to be useful. For example, when access to markets is restricted or unduly influenced by temporary monopoly or monopsony conditions, or when no market actually exists as of the date of the statement of financial position, alternative measures will be called for. In such circumstances, it might be necessary to refer to such indicators as the most recent market prices for the class of asset at issue, market prices for similar assets (e.g., different varieties of the same crop), sector benchmarks (e.g., relating value of a dairy farm to the kilograms of milk solids or fat produced), net present value of expected future cash flows discounted at a risk-class rate, or net realizable values for short-cycle products for which most growth has already occurred. Last and probably least useful would be historical costs, which might be particularly suited to biological assets that have thus far experienced little transformation.

One practical problem arises when an indirect method of valuation implicitly values both the crop and the land itself, taken together as a whole. IAS 41 indicates that such valuations must be allocated to the different assets to give a better indication of the future economic benefits each will confer. If a combined market price, for example, can be obtained for the land plus the immature growing crops situated thereon, and a quotation for the land alone can also be obtained, this will permit a fair value assessment of the immature growing crops (while the land itself will generally be presented on the statement of financial position at cost, not fair value, under IAS 16). Another technique would involve the subdivision of the assets into classes based on age, quality, or other traits, and the valuation of each subgroup by reference to market prices. While these methods may involve added effort, IAS 41 concludes that the usefulness of the resulting financial statements will be materially enhanced if this is done.

Increases in fair value due to the growth of the biological asset is only one-half of the accounting equation, of course, since there will normally have been cost inputs incurred to foster the growth (e.g., applications of fertilizer to the fields, etc.). Under the provisions of IAS 41, costs of producing and harvesting biological assets are to be charged to expense as incurred. This is necessary, since if costs were added to the assets' carrying amount (analogous to interest on borrowings in connection with long-term construction projects) and the assets were then also adjusted to fair value, there would be risk of double-counting cost or value increases. As mandated, however, value increases due to either price changes or growth, or both, will be taken into current income, where costs of production will be appropriately matched against them, resulting in a meaningful measure of the net result of periodic operations.

Recognition and Measurement

The recognition and measurement requirements of IAS 41 are as follows:

1. Biological assets are to be measured at their fair value, less estimated costs to sell, except where fair value cannot be measured reliably. In the latter instance, historical cost is to be used.
2. Agricultural produce harvested from an entity's biological assets should be measured at fair value less estimated costs to sell at the point of harvest. That amount effectively becomes the cost basis, to which further processing costs may be added, as the conditions warrant, with accounting thereafter guided by IAS 2, *Inventories,* or other applicable standard.
3. The presumption is that fair value can be measured reliably for a biological asset. That presumption can be rebutted, only at the time of initial recognition, for a biological asset for which market-determined prices or values are not available and for which alternative estimates of fair value are determined to be clearly unreliable. Once the fair value of such a biological asset becomes reliably measurable, it must be measured at its fair value less estimated costs to sell.
4. If an active market exists for a biological asset or for agricultural produce, the quoted price in that market is the appropriate basis for determining the fair value of that asset. If an active market does not exist, however, the reporting entity should use market-determined prices or values, such as the most recent market transaction price, when available.
5. Under certain circumstances, market-determined prices or values may not be available for an asset, as it exists in its current condition. In these circumstances, the entity should use the present value of expected net cash flows from the asset discounted at a current market-determined pretax rate, in determining fair value.
6. The gain or loss which is reported upon initial recognition of biological assets, and also those arising from changes in fair value less estimated point-of-sales costs, should be included in net profit or loss for the period in which the gain or loss arises. That is, these are reported in current period results of operations, and not taken directly into equity.
7. The gain or loss arising from the initial recognition of agricultural produce should be included in net profit or loss for the period in which it arises.
8. Land is to be accounted for under IAS 16, *Property, Plant, and Equipment,* or IAS 40, *Investment Property,* as is appropriate under the circumstances. Biological assets that are physically attached to land are recognized and measured at their fair value less estimated point-of-sales costs, separately from the land.

9. If the entity receives an unconditional government grant related to a biological asset measured at its fair value less estimated point-of-sales costs, the grant should be recognized as income when it first becomes receivable. If the grant related to a biological asset measured at its fair value less estimated costs to sell is conditional, including grants which require an entity not to engage in specified agricultural activity, the grant should be recognized in income when the conditions attaching to it are first met.

10. For government grants pertaining to biological assets which are measured at cost less accumulated depreciation and any accumulated impairment losses, IAS 20, *Accounting for Government Grants and Disclosure of Government Assistance,* should be applied. (See Chapter 21.)

11. Some contracts for the sale of biological assets or agricultural produce are not within the scope of IAS 39, *Financial Instruments: Recognition and Measurement,* because the reporting entity expects to deliver the commodity, rather than settle up in cash. Under IAS 41, such contracts are to be measured at fair value until the biological assets are sold or the produce is harvested.

Agricultural Produce (Measurement)

Agricultural produce is distinguished from biological assets and is not to be measured at fair value other than at the point of harvest, which is the point where biological assets become agricultural produce. For example, when crops are harvested they become agricultural produce and are initially valued at the fair value as of the date of harvest, at the location of harvest (i.e., the value of harvested crops at a remote point of delivery would not be a pertinent measure). If there has been a time interval between the last valuation and the harvest, the value as of the harvest date should be determined or estimated; any increase or decrease since the last valuation would be taken into earnings.

PRESENTATION AND DISCLOSURES

Financial Statement Presentation

Statement of financial position. IAS 41 requires that the carrying amount of biological assets be presented separately on the face of the statement of financial position (i.e., not included with other, nonbiological assets). Preparers are encouraged to describe the nature and stage of production of each group of biological assets in narrative format in the notes to the financial statements, optionally quantified. Consumable biological assets are to be differentiated from bearer assets, with further subdivisions into mature and immature subgroups for each of these broad categories. The purpose of these disclosures is to give the users of the financial statements some insight into the timing of future cash flows, since the mature subgroups will presumably be realized through market transactions in the near future, and the pattern of cash flows resulting from bearer assets differs from those deriving from consumables.

Statement of comprehensive income. The changes in fair value should be presented on the face of the statement of comprehensive income, ideally broken down between groups of biological assets. However, group level detail may be reserved to the notes to the financial statements.

IAS 1 permits the presentation of expenses in accordance with either a natural classification (e.g., materials purchases, depreciation, etc.) or a functional basis (cost of sales, administrative, selling, etc.). The draft standard on agriculture had urged that the natural classification of income and expenses be adopted for the statement of comprehensive income. Sufficient detail is to be included in the face of the statement of comprehensive income to support an analysis of operating performance. However, these are recommendations, not strict requirements.

Disclosures. IAS 41 establishes disclosure requirements for biological assets measured at cost less any accumulated depreciation and any accumulated impairment losses (i.e., for those exceptional biological assets which are **not** being carried at fair value). The disclosures are as follows:

1. A separate reconciliation of changes in the carrying amount of those biological assets;
2. A description of those biological assets;
3. An explanation of why fair value cannot be measured reliably;
4. A statement of the range of estimates within which fair value is highly likely to lie (if this is possible to give);
5. The amount of any gain or loss recognized on disposal of the biological assets;
6. The depreciation method used;
7. The useful lives or the depreciation rates used; and
8. The gross carrying amount and the accumulated depreciation at the beginning and end of the reporting period.

In addition to the foregoing, these disclosures are required:

1. If the fair value of biological assets previously measured at cost less any accumulated depreciation and any accumulated impairment losses subsequently becomes reliably measurable, the reporting entity must disclose a description of the biological assets, and explanation of how fair value has become reliably measurable, and the effect of the change in accounting method; and
2. Information about any significant decreases in the expected level of government grants related to agricultural activity covered by IAS 41.

Furthermore an entity shall present a reconciliation of changes in the carrying amount of biological assets between the beginning and the end of the current period. The reconciliation shall include

1. The gain or loss arising from changes in fair value less costs to sell;
2. Increases due to purchases;
3. Decreases attributable to sales and biological assets classified as held for sale (or included in a disposal group that is classified as held for sale) in accordance with IFRS 5;
4. Decreases due to harvest;
5. Increases resulting from business combinations;
6. Net exchange differences arising on the translation of financial statements into a different presentation currency, and on the translation of a foreign operation into the presentation currency of the reporting entity; and
7. Other changes.

The normally anticipated disclosures regarding the nature of operations, which are necessary to comply with IAS 1, also apply to entities engaging in biological and agricultural operations. These disclosures could incorporate, either in narrative form or as quantified terms, information about the groups of biological assets, the nature of activities regarding each of these groups, the maturity or immaturity for intended purposes of each group, the relative significance of different groups by reference to nonmonetary amounts (e.g., numbers of animals, acres of trees) dedicated to each, and nonfinancial measures or estimates of the physical quantities of each group of assets at the date of the statement of financial position and the output of agricultural produce during the reporting period.

Good practice, necessary to make the financial statements meaningful for users, would dictate that disclosures be made of

1. The measurement bases used to derive fair values;
2. Whether an independent appraiser was utilized;
3. Where relevant, the discount rate employed to compute net present values, along with the number of years' future cash flows assumed;
4. Additional details about the changes in fair value from the prior period, where needed;
5. Any restrictions on title and any pledging of biological assets as security for liabilities;
6. Commitments for further development or acquisitions of biological assets;
7. Specifics about risk management strategies employed by the entity (note that the use of hedging is widespread. The futures market, now heavily employed to control financial risks, was developed originally for agricultural commodities); and
8. Activities which are unsustainable, along with estimated dates of cessation of those activities.

Other possible disclosures include the carrying amount of agricultural land (at either historical cost or revalued amount) and of agricultural produce (governed by IAS 2, and subject to separate classification in the statement of financial position).

OTHER ISSUES

Agricultural Land

Agricultural land is not deemed a biological asset; thus, the principles espoused in IAS 41 for biological and agricultural assets do not apply to land. The requirements of IAS 16, which are applicable to other categories of property, plant and equipment, apply equally to agricultural land. The use of the allowed alternative method (i.e., revaluation), particularly for land-based systems such as orchards, plantations, and forests, where the fair value of the biological asset was determined from net realizable values which included the underlying land, would be logical and advisable, but is not actually a requirement. It would also enhance the usefulness of the financial statements if land held by entities engaged in agricultural activities is further classified in the statement of financial position according to specific uses. Alternatively, this information can be conveyed in the notes to the financial statements.

Intangible Assets Related to Agriculture

Under IAS 38, intangible assets may be carried at cost or at revalued amounts, but only to the extent that active markets exist for the intangibles. In general, it is not expected that such markets will exist for commonly encountered classes of intangible assets. On the other hand, agricultural activities are expected to frequently involve intangibles such as water rights, production quotas, and pollution rights, and it is anticipated that for these intangibles active markets may in fact exist.

To enhance the internal consistency of financial statements of entities engaged in biological and agriculture operations, if intangibles which pertain to the entity's agricultural activities have active markets, these should be presented in the statement of financial position at their fair values. This is not, however, an actual requirement.

Government Grants

IAS 20 addresses the accounting for government grants, whether received with conditions attached or not, and whether received in cash or otherwise. As noted above, IAS 41 effectively amends this in the case of reporting by entities receiving an unconditional government grant related to a biological asset that is measured at its fair value less estimated costs to sell. Such grants are recognized in profit or loss when the grant becomes receivable. For grants which are conditional, recognition in income will occur when there is reasonable assurance that the conditions have been met. If conditional grants are received before the conditions have been met, the grant should be recognized as a liability, not as revenue. For grants received in the form of nonmonetary assets, fair value is to be assessed in order to account for the grant.

US GAAP COMPARISON

US GAAP provides specific incremental guidance for the accounting, reporting, and disclosure of agricultural activities. Agricultural products and activities include animals (livestock) and plants. However, ASC 905 does not apply to growers of timber, growers of pineapple and sugarcane in tropical regions, raisers of animals for competitive sports, nor merchants or noncooperative processors of agricultural products that purchase commodities from growers, contract harvesters, or others serving agricultural producers.

The carrying amount of agricultural products is historical cost. For assets deemed property, plant, and equipment, depreciation is systematic and rational based on its utility. Permanent improvements to land, such as grading, are not depreciated because of their utility does not diminish with time. Short-lived animals, such as chickens, are classified as inventory. The costs of reclaiming productive capacity from the land that relates specifically to the current year harvest are accrued as part of the costs, even though these costs will benefit subsequent year's harvest. Costs involved in raising a progeny to a productive state (i.e., a calf to the point it produces milk) are accumulated as part of the costs and depreciated when the livestock reaches maturity.

Market prices for valuing crops or livestock are only used in valuing inventory or PP&E in exceptional circumstances when it is not practicable to determine an appropriate cost basis for products. Per ASC 905-330-30-1, a market basis is acceptable if the products meet all of the following criteria: (1)The products have immediate marketability at quoted market prices that cannot be influenced by the producer, (2) The products have characteristics of unit interchangeability, (3) The products have relatively insignificant costs of disposal.

US GAAP also provides guidance for Agricultural Cooperatives. An agricultural cooperative is an organization which performs any of following on behalf of its patrons: sale, processing, marketing, and other activities. Cooperatives can provide services for nonpatrons, but the results and financial positions must be separately presented. Cooperatives generally distribute all profits to patrons, except for retains, which are reserves to insulate the cooperative from financial shocks. Revenue is recorded by patrons whenever title passes to the cooperative. If title does not pass, the revenue is accounted for on a consignment basis, with revenue deferred until sale to the third-party buyer takes place. The equity section of an agricultural cooperative must separate earnings and balance between patrons and nonpatrons. This is because the cooperative's mission is to perform service on behalf of the patrons, and each patron may have different rights and obligations, although bylaws or other agreements generally govern most of the activities. Frequently, cooperatives pool products from patrons and remit proceeds to each patron based on the volume sold.

Investments by patrons in cooperatives are accounted for under the cost method or the equity method if it has significant influence (per applicable US GAAP). The investment balance includes retains. The investment balance is reduced if cooperative losses will likely not be recovered by the patron.

32 EXTRACTIVE INDUSTRIES

INTRODUCTION

IFRS 6 which deals with the accounting for exploration for, and evaluation of, mineral resources, which deals with somewhat limited issues, and the IASB, assisted by a task force consisting of national standard setters, has continued to examine other related matters.

Ongoing research is considering all issues associated with accounting for "upstream" extractive activities. Specifically, this is intended to address the treatment of

1. Reserves/resources—which will include determining whether

    a. Reserves/resources can or should be recognized as assets on the statement of financial position;
    b. Predevelopment costs incurred following the discovery of reserves/resources should be capitalized or expensed if reserves/resources are not recognized;
    c. Predevelopment costs incurred prior to the discovery of reserves/resources should be capitalized or expensed; and
    d. Reserves/resources information should be disclosed—and if so, what information.

2. Other issues arising from the application of IFRS by entities conducting extractive activities.

In April 2010, the IASB published the results of an international research project on a possible future IFRS for extractive activities in the form of a discussion paper—*Extractive Activities*. This chapter reports both on IFRS 6 and possible future developments.

Sources of IFRS
IFRS 6

DEFINITIONS OF TERMS

Exploration and evaluation assets. Exploration and evaluation expenditures recognized as assets in accordance with the reporting entity's accounting policy.

Exploration and evaluation expenditures. Expenditures incurred by a reporting entity in connection with the exploration for and evaluation of mineral resources, before the technical feasibility and commercial viability of extracting a mineral resource have been demonstrated.

Exploration for and evaluation of mineral resources. The search for mineral resources, including minerals, oil, natural gas, and similar nonregenerative resources after the entity has obtained legal rights to explore in a specific area, as well as the determination of the technical feasibility and commercial viability of extracting the mineral resource.

EXPLORATION AND EVALUATION OF MINERAL RESOURCES

Background

In mid 2005, the IASB issued IFRS 6, *Exploration for and Evaluation of Mineral Resources*, which proposed an interim solution, designed to facilitate compliance with IFRS by entities reporting exploration and evaluation assets, without making substantial changes to existing accounting practices. The reasons cited by the IASB for the development of an interim standard addressing exploration for and evaluation of mineral resources were as follows:

1. There were no extant IFRS that specifically addressed the exploration for and evaluation of mineral resources, which had been excluded from the scope of IAS 38. Furthermore, mineral rights and mineral resources such as oil, natural gas and similar nonregenerative resources were excluded from the scope of IAS 16. Accordingly, a reporting entity having such assets and activities is required to determine accounting policies for such expenditures in accordance with IAS 8.
2. There were alternative views on how the exploration for and evaluation of mineral resources and, particularly, the recognition of exploration and evaluation assets, were required to be accounted for under IFRS.
3. Accounting practices for exploration and evaluation expenditures under various national GAAP standards were quite diverse, and often differed from practices in other sectors for items that could have been considered similar (e.g., the accounting practices for research costs under IAS 38).
4. Exploration and evaluation expenditures represented a significant cost to entities engaged in extractive activities.
5. While relatively few entities incurring exploration and evaluation expenditures were reporting under IFRS at the time (circa 2005), many more were expected to do so, particularly given the EU mandate for publicly listed entities to report consolidated results in conformity with IFRS, which became effective in 2005, as well as the rapidly growing worldwide acceptance of IFRS.

IFRS 6 in Greater Detail

IFRS 6 sets forth a set of generalized principles that define the main issues for reporting entities that have activities involving the exploration for and evaluation of mineral resources. These principles are as follows:

1. IFRS fully applies to these entities, except when they are specifically excluded from the scope of a given standard.
2. Reporting entities may continue employing their existing accounting policies to account for exploration and evaluation assets, but any change in accounting will have to qualify under the criteria set forth by IAS 8.
3. A reporting entity that recognizes exploration and evaluation assets must assess those assets for impairment annually, in accordance with IAS 36. However, the entity may conduct the assessment at the level of "a cash-generating unit for exploration and evaluation assets," rather than at the level otherwise required by IAS 36. As set forth by IFRS 6, this is a higher level of aggregation than would have been the case under a strict application of the criteria in IAS 36.

Thus, according to IFRS 6, entities that have assets used for exploration and evaluation of mineral resources are to report under IFRS, but certain assets may be subject to alternative measurement requirements. The adoption of new, specialized requirements will be optional, at least at this time. The next phase of the extractive industries project may result in new requirements.

Cash-generating units for exploration and evaluation assets. The most significant aspect of IFRS 6 concerns its establishment of a unique definition of *cash-generating units* for impairment testing. It created a different level of aggregation for mineral exploration and evaluation assets, when compared to all other assets subject to impairment considerations under IAS 36. The reason for this distinction is that the IASB was concerned that requiring entities to use the standard definition of a cash-generating unit, as set forth by IAS 36, when assessing exploration and evaluation assets for impairment might have negated the effects of the other aspects of the proposal, thereby resulting in the inappropriate recognition of impairment losses under certain circumstances. Specifically, the IASB was of the opinion that the standard definition of a cash-generating unit could cause there to be uncertainty about whether the reporting entity's existing accounting policies were consistent with IFRS, because exploration and evaluation assets would often not be expected to

1. Be the subject of future cash inflow and outflow projections relating to the development of the project, on a reasonable and consistent basis, without being heavily discounted because of uncertainty and lead times;
2. Have a determinable net selling price; or
3. Be readily identifiable with other assets that generate cash inflows as a specific cash-generating unit.

In the IASB's view, the implications of the foregoing matters were that an exploration and evaluation asset would often be deemed to be impaired, inappropriately, if the IAS 36 definition of a cash-generating unit was applied without at least the potential for modification.

Given the foregoing concern, in the draft standard the IASB had proposed a unique definition of a cash-generating unit for exploration and evaluation assets. The cash-generating unit for exploration and evaluation assets was to be the cash-generating unit that represents the smallest identifiable group of assets that, together with exploration and evaluation assets, generates cash inflows from continuing use to which impairment tests were applied by the entity under the accounting policies applied for its most recent annual financial statements. The entity would be permitted to elect, under the proposed rules, to apply either the IAS 36 definition of a cash-generating unit, or the special definition above. The election would have to be made when the proposed IFRS was first applied. Beyond the choice of definition of the cash-generating unit, the mechanics of the impairment test itself would be as set forth at IAS 36.

During the development of IFRS 6, the IASB expressed concern that the availability of a choice in defining cash-generating units might impair the reliability and relevance of financial statements. To limit this risk, it proposed that a cash-generating unit for exploration and evaluation assets could be no larger than a segment, as defined by then-extant standard IAS 14.

As adopted, IFRS 6 mandates the proposed approach to impairment testing. Specifically, the standard provides that the reporting entity is to determine an accounting policy for allocating exploration and evaluation assets to cash-generating units or groups of cash-generating units for the purpose of assessing those assets for impairment as that need arises. Accordingly, each cash-generating unit or group of units to which an exploration and evaluation asset is allocated is not to be larger than an operating segment, determined in accordance with IFRS 8 (see discussion of IFRS 8 in Chapter 28). The level identified by the entity for the purposes of testing exploration and evaluation assets for impairment can comprise one or more cash-generating units.

IFRS 6 provides that exploration and evaluation assets are to be assessed for impairment when facts and circumstances suggest that the carrying amount of an exploration and evaluation asset might exceed the recoverable amount, as with other impairment testing prescribed by IAS 36. When facts and circumstances indicate that the carrying amount might exceed the respective recoverable amount, the reporting entity is required to measure, present, and disclose any resulting impairment loss in accordance with IAS 36, with the exception that the extent of aggregation may be greater than for other assets.

In addition to the criteria set forth in IAS 36, IFRS 6 identifies certain indications that impairment may have occurred regarding the exploration and evaluation assets. It states that one or more of the following facts and circumstances indicate that the reporting entity should test exploration and evaluation assets for impairment:

1. The period for which the entity has the right to explore in the specific area has expired during the period or will expire in the near future, and is not expected to be renewed.
2. Substantive expenditure by the entity on further exploration for and evaluation of mineral resources in the specific area is neither budgeted nor planned.
3. Exploration for and evaluation of mineral resources in the specific area have not resulted in the discovery of commercially viable quantities of mineral resources, and accordingly the reporting entity decided to discontinue such activities in the specific area.
4. Sufficient data exist to suggest that, although a development in the specific area is likely to proceed, the carrying amount of the exploration and evaluation asset is unlikely to be recovered in full from successful development or by sale.

If testing identifies impairment, the consequent adjustment of carrying amounts to the lower, impaired value results in a charge to current operating results, just as described by IAS 36 (discussed in Chapter 9).

Assets subject to IFRS 6 categorization. IFRS 6 provides a listing of assets that would fall within the definition of exploration and evaluation expenditures. These assets are those that are related to the following activities:

1. Acquisition of rights to explore;
2. Topographical, geological, geochemical, and geophysical studies;
3. Exploratory drilling;
4. Trenching;
5. Sampling; and

6. Activities in relation to evaluating technical feasibility and commercial viability of extracting a mineral resource.

The qualifying expenditures notably *exclude* those that are incurred in connection with the development of a mineral resource once technical feasibility and commercial viability of extracting a mineral resource have been established. Additionally, any administration and other general overhead costs are explicitly excluded from the definition of qualifying expenditures.

Availability of cost or revaluation models. Consistent with IAS 16, IFRS 6 requires initial recognition of exploration and evaluation assets based on actual cost, but subsequent recognition can be effected under either the historical cost model or the revaluation model. The standard does not offer guidance regarding accounting procedures, but it is presumed that those set forth under IAS 16 would be applied (e.g., regarding recognition of impairment and recoveries of previously recognized impairments). (See discussion in Chapter 9.)

Financial statement classification. IFRS 6 provides that the reporting entity is to classify exploration and evaluation assets as tangible or intangible according to the nature of the assets acquired, and apply the classification consistently. It notes that certain exploration and evaluation assets, such as drilling rights, have traditionally been considered intangible assets, while other assets have historically been identified as tangible (such as vehicles and drilling rigs). The standard states that, to the extent that a tangible asset is consumed in developing an intangible asset, the amount reflecting that consumption (that would otherwise be reported as depreciation) becomes part of the cost of the intangible asset. Using a tangible asset to develop an intangible asset, however, does not warrant classifying the tangible asset as an intangible asset.

In the statement of financial position, exploration and evaluation assets are to be set forth as a separate class of long-lived assets.

IFRS 6 only addresses exploration and evaluation. It holds that once the technical feasibility and commercial viability of extracting a mineral resource has been demonstrated, exploration and evaluation assets are no longer to be classified as such. At that point, the exploration and evaluation assets are to be assessed for impairment, and any impairment loss recognized, before reclassification of any remainder as operating or other asset classes.

Disclosure requirements under IFRS 6. A reporting entity is required to disclose information that identifies and explains the amounts recognized in its financial statements that pertain to the exploration for and evaluation of mineral resources. This could be accomplished by disclosing

1. Its accounting policies for exploration and evaluation expenditures, including the recognition of exploration and evaluation assets.
2. The amounts of assets, liabilities, income, and expense (and, if a statement of cash flows using the direct method is presented, cash flows) arising from the exploration for and evaluation of mineral resources.

The Exposure Draft preceding IFRS 6 had proposed that the mandatory disclosures identify the level at which the entity assesses exploration and evaluation assets for impairment. While this is not set forth in IFRS 6, it is obviously a good practice, and is therefore strongly recommended by the authors.

FUTURE DEVELOPMENTS

Extractive Industry Discussion Paper

In April 2010, the IASB published the discussion paper—*Extractive Activities*. Where relevant, the IASC Issues Paper and comments received in response were considered by the project team in developing this discussion paper. The Discussion Paper does not represent the views of the IASB, but rather those of the project team. After considering the responses received on the Discussion Paper, the IASB will decide whether to add this project to its active agenda.

The Discussion Paper addresses the following four questions:

1. How to estimate and classify the quantities of minerals or oil and gas discovered;
2. How to account for minerals or oil and gas properties;
3. How minerals or oil and gas properties should be measured; and
4. What information about extractive activities should be disclosed.

In summary, the Paper proposes to

- Introduce mineral reserve and resource definitions based on industry practice
- Eliminate "phase accounting"—separate accounting for exploration and evaluation, development, production and so on—in favor of one asset, either a "mineral asset" or "oil and gas asset"
- Account for mining and oil and gas projects using a "unit of account" which is effectively the "area of interest" accounting commonly used in Australia under current standards
- Require measurement based on historical cost, but countenancing the possibility of using another measure such as current value or (more likely) fair value
- Retain a modified impairment approach to assets in the exploration and evaluation stage
- Introduce extensive disclosures, including a form of "standardized value for reserves/resources and possibly responding to the "publish what you pay" lobby

IFRIC 20, *Stripping Costs in the Production Phase of a Surface Mine*

In August 2011, the IASB published the near final draft of IFRIC 20, *Stripping Costs in the Production Phase of a Surface Mine.*

The proposed IFRIC addresses the following three questions:

1. How and what production stripping costs to recognize as an asset;
2. How to initially measure the stripping activity asset; and
3. How to subsequently measure the stripping activity asset.

In summary, the IFRIC proposes that

- When benefits from the stripping activity are realized in the form of inventory produced, the principles of IAS 2 Inventories shall be applied. However, to the extent that the benefit is the improved access to ore, the entity shall recognize these costs as a noncurrent asset. This noncurrent asset will be known as the "stripping activity asset."
- The stripping activity asset will be accounted for as part of an existing asset (an enhancement of an existing asset) and will be classified as either tangible or intangible according to the nature of the existing asset of which it forms a part.

- The stripping activity asset will be initially measured at cost.
- The stripping activity asset will be subsequently measured at cost or revalued amount less depreciation or amortization and less impairment losses, in the same way as the existing asset of which it is a part.
- The stripping activity asset will be depreciated or amortized on a systematic basis, over the expected useful life of the identified component of the ore body that becomes more accessible as a result of the stripping activity.

If approved, this IFRIC will become effective for annual periods beginning on or after January 1, 2013.

US GAAP COMPARISON

US GAAP separately addresses, specifically for Oil and GAS Producing Companies, accounting for the acquisition of property, exploration, development, production, and support equipment and facilities.

33 ACCOUNTING FOR INSURANCE CONTRACTS

INTRODUCTION

IFRS 4, *Insurance Contracts,* addresses mainly the identification of insurance contracts and limited other recognition and measurement issues. IFRS 4 addresses the identification of insurance contracts by an entity that issues these contracts—which is not limited to insurance companies. It applies to insurance contracts issued, reinsurance contracts held, and financial instruments issued with a discretionary participation feature. The matter of the actual accounting for insurance contracts is not addressed in this standard, but it is discussed in the recently issued Exposure Draft and will be the subject of the planned new standard.

Sources of IFRS
IFRS 4

DEFINITIONS OF TERMS

Cedant. The policyholder under a reinsurance contract.

Deposit component. A contractual component that is not accounted for as a derivative under IFRS 9 and would be within the scope of IFRS 9 if it were a separate instrument.

Direct insurance contract. An insurance contract that is not a reinsurance contract.

Discretionary participation feature. A contractual right to receive, as a supplement to guaranteed benefits, additional benefits

1. That are likely to be a significant portion of the total contractual benefits;
2. Whose amount or timing is contractually at the discretion of the issuer; and
3. That are contractually based on

   a. The performance of a specified pool of contracts or a specified type of contract;
   b. The profit or loss of the company, fund or other entity that issues the contract.

Fair value. The amount for which an asset could be exchanged, or a liability settled, between knowledgeable, willing parties in an arm's length transaction.

Financial guarantee contract. A contract that requires the issuer to make specified payments to reimburse the holder for a loss it incurs because a specified debtor fails to make payment when due in accordance with the original or modified terms of a debt instrument.

Financial risk. The risk of a possible future change in one or more of a specified interest rate, financial instrument price, commodity price, foreign exchange rate, index of prices or rates, credit rating or credit index or other variable, provided in the case of a non-financial variable that the variable is not specific to a party to the contract.

Guaranteed benefits. Payments or other benefits to which a particular policyholder or investor has an unconditional right that is not subject to the contractual discretion of the issuer.

Guaranteed element. An obligation to pay guaranteed benefits, included in a contract that contains a discretionary participation feature.

Insurance asset. An insurer's net contractual rights under an insurance contract.

Insurance contract. A contract under which one party (the insurer) accepts significant insurance risk from another party (the policyholder) by agreeing to compensate the policyholder if a specified uncertain future event (the insured event) adversely affects the policyholder.

Insurance liability. An insurer's net contractual obligations under an insurance contract.

Insurance risk. Risk, other than financial risk, transferred from the holder of a contract to the issuer.

Insured event. An uncertain future event that is covered by an insurance contract and creates insurance risk.

Insurer. The party that has an obligation under an insurance contract to compensate a policyholder if an insured event occurs.

Liability adequacy test. An assessment of whether the carrying amount of an insurance liability needs to be increased (or the carrying amount of related deferred acquisition costs or related intangible assets decreased), based on a review of future cash flows.

Policyholder. A party that has a right to compensation under an insurance contract if an insured event occurs.

Reinsurance assets. A cedant's net contractual rights under a reinsurance contract.

Reinsurance contract. An insurance contract issued by one insurer (the reinsurer) to compensate another insurer (the cedant) for losses on one or more contracts issued by the cedant.

Reinsurer. The party that has an obligation under a reinsurance contract to compensate a cedant if an insured event occurs.

Unbundle. Account for the components of a contract as if they were separate contracts.

INSURANCE CONTRACTS

An insurance contract is an arrangement under which one party (the insurer) accepts significant insurance risk by agreeing with another party (the policyholder) to compensate the policyholder or other beneficiary if a specified uncertain future event (the insured event) adversely affects the policyholder or other beneficiary (other than an event that is only a change in one or more of a specified interest rate, security price, commodity price, foreign exchange rate, index of prices or rates, a credit rating or credit index, or similar variable—

which would continue to be accounted for under IAS 39 as derivative contracts). A contract creates sufficient insurance risk to qualify as an insurance contract only if there is a reasonable possibility that an event affecting the policyholder or other beneficiary will cause a significant change in the present value of the insurer's net cash flows arising from that contract. In considering whether there is a reasonable possibility of such significant change, it is necessary to consider the probability of the event and the magnitude of its effect. Also, a contract that qualifies as an insurance contract at inception or later remains an insurance contract until all rights and obligations are extinguished or expire. If a contract did not qualify as an insurance contract at inception, it should be subsequently reclassified as an insurance contract if, and only if, a significant change in the present value of the insurer's net cash flows becomes a reasonable possibility.

A range of other arrangements, which share certain characteristics with insurance contracts, would be excluded from any imposed insurance contracts accounting standard, since they are dealt with under other IFRS. These include financial guarantees (including credit insurance) measured at fair value; product warranties issued directly by a manufacturer, dealer, or retailer; employers' assets and liabilities under employee benefit plans (including equity compensation plans); retirement benefit obligations reported by defined benefit retirement plans; contingent consideration payable or receivable in a business combination; and contractual rights or contractual obligations that are contingent on the future use of, or right to use, a nonfinancial item (for example, certain license fees, royalties, lease payments, and similar items).

IFRS 4 applies to all insurance contracts, including reinsurance. Thus, the standard does not relate only to insurance companies, strictly defined. However, it does not apply to other assets and liabilities of issuers of insurance contracts, although other IFRS do apply. Insurance assets and liabilities will be subject to recognition when contractual rights and obligations, respectively, are created under the terms of the contract. When these no longer exist, derecognition will take place.

IFRS 4 does not apply to product warranties issued directly by a manufacturer, dealer or retailer; employers' assets and liabilities under employee benefit plans and retirement benefit obligations reported by defined benefit retirement plans; contractual rights or obligations that are contingent on the future use of or right to use a nonfinancial item, as well as lessee's residual value guarantees on finance leases; financial guarantees entered into or retained on transferring financial assets or financial liabilities within the scope of IAS 39; contingent consideration payable or receivable in a business combination; or direct insurance contracts that an entity holds as a policyholder.

Insurance risk. IFRS 4 sets forth the accounting and financial reporting requirements which will now be applicable to all insurance contracts (including reinsurance contracts) that are issued by the reporting entity, and to reinsurance contracts that the reporting entity holds, except for specified contracts which are covered by other standards. IFRS 4 does not apply to other assets and liabilities of an insurer (e.g., financial assets and financial liabilities which are addressed by IAS 39), nor does it address accounting or financial reporting by policyholders. The standard uses the term "insurer" to denote the party accepting liability as an insurer, whether or not the entity is legally or statutorily an insurance company.

IFRS 4 replaces what had been an indirect definition of an insurance contract under IAS 32 with a positive definition based on the transfer of significant insurance risk from the policyholder to the insurer. This definition covers most motor, travel, life, annuity, medical, property, reinsurance, and professional indemnity contracts. Some catastrophe bonds and weather derivatives would also qualify, as long as payments are linked to a specific climatic or other insured future event that would adversely affect the policyholder. On the other hand, policies that transfer no significant insurance risk—such as some savings and pensions plans—will be deemed financial instruments, addressed by IAS 39, regardless of their legal form. IAS 39 also applies to contracts that principally transfer financial risk, such as credit derivatives and some forms of financial reinsurance.

There may be some difficulty in classifying the more complex products (including certain hybrids). To facilitate this process, the IASB has explained that insurance risk will be deemed *significant* only if an insured event could cause an insurer to pay significant additional benefits in *any* scenario, apart from a scenario that lacks commercial substance (which in the Exposure Draft preceding IFRS 4 was denoted as a "plausible" event). As a practical matter, reporting entities should compare the cash flows from (1) the occurrence of the insured event against (2) all other events. If the cash flows under the former are significantly larger than under the latter, significant insurance risk is present.

For example, when the insurance benefits payable upon death are significantly larger than the benefits payable upon surrender or maturity, there is significant insurance risk. The significance of the additional benefits is to be measured irrespective of the probability of the insured event, if the scenario has commercial substance. Reporting entities have to develop internal quantitative guidance to ensure the definition is applied consistently throughout the entity. To qualify as significant, the insurance risk also needs to reflect a *preexisting* risk for the policyholder, rather than having arisen from the terms of the contract.

This requirement would specifically exclude from the cash flow comparison features such as waivers of early redemption penalties within investment plans or mortgages in the event of death. Since it is the contract itself that brought the charges into place, the waiver does not represent an additional benefit received for the transfer of a preexisting insurance risk.

The application of this IFRS 4 definition may result in the redesignation of a significant fraction of existing insurance contracts as investment contracts. In other situations, the impact could be the opposite. For example, a requirement to pay benefits earlier if an insured event occurs could make a contract insurance; this means that many pure endowment contracts are likely to meet the definition of insurance. All told, insuring entities will need to set clear, consistent, and justifiable contract classification criteria and rigorously apply these.

RECOGNITION AND MEASUREMENT GUIDANCE

Adequacy of insurance liabilities. IFRS 4 imposes a *liability adequacy test*, which requires that at each reporting (i.e., statement of financial position) date the "insurer" must assess whether its recognized insurance liabilities are adequate, using then-current estimates of future cash flows under the outstanding insurance contracts. If as a result of that assessment it is determined that the carrying (i.e., book) amount of insurance liabilities (less related deferred acquisition costs and related intangible assets, if appropriate—see discussion below) is insufficient given the estimated future cash flows, the full amount of such deficiency must be reported currently in earnings.

The standard defines minimum requirements for the adequacy test that is to be applied to the liability account. These minimum requirements are that

1. The test considers the current estimates of all contractual cash flows, and of such related cash flows as claims handling costs, as well as cash flows that will result from embedded options and guarantees.
2. If the test shows that the liability is inadequate, the entire deficiency is recognized in profit or loss.

In situations where the insuring entity's accounting policies do not require a liability adequacy test, or provides for a test that does not meet the minimum requirements noted above, then the entity is required under IFRS 4 to

1. Determine the carrying amount of the relevant insurance liabilities, less the carrying amount of

   a. Any related deferred acquisition costs; and
   b. Any related intangible assets, such as those acquired in a business combination or portfolio transfer.

2. Determine whether the carrying amount of the relevant net insurance liabilities is less than the carrying amount that would be required if the relevant insurance liabilities were within the scope of IAS 37.

The IAS 37 based amount is the required minimum liability to be presented. Therefore, if the current carrying amount is less, the insuring entity must recognize the entire shortfall in current period earnings. The corresponding credit to this loss recognition will either decrease the carrying amount of the related deferred acquisition costs or related intangible assets or increase the carrying amount of the relevant insurance liabilities, or both, dependent upon the facts and circumstances.

In applying the foregoing procedures, any related reinsurance assets are not considered, because an insuring entity accounts for these separately, as noted later in this discussion.

If an insuring entity's liability adequacy test meets the minimum requirements set forth above, this test is applied at the level of aggregation specified above. On the other hand, if the liability adequacy test does not meet the stipulated minimum requirements, the comparison must instead be made at the level of a portfolio of contracts that are subject to broadly similar risks and which are managed together as a single portfolio.

For purposes of comparing the recorded liability to the amount required under IAS 37, it is acceptable to reflect future investment margins only if the carrying (i.e., book) amount of the liability also reflects those same margins. Future investment margins are defined under IFRS 4 as being employed if the discount rate used reflects the estimated return on the insuring entity's assets, or if the returns on those assets are projected at an estimated rate of return, and discounted at a different rate, with the result included in the measurement of the liability. There is a rebuttable presumption that future investment margins should not be used, however, although exceptions (see below) can exist.

Impairment testing of reinsurance assets. When an insuring entity obtains reinsurance (making it the *cedant*), an asset is created in its financial statements. As with other assets, the reporting entity must consider whether an impairment has occurred as of the reporting (statement of financial position) date. Under IFRS 4, a reinsurance asset is impaired only when there is objective evidence that the cedant may not receive all amounts due to it under the terms of the contract, as a consequence of an event that occurred after initial recognition of the reinsurance asset, and furthermore, the impact of that event is reliably measurable in terms of the amounts that the cedant will receive from the reinsurer.

When the reinsurance asset is found to be impaired, the carrying value is adjusted downward and a loss is recognized in current period earnings for the full amount.

Selection of accounting principles. IFRS requires certain accounting practices to be adopted with regard to insurance contracts, but also allows other, existing procedures to remain in place under defined conditions. An insuring entity may, under provisions of IFRS 4, change accounting policies for insurance contracts only if such change makes the financial statements more relevant to the economic decision-making needs of users and no less reliable, or more reliable and no less relevant to those needs. Relevance and reliability are to be assessed by applying the criteria set forth in IAS 8.

To justify changing its accounting policies for insurance contracts, an insuring entity must demonstrate that the change brings its financial statements nearer to satisfying the criteria of IAS 8, but the change does not necessarily have to achieve full compliance with those criteria. The standard addresses changes in accounting policies in the context of current interest rates; continuation of existing reporting practices; prudence; future investment margins; and "shadow accounting." These are discussed in the following paragraphs.

Regarding interest rates, IFRS 4 provides that an insuring entity is permitted, although it is not required, to change its accounting policies such that it remeasures designated insurance liabilities to reflect current market interest rates, and recognizes changes in those liabilities in current period earnings. It may also adopt accounting policies that require other current estimates and assumptions for the designated liabilities. IFRS 4 permits an insuring entity to change its accounting policies for designated liabilities, without consistently applying those policies to all similar liabilities, as the requirements under IAS 8 would suggest. If the insuring entity designates liabilities for this policy choice, it must continue to apply current market interest rates consistently in all periods to all these liabilities until they are later eliminated.

An unusual feature of IFRS 4 is that it offers affected reporting entities the option to continue with their existing accounting policies. Specifically, an insuring entity is allowed to continue the following practices if in place prior to the effective date of IFRS 4:

1. Measuring insurance liabilities on an *undiscounted* basis.
2. Measuring contractual rights to future investment management fees at an amount that exceeds their fair value as implied by a comparison with current fees charged by other market participants for similar services. It is likely that the fair value at inception of those contractual rights equals the origination costs paid, unless future investment management fees and related costs are out of line with market comparables.
3. Employing nonuniform accounting policies for the insurance contracts (and related deferred acquisition costs and intangible assets, if any) of subsidiaries, except as permitted by the above-noted interest provision. If those accounting policies are not uniform, the insuring entity may change them if the change does not make the accounting policies more diverse, and also satisfies the other requirements of the standard.

The concept of *prudence*, as set forth in IFRS 4, is meant to excuse an insuring entity from a need to change its accounting policies for insurance contracts in order to eliminate excessive prudence (i.e., conservatism). However, if the insuring entity already measures its insurance contracts with sufficient prudence, it is not permitted to introduce additional prudence following adoption of IFRS 4.

The matter of *future investment margins* requires some explanation. Under IFRS 4 it is clearly preferred that the measurement of insurance contracts should not reflect future investment margins, but the standard does not require reporting entities to change accounting policies for insurance contracts to eliminate future investment margins. On the other hand, adopting a policy that would reflect this is presumed to be improper (the standard states that there is a rebuttable presumption that the financial statements would become less relevant and reliable if an accounting policy that reflects future investment margins in the measurement of insurance contracts is adopted, unless those margins affect the contractual payments). The standard offers two examples of accounting policies that reflect those margins. The first is using a discount rate that reflects the estimated return on the insurer's assets, while the second is projecting the returns on those assets at an estimated rate of return, discounting those projected returns at a different rate and including the result in the measurement of the liability.

IFRS 4 states that the insuring entity could possibly overcome this rebuttable presumption if the other components of a change in accounting policies increase the relevance and reliability of its financial statements sufficiently to outweigh the decrease in relevance and reliability caused by the inclusion of future investment margins. As an example, it cites the situation where the existing accounting policies for insurance contracts involve excessively prudent (i.e., conservative) assumptions set at inception, and a statutory discount rate not directly referenced to market conditions, and ignore some embedded options and guarantees. This entity might make its financial statements more relevant and no less reliable by switching to a comprehensive investor-oriented basis of accounting that is widely used and involves current estimates and assumptions; a reasonable (but not excessively prudent) adjustment to reflect risk and uncertainty; measurements that reflect both the intrinsic value and time value of embedded options and guarantees; and a current market discount rate, even if that discount rate reflects the estimated return on the insuring entity's assets.

The actual ability to overcome IFRS 4's rebuttable presumption is fact dependent. Thus, in some measurement approaches, the discount rate is used to determine the present value of a future profit margin, which is then attributed to different periods using a formula. In such approaches, the discount rate affects the measurement of the liability only indirectly, and the use of a less appropriate discount rate has a limited or no effect on the measurement of the liability at inception. In yet other approaches, the discount rate determines the measurement of the liability directly, and because the introduction of an asset-based discount rate has a more significant effect, it is highly unlikely that an insurer could overcome the rebuttable presumption noted above.

Finally, there is the matter of *shadow accounting*. According to IFRS 4, an insurer is permitted, but not required, to change its accounting policies so that a recognized but unrealized gain or loss on an asset affects those measurements in the same way that a realized gain or loss does. This is because, under some accounting models, realized gains or losses on an insurer's assets have a direct effect on the measurement of some or all of (1) its insurance liabilities, (2) related deferred acquisition costs, and (3) related intangible assets. IFRS 4 provides that the related adjustment to the insurance liability (or deferred acquisition costs or intangible assets) may be recognized in equity if, and only if, the unrealized gains or losses are recognized directly in equity.

Unbundling. Specific requirements pertain to *unbundling* of elements of insurance contracts, and dealing with embedded derivatives, options and guarantees.

Unbundling refers to the accounting for components of a contract as if they were separate contracts. Some insurance contracts consist of an insurance component and a deposit component. IFRS 4 in some cases requires the reporting entity to unbundle those components, and in other fact situations provides the entity with the option of unbundled accounting. Specifically, unbundling is *required* if both the following conditions are met:

1. The insuring entity can measure the deposit component (inclusive of any embedded surrender options) separately, *and*
2. The insuring entity's accounting policies do not otherwise require it to recognize all obligations and rights arising from the deposit component.

On the other hand, unbundling is permitted, but not required, if the insuring entity can measure the deposit component separately but its accounting policies require it to recognize all obligations and rights arising from the deposit component, regardless of the basis used to measure those rights and obligations.

Unbundling is actually prohibited if an insuring entity cannot measure the deposit component separately.

If unbundling is applied to a contract, the insuring entity applies IFRS 4 to the insurance component of the contract, while using IAS 39 to account for the deposit component of that contract.

Recognition. IFRS 4 prohibits the recognition of a liability for any provisions for possible future claims, if those claims arise under insurance contracts that are not in existence at the reporting date. Catastrophe and equalization provisions are thus prohibited, because they do not reflect loss events that have already occurred and, therefore, recognition would be inconsistent with IAS 37. Loss recognition testing is required for losses already incurred at each date of the statement of financial position, as described above. An insurance liability (or a part of an insurance liability) is to be removed from the statement of financial position only when it is extinguished (i.e., when the obligation specified in the contract is discharged or canceled, or expires).

In terms of display, offsetting of reinsurance assets against the related insurance liabilities is prohibited, as is offsetting of income or expense from reinsurance contracts against the expense or income from the related insurance contracts.

Discretionary participation features in insurance contracts. Insurance contracts sometimes contain a discretionary participation feature, as well as a guaranteed element. (That is, some portion of the return to be accrued to policyholders is at the discretion of the insuring entity.) Under the provisions of IFRS 4, the issuer of such a contract may, but is not required to, recognize the guaranteed element separately from the discretionary participation feature. If the issuer does not recognize them separately, it must classify the entire contract as a liability. If, on the other hand, the issuer classifies them separately, it will classify the guaranteed element as a liability. If the entity recognizes the discretionary participation feature separately from the guaranteed element, the discretionary participation feature can be classified either as a liability or as a separate component of equity; the standard does not specify how the decision should be reached. In fact, the issuer may even split that feature into liability and equity components, if a consistent accounting policy is used to determine that split.

When there is a discretionary participation feature which is reported in equity, the reporting entity is permitted to recognize all premiums received as revenue, without separating any portion that relates to the equity component. Changes in the guaranteed element and in the portion of the discretionary participation feature classified as a liability are to be reported in earnings, while changes in the part of the discretionary participation feature classified as equity are to be accounted for as an allocation of earnings, similar to how minority interest is reported.

Embedded derivatives. If the contract contains an embedded derivative within the scope of IAS 39, that standard must be applied to that embedded derivative.

DISCLOSURE

Under the provisions of IFRS 4, insuring entities must disclose information that identifies and explains the amounts in its financial statements arising from insurance contracts. This is accomplished by disclosure of accounting policies for insurance contracts and related assets, liabilities, income and expense; of recognized assets, liabilities, income and expense (and, if it presents its statement of cash flows using the direct method, cash flows) arising from insurance contracts. Additionally, if the insuring entity is a cedant, it must also disclose gains and losses recognized in profit or loss on buying reinsurance; and, if the cedant defers and amortizes gains and losses arising on buying reinsurance, the amortization for the period and the amounts remaining unamortized at the beginning and end of the period.

Disclosure is also required of the process used to determine the assumptions that have the greatest effect on the measurement of the recognized amounts described above. When practicable, quantified disclosure of those assumptions is to be presented as well. The effect of changes in assumptions used to measure insurance assets and insurance liabilities is required, reporting separately the effect of each change that has a material effect on the financial statements.

Finally, reconciliation of changes in insurance liabilities, reinsurance assets and, if any, related deferred acquisition costs are mandated by IFRS 4.

Regarding the amount, timing, and uncertainty of cash flows, the entity is required to disclose information that helps users to understand these matters as they result from insurance contracts. This is accomplished if the insuring entity discloses its objectives in managing risks arising from insurance contracts and its policies for mitigating those risks.

FUTURE DEVELOPMENTS

Phase II of the IASB Insurance Project

The bulk of the materials contained in the DSOP on insurance, which was issued by the IASC in 2001, will, if endorsed by the IASB, become part of the standard(s) that is being developed in Phase II of the Insurance Project. The IASB issued a Discussion Paper in May 2007, which was subsequently followed up by an Exposure Draft issued in July 2010. The lengthy deliberations suggest the complexity of the issues and the controversy anticipated to follow any firm decisions the IASB will make. The US standard setter, FASB, on September 17, 2010, issued for public comment a Discussion Paper, *Preliminary Views on Insurance Contracts*.

The IASB ED proposes a comprehensive measurement approach for all types of insurance contracts issued by entities (and reinsurance contracts held by entities), with a modified approach for some short-duration contracts. The approach is based on the principle that insurance contracts create a bundle of rights and obligations that work together to generate a package of cash inflows (premiums) and outflows (benefits and claims). An insurer would apply to that package of cash flows a measurement approach that uses the following building blocks:

1. A current estimate of the future cash flows
2. A discount rate that adjusts those cash flows for the time value of money
3. An explicit risk adjustment
4. A residual margin

The FASB DP proposes to combine the explicit risk adjustment and the residual margin in a composite margin. For most short-duration contracts, the IASB proposes a modified version of the measurement approach.

1. During the coverage period, the insurer would measure the contract using an allocation of the premium received, on a basis largely similar to existing practice.
2. The insurer would use the building block approach to measure claims liabilities for insured events that have already occurred.

The IASB has updated a summary of how the proposals in the Exposure Draft Insurance Contracts (ED) would change as a result of the IASB's and FASB's tentative decisions, and is planning to continue their discussion of this subject later in 2011. It is expected that the draft will be reexposed in 2012.

US GAAP COMPARISON

The US GAAP guidance on insurance contracts covers insurance activities, acquisition costs, claim costs and liabilities for future policy benefits, policyholder dividends, and separate accounts. Four methods of recognition for premium revenue and contract liabilities are developed: short-duration contract accounting and three methods for long-duration contract accounting, which are traditional, universal life, and participating contracts. Generally, the four methods reflect the nature of the insurance entity's obligations and policyholder rights under the provisions of the contract.

Short duration contracts, which are for a short period, usually one year, generally require revenue recognition on a straight line-basis. Long-duration contracts, in most cases, require offsetting of receivables or cash against unrecognized revenue. This revenue is recognized commensurate with the risk insured. Another feature of long-duration contract accounting is that for each reporting period, liabilities for coverage risk are assessed and increased if needed. The offset is recognized in the current period expense.

US GAAP also covers accounting for reinsurance contracts. These arrangements transfer some or all of the risk of insurance to a third party (not the insured). Generally, the accounting is similar to insurance contracts, although there are specific criteria for determining if the original insurer has transferred the risks to the reinsurer.

The revenue for financial guarantee contracts are recognized by multiplying the present value of the fees by the ratio of the principle coverage for the period by the sum of the principle amounts guaranteed over the life of the contract. For contracts that accrete coverage, this can result in different revenue for each period.

The concept of separate accounts specifies accounting when assets are specifically segregated for a particular policy holder, for example, variable annuity contracts that guarantee some minimum level of benefits.

INTRODUCTION

Interim financial reports are financial statements covering periods of less than a full fiscal year. Most commonly such reports will be for a period of three months (which are referred to as quarterly financial reports), although in some jurisdictions, tradition calls for semiannual financial reporting. The purpose of quarterly or other interim financial reports is to provide financial statement users with more timely information for making investment and credit decisions, based on the expectation that full-year results will be a reasonable extrapolation from interim performance. Additionally, interim reports can yield significant information concerning trends affecting the business and seasonality effects, both of which could be obscured in annual reports.

The basic objective of interim reporting is to provide frequent and timely assessments of an entity's performance. However, interim reporting has inherent limitations. As the reporting period is shortened, the effects of errors in estimation and allocation are magnified. The proper allocation of annual operating expenses to interim periods is also a significant concern. Because the progressive tax rates of most jurisdictions are applied to total annual income and various tax credits may arise, the accurate determination of interim period income tax expense is often difficult. Other annual operating expenses may be concentrated in one interim period, yet benefit the entire year's operations. Examples include advertising expenses and major repairs or maintenance of equipment, which may be seasonal in nature. The effects of seasonal fluctuations and temporary market conditions further limit the reliability, comparability, and predictive value of interim reports. Because of this reporting environment, the issue of independent auditor association with interim financial reports remains problematic.

Two distinct views of interim reporting have been advocated, particularly by US and UK standard setters, although some believe that this distinction is more apparent than real. The first view holds that the interim period is an integral part of the annual accounting period (the *integral* view), while the second views the interim period as a unique accounting period of its own (the *discrete* view). Depending on which view is accepted, expenses would either be recognized as incurred, or would be allocated to the interim periods based on forecasted annual activity levels such as sales volume. The integral approach would require more use of estimation, and forecasts of full-year performance would be necessary antecedents for the preparation of interim reports.

Sources of IFRS
IAS 1, 34   *IFRIC* 10
IASB's Framework for the Preparation and Presentation of Financial Statements

DEFINITIONS OF TERMS

Estimated annual effective tax rate. An expected annual tax rate which reflects estimates of annual earnings, tax rates, tax credits, etc.

Interim financial report. An interim financial report refers to either a complete set of financial statements for an interim period (prepared in accordance with the requirements of IAS 1), or a set of condensed financial statements for an interim period (prepared in accordance with the requirements of IAS 34).

Interim period. A financial reporting period shorter than a full financial year (e.g., a period of three or six months).

Last-twelve-months reports. Financial reporting for the twelve-month period which ends on a given interim date.

Seasonality. The normal, expected occurrence of a major portion of revenues or costs in one or two interim periods.

Year-to-date reports. Financial reporting for the period which begins on the first day of the fiscal year and ends on a given interim date.

ALTERNATIVE CONCEPTS OF INTERIM REPORTING

The argument is often made that interim reporting is generically unlike financial reporting covering a full fiscal year. Two distinct views of interim reporting have developed, representing alternative philosophies of financial reporting. Under the first view, the interim period is considered to be an integral part of the annual accounting period. This view directs that annual operating expenses are to be estimated and then allocated to the interim periods based on forecasted annual activity levels, such as expected sales volume. When this approach is employed, the results of subsequent interim periods must be adjusted to reflect prior estimation errors.

Under the second view, each interim period is considered to be a discrete accounting period, with status equal to a fiscal year. Thus, no estimations or allocations that are different from those used for annual reporting are to be made for interim reporting purposes. The same expense recognition rules should apply as under annual reporting, and no special interim accruals or deferrals are to be permitted. Annual operating expenses are recognized in the interim period in which they are incurred, irrespective of the number of interim periods benefited, unless deferral or accrual would be called for in the annual financial statements.

Proponents of the integral view argue that the unique expense recognition procedures are necessary to avoid creating possibly misleading fluctuations in period-to-period results. Using the integral view results in interim earnings which are hopefully more indicative of annual earnings and, thus, useful for predictive and other decision-making purposes. Proponents of the discrete view, on the other hand, argue that the smoothing of interim results for purposes of forecasting annual earnings has undesirable effects. For example, a turning point in an earnings trend that occurred during the year may be obscured.

Yet others have noted that the distinction between the integral and the discrete approaches is arbitrary and, in fact, rather meaningless. These critics note that interim periods bear the same relationship to full years as fiscal years do to longer intervals in the life cycle of a business, and that all periodic financial reporting necessitates the making of estimates and allocations. Direct costs and revenues are best accounted for as incurred and earned, respectively, which equates a discrete approach in most instances, while many indirect costs are more likely to require that an allocation process be applied, which is suggestive of an integral approach. In short, a mix of methods will be necessary as dictated by the nature of the cost or revenue item being reported upon, and neither a pure integral nor a pure discrete approach could be utilized in practice. The IFRS on interim financial reporting, IAS 34, does, in fact, adopt a mix of the discrete and the integral views, as described more fully below.

OBJECTIVES OF INTERIM FINANCIAL REPORTING

The purpose of interim financial reporting is to provide information that will be useful in making economic decisions (as, of course, is the purpose of annual financial information). Furthermore, interim financial reporting is expected to provide information specifically about the financial position, performance, and change in financial position of an entity. The objective is general enough to embrace the preparation and presentation of either full financial statements or condensed information.

While accounting is often criticized for looking at an entity's performance through the rearview mirror, in fact it is well understood by standard setters that to be useful, such information must provide insights into future performance. As outlined in the objective of the IASB's standard on interim financial reporting, IAS 34, the primary, but not exclusive, purpose of timely interim period reporting is to provide interested parties (e.g., investors and creditors) with an understanding of the entity's earnings-generating capacity and its cash-flow-generating capacity, which are clearly future-oriented. Furthermore, the interim data is expected to give interested parties not only insights into such matters as seasonal volatility or irregularity, and provide timely notice about changes in patterns or trends, both as to income or cash-generating behavior, but also into such balance-sheet-based phenomena as liquidity.

In reaching the positions set forth in the standard, the International Accounting Standards Committee (IASC, predecessor of the IASB) had considered the importance of interim reporting in identifying the turning points in an entity's earnings or liquidity. It was concerned that the integral approach to interim reporting can mask these turning points and thereby prevent users of the financial statements from taking appropriate actions. If this observation is correct, this would be an important reason to endorse the discrete view. In fact, the extent to which application of an integral approach masks turning points is probably related to the extent of "smoothing" applied to revenue and expense data.

It seems quite reasonable that interim reporting in conformity with the integral view, if done sensitively, could reveal turning points as effectively as would reports prepared under the discrete approach. As support for this assertion, one can consider national economic statistics (e.g., gross national product, unemployment), which are most commonly reported on seasonally adjusted bases, which is analogous to the consequence of utilizing an integral approach to interim reporting of entity financial information. Such economic data is often quite effective at highlighting turning points and is accordingly employed far more typically than is unadjusted monthly data, which would be roughly comparable to reporting under the discrete approach.

While the objectives of interim reporting are highly consistent with those of annual financial reporting, there are further concerns. These involve matters of cost and timeliness, as well as questions of materiality and measurement accuracy. In general, the belief has been that to be truly useful, the information must be produced in a more timely fashion than is often the case with annual reports (although other research suggests that users' tolerance for delayed information is markedly declining in all arenas), and that some compromises in terms of accuracy may be warranted in order to achieve greater timeliness.

APPLICATION OF ACCOUNTING POLICIES

There is no requirement under IFRS that entities must prepare interim financial statements. Furthermore, even if annual financial statements are prepared in accordance with IFRS, the reporting entity is free to present interim financial statements on bases other than IFRS, as long as they are not misrepresented as being IFRS compliant.

If interim financial statements are IFRS-based, IAS 34 states that interim financial data should be prepared in conformity with accounting policies used in the most recent annual financial statements. The only exception noted is when a change in accounting policy has been adopted since the last year-end financial report was issued. The standard also stipulates that the definitions of assets, liabilities, income, and expenses for the interim period are to be identical to those applied in annual reporting situations.

While IAS 34, in many instances, is quite forthright about declaring its allegiance to the discrete view of interim financial reporting, it does incorporate a number of important exceptions to the principle.

Consistency. The standard logically states that interim period financial statements should be prepared using the same accounting principles that had been employed in the most recent annual financial statements. This is consistent with the idea that the latest annual report provides the frame of reference that will be employed by users of the interim information. The fact that interim data is expected to be useful in making projections of the forthcoming full-year's reported results of operations makes consistency of accounting principles between the interim period and prior year important, since the projected results for the current year will undoubtedly be evaluated in the context of year-earlier performance. Unless the accounting principles applied in both periods are consistent, any such comparison is likely to be impeded.

The decision to require consistent application of accounting policies across interim periods and in comparison with the earlier fiscal year is a logical implication of the view of interim reporting as being largely a means of predicting the next fiscal year's results. It is also driven by the conclusion that interim reporting periods stand alone (rather than being merely an integral portion of the full year). To put it differently, when an interim period is seen as an integral part of the full year, it is easier to rationalize applying different accounting policies to the interim periods, if doing so will more meaningfully present the results of the portion of the full year within the boundaries of the annual reporting period. For example, deferral of certain costs at interim statement of financial position dates, notwithstanding the fact that such costs could not validly be deferred at year-end, might theoretically serve the purpose of providing a more accurate predictor of full-year results.

On the other hand, if each interim period is seen as a discrete unit to be reported upon without having to serve the higher goal of providing an accurate prediction of the full-year's expected outcome, then a decision to depart from previously applied accounting principles is less easily justified. Given IAS 34's clear preference for the discrete view of interim financial reporting, its requirement regarding consistency of accounting principles is entirely logical.

Consolidated reporting requirement. The standard also requires that, if the entity's most recent annual financial statements were presented on a consolidated basis, then the interim financial reports in the immediate succeeding year should also be presented similarly. This is entirely in keeping with the notion of consistency of application of accounting policies. The rule does not, however, either preclude or require publishing additional "parent company only" interim reports, even if the most recent annual financial statements did include such additional financial statements.

Materiality As Applied to Interim Financial Statements

Materiality is one of the most fundamental concepts underlying financial reporting. At the same time, it has largely been resistant to attempts at precise definition. Some IFRS do require that items be disclosed if material or significant, or if of "such size" as would warrant separate disclosure. Guidelines for performing an arithmetical calculation of a threshold for materiality (in order to measure "such size") is not prescribed in IAS 1, or for that matter in any other IFRS. Rather, this determination is left to the devices of each individual charged with responsibility for financial reporting.

IAS 34 advanced the notion that materiality for interim reporting purposes may differ from that defined in the context of an annual period. This follows from the decision to endorse the discrete view of interim financial reporting, generally. Thus, for example, discontinuing operations would have to be evaluated for disclosure purposes against whatever benchmark, such as gross revenue, is deemed appropriate as that item is being reported in the interim financial statements—not as it was shown in the prior year's financial statements or is projected to be shown in the current full-year's results.

The effect of the foregoing would normally be to lower the threshold level for reporting such items. Thus, it is deemed likely that some items separately set forth in the interim financials may not be so presented in the subsequent full-year's annual report that includes that same interim period.

The objective is not to mislead the user of the information by failing to include a disclosure that might appear to be material within the context of the interim report, since that is the user's immediate frame of reference. If later the threshold is raised and items previously presented are no longer deemed worthy of such attention, this is not thought to create a risk of misleading the user, in contrast to a failure to disclose an item in the interim financial statements that measured against the performance parameters of the interim period might appear significant.

Example of interim period materiality consideration

To illustrate, assume that Xanadu Corp. has gross revenues of €2.8 million in the first fiscal quarter and will, in fact, go on to generate revenues of €12 million for the full year. Traditionally, for this company's financial reporting, materiality is defined as 5% of revenues. If in the first quarter income from discontinued operations amounting to €200,000 is earned, this should be separately set forth in the quarterly financial statements since it exceeds the defined 5% threshold for materiality. If there are no other discontinued operations results for the balance of the year, it might validly be concluded that disclosure in the year-end financials may be omitted, since the €200,000 income item is not material in the context of €12 million of full year revenues. Thus, Xanadu's first quarter report might detail the discontinued operations, but that is later subsumed in continuing operations in the annual financial statements.

PRESENTATION

Content of an interim financial report. Instead of repeating information previously presented in annual financial statements, interim financial reports should preferably focus on new activities, events, and circumstances that have occurred since the date of publication of the latest complete set of financial statements. IAS 34 recognizes the need to keep financial statement users informed about the latest financial condition of the reporting entity, and has thus moderated the presentation and disclosure requirements in the case of interim financial reports. Thus, in the interest of timeliness and with a sensitivity to cost considerations, and also to avoid repetition of information previously (and recently) reported, the standard allows an entity, at its option, to provide information relating to its financial position in a condensed format, in lieu of comprehensive information provided in a complete set of financial statements prepared in accordance with IAS 1. The minimum requirements as to the components of the interim financial statements to be presented (under this option) and their content are discussed later.

IAS 34 sets forth the following three important aspects of interim financial reporting:

- That by permitting presentation of condensed financial information, the standard is not intended to either prohibit or discourage the reporting entity from presenting a complete set of interim financial statements, as defined by IAS 1;
- That even when the choice is made to present condensed interim financial statements, if an entity chooses to add line items or additional explanatory notes to the condensed financial statements, over and above the minimum prescribed by this standard, the standard does not, in any way, prohibit or discourage the addition of such extra information; and
- That the recognition and measurement guidance in IAS 34 applies equally to a complete set of interim financial statements as to condensed interim financial statements. Thus, a complete set of interim financial statements would include not only the disclosures specifically prescribed by this standard, but also disclosures required by other IFRS. For example, disclosures required by IFRS 7, such as those pertaining to interest rate risk or credit risk, would need to be incorporated in a complete set of interim financial statements, in addition to the selected note disclosures prescribed by IAS 34.

Minimum components of an interim financial report. IAS 34 sets forth minimum requirements in relation to condensed interim financial reports. The standard mandates that the following financial statements components be presented when an entity opts for the condensed format:

- A condensed statement of financial position;
- A condensed statement of comprehensive income, either as

  - A condensed single statement; or
  - A condensed separate statement of profit or loss and a condensed statement of comprehensive income;

- A condensed statement of changes in equity;
- A condensed statement of cash flows; and
- Selected explanatory notes.

Form and content of interim financial statements.

1. IAS 34 mandates that if an entity chooses to present the "complete set of (interim) financial statements" instead of opting for the allowed method of presenting only "condensed" interim financial statements, then the form and content of those statements should conform to the requirements set by IAS 1 for a complete set of financial statements.
2. However, if an entity opts for the condensed format approach to interim financial reporting, then IAS 34 requires that, at a minimum, those condensed financial statements include each of the headings and the subtotals that were included in the entity's most recent annual financial statements, along with selected explanatory notes, as prescribed by the standard.

   It is interesting to note that IAS 34 mandates expansiveness in certain cases. The standard notes that extra line items or notes may need to be added to the minimum disclosures prescribed above, if their omission would make the condensed interim financial statements misleading. This concept can be best explained through the following illustration:

   > At December 2011, an entity's comparative statement of financial position had trade receivables that were considered doubtful, and hence, were fully reserved as of that date. Thus, on the face of the statement of financial position as of December 31, 2011, the amount disclosed against trade receivables, net of provision, was a zero balance (and the comparative figure disclosed as of December 31, 2010, under the prior year column was a positive amount, since at that earlier point of time, that is, at the end of the previous year, a small portion of the receivable was still considered collectible). At December 31, 2011, the fact that the receivable (net of the provision) ended up being presented as a zero balance on the face of the statement of financial position was well explained in the notes to the annual financial statements (which clearly showed the provision being deducted from the gross amount of the receivable that caused the resulting figure to be a zero balance that was then carried forward to the statement of financial position). If at the end of the first quarter of the following year the trade receivables were still doubtful of collection, thereby necessitating creation of a 100% provision against the entire balance of trade receivables as of March 31, 2012, and the entity opted to present a condensed statement of financial position as part of the interim financial report, it would be misleading in this case to disclose the trade receivables as of March 31, 2012, as a zero balance, without adding a note to the condensed statement of financial position explaining this phenomenon.

3. IAS 34 requires disclosure of earnings per share (both basic EPS and diluted EPS) on the face of the interim statement of comprehensive income. This disclosure is mandatory whether condensed or complete interim financial statements are presented. However, since EPS is only required (by IAS 33) for publicly held companies, it is likewise only mandated for interim financial statements of such reporting entities.
4. IAS 34 mandates that an entity should follow the same format in its interim statement showing changes in equity as it did in its most recent annual financial statements.
5. IAS 34 requires that an interim financial report be prepared on a consolidated basis if the entity's most recent annual financial statements were consolidated statements. Regarding presentation of separate interim financial statements of the parent company in addition to consolidated interim financial statements, if they were included in the most recent annual financial statements, this standard neither requires nor prohibits such inclusion in the interim financial report of the entity.

Significant events and transactions. While a number of notes would potentially be required at an interim date, there could clearly be far less disclosure than is prescribed under other IFRS. IAS 34 reiterates that it is superfluous to provide the same notes in the interim financial report that appeared in the most recent annual financial statements, since financial statement users are presumed to have access to those statements in all likelihood. To the contrary, the interim financial report provides an explanation of events and transactions that are significant to an understanding of the changes in financial position and performance of the entity since the last annual reporting. This information updates the relevant information presented in the most recent annual financial report. In keeping with this line of thinking, the following is a nonexhaustive list of events and transactions that are disclosed, if they are significant:

1. The write-down of inventories to net realizable value and any reversal.
2. Losses from the impairment of financial assets, property, plant, and equipment, intangible or other assets and any reversal.
3. The reversal of any provision for restructuring cost.
4. Acquisitions and disposal of property, plant, and equipment.
5. Commitments for the purchase of property, plant, and equipment.
6. Litigation settlements.
7. Corrections of prior period errors.
8. Changes in the business or economic circumstances that effect the entity's financial assets and liabilities (recognized at fair value or amortized cost).
9. Any loan default or breach of a loan agreement that has not been remedied.
10. Related-party transactions.
11. Transfers between levels of the fair value hierarchy used for the measuring of financial instruments.
12. Changes in the classification of financial assets due to changes in purpose or use.
13. Changes in contingent liabilities and contingent assets.

Other disclosures. The following additional disclosure must also be provided in the notes to the interim financial statements on a financial year-to-year basis:

1. A statement that the same accounting policies and methods of computation are applied in the interim financial statements compared with the most recent annual financial statements, or if those policies or methods have changed, a description of the nature and effect of the change;

2. Explanatory comments about seasonality or cyclicality of interim operations;
3. The nature and magnitude of significant items affecting interim results that are unusual because of nature, size, or incidence;
4. Dividends paid, either in the aggregate or on a per-share basis, presented separately for ordinary (common) shares and other classes of shares;
5. The following segment information:

   - Revenues from external customers and intersegment revenue if reported to the chief operating decision maker;
   - A measure of profit or loss;
   - Total assets (if a significant change from the annual financial statements);
   - A description of any change in the basis of segmentation or in the basis of measuring segment profits;
   - A reconciliation of the total segments' profit or loss to the entity's profit or loss before tax and discontinued operations (or after tax if used).

6. Any events occurring subsequent to the end of the interim period;
7. Issues, repurchases, and repayments of debt and equity securities;
8. The nature and quantum of changes in estimates of amounts reported in prior interim periods of the current financial year, or changes in estimates of amounts reported in prior financial years, if those changes have a material effect in the current interim period; and
9. The effect of changes in the composition of the entity during the interim period, like business combinations, acquisitions, or disposal of subsidiaries, and long-term investments, restructuring, and discontinuing operations.

Finally, in the case of a complete set of interim financial statements, the standard allows additional disclosures mandated by other IFRS. However, if the condensed format is used, then additional disclosures required by other IFRS are *not* required.

Comparative interim financial statements. IAS 34 endorses the concept of comparative reporting, which is generally acknowledged to be more useful than is the presentation of information about only a single period. IAS 34 furthermore mandates not only comparative (condensed or complete) interim statements of comprehensive income (e.g., the second quarter of 2012 presented together with the second quarter of 2011), but the inclusion of year-to-date information as well (e.g., the first half of 2012 and also the first half of 2011). Thus, an interim statement of comprehensive income would ideally be comprised of four columns of data. On the other hand, in the case of the remaining components of interim financial statements (i.e., statement of financial position, statement of cash flows, and statement of changes in equity), the presentation of two columns of data would meet the requirements of IAS 34. Thus, the other components of the interim financial statements should present the following data for the two periods:

- The statement of financial position as of the end of the current interim period and a comparative statement of financial position as of the end of the immediately preceding fiscal year (*not* as of the comparable year-earlier date);
- The statement of cash flows cumulatively for the current financial year to date, with a comparative statement for the comparable year-to-date period of the immediately preceding financial year; and
- IAS 34 requires that the statement showing changes in equity cumulatively for the current financial year to date be presented, with a comparative statement for the comparable year-to-date period of the immediately preceding financial year.

The following illustration should amply explain the above-noted requirements of IAS 34.

XYZ Limited presents quarterly interim financial statements and its financial year ends on December 31 each year. For the second quarter of 2012, XYZ Limited should present the following financial statements (condensed or complete) as of June 30, 2012:

1. A statement of comprehensive income with four columns, presenting information for the three-month periods ended June 30, 2012, and June 30, 2011; and for the six-month periods ended June 30, 2012, and June 30, 2011
2. A statement of financial position with two columns, presenting information as of June 30, 2012, and as of December 31, 2011
3. A statement of cash flows with two columns presenting information for the six-month periods ended June 30, 2012, and June 30, 2011
4. A statement of changes in equity with two columns presenting information for the six-month periods ended June 30, 2012, and June 30, 2011

IAS 34 recommends that, for highly seasonal businesses, the inclusion of additional statement of comprehensive income columns for the twelve months ending on the date of the most recent interim report (also referred to as rolling twelve-month statements) would be deemed very useful. The objective of recommending rolling twelve-month statements is that seasonality concerns would be thereby eliminated, since by definition each rolling period contains all the seasons of the year. (Rolling statements, however, cannot correct cyclicality that encompasses more than one year, such as that of secular business expansions and recessions.) Accordingly, IAS 34 encourages companies affected by seasonality to consider including these additional statements, which could result in an interim statement of comprehensive income comprising six or more columns of data.

RECOGNITION ISSUES

General concepts. The definitions of assets, liabilities, income, and expense are the same for interim period reporting as at year-end reporting. These items are defined in the IASB's *Framework*. The effect of stipulating that the same definitions apply to interim reporting is to further underscore the concept of interim periods being discrete units of time upon which the statements report. For example, given the definition of assets as resources generating future economic benefits for the entity, expenditures that could not be capitalized at year-end because of a failure to meet this definition could similarly not be deferred at interim dates. Thus, by applying the same definitions at interim dates, IAS 34 has mandated the same recognition rules as are applicable at the end of full annual reporting periods.

However, while the overall implication is that identical recognition and measurement rules are to be applied to interim financial statements, there are a number of exceptions and modifications to the general rule. Some of these are in simple acknowledgment of the limitations of certain measurement techniques, and the recognition that applying those definitions at interim dates might necessitate interpretations different from those useful for annual reporting. In other cases, the standard clearly departs from the discrete view, since such departures are not only wise, but probably fully necessary. These specific recognition and measurement issues are addressed below.

Recognition of annual costs incurred unevenly during the year. It is frequently observed that certain types of costs are incurred in uneven patterns over the course of a fiscal year, while not being driven strictly by variations in volume of sales activity. For example, major expenditures on advertising may be prepaid at the inception of the campaign; tooling for new product production will obviously be heavily weighted to the preproduction and early production stages. Certain discretionary costs, such as research and development, will not bear any predictable pattern or necessary relationship with other costs or revenues.

If an integral view approach had been designated by IAS 34, there would be potent arguments made in support of the accrual or deferral of certain costs. For instance, if a major expenditure for overhauling equipment is scheduled to occur during the final interim period, logic could well suggest that the expenditure should be anticipated in the earlier interim periods of the year, if those periods were seen as integral parts of the fiscal year. Under the discrete view adopted by the standard, however, such an accrual would be seen as an inappropriate attempt to smooth the operating results over all the interim periods constituting the full fiscal year. Accordingly, such anticipation of future expenses is prohibited, unless the future expenditure gives rise to a true liability in the current period, or meets the test of being a contingency which is probable and the magnitude of which is reasonably estimable.

For example, many business entities grant bonuses to managers only after the annual results are known; even if the relationship between the bonuses and the earnings performance is fairly predictable from past behavior, these remain discretionary in nature and need not be granted. Such a bonus arrangement would not give rise to a liability during earlier interim periods, inasmuch as the management has yet to declare that there is a commitment that will be honored. (Compare this with the situation where managers have contracts specifying a bonus plan, which clearly would give rise to a legal liability during the year, albeit one which might involve complicated estimation problems. Also, a bonus could be anticipated for interim reporting purposes if it could be considered a constructive obligation, for example, based upon past practice for which the entity has no realistic alternative, and assuming that a realistic estimate of that obligation can be made).

Another example involves contingent lease arrangements. Often in operating lease situations the lessee will agree to a certain minimum or base rent, plus an amount that is tied to a variable such as sales revenue. This is typical, for instance, in retail rental contracts, such as for space in shopping malls, since it encourages the landlord to maintain the facilities in an appealing fashion so that tenants will be successful in attracting customers. Only the base amount of the periodic rental is a true liability, unless and until the higher rent becomes payable as defined sales targets are actually achieved. If contingent rents are payable based on a sliding scale (e.g., 1% of sales volume up to €500,000, then 2% of amounts up to €1.5 million, etc.), the projected level of full-year sales should not be used to compute rental accruals in the early periods; rather, only the contingent rents payable on the actual sales levels already achieved should be so recorded.

The foregoing examples were clearly categories of costs that, while often fairly predictable, would not constitute a legal obligation of the reporting entity until the associated conditions were fully met. There are, however, other examples that are more ambiguous. Paid vacation time and holiday leave are often enforceable as legal commitments, and if this is so, provision for these costs should be made in the interim financial statements. In other cases, as when company policy is that accrued vacation time is lost if not used by the end of a defined reporting year, such costs might not be subject to accrual under the discrete view. The facts of each such situation would have to be carefully analyzed to make a proper determination.

Revenues received seasonally, cyclically, or occasionally. IAS 34 is clear in stipulating that revenues such as dividend income and interest earned cannot be anticipated or deferred at interim dates, unless such practice would be acceptable under IFRS at year-end. Thus, interest income is typically accrued, since it is well established that this represents a contractual commitment. Dividend income, on the other hand, is not recognized until declared, since even when highly predictable based on past experience, these are not obligations of the paying corporation until actually declared.

Furthermore, seasonality factors should not be smoothed out of the financial statements. For example, for many retail stores a high percentage of annual revenues occur during the holiday shopping period, and the quarterly or other interim financial statements should fully reflect such seasonality. That is, revenues should be recognized as they occur.

Income taxes. The fact that income taxes are assessed annually by the taxing authorities is the primary reason for reaching the conclusion that taxes are to be accrued based on the estimated average annual effective tax rate for the full fiscal year. Further, if rate changes have been enacted to take effect later in the fiscal year (while some rate changes take effect in midyear, more likely this would be an issue if the entity reports on a fiscal year and the new tax rates become effective at the start of a calendar year), the expected effective rate should take into account the rate changes as well as the anticipated pattern of earnings to be experienced over the course of the year. Thus, the rate to be applied to interim period earnings (or losses, as discussed further below) will take into account the expected level of earnings for the entire forthcoming year, as well as the effect of enacted (or substantially enacted) changes in the tax rates to become operative later in the fiscal year. In other words, and as the standard puts it, the estimated average annual rate would "reflect a blend of the progressive tax rate structure expected to be applicable to the full year's earnings including enacted or substantially enacted changes in the income tax rates scheduled to take effect later in the financial year."

IAS 34 addresses in detail the various computational aspects of an effective interim period tax rate which are summarized in the following paragraphs.

Multiplicity of taxing jurisdictions and different categories of income. Many entities are subject to a multiplicity of taxing jurisdictions, and in some instances the amount of income subject to tax will vary from one to the next, since different laws will include and exclude disparate items of income or expense from the tax base. For example, interest earned on government-issued bonds may be exempted from tax by the jurisdiction that issued them, but be defined as fully taxable by other tax jurisdictions the entity is subject to. To the extent feasible, the appropriate estimated average annual effective tax rate should be separately ascertained for each taxing jurisdiction and applied individually to the interim period pretax income of each jurisdiction, so that the most accurate estimate of income taxes can be developed at each interim reporting date. In general, an overall estimated effective tax rate will not be as satisfactory for this purpose as would a more carefully constructed set of estimated rates, since the pattern of taxable and deductible items will fluctuate from one period to the next.

Similarly, if the tax law prescribes different income tax rates for different categories of income (such as the tax rate on capital gains which usually differs from the tax rate applicable to business income in many countries), then to the extent practicable, a separate tax rate should be applied to each category of interim period pretax income. The standard, while mandating such detailed rules of computing and applying tax rates across jurisdictions or across categories of income, recognizes that in practice such a degree of precision may not be achievable in all cases. Thus, in all such cases, IAS 34 softens its stand and allows usage of a "weighted-average of rates across jurisdictions or across categories of income" provided "it is a reasonable approximation of the effect of using more specific rates."

Tax credits. In computing an expected effective tax rate for a given tax jurisdiction, all relevant features of the tax regulations should be taken into account. Jurisdictions may provide for tax credits based on new investment in plant and machinery, relocation of facilities to backward or underdeveloped areas, research and development expenditures, levels of export sales, and so forth, and the expected credits against the tax for the full year should be given consideration in the determination of an expected effective tax rate. Thus, the tax effect of new investment in plant and machinery, when the local taxing body offers an investment credit for qualifying investment in tangible productive assets, will be reflected in those interim periods of the fiscal year in which the new investment occurs (assuming it can be forecast to occur later in a given fiscal year), and not merely in the period in which the new investment occurs. This is consistent with the underlying concept that taxes are strictly an annual phenomenon, but it is at variance with the purely discrete view of interim financial reporting.

IAS 34 notes that, although tax credits and similar modifying elements are to be taken into account in developing the expected effective tax rate to apply to interim earnings, tax benefits which will relate to onetime events are to be reflected in the interim period when those events take place. This is perhaps most likely to be encountered in the context of capital gains taxes incurred in connection with occasional dispositions of investments and other capital assets; since it is not feasible to project the rate at which such transactions will occur over the course of a year, the tax effects should be recognized only as the underlying events transpire.

While in most cases tax credits are to be handled as suggested in the foregoing paragraphs, in some jurisdictions tax credits, particularly those that relate to export revenue or capital expenditures, are in effect government grants. The accounting for government grants is set forth in IAS 20; in brief, grants are recognized in income over the period necessary to properly match them to the costs which the grants are intended to offset or defray. Thus, compliance with both IAS 20 and IAS 34 would necessitate that tax credits be carefully analyzed to identify those which are, in substance, grants, and then accounting for the credit consistent with its true nature.

Tax loss tax credit carrybacks and carryforwards. When an interim period loss gives rise to a tax loss carryback, it should be fully reflected in that interim period. Similarly, if a loss in an interim period produces a tax loss carryforward, it should be recognized immediately, but only if the criteria set forth in IAS 12 are met. Specifically, it must be deemed probable that the benefits will be realizable before the loss benefits can be given formal recognition in the financial statements. In the case of interim period losses, it may be necessary to assess not only whether the entity will be profitable enough in future fiscal years to utilize the tax benefits associated with the loss, but, furthermore, whether interim periods later in the same year will provide earnings of sufficient magnitude to absorb the losses of the current period.

IAS 12 provides that changes in expectations regarding the realizability of benefits related to net operating loss carryforwards should be reflected currently in tax expense. Similarly, if a net operating loss carryforward benefit is not deemed probable of being realized until the interim (or annual) period when it in fact becomes realized, the tax effect will be included in tax expense of that period. Appropriate explanatory material must be included in the notes to the financial statements, even on an interim basis, to provide the user with an understanding of the unusual relationship between pretax accounting income and the provision for income taxes.

Volume rebates or other anticipated price changes in interim reporting periods. IAS 34 prescribes that where volume rebates or other contractual changes in the prices of goods and services are anticipated to occur over the annual reporting period, these should be anticipated in the interim financial statements for periods within that year. The logic is that the effective cost of materials, labor, or other inputs will be altered later in the year as a consequence of the volume of activity during earlier interim periods, among others, and it would be a distortion of the reported results of those earlier periods if this were not taken into account. Clearly this must be based on estimates, since the volume of purchases, etc., in later portions of the year may not materialize as anticipated. As with other estimates, however, as more accurate information becomes available this will be adjusted on a prospective basis, meaning that the results of earlier periods should not be revised or corrected. This is consistent with the accounting prescribed for contingent rentals and is furthermore consistent with IAS 37's guidance on provisions.

The requirement to take volume rebates and similar adjustments into effect in interim period financial reporting applies equally to vendors or providers, as well as to customers or consumers of the goods and services. In both instances, however, it must be deemed probable that such adjustments have been earned or will occur, before giving recognition to them in the financials. This high a threshold has been set because the definitions of assets and liabilities in the IASB's *Framework* require that they be recognized only when it is probable that the benefits will flow into or out from the entity. Thus, accrual would only be appropriate for contractual price adjustments and related matters. Discretionary rebates and other price adjustments, even if typically experienced in earlier periods, would not be given formal recognition in the interim financials.

Depreciation and amortization in interim periods. The rule regarding depreciation and amortization in interim periods is more consistent with the discrete view of interim reporting. Charges to be recognized in the interim periods are to be related to only those assets actually employed during the period; planned acquisitions for later periods of the fiscal year are not to be taken into account.

While this rule seems entirely logical, it can give rise to a problem that is not encountered in the context of most other types of revenue or expense items. This occurs when the tax laws or financial reporting conventions permit or require that special allocation formulas be used during the year of acquisition (and often disposition) of an asset. In such cases, depreciation or amortization will be an amount other than the amount that would be computed based purely on the fraction of the year the asset was in service. For example, assume that convention is that one-half year of depreciation is charged during the year the asset is acquired, irrespective of how many months it is in service. Further assume that a particular asset is acquired at the inception of the fourth quarter of the year. Under the requirements of IAS 34, the first three quarters would not be charged with any depreciation expense related to this asset (even if it was known in advance that the asset would be placed in service in the fourth quarter). However, this would then necessitate charging fourth quarter operations with one-half year's (i.e., two quarters') depreciation, which arguably would distort that final period's results of operations.

IAS 34 does address this problem area. It states that an adjustment should be made in the final interim period so that the sum of interim depreciation and amortization equals an independently computed annual charge for these items. However, since there is no requirement that financial statements be separately presented for a final interim period (and most entities, in fact, do not report for a final period), such an adjustment might be implicit in the annual financials, and presumably would be explained in the notes if material (the standard does not explicitly require this, however).

The alternative financial reporting strategy, that is, projecting annual depreciation, including the effect of asset dispositions and acquisitions planned for or reasonably anticipated to occur during the year, and then allocating this ratably to interim periods, has been rejected. Such an approach might have been rationalized in the same way that the use of the effective annual tax rate was in assigning tax expense or benefits to interim periods, but this has not been done.

Inventories. Inventories represent a major category for most manufacturing and merchandising entities, and some inventory costing methods pose unique problems for interim financial reporting. In general, however, the same inventory costing principles should be utilized for interim reporting as for annual reporting. However, the use of estimates in determining quantities, costs, and net realizable values at interim dates will be more pervasive.

Two particular difficulties are addressed in IAS 34. These are the matters of determining net realizable values at interim dates and the allocation of manufacturing variances.

Regarding net realizable value determination, the standard expresses the belief that the determination of NRV at interim dates should be based on selling prices and costs to complete at those dates. Projections should therefore not be made regarding conditions which possibly might exist at the time of the fiscal year-end. Furthermore, write-downs to NRV taken at interim reporting dates should be reversed in a subsequent interim reporting period only if it would be appropriate to do so at the end of the financial year.

The last of the special issues related to inventories that are addressed by IAS 34 concerns allocation of variances at interim dates. When standard costing methods are employed, the resulting variances are typically allocated to cost of sales and inventories in proportion to the monetary magnitude of those two captions, or according to some other rational system. IAS 34 requires that the price, efficiency, spending, and volume variances of a manufacturing entity are recognized in income at interim reporting dates to the extent those variances would be recognized at the end of the financial year. It should be noted that some national standards have prescribed deferral of such variances to year-end based on the premise that some of the variances will tend to offset over the course of a full fiscal year, particularly if the result of volume fluctuations due to seasonal factors. When variance allocation is thus deferred, the full balances of the variances are placed onto the statement of financial position, typically as additions to or deductions from the inventory accounts. However, IAS 34 expresses a preference that these variances be disposed of at interim dates (instead of being deferred to year-end) since to not do so could result in reporting inventory at interim dates at more or less than actual cost.

Example of interim reporting of product costs

Dakar Corporation encounters the following product cost situations as part of its quarterly reporting:

- It only conducts inventory counts at the end of the second quarter and end of the fiscal year. Its typical gross profit is 30%. The actual gross profit at the end of the second quarter is determined to have been 32% for the first six months of the year. The actual gross profit at the end of the year is determined to have been 29% for the entire year.
- It determines that, at the end of the second quarter, due to peculiar market conditions, there is a net realizable value (NRV) adjustment to certain inventory required in the amount of €90,000. Dakar expects that this market anomaly will be corrected by year-end, which indeed does occur in late December.
- It suffers a decline of €65,000 in the market value of its inventory during the third quarter. This inventory value increases by €75,000 in the fourth quarter.
- It suffers a clearly temporary decline of €10,000 in the market value of a specific part of its inventory in the first quarter, which it recovers in the second quarter.

Dakar uses the following calculations to record these situations and determine quarterly cost of goods sold:

	Quarter 1	Quarter 2	Quarter 3	Quarter 4	Full Year
Sales	€10,000,000	€8,500,000	€7,200,000	€11,800,000	€37,500,000
(1 – Gross profit percentage)	70%		70%		
Cost of goods, gross profit method	7,000,000		5,040,000		
Cost of goods, based on actual physical count		5,580,000[1]		9,005,000[2]	26,625,000
Temporary net realizable value decline in specific inventory[3]		90,000		(90,000)	0
Decline in inventory value with subsequent increase[4]			65,000	(65,000)	0
Temporary decline in inventory value[5]	10,000	(10,000)	0	0	0
Total cost of goods sold	€7,010,000	€5,660,000	€5,105,000	€8,850,000	€26,625,000

[1] *Calculated as [€18,500,000 sales × (1– 32% gross margin)] – €7,000,000 (Quarter 1 cost of sales)*

[2] *Calculated as [€37,500,000 sales × (1 – 29% gross margin)] – €17,620,000 (Quarters 1-3 cost of sales)*

[3] *Even though anticipated to recover, the NRV decline must be recognized.*

[4] *Full recognition of market value decline, followed by recognition of market value increase, but only in the amount needed to offset the amount of the initial decline.*

[5] *No deferred recognition to temporary decline in value.*

Example of interim reporting of other expenses

Dakar Corporation encounters the following expense situations as part of its quarterly reporting:

- Its largest customer, Festive Fabrics, has placed firm orders for the year that will result in sales of €1,500,000 in the first quarter, €2,000,000 in the second quarter, €750,000 in the third quarter, and €1,650,000 in the fourth quarter. Dakar gives Festive Fabrics a 5% rebate if Festive Fabrics buys at least €5 million of goods each year. Festive Fabrics exceeded the €5 million goal in the preceding year and was expected to do so again in the current year.
- It incurs €24,000 of trade show fees in the first quarter for a trade show that will occur in the third quarter.
- It pays €64,000 *in advance* in the second quarter for a series of advertisements that will run through the third and fourth quarters.
- It receives a €32,000 property tax bill in the second quarter that applies to the *following* twelve months.
- It incurs annual factory air filter replacement costs of €6,000 in the first quarter.
- Its management team is entitled to a year-end bonus of €120,000 if it meets a sales target of €40 million, prior to any sales rebates, with the bonus dropping by €10,000 for every million dollars of sales not achieved.

Dakar uses the following calculations to record these situations:

	Quarter 1	Quarter 2	Quarter 3	Quarter 4	Full year
Sales	€10,000,000	€8,500,000	€7,200,000	€11,800,000	€37,500,000
Deduction from sales	(75,000)[1]	(100,000)	(37,500)	(82,500)	(295,000)
Marketing expense			24,000[2]		24,000
Advertising expense			32,000[3]	32,000	64,000
Property tax expense		8,000[4]	8,000	8,000	24,000
Maintenance expense	1,500[5]	1,500	1,500	1,500	6,000
Bonus expense	30,000[6]	25,500	21,600	17,900	95,000

[1] *The sales rebate is based on 5% of the actual sales to the customer in the quarter when the sale is incurred. The actual payment back to the customer does not occur until the end of the year, when the €5 million goal is*

definitively reached. Since the firm orders for the full year exceed the threshold for rebates, the obligation is deemed probable and must be recorded.

² The €24,000 trade show payment is initially recorded as a prepaid expense and then charged to marketing expense when the trade show occurs.

³ The €64,000 advertising payment is initially recorded as a prepaid expense and then charged to advertising expense when the advertisements run.

⁴ The €32,000 property tax payment is initially recorded as a prepaid expense and then charged to property tax expense on a straight-line basis over the next four quarters.

⁵ The €6,000 air filter replacement payment is initially recorded as a prepaid expense and then charged to maintenance expense over the one-year life of the air filters.

⁶ The management bonus is recognized in proportion to the amount of revenue recognized in each quarter. Once it becomes apparent that the full sales target will not be reached, the bonus accrual should be adjusted downward. In this case, the downward adjustment is assumed to be in the fourth quarter, since past history and seasonality factors made non-achievement of the full goal unlikely until fourth quarter results were known. (Note: with other fact patterns, quarterly accruals may have differed.)

Foreign Currency Translation Adjustments at Interim Dates

Given the IASC's embracing of the discrete view regarding interim reporting, it is not surprising that the same approach to translation gains or losses as is mandated at year-end would be adopted in IAS 34. IAS 21 prescribes rules for translating the financial statements for foreign operations into either the functional currency or the presentation currency and also includes guidelines for using historical, average, or closing foreign exchange rates. It also lays down rules for either including the resulting adjustments in income or in equity. IAS 34 requires that consistent with IAS 21, the actual average and closing rates for the interim period be used in translating financial statements of foreign operations at interim dates. In other words, the future changes to exchanges rates (in the current financial year) are not allowed to be anticipated by IAS 34.

Where IAS 21 provides for translation adjustments to be recognized in the statement of comprehensive income in the period it arises, IAS 34 stipulates that the same approach be applied during each interim period. If the adjustments are expected to reverse before the end of the financial year, IAS 34 requires that entities not defer some foreign currency translation adjustments at an interim date.

Adjustments to Previously Reported Interim Data

While year-to-date financial reporting is not required, although the standard does recommend it in addition to normal interim period reporting, the concept finds some expression in the standard's position that adjustments *not* be made to earlier interim periods' results. By measuring income and expense on a year-to-date basis, and then effectively backing into the most recent interim period's presentation by deducting that which was reported in earlier interim periods, the need for retrospective adjustment of information that was reported earlier is obviated. However, there may be the need for disclosure of the effects of such measurement strategies when this results effectively in including adjustments in the most current interim period's reported results.

Example of interim reporting of contingencies

Dakar Corporation is sued over its alleged violation of a patent in one of its products. Dakar settles the litigation in the fourth quarter. Under the settlement terms, Dakar must retroactively pay a 3% royalty on all sales of the product to which the patent applies. Sales of the product were €150,000 in the first quarter, €82,000 in the second quarter, €109,000 in the third quarter, and €57,000 in the fourth quarter. In addition, the cumulative total of all sales of the product in prior years is €1,280,000. Under provisions of IAS 34, Dakar cannot restate its previously issued quarterly financial results to include the following royalty expense, so instead will report the royalties expense, including that for earlier years, in the fourth quarter:

	Quarter 1	Quarter 2	Quarter 3	Quarter 4	Full year
Sales related to lawsuit	€150,000	€82,000	€109,000	€57,000	€398,000
Royalty expense	0	0	0	11,940	11,940
Royalty expense related to prior year sales	0			38,400	38,400

Accounting Changes in Interim Periods

A change in accounting policy other than one for which the transition is specified by a new standard should be reflected by restating the financial statements of prior interim periods of the current year and the comparable interim periods of the prior financial year.

One of the objectives of this requirement of IAS 34 is to ensure that a single accounting policy is applied to a particular class of transactions throughout the entire financial year. To allow differing accounting policies to be applied to the same class of transactions within a single financial year would be troublesome since it would result in "interim allocation difficulties, obscured operating results, and complicated analysis and understandability of interim period information."

The recent amendment to IFRS 1 as part of the 2010 *Improvements to IFRS* clarified that, if a first-time adopter changes its accounting policies or its use of the exemptions in IFRS 1 after it has published an interim financial report in accordance with IAS 34, *Interim Financial Reporting,* but before its first IFRS financial statements are issued, it should explain those changes and update the reconciliations between previous GAAP and IFRS.

Use of estimates in interim periods. IAS 34 recognizes that preparation of interim financial statements will require a greater use of estimates than annual financial statements. Appendix C to the standard provides examples of use of estimates to illustrate the application of this standard in this regard. The Appendix provides nine examples covering areas ranging from inventories to pensions. For instance, in the case of pensions, the Appendix states that for interim reporting purposes, reliable measurement is often obtainable by extrapolation of the latest actuarial valuation, as opposed to obtaining the same from a professionally qualified actuary, as would be expected at the end of a financial year. Readers are advised to read the other illustrations contained in Appendix C of IAS 34 for further guidance on the subject.

Impairment of assets in interim periods. IAS 34 stipulated that an entity was to apply the same impairment testing, recognition, and reversal criteria at an interim period as it would at the end of its financial year. The frequency of interim financial reporting, however, was not to affect the annual financial statements. This prescription created unanticipated conflicts, since certain impairments were not, according to other standards, subject to later reversals.

One apparent conflict between IAS 34's directives and the IAS 36 requirement is that an impairment loss recognized on goodwill cannot be later reversed. If, for example, an impairment of goodwill were indicated in the first fiscal quarter, but at year-end that impairment no longer existed, it would be impossible to comply with the proscription against having interim reporting affect annual results unless the impairment in the first quarter were reversed later in the year.

Another apparent conflict pertained to the IAS 39 mandate that impairments recognized on financial assets carried at cost (e.g., unquoted equity instruments) could not be reversed. Furthermore, IAS 39 also stipulated that losses on available-for-sale equity securities, if recognized in profit or loss (i.e., those losses deemed other than temporary in nature), could not later be reversed into income.

To resolve these specific conflicts (and no others), IFRIC Interpretation 10, *Interim Financial Reporting and Impairment*, directs that impairments of goodwill recognized in interim periods may not be later reversed, even if at year's end no impairment would otherwise have been reported. This interpretation therefore brings to an end the IAS 34-based mandate that the frequency of interim reporting cannot itself impact annual financial reporting.

IFRIC 10 also applies to losses recognized regarding equity securities classified as available-for-sale under IAS 39. That standard directs that, once written down as impaired by means of a charge against earnings, a subsequent increase in the fair value of available-for-sale equity securities, and for financial assets carried at cost (e.g., unquoted equity securities for which fair value cannot be reliably measured) cannot be recognized through income. For example, if an impairment is recognized in the second quarter of an entity's fiscal year, but the security's fair value has recovered by year's end, IAS 39 prohibits reporting the value increase in earnings. This conflicts with the IAS 34 prescription that frequency of interim reporting is not to affect annual results of operations. IFRIC 10 stipulates that an impairment loss recognized in connection with available-for-sale equity securities or financial instruments carried at cost cannot be reversed in subsequent interim periods. This is thus yet another mandate that conflicts with, and supersedes, the fundamental principle of IAS 34.

IFRS 9, issued in October 2010, amended a number of paragraphs under IFRIC 10. The revision of IFRIC 10 states that entities may not reverse an impairment loss recognized in a previous interim period in respect of goodwill. However, this restriction will not extend to other areas of potential conflict between IAS 34 and other standards.

Interim financial reporting in hyperinflationary economies. IAS 34 requires that interim financial reports in hyperinflationary economies be prepared using the same principles as at the financial year-end. Thus, the provisions of IAS 29 would need to be complied with in this regard. IAS 34 stipulates that in presenting interim data in the measuring unit, entities should report the resulting gain or loss on the net monetary position in the interim period's statement of comprehensive income. IAS 34 also requires that entities do not need to annualize the recognition of the gain or loss or use estimated annual inflation rates in preparing interim period financial statements in a hyperinflationary economy.

Examples of Financial Statement Disclosures

Roche Group consolidated income statement for the six months ended June 30, 2010

in millions of CHF	*Pharmaceuticals*	*Diagnostics*	*Corporate*	*Group*
Sales[2]	19,386	5,250	-	24,636
Royalties and other operating income[2]	784	94	-	878
Cost of sales	(4,369)	(2,501)	-	(6,970)
Marketing and distribution	(3,292)	(1,254)	-	(4,546)
Research and development[2]	(4,036)	(435)	-	(4,471)
General and administration	(464)	(207)	(200)	(871)
Operating profit before exceptional items[2]	**8,009**	**947**	**(200)**	**8,756**
Changes in Group organization[2]	(278)	-	-	(278)
Operating profit[2]	**7,731**	**947**	**(200)**	**8,478**
Associates				-
Financial income[5]				302
Financing costs[5]				(1,508)
Profit before taxes				**7,272**
Income taxes[4]				(1,800)
Income taxes on exceptional items[5]				93
Net income				**5,565**

in millions of CHF	Pharmaceuticals	Diagnostics	Corporate	Group
Attributable to				
• Roche shareholders				5,468
• Noncontrolling interests				97

Earnings per share and nonvoting equity security

Basic (CHF)	6.99
Diluted (CHF)	6.97

Roche Group consolidated income statement for the six months ended June 30, 2009

in millions of CHF	Pharmaceuticals	Diagnostics	Corporate	Group
Sales[2]	19,104	4,902	-	24,006
Royalties and other operating income[2]	1,047	69	-	1,118
Cost of sales	(4,648)	(2,452)	-	(7,100)
Marketing and distribution	(3,342)	(1,225)	-	(4,567)
Research and development[2]	(4,058)	(460)	-	(4,518)
General and administration	(640)	(190)	(137)	(967)
Operating profit before exceptional items[2]	**7,463**	**644**	**(137)**	**7,970**
Major legal cases[11]	(421)	-	-	(421)
Changes in Group organization[2]	(1,942)	-	-	(1,942)
Operating profit[2]	**5,100**	**644**	**(137)**	**5,607**
Associates				-
Financial income[5]				494
Financing costs[5]				(1,035)
Exceptional financing costs[5]				(365)
Profit before taxes				**4,691**
Income taxes[4]				(1,678)
Income taxes on exceptional items[5]				1,088
Net income				**4,051**
Attributable to				
• Roche shareholders				3,479
• Noncontrolling interests				578

Earnings per share and nonvoting equity security

Basic (CHF)	4.04
Diluted (CHF)	4.00

Roche Group consolidated statement of comprehensive income

in millions of CHF	Six months ended June 30 2010	2009
Net income recognized in income statement	**5,565**	**4,051**
Other comprehensive income		
Available-for-sale investments	(22)	259
Cash flow hedges	(146)	(9)
Currency translation of foreign operations	(1,394)	2,610
Defined benefit postemployment plans	(362)	733
Other comprehensive income, net of tax	**(1,924)**	**3,593**
Total comprehensive income	**3,641**	**7,644**

	Six months ended June 30	
	2010	*2009*
Attributable to		
• Roche shareholders	3,977	6,684
• Noncontrolling interests	264	960
Total	**3,641**	**7,644**

Roche Group consolidated statement of cash flows

	Six months ended June 30	
in millions of CHF	*2010*	*2009*
Cash flows from operating activities		
Cash generated from operations[11]	10,584	9,670
(Increase) decrease in net working capital	(2,299)	(1,168)
Payments made for defined benefit postemployment plans	(155)	(319)
Utilization of provisions	(970)	(419)
Other operating cash flows	-	165
Cash flows from operating activities, before income taxes paid	**7,741**	**7,936**
Income taxes paid	(1,584)	(488)
Total cash flows from operating activities	**6,177**	**7,450**
Cash flows from investing activities		
Purchase of property, plant, and equipment	(1,295)	(1,246)
Purchase of intangible assets	(89)	(97)
Disposal of property, plant, and equipment	59	77
Disposal of intangible assets	-	-
Disposal of products	20	33
Business combinations[7]	(179)	(84)
Divestments of subsidiaries	-	-
Interest and dividends received	38	268
Sales of marketable securities	26,740	13,186
Purchases of marketable securities	(17,164)	(12,714)
Other investing cash flows	78	(922)
Total cash flows from investing activities	**8,283**	**(899)**
Cash flows from financing activities		
Proceeds from issue of bonds and notes[12]	-	48,197
Redemption and repurchase of bonds and notes[12]	(5,438)	-
Increase (decrease) in commercial paper[12]	193	67
Increase (decrease) in other debt	(23)	(150)
Hedging and collateral arrangements[12]	(2,711)	2,487
Change in ownership interest in subsidiaries		
• Genentech[2]	-	(52,708)
• Memory[7]	-	(6)
Equity contribution by noncontrolling interests	14	-
Interest paid	(1,529)	(119)
Dividends paid	(5,214)	(4,353)
Equity-settled equity compensation plans, net of transactions in own equity instruments	(210)	(162)
Other financing cash flows	-	-
Total cash flows from financing activities	**(14,918)**	**(6,747)**
Net effect of currency translation on cash and cash equivalents	(5)	(1,591)
Increase (decrease) in cash and cash equivalents	**(463)**	**(1,797)**
Cash and cash equivalents at beginning of period	2,442	4,915
Cash and cash equivalents at end of period	**1,979**	**3,129**

Roche Group consolidated statement of changes in equity

in millions of CHF	Share capital	Retained earnings	Fair value	Hedging	Reserves transaction	Total	Noncontrolling interests	Total equity
Six months ended June 30, 2009								
At January 1, 2009	160	52,081	(231)	9	(7,540)	44,479	9,343	53,822
Net income	-	3,473	-	-	-	3,473	578	4,051
Available-for-sale investments	-	-	254	-	-	254	5	259
Cash flow hedges	-	-	-	(24)	-	(24)	15	(9)
Currency translation of foreign operations	-	-	(17)	(1)	2,266	2,248	362	2,610
Defined benefit postemployment plans	-	733	-	-	-	733	-	733
Total comprehensive income	-	**4,206**	**237**	**(25)**	**2,266**	**6,684**	**960**	**7,644**
Business combinations[7]	-	-	-	-	-	-	4	4
Dividends	-	(4,300)	-	-	-	(4,300)	(54)	(4,354)
Equity comprehensive plans, net of transactions in own equity instruments	-	305	-	-	-	305	177	482
Changes in ownership interests in subsidiaries								
• Genentech[2]	-	(43,777)	-	-	-	(43,777)	(8,464)	(52,241)
• Memory[7]	-	(2)	-	-	-	(2)	(4)	(6)
Changes in noncontrolling interests	-	(17)	-	-	-	(17)	17	-
At June 30, 2009	**160**	**8,496**	**6**	**(16)**	**(5,274)**	**3,372**	**1,979**	**5,351**
Six months ended June 30, 2010								
At January 1, 2010	**160**	**11,835**	**99**	**65**	**(4,793)**	**7,366**	**2,048**	**9,414**
Net income	-	5,468	-	-	-	5,468	97	5,565
Available-for-sale investments	-	-	(22)	-	-	(22)	-	(22)
Cash flow hedges	-	-	-	(146)	-	(146)	-	(146)
Currency translation of foreign operations	-	-	9	1	(1,571)	(1,561)	167	(1,394)
Defined benefit postemployment plans	-	(362)	-	-	-	(362)	-	(362)
Total comprehensive income	-	**5,106**	**(13)**	**(145)**	**(1,571)**	**3,377**	**264**	**3,641**
Dividends	-	(5,144)	-	-	-	(5,144)	(65)	(5,209)
Equity comprehensive plans, net of transactions in own equity instruments	-	(59)	-	-	-	(59)	-	(59)
Changes in noncontrolling interests	-	-	-	-	-	-	-	-
Equity contribution by noncontrolling interests	-	-	-	-	-	-	14	14
Other movements	-	(90)	68	22	-	-	-	-
At June 30, 2010	**160**	**11,648**	**154**	**(58)**	**(6,364)**	**5,540**	**2,261**	**7,801**

1. Accounting policies

Basis of preparation of financial statements

These financial statements are the unaudited interim consolidated financial statements (hereafter "the Interim Financial Statements") of Roche Holding Ltd, a company registered in Switzerland, and its subsidiaries (hereafter "the Group") for the six-month period ended June 30, 2010 (hereafter "the interim period"). They are prepared in accordance with International Accounting Standard 34 (IAS 34), *Interim Financial Reporting*. These Interim Financial Statements should be read in conjunction with the Consolidated Financial Statements for the year ended December 31, 2009 (hereafter "the Annual Financial Statements"), as they provide an update of previously reported information. They were approved for issue by the Board of Directors on July 21, 2010.

The Interim Financial Statements have been prepared in accordance with the accounting policies and methods of computation set out in the Annual Financial Statements, except for the accounting policy changes described below made after the date of the Annual Financial Statements. The presentation of the Interim Financial Statements is consistent with the Annual Financial Statement, except where noted below. Where necessary, comparative information has been reclassified or expanded from the previously reported Interim Financial Statements or in these Interim Financial Statements.

The preparation of the Interim Financial Statements requires management to make estimates and assumptions that affect the reported amounts of revenues, expenses, assets, liabilities, and the disclosure of contingent liabilities at the date of the Interim Financial Statements. If in the future such estimates and assumptions, which are based on management's best judgment at the date of the Interim Financial Statements, deviate from the actual circumstances, the original estimates and assumptions will be modified as appropriate in the period in which the circumstances change.

The Group operates in industries where significant seasonal or cyclical variations in total sales are not experienced during the financial year. Income tax expense is recognized based upon the best estimate of the weighted-average income tax rate expected for the full financial year.

The Group has two divisions, Pharmaceuticals and Diagnostics. Revenues are primarily generated from the sale of prescription pharmaceutical products and diagnostic instruments, reagents and consumables, respectively. Both divisions also derive revenue from the sale or licensing of products or technology to third parties. Certain headquarter activities are reported as "Corporate." These consist of corporate headquarters, including the Corporate Executive Committee, corporate communications, corporate human resources, corporate finance, including treasury, taxes and pension fund management, corporate legal and corporate safety and environmental services. Subdivisional information for Roche Pharmaceuticals and Chugai, the previously aggregated operating segments within the Pharmaceuaticals Division, is also presented.

Changes in accounting policies

In 2008 the Group early adopted the revised versions of IFRS 3, *Business Combinations* and IAS 27, *Consolidated and Separate Financial Statements,* which are required to be implemented from January 1, 2010, at the latest. In 2010 the Group has implemented various amendments to existing standards and interpretations, which have no material impact on the Group's overall results and financial position.

The Group is currently assessing the potential impacts of the other new and revised standards and interpretations that will be effective from January 1, 2011, and beyond, and which the Group has not early adopted. The Group does not anticipate that these will have a material impact on the Group's overall results and financial position.

2. Operating segment information

Divisional information

in millions of CHF
Six months ended June 30

	Pharmaceuticals 2010	Pharmaceuticals 2009	Diagnostics 2010	Diagnostics 2009	Corporate 2010	Corporate 2009	Group 2010	Group 2009
Revenues from external customers								
Sales	19,396	19,104	5,250	4,902	-	-	24,636	24,006
Royalties and other operating income	794	1,047	94	69	-	-	878	1,116
Total	**20,170**	**20,151**	**5,344**	**4,971**	**-**	**-**	**25,514**	**25,122**
Revenues from other operating segments								
Sales	2	3	7	5	-	-	9	8
Royalties and other operating income	-	-	-	-	-	-	-	-
Elimination of interdivisional revenue							(9)	(8)
Total	**2**	**3**	**7**	**5**	**-**	**-**	**-**	**-**
Segment results								
Operating profit before exceptional items	8,009	7,468	947	644	(200)	(137)	8,756	7,970
Major legal cases	-	(421)	-	-	-	-	-	(421)
Changes in Group organization	(278)	(1,942)	-	-	-	-	(278)	(1,942)
Operating profit	**7,731**	**5,100**	**947**	**644**	**(200)**	**(137)**	**8,478**	**5,607**
Capital expenditure								
Business combinations	-	57	257	50	-	-	257	107
Additions to property, plant, and equipment	569	671	540	484	49	1	1,158	1,156
Additions to intangible assets	52	96	19	1	-	-	71	97
Total capital expenditure	**621**	**824**	**816**	**535**	**49**	**1**	**1,486**	**1,360**
Research and development								
Research and development costs	4,036	4,058	435	460	-	-	4,471	4,518
Other segment information								
Depreciation of property, plant, and equipment	591	600	389	942	4	3	974	945
Amortization of intangible assets	90	162	221	294	-	-	311	396
Impairment of property, plant, and equipment	49	1,049	-	-	-	-	49	1,049
Impairment of goodwill	-	-	-	-	-	-	-	-
Impairment of intangible assets	102	174	17	11	6	-	102	195
Equity compensation plan expenses	129	383	17	15	6	7	152	405

Pharmaceuticals subdivisional information

in millions of CHF	Roche Pharmaceuticals		Chugai		Pharmaceuticals DMsion	
Six months ended June 30	*2010*	*2009*	*2010*	*2009*	*2010*	*2009*
Revenue from external customers						
Sales	17,325	16,920	2,061	2,184	19,396	19,104
Royalties and other operating income	780	998	4	49	784	1,047
Total	**18,105**	**17,918**	**2,065**	**2,233**	**20,170**	**20,151**
Revenues from other operating segments						
Sales	700	719	88	21	788	740
Royalties and other operating income	8	7	22	21	30	28
Elimination of income within division					(816)	(765)
Total	**708**	**726**	**110**	**42**	**2**	**3**
Segment results						
Operating profit before exceptional items	7,892	7,073	326	474	8,218	7,547
Elimination of interdivisional profit					(209)	(84)
Subtotal	7,892	7,073	326	474	8,009	7,463
Major legal cases	-	(421)	-	-	-	(421)
Changes in Group organization	(278)	(1,942)	-	-	(278)	(1,942)
Operating profit	**7,614**	**4,710**	**326**	**474**	**7,731**	**5,100**
Capital expenditure						
Business combinations	-	57	-	-	-	57
Additions to property, plant, and equipment	492	590	77	91	569	671
Additions to intangible assets	52	96	-	-	52	96
Total capital expenditure	**544**	**733**	**77**	**91**	**621**	**824**
Research and development						
Research and development costs	3,663	3,741	389	342	4,052	4,083
Elimination of costs within division					(16)	(25)
Total	**3,663**	**3,741**	**389**	**342**	**4,036**	**4,058**
Other segment information						
Depreciation of property, plant, and equipment	505	540	76	60	581	600
Amortization of intangible assets	58	126	37	36	90	162
Impairment of property, plant, and equipment	49	1,049	-	-	49	1,049
Impairment of goodwill	-	-	-	-	-	-
Impairment of intangible assets	102	174	-	-	102	174
Equity compensation plan expenses	128	382	1	1	129	383

3. Genentech

Genetech transaction

On March 12, 2009, Roche entered into a merger agreement with Genentech pursuant to which the Group made a successful tender offer to purchase all of the shares of Genentech not already owned by the Group for USD 95.00 per share in cash (the "Genetech transaction"). As a result, Genetech became a wholly owned subsidiary of the Group, effective March 26, 2009.

The cash consideration for the purchase of all public shares, including shares issuable under Genentech's outstanding employee stock option plans and payment of related fees and expenses, amounted to approximately 47 billion US dollars, as set out in the table below. These amounts have been recorded to equity as a change in ownership interest in subsidiaries in 2009.

Genetech transaction

	USD millions	*CHF millions*
Purchase of publicly held shares	44,400	49,774
Settlement of outstanding employee stock options	2,412	2,704
Directly attributable transaction costs	205	230
Total cash consideration	**47,017**	**52,708**
Income tax effects	(417)	(467)
Change in ownership interest in subsidiaries	46,600	52,241

Translated at spot rate on date of transaction (March 26, 2009) 1 USD – 1.12 CHF

4. Chugai

The common stock of Chugai is publicly traded and is listed on the Tokyo Stock Exchange under the stock code "TSE: 4519." At June 30, 2010, the Group's interest in Chugai was 61.6% (December 31, 2009: 61.6%). Chugai prepares financial statements in conformity with accounting principles generally accepted in Japan (JGAAP). These are filed on a quarterly basis with the Tokyo Stock Exchange. Due to certain consolidation entries and differences in the requirements of International Financial Reporting Standards (IFRS) and JGAAP, there are differences between Chugai's stand-alone results on a JGAAP basis and the results of Chugai as consolidated by the Roche Group in accordance with IFRS.

Dividends

The dividends distributed to third parties holding Chugai shares during the interim period totaled 57 million Swiss francs (2009: 47 million Swiss francs) and have been recorded to equity. Dividends paid by Chugai to Roche are eliminated on consolidation as intercompany items.

5. Financial income and financing costs

Financial income

	Six months ended June 30	
in millions of CHF	*2010*	*2009*
Gains on sale of equity securities	90	97
(Losses) on sale of equity securities	(3)	(2)
Divided income	1	1
Gains (losses) on equity security derivatives, net	3	1
Write-downs and impairments of equity securities	(10)	(2)
Net income from equity securities	**81**	**35**
Interest income	31	137
Gains on sale of debt securities	1	-
(Losses) on sale of debt securities	(1)	(9)
Gains (losses) on debt security derivatives, net	-	20
Gains (losses) on financial assets at fair-value-through-profit-or-loss, net	-	-
Write-downs and impairments of long-term loans	-	(3)
Net interest income and income from debt securities	**31**	**145**
Expected return on plan assets of defined benefit plans	286	257
Foreign exchange gains (losses) net	288	(742)
Gains (losses) on foreign currency derivatives, net	(369)	790
Net foreign exchange gains (losses)	**(81)**	**48**
Net other financial income (expense)	(15)	(1)
Total financial income	**302**	**484**

Financing costs

in millions of CHF	Six months ended June 30	
	2010	*2009*
Interest expense	(994)	(694)
Amortization of debt discount[13]	(26)	(17)
Gains (losses) on debt derivatives, net	(1)	1
Gains (losses) on redemption and repurchase of bonds and notes, net[12]	(144)	-
Gains (losses) on financial liabilities at fair-value-through-profit-or-loss, net[12]	-	6
Time cost of provisions	(7)	(11)
Interest cost of defined benefit plans	(336)	(890)
Total financing costs	**(1,508)**	**(1,035)**

Net financial income

in millions of CHF	Six months ended June 30	
	2010	*2009*
Financial income	302	484
Financing costs	(1,508)	(1,035)
Net financial income	**(1,206)**	**(551)**
Financial result from Treasury management	(1,156)	(478)
Financial result from Pension management	(50)	(73)
Net financial income	**(1,206)**	**(551)**

Exceptional financing costs

As described in Note 3, effective March 26, 2009, the Group purchased all publicly owned shares of Genentech for USD 95.00 per share in cash, with the total cash consideration of the transaction, including shares issuable under Genentech's outstanding employee stock option plans and payment of related fees and expenses, being approximately 52.7 billion Swiss francs.

In order to execute this transaction, the Group liquidated certain debt securities into cash in the interim period of 2009. This resulted in a net loss on these transactions of 226 million Swiss francs. Furthermore, due to the prevailing financial conditions at that time, the Group issued bonds and notes in advance of the transaction totaling 48.2 billion Swiss francs through a series of debt offerings, as described in Note 27 to the Annual Financial Statements. The interest expense on these instruments for the bridging period between their issue and the completion of the Genetech transaction on March 26, 2009, was 139 million Swiss francs.

Exceptional financing costs

in millions of CHF	Six months ended June 30	
	2010	*2009*
Gain (loss) on liquidation of debt securities)	-	(226)
Interest expense incurred on newly issued bonds and notes during bridging period	-	(139)
Total exceptional financing costs	**-**	**(365)**

6. Income taxes

Income tax expenses

in millions of CHF	Six months ended June 30	
	2010	*2009*
Current income taxes	(1,604)	(1,744)
Adjustments recognized for current tax of prior periods	13	75
Deferred income taxes	(209)	(9)
Total income tax (expense)/benefit	**(1,800)**	**(1,678)**

Exceptional income taxes

As described in Note 8, the Group incurred exceptional expenses totaling 278 million Swiss francs (2009: 1,942 million Swiss francs) in connection with the Genetech transaction and the related reorganizations in the Group's pharmaceuticals business. Furthermore, as described in Note 5, the Group incurred exceptional financing costs in the interim period of 2009 totaling 365 million Swiss francs in connection with the financing of the Genentech transaction. As disclosed in Note 11, expenses incurred in respect of major legal cases for the interim period of 2009 were 421 million Swiss francs. The income tax effects of these items, as shown in the table below, are disclosed separately in the income statement in order to fairly present the Group's results in the overall context of the Genentech transaction and related reorganizations in the Group's Pharmaceuticals Division. In the interim period of 2009 an income tax benefit of 147 million Swiss francs was recorded in respect of Genentech's stock options plans that was clearly attributable to the Genentech transaction, and therefore has been allocated as part of exceptional income taxes.

Exceptional income tax expenses

	Six months ended June 30	
in millions of CHF	2010	2009
Current income taxes	95	122
Deferred income taxes	(2)	916
Total income tax (expense)/benefit on exceptional items	**93**	**1,038**

Reconciliation of the Group's effective tax rate

	2010			2009		
Six months ended June 30	Profit before tax *(mCHF)*	Income taxes *(mCHF)*	Tax rate *(%)*	Profit before tax *(mCHF)*	Income taxes *(mCHF)*	Tax rate *(%)*
Group's effective tax rate before exceptional items	7,550	(1,800)	29.8	7,419	(1,678)	22.6
Major legal cases[11]	-	-	-	(421)	163	39.7
Changes in Group organization[5]	(278)	93	33.5	(1,942)	814	41.9
Exceptional financing costs[5]	-	-	-	(365)	61	16.7
Group's effective tax rate	**7,272**	**(1,707)**	**23.5**	**4,691**	**(640)**	**13.6**

7. Business combinations

Acquisitions—2010

Effective May 28, 2010, the Group acquired a 100% controlling interest in Medingo Ltd. ("Medingo"), a majority-owned subsidiary of the Elron group, based in Israel. Medingo is engaged in the development of a semidisposable insulin patch pump and is reported as part of the Diagnostics operating segment. The acquisition broadens the Group's portfolio of innovative insulin delivery technologies and strengthens its position in the diabetes care business. The total purchase consideration was 210 million Swiss francs, of which 178 million Swiss francs was paid in cash and 32 million Swiss francs from a contingent consideration arrangement. The payment from this arrangement is based on the achievement of four separate performance milestones that may arise between 2012 and 2014 and the range of outcomes, undiscounted, is between zero and 42 million US dollars, equivalent to 45 million Swiss francs at June 30, 2010 exchange rates. A liability of 32 million Swiss francs was recognized at the acquisition date, based on management's best estimate of the probability-adjusted expected cash outflow from the arrangement. As at June 30, 2010, the amount recognized for this arrangement was unchanged, based on the most recent management estimates.

The purchase consideration has been allocated as follows:

Acquisitions—2010: net assets acquired

in millions of CHF	Carrying value prior to acquisition	Fair value adjustments	Carrying value upon acquisition
Property, plant, and equipment	2	-	2
Goodwill	-	-	-
Intangible assets			
• Product intangibles: in use	-	178	178
• Marketing intangibles	-	-	-
• Product intangibles: not available for use	-	-	-
Inventories	-	-	-
Deferred income taxes	-	(45)	(45)
Cash	-	-	-
Other net assets (liabilities)	(2)	-	(2)
Net identifiable assets (liabilities)	-	**133**	**133**
Noncontrolling interests			-
Goodwill			77
Purchase consideration			**210**

Goodwill represents a control premium and synergies that can be obtained from the Group's existing business. None of the goodwill recognized is expected to be deductible for income tax purposes.

The fair value of other net assets (liabilities) does not include any receivables.

Directly attributable transaction costs of 1 million Swiss francs were incurred in this acquisition. These are reported within general and administration expenses in the current period as part of the operating result of the Diagnostics operating segment.

Acquisitions—2010: impact on results

in millions of CHF	Revenues from external customers	Inventory fair value adjustment	Amortization of intangible assets	Operating profit	Net income
Impact on reported results					
Medingo	-	-	**(1)**	**(3)**	**(2)**
Estimated impact on results if acquisition assumed effective January 1, 2010					
Medingo	-	-	**(7)**	**(16)**	**(12)**

The above figures exclude directly attributable transaction costs of 1 million Swiss francs. Corresponding tax impacts are also excluded.

Acquisitions—2010: net cash outflow

in millions of CHF	Cash consideration paid	Cash in acquired company	Net cash outflow
Acquisitions	(178)	-	(179)

Acquisitions—2009

Effective January 1, 2009, the Group acquired an 89.6% controlling interest in Memory Pharmaceuticals Corp. ("Memory") for a cash consideration of 48 million Swiss francs. Subsequent to the effective date of the acquisition, the Group purchased the remaining shares in Memory held by third parties to give the Group a 100% interest in Memory. The additional cash consideration was 6 million Swiss francs, which has been recorded to equity as a change in ownership interest in subsidiaries. There were other minor business combinations in the Diagnostics business with a total purchase consideration of 57 million Swiss francs, of which 55 million Swiss francs was in cash and 2 million Swiss francs from a contingent consideration arrangement. These transactions are fully described in Note 7 to the Annual Financial Statements.

Acquisitions—2009: net cash outflow

in millions of CHF	*Cash consideration paid*	*Cash in acquired company*	*Net cash outflow*
Acquisitions	(103)	19	(94)

The above cash consideration paid does not include the subsequent payment of 6 million Swiss francs to purchase the remaining shares in Memory held by third parties to give the Group a 100% interest in Memory. This is reported as financing cash flow in the statement of cash flows within the heading "Change in ownership interest in subsidiaries."

8. Changes in Group organization

On July 21, 2008, the Group announced an offer to purchase all outstanding shares of Genentech. Following the closing of the transaction, Genentech's South San Francisco site would become the headquarters of the Group's combined pharmaceuticals operations in the United States. On July 21, 2008, the Group also announced that Roche's pharmaceuticals business in the US would close manufacturing operations at its site in Nutley, New Jersey, and commercial operations would be moved to Genentech. The research site at Palo Alto, California, would be closed with the research activities being transferred to Nutley and to Genentech. Subsequent to these announcements, initial restructuring activities started at the Nutley and Palo Alto sites in 2008.

As described in Note 3, the Genentech transaction was completed effective March 26, 2009. Following this the Pharmaceuticals Division initiated a detailed integration program to align the Genentech business and the rest of Roche's pharmaceuticals business. Genentech's South San Francisco site is being established as the headquarters of the pharmaceuticals business in the US, including commercial operations for the US market. Genentech Research and Early Development is being set up as an autonomous unit while Genentech's late-stage development activities are being integrated with the global Pharmaceuticals Division network. The integration program includes prioritizing projects within the shared portfolio and eliminating activities that are either duplicated or no longer required, notably in the administration function.

Following the completion of the transaction, the Pharmaceuticals Division carried out a detailed reassessment of its global manufacturing network, with particular emphasis on its biotech manufacturing facilities. As a result several manufacturing facilities and construction projects are being discontinued, notably a bulk drug production unit on part of the site at Vacaville in California.

The Group currently anticipates that these restructuring activities will be substantially completed by the end of 2010. The total cost is expected to be in the order of 3.3 billion Swiss francs, which includes 2.7 billion Swiss francs that were incurred in 2008 and 2009. Of this total of 3.3 billion Swiss francs approximately 2.0 billion Swiss francs is noncash.

During the interim period significant costs were incurred as described below. These are disclosed separately in the income statement due to the materiality of the amounts and in order to fairly present the Group's results. Costs of other restructuring programs that are less material and do not fundamentally change the Group's organization are expensed in the current period and reported within the respective functional expense.

Changes in Group organization

	Six months ended June 30	
in millions of CHF	*2010*	*2009*
Employee-related costs		
Termination costs	37	149
Pensions and other postemployment benefits	--	(31)
Genentech Employee Retention Program expenses	--	20

	Six months ended June 30	
	2010	2009
Genentech stock options: accelerated vesting expenses	--	236
Other retention plans and other employee benefits	--	29
Other employee-related costs	52	31
Total employee-related costs	**95**	**433**
Site closure costs		
Impairment of property, plant, and equipment	20	1,049
Accelerated depreciation of property, plant, and equipment	40	48
Other site closure costs	35	181
Total site closure costs	95	1,278
Impairment of intangible assets	--	174
Other reorganization expenses	88	57
Total	**278**	**1,942**

The total income tax benefit recorded in respect of changes in Group organization was 93 million Swiss francs (2009: 814 million Swiss francs).

9. Goodwill]

Goodwill: movements in carrying value of assets

in millions of CHF
Six months ended June 30, 2010

At January 1, 2010	8,261
Business combinations	77
Impairment charge	--
Currency transaction effects	100
At June 30, 2010	**8,438**
Allocation by operating segment	
Roche Pharmaceuticals	2,206
Chugai	135
Diagnostics	6,097
Total Group	**8,438**

There are no accumulated impairment losses in goodwill.

10. Intangible assets

Intangible assets: movements in carrying value of assets

in millions of CHF	Product intangibles: in use	Product intangibles: not available for use	Marketing intangibles	Technology intangibles	Total
Six months ended June 30, 2010					
At January 1, 2010	3,529	2,304	21	152	6,005
Business combinations	178	--	--	--	178
Additions	4	51	--	16	71
Disposals	--	--	--	--	--
Transfers	44	(9)	--	(35)	--
Amortization charge	(297)	--	(2)	(12)	(311)
Impairment charge	--	(102)	--	--	(102)
Currency translation effects	5	62	(2)	2	67
At June 20, 2010	**3,462**	**2,306**	**17**	**123**	**5,908**

in millions of CHF	Product intangibles: in use	Product intangibles: not available for use	Marketing intangibles	Technology intangibles	Total
Allocation by division					
Pharmaceuticals	892	1,738	--	107	2,797
Diagnostics	2,570	568	17	16	3,171
Total Group	**3,462**	**2,306**	**17**	**123**	**5,909**

Classification of amortization and impairment expenses

in millions of CHF	Six months ended June 30, 2010 Amortization	Impairment	Six months ended June 30, 2009 Amortization	Impairment
Cost of sales				
Pharmaceuticals	90	--	141	--
Diagnostics	217	--	229	11
Marketing and distribution				
Diagnostics	2	--	1	--
Research and development				
Pharmaceuticals	10	102	21	--
Diagnostics	2	--	4	--
Changes in Group organization				
Pharmaceuticals	--	--	--	174
Total	**311**	**102**	**396**	**185**

Impairment of intangible assets

Impairment charges arise from changes in the estimates of the future cash flows expected to result from the use of an asset and its eventual disposal. Factors such as the presence or absence of competition, technical obsolescence, or lower than anticipated sales for products with capitalized rights could result in shortened useful lives or impairment.

2010. In the Pharmaceuticals operating segment a net impairment charge of 102 million Swiss francs was recorded. An impairment charge of 71 million Swiss francs was recorded, which relates to a decision to stop development of one compound with an alliance partner. The assets concerned, which were not yet being amortized, were fully written down by these charges. A further charge of 47 million Swiss francs was recorded, resulting from a portfolio prioritization decision on a project acquired as part of a previous business combination. The asset concerned, which was not yet being amortized, was written down to its recoverable value of 95 million Swiss francs. A reversal of previously recorded impairment loss of 16 million Swiss francs was recorded, which follows from the latest clinical data assessment of the project concerned.

2009. In the Pharmaceuticals operating segment an impairment charge of 174 million Swiss francs was recorded, which relates to the Pharmaceuticals Division reorganization (see Note 8). In the Diagnostics operating segment an impairment charge of 11 million Swiss francs was recorded, which relates to reduced revenue expectations of a project with an alliance partner. The assets concerned were fully written down by these charges.

11. Provisions and contingent liabilities

Provisions

in millions of CHF	June 30, 2010	December 31, 2009
Legal provisions	529	549
Environmental provisions	249	247
Restructuring provisions	436	592
Employee provisions	270	278
Other provisions	766	712
Total provisions	**2,250**	**2,318**

in millions of CHF	June 30, 2010	December 31, 2009
Of which		
Current portion	1,539	1,618
Noncurrent portion	711	700
Total provisions	**2,250**	**2,318**

Payments in the interim period from previously recorded provisions totaled 370 million Swiss francs (2009: 413 million Swiss francs).

Major legal cases

Income (expense) from major legal cases is disclosed separately in the income statement due to the materiality of the amounts and in order to fairly present the Group's results. There were no such items in the interim period. In the interim period of 2009 provisions for major legal cases were increased by 421 million Swiss francs, based on management's estimates at the time of the ultimate liabilities that were expected to arise, taking into account that development of the various litigation and arbitration processes and any negotiations to resolve these cases.

Other than as described below, no significant changes in the Group's contingent liabilities have occurred since the approval of the Annual Financial Statements by the Board of Directors.

On June 28, 2008, Mr. Ubaldo Bao Martinez filed a lawsuit against the Porriño Town Council and Genentech España S.L. in the Contentious Administrative Court Number One of Pontevedra, Spain. The lawsuit challenged the Town Council's decision to grant licenses to Genentech España S.L. for the construction and operation of a warehouse and and biopharmaceutical manufacturing facility in Parriño, Spain. On January 16, 2008, the Administrative Court ruled in favor of Mr. Bao on one of the claims in the lawsuit and ordered the closing and demolition of the facility, subject to certain further legal proceedings. On February 12, 2008, Genentech España S.L. and the Town Council filed appeals of the Administrative Court decision at the High Court in Galicia, Spain. On March 16, 2010, Genetech received notice that it prevailed over Mr. Bao on the appeal. This decision revokes the January 2008 ruling in its entirety.

There have been certain procedural developments in the other significant litigation matters described in Note 25 to the Annual Financial Statements. However, these do not significantly affect the assessment of the Group's management concerning the adequacy of the total provisions recorded for legal proceedings.

12. Debt

Debt: movements in carrying value of recognized liabilities

in millions of CHF
Six months ended June 30, 2010

At January 1, 2010	42,416
Proceeds from issue of bonds and notes	--
Redemption and repurchase of bonds and notes	(5,438)
Increase (decrease) in commercial paper	193
Increase (decrease) in other debt	(23)
(Gains) losses on redemption and repurchase of bonds and notes, net[5]	144
Amortization of debt discount[5]	26
(Gains) losses on financial liabilities at fair-value-through-profit or loss, net[5]	--
Currency translation effects and other	(878)
At June 30, 2010	**36,440**
Consisting of	
Bonds and notes	35,539
Commercial paper	474
Amounts due to banks and other financial institutions	125
Genentech leasing obligations	281
Finance lease obligations	2
Other borrowings	19
Total debt	**36,440**

Wiley IFRS 2012

Reported as
     Long-term debt   31,454
     Short-term debt   4,986
Total debt   **36,440**

Issuance of bonds and notes—2010

The Group did not issue any bonds or notes during the interim period of 2010.

Issuance of bonds and notes—2009

The Group financed the Genetech transaction (see Note 3) by a combination of the Group's own funds, bonds, notes, and commercial paper. The Group raised net proceeds of 48.2 billion Swiss francs through a series of debt offerings, as described in Note 27 to the Annual Financial Statements. All newly issued debt is senior, unsecured, and has been guaranteed by Roche Holding Ltd.

Cash inflows from issuance of bonds and notes

	Six months ended June 30	
in millions of CHF	*2010*	*2009*
US dollar denominated notes	--	21,681
European Medium Term Note program euro and sterling denominated notes	--	18,556
Swiss franc denominated bonds	--	7,960
Total	**--**	**48,197**

Currency swaps. Subsequent to the debt issuances, the proceeds of all of the European Medium Term Note program notes and 6,485 million Swiss francs of the Swiss franc denominated bonds were swapped into US dollars. As a result, in these financial statements, the notes have economic characteristics similar to US dollar denominated bonds and notes.

Collateral agreements. Collateral agreements were entered with the derivative counterparties to the above currency swaps to mitigate counterparty risk. As the fair value of the derivative instruments moved down during the first half of 2010 due to a stronger US dollar, a total of 2.0 billion Swiss francs cash collateral was delivered by the Group during the interim period (2009 interim period: 1.3 billion Swiss francs delivered to the Group). This collateral is recorded as a decrease in cash and a corresponding increase in current assets. The carrying value of current assets in respect to these agreements is 0.5 billion Swiss francs (December 31, 2009: accrued liabilities of 1.5 billion Swiss francs). The realized loss on derivatives in the interim period was 0.7 billion Swiss francs (2009: realized gain of 1.2 billion Swiss francs) and relates mainly to hedges on the non-US dollar denominated bonds and notes.

Repayment and redemption of bonds and notes — 2010

Redemption of US dollar denominated notes. On the due date of February 25, 2010, the Group redeemed notes with a principal of 3 billion US dollars at the original issue amount plus accrued original issue discount (OID). The effective interest rate of these notes was 3 months LIBOR plus 1.13%. The cash outflow was 3.244 million Swiss francs and there was no gain or loss recorded on the redemption.

Redemption of European Medium Term Note program notes. On the due date of March 4,2010, the Group redeemed notes with a principal of 1.5 billion euros at the original issue amount plus accrued original issue discount (OID). The effective interest rate of these notes was 3 months EURIBOR plus 1.05% (plus 0.92% including hedging). The cash outflow was 2,194 million Swiss francs and there was no gain or loss recorded on the redemption.

Cash outflows from repayment and redemption of bonds and notes

	Six months ended June 30	
in millions of CHF	*2010*	*2009*
US dollar denominated notes	3,244	--
European Medium Term Note program euro and sterling denominated notes	2,194	--
Total	**5,438**	**--**

Early redemption of US dollar denominated notes. On June 29, 2010, the Group resolved to exercise its option to call for redemption the US dollar denominated 4.50% fixed rate notes due March 1, 2012, with a principal of 2.5 billion US dollars. The Group will redeem these notes on September 9, 2010, at an amount equal to the sum of the present values of the remaining scheduled payments of these notes discounted to the redemption date at the US Treasury rate plus 0.50% together with accrued and unpaid interest on the principal. The US Treasury rate will be determined by an independent investment banker on the third business day preceding the redemption. A cash outflow of approximately 2,626 million US dollars, plus accrued interest, is expected on redemption. The Group has revised the carrying value of these notes to take into account the changes to the amounts and timings of the estimated cash flows. The revised carrying value of these notes at June 30, 2010, is 2,623 million US dollars (2,839 million Swiss Francs). The increase in carrying value of 133 million US dollars (144 million Swiss francs) is recorded within financing costs (see Note 5) as a loss on redemption. The effective interest rate of these notes before the redemption is 4.84%.

Subsequent to the end of the interim period, the Group redeemed the Genetech Senior Notes with a due date of July 15, 2010, at the original issue amount plus accrued original issue discount (OID). The effective interest rate of these bonds was 4.53%. The cash outflow was 500 million US dollars and there was no gain or loss recorded on the redemption.

Repayment and redemptions of bonds and notes — 2009

There were no repayments or redemptions of bonds and notes during the interim period of 2009.

Commercial paper

Roche Holdings, Inc. commercial paper program. In March 2009 the Group established a commercial paper program under which it can issue up to 7.5 billion US dollars of unsecured commercial paper notes guaranteed by Roche Holding Ltd. Committed credit lines of 2.5 billion euros and 950 million US dollars are available as back-stop lines. Maturity of the notes under the program cannot exceed 365 days from the date of issuance. At June 30, 2010, unsecured commercial paper notes with a principal of 438 million US dollars and an interest rate of 0.20% were outstanding.

Movements in obligations under commercial paper programs

(in millions of CHF)	*Six month ended June 30, 2010*
January 1, 2010	270
Cash proceeds (payments), net	193
Currency translation effects	11
June 30, 2010	**474**

13. Equity

The Group completed the purchase of the noncontrolling interest in Genentech effective March 26, 2009, as described in Note 3. Based on the revised International Accounting Standard 27, *Consolidated and Separate Financial Statements* (IAS 27), which was adopted by the Group in 2008, this transaction was accounted for in full as an equity transaction. As a consequence, the carrying amount of the consolidated equity of the Group was reduced in the interim period of 2009 by 52.2 billion Swiss francs, of which 8.4 billion Swiss francs was allocated to eliminate the book value of Genetech noncontrolling interest. This accounting effect significantly impacts the Group's net equity, but has no effect on the Group's business or its dividend policy.

Share capital and nonvoting equity securities (*Genusascheine*)

The authorized and called-up share capital of the Group and the number of issued nonvoting equity securities have not changed during the interim period. The weighted-average number of shares and nonvoting equity securities in issue during the interim period was 856 million (2009: 859 million).

Dividends

On March 2, 2010, the shareholders approved the distribution of a dividend of 6.00 Swiss francs per share and nonvoting equity security (2009: 5.00 Swiss francs) in respect of the 2009 business year. The distribution to holders of outstanding shares and nonvoting equity securities totaled 5,144 million Swiss francs (2009: 4,300 million Swiss francs) and has been recorded against retained earnings in 2010.

Own equity instruments

Nonvoting equity securities and derivative instruments are held for the Group's potential conversion obligations that may arise from the Roche Option Plan, Roche Stock-Settled Stock Appreciation Rights and Roche Restricted Stock Unit Plan. These mainly consist of call options that are exercisable at any time up to their maturity.

Own equity instruments in equivalent number of nonvoting equity securities

	June 30, 2010 (millions)	December 31, 2009 (millions)
Nonvoting equity securities	7.4	6.7
Derivative instruments	9.4	7.4
Total	**16.8**	**14.1**

The Group holds none of its own shares.

14. Statement of cash flows

Cash generated from operations

in millions of CHF	2010	2009
Net Income	5,565	4,051
Add back non-operating (income) expense		
Associated	--	--
Financial income	(302)	(494)
Financing costs	1,508	1,035
Exceptional financing costs	--	365
Income taxes	1,800	1,678
Income taxes on exceptional items	(93)	(1,038)
Operating profit	**8,478**	**5,607**
Depreciation of property, plant, and equipment	974	945
Amortization of intangible assets	311	396
Impairment of property, plant, and equipment	49	1,049
Impairment of intangible assets	102	185
Operating expenses for defined benefit postemployment plans	132	148
Operating expense for equity-settled equity compensation plans	158	411
Net (income) expense for provisions	340	935
Other adjustments	20	(6)
Cash generated from operations	**10,564**	**(9,670)**

Six months ended June 30,

US GAAP COMPARISON

While both US GAAP and IFRS require interim reporting for public companies, there are significant differences with regard to how and when the elements of the financial statements are recognized and measured.

US GAAP requires that product-related or variable costs be recognized in full in the interim period as they are incurred, the same way that is required for annual financial statements. Additionally, generally, practice and policies applied in annual periods shall be applied at interim periods. However, for other expenses, when the expenditure can be shown to clearly benefit a future period, the expense is deferred and recognized in the subsequent period. This is referred to as *smoothing*. Smoothing is done pursuant to the notion that an interim period is integral to the full fiscal period. IFRS regards each interim period as a discrete period. In other words under US GAAP, except for seasonal effects, each period should be predictive of the remaining periods of the fiscal year. Seasonal effects are disclosed. Entities are encouraged to present rolling full-year results for material seasonal effects if doing so would improve comparability. However, if an expense is unusual or cannot be reasonably attributed to future periods, it is not deferred. Allocations of these costs to current and future periods cannot be arbitrary. The effective income tax rate is based on full-year income estimates. Changes in income tax rates are recognized in the current interim period, unless it was attributed to an error.

US GAAP, unlike IFRS, does not allow decreases in inventory value recorded in annual financial statements to be reversed. However, for interim reporting, if the price of inventory rises in a subsequent interim period within the same fiscal year, a reversal gain is recognized. The LIFO method of inventory cost flow is prohibited under IFRS, but not under US GAAP. When a LIFO-layer liquidation is expected to be restored by the end of the year, a debit to inventory is made with a offset to current liabilities in the interim period.

Materiality of an adjustment is determined with regard to the expected income for the fiscal year. IFRS uses the current interim period results. Similar to IFRS, costs that are accrued during the year because the amount is based on full year activities (e.g. sales and purchase discounts, bonuses) are estimated and recognized at each interim period.

35 INFLATION AND HYPERINFLATION

INTRODUCTION

While the use of fair value as a measurement attribute for purposes of financial statement presentation has become increasingly popular in recent years, accounting principles—both most national GAAP and IFRS—still remain substantially grounded in historical costing.

In periods of price stability, the use of historical cost information does not do much of a disservice to understanding the reporting entity's financial position and results of operations. However, in times of price instability—or, in the case of long-lived assets, even in periods of modest changes in prices over long stretches of time—financial reporting can be distorted. Over many decades, a wide variety of solutions to this problem have been proposed, and, in certain periods of rampant inflation, some of these have even been put into practice.

Thus, although presentation of inflation-adjusted financial statements is no longer required, for entities choosing to present such financial data, this guidance continues to be pertinent.

IAS 29 addresses financial reporting in *hyperinflationary* economies. While, in general, this applies the same principles as are employed when using general price level accounting, the objective is to convert the financial statements of entities operating under conditions that render unadjusted financial statements of little or no value into meaningful measures of financial position and performance. Fortunately, over recent years there have been very few nations suffering from hyperinflation, but as with more moderate inflationary cycles, these have hardly disappeared from the economic horizon, and of course the possibility for renewed inflation in the future remains. Since there is some current need for this guidance, and the possibility of more need over time, this will also be explained in some detail in the present chapter.

Sources of IFRS		
IAS 29	*IFRS* 1	*IFRIC* 7

DEFINITIONS OF TERMS

Common dollar reporting. Synonymous with general price level or constant dollar financial reporting.

Constant dollar accounting. An accounting model that treats dollars of varying degrees of purchasing power essentially in the manner that foreign currencies are treated; dollars are translated into current purchasing power units and presented in restated financial statements. Constant dollar accounting converts all nonmonetary assets and equities from historical to current dollars by applying an index of general purchasing power. Specific value changes are ignored, and thus there are no holding gains or losses recognized. Monetary items are brought forward without adjustment, and these accounts (cash, claims to fixed amounts of cash, and obligations to pay fixed amounts of cash) therefore do give rise to purchasing power gains or losses. Constant dollar accounting does not attempt to address value changes.

Current cost accounting. An accounting model that attempts to measure economic values and changes therein, whether or not realized in the traditional accounting sense. In current cost accounting financial statements, nonmonetary items are reflected at current value amounts, measured variously by replacement cost, exit value, fair market value, net present value, or by other methodologies. Current cost based statements of earnings will report as operating income the amount of resources that are available for distribution (to shareholders and others) without impairing the entity's ability to replace assets as they are sold or consumed in the operation of the business. Holding gains may or may not also be reportable as a component of income, although these are never deemed to be distributable unless the entity is liquidating itself. In a pure current cost accounting system, no purchasing power gains or losses are given recognition, but hybrid models have been proposed under US GAAP and IAS, which do recognize these as well as specific price changes.

Distributable (replicable) earnings. The amount of resources that could be distributed (e.g., by dividends to shareholders) from the current period's earnings without impairing the entity's operating capacity versus its level at the beginning of the period. This parallels the classic definition of economic income. It is generally conceded that current cost would provide the best measure of distributable earnings. Traditional historical cost based financial reporting, on the other hand, does not attempt to measure economic income, but rather, seeks to match actual costs incurred against revenues generated; the result in many cases is that this measure of income will exceed real economic earnings.

Exit value. Also known as net realizable value, this is the measure of the resources that could be obtained by disposing of a specified asset, often for scrap or salvage value. Valuing assets at exit value is not generally valid as a measure of current cost, since value in use usually exceeds exit value, and most assets held by the entity will not be disposed of; however, for assets that are not to be replaced in the normal course of business, exit value may be a meaningful measure.

Fair value. Fair market value, or market value. For certain specialized properties, such as natural resources, this may be the most meaningful measure of current cost.

Gains/losses on net monetary items. Synonymous with general purchasing power gains and losses.

Holding gains/losses. In general, the increase or decrease in the current cost of non-monetary assets (plant assets and inventories, for the most part) during a period. Notwithstanding the gain/loss terminology, such items are not generally recognized as part of income but rather as part of stockholders' equity, although practice varies. Holding gains are not distributable to shareholders without impairing operating capacity. In some models, only the excess of specific price changes over general price level changes are deemed to be holding gains/losses.

Hyperinflation. The condition in an economy in which there is such extreme inflation that historical cost financial statements become meaningless; characterized by a general aversion of the population to holding monetary assets, the conducting of business in ways that provide some protection against inflation, such as denominating transactions in a stable foreign currency or indexing to compensate for price changes, and a cumulative inflation rate over three years approaching 100%.

Inventory profits. The overstatement of income resulting from charging cost of sales at historical levels instead of at replacement costs; during periods of rapid inflation, historical cost based income will exceed real, economic earnings (distributable or replicable earnings); this is partly the result of inventory profits. Not all entities are affected similarly.

Monetary items. Claims to, or obligations to pay, fixed sums of cash or its equivalent. Examples are accounts receivable and accounts payable. If constant dollar accounting is employed, net monetary assets or liabilities will create purchasing power gains or losses in periods of changing general prices, since such fixed claims to cash or obligations to pay cash gain or lose value as the general purchasing power of the currency grows or shrinks.

Net present value. The future cash flows that will be generated by operation of an asset, discounted by a relevant factor such as the opportunity cost of capital, to an equivalent present value amount. This is a surrogate measure for economic value (deprival value) that is useful in certain circumstances (e.g., determining the future net cash flow of income producing real estate). For other assets, such as machinery, this is difficult to compute because future cash flows are difficult to forecast and because the assets are part of integrated processes generating cash flows that cannot be attributed to each component.

Net realizable value. Generally used in accounting to denote the amount that could be realized from an immediate disposition of an asset; also known as exit value. Net realizable value is sometimes used for current costing purposes if the asset in question is not intended to be held beyond a brief period.

Nonmonetary items. Items that are neither claims to, nor obligations to pay, fixed sums of cash or its equivalent. Examples are inventories and plant assets. When constant dollar accounting is employed, all nonmonetary items are adjusted to current dollar equivalents by application of a general measure of purchasing power changes. If current cost accounting is employed, nonmonetary items are recorded at current economic values (measured by replacement cost, deprival value, etc.); nonmonetary equity accounts may be explicitly adjusted or the necessary balancing amounts can be imputed. Holding gains and losses result from applying current cost measures to nonmonetary items.

Purchasing power gains/losses. The economic benefit or detriment that results when an entity has claims to fixed amounts of cash (monetary assets) or has obligations to pay fixed sums (monetary liabilities) during periods when the general purchasing power of the monetary unit is changing. An excess of monetary assets over monetary liabilities coupled with rising prices results in a purchasing power loss; an excess of monetary liabilities results in a gain. These are reversed if prices are declining.

Realized holding gains/losses. Holding gains/losses can be realized or unrealized. If an appreciated item of inventory is sold, the holding gain is realized; if unsold at period end, it is unrealized. Historical cost based accounting does not recognize unrealized holding gains/losses (with some exceptions), and realized holding gains/losses are merged with other operating income and not given separate recognition.

Recoverable amount. The amount that could be obtained either from the continued use of an asset (the net present value of future cash flows) or from its disposal (exit or net realizable value).

Replacement cost. The lowest cost that would be incurred to replace the service potential of an asset in the normal course of the business.

Reproduction cost. The cost of acquiring an asset identical to the one presently in use. The distinction between reproduction cost and replacement cost is that operating efficiencies and technological changes may have occurred and the nominally identical asset would have a different productive capacity. Typically, replacement costs are lower than reproduction costs, and use of the latter would tend to overstate the effects of inflation.

Unrealized holding gains/losses. Holding gains or losses that have yet to be realized through an arm's-length transaction.

Value in use. Also known as value to the business, this is defined as the lesser of current cost or net recoverable amount.

RECOGNITION AND MEASUREMENT

Historical Review of Inflation Accounting

Accounting practice today, on virtually a worldwide basis, relies heavily on the historical cost measurement strategy, whereby resources and obligations are given recognition as assets and liabilities, respectively, at the original (dollar, yen, euro, rand etc.) amount of the transaction from which they arose. Once recorded, these amounts are not altered to reflect changes in value, except to the limited extent that various national GAAP standards or IFRS require recognition of impairments (e.g., lower of cost or fair value for inventories, etc.). Most long-lived assets such as buildings are depreciated against earnings on a rational basis over their estimated useful lives, while short-lived assets are expensed as physically consumed. Liabilities are maintained at cost until paid off or otherwise discharged.

It is useful to recall that before the historical cost model of financial reporting achieved nearly universal adoption, various alternative recognition and measurement approaches were experimented with. Fair value accounting was in fact widely employed in the nineteenth and early twentieth centuries, and for some regulatory purposes (especially in setting utility service prices, where regulated by governmental agencies) remained in vogue until somewhat more recently.

Why inflation undermines historical cost financial reporting. Actual and potential investors and creditors, as well as entity managers and others, desire accounting information to support their decision-making needs. Financial statements that ignore the effects of general price level changes as well as changes in specific prices are inadequate for several reasons.

1. Reported profits often exceed the earnings that could be distributed to shareholders without impairing the entity's ability to maintain the present level of operations, because inventory profits are included in earnings and because depreciation charges are not adequate to provide for asset replacements.
2. Statements of financial position fail to reflect the economic value of the business, because plant assets and inventories, especially, are recorded at historical values that may be far lower than current fair values or replacement costs.
3. Future earnings prospects are not easily projected from historical cost based earnings reports.
4. The impact of changes in the general price level on monetary assets and liabilities is not revealed, yet can be severe.
5. Because of the foregoing deficiencies, future capital needs are difficult to forecast, and in fact may contribute to the growing leveraging (borrowing) by many entities, which adds to their riskiness.
6. Distortions of real economic performance lead to social and political consequences ranging from suboptimal capital allocations to ill-conceived tax policies and public perceptions of corporate behavior.

Example

A business starts with one unit of inventory, which cost €2 and which at the end of the period is sold for €10 at a time when it would cost €7 to replace that very same unit on the display shelf. Traditional accounting would measure the earnings of the entity at €10 – €2 = €8, although clearly the business is only €3 "better off" at the end of the period than at the beginning, since real economic resources have only grown by €3 (after replacing the unit sold there is only that amount of extra resource available). The illusion that there was profit of €8 could readily destroy the entity if, for example, dividends of more than €3 were withdrawn or if fiscal policy led to taxes of more than €3 on the €8 profit.

On the other hand, if the financial report showed only €3 profit for the period, there could be several salutary effects. Owners' expectations for dividends would be tempered, the entity's real capital would more likely be preserved, and projections of future performance would be more accurate, although projections must always be fine-tuned since the past will never be replicated precisely.

The failure of the historical cost statement of financial position to reflect values is yet another major deficiency of traditional financial reporting. True, accounting was never intended to report values per se, but the excess of assets over liabilities has always been denoted as net worth, and to many that clearly connotes value. Similarly, the alternative titles for the statement of financial position, balance sheet, and statement of financial condition, strongly suggest value to the lay reader. The confusion largely stems from a failure to distinguish *realized* from *unrealized* value changes; if this distinction were carefully maintained, the statement of financial position could be made more useful while remaining true to its traditions.

General vs. specific price changes. An important distinction to be understood is that between general and specific price changes, and how the effects of each can be meaningfully reported on in financial statements. Changes in specific prices, as with the inventory example above, should not be confused with changes in the general level of prices, which give rise to what are often referred to as purchasing power gains or losses, and result from holding net monetary assets or liabilities during periods of changing general prices. As most consumers are well aware, during periods of general price inflation, holding net monetary assets typically results in experiencing a loss in purchasing power, while a net liability position leads to a gain, as obligations are repaid with "cheaper" dollars. Among other effects, prolonged periods of general price inflation motivates entities to become more leveraged (more in-debted to others) because of these purchasing power gains, although in reality creditors are aware of this and adjust interest rates to compensate.

Specific prices may change in ways that are notably different from the trend in overall prices, and they may even move in opposite directions. This is particularly true of basic commodities such as agricultural products and minerals, but may also be true of manufac-tured goods, especially if technological changes have great influence. For example, even during the years of rampant inflation during the 1970s some commodities, such as copper, were dropping in price, and certain goods, such as computer memory chips, were also de-clining even in nominal prices. For entities dealing in either of these items, holding invento-ries of these *nonmonetary* goods (usually a hedge against price inflation) would have pro-duced large economic losses during this time. Thus, not only the changes in general prices, but also the changes in specific prices, and very important, the interactions between these can have major effects on an entity's real wealth. Measurement of these phenomena should be within the province of accounting.

Experiments and proposals for inflation accounting. Over the past fifty years there have been a number of proposals for pure price level accounting, financial reporting that would be sensitive to changes in specific prices, and combinations of these. There have been proposals (academic proposals) for comprehensive financial statements that would be ad-justed for inflation, as well as for supplemental disclosures that would isolate the major in-flation effects without abandoning primary historical cost based statements (generally, the professional proposals and regulatory requirements were of this type). To place the former requirements of the now-withdrawn standard IAS 15 in context, a number of its more promi-nent predecessors will be reviewed in brief.

Price level accounting concepts and proposals. At its simplest, price level accounting views any given currency at different points in time as being analogous to different curren-cies at the same point in time. That is, 1955 US dollars have the same relationship to 2010 dollars as 2010 Swiss francs have to 2010 dollars or euros. They are "apples and oranges" and cannot be added or subtracted without first being converted to a common measuring unit. Thus, "pure" price level accounting is held to be within the mainstream historical cost tradi-tion and is merely a translation of one currency into another for comparative purposes. A broadly based measure of all prices in the economy should be used in accomplishing this (often, a consumer price index of some sort is employed).

Consider a simple example. Assume that the index of general prices was as follows:

January 1, 1988	65
January 1, 2000	100
January 1, 2011	182
December 31, 2011	188

Also assume the following items selected from the December 31, 2011 statement of fi-nancial position:

	Historical cost	Price level adjusted cost
Cash	€ 50,000	€ 50,000
Inventories (purchased 1/1/11)	350,000	
× 188/182		361,538
Land (acquired 1/1/88)	500,000	
× 188/65		1,446,154
Machinery (purchased 1/1/00)	300,000	

× 188/100		564,000
Accumulated depreciation	(200,000)	
× 188/100		(376,000)
Book value of assets	1,000,000	2,045,692
Less monetary liabilities	(500,000)	(500,000)
Net assets	€ 500,000	€1,545,692

In the foregoing, all nonmonetary items were adjusted to "current dollars" using the same index of general prices. This is not based on the notion that items such as inventory and machinery actually experienced price changes of that magnitude, but on the idea that converting these to current dollars is a process akin to converting foreign currency denominated financial statements. The implication is that the historical cost statement of financial position, showing net assets of €500,000, is equivalent to a statement of financial position that reports some items in British pounds sterling, some in US dollars, some in Mexican pesos, and so on. The price level adjusted statement of financial position, by contrast, is deemed to be equivalent to a statement of financial position in which all items have been translated into euros.

This analogy is a weak one, however. Not only are such statements essentially meaningless, they can also be misleading from a policy viewpoint. For example, during a period of rising prices, an entity holding more monetary assets than monetary liabilities will report an economic loss due to the decline in the purchasing power of its net monetary assets. Nonmonetary assets, of course, are adjusted for price changes and thus appear to be immune from purchasing power gains or losses. The implication is that holding nonmonetary assets is somehow preferable to holding monetary assets.

In the foregoing example, the net monetary liabilities at year-end are €500,000 – €50,000 = €450,000. Assuming the same net monetary liability position at the beginning of 2011, the gain experienced by the entity (due to owning monetary debt during a period of depreciating currency) would be given as

$$(€450,000 × 188/182) - €450,000 = €14,835$$

This suggests that the entity has experienced a gain, at the obvious expense of its creditors, which have incurred a corresponding loss, in the amount of €14,835. This fails entirely to recognize that creditors may have demanded an inflation adjusted rate of return based on actual past and anticipated future inflationary behavior of the economy; if this were addressed in tandem with the computed purchasing power gain, a truer picture would be given of the real wisdom of the entity's financial strategy.

Furthermore, the actual price level protection afforded by holding investments in nonmonetary assets is a function of the changes in their specific values. If the replacement value of the inventory had declined, for example, during 2011, having held this inventory during the year would have been an economically unwise maneuver. Land that cost €500,000 might, due to its strategic location, now be worth €2.5 million, not the indicated €1.4 million, and the machinery might be obsolete due to technological changes, and not worth the approximately €190,000 suggested by the price level adjusted book value. In fairness, of course, the advocates of price level accounting do not claim that these adjusted amounts represent *values*. However, the utility of these adjusted captions from the statement of financial position for decision makers is difficult to fathom and the potential for misunderstanding is great.

Current value models and proposals. By whatever name it is referred to, current value (replacement cost, current cost) accounting is really based on a wholly different concept than is price level (constant dollar) accounting. Current value financial reporting is far more closely tied to the original intent of the accounting model, which is to measure entity economic wealth and the changes therein from period to period. This suggests essentially a "statement of financial position orientation" to income measurement, with the difference between net worth (as measured by current values) at year beginning and year-end being, after adjustment for capital transactions, the measure of income or loss for the intervening period. How this is further analyzed and presented in the statement of comprehensive income (as realized and unrealized gains and losses) or even whether some of these changes even belong in the statement of comprehensive income (or instead, are reported in a separate statement of movements in equity, or are taken directly into equity) is a rather minor bookkeeping concern.

Although the proliferation of terminology of the many competing proposals can be confusing, four candidates as measures of current value can readily be identified: economic value, net present value, net realizable value (also known as exit value), and replacement cost (which is a measure of entry value). A brief explanation will facilitate the discussion of the IAS requirements later in this chapter.

Economic value is usually understood to mean the equilibrium fair market value of an asset. However, apart from items traded in auction markets, typically only securities and raw commodities, direct observation of economic value is not possible.

Net present value is often suggested as the ideal surrogate for economic value, since in a perfect market values are driven by the present value of future cash flows to be generated by the assets. Certain types of assets, such as rental properties, have predictable cash flows and in fact are often priced in this manner. On the other hand, for assets such as machinery, particularly those that are part of a complex integrated production process, determining cash flows is difficult.

Net realizable values (NRV) are more familiar to most accountants, since there are numerous instances when references to NRV must be made to ascertain whether asset write-downs are to be required. NRV is a measure of "exit values" since these are the amounts that the organization would realize on asset disposition, net of all costs; from this perspective, this is a conservative measure (exit values are lower than entry values in almost all cases, since transactions are not costless), but also is subject to criticism since under the going concern assumption it is not anticipated that the entity will dispose of all its productive assets at current market prices, indeed, not at any prices, since these assets will be retained for use in the business.

The biggest failing of this measure, however, is that it does not assist in measuring economic income, since that metric is intended to reveal how much income an entity can distribute to its owners, and so on, while retaining the ability to replace its productive capacity as needed. In general, an income measure based on exit values would overstate earnings (since depreciation and cost of sales would be based on lower exit values for plant assets and inventory) when compared with an income measure based on entry values. Thus, while NRV is a familiar concept to many accountants, this is not the ideal candidate for a current value model.

Replacement cost is intended as a measure of entry value and hence of the earnings reinvestment needed to maintain real economic productive capacity. Actually, competing proposals have engaged in much hairsplitting over alternative concepts of entry value, and this deserves some attention here. The simplest concept of replacement value is the cost of replacing a specific machine, building, and so on, and in some industries it is indeed possible to determine these prices, at least in the short run, before technology changes occur. However, in many more instances (and in the long run, in all cases) exact physical replacements are not available, and even nominally identical replacements offer varying levels of productivity enhancements that make simplistic comparisons distortive.

As a very basic example, consider a machine with a cost of €40,000 that can produce 100 widgets per hour. The current price of the replacement machine is €50,000, that superficially suggests a specific price increase of 25% has occurred. However, on closer examination, it is determined that while nominally the same machine, some manufacturing enhancements have been made (e.g., the machine will require less maintenance, will require fewer labor inputs, runs at a higher speed, etc.) which have altered its effective capacity (considering reduced downtime, etc.) to 110 widgets per hour. Clearly, a naive adjustment for what is sometimes called "reproduction cost" would overstate the machine's value on the statement of financial position and overstate periodic depreciation charges, thereby understating earnings. A truer measure of the replacement cost of the service potential of the asset, not the physical asset itself, would be given as

$$€40,000 \times (50,000/40,000) \times 100/110 = €45,454$$

That is, the service potential represented by the asset in use has a current replacement cost of €45,454, considering that a new machine costs 25% more but is 10% more productive.

Consider another example: An integrated production process uses machines A and B, which have reproduction costs today of €40,000 and €45,000, respectively. However, management plans to acquire a new type of machine, C, which at a cost of €78,000 will replace both machines A and B and will produce the same output as its predecessors. The combined reproduction cost of €85,000 clearly overstates the replacement cost of the service potential of the existing machines in this case, even if there had been no technological changes affecting machines A and B.

Limitations on replacement cost. While entry value is clearly the most logical of the alternative measures discussed thus far, under certain circumstances one of the other candidates would be preferable as a measure to use in current cost financial reporting. For example, consider a situation in which the value in use (economic value or net present value of future cash flows) is lower than replacement cost, due to changing market conditions affecting pricing of the entity's output. In such a circumstance, although the entity may continue to use the machines on hand and to sell the output profitably, it would not contemplate replacement of the asset, instead viewing it as a "cash cow." If current cost financial statements were to be developed that incorporated depreciation based on the replacement cost of the machine, earnings would be understated, since actual replacement is not to be provided for. A number of other hypothetical circumstances could also be presented; the end result is that a series of decision rules can be developed to guide the selection of the best measure of current cost. These are summarized in the following table, where NRC stands for net replacement cost, which is synonymous with current cost; NRV is net realizable value or exit value; and EV is the same as net present value.

Conditions	Value to the business
EV > NRC > NRV	NRC
NRC > EV > NRV	EV
NRC > NRV > EV	NRV
EV > NRV > NRC	NRC
NRV > EV > NRC	NRC
NRV > NRC > EV	NRC

Measuring Income under the Replacement Cost Approach

There are two reasons to employ replacement cost accounting: (1) to compute a measure of earnings that can probably be replicated on an ongoing basis by the entity and approximates real economic wealth creation, and (2) to present a statement of financial position that presents the economic condition of the entity at a point in time. Of these, the first is by far the more important objective, since decision makers' use of financial statements is largely oriented toward the future operations of the business, in which they are lenders, owners, managers, or employees.

Given the foregoing, the principal use of replacement cost information will be to assist in computing current period earnings on a true economic basis. The statement of comprehensive income items which on the historical cost basis are most distortive, in most cases, are depreciation and cost of sales. Historical cost depreciation can be based on asset prices that are ten to forty years old, during which time even modest price changes can compound to very sizable misrepresentations. Cost of sales will not typically suffer from compounding over such a long period, since turnover for most businesses will be in a matter of months, but since cost of sales will account for a much larger part of the entity's total costs than does depreciation, it can still have a major impact.

Thus, current cost/replacement cost/current value earnings are typically computed by adjusting historical cost income by an allowance for replacement cost depreciation and cost of sales. Typically, these two adjustments will effectively derive a modified earnings amount that closely approximates economic earnings. This modified amount can be paid out as dividends or otherwise disbursed, while leaving the entity with the ability to replace its productive capacity and continue to operate at the same level as it had been. (This does not, however, address the matter of purchasing power that may have been gained or lost by holding net monetary assets or liabilities during the period, which requires yet another computation.)

Determining current costs. In practice, replacement costs are developed by applying one or more of four principal techniques: indexation, direct pricing, unit pricing, and functional pricing. Each has advantages and disadvantages, and no single technique will be applicable to all fact situations and all types of assets. The following are useful in determining current costs of plant assets.

Indexation is accomplished by applying appropriate indices to the historical cost of the assets. Assuming that the assets in use were acquired in the usual manner (bargain purchases and other such means of acquisition will thwart this effort, since any index when applied to a nonstandard base will result in a meaningless adjusted number) and that an appropriate index can be obtained or developed (which incorporates productivity changes as well as price variations), this will be the most efficient approach to employ. For many categories of manufactured goods, such as machinery and equipment, this technique has been widely used with excellent results. One concern is that many published indices actually address only reproduction costs, and if not adjusted further, the likely outcome will be that costs are overstated and adjusted earnings will be artificially depressed.

Direct pricing, as the name suggests, relies on information provided by vendors and others having data about the selling prices of replacement assets. To the extent that these are list prices that do not reflect actual market transactions, these must be adjusted, and the same concern with productivity enhancements mentioned with reference to indexation must also be addressed. Since many entities are in constant, close contact with their vendors, obtaining such information is often straightforward, particularly with regard to machinery and other equipment.

Unit pricing is the least commonly employed method but can be useful when estimating the replacement cost of buildings. This is the bricks-and-mortar approach, which relies on statistical data about the per-unit cost of constructing various types of buildings and other assets. For example, construction cost data may suggest that single-storey light industrial buildings in cold climates (e.g., Europe) with certain other defined attributes may have a current cost of €47 per square foot, or that a first-class high-rise urban hotel in England has a construction cost of €125,000 per room. By expanding these per-unit costs to the scale of the entity's facilities, a fairly accurate replacement cost can be derived. There are complications; for example, costs are not linearly related to size of facility due to the presence of fixed costs, but these are widely understood and readily dealt with. Unit pricing is typically not meaningful for machinery or equipment, however.

Functional pricing is the most difficult of the four principal techniques and is best reserved for highly integrated production processes, such as refineries and chemical plants, where attempts to price individual components would be exceptionally difficult. For example, a plant capable of producing 400,000 tons of polyethylene annually could be priced as a unit by having an engineering estimate made of the cost to construct similar capacity in the current environment. Clearly, this is not a merely mechanical effort, as indexation in particular is likely to be, but demands the services of a skilled estimator. Technological issues are neatly avoided since the focus is on creating a new plant with defined output capacity, using whatever mix of components would be most cost-effective. This technique has been widely employed in actual practice.

Inventory costing problems. For a merchandising concern, direct pricing is likely to be an effective technique to assist in developing cost of sales on a current cost basis. Manufacturing firms, on the other hand, will need to build up replacement cost basis cost of goods manufactured and sold by separately analyzing the cost behavior of each major cost element (e.g., labor contracts, overhead expenses, and raw materials prices). It is unlikely that these will have experienced the same price movements, and therefore an averaging approach would not be sufficiently accurate. Also, as product mix changes over time, the entity may be subject to varying influences from one period to the next. Finally, the inventory costing method used (e.g., weighted–average vs. FIFO) will affect the extent of adjustment to be made, with (assuming that costs trend upward over time) relatively greater adjustments made to cost of sales determined on the FIFO basis, since relatively older costs are included in the GAAP statement of comprehensive income. Note that the now-banned LIFO method would have had an even more dramatically distorting effect on the statement of financial position.

Whatever assortment of methods is used, the end product is a restated inventory of plant assets, depreciation on which must then be computed. For the current cost earnings data to be comparable with the historical cost financial statements, it is usually recommended that no other decisions be superimposed. For example, no changes in asset useful lives should be made, for to do so would exacerbate or ameliorate the impact of the replacement cost depreciation and make interpretation very difficult for anyone not intimately familiar with the company. Some ancillary costs may need to be adjusted in computing cost of sales and depreciation on the revised basis. For example, if the only replacement machines available will reduce the need for skilled labor, the (higher) replacement cost depreciation should be reduced by related cost savings, if accurately predictable. There are literally scores of similar issues to be addressed, and indeed entire volumes have been written providing detailed guidance on how to apply current cost measures.

Examples of current costing adjustments to depreciation and cost of sales

Example 1

Hapsburg Corp. is a wholesale distributor for a single product. For 2011, the company reports sales of €35,000,000, representing sales of 600,000 units of its single product. The traditional statement of comprehensive income reports cost of sales as follows:

	(000 omitted)
Beginning inventory	€ 8.8
Purchases, net	25.7
Ending inventory	(6.5)
Cost of goods sold	€28.0

Reference to purchase orders reveals the fact that product cost early in 2011 was €42 per unit and was €55 per unit late in December of that year. The company employs FIFO accounting.

Since there is no evidence presented to the effect that net realizable value of the product is below current replacement cost, current cost can be used without modification.

Beginning current cost	€42.0
Ending current cost	€55.0
Average	€48.5

Total cost of sales for the period, on a replacement cost basis, is therefore €55 × 600,000 units = €33,000,000.

Example 2

In the following example, deprival value is, for one product line, better measured by net realizable value than by replacement cost. The company, St. Ignatz Mfg. Co., manufactures and sells two products, A and B. Product A has been a declining item for several years, and management now believes that it must close this line due to the shrinking market share, which will not support higher costs. St. Ignatz will continue to produce Product B and may possibly expand into new products in the future.

Company records show the following results in 2011:

	(000,000 omitted)		
	Product A	*Product B*	*Total*
Sales	€19.50	€40.50	€60.00
Cost of sales			
Beginning inventory	12.50	6.80	
Purchases	8.70	20.00	
Ending inventory	(3.00)	(5.40)	
Cost of sales	18.20	21.40	39.60
Gross profit	€ 1.30	€19.10	20.40
All other expenses			(18.80)
Net income			€ 1.60

The company's manufacturing records show the following data:

Current costs, beginning of year	€52.00	€75.00
Current costs, ending of year	63.00	79.00
Current costs, average	57.50	77.00

Sales in 2011 comprised 390,000 units of Product A and 540,000 units of Product B. Management believes that the market for Product A cannot support further price increases, and thus the remaining inventory will probably be sold at a loss. Selling expenses are estimated at €6 per unit.

Product A has a recoverable value lower than current manufacturing costs. The net recoverable amount is given by the selling price per unit less selling expenses: €50 – €6 = €44 per unit. Current cost of sales is €44 × €390,000 = €17,160,000. Note that recoverable amount, not replacement cost, is used.

Product B has an average current cost of €77 per unit, so 2011 cost of sales on a current cost basis is €77 × €540,000 = €41,580,000.

Total cost of sales on the current cost basis is therefore €17,160,000 + €41,580,000 = €58,740,000.

Example 3

Jacquet Corp. reports depreciation of €16,510 for 2011 in its historical cost based financial statements prepared on the basis of IFRS. A summary of plant assets reveals the following:

Asset class	Total depreciable cost*	Useful life (yr.)	Depreciation rate (%)**
A	€24,000	8	12 1/2
B	50,000	10	10
C	45,000	12	8 1/3
D	60,000	15	6 2/3
E	19,000	25	4

*Depreciable cost is historical cost less salvage value.
**Depreciation rate is 1/useful life.

Management employs appraisals and other methods, including information from vendors and indices, to develop current cost data as shown below.

	Current costs		
Asset class	1/1/11	12/31/11	Average
A	€28,000	€31,000	€29,500
B	56,000	60,000	58,000
C	55,000	60,000	57,500
D	62,000	68,000	65,000
E	30,000	33,000	31,500

From this information the current cost depreciation for the year 2011 can be computed as follows:

Asset class	Depreciation rate (%)	Average current cost	Depreciation
A	12 1/2	€29,500	€ 3,687.50
B	10	58,000	5,800.00
C	8 1/3	57,500	4,792.00
D	6 2/3	65,000	4,333.00
E	4	31,500	1,260.00
			€19,872.50

Note that the replacement cost basis depreciation for the year is €3,362.50 greater than was the historical cost depreciation.

Purchasing power gains or losses in the context of current cost accounting. Thus far, general price level (or purchasing power or constant dollar) accounting has been viewed as a reporting concept totally separate from current value (or current cost or replacement cost) accounting. As noted, advocates of price level adjustments have argued that these are not attempts to measure value, as current cost accounting is, but merely to "translate" old dollars into current dollars. For their part, advocates of current value accounting have generally been more focused on deriving a measure of the "replicable" economic earnings of the entity, usually with no mention of the fact that changing specific prices of productive assets exist against a backdrop of changing general price levels.

FINANCIAL REPORTING IN HYPERINFLATIONARY ECONOMIES

Hyperinflation is a condition that is difficult to define precisely, as there is not a clear demarcation between merely rampant inflation and true hyperinflation. However, in any given economic system, when the general population has so lost faith in the stability of the local economy that business transactions are commonly either denominated in a stable reference currency of another country, or are structured to incorporate an indexing feature intended to compensate for the distortive effects of inflation, this condition may be present. As a benchmark, when cumulative inflation over three years approaches or exceeds 100%, it must be conceded that the economy is suffering from hyperinflation.

Hyperinflation is obviously a major problem for any economy, as it creates severe distortions and, left unaddressed, results in uncontrolled acceleration of the rate of price changes, ending in inevitable collapse as was witnessed in post–World War I Germany. From a financial reporting perspective, there are also major problems, since even over a brief interval such as a year or even a quarter, the statement of comprehensive income will contain transactions with such a variety of purchasing power units that aggregation becomes meaningless, as would adding dollars, francs, and marks. This is precisely the problem discussed earlier in this chapter, but raised to an exponential level.

In a truly hyperinflationary economy, users of financial statements are unable to make meaningful use of such statements unless they have been recast into currency units having purchasing power defined by prices at or near the date of the statements. Unless this common denominator is employed, the financial statements are too difficult to interpret for purposes of making management, investing, and credit decisions. Although some sophisticated users, particularly in those countries where hyperinflation has been endemic, such as some of the South American nations, including Brazil and Argentina, and for certain periods nations such as Israel, are able to apply rules of thumb to cope with this problem, in general modifications must be made to general-purpose financial statements if they are to have any value.

Under international accounting standards, if hyperinflation is deemed to characterize the economy, a form of price level accounting must be applied to the financial statements to conform to generally accepted accounting principles. IAS 29 requires that all the financial statements be adjusted to reflect year-end general price levels, which entails applying a broad-based index to all nonmonetary items on the statement of financial position and to all transactions reported in the statement of comprehensive income and the statement of cash flows.

Severe Hyperinflation According to IFRS 1

In 2010 the Board was asked to clarify how an entity should resume presenting financial statements in accordance with IFRS after a period of severe hyperinflation, during which the entity had been unable to comply with IAS 29, *Financial Reporting in Hyperinflationary Economies*. It should be noted that an entity would be unable to comply with IAS 29 if a reliable general price index is not available to all entities with that same functional currency, and exchangeability between the currency and a relatively stable foreign currency does not exist. However, once the functional currency changes to a nonhyperinflationary currency, or the currency ceases to be severely hyperinflationary, an entity would be able to start applying IFRS to subsequent transactions.

Sufficient guidance in these circumstances was not provided by the IFRS. Therefore IFRS 1 was amended to provide guidance on how an entity can present IFRS financial statements after its currency ceases to be severely hyperinflationary, by presenting an opening IFRS statement of financial position on or after the functional currency normalization date.

It was believed that allowing an entity to apply the exemption when presenting an opening IFRS statement of financial position after, and not just on, the functional currency normalization date, would address practical concerns that may arise if the functional currency normalization date and the entity's date of transition to IFRS are different. This amendment would also be available to entities that were emerging from a period of severe hyperinflation but had not applied IFRS in the past.

IFRS 1 permits an entity emerging from a period of severe hyperinflation to elect to measure its assets and liabilities at fair value. That fair value could then be used as the deemed cost in its opening IFRS statement of financial position. This approach expands the scope of the deemed cost exemptions in IFRS 1 to enable them to be applied in these specific circumstances. However, because severe hyperinflation is a specific set of circumstances, the Board wanted to ensure that the fair value measurement option was applied only to those assets and liabilities that were held before the functional currency normalization date, and not to other assets and liabilities held by the entity at the time it made the transition to IFRS. Furthermore, where a parent entity's functional currency has been subject to severe hyperinflation, but its subsidiary company's functional currency has not been subject to severe hyperinflation, IFRS 1 does not require such a subsidiary company to apply this exemption.

Any adjustments arising on electing to measure assets and liabilities at fair value in the opening IFRS statement of financial position arise from events and transactions before the date of transition to IFRS. Thus, an entity should recognize those adjustments directly in retained earnings (or, if appropriate, in another category of equity) at the date of transition to IFRS.

Entities are required to prepare and present comparative information in accordance with IFRS. Furthermore it should be noted that the preparation of information in accordance with IFRS for periods before the functional currency normalization date may not be possible; hence the exemption refers to a date of transition on or after the functional currency normalization date. This may lead to a comparative period of less than 12 months. Entities should consider whether disclosure of non-IFRS comparative information and historical summaries would provide useful information to users of financial statements. In all such cases entities should explain the transition to IFRS.

Restating Historical Cost Financial Statements under Hyperinflation Conditions

The precise adjustments to be made depend on whether the financial reporting system is based on historical costs or on current costs. Although in both cases the goal is to restate the financial statements into the measuring unit that exists at the date of the statement of financial position, the mechanics will vary to some extent.

If the financial reporting system is based on historical costing, the process used to adjust the statement of financial position can be summarized as follows:

1. Monetary assets and liabilities are already presented in units of year-end purchasing power and receive no further adjustment. (See the appendix for a categorization of different assets and liabilities as to their status as monetary or nonmonetary.)
2. Monetary assets and liabilities that are linked to price changes, such as indexed debt securities, are adjusted according to the terms of the contractual arrangement. This does not change the characterization of these items as monetary, but it does serve to reduce or even eliminate the purchasing power gain or loss that would have other-

wise been experienced as a result of holding these items during periods of changing general prices.

3. Nonmonetary items are adjusted by applying a ratio of indices, the numerator of which is the general price level index at the date of the statement of financial position and the denominator of which is the index as of the acquisition or inception date of the item in question. For some items, such as plant assets, this is a straightforward process, while for others, such as work in process inventories, this can be more complex.

4. Certain assets cannot be adjusted as described above, because even in nominally historical cost financial statements these items have been revised to some other basis, such as fair value or net realizable amounts. For example, under the allowed alternative method of IAS 16, property, plant, and equipment can be adjusted to fair value. In such a case, no further adjustment would be warranted, assuming that the adjustment to fair value was made as of the latest date of the statement of financial position. If the latest revaluation was as of an earlier date, the carrying amounts should be further adjusted to compensate for changes in the general price level from that date to the date of the statement of financial position, using the indexing technique noted above.

5. Consistent with the established principles of historical cost accounting, if the restated amounts of nonmonetary assets exceed the recoverable amounts, these must be reduced appropriately. This can easily occur, since (as discussed earlier in this chapter) specific prices of goods will vary by differing amounts, even in a hyperinflationary environment, and in fact some may decline in terms of current cost even in such cases, particularly when technological change occurs rapidly. Since the application of price level accounting, whether for ordinary inflation or for hyperinflation, does not imply an abandonment of historical costing, being a mere translation into more timely and relevant purchasing power units, the rules of that mode of financial reporting still apply. Generally accepted accounting principles require that assets not be stated at amounts in excess of realizable amounts, and this constraint applies even when price level adjustments are reflected.

6. Equity accounts must also be restated to compensate for changing prices. Paid-in capital accounts are indexed by reference to the dates when the capital was contributed, which are usually a discrete number of identifiable transactions over the life of the entity. Revaluation accounts, if any, are eliminated entirely, as these will be subsumed in restated retained earnings. The retained earnings account itself is the most complex to analyze and in practice is often treated as a balancing figure after all other statement of financial position accounts have been restated. However, it is possible to compute the adjustment to this account directly, and that is the recommended course of action, lest other errors go undetected. To adjust retained earnings, each year's earnings should be adjusted by a ratio of indices, the numerator being the general price level as of the date of the statement of financial position, and the denominator being the price level as of the end of the year for which the earnings were reported. Reductions of retained earnings for dividends paid should be adjusted similarly.

7. IAS 29 addresses a few other special problem areas. For example, the standard notes that borrowing costs typically already reflect the impact of inflation (more accurately, interest rates reflect inflationary expectations), and thus it would represent a form of double counting to fully index capital asset costs for price level changes when part of the cost of the asset was capitalized interest, as defined in IAS 23 as an allowed alternative method (which under revised IAS 23, effective 2009, is the only

permitted method). As a practical matter, interest costs are often not a material component of recorded asset amounts, and the inflation-related component would only be a fraction of interest costs capitalized. However, the general rule is to delete that fraction of the capitalized borrowing costs which represents inflationary compensation, since the entire cost of the asset will be indexed to current purchasing units.

To restate the current period's statement of comprehensive income, a reasonably accurate result can be obtained if revenue and expense accounts are multiplied by the ratio of end-of-period prices to average prices for the period. Where price changes were not relatively constant throughout the period, or when transactions did not occur ratably, as when there was a distinct seasonal pattern to sales activity, a more precise measurement effort might be needed. This can be particularly important when a devaluation of the currency took place during the year.

While IAS 29 addresses the statement of cash flows only perfunctorily (its issuance was prior to the revision of IAS 7), this financial statement must also be modified to report all items in terms of year-end purchasing power units. For example, changes in working capital accounts, used to convert net income into cash flow from operating activities, will be altered to reflect the real (i.e., inflation-adjusted) changes.

To illustrate, if beginning accounts receivable were €500,000 and ending receivables were €650,000, but prices rose by 40% during the year, the apparent €150,000 increase in receivables (which would be a use of cash) is really a €50,000 decrease [(€500,000 × 1.4 = €700,000) − €650,000], which in cash flow terms is a source of cash. Other items must be handled similarly. Investing and financing activities should be adjusted on an item-by-item basis, since these are normally discrete events that do not occur ratably throughout the year.

In addition to the foregoing, the adjusted statement of comprehensive income will report a gain or loss on net monetary items held. As an approximation, this will be computed by applying the change in general prices for the year to the average net monetary assets (or liabilities) outstanding during the year. If net monetary items changed materially at one or more times during the year, a more detailed computation would be warranted. In the statement of comprehensive income, the gain or loss on net monetary items should be associated with the adjustment relating to items that are linked to price level changes (indexed debt, etc.) as well as with interest income and expense and foreign exchange adjustments, since theoretically at least, all these items contain a component that reflects inflationary behavior.

Restating Current Cost Financial Statements under Hyperinflation Conditions

If the financial reporting system is based on current costing (as described earlier in the chapter), the process used to adjust the statement of financial position can be summarized as follows:

1. Monetary assets and liabilities are already presented in units of year-end purchasing power and receive no further adjustment. (See the appendix for a categorization of different assets and liabilities as to their status as monetary or nonmonetary.)
2. Monetary assets and liabilities that are linked to price changes, such as indexed debt securities, are adjusted according to the terms of the contractual arrangement. This does not change the characterization of these items as monetary, but it does serve to reduce or even eliminate the purchasing power gain or loss that would have otherwise been experienced as a result of holding these items during periods of changing general prices.
3. Nonmonetary items are already stated at year-end current values or replacement costs and need no further adjustments. Issues related to recoverable amounts and other

complications associated with price level adjusted historical costs should not normally arise.

4. Equity accounts must also be restated to compensate for changing prices. Paid-in capital accounts are indexed by reference to the dates when the capital was contributed, which are usually a discrete number of identifiable transactions over the life of the entity. Revaluation accounts are eliminated entirely, as these will be subsumed in restated retained earnings. The retained earnings account itself will typically be a "balancing account" under this scenario, since detailed analysis would be very difficult, although certainly not impossible, to accomplish.

The current cost statement of comprehensive income, absent the price level component, will reflect transactions at current costs as of the transaction dates. For example, cost of sales will be comprised of the costs as of each transaction date (usually approximated on an average basis). To report these as of the date of the statement of financial position, these costs will have to be further inflated to year-end purchasing power units, by means of the ratio of general price level indices, as suggested above.

In addition to the foregoing, the adjusted statement of comprehensive income will report a gain or loss on net monetary items held. This will be similar to that discussed under the historical cost reporting above. However, current cost statements of comprehensive income, if prepared, already will include the net gain or loss on monetary items held, which need not be computed again.

To the extent that restated earnings differ from earnings on which income taxes are computed, there will be a need to provide more or less tax accrual, which will be a deferred tax obligation or asset, depending on the circumstances.

Comparative Financial Statements

Consistent with the underlying concept of reporting in hyperinflationary economies, all prior-year financial statement amounts must be updated to purchasing power units as of the most recent date of the statement of financial position. This will be a relatively simple process of applying a ratio of indices of the current year-end price level to the year earlier price level.

Other Disclosure Issues

IAS 29 requires that when the standard is applied, the fact that hyperinflation adjustments have been made be noted. Furthermore, the underlying basis of accounting, historical cost or current cost, should be stipulated, as should the price level index that was utilized in making the adjustments.

Economies Which Cease Being Hyperinflationary

When application of IAS 29 is discontinued, the amounts reported in the last statement of financial position that had been adjusted become, effectively, the new cost basis. That is, previously applied adjustments are not reversed, since an end to a period of hyperinflation generally means only that prices have reached a plateau, not that they have deflated to earlier levels.

Guidance on Applying the Restatement Approach

IFRIC issued an Interpretation of IAS 29 (IFRIC 7, *Applying the Restatement Approach*) that addresses the matter of differentiating between monetary and nonmonetary items. IAS 29 requires that when the reporting entity identifies the existence of hyperinflation in the economy of its functional currency, it must restate its financial statements for the effects of inflation. The restatement approach distinguishes between monetary and nonmonetary items, but in practice it has been noted there is uncertainty about how to restate the financial statements for the first time, particularly with regard to deferred tax balances, and concerning comparative information for prior periods. IFRIC 7 addresses these matters.

Under IFRIC 7, it is required that, in the first year that an entity identifies the existence of hyperinflation, it would start applying IAS 29 as if it had always applied that standard—that is, as if the economy had always been hyperinflationary. Therefore, it must recreate an opening statement of financial position at the beginning of the earliest annual accounting period presented in the restated financial statements, for the first year it applies IAS 29.

The implication of this Interpretation is that restatements of nonmonetary items that are carried at historical cost are effected as of the dates of first recognition (e.g., acquisition). The restatements cannot be effected merely from the opening date of the statement of financial position (which would commonly be at the beginning of the comparative financial statement year). For example, if the year-end 2011 statement of financial position is the first one under IAS 29, with two-year comparative reporting employed, but various plant assets acquired, say, in 2005, the application of IFRIC 7 would require restatements for price level changes from 2005 to year-end 2011.

Nonmonetary assets that are not reported at historical costs (e.g., plant assets revalued for IFRS-basis financial reporting, per IAS 16) require a different mode of adjustment. In this situation, the restatements are applied only for the period of time elapsed since the latest revaluation dates (which should, per IAS 16, be recent dates in most instances). For example, if revaluation was performed at year-end 2009, then only the period from year-end 2009 to year-end 2011 would be subject to adjustment, as the year-end 2009 revaluation already served to address hyperinflation occurring to that date.

IFRIC 7 provides that if detailed records of the acquisition dates for items of property, plant, and equipment are not available or are not capable of estimation, the reporting entity should use an independent professional assessment of the fair value of the items as the basis for restatement. Likewise, if a general price index is not available, it may be necessary to use an estimate based on the changes in the exchange rate between the functional currency and a relatively stable foreign currency, for example, when the entity restates its financial statements.

IFRIC 7 also provides specific guidance on the difficult topic of deferred tax balances in the *opening* statement of financial position of the entity subject to IAS 29 restatement. A two-step computational procedure is required to effect the restatement of deferred tax assets and liabilities. First, deferred tax items are remeasured in accordance with IAS 12, *after* having restated the nominal carrying amounts of all other nonmonetary items in the opening statement of financial position as of that (opening statement of financial position) date. Second, the remeasured deferred tax assets and/or liabilities are restated for hyperinflation's effects from the opening date of the statement of financial position to the reporting date (the most recent date of the statement of financial position).

After restatement of the financial statements has been accomplished, the corresponding amounts (i.e., comparatives) in any later statements of financial position are restated by applying changes in the measuring unit only to the restated amounts in the immediately preceding statement of financial position.

Example of Financial Statements

Meikles

2.   Basis of preparation

The Group's financial statements have been prepared in accordance with International Financial Reporting Standards (IFRS). The financial statements are prepared from statutory records that are maintained under the historical cost convention as modified by the revaluation of property, plant, and equipment, biological assets, and financial instruments which are measured at fair value in the opening statement of financial position.

2.1   Transition to IFRS

The Group is resuming presentation of IFRS financial statements after the Group issued financial statements in the prior reporting period ended December 31, 2009, which could not include an explicit and unreserved statement of compliance with IFRS due to the effects of severe hyperinflation. As discussed in note 2.5, the group has early adopted the amendments to IFRS 1 and is therefore applying that standard in returning to compliance with IFRS. The Group's functional currency for the period before January 1, 2009, the Zimbabwe dollar (ZW$) was subject to sever hyperinflation because it had both the following characteristics:

- A reliable general price index was not available to all entities with transactions and balances in ZW$ because the Zimbabwe Central Statistical office did not release the consumer price indices from August 1, 2008, while the existence of market distortions made measurement of inflation by alternative means unreliable; and
- Exchangeability between the ZW$ and a relatively stable foreign currency did not exist.

The Group's functional currency ceased to be subject to severe hyperinflation from January 1, 2009, when the Group changed its functional currency from ZW$ to US$.

2.2   Exemption for fair value as deemed cost

The Group elected to measure certain items of property, plant, and equipment, biological assets, bank balances and cash, inventories, other financial assets, other financial liabilities and trade, and other payables at fair value and to use the fair values as the deemed cost of those assets and liabilities in the opening statement of financial position as of January 1, 2009.

2.3   Comparative financial information

The financial statements comprise three statements of financial position, and two statements of comprehensive income, two statements of changes in equity and two statements of cash flow as a result of the retrospective application of the amendments to IFRS 1. The comparative statements of comprehensive income, changes in equity and cash flows are for twelve months.

2.4   Reconciliation to previous basis of preparation

The Group's financial statements for the prior period ended December 31, 2009, claimed compliance with IFRS, except certain of the requirements of IAS 1, *Presentation of Financial Statements*, IAS 21, *The Effects of Changes in Foreign Exchange Rates*, and IAS 29, *Financial Reporting in Hyperinflationary Economies*. Certain prior year errors were identified during the period and a reconciliation of the amounts previously stated in the December 31, 2009 financial statements and the comparative amounts as presented in this report is given in note 32.

2.5   Application of new and revised International Financial Reporting Standards (IFRS)

2.5.1 New and revised IFRS affecting amounts reported in the current period and/or prior years

The following new and revised IFRS have been applied in the current period and have affected the amounts reported in these financial statements. Details of other new and revised IFRS applied in these financial statements that have had no material effect on the financial statements are set out in section 2.5.2.

32. Prior year adjustments

32.1 Opening balances of property, plant, and equipment

During the period errors were identified on the January 1, 2009 carrying amounts of certain property, plant, and equipment for the stores and agricultural operations. The assets were omitted from the valuation exercise carried out at January 1, 2009, when the functional currency was changed from ZW$ to US$. This has been corrected by the restatement of the 2009 comparatives included in these financial statements.

32.2 Opening balances of biological assets, other receivables and nursery stocks

During the period, it was discovered that the carrying amounts of certain biological assets of the agricultural segment were understated while certain receivables and nursery stocks were incorrectly valued at January 1, 2009, resulting in a misstatement of the opening carrying amounts. The error has been corrected in the comparative statements of financial position.

Presented below are only those statements of comprehensive income and statements of financial position items which have been impacted by the prior year adjustments.

Prior year adjustments

Statement of comprehensive income

	December 31, 2009 previously stated US $	Adjustments of property, plant and equipment US $	Adjustments to biological assets US $	December 31, 2009 restated US $
Other operating costs	(16,067,056)	(862,866)	--	(16,929,922)
Fair value adjustments	(35,712)	--	2,116,946	2,081,234
Income tax	5,449,453	384,330	(545,114)	5,288,669
Loss for the year from continuing operations	(3,747,889)	(478,536)	1,571,832	(2,654,593)
Total comprehensive loss for the year	(3,824,645)	(478,536)	1,571,832	(2,731,349)

Statements of financial position

January 1, 2009	January 1, 2009 as previously stated US $	Adjustments of property, plant and equipment US $	Adjustments to inventories US $	Adjustments to trade and other receivables US $	January 1, 2009 restated US $
Property, plant, and equipment	89,650,542	4,720,754	--	--	94,371,296
Inventories	5,565,764	--	(502,194)	--	5,063,570
Trade and other receivables	10,280,439	--	--	(152,007)	10,128,432
Total assets	200,489,141	4,720,754	(502,194)	(152,007)	204,555,694
Nondistributable reserves	(148,118,994)	(3,476,943)	502,194	152,007	(150,941,736)
Deferred tax liability	(23,074,660)	(1,243,811)	--	--	(24,318,471)
Total equity and liabilities	(200,489,141)	(4,720,754)	502,194	152,007	(204,555,694)
December 31, 2009					
Property, plant, and equipment	76,672,807	4,720,754	(862,866)	--	80,530,695
Biological assets	4,193,614	--	--	2,116,946	6,310,560
Inventory	17,617,464	(502,194)	--	--	17,115,270
Trade and other receivables	7,485,896	(152,007)	--	--	7,333,889
Total assets	271,429,262	4,066,553	(862,866)	2,116,946	276,749,895
Non-distributable reserves	(107,160,978)	(2,822,742)	--	--	(109,983,720)
Accumulated loss	22,418,679	--	478,536	(1,571,832)	21,325,383
Deferred tax	(13,941,913)	(1,243,811)	384,330	(545,114)	(15,346,508)
Total equity and liabilities	(271,429,262)	(4,066,553)	862,866	(2,116,946)	(276,749,895)

32.3 Prior year costs reclassification

Certain prior year costs have been reclassified to conform to current year presentation.

US GAAP COMPARISON

US GAAP does not generally permit inflation-adjusted financial statements. However, under US GAAP entities under hyperinflation conditions are deemed to use a functional currency of a highly inflationary economy if the cumulative inflation rate for three years exceeds 100%, No such bright-line exists under IFRS to identify hyperinflation. A 100% cumulative inflation rate over three years is only an indicator that must be considered.

Under US GAAP, subsidiaries (both consolidated or equity-method accounted) that use highly inflationary currencies must substitute the hyperinflation currency with a reporting currency. Accordingly, remeasurement effects from the transaction currency into the reporting currency are recognized in profit and loss. If the currency of a subsidiary ceases to be highly inflationary, the reporting currency at the date of change shall be translated into the local currency at current exchange rates.

APPENDIX:
MONETARY VS. NONMONETARY ITEMS

Item	Monetary	Nonmonetary	Requires analysis
Cash on hand, demand deposits, and time deposits	x		
Foreign currency and claims to foreign currency	x		
Securities			
Common stock (passive investment)		x	
Preferred stock (convertible or participating) and convertible bonds			x
Other preferred stock or bonds	x		
Accounts and notes receivable and allowance for doubtful accounts	x		
Mortgage loan receivables	x		
Inventories		x	
Loans made to employees	x		
Prepaid expenses			x
Long-term receivables	x		
Refundable deposits	x		
Advances to unconsolidated subsidiaries	x		
Equity in unconsolidated subsidiaries		x	
Pension and other funds			x
Property, plant, and equipment and accumulated depreciation		x	
Cash surrender value of life insurance	x		
Purchase commitments (portion paid on fixed-price contracts)		x	
Advances to suppliers (not on fixed-price contracts)	x		
Deferred income tax charges	x		
Patents, trademarks, goodwill, and other intangible assets		x	
Deferred life insurance policy acquisition costs	x		
Deferred property and casualty insurance policy acquisition costs		x	
Accounts payable and accrued expenses	x		
Accrued vacation pay			x
Cash dividends payable	x		
Obligations payable in foreign currency	x		
Sales commitments (portion collected on fixed-price contracts)		x	
Advances from customers (not on fixed-price contracts)	x		
Accrued losses on purchase commitments	x		
Deferred revenue			x
Refundable deposits	x		
Bonds payable, other long-term debt, and related discount or premium	x		
Accrued pension obligations			x
Obligations under product warranties		x	
Deferred income tax obligations	x		
Deferred investment tax credits		x	
Life or property and casualty insurance policy reserves	x		
Unearned insurance premiums		x	
Deposit liabilities of financial institutions	x		

36 FIRST-TIME ADOPTION OF INTERNATIONAL FINANCIAL REPORTING STANDARDS

INTRODUCTION

When a reporting entity undertakes the preparation of its financial statements in accordance with International Financial Reporting Standards (IFRS) for the first time, a number of implementation questions must be addressed and resolved. These questions relate to recognition, classification, and measurement, as well as presentation and disclosure issues. Consequently, the IASB decided to promulgate a standard on this subject as its maiden pronouncement, notwithstanding the limited guidance issued by its predecessor, the IASC.

In principle, IFRS 1 requires companies implementing international standards to apply retrospectively all IFRS effective at the end of the company's first IFRS reporting period to all comparative periods presented, as if they had always been applied. However, the standard provides a number of mandatory exceptions and optional exemptions to the requirement for a full retrospective application of IFRS, which override the transitional provisions included in other IFRS. These exceptions and exemptions cover primarily two types of situations: (1)

those requiring judgments by management about past conditions after the outcome of a particular situation is already known, and (2) those in which the cost of a full retrospective application of IFRS would exceed the potential benefit to investors and other users of the financial statements. In addition, the standard specifies certain disclosure requirements.

IFRS 1 provides guidance that all companies must follow on initial adoption of IFRS. Although IFRS is considered a more principles-based framework, the provisions of IFRS 1 are rather rules-based and must be followed as written. The standard is quite complex and companies in transition to IFRS must carefully analyze it in order to determine the most appropriate accounting treatment and take advantage of an opportunity to reassess all financial reporting.

Sources of IFRS
IFRS 1
The Conceptual Framework for Financial Reporting

DEFINITIONS OF TERMS

Date of transition to IFRS. This refers to the beginning of the earliest period for which an entity presents full comparative information under IFRS in its "first IFRS financial statements" (defined below).

Deemed cost. An amount substituted for "cost" or "depreciated cost" at a given date. In subsequent periods, this value is used as the basis for depreciation or amortization.

Fair value. The amount for which an asset could be exchanged, or a liability settled, between knowledgeable, willing parties in an arm's-length transaction.

First IFRS financial statements. The first annual financial statements in which an entity adopts IFRS by making an explicit and unreserved statement of compliance with IFRS.

First IFRS reporting period. The latest reporting period covered by an entity's first IFRS financial statements that contains an explicit and unreserved statement of compliance with IFRS.

First-time adopter (of IFRS). An entity is referred to as a first-time adopter in the period in which it presents its first IFRS financial statements.

International Financial Reporting Standards (IFRS). The standards issued by the International Accounting Standards Board (IASB). More generally, the term connotes the currently outstanding standards (IFRS), the interpretations issued by the IFRS Interpretations Committee (IFRIC), as well as all still-effective previous standards (IAS) issued by the predecessor International Accounting Standards Committee (IASC), and the interpretations issued by the IASC's Standing Interpretations Committee (SIC).

Opening IFRS statement of financial position. The statement of financial position prepared in accordance with the requirements of IFRS 1 as of the "date of transition to IFRS." IFRS 1 requires that a first-time adopter *prepare* and *present* an opening statement of financial position. Thus, this statement is *published* along with the "first IFRS financial statements."

Previous GAAP. This refers to the basis of accounting (e.g., national standards) a first-time adopter used immediately prior to IFRS adoption.

Reporting date. The end of the latest period covered by financial statements or by an interim financial report.

FIRST-TIME ADOPTION GUIDANCE

Objective and Scope of IFRS 1

IFRS 1 applies to an entity that presents its *first IFRS financial statements.* It specifies the requirements that an entity must follow when it first adopts IFRS as the basis for preparing its general-purpose financial statements. IFRS 1 refers to these entities as *first-time adopters.*

The objective of this standard is to ensure that an entity's first IFRS financial statements, including interim financial reports, present high-quality information that:

1. Is transparent and comparable over all periods presented;
2. Provides a suitable starting point for accounting in accordance with IFRS; and
3. Can be prepared at a cost that does not exceed the benefits accruing.

First-time IFRS adopters' financial statements should be comparable over time and between entities applying IFRS for the first time, as well as those already applying IFRS.

Per IFRS 1, an entity must apply the standard in its first IFRS financial statements and in *each interim financial report* it presents under IAS 34, *Interim Financial Reporting,* for a part of the period covered by its first IFRS financial statements. For example, if 2012 is the first annual period for which IFRS financial statements are being prepared, the quarterly or semiannual statements for 2012, if presented, must also comply with IFRS.

According to the standard, an entity's first IFRS financial statements refer to the first annual financial statements in which the entity adopts IFRS by making an *explicit and unreserved statement* (in the financial statements) of compliance with IFRS (with *all* IFRS!). IFRS-compliant financial statements presented in the current year would qualify as first IFRS financial statements if the reporting entity presented its most recent previous financial statements:

- Under national GAAP or standards that were inconsistent with IFRS in all respects;
- In conformity with IFRS in all respects, but without an explicit and unreserved statement to that effect;
- With an explicit statement that the financial statements complied with certain IFRS, but not with all applicable standards;
- Under national GAAP or standards that differ from IFRS but using some individual IFRS to account for items which were not addressed by its national GAAP or other standards;
- Under national GAAP or standards, but with a reconciliation of selected items to amounts determined under IFRS.

Other examples of situations where an entity's current year's financial statements would qualify as its first IFRS financial statements are when

- The entity prepared financial statements in the previous period under IFRS but the financial statements had been identified as being "for internal use only" and had not been made available to the entity's owners or any other external users;
- The entity presented IFRS-compliant financial reporting in the previous period under IFRS for consolidation purposes without preparing a complete set of financial statements as mandated by IAS 1, *Presentation of Financial Statements;* and
- The entity did not present financial statements for the previous periods at all.

The following example would help illustrate the implications of this requirement of the standard.

> Excellent Inc., incorporated in Mysteryland, is a progressive multinational corporation that has always presented its financial statements under the national GAAP of the country of incorporation, with additional disclosures made in its footnotes. The supplementary data included value-added statements and a reconciliation of major items on its statement of financial position to International Financial Reporting Standards (IFRS). Excellent Inc. has significant borrowings from international financial institutions, and these have certain restrictive financial covenants—such as a defined upper limit on the ratio of external debt to equity, and minimum annual return on investments. In order to monitor compliance with these covenants, Excellent Inc. also prepared a separate set of financial statements in accordance with IFRS, but these were never made available to the international financial institutions or to the shareholders of Excellent Inc.
>
> With the growing global acceptance that IFRS had been receiving in recent years, the finance minister of Mysteryland attempted to have the country adopt IFRS as its national GAAP, but this was vetoed by the nation's accounting standard setters. Mysteryland's accession to membership in the WTO is being planned for 2012, and the country is taking steps to gain recognition as a global economic player. Mysteryland was invited to participate in the World Economic Forum, and to publicize his country's commitment to globalization, the finance minister announces at this event that his country would adopt IFRS as its national GAAP beginning in 2012. This announcement was subsequently ratified by Mysteryland's parliament (and later by its national standard-setting body) and thus it was publicly announced that IFRS would be adopted as the country's national GAAP from 2012.
>
> Excellent Inc. had always presented its financial statements under its national GAAP but had also voluntarily provided a reconciliation of major items on its statement of financial position to IFRS in its footnotes, and "for internal purposes" had also prepared a separate set of financial statements under IFRS. Despite these previous overtures towards IFRS compliance, in the year 2012—when Excellent Inc. moves to IFRS as its national GAAP and presents its financial statements to the outside world under IFRS, with an explicit and unreserved statement that these financial statements comply with IFRS—it will nonetheless be considered a first-time adopter and will have to comply with the requirements of IFRS 1.

In cases when the reporting entity's financial statements in the previous year contained an explicit and unreserved statement of compliance with IFRS, but in fact did not fully comply with all accounting policies under IFRS, such an entity would *not* be considered a first-time adopter for the purposes of IFRS 1. The disclosed or undisclosed departures from IFRS in previous year's financial statements of this entity would be treated as an "error" under IFRS 1, which warrants correction made in the manner prescribed by IAS 8, *Accounting Policies, Changes in Accounting Estimates and Errors*. In addition, an entity making changes in accounting policies as a result of specific transitional requirements in other IFRS is also not considered a first-time adopter.

IFRS 1 identifies three situations in which IFRS 1 would *not* apply. These exceptions include, for example, when an entity

1. Stops presenting its financial statements under national requirements (i.e., its national GAAP) along with another set of financial statements that contained an explicit or unreserved statement of compliance with IFRS;
2. Presented its financial statements in the previous year under national requirements (its national GAAP) and those financial statements contained (improperly) an explicit and unreserved statement of IFRS compliance; or
3. Presented its financial statements in the previous year that contained an explicit and unreserved statement of compliance with IFRS, and its auditors qualified their report on those financial statements.

Key Dates

In transition to IFRS, two important dates that must be clearly determined are the first IFRS *reporting date* and *transition date*. "Reporting date" for an entity's first IFRS financial statements refers to the end of the latest period covered by the annual financial statements, or interim financial statements, if any, that the entity presents under IAS 34 for the period covered by its first IFRS financial statements. This is illustrated in the following examples:

Example 1: Xodus Inc. presents its first annual financial statements under IFRS for the calendar year 2012, which include an explicit and unreserved statement of compliance with IFRS. It also presents full comparative financial information for the calendar year 2011. In this case, the latest period covered by these annual financial statements would end on December 31, 2012, and the *reporting date* for the purposes of IFRS 1 is December 31, 2012 (presuming the entity does not present financial statements under IAS 34 for interim periods within calendar year 2012).

Example 2: Alternatively, if Xodus Inc. decides to present its first IFRS interim financial statements for the first quarter ended March 31, 2013, in addition to the first IFRS annual financial statements for the year ended December 31, 2012, the *reporting date* may no longer be December 31, 2012; it is dependent upon how the interim financial statements are prepared. If the interim financial statements for the three months ended March 31, 2013, were prepared in accordance with IAS 34, then the reporting date would be March 31, 2013 (instead of December 31, 2012). If however, the interim financial statements for the first quarter ended March 31, 2013, were not prepared in accordance with IAS 34, then the reporting date would continue to be December 31, 2012 (and not March 31, 2013).

Example 3: Similarly, if Xodus Inc. decides to present its first IFRS interim financial statements in accordance with IAS 34 for the six months ended December 31, 2012, in addition to the first IFRS annual financial statements for the year ended June 30, 2013, the *reporting date* would be December 31, 2012 (and not June 30, 2013).

"Transition date" refers to the beginning of the earliest period for which an entity presents full comparative information under IFRS as part of its first IFRS financial statements. Thus the date of transition to IFRS depends on two factors: first, the date of adoption of IFRS and second, the number of years of comparative information that the entity decides to present along with the financial information of the year of adoption. In accordance with IFRS 1, at least one year of comparative information is required. The "first IFRS reporting period" is the latest reporting period covered by an entity's first IFRS financial statements.

The financial reporting requirements under IFRS 1 are presented below. Assume that Adaptability, Inc. decides to implement IFRS in 2012 and to present comparative information for one year only. The end of Adaptability's first IFRS reporting period is December 31, 2012. The last reporting period under previous GAAP is 2011. The example below illustrates reporting requirements under IFRS 1 applicable to this entity.

Example

Transition date   Reporting date

I---I------------------I---I

1/1/11   12/31/11   03/31/12   12/31/12

- Adaptability, Inc. must prepare and present an opening IFRS statement of financial position at the date of transition to IFRS, that is the beginning of business on January 1, 2011 (or, equivalently, close of business on December 31, 2010). Its last reporting period under "previous GAAP" is 2011 and end of comparative period is on December 31, 2011.
- Adaptability, Inc. will produce its first IFRS financial statements for the annual period ending December 31, 2012. Its first IFRS reporting period is 2012.

- Adaptability, Inc. will prepare and present its statement of financial position for December 31, 2012 (including comparative amounts for December 31, 2011), statement of comprehensive income, statement of changes in equity and statement of cash flows for the year ending December 31, 2012 (including comparative amounts for 2011) and disclosures (including comparative amounts for 2011).

Adaptability, Inc. has quarterly reporting requirements; the entity will comply with IAS 34 and present the first IFRS-compliant interim report—the March 31, 2012 quarterly report. Consequently, the first IFRS reporting date is March 31, 2012.

If Adaptability, Inc. would be required (or choose) to present two years of comparative information under IFRS, the transition date would be January 1, 2010.

Steps in Transition to IFRS

Transition to IFRS involves the following steps:

- Selection of accounting policies that comply with IFRS.
- Preparation of an opening IFRS balance sheet at the date of transition to IFRS as the starting point for subsequent accounting under IFRS.

  - *Recognize* all assets and liabilities whose recognition is required under IFRS;
  - *Derecognize* items as assets or liabilities if IFRS does not permit such recognition;
  - *Reclassify* items in the financial statements in accordance with IFRS; and
  - *Measure* all recognized assets and liabilities according to principles set forth in IFRS.

- Presentation and disclosure in an entity's first IFRS financial statements and interim financial reports.

Selection of Accounting Policies

IFRS 1 stipulates that an entity should use the same accounting policies throughout all periods presented in its first IFRS financial statements, and also in its opening IFRS statement of financial position. Furthermore, the standard requires that those accounting policies must comply with each IFRS effective at the "reporting date" (as explained before) for its first IFRS financial statements, with certain exceptions. It requires full retrospective application of all IFRS effective at the reporting date for an entity's first IFRS financial statements, except under certain defined circumstances wherein the entity is prohibited by IFRS from applying IFRS retrospectively (mandatory exceptions) or it may elect to use one or more exemptions from some requirements of other IFRS (optional exemptions). Both concepts are discussed later in this chapter.

If a new IFRS has been issued on the reporting date, but application is not yet mandatory, although reporting entities have been encouraged to apply it before the effective date, the first-time adopter is permitted, but not required, to apply it as well. As stated before, an entity's first reporting date under IFRS refers to the end of the latest period covered by the first annual financial statements in accordance with IFRS, or interim financial statements, if any, that the entity presents under IAS 34. For example, if an entity's first IFRS reporting date is December 31, 2014, consequently

- First IFRS financial statements must comply with IFRS in effect at December 31, 2014; and

- Opening statement of financial position at January 1, 2013, and comparative information presented for 2013, must comply with IFRS effective at December 31, 2014 (at the end of the first IFRS reporting period).

On first-time adoption of IFRS, the first most important step that an entity has to make is the selection of accounting policies that comply with IFRS. Management must select initial IFRS accounting policies based on relevance and reliability as these choices will affect the company's financial reporting for years to come. While many accounting policy choices will simply reflect relevant circumstances (e.g., method of depreciation, percentage of completion vs. completed contract accounting), other choices will not depend on circumstances but result from IFRS flexibility (e.g., options for recognizing actuarial gains and losses, or option to designate nontrading instruments as available-for-sale).

The several areas where a choice of accounting policies under IFRS exists include

- IFRS 1—Optional exemptions from the full retrospective application of IFRS for some types of transactions on first-time IFRS adoption (See Optional exemptions from other IFRS);
- IFRS 3—In acquisitions of less than 100%, option to measure noncontrolling interest at fair value or proportionate share of the acquiree's identifiable net assets (this choice will result in recognizing 100% of goodwill or only parent's share of goodwill);
- IFRS 4—Remeasure insurance liabilities to fair value during each accounting period;
- IAS 1—

    a. Present one statement of comprehensive income or separate income statement and comprehensive income statement;
    b. Presentation of expenses in the income statement by nature or by function;

- IAS 2—

    a. Value inventories at FIFO or weighted-average;
    b. Measure certain inventories, for example agricultural produce, minerals and commodities, at net realizable value rather than cost;

- IAS 7—

    a. Direct or indirect method for presenting operating cash flows;
    b. Classify interest and dividends as operating, investing, or financing;

- IAS 16—Measure property, plant, and equipment using the cost-depreciation model or the revaluation through equity model;
- IAS 19—Many options available for recognizing actuarial gains and losses (immediately in profit or loss, immediately in equity, or different methods of spreading the cost);
- IAS 20—Various options of accounting for government grants;
- IAS 27, IAS 28, IAS 31—Cost or fair value model for investments in subsidiaries, associates, joint ventures in *separate* financial statements;
- IAS 31—Equity method or proportionate consolidation for joint ventures;
- IAS 38—The cost-depreciation model or revaluation through equity model for intangible assets with quoted market prices;
- IAS 39—

    a. Optional hedge accounting;

b. Option to designate individual financial assets and financial liabilities to be measured at fair value through P&L;

c. Option to designate nontrading instruments as available-for-sale;

d. Option to reclassify out of fair-value-through-profit or loss, and out of available-for-sale categories;

e. Option to adjust the carrying amount of a hedged item for gains and losses on the hedging instrument;

f. Option of trade date or settlement date accounting;

g. Option to separate an embedded derivative or account for the entire contract at fair-value-through-profit or loss.

- IAS 40—

   a. The cost-depreciation model or fair value model for investment property;

   b. Option to classify land use rights as investment property.

A first-time adopter is not allowed to apply different versions of IFRS that were effective at earlier periods. With the passage of time, IFRS have been revised or amended several times and in some instances the current version of IFRS is vastly different from the earlier versions that were either superseded or amended. In a very important decision, IFRS 1 requires a first-time adopter to use the current version of IFRS (or future standards, if early adoption permitted), without considering the superseded versions. This obviates the need to identify varying iterations of the standards that would have guided the preparation of the entity's financial statements at each prior reporting date, which would have been a very time-consuming and problematic task. This means that the comparative financial statements accompanying the first IFRS-compliant reporting may differ—perhaps materially—from what would have been presented in those earlier periods had the entity commenced reporting consistent with IFRS at an earlier point in time. Entities can early adopt new standards if early adoption is permitted by the standards, but cannot apply standards that are not published at the first IFRS reporting period.

The IASB's original thinking was to grant the first-time adopter an option to elect application of IFRS *as if it had always applied IFRS* (i.e., from the entity's inception). However, to have actualized this, the first-time adopter would have had to consider the various iterations of IFRS that had historically existed over the period of time culminating with its actual adoption of IFRS. Upon reflection, this would have created not merely great practical difficulties for preparers, but would have negatively impacted comparability among periods and across reporting entities. Thus, IFRS 1 as promulgated offers no such option.

The recent amendment to IFRS 1 as part of the 2010 *Improvement to IFRS* clarified that, if a first-time adopter changes its accounting policies or its use of the exemptions in IFRS 1 after it has published an interim financial report in accordance with IAS 34, *Interim Financial Reporting,* but before its first IFRS financial statements are issued, it should explain those changes and update the reconciliations between previous GAAP and IFRS. The requirements in IAS 8 do not apply to such changes.

Opening IFRS Statement of Financial Position

A first-time adopter must prepare and present an opening IFRS statement of financial position at the date of transition to IFRS. This statement serves as the starting point for the entity's accounting under IFRS. Logically, preparation of an opening statement of financial position is a necessary step in order to accurately restate the first year's statements of comprehensive income, changes in equity, and cash flows.

The following example will clarify the date of the opening statement of financial position:

> Adaptability Inc. decided to adopt IFRS in its annual financial statements for the fiscal year ending December 31, 2012, and to present comparative information for the year 2011. Thus, the beginning of the earliest period for which the entity should present full comparative information under IFRS would be January 1, 2011. Accordingly, the opening IFRS statement of financial position for purposes of compliance with IFRS 1 would be that as of the beginning of business on January 1, 2011 (equivalent to the closing of business on December 31, 2010).
>
> Alternatively, if Adaptability Inc. decided (or was required, e.g., by the stock listing authorities) to present two years of comparative information (i.e., for both 2010 and 2011), as well as for the current year 2012, then the beginning of the earliest period for which the entity would present full comparative information would be January 1, 2010 (equivalent to close of business on December 31, 2009). Accordingly, the opening IFRS statement of financial position for purposes of compliance with IFRS 1 would be that as of January 1, 2010, under these circumstances.

The opening statement of financial position, prepared at the transition date, must be based on standards applied at the end of the first reporting period. This implies that advance planning will be required for several items, including hedging, and that the opening statement of financial position cannot be finalized until the end of the first IFRS reporting period (reporting date). The following provides an example of IFRS to be applied in the opening statement of financial position:

> ABC entity's first IFRS reporting period will end on December 31, 2011, and its transition date is January 1, 2010, since only one comparative period will be presented. In the first IFRS financial statements ABC will apply IFRS 7, as amended in 2010, in all periods presented in the first IFRS financial statements. The amendment in question clarifies the intended interaction between qualitative and quantitative disclosures of the nature and extent of risks arising from financial instruments and removed some disclosure items which were seen to be superfluous or misleading and was effective for all accounting periods beginning on or after January 1, 2011.

In preparing the opening IFRS statement of financial position in transition from previous GAAP to IFRS, several adjustments to the financial statements are required. A first-time IFRS adopter should apply the following (except in cases where IFRS 1 prohibits retrospective application or grants certain exemptions):

1. *Recognize* all assets and liabilities whose recognition is required under IFRS. It is expected that many companies will recognize additional assets and liabilities under IFRS reporting, when compared with the national GAAP formerly employed. Areas which may result in this effect include

   - Defined benefit pension plans (IAS 19)
   - Deferred taxation (IAS 12)
   - Assets and liabilities under certain finance leases (IAS 17)
   - Provisions where there is a legal or constructive obligation (IAS 37)
   - Derivative financial instruments (IAS 39)
   - Internal development costs (IAS 38)
   - Share-based payments (IFRS 2)

2. *Derecognize* items as assets or liabilities if IFRS does not permit such recognition. Some assets and liabilities recognized under an entity's previous (national) GAAP will have to be derecognized. For example

   - Provisions where there is no legal or constructive obligation (e.g., general reserves, postacquisition restructuring) (IAS 37)

- Internally generated intangible assets (IAS 38)
- Deferred tax assets where recovery is not probable (IAS 12)

3. *Reclassify* items that it recognized under previous GAAP as one type of asset, liability, or component of equity, but are a different type of asset, liability, or component of equity under IFRS. Assets and liabilities that might be reclassified to conform to IFRS include

- Investments accounted for in accordance with IAS 39
- Certain financial instruments previously classified as equity
- Any assets and liabilities that have been offset where the criteria for offsetting in IFRS are not met—for example, the offset of an insurance recovery against a provision
- Noncurrent assets held-for-sale (IFRS 5)
- Noncontrolling interest (IAS 27)

4. *Measure* all recognized assets and liabilities according to principles set forth in IFRS. This remeasurement may be required when the accounting basis is the same but measured differently (e.g., cost basis under IFRS may not be the same as under US GAAP), when the basis is changed (e.g., from cost to fair value), or there are differences in the applicability of discounting (e.g., provisions or impairments). Assets and liabilities that might have to be measured differently include

- Receivables (IAS 18)
- Inventory (IAS 2)
- Employee benefit obligations (IAS 19)
- Deferred taxation (IAS 12)
- Financial instruments (IAS 39)
- Provisions (IAS 37)
- Impairments of property, plant, and equipment, and intangible assets (IAS 36)
- Assets held for disposal (IFRS 5)
- Share-based payments (IFRS 2)

The following comprehensive example illustrates the practical application of the four rules outlined above:

Situation

ABC Inc. presented its most recent financial statements under the national GAAP through 2011. It adopted IFRS from 2012 and is required to prepare an opening IFRS statement of financial position as at January 1, 2011. In preparing the IFRS opening statement of financial position, ABC Inc. noted the following:

Under its previous GAAP, ABC Inc. sold certain financial receivables as well as trade receivables for the amount of $250,000 to special-purpose entities (SPEs) that are not consolidated although they conduct activities on behalf of the Group. In addition, ABC Inc. was using the last-in first-out (LIFO) method to account for certain inventories, and, consequently, reported the carrying value of inventory reduced by $150,000, as compared to the value under the FIFO method. Furthermore, it had not discounted to present value long-term provisions for warranty of $100,000 although the effect from discounting would be material ($10,000). Finally, all research and development costs of $500,000 (of which total $300,000 relates to research costs) for the invention of new products were expensed when incurred.

Solution

In order to prepare the opening IFRS statement of financial position at January 1, 2011, ABC Inc. would need to make the following adjustments to its statement of financial position at December 31, 2010, presented under its previous GAAP:

1. SIC 12 requires ABC Inc. to consolidate a SPE where it is deemed to control it. Indicators of control include the SPE conducting activities on behalf of the Group and/or the Group holding the majority of the risks and rewards of the SPE. Thus, SPEs should be consolidated and $250,000 of receivables is recognized under IFRS;
2. IAS 2 prohibits the use of LIFO. Consequently, the Group adopted the FIFO method and had to increase inventory by $150,000 under IFRS;
3. IAS 37 states that long-term provisions must be discounted to their present value if the effect from discounting is material. As a result, the Group adjusted the amount of provisions for warranty by $10,000, the effect from discounting;
4. IAS 38 allows that development costs are capitalized as intangible assets if the technical and economic feasibility of a project can be demonstrated. Thus, $200,000 incurred on development costs should be capitalized as an intangible asset under IFRS.

Mandatory Exceptions to the Retrospective Application of other IFRS

IFRS 1 *prohibits* retrospective application of some aspects of other IFRS when a judgment would have been required about the past and the outcome is known on first-time adoption. For example, practical implementation difficulties could arise from the retrospective application of aspects of IAS 39 or could lead to selective designation of some hedges to report a particular result. Mandatory exceptions relate to estimates, derecognition of nonderivative financial assets and nonderivative financial liabilities, hedge accounting, and noncontrolling interests.

Estimates. An entity's estimates under IFRS at the date of transition to IFRS should be consistent with estimates made for the same date under its previous GAAP (after adjustments to reflect any difference in accounting policies), unless there is objective evidence that those estimates were in error, as that term is defined under IFRS. Especially, such estimates as those of market prices, interest rates or foreign exchange rates should reflect market conditions at the date of transition to IFRS. Revisions based on information developed after the transition date should only be recognized as income or expense (reflected in results of operations) in the period when the entity made the revision, and may not be "pushed back" to the opening IFRS statement of financial position prepared at the transition date at which, historically, the new information had not been known. Any information an entity receives after the date of transition to IFRS about estimates it made under previous GAAP should be treated as a *nonadjusting* event after the date of the statement of financial position, and accorded the treatment prescribed by IAS 10, *Events after the Reporting Period.*

For example, ABC Inc. recognized a provision for legal claims of $800 in accordance with previous GAAP at the date of transition to IFRS on January 1, 2011. The settlement amount is $900, which is known on June 11, 2012, and requires the revision of this estimate. The entity should not reflect that new information in its opening IFRS statement of financial position (unless the estimate needs adjustment for any differences in accounting policies or there is objective evidence that the estimate was in error, in accordance with IAS 8). Instead, ABC Inc. will reflect that new information as an expense of $100 in profit or loss for the year ended December 31, 2012.

Derecognition of nonderivative financial assets and nonderivative financial liabilities (IAS 39). If a first-time adopter derecognized nonderivative financial assets or nonderivative financial liabilities under its previous GAAP, it should not recognize those assets and liabilities under IFRS, unless they qualify for recognition as a result of a later transaction or event. However, an entity may apply the derecognition requirements retrospectively, from a date of the entity's choice, if the information needed to apply IAS 39 to derecognized items as a result of past transactions was obtained at the time of initially accounting for those transactions.

A first-time adopter should recognize all derivatives and other interests retained after derecognition and still existing, and consolidate all special-purpose entities (SPEs) that it controls at the date of transition to IFRS (even if the SPE existed before the date of transition to IFRS or holds financial assets or financial liabilities that were derecognized under previous GAAP).

Hedge accounting (IAS 39). A first-time adopter is required, at the date of transition to IFRS, to measure all derivatives at fair value and eliminate all deferred losses and gains on derivatives that were reported under its previous GAAP. However, a first-time adopter is not permitted to reflect a hedging relationship in its opening IFRS statement of financial position if it does not qualify for hedge accounting under IAS 39. But if an entity designated a net position as a hedged item under its previous GAAP, it may designate an individual item within that net position as a hedged item under IFRS, provided it does so prior to the date of transition to IFRS. Transitional provisions of IAS 39 apply to hedging relationships of a first-time adopter at the date of transition to IFRS.

Noncontrolling interests (IFRS 3). A first-time adopter should apply the following requirements prospectively from the date of transition to IFRS:

- Attribution of total comprehensive income to the owners of the parent and to the noncontrolling interests even if this results in the noncontrolling interests having a deficit balance;
- Accounting for changes in the parent's ownership interest in a subsidiary that do not result in a loss of control; and
- Accounting for a loss of control over a subsidiary, and the related requirements of IFRS 5.

OPTIONAL EXEMPTIONS

IFRS 1 allows a first-time adopter to elect to use one or more optional (voluntary) exemptions from the retrospective application of other IFRS. Optional exemptions from the retrospective application of other IFRS are granted on first-time adoption in specific areas where the cost of complying with the requirements of IFRS 1 would be likely to exceed the benefits to users of financial statements or where the retrospective application is impractical. A parent company and all of its subsidiaries must analyze these exemptions to determine which exemptions to apply and how to apply them, but it should be emphasized that the exemptions do not impact future accounting policy choices and cannot be applied by analogy to other items.

The application of these optional exemptions is explained in detail below. A first-time adopter of IFRS may elect to use exemptions from the general measurement and restatement principles in one or more of the following instances:

Business combinations (IFRS 3, *Business Combinations*). IFRS 1 exempts the first-time adopter from mandatory retrospective application in the case of business combinations that occurred before the date of transition to IFRS. That is, requirements under IFRS 3 can be applied in accounting for combinations that occurred before the transition date under IFRS, but this *need not be done.* Thus, under IFRS 1, an entity may elect to use previous national GAAP accounting relating to such business combinations. The IASB provided this exemption because, if retrospective application of IFRS 3 had been made obligatory, it could have forced entities to estimate (or make educated guesses) about conditions that presumably prevailed at the respective dates of past business combinations. This would have been particularly challenging where data from past business combinations had not been preserved. The use of such estimates could have adversely affected the relevance and reliability of the financial statements, and was thus seen as a situation to be avoided.

In evaluating responses to the draft of its standard on first-time adoption of IFRS, the IASB concluded that notwithstanding the fact that restatement of past business combinations to conform with IFRS was conceptually preferable, a pragmatic assessment of cost versus benefit weighed in favor of *permitting* but *not requiring* such restatement. However, the IASB did place an important limitation on this election: if a first-time adopter having multiple acquisition transactions restates *any* business combination, it must restate *all* business combinations that took place subsequent to the date of that restated combination transaction. First-time adopters thus cannot "cherry pick" among past business combinations to apply IFRS opportunistically to certain of them.

For instance, if ABC Inc., a first-time adopter, did not seek this exemption, and instead opted to apply IFRS 3 retrospectively, and restated a major business combination that took place three years ago, then, under this requirement of IFRS 1, ABC Inc. is required to restate all business combinations that took place subsequent to the date of that major business combination to which it applied IFRS 3 retrospectively. Earlier combinations would *not* have to be restated, however.

If the entity employs the exemption under IFRS 1 and does not apply IFRS 3 retrospectively to a past business combination, it must observe these rules.

1. The first-time adopter should preserve the same classification (an *acquisition* or a *uniting of interests*) as was applied in its previous GAAP financial statements.
2. The first-time adopter should recognize all assets and liabilities at the date of transition to IFRS that were acquired or assumed in a past business combination, except

   a. Certain financial assets and financial liabilities that were derecognized under its previous GAAP; and
   b. Assets (including goodwill) and liabilities that were not recognized in the acquirer's consolidated statement of financial position under previous GAAP and also would not qualify for recognition under IFRS in the separate statement of financial position of the acquiree.

   Any resulting change should be recognized by the first-time adopter in retained earnings (or another component of equity, if appropriate) unless the change results from the recognition of an intangible asset that was previously incorporated within goodwill.
3. The first-time adopter should derecognize (i.e., exclude) from its opening IFRS statement of financial position any item recognized under previous GAAP that does not qualify for recognition, either as an asset or liability, under IFRS. The resulting change from this derecognition should be accounted by the first-time adopter as follows: first, if the first-time adopter had classified a past business combination as an acquisition and recognized as an intangible asset an item that does not qualify for recognition as an asset under IAS 38, it should reclassify that item (and any related deferred tax and noncontrolling interests) as part of goodwill (unless it deducted goodwill from equity, instead of presenting it as an asset, under its previous GAAP); and second, the first-time adopter should recognize all other resulting changes in retained earnings.

4. In cases where IFRS require subsequent measurement of some assets and liabilities on a basis other than original cost, such as fair value, the first-time adopter should measure these assets and liabilities on that basis in its opening IFRS statement of financial position, even if these assets and liabilities were acquired or assumed in a past business combination. Any resulting change in the carrying amount should be recognized by the first-time adopter in retained earnings (or another component of equity, if appropriate), instead of as an adjustment to goodwill.

5. Subsequent to the business combination, the carrying amount under previous GAAP of assets acquired and liabilities assumed in the business combination should be treated as their *deemed cost* under IFRS at that date. If IFRS require a cost-based measurement of those assets and liabilities at a later date, deemed cost should be used instead (e.g., as the basis for cost-based depreciation or amortization from the date of the business combination).

6. If assets acquired or liabilities assumed were not recognized in a past business combination under the previous GAAP, the first-time adopter should recognize and measure them in its consolidated statement of financial position on the basis that IFRS would require in the separate statement of financial position of the acquiree.

7. The carrying amount of goodwill in the opening IFRS statement of financial position should be its carrying amount under previous GAAP at the date of transition to IFRS, after the following adjustments:

   a. The carrying amount of goodwill should be increased due to a reclassification that would be needed for an intangible asset recognized under previous GAAP but which does not qualify as an intangible asset under IAS 38. Similarly, the carrying amount of goodwill should be decreased due to inclusion of an intangible asset as part of goodwill under previous GAAP but which requires separate recognition under IFRS.

   b. If the purchase consideration of a past business combination was based on a contingency which was resolved prior to the date of transition to IFRS, and a reliable estimate of the adjustment relating to the contingency can be made and it is probable that a payment will be made, the first-time adopter should adjust the carrying amount of goodwill by that amount. Similarly, if a previously recognized contingency can no longer be measured reliably, or its payment is no longer probable, the first-time adopter should adjust the carrying amount of goodwill accordingly.

   c. Whether or not there is evidence of impairment of goodwill, the first-time adopter should apply IAS 36 in testing goodwill for impairment, if any, and should recognize the resulting impairment loss in retained earnings (or, if so required by IAS 36, in revaluation surplus).

   The impairment test should be based on conditions at the date of transition to IFRS.

8. No other adjustments are permitted by IFRS 1 to the carrying amount of goodwill at the date of transition to IFRS. Thus, adjustments such as the following *cannot* be made:

   a. Excluding in-process research and development acquired in that business combination,

   b. Adjusting previous amortization of goodwill, or

   c. Reversing adjustments to goodwill that IFRS 3 would not permit but which were appropriately made under previous GAAP.

9. If under its previous GAAP a first-time adopter did not consolidate a subsidiary acquired in a business combination (i.e., because the parent did not treat it as a subsidiary under previous GAAP), the first-time adopter should adjust the carrying amounts of the subsidiary's assets and liabilities to the amounts that IFRS would require in the subsidiary's separate statement of financial position. The deemed cost of goodwill would be equal to the difference at the date of transition to IFRS between the parent's interest in those adjusted carrying amounts and the cost in the parent's separate financial statements of its investment in the subsidiary.

10. The above adjustments to recognized assets and liabilities should also flow through to noncontrolling interests and deferred assets.

IFRS 1 states that these exemptions for past business combinations also apply to past acquisitions of investments in associates and in joint ventures. Furthermore, the date chosen for electing to apply IFRS 3 retrospectively to past business combinations applies equally to all such investments.

For example, ABC Inc., a first-time adopter, has a transition date of January 1, 2012. ABC acquired entity DEF on June 1, 2011. Under previous GAAP, in accounting for this acquisition, ABC (1) did not separately recognize development costs of $100 at 1/1/12; (2) recognized a general restructuring provision of $200, which was 75% outstanding at 1/1/12; did not recognize a deferred tax asset of $50 resulting from temporary differences associated with assets acquired and liabilities assumed. In transition to IFRS, ABC elects not to restate previous business combinations. At the date of transition, ABC has to make the following adjustments: (1) recognize development costs of $100, with the adjustment taken to goodwill; (2) derecognize the general restructuring provision of $200, with the adjustment recognized in retained earnings; (3) recognize a deferred tax asset of $50, with the adjustment recognized in retained earnings.

In addition, the concept of "push-down accounting," required under SEC guidance in special circumstances, does not exist in IFRS. It means that previous revaluations to fair value at acquisition made by subsidiaries in order to apply push-down accounting need to be reversed in transition to IFRS, but those revaluations can be used as deemed cost of property, plant, and equipment, certain intangible assets, and investment property.

Share-based payment transactions (IFRS 2, *Share-Based Payment*). On first-time IFRS adoption an entity is encouraged, but not required, to apply IFRS 2 to equity instruments that were granted on or before November 7, 2002. In addition, the adopter is also encouraged, but not required, to apply IFRS 2 to equity instruments that were granted after November 7, 2002, and vested before the later of (1) the date of transition to IFRS, and (2) January 1, 2005; and to liabilities arising from share-based payment transactions that were (1) settled before the date of transition to IFRS; or (2) settled before January 1, 2005. But the latter option can only be applied if the entity has disclosed publicly the fair value of those equity instruments, determined at the measurement date.

Additionally, a first-time adopter is encouraged, but not required, to apply IFRS 2 to liabilities arising from share-based payment transactions that were (1) settled before the date of transition to IFRS, or (2) settled before January 1, 2005. The adopter is not required to present comparative information for liabilities presented under IFRS 2 for a period or date that is earlier than November 7, 2002.

Insurance contracts (IFRS 4, *Insurance Contracts*). A first-time adopter may apply the transitional provisions in IFRS 4. The standard restricts changes in accounting policies for insurance contracts, including those made by a first-time adopter.

Deemed cost. An entity may elect to measure an item of property, plant, and equipment at fair value at the date of its transition to IFRS and use the fair value as its deemed cost at that date. In accordance with IFRS 1, "deemed cost" is an amount substituted for "cost" or "depreciated cost" at a given date, and this value is subsequently used as the basis for depreciation or amortization. A first-time adopter may elect to use a previous GAAP revaluation of an item of property, plant, and equipment at, or before, the date of transition to IFRS as deemed costs at the date of revaluation if the revaluation amount, when determined, was broadly comparable to either fair value or cost (or depreciated cost under IFRS adjusted for changes in general or specific price index).

These elections are equally available for investment property measured under the cost model and intangible assets that meet the recognition criteria and the criteria for revaluation (including the existence of an active market).

For example, ABC Inc., a first-time adopter, has a transition date of January 1, 2012. ABC revalued buildings under previous GAAP and on the last revaluation date at 12/31/08, the buildings were valued at $500. Depreciation of $60 has been charged since the revaluation and the expected remaining useful life is 20 years. At 1/1/12 ABC had a cumulative balance in the revaluation reserve of $100. At the date of transition to IFRS, ABC elects the deemed cost exemption. ABC makes the following adjustments to its opening IFRS statement of financial position: (1) buildings are recognized at the deemed cost of $500; (2) the revaluation reserve of $100 is taken to retained earnings; (3) accumulated depreciation of $6 must be recognized for the period 12/31/08 to 1/1/12 [$(500 - 60)/20 = 22$ annually; $(22 \times 3 = 66) - 60 = 6$]

If a first-time adopter has established a deemed cost under previous GAAP for any of its assets or liabilities by measuring them at their fair values at a particular date because of the occurrence of an event such as privatization or an initial public offering (IPO), it is allowed to use such an event-driven fair value as deemed cost for IFRS at the date of that measurement. The May 2010 *Improvements to IFRS* amended IFRS 1 to clarify that a first-time adopter is also permitted to use an event-driven fair value as "deemed cost" at the measurement date for measurement events that occurred after the date of transition to IFRS but during the period covered by the first IFRS financial statements. Any resulting adjustment is recognized directly in equity at the measurement date.

First-time adopters must assess available options under IAS 16 and determine which options would be beneficial in adopting IFRS. For example, the first IFRS financial statements must present property, plant, and equipment as if the requirements of IAS 16 had always been applied. While the "component approach" to depreciation is allowed but rarely used under US GAAP, this approach is required under IFRS and may result in significant adjustments in conversion for US adopters. (See Chapter 9, Property, Plant, and Equipment.)

It is common in some countries to account for exploration and development costs for properties in development or production in cost centers that include all properties in a large geographical area (often referred to as "full cost accounting"). Since this approach is not allowed under IFRS, the process of remeasuring the assets on the first-time adoption of IFRS would likely be tedious and expensive. The amendments to IFRS 1, in effect for annual periods beginning on or after January 1, 2010, would allow an entity that used full cost accounting under its previous GAAP to measure exploration and evaluation assets, as well as oil and gas assets in the development or production phases, at the date of transition to IFRS, at the amount determined under the entity's previous GAAP.

The amendments allow an entity that used such accounting under previous GAAP to elect to measure oil and gas assets at the date of transition on the following basis:

(1) Exploration and evaluation assets at the amount determined under previous GAAP; and

(2) Assets in the development or production phases at the amount determined for the cost center under previous GAAP, and then, this amount is allocated pro rata to the underlying assets, using reserve volumes or reserve values as of that date.

To avoid the use of deemed costs resulting in an oil and gas asset being measured at more than its recoverable amount, the first-time adopter should test exploration and evaluation assets and assets in the development and production phases for impairment at the date of transition to IFRS in accordance with IFRS 6, *Exploration for and Evaluation of Mineral Resources*, or IAS 36, *Impairments of Assets*, and, if necessary, reduce the amount determined in accordance with (1) and (2). This paragraph considers only those oil and gas assets that are used in the exploration, evaluation, development or production of oil and gas.

In addition, in the May 2010 *Improvements to IFRS*, the IASB amended IFRS 1 to allow entities with rate-regulated activities that hold, or previously held, items of property, plant, and equipment or intangible assets for use in such operations (and recognized separately as regulatory assets) that may not be eligible for capitalization under IFRS to recognize such items and to elect to use the previous GAAP carrying amount of such items as their deemed cost at the date of transition to IFRS. This exemption is available on an item-by-item basis, but entities are required to immediately (at the date of transition to IFRS) test for impairment in accordance with IAS 36 each item for which this exemption is used. (See discussion of rate-regulated activities in Chapter 32, Extractive Industries.)

Leases. In accordance with IFRIC 4, *Determining Whether an Arrangement Contains a Lease*, a first-time adopter may determine whether an arrangement existing at the date of transition to IFRS contains a lease on the basis of facts and circumstances existing at that date.

IFRS 1 exempts entities with existing leasing contracts that made, under previous GAAP, the same determination as that required by IFRIC 4, but that assessment was at a date other than that required by IFRIC 4, from reassessing the classification of those contracts when adopting IFRS.

Employee benefits. IFRS 1 provides a first-time adopter with the option to restate to zero all cumulative actuarial gains and losses on defined benefit plans at the transition date. Under IAS 19 an entity may have unrecognized actuarial gains or losses when it uses the "corridor approach" defined under that standard. Prior GAAP may not have provided similar treatment, however. Retrospective application of IAS 19 would necessitate splitting the cumulative gains and losses, from inception of the plan until the date of transition to IFRS, into a recognized and an unrecognized portion. This would necessitate an enormously complicated analysis in some situations.

IFRS 1 allows a first-time adopter to elect to recognize all cumulative actuarial gains and losses at the date of transition to IFRS, even if it uses the corridor approach for subsequent actuarial gains or losses. IFRS 1 does mandate, however, that if an election is made for one employee benefit plan, it should apply to all other employee plans of that reporting entity.

Cumulative translation differences. A first-time IFRS adopter has the option to reset to zero all cumulative translation differences arising on monetary items that are part of a company's net investment in a foreign operations existing at the transition date. IAS 21 requires an entity to classify certain translation differences as a separate component of equity, and upon disposal of the foreign operation to transfer the cumulative translation difference relating to the foreign operation to the statement of comprehensive income as part of the gain or loss on disposal.

Under IFRS 1, a first-time adopter is exempted from a transfer of the cumulative translation adjustment that existed on the date of transition to IFRS. If it elects this exemption, the cumulative translation adjustment for all foreign operations would be deemed to be zero at the date of transition to IFRS. The gain or loss on subsequent disposal of any foreign operation should exclude translation differences that arose before the date of transition to IFRS, but would include all subsequent translation adjustments recognized in accordance with IAS 21.

A company in transition to IFRS may also need to change the functional currency of one or more subsidiaries under IAS 21, because, for example, due to differences in existing guidance in this respect. This could possibly create the need to revalue property, plant, and equipment on first-time adoption rather than restating nonmonetary assets measured at historical cost, which could be onerous.

Investments in subsidiaries, jointly controlled entities, and associates. In accordance with IAS 27 a company may value its investments in subsidiaries, jointly controlled entities and associates either at cost or in accordance with IAS 39. Under IFRS 1, a first-time adopter electing deemed cost to account for these investments may choose either fair value, determined in accordance with IAS 39, at the entity's date of transition to IFRS, or carrying amount under previous GAAP at that date.

Assets and liabilities of subsidiaries, associates, and joint ventures. IFRS 1 provides exemptions under two circumstances as follows:

1. If a subsidiary becomes a first-time adopter later than its parent, the subsidiary must, in its separate (stand-alone) financial statements, measure its assets and liabilities at either

   a. The carrying amounts that would be included in its parent's consolidated financial statements, based on its parent's date of transition to IFRS (if no adjustments were made for consolidation procedures and for the effect of the business combination in which the parent acquired the subsidiary), or
   b. The carrying amounts required by the other provisions of IFRS 1, based on subsidiary's date of transition to IFRS.

A similar choice can be made by associates or joint ventures that adopt IFRS later than the entity that exercises significant influence or joint control over them.

2. If a reporting entity (parent) becomes a first-time adopter after its subsidiary (or associate or joint venture) does, the entity is required, in its consolidated financial statements, to measure the assets and liabilities of the subsidiary (or associate or joint venture) at the same carrying amounts as in the separate (stand-alone) financial statements of the subsidiary (or associate or joint venture), after adjusting for consolidation and equity accounting adjustments and for effects of the business combination in which an entity acquired the subsidiary. In a similar manner, if a parent becomes a first-time adopter for its separate financial statements earlier or later than for its consolidated financial statements, it shall measure its assets and liabilities at the same amounts in both financial statements, except for consolidation adjustments.

In cases where a subsidiary decided to elect different exemptions from those the parent selects for the preparation of consolidated financial statements, this may create permanent differences between the subsidiaries' and parents' books, requiring adjustments in consolidation. This exemption does not impact the requirement in IAS 1 that uniform accounting policies must be applied in the consolidated entities for all entities within a group.

Compound financial instruments. If an entity has issued a compound financial instrument, such as a convertible debenture, with characteristics of both debt and equity, IAS 32 requires that at inception, it should split and separate the liability component of the compound financial instrument from equity. If the liability portion no longer is outstanding at the date of adoption of IFRS, a retrospective and literal application of IAS 32 would require separating two portions of equity. The first portion, which is in retained earnings, represents the cumulative interest accreted on the liability component. The other portion represents the original equity component of the instrument, and would be in paid-in capital.

IFRS 1 exempts a first-time adopter from this split accounting if the former liability component is no longer outstanding at the date of transition to IFRS. This exemption can be significant to companies that routinely issue compound financial instruments.

Designation of previously recognized financial instruments. IFRS 1 permits a first-time adopter to designate a financial asset as available-for-sale and a financial instrument (provided it meets certain criteria) as a financial asset or financial liability at fair value through profit or loss at the *date of transition* to IFRS. IAS 39 requires such designation to be made on *initial* recognition.

Fair value measurement of financial assets or financial liabilities at initial recognition. A first-time adopter may apply requirements of IAS 39 regarding (1) the best evidence of the fair value of a financial instrument at initial recognition, and (2) the subsequent measurement of the financial asset or financial liability and the subsequent recognition of gains and losses, prospectively to transactions entered into on or after date of transition to IFRS.

Decommissioning liabilities included in the cost of property, plant, and equipment. IFRS 1 provides that a first-time adopter need not comply with the requirements of IFRIC 1, *Changes in Existing Decommissioning, Restoration and Similar Liabilities,* for changes in such liabilities that occurred before the date of transition to IFRS. Adjustments to liabilities on first-time IFRS adoption arise from events and transactions before the date of transition to IFRS and are generally recognized in retained earnings. For entities using this exemption, certain measurements and disclosures are required. If a first-time adopter uses these exemptions, it should

1. Measure the liability at the date of transition in accordance with IAS 37;
2. Estimate the amount of the liability (that is within the scope of IFRIC 1) that would have been included in the cost of the related asset when the liability was first incurred, by discounting the liability to that date using its best estimate of the historical risk-adjusted discount rate(s) that would have applied for that liability over the intervening period; and
3. Calculate the accumulated depreciation on that amount, as of the date of transition to IFRS, on the basis of the current estimate of the useful life of the asset, using the depreciation policy in accordance with IFRS.

In addition, an entity that uses the exemption in IFRS 1 to value at deemed cost determined under previous GAAP oil and gas assets in the development or production phases in cost centers that include all properties in a large geographical area should, instead of following the above rules (1-3) or IFRIC 1

1. Measure decommissioning, restoration and similar liabilities as of the date of transition to IFRS under IAS 37; and
2. Recognize directly in retained earnings any difference between that amount and the carrying amount of those liabilities at the date of transition determined under previous GAAP.

Service concession arrangements. A first-time adopter may apply the transitional provisions of IFRIC 12.

Borrowing costs. IFRS 1 permits a first-time adopter to apply the transitional provisions included in IAS 23 (as revised in 2007). The effective date in IAS 23 should be interpreted as the later of July 1, 2009, or the date of transition to IFRS.

Based on the experience of EU and Australian companies, exceptions most likely to be elected by first-time adopters include those pertaining to the following: business combinations, deemed cost, employee benefits, share-based payment and cumulative translation differences.

These exemptions from the full retrospective application of IFRS should benefit first-time adopters, by reducing the cost of implementing IFRS. Entities should evaluate potential impacts of electing to use the proposed exemptions, including implications for information systems, taxes, and reported results of operations.

Severe hyperinflation. IFRS 1 permits a first-time adopter to, if it has a functional currency that was, or is, the currency of a hyperinflationary economy, it shall determine whether it was subject to severe hyperinflation before the date of transition to IFRS.

The currency of a hyperinflationary economy is subject to severe hyperinflation if it has both of the following characteristics:

1. A reliable general price index is not available to all entities with transactions and balances in the currency.
2. Exchangeability between the currency and a relatively stable foreign currency does not exist.

The functional currency of an entity ceases to be subject to severe hyperinflation on the functional currency normalization date. That is the date when the functional currency no longer has either, or both, of the characteristics in the above paragraph, or when there is a change in the entity's functional currency to a currency that is not subject to severe hyperinflation. When an entity's date of transition to IFRS is on, or after, the functional currency normalization date, the entity may elect to measure all assets and liabilities held before the functional currency normalization date at fair value on the date of transition to IFRS. The entity may use that fair value as the deemed cost of those assets and liabilities in the opening IFRS statement of financial position.

When the functional currency normalization date falls within a 12-month comparative period, the comparative period may be less than 12 months, provided that a complete set of financial statements as required by IAS 1 is provided for that shorter period.

PRESENTATION AND DISCLOSURE

IFRS 1 does not provide exemptions from the presentation and disclosure requirements in other IFRS.

Comparative information. A first-time adopter must prepare and present an opening statement of financial position as of its transition date, in accordance with IFRS in effect as of the company's first reporting date. At least one year of comparative financial statement information has to be presented. To comply with IAS 1, *Presentation of Financial Statements*, an entity's first IFRS financial statements should include at least three statements of financial position, two statements of comprehensive income, two separate income statements (if presented), two statements of cash flows and two statements of changes in equity and related notes, including comparative information.

If an entity also presents historical summaries of selected data for periods prior to the first period that it presents full comparative information under IFRS, and IFRS does not require the summary data to be in compliance with IFRS, such data should be labeled prominently as not being in compliance with IFRS and also disclose the nature of the adjustment that would make that data IFRS-compliant.

Reconciliations. A first-time adopter must explain how the transition to IFRS affected its reported financial position, financial performance, and cash flows. In order to comply with the above requirement, reconciliation of equity and profit and loss as reported under previous GAAP to IFRS should be included in the entity's first IFRS financial statements. Specifically, an entity should include a reconciliation of its equity reported under previous GAAP to its equity under IFRS, for both of the following dates: (1) the date of transition to IFRS, and (2) the end of the latest period presented in the entity's most recent annual financial statements under previous GAAP. Consequently, IFRS 1 requires the following reconciliations to be presented in first IFRS financial statements:

- Reconciliations of the entity's equity reported under previous GAAP to its equity restated under IFRS for both of the following dates:

  - The date of transition to IFRS; and
  - The end of the latest period presented in the entity's most recent annual financial statements under previous GAAP.

- A reconciliation of the entity's total comprehensive income reported in most recent financial statements under previous GAAP to its comprehensive income under IFRS for the same period. The starting point for that reconciliation should be the amount of comprehensive income reported under previous GAAP for the same period. If an entity did not report such a total, the reconciliation starts with profit or loss under previous GAAP.

- In addition to the reconciliations of its equity and comprehensive income, if the entity recognized or reversed any impairment losses for the first time in preparing its opening IFRS statement of financial position, the disclosures that would have been required in accordance with IAS 36, if the entity had recognized or reversed those impairment losses in the period beginning with the date of transition to IFRS.

Consequently, for an entity adopting IFRS for the first time in its December 31, 2012, financial statements, the reconciliation of equity would be required as of January 1, 2011, and December 31, 2011; and the reconciliation of comprehensive income for the year 2011. These reconciliations must provide sufficient detail enabling users to understand material adjustments to the statement of financial position and comprehensive income. Material adjustments to the statement of cash flows should also be disclosed. For all reconciliations, entities must distinguish the changes in accounting policies from corrections of errors.

Other disclosures. IFRS 1 requires first-time adopters to present other disclosures, including

- Entities that designated a previously recognized financial asset or financial liability as a financial asset or financial liability at fair value through profit or loss, or a financial asset as available for sale, should disclose the fair value designated into each category when this designation was made and the carrying amount in the previous financial statements.
- Entities that recognized or reversed any impairment losses for the first time in preparing opening IFRS statement of financial position need to present the disclosures required by IAS 36 as if those impairment losses or reversals had been recognized in the first period beginning with the date of transition to IFRS.

- Entities that used fair values in their opening IFRS statement of financial position as deemed cost for an item of property, plant, and equipment, an investment property or an intangible asset, should disclose for each line item in the opening IFRS statement of financial position the aggregate of those fair values and the aggregate adjustments made to the carrying amounts reported under previous GAAP.
- Also, entities that apply the exemption to measure oil and gas assets in the development or production phases at the amount determined for the cost center under previous GAAP (and this amount is allocated pro rata to the underlying assets, using reserve volumes or reserve values as of that date) should disclose that fact and the basis on which carrying amounts determined under previous GAAP were allocated.

Interim reporting. An entity adopting IFRS in an interim report (e.g., in quarterly or half-yearly financial statements) that is presented in accordance with IAS 34 is required to comply with IFRS 1, adopt IFRS effective at the end of the interim period, and prepare comparative financial information for interim periods. This is illustrated in the following example:

> Xodus Inc. decides to present its first IFRS interim financial statements for the three months ended March 31, 2012, in accordance with IAS 34, within its first IFRS reporting period ending on December 31, 2011. Consequently, the first reporting date is March 31, and the company will be required to provide comparative IFRS financial information for the quarterly periods. If the company decided to present comparative information for one year only, then the March 31, 2011, comparatives would have to be presented.

In accordance with IFRS 1, entities must be able to generate profit or loss statements also for interim periods and prepare certain reconciliations between amounts reported under previous GAAP and IFRS. In addition to satisfying the requirements of IAS 34, if an entity presented an interim financial report for the comparable interim period of the preceding financial year, the following reconciliations must be included:

- A reconciliation of the entity's equity reported under previous GAAP at the end of that comparable interim period, to its equity restated under IFRS at that date; and
- A reconciliation of the entity's comprehensive income reported under previous GAAP for that comparable interim period (if an entity did not report such a total, reconciliation of profit or loss under previous GAAP) to its restated comprehensive income under IFRS for the same period.

In addition to the reconciliations listed above, an entity's first interim financial report prepared under IAS 34 for part of the period covered by its first IFRS financial statements should also include reconciliations and other disclosures for the fiscal year. Also, IAS 34 requires an entity to disclose "any events or transactions that are material to an understanding of the current interim report."

It is anticipated, and recommended, that transition-period disclosures be presented as a complete package, covering

- A full set of restated financial statements (statements of financial position, comprehensive income, cash flows and changes in equity);
- Notes explaining the restatement, including reconciliations from amounts reported under previous GAAP to restated amounts under IFRS; and
- Notes on the accounting policies to be applied under IFRS and exemptions applied at transition.

Additional footnote detail in the annual financial statements for the first year IFRS is applied may also be useful. At a minimum, however, to provide a thorough understanding of the transition, it will be advisable to identify all the relevant factors considered by the preparer (the reporting entity) in converting to IFRS, in the transition disclosure package itself.

Options *With* and *Within* the Accounting Standards

An entity adopting IFRS for the first time may have a choice among accounting standards as well as accounting policies as a result of (1) options with accounting standards (newly issued IFRS), and (2) options within accounting standards.

In conformity with IFRS 1, an entity should adopt IFRS issued and effective at the reporting date of the entity's first IFRS financial statements. Some IFRS may not be issued as of the date of an entity's transition to IFRS but will be effective at the reporting date. It is also possible to adopt a standard whose application is not yet mandatory for the reporting period but whose early adoption is permitted. The IASB has a number of projects currently on its agenda where standards are expected to be finalized in the near future with application dates beyond that date, including those dealing with such matters as derecognition, liabilities, fair value measurement and accounting for income taxes.

On first-time adoption of IFRS, an entity must choose which accounting policies will be adopted. IFRS require an entity to measure some assets and liabilities at fair value, and some others (for example, pension liabilities) at net realizable value or other forms of current value that reflect explicit current projections of future cash flows. An entity will have a choice between different options of accounting policies within accounting standards that may be applied in preparing its first IFRS financial statements. Examples of areas where options within IFRS exist include cost versus revaluation model of accounting for property, plant, and equipment and intangible assets (IAS 16, IAS 38); cost versus fair value model of accounting for investment property (IAS 40); proportionate consolidation versus equity accounting of jointly controlled entities (IAS 31); and fair value versus proportionate share of the acquiree's identifiable net assets to measure noncontrolling interest in consolidated financial statements (IFRS 3). There are several other areas where there is a choice of accounting policies under IFRS which may have a significant impact on an entity's future results. Once an accounting policy is adopted, opportunities to change may be restricted to justified situations where the change would result in a more appropriate presentation.

In many respects, entities are given a "fresh start" and are required to redetermine their accounting policies under IFRS, fully restating past comparative information. The limited optional exceptions also present some opportunities for entities to determine optimal outcomes.

Transition from US GAAP to IFRS: The Case of DaimlerChrysler

DaimlerChrysler (former Daimler Benz, today Daimler AG) adopted US GAAP in 1998 for purposes of listing on the NYSE. Since it reported under US GAAP in 2005, DaimlerChrysler (DC) was exempted until 2007 from implementing the EU Regulation on adopting IFRS. In May 2007, DC announced that it would sell 80.1% of its stake in the Chrysler Group. Although the company no longer operates the Chrysler Group, it continues to trade on the NYSE and to carry US-issued debt. In November 2007, the SEC eliminated the requirement for foreign registrants reporting under IFRS to reconcile their financial statements to US GAAP. In 2007, DC had to implement IFRS and its 2007 financial statements were prepared in accordance with IFRS, as issued by the IASB and endorsed by the EU.

DC followed the provisions of IFRS 1, *First-Time Adoption of IFRS*, to prepare its opening IFRS statement of financial position at the transition date. In accordance with

IFRS 1, DC's *date of transition* to IFRS, on which the opening IFRS statement of financial position was prepared, was January 1, 2005, since the company presented two years of comparative financial statements (2005 and 2006). As required by IFRS 1, each IFRS effective at the reporting date of DC's first IFRS-compliant financial statements (December 31, 2007) were retrospectively applied.

Certain of DC's IFRS accounting policies applied in the opening statement of financial position differed from its US GAAP policies applied on that date. The resulting adjustments which arose from events and transactions before the date of transition to IFRS were recognized directly in retained earnings (or another category of equity where appropriate, as of January 1, 2005). The impacts of IFRS adoption on the financial statements are presented in Examples 1-2 below along with the footnote, Example 3, taken from the reissued 2006 report which provides explanation of the differences between IFRS and US GAAP that had major impacts on the financial reports.

Example 1: Statement of Financial Position Impacts of DaimlerChrysler's Transition to IFRS

Reconciliations of DaimlerChrysler's equity reported under US GAAP to its equity under IFRS at the transition date (January 1, 2005) and at the end of two comparative periods, 2005 and 2006, presented under US GAAP.

(in millions of €)	*At December 31, 2006*	*At December 31, 2005*	*At January 1, 2005*
Stockholders' equity under US GAAP (as reported)	34,155	36,449	33,522
Adjustments	154	131	169
Stockholders' equity under US GAAP (adjusted)	34,309	36,580	33,691
Minority interest (a)	663	653	909
Stockholders' equity under US GAAP (adjusted) and minority interest	34,972	37,233	34,600
Development costs (b)	5,066	5,142	4,710
Borrowing costs (c)	(843)	(977)	(910)
Investment in EADS (d)	810	1,142	972
Inventories (LIFO) (e)	477	495	349
Transfer of financial assets/leveraged leases (f)	(517)	(556)	(552)
Pension and other postemployment benefits (g)	(752)	(7,670)	(7,728)
Provisions (h)	321	764	678
Other adjustments (i)	(677)	(872)	(740)
Income taxes (j)	(1,408)	1,359	1,392
Total reconciling items	2,477	(1,173)	(1,829)
Equity under IFRS	37,449	36,060	32,771

Example 2: Income Statement Impacts of DaimlerChrysler's Transition to IFRS

Reconciliation of DaimlerChrysler's net income reported under US GAAP to its net profit under IFRS for two comparative periods, 2005 and 2006, presented under US GAAP.

(in millions of €)	*2006*	*2005*
Net income under US GAAP (as reported)	3,227	2,846
Adjustments	19	(43)
Net income under US GAAP (adjusted)	3,246	2,803
Minority interest (a)	56	74
Net income under US GAAP (adjusted) including minority interest	3,302	2,877
Development costs (b)	145	274
Borrowing costs (c)	47	52
Investment in EADS (d)	(468)	165
Inventories (LIFO) (e)	12	55
Transfer of financial assets/leveraged leases (f)	(61)	(4)
Pension and other postemployment benefits (g)	1,558	1,081
Provisions (h)	(374)	24
Other adjustments (i)	212	60
Income taxes (j)	(590)	(369)
Total reconciling items	481	1,338
Net profit under IFRS	3,783	4,215

Example 3: Required Explanation

An explanation of how the transition from US GAAP to IFRS has affected DaimlerChrysler's earnings, financial position and cash flows is presented in the following tables and notes that accompany the tables.

a. **Minority interest.** Under IFRS, minority interests are included in equity, and net profit includes the portion allocated to the minority interest holders. Under US GAAP, minority interests are classified outside of stockholders' equity and net income only includes the income attributable to the shareholders of DaimlerChrysler AG. The amounts of the reconciling items (b) – (j) presented in the tables above also include the amounts allocable to minority interest holders.

b. **Development costs.** Under US GAAP, with the exception of certain software development costs, all development costs are expensed as incurred in accordance with SFAS 2, *Accounting for Research and Development Costs.* Under IFRS, development costs are capitalized as intangible assets if the technical and economic feasibility of a project can be demonstrated. These costs are subsequently amortized on a straight-line basis over the expected useful lives of the products for which they were incurred (i.e., they become a part of the production costs in which the component for which such costs were incurred is used). Once these vehicles are sold, the amortization of development costs is included in cost of sales.

c. **Borrowing costs.** US GAAP requires in SFAS 34, *Capitalization of Interest*, that interest incurred as part of the cost of constructing property, plant, and equipment prior to its use, sale, or lease, be capitalized and amortized over the expected useful lives of the assets. Under IFRS, the Group expenses such interest when incurred in accordance with the option currently provided in IAS 23, *Borrowing Costs.*

d. **Investment in EADS.** Differences between US GAAP and IFRS also affect the carrying amount and DaimlerChrysler's equity in the earnings of EADS, a significant equity investee. DaimlerChrysler accounts for its investment in EADS at a three-month time-lag. Under US GAAP, transactions and events that occur during the intervening period between September 30, 2006, and DaimlerChrysler's reporting date do not result in adjustments, but are disclosed if significant. Under IFRS, the financial information of EADS has to be adjusted for significant transactions and events that occurred after September 30, 2006, but before DaimlerChrysler's reporting date. EADS recorded significant charges in the fourth quarter of 2006, primarily in connection with problems with the A380 program and resulting delivery delays and the decision to launch the industrial program for the new A350XWB aircraft family.

In 2003, under US GAAP, DaimlerChrysler determined that the decline in fair value below the carrying value of its investment in EADS was other than temporary and reduced the carrying value by €1.96 billion to its market value. The fair value was determined using the quoted market price, which approximated €3.5 billion at that time. Under IFRS, the investment would not have been considered impaired because the fair value would have been determined using the higher of fair value or value in use, which at that time exceeded the carrying amount.

e. **Inventories (LIFO).** Under US GAAP, the Group accounted for certain inventories of US subsidiaries using the last-in, first-out principle (LIFO). Under IFRS, the use of LIFO is prohibited, as set forth in IAS 2, *Inventories*.

f. **Transfer of financial assets/leveraged leases.** As part of its financing activities, the Group regularly sells certain financial receivables from its financial services business as well as trade receivables to special-purpose entities (SPEs) and other third parties ("transfer of financial assets"). Under IFRS, the SPEs are typically consolidated by the transferor while under US GAAP these SPEs are considered as "qualifying special-purpose entities" and are not consolidated. In addition, as a result of differences between US GAAP and IFRS criteria for the derecognition of receivables, certain transferred receivables to parties "other than qualifying special-purpose entities" did not qualify for derecognition under IFRS while they are derecognized under US GAAP.

In the US GAAP financial statements, transferred receivables meeting the derecognition conditions are removed from the balance sheet, any consideration received including retained interests is recognized, and gains or losses from the sale of such receivables are recognized in income. In contrast, in the IFRS consolidated balance sheets as of December 31, 2006 and 2005, receivables of €21.7 billion and €21.3 billion (primarily receivables from financial services), respectively, and liabilities of €21.7 billion and €21.3 billion (primarily financing liabilities), respectively, were reported which are not recorded on the balance sheets in accordance with US GAAP.

Under US GAAP, investments in leveraged leases are recorded on a net basis, (i.e. nonrecourse financing has been offset against the rental receivable of the lessor). The investment in leveraged leases is included in the line item receivables from financial services in the consolidated balance sheets. Revenue from leveraged leases is recognized under the effective interest method using an after-tax rate of return on the net investment. Under IFRS, investments in leveraged leases are generally recorded on a gross basis on the consolidated balance sheet as receivables from financial services, including the unguaranteed residual value, while the related nonrecourse debt is presented as a financial liability. Interest on the receivable is recognized as revenue based on a constant rate of return before taxes, at the rate implicit in the lease. As a result, in the IFRS consolidated balance sheets as of December 31, 2006 and 2005, the Group reported additional receivables from financial services of €1.5 billion and €2.0 billion and liabilities of €1.8 billion and €2.3 billion, respectively, compared to the US GAAP carrying amounts. In addition, certain investments in leveraged cross-border leases are not accounted for as leases at all under IFRS, but represent financial instruments for which revenue is recognized based on their rate of return before income taxes.

g. **Pensions and other postemployment benefits.** The Group recorded directly in equity (retained earnings) in the opening IFRS balance sheet as of January 1, 2005, the unrecognized actuarial net gains and losses relating to the Group's pension and other postemployment benefit plans.

The Group also adopted the recognition option for actuarial gains and losses provided under IAS 19, *Employee Benefits*, under which the Group does not immediately recognize actuarial gains and losses in income. Instead, the actuarial gains and losses are only recognized in the income statement starting in the following year when they exceed 10% of the greater of the present value of defined benefit obligations or the fair value of the plan assets applied on a plan-to-plan basis (corridor). While the same policy is applied under US GAAP, the amount of the corridor is different as a result of the election made at transition date to IFRS.

Under US GAAP, SFAS 87, *Employers' Accounting for Pensions*, required an additional minimum pension liability in case the accrued pension liability was lower than the excess of the accumulated benefit obligation (not including salary increases) over the fair value of plan assets as of the date of the opening balance sheet (January 1, 2005) and as of December 31, 2005. In this case, an intangible asset was capitalized up to the amount of unrecognized prior service cost from retroactive plan amendments, with any excess recognized in other comprehensive income (loss). IFRS does not provide for the recognition of any additional minimum pension liability.

As of December 31, 2006, the Group adopted the recognition provisions of SFAS 158, *Employers' Accounting for Defined Benefit Pension and Other Postretirement Plans,* under US GAAP. According to these provisions, the Group recognized the funded status of its pension and other postretirement benefit plans on its balance sheet as of December 31, 2006, with an offsetting amount recorded in accumulated other comprehensive income (loss).

Plan amendments resulted in an increase in the projected benefit obligation and a decrease in the accumulated postemployment benefit obligation. Under US GAAP, these changes are amortized over the remaining years of service, or estimated life expectancy for inactive employees, beginning in the following financial year. Under IFRS, the changes regarding vested benefits are recognized immediately in the income statement; the portion for nonvested benefits is required to be amortized until the obligations become vested.

h. **Provisions.** In accordance with IFRS, long-term provisions must be discounted to their present value if the effect from discounting is material. Under US GAAP, discounting is only permissible for specific types of provisions if the amount and timing of the cash flows can be reasonably predicted.

This item also includes differences between US GAAP and IFRS relative to the accounting for early retirement agreements concluded in the framework of the German Altersteilzeit benefits. Under US GAAP, all payments during the inactive phase are accrued with a corresponding charge to earnings over the period from reaching an early retirement agreement to the end of the employment. Under IFRS, however, the incremental benefit payments are fully recognized as expenses at the time the early retirement agreement is signed. In 2006, DaimlerChrysler changed its estimates of the effects of employee bonuses and other benefits upon adoption of EITF 05-5, *Accounting for Early Retirement or Postemployment Programs with Specific Features (Such As Terms Specified in Altersteilzeit Early Retirement Arrangements)*, and recognized a gain of €166 million, or €102 million, net of taxes.

i. **Other adjustments.** Other adjustments consist of a number of individually small different recognition and measurement provisions, including the effects of the elections to adjust retained earnings at the transition date for accumulated foreign currency translation differences upon transition to IFRS on gains or losses from disposals of foreign operations, the recognition of gains from sales of real estate leased back under the terms of operating leases, puttable minority interest and other items.

j. **Income taxes.** The adjustments for income taxes are mainly due to the tax effects of differences between IFRS and US GAAP.

This reconciliation item also includes adjustments owing to the use of different tax rates in the elimination of intercompany profits, different valuation allowances on deferred taxes and differences in recognition of uncertain income tax benefits.

For the elimination of intercompany profits, the deferred tax effects under IFRS are calculated by using the buyer's tax rate as set forth in IAS 12, *Income Taxes*, whereas under US GAAP, SFAS 109, *Accounting for Income Taxes*, requires the use of the seller's tax rate.

The differing valuation allowances, mainly for state and local taxes in the United States of America, are a result of the varying temporary differences under US GAAP compared to IFRS.

Until December 31, 2006, DaimlerChrysler recognized in its US GAAP financial statements the benefit of an uncertain income tax position only when it was probable that the tax position would be sustained based solely on the technical merits of the position and the application of the law. Under IFRS, the potential tax exposure from an uncertain income tax position has to be determined by using the best estimate of the probable amount which results in the recognition of the benefit from a tax position when it is more likely than not that it will be realized.

Information on the statement of cash flows. The presentation of cash flows between IFRS and US GAAP differs primarily because of investments in development projects which are capitalized and reported as investing activities under IFRS, accounting for transfers of receivables which fail derecognition under IFRS and are presented as a secured borrowing under IFRS and inventory-related operating leases between DaimlerChrysler and a customer which are presented as operating activities under IFRS.

(in millions of €)	*2006*	*2005*
Cash provided by operating activities under US GAAP	14,016	12,353
Difference	321	(1,321)
Cash provided by operating activities under IFRS	14,337	11,032
Cash used for investing activities under US GAAP	(14,581)	(11,222)
Differences	(1,276)	985
Cash used for investing activities under IFRS	(15,857)	(10,237)
Cash provided by (used for) financing activities under US GAAP	496	(1,513)
Differences	1,900	229
Cash provided by (used for) financing activities under IFRS	2,396	(1,284)

Example 4: First-time adoption by Meikles Group

2. Basis of Preparation

The Group's financial statements have been prepared in accordance with International Financial Reporting Standards (IFRS). The financial statements are prepared from statutory records that are maintained under the historical cost convention as modified by the revaluation of property, plant, and equipment, biological assets, and financial instruments which are measured at fair value in the opening statement of financial position.

2.1 Transition to IFRS

The Group is resuming presentation of IFRS financial statements after the Group issued financial statements in the prior reporting period ended December 31, 2009, which could not include an explicit and unreserved statement of compliance with IFRS due to the effects of severe hyperinflation. As discussed in note 2.5, the group has early adopted the amendments to IFRS 1 and is therefore applying that standard in returning to compliance with IFRS. The Group's functional currency for the period before January 1, 2009, the Zimbabwe dollar (ZW$) was subject to sever hyperinflation because it had both the following characteristics:

- A reliable general price index was not available to all entities with transactions and balances in ZW$ because the Zimbabwe Central Statistical office did not release the consumer price indices from August 1, 2008, while the existence of market distortions made measurement of inflation by alternative means unreliable; and
- Exchangeability between the ZW$ and a relatively stable foreign currency did not exist.

The Group's functional currency ceased to be subject to severe hyperinflation from January 1, 2009, when the Group changed its functional currency from ZW$ to US$.

2.2 Exemption for Fair Value as Deemed Cost

The Group elected to measure certain items of property, plant, and equipment, biological assets, bank balances and cash, inventories, other financial assets, other financial liabilities, and trade and other payables at fair value and to use the fair values as the deemed cost of those assets and liabilities in the opening statement of financial position as of January 1, 2009.

2.3 Comparative Financial Information

The financial statements comprise three statements of financial position, and two statements of comprehensive income, two statements of changes in equity and two statements of cash flows, as a result of the retrospective application of the amendments to IFRS 1. The comparative statements of comprehensive income, changes in equity and cash flows are for twelve months.

2.4 Reconciliation to Previous Basis of Preparation

The Group's financial statements for the prior period ended December 31, 2009, claimed compliance with IFRS, except certain of the requirements of IAS 1, *Presentation of Financial Statements*, IAS 21, *The Effects of Changes in Foreign Exchange Rates*, and IAS 29, *Financial Reporting in Hyperinflationary Economies*. Certain prior year errors were identified during the period and a reconciliation of the amounts previously stated in the December 31, 2009 financial statements and the comparative amounts as presented in this report is given in Note 32.

32. Prior Year Adjustments

32.1 Opening balances of property, plant, and equipment

During the period errors were identified on the January 1, 2009 carrying amounts of certain property, plant, and equipment for the stores and agricultural operations. The assets were omitted from the valuation exercise carried out at January 1, 2009, when the functional currency was changed from ZW$ to US$. This has been corrected by the restatement of the 2009 comparatives included in these financial statements.

32.2 Opening Balances of Biological Assets, Other Receivables and Nursery Stocks

During the period, it was discovered that the carrying amounts of certain biological assets of the agricultural segment were understated while certain receivables and nursery stocks were incorrectly valued at January 1, 2009, resulting in a misstatement of the opening carrying amounts. The error has been corrected in the comparative statements of financial position.

Presented below are only those statements of comprehensive income and statements of financial position items which have been impacted by the prior year adjustments.

32.3 Prior Year Costs Reclassification

Certain prior year costs have been reclassified to conform to current year presentation.

34. Prior Year Adjustments (continued)

Statement of comprehensive income

	December 31, 2009 previously stated US $	Adjustments of property, plant, and equipment US $	Adjustments to biological assets US $	December 31, 2009 restated US $
Other operating costs	(16,067,056)	(862,866)	--	(16,929,922)
Fair value adjustments	(35,712)	--	2,116,946	2,081.234
Income tax	5,449,453	384,330	(545,114)	5,288,669
Loss for the year from continuing operations	(3,747,889)	(478,536)	1,571,832	(2,654,593)
Total comprehensive loss for the year	(3,824,645)	(478,536)	1,571.832	(2,731.349)

Statements of financial position

January 1, 2009	January 1, 2009 as previously stated US $	Adjustments of property, plant and equipment US $	Adjustments to inventories US $	Adjustments to trade and other receivables US $	January 1, 2009 restated US $
Property, plant and equipment	89,650,542	4,720,754	--	--	94,371,296
Inventories	5,565,764	--	(502,194)	--	5,063,570
Trade and other receivables	10,280,439	--	--	(152,007)	10,128,432
Total assets	200,489,141	4,720,754	(502,194)	(152,007)	204,555,694
Non-distributable reserves	(148,118,994)	(3,476,943)	502,194	152,007	(150,941.736)
Deferred tax liability	(23,074,660)	(1,243,811)	--	--	(24,318,471)
Total equity and liabilities	(200,489,141)	(4,720,754)	502,194	152,007	(204,555,694)

December 31, 2009	December 31, 2009 as previously stated US $	January 1, 2009 net adjustments as above US $	Adjustments of property, plant, and equipment US $	Adjustments to biological assets US $	December 31, 2009 restated US $
Property, plant, and equipment	76,672,807	4,720,754	(862,866)	--	80,530,695
Biological assets	4,193,614	--	--	2,116,946	6,310,560
Inventory	17,617,464	(502,194)	--	--	17,115,270
Trade and other receivables	7,485,896	(152,007)	--	--	7,333,889
Total assets	271,429,262	4,066,553	(862,866)	2,116,946	276,749,895
Nondistributable reserves	(107,160,978)	(2,822,742)	--	--	(109,983,720)
Accumulated loss	22,418,679	--	478,536	(1,571,832)	21,325,383
Deferred tax	(13,941,913)	(1,243,811)	384,330	(545,114)	(15,346,508)
Total equity and liabilities	(271,429,262)	(4,066,553)	862,866	(2,116,946)	(276,749,895)

APPENDIX A:
DISCLOSURE CHECKLIST

This checklist provides a reference to the disclosures common to the financial statements of entities that are complying with International Financial Reporting Standards (IFRS), including those set forth by the International Accounting Standards (IAS) promulgated by the IASC earlier. These disclosures are set forth by IFRS/IAS and IFRIC/SIC and are effective for periods beginning after December 31, 2010. Certain changes have been mandated but will not become mandatorily effective until years beginning in 2011, and are identified as such. Changes which have been proposed but which have not been promulgated are not incorporated in this checklist. Superseded disclosures have been excluded.

DISCLOSURE CHECKLIST INDEX

General

Statement of Financial Position

GENERAL

A. Identification of Financial Statements and Basis of Reporting

1. The financial statements should be identified clearly and distinguished from other information in the same published document. In addition, the following information shall be displayed prominently, and repeated when it is necessary for a proper understanding of the information presentation:

   a. Name of the entity whose financial statements are being presented, or other means of identification, and any change in that information from the preceding statement of financial position;

   b. Disclosure whether the financial statements cover the individual entity or a group of entities;

   c. The accounting policies, including measurement bases and other policies necessary to an understanding of the financial statements;

   d. Presentation currency as defined in IAS 21;

   e. When presentation currency differs from functional currency, state this fact, disclose the functional currency and the reason for using a different presentation currency;

   f. Level of rounding used in presentation of the figures in the financial statements;

   g. Statement of financial position date or the period covered by the financial statements, whichever is appropriate to that component of financial statement; and

   h. Identify each component of the financial statements.

   (IAS 1, Para 49, 51 & 112; IAS 21, Para 53)

2. An entity shall disclose the following, if not disclosed elsewhere in information published in the financial statements:

   a. Entity's country of incorporation, domicile and legal form;

   b. Address of its registered office or principal place of business if different from the registered office;

   c. Name of the reporting entity's parent and the ultimate parent of the group;

   d. Description of the nature of the entity's operations and its principal activities; and

   e. If it is a limited life entity, information regarding the length of its life.

   (IAS 1, Para 138)

3. An entity shall disclose the following relating to the company's management of capital to enable users of its financial statements to evaluate the entity's objectives, policies and processes for managing capital:

   a. Qualitative information regarding its objectives, policies and processes to manage capital;

   b. A summary of the quantitative data concerning what the company manages as capital;

   c. Any changes in (a) and (b) from the previous period;

   d. Whether during the period it complied with any externally imposed capital requirements to which it is subject; and

   e. When the entity has not complied with such externally imposed capital requirements, the consequences of such noncompliance.

(The entity bases these disclosures on the information provided internally to key management personnel.)

(IAS 1, Para 134 and 135)

B.   Compliance with International Financial Reporting Standards

1. Financial statements shall present fairly the financial position, financial performance and the cash flows of the entity. Fair presentation requires the faithful presentation of the transactions, other events, and conditions in accordance with the definitions and recognition criteria for assets, liabilities, income, and expenses set out in the *Framework*. The application of IFRS, with additional disclosure when necessary, is presented to result in financial statements that achieve a fair presentation.

(IAS 1, Para 15)

2. An entity whose financial statements comply with IFRS shall make an explicit and unreserved statement of such compliance in the notes. Financial statements shall not be described as complying with IFRS unless they comply with all the requirements of IFRS.

(IAS 1, Para 16)

3. In virtually all circumstances, an entity achieves a fair presentation by compliance with applicable IFRS. A fair presentation also requires an entity

    a. To select and apply accounting policies in accordance with IAS 8, *Accounting Policies, Changes in Accounting Estimates, and Errors*. IAS 8 sets out a hierarchy of authoritative guidance that management considers in the absence of an IFRS that specifically applies to an item;
    b. To present information, including accounting policies, in a manner that provides relevant, reliable, comparable and understandable information;
    c. To provide additional disclosures when compliance with the specific requirements in IFRS is insufficient to enable users to understand the impact of particular transactions, other events and conditions on the entity's financial position and financial performance.

(IAS 1, Para 17)

4. An entity cannot rectify inappropriate accounting policies either by disclosure of the accounting policies used or by notes or explanatory material.

(IAS 1, Para 18)

5. In extremely rare circumstances in which management concludes that compliance with a requirement in a Standard or an Interpretation would be so misleading that it would conflict with the objective of financial statements set out in the *Framework*, the entity shall depart from that requirement in the manner set out in IAS 1, paragraph 20 (see below) if the relevant regulatory framework requires, or otherwise does not prohibit, such a departure.

(IAS 1, Para 19)

6. When an entity departs from a requirement of a Standard or an Interpretation in accordance with IAS 1, paragraph 17, it shall disclose

a. That management has concluded that the financial statements present fairly the entity's financial position, financial performance and cash flows;

b. That it had complied with applicable Standards and Interpretations, except that it had departed from a particular requirement to achieve a fair presentation;

c. The title of the Standard or Interpretation from which the entity has departed, the nature of the departure, including the treatment that the Standard or Interpretation would require, the reason why the treatment would be so misleading in the circumstances that it would conflict with the objective of financial statements set out in the *Framework*, and the treatment adopted; and

d. For each period presented, the financial impact of the departure on each item in the financial statements that would have been reported in complying with the requirement.

(IAS 1, Para 20)

7. When an entity has departed from a requirement of an IFRS in a prior period, and that departure affects the amounts recognized in the financial statements for the current period, it shall make the disclosures set out in IAS 1, Paragraphs 20(c) and (d). This applies when an entity departed in a prior period from a requirement in an IFRS for the measurement of assets or liabilities and that departure affects the measurement of changes in assets and liabilities recognized in the current period's financial statements.

(IAS 1, Para 21, 22)

8. When in extremely rare circumstances in which management concludes that compliance with a requirement of the Standard or Interpretation would be misleading and that it would conflict with the objective of the financial statements set out in the *Framework*, but the regulatory framework prohibits departure from the requirement, the entity shall, to the maximum extent possible, reduce the perceived misleading aspects of compliance by disclosing the following:

a. The title of the Standard or Interpretation in question, the nature of the requirement, and the reason why the management has concluded that complying with the requirement is so misleading in the circumstances that it conflicts with the objective of the financial statement set out in the *Framework*; and

b. For each period presented, the adjustment to each item of the financial statements that the management has concluded would be necessary to achieve a fair presentation.

(IAS 1, Para 23)

9. For the purpose of paragraphs 19–23, an item of information would conflict with the objective of financial statements when it does not represent faithfully the transactions, other events and conditions that it either purports to represent or could reasonably be expected to represent and, consequently, it would be likely to influence economic decisions made by users of financial statements. When assessing whether complying with a specific requirement in an IFRS would be so misleading that it would conflict with the objective of financial statements set out in the *Framework*, management considers

a. Why the objective of financial statements is not achieved in the particular circumstances; and

b. How the entity's circumstances differ from those of other entities that comply with the requirement. If other entities in similar circumstances comply with the requirement, there is a rebuttable presumption that the entity's compliance with the requirement would not be so misleading that it would conflict with the objective of financial statements set out in the *Framework.*

(IAS 1, Para 24)

C. Changes in Accounting Policies, Changes in Accounting Estimates and Errors

1. When initial application of a Standard or an Interpretation has an effect on the current period or any prior period, it would have such an effect except that it is impracticable to determine the amount of the adjustment, or might have an effect on future periods, an entity shall disclose

   a. The title of the Standard or Interpretation;
   b. When applicable, that the change in accounting policy is made in accordance with its transitional provisions;
   c. The nature of change in accounting policy;
   d. When applicable, a description of the transitional provisions;
   e. When applicable, the transitional provisions that might have an effect on future periods;
   f. For current period and each prior period presented, to the extent practicable, the amount of the adjustment

      (1) For each financial statement line item affected; and
      (2) If IAS 33, *Earnings per Share,* applies to the entity, for basic and diluted earnings per share;

   g. The amount of the adjustment relating to periods before those presented, to the extent practicable; and
   h. If retrospective application required by IAS 8, paragraph 19(a) or (b) is impracticable for a particular prior period, or for periods before those presented, the circumstances that led to the existence of that condition and a description of how and from when the change in accounting policy has been applied.

   (Financial statements of subsequent periods need not repeat these disclosures.)

(IAS 8, Para 28)

2. When a voluntary change in accounting policy has an effect on the current period or any prior period, would have an effect on that period except that it is impracticable to determine the amount of the adjustment, or might have an effect on future periods, an entity shall disclose

   a. The nature of change in accounting policy;
   b. The reasons why applying the new accounting policy provides reliable and more relevant information;
   c. For the current period and each prior period presented, to the extent practicable, the amount of the adjustment

      (1) For each financial statement line item affected; and
      (2) If IAS 33 applies to the entity, for basic and diluted earning per share;

d. The amount of the adjustment relating to periods before those presented, the circumstances that led to the existence of that condition and description of how and from when the change in accounting policy has been applied; and

e. If retrospective application is impracticable for a particular prior period, or for periods before those presented, the circumstances that led to the existence of that condition and a description of how and from when the change in accounting policy has been applied.

(Financial statements of subsequent periods need not repeat these disclosures.)

(IAS 8, Para 29)

3. When an entity has applied a new Standard or Interpretation that has been issued but is not yet effective, the entity shall disclose

a. This fact; and

b. Known or reasonably estimable information relevant to assessing the possible impact that application of the new Standard or Interpretation will have on entity's financial statements in the period of application.

(IAS 8, Para 30)

4. In complying with paragraph 30, an entity considers disclosing

a. The title of the new IFRS;

b. The nature of the impending change or changes in accounting policy;

c. The date by which application of the IFRS is required;

d. The date as at which it plans to apply the IFRS initially; and

e. Either

(1) A discussion of the impact that initial application of the IFRS is expected to have on the entity's financial statements; or

(2) If that impact is not known or reasonably estimable, a statement to that effect.

(IAS 8, Para 31)

5. An entity shall disclose the nature and amount of a change in an accounting estimate that has an effect in the current period or is expected to have an effect in future periods when it is impracticable to estimate that effect.

(IAS 8, Para 39)

6. If the amount of the effect in future periods is not disclosed because estimating it is impracticable, an entity shall disclose that fact.

(IAS 8, Para 40)

7. In correcting material prior period errors, as outlined in IAS 1, paragraph 42, an entity shall disclose the following:

a. The nature of the prior period error;

b. For each prior period presented, to the extent practicable, the amount of correction

(1) For each financial statement line item affected;

(2) If IAS 33 applies to the entity, for basic and diluted earnings per share;

   c. The amount of correction at the beginning of the earliest prior period presented; and

   d. If retrospective restatement is impracticable for a particular prior period, the circumstances that led to the existence of that condition and description of how and from when the error has been corrected.

(Financial statements of the subsequent periods need not repeat these disclosures.)

(IAS 8, Para 49)

8. A prior period error shall be corrected by retrospective restatement except to the extent that it is impractical to determine either the period-specific effects or the cumulative effect of the error.

(IAS 8, Para 43)

9. When it is impracticable to determine the period-specific effects of an error on comparative information for one or more prior periods presented, the entity shall restate the opening balances of assets, liabilities and equity for the earliest period for which retrospective restatement is practical.

(IAS 8, Para 44)

10. When it is impracticable to determine the cumulative effect, at the beginning of the current period, of an error on all prior periods, the entity shall restate the comparative information to correct the error prospectively from the earliest date practicable.

(IAS 8, Para 45)

11. In some circumstances, it is impracticable to adjust comparative information for one or more prior periods to achieve comparability with the current period. For example, data may not have been collected in the prior period(s) in a way that allows either retrospective application of a new accounting policy (including, for the purpose of paragraphs 51–53, its prospective application to prior periods) or retrospective restatement to correct a prior period error, and it may be impracticable to recreate the information.

(IAS 8, Para 50)

12. It is frequently necessary to make estimates in applying an accounting policy to elements of financial statements recognized or disclosed in respect of transactions, other events or conditions. Estimation is inherently subjective, and estimates may be developed after the reporting period. Developing estimates is potentially more difficult when retrospectively applying an accounting policy or making a retrospective restatement to correct a prior period error, because of the longer period of time that might have passed since the affected transaction, other event, or condition occurred. However, the objective of estimates related to prior periods remains the same as for estimates made in the current period, namely, for the estimate to reflect the circumstances that existed when the transaction, other event, or condition occurred.

(IAS 8, Para 51)

13. Therefore, retrospectively applying a new accounting policy or correcting a prior period error requires distinguishing information that

a. Provides evidence of circumstances that existed on the date(s) as at which the transaction, other event, or condition occurred, and

b. Would have been available when the financial statements for that prior period were authorized for issue from other information. For some types of estimates (e.g., an estimate of fair value not based on an observable price or observable inputs), it is impracticable to distinguish these types of information. When retrospective application or retrospective restatement would require making a significant estimate for which it is impossible to distinguish these two types of information, it is impracticable to apply the new accounting policy or correct the prior period error retrospectively.

(IAS 8, Para 52)

14. Hindsight should not be used when applying a new accounting policy to, or correcting amounts for, a prior period, either in making assumptions about what management's intentions would have been in a prior period or estimating the amounts recognized, measured, or disclosed in a prior period. For example, when an entity corrects a prior period error in calculating its liability for employees' accumulated sick leave in accordance with IAS 19, *Employee Benefits*, it disregards information about an unusually severe influenza season during the next period that became available after the financial statements for the prior period were authorized for issue. The fact that significant estimates are frequently required when amending comparative information presented for prior periods does not prevent reliable adjustment or correction of the comparative information.

(IAS 8, Para 53)

D. Related-Party Disclosures

1. Relationships between parents and subsidiaries shall be disclosed irrespective of whether there have been transactions between those related parties. An entity shall disclose the name of the entity's parent and, if different, the ultimate controlling party. If neither the entity's parent nor the ultimate controlling party produces financial statements available for public use, the name of the next most senior parent that does so shall also be disclosed.

(IAS 24, Para 13)

2. If there have been transactions between related parties, an entity shall disclose the nature of the related-party relationship as well as the information about the transactions and outstanding balances necessary for an understanding of the potential effect of the relationship on the financial statements. These disclosure requirements are in addition to the requirements in IAS 24, paragraph 16, to disclose key management personnel compensation. At a minimum, disclosure shall include

a. The nature of related-party relationships;

b. Types of transactions (for example, goods or services sold/purchased, management services, directors' remuneration, loans, and guarantees);

c. The amount of the transactions;

d. The amount of outstanding balances; and

   (1) Their terms and conditions, including whether they are secured, and the nature of the consideration to be provided in settlement; and

   (2) Details of any guarantees given or received;

e. Provisions for doubtful debt related to the amount of outstanding balances; and

f. The expense recognized during the period in respect of bad or doubtful debts due from related parties.

The disclosure required by above paragraph shall be made separately for each of the following categories:

(1) The parent;
(2) Entities with joint control or significant influence over the entity;
(3) Subsidiaries;
(4) Associates;
(5) Joint ventures in which the entity is a venturer;
(6) Key management personnel of the entity or its parent; and
(7) Other related parties.

(IAS 24, Para 18 & 19)

3. Items of similar nature may be disclosed in aggregate except when separate disclosure is necessary for an understanding of the effects of the related-party transactions on the financial statements of the entity.

(IAS 24, Para 24)

4. An entity shall disclose key management personnel compensation in total and for each of the following categories:

a. Short-term employee benefits;
b. Postemployment benefits;
c. Other long-term benefits;
d. Termination benefits; and
e. Share-based payments.

(IAS 24, Para 17)

5. A reporting entity is exempt from the disclosure requirements of paragraph 18 in relation to related-party transactions and outstanding balances, including commitments, with

a. A government that has control, joint control or significant influence over the reporting entity; and
b. Another entity that is a related party because the same government has control, joint control or significant influence over both the reporting entity and the other entity.

(IAS 24, Para 25)

6. If a reporting entity applies the exemption in paragraph 25, it shall disclose the following about the transaction and related outstanding balances referred to in paragraph 25:

a. The name of the government and the nature of its relationship with the reporting entity (e.g., control, joint control or significant influence);
b. The following information in sufficient detail to enable users of the entity's financial statements to understand the effect of related-party transactions on its financial statements:

(1) The nature and amount of each individually significant transaction; and

(2) For other transactions that are collectively, but not individually, significant, a qualitative or quantitative indication of their extent. Types of transactions include those listed in paragraph 21.

(IAS 24, Para 26)

7. In using its judgment to determine the level of detail to be disclosed in accordance with the requirements in paragraph 26 (b), the reporting entity shall consider the closeness of the related-party relationship and other factors relevant in establishing the level of significance of the transaction such as whether it is

a. Significant in terms of size;
b. Carried out on nonmarket terms;
c. Outside normal day-to-day business operations, such as the purchase and sale of business;
d. Disclosed to regulatory or supervisory authorities;
e. Reported to senior management;
f. Subject to shareholder approval.

(IAS 24, Para 27)

8. To enable users of financial statements to form a view about the effects of related-party relationships on an entity, it is appropriate to disclose the related-party relationship when control exists, irrespective of whether there have been transactions between the related parties.

(IAS 24, Para 14)

E. Contingent Liabilities and Contingent Assets

1. An entity should disclose for each class of contingent liability, unless the possibility of any outflow in settlement is remote, a brief description of the nature of the contingent liability. If practicable, an entity should also disclose an estimate of its financial effects, an indication of the uncertainties relating to the amount or timing of the outflow, and the possibility of any reimbursement.

(IAS 37, Para 86)

2. An entity should show a brief description of the nature of the contingent assets at the statement of financial position date, where an inflow of economic benefits is probable. Where practical, an estimate of the financial effect should be disclosed.

(IAS 37, Para 89)

3. Where an entity does not disclose any information required by IAS 37, para 86, and IAS 37, para 89, because it is not practical to do so, that fact should be disclosed.

(IAS 37, Para 91)

a. When provisions and contingent liabilities arise from a single event, the relationship between the provision and the contingent liability should be made clear.

(IAS 37, Para 88)

b. Disclose contingencies arising from postemployment benefit obligations and termination benefits.

(IAS 19, Para 125 & 141)

4. In extremely rare circumstances, if disclosures of some or all of the information required by IAS 37, paragraphs 84-89, would prejudice seriously the position of the entity in a dispute with other parties, on the subject matter of the provision, contingent liability, or contingent asset, an entity need not disclose such information. Instead, in such cases it should disclose the general nature of the dispute, along with the fact that, and reason why, the information has not been disclosed by the entity.

(IAS 37, Para 92)

F. Events After the Date of the Statement of Financial Position

1. When nonadjusting events after the statement of financial position date are so significant that nondisclosure would affect the ability of the users of the financial statements to make proper evaluations and decisions, an entity should disclose the nature of the event and an estimate of its financial effect. Such disclosure is required for each significant category of nonadjusting post-balance-sheet event. If such an estimate is not possible, a statement to that effect should be made.

(IAS 10, Para 21)

2. The date when the financial statements were authorized for issue and who gave the authorization should be disclosed by an entity. If the entity's owners or others have the power to amend the financial statements after issuance, the entity should disclose that fact.

(IAS 10, Para 17)

3. If an entity receives information after the statement of financial position date that existed at the statement of financial position date, the entity should update the disclosures that relate to these conditions, based on the new information received.

(IAS 10, Para 19)

4. In respect of loans classified as current liabilities, if the following events occur between the statement of financial position date and the date financial statements are authorized for issue, those events qualify for disclosures of nonadjusting events in accordance with IAS 10:

   a. Refinancing on a long-term basis;
   b. Rectification of a breach of a long-term loan agreement; and
   c. The receipt from the lender of a period of grace to rectify a breach of a long-term loan agreement ending at least twelve months after the statement of financial position date.

(IAS 1, Para 76)

5. Disclose income tax consequences of dividends proposed or declared after the statement of financial position date, but before the financial statements were authorized for issue; if payable at a rate different than normal due to being paid out as dividends, disclose nature of income tax effects and estimated amount.

(IAS 12, Para 81 & 82)

6. If an entity declares dividends to equity shareholders after the balance sheet date, the entity shall not recognize those dividends as a liability at the statement of financial position date.

(IAS 10, Para 12)

G. Comparative Information

1. In the case of provisions, comparative information is not required for the reconciliation of carrying amount at the beginning and end of the period.

   (IAS 37, Para 84)

2. Except when a Standard or an Interpretation permits or requires otherwise, comparative information shall be disclosed in respect of the previous period for all amounts reported in the financial statements. Comparative information shall be included for narrative and descriptive information when it is relevant to an understanding of the current period's financial statements.

   (IAS 1, Para 38)

3. An entity disclosing comparative information shall present, as a minimum, two statements of financial position, two of each of the other statements, and related notes. When an entity applies an accounting policy retrospectively or makes a retrospective restatement of items in its financial statements or when it reclassifies items in its financial statements, it shall present, as a minimum, three statements of financial position, two of each of the other statements, and related notes. An entity presents statements of financial position as at

   a. The end of the current period;
   b. The end of the previous period (which is the same as the beginning of the current period); and
   c. The beginning of the earliest comparative period.

   (IAS 1, Para 39)

4. In some cases, narrative information provided in the financial statements for the previous period(s) continues to be relevant in the current period. For example, an entity discloses in the current period details of a legal dispute whose outcome was uncertain at the end of the immediately preceding reporting period and that is yet to be resolved. Users benefit from information that the uncertainty existed at the end of the immediately preceding reporting period, and about the steps that have been taken during the period to resolve the uncertainty.

   (IAS 1, Para 40)

5. When the presentation and classification of items in the financial statements is amended, comparative amounts should be reclassified unless the reclassification is impracticable. When comparative amounts are reclassified, an entity shall disclose

   a. The nature of the reclassification;
   b. The amount of each item or class of items that is reclassified; and
   c. The reason for the reclassification.

   (IAS 1, Para 41)

6. When it is impracticable to reclassify comparative amounts, an entity shall disclose

   a. The reason for not reclassifying the amounts; and
   b. The nature of the adjustment that would have been made if the amounts had been reclassified.

   (IAS 1, Para 42)

H. Going Concern

1. When preparing financial statements, management shall make an assessment of an entity's ability to continue as a going concern. An entity shall prepare financial statements on a going concern basis unless management either intends to liquidate the entity or to cease trading, or has no realistic alternative but to do so. When management is aware, in making its assessment, of material uncertainties related to events or conditions that may cast significant doubt upon the entity's ability to continue as a going concern, the entity shall disclose those uncertainties. When an entity does not prepare financial statements on a going concern basis, it shall disclose that fact, together with the basis on which it prepared the financial statements and the reason why the entity is not regarded as a going concern.

(IAS 1, Para 25 and IAS 10, Para 14)

2. In assessing whether the going concern assumption is appropriate, management takes into account all available information about the future, which is at least, but is not limited to, twelve months from the end of the reporting period. The degree of consideration depends on the facts in each case. When an entity has a history of profitable operations and ready access to financial resources, the entity may reach a conclusion that the going concern basis of accounting is appropriate without detailed analysis. In other cases, management may need to consider a wide range of factors relating to current and expected profitability, debt repayment schedules and potential sources of replacement financing before it can satisfy itself that the going concern basis is appropriate.

(IAS 1, Para 26)

I. Current/Noncurrent Distinction

1. An entity shall present current and noncurrent assets, and current and noncurrent liabilities, as separate classifications on the face of the statement of financial position except when a presentation based on liquidity provides information that is reliable and more relevant. When that exception applies, all assets and liabilities shall be presented broadly in order of liquidity.

(IAS 1, Para 60)

2. Whether an entity chooses a classified presentation of the statement of financial position with current/noncurrent distinction, or it presents an unclassified statement of financial position, it should disclose, for each asset and liability item that combines amounts expected to be recovered or settled both before and after twelve months from the statement of financial position date, the amount expected to be recovered or settled after more than twelve months.

(IAS 1, Para 61)

3. When an entity supplies goods or services within a clearly identifiable operating cycle, separate classification of current and noncurrent assets and liabilities in the statement of financial position provides useful information by distinguishing the net assets that are continuously circulating as working capital from those used in the entity's long-term operations. It also highlights assets that are expected to be realized within the current operating cycle, and liabilities that are due for settlement within the same period.

(IAS 1, Para 62)

4. For some entities, such as financial institutions, a presentation of assets and liabilities in increasing or decreasing order of liquidity provides information that is reliable and more relevant than a current/noncurrent presentation because the entity does not supply goods or services within a clearly identifiable operating cycle.

(IAS 1, Para 63)

5. In applying paragraph 60, an entity is permitted to present some of its assets and liabilities using a current/noncurrent classification and others in order of liquidity when this provides information that is reliable and more relevant The need for a mixed basis of presentation might arise when an entity has diverse operations.

(IAS 1, Para 64)

J. Uncertainties

1. Entities are encouraged to disclose, outside the financial statements, a financial review by management, setting forth information about the principal uncertainties they face. Such a report may provide a review of

   a. The main factors that influence and determine financial performance, including changes in environment in which the entity operates, the entity's response to those changes and their effect;
   b. The entity's sources of funding and its target ratio of liabilities to equity; and
   c. The entity's resources not recognized in the statement of financial position in accordance with IFRS.

(IAS 1, Para 13)

K. Judgments and Estimations

1. An entity shall disclose, in the summary of significant accounting policies or other notes, the judgments, apart from those involving estimations, management has made in the process of applying the entity's accounting policies that have the most significant effect on the amounts recognized in the financial statements.

(IAS 1, Para 122)

2. An entity shall disclose in the notes information about the key assumptions concerning the future, and other major sources of estimation uncertainty at the reporting date, that have a significant risk of causing a material adjustment to the carrying amounts of assets and liabilities within the next financial year. In respect of those assets and liabilities, the notes shall include details of their nature and their carrying amount as at the statement of financial position date.

(IAS 1, Para 125)

L. First-Time Adoption of IFRS

1. IFRS 1 does not exempt a first-time adopter from the presentation and disclosure requirements of other IFRS—thus a first-time adopter should provide all disclosures required by other IFRS.

(IFRS 1, Para 20)

2. To comply with IAS 1, an entity's first IFRS financial statements shall include at least three statements of financial position, two statements of comprehensive income, two separate income statements (if presented), two statements of cash flows and two

statements of changes in equity and related notes, including comparative information.

(IFRS 1, Para 21)

3. If an entity presents historical summaries of selected data for periods before the first period for which it presents full comparative information under IFRS, or if it presents comparative information under previous GAAP as well as comparative information required by IFRS 1, then it shall

   a. Label the previous GAAP information prominently as not being prepared under IFRS; and
   b. Disclose the nature of the main adjustments that would be required to make it comply with IFRS (quantifying those adjustments is not required).

(IFRS 1, Para 22)

4. A first-time adopter shall present reconciliation (of equity and profit or loss presented under previous GAAP to corresponding amounts presented under IFRS) to explain how the transition from previous GAAP to IFRS affected its reported financial position, financial performance and cash flows.

(IFRS 1, Para 23)

   a. First-time IFRS financial statements should include reconciliations of equity under prior GAAP and IFRS as of date of transition and end of most recently presented financial statements under prior GAAP.
   b. First-time IFRS financial statements should include reconciliations of results of operations under prior GAAP and IFRS for the most recently presented financial statements under prior GAAP.
   c. If any impairment losses were recognized or reversed for first time in preparing an opening IFRS statement of financial position, the IAS 36 disclosures that would have been required if these would have been recognized in the period beginning with the transition date should be disclosed.

(IFRS 1, Para 24)

5. IAS 8 does not apply to the changes in accounting policies an entity makes when it adopts IFRS or to changes in those policies until after it presents its first IFRS financial statements. Therefore, IAS 8's requirements about changes in accounting policies do not apply in an entity's first IFRS financial statements. If during the period covered by its first IFRS financial statements an entity changes its accounting policies or its use of the exemptions contained in this IFRS, it shall explain the changes between its first IFRS interim financial report and its first IFRS financial statements, in accordance with paragraph 23, and it shall update the reconciliations required by paragraph 24(a) and (b).

(IFRS 1, Para 27, 27A)

6. If an entity did not present financial statements for previous periods, its first IFRS financial statements shall disclose that fact.

(IFRS 1, Para 28)

7. If an entity uses fair values in its opening IFRS statement of financial position as deemed costs for items of property, plant, and equipment, investment property or in-

tangible assets, then its opening IFRS statement of financial position shall disclose, for each line item (in the opening statement of financial position)

a. The aggregate of those fair values; and
b. The aggregate adjustment to the carrying amounts reported under previous GAAP.

(IFRS 1, Para 30)

8. If a first-time adopter presents interim financial reports under IAS 34 for part of the period covered by its first IFRS financial statements, it shall

a. Present reconciliation of equity and profit and loss under previous GAAP at the end of an interim period to corresponding amounts in total comprehensive income under IFRS at a comparable date (this reconciliation is in addition to the reconciliation required to be presented in 4. above).
b. If an entity changes its accounting policies or its use of the exemptions contained in this IFRS, it shall explain the changes in each such interim financial report in accordance with 5. above and update the reconciliations required by 4. above.

(IFRS 1, Para 32)

c. If a first-time adopter in its most recent annual financial statements under previous GAAP did not disclose information material to an understanding of the current interim period, its interim financial report shall disclose that information or include a cross-reference to another published document that includes it.

(IFRS 1, Para 33)

M. Share-Based Payment

1. An entity shall disclose information that enables users of the financial statements to understand the nature and extent of share-based payment arrangements that existed during the period.

(IFRS 2, Para 44)

2. The entity shall disclose at least the following:

a. A description of each type of share-based payment arrangement at any time during the period, including the general terms and condition of each arrangement, such as vesting requirement, the maximum term of options granted, and the method of settlement. An entity having similar type of share-based payment arrangements shall aggregate this information unless separate disclosure is required to satisfy the principle in IFRS 2, paragraph 44.
b. The number and weighted-average exercise prices of share options for each of the following group of options:

   (1) Outstanding at the beginning of the period;
   (2) Granted during the period;
   (3) Forfeited during the period;
   (4) Exercised during the period;
   (5) Expired during the period;
   (6) Outstanding at the end of the period; and
   (7) Exercisable at the end of the period.

c. If share options exercised during the period, the weighted-average prices at the date of exercise. If share options exercised regularly during the period, than the entity may disclose weighted-average share price during the period.

d. For share options outstanding at the end of the period, the range of the prices and weighted-average remaining contractual life. If the range of the prices is wide, the outstanding options shall be divided into ranges that are meaningful for assessing the number and timing of additional shares that may be issued and the cash that may be received upon exercise of those options.

(IFRS 2, Para 45)

3. An entity shall disclose information that enables users of the financial statements to understand how the fair value of the goods and services received, or the fair value of the equity instruments granted, during the period was determined.

(IFRS 2, Para 46)

4. If the entity has measured the fair value of goods or services received as consideration for equity instruments of the entity indirectly, by reference to the fair value of the equity instruments granted, to give to the principle in IFRS 2, paragraph 46, the entity shall disclose at least the following:

a. For share options granted during the period, the fair value at the measurement date and how that fair value was measured, including

   (1) The option pricing model used and the inputs to that model, including the weighted-average share price, exercise price, expected volatility, option life, expected dividend and risk-free interest rate and any other inputs to the model, including the method used and assumptions made to incorporate the effects of expected early exercise;

   (2) How expected volatility was determined, including an explanation of the extent to which expected volatility was based on historical volatility; and

   (3) Whether and how any other features of the option grant were incorporated into the measurement of fair value, such as market condition.

b. For other equity instruments granted during the period, the number and the weighted-average fair value of those equity instruments at the measurement, and information on how that fair value was measured, including

   (1) If fair value was not measured on the basis of an observable market price, how it was determined;

   (2) Whether and how expected dividends were incorporated into the measurement of fair value; and

   (3) Whether and how any other features of the equity instruments granted were incorporated into the measurement of fair value.

c. For share-based payment arrangements that were modified during the period

   (1) An explanation of those modifications;

   (2) The incremental fair value granted (as a result of those modifications); and

   (3) Information on how the incremental fair value granted was measured, consistently with the requirements set out in a. and b. above, where applicable.

(IFRS 2, Para 47)

5. If the entity has directly measured the fair value of the goods and services received during the period, the entity shall disclose how that fair value was determined.

(IFRS 2, Para 48)

a. If the assumption that fair value of goods or services exchanged for shares, other than employee services, can be measured has been rebutted, this must be stated together with an explanation.

(IFRS 2, Para 49)

6. An entity shall disclose information that enables users of the financial statements to understand the effect of share-based payment transaction on the entity's profit or loss of the period and on its financial position.

(IFRS 2, Para 50)

7. To give effect to IFRS 2, paragraph 50, the entity shall disclose at least the following:

a. The total expenses recognized for the period arising from share-based payment transactions in which goods or services received did not qualify for recognition as assets and hence were recognized immediately as an expense, including separate disclosure of that portion of the total expense that arises from transactions accounted for as equity-settled share-based payment transactions;

b. For liabilities arising from share-based payment transaction

(1) The total carrying amount at end of the period; and
(2) The total intrinsic value at the end of the period of liabilities for which the counterparty's right to cash or other assets had vested by the end of the period.

(IFRS 2, Para 51)

8. If the information required to be disclosed by this IFRS does not satisfy the principles in IFRS 2, paragraphs 44, 46, and 50, the entity shall disclose such additional information as is necessary to satisfy them.

(IFRS 2, Para 52)

N. Insurance Contracts

1. An insurer shall disclose information that identifies and explains the amount in its financial statements arising from insurance contracts.

(IFRS 4, Para 36)

2. To comply with IFRS 4, paragraph 36, an insurer shall disclose

a. Its accounting policies for insurance contracts and related assets and liabilities, income and expense;

b. The recognized assets, liabilities, income and expense (and, if it presents its cash flow statement using the direct method, cash flows) arising from insurance contracts. Furthermore, if the insurer is a cedant, it shall disclose

(1) Gains and losses recognized in profit or loss on buying reinsurance;
(2) If the cedant differs and amortizes gains and losses arising on buying reinsurance, the amortization for the period and the amounts remaining unamortized at the beginning and at the end of the period.

c. The process used to determine the assumptions that have the greatest effect on the measurement of the recognized amounts described in b. When practicable, an insurer shall also give quantified disclosures of those assumptions;

d. The effect of changes in assumption used to measure insurance assets and insurance liabilities, showing separately the effect of each change that has a material effect on the financial statements; and

e. Reconciliation of changes in insurance liabilities, reinsurance assets and if any, related deferred acquisition costs.

(IFRS 4, Para 37)

3. An insurer shall give the information to understand the amount, timing and uncertainty of future cash flows from insurance contracts.

(IFRS 4, Para 38)

4. To comply with IFRS 4, paragraph 38, an insurer shall disclose

a. Its objectives in managing risks arising from insurance contracts and its policies for mitigating those risks;

b. Information about insurance risk (both before and after risk mitigation by reinsurance), including information about

(1) The sensitivity of profit or loss and equity to changes in variables that have material effect on them;

(2) Concentrations of insurance risk;

(3) Actual claims compared with previous estimates (i.e., claim development). The disclosure about claims development shall go back to the period when the earliest material claim arose for which there is still uncertainty about the amount and timing of the claims payment, but need not go back more than ten years. An insurer need not disclose this information for claims for which uncertainty about the amount and timing of claims payments is typically resolved within one year.

c. The information about interest rate risk and credit risk that IFRS 7 would require if the insurance contracts were within the scope of IFRS 7;

d. Information about exposures to interest rate risk or market risk under embedded derivatives contained in a host insurance contract if the insurer is not required to, and does not, measure the embedded derivatives at fair value.

(IFRS 4, Para 39)

5. An entity need not apply the disclosure requirements in this IFRS to comparative information that relates to the annual period beginning before January 1, 2005, except for the disclosure required by IFRS 4, paragraph 37(a) and (b) about accounting policies, and recognized assets, liabilities, income and expense (and cash flow if direct method is used).

(IFRS 4, Para 42)

6. If it is impracticable to apply a particular requirement to comparative information that relates to annual periods beginning January 1, 2005, an entity shall disclose that fact. Applying the liability adequacy test to such comparative information might sometimes be impracticable, but it is highly unlikely to be impracticable to apply other requirements to such comparative information.

(IFRS 4, Para 43)

7. When an entity first applies this IFRS and if it is impracticable to prepare information about claim development that occurred before the beginning of the earliest period for which an entity presents full comparative information that complies with this IFRS, the entity shall disclose this fact.

(IFRS 4, Para 44)

O. Deemed Cost

1. Similarly, if an entity uses a deemed cost in its opening IFRS statement of financial position for an investment in a subsidiary, jointly controlled entity or associate in its separate financial statements (see paragraph D15), the entity's first IFRS separate financial statements shall disclose

   a. The aggregate deemed cost of those investments for which deemed cost is their previous GAAP carrying amount;
   b. The aggregate deemed cost of those investments for which deemed cost is fair value; and
   c. The aggregate adjustment to the carrying amounts reported under previous GAAP.

(IFRS 1, Para 31)

2. If an entity uses the exemption in paragraph D8A(b) for oil and gas assets or paragraph D8B for operations subject to rate regulation, it shall disclose that fact and the basis on which carrying amounts were determined under previous GAAP.

(IFRS 1, Para 31A, B)

3. If an entity elects to measure assets and liabilities at fair value and to use that fair value as the deemed cost in its opening IFRS statement of financial position because of severe hyperinflation (see paragraphs D26–D30), the entity's first IFRS financial statements shall disclose an explanation of how, and why, the entity had, and then ceased to have, a functional currency that has both of the following characteristics:

   a. A reliable general price index is not available to all entities with transactions and balances in the currency.
   b. Exchangeability between the currency and a relatively stable foreign currency does not exist.

(IFRS 1, Para 31C)

STATEMENT OF FINANCIAL POSITION

A. Minimum Disclosures on the Face of the Statement of Financial Position

1. The face of the statement of financial position should include, as a minimum, the following categories:

   a. Property, plant, and equipment;
   b. Investment property;
   c. Intangible assets;
   d. Financial assets (excluding amounts shown under e., h., and i.);
   e. Investments accounted for using the equity method;
   f. Biological assets;
   g. Inventories;

h. Trade and other receivables;
i. Cash and cash equivalents;
j. The total of assets classified as held-for-sale and assets included in disposal groups classified as held-for-sale in accordance with IFRS 5;
k. Trade and other payables;
l. Provisions;
m. Financial liabilities (excluding amounts shown under (k) and (l));
n. Liabilities and assets for current tax, as defined in IAS 12, *Income Taxes;*
o. Deferred tax liabilities and deferred tax assets, as defined in IAS 12;
p. Liabilities included in disposal groups classified as held-for-sale in accordance with IFRS 5;
q. Noncontrolling interest, and presented within equity;
r. Issued capital and reserves attributable to owners of the parent.

(IAS 1, Para 54)

B. Additional Line Items on the Face of the Statement of Financial Position

1. Additional line items, headings and subtotals should be presented on the face of the statement of financial position when an IFRS requires it, or when such presentation is necessary to present fairly the entity's financial position.

(IAS 1, Para 55)

C. Further Subclassifications of Line Items Presented

1. An entity shall disclose either on the face of the statement of financial position or in the notes further subclassifications of the line items presented, classified in a manner appropriate to the entity's operations. The detail provided in subclassifications depends on the requirement of IFRS and on the size, nature, and function of the amounts involved.

(IAS 1, Para 77, 78)

D. Inventories

1. The accounting policies and the cost formula used in inventory valuation.

(IAS 2, Para 36[a])

2. Total carrying amount and the breakdown of the carrying amount by appropriate subclassifications, such as merchandise, production supplies, work in progress, and finished goods.

(IAS 2, Para 36[b] & 37)

3. Carrying amount of inventories at fair value less cost to sell.

(IAS 2, Para 36[c])

4. Carrying amount of inventories pledged as securities.

(IAS 2, Para 36[h])

5. The amount of any reversal of any write-down that is recognized as a reduction in the amount of inventories recognized as expense in the period in accordance with paragraph 34.

(IAS 2, Para 36 [f])

6. The financial statement shall disclose

   a. The amount of inventories recognized as an expense during the period.

   (IAS 2, Para 36(d))

7. When inventories are sold, the carrying amount of those inventories shall be recognized as an expense in the period in which the related revenue is recognized. The amount of any write-down of inventories to net realizable value and all losses of inventories shall be recognized as an expense in the period the write-down or loss occurs. The amount of any reversal of any write-down of inventories arising from an increase in net realizable value shall be recognized as a reduction in the amount of inventories recognized as an expense in the period in which the reversal occurs.

   (IAS 2, Para 34)

8. The financial statement shall disclose

   a. The amount of any write-down of inventories recognized as an expense in the period in accordance with paragraph 34;
   b. The circumstances or events that led to the reversal of a write-down of inventories in accordance with paragraph 34.

   (IAS 2, Para 36[e] & [g]))

E. Property, Plant, and Equipment (PP&E)

1. In respect of each class (i.e., groupings of assets of a similar nature and use) of PP&E, the following disclosures are required:

   a. Measurement basis/bases used for the determination of the gross carrying amount; if more than one basis has been employed, then also the gross carrying amount determined in accordance with that basis in each category;
   b. The depreciation method(s) used;
   c. Either the useful lives or the depreciation rates used;
   d. The gross carrying amount and the accumulated depreciation at the beginning and the end of the period;
   e. A reconciliation of the carrying amount at the beginning and the end of the period disclosing

      (1) Additions;
      (2) Assets classified as held-for-sale or included in a disposal group classified as held-for-sale in accordance with IFRS 5, *Noncurrent Assets Held-for-Sale and Discontinued Operations,* and other disposals;
      (3) Acquisitions by means of business combinations;
      (4) Increases/decreases resulting from revaluations and from impairment losses recognized or reversed directly in equity (if any);
      (5) Impairment losses recognized in profit or loss (if any);
      (6) Impairment losses reversed in profit or loss (if any);
      (7) Depreciation;
      (8) Net exchange differences arising from translation of financial statements of a foreign entity (in accordance with IAS 21); and
      (9) Other changes, if any.

   (IAS 16, Para 73)

2. Additional disclosures to be made include the following:

    a. The existence and amount of restrictions on title, and PP&E pledged as security for liabilities;

    b. If it is not disclosed separately on the face of the income statement, the amount of compensation from third parties for items of P&PE that were impaired, lost or given up that is included in profit or loss;

    c. The amount of expenditures in respect of PP&E in the course of construction; and

    d. The amount of outstanding commitments for acquisition of PP&E.

(IAS 16, Para 74)

3. It is also necessary to disclose

    a. Depreciation, whether recognized in profit or loss or as a part of the cost of other assets, during a period; and

    b. Accumulated depreciation at the end of the period.

(IAS 16, Para 75)

4. In case items of PP&E are stated at revalued amounts, disclose the following information:

    a. The effective date of revaluation;

    b. Whether an independent party prepared the valuation;

    c. The methods and significant assumptions applied in estimating the item's fair value;

    d. The extent to which the item's fair value was determined directly by reference to observable prices in an active market or in a recent market transaction at arm's length or were estimated using other valuation techniques;

    e. The carrying amount of each class of PP&E that would have been included in the financial statements had the assets been carried under the cost model; and

    f. The revaluation surplus, including the movement for the period in that account and disclosure of any restrictions on the distribution of the balance in the revaluation surplus account to shareholders.

(IAS 16, Para 77)

5. An entity should disclose information on impaired property, plant, and equipment under IAS 36 in addition to information required under IAS 16, para 73[e] (iv to vi)

(IAS 16, Para 78)

6. Other recommended disclosures (entities are encouraged to disclose these amounts)

    a. The carrying amount of temporarily idle PP&E;

    b. The gross carrying amount of fully depreciated PP&E still in use;

    c. The carrying amount of PP&E retired from active use and not classified as held-for-sale; and

    d. In cases where items of PP&E are carried at cost model the fair value of PP&E if it is materially different from the carrying amount.

(IAS 16, Para 79)

F. Intangible Assets

1. In the case of each class of intangible assets, distinguishing between internally generated intangible assets and other intangible assets, the financial statements should disclose

   a. The useful lives of the amortization rates used, and whether the useful lives are indefinite or finite;
   b. The amortization methods used for intangibles with finite useful lives;
   c. The gross carrying amount and the accumulated amortization (aggregated with accumulated impairment) at the beginning and at the end;
   d. The line item(s) of the income statement in which the amortization of intangible assets is included;
   e. A reconciliation of the carrying amount at the beginning and the end of the period showing

      (1) Additions, indicating separately those from internal development, those acquired separately, and through business combinations;
      (2) Assets classified as held-for-sale or included in a disposal group classified as held-for-sale in accordance with IFRS 5, and other disposals;
      (3) Increases or decreases resulting from revaluations and from impairment losses recognized or reversed directly in equity (if any);
      (4) Impairment losses recognized in profit or loss (if any);
      (5) Impairment losses reversed in profit or loss (if any);
      (6) Amortization recognized;
      (7) Net exchange differences arising on translation of financial statements of a foreign entity; and
      (8) Other changes in carrying amount.

      (IAS 38, Para 118)

2. Additional disclosures with respect to intangibles are the following:

   a. An intangible asset assessed as having an indefinite useful life, the carrying amount of that asset, and the reasons supporting the assessment of an indefinite useful life. In giving these reasons, the entity shall describe the factor(s) that play a significant role in determining that the asset has an indefinite useful life.
   b. In the case of an individual intangible asset that is material to the financial statements as a whole, a description, the carrying amount, and the remaining amortization period;
   c. In the case of intangible assets acquired by way of a government grant and initially recognized at fair value: the fair value initially recognized for these assets, their carrying amounts, and whether they are carried under the cost model or the revaluation model for subsequent measurements;
   d. The existence and the carrying amount of intangible assets pledged as security for liabilities; and
   e. The amount of commitments for the acquisition of intangible assets.

   (IAS 38, Para 122)

3. In the case of intangible assets carried under the allowed at revalued amounts, the following disclosures are prescribed:

a. By class of intangible assets: the effective date of the revaluation, the current carrying amount and the carrying amount of revalued intangible assets carried under the cost model (i.e., at cost less accumulated amortization); and

b. The quantum of revaluation surplus that relates to intangible assets at the beginning and the end of the period, indicating the changes during the period and any restrictions on the distributions of the balance to shareholders;

c. The methods and significant assumptions applied in estimating the assets' fair values.

(IAS 38, Para 124)

4. It may be necessary to aggregate the classes of revalued assets into larger classes for disclosure purposes. However, classes are not aggregated if this would result in the combination of a class of intangible assets that includes amounts measured under both the cost and revaluation models.

(IAS 38, Para 125)

5. The financial statements should disclose the aggregate amount of research and development expenditure recognized as an expense during the period.

(IAS 38, Para 126)

6. An entity is encouraged, but not required, to disclose the following information:

a. A description of any fully amortized intangible assets that are still in use; and

b. A brief description of significant intangible assets controlled by the entity but not recognized as assets because they do not meet the recognition criteria in this Standard or because they were acquired or generated before the version of IAS 38 issued in 1998 was effective.

(IAS 38, Para 128)

7. Provide a reconciliation of goodwill carrying value, showing gross carrying amount and any impairment loss, as of beginning of period; any additions; any adjustments arising from recognition of deferred taxes subsequent to acquisition date; disposals; impairment losses during period; net exchange differences during period in accordance with IAS 21; other changes in the carrying amount; and gross amount and accumulated impairment loss as of end of period.

(IFRS 3, Para B67(d))

G. Other Long-Term Assets (Consolidated Financial Statement and Investment in Subsidiaries)

1. The following items should be disclosed separately:

a. The reasons why the ownership, directly or indirectly through subsidiaries, of more than one-half of the voting, or potential voting power of an investee, does not constitute control.

(IAS 27, Para 41[b])

2. A parent need not present consolidated financial statements if and only if

a. The parent is itself a wholly owned subsidiary, or is a partially owned subsidiary of another entity and its other owners, including those not otherwise entitled to vote, have been informed about, and do not object to, the parent not presenting consolidated financial statements;

b. The parent's debt or equity instrument is not traded in a public market (a domestic or foreign exchange or an over the counter market, including local and regional markets);

c. The parent did not file, nor is it in the process of filing, its financial statements with a securities commission or other regulatory organization for purpose of issuing any class of instruments in a public market; and

d. The ultimate or any intermediate parent of the parent produces consolidated financial statements available for public use that comply with IFRS.

(IAS 27, Para 10)

3. Consolidated financial statements are to be prepared using uniform accounting policies for like transactions and other events in similar circumstances.

(IAS 27, Para 24)

4. Noncontrolling interests shall be presented in the consolidated statement of financial position within equity, separately from the equity of the owners of the parent.

(IAS 27, Para 27)

5. The following disclosures shall be made in consolidated financial statements:

a. The nature of the relationship between the parent and the subsidiary, when the parent does not own, directly or indirectly through subsidiaries, more than one-half of the voting power;

b. The reasons why the ownership of more than half of the voting power of an investee does not constitute control;

c. The reporting date of the financial statements of a subsidiary, when such financial statements are used to prepare consolidated financial statements and are of a reporting date for a period that is different from that of the parent, and the reason for using the different reporting date or period.

d. The nature and extent of any significant restrictions (e.g., resulting from borrowing arrangements or regulatory requirements) on the ability of subsidiaries to transfer funds to the parent in the form of cash dividends or to repay loans or advances.

e. A schedule that shows the effect of any changes in parent's ownership interest in a subsidiary that do not result in a loss of control on the equity attributable to owners of the parent;

f. If control of a subsidiary is lost, the parent shall disclose the gain or loss, if any, recognized in accordance with paragraph 34, and

   (1) The portion of that gain or loss attributable to recognizing any investment retained in the former subsidiary at its fair value at the date when control is lost; and

   (2) The line item(s) in the statement of comprehensive income in which the gain or loss is recognized (if not presented separately in the statement of comprehensive income).

(IAS 27, Para 41)

6. When separate financial statements are prepared for a parent that, in accordance with IAS 27, paragraph 10, elects not to prepare consolidated financial statements, those separate financial statements shall disclose

a. The fact that the financial statements are separate financial statements; that the exemption from consolidation has been used; the name and country of incorporation or residence of the entity whose consolidated financial statements that comply with International Financial Reporting Standards have been produced for public use; and the address where those consolidated financial statements are obtainable;

b. A list of significant investments in subsidiaries, jointly controlled entities and associates, including the name, country or incorporation or residence, proportion of ownership interest, and, if different, proportion of voting power held; and

c. A description of the method used to account for the investments listed under b.

(IAS 27, Para 42)

7. When a parent (other than a parent covered by paragraph 42), venturer with an interest in a jointly controlled entity, or an investor in an associate prepares separate financial statements, those separate financial statements shall disclose

a. The fact that the statements are separate financial statements and the reasons why those statements are prepared if not required by law;

b. A list of significant investments in subsidiaries, jointly controlled entities and associates, including the name, country of incorporation or residence, proportion of ownership interest and, if different, proportion of voting power held;

c. A description of a method used to account for the investments listed under b.; and shall identify the financial statements prepared in accordance with IAS 27, paragraph 9, IAS 28 and IAS 31, to which they relate.

(IAS 27, Para 43)

H. Investments in Associates

1. Investments in associates accounted for using the equity method should be classified as noncurrent assets and separately set forth in the statement of financial position. The investor's share of profit or losses of such investments should be disclosed as a separate item in the income statement. The carrying amount of those investments and the investor's share of any discontinued operations of such associates should be disclosed.

(IAS 28, Para 38)

2. The fact that the investor's share of investee's carrying value includes an amount analogous to goodwill, and any accumulated impairment should be stated.

(IAS 28, Para 23)

3. The following disclosures shall be made:

a. The fair value of investments in associates for which there are published price quotations;

b. Summarized financial information of associates, including the aggregated amounts of assets, liabilities, revenues, and profit or loss;

c. The reasons why the presumption that an investor does not have significant influence is overcome if the investor holds, directly or indirectly though subsidiaries, less than 20% of the voting or potential voting power of the investee but concludes that it has significant influence;

    d. The reasons why the presumption that an investor has significant influence is overcome if the investor holds, directly or indirectly through subsidiaries, 20% or more of the voting or potential voting power of the investee but concludes that it does not have significant influence;

    e. The reporting date of the financial statements of an associate, when such financial statements are used in applying the equity method and are as of a reporting date or for a period that is different from that of the investor, and the reason for using a different reporting date or different period;

    f. The nature and extent of any significant restrictions on the ability of associates to transfer funds to the investor in the form of cash dividends, or repayments of loans or advances;

    g. The unrecognized share of losses of an associate, both for the period and cumulatively, if an investor has discontinued recognition of its share of losses of an associate;

    h. The fact that an associate is not accounted for using the equity method;

    i. Summarized financial information of associates, either individually or in groups, that are not accounted for using the equity method, including the amounts of total assets, total liabilities, revenues and profit or loss.

(IAS 28, Para 37)

4. The investor's share of changes recognized in other comprehensive income by the associate shall be recognized by the investor in other comprehensive income.

(IAS 28, Para 39)

5. In accordance with IAS 37, *Provisions, Contingent Liabilities, and Contingent Assets,* the investor shall disclose

    a. Its share of the contingent liabilities of an associate incurred jointly with other investors; and

    b. Those contingent liabilities that arise because that investor is severally liable for all or part of the liabilities of the associate.

(IAS 28, Para 40)

I.   Investments in Joint Ventures

1. The venturer is to disclose a listing and description of interests in significant joint ventures and proportions held in each, and aggregate current assets, noncurrent assets, current liabilities, noncurrent liabilities, income and expense related to interests in joint ventures.

(IAS 31, Para 56)

2. Separately from other contingent liabilities, disclose contingent liabilities arising from interest in joint ventures and share in each incurred jointly with other venturers; shares in contingent liabilities of the joint ventures themselves for which there are contingent obligations; and contingent liabilities arising in connection with contingent liability for obligations of the other venturers.

(IAS 31, Para 54)

3. Separately from other commitments, disclose capital commitments arising in connection with joint obligations with other venturers, and share of capital commitments of the joint ventures themselves.

(IAS 31, Para 55)

4. The venturer shall disclose the method used to recognize its interests in jointly controlled entities.

(IAS 31, Para 57)

J. Investment Property

1. In certain cases investment property will be property that is owned by the reporting entity and leased to others under operating-type lease arrangements. The disclosure requirement set forth in IAS 17 continue unaltered by IAS 40. (In addition IAS 40 stipulates a number of new disclosure requirements set out below.)

(IAS 40, Para 74)

2. An entity shall disclose

   a. Whether it applies the fair value model or cost model;
   b. If it applies fair value model, whether and in what circumstances the property held under operating leases are classified and accounted for as investment property;
   c. When classification is difficult, an entity that holds an investment property will need to disclose the criteria used to distinguish investment property from owner-occupied property and from property held for sale in the ordinary course of business;
   d. The method and any significant assumptions that were used in ascertaining the fair values of the investment properties are to be disclosed as well. Such disclosure should also include a statement about whether the determination of fair value was supported by market evidence or it relied heavily on other factors (which the entity needs to disclose as well) due to the nature of the property and the absence of comparable market data;
   e. If investment property has been revalued by an independent valuer having recognized and relevant qualifications and who has recent experience with properties having similar characteristics of location and type, the extent to which the fair value of investment property is based on valuation by such an independent valuer, if there is no such valuation, the fact should be disclosed as well;
   f. The amounts recognized in profit or loss for

      (1) Rental income from investment property;
      (2) Direct operating expenses including repairs and maintenance arising from investment property that generated rental income during the period;
      (3) Direct operating expenses including repairs and maintenance arising from investment property that did not generate rental income during the period; and
      (4) The cumulative change in fair value recognized in profit or loss on a sale of investment property from a pool of assets in which the cost model is used.

   g. The existence and the amount of any restrictions which may potentially affect the reliability of investment property or the remittance of income and proceeds from disposal to be received; and
   h. Material contractual obligations to purchase or build investment property or for repairs, maintenance, or improvements thereto.

(IAS 40, Para 75)

3. Disclosure applicable to investment property measured using the fair value model

    a. In addition to the disclosures outlined in IAS 40, paragraph 75, the standard requires that an entity that uses the fair value model should also disclose a reconciliation to be presented between the beginning and end of the period, of the carrying amount of investment property, from business combinations, and those derived from capitalized expenditures. It will also identify assets classified as held-for-sale or included in a disposal group classified as held-for-sale in accordance with IFRS 5 and other disposals, gains, or losses from fair value adjustment, the net exchange differences, if any, arising from the translation of the financial statements of a foreign entity, transfers to and from inventories and owner-occupied properties and any other movements.

(It will not be required that comparative reconciliation data be presented for prior periods.)

For the purposes of paragraph 76's reconciliation the entity shall disclose the following:

    (1) Additions, disclosing separately those additions resulting from acquisitions and those resulting from subsequent expenditure recognized in the carrying amount of an asset;

    (2) Additions resulting from acquisitions through business combinations;

    (3) Assets classified as held-for-sale or included in a disposal group classified as held-for-sale in accordance with IFRS 5 and other disposals;

    (4) Net gains or losses from fair value adjustments;

    (5) The net exchange differences arising on the translation of the financial statements into a different presentation currency, and on translation of a foreign operation into the presentation currency of the reporting entity;

    (6) Transfers to and from inventories and owner-occupied property; and

    (7) Other changes.

    b. Under exceptional circumstances, due to lack of reliable fair value, when an entity measures investment property using the cost model under IAS 16, the above reconciliation should disclose amounts separately for that investment property from amounts relating to other investment property. In addition, an entity should also disclose

    (1) A reconciliation—relating to that investment property separately—of the carrying amount at the beginning and end of the period;

    (2) A description of such a property;

    (3) An explanation of why fair value cannot be reliably measured;

    (4) If possible, the range of estimates within which fair value is highly likely to lie; and

    (5) On disposal of such an investment property, the fact that the entity has disposed of investment property not carried at fair value along with its carrying amount at the time of disposal and the amount of gain or loss recognized.

(IAS 40, Para 76 & 78)

4. Disclosures applicable to investment property measured using the cost model

    a. In addition to the disclosure requirements outlined in IAS 40, para 75, the standard requires that an entity that applies the cost model should also disclose the depreciation methods used, the useful lives or the depreciation rates used, and the gross carrying amount and the accumulated depreciation (aggregated with accumulated impairment losses) at the beginning and end of the period. It should also disclose a reconciliation of the carrying amount of investment property at the beginning and the end of the period showing the following details: additions resulting from acquisitions, those resulting from business combinations, and those deriving from capitalized expenditures subsequent to the property's initial recognition. It should also disclose assets classified as held for sale or included in a disposal group classified as held-for-sale under IFRS 5 and other disposals, depreciation, impairment losses recognized and reversed, the net exchange differences, if any, arising from the translation of the financial statements of a foreign entity to the presentation currency of the reporting entity, transfers to and from inventories and owner-occupied properties, and any other movements.

b. The fair value of investment property carried under the cost model should also be disclosed. In exceptional cases, when the fair value of the investment property cannot be reliably estimated, the entity should also disclose

(1) A description of such property;
(2) An explanation of why fair value cannot be reliably measured; and
(3) If possible, the range of estimates within which fair value is highly likely to lie.

(IAS 40, Para 79)

5. When a valuation obtained for investment property is adjusted significantly for the purpose of the financial statements, for example to avoid double-counting of assets or liabilities that are recognized as separate assets and liabilities as described in paragraph 50, the entity shall disclose a reconciliation between the valuation obtained and the adjusted valuation included in the financial statements, showing separately the aggregate amount of any recognized lease obligations that have been added back, and any other significant adjustments.

(IAS 40, Para 77)

K. Financial Instruments

1. When IFRS 7 requires disclosures by class of instrument, the entity shall group financial instruments into classes that are appropriate to the nature of the information disclosed and that take into account the characteristics of those financial instruments. Sufficient information must be provided to permit reconciliation to the line items presented in the statement of financial position.

(IFRS 7, Para 6)

2. An entity shall disclose information that enables users of its financial statements to evaluate the significance of financial instruments for its financial position and performance.

(IFRS 7, Para 7)

3. The carrying amounts of each of the following categories, as defined in IAS 39, is to be disclosed either on the face of the statement of financial position or in the notes:

a. Financial assets reported at fair value through profit or loss, showing separately

(1) Those designated as such upon initial recognition; and
(2) Those classified as held-for-trading in accordance with IAS 39.

b. Financial liabilities reported at fair value through profit or loss, showing separately

(1) Those designated for such accounting upon acquisition under the fair value option; and
(2) Those classified as held-for-trading purposes.

c. Financial liabilities measured at amortized cost;
d. Financial assets measured at amortized cost;
e. Financial assets measured at fair value through other comprehensive income.

(IFRS 7, Para 8)

4. For financial assets or liabilities carried at fair value through profit or loss, if the entity has designated as measured at fair value a financial asset (or group of assets) that would otherwise be measured at amortized cost, it shall disclose:

a. The maximum exposure to credit risk (see paragraph 36(a)) of the financial asset (or group of financial assets) at the end of the reporting period;
b. The amount by which any related credit derivatives or similar instruments mitigate that maximum exposure to credit risk;
c. The amount of change, during the period and cumulatively, in the fair value of the financial asset (or group of financial assets) that is attributable to changes in the credit risk of the financial asset determined either

(1) As the amount of change in its fair value that is not attributable to changes in market conditions that give rise to market risk, or
(2) Using an alternative method the entity believes more faithfully represents the amount of change in its fair value that is attributable to changes in the credit risk of the asset.

d. The amount of the change in the fair value of any related credit derivatives or similar instruments that has occurred during the period and cumulatively since the financial asset was designated at fair value to be reported through profit or loss.

(IFRS 7, Para 9)

5. If the entity has designated a financial liability to be reported at fair value through profit or loss in accordance with paragraph 9 of IAS 39, it is to disclose

a. The amount of change, during the reporting period and cumulatively, in the fair value of the financial liability that is attributable to changes in the credit risk of that liability determined either

(1) As the amount of change in its fair value that is not attributable to changes in market conditions that give rise to market risk; or
(2) Using an alternative method the entity believes more faithfully represents that amount of change in its fair value that is attributable to changes in the credit risk of the liability.

b. The difference between the financial liability's carrying amount and the amount the entity would be contractually required to pay at maturity to the holder of the obligation.

(IFRS 7, Para 10)

6. Disclosure is to be made of

   a. The methods used to determine the amount of change that is attributable to changes in credit risk in compliance with the requirements of IFRS 7, paragraphs 9(c) and 10(a); and

   b. If it is believed that the disclosure given to comply with the requirements of IFRS 7 paragraphs 9(c) or 10(a) does not faithfully represent the change in the fair value of the financial asset or financial liability attributable to changes in its credit risk, the reasons for reaching this conclusion and the factors believed to be relevant.

   (IFRS 7, Para 11)

7. If an entity has designated investments in equity instruments to be measured at fair value through other comprehensive income, it shall disclose;

   a. Which investments in equity instruments have been designated to be measured at fair value through other comprehensive income;

   b. The reasons for using this presentation alternative;

   c. The fair value of each such investment at the end of the reporting period;

   d. Dividends recognized during the period, showing separately those related to investments derecognized during the reporting period and those related to investments held at the end of the reporting period; and

   e. Any transfers of the cumulative gain or loss within equity during the period including the reason for such transfers.

   (IFRS 7, Para 11A)

8. If an entity derecognized investments in equity instruments measured at fair value through other comprehensive income during the reporting period, it shall disclose

   a. The reasons for disposing of the investments;

   b. The fair value of the investments at the date of derecognition; and

   c. The cumulative gain or loss on disposal.

   (IFRS 7, Para 11B)

9. An entity shall disclose if, in the current or previous reporting periods, it has been reclassified any financial assets in accordance with paragraph 4.9 of IFRS 9. For any such event, an entity shall disclose

   a. The date of reclassification;

   b. A detailed explanation of the change in business model and a qualitative description of its effect on the entity's financial statements;

   c. The amount reclassified into and out of each category.

   (IFRS 7, Para 12B)

10. For each reporting period following reclassification until derecognition, an entity shall disclose for assets reclassified so that they are measured at amortized cost in accordance with paragraph 4.9 of IFRS 9

    a. The effective interest rate determined on the date of reclassification; and

    b. The interest income or expense recognized.

    (IFRS 7, Para 12C)

11. If an entity has reclassified financial assets so that they are measured at amortized cost since its last annual reporting date, it shall disclose

    a. The fair value of the financial assets at the end of the reporting period; and
    b. The fair value gain or loss that would have been recognized in profit or loss during the reporting period if the financial assets had not been reclassified.

    (IFRS 7, Para 12D)

12. An entity may have transferred financial assets in such a way that part or all of the financial assets do not qualify for derecognition (see paragraphs 15-37 of IAS 39). The entity shall disclose for each class of such financial assets

    a. The nature of the assets not derecognized;
    b. The nature of the risks and rewards of ownership to which the entity remains exposed;
    c. When the entity continues to recognize all of the assets, the carrying amounts of the assets and of the associated liabilities; and
    d. When the entity continues to recognize the assets to the extent of its continuing involvement, the total carrying amount of the original assets, the amount of the assets that the entity continues to recognize, and the carrying amount of the associated liabilities.

    (IFRS 7, Para 13)

13. When collateral has been put up by the entity, disclosure is required of

    a. The carrying amount of financial assets the entity has pledged as collateral for either liabilities or contingent liabilities, including amounts that have been reclassified in the statement of financial position separately from other assets because the transferee has the right to sell or repledge, in accordance with IAS 39, paragraph 37(a); and
    b. The terms and conditions relating to the pledge.

    (IFRS 7, Para 14)

14. When collateral has been received by the entity, disclosure is required of

    a. The fair value of collateral held;
    b. The fair value of any such collateral sold or repledged, and whether the entity has an obligation to return it; and
    c. The terms and conditions associated with the entity's use of the collateral.

    (IFRS 7, Para 15)

15. When financial assets are impaired by credit losses and the entity records the impairment in a separate account (e.g., an allowance account used to record individual impairments or a similar account used to record a collective impairment of assets) rather than directly reducing the carrying amount of the asset, it shall disclose a reconciliation of changes in that account during the period for each class of financial assets.

    (IFRS 7, Para 16)

16. If the reporting entity has issued a compound financial instrument (i.e., an instrument that contains both a liability and an equity component), *and* the instrument has mul-

tiple embedded derivatives whose values are interdependent (e.g., a callable convertible debt instrument), it is to disclose the existence of those features.

(IFRS 7, Para 17)

17. For loans payable recognized at the reporting date, the entity is to disclose

    a. Details of any defaults occurring during the period as to principal, interest, sinking fund, or redemption terms of those loans payable;
    b. The carrying amount of the loans payable in default at the reporting date; and
    c. Whether the default was remedied, or whether the terms of the loans payable were renegotiated, before the financial statements were authorized for issuance.

(IFRS 7, Para 18)

18. If, during the period, there were breaches of loan agreement terms other than those described in IFRS 7, paragraph 18, disclosure is to be made of the same information as required by paragraph 18, if those breaches permitted the lender to demand accelerated repayment (unless the breaches were remedied, or the terms of the loan were renegotiated, on or before the reporting date).

(IFRS 7, Para 19)

19. For each class of financial assets and financial liabilities, the entity is to disclose the fair value of that class of assets and liabilities in a way that permits it to be compared with its carrying amount. It is to disclose

    a. The methods and, when a valuation technique is used, the assumptions applied in determining fair values of each class of financial assets or financial liabilities. If there has been a change in valuation technique, the entity must disclose the extent of this change and the reasons for such a change.

(IFRS 7, Para 27)

20. If a difference exists between the fair value at initial recognition and the amount that would be determined at that date using a valuation technique, disclosure must be made, by class of financial instrument, of

    a. The entity's accounting policy for recognizing that difference in profit or loss to reflect a change in factors (including time) that market participants would consider in setting a price;
    b. The aggregate difference yet to be recognized in profit or loss at the beginning and end of the period, together with a reconciliation of changes in the balance of this difference.

(IFRS 7, Para 28)

21. Disclosures of fair value are not required

    a. When the carrying amount is a reasonable approximation of fair value, for example, for financial instruments such as short-term trade receivables and payables;
    b. For derivatives linked to investments in equity instruments that do not have a quoted market price in an active market that are measured at cost in accordance with IAS 39 because their fair value cannot be measured reliably; or
    c. For a contract containing a discretionary participation feature (as described in IFRS 4) if the fair value of that feature cannot be measured reliably.

(IFRS 7, Para 29)

22. For an investment in equity instruments that do not have a quoted market price in an active market, or derivatives linked to such equity instruments, that is measured at cost because its fair value cannot be measured reliably, or for a contract continuing a discretionary participation feature, if the fair value of that feature cannot be measured reliably, the entity is to disclose information to help users of the financial statements make their own judgments about the extent of possible differences between the carrying amount of those financial assets or financial liabilities and their fair value, including

    a. The fact that fair value information has not been disclosed for these instruments because their fair value cannot be measured reliably;
    b. A description of the financial instruments, their carrying amount, and an explanation of why fair value cannot be measured reliably;
    c. Information about the market for the instruments;
    d. Information about whether and how the entity intends to dispose of the financial instruments; and
    e. If financial instruments whose fair value previously could not be reliably measured are derecognized, that fact, their carrying amount at the time of derecognition, and the amount of gain or loss recognized.

    (IFRS 7, Para 30)

23. The reporting entity is to disclose qualitative and quantitative information that enables users of its financial statements to evaluate the nature and extent of risks arising from financial instruments to which the entity is exposed at the reporting date.

    (IFRS 7, Para 31)

24. For each type of risk arising from financial instruments, the entity shall disclose the following qualitative matters:

    a. The exposures to that risk and how they arise;
    b. The entity's objectives, policies and processes for managing the risk and the methods used to measure the risk; and
    c. Any changes in these items from what was reported in the previous period.

    (IFRS 7, Para 33)

25. For each type of risk arising from financial instruments, the entity shall disclose the following quantitative matters:

    a. Summary quantitative data about the reporting entity's exposure to that risk at the reporting date. This disclosure is to be based on the information provided internally to key management personnel of the entity (e.g., the entity's board of directors or chief executive officer).
    b. Additional disclosures (see below), to the extent not provided in accordance with the preceding paragraph;
    c. Concentrations of risk if not apparent from the preceding disclosures, which should include

       (1) A description of how management determines concentrations;
       (2) A description of the shared characteristics that identifies each concentration (e.g., counterparty, geographical area, currency or market); and
       (3) The amount of the risk exposure associated with all financial instruments sharing that characteristic.

    (IFRS 7, Para 34)

26. If the quantitative data disclosed as at the reporting date are unrepresentative of an entity's exposure to risk during the period, an entity shall provide further information that is representative.

(IFRS 7, Para 35)

27. Regarding *credit risk*, the entity is to disclose, by class of financial instrument, the following:

    a. The amount that best represents its maximum exposure to credit risk at the reporting date, without taking account of collateral held or other credit enhancements, this disclosure is not required for financial instruments whose carrying amount best represents the maximum exposure to credit risk;
    b. A description of collateral held as security and other credit enhancements and their financial effect (e.g., a quantification of the extent to which collateral and other credit enhancements mitigate credit risk) in respect of the amount that best represents the maximum exposure to credit risk (whether disclosed in accordance with (a) or represented by the carrying amount of a financial instrument); and
    c. Information about the credit quality of financial assets that are neither past due nor impaired.

(IFRS 7, Para 36)

28. By class of financial asset, the following must be disclosed:

    a. An analysis of the age of financial assets that are past due as of the reporting date, but which are not impaired;
    b. An analysis of financial assets that are individually determined to be impaired as of the reporting date, including the factors that were considered in determining the condition of impairment.

(IFRS 7, Para 37)

29. When the reporting entity obtains financial or nonfinancial assets during the period by taking possession of collateral it holds as security, or by calling on other credit enhancements (e.g., guarantees), and such assets meet the recognition criteria of IFRS, the entity is to disclose for such assets held at the reporting date

    a. The nature and carrying amount of the assets; and
    b. When the assets are not readily convertible into cash, the entity's policies for disposing of such assets, or for using them in its operations.

(IFRS 7, Para 38)

30. Regarding *liquidity risk*, the entity is to disclose, by class of financial instrument, the following:

    a. A maturity analysis for nonderivative financial liabilities (including issued financial guarantee contracts) that shows the remaining contractual maturities;
    b. A maturity analysis for derivative financial liabilities, which will include the remaining contractual maturities for those derivative financial liabilities for which contractual maturities are essential for an understanding of the timing of the cash flows; and
    c. A description of how it manages the liquidity risk inherent in the foregoing item(s).

(IFRS 7, Para 39)

31. Regarding *market (interest rate)* risk, the entity is to disclose, by class of financial instrument, the following (unless a sensitivity analysis is presented, as discussed below, that reports on interdependencies among risk variables):

    a. A sensitivity analysis for *each* type of market risk to which the entity is exposed at the reporting date, showing how profit or loss and equity would have been affected by changes in the relevant risk variable that were reasonably possible at that date;
    b. The methods and assumptions used in preparing the sensitivity analysis; and
    c. Changes from the previous period in the methods and assumptions used, and the reasons for such changes.

    (IFRS 7, Para 40)

32. A sensitivity analysis, such as value-at-risk, that reflects interdependencies between risk variables (e.g., between interest rates and exchange rates) if used to manage financial risks, may be used in place of the analysis specified in item 31, above. In such instance, disclosure must be made of

    a. An explanation of the method used in preparing the sensitivity analysis, and of the main parameters and assumptions underlying the data provided; and
    b. An explanation of the objective of the method used and of limitations that may result in the information not fully reflecting the fair value of the assets and liabilities involved.

    (IFRS 7, Para 41)

33. When the sensitivity analyses employed (either approaches noted in the foregoing) are unrepresentative of a risk inherent in a financial instrument, disclosure must be made of that fact and the reason the sensitivity analyses are deemed to be unrepresentative.

    (IFRS 7, Para 42)

34. An entity is permitted to designate a previously recognized financial asset/liability as a financial asset/liability measured at fair value through profit or loss in accordance with paragraph D19/D19A of IAS 1. The entity shall disclose the fair value of financial assets so designated at the date of designation and their classification and carrying amount in the previous financial statements.

    (IAS 1, Para 29, 29A)

35. An entity must provide qualitative disclosures in the context of quantitative disclosures which enables users to link related disclosures and hence form an overall picture of the nature and extent of risks arising from financial instruments, to enable users to better understand the risks.

    (IFRS 1, Para 32A)

36. To make the disclosures required by paragraph 27B an entity must classify fair value measurements using a fair value hierarchy that reflects the significance of the inputs used in making the measurements. The fair value hierarchy levels must be categorized in the following levels:

    a. The quoted prices (unadjusted) in active markets for identical assets or liabilities (Level 1);

b. Inputs other than quoted prices included within Level 1 that are observable for the asset or liability, either directly (i.e., as prices) or indirectly (i.e., derived from prices) (Level 2); and

c. Inputs for the asset or liability that are not based on observable market data (unobservable inputs) (Level 3).

The level in the fair value hierarchy within which the fair value measurement is categorized in its entirety must be determined on the basis of the lowest level input that is significant to the fair value measurement in its entirety. For this purpose, the significance of an input is assessed against the fair value measurement in its entirety. If a fair value measurement uses observable inputs that require significant adjustment based on unobservable inputs, that measurement is a Level 3 measurement. Assessing the significance of a particular input to the fair value measurement in its entirety requires judgment, considering factors specific to the asset or liability.

(IFRS 7, Para 27A)

37. For fair value measurements recognized in the statement of financial position an entity shall disclose for each class of financial instruments (these disclosures are recommended to be disclosed in a tabular format)

a. The level in the fair value hierarchy into which the fair value measurements are categorized in their entirety, segregating fair value measurements in accordance with the levels defined in the preceding paragraph;

b. Any significant transfers between Level 1 and Level 2 of the fair value hierarchy and the reasons for those transfers. Transfers into each level shall be disclosed and discussed separately from transfers out of each level. For this purpose, significance shall be judged with respect to profit or loss, and total assets or total liabilities;

c. For fair value measurements in Level 3 of the fair value hierarchy, a reconciliation from the beginning balances to the ending balances, disclosing separately changes during the period attributable to the following:

(1) Total gains or losses for the period recognized in profit or loss, and a description of where they are presented in the statement of comprehensive income or the separate income statement (if presented);

(2) Total gains or losses recognized in other comprehensive income;

(3) Purchases, sales, issues and settlements (each type of movement disclosed separately); and

(4) Transfers into or out of Level 3 (e.g., transfers attributable to changes in the observability of market data) and the reasons for those transfers. For significant transfers, transfers into Level 3 must be disclosed and discussed separately from transfers out of Level 3.

d. The amount of total gains or losses for the period in (c)(1) above included in profit or loss that are attributable to gains or losses relating to those assets and liabilities held at the end of the reporting period and a description of where those gains or losses are presented in the statement of comprehensive income or the separate income statement (if presented); and

e. For fair value measurements in Level 3, if changing one or more of the inputs to reasonably possible alternative assumptions would change fair value significantly, the entity shall state that fact and disclose the effect of those changes. The entity shall disclose how the effect of a change to a reasonably possible alternative assumption was calculated. For this purpose, significance must be judged with respect to profit or loss, and total assets or total liabilities, or, when changes in fair value are recognized in other comprehensive income, total equity.

(IFRS 7, Para 27B)

L. Provisions

1. For each class of provision, for the current year only (comparative presentation not required)

   a. The carrying amount at the beginning and end of the period;
   b. Exchange differences from translation of foreign entities' financial statements;
   c. Provisions acquired through business combinations;
   d. Additional provisions made during the current period, including increases to existing provisions;
   e. Amounts utilized (i.e., incurred and charged against the provision) during the period;
   f. Unused amounts reversed during the period;
   g. The increase during the period in the discounted amount resulting from the passage of time and the effect of any change in discount rate; and
   h. The carrying amount at the end of the period.

   (IAS 37, Para 84)

2. For each class of provision an entity should disclose the following:

   a. A brief description of the nature of the obligation and the expected timing of resulting outflows of economic benefits;
   b. An indication of any uncertainties about the amount or timing of those outflows. Where necessary, disclosure of major assumptions made concerning future events; and
   c. The amount of any expected reimbursement, disclosing any asset that has been recognized for that expected reimbursement.

   (IAS 37, Para 85)

3. Unless the possibility of any outflow in settlement is remote, an entity shall disclose for each class of contingent liability at the statement of financial position date a brief description of the nature of contingent liability and, where practicable

   a. An estimate of its financial effect;
   b. An indication of the uncertainties relating to the amount or timing of any outflow; and
   c. The possibility of any reimbursement.

   (IAS 37, Para 86)

4. Where an inflow of economic benefits is probable, an entity shall disclose a brief description of the nature of the contingent assets at the statement of financial position date, and where practicable, an estimate of their financial effect, measured using the principles set out in IAS 37, paragraphs 36-52.

   (IAS 37, Para 89)

5. In *extremely rare circumstances*, if some or all disclosures as outlined in IAS 37, paragraphs 84 and 85, are expected to prejudice seriously the position of the entity in a dispute with other parties, an entity need not disclose such information. Instead, it should disclose the general nature of the dispute, along with the fact that, and reason why, the information has not been disclosed.

(IAS 37, Para 92)

M. Deferred Tax Liabilities and Assets

1. The following shall be disclosed separately:

   a. The aggregate current and deferred tax relating to items that are charged or credited to equity;
   b. An explanation of the relationship between tax expense (income) and accounting profit in either or both of the following forms:

      (1) A numerical reconciliation between tax expense (income) and accounting profit multiplied by the applicable tax rate(s) is (are) computed; or
      (2) A numerical reconciliation between average effective tax rate and the applicable tax rate, disclosing also the basis on which the applicable tax rate is computed;

   c. An explanation of changes in the applicable tax rate(s) compared to the previous accounting period;
   d. The amount (and expiration date, in any) of deductible temporary differences, unused tax losses, and unused tax credits for which no deferred tax asset is recognized in the statement of financial position;
   e. The aggregate amount of temporary differences associated with investments in subsidiaries, branches and associates and interests in joint ventures, for which deferred tax liabilities have not been recognized;
   f. In respect of each temporary difference, and in respect of each type of unused tax credits

      (1) The amount of deferred tax assets and liabilities recognized in the statement of financial position for each period presented;
      (2) The amount of deferred tax income or expense recognized in the income statement, if this is not apparent from changes in the amounts recognized in the statement of financial position for each period presented;
      (3) In respect of discontinued operations, the tax expense relating to

         (a) The gain or loss on discontinuance; and
         (b) The profit or loss from the ordinary activities of the discontinued operation for the period, together with the corresponding amounts for each prior period presented;

   g. The amount of income tax consequences of dividends to shareholders of the entity that were proposed or declared before the financial statements were authorized for issue, but are not recognized as a liability in the financial statements;
   h. If a business combination in which the entity is the acquirer causes a change in the amount recognized for its preacquisition deferred tax asset, the amount of that change; and
   i. If the deferred tax benefits acquired in a business combination are not recognized at the acquisition date but are recognized after the acquisition date, a description

of the event or change in circumstances that caused the deferred tax benefits to be recognized.

(IAS 12, Para 81)

2. An entity shall disclose the amount of deferred tax asset and the nature of the evidence supporting its recognition, when

a. The utilization of the deferred tax asset is dependent on future taxable profits in excess of the profits arising from the reversal of existing taxable temporary differences; and

b. The entity has suffered a loss in either the current or preceding period in the jurisdiction to which the deferred tax relates.

(IAS 12, Para 82)

3. In the circumstances described in this paragraph set out below, an entity shall disclose the nature of the potential income tax consequences that would result from the payment of dividends to its shareholders. In addition, the entity shall disclose the amounts of the potential income tax consequences not practically determinable. In some jurisdictions, income taxes are payable at a higher or lower rate if part or all of the net profit or retained earnings is paid out as a dividend to shareholders of the entity. In these circumstances, current and deferred tax assets and liabilities are measured at the tax rate applicable to undistributed profits.

(IAS 12, Para 82A & 52A)

4. Current tax assets and tax liabilities should not be offset unless there is a legally enforceable right of offset and the entity intends to settle on a net basis, or to realize the asset and settle the liability simultaneously and they apply to the same taxable entity.

(IAS 12, Para 71)

5. Deferred tax assets and tax liabilities relating to different jurisdictions should be presented separately.

(IAS 12, Para 74)

6. Deferred tax assets and tax liabilities relating to different entities in a group which are taxed separately by the taxation authorities should not be offset unless there is a legally enforceable right of offset.

(IAS 12, Para 74)

7. When utilization of the deferred tax asset is dependent upon future taxable profits in excess of amounts arising from the reversal of existing taxable temporary differences, and the entity has incurred losses in either the current or preceding period in the tax jurisdiction to which the deferred tax asset relates, the amount of deferred tax asset should be disclosed together with the nature of any evidence supporting its recognition.

(IAS 12, Para 82)

N. Employee Benefits—Defined Benefit Pension and Other Postretirement Benefit Programs

1. The entity's accounting policy for recognizing actuarial gains and losses.
2. A general description of the type of plan.

3. A reconciliation of opening and closing balances of the present value of the defined benefit obligation, showing separately, as applicable, the effects during the period attributable to each of the following:

   a. The current service cost;
   b. The interest cost;
   c. Contributions by plan participants;
   d. Actuarial gains and losses;
   e. Foreign currency exchange rate changes on plans measured in a currency different from the entity's presentation currency;
   f. The benefits paid;
   g. The past service cost;
   h. The effect of business combinations;
   i. The effect of any curtailments; and
   j. The effect of any settlements.

4. An analysis of the defined benefit obligation into amounts arising from plans that are wholly unfunded and those amounts arising from plans that are wholly or partly funded.

5. A reconciliation of the opening and closing balances of the fair value of plan assets and of the opening and closing balances of any reimbursement right recognized as an asset in accordance with paragraph 104A showing separately, if applicable, the effects during the period attributable to each of the following:

   a. The expected return on plan assets;
   b. The actuarial gains and losses;
   c. The effect of foreign currency exchange rate changes on plans measured in a currency different from the entity's presentation currency;
   d. Contributions by the employer;
   e. Contributions by plan participants;
   f. Any benefits paid;
   g. The effect of any business combinations; and
   h. Any settlements.

6. A reconciliation of the present value of the defined benefit obligation in (3) and the fair value of the plan assets in (5) to the assets and liabilities recognized in the statement of financial position, showing at least

   a. The net actuarial gains or losses not recognized in the statement of financial position (see IAS 19, paragraph 92);
   b. The past service cost not recognized in the statement of financial position (see IAS 19, paragraph 96);
   c. Any amount not recognized as an asset, because of the limit in IAS 19, paragraph 58(b);
   d. The fair value at the statement of financial position date of any reimbursement right recognized as an asset in accordance with IAS 19, paragraph 104A (with a brief description of the link between the reimbursement right and the related obligation); and
   e. Any other amounts recognized in the statement of financial position.

7. The total expense recognized in profit or loss for each of the following, and the line item(s) in which they are included

    a. Current service cost;

    b. Interest cost;

    c. Expected return on plan assets;

    d. Expected return on any reimbursement right recognized as an asset in accordance with IAS 19, paragraph 104A;

    e. Actuarial gains and losses;

    f. Past service cost;

    g. The effect of any curtailment or settlement; and

    h. The effect of the limit in IAS 19, paragraph 58(b).

8. The total amount recognized in the statement of recognized income and expense for each of the following:

    a. Actuarial gains and losses; and

    b. The effect of the limit set forth at IAS 19, paragraph 58(b).

9. For entities that recognize actuarial gains and losses in the statement of recognized income and expense in accordance with IAS 19, paragraph 93A, the cumulative amount of actuarial gains and losses recognized in the statement of recognized income and expense.

10. For each major category of plan assets, to include, but not be limited to, equity instruments, debt instruments, property, and all other assets, the percentage or amount that each major category constitutes of the fair value of the total plan assets.

11. The amounts included in the fair value of plan assets for

    a. Each category of the entity's own financial instruments; and

    b. Any property occupied by, or other assets used by, the entity.

12. A narrative description of the basis used to determine the overall expected rate of return on assets, including the effect of the major categories of plan assets.

13. The actual return on plan assets, as well as the actual return on any reimbursement right recognized as an asset in accordance with IAS 19, paragraph 104A.

14. The principal actuarial assumptions used as at the statement of financial position date, including, when applicable

    a. The discount rates;

    b. The expected rates of return on any plan assets for the periods presented in the financial statements;

    c. The expected rates of return for the periods presented in the financial statements on any reimbursement right recognized as an asset in accordance with IAS 19, paragraph 104A;

    d. The expected rates of salary increases (and of changes in an index or other variable specified in the formal or constructive terms of a plan as the basis for future benefit increases);

    e. Medical cost trend rates; and

    f. Any other material actuarial assumptions used.

An entity is also to disclose each actuarial assumption in absolute terms (for example, as an absolute percentage), and not just as a margin between different percentages or other variables.

15. The effect of an increase of one percentage point and the effect of a decrease of one percentage point in the assumed medical cost trend rates on

    a. The aggregate of the current service cost and interest cost components of net periodic postemployment medical costs; and

    b. The accumulated postemployment benefit obligation for medical costs.

For the purposes of this disclosure, all other assumptions are to be held constant. For plans operating in a high-inflation environment, the disclosure shall be the effect of a percentage increase or decrease in the assumed medical cost trend rate of a significance similar to one percentage point in a low-inflation environment.

16. The amounts for the current annual period and previous four annual periods of

    a. The present value of the defined benefit obligation, the fair value of the plan assets and the surplus or deficit in the plan; and

    b. The experience adjustments arising on

       (1) The plan liabilities expressed either as

         (a) An amount or

         (b) A percentage of the plan liabilities at the statement of financial position date, and

       (2) The plan assets expressed either as

         (a) An amount or

         (b) A percentage of the plan assets at the statement of financial position date.

17. The employer's best estimate, as soon as it can reasonably be determined, of contributions expected to be paid to the plan during the annual period beginning after the statement of financial position date.

(IAS 19, Para 120A)

O. Employee Benefits—Other Benefit Plans

1. For defined contribution pension plans and similar arrangements, the amount recognized as expense for the period being reported upon must be disclosed.

(IAS 19, Para 46)

2. For long-term compensated absences, long-term disability plans, profit sharing or bonus arrangements or deferred compensation plans payable more than twelve months after the end of the period in which benefits are earned, and similar types of benefit plans, any disclosures which would be mandated by other international standards, such as IAS 1, IAS 8, and IAS 24 (there being no specific disclosures required by IAS 19).

(IAS 19, Para 131)

3. If there is uncertainty regarding the number of employees who will accept an offer of termination benefits, the entity is to disclose information about the resulting contingent liability, unless the possibility of an outflow in settlement is remote. If material, the nature and amount of the expense arising from termination benefits is to be disclosed. Termination benefits for key management personnel, as required by IAS 24, should also be disclosed.

(IAS 19, Para 141-143)

4. For short-term employee benefits, such as short-term compensated absences and profit sharing or bonus arrangements to be paid within twelve months after the end of the period in which the employees render the related services, any disclosures which would be required by other international accounting standards, such as IAS 24, must be made.

(IAS 19, Para 23)

P. Leases—from the Standpoint of a Lessee

1. For finance leases

In addition to requirements of IFRS 7, make the following disclosures for finance leases:

    a. For each class of asset, the net carrying amount at statement of financial position date;

    b. A reconciliation between the total of minimum lease payments at the statement of financial position date, and their present value. In addition, an entity should disclose the total of the minimum lease payments at the statement of financial position date, their present value, for each of the following periods:

        (1) Due in one year or less,

        (2) Due in more than one but no more than five years, and

        (3) Due in more than five years.

    c. Contingent rents recognized as expense for the period;

    d. The total of minimum sublease payments to be received in the future under non-cancelable subleases as of the statement of financial position date;

    e. A general description of the lessee's significant leasing arrangements including, but not necessarily limited to the following:

        (1) The basis for determining contingent rentals;

        (2) The existence and terms of renewal or purchase options and escalation clauses; and

        (3) Restrictions imposed by lease arrangements such as on dividends or assumptions of further debt or further leasing.

(IAS 17, Para 31)

2. For operating leases, including those arising from sale-leaseback transactions

Lessees should, in addition to the requirements of IFRS 7, make the following disclosures for operating leases:

    a. Total of the future minimum lease payments under noncancelable operating leases for each of the following periods:

        (1) Due in one year or less;

        (2) Due in more than one year but no more than five years; and

        (3) Due in more than five years.

    b. The total of future minimum sublease payments expected to be received under noncancelable subleases at the statement of financial position date;

    c. Lease and sublease payments included in profit or loss for the period, with separate amounts of minimum lease payments, contingent rents, and sublease payments;

d. A general description of the lessee's significant leasing arrangements including, but not necessarily limited to the following:

(1) The basis for determining contingent rentals;
(2) The existence and terms of renewal or purchase options and escalation clauses; and
(3) Restrictions imposed by lease arrangements such as on dividends or assumption of further debt or on further leasing.

(IAS 17, Para 35)

Q. Leases—from the Standpoint of a Lessor

1. For finance leases

Lessors under finance leases are required to disclose, in addition to disclosures under IFRS 7, the following:

a. A reconciliation between the total gross investment in the lease at the statement of financial position date, and the present value of minimum lease payments receivable as of the statement of financial position date, categorized into

(1) Those due in one year or less;
(2) Those due in more than one year but not more than five years; and
(3) Those due beyond five years.

b. Unearned finance income.
c. The accumulated allowance for uncollectible minimum lease payments receivable.
d. Total contingent rentals included in income.
e. A general description of the lessor's significant leasing arrangements.

(IAS 17, Para 47)

2. For operating leases

For lessors under operating leases the following expanded disclosures are prescribed:

a. Future minimum lease payments under noncancelable operating leases, in the aggregate and classified into

(1) Those due in no more than one year;
(2) Those due in more than one but not more than five years; and
(3) Those due in more than five years.

b. Total contingent rentals included in income for the period.
c. A general description of leasing arrangements to which it is a party.

(IAS 17, Para 56)

R. Lease—Substance of the Transaction Involving the Legal Form

1. All aspects of an arrangement that does not, in substance, involve a lease under IAS 17 should be considered in determining the appropriate disclosures that are necessary to understand the arrangement and the accounting treatment adopted. An entity should disclose the following in *each period* that an arrangement exists:

    a. A description of the arrangement including

        (1) The underlying asset and any restrictions on its use;

        (2) The life and other significant terms of the arrangement;

        (3) The transactions that are linked together, including any options; and

    b. The accounting treatment applied to any fee received;

    c. The amount of fees recognized as income in the period; and

    d. The line item of the income statement in which the fee income is included.

(SIC 27, Para 10)

2. The disclosures required in accordance with SIC 27, paragraph 10, above, should be provided individually for each arrangement or in aggregate for each class of arrangement. (A "class" is a grouping of arrangements with underlying assets of a similar nature [e.g., power plants]).

(SIC 27, Para 11)

S. Stockholders' Equity

1. The following disclosures should be made by an entity either on the face of the statement of financial position or in the notes:

    a. For each class of share capital

        (1) The number of shares authorized;

        (2) The number of shares issued and fully paid, and issued but not fully paid;

        (3) Par value per share, or the fact that the shares have no par value;

        (4) A reconciliation of the number of shares outstanding at the beginning of the year to the number of shares outstanding at the end of the year;

        (5) The rights, preferences and restrictions attaching to each class of shares, including restrictions on the distribution of dividends and the repayment of capital;

        (6) Shares held by the entity itself or by subsidiaries or associates of the entity; and

        (7) Shares reserved for future issuance under options and sales contracts, including terms and amounts.

    b. For reserves within the owners' equity, a description, nature, and purpose of each reserve.

(IAS 1, Para 79)

2. An entity without share capital, such as a partnership or trust, should disclose information equivalent to that required above, showing movements during the year in each category of equity interest and the rights, preferences, and restrictions attaching to each category of equity interest.

(IAS 1, Para 80)

3. Treasury shares require the following disclosures:

    a. The amount of reductions to equity for treasury shares should be disclosed separately. This disclosure could be either on the face of the statement of financial position or in the notes to the financial statements.

    b. Where the entity, or its subsidiary, reacquires its own shares from parties able to control or exercise significant influence over the entity, this should be disclosed as a related-party transaction under IAS 24.

(IAS 32, Para 34)

4. Transaction costs issuing equity instruments or of acquiring them should be accounted for as a deduction from equity and separately disclosed. The related income taxes recognized directly in equity should also be included in the disclosure of the aggregate amount of current and deferred income tax credited or charged to equity.

(IAS 32, Para 35)

STATEMENT OF COMPREHENSIVE INCOME

A. Minimum Disclosures on the Face of the Income Statement

1. Minimum disclosures on the face of the statement of comprehensive income should include the following:

    a. Revenue;
    b. Gains and losses arising from the derecognition of financial assets measured at amortized cost;
    c. Finance costs;
    d. Share of profits and losses of associates and joint ventures accounted for using the equity method;
    e. If a financial asset is reclassified so that it is measured at fair value, any gain or loss arising from a difference between the previous carrying amount and its fair value at the reclassification date (as defined by IFRS 9);
    f. Tax expense;
    g. A single amount which will include (1) posttax profit/loss of discontinued operation and (2) posttax gain or loss recognized on the measurement to fair value less costs to sell or on the disposal of the assets or disposal groups constituting the discontinued operation;
    h. Profit or loss;
    i. Each component of other comprehensive income classified by nature(excluding amounts in j.;
    j. Share of the other comprehensive income of associates and joint ventures accounted for using the equity method; and
    k. Total comprehensive income.

(IAS 1, Para 82)

2. The following items shall be disclosed on the face of the statement of comprehensive income as allocations of the profit or loss for the period:

    a. Profit or loss attributable to noncontrolling interests;
    b. Profit or loss attributable to owners of the parent; and
    c. Total comprehensive income for the period attributable to

        (1) Noncontrolling interests; and
        (2) Owners of the parent.

(IAS 1, Para 83)

3. Additional line items, headings and subtotals should be presented on the face of the statement of comprehensive income when required by an IAS or when such a presentation is necessary in order to fairly present the entity's financial performance.

(IAS 1, Para 85)

4. All items of income and expense in a period are to be included in profit or loss unless an IFRS requires or permits otherwise.

(IAS 1, Para 88)

5. The amount of income tax relating to each component of other comprehensive income, including reclassification adjustments, are to be disclosed either in the statement of comprehensive income or in the notes.

(IAS 1, Para 90 and IAS 12, Para 81)

6. Reclassification adjustments relating to components of other comprehensive income are to be disclosed.

(IAS 1, Para 92)

7. An entity shall present all items of income and expense recognized in a period:

   a. In a single statement of comprehensive income; or
   b. In two statements: a statement displaying components of profit or loss(separate income statement) and a second statement beginning with profit or loss and displaying components of other comprehensive income (statement of comprehensive income.

(IAS 1, Para 81)

B. Investment Property

1. General disclosures

   a. Whether it applies the fair value model or cost model.
   b. If it applies fair value model, whether and in what circumstances the property held under operating leases are classified and accounted for as investment property.
   c. When classification is difficult, an entity that holds an investment property will need to disclose the criteria used to distinguish investment property from owner-occupied property and from property held for sale in the ordinary course of business.
   d. The method and any significant assumptions that were used in ascertaining the fair values of the investment properties are to be disclosed as well. Such disclosure should also include a statement about whether the determination of fair value was supported by market evidence or it relied heavily on other factors (which the entity needs to disclose as well) due to the nature of the property and the absence of comparable market data;
   e. If investment property has been revalued by an independent valuer having recognized and relevant qualifications and who has recent experience with properties having similar characteristics of location and type, the extent to which the fair value of investment property is based on valuation by such an independent valuer, if there is no such valuation, the fact should be disclosed as well;
   f. Amounts included in the statement of comprehensive income for

    (1) Rental income from investment property;

    (2) Direct operating expenses including repairs and maintenance arising from investment property that generated rental income during the period;

    (3) Direct operating expenses including repairs and maintenance arising from investment property that did not generate rental income during the period; and

    (4) The cumulative change in fair value recognized in profit or loss on a sale of investment property from a pool of assets in which the cost model is used.

  g. The existence and the amount of any restrictions which may potentially affect the reliability of investment property or the remittance of income and proceeds from disposal to be received; and

  h. Material contractual obligations to purchase or build investment property or for repairs, maintenance, or improvements thereto.

(IAS 40, Para 75)

2. In the case of investment property carried under the fair value model, as part of the reconciliation of the carrying amount of the investment at the beginning and the end of the period, the entity should disclose the following:

  a. Additions, comprising additions from acquisitions and from subsequent expenditure recognized in the carrying amount of an asset;

  b. Additions following from acquisitions through business combination;

  c. Assets held for sale or included in a disposal group held for sale in accordance with IFRS 5 and any other disposal;

  d. Net profit or losses incurred from fair value adjustment;

  e. Exchange differences arising on the translation of financial statements into a different presentation currency of the reporting entity;

  f. Transfers to and from inventories and owner-occupied property; and

  g. Any other changes.

(IAS 40, Para 76)

3. In the case of investment property carried under the cost model, as part of the reconciliation of the carrying amount of the investment at the beginning and at the end of the period, the depreciation, the amount of impairment losses recognized and reversed and the net exchange differences arising from the translation of the financial statements of a foreign entity and any additions resulting from acquisitions and from subsequent expenditure recognized as an asset and from acquisitions through business combinations and assets classified as held-for-sale or included in a disposal group classified as held-for-sale in accordance with IAS 36, transfers to and from inventories and owner-occupied property and other changes.

(IAS 40, Para 79d)

C. Income Taxes

1. Tax expense related to profit or loss from ordinary activities should be presented on the face of the statement of comprehensive income.

(IAS 12, Para 77)

2. The major components of tax expense should be presented separately. These commonly would include the following:

   a. Current tax expense;

   b. Any adjustments recognized in the period for current tax of prior periods;

   c. The amount of deferred tax expense relating to the origination and the reversal of timing differences;

   d. The amount of deferred tax expense relating to changes in tax rates or the imposition of new taxes;

   e. The amount of the benefit arising from a previously unrecognized tax loss, tax credit, or temporary difference of a prior period that is used to reduce current taxes;

   f. The amount of a benefit from a previously unrecognized tax loss, tax credit, or temporary difference of a prior period that is used to reduce deferred taxes;

   g. Deferred tax expense related to a write-down of a deferred tax asset or the reversal of a write-down; and

   h. The amount of tax expense relating to changes in accounting policies and correction of fundamental errors, accounted for consistent with the allowed alternative method under IAS 8, because they cannot be applied retrospectively.

(IAS 12, Para 79 & 80)

3. The following shall be disclosed separately:

   a. The aggregate current and deferred tax relating to items that are charged or credited to equity;

   b. An explanation of the relationship between tax expense (income) and accounting profit in either or both of the following forms:

      (1) A numerical reconciliation between tax expense (income) and accounting profit multiplied by the applicable tax rate(s) is (are) computed; or

      (2) A numerical reconciliation between average effective tax rate and the applicable tax rate, disclosing also the basis on which the applicable tax rate is computed;

   c. An explanation of changes in the applicable tax rate(s) compared to the previous accounting period;

   d. The amount (and expiration date, in any) of deductible temporary differences, unused tax losses, and unused tax credits for which no deferred tax asset is recognized in the statement of financial position;

   e. The aggregate amount of temporary differences associated with investments in subsidiaries, branches and associates and interests in joint ventures, for which deferred tax liabilities have not been recognized.

   f. In respect of each temporary difference, and in respect of each type of unused tax credits

      (1) The amount of deferred tax assets and liabilities recognized in the statement of financial position for each period presented;

      (2) The amount of deferred tax income or expense recognized in the income statement, if this is not apparent from changes in the amounts recognized in the statement of financial position for each period presented;

      (3) In respect of discontinued operations, the tax expense relating to

         (a) The gain or loss on discontinuance; and

         (b) The profit or loss from the ordinary activities of the discontinued operation for the period, together with the corresponding amounts for each prior period presented;

g. The amount of income tax consequences of dividends to shareholders of the entity that were proposed or declared before the financial statements were authorized for issue, but are not recognized as a liability in the financial statements;

h. If a business combination in which the entity is the acquirer causes a change in the amount recognized for its preacquisition deferred tax asset, the amount of that change; and

i. If the deferred tax benefits acquired in a business combination are not recognized at the acquisition date but are recognized after the acquisition date, a description of the event or change in circumstances that caused the deferred tax benefits to be recognized.

(IAS 12, Para 81)

D. Extraordinary Items

1. An entity shall not present any items of income or expense as extraordinary items, in the statement of comprehensive income or the separate income statement (if presented), or in the notes.

(IAS 1, Para 87)

E. Noncurrent Assets Held for Sale and Discontinued Operations

1. An entity shall present and disclose information that enables users of the financial statements to evaluate the financial effects of discontinued operations and disposals of noncurrent assets (or disposal groups).

(IFRS 5, Para 30)

2. An entity shall disclose

a. A single amount on the face of the income statement comprising the total of

(1) The posttax profit or loss of discontinuing operations; and;

(2) The posttax gain or loss recognized on the measurement to fair value less costs to sell or on the disposal of the assets or disposal group(s) constituting the discontinued operation.

b. An analysis of the single amount in a. into

(1) The revenue, expenses and pretax profit or loss of discontinued operations;

(2) The related income tax expense as required by IAS 12, paragraph 81(h);

(3) The gain or loss recognized on the measurement to fair value less costs to sell or on the disposal of the assets or disposal group(s) constituting the discontinued operation; and

(4) The related income tax expense as required by IAS 12, paragraph 81(h). The analysis may be presented in the notes or on the face of the income statement. If it is presented on the face of the income statement it shall be presented in a section identified as relating to discontinued operations (i.e., separately from continuing operations). The analysis is not required for disposal groups that are newly acquired subsidiaries that meet the criteria to be classified as held-for-sale on acquisition.

c. The net cash flows attributable to the operating, investing, and financing activities of discontinued operations. These disclosures may be presented either in the notes or on the face of the financial statements. These disclosures are not required for disposal groups that are newly acquired subsidiaries that meet the criteria to be classified as held-for-sale on acquisition.

    d. The amount of income from continuing operations and from discontinued operations attributable to owners of the parent. These disclosure may be presented either in the notes or in the statement of comprehensive income.

(IFRS 5, Para 33)

3. An entity shall re-present the disclosures in IFRS 5, paragraph 33 for prior periods presented in the financial statements so that the disclosures relate to all operations that have been discontinued by the statement of financial position date for the latest period presented.

(IFRS 5, Para 34)

4. An entity shall present a noncurrent asset classified as held-for-sale and the assets of a disposal group classified as held-for-sale separately from other assets in the statement of financial position. The liabilities of the disposal group classified as held-for-sale shall be presented separately from other liabilities in the statement of financial position. Those assets and liabilities shall not be offset and presented as a single amount. The major classes of assets and liabilities classified as held-for-sale shall be separately disclosed either on the face of the statement of financial position or in the notes. An entity shall present separately any cumulative income or expense recognized directly as equity relating to a noncurrent asset classified as held-for-sale.

(IFRS 5, Para 38)

5. If the disposal group is a newly acquired subsidiary that meets the criteria to be classified as held-for-sale on acquisition, disclosure of the major classes of assets and liabilities is not required.

(IFRS 5, Para 39)

6. An entity shall not reclassify or re-present amounts presented for noncurrent assets or for the assets and liabilities of disposal groups classified as held-for-sale in the statement of financial position for prior periods to reflect the classification in the statement of financial position for the latest period presented.

(IAS 5, Para 40)

7. An entity shall disclose the following information in the notes in the period in which a noncurrent asset (disposal group) has been either classified as held-for-sale or sold:

    a. A description of the noncurrent asset (or disposal group);

    b. A description of the facts and circumstances of the sale, or leading to the expected disposal, the expected manner and timing of that disposal;

    c. The impairment gain or loss recognized in accordance with IFRS 5, and if not separately presented on the face of the income statement, the caption in the income statement that includes that gain or loss; and

    d. If applicable, the segment in which the noncurrent asset (or disposal group) is presented in accordance with IFRS 8, *Operating Segments*.

(IFRS 5, Para 41)

8. If, as per IFRS 5, an entity changes to the plan of sale, it shall disclose, in the period of the decision to change the plan to sell the noncurrent asset (or disposal group), a

description of the facts and circumstances leading to the decision and the effect of the decision on the results of operations for the period and any prior periods presented.

(IFRS 5, Para 42)

F. Segment Data

1. General information about segments

   a. Factors used to identify the entity's reportable segments, including the basis of organization (for example, whether management has chosen to organize the entity around differences in products and services, geographical areas, regulatory environments, or a combination of factors and whether operating segments have been aggregated), and

   b. Types of products and services from which each reportable segment derives its revenues.

   (IFRS 8, Para 22)

2. Information about profit or loss, assets and liabilities

   a. The reporting entity is to report a measure of profit or loss and total assets for each reportable segment.

   b. It is to report a measure of liabilities for each reportable segment if such an amount is regularly provided to the chief operating decision maker.

   c. It also is to disclose the following about each reportable segment if the specified amounts are included in the measure of segment profit or loss reviewed by the chief operating decision maker, or are otherwise regularly provided to the chief operating decision maker, even if not included in that measure of segment profit or loss:

      (1) Revenues from external customers;
      (2) Revenues from transactions with other operating segments of the same entity;
      (3) Interest revenue;
      (4) Interest expense;
      (5) Depreciation and amortization;
      (6) Material items of income and expense disclosed in accordance with IAS 1;
      (7) The entity's interest in the profit or loss of associates and joint ventures accounted for by the equity method;
      (8) Income tax expense or income; and
      (9) Material noncash items other than depreciation and amortization.

   d. An entity is to report interest revenue separately from interest expense for each reportable segment unless a majority of the segment's revenues are from interest and the chief operating decision maker relies primarily on net interest revenue to assess the performance of the segment and make decisions about resources to be allocated to the segment. In that situation, an entity may report that segment's interest revenue net of its interest expense and disclose that it has done so.

   (IFRS 8, Para 23)

   e. The reporting entity is to disclose the following about each reportable segment if the specified amounts are included in the measure of segment assets reviewed by the chief operating decision maker or are otherwise regularly provided to the chief operating decision maker, even if not included in the measure of segment assets:

(1) The amount of investment in associates and joint ventures accounted for by the equity method, and

(2) The amounts of additions to noncurrent assets other than financial instruments, deferred tax assets, postemployment benefit assets and rights arising under insurance contracts.

(IFRS 8, Para 24)

3. Reconciliations of the totals of segment revenues, reported segment profit or loss, segment assets, segment liabilities and other material segment items to corresponding entity amounts as follows:

a. The total of the reportable segments' revenues to the entity's revenue.

b. The total of the reportable segments' measures of profit or loss to the entity's profit or loss before tax expense (tax income) and discontinued operations. However, if an entity allocates to reportable segments items such as tax expense (tax income), the entity may reconcile the total of the segments' measures of profit or loss to the entity's profit or loss after those items.

c. The total of the reportable segments assets to the entity's assets.

d. The total of the reportable segments liabilities to the entity's liabilities if segment liabilities are reported in accordance with paragraph 23.

e. The total of the reportable segments amounts for every other material item of information disclosed to the corresponding amount for the entity.

All material reconciling items shall be separately identified and described.

(IFRS 8, Para 28)

4. Entity-wide disclosures:

a. Information about products and services. Revenues from external customers for each product and service, or each group of similar products and services, are to be identified, unless the necessary information is not available and the cost to develop it would be excessive, in which case that fact shall be disclosed. The amounts of revenues reported are to be based on the financial information used to produce the entity's financial statements.

(IFRS 8, Para 32)

b. Information about geographic areas. The reporting entity is to disclose the following geographical information, unless the necessary information is not available and the cost to develop it would be excessive:

(1) Revenues from external customers (a) attributed to the entity's country of domicile and (b) attributed to all foreign countries in total from which the entity derives revenues. If revenues from external customers attributed to an individual foreign country are material, those revenues are to be disclosed separately. An entity is required to disclose the basis for attributing revenues from external customers to individual countries.

(2) Noncurrent assets other than financial instruments, deferred tax assets, postemployment benefit assets, and rights arising under insurance contracts (a) located in the entity's country of domicile and (b) located in all foreign

countries in total in which the entity holds assets. If assets in an individual foreign country are material, those assets shall be disclosed separately. If a classified statement of financial position is not presented (i.e., if liquidity ordering is utilized), noncurrent assets are to be defined as assets that include amounts expected to be recovered more than twelve months after the reporting date.

(IFRS 8, Para 33)

c. Information about major customers. Information about the extent of the reporting entity's reliance on its major customers must be provided. If revenues from transactions with a single external customer amount to 10% or more of the entity's revenues, it is to disclose that fact, the total amount of revenues from each such customer, and the identity of the segment or segments reporting the revenues. The entity need not disclose the identity of a major customer or the amount of revenues that each segment reports from that customer. For the purposes of this requirement under IFRS 8, a group of entities known to be under common control is to be considered a single customer, and a government (national, state, provincial, territorial, local or foreign) and entities known to be under the control of that government are to be considered a single customer.

(IFRS 8, Para 34)

G. Construction Contracts

1. An entity which accounts for construction contracts in accordance with IAS 11 should disclose the following in its financial statements:

   a. The amount of contract revenue recognized as revenue in the period;
   b. The methods used to determine the contract revenue recognized in the period; and
   c. The methods used to determine the stage of completion for contracts in progress.

(IAS 11, Para 39)

2. Each of the following should be disclosed for the contracts in progress:

   a. The aggregate amount of costs incurred and recognized profits (net of any recognized losses) to date;
   b. The amount of advances received; and
   c. The amount of retentions.

(IAS 11, Para 40)

3. On the statement of financial position, present gross amounts due from customers as an asset, and gross amounts due to customers for contract work as a liability.

(IAS 11, Para 42)

H. Foreign Currency Translation

1. Disclosure is required of the following:

   a. The amount of exchange differences included in net profit or loss for the period;
   b. Net exchange differences classified as a separate component of equity, and a reconciliation of the amount of such exchange differences at the beginning and the end of the period.

(IAS 21, Para 52)

2. If the reporting currency is different from the currency of the country in which the entity is domiciled, disclosure is required of the following:

    a. The reason for using a different currency; and
    b. The reason for any change in the reporting currency.

    (IAS 21, Para 53)

3. When there is a change in classification of a significant foreign operation or a change in functional currency, the following disclosures are required:

    a. The nature of the change; and
    b. The reason for the change.

    (IAS 21, Para 54)

4. When an entity presents its financial statements in a currency that is different from its functional currency, it shall describe the financial statements as complying with IFRS only if they comply with all the requirements of each applicable Standard and each applicable Interpretation of those Standards including the translation method.

    (IAS 21, Para 55)

5. When an entity displays its financial statements or other financial information in a currency that is different from either its functional currency or its presentation currency and the requirements of IAS 21, paragraph 21, are not met, it shall

    a. Clearly identify the information as supplementary information to distinguish it from the information that complies with IFRS;
    b. Disclose the currency in which the supplementary information is displayed; and
    c. Disclose the entity's functional currency and the method of translation used to determine the supplementary information.

    (IAS 21, Para 57)

I. Business Combinations

1. An acquirer shall disclose information that enables users of its financial statements to evaluate the nature and financial effect of business combinations that were effected

    a. During the period;
    b. After the statement of financial position date but before the financial statements are authorized for issue.

    (IFRS 3, Para 59)

2. The acquirer shall disclose the following information for each business combination that was effected during the period:

    a. The names and descriptions of the combining entities or businesses;
    b. The acquisition date;
    c. The percentage of voting equity interests acquired;
    d. The primary reasons for the business combination and a description of how the acquirer obtained control of the acquiree.
    e. A qualitative description of the factors that make up the goodwill recognized, such as expected synergies from combining operations of the acquiree and the acquirer, intangible assets that do not qualify for separate recognition or other factors.

f. The acquisition-date fair value of the total consideration transferred and the acquisition-date fair value of each major class of consideration, such as

   (1) Cash;
   (2) Other tangible or intangible assets, including a business or subsidiary of the acquirer;
   (3) Liabilities incurred, for example, a liability for contingent consideration; and
   (4) Equity interests of the acquirer, including the number of instruments or interests issued or issuable and the method of determining the fair value of those instruments or interests.

g. For contingent consideration arrangements and indemnification assets

   (1) The amount recognized as of the acquisition date;
   (2) A description of the arrangement and the basis for determining the amount of the payment; and
   (3) An estimate of the range of outcomes (undiscounted) or, if a range cannot be estimated, that fact and the reasons why a range cannot be estimated. If the maximum amount of the payment is unlimited, the acquirer shall disclose that fact.

h. For acquired receivables (these shall be provided by major class of receivable, such as loans, direct finance leases and any other class of receivables)

   (1) The fair value of the receivables;
   (2) The gross contractual amounts receivable; and
   (3) The best estimate at the acquisition date of the contractual cash flows not expected to be collected.

i. The amounts recognized as of the acquisition date for each major class of assets acquired and liabilities assumed.
j. For each contingent liability recognized, the information required in paragraph 85 of IAS 37, *Provisions, Contingent Liabilities, and Contingent Assets.* If a contingent liability is not recognized because its fair value cannot be measured reliably, the acquirer shall disclose

   (1) The information required by paragraph 86 of IAS 37; and
   (2) The reasons why the liability cannot be measured reliably.

k. The total amount of goodwill that is expected to be deductible for tax purposes.
l. For transactions that are recognized separately from the acquisition of assets and assumption of liabilities in the business combination in accordance with paragraph 51

   (1) A description of each transaction;
   (2) How the acquirer accounted for each transaction;
   (3) The amounts recognized for each transaction and the line item in the financial statements in which each amount is recognized; and
   (4) If the transaction is the effective settlement of a preexisting relationship, the method used to determine the settlement amount.

m. The disclosure of separately recognized transactions required by (l) shall include the amounts of acquisition-related costs and, separately, the amount of those costs recognized as an expense and the line item or items in the statement of comprehensive income in which those expenses are recognized. The amount of any issue costs not recognized as expenses and how they were recognized shall also be disclosed.

n. In a bargain purchase

    (1) The amount of any gain recognized in accordance with paragraph 34 and the line item in the statement of comprehensive income in which the gain is recognized; and

    (2) A description of the reasons why the transaction resulted in a gain.

o. For each business combination in which the acquirer holds less than 100% of the equity interests in the acquiree at the acquisition date

    (1) The amount of the noncontrolling interest in an acquiree recognized at the acquisition date and the measurement basis for that amount; and

    (2) For each noncontrolling interest in an acquiree measured at fair value, the valuation techniques and key model inputs used for determining that value.

p. In a business combination achieved in stages

    (1) The acquisition-date fair value of the equity interest in the acquiree held by the acquirer immediately before the acquisition date; and

    (2) The amount of any gain or loss recognized as a result of re-measuring to fair value the equity interest in the acquiree held by the acquirer before the business combination and the line item in the statement of comprehensive income in which that gain or loss is recognized.

q. The amounts of revenue and profit or loss of the acquiree since the acquisition date included in the consolidated statement of comprehensive income for the reporting period.

r. The revenue and profit or loss of the combined entity for the current reporting period as though the acquisition date for all business combinations that occurred during the year had been as of the beginning of the annual reporting period.

(IFRS 3, Para B64-B67)

3. The information required to be disclosed by IFRS 3, paragraph 67, shall be disclosed in aggregate for business combinations effected during the reporting period that are individually immaterial.

(IFRS 3, Para B65)

4. If the initial accounting for a business combination that was effected during the period was determined only provisionally as described in IFRS 3, the fact should be also disclosed together with an explanation of why this is the case.

(IFRS 3, Para B67)

5. An acquirer shall disclose information that enables its users to evaluate the financial effects of gains, losses, error corrections, and other adjustments recognized in the current period that relate to business combinations that were effected in the current or in previous periods.

(IFRS 3, Para 61)

6. The acquirer shall disclose the following information for each material business combination or in the aggregate for individually immaterial business combinations that are material collectively:

a. If the initial accounting for a business combination is incomplete for particular assets, liabilities, noncontrolling interests or items of consideration and the amounts recognized in the financial statements for the business combination thus have been determined only provisionally

  (1) The reasons why the initial accounting for the business combination is incomplete;
  (2) The assets, liabilities, equity interests or items of consideration for which the initial accounting is incomplete; and
  (3) The nature and amount of any measurement period adjustments recognized during the reporting period in accordance with paragraph 49.

b. For each reporting period after the acquisition date until the entity collects, sells or otherwise loses the right to a contingent consideration asset, or until the entity settles a contingent consideration liability or the liability is cancelled or expires

  (1) Any changes in the recognized amounts, including any differences arising upon settlement;
  (2) Any changes in the range of outcomes (undiscounted) and the reasons for those changes; and
  (3) The valuation techniques and key model inputs used to measure contingent consideration.

c. For contingent liabilities recognized in a business combination, the acquirer shall disclose the information required by paragraph 84 and 85 of IAS 37 for each class of provision.

d. Disclose a reconciliation of the carrying amount of goodwill at the beginning and the end of the period, showing separately

  (1) The gross amount and accumulated impairment losses at the beginning of the period;
  (2) Additional goodwill recognized during the period except goodwill included in a disposal group that, on acquisition, meets the criteria to be classified as held for sale in accordance with IFRS 5;
  (3) Adjustments resulting from the subsequent recognition of deferred tax assets during the period in accordance with IFRS 3, paragraph 65;
  (4) Goodwill included in disposal group classified as held for sale in accordance with IFRS 5 and goodwill derecognized during the period without having been previously included in a disposal group classified for sale;
  (5) Impairment losses recognized during the period in accordance with IAS 36;
  (6) Net exchange differences arising during the period in accordance with IAS 21, *The Effects of Changes in Foreign Exchange Rates*;
  (7) Any other changes in the carrying amount during the period; and
  (8) The gross amount and accumulated impairment losses at the end of the period.

e. The amount and an explanation of any gain or loss recognized in the current reporting period that both

(1) Relates to the identifiable assets acquired or liabilities assumed in a business combination that was effected in the current or previous reporting period; and

(2) Is of such a size, nature, or incidence that disclosure is relevant to understand the combined entity's financial statements.

(IFRS 3, Para B67)

J. Earnings Per Share

1. When an entity presents consolidated financial statements prepared in accordance with IAS 27, the disclosures required by this standard need be presented only on the basis of the consolidated information. An entity that chooses to disclose earnings per share based on its separate financial statements shall present such earnings per share information only in its statement of comprehensive income. An entity shall not present such earnings per share information in the consolidated financial statements.

(IAS 33, Para 4)

2. Entities should present both basic EPS and diluted EPS on the face of the statement of comprehensive income for each class of ordinary shares that has a different right to share in the net profit/(loss) for the period. Equal prominence should be given to both the basic EPS and diluted EPS figures for all periods presented.

(IAS 33, Para 66)

3. Entities should present basic EPS and diluted EPS even if the amounts disclosed are negative.

(IAS 33, Para 69)

4. Where relevant, EPS from continuing operations should be presented also.

(IAS 33, Para 66)

5. Entities should disclose amounts used as the numerator in calculating basic EPS and diluted EPS along with a reconciliation of those amounts to the net profit or loss for the period. Disclosure is also required of the weighted-average number of ordinary shares used as the denominator in calculating basic EPS and diluted EPS along with a reconciliation of these denominators to each other.

(IAS 33, Para 70[a] & 70[b])

6. a. In addition to the disclosure of the figures for basic EPS and diluted EPS, as required above, if an entity discloses per share amounts using a reported component of net profit, other than net profit or loss for the period attributable to ordinary shareholders, such amounts should be calculated using weighted-average number of ordinary shares determined in accordance with the requirements of IAS 33; this will ensure comparability of the per share amounts disclosed;

b. In cases where an entity discloses the above per share amounts using a component of net profit not reported as a line item in the income statement, a reconciliation is mandated by the standard, which should reconcile the difference between the component of net income used with a line item reported in the income statement; and

c. When additional disclosure is made by an entity of the above per share amounts, basic and diluted per share amounts should be disclosed with equal prominence (just as basic EPS and diluted EPS figures are given equal prominence).

(IAS 33, Para 73)

7. Entities are encouraged to disclose the terms and conditions of financial instruments or contracts generating potential ordinary shares, since such terms and conditions may determine whether or not any potential ordinary shares are dilutive and, if so, the effect on the weighted-average number of shares outstanding and any consequent adjustments to the net profit attributable to the ordinary shareholders.

(IAS 33, Para 72)

8. If changes (resulting from bonus issue or share split, etc.) in the number of ordinary or potential ordinary shares occur, after the statement of financial position date but before issuance of the financial statements, and the per share calculations reflect such changes in the number of shares, such a fact should be disclosed.

(IAS 33, Para 70[d])

9. An entity shall disclose the instruments (including contingently issuable shares) that could potentially dilute basic earnings per share in the future, but were not included in the calculation of diluted earnings per share because they are antidilutive for the period(s) presented.

(IAS 33, Para 70[c])

10. An entity that reports a discontinued operation shall disclose the basic and diluted amounts per share for the discontinued operation either in the statement of comprehensive income or in the notes.

(IAS 33, Para 68)

K. Impairments of Assets

1. For each class of assets, the financial statements should disclose

a. The amount of impairment losses recognized in the income statement during the period and the line item(s) of the income statements in which those impairment losses are included;
b. The amount of reversals of impairment losses recognized in the income statement during the period and the line item(s) of the income statement in which those impairment losses are reversed;
c. The amount of impairment losses on revalued assets recognized directly in equity during the period; and
d. The amount of reversals of impairment losses on revalued assets recognized directly in equity during the period.

(IAS 36, Para 126)

2. If impairment loss for an asset (including goodwill) or a cash-generating unit is recognized or reversed during the period and is **material** to the financial statements as a whole, an entity should disclose

a. Events and circumstances that led to the recognition or reversal of the impairment loss;

b. Amount of the impairment loss recognized or reversed;

c. For an individual asset, its nature and the primary reportable segment to which it belongs, based on the entity's primary format (as defined in IFRS 8, if that IFRS applies to the entity);

d. For a cash-generating unit, a description of the cash-generating unit, the amount of the impairment loss recognized or reversed by the class of assets and by the reportable segment based on the entity's primary format (as defined by IFRS 8, if that IFRS applies to the entity) and if the aggregation of assets for identifying the cash-generating unit has changed since the previous estimate of the cash-generating unit's recoverable amount (if any), the entity should describe the current and former manner of aggregating assets and the reasons for the change;

e. Whether the recoverable amount of the asset (cash-generating unit) is its net selling price or its value in use;

f. The basis used to determine fair value less sell (such as with reference to an active market or any other manner) in case the recoverable amount is fair value less cost to sell; and

g. If recoverable amount is value in use, the discount rate(s) used in the current estimate and previous estimate (if any) of value in use.

(IAS 36, Para 130)

3. If impairment losses are recognized (reversed) during the period in aggregate in the financial statements of the entity as a whole, an entity should disclose a brief description of the following:

a. The main classes of assets affected by impairment losses and reversals of impairment losses; and

b. The main events and circumstances that led to the recognition (reversal) of these impairment losses.

(IAS 36, Para 131)

4. If any portion of goodwill acquired in a business combination effected during the current period was not allocated to a cash-generating unit at the statement of financial position date, per IAS 36, para 84, the amount of the unallocated goodwill is to be disclosed, with an explanation of why it remains unallocated.

(IAS 36, Para 133)

5. For each cash-generating unit with material amounts of indefinite-life intangibles or goodwill

a. Disclose the carrying amount of goodwill; the carrying amount of indefinite-life intangibles; and the basis on which recoverable amounts were determined.

b. If the recoverable amounts were based on value in use, describe key assumptions made by management affecting the cash flow projections, management's approach to value determination for each key assumption, the period over which cash flows were projected with an explanation, as necessary, for projections over greater than five years, and the growth rate used to project cash flows and discount rates applied, with explanations for any that exceed the entity's historical long-term growth rate.

c. If the recoverable amounts were based on fair value less costs to sell, disclose methodology used to determine such amounts where not based on observable market data; describe each key assumption and management's approach to determining values assigned to key assumptions; where discounted cash flows method is used, the entity shall disclose the period over which management has projected cash flows, the growth rate used, and discount rates used.

d. When a reasonably possible change in a key assumption could cause the carrying value of the cash-generating unit to exceed its recoverable amount, disclose the amount by which the aggregate recoverable amounts exceed carrying values, the value(s) assigned to key assumption(s), and the amount by which the value assigned to assumption(s) would need to change to cause the recoverable amounts to equal the carrying amounts.

(IAS 36, Para 134)

6. If some or all of the carrying amount of goodwill or intangible assets with indefinite useful lives is allocated across multiple cash-generating units (groups of units), and the amount so allocated to each unit (group of units) is not significant in comparison with the entity's total carrying amount of goodwill or intangible assets with indefinite useful lives, that fact shall be disclosed, together with the aggregate carrying amount of goodwill or intangible assets with indefinite useful lives allocated to those units (groups of units). In addition, if the recoverable amounts of any of those units (groups of units) are based on the same key assumptions(s) and the aggregate carrying amount of goodwill or intangible assets with indefinite useful lives allocated to them is significant in comparison with the entity's total carrying amount of goodwill or intangible assets with indefinite useful lives, an entity shall disclose that fact, together with

a. The aggregate carrying amount of goodwill allocated to those units (groups of units).
b. The aggregate carrying amount of intangible assets with indefinite useful lives allocated to those units (groups of units).
c. A description of the key assumption(s).
d. A description of management's approach to determining the value(s) assigned to the key assumption(s), whether those value(s) reflect past experience or, if appropriate, are consistent with external sources of information, and, if not, how and why they differ from past experience or external sources of information.
e. If a reasonably possible change in the key assumption(s) would cause the aggregate of the units' (groups of units') carrying amounts to exceed the aggregate of their recoverable amounts

(1) The amount by which the aggregate of the units' (groups of units') recoverable amounts exceeds the aggregate of their carrying amounts.
(2) The value(s) assigned to the key assumption(s).
(3) The amount by which the value(s) assigned to the key assumption(s) must change, after incorporating any consequential effects of the change on the other variables used to measure recoverable amount, in order for the aggregate of the units' (group of units') recoverable amounts to be equal to the aggregate of their carrying amounts.

(IAS 36, Para 135)

7. If not disclosed separately in the statement of comprehensive income, compensation from third parties for items of property, plant, and equipment that were impaired, lost, or given up that is included in profit or loss should be disclosed.

(IAS 16, Para 74)

L. Financial Instruments

1. The entity is to disclose the following items of income, expense, gains or losses either on the face of the financial statements or in the notes:

    a. Net gains or net losses on

        (1) Financial assets and financial liabilities reported at fair value with changes recognized through profit or loss, showing separately those on financial assets or financial liabilities designated as such upon initial recognition, and those on financial assets or financial liabilities that are classified as held-for-trading;
        (2) Financial assets and liabilities measured at amortized cost; and
        (3) Financial assets and liabilities measured at fair value through other comprehensive income.

    b. The total interest income and total interest expense (calculated by means of the effective interest method) for financial assets or financial liabilities that are not carried at fair value with changes reported currently through profit or loss;

    c. Fee income and expense (other than amounts included in determining the effective interest rate) arising from

        (1) Financial assets or financial liabilities that are not carried at fair value with changes recognized currently through profit or loss; and
        (2) Trust and other fiduciary activities that result in the holding or investing of assets on behalf of individuals, trusts, retirement benefit plans, and other institutions.

    d. Interest income on impaired financial assets accrued in accordance with IAS 39; and

    e. The amount of any impairment loss for each class of financial asset.

(IFRS 7, Para 20)

STATEMENT OF CASH FLOWS

A. Basis of Presentation

1. A statement of cash flows should be prepared in accordance with IAS 7 and presented as an integral part of an entity's financial statements for each period for which the financial statements are presented.

(IAS 7, Para 1)

2. The statement of cash flows should report cash flows during the period, classified by

    a. Operating activities;
    b. Investing activities; and
    c. Financing activities.

(IAS 7, Para 10)

B. Format

1. Cash flows from operating activities should be reported using either

    a. The direct method, under which major classes of gross cash receipts and gross cash payments are disclosed; **or**

   b. The indirect method, wherein net profit or loss for the period is adjusted for the following:

   (1) The effects of noncash transactions;
   (2) Any deferrals or accruals of past or future operating cash receipts or payments; and
   (3) Items of income or expense related to investing or financing cash flows.

(IAS 7, Para 18)

2. An entity should generally report (separately) major gross cash receipts and payments from investing and financing activities.

(IAS 7, Para 21)

3. Under the following circumstances, however, an entity's[1] cash flows arising from operating, investing, or financing activities may be reported on a net basis:

   a. Cash receipts and payments on behalf of customers when the cash flows reflect the activities of the customer rather than those of the entity; and
   b. Cash receipts and payments for items in which the turnover is quick, the amounts are large, and maturities are short.

(IAS 7, Para 22)

4. Cash flows from interest received and dividends received and dividends paid should be classified consistently (from period to period) as either

   a. Operating activities;
   b. Investing activities; or
   c. Financing activities.

Each of these items should be disclosed separately.

(IAS 7, Para 31)

5. In relation to cash and cash equivalents, a cash flow statement should

   a. Disclose the policy which it adopts in determining the components;
   b. Disclose the components; and
   c. Present a reconciliation of the amounts in its statement of cash flows with similar items reported in the statement of financial position.

(IAS 7, Para 45 & 46)

6. The effect of exchange rate changes on cash and cash equivalents held or due in foreign currency should be presented separately from cash flows from operating, investing, and financing activities.

(IAS 7, Para 28)

---

[1] *Cash flows of financial institutions may be reported on a net basis under the following cases:*

   1. Cash flows from the acceptance and repayment of deposits with fixed maturity dates;
   2. Placement of deposits with and withdrawal of deposits from other financial institutions; and
   3. Cash advances and loans made to customers and the repayment of those advances and loans.

(IAS 7, Para 24)

7. Noncash transactions arising from investing and financing activities should be excluded from the statement of cash flows. Such transactions do not require the use of cash and cash equivalents and thus should be disclosed elsewhere in the financial statements by way of a note that provides all the relevant information about these activities.

(IAS 7, Para 43)

8. Cash payments and receipts relating to taxes on income should be separately disclosed and classified as cash flows from operating activities unless they could specifically be identified with financing and/or investing activities.

(IAS 7, Para 35)

9. In relation to acquisitions or disposals of subsidiaries or other business units which should be presented separately and classified as investing activities, an entity should disclose the following:

    a. The total consideration paid or received;
    b. Portion of the consideration discharged by cash and cash equivalents;
    c. Amount of cash and cash equivalents acquired or disposed; and
    d. Amount of assets and liabilities (other than cash or cash equivalents) summarized by major category.

(IAS 7, Para 40)

10. Significant cash and cash equivalent balances held by the entity which are not available for use by the group should be disclosed by the entity along with a commentary by management.

(IAS 7, Para 48)

C. Additional Recommended Disclosures

Additional disclosures which may be relevant to financial statement users in understanding an entity's financial position and liquidity have been encouraged by IAS 7 and include the following:

1. The amount of undrawn borrowing facilities including disclosure of restrictions, if any, as to their use;
2. The aggregate amount of cash flows related to interests in joint ventures reported using the proportionate consolidation;
3. The aggregate amount of cash flows that represent increases in operating capacity separately from those cash flows that are required to maintain the operating capacity; and
4. Disclosure of segmental cash flow information in order to provide financial statement users better information about the relationship of cash flows of the business as a whole vis-à-vis cash flows from its segments.

(IAS 7, Para 50)

STATEMENT OF CHANGES IN EQUITY

A. Statement of Changes in Equity

1. As a separate component of its financial statements, an entity should present a statement showing the following items:

   a. Total comprehensive income for the period, showing separately the total amounts attributable to owners of the parent and to noncontrolling interest;
   b. For each component of equity, the effects of retrospective application or retrospective restatement recognized in accordance with IAS 8; and
   c. For each component of equity, a reconciliation between the carrying amount at the beginning and the end of the period, separately disclosing changes resulting from, profit or loss, other comprehensive income, and transactions with owners in their capacity as owners, showing separately contributions by and distributions to owners and changes in ownership interests in subsidiaries that do not result in a loss of control.

   (IAS 1, Para 106)

2. An entity shall present for each component of equity, an analysis of other comprehensive income by item, in either the statement of changes in equity or in the notes.

   (IAS 1, Para 106A)

3. Either in the statement of changes in equity or in the notes, the amount of dividends recognized as distributions to owners during the period, and the related amount of dividends per share amounts.

   (IAS 1, Para 107)

NOTES TO THE FINANCIAL STATEMENTS

A. Structure of the Notes

1. The notes to the financial statements should

   a. Present information regarding the basis of preparation of the financial statements and the specific accounting policies selected and applied for significant transactions and events;
   b. Disclose information required by IAS which is not presented elsewhere in the financial statements; and
   c. Provide additional information which is not presented on the face of the financial statements but which is necessary for a fair presentation.

   (IAS 1, Para 112)

2. The notes to the financial statements should be presented in a systematic manner. Each item on the face of the statement of financial position, income statement and cash flow statement should be cross-referenced to any related information in the notes to the financial statements.

   (IAS 1, Para 113)

3. The following order of presentation of the notes is normally adopted which assists users of financial statements in understanding them and comparing them with those of other entities:

    a. Statement of compliance with IFRS;
    b. Summary of significant accounting policies applied;
    c. Supporting information for items presented in the statements of financial position and of comprehensive income, in the separate income statement (if presented), and in the statements of changes in equity and of cash flows, in the order in which each statement and each line item is presented; and
    d. Other disclosures, including

        (1) Contingencies and commitments and other financial disclosures; and
        (2) Nonfinancial disclosures.

    (IAS 1, Para 114)

4. An entity shall disclose in the notes

    a. The amount of dividends proposed or declared before the financial statements were authorized for issue but not recognized as a distribution to equity holders during the period, and the related amount per share; and
    b. The amount of any cumulative preference share not recognized.

    (IAS 1, Para 137)

B. Accounting Policies

1. The accounting policies section of the notes to the financial statements should describe the following:

    a. The measurement basis/bases used in preparing the financial statements; and
    b. Other accounting policies used that are relevant to an understanding of the financial statements.

    (IAS 1, Para 117)

2. Examples of accounting policies that an entity may consider presenting include, but are not restricted to, the following:

    a. Revenue recognition;
    b. Basis of consolidation of subsidiaries and method of accounting for investments in associates;
    c. Business combinations;
    d. Joint ventures;
    e. Recognition and depreciation/amortization of tangible and intangible assets;
    f. Capitalization of borrowing costs and other expenditures;
    g. Construction contracts;
    h. Investment properties;
    i. Financial instruments and investments;
    j. Hedge accounting;
    k. Leases;
    l. Research and development costs;
    m. Inventories;
    n. Taxes, including deferred taxes;
    o. Provisions;

    p. Employee benefit costs;
    q. Foreign currency translation and hedging;
    r. Definition of business and geographical segments and the basis for allocation of costs between segments;
    s. Definition of cash and cash equivalents;
    t. Inflation accounting; and
    u. Government grants.

C. Service Concession Arrangements

1. All aspects of a service concession arrangement should be taken into account in determining the appropriate disclosures in the notes. Both a concession operator and a concession provider should disclose the following *in each period:*

    a. A description of the service concession arrangement;
    b. Significant terms of the arrangement that may affect the amount, timing, and certainty of future cash flows (e.g., period of concession, repricing dates, and the basis upon which the repricing or renegotiation is determined);
    c. The nature and extent (e.g., the quantity, time period, or amount as appropriate) of

        (1) Rights to use specified assets;
        (2) Obligations to provide or rights to expect provision of services;
        (3) Obligations to acquire or build items of property, plant, and equipment;
        (4) Obligations to deliver or rights to receive specified assets at the end of the concession period;
        (5) Renewal and termination options; and
        (6) Other rights and obligations (e.g., major overhauls); and

    d. Changes in the arrangement taking place during the period and how the service arrangement has been classified.

2. The above-mentioned disclosures should be provided individually for each service concession arrangement or in aggregate for each class of service concession arrangements. A "class" is a grouping of service concession arrangements involving services of a similar nature (e.g., toll collections, telecommunications, and water treatment services).
3. An operator shall disclose the amount of revenue and profits or losses recognized in the period on exchanging construction services for a financial asset or an intangible asset.

(SIC 29, Para 6, 6A & 7)

INTERIM FINANCIAL STATEMENTS

A. Minimum Components of an Interim Financial Report

1. An interim financial report should include, at a minimum, the following components:

    a. A condensed statement of financial position;
    b. A condensed statement of comprehensive income, presented either as a condensed single statement, or a condensed separate income statement and a condensed statement of comprehensive income;

    c. A condensed statement of changes in equity;

    d. A condensed cash flow statement; and

    e. Selected set of explanatory/footnote disclosures.

(IAS 34, Para 8)

2. If an entity presents the components of profit or loss in a separate income statement as described in paragraph 81 of IAS 1 (as revised in 2007), it presents interim condensed information from that separate statement.

(IAS 34, Para 8A)

B. Form and Content of Interim Financial Statements

1. If an entity chooses the "complete set of (interim) financial statements" route, instead of opting for the shortcut method of presenting only "condensed" interim financial statements, then the form and content of those statements should conform to the requirements of IAS 1 for a complete set of financial statements.

(IAS 34, Para 9)

2. However, if an entity opts for the condensed format of interim financial reporting, then IAS 34 requires that, at a minimum, those condensed financial statements should include

    a. Each of the headings, and

    b. Subtotals that were included in the entity's most recent annual financial statements, along with selected explanatory notes, prescribed by the Standard.

(Additional line items or notes should be included if their omission would make the condensed interim financial statements misleading.)

(IAS 34, Para 10)

3. Basic and diluted earnings per share should be presented on the face of an income statement, complete or condensed, for an interim period.

(IAS 34, Para 11)

4. If an entity presents the components of profit or loss in a separate income statement as described in paragraph 81 of IAS 1 (as revised in 2007), it presents basic and diluted earnings per share in that separate statement.

(IAS 34, Para 11A)

5. An interim financial report should be prepared on a consolidated basis if the entity's most recent annual financial statements were consolidated statements. As regards presentation of separate interim financial statements of the parent company in addition to consolidated interim financial statements, if they were included in the most recent annual financial statements, this Standard neither requires nor prohibits such inclusion in the interim financial report of the entity.

(IAS 34, Para 14)

C. Selected Explanatory Notes

1. An entity shall include in its interim financial report an explanation of events and transactions that are significant to an understanding of the changes in financial position and performance of the entity since the end of the last annual reporting period.

Information disclosed in relation to those events and transactions shall update the relevant information presented in the most recent annual financial report.

(IAS 34, Para 15)

2. When an event or transaction is significant to an understanding of the changes in an entity's financial position or performance since the last annual reporting period, its interim financial report should provide an explanation of and an update to the relevant information included in the financial statements of the last annual reporting period.

(IAS 34, Para 15C)

3. The minimum disclosures required to accompany the condensed interim financial statements are the following:

   a. A statement that the same accounting policies and methods of computation are applied in the interim financial statements compared with the most recent annual financial statements or if those policies or methods have changed, a description of the nature and effect of the change;
   b. Explanatory comments about seasonality or cyclicality of interim operations;
   c. The nature and magnitude of significant items affecting interim results that are unusual because of nature, size, or incidence;
   d. The nature and amount of changes in estimates of amounts reported in prior interim periods of the current financial year or changes in estimates of amounts reported in prior financial years, if those changes have a material effect in the current interim period.
   e. Issuances, repurchases, and repayments of debt and equity securities;
   f. Dividends paid, either in the aggregate or on a per share basis, presented separately for ordinary (common) shares and other classes of shares;
   g. The following segments information (disclosure of segment information is required in an entity's interim financial report only if IFRS 8, *Operating Segments,* requires the entity to disclose segment information in its annual financial statements):

      (1) Revenues from external customers, if included in the measure of segment profit or loss reviewed by the chief operating decision maker or otherwise regularly provided to the chief operating decision maker;
      (2) Intersegment revenues, if included in the measure of segment profit or loss reviewed by the chief operating decision maker or otherwise regularly provided to the chief operating decision maker;
      (3) A measure of segment profit or loss;
      (4) Total assets for which there has been a material change from the amount disclosed in the last annual financial statements;
      (5) A description of differences from the last annual financial statements in the basis of segmentation or in the basis of measurement of segment profit or loss; and
      (6) A reconciliation of the total of the reportable segments' measures of profit or loss to the entity's profit or loss before tax expense (tax income) and discontinued operations. However, if an entity allocates to reportable segments items such as tax expense (tax income), the entity may reconcile the total of the segments' measures of profit or loss to profit or loss after those items. Material reconciling items shall be separately identified and described in that reconciliation.

h. Any significant events occurring subsequent to the end of the interim period; and

i. The effect of changes in the composition of the entity during the interim period like business combinations, acquisitions or disposal of subsidiaries and long-term investments, restructuring, and discontinuing operations.

(IAS 34, Para 16A)

4. If an entity's interim financial report is in compliance with this Standard, that fact shall be disclosed. An interim financial report shall not be described as complying with IFRSs unless it complies with all the requirements of IFRS.

(IAS 34, Para 19)

5. If an estimate of an amount reported in an interim period is changed significantly during the final interim period of the financial year but a separate financial report is not published for that final interim period, the nature and amount of that change in estimate shall be disclosed in a note to the annual financial statements for that financial year.

(IAS 34, Para 26)

INSURANCE CONTRACTS

1. An insurer shall disclose information that identifies and explains the amount in its financial statements arising from insurance contracts.

(IFRS 4, Para 36)

2. To comply with IFRS 4, paragraph 36, an insurer shall disclose

a. Its accounting policies for insurance contracts and related assets and liabilities, income, and expense;

b. The recognized assets, liabilities, income, and expense (and, if it presents its cash flow statement using the direct method, cash flows) arising from insurance contracts. Furthermore, if the insurer is a cedant, it shall disclose

(1) Gains and losses recognized in profit or loss on buying reinsurance; and

(2) If the cedant differs and amortizes gains and losses arising on buying reinsurance, the amortization for the period and the amounts remaining unamortized at the beginning and at the end of the period.

c. The process used to determine the assumptions that have the greatest effect on the measurement of the recognized amounts described in b. When practicable, an insurer shall also give quantified disclosures of those assumptions.

d. The effect of changes in assumption used to measure insurance assets and insurance liabilities, showing separately the effect of each change that has a material effect on the financial statements.

e. Reconciliation of changes in insurance liabilities, reinsurance assets and if any, related deferred acquisition costs.

(IFRS 4, Para 37)

3. An insurer shall give the information to understand the amount, timing, and uncertainty of future cash flows from insurance contracts.

(IFRS 4, Para 38)

4. To comply with IFRS 4, paragraph 38, an insurer shall disclose

   a. Its objectives in managing risks arising from insurance contracts and its policies for mitigating those risks.
   b. Information about insurance risk (both before and after risk mitigation by reinsurance), including information about

      (1) The sensitivity of profit or loss and equity to changes in variables that have material effect on them;
      (2) Concentrations of insurance risk; and
      (3) Actual claims compared with previous estimates (i.e., claim development). The disclosure about claims development shall go back to the period when the earliest material claim arose for which there is still uncertainty about the amount and timing of the claims payment, but need not go back more than ten years. An insurer need not disclose this information for claims for which uncertainty about the amount and timing of claims payments is typically resolved within one year.

   c. The information about interest rate risk and credit risk that IAS 32 would require if the insurance contracts were within the scope of IAS 32; and
   d. Information about exposures to interest rate risk or market risk under embedded derivatives contained in a host insurance contract, if the insurer is not required to, and does not, measure the embedded derivatives at fair value.

   (IFRS 4, Para 39)

5. An entity need not apply the disclosure requirements in this IFRS to comparative information that relates to the annual period beginning before January 1, 2005, except for the disclosure required by IFRS 4, paragraph 37(a) and (b) about accounting policies, and recognized assets, liabilities, income and expense (and cash flow if direct method is used).

   (IFRS 4, Para 42)

6. If it is impracticable to apply a particular requirement to comparative information that relates to annual periods beginning January 1, 2005, an entity shall disclose that fact. Applying the liability adequacy test to such comparative information might sometimes be impracticable, but it is highly unlikely to be impracticable to apply other requirements to such comparative information.

   (IFRS 4, Para 43)

7. When an entity first applies this IFRS and if it is impracticable to prepare information about claim development that occurred before the beginning of the earliest period for which an entity presents full comparative information that complies with this IFRS, the entity shall disclose this fact.

   (IFRS 4, Para 44)

AGRICULTURE

A. General

1. An entity should disclose the aggregate gain or loss arising during the current period on initial recognition of biological assets and agricultural produce and from the change in fair value less estimated point-of-sale costs of biological assets.

(IAS 41, Para 40)

2. An entity should provide a description of each group of biological assets disclosed by the entity.

(IAS 41, Para 41)

3. If not disclosed elsewhere in information published with the financial statements, an entity should describe

   a. The nature of its activities involving each group of biological assets; and
   b. Nonfinancial measures or estimates of the physical quantities of

      (1) Each group of the entity's biological assets at the end of the period; and
      (2) Output of agricultural produce during the period.

(IAS 41, Para 46)

4. An entity should disclose the methods and significant assumptions applied in determining the fair value of each group of agricultural produce at the point of harvest and each group of biological assets.

(IAS 41, Para 47)

5. An entity should disclose the fair value less estimated point-of-sale costs of agricultural produce harvested during the period, determined at the point of harvest.

(IAS 41, Para 48)

6. An entity should disclose

   a. The existence and carrying amounts of biological assets whose title is restricted, and the carrying amounts of biological assets pledged as security for liabilities;
   b. The amount of commitments for the development or acquisition of biological assets; and
   c. Financial risk management strategies related to agricultural activity.

(IAS 41, Para 49)

7. An entity should present a reconciliation of changes in the carrying amount of biological assets between the beginning and the end of the current period. Comparative information is not required. The reconciliation should include

   a. The gain or loss arising from changes in fair value less estimated point-of-sale costs;
   b. Increases due to purchases;
   c. Decreases due to sales;
   d. Decreases due to harvest;
   e. Increases resulting from business combinations;

f. Net exchange differences arising on the translation of financial statements of a foreign entity; and

g. Other changes.

(IAS 41, Para 50)

8. The fair value less costs to sell of a biological asset can change due to both physical changes and price changes in the market. Separate disclosure of physical and price changes is useful in appraising current period performance and future prospects, particularly when there is a production cycle of more than one year. In such cases, an entity is encouraged to disclose, by group or otherwise, the amount of change in fair value less costs to sell included in profit or loss due to physical changes and due to price changes. This information is generally less useful when the production cycle is less than one year (for example, when raising chickens or growing cereal crops).

(IAS 41, Para 51)

B. Additional Disclosure for Biological Assets Where Fair Value Cannot Be Measured Reliably

1. If an entity measures biological assets at their cost less any accumulated depreciation and any accumulated impairment losses at the end of the period, the entity should disclose for such biological assets

a. A description of the biological assets;

b. An explanation of why fair value cannot be measured reliably;

c. If possible, the range of estimates within which fair value is highly likely to lie;

d. The depreciation method used;

e. The useful lives or the depreciation rates used; and

f. The gross carrying amount and the accumulated depreciation (aggregated with accumulated impairment losses) at the beginning and end of the period.

(IAS 41, Para 54)

2. If, during the current period, an entity measures biological assets at their cost less any accumulated depreciation and any accumulated impairment losses, an entity should disclose any gain or loss recognized on disposal of such biological assets and the reconciliation required by IAS 41, para 50, should disclose amounts related to such biological assets separately. In addition, the reconciliation should include the following amounts included in net profit or loss related to those biological assets:

a. Impairment losses;

b. Reversals of impairment losses; and

c. Depreciation.

(IAS 41, Para 55)

3. If the fair value of biological assets previously measured at their cost, less any accumulated depreciation and any accumulated impairment losses, becomes reliably measurable during the current period, an entity should disclose for those biological assets

a. A description of the biological assets;

b. An explanation of why fair value has become reliably measurable; and

c. The effect of the change.

(IAS 41, Para 56)

C. Government Grants

1. An entity should disclose the following related to agricultural activity covered by this Standard:

   a. The nature and extent of government grants recognized in the financial statements;
   b. Unfulfilled conditions and other contingencies attaching to government grants; and
   c. Significant decreases expected in the level of government grants.

   (IAS 41, Para 57)

EXPLORATION FOR AND EVALUATION OF MINERAL RESOURCES

1. An entity shall disclose information that identifies and explains the amounts recognized in its financial statements arising from the exploration for and evaluation of mineral resources.

   (IFRS 6, Para 23)

2. To comply with paragraph 23, IFRS 6, an entity shall disclose

   a. Its accounting policies for explorations and evaluation of expenditures including the recognition of exploration and evaluation assets; and
   b. The amounts of assets, liabilities, income and expense, and operating and investing cash flows arising from the exploration for and evaluation of mineral resources.

   (IFRS 6, Para 24)

3. An entity shall treat exploration and evaluation assets as a separate class of assets and make the disclosures required by either IAS 16 or IAS 38 consistent with how the assets are classified.

   (IFRS 6, Para 25)

4. Exploration and evaluation assets shall be assessed for impairment when facts and circumstances suggest that the carrying amount of an exploration and evaluation asset may exceeds its recoverable amount. When facts and circumstances suggest that the carrying amount exceeds the recoverable amount, an entity shall measure, present, and disclose any resulting impairment loss in accordance with IAS 36.

   (IFRS 6, Para 18)

INDEX